Administrative Law and Regulatory Policy

Administrative Law and Regulatory Policy

Problems, Text, and Cases

Sixth Edition

Stephen G. Breyer
Associate Justice
United States Supreme Court

Richard B. Stewart
Emily Kempin Professor of Law
New York University

Cass R. Sunstein
Karl N. Llewellyn Distinguished Service
Professor of Jurisprudence
University of Chicago School of Law
and Department of Political Science

Adrian Vermeule
Bernard D. Meltzer Professor of Law
University of Chicago School of Law

111 Eighth Avenue, New York, NY 10011
http://lawschool.aspenpublishers.com

Aspen Publishers
Attn: Permissions Department
111 Eighth Avenue, 7th Floor
New York, NY 10011-5201

Printed in the United States of America

1 2 3 4 5 6 7 8 9 0

ISBN 0-7355-5606-7

Library of Congress Cataloging-in-Publication Data

Administrative law and regulatory policy : problems, text, and cases / Stephen G. Breyer . . . [et al.]. – 6th ed.
    p. cm.
Includes bibliographical references and index.
ISBN 0-7355-5606-7 (alk. paper)
1. Administrative law – United States – Cases. I. Breyer, Stephen G., 1938-

   KF5402.A4 B74 2006
   342.73'06–dc22

2006002727

About Aspen Publishers

Aspen Publishers, headquartered in New York City, is a leading information provider for attorneys, business professionals, and law students. Written by preeminent authorities, our products consist of analytical and practical information covering both U.S. and international topics. We publish in the full range of formats, including updated manuals, books, periodicals, CDs, and online products.

Our proprietary content is complemented by 2,500 legal databases, containing over 11 million documents, available through our Loislaw division. Aspen Publishers also offers a wide range of topical legal and business databases linked to Loislaw's primary material. Our mission is to provide accurate, timely, and authoritative content in easily accessible formats, supported by unmatched customer care.

To order any Aspen Publishers title, go to *http://lawschool.aspenpublishers.com* or call 1-800-638-8437.

To reinstate your manual update service, call 1-800-638-8437.

For more information on Loislaw products, go to *www.loislaw.com* or call 1-800-364-2512.

For Customer Care issues, e-mail *CustomerCare@aspenpublishers.com*; call 1-800-234-1660; or fax 1-800-901-9075.

Aspen Publishers
a Wolters Kluwer business

To Louis I. Jaffe
Teacher, Scholar, Colleague, Friend

Summary of Contents

Contents

5. *"Common Law" Requirements: Clarity, Consistency, "Fairness"* 405

Appendix C: Negotiated Rulemaking and Alternative Dispute Resolution Act   *975*

Table of Abbreviations

The following acronyms are used throughout the text.

ABA   American Bar Association
AEC   Atomic Energy Commission
APA   Administrative Procedures Act
CAB   Civil Aeronautics Board
CBA   cost-benefit analysis
CFTC   Commodities Futures Trading Commission
CPSC   Consumer Product Safety Commission
CSC   Civil Service Commission
DEA   Drug Enforcement Administration
EEOC   Equal Employment Opportunity Commission
EPA   Environmental Protection Agency
FAA   Federal Aviation Administration
FCC   Federal Communications Commission
FDA   Food and Drug Administration
FERC   Federal Energy Regulatory Commission
FMC   Federal Maritime Commission
FPC   Federal Power Commission
FRC   Federal Radio Commission
FTC   Federal Trade Commission
HEW   Department of Health, Education, and Welfare
HHS   Department of Health and Human Services
ICC   Interstate Commerce Commission
NHTSA   National Highway Traffic Safety Administration
NIOSH   National Institute for Occupational Safety and Health
NIRA   National Industrial Recovery Act of 1933
NLRB   National Labor Relations Board
NRC   Nuclear Regulatory Commission
NRDC   National Resources Defense Council
NTSB   National Transportation Safety Board
OIRA   Office of Information and Regulatory Activities
OMB   Office of Management and Budget
OPA   Office of Price Administration
OSHA   Occupational Safety and Health Administration
OSH   Occupational Safety and Health Act
OSHRC   Occupational Safety and Health Review Commission
SEC   Securities and Exchange Commission

Table of Abbreviations

The following abbreviations are used throughout the text.

ABA	American Bar Association
AEC	Atomic Energy Commission
APA	Administrative Procedure Act
CAB	Civil Aeronautics Board
CFR	Code of Federal Regulations
CPSC	Consumer Product Safety Commission
CPSC	Consumer Product Safety Commission
CSC	Civil Service Commission
DEA	Drug Enforcement Administration
EEOC	Equal Employment Opportunity Commission
EPA	Environmental Protection Agency
FAA	Federal Aviation Administration
FCC	Federal Communications Commission
FDA	Food and Drug Administration
FMC	Federal Maritime Regulatory Commission
FMC	Federal Maritime Commission
FPC	Federal Power Commission
FRC	Federal Radio Commission
FTC	Federal Trade Commission
DHEW	Department of Health, Education, and Welfare
HHS	Department of Health and Human Services
ICC	Interstate Commerce Commission
NHTSA	National Highway Traffic Safety Administration
NIOSH	National Institute for Occupational Safety and Health
NIRA	National Industrial Recovery Act of 1933
NLRB	National Labor Relations Board
NRC	Nuclear Regulatory Commission
NRDC	Natural Resources Defense Council
NTSB	National Transportation Safety Board
OIRA	Office of Information and Regulatory Affairs
OMB	Office of Management and Budget
OPA	Office of Price Administration
OSHA	Occupational Safety and Health Administration
OSH	Occupational Safety and Health Act
OSHRC	Occupational Safety and Health Review Commission
SEC	Securities and Exchange Commission

xxxv

Preface to the Sixth Edition

The previous edition of this book was published in 2002 — too early, by far, to incorporate the significant rethinking of administrative law that has occurred in the aftermath of the attacks of September 11, 2001. A primary change in the present edition is to show some of the many links between the war on terrorism and the administrative state. We believe that it is impossible to understand the legal problems of the post-9/11 era without reference to the principles of administrative law, and we have revised this edition with that point in mind.

More generally, the last several years have seen a great deal of ferment in our favorite field. Issues of regulatory policy continue to be reconceived; new attention has been paid to the uses and limits of cost-benefit analysis, the theoretical foundations of health and safety regulation, the place of deregulation, and the proper treatment of changes from one administration to another. The new attention receives corresponding treatment in this book.

There are fresh debates too about the scope of judicial review of agency action, the power of the president, access to federal courts, and new methods of producing agency policies. As before, we have worked especially hard to give users of this book a sense of state-of-the-art debates now beginning in the courts and likely to play a large role in the future.

Although this is a substantial revision, we have maintained considerable continuity with prior editions of this book. The basic structure is the same, as is the basic goal: to study administrative law in a way that is informed by, and integrated with, an understanding of the issues of regulatory policy that lie beneath, and sometimes at the surface of, every doctrinal problem, however technical or abstract it may seem. In this way, we have sought to help the next generation of lawyers and law students with the endlessly fascinating problems of administrative law — some of them old, some of them new, some of them now barely on the horizon.

Justice Breyer has not participated in the preparation of the most recent editions of this book, but we have retained a great deal of material from the editions for which he was co-author. We are grateful to Matthew Spitzer, Dean of the University of Southern California Law School, who was a co-author on the previous two editions but whose administrative responsibilities prevented him from working on this revision. We have learned a great deal from Matt's excellent editorial work, as from his superb work in the field, and we have hopes that he might be able to rejoin this enterprise in the future. We are also grateful to James Hobbs for research assistance.

Cass R. Sunstein
Richard B. Stewart
Adrian Vermeule

February 2006

Preface to the First Edition

The traditional course on Administrative Law primarily concerns the delegation of power to administrative agencies, the procedures that the law requires them to follow, the legal requirements for obtaining judicial review of agency decisions, and the standards applied during that review. Critics of this course persistently and increasingly raise two important objections:

First, isn't such a course too abstract? Too remote from the substantive essence of agency decisionmaking? Aren't efforts to generalize across decisions arising out of many different agencies and substantive fields misleading? Don't those decisions often reflect no more than court efforts to deal with distasteful agency action on a case-by-case basis, perhaps masked by appeals to procedural principle? In a word, is it possible to understand these court decisions without understanding the substantive work of the agency?

Second, doesn't concentration on appellate court decisions mislead the student about what agencies do? The impact of judicial decisions on agency work may often be slight; and court review may constitute only a small part of the work of the lawyers who practice before the agency. Should future lawyers not be given a broader understanding of the many other factors that affect the impact that agency action has upon the world? See R. Rabin, Perspectives on Administrative Process 7-14 (1978).

This casebook represents an effort to preserve the essential virtues of the traditional course while adapting it to meet these objections. The materials are organized along traditional procedural lines, as updated to reflect the vast change that has overtaken this body of law in recent years. At the same time the book uses notes and problems systematically to survey regulation, as broadly conceived to deal not only with prices and entry, but also with health, safety, and the environment. It shows the interaction between substance and procedure; and (particularly in Chapter 8) it describes some of the bureaucratic and political factors at work.

Thus, this casebook might be used in two different ways. The teacher who wishes to emphasize the "administrative process" rather than "administrative procedure" might use this book to do so. It will introduce the future practitioner to the substance of much regulation, its interplay with procedural rules, the agency seen as a bureaucratic institution, and the basic steps for obtaining court review. The teacher of the traditional course might teach that course from this book as well, using the substantive notes and comments as supplementary aids.

We recommend that those emphasizing the substantive regulatory aspects of the book in their courses refer to the Teachers Manual, which is based on our teaching notes. The book's cases, questions, and problems are deliberately organized to elicit in class discussion the points and issues that the Manual contains.

The book provides sufficient material for a four-hour course. Those wishing to teach a three-hour course are advised to forgo selected substantive areas of regulation (such as utility rate regulation, food and drug regulation, FTC regulation of false advertising) or procedural topics (such as application of due process, privacy jurisdiction, Freedom of Information Act) or a combination thereof.

We wish to acknowledge the great debt we owe our predecessors, and we mention specifically Professors Clark Byse, Kenneth Gulp Davis, Walter Gelhorn, and Louis Jaffe. Our work is obviously based upon their achievement. We particularly acknowledge our debt to Louis Jaffe, who, in mastering the intellectual problems of judicial review, laid the foundation on which we erect our own view of administrative law. We also acknowledge our use of the work of many others too numerous to mention, though we wish to point out that the discussion of the Federal Trade Commission in Chapter 8 draws upon that in G. Robinson & E. Gellhorn, The Administrative Process (1974), though we put that discussion to somewhat different use.

We have also dealt with the perennial problem of footnoting in casebooks as follows: All footnotes in a chapter are numbered consecutively from its beginning to its end. Thus footnotes belonging to cases within the chapter will not bear their original footnote numbers. The footnotes attached to cases are those written by the court unless the note itself specifically indicates that it was written by the editors.

We gratefully acknowledge the research assistance of Linda Agerter, Dee Carlson, Kenneth Kettering, Kenneth Kleinman, Diane Millman, Joseph Post, Richard Rose, Cass Sunstein, Victor Thuronyi, Jeffrey Wohl, and Michael Young. Alan Morrison and Robert Pitovsky were generous in providing helpful comment and criticism. The unstinting work of our secretaries, Sue Campbell, Astrid Dodds, Cindy Dodge, Sarah Johnson, Karen Lee, Gayle McKeen, Angela O'Neill, and Shane Snowdon, was indispensable and very much appreciated.

April 1979

Acknowledgments

We wish to express our appreciation to the following authors, periodicals, and publishers for their permission to reproduce material from their publications:

Ackerman & Stewart, Reforming Environmental Law: The Democratic Case for Economic Incentives, 13 Colum J. Envtl. L. 171, 172-175, 178-179, 188-190 (1988)

ALI, Restatement of Judgments §§ 1, 27, 28, 83

E. Anderson, Value in Ethics and Economics 204-207, 209-210 (1993). Reprinted by permission of the publisher from Value in Ethics and Economics by Elizabeth Anderson, Cambridge, Mass.: Harvard University Press, Copyright © 1993 by the President and Fellows of Harvard College.

S. Breyer, Breaking the Vicious Circle 10-11, 18-23, 59-63 (1993). Reprinted by permission of the publisher from Breaking the Vicious Circle by Stephen Breyer, Cambridge, Mass.: Harvard University Press, Copyright © 1993 by the President and Fellows of Harvard College.

S. Breyer, On the Uses of Legislative History in Interpreting Statutes, 65 S. Cal. L. Rev. 845 (1992). Reprinted with permission of the *Southern California Law Review.*

Cass, Allocation of Authority Within Bureaucracies: Empirical Evidence and Normative Analysis, Volume 66:1, Boston University Law Review (1986) 18-21. Reprinted with permission. © 1986 Trustees of Boston University. Forum of original publication.

K. Davis, 1 Administrative Law Treatise 208-209, 211-212, 213-214 (2d ed. 1978)

E. Donald Elliott, Chevron Matters: How the Chevron Doctrine Redefined the Roles of Congress, Courts and Agencies in Environmental Law, 16 Vill. Envt'l L. J. 1, 11-13 (2005). Reprinted with permission. Copyright © 2005 Villanova University; E. Donald Elliott.

J. Graham, Making Sense of Risk: An Agenda for Congress, in Risks, Costs, and Lives Saved 183, 183-185, 192-193, 195, 199-200. From Risks, Costs, and Lives Saved: Getting Better Results from Regulation, edited by Robert W. Hahn. Copyright © 1996 The American Enterprise Institute for Public Policy Research, Washington D.C. Used by permission of Oxford University Press, Inc., and AEI Press.

L. Lave, Benefit Cost Analysis: Do the Benefits Exceed the Costs?, in Risks, Costs, and Lives Saved 104, 120-121. From Risks, Costs, and Lives Saved: Getting Better Results from Regulation, edited by Robert W. Hahn. Copyright © 1996 The American Enterprise Institute for Public Policy Research, Washington D.C. Used by permission of Oxford University Press, Inc., and AEI Press.

R. Noll, Regulation After Reagan, 12(3) Regulation 13-20 (1988)

A. Scalia, Back to Basics: Making Law Without Making Rules, Regulation 25, 26-27 (July/Aug. 1981)

A. Scalia, A Matter of Interpretation, 29-32 (1996)

D. Schoenbrod, Power Without Responsibility 9-10, 126, 129 (Yale University Press, 1993)

*Administrative Law
and Regulatory Policy*

1

Introduction

Modern government is administrative government. Much of modern life is a product, in large part, of the activities of administrative agencies. The range of administrative government is remarkably wide, including — for starters and for illustration — protection of national security, energy, air and water quality, prices of consumer goods, conditions in the workplace, airline safety, taxation, and civil rights.

More than 15 million local, state, and federal government employees, organized in a variety of bureaucratic structures, carry out a vast array of functions using many different tools and procedures. The enormous variety and complexity that characterize "government administration" pose hard questions of choice and organization for those providing an introduction to the administrative state as a whole.

A. The Book's Content and Organization

We have approached the question of choice by asking ourselves what we think students who might practice administrative law ought to know as an introduction to the field. We concluded the following:

First, they should understand the basic principles applied by the courts in reviewing agency decisions. Students should also know how to get into court to challenge agency decisions. They should understand such traditional principles as "reviewability," standing, ripeness, and exhaustion of remedies, which determine when or whether they can ask a court to review agency action.

Second, students should understand something about the goals and actual performance of the regulatory state, including regulatory aspirations, regulatory successes, and regulatory failures. To understand this, students should learn something about the substantive areas of law or policy with which agencies deal. Administrative law is interpenetrated with regulatory law, and so we try in this book to give a sense of the content of regulatory law. We have selected a range of examples designed to introduce students to the substance of "regulation," broadly conceived. These examples raise important questions of both theory and fact. We have stressed the need to understand the goals of regulation — to have a kind of "map" of the regulatory state — and also to have a sense of the actual experience of government regulation.

Third, students should have some acquaintance with the agency viewed as governmental bureaucracy. How does the agency work as an institution? Who are its personnel? How are they organized? How do they work? Moreover, any agency operates in a political environment. How are its actions affected by political influences? We try to give the student some feeling for the way bureaucratic and political factors affect an agency's ability to carry out its statutory mission.

1

Fourth, students should consider the efforts of Congress, the president, and the courts to alter traditional administrative law principles to impose new, different, fewer, or greater controls on agency policymaking. Since the early 1970s, there has been a strong sense that many agencies have failed to discharge their missions. In this book, we examine various diagnoses of agency "failure" and the efforts of various institutions, including (but emphatically not only) the courts, to remedy "failure."

Fifth, students should have a sense of the arguments that lawyers might make, before both agencies and courts, in order to turn administrative policy in their preferred direction. How can deregulation be defended or instead challenged? When can the Environmental Protection Agency be convinced to regulate more stringently, or less so? What are the possible limits of cost-benefit analysis? How can costs, or benefits, be characterized in a way that makes best sense?

In sum, we have tried to design an administrative law course that contains a range of substantive areas, that conveys a view of the agency as an operating unit, and that provides an understanding of the roles of Congress, the president, and the courts as possible instruments of redress for shortcomings in agency performance.

The book is organized by administrative law topics; examples of substantive regulation and benefit programs are developed in the context of these topics.

We begin in Chapter 2 with a discussion of the constitutional position of the administrative agency. We investigate the reasons behind the departure from the traditional tripartite model of government. Why did the courts fail to use constitutional principles to prevent this departure? As we shall see, the "administrative state" was born (though not without difficulty), and so we arrive at the question posed by Chapter 3: Have agencies proved capable of operating democratically, efficiently, effectively, and fairly? If not, what can be done about it? What empirical data can be brought to bear on this question? (Administrative law is hard to do or to evaluate in an empirical vacuum.) How might administrative law act as a corrective? Chapter 3 emphasizes the policymaking discretion of many administrative agencies — discretion that comes in part from open-ended delegations of authority and in part from their combining traditionally separate governmental powers. Chapter 3 also explores the wide variety of solutions proposed for problems of "agency failure."

Chapter 4 explores the heart of the traditional administrative law course: judicial review of agency factfinding, lawmaking, and policy determination. Chapter 5 considers certain judge-made ("common law") principles of fairness, such as principles of "consistency," that courts apply in reviewing agency decisions. Chapter 6 examines the law concerning two principal methods for making and applying agency policy, namely rulemaking and adjudication. It discusses the constitutional differences between the two methods; it sets forth the statutory and case law that governs them; and it considers the Constitution's "due process" requirement in respect to adjudication. Chapter 7 focuses on the internal workings of the agency, including the "separation of functions" requirement. Chapter 8 examines traditional doctrines of reviewability, standing, ripeness, and the like, which determine when and whether an individual can obtain review from a court.

B. What Is Administrative Law?

Most broadly, administrative law might be defined as legal control of government. More narrowly, we might say that administrative law consists of those legal principles that define the authority and structure of administrative agencies, specify the procedural formalities that agencies use, determine the validity of administrative decisions, and outline the role of reviewing courts and other organs of government in their relation to administrative agencies.

Each particular field of administration has its corresponding substantive and procedural law. Labor law, for example, deals with the substantive principles and procedures used by the National Labor Relations Board (NLRB) and other administrative agencies having responsibility over labor relations. Environmental law deals similarly with the actions and procedures of the Environmental Protection Agency (EPA), the Nuclear Regulatory Commission (NRC), the Department of Health and Human Services (HHS), the Food and Drug Administration (FDA), and other federal and state regulatory agencies with environmental responsibilities. The welfare state and the development of "public interest" advocacy has created such fields as welfare law, consumer protection law, and prison law.

Administrative law deals with the more general principles and rules that cut across the particular substantive fields to embrace all forms of administrative activity. These principles and rules include three basic bodies of law: (1) constitutional law; (2) statutory law, including above all the Administrative Procedure Act (APA); and (3) a form of federal common law, embodied in judicial decisions that do not have a clear constitutional or statutory source.

Administrative law can be a difficult and elusive subject, precisely because of its generality and abstraction from the substantive and procedural law governing specific areas of administration. It is hard to deal with administrative law without knowing a fair bit about the underlying issues of substantive law. An important theme of this book is that we cannot understand the significance of procedural requirements or principles of judicial review apart from the substantive responsibilities of particular agencies and the means available to those agencies for accomplishing their goals. And in applying general principles, courts are sensitive to the identity of the agency whose action is challenged, the reputation and quality of its personnel, its overall mission, the practical difficulties it faces in discharging that mission, the content of the particular action under challenge, and the respective equities of the agency and the affected private parties.

In short: Some courts trust some agencies; some courts distrust some agencies. The absence or lack of trust can matter a great deal to the ultimate outcome.

C. Regulation

The substantive examples used here illustrate typical problems that give rise to regulation and the major types of regulatory programs initiated to deal with those problems. Not every type of problem can be illustrated, nor can all be treated in equal detail. The following taxonomy of regulation is designed to help you understand the sense in which the substantive examples can be considered typical. It is especially important to distinguish among various categories of reasons for regulation. Does regulation promote economic efficiency? Does it redistribute resources, and if so why? Does it promote, or reflect, democracy in some way? How are interest groups involved?

1. Problems Thought to Call for Administrative Regulation

No government can avoid "regulation." The common law is emphatically a regulatory system. It depends on the creation and enforcement, by law, of a set of rights, notably those creating private property and freedom of contract. When understood as a regulatory system, the common law system is often praised; it is also often reviled. Sometimes, the common law system is thought to promote both liberty and economic efficiency; sometimes, it is thought to do neither, and to be undemocratic as well, simply because it is overseen by courts rather than by more accountable officials.

When the common law is under attack, a statutory regime, accompanied by some administrative institution, is a likely solution. This was a principal theme in the New Deal period of the early 1930s, led by President Franklin Delano Roosevelt, when the system of common law ordering was displaced to a significant degree by administrative agencies. In this section, we describe as "administrative regulation" those statutory regimes that displace common law ordering. Sometimes, we use the term "regulation" as a shorthand, but the terms should not disguise the fact that common law ordering is emphatically "regulation" too.

Note also that we focus on legitimate grounds for regulating, but well-organized private groups often seek, and obtain, regulation for their own selfish ends. Environmental law, nominally designed to clean the air, might be used to help farmers, eastern coal companies, and others with a large stake in the outcome. For a classic discussion, see Bruce Ackerman and William Hassler, Clean Coal/Dirty Air (1983). Price regulation, nominally designed to protect consumers, might actually help producers. While we will focus on legitimate reasons for regulation below, the idea that regulation may be a bow to powerful interest groups will play a major role in this book.

a. Market Failures, Economically Defined

One method of analyzing administrative regulation is to view it as an attempt to solve various problems of "market failure" identified by economists. Such a view, which of course is popular with economists, treats the marketplace as the norm and assumes that those who advocate administrative regulation must justify it, by showing that it is needed to achieve an important public objective that the marketplace cannot provide.

Many market "defects" fall within one of the following categories. For more detailed discussion, see Stephen Breyer, Regulation and Its Reform (1982); Anthony Ogus, Regulation (1996).

1. *The need to control monopoly power.* A traditional rationale for price and profit regulation is based on the need to control the exercise of economic power by a "natural monopolist." When economies of scale are so great as to make it inefficient for more than one firm to operate, that firm can increase its profits by restricting output and charging higher than competitive prices.

Under these conditions, regulation aims in part at "allocative efficiency." To the extent that prices are set at levels approximating those that would exist under competitive conditions, they more accurately reflect the comparative costs of real resources used. Consumers are not led by an artificially (monopolistically set) high price for Product A to substitute Product B, which in terms of real resources costs the economy more to produce. Unless prices are set so as to achieve allocative efficiency, there is waste. Raw materials might be combined to satisfy consumer desires more fully; instead, misled by faulty price signals, producers combine those raw materials into products that consumers want less. As long as one believes that, without regulation, the natural monopoly will raise prices substantially, one can reasonably argue that regulated prices will help to achieve allocative efficiency — that is to say, they will help to avoid wasting the world's limited supply of factors of production.

The economic debate about whether regulated prices will avoid allocative waste is complex. And there is much debate over whether apparent natural monopolies really qualify as such; maybe we can identify competitors once we better understand the relevant market. (Do cars compete with railroads, if railroads seem to be natural monopolies? What about airlines? Is cable television a natural monopoly in view of the existence of broadcast television, satellite television, VCRs, radio, and movies?) Note in any event that the rationale for regulation of monopoly power rests not on economic claims alone, but also on other objectives such as fairer income distribution, avoiding discrimination in price or service among customers, and distrust of the social and political (as well as the economic) power of an unregulated monopolist.

We shall explore regulation of the natural monopolist in Chapter 4, using electricity production as an example.

2. *The need to compensate for inadequate information.* For competitive markets to work well, consumers need information with which to evaluate competing products. If consumers lack important information, markets will fail. This idea has been used to support regulation of safety in consumer products and the workplace; of securities markets; of commercial advertising; and much more.

Of course, information is itself a commodity, whose supply reflects cost and demand. The optimal level of information is not full information; who would want to know everything about every possible good? But the market for information may be imperfect. Consumers as a class have an interest in obtaining information, but there may be no satisfactory way for them to share the costs of doing so. Many consumers may be unwilling to pay enough for information from which all will benefit; if so, the "free rider" problem will result in insufficient information. In addition, some products are so complex that individual consumers need the assistance of experts to evaluate them. The issue very much bears on risk regulation. Workers, for example, may lack information about risks that they face in the workplace; consumers may not know much about the dangers associated with certain products.

People also face cognitive and motivational problems in processing information — a point emphasized by behavioral economists. See Richard Thaler, Quasi-Rational Economics (1993). On the cognitive side, people often use heuristic devices that lead to erroneous judgments, especially in dealing with low probability events, about which people may reason poorly. The most well-known of these heuristics is the "availability" heuristic; people think that events are more likely when and if an example can come to mind. This heuristic can distort judgments, by making people neglectful of some risks and unduly fearful of others. See generally Heuristics and Biases: The Psychology of Intuitive Judgement (Thomas Gilovich et al. eds. 2001); Tversky and Kahneman, Judgment Under Uncertainty: Heuristics and Biases, 185 Science 1124 (1974).

On the motivational side, people are sometimes too optimistic, and sometimes they engage in wishful thinking. There is evidence that many people are, pervasively and in the face of the actual facts, "risk optimists"; that is, they tend to believe that they have below-average susceptibility to risks, whether or not this is the case. Consider the fact that the vast majority of people believe that they are better than the average driver and less likely to be involved in a serious accident. People may attempt to reduce "cognitive dissonance" by believing a risk is lower than it is in fact.

Government regulation is sometimes designed to compensate for inadequate information or to lower the costs to consumers or workers of obtaining adequate information. In particular, government action may be justified when (1) suppliers mislead consumers whose available legal remedies, such as private court actions, are expensive or impractical; (2) consumers cannot readily evaluate the information available, such as the potential effectiveness of a drug; or (3) the market on the supply side fails to furnish the information needed or demanded. In the last two instances, the government may seek to provide more or better information or to require producers to supply the information, as in the case of the financial and other disclosures mandated by the Securities and Exchange Commission (SEC), or risk disclosures required by the Occupational Safety and Health Administration (OSHA) or the EPA.

There is also a question whether a regulatory mandate might be justified — as in a flat ban on the use or sale of dangerous products — when information is inadequate or when it is expensive to provide adequate information. The simplest argument here is that products should be banned if, were the information provided, no or very few consumers would want it.

We shall discuss the SEC's work briefly; we shall discuss drug regulation in Chapter 6, and health and safety regulation in Chapter 4.

Collective action problems. Sometimes, individually rational private behavior will produce collective or public harm. Individuals, acting in their rational self-interest, will create a problem that could be solved if and only if they could ensure mutual cooperation.

The clearest cases involve public or collective goods, which are characterized by two features: nonrivalrous consumption (consumption by one person does not create more scarcity for other consumers) and nonexcludability (the good necessarily benefits a group of people, and no one person or subgroup can easily, or at all, be prevented from enjoying it). The standard example is the system of national defense. Once that system is in place, no one can be excluded from it, and the fact that one person is protected does not diminish the protection of others. For the reasons just given, information may qualify as a public good too. In the area of environmental protection, clean air and clean water have the characteristics of public goods: It is hard for one person to enjoy clean air and clean water without many other people enjoying them too.

In a standard formulation, a group of people may face a "prisoner's dilemma" in which rational individual behavior makes the relevant actors worse off than they would be if they could act cooperatively. See, e.g., Jon Elster, The Cement of Society (1993); R. Hardin, Collective Action (1982); Edna Ullmann-Margalit, The Emergence of Norms (1976). If it works well, regulation brings about the necessary cooperation. We discuss environmental problems in Chapter 4.

4. *The need to correct for "externalities"* — *or for the existence of "transactions costs" that make bargaining difficult.* In a traditional formulation, regulation is frequently justified by the need to compensate for the fact that the price of a product does not reflect costs that its production and use impose on society. For example, in an unregulated market the price of steel will not reflect the "externalities" (sometimes referred to as "spillover costs") that its manufacture imposes in the form of air pollution. Neither the manufacturer nor the consumer of its products bears these costs. As a result, the demand

for steel will be greater than it should be, because it is higher than it would be if buyers had to pay for the cost of its adverse side effects. Many regulatory statutes can be seen as an effort to respond to this problem.

This is a conventional way of seeing the problem; it has been refocused by the seminal work of Nobel Prize winner Ronald Coase. See Coase, The Problem of Social Cost, 3 J.L. & Econ. 1 (1960). Coase's suggestion, now accepted by many economists and economically inspired law professors, is that the harmful effects of pollution should not be seen as externalities. Those costs result both from the steel company's production process and the fact that people have chosen to live near the plant. On this view, the steel company is not imposing spillovers or externalities on the people who live near the plant; the problem results from a large number of acts and omissions on both sides. (Of course, it would be possible to generate a moral argument to suggest that one or another side is really "responsible" or "at fault.") An efficient result would come about if the various parties were able to bargain with one another to the solution that they jointly prefer. "Transactions costs" — the cost of coming together to reach agreement — prevent bargains from occurring. Thus, the problem of externalities might be seen as one of transactions costs; this is one of Coase's largest claims or contributions.

In theory, steel users and pollution sufferers might agree to share the cost of pollution reduction through the installation of antipollution equipment. In this way, it is easy to see the problem of externalities as an underlying problem of transaction costs. Bargaining is impracticable because of transaction costs; regulation is a way of correcting for that fact. Environmental regulation is the most obvious example of regulation designed to deal with externality problems or transactions costs. As noted, aspects of such regulation will be discussed in Chapter 4 and elsewhere.

b. Less Secure Economic Grounds

There are some less conventional economic arguments for administrative regulation.

1. *The need to control "windfall" profits.* "Rents" as "windfall profits" may result from sudden increases in commodity prices. The profits may benefit any firm that holds a stock of that commodity or controls any nonduplicable low-cost source of supply.

Thus, those who own large stocks of oil are in a position to obtain windfall profits when the OPEC countries raise the price of their new oil; those who have large stocks of coffee are in a similar position when the price of coffee goes up; owners of old natural gas, if free to raise their prices, could obtain a "windfall" when the costs of finding new natural gas rise; and those who own existing housing could reap windfall profits as long as construction costs rise faster than other costs. Such profits are common in competitive and noncompetitive industries alike. Ordinarily, they are not regulated, but when they are large in amount and do not reflect any particular talent or skill on the part of producers, there may be a demand for regulation. The object of the regulation is to transfer allegedly undeserved profits from producers (or owners) of the scarce resource to consumers (or taxpayers). This is not a conventional economic argument for regulation, because as stated, the argument does not refer to any inefficiency, or market failure, for which the law is a remedy.

We shall discuss the subject of rent control briefly in Chapter 3.

2. *The need to eliminate "excessive" competition.* A commonly advanced justification for the regulation of trucking companies, airplane companies, and shipping firms is the asserted need to control "excessive," "destructive," or "unfair" competition. This argument is made in various ways, but underlying each is the view that if prices are too low most of the competing firms will go out of business. Only one or two firms will survive, and they will have a free rein in setting prices. Products and services will end up being too costly.

One argument has historic roots. When airline regulation began in the mid-1930s, the airlines argued for protection against "excessive competition." Although they did not mention the large government subsidies they were then receiving, these subsidies may have led in part to their fear of "excessive" price cutting. The subsidy program gave each airline an incentive to increase its size by cutting its prices well below cost, making up the resulting loss in revenues by means of the subsidy. Protection was provided in the form of minimum price regulation by the now defunct Civil Aeronautics Board (CAB). Similarly, minimum price regulation of trucking — which came about for several reasons — was in part a response to claims by the railroads that it was "unfair" to regulate them while leaving the unregulated truckers free to compete for the railroads' most lucrative business.

A second rationale for regulating excessive competition arises in the case of industries with large fixed costs and cyclical demand. The firms in the industry, pricing at incremental cost during an economic downswing, may find they have insufficient revenue to continue production. Yet in some cases to close their plants is inefficient, since it is more expensive to reopen plants during the next upswing than to keep them open continuously. This rationale might be used to justify a "depression cartel" that sets price floors and allots market shares. It has not been used to justify existing regulation in the United States, except in agriculture.

A third rationale — articulated in the antitrust laws — relates to the possibility of "predatory" pricing. A dominant firm sets prices below variable costs, with the objective of driving its rivals out of business and then raising its prices and recouping its lost profits before any new firms, attracted by the higher prices, enter the industry.

In Chapter 6, we shall examine the case of airline regulation and deregulation, which — like trucking, ocean shipping, and milk production — have been supported on the grounds of excessive competition.

3. *The need to alleviate scarcity.* It is sometimes argued that regulation is needed to allocate an item in short supply. Sudden and dramatic price increases or sudden problems (for example, an oil boycott) have led to the claim that allocation through market prices will cause too sudden or too serious a hardship on many users. It is important to bear in mind that a shortage may be the result of an ongoing regulatory program (as has been asserted in the case of natural gas). A shortage may also reflect a deliberate decision to abandon the market and use regulatory allocation to achieve "public interest" objectives, which are often neither clear nor specific (for example, television licenses). We shall explore television and natural gas regulation in Chapter 5.

4. *Agency problems.* Sometimes a person other than the buyer makes purchasing decisions for the buyer, or helps to pay for the buyer's purchase, or both. Market forces may then be distorted, generally causing greater consumption than if the buyer had to make the purchase and pay for it entirely alone. Medical care is an example. When ethical or other institutional constraints, or direct supervision by the physician, fail to control the amount of such purchases, government regulation may be demanded to reduce the excessive use of medical resources.

c. Redistribution

Sometimes, regulation is justified not as a way of promoting efficiency but instead as a means of redistributing resources from one group to another. Statutes directly transferring resources to the poor, such as the Social Security Act, are the most obvious examples. Administrative agencies making transfer payments — as opposed to engaging in regulation of private conduct — are the most obvious examples of redistributive agencies. But sometimes redistributive measures are regulatory rather than direct transfers. Examples include the minimum wage law, the maximum hour law, and much of the Fair Labor Standards Act. Indeed, much of modern regulation can be understood as redistributive in character. Frequently, regulation makes some people better off while making other people worse off — and these effects are actively sought by those who support such laws.

But when is redistributive regulation justified in principle? Note at this point that regulation, such as minimum wage and maximum hour laws, does not directly transfer resources from those who are rich to those who are poor. From the point of view of those who want to help the poor, the distributive consequences of regulation might be unfortunate or even perverse — a point to which we shall shortly return.

On behalf of redistributive laws, unequal bargaining power, based on unequal starting points, is sometimes invoked as a rationale for regulation. Unequal bargaining power may overlap with absence of information; consider possible problems faced by workers relying on the market to reduce cancer risks. Sometimes, occupational safety and health regulation is justified on redistributive grounds, by pointing to the unequal positions of some workers. Also consider efforts to regulate large firms to protect small firms with whom they deal. Examples include state regulations prescribing standard forms for insurance policies and the development by the courts of the "contract of adhesion" doctrine. In some instances, Congress has granted small sellers an exemption from the antitrust laws, thereby allowing them to organize to deal more effectively with a large buyer. This was the justification offered for the antitrust exemption granted to agricultural and fishing cooperatives. It is also used to support both the exemption of trade unions from the antitrust laws and NLRB regulation to ensure collective bargaining rights.

But redistributive rationales for regulation should be taken with a grain of salt. The reason is simple and pragmatic: *It is not clear that efforts to redistribute resources through regulation work well or, indeed, work at all.* Many people claim, with much plausibility, that the minimum wage does not operate as a direct transfer of resources from employers to employees, but that it instead has complex distributive consequences, some of them unfortunate. Increases in the minimum wage, for example, may increase unemployment and raise prices. This is a disputed empirical question. For various views, see David Card and Alan Krueger, Myth and Measurement: The New Economics of the Minimum Wage (1995); Finis Welsh, Minimum Wage: Issues and Evidence (1978); Shaviro, The Minimum Wage, the Earned Income Tax Credit, and Optimal Subsidy Policy, 64 U. Chi. L. Rev. 405 (1997). Similarly, rent control laws do not simply redistribute resources to the poor or even to tenants at the expense of landlords; they help existing tenants, but they may hurt prospective tenants and also diminish the aggregate stock of available housing. The public interest argument may well be a disguise for the private interest of well-organized factions.

Of course, many statutes with redistributive goals should be seen as the product of political power wielded by self-interested private groups. In fact, this point is a cautionary one about any "public interest" argument for regulation.

d. Nonmarket or Collective Values

Departing from the economic model, some regulatory programs can be understood as an effort to promote nonmarket values, or democratic aspirations, or considered judgments on the part of some segments of society. Some people, for example, may want public affairs and educational programming on television, even though their own consumption patterns favor situation comedies; they may want environmental law to protect pristine areas whether or not they use public parks; they may support regulation to protect endangered species even if they do not take steps to visit or study such species. Social or cultural norms may encourage political participants to seek regulation of this kind even if there is no conventional market failure.

Thus some people argue that purely economic accounts of regulation involve a "category mistake"; they use economic thinking, best suited for the market domain, as the model for the political domain. See Mark Sagoff, The Economy of the Earth (1992); Lisa Heinzerling and Frank Ackerman, Priceless (2004); Stewart, Regulation in a Liberal State: The Role of Noncommodity Values, 92 Yale L.J. 1537 (1983). On this view, existing preferences should not be taken as sacrosanct or as given; government legitimately engages in a degree of preference-shaping. We will encounter this argument in connection with regulation of broadcasting and protection of the environment.

e. Disadvantage and Caste

Some regulatory programs have emerged as a result of efforts to overcome systematic forms of social disadvantage or caste-like features in contemporary society. Here too, government attempts to shape preferences, rather than take them as given; its goal is to make people less likely to treat people differently on the basis of some characteristic. Laws banning discrimination on the basis of race, sex, age, and disability are the most familiar examples. Each of these laws is accompanied by a complex system of administrative enforcement. Thus, civil rights law is in significant part administrative law. And there are controversial questions about whether such programs carry out their intended purposes. See, e.g., Richard Epstein, Forbidden Grounds (1992).

f. Planning

Government regulation is occasionally justified on the ground that without it the firms in an industry would not produce their products in an economically efficient manner. European governments have sometimes intervened to overcome conservative business practices by "nationalizing" an industry, such as steel. And regulatory agencies in the United States have sometimes sought to engage in industrywide "planning." Sometimes, the interest in planning is accompanied by a claim that economic markets are insufficiently democratic; perhaps administrators, responsive to the electorate, might be able to take account of considerations that markets disregard.

g. Paternalism

Finally, some kinds of regulation have an element of paternalism. They are at least partly justified on the grounds that government has a certain obligation to protect individuals from their own confusion and irresponsibility. An example is the requirement that motorcycle riders wear helmets (although, of course, arguments related to the public interest, including lack of information and spillovers, also support such a requirement). Similar motives play a significant role in such government decisions as the mandating of secondary school education. And paternalistic grounds for regulation play a role in control of risks.

Some support for paternalism might be found in research finding that at the time of decision, people systematically misunderstand what they will actually experience. See D. Kahneman, New Challenges to the Rationality Assumption, in The Rational Foundations of Economic Behavior (K. Arrow et al. eds., 1996). There is also a possibility that some people have not just "preferences" but "preferences about their preferences" — like Ulysses when threatened by the Sirens, people may seek the aid of external forces to protect themselves against their own misjudgment. See J. Elster, Ulysses and the Sirens (1981). See, on some of these issues, Sunstein and Thaler, Libertarian Paternalism Is Not an Oxymoron, 70 U. Chi. L. Rev. 1159 (2003); Jolls, Sunstein, and Thaler, A Behavioral Approach to Law and Economics, 50 Stan. L. Rev. 1467 (1998).

Bear in mind that many regulatory programs are said to have multiple justifications. With respect to regulation of workplace safety, for example, it can be argued that bargaining between employers and employees fails to take account of the interests of those not represented at the bargaining table, such as other citizens who help to pay the costs of government health and disability programs. This is an externalities rationale. On the other hand, one might believe that workers do not know enough about the risks of accidents to insist on adequate safety expenditures. On this view, there is an information defect in the market. One might also believe that occupation regulation will have good redistributive effects. Finally, workers may overlook the likely seriousness of accidents and health hazards. If regulation is an effort to give them what they ought to want, it rests on a paternalistic rationale. Because diverse ideas may underlie the same regulatory statute, we can say that such statutes are frequently "incompletely theorized" in the sense that a social judgment on behalf of the statute is unaccompanied by a complete account of what theory really underlies the statute.

Each rationale, of course, may suggest a different remedy. Identification of the most appropriate rationale will assist in choosing the regulatory tool best suited to the problem at hand.

2. The Classic Regulatory Tools

The great variety of regulatory problems makes it tempting to conclude that each program or system of regulation is unique. In a way this is true, but it is also quite misleading. As indicated above, the tools at the agency's disposal can be categorized. More importantly, many different regulatory programs can be grouped into a variety of different types. They include (1) cost-of-service ratemaking; (2) allocation in accordance with a public interest standard; (3) standard-setting; (4) historically based price-setting, or allocation; (5) screening or licensing; (6) fees or taxes; (7) provision of information; (8) subsidies; and (9) noncoercive efforts to produce cooperation through moral suasion or political incentives. Each of these types of regulation is typically accompanied by a particular set of significant characteristics. Recognize too that the various forms of classic regulation have certain characteristics in common because almost all such programs are created and operate subject to the following four constraints:

First, the regulator and regulated industries are likely to have an adversarial relationship because the regulator will often be in a position to compel an industry to act in ways it would not choose to act. This is less true, of course, with less aggressive forms of regulation.

Second, the regulator is an institutional bureaucracy operated by administrators or civil servants who may well prefer to design rules that they can administer with relative ease.

Third, new regulatory programs usually copy old ones. For example, the framers of the Federal Aviation Act in 1937 copied the language of the Motor Carrier Act of 1935, which stemmed from the Interstate Commerce Act of 1887, whose framers modeled their statute on the British Railroad Act of 1845. Those devising new programs have almost always been the prisoners of history.

Fourth, regulatory decisions are subject to the requirements of administrative law, usually including the APA. Agencies must usually act with an eye to being able to justify their decisions before a court of law, which may be asked to decide whether an agency's decision in a particular case was rational and was reached through fair procedures.

In this book, you will explore instances of each of these typical modes of regulation. Cost-of-service ratemaking is the most commonly used method for regulating prices in a wide variety of individual industries, ranging from trucking and natural gas production to hospitals. It is examined in the context of electricity regulation in Chapter 4. Allocation in accordance with a public interest standard is commonly used when the government wishes to hand out a commodity or a permission that is in short supply. It is examined in the context of television regulation (Chapter 5). It is often used as well when the government allocates trucking licenses, liquor licenses, or such commodities as natural gas. Historically based price regulation is examined in its most common context — a governmental effort to impose nationwide price controls (Chapter 2). This type of regulation has also been used to control oil prices and has been suggested as a method for controlling hospital costs. Licensing as screening is examined in the context of a drug regulation (Chapter 6). It is used when an agency must clear or certify a particular item as safe or fit to be sold. Standard-setting is examined specifically in the context of auto safety and OSHA safety regulation standards (airbags) in Chapter 4. It also recurs throughout many of the examples used in the book. Fees or taxes have played a role in occupational safety and environmental protection as well. Subsidies are used to regulate agricultural prices and occasionally in the environmental context. Information disclosure, done or compelled by the public, has played a role in securities regulation, product safety, occupational safety and health, and telecommunications. Cooperation and moral suasion, not strictly speaking a form of regulation, have played a role in many contexts, including communications (where the Federal Communications Commission (FCC) has argued for greater attention to educational programming for children) and environmental protection (where the EPA has urged voluntary reductions in toxic releases).

In examining instances of these regulatory techniques, we have made an effort to stress significant characteristics of the mode, that is to say, features or difficulties that tend to recur whenever the particular form of regulation is applied.

Because the book is organized in terms of administrative law topics, it may be helpful here to list the extent to which we explore examples of regulation, first categorized by their principal rationale, and then by type of regulatory program used:

Rationale	Example	Chapter
monopoly power	electricity	4
information defect	safety	4
spillovers, collective action problems	environment	4
windfall profit control	natural gas	5
excessive competition	airlines	6
scarcity	television	5

Mode of Regulation	Example	Chapter
cost-of-service ratemaking	electricity	4
historically based price regulation	economy-wide price controls	2
public interest allocation	television	5
screening	drugs	4, 6
standard-setting	auto airbags, carcinogens & other examples	4 & throughout
fees or taxes	communications, workers' compensation	6
subsidies	agriculture, environmental law	4
information disclosure	securities law, occupational safety	4
cooperation and moral suasion	communications, environmental law	4

3. The Historical Development of Administrative Government and Administrative Law

What follows is a brief historical survey of the development of administrative law in response to the rise of administrative government. As we will see, administrative law doctrine is closely entangled with high-level political disputes about the actual and appropriate role of government.

a. English Antecedents

The origins of American administrative law lie in the common law courts of England. In short, administrative law grew out of common law, and the common law has a large and continuing influence on American administrative law.

Officers of the Crown, such as bailiffs or sheriffs, were subject to damage liability if (1) an aggrieved citizen could establish that the officer had committed what was prima facie a common law wrong (such as trespass or battery) that (2) the officer was unable to justify by reference to statute or higher authority. This principle — of accountability of government officials to damage suits in the regular courts of law — was a fundamental element of the English lawyer's conception of the "rule of law." W. Dicey, The Law of the Constitution 189 (8th ed. 1915). But the common law damage remedy was often inadequate. The actions of government officials could not always be pigeonholed into the common law forms of action. In addition, courts sensitive to the need for some administrative flexibility built up doctrines of official privilege based on the exercise of discretionary authority. Even if a plaintiff prevailed, the defendant official might be unable to satisfy the judgment out of his own pocket, or damages might not afford fully adequate relief.

In response to these and other limitations, the common law courts began in the seventeenth century to refashion old writs and develop new ones for the specific purpose of controlling official action. For example, the writ of mandamus was developed to require officials to grant or restore to citizens entitlements, such as the incumbency of a public office, owing to them as of right. The writ of prohibition was used to preclude administrative authorities from exercising powers not within their jurisdiction. Courts refashioned the writ of certiorari to review particular decisions of administrative bodies and invalidate those decisions found to be without statutory warrant or otherwise in excess of the administrators' "jurisdiction."

These writs were used by the common lawyers to control a growing variety of administrative functions, including the responsibility of local authorities for relief of the poor, the efforts of commissions to drain fens and other wetlands for agriculture, and the governance of the colleges of Oxford and Cambridge. Judicial review of administrative action was also available in cases where administrative officials resorted to courts to enforce their orders. And the Chancellor's Court of Equity began to develop the injunctive remedy as a means of controlling unlawful official action when an irreparable injury could be shown. The common law courts, however, continued to play the leading role in checking official power.

This reliance on the independent judiciary was not an inevitable solution to the need in modern government for an institution — in addition to the overworked legislature and chief executive — for controlling administrative action. Some nations, such as Italy and France, have relied on well-staffed and specialized tribunals, comprised of high-ranking civil servants and located within the administrative bureaucracy itself, to control the actions of administrators. Indeed, in England during the sixteenth and seventeenth centuries the Tudor and Stuart monarchs had developed powerful administrative tribunals, founded on the asserted prerogative powers of the Crown, that were employed to control subordinate officials in their relation to the citizenry. These bodies — like the Court of Star Chamber and the Court of High Commission — might well have evolved into a bureaucratic version of administrative justice analogous to the present French Conseil d'Etat or the Italian Consiglio di Stato. But this line of development was cut short in Britain by the Glorious Revolution of 1688, the political triumph of parliamentary government, and the related celebration of the independent judiciary as an important check on executive power.

b. The American Experience to 1875

The American colonies inherited the English system of common law writs and the Chancellor's injunctive power as mechanisms for the control of administrative officials. This system of judicial remedies formed the central basis of administrative law in the state and federal courts during the first 100 years of the Republic. Our account here is brief and impressionistic.

The era 1775-1875 is often viewed as one of relatively uninhibited laissez-faire. But take this conventional view with many grains of salt; a great deal happened in this long period, and much of it did not involve laissez-faire. In fact, the idea of laissez-faire had its greatest currency not in this period but in the first two decades of the twentieth century, partly fueled by the "free labor!" rhetoric of the antislavery movement. Note in this regard that the Constitution was a self-conscious rejection of the Articles of Confederation, partly because of the widespread view that the national government was too weak. The Framers sought to create a more active and centralized government, one that would have an energetic executive, accompanied by administrative institutions (including the first cabinet departments). See F. Bourgin, The Great Challenge: The Myth of Laissez-Faire in the Early Republic (1989); see also S. Beer, To Make a Nation (1993). Alexander Hamilton spoke above all on behalf of this vision.

Moreover, even during the alleged heyday of laissez-faire, national and state governments played a substantial role in the economy. For example, the federal government imposed taxes (principally tariffs, which had an important effect on external trade, and excise taxes), distributed the public lands to homesteaders and railroads, granted patents, paid military pensions, regulated relations with native Americans, controlled immigration, regulated marine navigation and commerce, and operated the post office. State governments were even more active, promoting (often with state funds or grants of monopolies) the construction of railroads, canals, turnpikes, and other transportation infrastructure, and controlling commercial enterprises through hand-tailored corporate charters.

But certainly the role of administrative government in economic and social life was far less extensive and centralized than it is today. In fact, the publication of Adam Smith's Wealth of Nations in 1776 coincided with the progressive dismantlement of Britain's pervasive system of mercantilist control of the national economy, which was replaced by the central government and regulation of local product and labor markets by guilds. The principle of free and equal markets unfettered by government restrictions and grants of monopolistic "privilege" played a significant role in post-Revolutionary America. As a result, responsibility for the allocation of resources in the economy and the distribution of wages, rents, and profits was shifted to a large degree from administrative officials to the marketplace and to the judges who formulated the rules of tort, property, and contract that defined the grounds and terms of market exchange.

What was the place of administrative law in this era? The basic answer is that at the behest of aggrieved citizens, American courts adapted the traditional writs in an effort to exert a measure of control over the administrative officials responsible for these programs. From our perspective, the writ system appears a clumsy device, hedged with technicalities and exhibiting surprising gaps in the availability of effective relief. In applying these remedies, the courts relied on the concept of "jurisdiction" to establish a sharp distinction between those actions that were within administrators' authority, and therefore completely beyond further court review, from those actions that were in excess of "jurisdiction" and therefore subject to judicial invalidation. The doctrinal effort to draw a sharp division between the responsibilities of administrators and courts ignored the possibility, developed at great length in our own era, of a category of administrative discretion that is subject to limited and partial judicial control and reexamination. However, courts applied the notion of "jurisdiction" with flexibility to achieve substantial justice in particular cases, and the writ system appears to have worked tolerably well — given the relatively limited intrusiveness of administrative powers in the early decades of the Republic.

c. 1875 to 1930: The Rise of Administrative Regulation and the Traditional Model of Administrative Law

A decisive first step in the development of modern administrative law was the growth of administrative regulation in the latter half of the nineteenth century. This development first occurred at the state level, in the form of rate regulation of railroads, grain elevators, and other natural monopolies. The limitations of state regulation of interstate railroad operations led to the establishment in 1887 of the first great federal regulatory agency, the Interstate Commerce Commission (ICC) (abolished in 1995).

Conflicting views of Why create ICC.

Why was the ICC created? The political explanation is the subject of much controversy. A traditional view is that the ICC was created to protect shippers (especially small shippers) from the exercise of monopoly power and rate discrimination by larger carriers. Another view more broadly defined the problem of the "market failure" to include "destructive competition" and wasteful and duplicative services. In this view, the commission was established not merely to shift income from railroads to shippers, but to indicate a more general public interest in an efficient transportation system through planning by expert administrators. This view is reflected in the notion that the ICC was to be "independent" of politics and be composed of commissioners and staff experts in railroading. A revisionist view is that the commission was created and administered to advance the interests of the railroads by protecting them against the rigors of competition. Still others have asserted that the ICC was not "captured" by the railroads but by shippers, and that short-sighted and inept regulation fatally weakened the railroads by destroying innovation and denying them needed revenues.

These conflicting views are of some importance, for they reflect competing views about why legislatures create administration regulation. Why do agencies exist? What political forces bring them about? Similar competing interpretations can be found in debates over many other agencies, and skepticism about interest-group forces may represent the intellectual roots of the contemporary sense of administrative failure that we explore in Chapter 3. In any case, it is important to ask about the role of powerful private groups in the creation and operation of regulatory schemes.

Whatever the ultimate explanation for the creation of the ICC or other early regulatory bodies (such as the Federal Trade Commission (FTC), created in 1914), regulated firms often tried to use courts to block regulatory decisions. The decisions of federal and state courts — often using common law ideas to stop regulation — laid the foundations of modern administrative law. In many instances, the common law writ system was supplanted by statutory provisions providing for judicial review of the regulatory body's decision. Many statutes also provided for a trial-type hearing before the regulatory agency to develop a factual record that would serve as the basis for agency action. When such statutory provisions were absent, courts often insisted on a trial-type administrative hearing as a requirement of due process. Reviewing courts would then carefully scrutinize the agency's decision to determine whether, on the basis of the hearing record, the agency's factual findings were reasonable, whether the agency had acted within its statutory authority and had based its decision on legally relevant factors, and whether the decision was not arbitrary in the particular circumstances.

In this light, we can identify what we shall call the traditional model of administrative law, which evolved from statutory enactments and judicial decisions. The purpose of the traditional model was to control government intrusions into private liberty and property interests. The traditional model had four essential elements:

✗ Traditional Model

Transmission Belt.

1. *The legislature must authorize administrative sanctions on private persons through rules or standards that limit agency discretion.* This principle reflects the view that administrative officials possess no inherent powers over private liberty or property, and that official intrusions into such interests must be authorized by the legislature as the institutionalized mechanism of popular consent in representative government. One goal of this principle is to promote traditional rule-of-law values — evenhanded treatment, limited official discretion to exploit government powers for personal or arbitrary ends, and predictability.

2. *The procedures used by the agency must tend to ensure agency compliance with legislative directives.* To ensure that agencies actually adhere to statutory authority and dispense evenhanded justice, agency procedures must be designed to promote the accurate, impartial, and rational application of legislative directives to given cases or classes of cases. In cases involving enforcement of regulatory controls and sanctions, this requirement normally translated into trial-type hearings. In these hearings the person subject to regulation was entitled to present evidence and challenge the legal and factual basis of the agency's authority to act. The agency was then required to decide the matter exclusively on the basis of the record thus generated.

3. *Judicial review must be available to ensure that agencies use accurate and impartial decisionmaking procedures and comply with legislative directives.*

4. *Agency processes must facilitate the exercise of judicial review.* A democratic system need not rely on judicial review to ensure that the agency acts within its legislative mandate. Legislative oversight, media scrutiny, and internal bureaucratic checks might serve this purpose. But our system has placed heavy reliance on the independent judiciary to police official conformance to statutory authorization by reviewing both the factual and legal basis for administrative imposition of controls. This reliance on judicial review requires that agencies use procedures that will facilitate review, including development of an orderly administrative record and articulation by officials of the factual findings and legal conclusions that form the basis for agency actions.

These four elements of the traditional model at least theoretically serve to limit and legitimate administrative power by functioning as a "transmission belt" to ensure that particular agency actions have been legislatively authorized. In the early period, however, the courts deployed these elements in a spirit that was very often antagonistic or unsympathetic to administrative government. For example, the statutory authority of the ICC was narrowly construed, and the federal judiciary often paid little heed to the decisions of the FTC, viewing the agency as essentially a subordinate factfinder. The basic impact of hearing procedures and judicial review was to constrain the effective power of the new regulatory bodies to control business conduct.

This pattern undoubtedly reflected the courts' enthusiasm for the common law, their preference for free markets, and their distrust of the substantive judgments that underlay the rise of administrative agencies. They also reflected a more general judicial distrust of administrative agencies, which threatened to undermine long-standing notions of private right and also to circumvent separation-of-power safeguards. Importantly, regulatory agencies represented a large threat to established traditions that placed major reliance for resource allocation on private market exchanges and the common law decisions of judges — traditions that often favored business and allied financial interests. Congress and the states continued to create new regulatory agencies, even during the 1920s heyday of pro-business "normalcy."

d. The New Deal and Beyond: 1932-1945

Franklin Delano Roosevelt's New Deal was a watershed for the development of American administrative law. Indeed, the New Deal is sometimes described as a "constitutional moment" because it represented a fundamental rethinking of the preexisting constitutional structure. See Bruce Ackerman, We the People vol. 1 (1991). Whether or not it qualifies as a constitutional moment, the New Deal greatly revised the basic cornerstones of the Constitution: the previous conceptions of individual rights, federalism, and separation of powers (or checks and balances), including judicial review. Because of the centrality of the New Deal to modern administrative law, it is worth spending a little time on each of these revisions. A general treatment can be found in Cass R. Sunstein, The Second Bill of Rights (2004).

During the conditions of the Great Depression, the common law catalog of rights was thought to include too much and too little. It was thought to include too much because it protected, more strongly than it should, rights of property and freedom of contract from governmental revision. It was thought to protect too little because it did not include basic rights to individual "security." Thus, the New Dealers sought to add a range of social and economic guarantees. President Roosevelt attempted to summarize the point in his famous 1944 State of the Union address, where he called for a Second Bill of Rights, including the right to a good education; the right to earn enough to provide adequate food, clothing, and recreation; the right to adequate medical care; the right to a decent home; the right to a useful and remunerative job; and the right to adequate protection from the economic fears of old age, sickness, accident, and unemployment. "I ask Congress to explore the means for implementing this economic bill of rights — for it is definitely the responsibility of the Congress to do so." Views of this kind were part of, and helped lead to, a new conception of individual rights, one that departed significantly from the conception that underlay the traditional model.

Federalism was of course a central part of the original constitutional plan, with states being regarded as self-governing communities, and with the right of "exit" being seen as an important guarantor of individual liberty. In the New Deal period, however, states were not really regarded as arenas for self-government, and the right of exit from one state to another no longer appeared to be a safeguard against tyranny. On the contrary, states appeared to be dominated by powerful interest groups. They were seen, by many New Dealers, as ineffectual barriers to both economic efficiency and democratic self-government, with the right of exit preventing states from doing what needed to be done. If states tried to act, revenue-producing industries would simply leave; and this would deter states from acting. Thus, the New Deal produced a dramatic increase in national authority, with Congress and the president coming to have dramatically increased powers. Much of the authority traditionally enjoyed by states was rapidly transferred to the national government.

In some ways most important, the system of checks and balances and separation of powers seemed an obstacle to effective governance. See James Landis, The Administrative Process (1938). Businesses do not run themselves on the principle of separation of powers — why, many New Dealers asked, should governments? Finding such questions unanswerable, the New Dealers moved in two novel directions. First, they gave the president powers of lawmaking and adjudication. Second, they increased the size and importance of the "independent" regulatory commissions.

More particularly, the New Dealers created a host of new administrative agencies in Washington, sharply expanding the extent of intervention by the federal government in economic affairs and laying the foundations of a national welfare state. These developments of course responded to the dramatic collapse of the economy in the Great Depression, which — in the view of many people — demonstrated that the market could not be trusted to serve the social and economic welfare of the nation. Congress responded enthusiastically to the president's call for new regulatory authorities to manage the economy. A host of zealous lawyers and academics descended on the nation's capital with a strong belief in the inevitability and viability of centralized economic planning.

The new administration's most ambitious effort at pervasive economic planning, the *New New Deal Agencies* National Recovery Administration, fizzled and was eventually invalidated as unconstitutional by the Supreme Court. But other regulatory programs survived and grew, as a reconstituted Court ultimately sustained sweeping extensions of federal economic regulation under the commerce power of Congress. The SEC was created to regulate the nation's capital markets. The NLRB was authorized to encourage the formation of unions and the development of collective bargaining in industry. Federal minimum wage and maximum hour legislation, and a national program for state employment compensation, also had an impact on labor markets. The FCC and the CAB were established to oversee important sectors of the economy. Extensive government intervention in agricultural pricing and output was undertaken, and government control over banking was extended. The basic rationale of these and other measures was to "save capitalism from itself" by correcting the most obvious failures of the unregulated market while avoiding the socialist alternative of direct government ownership of business enterprise.

These new measures were bitterly assailed by many business leaders and members of *Criticisms* the corporate bar, who contended that administrators exercised an essentially lawless discretion in a highly biased fashion. The NLRB, for example, was attacked as blatantly antimanagement. It and other agencies were particularly criticized for combining prosecutorial and adjudicatory functions; lawyers representing business complained of prejudgment, one-sided factfinding, and other departures from the judicial ideal of disinterested decisionmaking. Critics of the administrative process, including the American Bar Association (ABA), sought to transfer the agencies' adjudicatory functions to independent tribunals and to impose detailed procedural checks and stringent judicial review on agency action.

On the other hand, defenders of the administrative process sought to justify the agencies' combination of functions and to minimize procedural formalities and judicial review. They argued that effective performance, and even salvation of the economy, required administrative controls involving expert knowledge, mixed powers, and discretionary management analogous to that exercised by business leaders. Successful administration was said to be incompatible with legalistic formalities and to involve technical issues beyond the undertaking of lay judges. In place of legalistic safeguards, defenders of the New Deal agencies relied on the expert professionalism of administrators and political control by the president to prevent potential abuses.

During the earlier years of the New Deal, the federal courts often sided with critics of *Early Federal Adjudication of Admin Agencies.* the new regulatory programs. They invalidated many of the authorizing statutes as unconstitutional, narrowly construed the powers of other agencies, and closely scrutinized particular regulatory decisions. These decisions provoked vocal political criticism from Congress, the administration, and the press. Many people argued that the federal courts, and particularly the Supreme Court, were obstructing the popular will and thwarting the economic survival of the nation. President Roosevelt devised a "court-packing" plan to expand the membership of the Supreme Court with nominees of his own selection. Although it did not ultimately succeed, the proposal's threat to the Court's autonomy may have helped persuade one or more "swing" votes on the Court to shift, resulting in decisions that sustained the constitutional validity of New Deal administrative programs. Attrition on the bench thereafter gave the president the opportunity to replace some of the most conservative members of the Court with people such as Hugo Black, a populist southern senator with a strong pro-New Deal voting record; William O. Douglas, former Chairman of the SEC; and Felix Frankfurter, public advocate and intellectual sparkplug of many New Deal programs.

In a relatively short time, the Supreme Court (and with it, much of the lower federal judiciary) swung from almost undisguised hostility toward the new programs of administration to conspicuous deference to the agencies and the president. The availability of judicial review of administrative action was curtailed, and particular agency decisions were frequently sustained with judicial obeisance to the mysteries of administrative expertise. The defenders of the administrative process appeared to have substantially succeeded in insulating agency decisions from judicial check.

e. 1945 to 1962: The Administrative Procedure Act (APA) and the Maturation of the Traditional Model of Administrative Law

The key point in this interim period is the development of a "working compromise" between New Deal enthusiasts and those most critical of new regulatory institutions. The compromise, embodied in the APA, consisted largely of procedural checks and judicial review as responses to the largest perceived problem: administrative discretion.

While the federal courts were becoming more deferential to the administrative process, critics of the New Deal gained political strength. The national sense of crisis faded, and the president's program showed far less than total success in reviving the economy. In 1940, Congress passed the Walter-Logan bill, which would have imposed standardized procedural requirements on federal agencies and mandated a broad availability and scope for judicial review of agency decisions. The bill, supported by the ABA, was vetoed by President Roosevelt, who said that it represented "repeated efforts by a combination of lawyers who desire to have all the processes of government conducted through lawsuits and of interests which desire to escape regulation."

Despite the veto, many people accepted the need for some form of legislation to respond to perceived unfairness in the administrative process and to rationalize disparate administrative practices along more consistent lines. In 1939, Roosevelt established the Attorney General's Committee on Administrative Procedure, chaired by Dean Acheson and composed of distinguished practitioners, judges, and academics. The committee's report, issued in 1941, was based on an extensive series of careful empirical studies of federal administrative agencies. A minority of the committee recommended legislation that would create more standardized procedures for federal agencies, would require more searching judicial review, and would separate adjudicatory from prosecutorial functions. The majority, while concurring in the need for standardizing legislation, favored greater scope for agency flexibility in organization and decisionmaking practices and sought to meet the "combination of functions" problem by creating independent hearing examiners to conduct adjudicatory hearings in the first instance.

After long congressional consideration, a compromise measure was adopted in 1946 as the Federal Administrative Procedure Act, now codified in 5 U.S.C. §§551 et seq. The provisions of the APA will be examined in greater detail in later chapters. Its principal elements are as follows.

Section 2 of the act, 5 U.S.C. §551, contains definitions establishing the act's terms and coverage. Section 3, 5 U.S.C. §552, establishes requirements for publication of certain rules and regulations in the Federal Register and requires agencies to make other important decisions and documents available to the public on request. These provisions were subsequently amended in 1966, 1974, and 1976 to require that all documents in the agency's possession, with certain enumerated exceptions, be made available to members of the public, and to require, again with enumerated exceptions, that meetings of multi-member agencies be open to the public.

Sections 4 through 8, 5 U.S.C. §§553-558, deal with the procedural formalities that agencies must observe in decisionmaking; these are discussed in detail in Chapters 5 and 6. The purpose of the APA was to define and systematize such formalities, although particular statutes and agency regulations may impose different or additional requirements. The act establishes a basic distinction between the promulgation of general regulations through rulemaking and case-by-case decisions through adjudication. Subject to certain exemptions, the basic procedure provided by the APA for rulemaking in §553 consists of publication of proposed rules in the Federal Register, followed by opportunity for interested persons to submit written or oral comments on the proposed rules. Where the relevant organic statute requires decision "on the record after opportunity for agency hearing," the APA provides in §§556-557 for modified trial-type hearing procedures in rulemaking.

In cases of adjudication where the relevant organic statute requires an agency to decide "on the record after opportunity for agency hearing," the APA requires trial-type hearings conducted by independent administrative law judges, followed by an appeal procedure to the head of the agency. Sections 554, 556-557 of the act also mandated a partial separation of functions between prosecuting staff and agency decisionmaking. These provisions were designed to meet criticisms of agency bias and combination of functions, while stopping short of a total separation of adjudicatory and other regulatory functions. On the other hand, when the relevant organic statute fails to require that adjudication be conducted "on the record after opportunity for agency hearing," the APA does not impose any procedural requirements.

Section 10 of the act, 5 U.S.C. §§701-706, deals with the availability, timing, form, and scope of judicial review. These provisions, which are discussed in Chapters 4 and 8, essentially codify preexisting judge-made principles of administrative law. However, §10(e), 5 U.S.C. §706, makes clear that reviewing courts not only must determine whether administrators complied with relevant statutes, but also must examine whether the agency's action was "arbitrary, capricious, an abuse of discretion." In cases of agency decision on the basis of a trial-type record, §706 also requires courts to determine whether the agency's factfindings are supported by "substantial evidence" in the record as a whole.

In the 20 years after the enactment of the APA, the courts adhered to the act's spirit of compromise between the extreme claims of the critics and the defenders of the new administrative process. Courts undertook somewhat stiffer scrutiny of agency factfinding than was characteristic in the later years of the New Deal. Modest efforts were made to promote a degree of consistency in agency policy and to avoid shifts in the law that might seriously prejudice expectations. Yet courts were careful to leave agencies a fair measure of discretion in the formulation and implementation of policy, and informal processes of communication and negotiation were left largely undisturbed. A cooperative accommodation between court and agency had evolved.

Studies of the administrative process multiplied during the postwar period. A Commission on Organization of the Executive Branch of the Government was twice convened under the chairmanship of former President Hoover. Its reports in 1949 and 1955 called for stronger presidential control over the "independent" commissions, greater use of principles of managerial efficiency, and streamlined procedural formalities in agency decisionmaking. Observers of the administrative process also expressed concern over the isolation of regulatory agencies from effective political control by the chief executive. Other critics complained of agency failure to formulate clear and consistent policies. Concern was expressed over the delay and high cost of administrative proceedings. Congress investigated charges of corruption and undue influence in the regulatory process, particularly in the FCC's award of valuable broadcast licenses. But there was no frontal attack on the very existence of the regulatory commissions. The general assumption was that marginal adjustments within the existing system would perfect the administrative state. This sense of stability was reinforced by the appearance of the first great treatises on modern administrative law. K. Davis, Administrative Law Treatise (1958); Louis Jaffe, Judicial Control of Administrative Action (1965).

f. 1962 to 1980: The Rights Revolution, Critique of Administrative Process and Administrative Substance, and "Public Interest" Administrative Law

Public trust in regulation and the administrative process began to disintegrate after 1962. The work of administrative agencies came under increasingly sharp attack on several fronts, and courts began to impose more stringent and far-reaching controls on the administrative process. Ironically, all this happened during an outburst of enthusiasm for regulatory solutions to public problems.

In terms of sheer output, the period between 1965 and 1975 represented the most creative one in Congress since the New Deal. The period marked a revolution in the category of legally protected rights. Congress and the president invoked the rhetorical power of the civil rights movement to create a number of new agencies involving race and sex discrimination — and, in addition, to produce new initiatives involving the environment, workers, the poor, and consumers. The period saw the creation of the Consumer Product Safety Commission (CPSC), Equal Employment Opportunity Commission (EEOC), National Highway Traffic Safety Administration (NHTSA), EPA, NRC, and OSHA. Hence the period is sometimes described as a "rights revolution." Consider Table 1-1.

Regulation in this period differed both substantively and institutionally from that in the 1930s. In the later period, the purpose of new institutions was not principally to stabilize the economy or to provide price and entry controls to establish business confidence. Far from facing a depression, the "rights revolution" occurred during an era of relative prosperity. The basic goals were to protect public health and safety from risks of various sorts — at work, in the air and water, and in consumer products — and to counteract discrimination against various disadvantaged groups. Moreover, in the 1960s and 1970s Congress largely abandoned the New Deal faith in administrative autonomy, often enacting relatively clear guidelines for agencies to follow and surrounding agencies with

TABLE 1-1
Representative Agencies Created in the 1960s and 1970s and in the New Deal Period

1960s and 1970s

Department of Energy (1977)
Office of Surface Mining (1977)
Nuclear Regulatory Commission (1975)
Materials Transportation Board (1975)
Mine Safety and Health Administration (1973)
Occupational Safety and Health Administration (1973)
Consumer Product Safety Commission (1972)
National Highway Traffic Safety Administration (1970)
Environmental Protection Agency (1970)
Equal Employment Opportunity Commission (1964)
United States Commission on Civil Rights (expansion;
  originally created 1957) (1960)

New Deal

Food and Drug Administration (expansion) (1938)
Federal Trade Commission (expansion) (1938)
Federal Communications Commission (1936)
Soil Conservation Service (1938)
Social Security Administration (1935)
Federal Power Commission (1935)
Securities and Exchange Commission (1934)
National Labor Relations Board (1934)
Federal Housing Administration (1934)
Public Works Administration (1933)
Tennessee Valley Authority (1933)
Civil Works Administration (1933)
Rural Electrification Administration (1933)
Civilian Conservation Corps (1933)
Federal Deposit Insurance Corporation (1933)
Federal Home Loan Bank Board (1932)

procedural requirements and even deadlines. These deadlines, often described as "hammers," sometimes threaten to overwhelm agencies with mandatory duties.

In this period, criticism of the administrative process had several strands. Consumer advocates, such as Ralph Nader, argued that agencies had been captured by the very firms they were supposed to regulate. In the view of such critics, agencies failed to act vigorously to protect the interests of consumers, workers, and other supposed beneficiaries of regulatory programs. The solutions offered by these critics to problems of agency indolence and "capture" included greater public openness in agency decisionmaking; statutory deadlines or "hammers," requiring agencies to do particular things by particular times; increased participation by "public interest" advocates for consumer, environmental, and other interests in agency decisionmaking; more formal decisionmaking procedures; stricter judicial scrutiny of agency action or inaction, including judicial requirements that agencies take

Capture criticism.

affirmative measures to protect the beneficiaries of regulatory policies; closer congressional scrutiny of agency policies; elimination of conflicts of interest by regulators with prior or subsequent ties to regulated industry; and (in some cases) elimination or modification of regulatory programs that primarily benefited regulated firms.

A different line of criticism focused on the administrative apparatus of the welfare and public service state. Beneficiaries of welfare programs and public services sought more in the way of procedural protection. Could welfare money, licenses, and other benefits be deemed "the new property"? Welfare agencies, public housing authorities, school officials, and other dispensers of public benefits had not traditionally been subject to procedural formalities or judicial control to the same extent as administrators engaged in regulating private activity through more traditional "coercive" controls or financial penalties. Critics claimed that the impact of these agencies on individual welfare and the dangers of arbitrary power are at least as great as in the case of traditional regulatory agencies. They urged that administrative law safeguards — such as trial-type hearings or other procedural formalities and thorough judicial review — should be extended to welfare recipients, public housing tenants, students, government employees, and so on.

A quite separate set of criticisms, directed against the regulatory agencies by economists, other social scientists, and some business leaders, began in the mid-1970s to advocate a large-scale reduction in the size and power of the administrative state. More particularly, these critics argued for (1) deregulation, (2) greater attention to cost and unintended harmful consequences of regulation, and (3) the consolidation of administrative programs. Deregulation might occur through abolishing regulatory programs and relying on markets and state government. Agencies might also be required to pay careful attention to the costs of their actions. Consolidation might occur, for example, through abolition of the FTC, whose antitrust authorities overlap with those of the Department of Justice, or through replacement of a myriad welfare programs with a single system of income redistribution (such as a negative income tax).

One version of this criticism held that regulatory programs are characteristically created and administered for the benefit of strategically placed and well-organized interests at the expense of the general public. In this view, regulatory programs are inefficient and involve a serious welfare loss for the society as a whole. For the most radical critics, any efforts to "reform" the administrative process are likely to be ineffectual. Accordingly, it was urged, the best solution is to abolish most or many administrative functions.

A second and milder version of this line of criticism held that certain kinds of administrative intervention are justified to correct serious market failures, particularly when consumers' information about goods and services is highly imperfect, or when there are important spillover effects, or when the distribution of wealth and income that results from market exchange is inequitable. However, it was asserted that the tools customarily used by administrators to alter market behavior — such as regulatory prohibitions, licensing, and other legalistic controls — are inappropriate, clumsy, and excessively costly. These critics complained of the resulting "mismatch" between various forms of "market failure"; see Stephen Breyer, Regulation and Its Reform (1982). They also urged that the tools used by administrators were the wrong ones and that command-and-control regulation should be replaced with more flexible, cheaper methods, particularly economic incentives. Rather than have a regulatory agency set a specific amount of permissible pollutants for each source, they would have administrators charge a fee for each pound of air or water pollution emitted, thereby affording greater flexibility to individual sources and ensuring a given overall level of cleanup at cheaper cost.

Legal Adjustments

In terms of legal doctrine, the courts responded through a number of important developments. Each of these represented a shift of traditional doctrines in favor of a greater measure of judicial control over agency decisionmaking.

First, courts extended the right to participate in agency decisions and to seek judicial review to welfare recipients, students, government contractors, and "public interest" representatives of consumers, environmentalists, the poor, and other loosely organized groups. By extending to these interests the rights of participation and judicial redress formerly enjoyed by regulated firms, the courts transformed the basic purpose of administrative law — from one of limiting governmental power to protect private interests (as defined by the common law) to one of representing relevant interests, by providing a system in which all of the various interests with a stake in agency policy have the right to participate and secure judicial review of the balance struck by the agency.

Second, courts extended the coverage and content of procedural formalities to require that actions once taken by administrators through informal means be more fully documented through a factual record, and that administrators employ procedural formalities to give interested parties an effective chance to ascertain and challenge the factual and analytical bases for agency decisions. Federal courts imposed greater procedural formalities on federal regulatory agencies and (often through due process rulings) on state and federal agencies involved in welfare and service functions such as education, administration of welfare programs, and public employment.

Third, courts expanded the availability of judicial review and broadened the scope of review by insisting that agencies more fully explain and document their decisions, and also by scrutinizing more closely the factual and analytic bases for such decisions.

At the same time, other institutions responded to the problems in other ways. At the end of the 1970s, Congress enacted laws that deregulated certain industries. In 1978, Congress abolished the most important forms of economic regulation (price and entry regulation) for domestic airlines. It also significantly liberalized economic regulation of trucking and railroads. It abolished price and entry regulation for long-distance telecommunications. It effectively abolished regulation of natural gas production, and it removed the price controls over oil and gas that it had introduced as a result of the oil price increases of the early and mid-1970s. At the same time, the government began to experiment with limited forms of economic incentives, such as "marketable" air pollution rights. By 1980, the government had responded, modestly or less modestly, to many of the critics who had seen certain traditional economic regulatory programs (particularly in transportation and communication) as unnecessary or harmful.

g. 1980 to ?: Presidential Administration and the Cost-Benefit State

The election of President Reagan signaled a new period, one that led to more formalized presidential oversight of administration and to considerable rethinking of the purposes and performance of administrative institutions. A central theme that emerged was that regulation (usually? too often?) costs much more than it should and that the benefits that it provides are far too small to be worth the public and private expense. Consider (but take with some grains of salt) Table 1-2 on pages 26-27, which has become an organizing theme in many administrative law circles. For an instructive criticism of Table 1-2, suggesting that it depends on contentious assumptions, see Heinzerling, Regulatory Costs of Mythic Proportions, 106 Yale L.J. 1981 (1998).

Regan Era Philosophy

TABLE 1-2
Cost-Effectiveness of Selected Regulations (from the Budget for
Fiscal Year 1992, Table C-2, Part 2, p. 370)

Regulation	Agency	Cost per premature death averted ($ millions 1990)
Unvented Space Heater Ban	CPSC	0.1
Aircraft Cabin Fire Protection Standard	FAA	0.1
Auto Passive Restraint/Seat Belt Standards	NHTSA	0.1
Steering Column Protection Standard	NHTSA	0.1
Underground Construction Standards	OSHA	0.1
Trihalomethane Drinking Water Standards	EPA	0.2
Aircraft Seat Cushion Flammability Standard	FAA	0.4
Alcohol and Drug Control Standards	FRA	0.4
Auto Fuel-System Integrity Standard	NHTSA	0.4
Standards for Servicing Auto Wheel Rims	OSHA	0.4
Aircraft Floor Emergency Lighting Standard	FAA	0.6
Concrete & Masonry Construction Standards	OSHA	0.6
Passive Restraints for Trucks & Buses (Proposed)	OSHA	0.7
Crane Suspended Personnel Platform Standard	NHTSA	0.7
Children's Sleepwear Flammability Ban	CPSC	0.8
Auto Side Door Support Standards	NHTSA	0.8
Side-Impact Standards for Autos (Dynamic)	NHTSA	0.8
Low Altitude Windshear Equipment & Training Standards	FAA	1.3
Electrical Equipment Standards (Metal Mines)	MSHA	1.4
Traffic Alert and Collision Avoidance (TCAS) Systems	FAA	1.5
Trenching and Excavation Standards	OSHA	1.5
Hazard Communication Standard	OSHA	1.6
Side-Impact Standards for Trucks, Buses, and MPVs (Proposed)	NHTSA	2.2
Grain Dust Explosion Prevention Standards	OSHA	2.8
Rear Lap/Shoulder Belts for Autos	NHTSA	3.2
Benzine NESHAP (Original: Fugitive Emissions)	EPA	3.4
Standards for Radionuclides in Uranium Mines	EPA	3.4
Ethylene Dibromide Drinking Water Standard	EPA	5.7
Benzene NESHAP (Revised: Coke Byproducts)	EPA	6.1
Asbestos Occupational Exposure Limit	OSHA	8.3
Benzene Occupational Exposure Limit	OSHA	8.9
Electrical Equipment Standards (Coal Mines)	MSHA	9.2
Arsenic Emission Standards for Glass Plants	EPA	13.5
Ethylene Oxide Occupational Exposure Limit	OSHA	20.5

Regulation	Agency	Cost per premature death averted ($ millions 1990)
Arsenic/Copper NESHAP	EPA	23.0
Hazardous Waste Listing for Petroleum Refining Sludge	EPA	27.6
Cover/Move Uranium Mill Tailings (Inactive Sites)	EPA	31.7
Benzene NESHAP (Revised: Transfer Operations)	EPA	32.9
Cover/Move Uranium Mill Tailings (Active Sites)	EPA	45.0
Acrylonitrile Occupational Exposure Limit	OSHA	51.5
Coke Ovens Occupational Exposure Limit	OSHA	63.5
Lockout/Tagout	OSHA	70.9
Asbestos Occupational Exposure Limit	OSHA	74.0
Arsenic Occupational Exposure Limit	OSHA	106.9
Asbestos Ban	EPA	110.7
Diethylstilbestrol (DES) Cattlefeed Ban	FDA	124.8
Benzene NESHAP (Revised: Waste Operations)	EPA	168.2
1,2 Dichloropropane Drinking Water Standard	EPA	653.0
Hazardous Waste Land Disposal Ban (1st 3rd)	EPA	4,190.4
Municipal Solid Waste Landfill Standards (Proposed)	EPA	19,107.0
Formaldehyde Occupational Exposure Limit	OSHA	86,201.8
Atrazine/Alachlor Drinking Water Standard	EPA	92,069.7
Hazardous Waste Listing for Wood-Preserving Chemicals	EPA	5,700,000.0

OMB Regulation

A key development in this period was the promulgation of Executive Order 12,291 (discussed in Chapter 2), which called for Office of Management and Budget (OMB) control of regulations with careful attention to the costs and benefits of proposed initiatives. The articulated goal of the executive order was to provide more coordination of the regulatory process, and at the same time to make sure that expensive regulations actually delivered regulatory benefits.

President Reagan's approach was challenged by many who thought it was motivated by the interests of powerful private groups concerned more with obstructing than improving administrative processes. But in Executive Order 12,866 (also discussed in Chapter 2) President Clinton endorsed the broad outlines and many of the specifics of President Reagan's approach. President George W. Bush, in many ways a sharp critic of President Clinton, has governed under President Clinton's Executive Order — without changing a single word. Hence, OMB oversight of regulation, with a view toward some form of cost-benefit balancing, appears to be fairly entrenched. In the last two decades and more, the president has asserted a more formal role as manager of administrative institutions. For a valuable overview, see Kagan, Presidential Administration, 114 Harv. L. Rev. 2245 (2001).

But the other branches have not been inactive. Congress has seriously considered substantial changes to regulatory and administrative law. Some of these changes would represent a substantial movement against the New Deal reformation of the constitutional structure — in the direction of a renewed emphasis on market ordering pursuant to the

Move toward Cost/benefit

common law; a reinvigoration of state as opposed to national authority; and decreased enthusiasm for discretionary policymaking by regulators, who would henceforth be limited by requirements of cost-benefit balancing and selection of least-cost solutions. More modest proposals would impose a general "supermandate" of cost-benefit analysis, effectively amending all statutes to require agencies to show that the benefits are worth the costs. Both agencies and courts have occasionally moved in this direction.

The enactment of major deregulatory reform programs has shifted the nation's regulatory emphasis away from price and entry controls in particular industries to more broadly applicable environmental, health, and safety regulation. A consensus favors such programs in some form. There is considerable debate, however, about just where they are needed, how they can be made effective, and how they can be conducted democratically and efficiently. What type of environmental regulation should we have? How can we effectively and rationally regulate health risks?

Since 1980, three developments have been of special importance. Government has shown an increasing interest in engaging in *quantitative* analysis, by looking at the magnitude of problems, not merely their existence. It has also shown a great interest in assessing *tradeoffs*, by examining costs and unintended side effects of regulation. At the same time, government has shown an interest in *smarter tools*, especially by replacing command-and-control regulation with information disclosure and economic incentives. All of these developments have played a role in the executive branch, Congress, and the federal courts, with some cases invalidating agency action as insufficiently responsive to the new interest in quantitative analysis, tradeoffs, and smarter tools.

Similarly, the debate over institutional arrangements has tended to shift from the best way to "control" regulatory bodies that are "out of control," to the topic of improving and coordinating related regulatory programs operated by different parts of the executive branch. How can we set reasonable priorities? To what extent should regulatory policy be controlled by the White House, or by OMB? To what extent should "political" judgment from the executive "center" control detailed judgments made at the more "expert" agency periphery? To what extent should Congress, through legislation or congressional hearings, "micromanage" agency decisionmaking? The executive branch has taken the lead here, especially through a series of executive orders implanting the president's will on the administrative state and often requiring close attention to consequences.

At the same time, the judicial developments of 1962-1980 — increased participation, increased procedural requirements, increasingly strong judicial review — have undergone significant revision and modification. These developments were criticized by many who claimed that they meant delay and that they wasted resources without providing an effective, sensible way to control agency policymaking. Others, including the Supreme Court, feared that the judiciary might usurp political policy choices that legislative or administrative officials, not judges, ought to make. Still others argued that courts lacked the competence to deal adequately with the complex problems of administrative government. At the same time, critics of the legal system in general provided reasons for fearing that American society (compared, say, with Japan) has too many lawyers, too much litigation, and too much preoccupation with distributional conflicts; these critics called for more cooperative advancement of the social and economic welfare of the nation. The Supreme Court has decided important cases that (1) give the agencies considerable freedom from judicial review when they decide not to take certain kinds of action, (2) limit the extent to which the courts can impose new procedural requirements on the agencies, and (3) require the courts to pay particular attention to agency interpretations of statutes. Rules of standing governing access to courts have become somewhat more restrictive. At the same time, lower federal courts have shown an unmistakable interest in ensuring agency attention to quantities, tradeoffs, and smarter tools; sometimes, they have exercised an aggressive role in combating what they apparently see as agency overzealousness.

It remains far too early to assess the consequences of the terrorist attacks of September 11, 2001, on federal administrative law. But those attacks have raised a host of fresh questions about judicial deference to presidential authority, questions that have produced new thinking about traditional doctrines in the context of threats to national security. The Court has already produced decisions that can well be understood as administrative law rulings.

The recent developments, and the increasing attention to legislative and administrative reforms, have raised a set of important questions — some old, some altogether new. How far is it possible to reconcile the needs of administrative government with judicial traditions of adversary hearings, impartial decisionmaking, and reasoned continuity in "the rule of law"? In light of the expense, delay, and limited competencies of adversary litigation, to what extent is it desirable or feasible to rely on the courts as a primary protection of citizens against arbitrary or unlawful administrative action? Once we understand regulatory goals and regulatory performance, what alternative institutional mechanisms should be developed? What is the role of administrative law when national security is at risk? How serious is the "failure" of the administrative process to live up to the bright hopes of New Deal and later champions of administrative intervention? Can the "failures" of the administrative process be solved by moderate alterations in institutional and procedural arrangements? By greater use of economic analysis and centralized review by the White House and OMB? By promoting nonjudicial mechanisms of negotiation and mediation? By decentralizing political and economic power to states, cities, and voluntary organizations? By more specific and wiser directives from Congress? In confronting these basic questions, the United States attempts to promote the economic and democratic goals that underlie the modern administrative state.

2

The Constitutional Position of the Administrative Agency

A. Introductory Note: Separation of Powers and (or) Checks and Balances

The American constitutional system is sometimes described as one of separation of powers. Equally often, it is described as one of checks and balances. The two descriptions point in different directions. The notion of checks and balances suggests intermingled authority (consider the president's role in lawmaking through the veto power); separation of powers suggests independence of authority. The idea of checks and balances is a much more accurate description of the Framers' understanding. But the idea of separation exerted a large influence too.

It has been a fundamental element of separation-of-powers doctrine, as developed by Locke and Montesquieu and refined by James Madison, that governmental intrusions on private liberty must be authorized by general rules formulated by a politically responsible group of officials. These officials are supposed to be separate from the officials responsible for executing the rules. Separation, so understood, is part and parcel of the ideal of the rule of law.

A central reason is that separation helps to promote uniformity and impartiality in the application of sanctions. If the executing officials had the power to decide when sanctions would be imposed, enforcement policies might reflect the private advantage or prejudice of those officials; policies would also be unpredictable. (One of Adolf Hitler's first goals was to acquire the power to rule by decree.) Compare a situation in which rules are general and formulated by officials who may find it difficult to estimate how their own interests will be affected by the disposition of particular cases. In that case, it is more likely that the policies adopted will more nearly reflect a broad social judgment about desirable policy than the officials' own private advantage. This likelihood is increased if the officials in question must seek reelection. Moreover, the requirement that policies be general promotes increased predictability, thus facilitating private planning and security. The principle of separation of lawmaking and law-applying powers also reduces the power that government can exert against citizens — and reduces the possibility that the entire power of government could be taken over by any one faction, a core concern of the founding generation. See The Federalist No. 10.

Thus, it follows, as a majority of the Court held in Youngstown Sheet & Tube Co. v. Sawyer, 343 U.S. 579 (1952), that, outside of certain narrowly defined foreign affairs and military situations, Congress must authorize any intrusions by executive officials on private liberty or property. The president cannot proceed on his own. Moreover, the doctrine against legislative "delegation" of legislative power (to, for example, an administrative agency or the president), reflected (though hardly ever enforced) in court decisions, requires that such authorization take the form of rules that control administrative decision. (Note that the German Constitutional Court is quite active in policing broad delegations of legislative power to the executive.) If a rule is too vague, there is a danger that the executing official will really be a lawmaker, and the salutary elements of predictability and electoral responsibility will be impaired.

The separation-of-powers principle also reserves a special role for an independent judiciary. The courts have traditionally exercised a reviewing function to ensure executive compliance with the applicable public law — policing executive officers' obedience to legislative commands and providing a further set of internal checks on governmental power used against the citizenry.

Many people think that these traditional principles have been threatened by the creation of administrative agencies that combine lawmaking, adjudicative, and executive functions. See, e.g., T. Lowi, The End of Liberalism (2d ed. 1977); D. Schoenbrod, Power Without Responsibility (1994). In fact, there is a vivid and influential narrative about the rise of the administrative state; one that sees successive breaches of Article I, Article II, and Article III of the Constitution through the creation of institutions that make law, enforce law, and interpret law. Certainly, agencies have been given the authority to promulgate legislative-type rules and simultaneously to apply these rules in given cases. They have also been invested with the power to investigate, prosecute, and decide individual controversies.

The question addressed in this chapter is how the combination of functions characteristic of modern administrative agencies can be reconciled with the structural principles underlying the Constitution. The Constitution, after all, describes and distinguishes "legislative Powers" in Article I (Congress), the "executive Power" in Article II (the president), and the "judicial Power" in Article III (the federal courts). While it recognizes the existence of executive departments, it contains no article expressly authorizing administrative agencies.

Sometimes, the Constitution has been criticized on just this ground. Defenders of the administrative process have rejected rigid ideas about separation of powers and checks and balances as anachronistic in an industrialized society, claiming, for example, that effectively to manage and control the complex modern economy, government must emulate techniques of integrated, expert, hierarchical management practiced by business corporations. Thus, in 1938 James Landis wrote:

> If in private life we were to organize a firm for the operation of an industry, it would scarcely follow Montesquieu's lines. . . . Yet the problems of operating a private industry resemble to a great degree those entailed by its regulation.

J. Landis, The Administrative Process 10 (1938). As you explore the constitutional questions, it is worthwhile to ask a pragmatic question: Would judicial enforcement of a certain understanding of the Constitution — requiring Congress to speak clearly, abolishing "independent" agencies — be likely to make the regulatory state work better or worse?

B. The Agency's Power to Legislate

Article I, §1 of the Constitution says that "all legislative powers . . . shall be vested in a Congress of the United States. . . ." Early cases stated that this legislative power, which the Constitution had delegated to Congress, could not be redelegated to others. As Justice Story put it, "The general rule of law is, that a delegated power cannot be delegated." Shankland v. Washington, 30 U.S. 390, 395 (1831). Justice Harlan, in Field v. Clark, 143 U.S. 649, 692 (1892), wrote, "[T]hat Congress cannot delegate legislative power . . . is a principle universally recognized as vital to the integrity and maintenance of the system of government ordained by the Constitution." We will see below, however, that these are general statements that may not decisively arbitrate between competing modern views about the constitutionality of broad or highly discretionary delegating statutes.

Such statutes became increasingly common in the late nineteenth and early twentieth centuries, perhaps due to increasing demands on the legislative agenda, which increased the benefits of delegation to nonlegislative agents. For the most part, the Supreme Court got out of the way of this development. The Court said in 1897 that although the power to prescribe rules "in the future . . . is a legislative act, . . . Congress . . . might commit to some subordinate tribunal this duty." ICC v. Cincinnati, New Orleans, & Texas Pacific Ry., 167 U.S. 479, 494 (1897). The Court went on to hold that the Interstate Commerce Act of 1887 did not give the Interstate Commerce Commission (ICC) this "power to exercise the legislative function of prescribing rates which shall control in the future." Id. at 505-506. But when Congress later specifically granted this authority in the Hepburn Act (1906), the courts simply assumed the constitutionality of its doing so.

Similar issues arose at the state level, as illustrated by the following case, which involved a state constitutional challenge to the Minnesota legislature's delegation of rate-setting authority to an administrative commission.

State ex rel. Railroad & Warehouse Commission v. Chicago, M. & St. P. Ry

38 Minn. 281, 37 N.W. 782 (1888)

[Groups of shippers complained to the Minnesota Railroad Commission that rates for milk carried on passenger trains to St. Paul and Minneapolis from Owatonna (71 miles/3¢ per 10 gallons), from Faribault (56 miles/3¢ per 10 gallons), from Northfield (43 miles/2½¢ per 10 gallons), and from Farmington (30 miles/2½¢ per 10 gallons) were unreasonably high. The commission agreed with respect to the Owatonna and Faribault rates. It held that a rate of 2½¢ per 10 gallons from all four towns would be equal and reasonable. The commission then brought a mandamus action in the state court to compel the railroad to obey its order.]

MITCHELL, J. The questions here presented are — First, the construction, and second, the constitutionality, of chapter 10. [It creates the Railroad and Warehouse Commission.] It provides that all charges by any common carrier for the transportation of passengers and property shall be equal and reasonable. . . . [It requires carriers to file tariffs and charge only the rates contained in the tariff.] [I]n case the Commission shall at any time find that any part of the tariffs of rates, fares, charges, or classifications, so filed and published . . . are in any respect unequal or unreasonable, it shall have the power . . . to compel any common carrier to . . . adopt such rate, fare, charge, or classification as said Commission shall declare to be reasonable and equal; . . .

The question that arises on the construction of the act is as to the nature and extent of the powers granted to the Commission in the matter of fixing rates. . . . If language means anything, it is perfectly evident that the expressed intention of the legislature is that the rates recommended and published by the Commission . . . should be not simply advisory, nor merely prima facie equal and reasonable, but final and conclusive as to what are lawful or equal and reasonable charges; that, in proceedings to compel compliance with the rates thus published, the law neither contemplates nor allows any issue to be made or inquiry had as to their equality and reasonableness in fact. . . . [In this respect the state act is unlike the federal Interstate Commerce Act, which allows the federal courts to review a commission decision as to reasonableness.] This brings us to the question of the validity of the act, that is the authority of the legislature to confer such powers upon this Commission. That the legislature itself has the power to regulate railroad charges is now too well settled to require either argument or citation of authority. . . . Railways had become practically the public highway system of the country. The situation was anomalous, being the first instance in history where a public highway system was at the same time owned by private parties, and exclusively used by those who owned it. This condition of things, emphasized by the reckless railway management of 15 years ago, led to legislation assuming to regulate and limit railway charges for the transportation of persons and property. Entrenched behind the doctrine that a charter is a contract, the railroad companies denied the power of the legislatures to do this; claiming the right to charge what they pleased for their services, subject only to the common-law rule that these charges should be in themselves reasonable; and this they claimed was a question for judicial, and not legislative, determination. The dispute was submitted to the arbitrament of the courts. The decisions in the so-called "Granger Cases," over 11 years ago, resulted in a complete victory for the right of legislative control. See Granger Cases, 94 U.S. 113-187.

[No] modern civilized community could long endure that their public highway system should be in the uncontrolled, exclusive use of private owners. The only alternative was either governmental regulation, or governmental ownership of the roads. . . .

[The Court went on to hold that it was constitutional for a statute to deny the courts the power to review a determination, either by an agency or by the legislature, setting certain specific rates as reasonable. This holding was later reversed by the U.S. Supreme Court as inconsistent with the due process clause of the fourteenth amendment. Chicago, M. & St. P. Ry. v. Minnesota, 134 U.S. 418 (1890). One apparent premise of this ruling is that rate regulation that did not secure the railroad an adequate return on its invested capital would amount to an unconstitutional "taking" of its property, and that judicial review was therefore constitutionally required to ensure the adequacy of the rates allowed by the commission. Alternatively, the ruling may reflect the more general principle that due process requires judicial review of administrative impositions and exactions to ensure that they conform to the agency's statutory authority and have therefore been legislatively authorized. In Chapter 4, we examine the court's effort to police the constitutional adequacy of regulated rates. In Chapter 8, we consider whether due process requires judicial review of agency conformance to statute, rendering statutes that preclude review unconstitutional.]

[The Court continued:] It is contended that the power to regulate rates, if it exists at all, is legislative, and therefore the act is void, because it delegates legislative power to a commission. [It] is often difficult to discriminate, in particular cases, between what is properly legislative, and what is or may be executive or administrative, duty. The authority that makes the laws has large discretion in determining the means through which they shall be executed; and the performance of many duties, which they may provide for by law, they may refer to some ministerial officer, specially named for the duty. Cooley, Const. Law, 114. It is not every grant of powers, involving the exercise of discretion and judgment, to executive or administrative officers, that amounts to a delegation of legislative power. The difference between the departments undoubtedly is that the legislative makes, the executive executes, and the judiciary construes, the law; but the maker of the law may commit something to the discretion of the other departments, and the precise boundary of this power is a subject of delicate and difficult inquiry, into which a court will not unnecessarily enter. . . . The principle is repeatedly recognized by all courts that the legislature may authorize others to do things which it might properly, but cannot conveniently or advantageously, do itself. . . . If this was not permissible, the wheels of government would often be blocked. . . . The statute books are full of legislation granting to officers large discretionary powers in the execution of laws, the validity of which has never been successfully assailed. We might mention as examples of this the grant of power to courts to adopt rules governing their own practice and process; the power given to boards for the control of public institutions to make contracts, fix prices, and adopt rules reasonably adapted to carry out the purposes of their creation. The power of taxation is legislative, but this does not require the legislature itself to assess the value of each man's property, or determine his share of the tax. . . . The true distinction is between the delegation of power to make the law, which necessarily involves a discretion as to what it shall be, and the conferring of an authority to discretion to be exercised under and in pursuance of the law. . . . It seems to us that the authority and discretion conferred upon this Commission is of the latter kind. [What] are equal and reasonable rates is a question depending upon an infinite and ever-changing variety of circumstances. What may be such on one road, or for one description of traffic, may not be such on or for another. What are reasonable one month may not be so the next. For a popular legislature that meets only once in two years, and then only for 60 days, to attempt to fix rates, would result only in the most ill-advised and haphazard action, productive of the greatest inconvenience and injustice, alike to the railways and the public. If such a power is to be exercised at all it can only be satisfactorily done by a board or commission, constantly in session, whose time is exclusively given to the subject, and who, after investigation of the facts, can fix rates with reference to the peculiar circumstances of each road, and each particular kind of business, and who can change or modify these rates to suit the ever-varying conditions of traffic. . . . [Whether] the charges of a railway in any particular case are or are not equal and reasonable is a fact left by the law for them to determine. . . .

Our opinion is that the act is not obnoxious to the objection made. Let the writ issue as prayed for.

Questions

1. Consider the following questions in relation to the *Chicago Railway* case:

   (a) Why should railroad rates be regulated at all? What kind of market failure might justify regulation? Consider the possibility that the legislature was responding to a natural monopoly or to unfairness in the form of discrimination among shippers. But consider the possibility that the railroad commission is really an effort to protect the selfish interests of well-organized private groups. Whose self-interest would be helped by a railroad commission — railroads or shippers?

(b) Why couldn't the problem of unreasonable rates be handled adequately through private lawsuits? Note that at common law innkeepers, carriers, and others serving the public were required to charge no more than a "reasonable" rate; overcharged customers could bring an action for damages. Why didn't this remedy obviate the need for regulation?

(c) If rate regulation is necessary, why shouldn't the legislature itself, using the expertise of its committees and subcommittees, set rates through a statute rather than delegating the job to an administrative agency?

(d) How and to what extent does delegation to an agency solve the institutional problems of relying on courts or the legislature to deal with unreasonable rates?

2. The relevant distances and rates involved were as follows:

Towns	Miles from Minneapolis	Railroad's rates (cents)	Commission's rates (cents)
Owatonna	71	3	2.5
Faribault	56	3	2.5
Northfield	43	2.5	2.5
Farmington	30	2.5	2.5

(a) How should the agency determine whether these rates are equal and reasonable?

(b) Should a legislature be required to give specific statutory guidance as to what factors the agency should take into account? How?

(c) If the legislature does not give clear directives to administrators, on what basis are courts to review the legal validity of agency decisions?

3. In the principal case, the statute precluded judicial review. How, if at all, does this bear on the nondelegation challenge? Consider the idea that judicial review can weaken a nondelegation challenge, because it places some constraints on agency discretion.

C. The Nondelegation Doctrine in Federal Law

By vesting all "legislative powers" in "a Congress of the United States," does the Constitution create a nondelegation doctrine? We will begin with the conceptual and textual issues, and then discuss the case law.

1. The Nondelegation Doctrine: Analytic and Textual Foundations

What might it mean to say that Constitution in general, or Article I's grant of legislative powers to Congress in particular, creates a "nondelegation" doctrine? For a thorough parsing of the possibilities, see Thomas W. Merrill, Rethinking Article I, Section 1: From

Nondelegation to Exclusive Delegation, 104 Colum. L. Rev. 2097 (2004). Consider the following positions on the meaning of "delegation":

(1) *The vesting of all legislative powers in Congress is not only an initial allocation, but also a final one. Congress cannot transfer its legislative powers to any other institution.* To be sure, no constitutional provision expressly says that Congress cannot choose to delegate its legislative power to others. But this is a time-honored principle of American law, going back at least to the 1831 *Shankland* case, as described above.

    This "nondelegation doctrine" is uncontroversial; everyone agrees with it. It is also deeply ambiguous. It is logically consistent with either of the two following additional views:

(2) *When Congress enacts a statute granting authority to the executive (or perhaps to private parties; see the notes to the* Schechter *case, below) the statute amounts to or effects a delegation of legislative power if the scope of the grant is too broad or if it vests too much discretion in the executive.* As we will see, this is what proponents of the "nondelegation doctrine" typically understand it to hold. A frequent confusion arises when people who subscribe to this position make arguments that only support the general, uncontroversial position described in (1) above. The problem is that there is also another position, equally consistent with (1). That other position is the following:

(3) *When Congress enacts a statute granting authority to the executive (or private parties), there is no "delegation" of legislative power no matter how broad the grant or how much discretion it confers.* Rather than *delegating* legislative power, Congress has *exercised* it, by enacting the relevant statute. So long as the grantee acts within the bounds of its statutory authority, the grantee is necessarily exercising executive power, not legislative power. The *Youngstown* principle dictates that (putting aside constitutional authority) the executive must stay within the bounds of its statutory authority. The flip-side of *Youngstown*, however, is that when the executive does stay within those bounds, it is taking care that the laws be faithfully executed, see U.S. Const. Art. II, sec. 3, and thus exercising executive power.

From one standpoint, this third position is a radical view that denies entirely that there is such a thing as a "nondelegation doctrine," if that phrase refers to Position (2) above. The appearance of radicalism may be misleading, however. Note that Position (3) is fully consistent with Position (1). Position (3) accepts that legislative power cannot be delegated; what it denies is that a grant of statutory authority to the executive can ever amount to such a delegation. According to Position (3), an appeal to the separation of powers or to the nondelegability of legislative powers cannot, by itself, justify Position (2), because Position (3) also holds that legislative power is nondelegable.

These analytic distinctions are consequential. The issue that tends to divide proponents of the nondelegation doctrine from critics is whether a statutory grant of authority can ever violate the nondelegation constraint. Positions (2) and (3) give directly opposing answers to that question. Position (2) answers "yes, if the grant is too discretionary or too broad;" Position (3) answers "no." Position (2) *cannot* be justified simply by asserting Position (1), with which no one disagrees.

Position (3) is advanced in Eric A. Posner & Adrian Vermeule, Interring the Nondelegation Doctrine, 69 U. Chi. L. Rev. 1721 (2002). Proponents of Position (2) have

Dispute b/w 2+3

vigorously criticized Position (3) on various grounds. See, e.g., Larry Alexander & Saikrishna Prakash, Reports of the Nondelegation Doctrine's Death Are Greatly Exaggerated, 70 U. Chi. L. Rev. 1297 (2003); Gary Lawson, Discretion as Delegation: The 'Proper' Understanding of the Nondelegation Doctrine, 73 Geo. Wash. L.R. 235 (2005). For a reply to the former work, see Eric A. Posner & Adrian Vermeule, Nondelegation: A Post-mortem, 70 U. Chi. L. Rev. 1331 (2003).

Prominent among these criticisms is the worry that Position (3) is an excessively formalistic view. It entails that the following statute would not be invalid on nondelegation grounds (although it might be on other grounds): "Congress hereby authorizes the President to make rules on any subject within the constitutional power of Congress." Is the possibility of such a statute disturbing, or is this an example of an implausible slippery-slope argument? What political mechanisms might work to prevent such a statute from being enacted? Note that, under conventional constitutional-law assumptions, Congress could always enact a later statute revoking the statutory grant. If the quoted statute were enacted, what could the judges do about it (under the rubric of the nondelegation doctrine)? Should constitutional rules be geared to minimize the probability that the worst-case scenario will come to pass, or is this like designing every house to withstand a meteor strike? Consider, in this regard, the early decision by the German legislature to confer on Adolf Hitler the power to rule by "decree"; this delegation made possible lawmaking exercises that would otherwise have been extremely cumbersome, and hence removed an important check on arbitrary rule. Note in this regard that the German Constitutional Court enforces the nondelegation doctrine. See D. Currie, The Constitution of the Federal Republic of Germany 125-134 (1995). Is the German experience highly illuminating, an outlier or atypical case, or something in between? For a comparative political science treatment suggesting that the German experience is not the norm, see John Carey & Matthew Shugart, eds., Executive Decree Authority (1998).

2. The Nondelegation "Doctrine" — Early History and Pre-1935 Supreme Court Decisions

It is often remarked that the Supreme Court last used the nondelegation doctrine to invalidate a federal statute in 1935. It is less often remarked that the Court first used the nondelegation doctrine to invalidate a statute in 1935. We might therefore say that in American law, the nondelegation doctrine has had only one good year.

The historical credentials of the nondelegation doctrine, in the sense of Position (2) above, are a matter of controversy. In its first year, Congress gave the president the power to grant licenses to trade with the Indian tribes "under such rules and regulations as the President shall prescribe," 1 Stat. 137. The first Congress also provided for military pensions "under such regulations as the President of the United States may direct," 1 Stat. 95, and gave considerable power to the secretary of the treasury to mitigate or remit fines and forfeitures. See 1 Stat. 123. How much weight should this history have in suggesting the existence, or content, of any prohibition on the delegation of legislative power, or on excessively discretionary statutory grants?

In any case, courts began to suggest the existence of a nondelegation prohibition, again in the sense of Position (2) above, at some time in the nineteenth century, although there is controversy about whether this development occurred early or late in the century. The later the development, the less impressive is the claim of the nondelegation doctrine to capture the original understanding of the Constitution, or to represent a longstanding tradition. One view suggests that the nondelegation doctrine has deep roots in Supreme Court precedent. See Lisa Schultz Bressman, Schecter Poultry at the Milennium: A Delegation Doctrine for the Administrative State, 109 Yale L.J. 1399, 1403 (2000). On another view, "the nondelegation [doctrine] was a legal theory of uncertain provenance that skulked around the edges of nineteenth-century constitutionalism." Posner & Vermeule, 69 U. Chi. L. Rev. at 1737.

Here again, part of the disagreement arises from confusions among Positions (1), (2), and (3) above. Position (1) — the simple idea that the legislative power is nondelegable — is indeed venerable. Is Position (2) equally so? Before its decisions in Panama Refining Co. v. Ryan, 293 U.S. 388 (1935), and A. L. A. Schechter Poultry Corp. v. United States, 295 U.S. 495 (1935), which we review below, the Supreme Court consistently sustained congressional statutes against the charge that they involved an unlawful delegation of legislative power to executive officials. Perhaps, however, the Court endorsed some version of a "nondelegation" doctrine in dictum.

The Brig Aurora, 11 U.S. (7 Cranch) 382 (1813), upheld a statute that revived certain previously expired statutory import restrictions on a determination by the president that either Great Britain or France had ceased violating the neutral commerce of the United States. The Court found nothing objectionable in conditioning the revival on an executive determination. The lawyer for one of the parties argued for a nondelegation doctrine; the Court's terse dismissal of the claim does not clearly accept, or reject, the existence of such a doctrine. As with all the other cases before 1935, the Court did not strike down any statute on nondelegation grounds.

Nondelegation Not used until 1935 to strike Down a statute.

Wayman v. Southard, 23 U.S. (10 Wheat.) 1 (1825), in relevant part, upheld a statute granting rulemaking authority to the federal courts. Marshall's opinion stated: "It will not be contended that Congress can delegate to the Courts, or to any other tribunals, powers which are strictly and exclusively legislative. But Congress may certainly delegate to others, powers which the legislature may rightfully exercise itself." Is this a statement of the nondelegation doctrine in the sense of Position (2) above; a statement of the nondelegation doctrine in the sense of Position (1), above; a statement of some other view; or a confusing mishmash? Compare Posner & Vermeule, 69 U. Chi. L. Rev. at 1738-1739 with Gary Lawson, Delegation and Original Meaning, 88 Va. L. Rev. 327, 355-61 (2002) Or does Wayman seem ambiguous on the crucial questions just because the justices were not focused on the issues that are of interest some 150 years later?

Field v. Clark, 143 U.S. 649 (1892), relied on the Brig Aurora case to uphold a statute that provided for imposition of a retaliatory tariff schedule on imports from nations that imposed duties on American products that the president "may deem to be reciprocally unequal and unreasonable." The president, the Court held, was not given legislative authority by the statute because his powers were limited to ascertaining a matter of contingent "fact" — the imposition by foreign nations of "reciprocally unequal and unreasonable" tariffs — on which the legislative provision for retaliatory tariff schedules was contingent. Is the determination whether duties are "reciprocally unequal and unreasonable" really one of fact? On the broader nondelegation issue, the doctrinal significance of Field v. Clark is that it clearly asserts Position (2) above — it clearly says, not merely that legislative power is nondelegable, but that a statutory grant of authority that gives the president excessive discretion amounts to a forbidden delegation.

Pos 2.

The "contingency" rationale proved inadequate in United States v. Grimaud, 220 U.S. 506 (1911), which sustained a statute giving the secretary of agriculture broad authority to "make provision for the protection against destruction and depradations upon the public forests and forest reservations," including authority to adopt "such rules and regulations . . . to regulate [the reservations'] occupancy and use, and to preserve the forests thereof from destruction." Violation of the regulations was made a criminal offense. The Court held that the statute did not delegate legislative authority but merely gave the secretary a "power to fill up the details."

An even more generous standard was applied in J. W. Hampton, Jr. & Co. v. United States, 276 U.S. 394 (1928), which upheld a statute giving the president power to revise the tariff duties specified in the statute whenever he determined that such revision was necessary to "equalize the costs of production in the United States and the principal competing country." While the Court justified the president's powers under the statute by reference to the contingency theory of Field v. Clark and the "filling up the details" principle of *Grimaud*, it rested on the broader ground that "[i]f Congress shall lay down by legislative act an intelligible principle to which the person or body authorized to [take action] is directed to conform, such legislative action is not a forbidden delegation of legislative power." The Court found that the notion of adjusting tariffs to "equalize the costs of production" constituted an "intelligible principle." Does it?

3. Panama Refining *and* Schechter

(a) A major piece of legislation, designed to help ease the Depression, was enacted during President Roosevelt's first "100 days" in office: the National Industrial Recovery Act (NIRA) of 1933. Its objective was to have representatives of management and labor in each industry meet and develop codes of "fair competition." In practice, this procedure was meant to stabilize wages and prices with the hope that, by arresting price and wage declines, business confidence would be restored and workers' purchasing power maintained. Many saw the act in broader terms as the vehicle for inaugurating comprehensive national planning of the economy, which they believed necessary to ensure future economic growth. Critics feared the development of a "corporate state," suggesting a parallel with the philosophy of Mussolini.

The NIRA, 48 Stat. 195 (1935), provided in part the following (emphasis added):

DECLARATION OF POLICY

Section 1. A national emergency productive of widespread unemployment and disorganization of industry, which burdens interstate and foreign commerce, affects the public welfare, and undermines the standards of living of the American people, is hereby declared to exist. It is hereby declared to be the policy of Congress to remove obstructions to the free flow of interstate and foreign commerce which tend to diminish the amount thereof; and to provide for the general welfare by promoting the organization of industry *for the purpose of cooperative action among trade groups*, to induce and maintain united action of labor and management under adequate governmental sanctions and supervision, to eliminate unfair competitive practices, to promote the fullest possible utilization of the present productive capacity of industries, *to avoid undue restriction of production* (except as may be temporarily required), to increase the consumption of industrial and agricultural products by increasing purchasing power, to reduce and relieve unemployment, to improve standards of labor, and otherwise to rehabilitate industry and to conserve natural resources.

Section 2. (a) To effectuate the policy of this title, the President is hereby authorized to establish such agencies . . . as he may find necessary, to prescribe their authorities, duties, responsibilities, and tenure. . . .

(b) The President may delegate any of his functions and powers under this title to such officers, agents, and employees as he may designate or appoint. . . .

(c) [The program is limited to a two-year time period.]

CODES OF FAIR COMPETITION

Section 3. (a) Upon the application to the President by one or more trade or industrial associations or groups, the President may approve a code or codes of fair competition for the trade or industry or subdivision thereof, represented by the applicant or applicants, if the President finds (1) that such associations or groups impose no inequitable restrictions on admission to membership therein and are truly representative of such trades or industries or subdivisions thereof, and (2) that such code or codes are not designed to promote monopolies or to eliminate or oppress small enterprises and will not operate to discriminate against them, and will tend to effectuate the policy of this title: Provided, That such code or codes shall not permit monopolies or monopolistic practices: Provided further, That where such code or codes affect the services and welfare of persons engaged in other steps of the economic process, nothing in this section shall deprive such persons of the right to be heard prior to approval by the President of such code or codes. The President may, as a condition of his approval of any such code, impose such conditions (including requirements for the making of reports and the keeping of accounts) for the protection of consumers, competitors, employees, and others, and in furtherance of the public interest, and may provide such exceptions to an exemption from the provisions of such code, as the President in his discretion deems necessary to effectuate the policy herein declared.

(b) After the President shall have approved any such code, the provisions of such code shall be the standards of fair competition for such trade or industry or subdivisions thereof. Any violation of such standards in any transaction in or affecting interstate or foreign commerce shall be deemed an unfair method of competition in commerce within the meaning of the Federal Trade Commission Act. . . .

Types of Regs under NIRA

(b) "In the course of its short life from August, 1933, to February, 1935, the Administration formulated and approved 546 codes and 185 supplemental codes filling 18 volumes and 13,000 pages; 685 amendments and modifications to these codes. It issued over 11,000 administrative orders interpreting, granting exemptions from, and establishing classifications under the provisions of individual codes; 139 administrative orders bearing generally upon administrative procedure. These codes of so-called fair competition were not uniform in content. They contained regulations of the greatest variety of practices. Most of them had *minimum wage* and *maximum hour* provisions. One or another of them had provisions for *minimum price* or prohibitions against *sales below 'cost'* (cost being a generalized figure that might be much above actual cost); provisions *controlling or restricting* production sometimes directly, sometimes by concealed devices; provisions *prohibiting exceptional* discounts, rebates and other *devices of price competition*; provisions regulating advertising, sales techniques, etc." L. Jaffe & N. Nathanson, Administrative Law, Cases and Materials 52 (4th ed. 1976) (emphasis added).

As a practical matter, a draft of each code would be written and presented to the government by a few powerful groups in each major industry. Other firms and interests would be notified, and a final draft would emerge out of negotiations among the parties.

(c) Panama Refining Co. v. Ryan, 293 U.S. 388 (1935), involved a challenge to the NIRA's Petroleum Code. The challengers won the major portion of their case when it was discovered that the official but unpublished version of the code, setting oil production quotas, through a mistake, contained no sentence making a violation of oil production quotas unlawful. (The fact that even government lawyers had difficulty finding the official version led to the creation of the *Federal Register* and the requirement that agency documents, to be valid, must be published there. See 49 Stat. 5400 (1935).)

The president, however, had also issued an Executive Order under §9(c) of the NIRA. This section stated that "the President is authorized to prohibit the transportation in interstate commerce" of oil produced in violation of state-imposed production quotas. The majority of the Court held this section unconstitutional because it did not provide a standard governing *when* the president was to exercise the authorized power. Justice Cardozo, the sole dissenter, argued that NIRA §1 delineated many such standards. He also found standards derivable from the context and background of the statute. Chief Justice Hughes replied that that was just the problem: NIRA §1 provided too many conflicting standards with no indication how the president was to choose among them. Nor had the president indicated how he had so chosen.

A. L. A. Schechter Poultry Corp. v. United States
295 U.S. 495 (1935)

Mr. Chief Justice HUGHES delivered the opinion of the Court.

Petitioners . . . were convicted in the . . . Eastern District of New York on eighteen counts of an indictment charging violations of what is known as the "Live Poultry Code." . . . By demurrer to the indictment . . . the defendants contended (1) that the Code had been adopted pursuant to an unconstitutional delegation by Congress of legislative power; . . .

The defendants are slaughterhouse operators. Schechter Poultry Corporation and Schechter Live Poultry Market are corporations conducting wholesale poultry slaughterhouse markets in Brooklyn, New York City. . . . They buy the poultry for slaughter and resale. After the poultry is trucked to their slaughterhouse markets in Brooklyn, it is there sold, usually within twenty-four hours, to retail poultry dealers and butchers who sell directly to consumers. The poultry purchased from defendants is immediately slaughtered, prior to delivery, by *schochtim* in defendant's employ. . . .

The "Live Poultry Code" [is a code of "fair competition" for those in the New York area live poultry industry. It] was promulgated under §3 of the National Industrial Recovery Act . . . [and] was approved by the President on April 13, 1934. . . .

The Code . . . provides that no employee, with certain exceptions, shall be permitted to work in excess of forty (40) hours in any one week, and that no employee, save as stated, "shall be paid in any pay period less than at the rate of fifty (50) cents per hour." . . . The minimum number of employees, who shall be employed by slaughterhouse operators, is fixed. . . .

Provision is made for administration through an "industry advisory committee," to be selected by trade associations and members of the industry, and a "code supervisor" to be appointed, with the approval of the committee, by agreement between the Secretary of Agriculture and the Administrator for Industrial Recovery. . . .

The seventh article, containing "trade practice provisions," prohibits various practices which are said to constitute "unfair methods of competition." . . .

Of the eighteen counts of the indictment upon which the defendants were convicted, . . . ten counts were for violation for the requirement (found in the "trade practice provisions") [that a wholesale seller could not allow a buyer to select particular chickens. Rather they had] . . . "to accept the run of any half coop, coop, or coops." . . .

[It was charged] that the defendants in selling to retail dealers and butchers had permitted "selections of individual chickens taken from particular coops and half coops."

. . . [One other count] charged the sale to a butcher of an unfit chicken. . . .

[The] Congress is not permitted to abdicate or to transfer to others the essential legislative functions with which it is vested. We have repeatedly recognized the necessity of adapting legislation to complex conditions involving a host of details with which the national legislature cannot deal directly. We pointed out in the *Panama Company* case that the Constitution has never been regarded as denying to Congress the necessary resources of flexibility and practicality. . . . But we said that the constant recognition of the necessity and validity of such provisions, and the wide range of administrative authority which has been developed by means of them, cannot be allowed to obscure the limitations of the authority to delegate, if our constitutional system is to be maintained.

[What] is meant by "fair competition" as the term is used in the Act? Does it refer to a category established in the law, and is the authority to make codes limited accordingly? Or is it used as a convenient designation for whatever set of laws the formulators of a code for a particular trade or industry may propose and the President may approve . . . as being wise and beneficent provisions for the government of the trade or industry in order to accomplish the broad purposes of rehabilitation, correction and expansion which are stated in the first section of Title I?

The Act does not define "fair competition." "Unfair competition," as known to the common law, is a limited concept. In recent years, its scope has been extended. . . .

The Federal Trade Commission Act (§5) introduced the expression "unfair methods of competition," which were declared to be unlawful. What are "unfair methods of competition" are thus to be determined in particular instances, upon evidence, in the light of particular competitive conditions and of what is found to be a specific and substantial public interest. To make this possible, Congress set up a special procedure. A Commission, a quasi-judicial body, was created. . . .

Quasi Judicial

In providing for codes, the National Industrial Recovery Act dispenses with this administrative procedure and with any administrative procedure of an analogous character. But the difference between the code plan of the Recovery Act and the scheme of the Federal Trade Commission Act lies not only in procedure but in subject matter. We cannot regard the "fair competition" of the codes as antithetical to the "unfair methods of competition" of the Federal Trade Commission Act. The "fair competition" of the codes has a much broader range and a new significance. . . .

For a statement of the authorized objectives and content of the "codes of fair competition" we are referred repeatedly to the "Declaration of Policy" in §1 of Title I of the Recovery Act. . . . That declaration embraces a broad range of objectives. . . .

Under §3, whatever "may tend to effectuate" these general purposes may be included in the "codes of fair competition." . . . [T]he purpose is clearly disclosed to authorize new and controlling prohibitions through codes of laws which would embrace what the formulators would propose, and what the President would approve, or prescribe, as wise and beneficent measures for the government of trades and industries in order to bring about their rehabilitation, correction and development, according to the general declaration of policy in §1. . . .

The Government urges that the codes will "consist of rules of competition deemed fair for each industry by representative members of that industry — by the persons most vitally concerned and most familiar with its problems." Instances are cited in which Congress has availed itself of such assistance; as e.g., in the exercise of its authority over

Argument over Meaning of "fair Competition"

the public domain, with respect to the recognition of local customs or rules of miners as to mining claims, or, in matters of a more or less technical nature, as in designating the standard height of drawbars. But would it be seriously contended that Congress could delegate its legislative authority to trade or industrial associations or groups so as to empower them to enact the laws they deem to be wise and beneficent for the rehabilitation and expansion of their trade or industries? Could trade or industrial associations or groups be constituted legislative bodies for that purpose because such associations or groups are familiar with the problems of their enterprises? And, could an effort of that sort be made valid by such a preface of generalities as to permissible aims as we find in §1 of Title I? The answer is obvious. Such a delegation of legislative power is unknown to our law and is utterly inconsistent with the constitutional prerogatives and duties of Congress.

The question, then, turns upon the authority which §3 of the Recovery Act vests in the President to approve.

[Accordingly,] we turn to the Recovery Act to ascertain what limits have been set to exercise of the President's discretion. *First*, the President, as a condition of approval, is required to find that the trade or industrial associations or groups which propose a code, "impose no inequitable restrictions on admission to membership" and are "truly representative." . . .

Second, the President is required to find that the code is not "designed to promote monopolies or to eliminate or oppress small enterprises and will not operate to discriminate against them." . . . But these restrictions leave virtually untouched the field of policy envisaged by §1. . . . The Act provides for the creation by the President of administrative agencies to assist him, but the action or reports of such agencies, or of his other assistants . . . have no sanction beyond the will of the President, who may accept, modify or reject them as he pleases. Such recommendations or findings in no way limit the authority which §3 undertakes to vest in the President with no other conditions than those there specified. And this authority relates to a host of different trades and industries, thus extending the President's discretion to all the varieties of laws which he may deem to be beneficial in dealing with the vast array of commercial and industrial activities throughout the country. . . .

Section 3 of the Recovery Act is without precedent. It supplies no standards for any trade, industry or activity. It does not undertake to prescribe rules of conduct to be applied to particular states of fact determined by appropriate administrative procedure. Instead of prescribing rules of conduct, it authorizes the making of codes to prescribe them. For that legislative undertaking, §3 sets up no standards, aside from the statement of the general aims of rehabilitation, correction and expansion described in §1. In view of the scope of that broad declaration, and of the nature of the few restrictions that are imposed, the discretion of the President in approving or prescribing codes, and thus enacting laws for the government of trade and industry throughout the country, is virtually unfettered. We think that the code-making authority thus conferred is an unconstitutional delegation of legislative power. . . .

Mr. Justice CARDOZO, concurring.

The delegated power of legislation which has found expression in this code is not canalized within banks that keep it from overflowing. It is unconfined and vagrant. . . .

Here, in the case before us, is an attempted delegation not confined to any single act nor to any class or group of acts identified or described by reference to a standard. Here in effect is a roving commission to inquire into evils and upon discovery correct them.

. . . If codes of fair competition are codes eliminating "unfair" methods of competition ascertained upon inquiry to prevail in one industry or another, there is no unlawful delegation of legislative functions when the President is directed to inquire into such practices and denounce them when discovered.

But there is another conception of codes of fair competition, their significance and function, which leads to very different consequences. . . . By this other conception a code is not to be restricted to the elimination of business practices that would be characterized by general acceptance as oppressive or unfair. It is to include whatever ordinances may be desirable or helpful for the well-being or prosperity of the industry affected. In that view, the function of its adoption is not merely negative, but positive; the planning of improvements as well as the extirpation of abuses. What is fair, as thus conceived, is not something to be contrasted with what is unfair or fraudulent or tricky. The extension becomes as wide as the field of industrial regulation. If that conception shall prevail, anything that Congress may do within the limits of the commerce clause for the betterment of business may be done by the President upon the recommendation of a trade association by calling it a code. This is delegation running riot. No such plenitude of power is susceptible of transfer. The statute, however, aims at nothing less, as one can learn both from its terms and from the administrative practice under it.

. . . It sets up a comprehensive body of rules to promote the welfare of the industry, if not the welfare of the nation, without reference to standards, ethical or commercial, that could be known or predicted in advance of its adoption. One of the new rules, the source of ten counts in the indictment, is aimed at an established practice, not unethical or oppressive, the practice of selective buying. . . .

Amalgamated Meat Cutters v. Connally

337 F. Supp. 737 (D.D.C. 1971)

[The Meat Cutters Union challenged the Economic Stabilization Act on grounds of excessive delegation.

In an important opinion by Judge Leventhal, the three-judge court sustained the constitutionality of the act. The opinion first lays down a standard for determining whether a given delegation of legislative power is permissible:]

[T]here is no forbidden delegation of legislative power "if Congress shall lay down by legislative act an intelligible principle" to which the official or agency must conform.

Concepts of control and accountability define the constitutional requirement. The principle permitting a delegation of legislative power, if there has been sufficient demarcation of the field to permit a judgment whether the agency has kept within the legislative will, establishes a principle of accountability under which compatibility with the legislative design may be ascertained not only by Congress but by the courts and the public. That principle was conjoined in *Yakus* [v. United States, 321 U.S. 414 (1944),] with a recognition that the burden is on the party who assails the legislature's choice of means for effecting its purpose, a burden that is met only if we could say that there is an absence of standard for the guidance of the Administrator's action so that it would be impossible in a proper proceeding to ascertain whether the will of Congress has been obeyed.

[The court then concluded that the act, read in light of its background, legislative history, and prior regulatory programs to control wages and prices, did furnish an "intelligible principle" by which a court could police its implementation. It stressed that "the

ESA Does include

standards of a statute are not to be tested in isolation" and derive "meaningful content from the purpose of the Act, its factual background, and the statutory context." Congress, the court found, contemplated a broad freeze of prices and wages, whose timing must necessarily be left to executive discretion, to halt "cost-push" inflation and check accompanying "inflationary psychology." The court also found significance in the limited duration of the authority granted the president.

The Meat Cutters Union contended, however, that, despite the limited duration of the delegated power, the delegation was invalid because it afforded the president a "blank check" for controlling domestic affairs that is intolerable in our constitutional system. The union stressed the absence in the act of a requirement, found in earlier price and wage control programs, that controls be "fair and equitable," and argued that the act therefore gave the president power arbitrarily to prefer certain social and economic constituencies at the expense of others. It pointed to the exemption from control in Executive Order 11,615 of the prices of raw agricultural products as an example of such an arbitrary preference. To this argument the court replied as follows:]

If the Act gives the President authority to be unfair and inequitable, as the Union claims, this legislative vessel may indeed founder on a constitutional rock. But we do not reach this constitutional issue because we do not think the Act can be given the extremist interpretation offered by the Union.

We take this view not only because of the doctrine that statutes are to be construed so as to avoid serious constitutional questions, but more directly because we do not think it can sensibly or fairly be said that this extremist approach was what was intended by the legislature. As we have already shown there is no lack of specificity in the constitutional sense in the standards of the Act for the initiation of controls, either in particular industries or sectors of the economy, or in the general wage-price freeze.

The problem that now concerns us is whether the Act has sufficient specificity to avoid the constitutional condemnation, of excessive "blank check" authority to the President, as to the period following the initial general price-wage freeze.

We do not think it can be said that the possibility of controls beyond the initial freeze was left without any standard other than the President's unfettered discretion, including the discretion to be unfair and inequitable. This is not a case where Congress indicated an intention to leave the matter wholly to the discretion of the President without any possibility of judicial review. The ultimate standard for follow-on controls replacing the freeze is a standard of fairness and equity. This standard of removal of "gross inequities" is voiced as an authority of the President in §202 of the Act. . . . We think there is fairly implicit in the Act the duty to take whatever action is required in the interest of broad fairness and avoidance of gross inequity, although presumably his range of discretion means there may be inequities that a President may remove that he is not compelled by law to remove.

This conclusion is supported by constitutional considerations and historic context. The 1942 statute on prices specifically articulated the "generally fair and equitable" standard. But the broad equity standard is inherent in a stabilization program. It was incorporated into the 1942 wage control measures providing for stabilization of wages and salaries. Fairness and equity are also furthered by the requirement that the Executive develop implementing standards, with deliberate criteria replacing the fortuities of a freeze.

It is not our purpose or function at this time to define the contours of the standard of broad fairness and avoidance of gross inequity. That would be appropriate if the taking or omission of specific action were challenged. But we reiterate that we cannot accept the contention of the Government that the court must pass on the constitutionality of the Act without any conception of its content. We take the intermediate course and rule that our judgment has two parts: first, that the statute does at least contain a standard of broad fairness and avoiding gross inequity, leaving to the future the implementation of that standard; second, that this statute is not unconstitutional as an excessive delegation of power by the legislature to the Executive for the limited term of months contemplated by Congress to follow the initiating general freeze.

. . . Another feature that blunts the "blank check" rhetoric is the requirement that any action taken by the Executive under the law, subsequent to the freeze, must be in accordance with further standards as developed by the Executive. This requirement, inherent in the Rule of Law and implicit in the Act, means that however broad the discretion of the Executive at the outset, the standard once developed limits the latitude of subsequent Executive action.

The importance in present context of this self-limiting aspect of Executive and agency discretion is brought out in Yakus v. United States, supra. After noting that the Constitution does not demand the impossible, that the essentials of the legislative functions are preserved with a determination of legislative policy, Chief Justice Stone continues: "It is no objection that the determination of facts and the inferences to be drawn from them in the light of the statutory standards and declaration of policy call for the exercise of judgment, and for the formulation of subsidiary administrative policy within the prescribed statutory framework."

The crucial paragraph of the opinion specifically relies on the reasoning of Executive administration as helping to supply the requisite specificity and precision:

> [T]he standards prescribed by the present Act, with the aid of the "statement of the considerations" required to be made by the Administrator, are sufficiently definite and precise to enable Congress, the courts and the public to ascertain whether the Administrator, in fixing the designated prices, has conformed to those standards. . . . Hence we are unable to find in them an unauthorized delegation of legislative power. [321 U.S. at 426.]

The requirement of subsidiary administrative policy, enabling Congress, the courts and the public to assess the Executive's adherence to the ultimate legislative standard, is in furtherance of the purpose of the constitutional objective of accountability. This 1970 Act gives broadest latitude to the Executive. Certainly there is no requirement of formal findings. But there is an ongoing requirement of intelligible administrative policy that is corollary to and implementing of the legislature's ultimate standard and objective. This requirement is underscored by the consideration that the exercise of wide discretion will probably call for "imaginative interpretation," leaving the courts to see whether the Executive, using its experience, "has fairly exercised its discretion within the vaguish, penumbral bounds" of the broad statutory standard.

In view of the administration of the prior two stabilization programs the Government cannot sensibly contend that the requirement of development of administrative standards is unattainable or would reduce to a futility the legislative objective of controlling inflation.

[Finally, the court discussed the pertinence of the Schechter decision:]

In Schechter, which held invalid the provisions of the National Industrial Recovery Act that authorized the fixing of codes of fair conduct, the "function of formulating the codes was delegated, not to a public official responsible to Congress or to the Executive, but to private individuals engaged in the industries to be regulated." Yakus v. United

States, supra, 321 U.S. at 424. . . . The "corporate state" aspects of the Blue Eagle codes that emerged in practice were made possible and reinforced by a legal context of authority to prescribe "codes of fair competition" that covered the entire range of economic life, going beyond even the broad subject matter before us.

Schechter has fairly been described as a ruling that administered "the hemlock of excessive delegation" in a case of "delegation run riot." We think the extremist pattern then before the Court cannot fairly be analogized to the anti-inflation statute, limited in life and passed in a context of experiences with similar legislation, that is before us for consideration.

Plaintiff's motion for injunctive relief must be denied.

[The court also noted that the act, unlike the NIRA, is subject to the APA's review provisions.]

Questions on *Schechter* and *Amalgamated Meat Cutters*

1. What goals are promoted by the nondelegation doctrine? A standard answer is political accountability. But this answer is far too simple. In both of the principal cases, the relevant authority would have been exercised by the president, who is certainly subject to electoral control. Most agencies that are given discretionary authority are subject, to a greater or lesser degree, to presidential oversight. Perhaps the problem lies in the phrase "to a greater or lesser degree." But a more subtle answer would be that the doctrine is designed to promote a distinctive kind of accountability — the kind of accountability that comes from requiring specific decisions from a deliberative body reflecting the views of representatives from various states of the union. The president is elected by a nationwide majority or plurality, while Congress is a summation of local majorities or pluralities.

On this view, the nondelegation doctrine should be associated less with accountability in the abstract than with the particular constitutional goal of ensuring a deliberative democracy, one that involves not only accountability but also reflectiveness. The vesting of lawmaking power in Congress is designed to ensure the combination of deliberation and accountability that comes from saying that government power cannot be brought to bear on individuals unless diverse representatives, from diverse places, have managed to agree on the details.

A closely related point has to do with the extent to which law, and particularly national legislation, can amount to an infringement on liberty. If no law may be brought to bear against the public unless diverse members of Congress have been able to agree on a particular form of words, then perhaps there is an important safeguard of freedom. The underlying idea is that people may not be subject to national legal constraints unless and until there has been specific legislative authorization for the constraints. This idea can in turn be associated with social contract theory, allowing people to maintain certain private law rights unless there has been explicit authorization for what would otherwise be a common law wrong.

The nondelegation doctrine is also said to promote rule-of-law values. It does this, first, by promoting planning by those subject to law, by giving them a sense of what is permitted and what is forbidden. It does this, second, by cabining the discretionary authority of enforcement officials, who might otherwise act abusively or capriciously. In all these ways, the nondelegation doctrine might be seen as a safeguard against the Framers' core concerns, self-interested representation and factional power.

These points can be collected with the suggestion that the nondelegation doctrine reflects the Constitution's commitment to dual-branch lawmaking, as reflected in

Article I, Section 7's provisions for bicameral lawmaking and presentment of bills to the president. That commitment cabins arbitrary power and promotes deliberation as well as accountability, by ensuring that governmental authority can be exercised only when both the legislature and the executive have made a particular decision to that effect. For relevant discussion, see David Schoenbrod, Power Without Responsibility (1997); Sunstein, Is the Clean Air Act Unconstitutional?, 98 Mich. L. Rev. 303, 335-337 (1999); John M. Manning, The Nondelegation Doctrine as a Canon of Avoidance, 2000 Sup Ct Rev 223.

The foregoing points go a long way toward justifying Position (1), the basic idea that legislative power is nondelegable. But on a skeptical view, it is unclear how, exactly, these values — accountability, deliberativeness, liberty — support a "nondelegation doctrine" in the sense of Position (2) above. There, the crucial idea is that statutes granting authority to the executive count as forbidden delegations when the grant is too discretionary or too broad. Why isn't it sufficient that the statute granting authority to the executive must itself be approved by Congress, and will thus itself embody the values promoted by Article I, Section 7? A deliberative, accountable, and liberty-respecting Congress will be a Congress that grants statutory authority to executive agents when, and only when, it is best that Congress should do so. To the extent that the nondelegation doctrine is premised on slippery-slope arguments and a deep distrust of Congress, it cannot also be justified by referring to Congress's advantages in deliberativeness and accountability. Those advantages will themselves make it unlikely that Congress will delegate when delegation is bad. The idea that Congress may be held accountable for enacting the delegating statutes themselves is a principal theme of J. Mashaw, Why Administrators Should Make Political Decisions, in J. Mashaw, Greed, Chaos, and Governance (1997).

2. How exactly are these two principal cases different? Consider the view that in *Schechter* there was in effect a delegation of lawmaking power to private groups. Is there any reason to be especially concerned about statutory grants of authority to nonexecutive agents? This might be an especially troubling practice if it represents a capitulation to the power of private factions.

Note, however, that this is not obviously a *nondelegation* problem. The nondelegation doctrine might be strictly about the question what Congress can give away, not who the constitutionally permissible recipients are. We might understand the problem in *Schechter* as one of the allocation of executive power, not legislative power; perhaps only public officials are constitutionally entitled to exercise the power to execute federal statutes. By the way, do state officials count? See Printz v. United States, 521 U.S. 898, 922 (Scalia, J., concurrring) (suggesting that law-execution authority cannot be vested in someone other than a federal executive officer subject to presidential control); cf. United States Telecom Assn. v. FCC, 359 F.3d 554 (D.C. Cir. 2004) (FCC may not subdelegate its power to make regulatory decisions to state agencies).

In any event, modern constitutional doctrine is quite permissive about delegations to private parties. See Currin v. Wallace, 306 U.S. 1 (1939) (upholding a statute providing that restrictions upon the production or marketing of agricultural commodities would take effect when approved by a prescribed majority of the affected farmers); United States v. Rock Royal Co-operative, 307 U.S. 533, 577 (1939) (upholding a statute that gave producers of specified commodities the right to veto marketing orders issued by the secretary of agriculture).

If there is a nondelegation problem in the picture, would it have been possible for the *Schechter* Court to have responded to this problem by construing the executive branch's authority narrowly, so as to avoid the delegation problem? Could the executive branch have construed its own authority narrowly?

3. How does a requirement of "subsidiary administrative policy" remedy a delegation problem? Consider the view that consistency and clarity from an agency can alleviate concerns from the standpoint of the rule of law by increasing predictability, but cannot alleviate concerns from the standpoint of electoral accountability because Congress is not, in fact, the relevant lawmaker. The Supreme Court has rejected this view in *American Trucking*, infra, and the Court's analysis there raises serious questions about the viability of the reasoning, if not the outcome, in *Amalgamated Meat Cutters*. After reading *American Trucking*, it will be useful to return to the issues in *Amalgamated Meat Cutters*.

4. If courts vigorously enforced the nondelegation doctrine, what, if any, problems would you foresee? We will deal with this question in some detail below.

Note on Historically Based Price Regulation

As *Amalgamated Meat Cutters* makes clear, during times of war the government has tried to control both wages and prices throughout the economy. That is because large amounts of productive capacity had to be used to make war materials, creating serious shortages of ordinary peacetime products and threatening inflation if the government permitted consumers freely to bid for the resulting short supply. But how can the government regulate the prices of the millions of different products that make up the entire economy?

Perhaps the only feasible system is a simple one. First, pick a date, say, August 15, 1942. Second, select a rigid rule, "Charge the same price that you charged on August 15, 1942." Third, moderate the rigid rule in recognition of the facts that many firms on that special date may have been involved in "special circumstances" (for example, a "special" low-priced "sale") and that some factor prices will inevitably rise (for example, food prices, import prices), and permit the firm to raise its price above the August 15 level by some factor x. X, for example, may consist of the firm's own justified cost increases since August 15, or it may consist of a percentage determined by average price increases in a region, an industry, or the economy as a whole among some, or all, factors. The resulting price rule takes the form "Charge the prices you charged on August 15 plus x."

Economists have disagreed about whether such a system should be used in peacetime to combat inflation or whether it ever works, even in wartime. The basic problem is that, as time goes on, more and more special circumstances develop. The government must calculate prices for new products; it must determine how to price the production that stems from new (higher cost) investment; it must consider firms' claims that special, higher cost factors of production warrant special price increases; it must consider firms' claims that, for special reasons, their prices were too low to begin with; it must consider whether price or profit incentives are needed to induce manufacture of new items, or of more items in short supply; it must consider whether firms' profits are too low, too high, or about right; it must consider how to allocate goods in respect to which "price ceilings" have created shortages. Moreover, when price controls have been applied nationwide, the government has had to take special steps to hold wages down; otherwise, increasing wages with fixed prices would soon destroy firms' profits. Finally, the government must find an administrative way to stop widespread evasion.

Consider here two related questions. The first is a legal question: How broad a delegation is required for the government to be able, effectively, to administer such a program? The 1970 law permitting the president to impose wage and price controls consisted, in essence, of the following three statutory sentences:

> The President is authorized to issue such orders and regulations as he may deem appropriate to stabilize prices, rents, wages, and salaries at levels not less than those prevailing on May 25, 1970. Such orders and regulations may provide for the making of such adjustments as may be necessary to prevent gross inequities. . . . The President may delegate the performance of any function under this title to such officers, departments, and agencies of the United States as he may deem appropriate.

Economic Stabilization Act of 1970, 84 Stat. 799 (1970).

Acting under this legal authority, the president established the Cost of Living Council, to which he delegated all his powers. He ordered that "prices, rents, wages, and salaries shall be stabilized for a period of 90 days from August 15, 1971, at levels not greater than the highest of those pertaining to a substantial volume of actual transactions by each individual, business, firm or other entity." (If no transaction occurred on that date, the ceiling is the highest price during the preceding 30-day period in which transactions did not occur.) No one "directly or indirectly" shall charge a higher price than those permitted. Food is exempt. Violation of a council regulation is a crime. Executive Order No. 11,615, 36 C.F.R. 600 (Aug. 15, 1971).

The council subsequently enacted more specific regulations, which we set forth below.

The second question is practical. How well do you think this system worked? Read the council's regulations.

PRICE STABILIZATION REGULATIONS

§300.5 *Definitions*. . . . "Price increase" means an increase in the unit price of a property or service or a decrease in the quality of substantially the same property or services.

"Profit margin" means the ratio that operating income (net sales less cost of sales and less normal and generally recurring costs of business operations, determined before nonoperating items, extraordinary items, and income taxes) bears to net sales as reported on the person's financial statement prepared in accordance with generally accepted accounting principles consistently applied. . . .

§300.11 *General rule*. (a) No person may charge a price with respect to any sale or lease of an item of property or a service after November 13, 1971, which exceeds the base price (or other price authorized under this part) for that item of property or that service. . . .

§300.12 *Manufacturers*. A manufacturer may charge a price in excess of the base price only to reflect increases in allowable costs that it incurred since the last price increase in the item concerned, or that it incurred after January 1, 1971, whichever was later, and that it is continuing to incur, reduced to reflect productivity gains, and only to the extent that the increased price does not result in an increase in its profit margin over that which prevailed during the base period. . . .

§300.13 *Retailers and wholesalers*. (a) General. A retailer or wholesaler may charge a price in excess of the base price whenever its customary initial percentage markup after November 13, 1971, with respect to property sold, is equal to or less than its last customary initial percentage markup before November 14, 1971, or, at its option, its customary initial percentage markup during its last fiscal year ending before August 15, 1971. However, the increased price may not result in an increase in its profit margin over that which prevailed during the base period. . . .

§300.409 *New property and new services.* . . . (b) Base price determination. A person offering a new property or a new service shall determine its base price as follows:

(1) Net operating profit markup — Manufacturer or service organization. A manufacturer or service organization shall apply the net operating profit markup it received on the most nearly similar property or service it sold or leased to the same market during the freeze base period to the total allowable unit costs of the new property or service. For the purposes of this subparagraph, "net operating profit market" means the ratio which the selling price bears to the total allowable unit costs of the property or service.

(2) Customary initial percentage markup — Retailer or wholesaler shall apply the customary initial percentage markup it received on the most nearly similar property or service it sold to the same market during the freeze base period to the allowable unit costs of the new property.

(3) Average price of comparable property or services. If the person did not offer a similar property or service for sale or lease to a particular market during the freeze base period, the base price for sales or leases to that market shall be the average price received in a substantial number of current transactions in that market by other persons selling or leasing comparable property or services in the same marketing area.

(4) Customary pricing practice. If none of the methods provided in subparagraphs (1) through (3) of this paragraph can be used and the new property or new service is not reasonably comparable to any property or service previously sold or leased by any person within the same marketing area or being sold or leased by the person concerned in current transactions in the same market, he may use any customary pricing practice he used during the freeze base period, or, if the person did not sell or lease any property or service before August 15, 1971, he may use any other pricing practice commonly used by other persons engaging in comparable business with the same market.

A Further Note on Historically Based Price Regulation

Even though it seems unlikely that the government will impose nationwide price controls in the near future, controls may be used for more limited purposes, as occurred with the regulation of oil prices during the 1970s. Many have advocated them as a "simplified" way to control railroad or electricity rates. Rather than examine the individual costs of the electricity company or the railroad (an examination that is time-consuming and costly, and which we shall study in Chapter 4), perhaps the regulator could devise a simple rule of the form "Charge your historical price plus x." If one could find an appropriate, simple way to determine x, then the regulator might have an easy way to decide if the regulated firm's rates were too high. These regulatory proposals are sometimes called "price caps."

When Congress deregulated many railroad rates, for example, it retained the rights of shippers to challenge rates as too high in areas where the railroads maintained "market dominance." 49 U.S.C. §10701a (1982). To provide a "simple" method for deciding whether a rate was too high, Congress also provided that the Interstate Commerce Commission (ICC) maintain a quarterly index of railroad costs. Once determined, the commission could multiply existing (or "base") rates by the average increase in those costs to determine a "proper" present rate. That is to say, this "index" of average increases in railroad costs could provide an x for adjusting historical rates to determine a proper ceiling.

This system works well as long as relative costs remain constant among the many different services that the regulated firm provides or incurs. But once those relative costs begin to change, the system begins to falter. Insofar as relative costs related to a particular service rise faster than (average railroad factor cost) inflation, the regulated company will begin to lose money on the related service; it will ask the regulator to make an exception permitting it to continue to provide the service profitably; in the absence of the exception, it will try to cut back the service, at least in respect to its quality. Insofar as relative costs related to a particular service rise slower than (average railroad factor cost) inflation, then (to the extent competition fails to force price cuts) the firm will find it possible to earn supernormal profits with respect to that service. See Judge Starr's discussion of these problems in Alabama Power Co. v. Interstate Commerce Commission, 852 F.2d 1361 (D.C. Cir. 1988).

The more time that passes, the more likely that significant changes in relative prices will occur; the more likely that the firm will respond to the incentives to which they give rise; the more likely one will find misallocation; the more likely the regulator will respond with ad hoc adjustments focusing on particular services and particular costs; and the more likely the "simplified" price control system will no longer be "simple." It will come to resemble the traditional, firm-specific, detailed, cost-based system we describe in Chapter 4.

In Great Britain, the government "privatized" previously nationalized electricity-generating companies. A nationally owned company, in principle, would set prices that led to reasonable, rather than exorbitant, profits. A privately owned firm operates without any such constraint. Therefore, Britain decided to regulate the prices charged by the new, private firms. It also decided to use a simplified "price cap" system for deciding whether prices are reasonable. It permits the private firms to charge the prices charged during a specific "base" period plus an upward adjustment to reflect economy-wide price inflation. See J. Vickers & G. Yarrow, Privatization: An Economic Analysis (1988); S. C. Littlechild, Regulations of British Telecommunications Profitability (London, HMSO 1983); UK Department of Energy, Draft Public Electricity Supply License (1990).

Industrial Union Department, AFL-CIO v. American Petroleum Institute (The Benzene Case)
448 U.S. 607 (1980)

Mr. Justice STEVENS announced the judgment of the Court and delivered an opinion, in which THE CHIEF JUSTICE and Mr. Justice STEWART joined and in Parts I, II, III-A, III-B, III-C, and III-E of which Mr. Justice POWELL joined.

[Industry challenged the adoption by the secretary of labor of a regulatory standard limiting occupational exposure to benzene. Under the Occupational Safety and Health Act, the Occupational Safety and Health Administration (OSHA), within the Department of Labor, is responsible for developing such standards.]

The Act delegates broad authority to the Secretary to promulgate different kinds of standards. The basic definition of an "occupational safety and health standard" is found in §3(8) [of the Occupational Safety and Health Act], which provides:

> The term "occupational safety and health standard" means a standard which requires conditions, or the adoption or use of one or more practices, means, methods, operations, or processes, reasonably necessary or appropriate to provide safe or healthful employment and places of employment. 84 Stat. 1591, 29 U.S.C. §652(8).

Where toxic materials or harmful physical agents are concerned, a standard must also comply with §6(b)(5), which provides:

> The Secretary, in promulgating standards dealing with toxic materials or harmful physical agents under this subsection, shall set the standard which most adequately assures, to the extent feasible, on the basis of the best available evidence, that no employee will suffer material impairment of health or functional capacity even if such employee has regular exposure to the hazard dealt with by such standard for the period of his working life. 84 Stat. 1594, 29 U.S.C. §655(b)(5).

Wherever the toxic material to be regulated is a carcinogen, the Secretary has taken the position that no safe exposure level can be determined and that §6(b)(5) requires him to set an exposure limit at the lowest technologically feasible level that will not impair the viability of the industries regulated. In this case, after having determined that there is a causal connection between benzene and leukemia (a cancer of the white blood cells), the Secretary set an exposure limit on airborne concentrations of benzene of one part benzene per million parts of air (1 ppm). . . .

Reading the two provisions together, the Fifth Circuit held that the Secretary was under a duty to determine whether the benefits expected from the new standard bore a reasonable relationship to the costs that it imposed. . . . The court noted that OSHA had made an estimate of the costs of compliance, but that the record lacked substantial evidence of any discernible benefits.

We agree with the Fifth Circuit's holding that §3(8) requires the Secretary to find, as a threshold matter, that the toxic substance in question poses a significant health risk in the workplace and that a new, lower standard is therefore "reasonably necessary or appropriate to provide safe or healthful employment and places of employment." Unless and until such a finding is made, it is not necessary to address the further question whether the Court of Appeals correctly held that there must be a reasonable correlation between costs and benefits, or whether, as the federal parties argue, the Secretary is then required by §6(b)(5) to promulgate a standard that goes as far as technologically and economically possible to eliminate the risk. . . .

I

The entire population of the United States is exposed to small quantities of benzene, ranging from a few parts per billion to 0.5 ppm, in the ambient air.

. . . [O]ne million workers are subject to additional low-level exposures as a consequence of their employment. The majority of these employees work in gasoline service stations, benzene production (petroleum refineries and coking operations), chemical processing, benzene transportation, rubber manufacturing, and laboratory operations.

Benzene is a toxic substance. . . . Persistent exposures at levels above 25-40 ppm may lead to blood deficiencies and diseases of the blood-forming organs, including aplastic anemia, which is generally fatal.

[As authorized by the act, the secretary in 1971 adopted as the federal standard the American National Standards Institute "consensus standard" for occupational exposure to benzene of 10 ppm averaged over an eight-hour period. The National Institute for Occupational Safety and Health (NIOSH), OSHA's research arm, concluded, on the basis of epidemiological studies correlating exposure levels of 150-600 ppm over extended periods and increased cancer incidence by exposed workers, that benzene caused leukemia. Although the studies failed to establish dose-response relations that would predict cancer incidence at lower exposure levels, NIOSH recommended that the exposure limit be set as low as possible.]

[OSHA proposed a "permanent" standard of 1 ppm. It] did not ask for comments as to whether or not benzene presented a significant health risk at exposures of 10 ppm or less. Rather, it asked for comments as to whether 1 ppm was the minimum feasible exposure limit. As OSHA's Deputy Director of Health Standards, Grover Wrenn, testified at the hearing, this formulation of the issue to be considered by the Agency was consistent with OSHA's general policy with respect to carcinogens. Whenever a carcinogen is involved, OSHA will presume that no safe level of exposure exists in the absence of clear proof establishing such a level and will accordingly set the exposure limit at the lowest level feasible. . . .

The permanent standard is expressly inapplicable to the storage, transportation, distribution, sale, or use of gasoline or other fuels subsequent to discharge from bulk terminals. This exception is particularly significant in light of the fact that over 795,000 gas station employees, who are exposed to an average of 102,700 gallons of gasoline (containing up to 2% benzene) annually, are thus excluded from the protection of the standard.

As presently formulated, the benzene standard is an expensive way of providing some additional protection for a relatively small number of employees. According to OSHA's figures, the standard will require capital investments in engineering controls of approximately $266 million, first-year operating costs (for monitoring, medical testing, employee training, and respirators) of $187 million to $205 million and recurring annual costs of approximately $34 million. 43 Fed. Reg. 5934 (1978). The figures outlined in OSHA's explanation of the costs of compliance to various industries indicate that only 35,000 employees would gain any benefit from the regulation in terms of a reduction in their exposure to benzene. Over two-thirds of these workers (24,450) are employed in the rubber-manufacturing industry. Compliance costs in that industry are estimated to be rather low with no capital costs and initial operating expenses estimated at only $34 million ($1,390 per employee); recurring annual costs would also be rather low, totaling less than $1 million. By contrast, the segment of the petroleum refining industry that produces benzene would be required to incur $24 million in capital costs and $600,000 in first-year operating expenses to provide additional protection for 300 workers ($82,000 per employee), while the petrochemical industry would be required to incur $20.9 million in capital costs and $1 million in initial operating expenses for the benefit of 552 employees ($39,675 per employee).

Although OSHA did not quantify the benefits to each category of worker in terms of decreased exposure to benzene, it appears from the economic impact study done at OSHA's direction that those benefits may be relatively small. Thus, although the current exposure limit is 10 ppm, the actual exposures outlined in that study are often considerably lower. For example, for the period 1970-1975 the petrochemical industry reported that, out of a total of 496 employees exposed to benzene, only 53 were exposed to levels between 1 and 5 ppm and only 7 (all at the same plant) were exposed to between 5 and 10 ppm. . . .

II

Any discussion of the 1 ppm exposure limit must, of course, begin with the Agency's rationale for imposing that limit. The written explanation of the standard fills 184 pages of the printed appendix. Much of it is devoted to a discussion of the voluminous evidence of the adverse effects of exposure to benzene at levels of concentration well above 10 ppm. This discussion demonstrates that there is ample justification for regulating occupational exposure to benzene and that the prior limit of 10 ppm, with a ceiling of 25 ppm (or a peak of 50 ppm) was reasonable. It does not however, provide direct support for the Agency's conclusion that the limit should be reduced from 10 ppm to 1 ppm.

The evidence in the administrative record of adverse effects of benzene exposure at 10 ppm is sketchy at best. [The Court reviewed the studies.]

[OSHA concluded] that some benefits were likely to result from reducing the exposure limit from 10 ppm to 1 ppm. This conclusion was based, again, not on evidence, but rather on the assumption that the risk of leukemia will decrease as exposure levels decrease. Although the Agency had found it impossible to construct a dose-response curve that would predict with any accuracy the number of leukemias that could be expected to result from exposures at 10 ppm, at 1 ppm, or at any intermediate level, it nevertheless "determined that the benefits of the proposed standard are likely to be appreciable."

It is noteworthy that at no point in its lengthy explanation did the Agency quote or even cite §3(8) of the Act. It made no finding that any of the provisions of the new standard were "reasonably necessary or appropriate to provide safe or healthful employment and *places* of employment."

III

[The Court noted industry's argument that OSHA's statute requires it to use a cost-benefit approach to setting standards, but concluded that it need not decide the issue.]

A

. . . . [W]e think it is clear that the statute was not designed to require employers to provide absolutely risk-free workplaces whenever it is technologically feasible to do so, so long as the cost is not great enough to destroy an entire industry. Rather, both the language and structure of the Act, as well as its legislative history, indicate that it was intended to require the elimination, as far as feasible, of significant risks of harm.

B

Therefore, before he can promulgate any permanent health or safety standard, the Secretary is required to make a threshold finding that a place of employment is unsafe — in the sense that significant risks are present and can be eliminated or lessened by a change in practices. . . .

In the absence of a clear mandate in the Act, it is unreasonable to assume that Congress intended to give the Secretary the unprecedented power over American industry that would result from the Government's view of §§(8) and 6(b)(5), coupled with OSHA's cancer policy. Expert testimony that a substance is probably a human carcinogen — either because it has caused cancer in animals or because individuals have contracted cancer following extremely high exposures — would justify the conclusion that the substance poses some risk of serious harm no matter how minute the exposure and no matter how many experts testified that they regarded the risk as insignificant. That conclusion would in turn justify pervasive regulation limited only by the constraint of feasibility. In light of the fact that there are literally thousands of substances used in the workplace that have been identified as carcinogens or suspect carcinogens, the Government's theory would give OSHA power to impose enormous costs that might produce little, if any, discernible benefit. If the Government were correct in arguing that neither §3(8) nor §6(b)(5) requires that the risk from a toxic substance be quantified sufficiently to enable the Secretary to characterize it as significant in an understandable way, the statute would make such a "sweeping delegation of legislative power" that it might be unconstitutional under the Court's reasoning in A. L. A. Schechter Poultry Corp. v. United States, 295 U.S. 495, 539 [(1935)] and Panama Refining Co. v. Ryan, 293 U.S. 388 [(1935)]. A construction of the statute that avoids this kind of open-ended grant should certainly be favored.

C

The legislative history also supports the conclusion that Congress was concerned, not with absolute safety, but with the elimination of significant harm. . . .

D

. . . As we read the statute, the burden was on the Agency to show, on the basis of substantial evidence, that it is at least more likely than not that long-term exposure to 10 ppm of benzene presents a significant risk of material health impairment. Ordinarily, it is the proponent of a rule or order who has the burden of proof in administrative proceedings. . . .

In this case OSHA did not even attempt to carry its burden of proof. . . .

Contrary to the Government's contentions, imposing a burden on the Agency of demonstrating a significant risk of harm will not strip it of its ability to regulate carcinogens, nor will it require the Agency to wait for deaths to occur before taking any action. First, the requirement that a "significant" risk be identified is not a mathematical straitjacket. It is the Agency's responsibility to determine, in the first instance, what it considers to be a "significant" risk. . . .

Second, OSHA is not required to support its finding that a significant risk exists with anything approaching scientific certainty. . . .

The judgment of the Court of Appeals remanding the petition for review to the Secretary for further proceedings is affirmed.

Mr. Justice POWELL, concurring in part and in the judgment. . . .

[Justice Powell found that OSHA had not relied solely on its assumption that no safe threshold exposure for a carcinogen exists, but had also claimed that the specific facts of record, including evidence of adverse health effects of levels of benzene exposure substantially higher than 10 ppm, established that the 1 ppm standard adopted was reasonably necessary to deal with a significant health risk. The Justice concluded that the record failed to establish "substantial evidence" for such a finding.]

. . . But even if one assumes that OSHA properly met this burden, I conclude that the statute also requires the agency to determine that the economic effects of its standard bear a reasonable relationship to the expected benefits. An occupational health standard is neither "reasonably necessary" nor "feasible," as required by statute, if it calls for expenditures wholly disproportionate to the expected health and safety benefits. . . . It is simply unreasonable to believe the Congress intended OSHA to pursue the desirable goal of risk-free workplaces to the extent that the economic viability of particular industries — or significant segments thereof — is threatened. . . .

[Such a policy] would impair the ability of American industries to compete effectively with foreign businesses and to provide employment for American workers.. . . Perhaps more significantly, however, OSHA's interpretation of §6(b)(5) would force it to regulate in a manner inconsistent with the important health and safety purposes of the legislation we construe today. Thousands of toxic substances present risks that fairly could be characterized as "significant." . . . Even if OSHA succeeded in selecting the gravest risks for earliest regulation, a standard-setting process that ignored economic considerations would result in a serious misallocation of resources and a lower effective level of safety than could be achieved under standards set with reference to the comparative benefits available at a lower cost. I would not attribute such an irrational intention to Congress.

In this case, OSHA did find that the "substantial costs" of the benzene regulations are justified. . . . But the record before us contains neither adequate documentation of this conclusion, nor any evidence that OSHA weighed the relevant considerations. . . .

Mr. Justice REHNQUIST, concurring in the judgment. . . .

In considering the alternative interpretations . . . [of the statute,] my colleagues manifest a good deal of uncertainty, and ultimately divide over whether the Secretary produced sufficient evidence that the proposed standard for benzene will result in any appreciable benefits at all. This uncertainty, I would suggest, is eminently justified, since I believe that this litigation presents the Court with what has to be one of the most difficult issues that could confront a decisionmaker: whether the statistical possibility of future deaths should ever be disregarded in light of the economic costs of preventing those deaths. I would also suggest that the widely varying positions advanced in the briefs of the parties and in the opinions of Mr. Justice Stevens, the Chief Justice, Mr. Justice Powell, and Mr. Justice Marshall demonstrate, perhaps better than any other fact, that Congress, the governmental body best suited and most obligated to make the choice confronting us in this litigation, has improperly delegated that choice to the Secretary of Labor and, derivatively, to this Court.

I

In this Second Treatise of Civil Government, published in 1690, John Locke wrote that "[t]he power of the legislative, being derived from the people by a positive voluntary grant and institution, can be no other than what that positive grant conveyed, which being only to make laws, and not to make legislators, the legislative can have no power to transfer their authority of making laws and place it in other hands." Two hundred years later, this Court expressly recognized the existence of and the necessity for limits on Congress' ability to delegate its authority to representatives of the Executive Branch: "That Congress cannot delegate legislative power to the President is a principle universally recognized as vital to the integrity and maintenance of the system of government ordained by the Constitution." Field v. Clark, 143 U.S. 649, 692 (1982).

The rule against delegation of legislative power is not, however, so cardinal a principle as to allow for no exception. The Framers of the Constitution were practical statesmen. . . .

[The Justice discussed the history of the doctrine that Congress may not delegate "legislative" powers to administrative agencies without adequate standards to guide its exercise.] . . .

Viewing the legislation at issue here in light of these principles, I believe that it fails to pass muster. Read literally, the relevant portion of §6(b)(5) is completely precatory, admonishing the Secretary to adopt the most protective standard if he can, but excusing him from that duty if he cannot. In the case of a hazardous substance for which a "safe" level is either unknown or impractical, the language of §6(b)(5) gives the Secretary absolutely no indication where on the continuum of relative safety he should draw his line. Especially in light of the importance of the interests at stake, I have no doubt that the provision at issue, standing alone, would violate the doctrine against uncanalized delegations of legislative power. For me the remaining question, then, is whether additional standards are ascertainable from the legislative history or statutory context of §6(b)(5) or, if not, whether such a standardless delegation was justifiable in light of the "inherent necessities" of the situation.

II

One of the primary sources looked to by this Court in adding gloss to an otherwise broad grant of legislative authority is the legislative history of the statute in question.

[The Justice reviewed the legislative history of §6(b)(5), which originally required OSHA to prevent injury to workers' health, without regard to feasibility. The words "to the extent feasible" were added during the Senate floor debates.]

. . . I believe that the legislative history demonstrates that the feasibility requirement, as employed in §6(b)(5), is a legislative mirage, appearing to some Members but not to others, and assuming any form desired by the beholder. . . .

In sum, the legislative history contains nothing to indicate that the language "to the extent feasible" does anything other than render what had been a clear, if somewhat unrealistic, standard largely, if not entirely, precatory. There is certainly nothing to indicate that these words, as used in §6(b)(5), are limited to technological and economic feasibility. . . .

III

[I]n some cases this Court has abided by a rule of necessity, upholding broad delegations of authority where it would be "unreasonable and impracticable to compel Congress to prescribe detailed rules" regarding a particular policy or situation. . . .

. . . But no need for such an evasive standard as "feasibility" is apparent in the present cases. In drafting §6(b)(5), Congress was faced with a clear, if difficult, choice between balancing statistical lives and industrial resources or authorizing the Secretary to elevate human life above all concerns save massive dislocation in an affected industry.

. . . That Congress chose, intentionally or unintentionally, to pass this difficult choice on to the Secretary is evident from the spectral quality of the standard it selected and is capsulized in Senator Saxbe's unfulfilled promise that "the terms that we are passing back and forth are going to have to be identified."

IV

As formulated and enforced by this Court, the nondelegation doctrine serves three important functions. First, and most abstractly, it ensures to the extent consistent with orderly governmental administration that important choices of social policy are made by

Congress, the branch of our Government most responsive to the popular will. . . . Second, the doctrine guarantees that, to the extent Congress finds it necessary to delegate authority, it provides the recipient of that authority with an "intelligible principle" to guide the exercise of the delegated discretion. . . . Third, and derivative of the second, the doctrine ensures that courts charged with reviewing the exercise of delegated legislative discretion will be able to test that exercise against ascertainable standards.

I believe the legislation at issue here fails on all three counts. . . . I would suggest that the standard of "feasibility" renders meaningful judicial review impossible.

We ought not to shy away from our judicial duty to invalidate unconstitutional delegations of legislative authority solely out of concern that we should thereby reinvigorate discredited constitutional doctrines of the pre-New Deal era. If the nondelegation doctrine has fallen into the same desuetude as have substantive due process and restrictive interpretations of the Commerce Clause, it is, as one writer has phrased it, "a case of death by association." J. Ely, Democracy and Distrust, A Theory of Judicial Review 133 (1980). Indeed, a number of observers have suggested that this Court should once more take up its burden of ensuring that Congress does not unnecessarily delegate important choices of social policy to politically unresponsive administrators. Other observers, as might be imagined, have disagreed.

If we are ever to reshoulder the burden of ensuring that Congress itself make the critical policy decisions, these are surely the cases in which to do it. It is difficult to imagine a more obvious example of Congress simply avoiding a choice which was both fundamental for purposes of the statute and yet politically so divisive that the necessary decision or compromise was difficult, if not impossible, to hammer out in the legislative forge. . . . When fundamental policy decisions underlying important legislation about to be enacted are to be made, the buck stops with Congress and the President insofar as he exercises his constitutional role in the legislative process. . . . Accordingly, for the reasons stated above, I concur in the judgment of the Court affirming the judgment of the Court of Appeals.

Mr. Justice MARSHALL, with whom Mr. Justice BRENNAN, Mr. Justice WHITE, and Mr. Justice BLACKMUN join, dissenting. . . .

The plurality's conclusion . . . is based on its interpretation of 29 U.S.C. §652(8), which defines an occupational safety and health standard as one "which requires conditions . . . reasonably necessary or appropriate to provide safe or healthful employment. . . ." According to the plurality, a standard is not "reasonably necessary or appropriate" unless the Secretary is able to show that it is "at least more likely than not," . . . that the risk he seeks to regulate is a "significant" one. . . . Nothing in the statute's language or legislative history, however, indicates that the "reasonably necessary or appropriate" language should be given this meaning. . . .

. . . Contrary to the plurality's suggestion, the Secretary did not rely blindly on some Draconian carcinogen "policy." . . .

In this case the Secretary found that exposure to benzene at levels above 1 ppm posed a definite albeit unquantifiable risk of chromosomal damage, nonmalignant blood disorders, and leukemia. . . .

In these circumstances it seems clear that the Secretary found a risk that is "significant" in the sense that the word is normally used [and he appropriately weighed costs and benefits]. . . .

Because the approach taken by the plurality is so plainly irreconcilable with the Court's proper institutional role, I am certain that it will not stand the test of time. In all likelihood, today's decision will come to be regarded as an extreme reaction to a regulatory scheme that, as the Members of the plurality perceived it, imposed an unduly harsh burden on regulated industries. But as the Constitution "does not enact Mr. Herbert Spencer's Social Statics," *Lochner v. New York*, 198 U.S. 45, 75 (1905) (Holmes, J., dissenting), so the responsibility to scrutinize federal administrative action does not authorize this Court to strike its own balance between the costs and benefits of occupational safety standards. I am confident that the approach taken by the plurality today, like that in *Lochner* itself, will eventually be abandoned, and that the representative branches of government will once again be allowed to determine the level of safety and health protection to be accorded to the American worker.

Note: The *Benzene* Problem

1. Why did Congress create the Occupational Safety and Health Administration? Consider the following possibilities. (a) Because workers lack the information necessary to make informed tradeoffs between health risks and other relevant values, such as wages. (b) Because even if workers have relevant information, they cannot be expected to use it well. People tend to process information poorly and to engage in various forms of wishful thinking. (c) Because Congress wanted to redistribute resources from employers to employees. (d) Because injuries to workers impose external harms on, for example, family members and taxpayers.

With respect to these possibilities, what difference would it make if empirical studies showed that employers must pay a significant "wage premium" for subjecting employees to workplace risks? W. Kip Viscusi, Risk by Choice (1983), makes this argument, with evidence. Consider also the view that occupational safety and health requirements are not likely to be a good redistributive strategy because the consequence of such requirements will be (a) to depress wages, (b) to increase unemployment, and (c) to increase prices, so that workers as a whole are not clearly helped on balance. See Rose-Ackerman, Progressive Law and Economics, 97 Yale L.J. 1083 (1989). There is evidence that worker compensation legislation resulted, in the nonunionized sector, in a dollar-for-dollar wage reduction for workers. See Price Fishback and Shawn Everett Kantor, A Prelude to the Welfare State: The Origins of Workers' Compensation (2000). Does this point suggest that occupational safety and health regulation might not be in workers' interests? Fishback and Kantor urge that notwithstanding dollar-for-dollar reduction, workers' compensation programs were generally good for workers.

2. Suppose it is decided that the national government has a legitimate role to play in promoting safe, or safer, workplaces. What exactly ought the national government to be doing? Consider the following possibilities. (a) It should conduct research about risks and ensure that employers disclose to workers existing information about workplace risks. (b) It should ban from the workplace those, and only those, risks that are so severe that no reasonable person would be willing to face them. (c) It should impose financial penalties on employers for causing injuries to workers. The penalties might go to employees; they might go to the treasury. The goal of the penalties would be to provide compensation and (optimal) deterrence. (d) It should require employers to reduce workplace injuries by a certain percentage or amount, and allow employers to decide exactly how to do this. (e) It should strengthen workers' associations to enable them to bargain collectively about risks in the workplace. (f) It should require employers to meet certain standards with respect to workplace conditions, including, for example, permissible exposure limits to carcinogens, use of ladders, location and use of toilet seats, and so forth.

　　Which of these possibilities would be better? Did Congress make any decisions about a, b, c, d, e, or f? Which did it exclude, and which did it prescribe? Consider the view that in enacting OSHA, Congress's largest failure was that it did not connect its perception of the problem at issue with its perception of the appropriate regulatory solution. The result is legislation that is not only vague but undirected — not directed to any particular understanding of the nature of the problem that was to be solved.

　　3. In the *Benzene Case*, the plurality held that OSHA must show that any risk it seeks to regulate is "significant." The plurality did not say that OSHA must use cost-benefit analysis, and indeed the Court subsequently held that the statute does not contemplate cost-benefit analysis. See American Textile Manufacturers' Inst. v. Donovan, 452 U.S. 490 (1981), page 356. But can an agency sensibly decide whether a risk is "significant" without also examining the cost of eliminating it? Suppose that a lifetime cancer risk from a certain substance is 1/1000, faced by 10,000 workers. Is that risk "significant"? Would the answer be different if the same lifetime cancer risk was faced by 10 million workers? To decide whether to eliminate the risk, would you like to know whether the cost is $1 million or $1 billion?

　　OSHA has said, by the way, that a lifetime risk of over 1.64/1000 is "significant," see Building & Constr. Trades Dept. v. Block, 838 F.2d 1258, 1265 (D.C. Cir. 1988), but that a risk of 0.6/100,000 "may be approaching a level that can be viewed as safe." Occupational Exposure to Formaldehyde, 52 Fed. Reg. 56,168, 46,234 (1987). Might this approach be criticized on the ground that OSHA appears not to be thinking about the size of the exposed population? It would seem sensible to think that a risk of 0.6 in 100,000 is insignificant if the exposed population has 10,000 people in it, but not if the exposed population has 200 million people in it. See James Hamilton & W. Kip Viscusi, Calculating Risks 91-108 (2000), for discussion of the importance of the size of the affected population.

　　4. In requiring OSHA to show a "significant risk," Justice Stevens uses a technique of statutory interpretation like that in *Amalgamated Meat Cutters*: He construes the statute a certain way to avoid a nondelegation problem. But it is not clear that the government's position would actually have created such a problem. If Congress said, "Eliminate all workplace risks, to the extent feasible," would there be a nondelegation issue? Wouldn't this somewhat draconian statute create limited administrative discretion? Consider the possibility that Justice Stevens has confused the existence of administrative *discretion* with the existence of administrative *power*. See also the lower court opinion in *American Trucking*, infra, suggesting that a statute that requires agencies to eliminate all risks, even tiny ones, would raise no nondelegation problem.

　　5. What would be the consequences if the Supreme Court adopted Justice Rehnquist's view in the *Benzene Case*? Would many statutes be invalidated? Note that Justice Rehnquist's special concern is that Congress did not choose whether to require cost-benefit balancing, or a showing of a "significant risk," or something else.

　　6. Does it matter whether agencies that have broad discretionary power are, in practice, doing better than agencies that have limited discretionary power? It is possible to think that agency performance and reputation cannot be predicted by asking whether Congress has sharply limited agency discretion — or, in other words, that the extent of agency discretion is not much connected with the extent to which agencies have actually made things work better rather than worse. Thus, for example, the Securities and Exchange Commission (SEC), which has a good deal of discretion, is generally well regarded, whereas the Department of Agriculture, which has limited discretion under many of its statutory provisions, tends not to be well regarded. Whether agencies have

good reputations, or seem to have successfully served the public interest, may well be quite independent of whether they have limited discretion. This is partly because legislative limitations on agency discretion may be confused, ill-considered, or reflective of the self-interest of powerful private groups. Do these points bear on the question whether the nondelegation doctrine should be revived?

4. Recent Developments

American Trucking Associations, Inc. v. Environmental Protection Agency

175 F.3d 1027 (D.C. Cir. 1999)

PER CURIAM:

The Clean Air Act requires EPA to promulgate and periodically revise national ambient air quality standards ("NAAQS") for each air pollutant identified by the agency as meeting certain statutory criteria. For each pollutant, EPA sets a "primary standard" — a concentration level "requisite to protect the public health" with an "adequate margin of safety" — and a "secondary standard" — a level "requisite to protect the public welfare."

In July 1997 EPA issued final rules revising the primary and secondary NAAQS for particulate matter ("PM") and ozone. Numerous petitions for review have been filed for each rule. [W]e find that the construction of the Clean Air Act on which EPA relied in promulgating the NAAQS at issue here effects an unconstitutional delegation of legislative power. . . . Although the factors EPA uses in determining the degree of public health concern associated with different levels of ozone and PM are reasonable, EPA appears to have articulated no "intelligible principle" to channel its application of these factors; nor is one apparent from the statute. The nondelegation doctrine requires such a principle. Here it is as though Congress commanded EPA to select "big guys," and EPA announced that it would evaluate candidates based on height and weight, but revealed no cut-off point. The announcement, though sensible in what it does say, is fatally incomplete. The reasonable person responds, "How tall? How heavy?"

EPA regards ozone definitely, and PM likely, as non-threshold pollutants, i.e., ones that have some possibility of some adverse health impact (however slight) at any exposure level above zero. For convenience, we refer to both as non-threshold pollutants; the indeterminacy of PM's status does not affect EPA's analysis, or ours. [Thus] the only concentration for ozone and PM that is utterly risk-free, in the sense of direct health impacts, is zero. Section 109(b)(1) says that EPA must set each standard at the level "requisite to protect the public health" with an "adequate margin of safety." These are also the criteria by which EPA must determine whether a revision to existing NAAQS is appropriate. . . . For EPA to pick any non-zero level it must explain the degree of imperfection permitted. The factors that EPA has elected to examine for this purpose in themselves pose no inherent nondelegation problem. But what EPA lacks is any determinate criterion for drawing lines. It has failed to state intelligibly how much is too much.

We begin with the criteria EPA has announced for assessing health effects in setting the NAAQS for non-threshold pollutants. They are "the nature and severity of the health effects involved, the size of the sensitive population(s) at risk, the types of health information available, and the kind and degree of uncertainties that must be addressed." Although these criteria, so stated, are a bit vague, they do focus the inquiry on pollution's effects on public health. And most of the vagueness in the abstract formulation melts away as EPA applies the criteria: EPA basically considers severity of effect, certainty of effect, and size of population affected.

Read in light of these factors, EPA's explanations for its decisions amount to assertions that a less stringent standard would allow the relevant pollutant to inflict a greater quantum of harm on public health, and that a more stringent standard would result in less harm. . . . Consider EPA's defense of the 0.08 ppm level of the ozone NAAQS. EPA explains that its choice is superior to retaining the existing level, 0.09 ppm, because more people are exposed to more serious effects at 0.09 than at 0.08. In defending the decision not to go down to 0.07, EPA never contradicts the intuitive proposition, confirmed by data in its Staff Paper, that reducing the standard to that level would bring about comparable changes. . . . In other words, effects are less certain and less severe at lower levels of exposure. This seems to be nothing more than a statement that lower exposure levels are associated with lower risk to public health.

Where (as here) statutory language and an existing agency interpretation involve an unconstitutional delegation of power, but an interpretation without the constitutional weakness is or may be available, our response is not to strike down the statute but to give the agency an opportunity to extract a determinate standard on its own. Doing so serves at least two of three basic rationales for the nondelegation doctrine. If the agency develops determinate, binding standards for itself, it is less likely to exercise the delegated authority arbitrarily. And such standards enhance the likelihood that meaningful judicial review will prove feasible. A remand of this sort of course does not serve the third key function of non-delegation doctrine, to "ensure[ ] to the extent consistent with orderly governmental administration that important choices of social policy are made by Congress, the branch of our Government most responsive to the popular will." The agency will make the fundamental policy choices. But the remand does ensure that the courts not hold unconstitutional a statute that an agency, with the application of its special expertise, could salvage. . . .

What sorts of "intelligible principles" might EPA adopt? Cost-benefit analysis . . . is not available under decisions of this court. . . . In theory, EPA could make its criterion the eradication of any hint of direct health risk. This approach is certainly determinate enough, but it appears that it would require the agency to set the permissible levels of both pollutants here at zero. No party here appears to advocate this solution, and EPA appears to show no inclination to adopt it. . . . EPA's past behavior suggests some readiness to adopt standards that leave non-zero residual risk. For example, it has employed commonly used clinical criteria to determine what qualifies as an adverse health effect. On the issue of likelihood, for some purposes it might be appropriate to use standards drawn from other areas of the law, such as the familiar "more probable than not" criterion.

Of course a one-size-fits-all criterion of probability would make little sense. There is no reason why the same probability should govern assessments of a risk of thousands of deaths as against risks of a handful of people suffering momentary shortness of breath. More generally, all the relevant variables seem to range continuously from high to low: the possible effects of pollutants vary from death to trivialities, and the size of the affected population, the probability of an effect, and the associated uncertainty range from "large" numbers of persons with point estimates of high probability, to small numbers and vague ranges of probability. This does not seem insurmountable. Everyday life compels us all to make decisions balancing remote but severe harms against a probability distribution of benefits; people decide whether to proceed with an operation that carries a 1/1000 possibility of death, and (simplifying) a 90 percent chance of cure and a 10 percent chance of no effect, and a certainty of some short-term pain and nuisance. To be sure, all that requires is a go/no-go decision, while a serious effort at coherence under §109(b)(1) would need to be more comprehensive. For example, a range of ailments short of death might need to be assigned weights. Nonetheless, an agency wielding the power over American life possessed by EPA should be capable of developing the rough equivalent of a generic unit of harm that takes into account population affected, severity and probability. Possible building blocks for such a principled structure might be found in the approach Oregon used in devising its health plan for the poor. In determining what conditions would be eligible for treatment under its version of Medicaid, Oregon ranked treatments by the amount of improvement in "Quality-Adjusted Life Years" provided by each treatment, divided by the cost of the treatment. Here, of course, EPA may not consider cost, and indeed may well find a completely different method for securing reasonable coherence. Alternatively, if EPA concludes that there is no principle available, it can so report to the Congress, along with such rationales as it has for the levels it chose, and seek legislation ratifying its choice. . . .

Whitman v. American Trucking Associations, Inc.

531 U.S. 457 (2001)

Justice SCALIA delivered the opinion of the Court.

Section 109(b)(1) of the CAA instructs the EPA to set "ambient air quality standards the attainment and maintenance of which in the judgment of the Administrator, based on [the] criteria [documents of §108] and allowing an adequate margin of safety, are requisite to protect the public health." The Court of Appeals . . . found that the EPA's interpretation (but not the statute itself) violated the nondelegation doctrine. We disagree.

[In] a delegation challenge, the constitutional question is whether the statute has delegated legislative power to the agency. Article I, §1, of the Constitution vests "[a]ll legislative Powers herein granted . . . in a Congress of the United States." This text permits no delegation of those powers, and so we repeatedly have said that when Congress confers decisionmaking authority upon agencies *Congress* must "lay down by legislative act an intelligible principle to which the person or body authorized to [act] is directed to conform." We have never suggested that an agency can cure an unlawful delegation of legislative power by adopting in its discretion a limiting construction of the statute. . . . The idea that an agency can cure an unconstitutionally standardless delegation of power by declining to exercise some of that power seems to us internally contradictory. The very choice of which portion of the power to exercise — that is to say, the prescription of the standard that Congress had omitted — would *itself* be an exercise of the forbidden legislative authority. Whether the statute delegates legislative power is a question for the courts, and an agency's voluntary self-denial has no bearing upon the answer.

We agree with the Solicitor General that the text of §109(b)(1) of the CAA at a minimum requires that "[f]or a discrete set of pollutants and based on published air quality criteria that reflect the latest scientific knowledge, [the] EPA must establish uniform national standards at a level that is requisite to protect public health from the adverse effects of the pollutant in the ambient air." Requisite, in turn, "mean[s] sufficient, but not more than necessary." These limits on the EPA's discretion are strikingly similar to the ones we approved in Touby v. United States, 500 U.S. 160 (1991), which permitted the Attorney General to designate a drug as a controlled substance for purposes of criminal drug enforcement if doing so was " 'necessary to avoid an imminent hazard to the public safety.'" They also resemble the Occupational Safety and Health Act provision requiring the agency to " 'set the standard which most adequately assures, to the extent feasible, on the basis of the best available evidence, that no employee will suffer any impairment of health' " — which the Court upheld [in the *Benzene Case*], and which even then-Justice Rehnquist, who alone in that case thought the statute violated the nondelegation doctrine, would have upheld if, like the statute here, it did not permit economic costs to be considered.

The scope of discretion §109(b)(1) allows is in fact well within the outer limits of our nondelegation precedents. In the history of the Court we have found the requisite "intelligible principle" lacking in only two statutes, one of which provided literally no guidance for the exercise of discretion, and the other of which conferred authority to regulate the entire economy on the basis of no more precise a standard than stimulating the economy by assuring "fair competition." We have, on the other hand, upheld the validity of §11(b)(2) of the Public Utility Holding Company Act of 1935, 49 Stat. 821, which gave the Securities and Exchange Commission authority to modify the structure of holding company systems so as to ensure that they are not "unduly or unnecessarily complicate[d]" and do not "unfairly or inequitably distribute voting power among security holders." We have approved the wartime conferral of agency power to fix the prices of commodities at a level that " 'will be generally fair and equitable and will effectuate the [in some respects conflicting] purposes of th[e] Act.'" Yakus v. United States, 321 U.S. 414, 420 (1944). And we have found an "intelligible principle" in various statutes authorizing regulation in the "public interest." In short, we have "almost never felt qualified to second-guess Congress regarding the permissible degree of policy judgment that can be left to those executing or applying the law."

It is true enough that the degree of agency discretion that is acceptable varies according to the scope of the power congressionally conferred. While Congress need not provide any direction to the EPA regarding the manner in which it is to define "country elevators," which are to be exempt from new- stationary-source regulations governing grain elevators, it must provide substantial guidance on setting air standards that affect the entire national economy. But even in sweeping regulatory schemes we have never demanded, as the Court of Appeals did here, that statutes provide a "determinate criterion" for saying "how much [of the regulated harm] is too much." In *Touby*, for example, we did not require the statute to decree how "imminent" was too imminent, or how "necessary" was necessary enough, or even — most relevant here — how "hazardous" was too hazardous. [It] is therefore not conclusive for delegation purposes that, as respondents argue, ozone and particulate matter are "nonthreshold" pollutants that inflict a continuum of adverse health effects at any airborne concentration greater than zero, and hence require the EPA to make judgments of degree. . . . Section 109(b)(1) of the CAA, which to repeat we interpret as requiring the EPA to set air quality standards at the level that is "requisite" — that is, not lower or higher than is necessary — to protect the public health with an adequate margin of safety, fits comfortably within the scope of discretion permitted by our precedent.

We therefore reverse the judgment of the Court of Appeals remanding for reinterpretation that would avoid a supposed delegation of legislative power.

Justice THOMAS, concurring.

[The] parties to this case who briefed the constitutional issue wrangled over constitutional doctrine with barely a nod to the text of the Constitution. Although this Court since 1928 has treated the "intelligible principle" requirement as the only constitutional limit on congressional grants of power to administrative agencies, the Constitution does not speak of "intelligible principles." Rather, it speaks in much simpler terms: "*All* legislative Powers herein granted shall be vested in a Congress." U.S. Const., Art. 1, §1 (emphasis added). I am not convinced that the intelligible principle doctrine serves to prevent all cessions of legislative power. I believe that there are cases in which the principle is intelligible and yet the significance of the delegated decision is simply too great for the decision to be called anything other than "legislative."

As it is, none of the parties to this case has examined the text of the Constitution or asked us to reconsider our precedents on cessions of legislative power. On a future day, however, I would be willing to address the question whether our delegation jurisprudence has strayed too far from our Founders' understanding of separation of powers.

Justice STEVENS, with whom Justice SOUTER joins, concurring in part and concurring in the judgment.

The Court has two choices. We could choose to articulate our ultimate disposition of this issue by frankly acknowledging that the power delegated to the EPA is "legislative" but nevertheless conclude that the delegation is constitutional because adequately limited by the terms of the authorizing statute. Alternatively, we could pretend, as the Court does, that the authority delegated to the EPA is somehow not "legislative power." Despite the fact that there is language in our opinions that supports the Court's articulation of our holding, I am persuaded that it would be both wiser and more faithful to what we have actually done in delegation cases to admit that agency rulemaking authority is "legislative power." . . .

It seems clear that an executive agency's exercise of rulemaking authority pursuant to a valid delegation from Congress is "legislative." As long as the delegation provides a sufficiently intelligible principle, there is nothing inherently unconstitutional about it. Accordingly, [I] would hold that when Congress enacted §109, it effected a constitutional delegation of legislative power to the EPA.

[A concurring opinion by Justice Breyer, not dealing with the nondelegation issue, is omitted.]

Questions on *American Trucking*

1. After *American Trucking*, what room remains for the nondelegation doctrine? Can you think of a statute, real or hypothetical, that the Court would actually strike down? Ask whether the Court's approach is or is not compatible with then-Justice Rehnquist's approach in the *Benzene Case*. Lower courts have continued to reject all nondelegation challenges in the wake of *American Trucking*, whether or not the president is thought to have independent constitutional power in the area. See, e.g., South Carolina Medical Assn. v. Thompson, 327 F.3d 246 (4th Cir. 2003) (upholding Health Insurance Portability and Accountability Act); Doe v. Bush, 323 F.3d 133 (1st Cir. 2003) (upholding congressional authorization to use military force in Iraq).

2. *American Trucking* is best understood against the background set by several decades of rethinking of the nondelegation doctrine. Many people have advocated a

return to a more stringent version of the doctrine as a way of ensuring that basic value judgments are made by the legislature, not by administrative agencies. See D. Schoenbrod, Power Without Responsibility (1995); Gellhorn, Returning to First Principles, 36 Am. U.L. Rev. 345, 349-352 (1987); Lowi, Two Roads to Serfdom: Liberalism, Conservatism and Administrative Power, 36 Am. U.L. Rev. 355 (1987); Scalia, A Note on the *Benzene Case*, 4 Reg. 25, 25 (July-Aug. 1980) ("Even with all its Frankensteinlike warts, knobs and (conceded) dangers, the unconstitutional delegation doctrine is worth hewing from the ice."). Some of these critics have argued that the Constitution simply does not tolerate a situation in which Congress gives open-ended discretion to the executive. Others have urged that the nondelegation doctrine could prevent the use of agency power for the benefit of private groups. Above all, they have emphasized the benefits, for private liberty and sound governance alike, of forcing legislatures to consider legislation more carefully.

But others have argued against revival of the doctrine. One class of arguments focuses on constitutional text, structure, and history, including judicial precedent, and suggests that there is simply no legal basis for a nondelegation doctrine (in the sense of a restriction on the discretion that statutes may lodge in the executive). We have canvassed the relevant considerations above.

Beyond the debate over the constitutional sources of the nondelegation doctrine, two other classes of arguments involve (1) whether such a doctrine would make government work better and (2) whether courts are capable of implementing and enforcing such a doctrine. Critics typically deny either (1) or (2), or both. "There are two principal reasons why the courts are justified in refusing to enforce this long somnolent doctrine in any but the most unusual and infrequent circumstances. The first is the absence of judicially manageable and defensible criteria to distinguish permissible delegations. The second is that requiring Congress to write detailed commands in statutes could well produce unsound and less responsible government." Stewart, Beyond Delegation Doctrine, 36 Am. U.L. Rev. 323 (1987).

For the critics, there is no evidence that the nondelegation doctrine would actually make government work better. In fact, they urge that the nondelegation doctrine would effectively increase the power of congressional committees, thus compromising political accountability. See the illuminating empirical analysis in David Epstein & Sharyn O'Halloran, Delegating Powers (1999). For more general statements of the view that a nondelegation doctrine has no functional justification, see Posner & Vermeule, 69 U. Chi. L. Rev. at 1743-1754; Pierce, Political Accountability and Delegated Power: A Response to Professor Lowi, 36 Am. U.L. Rev. 391 (1987); Mashaw, Prodelegation: Why Administrators Should Make Political Decisions, 1 J.L. Econ. & Org. 1 (1985).

Critics also express concern that the nondelegation doctrine, if revived, would put courts in an intolerable position. They urge that the question whether Congress has delegated legislative power is inevitably an issue of degree: How much discretion is too much discretion? See *Stewart*, supra. In this view, courts would inevitably produce constitutional doctrine that involves no clear lines but instead case-by-case judgment, in a way that would inevitably give rise to the appearance, and perhaps the reality, of opposition to the particular programs at issue. Justice Scalia himself has emphasized this issue. See Mistretta v. United States, 488 U.S. 361 (1988) (Scalia, J., concurring), as we take up below.

3. *American Trucking* firmly repudiates the analysis in *Amalgamated Meat Cutters*, and followed in subsequent lower court cases, to the effect that an agency can "save" an otherwise unconstitutional delegation through a narrowing construction that constrains

the agency's own discretion. Why did lower courts take this route, and why did the Supreme Court reject it? The simplest answer is that for the Supreme Court, the point of the nondelegation doctrine is to ensure that *Congress* create an "intelligible principle" — and that an agency's narrowing construction is neither here nor there.

An especially relevant case, involving OSHA, is International Union, UAW v. OSHA, 938 F.2d 1310 (D.C. Cir. 1991). There, the court was presented with a nondelegation attack on a regulation not involving toxic substances, and therefore issued solely under OSHA's seemingly open-ended authority to promulgate "reasonably necessary or appropriate" regulations. The court said that the Constitution would be violated if OSHA did not specify what it understood the "reasonably necessary or appropriate" language to mean — if, in other words, OSHA believed itself free to do whatever it chose. On remand, OSHA concluded that the "reasonably necessary or appropriate" language basically required it not to do cost-benefit analysis, but to regulate any "significant" risk in a way that put a high premium on worker safety. The agency attempted to specify, a bit, these various concepts. On remand, the D.C. Circuit upheld the agency's view. International Union, UAW v. OSHA, 37 F.3d 605 (D.C. Cir. 1994).

Does *American Trucking* suggest that the "reasonably necessary or appropriate" language is unconstitutional, because the agency is not permitted to save the statute through a narrowing construction? Evaluate the following argument: "Reasonably necessary or appropriate" could mean anything at all. Unlike the provision of the Clean Air Act involved in *American Trucking*, the OSHA language could call for cost-benefit balancing, or an analysis limited to health, or anything at all. For this reason, the "reasonably necessary or appropriate" provision lacks an intelligible principle and provides a constitutionally unacceptable blank check.

4. Does the Supreme Court really come to terms with the concerns of the lower court in *American Trucking*? To answer this question, it would seem to be necessary to ascertain the meaning of the phrase, "requisite to protect the public health." In the Court's view, this phrase requires that the agency regulate to the point that is no more, but also no less, than necessary. But what does this mean? For ozone, the EPA's regulatory impact analysis considered three options, of which the middle one, in Table 2-1 below, was chosen. But notice that a more stringent choice would have resulted in more protection of health, and that a less stringent choice would have resulted in less protection of health. What, in the statute as construed by the Court, limits the agency's ability to choose to do what it wants?

5. The American Trucking Association also argued, unsuccessfully, that the relevant provision of the Clean Air Act requires EPA to consider costs as well as benefits. Consider in this light two problems. (a) A statute requires an agency to balance costs and benefits, but it gives the agency no guidance on how to value benefits. Suppose, for example, that the statute does not, on its face, ban the agency from valuing a statistical life at $1 million, or $10 million, or $30 million. If the agency can make any of these choices, would the statute be unconstitutional, on *American Trucking*'s view of the nondelegation doctrine? (b) A statute allows an agency to decide whether to have, as its guiding criterion, a form of cost-benefit balancing or, instead, something like the statute as construed in *American Trucking*, which calls for regulation to the point "requisite to protect the public health." If the agency can choose the basic criterion in the statute, does *American Trucking* suggest that the statute is unconstitutional? If so, does this mean that the "reasonably appropriate or necessary" provision in OSHA is unconstitutional after all?

TABLE 2-1
Ozone: National Annual Health Incidence Reductions
Estimates are incremental to the current ozone NAAQS (year = 2010)

Endpoint[1]	Partial Attainment Scenario		
	0.08 5th Max High-End Est.	0.08 4th MaTBx Low- to High-End Est.	0.08 3rd Max High-End Est.
Ozone Health:			
1. Mortality	80	0-80	120
Hospital Admissions:			
2. all respiratory (all ages)	280	300-300	420
all respiratory (ages 65+)	2,300	2,330-2,330	1,570
pneumonia (ages 65+)	860	870-870	600
COPD (ages 65+)	260	260-260	200
emer. dept. visits for asthma	120	130-130	180
3. Acute Respiratory Symptoms (any of 19)	28,510	29,840-29,840	42,070
asthma attacks	60	60-60	90
MRADs	620	650-650	920
4. Mortality from air toxics	1	1-1	2
Ancillary PM Health:			
1. Mortality[2]: Short-term exposure	60	0-80	110
Long-term exposure	180	0-250	340
2. Chronic Bronchitis	400	0-530	690
Hospital Admissions:			
3. all respiratory (all ages)	70	0-90	120
all resp. (ages 65+)	50	0-60	80
pneumonia (ages 65+)	20	0-20	30
COPD (ages 65+)	10	0-20	20
4. congestive heart failure	10	0-20	20
5. ischemic heart disease	10	0-20	20
6. Acute Bronchitis	290	0-400	530
7. Lower Respiratory Symptoms	3,510	0-4,670	6,190
8. Upper Respiratory Symptoms	320	0-430	570
shortness of breath	800	0-1,220	1,660
asthma attacks	4,210	0-5,510	7,200
9. Work Loss Days	38,700	0-50,440	66,160
10. Minor Restricted Activity Days (MRADs)	322,460	0-420,300	551,300

[1] Only endpoints denoted with an * are aggregated into total benefits estimates.

[2] PM mortality estimates must be aggregated using either short-term exposure or long-term exposure, but not both, due to double-counting issues.

6. Compare Clinton v. New York, 524 U.S. 417 (1998), in which the Court struck down the Line Item Veto Act, which authorized the president to "cancel" certain appropriations that, in his view, should be vetoed as inconsistent with public policy. The Court held that the Act allowed the president to repeal or amend a statute on his own, without following the constitutionally specified procedures for repeal or amendment of a law. In response, it was urged that the president was really being given a delegation, one well within the boundaries of the nondelegation cases. To this the Court responded as follows: "The critical difference between this statute and all of its predecessors, however, is that unlike any of them, this Act gives the President the unilateral power to change the text of duly enacted statutes." Is this response too formalistic?

Note: Other Delegations

There has been no Supreme Court case since *Schechter* invalidating federal legislation on the ground of overly broad delegation. As *American Trucking* suggests, a number of decisions have upheld other delegations that seem fairly extreme. Yakus v. United States, 321 U.S. 414 (1944), discusssed in *American Trucking*, upheld a World War II price control statute authorizing the Office of Price Administration (OPA) "to stabilize prices and to prevent speculative, unwarranted, and abnormal increases in prices and rents." The statute required the administrator to set prices that were "generally fair and equitable," giving consideration to prices prevailing in October 1941. In Lichter v. United States, 334 U.S. 742 (1948), the Supreme Court sustained the validity of the Renegotiation Act, which provided for the recovery of "excessive profits" by government officers. When originally enacted, the law made no effort to guide the officers' determination of what was excessive; a later amendment contained a host of often conflicting "considerations" for the administrator to take into account.

In United States v. Southwestern Cable Co., 392 U.S. 157 (1968), the Court upheld a regulation of the Federal Communications Commission (FCC) forbidding Community Antenna Television Systems (CATV) to rebroadcast certain television signals outside of a particular area. The Court sustained the commission's authority to regulate CATV under the statutory provision making the Communications Act of 1934 applicable to "all interstate and foreign communication by wire or radio"; it held that the commission could make rules reasonably ancillary to its responsibilities to regulate television, although the only standard governing the FCC in its exercise of this power lies in the commission's authority to issue "such rules and regulations . . . not inconsistent with law" as "public convenience, interest or necessity requires." 47 U.S.C. §303(r). See also, e.g., National Broadcasting Co. v. United States, 319 U.S. 190 (1943) ("public interest" standard). If the FCC can act as the "public interest" requires, is its discretion limited at all? Can it regulate broadcasting aggressively, by requiring educational programming for children and programming related to the local community, and then deregulate, and then regulate again? If so, can it do whatever it wants? Can the commission and the courts develop a common law of telecommunications that effectively operates as a constraint on the commission's policy choices?

For another interesting (and extreme) example of delegation, see Arizona v. California, 373 U.S. 546 (1963) (upholding secretary of interior's power to allocate water from interstate river among various states). The Court has continued to sustain broad delegations concerning foreign relations and trade. See Federal Energy Administration v. Algonquin SNG, Inc., 426 U.S. 548 (1976).

On the other hand, state courts have occasionally applied the nondelegation doctrine to invalidate legislation. And in National Cable Television Assn. v. United States, 415 U.S. 336 (1974), the Supreme Court indicated (in dicta) that the nondelegation doctrine may have life when delegations of the taxing power are at issue. In the immediate aftermath of Justice Rehnquist's opinion in the *Benzene Case,* lower courts referred to the doctrine as "no longer . . . moribund," and there are occasional decisions suggesting that the doctrine still lives, not only in the area of statutory construction, but also as a tool for invalidation. See, e.g., Fort Worth & Denver Ry. Co. v. Lewis, 693 F.2d 432, 435 n.8 (5th Cir. 1982).

In an earlier case, the D.C. Circuit, in a per curiam opinion likely written by Justice (then Judge) Scalia, rejected the claim that the nondelegation doctrine prevents the delegation of certain "core" functions, such as Congress's power to make appropriations. The court wrote,

> We reject this "core functions" argument for several reasons. First, plaintiffs cite no case in which the Supreme Court has held any legislative power, much less that over appropriations, to be nondelegable due to its "core function" status. . . . Second, judicial adoption of a "core functions" analysis would be effectively standardless. No constitutional provision distinguishes between "core" and "non-core" legislative functions, so that the line would necessarily have to be drawn on the basis of the court's own perceptions of the relative importance of various legislative functions. Finally, if there were any nondelegable "core functions," there is no reason to believe that appropriations functions would be among them.

Synar v. United States, 626 F. Supp. 1374 (1986).

In Mistretta v. United States, 488 U.S. 361 (1988), the Court held constitutional a congressional delegation of power to write sentencing guidelines to a commission (in the judicial branch) composed of three federal judges, three academics, and one prison warden (appointed by the president, confirmed by the Senate). The guidelines would specify the length of time an offender should serve, depending on the offense committed and prior criminal record. The sentencing judge could depart from the guidelines in a particular case only where he or she found special circumstances. The majority of eight, citing authority such as *J. W. Hampton,* simply noted the detailed standards that Congress wrote into the statute, instructing the commission about what it must do. Justice Scalia dissented. He noted that the commission makes decisions that "are far from technical, but are heavily laden . . . with value judgments and policy assessments." He added,

> Petitioner's most fundamental and far-reaching challenge to the Commission is that Congress's commitment of such broad policy responsibility to any institution is an unconstitutional delegation of legislative power. It is difficult to imagine a principle more essential to democratic government than that upon which the doctrine of unconstitutional delegation is founded: Except in a few areas constitutionally committed to the Executive Branch, the basic policy decisions governing society are to be made by the Legislature. Our Members of Congress could not, even if they wished, vote all power to the President and adjourn sine die.
>
> But while the doctrine of unconstitutional delegation is unquestionably a fundamental element of our constitutional system, it is not an element readily enforceable by the courts. Once it is conceded, as it must be, that no statute can be entirely precise, and that some judgments, even some judgments involving policy considerations, must be left to the officers executing the law and to the judges applying it, the debate over the unconstitutional delegation becomes a debate not over a point of principle, but over a

question of degree. [T]he limits of delegation must be fixed according to common sense and the inherent "necessities" of government, and since the factors bearing upon those necessities are both multifarious and (in the nonpartisan sense) highly political, . . . it is small wonder that we have almost never felt qualified to second-guess Congress regarding the permissible degree of policy judgment that can be left to those executing or applying the law. [But, the] whole theory of *lawful* Congressional delegation is not that Congress is sometimes too busy or too divided and can therefore assign its responsibility of making law to someone else; but rather that a certain degree of discretion, and thus of law-making, *inheres* in most executive or judicial action, and it is up to Congress, by the relative specificity or generality of its statutory commands, to determine — up to a point — how small or how large that degree shall be.

Consequently, "the power to make law cannot be exercised by anyone other than Congress, except in conjunction with the lawful exercise of executive judicial power. . . . The lawmaking function of the Sentencing Commission is completely divorced from any responsibility for execution of the law or adjudication of private rights under the law." Hence Justice Scalia would have held the delegation unconstitutional.

Touby v. United States, 500 U.S. 160 (1991), upheld the constitutionality of provisions in the Controlled Substance Act authorizing the attorney general to designate, on an expedited, temporary basis, new "designer drugs," in addition to those listed in the statute, possession or sale of which is a crime. The Court found that the statutory standards — requiring the attorney general to consider the relevant extent and seriousness of abuse of a drug and the threat to public health — were constitutionally adequate even where it assumed (a question it did not decide) that more specific delegation standards are required in the criminal context. It also rejected contentions that combining in the attorney general the power to designate new drugs and the power to initiate prosecutions violates separation-of-powers principles, and that a provision barring direct judicial review of temporary listings violates nondelegation principles by depriving courts of the power to ensure that statutory standards are followed. It noted that direct judicial review is available following more elaborate procedures for "permanent" designation of a new drug. A concurring opinion asserted that a defendant in a prosecution could also obtain such review.

In Loving v. United States, 517 U.S. 748 (1996), the Court upheld a grant of power to the president to choose the "aggravating factors" that would permit a court martial to impose the death penalty on a member of the armed services who had been convicted of murder. The Court stressed the historical discretion of the president in overseeing the military, but also emphasized that recent cases had "without exception" permitted "delegations under standards phrased in sweeping terms." In Freedom to Travel Campaign v. Newcomb, 82 F.3d 1431 (9th Cir. 1996), a lower court upheld a statute allowing the president to extend a preexisting economic embargo by concluding that an extension is "in the national interest."

A few unusual cases have invoked the nondelegation doctrine to strike down legislation. In South Dakota v. Department of Interior, 69 F.3d 878 (8th Cir. 1995), a court of appeals struck down the Indian Reorganization Act insofar as that act authorized the secretary of the interior "in his discretion, to acquire . . . any interest in lands . . . within or without existing reservations . . . for the purpose of providing land for Indians." Although the legislative history suggested some restrictions on the secretary's discretion, the court thought the text was too open-ended. In Massieu v. Reno, 915 F. Supp. 681 (D.N.J. 1996), a district court struck down a provision of a federal deportation statute. The relevant provision says that "an alien whose presence or activities in the United States the Secretary of

State has reasonable ground to believe would have potentially serious adverse foreign policy consequences for the United States is deportable." 8 U.S.C. §1251(a)(4)(C)(i). The court held that this was an unacceptably open-ended grant of power.

Note on Nondelegation and Statutory Interpretation

American Trucking reaffirms that the nondelegation doctrine will rarely be invoked, if at all, to invalidate federal statutes on constitutional grounds. *American Trucking* does not reject the separate possibility that the nondelegation doctrine might live on as a canon of statutory construction. See Sunstein, Nondelegation Canons, 67 U. Chi. L. Rev. 315 (2000). The canon holds that, where fairly possible, statutes will be construed to avoid serious nondelegation questions. A "nondelegation canon" of this sort would be a special case of the broader idea that statutes should be construed to avoid serious constitutional questions. See Manning, The Nondelegation Doctrine as a Canon of Avoidance, supra.

We have already seen this idea in *Amalgamated Meat Cutters*, supra, and in Industrial Union Department, AFL-CIO v. American Petroleum Institute, 448 U.S. 607 (1980), widely known as "The Benzene Case." In Chapter 4, we discuss recent cases that invoke the nondelegation canon to override deference to agency interpretations of law; see especially FDA v. Brown & Williamson Tobacco, 529 U.S. 120, 161 (2000).

Is there a risk that this practice will allow courts to limit administrative power without taking the political heat that comes from straightforward constitutional invalidation of a statute? Might it not be better for the Court to strike down the relevant statutes, so as to encourage Congress to legislate with some particularity? If the nondelegation doctrine is beyond the capacity of the courts to enforce, or is infeasible, does the nondelegation canon fare any better? If it does, it may be because the stakes are lower at the level of statutory interpretation, or because the line-drawing problems that bedevil the constitutional doctrine are less severe. See Sunstein, Nondelegation Canons, supra.

Concluding Questions

Would it be desirable, as a matter of democratic theory or practical policy, for Congress to write more detailed statutes? For Congress to make more policy judgments itself?

(a) Should Congress have done so when delegating the power to control prices?

(b) Is it desirable for Congress to write statutes involving health, safety, or the environment in detail? What kind of detail? Congress might specify means, ends, or both. Should Congress specify, for example, how much sulfur dioxide each smokestack may emit? Should Congress specify what cleanup technology each firm should use? Should it specify how clean air or water in each geographical area ought to be? Should Congress simply specify a bottom line object — reduce pollution, saving *x* lives at a cost of no more than *y* dollars — and leave the rest to the Environmental Protection Agency (EPA)? See B. Ackerman & W. Hassler, Clean Coal/Dirty Air (1983).

D. The Executive and the Agencies

If Congress does not control agency discretion, perhaps the president will do so; this is Justice Scalia's suggestion, and hope, in the *Mistretta* case. Perhaps the president should see that agencies make intelligent, fair, and effective decisions; perhaps the president should ensure that agencies follow his will; perhaps the president should make certain that regulatory policies are properly coordinated. For a general catalogue and discussion, see Kagan, Presidential Administration, 114 Harv. L. Rev. 2245 (2001).

Of course, most, if not all, of the regulators and agency heads work for the president anyway, don't they? So just what is the issue? Is it simply one of an employer watching more closely the activities of its employees? Is the problem the obvious one that affects any large private firm — that the chief has too much to do to supervise everyone? Or are there good reasons to insulate some agencies from presidential management?

In considering these questions, note that there is a serious "coordination problem" within the federal government. The need for coordination arises out of the many thousands of different civil servants, bureaus, divisions, and appointed officials with overlapping responsibilities, or with authority that, when exercised, may affect the responsibilities of other agencies. For example, in recent years at least 16 different federal agencies have borne some responsibility for energy prices and supply. In many areas, there are potential conflicts and overlaps of duties. One agency may be controlling lead paint, while another is controlling lead emissions from gasoline, and yet another is attempting to ensure urban development that protects children from living in high-lead areas. One agency might try to guarantee hospital patient safety by requiring that all syringes be disposable, while a second agency worries about inadequate ability to dispose of solid waste, while yet a third is concerned about the increased number of disposable syringes that escape from waste disposal sites and wash up on beaches. Each of these different agencies or bureaus may operate under different statutes granting differing degrees of legal authority under different kinds of restrictions.

The problem of coordinating and reviewing agency decisions, even within the executive branch, is made more difficult by a *legal* circumstance and by a political circumstance. The legal circumstance consists of the fact that many statutes give the *legal* power to make regulatory decisions not to the president, but to the head of an agency, to a cabinet secretary, to a board, or to a commission. The *political* circumstance consists of the fact that the constituencies affected by a particular regulatory decision often have an ongoing relationship with both Congress and the special agency, but not necessarily with the White House. Trade unions, employers' groups, the Department of Labor, and the relevant congressional labor committees often work with each other on many different detailed regulatory matters. These groups deal with the White House less often, and typically do so on matters of grander scope than are at issue in most regulatory decisions. All these groups are likely to be better informed about the details of a particular matter than the White House. None of these groups is likely to want the White House to interfere too often with the general working relationships they have established with each other.

The consequent balkanization of the executive branch, fragmenting into numerous subbranches, is exacerbated by Congress's growing tendency to create more and more subcommittees, each of which provides some check on agency action and simultaneously offers a degree of political visibility to its director. Different subcommittees, however, may have different views about "correct" policy; different subcommittees may support different agencies, or different internal bureaus of different agencies, in respect to policy decisions that will affect others. Can the EPA, for example, adequately coordinate its own internal policies, let alone its policies that affect other agencies, when it must report to 34 different Senate and House committees and subcommittees? The administrator of the EPA is not infrequently in the position of having to testify before, and please, a wide range of committees and subcommittees, all with quite different agendas and commitments.

Aware of these special needs and problems, those who have called for closer presidential control of agency action have urged that the president, or those parts of the federal government that respond more directly and immediately to the president's wishes, should be given more direct authoritative control over the detailed decisions that the agencies make.

1. The Old Learning

For much of this century, the president's control over "the administration" — understood as the set of agencies that implemented federal law — was governed by two Supreme Court decisions. The two decisions appeared to contradict one another and contained a high degree of ambiguity and vagueness.

Myers v. United States
272 U.S. 52 (1926)

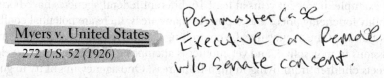

Postmaster Case
Executive can Remove
w/o Senate consent.

[Myers was appointed postmaster for a four-year term at Portland, Oregon, under a statute providing that postmasters "shall be appointed and may be removed by the President and with the advice and consent of the Senate." President Wilson removed him from office, prior to the expiration of his term, without the consent of the Senate. In this suit for back pay, the government claimed Myers's removal was lawful because it is unconstitutional to limit the president's power to remove an executive branch official by requiring the Senate's agreement.

The Court agreed with the government. Chief Justice Taft wrote that the power to remove subordinates is inherently part of the executive power, which Article II, §1, of the Constitution vests "in a President of the United States."

Chief Justice Taft wrote:]

Made responsible under the Constitution for the effective enforcement of the law, the President needs as an indispensable aid to meet it the disciplinary influence upon those who act under him of a reserve power of removal. . . . The highest and most important duties which his subordinates perform are those in which they act for him. In such cases they are exercising not their own but his discretion. . . .

In all such cases, the discretion to be exercised is that of the President in determining the national public interest and in directing the action to be taken by his executive subordinates to protect it. In this field his cabinet officers must do his will. He must place in each member of his official family, and his chief executive subordinates, implicit faith. The moment that he loses confidence in the intelligence, ability, judgment, or loyalty of any one of them, he must have the power to remove him without delay. To require him to file charges and submit them to the consideration of the Senate might make impossible that unity and co-ordination in executive administration essential to effective action.

The duties of the heads of departments and bureaus in which the discretion of the President is exercised and which we have described are the most important in the whole field of executive action of the Government. There is nothing in the Constitution which permits a distinction between the removal of the head of a department or a bureau, when he discharges a political duty of the President or exercises his discretion, and the removal of executive officers engaged in the discharge of their normal duties. The imperative

Const. is silent on Removal, thus since Power to Remove is so vital, we must. Read it to exist.

reasons requiring an unrestricted power to remove the most important of his subordinates in their most important duties must, therefore, control the interpretation of the Constitution as to all appointed by him.

But this is not to say that there are not strong reasons why the President should have a like power to remove his appointees charged with other duties than those above described. The ordinary duties of officers prescribed by statute come under the general administrative control of the President by virtue of the general grant to him of the executive power, and he may properly supervise and guide their construction of the statutes under which they act in order to secure that unitary and uniform execution of the laws which Article II of the Constitution evidently contemplated in vesting general executive power in the President alone. Laws are often passed with specific provision for the adoption of regulations by a department or bureau head to make the law workable and effective. The ability and judgment manifested by the official thus empowered, as well as his energy and stimulation of his subordinates, are subjects which the President must consider and supervise in his administrative control. Finding such officers to be negligent and inefficient, the President should have the power to remove them. Of course there may be duties so peculiarly and specifically committed to the discretion of a particular officer as to raise a question whether the President may overrule or revise the officer's *exception* interpretation of his statutory duty in a particular instance. Then there may be duties of a quasi-judicial character imposed on executive officers and members of executive tribunals whose decisions after hearing affect interests of individuals, the discharge of which the President cannot in a particular case properly influence or control. But even in such a case he may consider the decision after its renditions, as a reason for removing the officer, on the ground that the discretion regularly entrusted to that officer by statute has not been on the whole intelligently or wisely exercised. Otherwise he does not discharge his own constitutional duty of seeing that the law be faithfully executed.

[The Chief Justice conceded that Congress could limit the power of the president to remove inferior officers — say, by creating a Civil Service, with removal only for cause. But it *Congress could limit to inferior officers* can do so only because the Constitution, Article II, §2, allows Congress to "vest the appointment of such inferior officers as they think proper, in the President alone, in the courts of law, or in the heads of departments." In any event, Congress had not vested "in the President alone" the power to appoint Myers; hence his appointment must be considered a major one, and his removal must, constitutionally, be left to the discretion of the president.]

[Justices Holmes, Brandeis, and McReynolds dissented.]

Humphrey's Executor v. United States

295 U.S. 602 (1935)

FTC Case — FDR Desires Removal.

[The Federal Trade Commission (FTC) was created in 1914 to enforce (concurrently with the Justice Department) certain provisions of the antitrust laws and to define and eliminate "unfair methods of competition." Proponents of the bill wanted "a nonpartisan organization, which moves absolutely free from the interference of either Congress or the President." 51 Cong. Rec. 11235 (1914). In its early years the commission brought few major cases. President Franklin D. Roosevelt believed that his predecessors had deliberately appointed commissioners who did not believe in the legislative purposes of the Trade Commission Act. He therefore sought to replace Commissioner Humphrey. He felt that, in doing so, he would be able to make the FTC act more effectively.]

Mr. Justice SUTHERLAND delivered the opinion of the Court. . . .

William E. Humphrey . . . was nominated by President Hoover . . . as a member of the Federal Trade Commission, and was confirmed. . . . He was commissioned for a term of seven years expiring September 25, 1938; . . . On July 25, 1933, President Roosevelt addressed a letter to the commissioner asking for his resignation, on the ground "that the aims and purposes of the Administration with respect to the work of the Commission can be carried out most effectively with personnel of my own selection," but disclaiming any reflection upon the commissioner personally or upon his services. The commissioner replied, asking time to consult his friends. After some further correspondence upon the subject, the President on August 31, 1933, wrote the commissioner expressing the hope that the resignation would be forthcoming and saying: "You will, I know, realize that I do not feel your mind and my mind go along together on either the policies or the administering of the Federal Trade Commission, and, frankly, I think it is best for the people of this country that I should have a full confidence." The Commissioner declined to resign; and on October 7, 1933, the President wrote him: "Effective as of this date you are hereby removed from the office of Commissioner of the Federal Trade Commission."

Humphrey never acquiesced in this action, but continued thereafter to insist that he was still a member of the commission, entitled to perform its duties and receive the compensation provided by law. [In this suit for back pay the Court of Claims certified two questions to the Supreme Court:]

1. Do the provisions of section 1 of the Federal Trade Commission Act, stating that "any commissioner may be removed by the President for inefficiency, neglect of duty, or malfeasance in office," restrict or limit the power of the President to remove a commissioner except upon one or more of the causes named? [The Supreme Court answered yes.]

If the foregoing question is answered in the affirmative, then —

2. If the power of the President to remove a commissioner is restricted or limited as shown by the foregoing interrogatory and the answer made thereto, is such a restriction or limitation valid under the Constitution of the United States?

. . . To support its contention that the removal provision of §1 . . . is an unconstitutional interference with the executive power of the President, the government's chief reliance is Myers v. United States, 272 U.S. 52 [(1926)]. [T]he narrow point actually decided was only that the President had power to remove a postmaster of the first class, without the advice and consent of the Senate as required by act of Congress. In the course of the opinion of the court, expressions occur which tend to sustain the government's contention, but these are beyond the point involved and, therefore, do not come within the rule of stare decisis. In so far as they are out of harmony with the views here set forth, these expressions are disapproved. . . .

The office of a postmaster is so essentially unlike the office now involved that the decision in the Myers case cannot be accepted as controlling our decision here. A postmaster is an executive officer restricted to the performance of executive functions. He is charged with no duty at all related to either the legislative or judicial power. The actual decision in the Myers case finds support in the theory that such an officer is merely one of the units in the executive department and, hence, inherently subject to the exclusive and illimitable power of removal by the Chief Executive, whose subordinate and aid he is. [T]he necessary reach of the decision goes far enough to include all purely executive officers. It

They Mark FTC as Quasi legislative. Prez can't remove as in Meyer ✓

goes no farther; — much less does it include an officer who occupies no place in the executive department and who exercises no part of the executive power vested by the Constitution in the President.

The Federal Trade Commission is an administrative body created by Congress to carry into effect legislative policies embodied in the statute in accordance with the legislative standard therein prescribed, and to perform other specified duties as a legislative or as a judicial aid. Such a body cannot in any proper sense be characterized as an arm or an eye of the executive. Its duties are performed without executive leave and, in the contemplation of the statute must be free from executive control. [T]he commission acts in part quasi-legislatively and in part quasi-judicially. . . .

The fundamental necessity of maintaining each of the three general departments of government entirely free from the control or coercive influence, direct or indirect, of either of the others, has often been stressed and is hardly open to serious question.

The power of removal here claimed for the President falls within this principle, since its coercive influence threatens the independence of a commission, which is not only wholly disconnected from the executive department, but which, as already fully appears, was created by Congress as a means of carrying into operation legislative and judicial powers, and as an agency of the legislative and judicial departments. . . .

The result of what we now have said is this: Whether the power of the President to remove an officer shall prevail over the authority of Congress to condition the power by fixing a definite term and precluding a removal except for cause, will depend upon the character of the office; the *Myers* decision, affirming the power of the President alone to make the removal, is confined to purely executive officers; and as to officers of the kind here under consideration, we hold that no removal can be made during the prescribed term for which the officer is appointed, except for one or more of the causes named in the applicable statute.

Removal Power based on character of office.

Weiner v. United States

357 U.S. 349 (1958)

(Pre 1937 — FDR vs. Court here?)

— goes beyond Humphry to say even w/o removal Limits, good cause is implied.

Mr. Justice FRANKFURTER delivered the opinion of the Court.

This is a suit for back pay, based on petitioner's alleged illegal removal as a member of the War Claims Commission. . . . By the War Claims Act of 1948, Congress established that Commission with "jurisdiction to receive and adjudicate according to law," claims for compensating internees, prisoners of wars, and religious organizations, and who suffered personal injury or property damage at the hands of the enemy in connection with World War II. The Commission was to be composed of three persons, at least two of whom were to be members of the bar, to be appointed by the President, by and with the advice and consent of the Senate. The Commission was to wind up its affairs not later than three years after the expiration of the time for filing claims, . . . and Congress made no provisions for removal of a Commissioner.

Having been duly nominated by President Truman, the petitioner . . . took office on June 8, following. On his refusal to heed a request for his resignation, he was, on December 10, 1953, removed by President Eisenhower. . . .

Controversy pertaining to the scope and limits of the President's power of removal fills a thick chapter of our political and judicial history. The long stretches of its history . . . were laboriously traversed in Myers v. United States, 272 U.S. 52 [(1926)]. . . . Speaking through a Chief Justice who himself had been President, the Court did not restrict itself to the immediate issue before it, the President's inherent power to remove a postmaster, obviously an executive official. [T]he Court announced that the President had inherent constitutional power of removal also of officials who have "duties of a quasi-judicial character . . . whose decisions after hearing affect interests of individuals, the discharge of which the President cannot in a particular case properly influence or control." Myers v. United States, supra, at 135. This view of presidential power was deemed to flow from his "constitutional duty of seeing that the laws be faithfully executed." Ibid.

The assumption was short-lived. . . . In Humphrey's Executor v. United States, 295 U.S. 602 [(1935)], [the Court] narrowly confined the scope of the Myers decision to include only "all purely executive officers." 295 U.S., at 628. The Court explicitly "disapproved" the expressions in Myers supporting the President's inherent constitutional power to remove members of quasi-judicial bodies. . . .

Humphrey's case was a cause célèbre — and not least in the halls of Congress. And what is the essence of the decision in Humphrey's case? It drew a sharp line of cleavage between officials who were part of the Executive establishment and were thus removable by virtue of the President's constitutional powers, and those who are members of a body "to exercise its judgment without the leave or hindrance of any other official or any department of the government," 295 U.S., at 625-626, as to whom a power of removal exists only if Congress may fairly be said to have conferred it. This sharp differentiation derives from the difference in functions between those who are part of the Executive establishment and those whose tasks require absolute freedom from Executive interference. . . .

Thus, the most reliable factor for drawing an inference regarding the President's power of removal in our case is the nature of the function that Congress vested in the War Claims Commission. What were the duties that Congress confided to this Commission? . . .

. . . The Commission was established as an adjudicating body with all the paraphernalia by which legal claims are put to the test of proof, with finality of determination "not subject to review by any other official of the United States or by any court by mandamus or otherwise." . . .

. . . Congress could, of course, have given jurisdiction over these claims to the District Courts or to the Court of Claims. The fact that it chose to establish a Commission to "adjudicate according to law" the classes of claims defined in the statute did not alter the intrinsic judicial character of the task with which the Commission was charged. . . . If, as one must take for granted, the War Claims Act precluded the President from influencing the Commission in passing on a particular claim, a fortiori must it be inferred that Congress did not wish to have hang over the Commission the Damocles' sword of removal by the President for no reason other than he preferred to have on that Commission men of his own choosing. . . . Judging the matter in all the nakedness in which it is presented, namely, the claim that the President could remove a member of an adjudicatory body like the War Claims Commission merely because he wanted his own appointees on such a Commission, we are compelled to conclude that no such power is given to the President directly by the Constitution, and none is impliedly conferred upon him by statute simply because Congress said nothing about it. The philosophy of Humphrey's Executor, in its explicit language as well as its implications, precludes such a claim.

The judgment is reversed.

Notes and Questions

1. *Humphrey's Executor* holds that Congress may create "independent" regulatory agencies. The ICC, established in 1887, is ordinarily considered the first such agency. Its several members are appointed by the president, but their terms do not coincide with his. They were intended to be experts who would independently administer the Interstate Commerce Act. The independent agency model was copied when the FTC was created in 1914.

The independent agency grew in popularity during the New Deal period, which saw the establishment of the Civil Aeronautics Board (CAB), the National Labor Relations Board (NLRB), the Federal Power Commission (FPC), and the SEC. Many others have been created since, though during the "rights revolution" of the 1960s and 1970s — the next burst of legislative creation of agencies after the New Deal — the independent agency form was not especially popular.

2. What provisions of the Constitution does the Court invoke in *Myers*? Does the vesting of executive power in the president compel the Court's conclusion? Does the provision requiring the president to "take Care" that the laws be faithfully executed? Or is removal an inherently executive act?

What policies underlie the constitutional commitment, as understood in *Myers*, to a strongly "unitary" executive branch? Consider the possibility that unitariness helps ensure both coordination of a mass of legislation and political accountability — because everyone will know who is responsible if things go wrong — and also promotes expedience in government — because one person can act more quickly than six. These policies played a key role in the framers' decision to create some kind of unitary executive. See The Federalist No. 47. But are there reasons to think that unitariness in execution of the laws may cause serious problems? Why does Congress ever create independent regulatory commissions?

3. Consider several differences between *Myers* and *Humphrey's Executor.*

(a) The FTC commissioners are high-level policymakers, unlike the postmaster in *Myers.*

(b) In *Myers*, Congress did not merely create independent officers; it reserved for itself a role in removal.

(c) The FTC performs quasi-judicial functions (it acts like a court of appeals) and also quasi-legislative functions (it compiles reports for Congress; note that by saying that the FTC performs quasi-legislative functions, the Court was not referring to rulemaking). This cannot be said of the postmaster. The *Humphrey's Executor* Court seized on this last point. Why is that point so important?

4. There is a vigorous textual and historical debate over the legitimacy of independent regulatory agencies. The Constitution vests executive power in the president alone; it makes no explicit provision for "independent" officers. Is this powerful textual evidence against *Humphrey's Executor*? It might be thought that the Constitution self-consciously creates one executive and deprives Congress of authority to create otherwise. Can the text bear this much weight? See Calabresi & Prakash, The President's Power to Execute the Law, 104 Yale L.J. 541 (1994); Calabresi & Rhodes, The Structural Constitution, 105 Harv. L. Rev. 1153 (1992); Miller, Independent Agencies, 1986 Sup. Ct. Rev. 41.

Some people argue that the early history strongly supports the view that the Constitution creates a unitary executive, in which the president has plenary power of discharge of high-level employees. Especially important here is the so-called Decision of

1789, by which Congress decided to place the Departments of War, Treasury, and Foreign Affairs under the president; there can be no question that this decision was informed by an understanding of constitutional requirements. Other people have argued that the original Constitution was quite ambiguous, and that the vesting of the "executive" power signaled no decision to forbid Congress from creating administrators free from presidential control. Thus, there is some evidence that the founding generation believed that Congress would have considerable discretion over the structure of what we now call the executive branch. Some of the early practices, involving the relatively independent comptroller of the currency, provide support for the judgment in *Humphrey's Executor* itself. In fact, there is reason to believe that Congress created a relatively independent comptroller because it believed that the comptroller exercised both legislative and judicial authority, in a way that provides some historical support for the outcome in *Humphrey's Executor*. See G. Casper, Separating Power (1997); Lessig & Sunstein, The President and the Administration, 94 Colum. L. Rev. 1 (1994). If it is the case that many members of Congress thought that Congress could create independent officers, does it follow that *Humphrey's Executor* was right?

5. There is also a vigorous debate over the relevance of changed circumstances to the question whether Congress can immunize some officers from presidential control. It is possible to think that even if Congress lacked this power at the time of the founding, Congress should be taken to have this power now, so as to ensure that the executive branch does not become unduly powerful in an area in which agencies exercise far more authority than the Framers anticipated. On this view, the downfall of the nondelegation doctrine, the New Deal, and the rise of increased national authority call for an act of "translation" that gives Congress the power to create independent agencies to maintain fidelity with the Framers' commitment to dividing governmental authority. See Greene, Checks and Balances in an Era of Presidential Lawmaking, 61 U. Chi. L. Rev. 123 (1993).

Others argue in the opposite direction. They say that the rise of administrative agencies calls for more, not less, in the way of presidential direction, and precisely in the interest of the founding commitments to coordination and accountability in government. See Lessig & Sunstein, supra.

6. Just what is the "constitutional position" of the independent agencies? Are they, as a 1937 presidential commission wrote, "in reality miniature independent governments, . . . a headless 'fourth branch' of the Government"? Note that the holding of *Humphrey's Executor* is quite narrow. The Court did not specify what kind of power the president had over the FTC; it only said that commissioners were not "at-will" employees, like the secretary of state. We will return to some of these questions after examining the modern doctrine.

7. Is the judgment in *Humphrey's Executor* under the influence of the Progressive Era belief in the capacity of impartial experts to discern the public interest? If we do not share that belief, might we nonetheless want some agencies to be independent of the president? Why?

8. Note that notwithstanding the apparent embrace of presidential authority in *Myers*, the Court leaves Congress with some residual authority. The Civil Service Act, according to the Court, is constitutional. Moreover, adjudicative decisions can apparently be insulated from presidential influence. And Congress is permitted to prevent the president from "overruling" certain decisions vested by Congress in agency heads. What justifies these exceptions? Are they consistent with Article II as understood in *Myers* itself?

Might it be argued that so long as the president can discharge high-level policymakers, the essentials of Article II power have been retained?

2. Modern Developments

For several decades *Myers* and *Humphrey's Executor* dominated the law with respect to the relationship between the president and administrative agencies. Actual governmental practice reflected not new Supreme Court decisions, but political forces and diverse readings of these two ambiguous holdings — with Congress and the president understanding the decisions in very different ways. In the modern era, a new set of claims has been made, and a new synthesis appears to have emerged. The story begins with the legislative veto.

a. The Legislative Veto

The legislative veto essentially is a clause in a statute that says that a particular executive action (and by "executive" we mean to include the so-called independent agencies discussed below) will take effect only if Congress does not nullify it by resolution within a specified period of time. Variations in detail are possible: The resolution might have to be passed by one house of Congress, both houses, or simply by a committee. The action itself might take effect while Congress debates, or it might rest in limbo. But whatever the details, three elements are essential:

1. a statutory delegation of power to the Executive;
2. an exercise of that power by the Executive;
3. a reserved power in the Congress to nullify that exercise of authority.

Thus, Congress might delegate to the president the authority to commit armed forces to action overseas; it might delegate to the attorney general the authority to suspend the deportation of those not legally entitled to remain in the United States; it might delegate to the FTC the authority to regulate trade practices by rule. And, in each instance, it might reserve to itself the power to nullify an individual act taken pursuant to the delegated authority.

Apparently, the first time Congress enacted a veto clause was in 1932 when it gave President Hoover the authority to reorganize executive departments subject to a one-house veto. Between 1932 and 1980, veto clauses proliferated like water lilies on a pond (or algae in a swimming pool, depending on one's point of view).

The basic goal of the legislative veto was to allow Congress an opportunity to oversee, or veto, agency decisions, especially if agencies acted under statutes that gave them broad discretion amounting, in practice, to a form of lawmaking. Advocates of the veto argued that it allowed Congress to reclaim some of its original constitutional responsibilities.

Immigration & Naturalization Service v. Chadha

462 U.S. 919 (1983)

[Chadha, an East Indian born in Kenya, remained in the United States after his visa expired. He was ordered deported. The attorney general suspended his deportation, allowing him to remain in the United States, for reasons of hardship. Immigration and Nationality Act §244, 8 U.S.C. §1254. However, §244(c)(2) provides:

> (2) In the case of an alien specified in paragraph (1) of subsection (a) of this subsection — if during the session of the Congress at which a case is reported, or prior to the close of the session of the Congress next following the session at which a case is reported, either the Senate or the House of Representatives passes a resolution stating in substance that it does not favor the suspension of such deportation, the Attorney General shall thereupon deport such alien or authorize the alien's voluntary departure at his own expense under the order of deportation in the manner provided by law. If, within the time above specified, neither the Senate nor the House of Representatives shall pass such a resolution, the Attorney General shall cancel deportation proceedings.

The House of Representatives enacted a resolution overturning the attorney general's decision. There was no public hearing, report, or meaningful statement of reasons on a committee recommendation in favor of the resolution, which was passed without a recorded vote.]

Mr. Chief Justice BURGER delivered the opinion of the Court. . . .

III

A

We turn now to the question whether action of one House of Congress under §224(c)(2) violates strictures of the Constitution. [The] wisdom [of the statute] is not the concern of the courts; . . . The fact that a given law or procedure is efficient, convenient, and useful in facilitating functions of government, standing alone, will not save it if it is contrary to the Constitution. . . .

Explicit and unambiguous provisions of the Constitution prescribe and define the respective functions of the Congress and of the Executive in the legislative process. Since the precise terms of those familiar provisions are critical to the resolution of this case, we set them out verbatim. Art. I provides:

> All legislative Powers herein granted shall be vested in a Congress of the United States, which shall consist of a Senate *and* a House of Representatives. Art. I, §1. (Emphasis added.)
>
> Every Bill which shall have passed the House of Representatives *and* the Senate, *shall*, before it become a Law, be presented to the President of the United States; . . . Art. I, §7, cl. 2. (Emphasis added.)
>
> *Every* Order, Resolution, or Vote to which the Concurrence of the Senate and House of Representatives may be necessary (except on a question of Adjournment) *shall* be presented to the President of the United States; and before the Same shall take Effect, *shall* be approved by him, or being disapproved by him, *shall* be repassed by two thirds of the Senate and House of Representatives, according to the Rules and Limitations prescribed in the Case of a Bill. Art. I, §7, cl. 3. (Emphasis added.)

These provisions of Art. I are integral parts of the constitutional design for the separation of powers. We have recently noted that "[t]he principle of separation of powers was not simply an abstract generalization in the minds of the Framers: it was woven into the documents that they drafted in Philadelphia in the summer of 1787." . . .

The Presentment Clauses

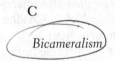

The records of the Constitutional Convention reveal that the requirement that all legislation be presented to the President before becoming law was uniformly accepted by the Framers. Presentment to the President and the Presidential veto were considered so imperative that the draftsmen took special pains to assure that these requirements could not be circumvented. . . .

The President's role in the lawmaking process also reflects the Framers' careful efforts to check whatever propensity a particular Congress might have to enact oppressive, improvident, or ill-considered measures. The President's veto role in the legislative process was described later during public debate on ratification: "It establishes a salutary check upon the legislative body, calculated to guard the community against the effects of faction, precipitancy, or of any impulse unfriendly to the public good which may happen to influence a majority of that body. . . ."

The Court also has observed that the Presentment Clauses serve the important purpose of assuring that a "national" perspective is grafted on the legislative process:

> The President is a representative of the people just as the members of the Senate and of the House are, and it may be, at some times, on some subjects, that the President elected by all the people is rather more representative of them all than are the members of either body of the Legislature whose constituencies are local and not countrywide. . . . Myers v. United States, [272 U.S. 52, 123 (1926)].

C

Bicameralism

The bicameral requirement of Art. I, §§1, 7 was of scarcely less concern to the Framers than was the Presidential veto and indeed the two concepts are interdependent. By providing that no law could take effect without the concurrence of the prescribed majority of the Members of both Houses, the Framers reemphasized their belief, already remarked upon in connection with the Presentment Clauses, that legislation should not be enacted unless it has been carefully and fully considered by the Nation's elected officials.

Hamilton argued that a Congress comprised of a single House was antithetical to the very purposes of the Constitution — [such as the need to check the passions of legislative bodies and the "great compromise" between big and small states]. . . .

We see therefore that the Framers were acutely conscious that the bicameral requirement and the Presentment Clauses would serve essential constitutional functions. The President's participation in the legislative process was to protect the Executive Branch from Congress and to protect the whole people from improvident laws. The division of the Congress into two distinctive bodies assures that the legislative power would be exercised only after opportunity for full study and debate in separate settings. The President's unilateral veto power, in turn, was limited by the power of two thirds of both Houses of Congress to overrule a veto thereby precluding final arbitrary action of one person. . . . It emerges clearly that the prescription for legislative action in Art. I, §§1, 7 represents the Framers' decision that the legislative power of the Federal government be exercised in accord with a single, finely wrought and exhaustively considered, procedure.

IV

The Constitution sought to divide the delegated powers of the new federal government into three defined categories, legislative, executive and judicial, to assure, as nearly as possible, that each Branch of government would confine itself to its assigned responsibility. The hydraulic pressure inherent within each of the separate Branches to exceed the outer limits of its power, even to accomplish desirable objectives, must be resisted.

Although not "hermetically" sealed from one another, the powers delegated to the three Branches are functionally identifiable. When any Branch acts, it is presumptively exercising the power the Constitution has delegated to it. See Hampton & Co. v. United States, 276 U.S. 394, 406 (1928). When the Executive acts, it presumptively acts in an executive or administrative capacity as defined in Art. II. And when, as here, one House of Congress purports to act, it is presumptively acting within its assigned sphere. . . .

Examination of the action taken here by one House pursuant to §244(c)(2) reveals that it was essentially legislative in purpose and effect. . . .

The legislative character of the one-House veto in this case is confirmed by the character of the Congressional action it supplants. Neither the House of Representatives nor the Senate contends that, absent the veto provision in §244(c)(2), either of them, or both of them acting together, could effectively require the Attorney General to deport an alien once the Attorney General, in the exercise of legislatively delegated authority, had determined the alien should remain in the United States. Without the challenged provision in §244(c)(2), this could have been achieved, if at all, only by legislation requiring deportation. Similarly, a veto by one House of Congress under §244(c)(2) cannot be justified as an attempt at amending the standards set out in §244(a)(1), or as a repeal of §244 as applied to Chadha. Amendment and repeal of statutes, no less than enactment, must conform with Art. I.

The nature of the decision implemented by the one-House veto in this case further manifests its legislative character. After long experience with the clumsy, time-consuming private bill procedure, Congress made a deliberate choice to delegate to the Executive Branch, and specifically to the Attorney General, the authority to allow deportable aliens to remain in this country in certain specified circumstances. It is not disputed that this choice to delegate authority is precisely the kind of decision that can be implemented only in accordance with the procedures set out in Art. I. Disagreement with the Attorney General's decision on Chadha's deportation — that is, Congress' decision to deport Chadha — no less than Congress' original choice to delegate to the Attorney General the authority to make that decision, involves determination of policy that Congress can implement in only one way: bicameral passage followed by presentment to the President. Congress must abide by its delegation of authority until that delegation is legislatively altered or revoked.

Finally, we see that when the Framers intended to authorize either House of Congress to act alone and outside of its prescribed bicameral legislative role, they narrowly and precisely defined the procedure. There are but four provisions in the Constitution, explicit and unambiguous, by which one House may act alone with the unreviewable force of law, not subject to the President's veto:

(a) The House of Representatives alone was given the power to initiate impeachments. Art. I, §2, cl. 6;

(b) The Senate alone was given the power to conduct trials following impeachment on charges initiated by the House and to convict following trial. Art. I, §3, cl. 5;

(c) The Senate alone was given final unreviewable power to approve or to disapprove presidential appointments. Art. II, §2, cl. 2;

(d) The Senate alone was given unreviewable power to ratify treaties negotiated by the President. Art. II, §2, cl. 2. . . .

This is not one of those

Since it is clear that the action by the House under §244(c)(2) was not within any of the express constitutional exceptions authorizing one House to act alone, and equally clear that it was an exercise of legislative power, that action was subject to the standards prescribed in Article I. The bicameral requirement, the Presentment Clauses, the President's veto, and Congress' power to override a veto were intended to erect enduring checks on each Branch and to protect the people from the improvident exercise of power by mandating certain prescribed steps. To preserve those checks, and maintain the separation of powers, the carefully defined limits on the power of each Branch must not be eroded. To accomplish what has been attempted by one House of Congress in this case requires action in conformity with the express procedures of the Constitution's prescription for legislative action: passage by a majority of both Houses and presentment to the President.

[Justice Powell concurred in the result. He argued that the Congress here "adjudicated" Chadha's individual case, thereby invading the province that the Constitution reserved for the Judiciary.]

Mr. Justice WHITE, dissenting.

Kills lots of legislative vetos.

Today the Court not only invalidates §244(c)(2) of the Immigration and Nationality Act, but also sounds the death knell for nearly 200 other statutory provisions in which Congress has reserved a "legislative veto." For this reason, the Court's decision is of surpassing importance. And it is for this reason that the Court would have been well-advised to decide the case, if possible, on the narrower grounds of separation of powers, leaving for full consideration the constitutionality of other congressional review statutes operating on such varied matters as war powers and agency rulemaking, some of which concern the independent regulatory agencies. . . .

The power to exercise a legislative veto is not the power to write new law without bicameral approval or presidential consideration. The veto must be authorized by statute and may only negative what an Executive department or independent agency has proposed. On its face, the legislative veto no more allows one House of Congress to make laws than does the presidential veto confer such power upon the President. . . .

was passed originally . . .

The terms of the Presentment Clauses suggest only that bills and their equivalent are subject to the requirements of bicameral passage and presentment to the President. . . . Its purpose was to prevent Congress from circumventing the presentation requirement in the making of new legislation. . . .

There is no record that the Convention contemplated, let alone intended, that these Article I requirements would someday be invoked to restrain the scope of Congressional authority pursuant to duly-enacted law. . . .

Why can't Congress pass this kind of Law?

When the Convention did turn its attention to the scope of Congress' lawmaking power, the Framers were expansive. The Necessary and Proper Clause, Art. I, §8, cl. 19, vests Congress with the power "to make all laws which shall be necessary and proper for carrying into Execution the foregoing Powers [the enumerated powers of §8], and all other Powers vested by this Constitution in the government of the United States, or in any Department or Officer thereof." It is long-settled that Congress may "exercise its best judgment in the

Necessary + Proper?

selection of measures, to carry into execution the constitutional powers of the government," and "avail itself of experience, to exercise its reason, and to accommodate its legislation to circumstances." McCulloch v. Maryland, 4 Wheat. 316, 415-416, 420 (1819). . . .

If Congress may delegate lawmaking power to independent and executive agencies, it is most difficult to understand Article I as forbidding Congress from also reserving a check on legislative power for itself. Absent the veto, the agencies receiving delegations of legislative or quasi-legislative power may issue regulations having the force of law without bicameral approval and without the President's signature. It is thus not apparent why the reservation of a veto over the exercise of that legislative power must be subject to a more exacting test. In other cases, it is enough that the initial statutory authorizations comply with the Article I requirements.

Nor are there strict limits on the agents that may receive such delegations of legislative authority so that it might be said that the legislature can delegate authority to others but not to itself. While most authority to issue rules and regulations is given to the executive branch and the independent regulatory agencies, statutory delegations to private persons have also passed this Court's scrutiny. In Currin v. Wallace, 306 U.S. 1 (1939), the statute provided that restrictions upon the production or marketing of agricultural commodities was to become effective only upon the favorable vote by a prescribed majority of the affected farmers. United States v. Rock Royal Co-operative, 307 U.S. 533, 577 (1939), upheld an act which gave producers of specified commodities the right to veto marketing orders issued by the Secretary of Agriculture. Assuming *Currin* and *Rock Royal Co-operative* remain sound law, the Court's decision today suggests that Congress may place a "veto" power over suspensions of deportation in private hands or in the hands of an independent agency, but is forbidden from reserving such authority for itself. . . .

If the effective functioning of a complex modern government requires the delegation of vast authority which, by virtue of its breadth, is legislative or "quasi-legislative" in character, I cannot accept that Article I — which is, after all, the source of the non-delegation doctrine — should forbid Congress from qualifying that grant with a legislative veto. . . .

The Court also takes no account of perhaps the most relevant consideration: However resolutions of disapproval under §244(c)(2) are formally characterized, in reality, a departure from the status quo occurs only upon the concurrence of opinion among the House, Senate, and President. Reservations of legislative authority to be exercised by Congress should be upheld if the exercise of such reserved authority is consistent with the distribution of and limits upon legislative power that Article I provides. . . .

The central concern of the presentation and bicameralism requirements of Article I is that when a departure from the legal status quo is undertaken, it is done with the approval of the President and both Houses of Congress — or, in the event of a presidential veto, a two-thirds majority in both Houses. This interest is fully satisfied by the operation of §244(c)(2). The President's approval is found in the Attorney General's action in recommending to Congress that the deportation order for a given alien be suspended. The House and the Senate indicate their approval of the Executive's action by not passing a resolution of disapproval within the statutory period. Thus, a change in the legal status quo — the deportability of the alien — is consummated only with the approval of each of the three relevant actors. The disagreement of any one of the three maintains the alien's pre-existing status: the Executive may choose not to recommend suspension; the House and Senate may each veto the recommendation. The effect of the rights and obligations of the affected individuals and upon the legislative system is precisely the same as if a private bill were introduced but failed to receive the necessary approval. . . .

It may be objected that Congress cannot indicate its approval of legislative change by inaction. In the Court of Appeals' view, inaction by Congress "could equally imply endorsement, aquiescence, passivity, indecision or indifference," . . . and the Court appears to echo this concern. . . . This objection appears more properly directed at the wisdom of the legislative veto than its constitutionality. The Constitution does not and cannot guarantee that legislators will carefully scrutinize legislation and deliberate before acting. . . .

I do not suggest that all legislative vetoes are necessarily consistent with separation-of-powers principles. A legislative check on an inherently executive function, for example that of initiating prosecutions, poses an entirely different question. But the legislative veto device here — and in many other settings — is far from an instance of legislative tyranny over the Executive. It is a necessary check on the unavoidably expanding power of the agencies, both executive and independent, as they engage in exercising authority delegated by Congress.

Notes and Questions

1. Is *Chadha* consistent with the nondelegation cases, which appear to allow the executive to "legislate"? What about the judiciary's apparent "legislative" power in interpreting open-ended statutes such as the antitrust laws? Can Justice White's opinion be read to suggest that the legislative veto is a constitutionally desirable quid pro quo for the downfall of the nondelegation doctrine? *Too Formalistic Decision?*

An underlying question is whether the decision in *Chadha* should be accused of being excessively "formalistic." On one view, the Supreme Court should not treat the Constitution as a set of rigid, formal instructions, at least when circumstances have changed radically since the founding. Justice White's opinion might be seen as a less formal effort to keep faith with founding commitments under new conditions by allowing Congress to assume something closer to its original constitutional role. See Elliott, INS v. Chadha: The Administrative Constitution, the Constitution, and the Legislative Veto, 1983 Sup. Ct. Rev. 125. Thus we can see the debate over *Chadha* as reflecting a debate over two styles of constitutional interpretations — one stressing text and original understanding, the other stressing broad purposes. See Strauss, Formal and Functional Approaches to Separation of Powers Questions, 72 Cornell L. Rev. 488 (1987).

On the other hand, there is evidence that in practice, the legislative veto increased the power of self-interested private groups over regulatory law, precisely by circumventing the original constitutional checks of bicameralism and presentment to the president. See Bruff & Gellhorn, Congressional Control of Administrative Regulation, 90 Harv. L. Rev. 1369, 1372-1381 (1977). Does this evidence suggest that *Chadha* is right after all, because a purposive or structural understanding of the Constitution supports, and does not undermine, a textual or historical approach? See generally Sunstein, Constitutionalism After the New Deal, 101 Harv. L. Rev. 421, 491-501 (1987).

2. "The failure to veto shows that the three bodies — the President, the Senate, and the House — agree. That is sufficient for purposes of the Constitution." Argue for and against this proposition.

3. In what sense is the legislative veto dead? Congress unquestionably retains a host of traditional weapons in its legislative and political arsenal that can accomplish *some* of the veto's objectives. Consider, first and foremost, legislation enacted in 1996 and supported by President Clinton that requires agencies to submit certain regulations to Congress and that creates a 60-day period in which the full Congress may "veto" any

regulation of which it disapproves. 7 U.S.C. §§801 et seq. Is this a desirable measure? Is it mostly symbolic, because Congress can in any case veto laws by acting through the constitutionally authorized channels? What effect is it likely to have? How might it compare to the legislative veto?

Note that this so-called congressional review mechanism was used only once in its first five years, to overturn the Clinton Administration's occupational safety and health regulation involving "ergonomics," which covered back injuries, carpal tunnel syndrome, and similar problems on the job. Some people think that the congressional override worked well, because the regulation was ill-considered, would cost a great deal, and would have few benefits. But critics complain that the regulation was developed over a period of years and that Congress overturned it without holding hearings or considering the relevant evidence. In their view, a serious problem with the system for congressional review is that it lacks the ordinary protections of the committee structure.

Other possible alternatives include Congress's power to provide that the legislation delegating authority to the executive expires every so often. To continue to exercise that authority, the executive would have to seek congressional approval, at which point past agency behavior that Congress disliked would become the subject of serious debate. Moreover, Congress might sometimes tailor its statutes more specifically, limiting executive power. In practice, though not in law, Congress typically requires the president, before taking action, to consult with congressional representatives whose views would carry significant political weight.

Note that in 1996, Speaker of the House Newt Gingrich created a "Corrections Day" to be held on the second and fourth Monday of every month, by which Congress corrects perceived mistakes in legislation or regulation. Finally, each year Congress considers the agency's budget. If a significant group of legislators strongly opposes a particular agency decision, it might well succeed in including a sentence in the appropriations bill denying the agency funds to enforce that decision.

Congress could also enact "confirmatory law" provisions that would condition the legal effect of exercises of delegated authority on subsequent enactment of a confirming statute. For example, the Transportation Department might propose a new auto safety rule that could go into effect only after Congress enacted an authorizing statute (with opportunity for veto by the president — a superfluous safeguard in most cases because the department presumably would not have proposed the regulation over White House opposition). But this strategy would drastically — and perhaps unworkably — undermine executive or agency power, for it is much harder to enact a new law than to decline to exercise a veto. Moreover, it might effectively preclude judicial review of agency initiatives on all grounds other than the unconstitutionality of the statute authorizing the initiative — largely eliminating administrative law! For general discussion of congressional efforts to discipline the regulatory state, especially in the aftermath of the 1994 Contract with America, see Sunstein, Congress, Constitutional Moments, and the Cost-Benefit State, 48 Stan. L. Rev. 247 (1996).

4. In considering other statutes containing legislative vetos, many courts have held the statutes to be constitutional because the invoked legislative veto was "severable" from the rest of the statute (that is, Congress would have passed the statute without the veto had it known that the veto could not constitutionally be used). The Supreme Court, upholding the severability of a one-house veto provision in the Airline Deregulation Act of 1978, repeated the traditional test of severability, namely, "unless it is evident that the legislature would not have enacted those provisions which are within its power, independently

of that which is not, the involved part may be dropped if what is left is fully operative as law." Alaska Airlines v. Brock, 480 U.S. 678, 684 (1987). The circuit courts of appeals have split over the question whether, in the absence of a legislative veto clause, "it is evident" that Congress would have enacted the Reorganization Act of 1985 (giving the president power to reorganize executive departments, including the Equal Employment Opportunity Commission (EEOC)). Compare EEOC v. CBS, 743 F.2d 969 (2d Cir. 1984) (finding the clause nonseverable and therefore denying EEOC the power to enforce the Age Discrimination Act), with Muller Optical Co. v. EEOC, 743 F.2d 380 (6th Cir. 1984) (same).

5. An especially important aspect of *Chadha* is its suggestion that the problem with the legislative veto was its "encroachment" on executive prerogatives. This view suggested the possibility of a rebirth of constitutional "formalism," which might endanger the independent agencies and even lead to a revival of the nondelegation doctrine. More modestly, it suggested a possible rethinking of *Myers* and *Humphrey's Executor*, as we shall now see.

Bowsher v. Synar
478 U.S. 714 (1986)

Chief Justice BURGER delivered the opinion of the Court.

[The basic question is whether Congress may constitutionally delegate to the comptroller general the power to review estimates of likely budget deficits, to determine whether the estimated deficit will exceed a specified amount, and if so, to determine program by program, according to statutorily specified rules, how much appropriated money the president must "sequester" (that is, not spend).] The relevant appointment statutes provide that the President appoint the Comptroller General from a list of these individuals recommended by the Speaker of the House and the Senate President pro tempore, 31 U.S.C. 703(a)(2). He must be confirmed by the Senate. He may be removed "at any time" by Joint Resolution of Congress (which requires a Presidential signature or a two-thirds Congressional override of his veto) for the following: "(i) permanent disability; (ii) inefficiency; (iii) neglect of duty; (iv) malfeasance; or (v) a felony or conduct involving moral turpitude." 31 U.S.C. 703(e)(1). . . .

We noted recently that "[t]he Constitution sought to divide the delegated powers of the new Federal Government into three defined categories, Legislative, Executive, and Judicial." . . .

That this system of division and separation of powers produces conflicts, confusion, and discordance at times is inherent, but it was deliberately so structured to assure full, vigorous and open debate on the great issues affecting the people and to provide avenues for the operation of checks on the exercise of government power.

The Constitution does not contemplate an active role for Congress in the supervision of officers charged with the execution of the laws it enacts. The President appoints "Officers of the United States" with the "Advice and Consent of the Senate. . . ." Article II, 2. Once the appointment has been made and confirmed, however, the Constitution explicitly provides for removal of Officers of the United States by Congress only upon impeachment by the House and trial by the Senate [which] can rest only on "Treason, Bribery or other high Crimes and Misdemeanors." Article II, 4. A direct Congressional role in the removal of officers charged with the execution of the laws beyond this limited one is inconsistent with separation of powers. . . .

[W]e conclude that Congress cannot reserve for itself the power of removal of an officer charged with the execution of the laws except by impeachment. To permit the execution of the laws to be vested in an officer answerable only to Congress would, in practical terms, reserve in Congress control over the execution of the laws. As the District Court observed, "Once an officer is appointed, it is only the authority that appointed him . . . that he must fear, and in the performance of his function, obey." The structure of the Constitution does not permit Congress to execute the laws; it follows that Congress cannot grant to an officer under its control what it does not possess. . . .[4]

Appellants urge that the Comptroller General performs his duties independently and is not subservient to Congress. We agree with the District Court that this contention does not bear close scrutiny.

The critical factor lies in the provisions of the statute defining the Comptroller General's office relating to removability. Although the Comptroller General is nominated by the President from a list of three individuals recommended by the Speaker of the House of Representatives and the President pro tempore of the Senate, see 31 U.S.C. 703(a)(2), and confirmed by the Senate, he is removable only at the initiation of Congress. He may be removed not only by impeachment but also by Joint Resolution of Congress "at any time" resting on any one of the following bases:

    (i)   permanent disability;
    (ii) inefficiency;
    (iii) neglect of duty;
    (iv) malfeasance; or
    (v)   a felony or conduct involving moral turpitude.

31 U.S.C. 703(e)(1).

This provision was included, as one Congressman explained in urging passage of the Act, because Congress "felt that [the Comptroller General] should be brought under the sole control of Congress, so that Congress at the moment when it found he was inefficient and was not carrying on the duties of his office as he should and as the Congress expected, could remove him without the long, tedious process of a trial by impeachment." 61 Cong. Rec. 1081 (1921).

The removal provision was an important part of the legislative scheme. . . .

This much said, we must also add that the dissent is simply in error to suggest that the political realities reveal that the Comptroller General is free from influence by Congress. . . . The Comptroller General heads the General Accounting Office, "an instrumentality of the United States Government independent of the executive departments." 31 U.S.C. 702(a). . . . [I]t is clear the Congress has consistently viewed the Comptroller General as an officer of the Legislative Branch. . . .

Against this background, we see no escape from the conclusion that, because Congress has retained removal authority over the Comptroller General, he may not be entrusted with executive powers. The remaining question is whether the Comptroller General has been assigned such powers in the Balanced Budget and Emergency Deficit Control Act of 1985. . . .

---

[4] Appellants are wide of the mark in arguing that an affirmance in this case requires casting doubt on the status of "independent" agencies because no issues involving such agencies are presented here. The statutes establishing independent agencies typically specify either that the agency members are removable by the President for specified causes . . . or else do not specify a removal procedure. . . . This case involves nothing like these statutes, but rather a statute that provides for direct Congressional involvement over the decision to remove the Comptroller General. . . .

Since Congress Keeps Removal power, Comptroller can't have exec powers, but since he does, congress can't remove

The primary responsibility of the Comptroller General under the instant Act is the preparation of a report. [This report effectively determines how the President must cut the budget. The President, under the statute "may not modify or recalculate any of the estimates in amounts or percentages set forth in the report." Hence, the Comptroller's function under the Gramm-Rudman Act is executive in nature.] . . . By placing the responsibility for execution of the Balanced Budget and Emergency Deficit Control Act in the hands of an officer who is subject to removal only by itself, Congress in effect has retained control over the execution of the Act and has intruded into the executive function. The Constitution does not permit such intrusion. . . .

[Justices Stevens and Marshall concurred. Justice Stevens drew attention to the fact that, in light of history and the nature of many of his statutory responsibilities, the comptroller general has long been considered an agent of Congress.

Justice White dissented. He attacked the Court's willingness to interpose its distressingly formalistic view of separation of powers as a bar to the attainment of governmental objectives through the means chosen by the Congress and the president in the legislative process established by the Constitution. He said:]

The Act vesting budget-cutting authority in the Comptroller General represents Congress' judgment that the delegation of such authority to counteract ever-mounting deficits is "necessary and proper" to the exercise of the powers granted the Federal government by the Constitution; and the President's approval of the statute signifies his unwillingness to reject the choice made by Congress. Cf. Nixon v. Administrator of General Services, 433 U.S., at 441. Under such circumstances, the role of this Court should be limited to determining whether the Act so alters the balance of authority among the branches of government as to pose a genuine threat to the basic division between the lawmaking power and the power to execute the law. Because I see no such threat, I cannot join the Court in striking down the Act.

[Justice Blackmun also dissented. He said that Congress's "removal authority" should be held unconstitutional and severed from the rest of the statute, which, without that removal authority, would plainly be constitutional.]

Mistretta v. United States

488 U.S. 361 (1989)

[The Supreme Court, Justice Scalia alone dissenting, considered and upheld the constitutionality of the United States Sentencing Commission, a body composed of seven members, statutorily located in the "judicial branch," with the legal power to write sentencing guidelines that are binding on federal judges who sentence criminal defendants. Congress wrote fairly detailed standards in the statute. It also provided that the president could remove members for "cause." The Court held that the delegation of power did not violate the nondelegation doctrine. It went on to discuss the question of separation of powers.]

Separation of Powers — Having determined that Congress has set forth sufficient standards for the exercise of the Commission's delegated authority, we turn to Mistretta's claim that the Act violates the constitutional principle of separation of powers. . . .

In applying the principle of separated powers in our jurisprudence, we have sought to give life to Madison's view of the appropriate relationship among the three coequal Branches. Accordingly, we have recognized, as Madison admonished at the founding, that while our Constitution mandates that "each of the three general departments of government [must remain] entirely free from the control or coercive influence, direct or indirect, of either of the others," . . . the Framers did not require — and indeed rejected — the notion that the three Branches must be entirely separate and distinct. . . .

In adopting this flexible understanding of separation of powers, we simply have recognized Madison's teaching that the greatest security against tyranny — the accumulation of excessive authority in a single branch — lies not in a hermetic division between the Branches, but in a carefully crafted system of checked and balanced power within each Branch. . . .

It is this concern of encroachment and aggrandizement that has animated our separation-of-powers jurisprudence and aroused our vigilance against the "hydraulic pressure inherent within each of the separate Branches to exceed the outer limits of its power." . . . Accordingly, we have not hesitated to strike down provisions of law that either accrete to a single branch powers more appropriately diffused among separate branches or that undermine the authority and independence of one or another coordinate branch. . . .

Mistretta argues that the Act suffers from each of these constitutional infirmities. He argues that Congress, in constituting the Commission as it did, effected an unconstitutional accumulation of power within the Judicial Branch while at the same time undermining the Judiciary's independence and integrity.

When this Court is asked to invalidate a statutory provision that has been approved by both Houses of the Congress and signed by the President, particularly an Act of Congress that confronts a deeply vexing national problem, it should only do so for the most compelling constitutional reasons. . . . Although the unique composition and responsibilities of the Sentencing Commission give rise to serious concerns about a disruption of the appropriate balance of governmental power among the coordinate Branches, we conclude, upon close inspection, that petitioner's fears for the fundamental structural protections of the Constitution prove, at least in this case, to be "more smoke than fire," and do not compel us to invalidate Congress' considered scheme for resolving the seemingly intractable dilemma of excessive disparity in criminal sentencing. . . .

Location of the Commission — The Sentencing Commission unquestionably is a peculiar institution within the framework of our Government. Although placed by the Act in the Judicial Branch, it is not a court and does not exercise judicial power. Rather, the Commission is an "independent" body comprised of seven voting members including at least three federal judges, entrusted by Congress with the primary task of promulgating sentencing guidelines. 28 U.S.C. 991(a). Our constitutional principles of separated powers are not violated, however, by mere anomaly or innovation. . . . Congress' decision to create an independent rulemaking body to promulgate sentencing guidelines and to locate that body within the Judicial Branch is not unconstitutional unless Congress has vested in the Commission powers that are more appropriately performed by the other Branches or that undermine the integrity of the Judiciary.

According to express provision of Article III, the judicial power of the United States is limited to "Cases" and "Controversies." . . . Nonetheless, we have recognized significant exceptions to this general rule and have approved the assumption of some nonadjudicatory activities by the Judicial Branch. . . . None of our cases indicate that rulemaking per se is a function that may not be performed by an entity within the Judicial Branch, either because rulemaking is inherently nonjudicial or because it is a function exclusively committed to the Executive Branch. On the contrary, we specifically have held that Congress, in some circumstances, may confer rulemaking authority on the Judicial Branch. . . .

Our approach to other nonadjudicatory activities that Congress has vested either in federal courts or in auxiliary bodies within the Judicial Branch has been identical to our approach to judicial rulemaking: consistent with the separation of powers, Congress may delegate to the Judicial Branch nonadjudicatory functions that do not trench upon the prerogatives of another Branch and that are appropriate to the central mission of the Judiciary. . . .

The sentencing function long has been a peculiarly shared responsibility among the Branches of government and has never been thought of as the exclusive constitutional province of any one Branch. . . .

[The Court went on to describe the special nature of sentencing at some length. It concluded that, given] the consistent responsibility of federal judges to pronounce sentence within the statutory range established by Congress, we find that the role of the Commission in promulgating guidelines for the exercise of that judicial function bears considerable similarity to the role of this Court in establishing rules of procedure under the various enabling acts. . . .

In sum, since substantive judgment in the field of sentencing has been and remains appropriate to the Judicial Branch, and the methodology of rulemaking has been and remains appropriate to that Branch, Congress' considered decision to combine these functions in an independent Sentencing Commission and to locate that Commission within the Judicial Branch does not violate the principle of separation of powers. . . .

COMPOSITION OF THE COMMISSION

[5] We now turn to petitioner's claim that Congress' decision to require at least three federal judges to serve on the Commission and to require those judges to share their authority with nonjudges undermines the integrity of the Judicial Branch. . . .

[The Court analyzed the nature of the work and found that service on the Commission would not significantly interfere with judges' ability to carry out their normal work.]

PRESIDENTIAL CONTROL

The Act empowers the President to appoint all seven members of the Commission with the advice and consent of the Senate. The Act further provides that the President shall make his choice of judicial appointees to the Commission after considering a list of six judges recommended by the Judicial Conference of the United States. The Act also grants the President authority to remove members of the Commission, although "only for neglect of duty or malfeasance in office or for other good cause shown." 28 U.S.C. 991(a). . . .

The notion that the President's power to appoint federal judges to the Commission somehow gives him influence over the Judicial Branch or prevents, even potentially, the Judicial Branch from performing its constitutionally assigned functions is fanciful. We have never considered it incompatible with the functioning of the Judicial Branch that the President has the power to elevate federal judges from one level to another or to tempt judges away from the bench with Executive Branch positions. The mere fact that the President within his appointment portfolio has positions that may be attractive to federal judges does not, of itself, corrupt the integrity of the Judiciary. Were the impartiality of the Judicial Branch so easily subverted, our constitutional system of tripartite government would have failed long ago. We simply cannot imagine that federal judges will comport their actions to the wishes of the President for the purpose of receiving an appointment to the Sentencing Commission.

The President's removal power over Commission members poses a similarly negligible threat to judicial independence. The Act does not, and could not under the Constitution, authorize the President to remove, or in any way diminish the status of Article III judges, as judges. Even if removed from the Commission, a federal judge appointed to the Commission would continue, absent impeachment, to enjoy tenure "during good behavior" and a full judicial salary. U.S. Const., Art. III, §1. Also, the President's removal power under the Act is limited. In order to safeguard the independence of the Commission from executive control, Congress specified in the Act that the President may remove the Commission members only for good cause. Such congressional limitation on the President's removal power, like the removal provisions upheld in Morrison v. Olson and Humphrey's Executor v. United States, are specifically crafted to prevent the President from exercising "coercive influence" over independent agencies. . . .

In other words, since the President has no power to affect the tenure or compensation of Article III judges, even if the Act authorized him to remove judges from the Commission at will, he would have no power to coerce the judges in the exercise of their judicial duties. In any case, Congress did not grant the President unfettered authority to remove Commission members. Instead, precisely to ensure that they would not be subject to coercion even in the exercise of their nonjudicial duties, Congress insulated the members from Presidential removal except for good cause. Under these circumstances, we see no risk that the President's limited removal power will compromise the impartiality of Article III judges serving on the Commission and, consequently, no risk that the Act's removal provision will prevent the Judicial Branch from performing its constitutionally assigned function of fairly adjudicating cases and controversies. . . .

We conclude that in creating the Sentencing Commission — an unusual hybrid in structure and authority — Congress neither delegated excessive legislative power nor upset the constitutionally mandated balance of powers among the coordinate Branches. The Constitution's structural protections do not prohibit Congress from delegating to an expert body located within the Judicial Branch the intricate task of formulating sentencing guidelines consistent with such significant statutory direction as is present here. Nor does our system of checked and balanced authority prohibit Congress from calling upon the accumulated wisdom and experience of the Judicial Branch in creating policy on a matter uniquely within the ken of judges. Accordingly, we hold that the Act is constitutional.

Questions: The Status of Independent Agencies and Independent Officials

1. The president is precluded by the statutes that create the civil service system from removing most civil servants without cause. Why does everyone seem to agree that this limitation on the president's power is constitutional?

2. *Humphrey's Executor* legitimates the existence of independent regulatory commissions, defined as those agencies whose heads do not serve at the pleasure of the president. (We offer more details below.) Under President Reagan, the White House and the Department of Justice challenged the whole idea of independent agencies as inconsistent with the constitutional structure. In *Bowsher*, the Court attempted to avoid that issue, by suggesting that the problem in *Bowsher* was not mere independence (which is constitutional) but "encroachment" and "aggrandizement" (which are not). Thus, the key to

Bowsher was the fact that the comptroller general was not simply independent of the president but also, and more importantly, subject to congressional control.

In *Mistretta*, the Court suggested that the constitutional status of the independent agencies, and hence the holding in *Humphrey's Executor*, are quite secure — that the difference between *Bowsher* and *Humphrey's Executor* is that the former case involved a congressional agent, and hence encroachment, but that the latter case involved an independent agent. In this way *Bowsher* appears to reread *Myers*; the *Bowsher* Court emphasizes, as the *Myers* Court did not, that the arrangement in *Myers* involved not an independent officer but one with respect to whom the president and the Senate shared removal authority. Thus, *Bowsher* and *Myers* are cases of encroachment, whereas *Humphrey's* is one of independence.

From the constitutional point of view, why does this matter? Why is "independence" — whatever that may mean in practice and in law — any less troublesome than encroachment? What constitutional values are particularly endangered by encroachment? Consider the view that encroachment is a greater threat to the system of "dual branch lawmaking" because it effectively concentrates both the power to make law and the power to enforce law in a single official. But if this is a problem, why shouldn't the Court revive the nondelegation doctrine?

3. Does *Bowsher* really sidestep the question of the constitutional status of independent agencies? Consider the fact that the language governing Congress's power over the comptroller general is *nearly identical* to the language governing the president's power over independent commissioners. If the comptroller general is basically Congress's employee because of the language of the governing statute, why aren't independent commissioners basically the president's employees because of the language of the governing statute? This question raises an issue of interpretation. If the president is allowed to fire the members of independent agencies for inefficiency, neglect of duty, or malfeasance in office, what authority exactly does he have over those members?

Suppose that the president tries to fire a member of the FCC for one of the following reasons: (a) corruption; (b) laziness and absenteeism; (3) an inability to understand the nature of the emerging telecommunications market; (4) an unwarranted and excessive belief in the magic of laissez-faire; (5) indifference to the need to protect the public interest by ensuring educational programming for children or by allowing free air time for candidates for national office; (6) consistent rejection of the positions of the president. Which, if any, of these grounds for discharge is illegitimate under a provision that allows the president to discharge for inefficiency, malfeasance, or neglect of duty?

4. How strongly does *Mistretta* suggest that *Humphrey's Executor* remains good law? What about independent officials and institutions not part of the "independent agencies"?

(a) Section 5 of the Department of Transportation Act, 80 Stat. 835 (1966), established "within the Department a [five-member] National Transportation Safety Board" that investigates accidents and hears appeals in cases involving, for example, revocations of licenses to fly. The statute states that the president shall appoint its members to five-year terms, with the Senate's advice and consent, and can remove them only for "inefficiency, neglect of duty or malfeasance." Is this limitation on removal power constitutional?

(b) The administrator of the Federal Aviation Administration (FAA) makes initial decisions to award or to revoke a license to fly. Prior to 1968, the FAA was an "independent agency" in the sense of being located outside any of the traditional departments. It was then transferred to the Department of Transportation. The statute is silent as to the administrator's term of office or removal. Can the president remove the administrator without cause?

(c) The secretary of agriculture has authority under the Packers & Stockyards Act of 1921 to determine, after hearing, whether a packer is guilty of enumerated unlawful practices. And he can prescribe, after a hearing, just and reasonable rates. His authority under this act is similar to that of, say, the CAB in relation to airline rates. Can Congress constitutionally enact a statute prohibiting the president from removing the secretary without cause?

5. In Morrison v. Olson, 487 U.S. 654 (1988), the Supreme Court upheld a statute that gave a court the power to appoint an "independent counsel" who would investigate crime and prosecute high-level political officials. The president can remove the counsel only for "good cause." Olson argued that under the cases, the independent counsel was clearly a constitutionally impermissible agent because she exercised executive power without plenary presidential control. No previous case had allowed that arrangement. The Court responded that the existence of the independent counsel would not prevent the president from exercising his constitutionally specified functions. The Court emphasized that the independent counsel was not entirely an independent agent, because she could be fired for "good cause," which the Court did not define.

Justice Scalia wrote an impassioned dissent, suggesting that *Humphrey's Executor* had held that Congress could create independent agencies if and only if the commissioners exercised quasi-judicial and quasi-legislative functions, whereas the independent counsel was a prosecutor exercising unambiguously executive powers. In his view, *Morrison* was unacceptable because it allowed Congress to insulate executive officers from presidential control, subject only to an open-ended balancing test.

In the aftermath of the impeachment of President Clinton, the Independent Counsel Act was allowed to expire, in part because of a fear of the risks supposedly posed by a genuinely independent counsel, armed with a large budget and a narrow target. But the decision in Morrison v. Olson retains general importance. See, e.g., FEC v. NRA Political Victory Fund, 6 F.3d 821 (D.C. Cir. 1993), upholding the Federal Election Commission, and concluding that the FEC was not an unconstitutional independent agency because the president should be taken to have the authority to remove an FEC member for cause, and perhaps at will.

6. Consider Metropolitan Washington Airports Auth. v. Citizens for the Abatement of Airport Noise, Inc., 501 U.S. 252 (1992). MWAA was created by a congressionally approved compact between the District of Columbia and Virginia to lease National and Dulles airports from the federal government and operate them. The congressional statute approving the compact required creation of a Board of Review with veto power over major MWAA decisions; the Board must consist of nine members of Congress selected by Congress from designated committees with oversight responsibility for aviation matters, but serving in their "individual" capacities. The Court held (6–3) that the Board was a constitutionally invalid "encroachment" by Congress. If the powers of the Review Board were deemed "executive," *Bowsher* forbids the vesting of such powers in agents of Congress. If they were deemed "legislative," *Chada* requires that such powers be exercised through the normal legislation process. "One might argue that the provision for a Board of Review is the kind of practical accommodation between the Legislature and the Executive that should be permitted in a 'workable government.' . . . However, the statutory scheme challenged today provides a blueprint for extensive expansion of the legislative power beyond its constitutionally defined role. . . . Congress could . . . use similar expedients to enable its Members or its agents to retain control, outside the ordinary legislative process,

of the activities of state grant recipients charged with executing virtually every aspect of national policy." See also Hechinger v. Metropolitan Washington Airports Auth., 36 F.3d 97 (D.C. Cir. 1994) (striking down an effort to create an airport board containing people chosen from a list supplied by House and Senate leaders).

7. Can you reconcile *Myers, Humphrey's Executor, Weiner, Bowsher, Morrison,* and *Mistretta*? Consider:

(a) What is the "headless fourth branch" of government? Does the Supreme Court still recognize the existence of such an entity? Under the more recent cases, is there a constitutional threat to the existence of the independent agencies? See FTC v. American National Cellular, 810 F.2d 1511 (9th Cir. 1987) (holding that there is no such threat).

(b) If the FTC is really an executive branch agency, why does the Constitution permit Congress to limit the president's removal powers? How and why do these labels matter?

(c) If the FTC is really an executive branch agency and Congress can limit the president's removal powers because it has good reason for doing so, then why is the comptroller general not "really" an executive branch official? That is, if executive branch agencies and officials come in "many shapes and sizes," why isn't one of those called the "comptroller general"? If the answer has to do with Congress's power to remove the comptroller, just why is that so important?

(d) Is *Bowsher* really an "inside the Capitol beltway" decision resting on the well-known-to-political-insiders fact that Congress tells the comptroller general what to do, irrespective of what the statute says? Would it not have been somewhat more difficult for the Supreme Court to find that sentencing commissioners could serve in the executive branch than in the judicial branch? Why did the Court not discuss this possibility? Did it forget about *Bowsher*?

(e) Compare the attitude of the Court toward the separation-of-powers question in *Chadha* and *Mistretta*. Can one say that the Court has experimented with, but abandoned, formal restrictions, that it now has a more flexible attitude, and that the Congress's determinations about where to place a power will now normally prevail? The more flexible attitude might be justified, if it is to be justified, on (a) historical grounds, (b) grounds that point to the transformed nature of modern government, or (c) grounds that point to the limited power of the Supreme Court to limit or oversee legislative experimentation. See generally Strauss, Formal and Functional Approaches to Separation of Powers Questions — A Foolish Inconsistency?, 72 Cornell L. Rev. 488 (1987).

Thus we can imagine four kinds of positions: (a) an originalist view that would invalidate independent agencies, see Calabresi & Prakash, The President's Power to Execute the Law, 104 Yale L.J. 541 (1994); (b) an originalist view that would uphold independent agencies, see Lessig & Sunstein, The President and the Administration, 94 Colum. L. Rev. 1 (1994); (c) a view emphasizing changed circumstances that would invalidate independent agencies even if they were constitutionally acceptable at the founding; (d) a view emphasizing changed circumstances that would uphold independent agencies even if they were constitutionally unacceptable at the founding, see Greene, supra. This statement of the various positions leaves open the question of what "independent" precisely means, in practice or in law, a question that we will take up shortly.

(f) Here are two efforts to reconcile the cases:

(i) The cases, with one exception, suggest that the Court will uphold legislation delegating power to a branch, provided: (1) the power is at least arguably related to the basic function of that branch; (2) the specific text of the Constitution does not forbid the delegation; and (3) the delegation of the power to one branch does not unreasonably interfere with the ability of a different branch to carry out its constitutionally mandated duties. If one is prepared to overlook some of the analysis (say, by reading *Humphrey's Executor* as not being about a "headless fourth branch" but as being about "executive agencies com[ing] in many different shapes and sizes") and if one assumes that *Mistretta*, rather than *Bowsher*, represents the future, then the Court seems willing to apply these principles and not very restrictively.

(ii) The Court has now said, very simply, that independence is acceptable, but that encroachment and aggrandizement are not. In *Humphrey's Executor*, *Mistretta*, and *Morrison*, the Court allowed Congress to create independent officials. In *Myers*, *Bowsher*, and *Chadha*, the Court said that Congress could not entangle itself in the process of execution or implementation of the laws. Hence the key question, for the future, is whether there is independence (which is acceptable so long as the president can exercise his constitutional functions) or encroachment and aggrandizement (which are constitutionally unacceptable).

Either support these propositions with examples or argue against them. Does either view suggest a sensible and clear direction for future doctrine? To what constitutional principles are they responsive, if any?

Note: The "Independent" and "Executive" Agencies

The traditional and prominent independent agencies are the CAB, FCC, FMC, FRB, FTC, ICC, NLRB, NRC, FERC, and SEC. These agencies are independent *because Congress has limited the president's authority to remove their leaders.* How, if at all, do these "alphabet" agencies enjoy a constitutional or legal position somehow distinct from other bureaucratic units more clearly within the executive branch?

1. *From a strictly legal point of view:*

(a) The simple point is that Congress sometimes limits presidential removal authority and in that way creates a measure of independence. But whether the agency is or is not "within an executive department" is not determinative of whether Congress can limit the president's power to remove an agency head without cause, is it? Surely the cases do not mean to distinguish agencies on the basis of their positions in an organizational chart. Might not Congress, as with the Transportation Safety Board, limit the president's power to remove the heads of some "executive offices" as it has done with his power to remove the heads of certain of these "independent" agencies?

(b) Is the president legally prevented from "dictating policy" to an "independent" agency? Many presidents would be surprised to hear this; many presidents think that they have some power to control the policies of the FCC, the NLRB, and the FTC. Does any decision really say that the president cannot give policy guidance to independent agencies, or attempt to push those agencies in his preferred directions? The conventional wisdom has been that the president has quite limited power here, as a matter of law. More recently, decisions of lower courts have seemingly taken the opposite view, suggesting that the Article II Vesting Clause and the Take Care Clause create broad presidential power to dictate policy to officials. See Building and Construction Trades Department v. Allbaugh, 295 F.3d 28 (D.C. Cir. 2002). This reasoning might extend even to independent agencies. However, *Allbaugh* does not explicitly address the question of presidential control of independent agencies, and the opinion is limited by a vague proviso that inferior officers are "duty-bound to give effect to the President's direction, to the extent allowed by the law."

(c) In a sense, the president is also often prevented from "dictating policy" to units within the executive branch. The president cannot dictate policy to any unit insofar as that policy runs counter to the statute under which the unit operates. But, more importantly, certain units within the executive branch exercise delegated authority under statute, at least theoretically free from presidential power to dictate the ultimate decision. See *Myers*, supra. It seems questionable, for example, whether the president could directly overrule the FAA's decision to grant a license to fly — despite the fact that the FAA is part of the Department of Transportation — for Congress has delegated the authority to license to the administrator, not to the president. Moreover, Congress stated that the administrator "shall not submit his decisions for the approval of, nor be bound by, the decisions or recommendations of any committee, board, or other organization created by Executive Order."

There is no authoritative answer to the question whether and in what sense the president can order executive branch officials to do what he wishes. *Myers* seems to suggest that Congress has the power to confer the power of decision on those officials — and to allow the president to fire them if they do something to which he objects. But see Kagan, Presidential Administration, supra, for the argument that statutes conferring power on executive branch officials should ordinarily be construed to assume that where the president wishes to insist on a particular outcome, he is entitled to do so. The Department of Justice has occasionally raised questions about the *Myers* dicta and suggested that the president can displace the agency head's decision if he wishes.

2. *From a practical point of view:*

(a) Regardless of what the statute says, the president can often determine who will run an "independent" agency. Unfilled vacancies, resignations, and "throwing in the towel" often allow a new president quickly to gain control of an administrative body. Although FCC commissioners are appointed for seven-year terms, one of those commissioners is by virtue of executive reorganization provisions selected by the president as chair — a far more important job. And he serves as chair at the president's pleasure — a fact that may make him susceptible to the president's policy views. These independent agencies generally come into line, sooner or later, with the president's views. The NLRB, for example, moves, as a practical matter, with the political party of the president; the same is true for the FCC.

Alternatively, there are executive department officials that the president, for political reasons, cannot remove from office (consider J. Edgar Hoover at the FBI or Frances Knight at the Passport Office). Thus these officials can serve and make policy almost totally insulated from the president's views. This insulation is not necessarily detrimental. Consider how disturbing it would be if the president told his attorney general whom to prosecute in particular cases. These examples should simply point out that "organizational position" does not necessarily correspond with "policy independence" either legally or practically.

(b) The president has other ways to affect the policies of "independent agencies." The Department of Justice, for example, frequently intervenes in agency proceedings. Except in a few limited situations, the department will also represent the agency in court, and thus may influence its views. Further, the president controls budget requests. Since the Budget and Accounting Act of 1921, agency budget requests must be reviewed — along with all executive department requests — by the Office of Management and Budget, which may modify them. 31 U.S.C. §§16 et seq. (There are a few exceptions, including the Consumer Product Safety Commission.)

Moreover, the president retains some control over the selection of certain agency personnel. Some agencies have an unwritten policy of consulting with the White House over high-level appointments, especially where the chair is politically indebted to the president or a White House sponsor. The power to allocate "supergrades," the higher-paid positions without which an agency is virtually immobilized, is vested in the Civil Service Commission (CSC), the members of which are all appointed by the president. 15 U.S.C. §§1101, 1103. This power over personnel is not inconsiderable and has been used to influence, perhaps even to coerce "independent" agencies.

Finally, the president can influence agency policy and structure through his control over the introduction of substantive legislation and through reorganization of the government. All legislation proposed by the president or the agencies must be cleared through the Office of Management and Budget (OMB), although often an agency will independently approach a member of Congress with suggestions. Since 1970, Congress has authorized sweeping powers to the president to reorganize the government; President Nixon initially created the EPA through such a reorganization scheme.

On the other hand, Congress, executive branch officials, and the public often refer to certain agencies, such as the FCC or FTC, as "independent." This matters, at least psychologically, and probably more than that. Presumably, the solicitor general pays them greater deference than an executive department when he formulates a legal position for the government; OMB may treat their budget requests or legislative recommendations with greater respect. There is anecdotal evidence that the FCC and the FTC consider themselves to have a significant degree of policymaking autonomy from the president. Consider as well the fact that several presidents have been reluctant to allow OMB to oversee the process of regulation by independent agencies, even when such presidents (above all President Reagan) made serious efforts to oversee and coordinate national policy. Members of Congress, even those of the president's own party, have typically asserted that the independent agencies are not for presidential or OMB supervision.

3. *As a test case:*

You are a legal advisor to a newly elected president, one who is not entirely thrilled with the policies of his predecessor. You might, for example, work for President George W. Bush, who might well seek to change the policies of (for example) the Federal Trade Commission, the National Labor Relations Board, and the Federal Communications Commission. Can you write a brief memorandum, indicating what steps might lawfully be taken to ensure that these and other changes will do what the new president wants?

3. *Presidential Control of the Regulatory State*

Since the 1970s, many people have argued that the White House itself, or OMB, should examine and coordinate detailed agency regulatory policies more closely than in the past. OMB should act not simply as a "budget" agency, but also as a general "managing" agency within the executive branch. Precisely how this should be done is much debated. Should the president or his staff be given by statute the legal power to oversee policy, to make many of the regulatory decisions, to promulgate or withdraw rules or policies, even if statutes now vest these powers in various individual agencies? Should there be intergovernmental committee meetings at which different agency heads simply seek to coordinate their policies? Should OMB review regulatory proposals and try to coordinate them with administration policy and with other agencies, perhaps testing their merits through the application of cost-benefit analysis?

Since the 1970s, every president has agreed that some centralized review is important, and they have created a review system that has emphasized both coordination and cost effectiveness. President Nixon created a "Quality of Life" review group to review, inter alia, environmental, health, safety, and consumer protection programs. President Ford issued Executive Order 11,821 requiring agencies considering major actions to issue Inflation Impact Statements, which OMB reviewed. President Carter issued Executive Order 12,044, which required detailed analysis of proposed regulatory rules and review of such analyses by the Executive Office of the President. He also created a Regulatory Analysis Review Group composed of representatives from the major regulating agencies; using OMB staff and the Council of Economic Advisors, it reviewed agency proposals likely to have a significant economic impact. Carter created a Regulatory Council as well, which consisted of the heads of major agencies, which published a semiannual calendar of proposed regulatory activities and which provided analyses of about 150 major proposed rules each year.

During the 1980s Presidents Reagan and Bush continued and greatly expanded the system for centralized White House review of proposed agency actions, with the boldest and most important initiatives coming from President Reagan. President Clinton continued their basic model. For detailed discussion, see T. McGarrity, Regulation (1993); Pildes & Sunstein, Reinventing the Regulatory State, 62 U. Chi. L. Rev. 1 (1996). The review now takes place in OMB, in the Office of Information and Regulatory Activities (OIRA). Its administrator is a high-ranking politically appointed official. OIRA's staff has typically consisted of about 40 professionals, many of whom are relatively young, more than half of whom have degrees in public administration, finance, or economics, and only a handful of whom are lawyers. During the last decade there has been an effort to speed up the process and to ensure earlier OIRA consultation, so as to minimize the need to return rules for reconsideration.

Note too that through official memoranda and executive orders, the president can do a great deal to push the executive branch (and possibly independent agencies) in his preferred directions. President George W. Bush, for example, issued an executive order requiring agencies to give careful consideration to the effects of their actions on the nation's need for energy. For an argument that "presidential control of administration . . . expanded significantly during the Clinton Presidency," see Kagan, Presidential Administration, 114 Harv. L. Rev. 2245, 2281 (2001). Kagan orients her analysis with two examples. The first is President Clinton's press conference, announcing publication of a proposed rule to reduce youth smoking. Though the regulation was issued by the FDA, President Clinton described it as his own. Id. at 2283. The second example involved a public announcement that President Clinton would "direct the Secretary of Labor" to issue a regulation allowing states to offer paid leave to new mothers and fathers. Id. at 2284. (Recall that there is a question whether the president has the authority to "direct" a cabinet head to do any such thing.) Kagan explains how memoranda to the heads of departments, and less formal public statements of various sorts, served to put the president's stamp firmly on regulation.

Is all this lawful? The major constitutional source of legal authority for presidential control consists of Article II's statements that the "executive Power shall be vested in a President," that the president "shall take care that the laws be faithfully executed," and that he "may require the Opinion, in writing, of the principal Officer in each of the executive Departments, upon any Subject relating to the Duties of their respective offices." Other legal authority for OMB, hence for OIRA, proceeds from two executive orders and the Paperwork Reduction Act.

Could you argue that White House control of rulemaking is unlawful? Could the White House require independent agencies to submit to the process of review? Could President George W. Bush tell the FCC to issue a new rule, relieving television broadcasters of the obligation to provide three hours of programming for children each week? Consider these questions as you read the materials to follow.

a. Executive Order 12,291 — Regulatory Analysis   *Reports & Analyses*

Under Presidents Reagan and Bush, Executive Order 12,291, 46 Fed. Reg. 13193 (1980), governed regulations issued by federal executive agencies, expressly excluding "independent" agencies," and regulations governed by the formal rulemaking requirements of the APA or relating to military and foreign affairs functions or to agency organization, management, or personnel.

Section 2 of the order required that when agencies promulgate new regulations, review existing regulations, or develop legislative proposals concerning regulation, they must adhere to the following requirements "to the extent permitted by law":

Regular Rules

(a) Administrative decisions shall be based on adequate information concerning the need for and consequences of proposed government action;
(b) Regulatory action shall not be undertaken unless the potential benefits to society from the regulation outweigh the potential costs to society;
(c) Regulatory objectives shall be chosen to maximize the net benefits to society;
(d) Among alternative approaches to any given regulatory objective, the alternative involving the least net cost to society shall be chosen. . . .

Major Rules

Section 3 of the order imposed special decisionmaking procedures for "major" rules, defined as those that will have an annual effect on the economy of $100 million or more or will result in "major" price or cost increases or "significant" adverse effects on competition, employment, investment, productivity, innovation, or U.S. competition in world markets. Prior to issuing a notice of proposed rulemaking of or adoption of a final major rule, an agency must prepare, "and to the extent permitted by law consider," a Regulatory Impact Analysis containing the following information:

(1) A description of the potential benefits of the rule, including any beneficial effects that cannot be quantified in monetary terms, and the identification of those likely to receive the benefits;
(2) A description of the potential costs of the rule, including any adverse effects that cannot be quantified in monetary terms, and the identification of those likely to bear the costs;
(3) A determination of the potential net benefits of the rule, including an evaluation of effects that cannot be quantified in monetary terms;
(4) A description of alternative approaches that could substantially achieve the same regulatory goal at lower cost, together with an analysis of its potential benefit and costs and a brief explanation of the legal reasons why such alternatives, if proposed, could not be adopted; and
(5) Unless covered by the description required under paragraph (4) of this subsection, an explanation of any legal reasons why the rule cannot be based on the requirements set forth in Section 2 of this Order.

Analyses must be transmitted by the director of the OMB, who is to "review any issues raised under this Order or ensure that they are presented to the President." Agencies must withhold final action until they have received and responded to the OMB's views on the rule. Procedures for review of existing rules and publication of regulatory agendas are incorporated in the order along with procedural exceptions for emergency rules or those subject to statutory deadlines.

Section 9 of the order, entitled "Judicial Review," provides that "this Order is intended only to improve the internal management of the Federal government, and is not intended to create any right or benefit, substantive or procedural, enforceable at law by a party against the United States, its agencies, its officers or any person."

b. Executive Order 12,498 — Regulatory Planning

In 1985 President Reagan promulgated another important executive order designed to give the OMB power to coordinate regulatory planning. Executive Order 12,498, 50 Fed. Reg. 1036 (1985), Section 1 states that to develop an "administrative . . . Regulatory Program for each year," each agency subject to Executive Order 12,291 "shall submit to the Director of OMB a statement of its regulatory policies, goals and objectives for the coming year and information concerning all significant regulatory actions underway or planned." All regulatory actions must be "consistent with the goals of the agency and of the Administration" and "be appropriately implemented."

Section 2 states:

(a) The head of each agency shall submit to the Director an overview of the agency's regulatory policies, goals, and objectives for the program year and such information concerning all significant regulatory actions of the agency, planned or underway, including actions taken to consider whether to initiate rulemaking; requests for public comment; and the development of documents that may influence, anticipate, or could lead to the commencement of rulemaking proceedings at a later date, as the Director deems necessary to develop the Administration's Regulatory Program. This submission shall constitute the agency's draft regulatory program. . . .

(b) The overview portion of the agency's submission should discuss the agency's broad regulatory purposes, explain how they are consistent with the Administration's regulatory principles, and include a discussion of the significant regulatory actions, as defined by the Director, that it will take. The overview should specifically discuss the significant regulatory actions of the agency to revise or rescind existing rules.

Section 3 says that OMB's director shall review the agency's program to see if it is consistent with administration policy. If not, the director must state what must be done to achieve consistency. In the event of disagreement, the agency head or the director "may raise issue for further review by the President" or "either forum" (including the cabinet) that the president designates. After the program is finally worked out, should the agency "propose . . . to take a regulatory action that is materially different from the action described in the program," it must submit the proposal to OMB for review.

Absent unusual circumstances, such as new statutory or judicial requirements or unanticipated emergency situations, the director may, to the extent permitted by law, return for reconsideration any rule submitted for review under Executive Order 12,291 that would be subject to, but was not included in, the agency's final regulatory program for that year, or any other significant regulatory action that is materially different from those described in the administration's regulatory program for that year.

Section 4 states, "The Director of the Office of Management and Budget is authorized, to the extent permitted by law, to take such actions as may be necessary to carry out the provisions of this Order."

Section 5 states, "This Order is intended only to improve the internal management of the Federal government, and is not intended to create any right or benefit, substantive or procedural, enforceable at law by a party against the United States, its agencies, its officers or any person."

Executive Order 12,866: Regulatory Planning and Review
58 Fed. Reg. 51735 (1993)

The American people deserve a regulatory system that works for them, not against them: a regulatory system that protects and improves their health, safety, environment, and well-being and improves the performance of the economy without imposing unacceptable or unreasonable costs on society; regulatory policies that recognize that the private sector and private markets are the best engine for economic growth; regulatory approaches that respect the role of State, local, and tribal governments; and regulations that are effective, consistent, sensible, and understandable. We do not have such a regulatory system today.

With this Executive order, the Federal Government begins a program to reform and make more efficient the regulatory process. The objectives of this Executive order are to enhance planning and coordination with respect to both new and existing regulations; to reaffirm the primacy of Federal agencies in the regulatory decision-making process; to restore the integrity and legitimacy of regulatory review and oversight; and to make the process more accessible and open to the public. In pursuing these objectives, the regulatory process shall be conducted so as to meet applicable statutory requirements and with due regard to the discretion that has been entrusted to the Federal agencies.

Accordingly, by the authority vested in me as President by the Constitution and the laws of the United States of America, it is hereby ordered as follows:

SECTION 1. STATEMENT OF REGULATORY PHILOSOPHY AND PRINCIPLES

(a) *The Regulatory Philosophy.* Federal agencies should promulgate only such regulations as are required by law, are necessary to interpret the law, or are made necessary by compelling public need, such as material failures of private markets to protect or improve the health and safety of the public, the environment, or the well- being of the American people. In deciding whether and how to regulate, agencies should assess all costs and benefits of available regulatory alternatives, including the alternative of not regulating. Costs and benefits shall be understood to include both quantifiable measures (to the fullest extent that these can be usefully estimated) and qualitative measures of costs and benefits that are difficult to quantify, but nevertheless essential to consider. Further, in choosing among alternative regulatory approaches, agencies should select those approaches that maximize net benefits (including potential economic, environmental, public health and safety, and other advantages; distributive impacts; and equity), unless a statute requires another regulatory approach.

(b) *The Principles of Regulation.* To ensure that the agencies' regulatory programs are consistent with the philosophy set forth above, agencies should adhere to the following principles, to the extent permitted by law and where applicable:

(1) Each agency shall identify the problem that it intends to address (including, where applicable, the failures of private markets or public institutions that warrant new agency action) as well as assess the significance of that problem.

(2) Each agency shall examine whether existing regulations (or other law) have created, or contributed to, the problem that a new regulation is intended to correct

and whether those regulations (or other law) should be modified to achieve the intended goal of regulation more effectively.

(3) Each agency shall identify and assess available alternatives to direct regulation, including providing economic incentives to encourage the desired behavior, such as user fees or marketable permits, or providing information upon which choices can be made by the public.

(4) In setting regulatory priorities, each agency shall consider, to the extent reasonable, the degree and nature of the risks posed by various substances or activities within its jurisdiction.

(5) When an agency determines that a regulation is the best available method of achieving the regulatory objective, it shall design its regulation in the most cost-effective manner to achieve the regulatory objective. In doing so, each agency shall consider incentives for innovation, consistency, predictability, the costs of enforcement and compliance (to the government, regulated entities, and the public), flexibility, distributive impacts, and equity.

(6) Each agency shall assess both the costs and the benefits of the intended regulation and, recognizing that some costs and benefits are difficult to quantify, propose or adopt a regulation only upon a reasoned determination that the benefits of the intended regulation justify its costs.

(7) Each agency shall base its decisions on the best reasonably obtainable scientific, technical, economic, and other information concerning the need for, and consequences of, the intended regulation.

(8) Each agency shall identify and assess alternative forms of regulation and shall, to the extent feasible, specify performance objectives, rather than specifying the behavior or manner of compliance that regulated entities must adopt.

(9) Wherever feasible, agencies shall seek views of appropriate State, local, and tribal officials before imposing regulatory requirements that might significantly or uniquely affect those governmental entities. Each agency shall assess the effects of Federal regulations on State, local, and tribal governments, including specifically the availability of resources to carry out those mandates, and seek to minimize those burdens that uniquely or significantly affect such governmental entities, consistent with achieving regulatory objectives. In addition, as appropriate, agencies shall seek to harmonize Federal regulatory actions with related State, local, and tribal regulatory and other governmental functions.

(10) Each agency shall avoid regulations that are inconsistent, incompatible, or duplicative with its other regulations or those of other Federal agencies.

(11) Each agency shall tailor its regulations to impose the least burden on society, including individuals, businesses of differing sizes, and other entities (including small communities and governmental entities), consistent with obtaining the regulatory objectives, taking into account, among other things, and to the extent practicable, the costs of cumulative regulations.

(12) Each agency shall draft its regulations to be simple and easy to understand, with the goal of minimizing the potential for uncertainty and litigation arising from such uncertainty.

SECTION 2. ORGANIZATION

An efficient regulatory planning and review process is vital to ensure that the Federal Government's regulatory system best serves the American people.

(a) *The Agencies.* Because Federal agencies are the repositories of significant substantive expertise and experience, they are responsible for developing regulations and assuring that the regulations are consistent with applicable law, the President's priorities, and the principles set forth in this Executive order.

(b) *The Office of Management and Budget.* Coordinated review of agency rule-making is necessary to ensure that regulations are consistent with applicable law, the President's priorities, and the principles set forth in this Executive order, and that decisions made by one agency do not conflict with the policies or actions taken or planned by another agency. The Office of Management and Budget (OMB) shall carry out that review function. Within OMB, the Office of Information and Regulatory Affairs (OIRA) is the repository of expertise concerning regulatory issues, including methodologies and procedures that affect more than one agency, this Executive order, and the President's regulatory policies. To the extent permitted by law, OMB shall provide guidance to agencies and assist the President, the Vice President, and other regulatory policy advisors to the President in regulatory planning and shall be the entity that reviews individual regulations, as provided by this Executive order.

(c) *The Vice President.* The Vice President is the principal advisor to the President on, and shall coordinate the development and presentation of recommendations concerning, regulatory policy, planning, and review, as set forth in this Executive order. In fulfilling their responsibilities under this Executive order, the President and the Vice President shall be assisted by the regulatory policy advisors within the Executive Office of the President and by such agency officials and personnel as the President and the Vice President may, from time to time, consult.

Section 3. Definitions . . .

(e) "Regulatory action" means any substantive action by an agency (normally published in the *Federal Register*) that promulgates or is expected to lead to the promulgation of a final rule or regulation, including notices of inquiry, advance notices of proposed rulemaking, and notices of proposed rulemaking.

(f) "Significant regulatory action" means any regulatory action that is likely to result in a rule that may:

(1) Have an annual effect on the economy of $100 million or more or adversely affect in a material way the economy, a sector of the economy, productivity, competition, jobs, the environment, public health or safety, or State, local, or tribal governments or communities;

(2) Create a serious inconsistency or otherwise interfere with an action taken or planned by another agency;

(3) Materially alter the budgetary impact of entitlements, grants, user fees, or loan programs or the rights and obligations of recipients thereof; or

(4) Raise novel legal or policy issues arising out of legal mandates, the President's priorities, or the principles set forth in this Executive order. . . .

Section 6. Centralized Review of Regulations

The guidelines set forth below shall apply to all regulatory actions, for both new and existing regulations, by agencies other than those agencies specifically exempted by the Administrator of OIRA:

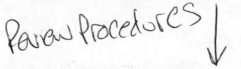
(a) *Agency Responsibilities.*

(1) Each agency shall (consistent with its own rules, regulations, or procedures) provide the public with meaningful participation in the regulatory process. In particular, before issuing a notice of proposed rulemaking, each agency should, where appropriate, seek the involvement of those who are intended to benefit from and those expected to be burdened by any regulation (including, specifically, State, local, and tribal officials). In addition, each agency should afford the public a meaningful opportunity to comment on any proposed regulation, which in most cases should include a comment period of not less than 60 days. Each agency also is directed to explore and, where appropriate, use consensual mechanisms for developing regulations, including negotiated rulemaking.

(2) Within 60 days of the date of this Executive order, each agency head shall designate a Regulatory Policy Officer who shall report to the agency head. The Regulatory Policy Officer shall be involved at each stage of the regulatory process to foster the development of effective, innovative, and least burdensome regulations and to further the principles set forth in this Executive order.

(3) In addition to adhering to its own rules and procedures and to the requirements of the Administrative Procedure Act, the Regulatory Flexibility Act, the Paperwork Reduction Act, and other applicable law, each agency shall develop its regulatory actions in a timely fashion and adhere to the following procedures with respect to a regulatory action:

(A) Each agency shall provide OIRA, at such times and in the manner specified by the Administrator of OIRA, with a list of its planned regulatory actions, indicating those which the agency believes are significant regulatory actions within the meaning of this Executive order. Absent a material change in the development of the planned regulatory action, those not designated as significant will not be subject to review under this section unless, within 10 working days of receipt of the list, the Administrator of OIRA notifies the agency that OIRA has determined that a planned regulation is a significant regulatory action within the meaning of this Executive order. The Administrator of OIRA may waive review of any planned regulatory action designated by the agency as significant, in which case the agency need not further comply with subsection (a)(3)(B) or subsection (a)(3)(C) of this section.

(B) For each matter identified as, or determined by the Administrator of OIRA to be, a significant regulatory action, the issuing agency shall provide to ORIA:

(i) The text of the draft regulatory action, together with a reasonably detailed description of the need for the regulatory action and an explanation of how the regulatory action will meet that need; and

(ii) An assessment of the potential costs and benefits of the regulatory action, including an explanation of the manner in which the regulatory action is consistent with a statutory mandate and, to the extent permitted by law, promotes the President's priorities and avoids undue interference with State, local, and tribal governments in the exercise of their governmental functions.

(C) For those matters identified as, or determined by the Administrator of OIRA to be, a significant regulatory action within the scope of section 3(f)(1), the agency shall also provide to OIRA the following additional information developed as part of the agency's decision-making process (unless prohibited by law):

(i) An assessment, including the underlying analysis, of benefits anticipated from the regulatory action (such as, but not limited to, the promotion of the efficient functioning of the economy and private markets, the enhancement of health and safety, the protection of the natural environment, and the elimination or reduction of discrimination or bias) together with, to the extent feasible, a quantification of those benefits;

(ii) An assessment, including the underlying analysis, of costs anticipated from the regulatory action (such as, but not limited to, the direct cost both to the government in administering the regulation and to businesses and others in complying with the regulation, and any adverse effects on the efficient functioning of the economy, private markets (including productivity, employment, and competitiveness), health, safety, and the natural environment), together with, to the extent feasible, a quantification of those costs; and

(iii) An assessment, including the underlying analysis, of costs and benefits of potentially effective and reasonably feasible alternatives to the planned regulation, identified by the agencies or the public (including improving the current regulation and reasonably viable nonregulatory actions), and an explanation why the planned regulatory action is preferable to the identified potential alternatives.

(D) In emergency situations or when an agency is obligated by law to act more quickly than normal review procedures allow, the agency shall notify OIRA as soon as possible and, to the extent practicable, comply with subsections (a)(3)(B) and (C) of this section. For those regulatory actions that are governed by a statutory or court-imposed deadline, the agency shall, to the extent practicable, schedule rulemaking proceedings so as to permit sufficient time for OIRA to conduct its review, as set forth below in subsection (b)(2) through (4) of this section.

(E) After the regulatory action has been published in the Federal Register or otherwise issued to the public, the agency shall:

(i) Make available to the public the information set forth in subsections (a)(3)(B) and (C);

(ii) Identify for the public, in a complete, clear, and simple manner, the substantive changes between the draft submitted to OIRA for review and the action subsequently announced; and

(iii) Identify for the public those changes in the regulatory action that were made at the suggestion or recommendation of OIRA.

(F) All information provided to the public by the agency shall be in plain, understandable language.

(b) *OIRA Responsibilities.* The Administrator of OIRA shall provide meaningful guidance and oversight so that each agency's regulatory actions are consistent with applicable law, the President's priorities, and the principles set forth in this Executive order and do not conflict with the policies or actions of another agency. OIRA shall, to the extent permitted by law, adhere to the following guidelines:

(1) OIRA may review only actions identified by the agency or by OIRA as significant regulatory actions under subsection (a)(3)(A) of this section.

(2) OIRA shall waive review or notify the agency in writing of the results of its review within the following time periods:

(A) For any notices of inquiry, advance notices of proposed rulemaking, or other preliminary regulatory actions prior to a Notice of Proposed Rulemaking, within 10 working days after the date of submission of the draft action to OIRA;

(B) For all other regulatory actions, within 90 calendar days after the date of submission of the information set forth in subsections (a)(3)(B) and (C) of this section, unless OIRA has previously reviewed this information and, since that review, there has been no material change in the facts and circumstances upon which the regulatory action is based, in which case, OIRA shall complete its review within 45 days; and

(C) The review process may be extended (1) once by no more than 30 calendar days upon the written approval of the Director and (2) at the request of the agency head.

(3) For each regulatory action that the Administrator of OIRA returns to an agency for further consideration of some or all of its provisions, the Administrator of OIRA shall provide the issuing agency a written explanation for such return, setting forth the pertinent provision of this Executive order on which OIRA is relying. If the agency head disagrees with some or all of the bases for the return, the agency head shall so inform the Administrator of OIRA in writing.

(4) Except as otherwise provided by law or required by a Court, in order to ensure greater openness, accessibility, and accountability in the regulatory review process, OIRA shall be governed by the following disclosure requirements:

(A) Only the Administrator of OIRA (or a particular designee) shall receive oral communications initiated by persons not employed by the executive branch of the Federal Government regarding the substance of a regulatory action under OIRA review;

(B) All substantive communications between OIRA personnel and persons not employed by the executive branch of the Federal Government regarding a regulatory action under review shall be governed by the following guidelines:

(i) A representative from the issuing agency shall be invited to any meeting between OIRA personnel and such person(s);

(ii) OIRA shall forward to the issuing agency, within 10 working days of receipt of the communication(s), all written communications, regardless of format, between OIRA personnel and any person who is not employed by the executive branch of the Federal Government, and the dates and names of individuals involved in all substantive oral communications (including meetings to which an agency representative was invited, but did not attend, and telephone conversations between OIRA personnel and any such persons); and

(iii) OIRA shall publicly disclose relevant information about such communication(s), as set forth below in subsection (b)(4)(C) of this section.

(C) OIRA shall maintain a publicly available log that shall contain, at a minimum, the following information pertinent to regulatory actions under review:

(i) The status of all regulatory actions, including if (and if so, when and by whom) Vice Presidential and Presidential consideration was requested;

(ii) A notation of all written communications forwarded to an issuing agency under subsection (b)(4)(B)(ii) of this section; and

(iii) The dates and names of individuals involved in all substantive oral communications, including meetings and telephone conversations, between OIRA personnel and any person not employed by the executive branch of the Federal Government, and the subject matter discussed during such communications.

(D) After the regulatory action has been published in the Federal Register or otherwise issued to the public, or after the agency has announced its decision not to publish or issue the regulatory action, OIRA shall make available to the public all documents exchanged between OIRA and the agency during the review by OIRA under this section.

(5) All information provided to the public by OIRA shall be in plain, understandable language.

SECTION 7. RESOLUTION OF CONFLICTS

To the extent permitted by law, disagreements or conflicts between or among agency heads or between OMB and any agency that cannot be resolved by the Administrator of OIRA shall be resolved by the President, or by the Vice President acting at the request of the President, with the relevant agency head (and, as appropriate, other interested government officials). Vice Presidential and Presidential consideration of such disagreements may be initiated only by the Director, by the head of the issuing agency, or by the head of an agency that has a significant interest in the regulatory action at issue. Such review will not be undertaken at the request of other persons, entities, or their agents.

Resolution of such conflicts shall be informed by recommendations developed by the Vice President, after consultation with the Advisors (and other executive branch officials or personnel whose responsibilities to the President include the subject matter at issue). The development of these recommendations shall be concluded within 60 days after review has been requested.

During the Vice Presidential and Presidential review period, communications with any person not employed by the Federal Government relating to the substance of the regulatory action under review and directed to the Advisors or their staffs or to the staff of the Vice President shall be in writing and shall be forwarded by the recipient to the affected agency(ies) for inclusion in the public docket(s). When the communication is not in writing, such Advisors or staff members shall inform the outside party that the matter is under review and that any comments should be submitted in writing.

At the end of this review process, the President, or the Vice President acting at the request of the President, shall notify the affected agency and the Administrator of OIRA of the President's decision with respect to the matter.

SECTION 8. PUBLICATION

Except to the extent required by law, an agency shall not publish in the Federal Register or otherwise issue to the public any regulatory action that is subject to review under section 6 of this Executive order until (1) the Administrator of OIRA notifies the agency that OIRA has waived its review of the action or has completed its review without any requests for further consideration, or (2) the applicable time period in section 6(b)(2) expires without OIRA having notified the agency that it is returning the regulatory action for further consideration under section 6(b)(3), whichever occurs first. If the terms of the preceding sentence have not been satisfied and an agency wants to publish or otherwise issue a regulatory action, the head of that agency may request Presidential consideration through the Vice President, as provided under section 7 of this order. Upon receipt of this request, the Vice President shall notify OIRA and the Advisors. The guidelines and time period set forth in section 7 shall apply to the publication of regulatory actions for which Presidential consideration has been sought.

SECTION 9. AGENCY AUTHORITY

Nothing in this order shall be construed as displacing the agencies' authority or responsibilities, as authorized by law.

SECTION 10. JUDICIAL REVIEW

Nothing in this Executive order shall affect any otherwise available judicial review of agency action. This Executive order is intended only to improve the internal management of the Federal Government and does not create any right or benefit, substantive or procedural, enforceable at law or equity by a party against the United States, its agencies or instrumentalities, its officers or employees, or any other person.

President Clinton's Regulatory Planning and Review Executive Order

19 Admin. L. News 8-9 (Winter 1994)

On September 30, 1993, President Clinton issued his long-awaited Executive Order to replace E.O. 12291, President Reagan's regulatory reform order. The similarities between the two orders are striking. Indeed, most of the differences merely codify practice under the Reagan order. Nevertheless, there are some material changes, and there is a substantially different tenor to the document.

Section 1 of E.O. 12866 states the Regulatory Philosophy and Principles President Clinton wishes agencies to follow. Agencies should only promulgate regulations when "necessary," and decisions as to whether and how to regulate should consider the cost and benefits of available regulatory alternatives, including the alternative of not regulating. Like the Reagan order, the Clinton order asks agencies to adopt approaches that "maximize net benefits" to society unless a law requires otherwise. [As with E.O. 12291, these principles apply "to the extent permitted by law."]

Section 3 is the definition section of the order. One potentially important change here is in the definition for "regulation." Under the Reagan order, the term was defined to include interpretive rules and statements of policy (sometimes called "non-legislative rules"), but the Clinton order [which is limited to rules or regulation "which the agency intends to have the force and effect of law"] has excluded such rules and policy statements from the definition of regulation and hence from the review function. This may create another incentive for agencies to utilize such rules instead of normal notice-and-comment rulemaking. What was defined as a "major rule" under the Reagan order is now a "significant regulatory action" [which includes rules which "may" have an annual effect on the economy of $100 million or more].

[T]he Regulatory Plan submitted by agencies to OIRA does not purport to lock agencies into that plan, nor does OIRA play the same oversight role of these plans as it did under E.O. 12498. Rather, OIRA's function seems to be more of a clearing-hou[se] and coordination role. Section 4 also provides for an entity that seems to be the descendant of the Council on Competitiveness. This new entity is denominated the Regulatory Working Group, consisting of representatives of agencies with significant regulatory responsibilities, the Vice President, and presidential advisors, and chaired by the

Administrator of OIRA. [Notably, the Clinton order requires the independent agencies to participate in the creation of an annual "unified regulatory agenda," and it requires independent agencies to submit an annual regulatory plan on which the Vice President may advise and consult. Are these requirements lawful?]

Section 5 relates to existing regulations. Like Presidents Reagan and Bush before him, President Clinton is requiring agencies to review existing regulations to eliminate regulations that do not meet the philosophy and principles of regulation outlined in the order. Agencies are required to create institutional review programs for periodic reviews. Again, shades of the Council on Competitiveness, the Working Group "and other interested entities" are to pursue the objectives of identifying and eliminating unnecessary existing regulations.

Section 6 contains the new rules for the centralized review of regulations. While most of E.O. 12291's review process remains, there are a number of new provisions. . . .

While E.O. 12291 required all proposed and final regulations to be sent to OIRA for review and comment before they were published in the Federal Register, E.O. 12866 does not require regulations that are not "significant regulatory actions" to be sent to OIRA at all. Agencies are to send lists of planned regulatory actions, both significant and otherwise to OIRA at specified times, and OIRA has 10 days to determine that a regulation the agency believes is not significant is significant. For those regulations that are significant, the review process seems indistinguishable from that conducted under the Reagan order for "major rules," including pre-publication submission of each proposed and final rule to OIRA for review and comment and the inclusion of a regulatory impact analysis requirement (although the term is not used) for regulations with over $100 million impact.

Under E.O. 12291, OIRA was required to complete its review within a limited period of time (never longer than 60 days). In practice, these limitations were often violated. Moreover, the order in essence allowed OIRA to toll the time periods by returning a rule to an agency for further review and comment. There was some criticism of the delay involved for several controversial rules, where some thought the review process was used for the purpose of delay. The Clinton order also imposes specified deadlines, but they are no longer than under the Reagan order (the longest period being 120 days). Moreover, under section 8 of the order, OMB can effectively toll that period by notifying the agency that OIRA is returning the rule for further consideration.

An aspect of practice under the Reagan order thought to create problems was so-called conduit communications, where persons would lobby OIRA (or the Council on Competitiveness) rather than (or in addition to) participating in the agency regulatory process. OIRA then could communicate those concerns, as if they were its own, to the agency. . . .

The order now requires that only the administrator of OIRA (or a particular designee) can receive oral communications from persons outside the executive branch, and no meeting with outside persons can take place without inviting a representative from the affected agency. Information about these contacts and communications must be made available to the public. Moreover, the order specifies that when OIRA returns a rule to an agency for further consideration, OIRA put its reasons in writing. After the regulatory actions have been published, OIRA is to make public all documents exchanged between the agency and OIRA.

Section 7 relates to conflict resolution. The Administrator of OIRA is primarily responsible for resolving conflicts between agency heads and OIRA. When the conflict cannot be resolved by the Administrator, the President or the Vice President (if requested by the President) shall resolve it. . . .

Note on Executive Order 12,866

Executive Order 12,866 contains somewhat different guidance from Executive Order 12,291. Its basic principles are more numerous and more detailed. It emphasizes that agencies should consider "qualitative" costs and benefits as well as amounts that can be quantified. Among the considerations that agencies shall consider are "distributional impacts" and "equity." It asks agencies to seek views of state, local, and tribal officials before imposing regulatory requirements on them. Moreover, Executive Order 12,866 encourages agencies to ask whether the problem that a regulation is designed to overcome is itself a product of an existing regulation; to identify alternatives to "direct" regulation, including provision of information and economic incentives; and to use performance standards rather than design standards. For discussion of various issues raised by Executive Order 12,866, see Pildes & Sunstein, Reinventing the Regulatory State, 62 U. Chi. L. Rev. 1 (1995).

Executive Order 12,866 was not used aggressively by OIRA, but was used as the springboard for President Clinton's "reinventing government" initiatives, which received special attention during congressional debates on regulatory reform. These various initiatives were designed to reduce paperwork burdens on the private sector and on local government; to increase flexibility, by allowing exemptions from regulatory requirements where special circumstances can be shown; and to increase the use of economic incentives in lieu of command and control regulation. See generally Vice President Al Gore, From Red Tape to Results — Creating a Government that Works Better and Costs Less, Report of the National Performance Review (1993). With respect to "reinventing government," the executive branch has issued numerous reports intended to reflect and to spur more cost-effective methods of implementation. It is important to see, however, that many federal agencies do not comply with the apparent requirements of cost-benefit balancing in existing executive orders. Robert Hahn has shown that compliance is episodic and that a great deal needs to be done to systematize the process. See Robert W. Hahn et al., Empirical Analysis: Assessing Regulatory Impact Analysis: The Failure of Agencies to Comply With Executive Order 12866, 23 Harv J. L. & Pub. Poly. 859 (2000).

d. The 1995 Unfunded Mandate Reform Act

The 1995 Unfunded Mandate Reform Act (UMRA) is a legislative response to complaints that federal regulatory programs impose financially burdensome regulatory and social assistance obligations on state and local governments without at the same time providing the necessary fiscal means to carry out these mandates. The act imposes several new requirements on agencies promulgating rules under notice and comment procedures. Unless otherwise prohibited by law, federal agencies, before promulgating a proposed or a final rule that includes a federal mandate that may result in the expenditure by state, local, or tribal governments, in the aggregate, or by the private sector, of more than $100 million yearly must prepare a "statement" that includes (1) an identification of the provision of federal law under which the rule is being promulgated; (2) a qualitative and quantitative cost-benefit analysis of the mandate; (3) a consideration of disproportionate effects of the mandate on particular regions of the country, types of communities, or segments of the private sector; (4) an estimate, if feasible and relevant, of the mandate's effect on the national economy and on such issues as productivity, economic growth, full employment, job creation, and international competitiveness; and (5) a description of the agency's consultation with local elected officials and a summary of their concerns and comments. A summary of this statement must be published with an agency's general notice of proposed rulemaking or final rule. (On these points we offer more details below.)

UMRA §401 authorizes courts to order agencies to issue the required statements. However, an agency's failure to issue the statement cannot be used as a basis for enjoining, invalidating, or otherwise affecting an agency rule. This section also allows a court to consider information generated as part of an agency's statement in reviewing a rule.

Finally, all agencies must "identify and consider a reasonable number of regulatory alternatives and from those alternatives select the least costly, most cost-effective, or least burdensome alternative that achieves the objectives of the rule." There is an exception if these steps are inconsistent with law or if the agency explains why it has not chosen that least-burdensome alternative. This provision could have significant consequences. In many cases, it is questionable whether an agency has chosen the cheapest means of accomplishing regulatory goals. Economic incentives may well be able to achieve those goals at much less expense than command-and-control alternatives. It follows that the UMRA provides the opportunity for a good deal of litigation — about whether existing statutes forbid the approach suggested by the act — and a good deal of rethinking of existing tools. Agencies may well be required to use economic incentives where they now use technological requirements.

Under §425 of the UMRA, federal agencies are required, unless exempted by Congress, to determine whether there are sufficient funds to carry out mandates under their jurisdictions. If the funds are insufficient, they must notify the appropriate congressional authorizing committees within 30 days of the beginning of the fiscal year. The agency can then submit a reestimate, based on consultations with state, local, and tribal governments, that the amount appropriated is sufficient to pay for the mandate. Alternatively, it must submit recommendations for implementing a less-costly mandate or making the mandate ineffective for the fiscal year. Congress then has 30 days to consider the recommendations under expedited procedures. If Congress takes no action within 60 days, the mandate will be abolished.

e. The Paperwork Reduction Act

Each year OMB reviews 3000 to 4000 agency requests to collect information. In considering these requests, OMB evaluates their likely usefulness against the burden they may impose on the public. Its authority to deny requests comes from the Paperwork Reduction Act, 44 U.S.C. §§3501-3520. The Supreme Court, in Dole v. United Steelworkers, 494 U.S. 26 (1990), described this act as follows:

> The Paperwork Reduction Act was enacted in response to one of the less auspicious aspects of the enormous growth of our federal bureaucracy: its seemingly insatiable appetite for data. Outcries from small businesses, individuals, and state and local governments, that they were being buried under demands for paperwork, led Congress to institute controls. Congress designated OMB the overseer of other agencies with respect to paperwork and set forth a comprehensive scheme designed to reduce the paperwork burden. The Act charges OMB with developing uniform policies for efficient information processing, storage and transmittal systems, both within and among agencies. OMB is directed to reduce federal collection of all information by set percentages, establish a Federal Information Locator System, and develop and

implement procedures for guarding the privacy of those providing confidential information. See 44 U.S.C. 3504, 3505, 3511 (1982 ed., Supp. V).

The Act prohibits any federal agency from adopting regulations which impose paperwork requirements on the public unless the information is not available to the agency from another source within the Federal Government, and the agency must formulate a plan for tabulating the information in a useful manner. Agencies are also required to minimize the burden on the public to the extent practicable. See 44 U.S.C. §3507(a)(1) (1982 ed., Supp. V). In addition, the Act institutes a second layer of review by OMB for new paperwork requirements. After an agency has satisfied itself that an instrument for collecting information — termed an "information collection request" — is needed, the agency must submit the request to OMB for approval. See 44 U.S.C. §3507(a)(2) (1982 ed., Supp. V.). If OMB disapproves the request, the agency may not collect the information. See 44 U.S.C. 3507(a)(3) (1982 ed.).

Typical information collection requests include tax forms, medicare forms, financial loan applications, job applications, questionnaires, compliance reports, and tax or business records. See S. Rep., at 3-4. These information requests share at least one characteristic: The information requested is provided to a federal agency, either directly or indirectly. Agencies impose the requirements on private parties in order to generate information to be used by the agency in pursuing some other purpose. For instance, agencies use these information requests in gathering background on a particular subject to develop the expertise with which to devise or fine-tune appropriate regulations, massing diffuse data for processing into useful statistical form, and monitoring business records and compliance reports for signs or proof of nonfeasance to determine when to initiate enforcement measures. . . . The Act applies to "information collection requests" by a federal agency which are defined as:

> a written report form, application form, schedule, questionnaire, reporting or recordkeeping requirement, collection of information requirement, or other similar method calling for the collection of information.

44 U.S.C. 3502(11) (1982 ed., Supp. V). "Collection of information," in turn, is defined as:

> the obtaining or soliciting of facts or opinions by an agency through the use of written report forms, application forms, schedules, questionnaires, reporting or recordkeeping requirements, or other similar methods calling for either —

(A) answers to identical questions posed to, or identical reporting or recordkeeping requirements imposed on, ten or more persons, other than agencies, instrumentalities, or employees of the United States; or

(B) answers to questions posed to agencies, instrumentalities, or employees of the United States which are to be used for general statistical purposes.

44 U.S.C. 3502(4).

The Supreme Court held that the act plainly does *not* apply to government regulations that require private persons to distribute information to other private persons, such as a rule requiring employers to tell employees about hazardous conditions in the workplace. Thus, the Department of Labor need not have OMB's formal approval to issue such a request.

f. Executive Branch Regulatory Management Process

As a result of the recent executive orders, the rule-writing process for important regulatory rules looks like Figure 2-1.

FIGURE 2-1

REGULATORY AGENCY   OFFICE OF MANAGEMENT AND BUDGET

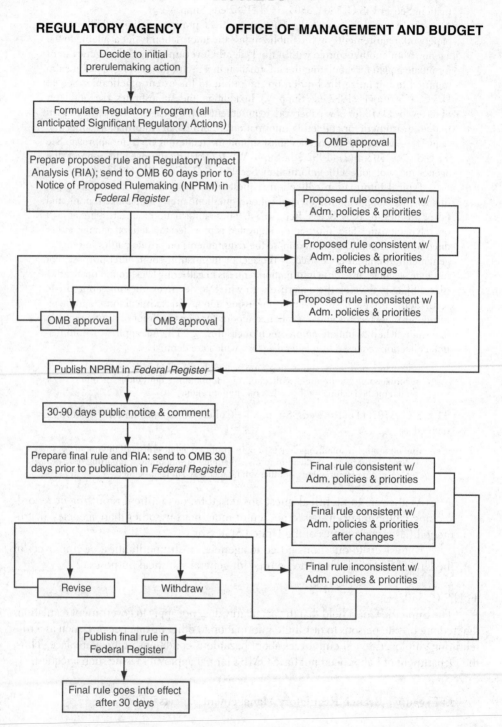

Source: General Accounting Office, Regulatory Review, Information on OMB's Review Process Fact Sheet for the House Govt. Operators' Comm., App. I, July 1989.

Notes and Questions

1. OIRA has said that the executive orders require the agencies basically to ask, and to answer, the following questions.

(a) Is there a genuine need for federal regulation? In particular, what "defect" is there in the free market that requires governmental intervention? What is the problem that the regulation seeks to cure, and why does the agency think a regulation will work better than the marketplace without it?

(b) If there is a need for governmental intervention, why will regulation work better than some less restrictive alternative, such as use of the "judicial system, . . . antitrust enforcement, workers compensation systems, and regulation at the State or local level"?

(c) What are the regulatory options, for example, should the agency set standards for a product's performance, or should it require the use of certain designed technology?

(d) What are the benefits likely to be achieved through each option? The agency should show causal connections between policy options and specific benefits. It should try to quantify benefits, using ranges of estimates, quantifying even nonmonetary benefits through use of "willingness-to-pay estimates" if possible. It should explain benefits that cannot be monetized.

(e) What are the likely costs of each option? The agency should calculate "incremental" costs, including "private-sector compliance costs, government administrative and enforcement costs, and costs of reallocating workers displaced as a result of the regulation."

(f) The agency should explain the assumption it uses to calculate costs and benefits where risk and uncertainty are involved. It should discount values for future costs and benefits to obtain a present value.

(g) In light of needs, alternatives, costs, and benefits, is the regulatory alternative chosen the best alternative?

2. Critics of OIRA — especially, but not only, under Presidents Reagan and Bush — raised the following sorts of objections, coming from very different directions.

(a) OIRA's analysis is weighted too heavily in favor of minimizing costs. The benefits of regulations are sometimes hard to measure; their costs are easier to demonstrate in terms of hard numbers. Who can quantify the value of saving a human life or of helping to preserve wildlife? What answer should OIRA make to this kind of argument?

(b) OIRA lacks the relevant expertise. Policy analysts are not safety or environmental experts. A scientist who has worked for years in, say, the Food and Drug Administration (FDA) or EPA is more likely to evaluate accurately the true costs, benefits, and risks of a regulation than is a recent graduate of a school of government. What answer should OIRA make?

(c) OIRA lacks sufficient staff. EPA with its staff of 10,000 sends its rules for review to four OIRA case officers. Forty analysts are no match for thousands of agency personnel. To supervise the work of the agency from a central location effectively would require hundreds or thousands of bureaucrats. It would involve creating a new bureaucracy that would rival the size of the old. OIRA's answer?

(d) OIRA lacks the necessary "political clout." Suppose an agency head, backed up by the cabinet secretary, says that it will ignore OIRA. What can OIRA do about it, even if the costs are high and the benefits low?

(e) OIRA unnecessarily delays the promulgation of important regulations.

(f) OIRA officials confer off the record with agency officials, and even with members of self-interested private groups. They may consider material that the agency has not seen (though OIRA has said it will make such material available on request). They may be susceptible to political pressure. The guarantees of a "public record" are missing. (We shall consider this question in later chapters.)

Assessment of these criticisms will inevitably be influenced by assessment of the substantive regulations that OIRA changes. For example, OIRA was criticized under President Reagan for leading EPA and OSHA to revise, and to make less stringent, regulations dealing with asbestos exposure and exposure to a suspected carcinogen called ethylene oxide. The revisions may have put lives at risk; alternatively, the revisions may have saved employers, employees, and the public vast amounts of money while proving a still more effective way of promoting safety. We obviously cannot know which is the proper characterization without knowing more about the substance of the particular regulations. Can one fairly praise or blame OIRA for its overall performance without some such idea about substance? Are there good "nonsubstantive" bases for evaluating OIRA's work? What are they? How important are they? For a valuable study, suggesting that economic analysis has actually had a range of good consequences, see Economic Analysis at EPA (R. Morgenstern ed. 1999).

Under President Clinton, the process of review was frequently criticized as too tepid and cautious. On this view, OIRA is not sufficiently aggressive in ensuring that agencies choose the least restrictive alternative or that the benefits are proportionate to the costs. There is indeed reason to think that OIRA became more of a procedural, or coordinating, institution and less of a substantive one. Much of the center of substantive change shifted to Vice President Gore's "reinventing government" initiatives. Is this a problem? If so, what should Congress do about it? See Cavanaugh, Hahn & Stavins, National Environmental Policy in the Clinton Years (2001), available at www.aei.brookings.org/publications/abstract.asp?pID = 152.

President George W. Bush's choice to head OIRA, John Graham, is a noted expert on risk analysis, and is expected to attempt a more substantive role for OIRA. Indeed, OIRA issued a number of "return letters" under Graham, asking agencies to reconsider proposed regulations, generally on the ground that they would fail a cost-benefit test or otherwise violate the principles set out in Executive Order 12866 (continuing in effect under President George W. Bush). For a set of return letters, see www.whitehouse.gov/omb/inforeg/return_letter.html. Graham also initiated a new device, called "prompt letters," which are intended to encourage agencies to act when action seems justified. See www.whitehouse.gov/omb/inforeg/prompt_letter.html.

One of those letters, to the Food and Drug Administration (FDA), involved mandatory disclosure of trans fatty acids in the Nutrition Facts panel of food. Drawing attention to evidence that trans fatty acids contribute to coronary heart disease (CHD), the letter noted that a disclosure rule seemed to be supported by the FDA's preliminary analysis, which estimated that, ten years after the effective date, the rule would prevent 7,600 to 17,100 cases of CHD and avert 2,500 to 5,600 deaths per year. Over a 20-year period, the FDA estimated the benefits of such a rule would range from $25 billion to $59 billion, while the costs would be $400 million to $850 million. The prompt letter strongly encouraged the FDA to issue a disclosure rule or to explain its failure to do so.

The other prompt letter, involving automatic external defibrillators (AEDs), was sent to the Occupational Safety and Health Administration (OSHA), with a firm request that the agency "consider whether promotion of AEDs should be elevated to a priority." The letter referred to an editorial in the New England Journal of Medicine, noting that only 2 percent to 5 percent of the 225,000 persons who have sudden and unexpected cardiac arrest each year outside a hospital are successfully resuscitated compared to the

17 percent to 38% success rates found with AEDs. The prompt letter observed that "some preliminary cost-effectiveness calculations" showed that "AEDs in the workplace might prove to be a very cost-effective intervention." Indeed AEDs, now mandated on air carriers by the Department of Transportation, are estimated to save nine lives per year, at the comparatively low price of $2.4 million in annual costs. The prompt letter suggested that OSHA should consider following the Department of Transportation's lead.

These "prompt letters" are a potentially important development. The idea of cost-benefit analysis has often been associated with dogmatic opposition to regulation. But cost-benefit analysis often can show, and has shown, that government action is worth-while — and indeed that government should do more.

Prompt Letters

3. The courts have said little about the legality of OIRA, even though the reviewing process is long-standing. It is apparently quite hard to develop a record that provides a clear basis for attacking OIRA involvement. A district court has held, not surprisingly, that "OMB has no authority to use its regulatory review under Executive Order 12,291 to delay promulgation of EPA regulations . . . beyond the date of a statutory deadline." EDF v. Thomas, 627 F. Supp. 566 (D.D.C. 1986). The Supreme Court, in Dole v. United Steelworkers, excerpted above, held that the Paperwork Reduction Act does not apply to "disclosure" rules, that is, rules requiring employers to disclose information to private parties or to the public (rather than to gather information for the agency). All of the relevant executive orders say that their requirements apply only "to the extent permit-ted by law." The orders do not purport to change any statutory mandate. They also try to insulate OMB review from judicial review. Cases involving OMB review therefore seem unlikely. Whether or not case law develops on the subject, the "OIRA development" is extremely important for administrative law.

4. Does the president have the power to require agencies to make cost-benefit analy-sis the basis for decision? Recall that the executive orders do not impose this requirement when statutes say otherwise. But suppose that a statute is ambiguous, and an agency does not want to make cost-benefit analysis the basis for decision; may the president overturn the agency's determination? The question may be less hypothetical than it seems. Recall International Union, UAW v. OSHA, 37 F.3d 605 (D.C. Cir. 1994), where OSHA appar-ently had the statutory authority to make cost-benefit analysis the basis for decision but refused. What if the president and OMB ordered OSHA to do so? Indeed, there is an oddity in the background of that very case, for OSHA was governed by President Clinton's executive order, which might have been taken to direct the agency to do precisely that. Does OSHA's ultimate decision suggest that President Clinton's executive order allows agencies more room to reject cost-benefit analysis than did Executive Order 12,291?

Or suppose that an agency decides to do cost-benefit analysis, but in accordance not with OMB's guidance but with its own judgments about how to value life and health and how to deal with lives lost in the future. Could the president require the agency to comply with what OMB wants to mandate?

Put cost-benefit analysis to one side. Could the president direct federal agencies to give special weight to environmental protection, energy problems, the alleviation of poverty, the prevention of unemployment, or racial harmony? Soon after his inaugura-tion, President George W. Bush did in fact issue an executive order, telling agencies to give special attention to energy-related issues.

5. What are the most important differences between Clinton's order and Reagan's orders? The most important similarities? Note that both require cost-benefit analysis, though Clinton's does so in somewhat softened form. Does Clinton's order demonstrate

that the criticisms of Reagan's orders were partisan, not principled — or, more fundamentally, that some form of cost-benefit balancing, operating under OMB, is an enduring part of the modern regulatory state? Consider the view that the language of the orders matters less than how they are applied and enforced. Consider also whether cost-benefit analysis is entirely open-ended, to be filled in as bureaucrats wish, or instead a more or less scientific tool that promises to discipline and improve agency decisions. Note also that President Clinton's order attempts to ensure more disclosure of commentaries between OIRA and agencies, and also to increase agency autonomy.

If you were president or a member of Congress, would you define "costs" and "benefits"? Would you support a specific number representing the appropriate expenditure per life saved (say, $7 million) or floors ($1 million?) and ceilings ($12 million?)? If administrators cannot realistically avoid assigning dollar amounts to human lives, why should Congress fail to provide guidance? Relevant discussion can be found in W. Kip Viscusi, Fatal Tradeoffs (1993), which uses labor market and consumer behavior to try to discern the value of human life for regulatory purposes. Compare E. Anderson, Value in Ethics and Economics (1993), which discusses issues of "incommensurability" in this context.

Should Executive Order 12,866 relieve the pressure for statutory changes designed to ensure that agencies do not impose excessively costly regulations? Or are statutory changes needed because some statutes now forbid such balancing?

6. We have noted that most people believe that under the law as it now stands, the president often cannot tell an agency directly what to do, even an agency the head of which "reports" to the president. OSHA, for example, says that the secretary of labor, not the president, shall issue health regulations. Do the executive orders violate this kind of statute by permitting the president, or the OMB or OIRA director, to exercise de facto power that the statute lodges elsewhere? Consider: The president has the constitutional authority to ask the secretary to submit reports. The president can discharge the secretary if he wishes. The Constitution gives the president, not the secretary, the power to execute the laws. Do these considerations convince you that a court should read OSHA's grant of power to the secretary as consistent with presidential (or OMB) review? In other words, should it be concluded that the president does, after all, have the authority to order agency heads to do what he wishes, so long as his wish is consistent with law?

Does all this matter? Couldn't the president just insist that the secretary do what he says on pain of dismissal? Or are there political reasons for believing the latter power is not a very effective check against "uncontrolled" Department of Labor decisionmaking?

7. The regulatory agenda requirement seems to have helped the public by creating a single place where any member of the public can learn just what the federal government is considering by way of regulatory action. It might be interesting to look at the agenda when you are next in a law library.

8. Should Congress or the president go much further than these executive orders? Consider the suggestion that many of the most serious problems in regulation stem from insufficient coordination and poor priority-setting. If this is so, perhaps some institution in government, expert in a wide range of areas, should have the authority to divert resources from small problems to large ones. Should the president be authorized to rationalize regulation in this general way? See S. Breyer, Breaking the Vicious Circle (1993), excerpted in Chapter 3; see also the criticisms and questions raised in Pildes & Sunstein, Reinventing the Regulatory State, 62 U. Chi. L. Rev. (1995), and in Heinzerling, Political Science, 62 U. Chi. L. Rev. 172 (1996).

E. The Agency's Power to Adjudicate

"The judicial Power of the United States shall be vested in one supreme Court and in such inferior Courts as the Congress shall from time to time ordain and establish. The Judges . . . shall hold their offices during good behaviour, and shall . . . receive . . . compensation, which shall not be diminished during their continuance in office." U.S. Const. art. III, §1.

Crowell v. Benson
285 U.S. 22 (1932)

Mr. Chief Justice HUGHES delivered the opinion of the Court.

This suit was brought in the District Court to enjoin the enforcement of an award made by Crowell, as deputy commissioner of the United States Employees' Compensation Commission, in favor of Knudsen and against Benson. The award was made under the Longshoremen's and Harbor Workers' Compensation Act and rested upon the finding of the deputy commissioner that Knudsen was injured while in the employ of Benson and performing service upon the navigable waters of the United States. The complainant alleged that the award was contrary to law for the reason that Knudsen was not at the time of his injury an employee of [Benson] and his claim was not "within the jurisdiction" of the deputy commissioner [and] that the Act was unconstitutional. . . .

[The Court held that the statute did not violate the due process clause.]

(2) The contention [that the statute unconstitutionally bestows judicial power upon a nonjudicial body] presents a distinct question. In Murray's Lessee v. Hoboken Land and Improvement Co., 18 How. 272, 284 [(1856)], this Court, speaking through Mr. Justice Curtis, said:

> To avoid misconstruction upon so grave a subject, we think it proper to state that we do not consider Congress can either withdraw from judicial cognizance any matter which, from its nature, is the subject of a suit at the common law, or in equity, or in admiralty; nor, on the other hand, can it bring under the judicial power a matter which, from its nature, is not a subject for judicial determination.

The question in the instant case, in this aspect, can be deemed to relate only to determinations of fact. . . . The Congress did not attempt to define questions of law, and the generality of the description leaves no doubt of the intention to reserve to the Federal court full authority to pass upon all matters which this Court had held to fall within that category. . . .

As to determinations of fact, the distinction is at once apparent between cases of private right and those which arise between the Government and persons subject to its authority in connection with the performance of the constitutional functions of the executive or legislative departments. The Court referred to this distinction in Murray's Lessee v. Hoboken Land and Improvement Co., . . . pointing out that "there are matters, involving public rights, which may be presented in such form that the judicial power is capable of acting on them, and which are susceptible of judicial determination, but which Congress may or may not bring within the cognizance of the courts of the United States, as it may deem proper." Thus the Congress, in exercising the powers confided to it, may establish "legislative" courts (as distinguished from "constitutional courts in which the judicial power conferred by the Constitution can be deposited") which are to form part of the government of territories or of the District of Columbia, or to serve as special tribunals "to examine and determine various matters, arising between the government and others, which from their nature do not require judicial determination and yet are susceptible of it." But "the mode of determining matters of this class is completely within congressional control. Congress may reserve to itself the power to decide, may delegate that power to executive officers, or may commit it to judicial tribunals." . . . Familiar illustrations of administrative agencies created for the determination of such matters are found in connection with the exercise of the congressional power as to interstate and foreign commerce, taxation, immigration, the public lands, public health, the facilities of the post office, pensions and payments to veterans.

The present case does not fall within the categories just described but is one of private right, that is, of the liability of one individual to another under the law as defined. But in cases of that sort, there is no requirement that, in order to maintain the essential attributes of the judicial power, all determinations of fact in constitutional courts shall be made by judges. On the common law side of the Federal courts, the aid of juries is not only deemed appropriate but is required by the Constitution itself. In cases of equity and admiralty, it is historic practice to call to the assistance of the courts, without the consent of the parties, masters and commissioners or assessors, to pass upon certain classes of questions, as, for example, to take and state an account or to find the amount of damages. While the reports of masters and commissioners in such cases are essentially of an advisory nature, it has not been the practice to disturb their findings when they are properly based upon evidence, in the absence of errors of law, and the parties have no right to demand that the court shall redetermine the facts thus found. In admiralty, juries were anciently in use not only in criminal cases but apparently in civil cases also. . . .

In deciding whether the Congress, in [allowing the deputy commissioner to determine the facts,] has exceeded the limits of its authority to prescribe procedure in cases of injury upon navigable waters, regard must be had, . . . not to mere matters of form but to the substance of what is required. The statute has a limited application, being confined to the relation of master and servant, and the method of determining the questions of fact . . . is necessary to its effective enforcement. The Act itself, where it applies, establishes the measure of the employer's liability, thus leaving open for determination the questions of fact as to the circumstances, nature, extent and consequences of the injuries sustained by the employee for which compensation is to be made in accordance with the prescribed standards. Findings of fact by the deputy commissioner upon such questions are closely analogous to the findings of the amount of damages that are made, according to familiar practice, by commissioners or assessors; and the reservation of full authority to the court to deal with matters of law provides for the appropriate exercise of the judicial function in this class of cases. For the purposes stated, we are unable to find any constitutional obstacle to the action of the Congress in availing itself of a method shown by experience to be essential in order to apply its standards to the thousands of cases involved, thus relieving the courts of a most serious burden while preserving their complete authority to insure the proper application of the law.

(3) What has been said thus far relates to the determination of claims of employees within the purview of the Act. A different question is presented where the determinations of fact are fundamental or "jurisdictional," in the sense that their existence is a condition precedent to the operation of the statutory scheme. These fundamental requirements are

that the injury occur upon the navigable waters of the United States and that the relation of master and servant exist.

[In] relation to these basic facts, the question is not the ordinary one as to the propriety of provision for administrative determinations. [It] is the question whether Congress may substitute for constitutional courts, in which the judicial power of the United States is vested, an administrative agency — in this instance a single deputy commissioner — for the final determination of the existence of the facts upon which the enforcement of the constitutional rights of the citizen depend. The recognition of the utility and convenience of administrative agencies for the investigation and finding of facts within their proper province, and the support of their authorized action, does not require the conclusion that there is no limitation of their use, and that the Congress could completely oust the courts of all determinations of fact by vesting the authority to make them with finality in its own instrumentalities or in the Executive Department. That would be to sap the judicial power as it exists under the Federal Constitution, and to estab-lish a government of a bureaucratic character alien to our system, wherever fundamental rights depend, as not infrequently they do depend, upon the facts, and finality as to facts becomes in effect finality in law. . . .

In cases brought to enforce constitutional rights the judicial power of the United States necessarily extends to the independent determination of all questions, both of fact and law, necessary to the performance of that supreme function. The case of confiscation is illustrative, the ultimate conclusion almost invariably depending upon the decisions of questions of fact. This court has held the owner to be entitled to "a fair opportunity for submitting that issue to a judicial tribunal for determination upon its own independent judgment as to both law and facts." Ohio Valley Water Co. v. Ben Avon Borough [253 U.S. 287 (1920)]. . . .

Jurisdiction in the Executive to order deportation exists only if the person arrested is an alien, and while, if there were jurisdiction, the findings of fact of the Executive Department would be conclusive, the claim of citizenship "is a denial of an essential jurisdictional fact" both in the statutory and the constitutional sense, and a writ of habeas corpus will issue "to determine the status." Persons claiming to be citizens of the United States "are entitled to a judicial determination of their claims," said this Court in Ng Fung Ho v. White, [259 U.S. 276, 285 (1922)] and in that case the cause was remanded to the Federal District Court "for trial in that court of the question of citizenship."

In the present instance, the argument that the Congress has constituted the deputy commissioner a fact-finding tribunal is unavailing, as the contention makes the unten-able assumption that the constitutional courts may be deprived in all cases of the deter-mination of facts upon evidence even though a constitutional right may be involved. [W]hen fundamental rights are in question, this Court has repeatedly emphasized "the difference in security of judicial over administrative action." Ng Fung Ho v. White. . . .

[The Court held the statute constitutional because it construed the statute to allow the federal court to determine for itself the existence of these fundamental or jurisdictional facts.]

Upon what record is the determination to be made? . . . We think that the essential independence of the exercise of the judicial power of the United States in the enforce-ment of constitutional rights requires that the Federal court should determine such an issue upon its own record and the facts elicited before it.

The argument is made that there are other facts besides the locality of the injury and the fact of employment which condition the action of the deputy commissioner. . . . But we think that there is a clear distinction between cases where the locality of the injury takes the cases out of the admiralty and maritime jurisdiction, or where the fact of employment being absent there is lacking under this statute any basis for the imposition of liability without fault, and those cases which fall within the admiralty and maritime jurisdiction and where the relation of master and servant in maritime employment exists. It is in the latter field that the provisions for compensation apply and that . . . the determination of the facts relating to the circumstances of the injuries received, as well as their nature and consequences may appropriately be subjected to the scheme of administration for which the Act provides. . . .

We are of the opinion that the District Court did not err in permitting a trial de novo on the issue of employment.

Decree affirmed.

Mr. Justice BRANDEIS, dissenting. . . .

The primary question for consideration is not whether Congress provided, or validly could provide, that determinations of fact by the deputy commissioner should be conclusive upon the district court. The question is: Upon what record shall the district court's review of the order of the deputy commissioner be based?

[Justice Brandeis challenged the Court's requirement of a totally new evidentiary hearing before the district court to create a record supplanting that developed at the administrative hearing. He pointed out that such a procedure would involve duplication and delay, and asserted that nothing in the Constitution prevented Congress from assigning to administrative agencies the exclusive power to collect the record evidence on which factual issues would be determined, even if these facts were labeled "constitutional" or "jurisdictional." Why, asks Justice Brandeis, are "constitutional facts" different from any other fact? Why can Congress not give an administrative agency the power to determine constitutional facts just as any other fact — or at least the power to collect the evidence on which the fact will be determined? He asserted that neither the due process clause nor any other provision in the Constitution requires de novo judicial review of the questions whether the injury occurred in or on navigable waters and whether an employer-employee relation existed, and challenged the logic of singling out these issues from statutory prerequisites for liability and according them special de novo treatment as "constitutional" or "jurisdictional" issues.]

The holding that the difference between the procedure prescribed by the Longshoremen's Act and these historic methods of hearing evidence transcends the limits of congressional power when applied to the issue of the existence of a relation of employment, as distinguished from that of the circumstances of an injury or the existence of a relation of dependency, seems to me without foundation in reality. Certainly, there is no difference to the litigant.

[Even if the employment relation is a "constitutional" issue,] I see no reason for making special exception as to issues of constitutional right, unless it be that under certain circumstances, there may arise difficulty in reaching conclusions of law without consideration of the evidence as well as the findings of fact. . . . I see no basis for a contention that the denial of the right to a trial de novo upon the issue of employment is in any manner subversive of the independence of the federal judicial power. Nothing in the Constitution, or in any prior decision of this Court to which attention has been called, lends support to the doctrine that a judicial finding of any fact involved in any civil proceeding to enforce a pecuniary liability may not be made upon evidence introduced before a properly constituted administrative tribunal, or that a determination so made may not be deemed an independent judicial determination. Congress has repeatedly exercised authority to confer upon the tribunals which it creates, be they administrative bodies or courts of limited jurisdiction, the power to receive evidence concerning the facts upon which the exercise of federal power must be predicated, and to determine whether those facts exist. The power of Congress to provide by legislation for liability under certain circumstances subsumes the power to provide for the determination of the existence of those circumstances. It does not depend upon the absolute existence in reality of any fact. . . .

By the Longshoremen's Act, Congress created fact-finding and fact-gathering tribunals, supplementing the courts and entrusted with power to make initial determinations in matters within, and not outside, ordinary judicial purview. The purpose of these administrative bodies is to withdraw from the courts, subject to the power of judicial review, a class of controversies which experience has shown can be more effectively and expeditiously handled in the first instance by a special and expert tribunal. The proceedings of the deputy commissioners are endowed with every substantial safeguard of a judicial hearing. Their conclusions are, as a matter of right, open to reexamination in the courts on all questions of law; and, we assume for the purposes of this discussion, may be open even on all questions of the weight of the evidence. . . .

The "judicial power" of Article III of the Constitution is the power of the federal government, and not of any inferior tribunal. There is in that Article nothing which requires any controversy to be determined as of first instance in the federal district courts. The jurisdiction of those courts is subject to the control of Congress. Matters which may be placed within their jurisdiction may instead be committed to the state courts. If there be any controversy to which the judicial power extends that may not be subjected to the conclusive determination of administrative bodies or federal legislative courts, it is not because of any prohibition against the diminution of the jurisdiction of the federal district courts as such, but because, under certain circumstances, the constitutional requirement of due process is a requirement of judicial process. An accumulation of precedents, already referred to, has established that in civil proceedings involving property rights determination of facts may constitutionally be made otherwise than judicially; and necessarily that evidence as to such facts may be taken outside of a court. I do not conceive that Article III has properly any bearing upon the question presented in this case.

. . . To permit a contest de novo in the district court of an issue tried, or triable, before the deputy commissioner will, I fear, gravely hamper the effective administration of the Act. The prestige of the deputy commissioner will necessarily be lessened by the opportunity of relitigating facts in the courts. The number of controverted cases may be largely increased. Persistence in controversy will be encouraged. And since the advantage of prolonged litigation lies with the party able to bear heavy expenses, the purpose of the Act will be in part defeated.

[T]he judgment of the Circuit Court should be reversed and the case remanded.

Questions

1. Why might Congress delegate the power to assess accident liability to an agency instead of a court? Consider the role of the following factors: saving time; applying expertise; ensuring that adjudication is undertaken by people sympathetic to prevailing political commitments. Which of these factors might justify a decision to give adjudicative power to people assessing the claims in Crowell v. Benson? To adjudicators in the context

of social security disability determinations? To adjudicators deciding questions involving labor-management relations?

2. What constitutional problems might arise when adjudicatory functions, formerly exercised by the courts, are delegated to an agency?

(a) Must Congress provide for a jury trial? (We take up this issue below.)

(b) What due process problems does this delegation raise?

(c) What Article III problems does this delegation raise? What are the underlying constitutional concerns? To what extent do the "due process" answers successfully resolve them?

3. Would Justice Brandeis's approach allow Congress to transfer all of the civil business of the federal district courts to administrative agencies?

4. What are the implications of *Crowell* for the scope of judicial review of agency decisions? Does the Constitution require that courts review all questions of law presented in agency decisions? If so, how should "questions of law" be defined in this context? Is the Chief Justice's model of agencies as nothing more than subordinate factfinding adjuncts of courts accurate or desirable? Note that in practice, agencies are really a lot more than special masters or subordinate factfinders; their determinations of fact are upheld unless they are unreasonable. We discuss this topic in detail in Chapter 4.

5. After *Crowell*, much (not all!) of the law governing the relationship between Article III and the administrative state could, and still can, be summarized in the following way: Congress is permitted to delegate adjudicatory functions to an administrative agency if and only if there is judicial review to ensure that the agency has followed the law and found the facts in a reasonable manner. Is this view consistent with the best reading of the text and purposes of article III? How should it be qualified?

1. The "Private Right/Public Right" Distinction and the Role of Article III Courts

Two years before *Crowell* the Supreme Court had held that Congress may not grant a court the power to award a radio license because awarding licenses is an "administrative" function that the federal Constitution, Article III, does not authorize courts to perform. Federal Radio Commission v. General Elec. Co., 281 U.S. 464 (1930). This holding indicates that constitutional separation-of-powers principles sometimes forbid de novo consideration, by a court, of "nonjudicial" administrative agency activities. Such "nonjudicial" activities, perhaps, are those that bear little analogy to historical judicial functions. Awarding licenses, like nineteenth-century grants of federal land, is not very much like adjudicating individual controversies through reference to a rule of law.

Crowell, and several other Supreme Court cases, deal with the converse question: Under what circumstances does Article III *require* a court to decide a matter? To what extent does it *forbid* Congress to take a matter away from Article III courts and give it to another official person or body for decision? To what extent does Article III require courts to review a decision of another body strictly, perhaps deciding factual or legal questions de novo?

The Supreme Court, in 1856, suggested that the nature of the right at stake, whether it be "public" or "private," may help answer these questions. It wrote:

> We do not consider Congress can either withdraw from judicial cognizance any matter which, from its nature, is the subject of a suit at common law, or in equity, or admiralty; nor, on the other hand, can it bring under the judicial power a matter which, from its nature, is not a subject for judicial determination. At the same time,

> there are matters, involving public rights, which may be presented in such form that
> the judicial power is capable of acting on them, and which are susceptible of judicial
> determination, but which Congress may or may not bring within the cognizance of
> the courts of the United States, as it may deem proper.

Murray's Lessee v. Hoboken Land & Improvement Co., 18 How. 272, 284 (1856). In *Crowell*, and in several other cases, the Supreme Court has referred to or used the concept of "public rights" in an effort to determine whether Congress can or cannot grant adjudicatory power to a nonjudicial body.

NORTHERN PIPELINE CONSTRUCTION CO. v. MARATHON PIPE LINE CO., 485 U.S. 50 (1982).

Justice Brennan, writing for a plurality (not a majority) of the Court, spelled out a rather formal separation-of-powers position that would tend to restrict, perhaps to a greater extent than *Crowell*, Congress's ability to delegate adjudicatory powers to non-Article III decisionmakers. The case involved bankruptcy judges rather than agencies. Still, bankruptcy judges are much like agency administrators for present constitutional purposes in that bankruptcy judges enjoy neither life tenure nor a constitutionally protected salary; hence, they are not *Article III* judges. The question in the case was whether Congress constitutionally could give those non-Article III judges the broad legal power to hear and to decide all legal controversies "arising in or related to" bankruptcy proceedings. To be specific, the statute gave bankruptcy courts jurisdiction over all "civil proceedings arising under" the federal bankruptcy law, "*or arising in or related to*" those bankruptcy proceedings. Could Congress constitutionally delegate to the non-Article III bankruptcy judge the legal power to decide an ordinary state law contract claim that Northern Pipeline, a company in the midst of bankruptcy reorganization, filed against Marathon? Permitting the bankruptcy court to decide such claims, rather than referring them to other courts for decision, would prove administratively useful, for a bankrupt company could thereby bring all its assets before the bankruptcy court (including those it had to sue to collect) without having to bring suits outside the bankruptcy court itself.

Justice Brennan wrote that the Constitution forbids Congress to grant this adjudicatory power to bankruptcy judges (even though Article III judges would review on appeal the bankruptcy judges' decisions). He noted that precedent permitted a delegation of adjudicatory power to non-Article III judges in three instances: (1) Congress may delegate that power to "territorial courts." (2) Congress may delegate that power to "courts martial." (3) Congress may delegate to "legislative courts and administrative agencies" the power "to adjudicate *cases involving 'public rights.'*" Justice Brennan said that "public rights" are rights that arise "between the government and others." He contrasted them with "private rights," which involve "the liability of one individual to another under the law as defined." The government need not have created public rights at all. In the nineteenth century, it need not have created rights to public lands for those who settled them; in the twentieth century it need not have created rights to welfare or social security for those in need. Since it need not have provided such rights against the government at all, why could it not permit administrative agencies or legislative courts to administer those rights that it did create (at least assuming the system is fair enough to survive any "due process" challenges)? Thus, Justice Brennan said it was established that, since Congress could commit public right matters "completely to non-judicial executive determination, . . . there can be no constitutional objection to Congress employing the less drastic expedient of committing their determination to a legislative court or an administrative agency."

Northern Pipeline's state law contract claim, however, was not a public right. It did not run between Northern and the government. Rather, it was a private right, involving the liability of one private individual to another under the "law as defined." Moreover, the statute "has impermissibly removed most, if not all, of the essential attributes of the judicial power" from Article III courts and vested them in non-Article III bankruptcy courts. Thus, Congress could not permit a non-Article III judge to adjudicate the claim.

But what about *Crowell*? Did that case not also involve private rights (between employer and employee)? Did Justice Brennan mean to overrule *Crowell*, casting doubt on the constitutional legitimacy of agency adjudications among private parties? He did not. To distinguish *Crowell*, Justice Brennan identified different kinds of private rights: those that *Congress* had created and other kinds of private rights (presumably common law rights or those that states had created). He said that, when Congress creates "a substantive federal right, . . . it possesses substantial discretion to prescribe the manner in which that right may be adjudicated — including the assignment to an adjunct of some functions historically performed by the judge." Congress can, "in determining that right, . . . create presumptions, or assign burdens of proof," or create "particularized tribunals to perform the specialized adjudicative tasks related to that right." But, "when the right adjudicated is not of Congressional creation," then Article III forbids "substantial inroads into functions that have traditionally been performed by the judiciary."

Justice Brennan also noted that *Crowell* itself required closer court supervision of the agency's adjudicatory decision than would likely occur in the bankruptcy context. "First, the agency in *Crowell* made only specialized, narrowly confined factual determinations regarding a particularized area of the law." By contrast, the bankruptcy court makes all relevant findings of fact in many areas of the law. Second, the agency in *Crowell* had to seek court enforcement of its orders. The bankruptcy court could enforce its own orders. Third, "while orders issued by the agency in *Crowell* were to be set aside if 'not supported by the evidence,' the judgments of the bankruptcy courts are apparently subject to review only under the more deferential 'clearly erroneous' standard."

In sum, in Justice Brennan's view, *Crowell* involves both (1) a private right that Congress created, and (2) greater Article III court participation and supervision. His view nonetheless is support for the position that constitutional separation-of-powers considerations require the supervisory framework that the Court erected in *Crowell*.

Justices Rehnquist and O'Connor did not accept Justice Brennan's analysis, but they agreed with his conclusion. They simply thought the claim (state law contract) was too traditionally judicial in nature for Congress to permit a nonjudicial body to resolve it.

Justices White, Powell, and Chief Justice Burger dissented. They took a more "functional" approach. They thought that the presence of appellate court review and the likely nonpolitical nature of the claims meant that traditional separation-of-powers concerns were satisfied. Appellate review guaranteed uniformity of, and conformity with, the law; the nonpolitical nature of the cases meant no undue executive or legislative efforts to influence the outcomes or any "dangerous accumulation of power in one of the political branches of government." Consequently, the purposes of "separation of powers" doctrine being served, the Constitution did not prohibit the delegation of adjudicatory power to a non-Article III tribunal.

COMMODITY FUTURES TRADING COMMISSION v. SCHOR, 478 U.S. 833 (1986). The legal question in this case is very similar to the *Marathon* question. Can Congress constitutionally grant to an agency, the Commodities Futures Trading Commission

(CFTC), the power to adjudicate ordinary state law contract claims between two individuals? The question arose in the following context: (1) Congress created a special, new proceeding, called a "reparations" proceeding, through which a disgruntled customer of a commodities broker could claim damages for the broker's violation of the Commodities Exchange Act. The proceeding takes place before the agency, which adjudicates the controversy. The disgruntled customer need not use this agency procedure, however, but has a choice either to use the agency reparations proceeding or to bring a claim based on a violation of the act directly in federal court. (2) If the customer uses the agency procedure, the act (as interpreted by the agency and the courts) permits the agency to adjudicate, at the same time, any related state law counterclaim that the broker wishes to bring against the customer. (3) Schor, a customer who had lost money trading in commodities, brought an agency reparations action against his broker. He claimed that the broker had cheated him in various ways that violated the Commodities Exchange Act. Conti, the broker, who said that Schor still owed him some of the money lost, brought an ordinary state law counterclaim for debt. Initially, Conti brought his state law claim in federal court (in a diversity action). Then Conti voluntarily dismissed his court claim (at Schor's request) and brought the same action as a counterclaim before the agency. (4) Schor lost. Conti won. Schor later argued that the agency could not constitutionally adjudicate the state law contract claim (citing *Marathon*). Justice O'Connor, writing for a seven-member majority, in effect repudiated the *Marathon* plurality and, in a sense, reaffirmed *Crowell*. She wrote:

> [Article III of the Constitution] directs that the "judicial Power of the United States shall be vested in one supreme Court and in such inferior Courts as the Congress may from time to time ordain and establish." . . . Although our precedents in this area do not admit of easy synthesis, they do establish that the resolution of claims such as Schor's cannot turn on conclusory reference to the language of Article III. . . . Rather, the constitutionality of a given congressional delegation of adjudicative functions to a non-Article III body must be assessed by reference to the purposes underlying the requirements of Article III. . . . This inquiry, in turn, is guided by the principle that "practical attention to substance rather than doctrinaire reliance on formal categories should inform application of Article III."
>
> Article III, serves both to protect "the role of the independent judiciary within the constitutional scheme of tripartite government," . . . and to safeguard litigants' "right to have claims decided before judges who are free from potential domination by other branches of government." [T]his guarantee serves to protect primarily personal, rather than structural, interests. [In respect to those "personal" interests,] precedents . . . demonstrate . . . that Article III does not confer on litigants an absolute right to the plenary consideration of every nature of claim by an Article III court [citing *Crowell*]. . . . Schor indisputably waived any personal right [he had to an Article III trial on the counterclaim when he asked Conti to dismiss his federal court suit and try the claim before the agency, and] even were there no evidence of an express waiver here, Schor's election to forgo his right to proceed in state or federal court on his claim and his decision to seek relief instead in a CFTC reparations proceeding constituted an effective waiver.
>
> [In respect to the "structural" interests, Article III] safeguards the role of the Judicial Branch . . . by barring congressional attempts "to transfer jurisdiction [to non-Article III tribunals] for the purpose of emasculating" constitutional courts . . . and thereby preventing "the encroachment or aggrandizement of one branch at the expense of the other." . . . To the extent that this structural principle is implicated in a given case, the parties cannot by consent [or waiver] cure the constitutional difficulty. [But, in measuring the scope of the constitutional threat,] the Court has declined to adopt formalistic and unbending rules.

[Rather, it has taken into account various factors, such as] the extent to which the "essential attributes of judicial power" are reserved to Article III courts, and, conversely, the extent to which the non-Article III forum exercises the range of jurisdiction and powers normally vested only in Article III courts, the origins and importance of the right to be adjudicated, and the concerns that drove Congress to depart from the requirements of Article III.

[In this instance, the] CFTC's adjudicatory powers depart from the traditional agency model in just one respect: the CFTC's jurisdiction over common law counterclaims. . . . The CFTC, like the agency in *Crowell*, deals only with a "particularized area of law," . . . whereas the jurisdiction of the bankruptcy courts found unconstitutional . . . extended broadly to "all civil proceedings arising under [the bankruptcy] title 11 or arising in or *related to* cases under title 11." [Court review of CFTC orders, in respect to matters of fact and of law, also follows the *Crowell* model. And,] the CFTC, unlike the bankruptcy courts . . . does not exercise "all ordinary powers of district courts." . . .

Of course, the nature of the claim has significance. . . . The counterclaim . . . is a "private" right for which state law provides the rule of decision. It is therefore a claim of the kind assumed to be at the "core" of matters normally reserved to Article III courts. . . . Yet this conclusion does not end our inquiry; [the label is not "talismanic," and the public right-private right distinction is not] determinative for Article III purposes. [Rather,] "the public rights doctrine reflects simply a pragmatic understanding that when Congress selects a quasi-judicial method of resolving matters that "could be conclusively determined by the Executive and Legislative Branches,' the danger of encroaching on the judicial powers" is less than when private rights, which are normally [and traditionally] within the purview of the judiciary, are relegated as an initial matter to administrative adjudication. . . . The risk that Congress may improperly have encroached on the federal judiciary is obviously magnified when Congress [withdraws from judicial cognizance such traditional matters as suits at common law, or in equity, or admiralty]. Accordingly, where private common law rights are at stake, our examination . . . has been searching. . . .

[Here, there is no substantial threat to the separation of powers. Congress left jurisdiction in the courts to decide such matters as well as placing it in the agency. It] seems self-evident that just as Congress may encourage parties to settle a dispute out of court or resort to arbitration without impermissible incursions on the separation of powers, Congress may make available a quasi-judicial mechanism through which willing parties may, at their option, elect to resolve their differences. This is not to say, of course, that if Congress created a phalanx of non-Article III courts without any Article III supervision or control and without evidence of valid and specific legislative necessities, the fact that the parties had the election to proceed in their forum of choice would necessarily save the scheme from constitutional attack. [But, here, there is an important, demonstrated need for the delegation.] [T]he CFTC's assertion of counterclaim jurisdiction is limited to that which is necessary to make the reparations procedure workable. [T]he purpose of the legislation [is] to furnish a prompt continuous, expert and inexpensive method for dealing with a class of questions of fact which are peculiarly suited to examination and determination by an administrative agency specially assigned to the task.

Justices Brennan and Marshall dissented. Justice Brennan relied upon the more formal analysis of his *Marathon* option. He did not see how Congress could "withdraw from [Article III] judicial cognizance any matter which, from its nature, is the subject of a suit at the common law." He argued that the

danger of the Court's balancing approach is . . . that as individual cases accumulate in which the Court finds that the short-term benefits of efficiency out-weigh the long-term benefits of judicial independence, the protections of Article III will be eviscerated.

> [T]he reasoning of this decision strongly suggests that, given "legislative necessity" and party consent, any federal agency may decide the state-law issues that are ancillary to federal issues within the agency's jurisdiction. Thus, . . . the potential impact of the Court's decision on federal court jurisdiction is substantial.

Justice Brennan also argued that "waiver" was not relevant, as "the structural and individual interests served by Article III are inseparable."

THOMAS v. UNION CARBIDE AGRICULTURAL PRODUCTS CO., 473 U.S. 568 (1984).   Here a unanimous Supreme Court found constitutional a congressional delegation to the EPA to adjudicate controversies among pesticide makers about how much compensation-for-information one should pay another. Justice Brennan noted that the right in question — the right of a pesticide maker who generates certain information (needed to register a pesticide) to compensation (for the cost of generating) from another maker of a similar pesticide who later borrows and uses that information — is a private right, *but a right created by congressional statute.* Justice Brennan thought that the need for the scheme and a degree of judicial supervision made the delegation a reasonable one. Justice O'Connor, writing for a majority, used a more "functional" analysis. She found the delegation constitutional and noted in particular the degree to which the agency adjudicatory process was integrated into a broader regulatory scheme.

Questions

Reconsider the *Crowell* analysis in light of the later cases.

1. Just what "personal interests" is Article III designed to protect? In answering this question, assume (as did Justice Brandeis) that the due process clauses of the fifth and fourteenth amendments secure a judicial forum to a litigant in any case where a different kind of forum would be fundamentally unfair (because, for example, the adjudicative official would be biased). If there are some such interests, why would Article III protect them only when private rights, but not when public rights, are involved? Is it more important for a litigant to secure an "impartial," constitutionally independent forum when seeking (a contractually promised) payment of a broker's fee than when seeking a welfare or social security disability payment? Why? What is the relationship between the public rights doctrine and the idea of sovereign immunity? Between the public rights doctrine and the idea that Congress need not create most statutory rights at all? See also Simpson v. Office of Thrift Supervision, 29 F.3d 1418 (9th Cir. 1994), upholding an agency's power to adjudicate a dispute in which it compelled an officer of a savings and loan to pay restitution to the savings and loan. In holding that there was no Article III violation, the court emphasized that Congress had provided for meaningful judicial review and also that the thrift regulation statutes create public rights.

Note also that there are independent limitations, not stemming from Article III, on agency power to adjudicate. For one such limitation, see Federal Maritime Commission v. South Carolina Ports Authority, 122 S. Ct. 1864 (2002) (state sovereign immunity precludes a federal agency from adjudicating a dispute between a private citizen and a state).

2. What are the "structural interests" with which Article III is concerned? Do they reflect the need to have judicial fora, with appellate channels leading to the Supreme Court, in order to create a uniform system of law? Could appellate courts alone not satisfy this need? Justice O'Connor, in *Schor,* makes clear that Congress could not create

"a phalanx of non-Article III tribunals equipped to handle the entire business of the Article III courts." Why not (assuming due process controls and appeals on questions of law)? Must we simply keep judges busy? Note that Justice O'Connor immediately qualified her statement by adding: (1) "without any Article III supervision or control," and (2) "without evidence of valid and specific legislative necessities." See Noriega-Perez v. United States, 179 F.3d 1166 (9th Cir. 1999). There the court held that *Schor* permitted an agency to adjudicate a civil dispute involving document fraud, emphasizing that Article III courts retained the ability to review the results, that the rights at issue were public rights, that the assignments to agencies promoted the legislative goal of increasing efficiency, and that only a narrow class of disputes was assigned to the agency. In the same vein, see Gulf Power Co. v. United States, 187 F.3d 1324 (11th Cir. 1999), allowing an agency to determine how much compensation was due someone whose property was taken in violation of the Fifth Amendment, because an Article III court was permitted to review the agency's decision. See also Simpson v. Office of Thrift Supervision, 29 F.3d 1418 (9th Cir. 1994) (allowing agency adjudication in the context of public rights and meaningful judicial review).

3. If one worries about Congress transferring the courts' workload elsewhere, why would one draw a distinction between public rights and private rights? After all, many traditional common law rights and remedies may be replaced by schemes of administrative rules and remedies, created by congressional statute. Such regulatory schemes may create a public body (the NLRB, the FTC) that adjudicates what sounds like a public matter (for example, a finding of an "unfair" labor or trade practice), but the benefit of which runs to other private individuals and that replaces what previously might have taken the form of a private suit (an employee versus an employer for breach of contract; a consumer versus a manufacturer for fraud). See L. Jaffe, Judicial Control of Administrative Action 90 (1965). One could fairly easily remove much of the work of the federal courts by creating administrative tribunals to adjudicate employment discrimination, civil rights violations, and similar controversies that have both a public and a private aspect.

4. Does the distinction between public rights and private rights reflect more than tradition? Recall from Chapter 1 that the New Dealers attacked the view that the common law was prepolitical or enjoyed any special status. For the New Dealers, the common law was a regulatory system, to be evaluated on pragmatic grounds: What effects did it have on the lives of those subject to it? When the Court suggests that public rights are "state-created" and thus privileges for Congress to dispense on such terms as it wishes, does it partake of pre-New Deal thinking about the line between prepolitical common law rights and more "artificial" statutory rights? If the answer is yes, is the Court's analysis supported or undermined? Why aren't all rights, strictly as a matter of fact, state-created? We will return to related issues in discussing the status of the "new property" in Chapter 6.

5. France enjoys a system of "administrative courts," the *Conseil d'Etat*, staffed by civil servants who work, during their careers, both as judges and as active members of the bureaucracy. They enjoy considerable expertise but not independence. Citizens' complaints against the government, and most other cases involving the government, must be brought in such courts; they cannot be brought in ordinary civil courts. Could the United States constitutionally create such a system?

6. Reconsider *Crowell's* asserted framework of judicial control: review of fact, review of law, review of procedure, redetermination of certain key facts. To what extent, where, and when, in your view, are such controls required by the Constitution?

See further on this subject: Fallon, Of Legislative Courts, Administrative Agencies, and Article III, 101 Harv. L. Rev. 916 (1988); Strauss, Formal and Functional Approaches to Separation of Powers Questions — A Foolish Inconsistency?, 72 Cornell L. Rev. 488 (1987).

2. The "Jurisdictional Fact" and "Constitutional Fact" Doctrines

Crowell holds that even though agencies may adjudicate otherwise private controversies (such as workers' compensation claims) subject to limited Article III court review, certain jurisdictional "facts" must be subject to de novo judicial review. The "jurisdictional fact" doctrine of *Crowell* has suffered much criticism, and doubts have often been expressed by judges and commentators alike as to its continued vitality. In fact, the Supreme Court has declined invitations to extend the doctrine. Lower courts almost uniformly confine the doctrine to the two specific jurisdictional findings listed in *Crowell*: the finding regarding the employment relationship and the finding that the injury occurred on navigable waters. Lower courts have also construed *Crowell* to give the trial court discretion concerning whether to conduct a trial de novo. Which, then, is more significant? The fact that the Court has declined the opportunities to overrule *Crowell*, thereby perhaps reserving the holding as an ace in the hole for some future contingency, or the fact that it has interred the doctrine, for all practical purposes, by not reversing the lower court decisions?

The requirement of de novo judicial determination of key factual issues, however, appears to still have vitality when important personal interests are involved. In *Crowell*, Chief Justice Hughes relied in part on Justice Brandeis's opinion for the Court in Ng Fung Ho v. White, 259 U.S. 276 (1922), which held that, in habeas corpus proceedings to test the validity of a deportation order, the petitioner was entitled to a de novo judicial trial on a claim of citizenship. The Court stated that the government could not constitutionally deport a citizen; administrative denial of a claim of citizenship was therefore "a denial of an essential jurisdictional fact." Brandeis apparently regretted this choice of language, and in *Crowell* he sought to distinguish Ng Fung Ho on the ground that the statute in question there did not provide for an administrative hearing and judicial review on the basis of the administrative record. He stated, "No question arose [in Ng Fung Ho] as to whether Congress might validly have provided for review exclusively upon the record made in the executive department; nor as to the scope of review which might have been permissible upon such record." 285 U.S. 22, 90 n.26a (1932). Consider also that Ng Fung Ho asserted that "[t]o deport one who . . . claims to be a citizen obviously deprives him of liberty. . . . It may result also in loss of both property and life, or of all that makes life worth living." 259 U.S. at 284.

Ng Fung Ho, involving deportation, did not present what *Crowell* would regard as a claim of private right. But it did present a claim that appears to be constitutional: the right of a citizen not to be deported. It suggests that courts have a special responsibility to examine the facts underlying federal constitutional claims. Would this responsibility be derived from the Article III powers of federal courts or from the more general dictates of due process, which would apply to state as well as to federal governments? The latter interpretation is suggested by Ohio Valley Water Co. v. Ben Avon Borough, 253 U.S. 287 (1920), in which the Supreme Court enunciated the "constitutional fact" doctrine. It held that the due process clause required a full judicial trial when a utility raised a claim of confiscation, asserting that municipal limitations on its rates deprived it of revenues adequate to yield a profit, and thereby took its property for public use without payment of just compensation. The court must determine both the law and the facts on its own independent judgment, and the prior hearings conducted by the agency seemingly are for naught. *Ben Avon* will be considered later, but it should be noted here that the case has had a powerful influence on state decisions. Massachusetts continued to follow the *Ben Avon* doctrine, primarily as an interpretation of the state constitution. Some eight states expressly follow *Ben Avon*, and at least nine others profess some degree of adherence to the doctrine.

Attempts to distinguish which factual situations may be subjected to trial de novo may ultimately collapse, as Justice Brandeis argued. Nevertheless, there are some decisions that the Supreme Court regards as so important that it is unwilling to defer to the judgment of administrative agencies or even to that of juries, in some cases. Consider the following areas of the law: libel of public figures, obscenity, and admissibility of "voluntary" confessions. In each of these areas, the Supreme Court has felt compelled to substitute its own independent judgment as to the facts in particular cases, and has explicitly admitted as much on occasion. See, e.g., Ashcraft v. Tennessee, 322 U.S. 143 (1944). The Court has rarely articulated the constitutional rationale for such independent judgment. Is independent judicial judgment required by due process or on the ground that judicial review, with its full panoply of adversary safeguards and tradition of judicial impartiality, is needed in order to protect constitutional rights adequately? Or does it stem from a special responsibility of Article III federal courts to safeguard the Constitution? The Court is obviously uncomfortable about its role in such cases and can cure the dilemma by fashioning a prophylactic rule, as in Miranda v. Arizona, or by appointing some alternative decisionmaker, as in Miller v. California. As yet, there appears to be no final solution to the problem of review of administrative findings of jurisdictional or constitutional facts.

3. *The Seventh Amendment as a Limitation on the Agency's Power to Adjudicate*

In the famous case of NLRB v. Jones & Laughlin Steel Corp., 301 U.S. 1 (1937), the NLRB found Jones & Laughlin guilty of discriminating against union members — an unfair labor practice — and ordered reinstatement and back pay. The company challenged the constitutionality of the National Labor Relations Act, but the Court upheld it as within the commerce power. The opinion also touched briefly on the seventh amendment question:

> Respondent complains that the Board not only ordered reinstatement but directed the payment of wages for the time lost. . . . It is argued that the requirement is equivalent to a money judgment and hence contravenes the Seventh Amendment with respect to trial by jury. The Seventh Amendment provides that "In suits at common law, where the value in controversy shall exceed twenty dollars, the right of trial by jury shall be preserved." The Amendment thus preserves the right which existed under the common law when the Amendment was adopted. Thus it has no application to cases where recovery of money damages is an incident to equitable relief even though damages might have been recovered in an action at law. It does not apply where the proceeding is not in the nature of a suit at common law.
>
> The instant case is not a suit at common law or in the nature of such a suit. The proceeding is one unknown to the common law. It is a statutory proceeding. Reinstatement of the employee and payment for time lost are requirements imposed

for violation of the statute and are remedies appropriate to its enforcement. The contention under the Seventh Amendment is without merit.

Id. at 48-49.

In Curtis v. Loether, 415 U.S. 189 (1974), the Court held that the seventh amendment requires a jury trial in an action for money damages under the Civil Rights Act of 1968 (making it illegal to discriminate in renting a house). Plaintiff (fearing jury sympathy for the defendant landlord) argued that a jury trial was not required because her cause of action was created by statute, not by the common law. The Court replied:

> Whatever doubt may have existed should now be dispelled. The Seventh Amendment does apply to actions enforcing statutory rights, and requires a jury trial upon demand, if the statute creates legal rights and remedies, enforceable in an action for damages in the ordinary courts of law.
>
> NLRB v. Jones & Laughlin Steel Corp., 301 U.S. 1 (1937), relied on by petitioner, lends no support to her statutory-rights argument. The Court there upheld the award of backpay without jury trial in an NLRB unfair practice proceeding, rejecting a Seventh Amendment claim on the ground that the case involved a "statutory proceeding" and "not a suit at common law or in the nature of such a suit." Id., at 48. *Jones & Laughlin* merely stands for the proposition that the Seventh Amendment is generally inapplicable in administrative proceedings, where jury trials would be incompatible with the whole concept of administrative adjudication and would substantially interfere with the NLRB's role in the statutory scheme. [This case upholds] congressional power to entrust enforcement of statutory rights to an administrative process or specialized court of equity free from the strictures of the Seventh Amendment. But when Congress provides for enforcement of statutory rights in an ordinary civil action in the district courts, where there is obviously no functional justification for denying the jury trial right, a jury trial must be available if the action involves rights and remedies of the sort typically enforced in an action at law.
>
> We think it is clear that a damages action under §812 is an action to enforce "legal rights" within the meaning of our Seventh Amendment decisions. . . .

Id. at 194-195.

In Atlas Roofing Co. v. Occupational Safety & Health Review Commn., 430 U.S. 442 (1977), the Court rejected a seventh amendment defense to administrative imposition of monetary penalties for regulatory violations. The Court invoked the distinction between private rights and public rights, and asserted:

> At least in cases in which "public rights" are being litigated — e.g., cases in which the Government sues in its sovereign capacity to enforce public rights created by statutes within the power of Congress to enact — the Seventh Amendment does not prohibit Congress from assigning the factfinding function and initial adjudication to an administrative forum with which the jury would be incompatible.

Id. at 450.

In Granfinanciera, S.A. v. Nordberg, 492 U.S. 33 (1989), the Supreme Court directly tied the "jury trial" question to the "Article III/delegation-of-adjudication" question. The Court considered a proceeding brought by a trustee in bankruptcy in a bankruptcy (non-Article III) court to obtain money that the bankrupt company had preferentially (and therefore unlawfully) paid to a creditor just before the company went bankrupt. Is the creditor entitled to a jury trial, or may the bankruptcy court try the claim (as bankruptcy courts have traditionally done) without a jury?

The Court held (6–3) that the "preference" claim was legal in nature; moreover, to require a jury trial would not "go far to dismantle" Congress's special bankruptcy "statutory scheme." Hence, the seventh amendment requires trial by jury. Justice Brennan, writing for the Court, returned to the public right-private right distinction, but with a special twist:

> [I]f a statutory cause of action is legal in nature, the question whether the Seventh Amendment permits Congress to assign its adjudication to a tribunal that does not employ juries as factfinders requires the same answer as the question whether Article III allows Congress to assign adjudication of that cause of action to a non-Article III tribunal. For if a statutory cause of action . . . is not a "public right" for Article III purposes, then Congress may not assign its adjudication to a specialized non-Article III court lacking "the essential attributes of the judicial power." Crowell v. Benson, . . . And if the action must be tried under the auspices of an Article III court, then the Seventh Amendment affords the parties a right to a jury trial whenever the cause of action is legal in nature. Conversely, if Congress may assign the adjudication of a statutory cause of action to a non-Article III tribunal, then the Seventh Amendment poses no independent bar to the adjudication of that action by a nonjury factfinder. . . .

How can Justice Brennan cite *Crowell*? After all, *Crowell* was a case involving *private rights*, wasn't it? It was not a case between "the government and others." The answer to this question may lie in the supervision that the courts provided the *Crowell* tribunal. Or, it may lie in the fact that the Supreme Court has suddenly redefined public rights. Justice Brennan went on to say that, since *Thomas*,

> the Federal Government need not be a party for a case to revolve around "public rights." . . . The critical question, in cases not involving the Federal Government, is whether Congress, acting for a valid legislative purpose . . . created a seemingly "private" right that is so closely integrated into a public regulatory scheme as to be a matter appropriate for agency resolution with limited involvement by the Article III judiciary. . . . If a statutory right is not closely intertwined with a federal regulatory program Congress has power to enact, and if that right neither belongs to nor exists against the Federal Government, then it must be adjudicated by an Article III court. If the right is legal in nature, then it carries with it the Seventh Amendment's guarantee of a jury trial.

Justice Scalia, concurring, denounced the Court's change in the meaning of the term "public right." He said that "what we meant by public rights were not rights important to the public, or rights created by the public, but rights *of the public* — that is, rights pertaining to claims brought by or against the United States." Since no such rights were involved in this case, and since the claim was a legal one, a jury trial was required. Moreover, in Justice Scalia's view, apparently, Congress cannot delegate the adjudication of "private rights" to agencies. He said that both *Thomas* and *Schor* (decided before he joined the Court) were in "error," without "constitutional basis." He added, dissenting,

> I do not think one can preserve a system of separation of powers on the basis of . . . intuitive judgments regarding "practical effects," no more with regard to the

assigned functions of the courts, . . . than with regard to the assigned functions of the Executive. . . . This central feature of the Constitution must be anchored in rules, not set adrift in some multifactored "balancing test" — and especially not in a test that contains as its last and most revealing factor "the concerns that drove Congress to depart from the requirements of Article III." *Schor.* . . .

Questions

1. Can *Crowell*'s Compensation Commission still adjudicate claims without a jury? In Justice Brennan's view? In Justice Scalia's? Are the rights at stake there public or private rights? How can one find out?

2. Did Justice Brennan adopt a "functional" view of Article III? What, other than functional considerations, will determine whether a delegation to an agency of adjudicatory power brings the matter within the *expanded* definition of "public right"?

3. What would Justice Brandeis think of the current state of the law? Professor Bator would read separation-of-powers doctrine as permitting transfers of adjudicative power to non-Article III tribunals so long as "it can be demonstrated that there is a reasoned basis for the judgment that dispensing with Article III restrictions has an appropriate and valid purpose connected with the achievement of a valid legislative program." Bator, The Constitution as Architecture, 65 Ind. L.J. 233, 258 (1990). Is this standard standardless? *Is* it unconnected with the Constitution? Would this standard adequately deal with the Supreme Court's expressed fear, that Congress might enact "wholesale" transfers of judicial power to non-Article III courts?

Concluding Note

In this chapter we have discussed the relation between the administrative state and Articles I, II, and III of the Constitution. It is worthwhile to ask whether the Supreme Court's analysis has been the same, or quite different, under the three articles. Consider the pessimist's view: The Court has allowed successive, large-scale departures from the constitutional settlement under intense pressure from powerful political forces and perceived practical necessities. Consider the optimist's view: The Court has kept basic faith with constitutional principles under all three articles, by using interpretive techniques that allow Congress, the president, and the federal judiciary to retain the most essential parts of their original constitutional authority under dramatically changed conditions. If the optimist's view is overstated, what doctrines are the strongest candidates for change? Would the changes make the administrative state work better or worse?

3

Administrative Discretion, Administrative Substance, and Regulatory Performance

The goal of this chapter is to explore the most fundamental criticisms of administrative procedure and administrative substance—criticisms based on the claim that agencies have excessive discretion or that they have not exercised their discretion wisely. The chapter will also survey a range of proposals aimed at improving agency performance.

It is important to see that there are two principal categories of complaints about the administrative state. The first category revolves around the fact that administrators generally have a lot of discretion. Some people think that realistically speaking, agencies are lawmakers, and that this is extremely troublesome in a system committed to checks and balances. In the view of these critics, *controls on administrative discretion* are the best or most natural solution. Here, the basic complaint is that administrative agencies, in their current form, create serious problems from the standpoint of democratic legitimacy.

The second category of complaints involves not regulatory discretion but regulatory outcomes. Here the basic complaint is that agencies have failed *to improve social or economic well-being.* Does the Environmental Protection Agency (EPA) perform its job well—for example, by significantly limiting air and water pollution and doing so at relatively low cost? Or is it sometimes subject to well-organized private groups, using environmental protection as a guise for political favors? Does the Equal Employment Opportunity Commission (EEOC) actually reduce discrimination? Has the Securities and Exchange Commission (SEC) improved or impaired the functioning of the securities market? How has the Federal Communications Commission (FCC) dealt with the new opportunities and problems created by recent developments in telecommunications? Has it helped consumers? Is it captured by broadcasters? How have its actions affected the democratic process?

Those who emphasize the perceived problem of excessive administrative discretion may or may not agree with those interested in good regulatory performance. Perhaps some agencies with broad discretionary power are performing well, in the sense that they are making life better for all or most people. Perhaps some agencies with narrowly confined authority, and little discretion, are performing badly, because they are limited by congressional instructions that reflect legislative ignorance or by the power of well-organized private groups that have influence over Congress. In this light we can see that some people think that the principal problem created by the administrative state is undue discretion and an absence of political legitimacy, whereas other people think that the principal problem is bad outcomes and bad regulation. It is possible for the two kinds of critics to agree in some areas—because agencies with a good deal of discretion are performing poorly—but they may sharply disagree in others.

A. Political Legitimacy and the Concentration of (Unchecked?) Power

The materials in the preceding chapter illustrate a basic fact: Courts have declined to impose significant constitutional checks on congressional creation of administrative agencies that combine powers traditionally distributed among the three branches that are explicitly recognized in the federal Constitution. Agencies have been permitted to exercise legislative-type power, to assume responsibility for adjudication formerly performed by courts, and to exercise prosecutorial and managerial functions while free from continuous and direct control by the chief executive. This state of affairs has created two basic difficulties at the level of constitutional or political theory.

The first difficulty is one of accountability or legitimacy. Of course administrators are not chosen by vote. Unlike legislators and the chief executive, administrators are not elected by the citizenry. Nor do they enjoy the courts' own distinctive guarantors of legitimacy of life tenure, insulation from partisan politics, and professional commitment to an ideal of principled decisionmaking. In the words of President Franklin Roosevelt's Committee on Administrative Management, they are effectively a "headless 'fourth branch'" of government. It is sometimes said that the administrative process in the United States suffers from a near-perpetual crisis of legitimacy, one that can erode public confidence in administrators and hinder the effective discharge of their duties.

During the New Deal, champions of the administrative process seemed to suppose that there was an objective "public interest" that could be ascertained and implemented by expert administrators, provided they were given generous powers. Today, there are many questions about the appropriate role of experts, and many people doubt whether "experts" can determine and execute what is in the public interest. Of course, facts and science matter a great deal; technical experts can provide a great deal of help in making good choices. Perhaps an understanding of the facts can produce broad agreement (on, for example, issues of motor vehicle safety) from people who disagree on many basic questions. But experts may have no special claim to wisdom with respect to the values at stake, and so administrative expertise can hardly be a full answer to the problem of agency legitimacy.

A second basic problem has to do with liberty. Administrative agencies combine powers previously distributed among the three traditional branches. Of course, the constitutional separation of powers among the branches of government was never intended to be watertight (see Chapter 2, section E); and the original system might be seen as one of checks and balances as well as, or more than, separation of powers. But there can be no doubt that agencies such as the Federal Trade Commission (FTC) and the National Labor Relations Board (NLRB) meld prosecuting, legislating, judging, and managing functions in a far more complete and systematic fashion than the original structure of the Constitution contemplated. One of the Framers' purposes in separating the powers of government among the various branches was to diminish the effective power that the government can exert against the citizenry—to prevent tyranny by dividing power and creating mutual constraints. In a metaphor, the original system allowed the sovereign people to pursue a strategy of "divide and conquer."

In the view of some critics, administrative agencies threaten this system of safeguards by combining powers in ways that avoid the original checks. Administrators may well have the power to exercise governmental authority so as to reallocate wealth and opportunities to their preferred specific social or economic groups. Agencies often reallocate wealth, not only directly, as in the administration of the Internal Revenue Code or the administrative allocation of scarce welfare resources such as public housing, but also indirectly, through regulatory policies that favor some consumers or firms at the expense of others. Because agency decisionmaking is sometimes not highly visible and is not directly subject to the electoral check, there is a danger that the redistributive authority of agencies will be exercised in favor of a limited group of organized interests with a special stake in an agency's policies.

Note, however, that no industrialized nation dispenses with some form of the regulatory-welfare state. In the early part of the century, James Landis wrote, "The administrative process is, in essence, our generation's answer to the inadequacy of the judicial and legislative processes." See J. Landis, The Administrative Process 46 (1938). Has not the verdict of history vindicated that view? There are at present about 90 *major* regulatory agencies in the federal government alone, and many more in state and local government. And it might be asked whether the problems of political legitimacy are in fact so serious for administrative agencies. Agencies are, after all, subject to some control from each of the three branches, and perhaps Congress is distinctly subject to the power of well-organized private interest groups. See J. Mashaw, Greed, Chaos, and Governance (1996), for an argument that often agencies, and not Congress, should make political choices.

If it is neither possible nor desirable to abolish administrative agencies and return to the tripartite frame of government celebrated in the eighteenth century, it may nonetheless be possible to serve the basic purposes of the Founders through new institutional arrangements. But how do we characterize those purposes in such a different world? And are these ideals merely anachronistic vestiges of an earlier era, wholly unrealistic today?

B. Criticisms of Administration

Few observers of the subject today share James Landis's undiluted optimism about the potential use of the administrative agency. Federal administrative agencies have been subjected to many criticisms coming from a variety of positions. Some critics complain that the process is insufficiently democratic—that it fails to reflect the Constitution's intended system of reflective deliberation among people who are accountable to the public as a whole. On this view, problems of "faction," lack of openness, and infrequent participation are major culprits. Economists are concerned with the inefficiency, waste, susceptibility to interest-group power, and shortages they see caused by many forms of regulation. Members of the business community complain of unreasonable administrative burdens, unpredictable law, excessive rigidity, and lack of coordination among agencies. Consumer groups and environmental organizations, among others, complain that regulation is ineffective, partly because agencies are "captured" by the very groups they are supposed to regulate. All this criticism centers around the charge that the agencies have failed effectively to discharge their mission of regulating given sectors of the economy in such a way as to promote the public interest. On this view, government failure follows market failure.

The chorus of criticisms should not be taken to obscure substantial success stories. The view that regulation has generally proved unsuccessful is far too crude. Consider a few examples. In the environmental arena, regulatory controls have helped to produce substantial decreases in both the levels and emissions of major air pollutants, including

sulfur dioxide, carbon monoxide, lead, and nitrogen dioxide. Lead is an especially dangerous substance, and ambient concentrations of lead have decreased especially dramatically, declining 96 percent since 1975; transportation emissions of lead decreased from
122.6 million metric tons in 1975 to 3.5 in 1986. Water pollution control has shown
significant successes as well. All sewage in the nation is treated before it is discharged, and
the treatment ordinarily brings water to a level safe for swimming. The Great Lakes are
much cleaner than they were in 1965. In 1970, about 25 percent of U.S. river miles were
safe for fishing and swimming; the number is now about 56 percent and growing. Ocean
dumping of sludge is now substantially eliminated in the United States.

Nor are successes limited to environmental protection. The risk of a fatal accident in
the workplace was reduced by 50 percent between 1970 and 1990, partly because of
workers' compensation, occupational safety and health, and other programs. Similarly,
automobile safety regulation appears to have significantly reduced deaths and serious
injuries. Automobiles are much safer for occupants, and many of the safety-improving
features of automobiles are a product of regulatory controls supported by cost-benefit
balancing. For example, the requirement that all cars have center-high mounted stop
lamps was shown to be highly effective in reducing rear-end collisions. More generally,
some observers calculate that highway fatalities would have been about 40 percent higher
in 1981 if not for governmental controls; in this view, the lives of about 34,000 passenger
car occupants were saved as a result of occupant safety standards set between 1966 and
1974. For automobile regulation in general, the ratio of benefits to costs is extremely high.
Indeed, some of the regulations pay for themselves in terms of health and related savings,
and the large number of deaths actually prevented is, of course, a bonus.

Most broadly, studies of the costs and benefits of regulatory initiatives show that a
number of other measures have produced health, safety, and other benefits at especially
low costs. Of course, it is not clear that government regulation in its current form passes a
global cost-benefit test. There is much indeterminacy in the data, and certainly many
regulatory efforts have been futile, self-defeating, counterproductive, or much worse.
Every detailed study shows a number of regulations that have saved lives at comparatively
low cost; see Table 3-1 on pages 151-152.

Regulatory successes are not limited to the areas of safety and health. The most
important civil rights initiative—the Voting Rights Act of 1965—appears to have broken
up the white monopoly on electoral processes in a number of states. Only two years after
passage of the act, the number of registered blacks in the 11 southern states increased
from 1.5 million to 2.8 million—an increase of nearly 90 percent. Though the evidence
is more disputed, many people argue that the Civil Rights Act of 1964 has also had important beneficial consequences. A careful study finds that the act had major effects on the
manufacturing sector in South Carolina. "Suddenly in 1965 the black share in employment begins to improve when Title VII legislation becomes effective and the Equal
Employment Opportunity Commission begins to press textile firms to employ blacks and
when Executive Order 11246 forbids discrimination by government contractors at the
risk of forfeit of government business." Heckman & Payner, Determining the Effect of
Federal Antidiscrimination Policy on the Economic Status of Blacks: A Study of South
Carolina, 79 Am. Econ. Rev. 138, 143 (1989). Many other studies reach a broadly similar
conclusion: that the federal effort to redress race and sex discrimination has had many
favorable consequences.

Our focus in this chapter, however, is on problems of administrative regulation, and
the excerpts that follow are intended to give a sampling of views on agency "failure." You

should assess critically the differences of opinion among the excerpts on whether the agencies have failed, the nature of the failure, and the locus of responsibility for failure. You should also consider what solutions might remedy these perceived failures. In particular, is failure attributable to the anomalous constitutional position of the agencies, which exercise combined powers without formal accountability? Can failure be eliminated by altered institutional arrangements? Do criticisms of administrative failure simply reflect a disagreement with Congress's policy judgments in directing agencies to deal with social problems, in which case the only remedy is to change those congressional policies through the political process?

R. Noll, Regulation After Reagan

12(3) Reg. 13-20 (1988)

Economists generally entered the study of regulation with the naive view that regulatory institutions were set up for the purpose of rectifying market failures. Unfortunately, and almost without exception, the early empirical studies—those commencing in the late 1950s and continuing into the 1970s—found that the effects of regulation correlated poorly with the stated goals of regulation. By the early 1970s the overwhelming majority of economists had reached consensus on two points. First, economic regulation did not succeed in protecting consumers against monopolies, and indeed often served to create monopolies out of workably competitive industries or to protect monopolies against new firms seeking to challenge their position. Second, in circumstances where market failures were of enduring importance (such as environmental protection), traditional standard-setting regulation was usually a far less effective remedy than the use of markets and incentives (such as emissions taxes or tradable emissions permits). . . .

THE PERFORMANCE EXPLANATION

. . . I will offer some key generalizations that reflect the consensus of the research literature on the effects of recent regulatory reforms.

- Economic deregulation reduced prices and costs in literally every industry in which it was tried. Prices fell because competition replaced monopoly and, more importantly, because deregulation caused efficient firms to grow at the expense of inefficient ones, and led some inefficient firms to improve.
- Economic deregulation did not cause every price to fall, because under regulation some prices purposely had been set below costs—with losses offset by higher prices elsewhere. Price increases are more likely to occur in rural areas and small towns, which historically had been favored in regulatory price setting.
- In only a few cases did a truly competitive market replace regulation. AT&T probably still retains market power in some long-distance markets and in some lines of telecommunications equipment, and the hub-and-spoke structure of the airline industry probably gives some airlines market power in their major hubs. In most cases, however, if the extent of competition is less than perfect, the reason is generally that policy interventions are not permitting as much competition as would emerge naturally. Remaining federal and, especially, state regulation limits competition, and other federal policies (such as those governing airport

construction, the awarding of landing and take-off slots, and merger approvals in the airline industry) have not accommodated healthy competition.

- In no case was overall industry safety or service quality adversely affected by economic deregulation. Nonetheless, some specific problems did emerge. In some cases the transition to less regulation caused intermittent reductions in service quality for some customers; in other cases the quality effect was ambiguous. For example, the replacement of less frequent jet service by more frequent commuter-aircraft service changed the nature of the product for some consumers in small cities, probably leaving some better off and others worse off, depending on their valuations of flight frequency in relation to comfort and the additional safety of larger airlines and aircraft.

- A substantial portion of the reductions in prices and costs following deregulation was due to the weakening of labor unions and the lowering of wages. Total employment in the former Bell System was cut, especially by the divested AT&T, in order to improve the system's competitive position in telecommunications. In transportation the power of unions was vastly undercut by the removal of entry barriers and the emergence of discount carriers, many of which are nonunion. Overall, however, deregulation increased employment by lowering prices and raising sales volume. More people are being employed at generally lower wages.

- In the environmental, health, and safety arena, especially during the 1980s, there has been little if any improvement in measures of environmental quality and illness and injuries related to products and workplaces. With very few exceptions, performance measures have changed only a few percent, one way or the other, over the past decade. The optimistic interpretation is that regulation arrested a deterioration in these measures. Advocates of these programs clearly sought more than this, however, and they express growing dissatisfaction with the progress that has been made.

- Environmental, health, and safety regulation has imposed substantial costs on a few key industries, such as chemicals, electric utilities, steel, and automobiles. These costs do not, however, loom large with respect to the performance of the national economy as evaluated with core macroeconomic indexes, such as productivity, balance of trade, employment, or inflation. From the vantage of economic analysis, regulatory effort in the environmental, health, and safety arena appears to be badly misallocated. Some pollutants and hazards are far more intensely regulated than others that are more serious. And some industries are regulated far more intensely than others that produce exactly the same pollutants. As a result, society could have spent far less to achieve the amount of progress that has been made or, alternatively, could have made far more progress at the costs that have been incurred. . . .

THE REAL EXPLANATION: POLITICS AS USUAL

[E]xtensive economic deregulation has taken place and there has been a noteworthy expansion of economic approaches to social regulation. With the single exception of the CAB [Civil Aeronautics Board], however, all of the regulatory institutions in existence in 1970 still exist today. The same economic interests still participate in the administrative processes of regulatory agencies and still lobby the members of Congress who sit on the relevant oversight committees. Even the airlines have the U.S. Department of Transportation, the House Energy and Commerce Committee, and the Senate Commerce, Science, and Transportation Committee, all of which still play important roles in shaping the industry. Consequently, all of the political forces that gave rise to regulation are still in place, leaving industries, unions, and favored communities the same forum for pleading their cases. The real test of regulatory reform now and in the years ahead is whether these interests will be able to undo what has been done thus far. . . .

[F]urther success will require that the next administration adopt a holistic approach to regulatory reform: actively pursuing policies to ease the transition to a less regulated economy, working with a bipartisan congressional coalition for regulatory reform, and taking effective actions to make certain that inefficient federal policies are not simply replaced by equally undesirable state regulations. All of this will require that the new administration adopt a coherent, broadly consistent approach to regulation, regarding it as something more than a group of discrete and unrelated specific problems to be solved by writing a better regulation.

C. R. Sunstein, Free Markets and Social Justice
322-326 (1997)

How has the American system of public law actually performed? Has it promoted economic prosperity and democratic governance? We now have considerable evidence on both scores. There have been many successes, and it would be a mistake to think that regulation has entirely failed in achieving its purposes. But much of the overall story is dismaying.

INEFFICIENCY

The current system is extraordinarily inefficient. The annual net cost of regulation has been estimated at between $400 and $500 billion. There is no question that we need not spend this amount for the gains we actually receive. A 1995 study suggests that better allocations of existing expenditures could save an additional 60,000 lives at no increased cost, and that with better allocations, we could save the same number of lives we now save with $31 billion in annual savings.

So-called economic regulation—calling for price and entry controls in various sectors of the economy—produced unnecessary and exorbitant costs for American consumers. Thus, it is estimated that airline deregulation yielded gains to airlines and travelers of about $15 billion annually. The corresponding numbers for trucking deregulation and railroad deregulation were $30 billion and $15 billion. The Natural Gas Act, which allowed government control of gasoline prices, certainly contributed to the dangerous gas shortages of the 1970s. The resulting inefficiencies led to decreases in industrial production, losses of hundreds of thousands of jobs, and reductions in the supply of gas for millions of Americans.

Nor are inefficiencies limited to the area of economic regulation. The Food and Drug Administration has delayed the entry of beneficial foods and drugs onto the market, significantly increasing risks to safety and health. The "drug lag" has been a serious problem for Americans. The EPA's fuel economy standards appear to have produced uncertain gains in light of the fact that manufacturers were in any case moving to smaller and more efficient cars; but fuel economy standards did lead to significant losses in lives as a result of producing more dangerous, lighter vehicles. The United States spent over a trillion dollars for pollution control between 1972 and 1995. Some studies suggest that alternative strategies could have achieved the same gains at less than one-quarter of the cost.

What is the cause of existing problems? A pervasive source of regulatory inefficiency in the United States is the use of rigid, highly bureaucratized "command-and-control" regulation, which dictates, at the national level, control strategies for hundreds, thousands, or millions of companies and individuals in an exceptionally diverse nation. Command-and-control regulation is a dominant part of American government in such areas as environmental protection and occupational safety and health regulation. . . .

In general, governmental specification of the "means" of achieving desired ends is a good way of producing inefficiency. Instead of permitting industry and consumers to choose the means—and thus to impose a form of market discipline on that question—government often selects the means in advance. The governmentally prescribed means is often the inefficient one. . . .

More generally, studies of the costs and benefits of regulatory programs show a crazy-quilt pattern, including both too much and too little regulation. Consider, for example, expenditures per life saved. Some programs pay for themselves in terms of health and related savings. The lives saved are purely a bonus, in the sense that they come for free. Other programs cost between $100,000 and $300,000 per life saved—surely an amount well worth spending. But still other programs cost $89 million per life saved, $92 million per life saved, even $132 million per life saved. To be sure, some disparities, even significant ones, might well be expected in a democracy. But it is difficult to believe that these differences reflect anything but interest-group power and irrationality of various sorts.

This brief summary should be sufficient to suggest that from the standpoint of efficiency, most of modern government is ill directed. There is no real effort at setting priorities. Some programs are not beneficial at all; others have unnecessary and costly side effects. We could obtain the same benefits much more cheaply.

Sometimes inefficiency in government, particularly when described by economists, seems a dry and technical matter. But the consequences of the status quo are anything but merely technical. They include a range of adverse effects on real human beings: excessively high prices, greater unemployment, lower benefits in terms of safety and health, greater mortality and morbidity, more poverty, and increased difficulty for American companies and workers attempting to compete in an increasingly international market.

DEMOCRACY

The New Deal aspired not only to greater efficiency but also to more in the way of democracy. The New Dealers hoped for a system in which citizens and representatives, operating through responsive but expert organs, would make deliberative decisions about the basic system of public law. In place of the undemocratic systems of common law ordering and judge-made constitutionalism, new regulatory institutions would be subject to political will and carry out public instructions. The new regime was to combine a high degree of accountability with a high degree of deliberation.

In practice, this democratic aspiration has often been defeated. People rarely have enough information to participate at all, or at all well, in the processes of government. The extraordinary concentration of regulation in Washington has hampered democratic deliberation both in localities and in the private sphere. The technical complexity of underlying issues has contributed to the power of well-organized interest groups over the regulatory process. Thus the New Deal has helped bring about a kind of Madisonian nightmare of government by faction.

Democratic failures are widespread. [Command-and-control regulation], for example, is severely deficient from the standpoint of a well-functioning political process. That approach ensures that citizens and representatives will be focusing their attention not on what levels of reduction are appropriate, but instead on the largely incidental and nearly impenetrable question of what technologies are now available. Because of its sheer complexity, this issue is not easily subject to democratic resolution and is not the relevant one for democratic politics, which is the appropriate degree and nature of environmental protection. . . .

The focus on the question of "means" also tends to increase the power of well-organized private groups, by allowing them to press environmental and regulatory law in the service of their own parochial ends. These ends include, for example, the promotion of ethanol, which is helpful to corn farmers though not necessarily to environmental protection; other fuels might well be preferable on environmental grounds. Ends favored by parochial interests also include governmentally compelled use of coal scrubbers, which is helpful to eastern coal though not necessarily to air quality. The use of already-clean coal might well be better. . . .

. . . Centralization at the national level diminishes opportunities for citizen participation. It promotes intense and unproductive struggles among well-organized factions. Education of citizens about the key issues—risk levels and risk comparisons—is at best episodic. In their capacity as consumers, citizens, workers, or users of the air and water, people are inadequately informed of the risks that they face. Public attention tends to be focused on particular incidents, which are gripping and sensationalistic but often misleading.

In these circumstances, it is difficult indeed to ensure that citizens and representatives will be involved in deliberating about different strategies for achieving social goals, or (what is more important) in identifying those goals in the first place. By directing attention to means, the current system also creates powerful incentives for interest groups to ensure that they are favored in the legislature or the bureaucracy. Thus current institutions cannot carry out Roosevelt's goal of linking the Hamiltonian commitment to an energetic executive with the Jeffersonian belief in self-government. The democratic aspirations of the New Deal have failed.

W. Kip Viscusi, Fatal Tradeoffs
249-251, 263-265, 285 (1992)

. . . Here I will review the guidelines for reform that emerged in the economic literature and policy debates of the 1970s. These guidelines will serve as the reference point for assessing the regulatory reforms of the 1980s.

First, economists recognized that there were often legitimate market failures that needed to be addressed. Environmental problems involve a classic case of externalities. Moreover, imperfect consumer and worker information may impede market provision of safety. Market forces involving risk are not, however, completely absent. A series of studies . . . documented labor market compensation for risk on the order of several hundred thousand dollars per statistical death for workers who had selected themselves into very high-risk jobs to as much as several million dollars per death for the more typical blue-collar worker. Because of these constructive market forces, it is essential to ascertain that there is a legitimate market failure before determining that a regulation is warranted.

The second general principle is that one should obtain an assessment of the costs and benefits of the regulatory policy. Initially, the concern was with regulatory costs. The steel and automobile industries, for example, were hit particularly hard. Since these basic industries were in decline and threatened by foreign competition, ensuring that excessive government regulation was not the causal factor in their demise became a prominent concern.

Regulatory impacts should, however, be measured correctly. In assessing these costs and benefits, what matters is the value of the expected payoffs that will accrue to society. One should use the mean of the probability distribution rather than focusing on worst-case scenarios or, as many agencies do, the upper end of the 95 percent confidence interval for the risk level.

Although assessing the impacts of policies is an essential prerequisite to sound policy choice, one must then utilize this information to select among policy alternatives. The third regulatory principle is that policy choices should be cost-effective. Available policy alternatives that can achieve the same benefits at less cost are preferable. Another example of an inefficient regulatory alternative was the imposition of a requirement for a technological solution to air pollution problems by mandating the installation of scrubbers, whereas a lower-cost method of achieving the same benefits by altering the type of coal used would have been sufficient.

A class of regulatory options viewed as being superior to existing regulations on cost-effectiveness grounds is that of performance-oriented alternatives. Performance standards for the guarding of machines, for example, would not only be less costly than OSHA specification standards but also would pertain to more types of machine designs, thus reducing machine guarding risks for a larger number of workers. Similarly, use of protective equipment to avert hearing loss resulting from excessive noise exposures would impose considerably lower compliance costs than changing the workplace environment. Although there are legitimate debates regarding the feasibility of such performance-oriented alternatives, due to the difficulties of monitoring compliance, the economic critics of regulatory agencies have urged these agencies to at least assess the merits of performance-oriented alternatives.

A fourth regulatory reform principle is that there should be an appropriate balancing of the benefits and costs of policies. Strict adherence to efficiency guidelines suggests that a benefit-cost test would be applicable, but the oversight process did not formally adopt this criterion until the 1980s. Even where a precise calculation of benefits and costs is not feasible, agencies should consider the overall merits of the policy and pursue only those policies that they judge to be in society's best interests. . . .

By far the most important need was for fundamental legislative reform to incorporate the opportunity for such balancing of cost and benefit considerations in the design of regulatory policy. Such changes are fundamental to any reform effort, since the legislative mandates will limit the degree to which regulatory oversight activities will be able to influence the policies of the regulatory agencies. Short-term efforts to alter regulatory policies by slowing the pace of regulation or altering the enforcement effort will not yield long-run changes in the regulatory approach. Ultimately, the agency's enabling legislation will determine the shape of these policies. . . .

[M]any of the regulations in the 1980s clearly pass a benefit-cost test. The policies of the FAA appear to be outstanding bargains. Their low costs-per-life-saved figures should not, however, be viewed as a regulatory success. A main contributor to this low figure is that the FAA valued the lives saved in airplane crashes using the present value of the lost earnings of the accident victims. This approach underestimates the value of life of airplane passengers by more than an order of magnitude. In one case, the FAA dismissed repairs of the DC-10 as being not worthwhile because of the low level of the risk, whereas a proper benefit-cost calculation indicates that the risk reductions were clearly desirable. Application of value-of-life principles and benefit-cost analysis would have led an agency to be more aggressive.

The cutoff in Table 3-1 for policies with benefits in excess of their costs is probably just below the regulation of benzene/fugitive emissions, with a cost per life saved of $2.8 million. Policies below that regulation in the table would not pass a benefit-cost test unless they protect populations with comparatively high values per life. OMB rejected none of the policies with lower costs per life, whereas they rejected eight policies with higher costs per life. OMB blocked some of the particularly inefficient regulations, although several regulations with very low efficacy were enacted. Indeed, the minimum tradeoff threshold for OMB to reject a regulation is quite high. None of the regulations in Table 3-1 with costs per life saved below $142 million were rejected. OMB's efficacy is apparently limited to the most extreme instances of regulatory excess. . . .

TABLE 3-1
The Cost of Various Risk-Reducing Regulations per Life Saved

Regulation	Year and status	Agency	Initial annual risk[a]	Annual lives saved	Cost per life saved (millions of 1984 $)
Pass benefit-cost test:					
Unvented space heaters	1980 F[b]	CPSC	2.7 in 10^5	63.000	$.10
Oil and gas well service	1983 P	OSHA-S	1.1 in 10^3	50.000	.10
Cabin fire protection	1985 F	FAA	6.5 in 10^8	15.000	.20
Passive restraints/belts	1984 F	NHTSA	9.1 in 10^5	1,850.000	.30
Underground construction	1989 F	OSHA-S	1.6 in 10^3	8.100	.30
Alcohol and drug control	1985 F	FRA	1.8 in 10^6	4.200	.50
Servicing wheel rims	1984 F	OSHA-S	1.4 in 10^5	2.300	.50
Seat cushion flammability	1984 F	FAA	1.6 in 10^7	37.000	.60
Floor emergency lighting	1984 F	FAA	2.2 in 10^8	5.000	.70
Crane suspended personnel platform	1988 F	OSHA-S	1.8 in 10^3	5.000	1.20
Concrete and masonry construction	1988 F	OSHA-S	1.4 in 10^5	6.500	1.40

Regulation	Year and status	Agency	Initial annual risk[a]	Annual lives saved	Cost per life saved (millions of 1984 $)
Hazard communication	1983 F	OSHA-S	4.0 in 10^5	200.000	1.80
Benzene/fugitive emissions	1984 F	EPA	2.1 in 10^5	0.310	2.80
Fail benefit-cost test:					
Grain dust	1987 F	OSHA-S	2.1 in 10^4	4.000	5.30
Radionuclides/ uranium mines	1984 F	EPA	1.4 in 10^4	1.100	6.90
Benzene	1987 F	OSHA-H	8.8 in 10^4	3.800	17.10
Arsenic/glass plant	1986 F	EPA	8.0 in 10^4	0.110	19.20
Ethylene oxide	1984 F	OSHA-H	4.4 in 10^5	2.800	25.60
Arsenic/copper smelter	1986 F	EPA	9.0 in 10^4	0.060	26.50
Uranium mill tailings, inactive	1983 F	EPA	4.3 in 10^4	2.100	27.60
Uranium mill tailings, active	1983 F	EPA	4.3 in 10^4	2.100	53.00
Asbestos	1986 F	OSHA-H	6.7 in 10^5	74.700	89.30
Asbestos	1989 F	EPA	2.9 in 10^5	10.000	10^4.20
Arsenic/glass manufacturing	1986 R	EPA	3.8 in 10^5	0.250	142.00
Benzene/storage	1984 R	EPA	6.0 in 10^7	0.043	202.00
Radionuclides/ DOE facilities	1984 R	EPA	4.3 in 10^6	0.001	210.00
Radionuclides/ elem. phosphorous	1984 R	EPA	1.4 in 10^5	0.046	270.00
Benzene/ethylben- zenol styrene	1984 R	EPA	2.0 in 10^6	0.006	483.00
Arsenic/low arsenic copper	1986 R	EPA	2.6 in 10^4	0.090	764.00
Benzene/maleic- anhydride	1984 R	EPA	1.1 in 10^6	0.029	820.00
Land disposal	1988 F	EPA	2.3 in 10^8	2.520	3,500.00
EDB	1989 R	OSHA-H	2.5 in 10^4	0.002	15,600.00
Formaldehyde	1987 F	OSHA-H	6.8 in 10^7	0.010	72,000.00

[a]Annual deaths per exposed population. An exposed population of 103 is 1,000, 104 is 10,000, etc.

[b]F, P, or R = Final, proposed, or rejected rule.

Source: John F. Morrall III (1986), p. 30. These statistics were updated by John F. Morrall III via unpublished communication with the author, July 10, 1990.

   The ultimate objective of social regulation policies is to influence health, safety, and environmental outcomes. Assessing the impact of the regulatory activities of the 1980s is not straightforward. Some of the ultimate costs of these regulations have not been fully transmitted throughout the economy. This is particularly true for situations involving noncompliance, phased schedules for compliance to accommodate industries in economic hardship, and regulations promulgated in the 1980s but with increasingly stringent requirements being imposed over time. A second complicating factor is that regulation is not the only influence on safety and environmental outcomes. Safety risk levels of all kinds have been declining throughout the century. As society has become wealthier, our preferences for safety are enhanced. Ideally, we would like to distinguish the effects of government regulation from the trends that otherwise would have taken place in the absence of regulation.

   Table 3-2 provides a summary of several death risk trends. One can view 1970 as marking the beginning of the decade of safety and environmental regulation. All three sets of death rates in Table 3-2 have been in decline since the 1930s. The rate of decline for work accidents was somewhat greater in the 1980s than in previous decades, while the rate of decline in motor vehicle accidents is a bit higher than in the 1970s. The 1980s rate of decline in home accidents, which reflects the activities of the CPSC and the FDA, was almost identical to that in the 1970s. Overall, death rates continued to drop in the 1980s at roughly the same pace as in previous decades. . . .

T. Tengs & J. Graham, The Opportunity Costs of Haphazard Social Investments in Life-Saving, Risks, Costs, and Lives Saved

167, 172-174, 176 (R. Hahn ed., 1996)

   . . . How many lives could we save if we were to spend the same amount of money but invest it in those interventions that, taken together, would save the greatest number of lives possible? Results indicate that if we hold investments constant at $21.4 billion and make funding decisions so as to maximize lives saved, we could save a total of 117,000 lives annually. That represents an additional 60,200 lives saved, or about twice as many

TABLE 3-2
Principal Death Risk Trends

	Annual rate of increase in death rates		
	Work (per 100,000 population)	Home (per 100,000 population)	Motor vehicle (per 100,000 population)
1930-1940	−1.8	−0.2	−3.3
1940-1950	−2.3	−2.2	−4.0
1950-1960	−2.8	−2.1	−3.5
1960-1970	−1.2	−1.7	−0.8
1970-1980	−1.6	−2.7	−3.4
1980-1990	−3.2	−2.4	−4.3

Source: Calculations by the author using death-rate data from the National Safety
    Council (1988), pp. 14-15, 70-71.

lives saved relative to the status quo. To accomplish those gains, we could simply invest in all interventions costing less than the marginal cost per life value of $7.57 million and in none of the interventions costing more than $7.57 million. On average, we would spend $183,000 per life saved.

By maximizing "lives saved," we are treating all premature deaths as equally undesirable, regardless of when they occur. Suppose that we instead took into account the age of death and considered the years of life that are saved when a premature death is averted. To do this, we substitute "years of life saved" as our measure of survival gains, so that when we avert the death of a forty-year-old who would have lived to age seventy-seven, we save approximately thirty-seven years of life. Here, results indicate that for $21.4 billion we could save 1,230,000 years of life annually. That represents an additional 636,000 life-years over the status quo, and we could achieve that result by investing in all interventions costing less than $607,000 per year of life saved. On average, we would spend $17,400 per year of life saved.

Next, we consider the question, How little could we spend while still maintaining our present level of survival benefits? Results indicate that if we hold life-years saved constant at 592,000 or lives saved constant at 56,700 and make funding decisions so as to minimize expenditures, we could save about $31.1 billion over the status quo. In fact, because there are many untapped investment opportunities that save both lives and money, the result would be a net monetary savings. That is, not only would we save the $21.4 billion that we are currently spending, but another $10 billion—all while maintaining our present level of survival benefits. . . .

This analysis demonstrates that retaining our present pattern of investments in the 185 life-saving interventions considered here results in the loss of $31.1 billion, 636,000 life-years, or 60,200 lives every year. That is, we could more than double the life-saving potential of our current investments. Alternatively, we could maintain our present level of risk reduction and, in addition, save money. . . .

S. Breyer, Breaking the Vicious Circle

10-11, 18-23 (1993)

Three serious problems currently plague efforts to regulate small, but significant, risks to our health. I call these problems *tunnel vision* (or "the last 10 percent"), *random agenda selection*, and *inconsistency.* . . .

Tunnel vision, a classic administrative disease, arises when an agency so organizes or subdivides its tasks that each employee's individual conscientious performance effectively carries single-minded pursuit of a single goal too far, to the point where it brings about more harm than good. In the regulation of health risks, a more appropriate label is "the last 10 percent," or "going the last mile." . . .

The resources available to combat health risks are not limitless. Consider such present-system cost estimates as a *New York Times* survey of experts predicting that total toxic waste cleanup costs will mushroom to $300-700 billion, a university study suggesting various toxic site cleanup costs of $245-700 billion, a Mitre Corporation estimate of total Superfund cleanup costs of as much as $1 trillion, and a Department of Energy estimate of its (quite separate) nuclear site cleanup costs of $240 billion. Compare these numbers with the total of $100-120 billion annually the federal government now spends to protect all aspects of the environment. If we take the $9.3 million spent on the New Hampshire waste dump cleanup as an indicator of the general problem of high costs in trying for that "last 10 percent" ($9.3 million times 26,000 toxic waste dumps is $242 billion), we have an answer to the question, "Does it matter if we spend too much over-insuring our safety?" The money is not, or will not be, there to spend, at least not if we want to address more serious environmental or social problems: the need for better prenatal care, vaccinations, and cancer diagnosis, let alone daycare, housing, and education. For example, one study suggests that vaccinating 18-month-olds against *Hemophilus* influenza Type b, the leading cause of bacterial meningitis, would save toddlers' lives at the comparatively tiny cost of $68,000 each. Similarly, a large-scale study conducted in the Netherlands found that a far-reaching mammography program would save thousands of lives at a cost of about $54,000 each. While several states have instituted limited-screening programs for breast cancer, there is no national effort to encourage and fund regular examinations. . . .

The literature also suggests a serious problem with the creation of regulatory agendas and with the establishment of rational priorities among the items that are included in those agendas. . . .

. . . In [one] report EPA managers provided their own views of proper program priority rankings and compared them with existing priorities. Subjects that risk managers ranked low, such as hazardous waste cleanup, had high funding priorities; subjects that they ranked high, such as indoor air pollution and global warming, had low funding priorities. In 1990 EPA's Science Advisory Board conducted a similar exercise and, after careful study, confirmed the risk managers' views. The general public's ranking of safety priorities is very different from these experts' views (see Table 3-3). Agency priorities and agendas may more closely reflect public rankings, politics, history, or even chance than the kind of priority list that environmental experts would deliberately create. To a degree, that is inevitable. But one cannot find any detailed federal governmental list that prioritizes health or safety risk problems so as to create a rational, overall agenda—an agenda that would seek to maximize attainable safety or to minimize health-related harms. . . .

TABLE 3-3
How the Public and EPA Rate Health Risks Associated with Environmental Problems

Public	EPA experts
1. Hazardous waste sites	Medium-to-low
2. Exposure to worksite chemicals	High
3. Industrial pollution of waterways	Low
4. Nuclear accident radiation	Not ranked
5. Radioactive waste	Not ranked
6. Chemical leaks from underground storage tanks	Medium-to-low
7. Pesticides	High
8. Pollution from industrial accidents	Medium-to-low
9. Water pollution from farm runoff	Medium
10. Tap water contamination	High
11. Industrial air pollution	High
12. Ozone layer destruction	High

Public	*EPA experts*
13. Coastal water contamination	Low
14. Sewage-plant water pollution	Medium-to-low
15. Vehicle exhaust	High
16. Oil spills	Medium-to-low
17. Acid rain	High
18. Water pollution from urban runoff	Medium
19. Damaged wetlands	Low
20. Genetic alteration	Low
21. Nonhazardous waste sites	Medium-to-low
22. Greenhouse effect	Low
23. Indoor air pollution	High
24. X-ray radiation	Not ranked
25. Indoor radon	High
26. Microwave oven radiation	Not ranked

Source: Frederick Allen, U.S. EPA, based on EPA report "Unfinished Business: A Comparative Assessment of Environmental Problems" (1987) and national public opinion polls by the Roper Organization in December 1987 and January 1988.

A final problem that the literature suggests is serious inconsistencies within and among both programs and agencies. First, agencies use different methods for estimating the effects of their regulations. Thus, a Resources for the Future expert, trying to estimate the number of cancer deaths EPA regulations might prevent, was forced to estimate about 6,400 lives saved using EPA's methods of calculation, but only about 1,400 using FDA's methods, a five-fold discrepancy.

Second, irrespective of different calculation methods, the values that regulators implicitly attach to the saving of a statistical life vary widely from one program or agency to another. OMB's 1992 study shows variations ranging from space heater regulations that save lives at a cost of $100,000 per life saved to bans on DES in cattle feed that require an expenditure of $125 million per statistical life. (OMB calculated that one minor regulation cost $5.7 trillion per life saved, which calculation probably means only that OMB thought it saved no one.) By way of comparison, statistical studies indicate that labor unions, when free to bargain about safety rules, will insist upon rules that value statistical lives saved at around $5-6 million. These estimates suggest that the nation could buy more safety by refocusing its regulatory efforts.

Third, one can find many examples of regulators' ignoring one program's safety or environmental effects upon another, which suggests a need for interprogram coordination. Proposed rules concerning disposal of sewage sludge, designed to save one statistical life every five years, would encourage waste incineration likely to cause two statistical cancer deaths annually. Rules designed to limit zinc in water raise the cost of using regular diapers, encouraging the use of disposable—and doubtfully "recyclable"—diapers, which are a major contributor to landfills. At one time, EPA's Office of Solid Waste and Emergency Response had designated trace levels of carbon tetrachloride and chloroform found in chlorofluorocarbons (CFCs) as hazardous waste, thus severely discouraging (with the threat of Superfund liability) the recycling of refrigerators, which contain CFCs, while EPA's Office of Air and Radiation was urging that refrigerators be recycled to save the ozone layer. The FDA, meanwhile, was and remains content with the use of the same CFCs in asthma inhalers. In 1989 the National Highway Traffic Safety Authority refused to make automobile fuel consumption standards less stringent, despite evidence that, by encouraging manufacturers to market smaller, less crash-resistant cars, the stringency of the regulations may have been costing hundreds of lives per year. According to Judge Stephen Williams, the NHTSA failed to address the lives-for-fuel tradeoff, instead "cowering behind bureaucratic mumbo-jumbo." Again, despite the controversies surrounding each individual example here cited, the instances are sufficient in number to produce an overall impression of an interprogram, interagency coordination problem.

Fourth, and perhaps most seriously, the regulation of small risks can produce inconsistent results, for it can cause more harm to health than it prevents. Sometimes risk estimates leave out important countervailing lethal effects, such as the effect of floating asbestos fibers on passersby or on asbestos removal workers (who, in fact, do not wear completely protective clothing). Sometimes the regulator does not, or cannot easily, take account of offsetting consumer behavior, as, for example, when a farmer, deprived of his small-cancer-risk artificial pesticide, grows a new, hardier crop variety that contains more "natural pesticides" which may be equally or more carcinogenic (99.99 percent of all pesticides in food, measured by weight, are "natural," according to one scientist, Bruce Ames).

At all times regulation imposes costs that mean less real income available to individuals for alternative expenditure. That deprivation of real income itself has adverse health effects, in the form of poorer diet, more heart attacks, more suicides. To obtain an order of magnitude, a sample of academic studies suggests, as a conservative estimate, that every $7.25 million spent on a cleanup regulation will, under certain assumptions, induce one additional fatality through this "income effect"; that a 1 percent increase in unemployment, sustained over five years, means 19,000 more heart attacks and 1,100 more suicides over that time; and that risk varies inversely with family income such that "a 1 percent change in income reduces mortality by about 0.05 percent on average." One need not take these studies as quantitatively accurate. They show only small negative income effects. Where regulation aims at large risks, this small counterproductive tendency is irrelevant; where regulation aims at tiny risks, however, these small negative offsetting consequences mean that a costly standard that seeks to save a few statistical lives more likely saves no lives at all, on balance.

Finally, the literature suggests many concrete possibilities for obtaining increased health, safety, and environmental benefits through reallocation of regulatory resources. Consider the following possible courses: advertising the cancer-causing potential of sunbathing, indoor smoke and pollution, and radon and subsidizing the creation of healthier indoor climates; encouraging changes in diet to avoid natural carcinogens; encouraging or requiring manufacturers to conduct "environmental audits." . . .

D. Schoenbrod, Power Without Responsibility
9-10, 126-129 (1993)

Delegation can shield our elected lawmakers from blame for harming the public not only when a regulatory program . . . such as the navel orange marketing order serves no legitimate public purpose, but also when a regulatory program should serve an important public purpose. Then the consequences of delegation for the public can be even greater because lawmakers can use delegation to escape blame both for failing to achieve that purpose and for imposing unnecessary costs. . . .

Congress and the president delegate for much the same reason that they continue to run budget deficits. With deficit spending, they can claim credit for the benefits of their expenditures yet escape blame for the costs. The public must pay ultimately of course, but through taxes levied at some future time by some other officials. The point is not that deficits always have bad economic consequences, but that they have the political consequence of allowing officials to duck responsibility for costs.

Likewise, delegation allows legislators to claim credit for the benefits which a regulatory statute promises yet escape the blame for the burdens it will impose, because they do not issue the laws needed to achieve those benefits. The public inevitably must suffer regulatory burdens to realize regulatory benefits, but the laws will come from an agency that legislators can then criticize for imposing excessive burdens on their constituents. Just as deficit spending allows legislators to appear to deliver money to some people without taking it from others, delegation allows them to appear to deliver regulatory benefits without imposing regulatory costs. . . .

By making impossible demands upon agency officials, statutes that delegate heap on them legal and political as well as psychological guilt. The Clean Air Act, for example, says that the law of air pollution should protect health and yet be sensitive to the economy. Similarly, statutes that delegate lawmaking authority over energy "institutionaliz[e] . . . inconsistent demands upon administrative agencies—for example, for both higher and lower gas prices and electric rates and more vigorous or more flexible regulation of coal and nuclear power." When statutes say what laws should achieve rather than what they are, agencies often cannot make law that achieves everything Congress says it should. Moreover, agencies cannot make all the laws and complete all the lawmaking procedures in the time and with the resources that Congress allows. . . .

When legislators place impossible demands on agencies, they give their constituents false hopes of cheap, effective regulatory protection. Legislators talk as if authorizing an agency to make laws to achieve popular goals is tantamount to Congress's guaranteeing the achievement of those goals. With such talk, legislators may be fooling their constituents or, still worse, fooling themselves. Regardless, the superficially rational processes that delegation launches take on a reality of their own. Lawmakers and EPA personnel speak of the planning concepts in the Clean Air Act, for example, as if they are natural objects and behave as if showing achievement of the act's goals on paper is the same as achieving them.

Wed to the official fantasy, lawmakers take actions that harm the public. As one example, the public would not have suffered the huge costs of bailing out the savings and loan associations but for the fantasy created by delegation that regulation would keep the savings and loans solvent. . . .

The savings and loan debacle is only one instance of legislators' using delegation to create illusions for which the public may well have to pay dearly. Congress guaranteed private pension plans in the expectation that such plans are generally made financially secure through agency law. Some analysts fear that the guarantees will cost the taxpayers billions of dollars. Congress will likely establish a national health plan whose financial integrity is based upon the assumption that an agency will use delegated power to reduce health care costs to an unrealistic extent.

M. Seidenfeld, A Civic Republican Justification for the Bureaucratic State

105 Harv. L. Rev. 25, 25-27 (1992)

Recently, commentators have proffered an alternative understanding of the constitutional constraints on government regulation—the "civic republican" theory of constitutional democracy. Modern civic republicans view the Constitution as an attempt to ensure that government decisions are a product of deliberation that respects and reflects the values of all members of society. Civic republicanism promises democratic government that does not exclude or coerce citizens whose backgrounds and values differ from those of mainstream society. The civic republican model rejects the pluralistic assertion that government can, at best, implement deals that divide political spoils according to the prepolitical preferences of interest groups. Instead, government's primary responsibility is to enable the citizenry to deliberate about altering preferences and to reach consensus on the common good. . . .

. . . I believe that civic republicanism provides a strong justification for the assignment of broad policymaking discretion to administrative agencies. . . . I contend that, on the whole, civic republicanism is consistent with broad delegations of political decision-making authority to officials with greater expertise and fewer immediate political pressures than directly elected officials or legislators. Moreover, given the current ethic that approves of the private pursuit of self-interest as a means of making social policy, reliance on a more politically isolated administrative state may be necessary to implement something approaching the civic republican ideal.

In sum, I view the civic republican conception as providing an essential justification for the modern bureaucratic state. This article argues that although the Congress, the president, and the courts retain an important reviewing function, having administrative agencies set government policy provides the best hope of implementing civic republicanism's call for deliberative decisionmaking informed by the values of the entire polity.

This thesis has several implications for public policy. First, it suggests that congressional and judicial efforts to limit agency discretion and thereby eliminate perceived problems with the legitimacy of agency policymaking are often misguided. Second, if administrative policy setting is to achieve the civic republican ideal, agency decisionmaking processes must proceed in a manner consistent with civic republican theory. Hence, my thesis suggests the need for numerous changes in administrative law. For example, Congress should amend the Administrative Procedure Act to require public involvement in the early stages of agency policy formulation. Congress should also require that its members and the White House staff reveal all of their interactions with agency personnel. Courts should abandon the rigid dichotomy that they draw between agency decisions of law and decisions of policy, and should review both for persuasiveness in light of pragmatic limitations. . . .

Administrative agencies—the so-called fourth branch of government—may be the only institutions capable of fulfilling the civic republican ideal of deliberative decisionmaking. Congress adheres primarily to pluralistic norms and responds most directly to factional influence. . . . [The] size, structure, and historically rooted decision-making procedures of Congress render the prospect of revitalization unlikely. Perhaps for this reason, another proponent of civic republicanism, Frank Michelman, has called upon the judiciary to define directly the values that underlie governmental policy and are embodied in law. Courts, however, are too far removed from the voice of the citizenry, and judges' backgrounds are too homogenous and distinct from those of many Americans to ensure that judicially defined policy will accord with the public values of the polity.

Administrative agencies, however, fall between the extremes of the politically overresponsive Congress and the overinsulated courts. Agencies are therefore prime candidates to institute a civic republican model of policymaking. Some recent administrative resolutions of tough policy choices illustrate the role that agencies can play. For example, although the American public, experts, and government officials all agreed that the United States should close some military bases, Congress was unable to close any, or even set the criteria for deciding which bases should be closed. Too many representatives found the prospect of a base closing in their district politically unacceptable. A special commission, however, was able to order base closings and do so in a fashion that took into account efficiency concerns, the need for national defense, and the economic dislocations in areas where bases will close.

I believe that the success achieved by the Defense Base Closure and Realignment Commission was not an anomaly. The place of administrative agencies in government—subordinate and responsible to Congress, the courts and the president—allows for the checks on agency decisionmaking that ensure politically informed discourse and prevent purely politically driven outcomes. The bureaucratic structure of administrative agencies and the processes by which they frequently decide questions of policy also foster deliberative government. Consequently, . . . the administrative state holds greater promise for a "civic republican resolution" to many questions of policy than either the judicial or legislative alternatives.

C. Alternative Remedies for Regulatory "Failure"

The problems with regulation and agency performance have spawned a host of suggestions for change or reform. Many of the cases studied in this course can be best understood as representing an effort by judges to deal with agency failures—though in doing so the judges must work within a framework of institutional and legal constraints.

Before turning to the many different legal doctrines developed as part of the judicial effort to oversee government agencies—doctrines that often concern procedure—you should consider some of the major alternative analyses of what is wrong with government regulatory agencies and how their failings might be overcome. These analyses have led to a variety of suggestions for reform, which can be roughly grouped as follows: (1) changes in substantive policy, (2) improved regulatory personnel, (3) changes in agency structure, (4) increased supervision or control over agencies, and (5) the development of new institutions.

1. Substantive Policy Change: Deregulation, Mismatch, and Economic Incentives

a. Changing Individual Programs

There are those who argue that most agency failings can be traced to the agency's legislative mandate. It has been given a job that it cannot do, or cannot do well.

(1) Deregulation

Should government engage in widespread deregulation? Many people think that many of the problems with administrative performance might be solved simply through this route. Perhaps a return to market ordering and common law principles would work far better. See generally Richard Epstein, Simple Rules for a Complex World (1996).

Consider, as a historic example, the old Civil Aeronautics Board (CAB), prior to the Airline Deregulation Act of 1978. The board was told to regulate the prices and profits of air carriers and to control entry into the industry. Yet the industry itself appeared quite competitive, consisting of ten major domestic carriers and many smaller carriers. Moreover, the economics of the industry were and are volatile. Board critics argued that there was no practical way for an agency to determine proper prices for firms in such an industry. Inevitably, the agency would have to set fixed prices that actually prevent firms from competing in price. The firms instead would compete in service, with better meals, wider seats, more frequent schedules, and emptier planes.

The result, from the consumers' point of view, was undesirable high prices. The only practical solution, according to these critics, was not to regulate at all, which is to say to operate under a framework like that of the common law—to return to a free marketplace and allow competition to determine prices, the range of service offered, and which firms offer it. Eventually Congress responded with widespread deregulation.

The first independent regulatory agency, the Interstate Commerce Commission (ICC), was abolished for related reasons; its critics believed that its principal effect was to prevent competition from operating effectively. Similarly, some have claimed that the many problems with the performance of the Federal Power Commission (FPC), the Federal Maritime Commission (FMC), and the Federal Trade Commission (FTC) stem from the fact that these agencies should not be regulating at all. The Occupational Safety and Health Administration (OSHA) has been subject to a similar set of arguments.

This school of thought advocates widespread "deregulation." In many areas, it sees the defects of government regulation as generally outweighing those of the marketplace. Government may, for example, be subject to powerful private interest groups; it may aggravate the very problem that it was meant to solve. Although unregulated workplaces or automobiles may be unsafe, regulated workplaces or automobiles, it is argued, are likely to be little safer and far more expensive to boot. In the environmental area, it is urged that "free market environmentalism," consisting of the creation of well-policed property rights, would be a substantial improvement. See T. Anderson & E. Leal, Free Market Environmentalism (1993); Adler, Free & Green: A New Approach to Environmental Protection, 24 Harv. J. L. & Pub. Poly. 653 (2001); P. Huber, Hard Green (1999).

As the last point suggests, the very term "deregulation" should be taken with many grains of salt. Any alternative to administrative regulation is likely to be another form of regulation, perhaps one policed by courts operating under traditional principles of tort, contract, and property. This is not a system lacking regulation. It is another, perhaps preferable, kind of regulatory system.

Putting this point to one side, it seems clear that greater reliance on markets would be desirable in many contexts. But it is possible to doubt whether deregulation can work as a total solution. For one thing, regulatory successes can be found in several areas, and hence the empirical findings do not always argue for deregulation. For another, there are many cases where administrative regulation seems clearly warranted by considerations of efficiency. As we have seen, collectively managed controls may also be necessary to deal effectively with problems involving "externalities" or (more accurately) transactions costs. In many areas, people seem to lack the necessary information; certainly this is a plausible judgment in areas involving risk to life and health. Cognitive and motivational defects may aggravate problems created by the sheer absence of facts.

Theoretically, some problems of air and water pollution might be handled through private liability rules administered by the courts. See Adler, supra. But there are serious difficulties in implementing such a scheme, and these difficulties suggest the need for some degree of centralized and specialized administrative direction. And in a complex industrial society permeated by technological changes with significant second- and third-order consequences, it is possible to come to the same judgment in many other fields, such as telecommunications. But see R. Epstein, supra, for an argument in favor of greater reliance on markets in telecommunication; see, in the same vein, P. Huber, Law and Disorder in Cyberspace (1997).

Those skeptical about deregulation often make arguments having little to do with economic efficiency. Some programs have redistributive goals—consider the Social Security Act, or statutes designed to help farmers—and deregulation would not, by itself, promote those goals. As we saw in Chapter 1, some regulatory statutes are founded in public aspirations or democratic judgments that reflect skepticism about private "preferences" as the criterion for law and policy. Some such statutes are rooted in noncommodity values that might be inadequately reflected in market outcomes. For example, free market environmentalism depends on the view that the market should be used for purposes of controlling environmental protection. On this view, the key question is how much people would pay for environmental amenities in their capacity as consumers. The answer to that question is taken to define people's "choices" and "values." But it is controversial to take private choices, expressed in the market domain, as definitional of choice. As consumers, people make choices that diverge from the choices they make as citizens. Market choices are limited by the available options and by the fact that each person must act as an individual. The appropriate kind and degree of environmental protection might be thought to raise issues to be discussed by citizens offering reasons for one or another view. This democratic conception of environmental protection—and of many areas of regulatory policy—competes with the market-oriented view. Consider too the context of communications regulation, where people might reasonably favor regulation that departs from their consumption choices to favor, for example, educational programming, public affairs programming, or free airtime for candidates for political office.

There are practical issues too. Existing regulatory systems have developed strong supporters among interest groups who have benefited from, or relied on, existing regulation. Hence, deregulation may not be practical even when it is desirable. Note, however, that this was said in the 1960s about much regulation of the transportation industry, which was substantially deregulated in the 1970s.

(2) Mismatch

A more cautious critique is sounded by those who blame many regulatory problems on a basic mismatch between the objective of a regulatory program and the tools used to achieve that objective. This approach attempts to classify several different types of economic problems, with which an unregulated market and a court system of private litigation allegedly cannot cope, that give rise to a demand for regulation. As we have already noted in Chapter 1, Section C.1, these include

(a) "Natural monopoly"—the need to control the prices and profits of a firm like the telephone company in an industry where it is wasteful to have more than one firm;

(b) Control of windfall profits ("rent control")—the desire to transfer large unearned windfalls, typically from producers (for example, landlords) to consumers (for example, renters);

(c) Externalities or transactions costs—the problem of a commodity or production process imposing costs (such as pollution) on the community when costs are not reflected in the price that buyers must pay for the product;

(d) Inadequate information—the inability of consumers to obtain enough information to make reasonable buying decisions;

(e) Various others—such as the need to rationalize efficiently small firms into larger production units, the need to compensate for the bad incentives that arise when the purchaser of a good (say medical care) does not herself pay for it, or the alleged if dubious need to prevent "excessive competition" or "predatory behavior."

Government has a number of weapons to deal with these problems. (1) It can attack them through more aggressive antitrust law enforcement designed to make the unregulated marketplace work more effectively. (2) It can use classic systems of regulation, which include "cost of service" ratemaking, allocation systems, or the writing of standards for products or workplaces. (3) It can impose taxes or provide subsidies designed either to transfer income or to discourage (or encourage) the use of a particular product or production process. (4) It can use systems of arbitration, or collective bargaining, or mediation to achieve agreed-on changes. (5) It can itself provide information. (6) It can itself operate a "nationalized" industry. (7) It can use moral suasion and attempt to promote voluntary or cooperative solutions.

According to the "mismatch" view, the major source of regulatory problems arises from a failure to match the weapon with the problem it is seeking to overcome. The weapon that should be selected is that which will interfere the least with the private marketplace and which will rely to the maximum feasible extent on incentives, rather than administrative rules, to cure the problem at hand. Thus, the problems of airlines or trucking might be better dealt with through increased antitrust enforcement. (This view has been accepted in the case of airlines, which were deregulated.) The problem necessitating natural gas regulation—windfall producer profits—would have been better dealt with through taxes.

Environmental problems might be ameliorated through increased use of tax, or other incentive, devices. In particular, major efforts are now being made in the environmental area to use more efficient, economically based methods of regulation. Many problems of industrial safety might be better dealt with through collective bargaining or increased information. Instead, the overuse of classic command-and-control regulatory techniques, in which administrators attempt to mandate specific private conduct in each of these areas, has led to many of the criticisms already noted. Many of the problems you will consider throughout the course fall within the mismatch matrix sketched above. You might try to determine the extent to which regulatory problems reflect a correctable mismatch. See S. Breyer, Regulation and Its Reform (1982).

Two difficulties with the mismatch approach are (1) the detailed knowledge of the industry or agency usually needed before a specific, detailed, improved mandate can be devised; and (2) the difficulty of obtaining the political consensus needed to enact major substantive change.

Government programs whose basic aim is to redistribute income or wealth have also been criticized for employing clumsy or inappropriate tools. As we have noted, regulation may be a poor way of redistributing income. The minimum wage, for example, is not a direct transfer from the rich to the poor; on the contrary, it has a complicated incidence of benefits and burdens, including, very plausibly, adverse effects on people thrown into unemployment. For a helpful, detailed discussion, see Shaviro, The Minimum Wage, the Earned Income Tax Credit, and Optional Subsidy Policy, 64 U. Chi. L. Rev. 405 (1997).

There are problems with nonregulatory redistributive programs as well. The federal government, for example, administers dozens of programs to confer benefits on various classes of beneficiaries. Sometimes these benefits take the form of cash—aid for families with dependent children, unemployment compensation, disability payments. But in many instances the benefits are distributed in kind—low-cost housing, food stamps, special educational programs for the disadvantaged, day-care facilities for working mothers, Medicaid. These often overlapping programs give rise to a vast, complex bureaucracy.

Many critics, from various political perspectives, would sweep away this system of special programs and benefits with a single system of cash payments based on income; the very poorest would get the highest payments, and payments would diminish proportionately as income rises, ceasing altogether at some legislatively fixed poverty level. Such "negative income tax" proposals would eliminate the need for many administrators and would perhaps lead to a more rational and equitable system of benefits. But the entire approach has been criticized as ignoring the special needs of various groups in the population. Moreover, the proposal has been opposed by beneficiary groups (some of whom would receive less under a negative income tax than under existing programs, especially when they are eligible for benefits under several programs), by members of Congress (many of whom have in part built their careers on specialized benefit programs), and by existing agencies (many of which would be abolished).

(3) Economic Incentives

In the last decade, a particular instance of the mismatch critique has received special attention. Many critics of regulation claim that government should switch from command-and-control to economic incentives. Government might, for example, require those who cause harm—polluters, owners of unsafe workplaces, perhaps broadcasters failing to carry out their responsibilities to the public—to pay a fee. Or government might provide licenses to those who cause harm and allow the licenses to be traded. Consider the following.

Ackerman & Stewart, Reforming Environmental Law: The Democratic Case for Economic Incentives

13 Colum. J. Env. L. 171, 172-175, 178-179, 188-190 (1988)

We propose, in short, to convince you that there *is* such a thing as a free lunch. A reform relying on market incentives is just plain better, in terms of all relevant public values, than the status quo. This is not to say, of course, that nobody will lose by the abandonment of our expensive, cumbersome and undemocratic system. The congressional committees, government bureaucracies, industry and environmental groups that have helped shape the status quo want to see it perpetuated. Nonetheless, we should not be too impressed by the "iron triangle" against change. As other efforts at regulatory reform suggest, these alliances can disintegrate with remarkable speed as their ideological underpinnings are eroded by a generation of sustained critique. Does a similar fate await environmental law? For twenty years now, we have learned how the present system fails to fulfill the brave hopes expressed by its founders in the 1960s. Rather than sticking with the old mistakes, we can do better, much better. . . .

The existing system of pollution regulation is primarily based on a best available control technology (BAT) strategy. If an industrial process generates some non-trivial risk, the responsible plant or industry must install whatever technology is available to reduce or eliminate the risk, so long as the costs of doing so will not shut down the relevant plant or industry. BAT requirements are largely determined through centralized uniform federal regulation. Under the Clean Water Act's BAT strategy, EPA adopts nationally uniform effluent limitations for some 500 different industries. A similar BAT strategy is used in the Clean Air Act for new industrial sources of air pollution, new automobile and industrial sources of toxic air pollutants. BAT strategies are also widely used in many fields of environmental regulation other than air and water pollution.

BAT was embraced by Congress and administrators in the early 1970s in order to impose immediate, readily-enforceable, federal controls on a relatively few, widespread pollutants, while avoiding widespread industrial shutdowns. Subsequent experience and analysis has demonstrated:

1. Uniform BAT requirements waste many billions of dollars annually by ignoring variations among plants and industries in the costs of reducing pollution and by ignoring geographic variations in pollution effects. A more cost-effective strategy of risk reduction could free up enormous resources for additional pollution reduction or other purposes.
2. BAT controls, and the litigation which they provoke, impose disproportionate penalties on new products and processes. A BAT strategy typically imposes far more stringent controls on new sources because there is no risk of shutdown. Also, new plants and products must run the gauntlet of lengthy regulatory and legal proceedings to win approval; the resulting uncertainty and delay discourage new investment. By contrast, existing products and processes can use the legal process to postpone or water down compliance requirements. Also, BAT strategies impose

disproportionate burdens on more productive and profitable industries because they can "afford" more stringent controls. This "soak the rich" approach penalizes growth and international competitiveness.

3. BAT controls can ensure the diffusion of established control technologies. But they do not provide strong incentives for the development of new, environmentally superior strategies and may actually discourage their development. Such innovations are essential if we are to maintain economic growth in the long run without simultaneously increasing pollution and other forms of environmental degradation.

4. BAT involves centralized, uniform determination of complex scientific, engineering and economic issues involving the feasibility of controls on hundreds of thousands of pollution sources. Such determinations impose massive information gathering burdens on administrators and provide a fertile ground for litigation, producing reams of technical data, complex adversary rulemaking proceedings and protracted judicial review. Given the high cost of regulatory compliance and the potential gains from litigation brought to defeat or delay regulatory requirements, it is often more cost effective for industry to invest in litigation rather than compliance.

5. A BAT strategy is inconsistent with intelligent priority setting. Simply regulating to the hilt whatever pollutants or problems happen to get on the regulatory agenda may preclude an agency from dealing adequately with other more serious problems that come to scientific attention later. The BAT strategy also tends to reinforce regulatory inertia. Foreseeing that "all or nothing" regulation of a given substance under BAT will involve very large administrative and compliance costs, and recognizing that resources are limited, agencies will seek to limit the number of substances on the agenda for regulatory action. . . .

A BAT system has an implicit environmental goal: achievement of the environmental quality level that would result if all sources installed BAT controls on their discharges. The usual means for implementing this goal are centralized, uniform regulations that command specific amounts of cleanup from specific polluters. When a polluter receives an air or water permit under existing law, the piece of paper does not content itself, in the manner of Polonius, with the vague advice that he "use the best available technology." Instead, the permit tries to be as quantitatively precise as possible, telling each discharger how much of each of the regulated pollutants he may discharge.

Reformers propose to build upon, and do not abandon, this basic permit system. Indeed, they have only two, albeit far-reaching, objections to the existing permit mechanism. First, existing permits are free. This is bad because it gives the polluter no incentive to reduce his wastes below the permitted amount. Second, permits are not transferable. This is bad because polluter A is obliged to cut back his own wastes even if it is cheaper for him to pay his neighbor B to undertake the extra cleanup instead.

The basic reform would respond to these deficiencies by allowing polluters to buy and sell each other's permits—thereby creating a powerful financial incentive for those who can clean up most cheaply to sell their permits to those whose treatment costs are highest. This reform will, at one stroke, cure many of the basic defects with existing command-and-control regulation. A system of tradable rights will tend to bring about a least-cost allocation of control burdens, saving billions of dollars annually. It will eliminate the disproportionate burdens that BAT imposes on new industries and more productive industries by treating all sources of the same pollutant on the same basis. It will provide positive economic rewards for the development by those regulated of environmental[ly] superior products and processes. It will . . . reduce the incentives for litigation and simplify the issues in controversy. . . .

So far we have been approaching reform in the much-maligned mode of the social engineer—offering to build you a better mousetrap, as it were, than the Rube Goldberg model now in operation. While we do not join in the fashionable disdain for such matters of "instrumental rationality," there is obviously more to political life than building efficient bureaucratic machines. The ultimate political questions involve ends, not means: How important is a healthy environment anyway? It isn't enough to say "very," since environmental quality is a very expensive good, which must compete with other precious public values as education, welfare, social security, etc. Somehow or other tough choices must be made: When should we stop pouring money into a clean environment to make room for a first-rate educational system or . . . How much is enough?

Our basic problem with the BAT system is that it discourages a serious political encounter with such questions. BAT focuses Congressional debate, as well as administrative and judicial proceedings, upon arcane technological questions which rapidly exhaust the time and energy that most politicians, let alone the larger public, are willing to spend on environmental matters. In contrast, the marketable permit system will allow the policymaking debate to take a far more intelligible shape. Rather than debating the difference between the "best available control technology" and "lowest achievable emission rate," citizens may focus upon a different question when the environmental acts come up for revision: During the next n years, should we instruct the EPA gradually to decrease (or increase) the number of pollution rights by x percent? Environmentalists will, of course, argue for big reductions; others, who are more impressed with the costs of control, for smaller reductions or even selective increases. But at least the Congressional debate would be encouraged to focus upon the fundamental question: Speaking broadly, do the American people believe existing environmental objectives to be too ambitious (in which case Congress should increase the number of rights) or do we think that we should further cut back on pollution (by cutting back on the number of rights)?

There is, of course, no single technocratic answer to this question. That's precisely why it should be *the* focus of political debate. The great virtue of the marketable permit program is that it puts the question in an operational form accessible to the general public.

An analogy from a very different policy area may be instructive. Imagine that the Labor Department refused to report an Unemployment Rate each month. Instead, when it was asked about the employment situation, it inundated its audience with stories about how workers in one or another industry might be displaced by one or another technology. While such stories are informative, wouldn't there be a great danger that the general public, and Congress, would miss the forest for the trees? The preeminent question, after all, that generalist decisionmakers can and should answer is how much overall unemployment is tolerable. And for this purpose, the unemployment rate functions as a key control variable. The same holds true in environmental policy: a vote on a proposal to change the overall number of pollution permits would be a vehicle for the democratic formulation of policy superior to any generated by the existing BAT regulatory system. . . .

Should Congress amend the Administrative Procedure Act (APA) so as to require, or permit, agencies to use economic incentives instead of command-and-control regulation? Consider the following proposal: "Notwithstanding any other provision of law, agencies shall be permitted [or required] to use economic incentives or other more flexible, cost-effective means of achieving regulatory goals." Some people fear that a provision of this kind would enable well-organized private groups to fend off even desirable regulation. They also suggest that the supporters of economic incentives understate the administrative burden that incentives impose on regulators—and overstate the problems introduced by command-and-control. See Latin, Ideal Versus Real Regulatory Efficiency, 37 Stan. L. Rev. 1267 (1985); for an overview, see Mintz, Economic Reform of Environmental Protection, 15 Harv. Envtl. L. Rev. 149 (1991).

Closely related to economic incentives are proposals for "contractual" solutions, which would enable regulators to waive regulatory requirements in return for an agreement, by a firm or a group of firms, to achieve the same regulatory goals in their own way. In the environmental area, for example, an industry might be permitted to "contract out" of a statutory requirement so long as it is able to provide the same, or more, in the way of environmental improvement. A popular book—in fact a surprise bestseller—pointed in this direction by suggesting that rigid law is preventing the regulatory and private sectors from devising commonsense methods for achieving social goals. See P. Howard, The Death of Common Sense: How Law Is Suffocating America (1995). The basic argument has received attention in high circles. See Al Gore, Common Sense Government (1995).

b. Generic Efforts to Bring about Substantive Reform

Several generic proposals would encourage substantive reform and, in particular, substantive change toward better informed or less restrictive methods of regulation. These proposals are of three sorts: (1) those that require cost-benefit analysis and/or comparative risk rankings; (2) those that encourage the agencies to adopt more competitive or less restrictive proposals by imposing an "impact statement" requirement; and (3) those that encourage Congress and the president to examine regulatory programs individually and in detail.

(1) Cost-Benefit Analysis, Least Burdensome Alternatives, and Comparative Risk Rankings

Many critics of the regulatory state, building on the problems discussed above, have argued that all agencies should be required to engage in cost-benefit analysis. For an overview, see Cost-Benefit Analysis (Matthew D. Adler & Eric Posner eds. 2001). Critics have also argued that agencies charged with risk regulation should rank risks, so as to engage in more sensible priority-setting. Some such proposals have been accompanied by requirements of "least burdensome" or "least restrictive" means (such as economic incentives). For an overview of such proposals, see C. R. Sunstein, Free Markets and Social Justice 348-381 (1997).

Cost-benefit requirements have been urged on economic, democratic, and what we might call "cognitive" grounds. The economic argument is that such requirements will (by definition) produce greater efficiency. The democratic argument is that the effects of regulation are often obscure, and a public catalogue of effects, under the rubric of cost-benefit analysis, can promote openness and visibility and give both the public and affected groups a clearer sense of what is at stake. The "cognitive" ground is that people have a hard time thinking sensibly about risks, and about the consequences of attempting to control them. In this view, cost-benefit analysis is a way of overcoming the cognitive difficulties and of ensuring that all of the consequences of regulation are placed before public officials. See Williams, Squaring the Vicious Circle, 53 Ad. L. Rev. 257 (2000); C.R. Sunstein, Risk and Reason (2002). Indeed, the emergence of the "cost-benefit state" seems to be a response to these economic, democratic, and cognitive concerns, at least for those who seek to use economic analysis to ensure better decisions.

Consider the following much-discussed language from a late draft of a 1996 Senate reform proposal, one that came quite close to enactment:

(a) The requirements of this section shall supplement, and not supersede, any other decisional criteria otherwise provided by law.

(b) [N]o final major rule . . . shall be promulgated unless the agency head publishes in the Federal Register a finding that

(1) the benefits from the rule justify the costs of the rule;

(2) the rule employs to the extent practicable flexible reasonable alternatives [that is, economic incentives] . . . ;

(3)(A) the rule adopts the least cost alternative . . .

(B) if scientific, technical, or economic uncertainties or nonquantifiable benefits . . . make a more costly alternative . . . appropriate and in the public interest and the agency head provides an explanation of those considerations, the rule adopts the least cost alternative of the reasonable alternatives necessary to take into account such uncertainties or benefits; and

(4) if a risk assessment is required . . .

(A) the rule is likely to significantly reduce the human health, safety, and environmental risks to be addressed; or

(B) if scientific, technical, or economic uncertainties or nonquantifiable benefits . . . preclude making the finding of subparagraph (A), promulgating the final rule is nevertheless justified for reasons stated in writing accompanying the rule. . . .

Various provisions of this kind have frequently been debated in Congress, and some version may be enacted before long.

Consider the following view.

J. Graham, Making Sense of Risk: An Agenda for Congress, in Risks, Costs, and Lives Saved

183, 183-185, 192-193, 195, 199-200 (R. Hahn ed., 1996)

OVERVIEW

The American people are suffering from what can be called "a syndrome of paranoia and neglect" about potential dangers to their health, safety, and the environment. This leads to a paradox that is becoming increasingly recognized. Large amounts of resources are devoted to slight or speculative dangers while substantial and well-documented dangers remain unaddressed. . . .

. . . We are paranoid in the sense that we devote large amounts of resources and attention to alleged dangers that are speculative (at best) and probably small (or even nonexistent). Examples of "overblown" hazards include soil and groundwater contamination at many abandoned hazardous waste sites, the pesticide residues on fruits and vegetables purchased in grocery stores, the benzene in the ambient air of urban and rural communities, and the residual chloroform found in drinking water after disinfection of water supplies through chlorination. None of those hazards constitutes a major public health problem, but the media and government agencies treat them as if they are.

Accompanying that paranoia is a disturbing degree of tolerance of well-documented and substantial dangers to public health and environmental quality. Examples of "neglected" hazards include violence in families and communities, deteriorating lead paint in older homes, inadequate use of basic preventive health services such as childhood immunizations, influenza vaccinations, and breast cancer screening, and hazardous lifestyles characterized by smoking, abuse of alcohol, high-fat diets, lack of physical exercise, and failure to use basic safety devices such as smoke detectors and lap/shoulder belts in cars. These are all major public health problems that receive less than their fair share of attention in media stories and public policy. . . .

RISK-BASED PRIORITY SETTING

Although the federal government undertakes numerous risk analyses each year, few of them address the "big picture" questions about how resources are allocated among various dangers. For example, why are we spending billions of dollars cleaning up lead in soil at industrial sites, where the probability of childhood exposure is low, when we spend few resources to protect urban children against the neurotoxic effects of ingesting deteriorating lead paint in old homes? In the absence of risk rankings, it is difficult for Congress, regulatory agencies, and the public to gain a sense of perspective about the relative importance of each new danger reported in the mass media.

To counteract the "risk-of-the-month" syndrome, Congress should require the executive branch to periodically rank hazards according to their seriousness and the available opportunities for cost-effective reduction. If such rankings were publicly available, reporters could frame questions and write stories about how newly alleged hazards might rank in seriousness relative to hazards that have already been ranked. . . .

When policy makers work to reduce risks, they should routinely quantify the target risks and consider what benefits and costs are anticipated to result from their favored policies. Legislators in particular need to recognize the need to assess risks, benefits, and costs before passing new laws. . . .

In the 1960s and 1970s Congress was understandably hesitant to require agencies to show that every risk regulation has marginal monetary benefits in excess of marginal monetary costs. Even today, despite twenty-five years of progress in the science of quantifying and monetizing risks, it would not be wise to impose a strict net-benefit test on rulemaking.

Many human health and environmental benefits remain difficult to quantify (for example, the monetary value of slightly improved visibility on summer days). Progress has been made in methods of "contingent valuation" of health and environmental benefits, but substantial obstacles remain in the confident application of those tools to risk regulation. At the same time, many of the more subtle economic effects of rules are difficult to quantify (such as the indirect impacts on industrial productivity and innovation). In addition, fairness and justice considerations may persuade us to adopt some rules that would "flunk" a strict net-benefit test. For instance, a proposed rule that does not satisfy a net-benefit test but promises a significant reduction in the risks and costs incurred by low-income and minority populations may be worth adopting on equity grounds.

While a strict net-benefit test is ill-advised, Congress should require agencies to make a plausible case that the benefits of a rule (quantitative and qualitative) bear a reasonable relationship to costs (quantitative and qualitative). *Reasonable relationship* is intended here as an intuitive narrative standard rather than a specific mathematical balance. Of course, what one person perceives to be intuitively reasonable may seem nutty to someone else. Various federal agencies are clearly operating under different norms about what kinds of investments in risk reduction are reasonable. . . .

What, specifically, does cost-benefit analysis (CBA) entail? Proponents tend to see CBA as a commonsense method for disciplining administrative power by calling for salutary balancing, while adversaries fear that CBA is a cold-hearted way of sacrificing human health and life for the sake of mere dollars. But this is too simple. In fact, there are two sorts of criticisms that might be made of a proposed framework for evaluating governmental performance. One sort of criticism is that the framework is wrong—that it ignores certain important variables or that it is founded on an indefensible theory of value. Another sort of criticism is that it is incompletely specified—that it is vague and hence that its meaning depends on further subsidiary judgments that have yet to be offered. If a framework is incompletely specified, it might be criticized not as wrong but as indeterminate and empty.

CBA is sometimes subject to the first kind of criticism to the extent that it purports to align values in the economists' preferred way, that is, via the single metric of aggregated private willingness to pay. Based on studies of risks in the workplace, the Environmental Protection Agency has recently valued a statistical life at between $4.8 million and $6.1 million. Consider the following numbers, from the regulatory impact analysis by the EPA for its regulation of particulates and ozone, all based on efforts to identify people's willingness to pay to prevent low-level risks:

Health Endpoint	Mean WTP Value per Incident (1990 $)
Mortality	
Life saved	$4.8 million
Life year extended	$120,000
Hospital Admissions	
All Respiratory Illnesses, all ages	$12,700
Pneumonia, age >65	$13,400
COPD, age >65	$15,900
Ischemic Heart Disease, age >65	$20,600
Congestive Heart Failure, age >65	$16,600
Emergency Visits for Asthma	$9,000
Chronic Bronchitis	$260,000
Upper Respiratory Symptoms	$19
Lower Respiratory Symptoms	$12
Acute Bronchitis	$45
Acute Respiratory Symptoms (any of 19)	$18
Asthma	$32

	Mean WTP *Value per Incident*
Health Endpoint	(1990 $)
Shortness of Breath	$5.30
Sinusitis and Hay Fever	not monetized
Work Loss Days	$83
Restricted Activity Days (RAD)	
Minor RAD	$38
Respiratory RAD	not monetized
Worker Productivity	$1 per worker per 10% change in ozone
Visibility: residential	$14 per unit decrease in deciview per household
Recreational	Range of $7.30 to $11 per unit decrease in deciview per household
Household Soiling Damage	$2.50 per household

From these numbers, the EPA is able to calculate the total benefits of health improvements from new regulation. But should regulatory goods really be assessed by asking people how much they would pay for them? Is the environment, for example, to be valued by asking about private willingness to pay? See Lisa Heinzerling & Frank Ackerman, Priceless (2004); Elizabeth Anderson, Value in Ethics and Economics (1993). Critics sometimes urge that regulation should be founded on citizen judgments, not on aggregated willingness to pay. See Marc Sagoff, The Economy of the Earth (1992). Or regulation may be rooted in distributive rather than allocative goals; consider the antidiscrimination laws as possible examples. We will deal with these aspects of cost-benefit analysis in greater detail in Chapter 4, below.

Other critics argue that a problem with CBA is that it is incompletely specified. Its meaning depends on how costs and benefits are characterized and on how issues of valuation are resolved. The least ambitious possibility is that cost-benefit criteria would be understood in a less technical and more commonsensical way, as an invitation to balancing a range of variables under statutes that had formerly been thought to be absolutist and hence to forbid balancing. On this view, a cost-benefit requirement would not be so ambitious as to call for use of purely economic criteria. Its more modest goal would be to ask administrators to look at costs, or adverse effects, as well as at benefits.

L. Lave, Benefit-Cost Analysis: Do the Benefits Exceed the Costs?, in Risks, Costs, and Lives Saved

104, 120-121 (R. Hahn ed., 1996)

. . . What should [former] EPA Administrator Carol Browner infer from a benefit-cost analysis of a new automobile emissions standard? Suppose she was informed that the analysis was done by a GS-9 with a B.A. or even an M.B.A. in six weeks with no supplementary budget? The analyses produced by government agencies often contain major flaws in theory, quantification, and analysis. We economists lose our credibility and risk ridicule by requiring analyses we know will have major flaws and by insisting that the option with the greatest *measured* net benefit is the optimal choice.

Myriad other problems occur in practice. We assume that market prices reflect a purely competitive market, even in concentrated industries. We assume that tastes do not change over time. We assume that many "small" externalities do not need to be included in the analysis because they are unimportant.

A benefit-cost analysis will reveal legions of uncertainties and gaps in knowledge. If they are displayed to the reader, they might create a bias toward concluding that the analysis is unworthy of confidence and would certainly lead to a long, unreadable report. If they are not highlighted, the public might have more confidence in the analysis than is warranted. In practice, what decision makers learn from benefit-cost analysis comes from the executive summary. But no one- or two-page summary can indicate the range of uncertainties and other qualifications that a decision maker must know to use the analysis intelligently. For example, global climate change issues are so awash in uncertainty that definitive actions are not possible. Because the analysis seems to be scientific, it is often presented as if disagreeing with the results is akin to asserting that two plus two do not equal four. I conclude that in neither theory nor practice does benefit-cost analysis have a legitimate claim to be the optimizing framework that many economists believe it is; our current attempts at benefit-cost analysis are probably biased.

Although we have no conceptual difficulty with how to incorporate nonmarket effects, we do not have accurate ways to incorporate them into current analyses. In short, I conclude that the estimated net benefit of current social issues may be biased and misleading; the deficiencies stem from both theory and practice. Even if we hired the best and brightest economists and gave them essentially unlimited resources, they could not carry out a benefit-cost analysis of complicated issues that would give a confident estimate of the net social benefit.

Consider, for example, an analysis of whether to build a nuclear power plant on Long Island, New York, or whether to open northern Alaska to the production of petroleum. Benefit-cost analysis requires hundreds of value judgments, most of them small and hidden. Which environmental effects are nontrivial will depend on whether the analyst believes that rocks have the same rights as people or whether she believes that nature is nasty and cruel. Does she favor draining swamps or extolling wetland? Even if both analyses were doing their best to be objective and neutral, their analyses would look very different. Our quest for technocratic neutrality leads to the conclusion that if benefit-cost analyses differ, one must be wrong. In fact, there is a range of uncertainty concerning the extent of physical effects and a range of uncertainty concerning valuation. Benefit-cost analyses could be quite different, and yet each could be equally valid in the sense that disparities are due to value differences in structuring and monetizing, although each structure could be equally valid from a technocratic viewpoint. That recognition leads to a shocking assertion. The same economist might do quite different benefit-cost analyses of the same issue, depending on who the client is. A principled analyst could produce analyses with quite different preferred options (the one with the largest net benefits).

A decision maker cannot interpret a benefit-cost analysis properly without knowing the values of the analyst and sponsoring organization. Although a different analysis could be an indication of technical inadequacy or misconduct, it could also result from value differences. A reviewer has the difficult task of determining whether an analysis is technically accurate and spelling out the values used. . . .

E. Anderson, Value in Ethics and Economics (1993)
204-207, 209-210 (1993)

The crucial assumption behind this economic analysis of environmental goods is that the ways people value the environment when acting in their roles as consumers and producers exhaust the ways they care about it. Only if this is true is it proper to make their valuations of the environment in their market choices normative for public choice. If people have concerns about the environment that cannot be adequately expressed through market norms and commodity consumption, willingness-to-pay statistics will not capture them. Cost-benefit analysts make three assumptions about how consumers value commodities which they apply to their evaluation of environmental amenities. First, consumers seek to advance their personal welfare in purchasing commodities. Therefore, if environmental goods are just like commodities, their value is instrumental and consists in their uses for promoting human welfare. Second, commodities advance an individual's welfare best when she can privately appropriate them for her personal use. This follows from the fact that their value is a kind of use-value, realized in subordinating it to an individual's purposes, which are assumed to be definable and satisfiable independent of others' purposes. When access to a good is not limited, individuals tend to use it at cross-purposes. The market price of a good reflects how much people value it for exclusive use. If environmental goods are just commodities, then inferred market prices for them will effectively capture how much individuals value them. Third, as mere use-values, commodities are indifferently substitutable for any other bundle of goods with the same market price. If environmental goods are mere commodities, they should be comprehensively subject to tradeoffs against other commodities. This norm contrasts with norms for valuing higher goods, which prohibit some tradeoffs between higher and lower goods.

Cost-benefit analysts also make a crucial assumption about the regard public policy should have for individuals' values. Respect for an individual's values in the market sphere is expressed by satisfying her wants in proportion to the amount of money she is willing to put behind them, without questioning her reasons for having those wants. If people value the environment just as they value pure commodities, then this is also thought to be the way public bodies should express respect for individual concerns about the environment. Each of these assumptions about the ways people value the environment, and about how we should treat people's values in public policy formation, are subject to challenge. . . .

Consider the difficulties encountered in attempting to force all our valuations of environmental goods into the instrumental mold. People appreciate many environmental goods for their beauty. Appreciation is a mode of intrinsic valuation. It is immediately directed toward the object of beauty, not toward ourselves. But some economists deny that any tenable distinction can be drawn between economic (useful) and aesthetic values. This forces them to maintain that things of beauty are only of instrumental value for the enjoyment humans derive from beholding them. This view commits the crude hedonistic error [of] taking the object of intrinsic value to be a favorable response rather than the object of a favorable response. The hedonistic account of the value of beautiful natural objects mistakenly assimilates its value to the mere use-values of amusement park rides, or consciousness altering drugs. In the latter case the experience alone matters. Any alteration of these things that produces the same or better experiences improves them. But when we contemplate a beautiful natural scene, and are struck by its grandeur or peacefulness, we experience it as worthy of our appreciation, not just as good for kicks. In appreciating a thing of natural beauty, we acknowledge that it possesses an integrity not to be violated, a unity of characteristics not to be modified merely for our pleasure or for ends not tied to its preservation in a flourishing natural state. This is why people who intrinsically care about the environment object to practices that use natural wonders for mere spectacle-seeking, as when chemicals are poured into geysers to stimulate eruptions, or magnificent caves decked out in lurid colored lights. Appreciation, as a higher mode of valuation than use, demands constraints on the ways we may use its objects. . . .

[Most] U.S. citizens believe that to treat the value of some environmental goods as reducible to a cash equivalent is itself to express an inappropriate attitude toward the environment. They do not view the choices at stake in the terms in which cost-benefit analysis frames them. In holding that environmental goods are worthy of consideration and appreciation, they reject the view that the satisfaction of human wants or the promotion of human welfare is the only proper end of public policy. Because market prices and willingness-to-pay statistics generally reflect individuals' valuations of things only as satisfying their private wants and interests, they do not capture all the ways people value environmental goods. The preferences people express in their roles as consumers therefore do not capture all the concerns they have. So people in their roles as citizens debating public policy do not and should not take the preferences they express in their market choices as normative for public purposes. . . .

(2) Statements of Effects or Impacts

The use of environmental impact statements to encourage agencies to take account of the environment has led regulatory reformers to propose other impact statement requirements, designed to influence the substantive direction of agency policy. The most significant proposals, perhaps part of a cost-benefit mandate, would encourage agencies to adopt less costly or less restrictive methods of regulation. President Ford, by executive order, required the agencies to write an "inflationary impact statement." The agency would determine how much its proposed action would raise costs and whether there were alternative, less costly ways of dealing with the problem. The most relevant and important of such requirements are more recent: Presidents Reagan, George H. W. Bush, and Clinton also required agencies to consider less restrictive alternatives and to use cost-benefit analyses. See Chapter 2. Early in his presidency, President George W. Bush issued an "energy impact statement" requirement, calling on all agencies to discuss the effect of their regulations on the supply of energy.

In a similar vein, the 1996 Unfunded Mandates Act requires agencies proposing significant regulatory actions to provide a statement that includes "a qualitative and quantitative assessment of the anticipated costs and benefits of the Federal mandate." The statement must include, among other things, a statement of compliance costs, any disproportionate budgetary effects, and estimates of effects on economic growth and employment. It also requires agencies to "identify and consider a reasonable number of regulatory alternatives and from those alternatives select the least costly, most cost-effective, or least burdensome alternative that achieves the objectives of the rule." There is an exception if these steps are inconsistent with law or if the agency explains why it has not chosen that least burdensome alternative.

In addition to focusing agencies on factors currently of interest to Congress, such statements may have an institutional consequence: they may provide a justification for the Office of Management and Budget (OMB), the Council of Economic Advisors, and the Department of Justice (Antitrust Division) to intervene in agency proceedings and to present their views. These agencies are institutionally disposed to stress the need for competition, the importance of incentives, the need to take account of costs, and the difficulties of classical regulation. Their presence in the proceeding can force the agency to take more serious account of these considerations.

Intervention based on the impact statement can also force the White House staff to pay attention to issues and decisions that might otherwise pass unnoticed. Involvement by the Council of Economic Advisors in some major regulatory proceedings, for example, has led the White House to develop a firm position, which, in turn, has strongly influenced the agency's decision toward less restrictive regulation. Finally, if the impact statement is reviewable in court, action that is unreasonable in terms of the statement can be set aside.

There are several major weaknesses of the impact statement approach. (1) It is difficult to find a single factor, or even a small number of factors, that all agencies would do better to focus on. Perhaps a general requirement of attention to costs and benefits is an exception to this proposition. (2) The final decision remains with the agency. (3) It is not difficult to write a plausible justification for almost any decision along the lines required by the statement. On this view, a general requirement of cost-benefit analysis (for example) may well prove empty in practice, if agencies have the freedom to value benefits and costs however they wish. Classical regulation, even when far too restrictive and undesirable, is never without plausible justification. In every instance one can find claims, evidence, and argument that will support regulation. Thus, it may not be difficult for agencies to reach a decision and then to write whatever impact statement is needed to justify it. In many agencies it is common practice first to reach a decision and then to have a special opinion-writing section compose a statement in justification. How might it be possible to respond to these concerns? A possible response would be that the objection is simply overstated—that an obligation to assess consequences, of whatever kind, will focus attention and discipline inquiry. For evidence to this effect, see Economic Analysis at EPA (R. Morgenstern ed. 1998).

(3) Encouraging Step-by-Step Reform

Many proposals call for step-by-step, detailed examination of individual administrative programs. Detailed congressional oversight, for example, helped bring about airline and trucking deregulation. Executive branch study, when combined with congressional support, also brought about major change in the railroad, banking, and telecommunications industries. But how can Congress and the executive be encouraged to continue to conduct this type of oversight and reform? A major proposal advocated as a way to do so is "sunset" legislation.

Sunset legislation is designed to force Congress to consider regulatory reform on an agency-by-agency basis. It provides that an agency, together with its rules and regulations, will simply cease to exist as of a certain date unless Congress specifically enacts legislation that extends the agency's life. The threat of extinction should lead Congress to reconsider the need for a regulatory program before it disappears. Typically, sunset legislation also provides a comprehensive set of criteria, which Congress, after investigation, is to use in determining whether the agency's life should be prolonged. Several states, including Colorado and Florida, have adopted sunset laws. In the last decade, sunset legislation has proved quite popular, and there is at least anecdotal evidence that it has succeeded in focusing congressional attention on programs that may need reform.

There are two major problems with the sunset approach. First, there is no guarantee that Congress will address itself seriously to the reform question and undertake the detailed work required. It may well simply reenact the old program automatically. Pressed by the demand for quick action, it may simply attack administrative waste without examining the fundamental objectives of the program. Second, the approach may condemn to extinction those agencies that are the subject of serious political controversy. It is far more difficult to pass legislation through Congress than to stop legislation from being passed. To give an obvious example, a few senators can filibuster and prevent a bill's enactment. Even without a filibuster, a determined minority can take advantage of time pressures, the committee system, and floor rules to delay or halt unfavorable legislation. The proponents of sunset laws seek to use this very fact to force serious reexamination of agencies. Yet the obverse side of the coin is that a minority within Congress could destroy a desirable agency. These defects suggest that the sunset approach needs modifications.

One such modification would have the president appoint a special committee, whose members would include the chairman of the Council of Economic Advisors, the attorney general, and perhaps members of Congress, to review regulatory programs individually and in detail on a ten-year schedule. The president would be required to send reform recommendations to Congress, where they would be automatically discharged from committee and voted upon on the floor after one year. This discharge provision is designed as a trigger to force those with political authority to take agency reform seriously because they know they will have to vote on it publicly. The committee's makeup might be designed to include persons who represent "procompetitive" institutions and thus are likely to favor a least restrictive alternative approach to regulation. Of course, one cannot predict whether the committee's meetings would be attended by only low-level staff, whether the recommendations would be significant, or whether reform could pass Congress.

2. Better Personnel

Some critics have explained the failure of regulation by claiming that government has not attracted people best equipped to handle regulatory responsibilities. The notion that agency performance would improve dramatically with better qualified personnel is seductive, for what organization's performance would not? James Landis pointed out in his report to President Kennedy: "The prime key to the improvement of the administrative process is the selection of qualified personnel. Good men make poor laws workable; poor men will wreak havoc with good laws." J. Landis, Report on Regulatory Agencies to the President-Elect, Subcomm. on Admin. Practice and Procedure, Senate Comm. on the Judiciary, 86th Cong., 2d Sess. (Comm. Print, 1960). The Ash Council in 1970 noted that the regulatory agencies had difficulty attracting and retaining "highly qualified personnel." President's Advisory Council on Executive Organization, A New Regulatory Framework: Report on Selected Independent Regulatory Agencies (Washington, D.C., 1971). The Senate Commerce Committee complained that many appointments to the FTC and the FCC over a 25-year period "can be explained in terms of powerful political connections and little else." Senate Comm. on Government Operations, "The Regulatory Appointments Process," in Study on Federal Regulation 1, 95th Cong., 1st Sess. (January 1997), at 7. And the Governmental Affairs Committee found that "the preeminent problem with the regulatory appointments process, as it has operated in the past, is that it has not consistently resulted in the selection of people best equipped to handle regulatory responsibilities. For much of the past 15 years, neither the White House nor the Senate has demonstrated a sustained commitment to high quality regulatory appointments." Id., at xxxi (finding number 1).

Occasionally, the appointment of a particular person leads to major change. President Carter, for example, appointed Alfred Kahn chairman of the CAB in 1977, knowing that Kahn favored deregulation of the airline industry. Kahn, operating within the broad language of the Federal Aviation Act, began to deregulate the airlines administratively. He also worked for and helped secure passage of new deregulating legislation. President Clinton appointed Reed Hundt the Chairman of the FCC, and Hundt was known for attempting to promote competition in many areas while at the same time encouraging producers of programming to attend to their public services obligations, above all to children.

Despite the occasional example, efforts to reform agencies by appointing "better people" have been criticized on two grounds: (1) "Better people" is a solution to any institutional problem, but the number of better people is limited. Even if they could be identified and attracted to agency administration, the nation is not necessarily better off than it would be if they administered medical clinics, disarmament conferences, or major corporations. (2) There is no practical proposal for a system more likely to achieve administration by better people. The president does not deliberately appoint poorly qualified people. Rather, the present system leads him to nominate appointees who are neither better nor worse than would be produced by any other selection method.

Some proposals are aimed at *encouraging better people to apply* for agency jobs. The Ash Council, for example, recommended that agency heads have more power and authority. Others have proposed lifetime tenure for commissioners. Still others propose higher salaries. Some have suggested a massive advertising campaign to publicize the jobs, explaining how complex and interesting they are. Common Cause has advocated the creation of a public interest talent bank.

A second type of proposal seeks to encourage the president to *select better people*. Thus, some have argued for a special office in the White House that would develop standards for selection, consult advisory committees, and then select on the basis of competence, experience, and integrity, not politics. Others, including Common Cause and the Senate Governmental Affairs Committee, have argued that Congress or a congressionally created commission or the Senate through its confirmation process should develop similar selection standards and then enforce them through a closer look at the president's nominee. Others seek an "independent" board to evaluate nominees.

Some people are skeptical, however, of the value of such proposals. As long as the president appoints and the Senate confirms, the appointment process will remain political. If the politics of the day favor the appointment of an experienced person of great integrity, that is likely to be done, in the presence or in the absence of advisory committees, standards, and "close looks." If not, it is unlikely that standards and so forth will make much difference. Indeed, the extent to which politicians heed the advice of advisory committees or of various members itself depends on political factors. And advisory committees, too, can develop politics of their own. It is difficult to find examples of advisory committees or standards improving a basically political selection process.

It is also very hard to develop a meaningful or administrable set of standards of government hiring. Those suggested tend to be embarrassingly general, such as the suggestion by the Governmental Affairs Committee that "by reason of background, training or experience, the nominee" be "affirmatively qualified for the office to which he or she is nominated." Furthermore, the commissions, committees, or others called on to participate or advise must themselves be selected.

A third type of proposal focuses on the *elimination of conflicts of interest.* Popular wisdom identifies a partial cause of regulation's failure with the fact that many regulators have a financial stake in the well-being of the industry or firms that they regulate. This stake may consist of the ownership of stock in companies affected by regulatory action. It may arise out of hoped-for future employment, for many commissioners and agency staff leave the agency for work in regulated industry, law firms, or other professional groups that serve the industry. Or it may arise out of past associations and loyalties because staff and commissioners often come from regulated companies or their law firms.

Reformers have typically proposed three approaches to the conflict-of-interest problem. One proposal would require top executive branch staff to file an annual public financial disclosure statement describing all of their sources of income, including gifts, honoraria, and their net worth including all property, companies, and organizations in which they hold a financial interest. At present, such statements are required only of top officials. Another proposal would require all top officials and employees to divest, unless granted a specific exemption, all financial interests in any company or organization that is affected in any way by any proceeding in which they are likely to participate. Still another proposal would require employees working for the government to sign contracts agreeing that for two years after leaving the government, they will not work for, represent, or accept any compensation from any company or organization that was affected by proceedings in which they personally participated.

Why have these suggestions not been welcomed by all those who believe in good government? Some point out that an effort to apply them strictly may make it that much more difficult to attract the highly qualified personnel that reformers typically claim are needed. Will top professionals accept jobs in the government if doing so requires them to sell all their investments, pay the resulting taxes, and reinvest in government securities? Others are concerned about privacy. What are the implications for privacy of working in an office where everyone—and the general public—knows one's net worth from day to day?

The most serious problem these proposals raise, however, concerns the government's need for expertise. The factual information base needed to carry on the many regulatory activities—ranging from determining how pollution controls ought to be implemented to how energy should be allocated—is enormous. Administrators possessing detailed knowledge of the industry—those familiar with its workings, problems, and standards—can often move far more quickly and effectively than those coming fresh to the problem. For example, it took the National Highway Transportation Safety Administration (NHTSA) more than seven years to determine what tire characteristics should appear on a tire's label and how they should be measured. The standard might never have been developed had the job of doing so not been placed in the hands of an agency official who had previously worked 35 years for a tire company. Those familiar enough with the industry to possess the necessary qualifications for appointment to many agencies are likely to have had some prior industry connection.

Moreover, if younger employees cannot look for future employment in the regulated industry or the law firms that serve it, will they seek jobs in regulatory agencies? Must they choose between permanent careers in government and careers totally outside it?

3. *Structural Change: Managerial Proposals*

Managerial proposals would reorganize lines of authority and accountability to make the agency a more efficient, responsible managerial unit. Some such proposals are designed to obtain a better mix of technocratic and political virtues, by putting both expertise and democratic judgments where they belong.

a. Putting Independent Agencies under the President

Perhaps the most persistent of the managerial restructuring proposals have been aimed not at all agencies but at the independent agencies. These agencies, such as the FCC and the FTC, are not directly responsible to the president (though as we have seen, there are lines of connection between the independent agencies and both Congress and the president). Criticisms of independent agency structure usually take one or more of the following forms: (1) adjudication and management functions should not be combined; (2) multimember boards cannot manage effectively; and (3) independence from the president breeds irresponsibility. In the last two decades, the third criticism has been the most prominent.

In 1937 the President's Committee on Administrative Management observed:

> For the purposes of management, boards and commissions have turned out to be failures. Their mechanism is inevitably slow, cumbersome, wasteful, and ineffective, and does not lend itself readily to cooperation with other agencies. Even strong men on boards find that their individual opinions are watered down in reaching board decisions. When freed from the work of management, boards are, however, extremely useful and necessary for consultation, discussion, and advice; for representation of diverse views and citizen opinion; for quasi-judicial action; and as a repository for corporate powers.
>
> The conspicuously well-managed administrative units in the Government are almost without exception headed by single administrators.
>
> President's Committee on Administrative Management, Report of the Committee (Washington, D.C., 1937). The First Hoover Commission concluded that chairmen are "too frequently merely presiding officers at commission meetings. No one has been responsible for planning and guiding the general program of commission activity." U.S. Commission on Organization of the Executive Branch of the Government, The Independent Regulatory Commissions: A Report with Recommendations 4 (Washington, D.C., 1949). Finding that administration by plural executives was universally regarded as inefficient, the commission noted that it was very difficult for a bureau chief to report to five or more masters. The Second Hoover Commission reached similar conclusions, as did the Landis Report in 1960. As a result of the Landis work, the agencies' structure was somewhat changed. The power of the chairman was increased and his term redefined so that he serves at the pleasure of the president.

An influential study of agency structure is that of the Ash Council in 1971. The Ash Council recommended that most commissions be headed by a single administrator directly responsible to the president. The council argued that collegial bodies are "inefficient mechanisms for formulating and implementing specific policy in a timely manner." They tend to "overjudicialize" agency procedures. They "are not an efficient form for managing operations." A single administrator "would be more visible to all concerned and therefore more easily held accountable for agency performance. . . . Agency policy and direction would more likely conform to the interest of the public, Congress and the executive branch and would result in a more expeditious and fair response to the regulated industries."

This sort of structural proposal is commonly advanced by study commissions viewing agencies from an administrative or business management perspective. Whether their implementation would in fact significantly improve agency performance, however, is questionable. Is it so clear, in principle, that a single head would improve the quality of a multimember agency's performance? Of course, a collegial body may provoke more policy disagreements than a single head. But whether such disagreements are desirable depends on the substantive policy at issue.

The other recommended structural change—that the president have authority to replace agency chiefs at will—rests on the view that independent agencies are less subject to democratic controls and more subject to selfish, well-organized private interests, largely because they are free of the insulating arm of the president. On this view, the independent agencies are hardly independent. A key problem is that the president feels less responsible for the actions of an independent agency. Here too, however, it is possible to doubt the significance of the change. Is it clear that agencies do better if they are placed under the president's continuing control?

Reconsider the treatment of this question in Chapter 2 and notice that the independent agencies are not really free from presidential authority. After a short period, most independent agencies—the National Labor Relations Board, the Federal Communications Commission, the Federal Trade Commission—tend to reflect the views of the incumbent president, at least to a substantial degree. Under President George W. Bush, for example, many of the nominally independent agencies tended to reflect his policies, in part because of his power to appoint the chair and to fill vacancies when they occur. In these circumstances, it is reasonable to wonder how much difference it would make if independent agencies were subjected to full presidential control.

b. Coordination

A related set of managerial proposals seeks to improve agency planning, coordination, and performance. OMB, for example, once claimed that it had "identified the single, most important problem in the regulatory process as the lack of consistent and effective policy oversight of regulatory decisions by the heads of regulatory agencies. . . . The officials who signed regulations often had no idea of what was in them. Those who wrote regulations were not held accountable for their actions." There has been a steady trend in the direction of greater presidential coordination, generally through OMB itself. President Clinton's Executive Order 12,866 is an illustration. See Kagan, Presidential Administration, 114 Harv. L. Rev. 2245 (2001); Pildes & Sunstein, Reinventing the Regulatory State, 62 U. Chi. L. Rev. 1 (1995), for a discussion of increased coordination of administrative judgments.

The goal of coordination purports to be responsive to several perceived defects in administrative performance. Perhaps coordination will increase predictability by publicizing agency directives in advance. Perhaps coordination will increase democratic accountability by funneling agency decisions through the White House or some institution close to the president's will. For a discussion of the record of OMB coordination under President Reagan, see T. McGarity, Rationalizing Regulation

(1985). For a discussion of the experience under President Clinton, see Kagan, Presidential Administration, supra.

c. Priority-Setting

Some of the excerpts above suggest that government does not engage in sufficient priority-setting—that it is driven by external forces suggesting, for the day, the week, or the month, that a certain problem is "urgent," without being able to get the kind of overview that would enable it to choose which problems deserve serious attention. This complaint is related to the general goal in the area of risk regulation of "comparative risk analysis," intended to enable officials and the public to evaluate risks not in isolation, but in comparison with one another.

Is there a possible institutional solution to this problem?

S. Breyer, Breaking the Vicious Circle
59-63 (1993)

Neither the courts nor Congress seem likely to provide real solutions to the problems of risk regulation. Major nonregulatory alternatives, deregulation, taxes, labeling, or greater public participation seem insufficient. Is it possible to find administrative help within the Executive Branch? Our problems are essentially problems of good government. Is there then a better-government or bureaucratic solution to the problems posed?

There are strong reasons for believing that an answer does lie in that direction. I shall describe a possible change in administrative organization that is not a cure-all, nor a definitive answer, but, I believe, is a constructive approach. Like more radical changes, such as the creation of OMB itself (and perhaps like the creation of the Senior Executive Service), its aim is to help to realize the hope for effective government implicit in any civil service able to attract honest, talented, and qualified administrators.

The suggestion has two parts: (1) establishment of a new career path that would provide a group of civil servants with experience in health and environmental agencies, Congress, and OMB; and (2) creation of a small, centralized administrative group, charged with a rationalizing mission, whose members would embark upon this career path. Such a proposal is likely to engender objections that the proposal sounds undemocratic, elitist, ineffective, politically unfeasible, and without any practical means of implementation. Before considering those objections, however, I wish to describe the essential characteristics of such a group, how it might draw on certain positive attributes of bureaucracies, the nature of its specific mission, and several examples of related institutional experience. . . .

[T]he design of any new administrative group would have to incorporate five features. First, the group must have a specified risk-related *mission* not the mission of "total safety" or "zero risk," or "maintaining economic productivity," but the mission of building an improved, coherent risk-regulating system, adaptable for use in several different risk-related programs; the mission of helping to create priorities within as well as among programs; and the mission of comparing programs to determine how better to allocate resources to reduce risks.

Second, the group must have *interagency jurisdiction*. Such jurisdiction is needed to bring about needed transfers of resources, say from toxic waste to vaccination or prenatal care; otherwise, efforts to overcome resource misallocation would remain somewhat theoretical, rather like discussions about transferring money spent on aircraft carriers to health care. Without such interagency jurisdiction, the group would find it difficult to overcome the tendencies of separate agencies simply to compromise differences through a single meeting leading to a single rule determined administratively rather than scientifically, as when EPA, CPSC, and FDA recently ironed out their rat-to-man "comparative body weight" versus "comparative surface area" disagreement simply by choosing a number — body weight raised to the 3/4 power — that split the difference. Without interagency jurisdiction, the group would find itself limited in its ability to find examples of comparable risk-related problems in different areas which it could use in building its system, to suggest priorities among programs, and to look for potentially creative ways to put health resources to work more effectively.

Third, the group must have a degree of *political insulation* to withstand various political pressures, particularly in respect to individual substances, that emanate from the public directly or through Congress and other political sources. At a minimum, a group's members must enjoy civil service protection.

Fourth, the group must have *prestige*. That prestige must both attract, and arise out of an ability to attract, a highly capable staff. A capable staff is one that understands science, some economics, administration, possibly law, and has the ability to communicate in a sophisticated way with experts in all these fields.

Fifth, the group must have the *authority* that will give it a practical ability to achieve results. Such authority may arise in part out of a legal power to impose its decisions. But it may also arise through informal contacts with line agency staffs, out of its perceived knowledge and expertise, out of "rationalizing" successes that indicate effectiveness, and out of the public's increased confidence that such successes may build.

In summary, my proposal is for a specific kind of group: mission oriented, seeking to bring a degree of uniformity and rationality to decision making in highly technical areas, with broad authority, somewhat independent, and with significant prestige. Such a group would make general and government-wide the rationalizing efforts in which EPA is currently engaged. Let me now turn to why the creation of such a group might help. . . .

DRAWING UPON THE VIRTUES OF BUREAUCRACY

The group I have in mind, composed of civil servants who are following the proposed career path, would draw strength from its ability to harness several virtues inherent in many administrative systems: rationalization, expertise, insulation, and authority.

1. *Rationalization*. Bureaucracies rationalize the problems and processes with which they work, allowing them to develop systems. For example, gradually over several decades, bureaucracies charged with setting rates for electricity, communications, and transportation have developed a complex but fairly uniform system of "cost of service ratemaking." That system does not consist simply of rules and regulations. Rather, the rules are accompanied by standards, practices, guidelines, prototypes, models, and informal procedures, all shaped to some extent by a general goal (that of replicating a competitive marketplace) but more directly guided by goals internal to the system (efficiency, fairness, fair return on investment). The system solves roughly similar problems in roughly similar ways irrespective of the particular regulatory program or regulated industry at issue.

The problems of health and safety risk regulation could well benefit from the development of a similar system. Such a system would recognize differences between, say, unusually high risks to specially placed individuals and risks to a general population. It would neither reduce all lives saved to a common dollar-value, nor claim incommensurable differences among different health programs and circumstances. Such a system would compare experience under different programs to create a uniform approach, while embodying that approach in models, examples, and paradigms that permit local variation. Ratemaking problems are somewhat simpler, yet they suggest a parallel.

2. *Expertise*. Bureaucracies develop expertise in administration, but also in the underlying subject matter. They normally understand that subject matter at least well enough to communicate with substantive experts, to identify the better experts, and to determine which insights of the underlying discipline can be transformed into workable administrative practices, and to what extent. A unified group charged with developing a system for addressing health risk regulation might bring together people familiar with science, risk analysis, economics, and administration—expertise that now is divided among different agencies, such as EPA and OMB.

3. *Insulation*. A civil service automatically offers a degree of insulation or protection both from politics and from public opinion. Of course, tenure rules tend to insulate its members, to some extent, from the force of public criticism. More important, administrators of a system can rationalize or justify particular results in particular cases in terms of the system's rules, practices, and procedures. Just as a doctor justifies a dose of bitter medicine by reference to medical theory and practice that indicate it will help the patient, so regulators explain and justify highly unpopular individual decisions, such as a decision that means a significant rate increase for the public. They do so through reference to the rules and practices of a system that, considered as a whole, helps the public by keeping rates within reason. Use of a coherent, well-worked-out system changes the focus of political questions. It becomes more difficult simply to ask, "Isn't this specific result terrible?" The relevant question becomes, "Is this a good *system*; and, if so, does the system generate this particular result?" Bureaucratic solutions, if sound and coherent, resting on well-constructed comparisons among different substances, offer administrators the promise of a modest increase in independence, through greater insulation from public criticism of individual decisions.

4. *Authority*. A bureaucratic solution offers the hope of creating authoritative decisions that may, in turn, help break the vicious circle. Respect for decisions as authoritative is not easy to create in this era of political distrust, an era that since 1970 has seen Americans' confidence in virtually every institution—government, business, the press (but, surprisingly, not the military)—plummet, and an era in which different political parties control Congress and the Executive Branch. Still, it seems to me that public respect depends not only upon the perception of public participation but also, in part, upon an organization's successful accomplishment of a mission that satisfies an important societal need. (Consider the rebound of confidence in the military during the 1980s.) If that is so, the authority or legitimacy of a particular regulatory action depends in part upon its technical sophistication and correctness, and in part upon its conformity with the law, and both parts help to determine the extent of public confidence in the regulator.

Insofar as a systematic solution produces technically better results, the decision will become somewhat more legitimate, and thereby earn the regulator a small additional amount of prestige, which may mean an added small amount of public confidence. Any such increase in trust may encourage greater legislative respect. As a central bureaucratic group attains a degree of prestige and develops contacts, Congressional committees may begin to ask it for advice in drafting legislation, thereby helping further to rationalize risk-regulation programs and expenditures. Congress might delegate it additional or broader regulatory authority. That authority may increase the agency's prestige, making it easier to attract better-trained personnel, who may in turn do a better technical job, which in turn may generate increased public confidence. These tendencies, even if only gradual, point in the right direction. . . .

This proposal has been criticized on the ground that it is too highly technocratic, placing too much emphasis on the purely technical characteristics of risk regulation, and too little on issues of value, which, it is said, appropriately lead to different treatment of quantitatively equivalent risks. Is this a serious criticism? See Heinzerling, Political Science, 62 U. Chi. L. Rev. 449 (1995); Pildes and Sunstein, Reinventing the Regulatory State, 62 U. Chi. L. Rev. 1, 86-89 (1995).

4. Supervisory Proposals

Not surprisingly, many proposals would restructure relationships within the government to give others more authority to supervise agency performance. Placing independent agencies within the domain of the president is part of such an approach; Justice Breyer's proposal can be seen as belonging in the same category. We trace here approaches that would give more supervisory power to Congress, to the president, and to the courts.

a. Congress

Some especially popular proposals are designed to empower Congress. Of these the most straightforward would be to require Congress to delegate with particularity, either by means of the nondelegation doctrine or through informal norms governing legislative performance. We have already discussed these proposals.

Another popular proposal would give one or both houses of Congress an opportunity to veto any major rule of an agency after it is promulgated but before it takes effect. We have discussed the legislative veto in detail in Chapter 2. But there are other proposals also designed to increase Congress's supervisory powers. Most important, Congress enacted a provision that forbids major regulations from taking effect until a 60-day period in which Congress may, with the ordinary possibility of presidential veto, overturn such regulations. See 5 U.S.C. §§801 et seq. As a result, regulations are in a sense mere "proposals" for congressional review. But note that inertia favors the agency proposal. If Congress fails to act, as it almost always does, the agency's decision stands. How is this enactment different from that of the legislative veto? From statutory specificity? From a reform that would make agency regulations into genuine "proposals," to go into effect only if Congress enacts them?

Congress also controls agencies through "oversight hearings," which threaten legislation and produce a good deal of publicity without necessarily leading to new law or even proposed legislation. Agency heads are sometimes fearful of oversight hearings (not least because they can be quite time-consuming), and the threat of a hearing might well affect agency behavior. Perhaps Congress should be encouraged to use its oversight power more frequently and effectively. Congressional oversight of airline and trucking regulation has helped bring about significant change. There are numerous examples of material effects from oversight hearings.

Yet how to institutionalize the process is unclear. The subcommittee of Congress directly charged with the responsibility of overseeing a particular agency's work sometimes finds it difficult to carry out detailed oversight. The very fact that the subcommittee is involved with the agency on a regular basis means that its members and staff develop an interest in preserving the regulatory status quo just as does the agency itself. The subcommittee and the agency deal with the same parties, they are subjected to the same arguments, and they may begin to see the issues in the same way. If this does not happen, the oversight committee may be unduly adversarial, unrepresentative of Congress as a whole, or engaged in oversight hearings not to produce better policy but to achieve political results for subcommittee chairs or selfish interests.

Some have suggested that the Congress should create an omnibus "risk regulation" committee, designed to ensure that agencies are engaging in sensible priority-setting and are entrusted with the task of overseeing statutes to make sure that they do not lead to costly regulation without significant gains. This proposal is a close cousin to Justice Breyer's proposal (pages 182-185). Others have suggested that the Budget Committee or the Appropriations Committee should carry out oversight and that they should do so by insisting that each agency justify its *entire* budget, not just the incremental increase, each year ("zero-based budgeting"). Still others have proposed a special Congressional Office on Regulatory Oversight, with a director and staff. Of course, the product of such an office would likely depend on the views of its chairman or majority. If such an office created an agenda, decided to develop a coherent overall intellectual framework, and carried out the painstaking, elaborate, and often unglamorous detailed work needed for individual agency investigation, reform might well come about. But there is nothing in the simple creation of the office that suggests this will necessarily happen.

b. The President

Proposals to strengthen the president's power to influence agency policies have been made by many who argue that the president has become unable to coordinate policies among the executive branch and independent agencies. As we have seen, presidents have moved very much in this direction on their own, and more centralized presidential oversight of the administrative process has been one of the most striking developments of the last two decades.

With the support of the American Bar Association (ABA), critics propose to go even further, with a statute that would allow the president to direct an agency to take up and decide any regulatory issue within a specified period of time, or to modify or reverse an agency rule or policy. In other words, the president, acting under certain procedural constraints, could reverse most agency policymaking. Presidential action might be subject to congressional review, either through a legislative veto process or by requiring Congress to renew the president's authority at regular intervals.

Why might a statute be required? If it is, the reason is that most regulatory statutes delegate power not to the president but to the agency head. Thus, many people believe that the president cannot, as a matter of law, overrule the agency head on a particular matter but can only dismiss a regulator who displeases him. Presidents are unwilling to fire a major public official except over a very important matter. It is disputed how much autonomy agency heads have in practice. The fact that presidential discharge is unlikely makes it possible for an agency head to resist the president if she or he is really determined to do so. On the other hand, it is not likely that an agency head will reject the president's judgment frequently or on matters of great significance.

In these circumstances, perhaps the proposed statute would allow the president to bring about increased policy coordination among agencies, to prevent major departures from executive branch policies, and to prevent actions that he would consider seriously mistaken. It would also involve him more directly in regulatory matters, providing increased opportunity for major change. On the other hand, the proposal has its problems. Perhaps the recent executive orders have accomplished most of the relevant tasks. Perhaps an explicit authority to this effect is unnecessary. And might such a statute mean that groups adversely affected by agency action simply come to the White House for a second opportunity to defeat it? A deeper question is this: Why is the president's policy likely to be so much more sensible than the agency's? The president may have higher-quality advice available from some sources, but the agency has many more facts at its disposal and is more familiar with them. Would the proposal require a much larger White House staff?

For detailed discussion of the experience under President Clinton, with a suggestion that we have entered a new era of genuinely presidential administration, see Kagan, supra.

c. The Courts

Periodically, it is suggested that problems with administrative discretion and administrative substance can be alleviated through more aggressive judicial review. Courts might attempt, for example, to ensure that regulation does not impose large costs for small gains or that selfish private groups have not produced apparently public-interested legislation. Sometimes it is suggested that a good deal might be accomplished by telling courts to ensure that agencies "do more good than harm." See H. Margolis, Dealing With Risk (1996). Margolis and others argue that this simple principle would help ensure that agencies focus on all rather than part of a problem, and that they avoid some of the problems discussed in this chapter.

We will discuss ideas of this sort in some detail. For the moment, the central question is whether courts have the competence, democratic legitimacy, or resources to examine agency decisions with care. From the perspective of regulatory policy, the effect of any proposal for increased judicial supervision is indeterminable. Judicial review may increase or decrease the extent of regulation; it may shift policy in all sorts of possible directions. By slowing down agency proceedings and examining more closely the relation of the agency decision to the authorizing statute, stricter review may mean less experimentation, less regulation, or a bias toward the status quo. See J. Mashaw and D. Harst, The Struggle for Auto Safety (1993). These questions and many others will arise frequently in the course.

5. New Institutions

Proposals have been made to create various new institutions designed to help overcome the problems of regulation. Justice Breyer's controversial proposal is directly addressed to the issue of better priority-setting; the following proposals are only tangentially relevant to the types of regulatory problems we have discussed.

a. An Administrative Court

The Ash Council recommended creating a separate administrative court, similar to the tax court, to review administrative decisions of the securities, energy, and transportation agencies. Forty years earlier the ABA had recommended the creation of a similar court that would handle agency adjudications and many of the agencies' licensing functions as well. The principal objectives of such proposals are (1) to secure better review of agency decisions and promote uniformity of decisionmaking processes and results among agencies; and (2) to relieve the agencies of many time-consuming adjudicatory tasks and allow them to concentrate on policymaking and managerial functions.

The critics of these proposals argue that these objectives would not be achieved. The court's limited jurisdiction might restrict its appeal to highly qualified judicial candidates. Moreover, to remove adjudications from the agencies is to remove much of their basic work. Familiarity with individual cases helps agencies determine proper policy, and the ability to make policy in individual adjudicatory proceedings gives the agencies flexibility. Thus, there is no guarantee that removal of the agencies' adjudicatory powers would produce better policies. To remove the agencies' power to award licenses and place it in a court may simply prevent agencies from coordinating complementary policies without curing the problems that make individual decisions so difficult. Finally, even if freeing agencies from their adjudicatory burden gives them more time to set policy, that policy will not necessarily be better. With more time, the FPC in the 1960s would have continued to hold down natural gas prices; the CAB's rate policies would have remained restrictive; and the FCC would have continued to find it impossible to devise fair and effective licensing rules.

b. A Technical Review Board

Some students of the regulatory process, noting the difficulty that agencies and courts have in making technical analyses, have proposed the creation of new institutions to perform or to evaluate technical work. One possibility, for example, is to create a board of experts in technical disciplines to act as advisors to agencies or judges. Others have urged the creation of a Science Court, composed of experts who would hear arguments and then issue a statement of the scientific facts relevant to a policy controversy. Such evaluations and advice make for better decisions and would help the courts decide when an agency decision was unreasonable.

Critics of these proposals have raised several questions. Who will serve on such panels? Why will they reach better results than an agency itself? Can controversy among experts be narrowed down or resolved easily? How often can one separate out from a major policy issue the "value" questions and the "factual" questions, the scientific questions that can be resolved and the scientific questions that cannot be resolved? Can a panel properly evaluate technical studies and judge whether they are being used properly or misused by the agency, without a thorough knowledge of the particular regulatory proceeding and issue? Will the panel become sufficiently familiar with the details of the regulatory proceeding? Would it prove nearly as useful to provide judges with scientifically trained law clerks who could help them evaluate the technical soundness of an agency's decision?

c. The Ombudsman

Many foreign countries, several states, and a number of American cities have successfully used ombudsmen to deal with complaints concerning abuse of governmental power. The ombudsman classically investigates, criticizes, publicizes, and recommends change in administrative practice, but he cannot himself change any administrative act.

Ombudsman-like functions are now performed at the federal level but not by an ombudsman. The power to examine agency procedures and practices, for example, rests in the hands of the congressional committees, OMB, and the Administrative Conference of the United States. The power to investigate and to prosecute criminal misbehavior on the part of public officials is vested in the Department of Justice. The obligation and the power to investigate citizen complaints—to cut through red tape to produce action and to correct individual instances of injustice belongs to individual senators and congressmembers, who help secure their own reelection by serving constituents in this way.

Proposals to create an ombudsman rest on the view that doing so would be inexpensive. It would provide a formal, visible method for citizens to complain, and the office would be, and would appear to be, nonpolitical. These facts and experience elsewhere suggest that an ombudsman will focus on individual instances of injustice and will affect only very indirectly the matters of substantive regulatory policy.

d. Strengthening Bureaucracy

In many other industrial democracies, including Britain, Germany, France, and Japan, there is a well-established administrative tradition that attracts and holds qualified individuals to government service. More insulated from legislative and judicial control than their U.S. counterparts, agencies in these countries develop strong technical competence and enjoy leeway to devise and carry out policies, often with greater continuity than is possible in the United States, where changes in presidential administration or Congress can produce abrupt policy and personnel changes. Far greater reliance in these other countries is placed on administrative rather than judicial control and review. In France, for example, a *Conseil d'Etat*, made up of administrators, decides both the wisdom and the lawfulness of many regulatory and administrative policies, and it hears the complaints of ordinary citizens as well. It can investigate matters itself, using an inquisitorial, rather than an adversary, system.

The New Deal period, of course, reflected considerable interest in the ideal of administrative expertise. This ideal came under a great deal of pressure in the 1960s and 1970s, with an insistence that regulatory problems often involved basic values and with doubt about the existence of a unitary or objective public interest that technocrats could discover. But the last decades have witnessed a rebirth of interest in expertise and expert solutions. One of the enduring goals of administrative law is the infusion of specialized knowledge into the political domain. How could government think well about telecommunications, occupational safety, natural gas regulation, or airline regulation without knowing an enormous amount of factual detail? See J. Mashaw, Greed, Chaos, and Governance (1997), for a recognition of some of the values promoted by autonomous administrative agencies. Justice Breyer's proposal (pages 182-185) also places a premium on expert knowledge.

But efforts to strengthen bureaucracy may well require major changes in existing attitudes. At least since Andrew Jackson's presidency, it has been an American principle that administration should be infused with a "popular" element. This infusion today occurs through presidential appointment of those who fill the top and middle policymaking and management positions. Political appointees change with changes in administrations and stay in their positions little more than two years. By contrast, in industrial democracies with a strong administrative tradition, political appointees occupy only the top positions in a ministry or department; other high policymaking and administrative positions are staffed by career officials. The prestige and power associated with such positions is a powerful attraction for able individuals to enter and remain in the civil service. Whether Americans would place sufficient trust in career officials, and would be willing to cut back on judicial as well as political control over their activities, is highly problematic. Yet the demands of modern administration arguably call for the competence, continuity, and relative independence that such a system secures.

Concluding Note

These questions raise large issues about the appropriate role of technocratic and political elements in the administrative state. How do the various criticisms of administrative process and administrative substance sort out those elements? Note that the answer partly depends on whether the problems with the administrative state are seen as problems of political legitimacy or instead as problems of real-world results. If the central problem is an absence of democratic controls or checks and balances, much more in the way of "political" elements certainly seems necessary. If the central problem is costly regulations doing too little good and squandering opportunities for beneficial regulation, perhaps much of the solution is technocratic in nature; perhaps it involves better regulatory tools. These points in turn raise the general question of the status of a claim that an agency decision is "political"—a claim that is sometimes meant as a sharp criticism of the agency but sometimes meant as an endorsement of the agency, a plea that courts, and lawyers, should keep their distance.

We end this chapter with a quotation from Karl N. Llewellyn, a distinguished professor of law at Columbia and the University of Chicago Law Schools. Unfortunately, Llewellyn never published the quotation, and memories of Llewellyn's colleagues point to two different versions of the quotation. Here is the first: "Technique without morals is a menace, but morals without technique is a mess." Here is the second: "Morals without technique is a mess, but technique without morals is a menace." It is interesting to ask which of these versions more accurately captures poor performance by American administrative agencies.

4

The Scope of Judicial Review — Questions of Fact, Law, and Policy

Administrative agencies exercise much of the authority formerly exercised by common law courts. When a court reviews the lawfulness of a particular agency decision, to what extent should it "respect," "defer," or give "weight" (perhaps controlling weight) to the agency's judgment? This central question of administrative law involves the proper relation of the courts to the administrative agencies. Should a court accept whatever conclusion an agency reaches? If it did so, judicial review would be meaningless; it would not exist at all. But if a court were to decide every question afresh, without deferring at all, we would lose many of the advantages of having administrative agencies.

In the first instance, and subject to constitutional limits, it is for Congress to choose the appropriate scope of judicial review. In developing governing principles, Congress and courts have arranged the kinds of questions under review into broad categories ("fact," "law," and, perhaps, "policy"). In elaborating these principles, courts have inevitably drawn analogies with the institution they know best, namely the courts themselves. Sometimes, they begin by analogizing the court-agency relation to the judge-jury or the appellate-trial court relation. But there is a question as to whether and to what extent these analogies provide a proper balance between the need for agency efficiency and democratic judgment (needs that typically argue against close judicial control) and the need to ensure fidelity to law (needs that may argue for close judicial control, though this is contested).

Consider, too, the vast number of different agencies, different government programs, and different statutes that bureaucratic administration might bring in these different contexts. Will highly general rules work well in the individual contexts of all these different programs? If not, might things be better, or worse, if judgments about scope of review are made on an ad hoc, case-by-case basis? There is a pervasive conflict, here as elsewhere in administrative law, between those who seek clear rules and those who believe that clear rules will inevitably go wrong when measured against the diversity and complexity of individual cases.

This chapter's basic question of the proper relation between court and agency is, in part, a theoretical question involving the proper place of each institution within the constitutional structure. It is also, however, a very practical question. Its answer helps to determine how effectively the administrative state can carry out its task of governing. Its answer also helps to determine the protection given the individual against abuse and unfairness at the hands of that same administrative state.

A. Review of Questions of Fact

1. *The* Universal Camera *Litigation*

NLRB v. Universal Camera Corp. (I)

179 F.2d 749 (2d Cir. 1950)

Before L. HAND, Chief Judge, and SWAN and FRANK, Circuit Judges.

L. HAND, Chief Judge.

This case arises upon a petition to enforce an order of the Labor Board, whose only direction that we need consider was to reinstate with back pay a "supervisory employee," named Chairman, whom the respondent discharged on January 24, 1944, avowedly for insubordination. If the Board was right, the discharge was in fact for giving testimony hostile to the respondent at a hearing conducted by the Board to determine who should be the representative of the respondent's "maintenance employees." Chairman was an assistant engineer, whose duties were to supervise the "maintenance employees," and he testified at the hearing in favor of their being recognized as a separate bargaining unit. The respondent opposed the recognition of such a unit, and several of its officers testified to that effect, among whom were Shapiro, the vice-president, Kende, the chief engineer, and Politzer, the "plant engineer." The examiner, who heard the witnesses, was not satisfied that the respondent's motive in discharging Chairman was reprisal for his testimony; but on review of the record a majority of the Board found the opposite, and on August 31, 1948, ordered Chairman's reinstatement. The respondent argues (1) that the majority's findings are subject to a more searching review under the New Act than under the Old; (2) that in the case at bar the findings cannot be supported, because they are not supported by "substantial evidence." . . .

The substance of the evidence was as follows. On November 30, 1943, Chairman and Kende testified at the hearing upon representation, after which Kende told Chairman that he [Chairman] had "perjured" himself; and on the stand in the proceeding at bar Kende testified that Chairman "was either ignorant of the true facts regarding the organization within the company . . . or . . . he was deliberately lying, not in one instance, but in many instances, all afternoon"; and "that there was definite doubt regarding his suitability for a supervisory position of that nature." The examiner believed the testimony of Chairman that two other employees, Goldson and Politzer, had cautioned him that the respondent would take it against him, if he testified for the "maintenance employees"; and Kende swore that he told another employee, Weintraub — the personnel manager — that he thought Chairman was a Communist. After Politzer reported to him on December second or third that this was a mistake, Kende told him to keep an eye on Chairman. From all this it is apparent that at the beginning of December Kende was hostile to Chairman; but he took no steps at that time to discharge him.

Nothing material happened until the very end of that month, when Chairman and Weintraub got into a quarrel, about disciplining a workman, named Kollisch. Chairman swore that Weintraub demanded that he discharge Kollisch for loafing; and Weintraub swore that he only demanded that Chairman put Kollisch to work. In any event high words followed; Chairman told Weintraub that he was drunk; Weintraub brought up a plant guard to put Chairman out of the premises, and the quarrel remained hot, until one, Zicarelli, a union steward, succeeded in getting the two men to patch up an apparent truce. Two days later Weintraub saw Politzer and told him that he had heard that Politzer was looking into Chairman's statement that Weintraub was drunk, and on this account Weintraub asked Politzer to discharge Chairman. Politzer testified that he answered that Chairman was going to resign soon anyway, and this the examiner believed. He did not, however, believe Politzer's further testimony that Chairman had in fact told Politzer that he was going to resign; he thought that Politzer either was mistaken in so supposing, or that he had made up the story in order to quiet Weintraub. Probably his reason for not believing this part of Politzer's testimony was that he accepted Chairman's testimony that ten days later Politzer intimated to Chairman that it would be well for him to resign, and Chairman refused. Whatever the reason, Weintraub did not, after his talk with Politzer, press the matter until January 24, 1944, when, learning that Chairman was still in the factory, he went again to Politzer and asked why this was. When Politzer told him that Chairman had changed his mind, Weintraub insisted that he must resign anyway, and, upon Politzer's refusal to discharge him, they together went to Kende. Weintraub repeated his insistence that Chairman must go, giving as the reason that his accusation of drunkenness had undermined Weintraub's authority. Kende took Weintraub's view and Politzer wrote out an order of dismissal. No one testified that at this interview, or any time after December first, any of the three mentioned Chairman's testimony at the representation hearing.

As we have said, the examiner was not satisfied that the Board had proved that Chairman's testimony at the representation proceeding had been an actuating cause of his discharge; but, not only did the majority of the Board reverse his ruling as to that, but they also overruled his finding that Politzer had told Weintraub on January first that Chairman was going to resign. They then found that Kende and Weintraub had agreed to bring about Chairman's discharge, at some undefined time after December first, because of Chairman's testimony; and that Weintraub's complaint on January 24 was to cover for affecting that purpose. Whether these findings were justified is the first, and indeed the only important, question of fact; and as a preliminary point arises the extent of our review.

This has been the subject of so much uncertainty that we shall not try to clarify it; but we must decide what change, if any, the amendment of 1947 has made. Section 10(e) now reads that the findings "shall be conclusive" "if supported by substantial evidence on the record considered as a whole"; and the original was merely that they should be conclusive, "if supported by evidence." . . . The most probable intent in adding the phrase, "on the record considered as a whole," was to overrule what Congress apparently supposed — perhaps rightly — had been the understanding of the courts: i.e. that, if any passage could be found in the testimony to support a finding, the review was to stop, no matter how much other parts of the testimony contradicted, or outweighed, it. . . . It appears to us that, had it been intended to set up a new measure of review by the courts, the matter would not have been left so at large. We cannot agree that our review has been "broadened"; we hold that no more was done than to make definite what was already implied.

Just what that review was is another and much more difficult matter — particularly, when it comes to deciding how to treat a reversal by the Board of a finding of one of its own examiners. Obviously no printed record preserves all the evidence, on which any judicial officer bases his finding; and it is principally on that account that, upon an appeal from the judgment of a district court, a court of appeals will hesitate to reverse. Its position must be: "No matter what you saw of the witnesses and what else you heard than these written words, we are satisfied from them alone that you were clearly wrong. Nothing which could have happened that is not recorded, could have justified your conclusion in the face of what is before us." That gives such findings great immunity, which the Rules extend even to the findings of masters, when reviewed by a district judge. The standing of an examiner's findings under the Labor Relations Act is not plain; but it appears to us at least clear that they were not intended to be as unassailable as a master's. The Old Act provided for "examiners," but they did not have to make reports, and, although §10(c) of the New Act requires them to do that, it does not undertake to say how persuasive their findings are to be. On the other hand, §8(a) of the Administrative Procedure Act provides that "on appeal from or review of" the decision of an "officer" who has presided at a hearing, "the agency shall . . . have all the powers which it would have in making the initial decision." It is clear that these words apply to the decisions of the "agency" upon the evidence; but nothing is said as to what effect the "agency" must give to the "officer's" finding; except that, if the text be read literally, it could be argued that the "agency" was to disregard it. The reports in Congress do not help very much. The Senate Report merely said that the findings "would be of consequence, for example, to the extent that material facts in any case depend on the determination of the credibility of witnesses as shown by their demeanor or conduct at the hearing." [We should not] assume that the Board must accept the finding, unless what is preserved in the record makes it "clearly erroneous." That would assimilate examiners to masters, and, if that had been intended, we should expect a plainer statement. On the other hand, [some decisions in other circuits] certainly do mean that, when the Board reverses a finding, it shall count in the court's review of the Board's substituted finding. . . . On the whole we find ourselves unable to apply so impalpable a standard without bringing greater perplexity into a subject already too perplexing. The weight to be given to another person's conclusion from evidence that has disappeared, depends altogether upon one's confidence in his judicial powers. The decision of a child of ten would count for nothing; that of an experienced master would count for much. Unless we set up some canon, universally applicable, . . . each case in this statute will depend upon what competence the Board ascribes to the examiner in question. . . . We hold that, although the Board would be wrong in totally disregarding his findings, it is practically impossible for a court, upon review of those findings which the Board itself substitutes, to consider the Board's reversal as a factor in the court's own decision. This we say, because we cannot find any middle ground between doing that and treating such a reversal as error, whenever it would be such, if done by a judge to a master in equity.

The foregoing discussion is relevant in the case at bar for the following reason. One ground why the evidence failed to convince the examiner of any agreement between Kende and Weintraub to discharge Chairman, was that he thought it quite as likely that the quarrel between Weintraub and Chairman at the end of December still rankled in Weintraub's mind, and induced him to insist upon Chairman's discharge on January 24, 1944. It became important in this view to explain why Weintraub waited for over three weeks; and this the examiner did explain because he believed that Politzer had told Weintraub that Chairman was going to resign. When the majority of the Board refused to accept this finding, they concluded that, since this left Weintraub's delay unexplained, his motive was to be related back to the quarrel of Kende and Chairman on November 30. We should feel obliged in our turn to reverse the reversal of this finding of a master, because the reasons given do not seem to us enough to overbear the evidence which the record did not preserve and which may have convinced the examiner. These were (1) that the examiner did not believe all that Politzer had said; and (2) that the finding was "irreconcilable with the other related facts and all the other evidence bearing on Politzer's behavior and attitude." It is no reason for refusing to accept everything that a witness says, because you do not believe all of it; nothing is more common in all kinds of judicial decisions than to believe some and not all. Nor can we find "other related facts" which were "irreconcilable" with believing that Politzer told Weintraub that Chairman was going to resign. Indeed, Chairman himself swore that on January 11, Politzer suggested to him that he resign, which affirmatively serves to confirm the examiner's findings that Politzer told Weintraub that Chairman would resign in order to placate him. However, as we have said, we think that we are altogether to disregard this as a factor in our review, which we should confine to the bare record; and on that we cannot say that Politzer's testimony had to be believed, in the face of Chairman's denial that he ever told him that he would resign.

There remains the question whether, with this explanation of Weintraub's delay missing, there was "substantial evidence" that the cause of Chairman's discharge was his testimony; and on that the Board had the affirmative; so that it is not enough that Kende and Weintraub might have agreed to find a means of getting rid of Chairman, or that Kende unassisted might have been awaiting an opportunity. Once more, if this was the finding of a judge, we should be in doubt whether it was sufficiently supported. When Weintraub went to Politzer on January 24, 1944, with his complaint at Chairman's continued presence in the factory, and when the two went to Kende because Politzer would not discharge Chairman, if Weintraub was acting in accordance with an agreement between Kende and himself, he was concealing the facts from Politzer. So too was Kende at the ensuing interview; indeed, we must assume that the two had arranged beforehand to keep Politzer in the dark, else Weintraub could scarcely have relied upon Kende to play his part. This appears to us to be constructed substantially out of whole cloth, so improbable is it that they should have gone to such devious means to deceive Politzer. On the other hand, although it is possible that Kende had been waiting for a proper occasion, independently of Weintraub, and that he seized upon Weintraub's complaint, being secretly actuated by his old grievance, we do not read the majority's decision as distinctly indicating that they meant so to find. But, if they did, unless we assume that Weintraub's complaint was trumped up ad hoc, to deceive Politzer, it becomes the merest guess that Kende did not find it alone a sufficient reason for his action, and reverted to his concealed spite.

Nevertheless, in spite of all this we shall direct the Board's order to be enforced. If by special verdict a jury had made either the express finding of the majority that there was an agreement between Kende and Weintraub, or the alternate finding, if there be one, that Kende without Weintraub's concurrence used Weintraub's complaint as an excuse, we should not reverse the verdict; and we understand our function in cases of this kind to be the same. Such a verdict would be within the bounds of rational entertainment. When all is said, Kende had been greatly outraged at Chairman's testimony; he then did propose to get him out of the factory; he still thought at the hearings that he was unfit to remain; and he had told Weintraub to keep watch on him. We cannot say that, with all these circumstances before him, no reasonable person could have concluded that Chairman's testimony was one of the causes of his discharge, little as it would have convinced us, were we free to pass upon the evidence in the first instance. . . .

An enforcement order will issue.

SWAN, Circuit Judge (dissenting).

In National Labor Relations Board v. A. Sartorius & Co., 2d Cir., 140 F.2d 203, 205, we said that "if an administrative agency ignores all the evidence given by one side in a controversy and with studied design gives credence to the testimony of the other side, the findings would be arbitrary and not in accord with the legal requirement." I think that is what the majority of the board has done in the case at bar. I would reverse its finding of motive and deny enforcement of the order.

Universal Camera Corp. v. NLRB
340 U.S. 474 (1951)

Mr. Justice FRANKFURTER delivered the opinion of the Court.

The essential issue raised by this case and its companion, Labor Board v. Pittsburgh Steamship Co., . . . is the effect of the Administrative Procedure Act and the legislation colloquially known as the Taft-Hartley Act on the duty of Courts of Appeals when called upon to review orders of the National Labor Relations Board. . . .

I

Want of certainty in judicial review of Labor Board decisions partly reflects the intractability of any formula to furnish definiteness of content for all the impalpable factors involved in judicial review. But in part doubts as to the nature of the reviewing power and uncertainties in its application derive from history, and to that extent an elucidation of this history may clear them away.

The Wagner Act provided: "The findings of the Board as to the facts, if supported by evidence, shall be conclusive." Act of July 5, 1935, §10(e), 49 Stat. 449, 454, 29 U.S.C. §160(e). This Court read "evidence" to mean "substantial evidence," Washington, V. & M. Coach Co. v. Labor Board, 301 U.S. 142, and we said that "[s]ubstantial evidence is more than a mere scintilla. It means such relevant evidence as a reasonable mind might accept as adequate to support a conclusion." Consolidated Edison Co. v. Labor Board, 305 U.S. 197, 229. Accordingly, it "must do more than create a suspicion of the existence of the fact to be established. [I]t must be enough to justify, if the trial were to a jury, a refusal to direct a verdict when the conclusion sought to be drawn from it is one of fact for the jury." Labor Board v. Columbian Enameling & Stamping Co., 306 U.S. 292, 300.

The very smoothness of the "substantial evidence" formula as the standard for reviewing the evidentiary validity of the Board's findings established its currency. But the inevitably variant applications of the standard to conflicting evidence soon brought contrariety of views and in due course bred criticism. Even though the whole record may have been canvassed in order to determine whether the evidentiary foundation of a determination by the Board was "substantial," the phrasing of this Court's process of review readily lent itself to the notion that it was enough that the evidence supporting the Board's result was "substantial" when considered by itself. It is fair to say that by imperceptible steps regard for the factfinding function of the Board led to the assumption that the requirements of the Wagner Act were met when the reviewing court could find in the record evidence which, when viewed in isolation, substantiated the Board's findings. Compare Labor Board v. Waterman Steamship Corp., 309 U.S. 206; Labor Board v. Bradford Dyeing Assn., 310 U.S. 318; and see Labor Board v. Nevada Consolidated Copper Corp., 316 U.S. 105. . . .

Criticism of so contracted a reviewing power reinforced dissatisfaction felt in various quarters with the Board's administration of the Wagner Act in the years preceding the war. The scheme of the Act was attacked as an inherently unfair fusion of the functions of prosecutor and judge. Accusations of partisan bias were not wanting. The "irresponsible admission and weighing of hearsay, opinion, and emotional speculation in place of factual evidence" was said to be a "serious menace." No doubt some, perhaps even much, of the criticism was baseless and some surely was reckless. What is here relevant, however, is the climate of opinion thereby generated and its effect on Congress. Protests against "shocking injustices" and intimations of judicial "abdication" with which some courts granted enforcement of the Board's orders stimulated pressures for legislative relief from alleged administrative excesses. [A distinguished committee (chaired by Dean Acheson) was appointed by the attorney general to study administrative law and procedures in the federal government and to make recommendations. Its staff conducted the first comprehensive study of the federal administrative process.]

The final report of the Attorney General's Committee was submitted in January, 1941. The majority concluded that "[d]issatisfaction with the existing standards as to the scope of judicial review derives largely from dissatisfaction with the fact-finding procedures now employed by the administrative bodies." Departure from the "substantial evidence" test, it thought, would either create unnecessary uncertainty or transfer to courts the responsibility for ascertaining and assaying matters the significance of which lies outside judicial competence. Accordingly, it recommended against legislation embodying a general scheme of judicial review.

Three members of the Committee [stated] that the "present system or lack of system of judicial review" led to inconsistency and uncertainty. They reported that under a "prevalent" interpretation of the "substantial evidence" rule "if what is called 'substantial evidence' is found anywhere in the record to support conclusions of fact, the courts are said to be obliged to sustain the decision without reference to how heavily the countervailing evidence may preponderate — unless indeed the stage of arbitrary decision is reached. Under this interpretation, the courts need to read only one side of the case and, if they find any evidence there, the administrative action is to be sustained and the record to the contrary is to be ignored." Their view led them to recommend that Congress enact principles of review applicable to all agencies not excepted by unique characteristics. One of these principles was expressed by the formula that judicial review could extend to "findings, inferences, or conclusions of fact unsupported, upon the whole record, by substantial evidence." [T]he phrase "upon the whole record" makes its first appearance in this recommendation of the minority of the Attorney General's Committee. This evidence of the close relationship between the phrase and the criticism out of which it arose is important, for the substance of this formula for judicial review found its way into the statute books when Congress with unquestioning — we might even say uncritical — unanimity enacted the Administrative Procedure Act.

One is tempted to say "uncritical" because the legislative history of the Act hardly speaks with that clarity of purpose which Congress supposedly furnishes courts in order to enable them to enforce its true will. On the one hand, the sponsors of the legislation indicated that they were reaffirming the prevailing "substantial evidence" test. But with equal clarity they expressed disapproval of the manner in which the courts were applying their own standard. The committee reports of both houses refer to the practice of agencies to rely upon "suspicion, surmise, implication, or plainly incredible evidence," and indicate that courts are to exact higher standards "in the exercise of their independent judgment" and on consideration of "the whole record."

Similar dissatisfaction with too restricted application of the "substantial evidence" test is reflected in the legislative history of the Taft-Hartley Act. [A]s the Senate Committee Report relates, "it was finally decided to conform the statute to the corresponding section of the Administrative Procedure Act where the substantial evidence test prevails. In order to clarify any ambiguity in that statute, however, the committee inserted the words "questions of fact, if supported by substantial evidence *on the record considered as a whole. . . .*"

It is fair to say that in all this Congress expressed a mood. And it expressed its mood not merely by oratory but by legislation. As legislation that mood must be respected, even though it can only serve as a standard for judgment and not as a body of rigid rules assuring sameness of application. Enforcement of such broad standards implies subtlety of mind and solidity of judgment. But it is not for us to question that Congress may assume such qualities in the federal judiciary.

From the legislative story we have summarized, two concrete conclusions do emerge. One is the identity of aim of the Administrative Procedure Act and the Taft-Hartley Act regarding the proof with which the Labor Board must support a decision. The other is that now Congress has left no room for doubt as to the kind of scrutiny which a Court of Appeals must give the record before the Board to satisfy itself that the Board's order rests on adequate proof. . . .

Whether or not it was ever permissible for courts to determine the substantiality of evidence supporting a Labor Board decision merely on the basis of evidence which in and of itself justified it, without taking into account contradictory evidence or evidence from which conflicting inferences could be drawn, the new legislation definitely precludes such a theory of review and bars its practice. The substantiality of evidence must take into account whatever in the record fairly detracts from its weight. This is clearly the significance of the requirement in both statutes that courts consider the whole record. . . .

To be sure, the requirement for canvassing "the whole record" in order to ascertain substantiality does not furnish a calculus of value by which a reviewing court can assess the evidence. Nor was it intended to negative the function of the Labor Board as one of those agencies presumably equipped or informed by experience to deal with a specialized field of knowledge, whose findings within that field carry the authority of an expertness which courts do not possess and therefore must respect. Nor does it mean that even as to matters not requiring expertise a court may displace the Board's choice between two fairly conflicting views, even though the court would justifiably have made a different choice had the matter been before it de novo. Congress has merely made it clear that a reviewing court is not barred from setting aside a Board decision when it cannot conscientiously find that the evidence supporting that decision is substantial, when viewed in the light that the record in its entirety furnishes, including the body of evidence opposed to the Board's view.

There remains, then, the question whether enactment of these two statutes has altered the scope of review other than to require that substantiality be determined in the light of all that the record relevantly presents. . . .

. . . . The adoption in these statutes of the judicially constructed "substantial evidence" test was a response to pressures for stricter and more uniform practice, not a reflection of approval of all existing practices. To find the change so elusive that it cannot be precisely defined does not mean it may be ignored. We should fail in our duty to effectuate the will of Congress if we denied recognition to expressed Congressional disapproval of the finality accorded to Labor Board findings by some decisions of this and lower courts, or even of the atmosphere which may have favored those decisions.

We conclude, therefore, that the Administrative Procedure Act and the Taft-Hartley Act direct that courts must now assume more responsibility for the reasonableness and fairness of Labor Board decisions than some courts have shown in the past. Reviewing courts must be influenced by a feeling that they are not to abdicate the conventional judicial function. Congress has imposed on them responsibility for assuring that the Board keeps within reasonable grounds. That responsibility is not less real because it is limited to enforcing the requirement that evidence appear substantial when viewed, on the record as a whole, by courts invested with the authority and enjoying the prestige of the Courts of Appeals. The Board's findings are entitled to respect; but they must nonetheless be set aside when the record before a Court of Appeals clearly precludes the Board's decision from being justified by a fair estimate of the worth of the testimony of witnesses or its informed judgment on matters within its special competence or both.

From this it follows that enactment of these statutes does not require every Court of Appeals to alter its practice. Some — perhaps a majority — have always applied the attitude reflected in this legislation. To explore whether a particular court should or should not alter its practice would only divert attention from the application of the standard now prescribed to a futile inquiry into the nature of the test formerly used by a particular court.

Our power to review the correctness of application of the present standard ought seldom to be called into action. Whether on the record as a whole there is substantial evidence to support agency findings is a question which Congress has placed in the keeping of the Courts of Appeals. This Court will intervene only in what ought to be the rare instance when the standard appears to have been misapprehended or grossly misapplied.

II

[The Supreme Court said that there was "substantial evidence on the record considered as a whole" to support the board's decision, assuming that the court of appeals could not consider the hearing examiner's report. It then addressed the question whether that report should be given any weight by a reviewing court.]

III

The Court of Appeals deemed itself bound by the Board's rejection of the examiner's findings because the court considered these findings not "as unassailable as a master's." 179 F.2d at 752. They are not. Section 10(c) of the Labor Management Relations Act provides that "If upon the preponderance of the testimony taken the Board shall be of the opinion that any person named in the complaint has engaged in or is engaging in any such unfair labor practice, then the Board shall state its findings of fact. . . ." 61 Stat. 147, 29 U.S.C. (Supp. III) §160(c). The responsibility for decision thus placed on the Board is wholly inconsistent with the notion that it has power to reverse an examiner's findings only when they are "clearly erroneous." Such a limitation would make so drastic a departure from prior administrative practice that explicitness would be required.

The Court of Appeals concluded from this premise "that, although the Board would be wrong in totally disregarding his findings, it is practically impossible for a court, upon review of those findings which the Board itself substitutes, to consider the Board's reversal as a factor in the court's own decision. This we say, because we cannot find any middle ground between doing that and treating such a reversal as error, whenever it would be such, if done by a judge to a master in equity." 179 F.2d at 753. Much as we respect the logical acumen of the Chief Judge of the Court of Appeals, we do not find ourselves pinioned between the horns of his dilemma.

We are aware that to give the examiner's findings less finality than a master's and yet entitle them to consideration in striking the account, is to introduce another and an unruly factor into the judgmatical process of review. But we ought not to fashion an exclusionary rule merely to reduce the number of imponderables to be considered by reviewing courts.

The Taft-Hartley Act provides that "The findings of the Board with respect to questions of fact if supported by substantial evidence on the record considered as a whole shall be conclusive." 61 Stat. 148, 29 U.S.C. (Supp. III) §160(e). Surely an examiner's report is as much a part of the record as the complaint or the testimony. According to the Administrative Procedure Act, "All decisions (including initial, recommended, or tentative decisions) shall become a part of the record. . . ." §8(b), 60 Stat. 242, 5 U.S.C. §1007(b).

It is therefore difficult to escape the conclusion that the plain language of the statutes directs a reviewing court to determine the substantiality of evidence on the record including the examiner's report. The conclusion is confirmed by the indications in the legislative history that enhancement of the status and function of the trial examiner was one of the important purposes of the movement for administrative reform. . . .

[The Court referred in passing to] the rather obscure provision that an agency which reviews an examiner's report has "all the powers which it would have in making the initial decision."

But [n]othing in the statutes suggests that the Labor Board should not be influenced by the examiner's opportunity to observe the witnesses he hears and sees and the Board does not. Nothing suggests that reviewing courts should not give to the examiner's report such probative force as it intrinsically commands. To the contrary, §11 of the Administrative Procedure Act contains detailed provisions designed to maintain high standards of independence and competence in examiners. Section 10(c) of the Labor Management Relations Act requires that examiners "shall issue . . . . a proposed report, together with a recommended order." Both statutes thus evince a purpose to increase the importance of the role of examiners in the administrative process. High standards of public administration counsel that we attribute to the Labor Board's examiners both due regard for the responsibility which Congress imposes on them and the competence to discharge it. . . .

We do not require that the examiner's findings be given more weight than in reason and in the light of judicial experience they deserve. The "substantial evidence" standard is not modified in any way when the Board and its examiner disagree. We intend only to recognize that evidence supporting a conclusion may be less substantial when an impartial, experienced examiner who has observed the witnesses and lived with the case has drawn conclusions different from the Board's than when he has reached the same conclusion. The findings of the examiner are to be considered along with the consistency and inherent probability of testimony. The significance of his report, of course, depends largely on the importance of credibility in the particular case. To give it this significance does not seem to us materially more difficult than to heed the other factors which in sum determine whether evidence is "substantial." . . .

We therefore remand the cause to the Court of Appeals. On reconsideration of the record it should accord the findings of the trial examiner the relevance that they reasonably command in answering the comprehensive question whether the evidence supporting the Board's order is substantial. But the court need not limit its reexamination of the case to the effect of that report on its decision. We leave it free to grant or deny enforcement as it thinks the principles expressed in this opinion dictate.

Judgment vacated and cause remanded.

Mr. Justice Black and Mr. Justice Douglas concur with part I and II of this opinion but as to part III agree with the opinion of the court below. . . .

NLRB v. Universal Camera Corp. (II)

190 F.2d 429 (2d Cir. 1951)

Before SWAN, Chief Judge, and FRANK and L. HAND, Circuit Judges.

L. HAND, Circuit Judge.

By a divided vote we decided this appeal last year upon the same record that is now before us, holding that the Board's order should be "enforced." The Supreme Court vacated our order and remanded the cause to us for reconsideration. . . .

. . . We had said that we could find no practical mesne between giving the findings of an examiner the immunity which a court must give to those of a master, and saying that, although the Board should no doubt treat them as having some evidentiary value, it was impossible for us to measure what that ought to be; and that therefore we would decide the appeal, as though there had been no findings. Although this went too far, again it is plain that the weight which we should insist that the Board should give them must be left at large; except that we must count them for something, and particularly when — as indeed we said at length in our first opinion — they were based on that part of the evidence which the printed words do not preserve. Often that is the most telling part, for on the issue of veracity the bearing and delivery of a witness will usually be the dominating factors, when the words alone leave any rational choice. Perhaps as good a way as any to state the change effected by the amendment is to say that we are not to be reluctant to insist that an examiner's findings on veracity must not be overruled without a very substantial preponderance in the testimony as recorded.

In the case at bar the examiner came to the conclusion that Chairman's discharge on January 24, 1944, was not because of his testimony two months before. He believed that Politzer had told Weintraub, a day or two after Weintraub's quarrel with Chairman at the end of December, that Chairman had said he was going to resign; and, although he did not believe that Chairman had in fact said so, he found that Politzer either thought he had, or told Weintraub that he had in the hope of s[m]oothing over their quarrel. We see nothing improbable in this story, nor can we find any contradiction of it in Chairman's testimony that on January 11th Politzer asked him if he was going to resign. Indeed, if Politzer had got the impression that Chairman was going to resign, Politzer might very naturally have followed it with an inquiry which to Chairman appeared like opening up a new subject. Be that as it may, we are satisfied, as we were before, that there was enough to justify the conclusion that, when Weintraub complained that Chairman was undermining his influence in the factory, Politzer put him off, presumably in the hope that time might soften his animosity. Hence, even were the Board's argument more cogent than it is, we can no longer agree that it was free to overrule the examiner's conclusion that Weintraub's delay in complaining to Kende was because he had been waiting for Chairman to resign. Once this is accepted as true, it becomes incredible that Chairman's dismissal on January 24, 1944, was in fulfillment of any joint plan between Kende and Weintraub. In our first opinion we gave our reasons for thinking so; and, as we read the Board's brief, it does not argue the contrary.

However, it does argue that, even if Kende and Weintraub had no such joint plan, the case against the respondent was proved, for it was enough if Kende independently and of his own motion seized upon Weintraub's complaint to vent his personal spleen upon Chairman. It is of course true that no one can be sure what may have actuated Kende at least in part; nothing is more difficult than to disentangle the motives of another's conduct — motives frequently unknown even to the actor himself. But for that very reason those parts of the evidence which are lost in print become especially pregnant, and the Board which had no access to them should have hesitated to assume that the examiner was not right to act upon them. A story may indeed be so unreasonable on its face that no plausibility in its telling will make it tenable, but this is seldom true and certainly was not true here. In appeals from the Board we have over and over again refused to upset findings which in cold type seemed to us extremely doubtful just because we were aware that we could not know what may have been the proper deciding factors. However limited should be the regard which the Board must give to the findings of its examiner, we cannot escape the conclusion that the record in the case at bar was such that the following findings of the examiner should have turned the scale; "the undersigned is not persuaded that Kende based his decision upon any animus against Chairman for testifying rather than on an evaluation of Weintraub's request based upon the merits." Indeed, it is at least doubtful whether the Board meant to overrule that finding except as it was involved in its own finding that Kende and Weintraub had a joint plan to oust Chairman. That it may not have meant more appears from the statement in note seven of its opinion: "the absence of direct and detailed evidence of such a conspiracy . . . does not militate against our conviction that it was actually because of Chairman's testimony at the Board hearing and only ostensibly because of the resurrected December 30th episode that Weintraub and Kende brought about Chairman's discharge. On the evidence before us we have no substantial doubt" (surely a very curious assurance) "that discrimination occurred." Be that as it may, upon a reexamination of the record as a whole, and upon giving weight to the examiner's findings — now in compliance with the Court's directions as we understand them — we think that our first disposition of the appeal was wrong, and we hold that the Board should have dismissed the complaint.

Order reversed; complaint to be dismissed.

FRANK, Circuit Judge (concurring).

Recognizing, as only a singularly stupid man would not, Judge Hand's superior wisdom, intelligence and learning, I seldom disagree with him, and then with serious misgivings. In this instance, I have overcome my misgivings because I think that his modesty has moved him to interpret too sweepingly the Supreme Court's criticism of our earlier opinion written by him. I read the Supreme Court's opinion as saying that we had obeyed the new statute with but one exception: We had wholly disregarded the examiner's finding which the Board rejected.

The Supreme Court . . . said of our earlier opinion that "it is clear" that this court "in fact did consider the 'record as a whole,' and did not deem itself merely the judicial echo of the Board." In interpreting the new statute, the Court relied upon and quoted Senator Taft's statement. "It does not go quite so far as the power given to a circuit court of appeals to review a district-court decision." And the Court, after saying that the new statute was not intended to "negative the function of the Labor Board" with reference to "findings within . . . a specialized field of knowledge," significantly added the following: "Nor does it mean that even as to matters not requiring expertise a court may displace

the Board's choice between two . . . conflicting views, even though the court would justifiably have made a different choice had the matter been before it."

I think, then, that we must thus conclude: (1) Except that we did not consider the
examiner's findings which differed from the Board's, we had not in this case disobeyed the
new statute; (2) that statute does not put us, vis-à-vis the Board, in the same position we
occupy with respect to a trial court; (3) even as to matters within the area of the Board's
so-called "expertise," we may not try Board cases de novo.

Concerning our error in disregarding the examiner's findings, Judge Hand, as I
understand him, interprets as follows the Supreme Court's ruling: The Board may never
reject an examiner's findings if it rests on his evaluation of the credibility of oral testimony
unless (1) that rejection results from the Board's rational use of the Board's specialized
knowledge or (2) the examiner has been absurdly naive in believing a witness. This, I
think, is somewhat more restrictive of the Board's powers than the Supreme Court
suggested, for it said: "The responsibility for decision thus placed on the Board is wholly
inconsistent with the notion that it has power to reverse an examiner's findings only when
they are 'clearly erroneous.'"

I would also, by way of caution, add this qualification (to which, judging from his opinions elsewhere, I gather Judge Hand will not demur): An examiner's finding binds the Board
only to the extent that it is a "testimonial inference," or "primary inference," i.e., an inference that a fact to which a witness orally testified is an actual fact because that witness so
testified and because observation of the witness induces a belief in that testimony. The
Board, however, is not bound by the examiner's "secondary inferences," or "derivative inferences," i.e., facts to which no witness orally testified but which the examiner inferred from
facts orally testified by witnesses whom the examiner believed. The Board may reach its
own "secondary inferences," and we must abide by them unless they are irrational; in that
way, the Board differs from a trial judge (in a juryless case) who hears and sees the witnesses,
for, although we are usually bound by his "testimonial inferences," we need not accept his
"secondary inferences" even if rational, but, where other rational "secondary inferences"
are possible, we may substitute our own. Since that is true, it is also true that we must not
interfere when the Board adopts either (1) its examiner's "testimonial inferences" and they
are not absurd, or (2) his rational "secondary inferences."

Except as noted above, I concur.

2. *Background Notes on* Universal Camera

Behind the labor legislation of the 1930s lay a long history of judicial hostility to
labor unions — and to the economic weapons used by labor in its struggle to organize. If
an employer could convince a court that a strike or boycott had "unlawful objectives" or
used "unlawful means," the court would order it enjoined. Critics claimed that the term
"unlawful" was used broadly by the courts to denote not something contrary to law but
any objective that the courts disapproved. The creation of the National Labor Relations
Board (NLRB) under the Wagner Act of 1935 was in part a response to this widely
acknowledged judicial hostility toward union activity. Faced with an avowed government
policy of actively promoting unionization and collective bargaining through reliance on a
labor board staffed by "enthusiasts burning with zeal for organized labor," many courts
exercised great restraint in overturning findings by the board. A series of ambiguous
Supreme Court decisions created confusion among the lower courts about whether they

should consider the entire record when ascertaining the substantiality of the labor board's position or only that evidence favorable to the board's decision.

No opinion of the Supreme Court explicitly said that the substantiality of evidence was to be determined by examining only evidence that supported the board decision, nor did all lower courts interpret the Court's decisions to require this. But during oral argument in NLRB v. Pittsburgh Steamship Co., 340 U.S. 498 (1951), the companion case to *Universal Camera*, Justice Frankfurter indicated his view that in fact the Supreme Court had been using the more deferential standard. Quoting from NLRB v. Nevada Consolidated Copper Corp., 316 U.S. 105 (1942), he said "'since upon examination of the record, we cannot say that the finding of fact of the Board is without support in the evidence' — that means if I find something in the evidence which supports it, my case is at an end. This is what I thought I had been doing." To which the government counsel who was arguing fervently that the Court had been using the whole record test all along could only reply, "I cannot contradict your Honor." Jaffe, Judicial Review: Substantial Evidence on the Whole Record, 64 Harv. L. Rev. 1233, 1236 (1951).

It is difficult to believe, however, that courts literally looked at only those portions of the record favorable to the board. Suppose a record contained evidence that (1) an employee testified in favor of a union at a labor board hearing, and (2) the employer subsequently discharged him. Would a court have sustained a board finding of an unfair labor practice if the employer introduced evidence showing that (3) ten years lapsed between the time of testimony and discharge, and (4) the employee was repeatedly drunk in the six months prior to discharge? Doesn't the reasonableness of inferring certain facts from given evidence inevitably depend on the presence or absence of other relevant evidence? Perhaps courts did not literally look only at evidence favorable to the board but were simply very deferential to the board's factfinding.

3. Allentown Mack: *Facts, Politics, and Law*

Allentown Mack Sales and Service v. National Labor Relations Board
522 U.S. 359 (1998)

Justice SCALIA delivered the opinion of the Court.

Under longstanding precedent of the National Labor Relations Board, an employer who believes that an incumbent union no longer enjoys the support of a majority of its employees has three options: to request a formal, Board-supervised election, to withdraw recognition from the union and refuse to bargain, or to conduct an internal poll of employee support for the union. The Board has held that the latter two are unfair labor practices unless the employer can show that it had a "good-faith reasonable doubt" about the union's majority support. We must decide whether the Board's standard for employer polling is rational and consistent with the National Labor Relations Act, and whether the Board's factual determinations in this case are supported by substantial evidence in the record.

I

Mack Trucks, Inc., had a factory branch in Allentown, Pennsylvania, whose service and parts employees were represented by Local Lodge 724 of the International

Association of Machinists and Aerospace Workers, AFL-CIO (Local 724). Mack notified its Allentown managers in May 1990 that it intended to sell the branch, and several of those managers formed Allentown Mack Sales & Service, Inc., the petitioner here, which purchased the assets of the business on December 20, 1990, and began to operate it as an independent dealership. From December 21, 1990, to January 1, 1991, Allentown hired 32 of the original 45 Mack employees.

During the period before and immediately after the sale, a number of Mack employees made statements to the prospective owners of Allentown Mack Sales suggesting that the incumbent union had lost support among employees in the bargaining unit. In job interviews, eight employees made statements indicating, or at least arguably indicating, that they personally no longer supported the union. In addition, Ron Mohr, a member of the union's bargaining committee and shop steward for the Mack Trucks service department, told an Allentown manager that it was his feeling that the employees did not want a union, and that "with a new company, if a vote was taken, the Union would lose." And Kermit Bloch, who worked for Mack Trucks as a mechanic on the night shift, told a manager that the entire night shift (then five or six employees) did not want the union.

On January 2, 1991, Local 724 asked Allentown Mack Sales to recognize it as the employees' collective-bargaining representative, and to begin negotiations for a contract. The new employer rejected that request by letter dated January 25, claiming a "good faith doubt as to support of the Union among the employees." The letter also announced that Allentown had "arranged for an independent poll by secret ballot of its hourly employees to be conducted under guidelines prescribed by the National Labor Relations Board." The poll, supervised by a Roman Catholic priest, was conducted on February 8, 1991; the union lost 19 to 13. Shortly thereafter, the union filed an unfair-labor-practice charge with the Board.

[The] Board [concluded] that Allentown "had not demonstrated that it harbored a reasonable doubt, based on objective considerations, as to the incumbent Union's continued majority status after the transition." The Board ordered Allentown to recognize and bargain with Local 724. . . .

II

[The Court rejected Allentown's argument that it is irrational to require the same factual showing to justify a poll as to justify an outright withdrawal of recognition, because that leaves the employer with no legal incentive to poll. The Court wrote:] While the Board's adoption of a unitary standard for polling, RM elections, and withdrawals of recognition is in some respects a puzzling policy, we do not find it so irrational as to be "arbitrary [or] capricious["] within the meaning of the Administrative Procedure Act. The Board believes that employer polling is potentially "disruptive" to established bargaining relationships and "unsettling" to employees, and so has chosen to limit severely the circumstances under which it may be conducted. The unitary standard reflects the Board's apparent conclusion that polling should be tolerated only when the employer might otherwise simply withdraw recognition and refuse to bargain. . . .

III

The Board held Allentown guilty of an unfair labor practice in its conduct of the polling because it "ha[d] not demonstrated that it held a reasonable doubt, based on objective considerations, that the Union continued to enjoy the support of a majority of the bargaining unit employees." We must decide whether that conclusion is supported by substantial evidence on the record as a whole. Put differently, we must decide whether on this record it would have been possible for a reasonable jury to reach the Board's conclusion. . . .

The question presented for review, therefore, is whether, on the evidence presented to the Board, a reasonable jury could have found that Allentown lacked a genuine, reasonable uncertainty about whether Local 724 enjoyed the continuing support of a majority of unit employees. In our view, the answer is no. The Board's finding to the contrary rests on a refusal to credit probative circumstantial evidence, and on evidentiary demands that go beyond the substantive standard the Board purports to apply. . . .

The Board adopted the ALJ's finding that 6 of Allentown's 32 employees had made "statements which could be used as objective considerations supporting a good-faith reasonable doubt as to continued majority status by the Union." [And] it presumably accepted the ALJ's assessment that "7 of 32, or roughly 20 percent of the involved employees" was not alone sufficient to create "an objective reasonable doubt of union majority support." The Board did not specify how many express disavowals would have been enough to establish reasonable doubt, but the number must presumably be less than 16 (half of the bargaining unit), since that would establish reasonable *certainty*. Still, we would not say that 20% first-hand-confirmed opposition (even with no countering evidence of union support) is alone enough to *require* a conclusion of reasonable doubt. But there was much more.

For one thing, the ALJ and the Board totally disregarded the effect upon Allentown of the statement of an eighth employee, Dennis Marsh, who said that "he was not being represented for the $35 he was paying." The ALJ, whose findings were adopted by the Board, said that this statement "seems more an expression of a desire for better representation than one for no representation at all." It seems to us that it is, more accurately, simply an expression of dissatisfaction with the union's performance — which *could* reflect the speaker's desire that the union represent him more effectively, but *could also* reflect the speaker's desire to save his $35 and get rid of the union. The statement would assuredly engender an *uncertainty* whether the speaker supported the union, and so could not be entirely ignored.

But the most significant evidence excluded from consideration by the Board consisted of statements of two employees regarding not merely their own support of the union, but support among the work force in general. Kermit Bloch, who worked on the night shift, told an Allentown manager "the entire night shift did not want the Union." The ALJ refused to credit this, because "Bloch did not testify and thus could not explain how he formed his opinion about the views of his fellow employees." Unsubstantiated assertions that other employees do not support the union certainly do not establish *the fact of that disfavor* with the degree of reliability ordinarily demanded in legal proceedings. But under the Board's enunciated test for polling, it is not the fact of disfavor that is at issue (the poll itself is meant to establish that), but rather the existence of a reasonable uncertainty on the part of the employer regarding that fact. On that issue, absent some reason for the employer to know that Bloch had no basis for his information, or that Bloch was lying, reason demands that the statement be given considerable weight.

Another employee who gave information concerning overall support for the union was Ron Mohr, who told Allentown managers that "if a vote was taken, the Union would lose" and that "it was his feeling that the employees did not want a union." The ALJ again objected irrelevantly that "there is no evidence with respect to how he gained this knowledge." In addition, the Board held that Allentown "could not legitimately rely on [the statement] as a basis for doubting the Union's majority status," because Mohr was "referring to Mack's existing employee complement, not to the individuals who were later hired by [Allentown]." This basis for disregarding Mohr's statements is wholly irrational. Local 724 had never won an election, or even an informal poll, within the actual unit of 32 Allentown employees. Its claim to represent them rested entirely on the Board's presumption that the work force of a successor company has the same disposition regarding the union as did the work force of the predecessor company, if the majority of the new work force came from the old one. The Board cannot rationally adopt that presumption for purposes of imposing the duty to bargain, and adopt precisely the opposite presumption (*i.e.*, contend that there is no relationship between the sentiments of the two work forces) for purposes of determining what evidence tends to establish a reasonable doubt regarding union support. Such irrationality is impermissible even if, as Justice Breyer suggests, it would further the Board's political objectives.

It must be borne in mind that the issue here is not whether Mohr's statement clearly establishes a majority in opposition to the union, but whether it contributes to a reasonable uncertainty whether a majority in favor of the union existed. We think it surely does. . . .

Accepting the Board's apparent (and in our view inescapable) concession that Allentown received reliable information that 7 of the bargaining-unit employees did not support the union, the remaining 25 would have had to support the union by a margin of 17 to 8 — a ratio of more than 2 to 1 — if the union commanded majority support. The statements of Bloch and Mohr would cause anyone to doubt that degree of support, and neither the Board nor the ALJ discussed any evidence that Allentown should have weighed on the other side. [We] think it quite impossible for a rational factfinder to avoid the conclusion that Allentown had reasonable, good-faith grounds to doubt — to be *uncertain about* — the union's retention of majority support.

IV

That conclusion would make this a fairly straightforward administrative-law case, except for the contention that the Board's factfinding here was not an aberration. Allentown asserts that, although "the Board continues to cite the words of the good faith doubt branch of its withdrawal of recognition standard," a systematic review of the Board's decisions will reveal that "it has in practice eliminated the good faith doubt branch in favor of a strict head count." The Board denies (not too persuasively) that it has insisted upon a strict head count, but does defend its factfinding in this case by saying that it has regularly rejected similarly persuasive demonstrations of reasonable good-faith doubt in prior decisions.

[It] is certainly conceivable that an adjudicating agency might consistently require a particular substantive standard to be established by a quantity or character of evidence so far beyond what reason and logic would require as to make it apparent that the *announced* standard is not *really* the effective one. And it is conceivable that in certain categories of cases an adjudicating agency which purports to be applying a preponderance standard of proof might so consistently demand in fact more than a preponderance, that all should be on notice from its case law that the genuine burden of proof is more than a preponderance. The question arises, then, whether, if that should be the situation that obtains here, we ought to measure the evidentiary support for the Board's decision against the standards consistently applied rather than the standards recited. As a theoretical matter (and leaving aside the question of legal authority), the Board could certainly have raised the bar for employer polling or withdrawal of recognition by imposing a more stringent requirement than the reasonable-doubt test, or by adopting a formal requirement that employers establish their reasonable doubt by more than a preponderance of the evidence. Would it make any difference if the Board achieved precisely the same result by formally leaving in place the reasonable-doubt and preponderance standards, but consistently applying them as though they meant something other than what they say? We think it would.

[Reasoned] decisionmaking, in which the rule announced is the rule applied, promotes sound results, and unreasoned decisionmaking the opposite. The evil of a decision that applies a standard other than the one it enunciates spreads in both directions, preventing both consistent application of the law by subordinate agency personnel (notably ALJ's), and effective review of the law by the courts. . . . If revision of the Board's standard of proof can be achieved thus subtly and obliquely, it becomes a much more complicated enterprise for a court of appeals to determine whether substantial evidence supports the conclusion that the required standard has or has not been met. [An] agency should not be able to impede judicial review, and indeed even political oversight, by disguising its policymaking as factfinding.

Because reasoned decisionmaking demands it, and because the systemic consequences of any other approach are unacceptable, the Board must be required to apply in fact the clearly understood legal standards that it enunciates in principle, such as good-faith reasonable doubt and preponderance of the evidence. Reviewing courts are entitled to take those standards to mean what they say, and to conduct substantial-evidence review on that basis. Even the most consistent and hence predictable Board departure from proper application of those standards will not alter the legal rule by which the agency's factfinding is to be judged. . . .

The Board can, of course, forthrightly and explicitly adopt counterfactual evidentiary presumptions (which are in effect substantive rules of law) as a way of furthering particular legal or policy goals — for example, the Board's irrebuttable presumption of majority support for the union during the year following certification. The Board might also be justified in forthrightly and explicitly adopting a rule of evidence that categorically excludes certain testimony on policy grounds, without reference to its inherent probative value. [That] is not the sort of Board action at issue here, however, but rather the Board's allegedly systematic undervaluation of certain evidence, or allegedly systematic exaggeration of what the evidence must prove. When the Board purports to be engaged in simple factfinding, unconstrained by substantive presumptions or evidentiary rules of exclusion, it is not free to prescribe what inferences from the evidence it will accept and reject, but must draw all those inferences that the evidence fairly demands. "Substantial evidence" review exists precisely to ensure that the Board achieves minimal compliance with this obligation, which is the foundation of all honest and legitimate adjudication. . . .

We conclude that the Board's "reasonable doubt" test for employer polls is facially rational and consistent with the Act. But the Board's factual finding that Allentown Mack Sales lacked such a doubt is not supported by substantial evidence on the record as a whole. The judgment of the Court of Appeals for the District of Columbia Circuit is therefore reversed, and the case is remanded with instructions to deny enforcement.

It is so ordered.

Chief Justice REHNQUIST, with whom Justice O'CONNOR, Justice KENNEDY, and Justice THOMAS join, concurring in part and dissenting in part.

I concur in the judgment of the Court and in Parts I, III, and IV. However, I disagree that the National Labor Relations Board's standard is rational and consistent with the National Labor Relations Act, and I therefore dissent as to Part II. . . .

Justice BREYER, with whom Justice STEVENS, Justice SOUTER, and Justice GINSBURG join, concurring in part and dissenting in part.

[To] decide whether an agency's conclusion is supported by substantial evidence, a reviewing court must identify the conclusion and then examine and weigh the evidence. [If] the majority is to overturn a court of appeals' "substantial evidence" decision, it must identify the agency's conclusion, examine the evidence, and then determine whether the evidence is so *obviously* inadequate to support the conclusion that the reviewing court must have seriously misunderstood the nature of its legal duty.

The majority opinion begins by properly stating the Board's conclusion, namely, that the employer, Allentown Mack Sales & Service, Inc., did not demonstrate that it "held a reasonable doubt, *based on objective considerations*, that the Union continued to enjoy the support of a majority of the bargaining unit employees." (emphasis added; internal quotation marks omitted). The opinion, however, then omits the words I have italicized and transforms this conclusion, rephrasing it as: "Allentown lacked a genuine, reasonable uncertainty about whether Local 724 enjoyed the continuing support of a majority of unit employees."

Key words of a technical sort that the Board has used in hundreds of opinions written over several decades to express what the Administrative Law Judge (ALJ) here called "*objective* reasonable doubt" have suddenly disappeared, leaving in their place what looks like an ordinary jury standard that might reflect not an agency's specialized knowledge of the workplace, but a court's common understanding of human psychology. . . .

[Allentown] sought to show that it had an "objective" good-faith doubt primarily by presenting the testimony of Allentown managers, who, in turn, reported statements made to them by 14 employees. The ALJ set aside the statements of 5 of those employees as insignificant for various reasons — for example because the employees were not among the rehired 32, because their statements were equivocal, or because they made the statements at a time too long before the transition. The majority does not take issue with the ALJ's reasoning with respect to these employees. The ALJ then found that statements made by six, and possibly seven, employees (22 percent of the 32) helped Allentown show an "objective" reasonable doubt. The majority does not quarrel with this conclusion. The majority does, however, take issue with the ALJ's decision not to count in Allentown's favor three further statements, made by employees Marsh, Bloch, and Mohr. The majority says that these statements *required* the ALJ and the Board to find for Allentown. I cannot agree.

Consider Marsh's statement. Marsh said, as the majority opinion notes, that " 'he was not being represented for the $35 he was paying.' " The majority says that the ALJ was wrong not to count this statement in the employer's favor. But the majority fails to mention that Marsh made this statement to an Allentown manager while the manager was interviewing Marsh to determine whether he would, or would not, be one of the 32 employees whom Allentown would reemploy. The ALJ, when evaluating all the employee statements, wrote that statements made to the Allentown managers during the job interviews were "somewhat tainted as it is likely that a job applicant will say whatever he believes the prospective employer wants to hear." In so stating, the ALJ was reiterating the Board's own normative general finding that employers should not "rely in asserting a good-faith doubt" upon "[s]tatements made by employees during the course of an interview with a prospective employer." . . .

I do not see how, on the record before us, one could plausibly argue that these relevant general findings of the Board fall outside the Board's lawfully delegated authority. The Board in effect has said that an employee statement *made during a job interview with an employer who has expressed an interest in a nonunionized work force* will often tell us precisely *nothing* about that employee's true feelings. That Board conclusion represents an exercise of the kind of discretionary authority that Congress placed squarely within the Board's administrative and fact-finding powers and responsibilities. Nor is it procedurally improper for an agency, rather like a common-law court (and drawing upon its accumulated expertise and exercising its administrative responsibilities) to use adjudicatory proceedings to develop rules of thumb about the likely weight assigned to different kinds of evidence.

[The] majority says that "reason demands" that Bloch's statement "be given considerable weight." But why? The Board, drawing upon both reason and experience, has said it will "view with suspicion and caution" one employee's statements "purporting to represent the views of other employees." . . . How is it unreasonable for the Board to provide this kind of guidance, about what kinds of evidence are more likely, and what kinds are less likely, to support an "objective reasonable doubt" (thereby helping an employer understand just when he may refuse to bargain with an established employee representative, in the absence of an employee-generated union decertification petition)? . . .

Finally, consider the Allentown manager's statement that Mohr told him that "if a vote was taken, the Union would lose." . . . One can find reflected in the majority opinion some of the reasons the ALJ gave for discounting the significance of Mohr's statement. The majority says of the ALJ's first reason (namely, that "'there is no evidence with respect to how'" Mohr "'gained this knowledge'") that this reason is "irrelevan[t]." But why so? The lack of any specifics provides some support for the possibility that Mohr was overstating a conclusion, say, in a job-preserving effort to curry favor with Mack's new managers. More importantly, since the absence of detail or support brings Mohr's statement well within the Board's pre-existing cautionary evidentiary principle (about employee statements regarding the views of other employees), it diminishes the reasonableness of any employer reliance. . . .

The majority's opinion will, I fear, weaken the system for judicial review of administrative action that this Court's precedents have carefully constructed over several decades.

For these reasons, I dissent.

4. Judicial Review of Agency Factfinding

(a) Why should there be *any* judicial review of factfinding by administrative agencies? Specialized factfinding competence was an important reason for the creation of many administrative agencies. Perhaps the role of the courts is to preserve the integrity of the statutes and other rules of law. Why not leave factfinding to the agencies, reserving only questions of law for reviewing courts?

The obvious answer, perhaps signaled by *Allentown*, is this: If administrative agencies were free to find whatever facts they pleased, without regard to the evidence or the reasonableness of inferences that might be drawn from the evidence, agencies could alter the operation of statutes or legal rules so as to change their meaning. For example, if the NLRB were free to "find," regardless of the evidence presented, that any employee discharge was motivated by anti-union bias, the National Labor Relations Act would be transformed into a legal guarantee of employee tenure. On the other hand, if the board were free to "find" a lack of anti-union motivation in discharges, no matter how blatant the evidence of such animus, the intended purposes of the act would be destroyed. It might seem to follow that if courts are to review effectively the fidelity and impartiality with which administrative agencies apply statutes or legal rules, they must also review agency factfinding.

Do you think that the *Allentown* Court's unusually aggressive approach reflected a concern that the NLRB was showing a pro-union bias? Do you think that the Court's concern might reflect an anti-union bias?

A fear of policymaking in the guise of factfinding does not mean that the courts should ordinarily decide each relevant factual issue independently or "de novo." After all, some relevant evidence (for example, the demeanor of witnesses) does not appear in the printed record. In addition, de novo judicial factfinding would destroy many of the reasons for creating administrative agencies in the first place. Speedy and cheap administrative resolution of controversies would be threatened. The ability of administrative agencies to draw specialized inferences based on their experience, or (more controversially) their political judgments, would be lost. The burden on reviewing courts imposed by millions of such administrative cases would be intolerable. Administrative agencies would become little more than evidence gatherers, and most decisional responsibility would be shifted to the judiciary.

It follows that neither extreme is ordinarily believed to be acceptable. (But can you think of unusual circumstances in which no review of facts would make sense? What if judges were almost always wrong, and agencies almost always right?) On the usual view, the problem is to define an appropriate ground between these extremes. The substantial evidence standard adopted in the Administrative Procedures Act (APA) and the Taft-Hartley Act represents one attempt to formulate such an intermediate position. But it is not easy to determine in the abstract precisely what the substantial evidence standard requires of a court reviewing administrative factfinding.

(b) The problem of judicial review of agency factfinding parallels the similar issues involved when judges review factfinding by juries or appellate courts review factfinding by trial judges.

One might ask what factors should lead a reviewing court to give greater (or lesser) deference to factfinding by administrative agencies as compared to either trial judges or juries. Some courts have equated the substantial evidence test with the standard used for the grant or denial of directed verdicts. In *Allentown* itself, the Court suggested that the standard used for reviewing jury verdicts is the same as the standard used under the substantial evidence test. But this has not always been thought to be true. In the oral argument for NLRB v. Pittsburgh Steamship Co., 340 U.S. 498 (1951), Justice Frankfurter explicitly rejected the analogy to the jury verdict standard:

> When you deal with a jury, you introduce a popular element into the administration of law. I would give a jury myself every possible leeway to believe in plausible stories, but when you deal with these matters where it is not a question of a jury, and with all due regard to the expertise and expertness of the NLRB, judges also have a good deal of experience in the world with these matters. . . .

Jaffe, Judicial Review: Substantial Evidence on the Whole Record, 64 Harv. L. Rev. 1233, 1246 (1951). Frankfurter suggests that judges give administrative agencies less leeway to find facts than they give juries. Yet might the opposite conclusion be equally well defended, on the ground that agencies are specialists? Might Congress not have intended the agency, which is usually subject to the president, to introduce a "popular" element as well as expertise into factfinding?

See also School District of Wisconsin Dells v. Z.S. Littlegorge, 295 F.3d 671 (7th Cir. 2002), for the court's striking suggestion that "the cognitive limitations that judges share with mere mortals may constitute an insuperable obstacle to making distinctions any finer than that of plenary versus deferential review." The court added that "the actual amount of deference given the finding of a lower court or an agency will often depend on the nature of the issue," not the announced standard of review. For strong supporting evidence, see Verkuil, An Outcomes Analysis of Scope of Review Standards, 44 Wm. & Mary L. Rev. 679 (2002).

Should reviewing courts give greater leeway to agencies than they give to trial judges' factfinding, which will be set aside if "clearly erroneous"? On the one hand, agencies can draw on specialized experience that trial judges lack. On the other hand, there is a greater danger that an agency with a strongly defined mission, such as the NLRB, will bend its assessment of the evidence to support outcomes that it prefers on grounds of general policy. How should these considerations be assessed? As the *Universal Camera* opinions indicate, it has generally been accepted that "substantial evidence" represents a narrower standard of review, permitting administrators greater discretion in factfinding, than that accorded to trial judges under the clearly erroneous standard. It might, however, be doubted whether the selection of the label "substantial evidence" instead of the label "clearly erroneous" has any practical significance.

(c) Both before and after *Universal Camera*, reviewing courts have shown deference to agency findings about the credibility of witnesses. The wisdom of this practice depends on how important one believes demeanor is as evidence in assessing credibility. In considering *Universal Camera* on remand, Judge Learned Hand indicated that demeanor is often "the most important part," but other judges have thought demeanor less weighty than the inherent probability of testimony in the light of general human experience, the interest of the witness in the case, and other background circumstances.

(d) To what extent can courts review factfinding that the agency justifies on the basis of its superior ability to draw inferences from evidence in a field where it is technically expert or has specialized experience? In *Allentown Mack*, the Court was skeptical of this idea, at least when the NLRB had not articulated some publicly stated basis for a presumption of one kind or another. But if technical expertise is involved, a reviewing judge might sustain agency factual findings that the judge would not be prepared, on the basis of his or her lay experience, to infer from the evidence in the record. Thus, in NLRB v. Stow Mfg. Co., 217 F.2d 900 (2d Cir. 1954), Judge Learned Hand found not even a "scintilla" of evidence to justify the board's conclusion that company practices had turned employees against the union, but nevertheless sustained the agency "because we are to attribute to the board an acquaintance with phenomena in this field, out of which it was reasonable to draw the conclusion that such practices in fact ordinarily do cause a change of votes." 217 F.2d at 905. Recall also Judge Hand's emphasis in his second *Universal Camera* opinion on the "Board's specialized experience [which] equips it with major premises inaccessible to judges." But if agency claims of "expertise" could always fill otherwise fatal gaps in the evidence, judicial review could easily become "a mere feint." Yet it is obviously difficult for judges who lack technical training to determine the validity of factual inferences drawn by specialized administrative agencies with respect to scientific or other technical issues. For most judges, the greater the apparent importance of specialized agency experience in evaluating data, the greater the deference they will accord to agency factual conclusions.

(e) It is not always easy to distinguish between agency factfinding and policymaking, as *Allentown Mack* itself suggests. An agency's decision about the facts may well reflect its judgments about policy — about how, for example, to resolve burdens of proof, and about to whom to allocate burdens of uncertainty. This point raises the possibility that an agency should receive deference on factfinding precisely because judgments about facts, in the face of uncertainty, might best be made by those whose policy judgments are subject to greater political control. Does this make sense in the context of the NLRB? Is there an argument the other way?

(f) Reviewing courts may, as a practical matter, give agencies greater or lesser leeway to find facts depending on the court's confidence in the agency, the judge's reaction to the underlying merits of the decision, the judge's confidence in her own ability to deal with technical matters, and the sheer bulk of the record. The same court in the same year may display wide variations in the deference accorded to agency findings, depending on the agency and issues involved. In *Universal Camera*, Justice Frankfurter asserted that Congress, by adopting the "substantial evidence on the whole record" standard of review, expressed a "mood" concerning the function of reviewing courts. Given the number of different factors that affect the deference paid by courts to agency factfinding, one must wonder whether one can speak more definitively than in terms of a "mood."

(g) In addition to adjudicating particular controversies like that in *Universal Camera* and *Allentown Mack*, agencies also make policy by formulating broad rules of general applicability in rulemaking proceedings or in the course of adjudication. For example, agencies adopt general rules defining the extent to which cable television systems should be allowed to offer competition to over-the-air broadcasters; agencies also examine rules regarding eligibility for assistance payments for those too disabled to work. These and many other "legislative" decisions made by agencies involve considerable analysis and interpretation of factual material as well as value choices. The extent to which courts will review the factual basis for such decisions — whether the scope of judicial review is the same as in the context of particular adjudications — is an issue examined below.

(h) Many people have expressed concern that *Allentown Mack* will signal a substantial change in the law. Consider the following thoughts: "It is extraordinarily rare for a district court or a circuit court to engage in the kind of detailed, intrusive, nondeferential, second guessing of an agency's basis for a finding of fact that is represented by the majority opinion in *Allentown*. The Supreme Court has never before engaged in that type of review." Richard J. Pierce, 2 Administrative Law Treatise 775 (2002). In Pierce's view, the Court's message could "have a dramatic transformative effect on administrative law. Agencies make tens of millions of findings of fact each year. . . . Where will the judiciary get the resources necessary to engage in the type of review illustrated by the majority opinion"? Id. at 776.

Could you argue that *Allentown Mack* is actually a case in which the agency's specialized competence was not really involved? Or that the case is really about the Court's distrust of the NLRB, in part because of a perception that the board was biased, in part because of a perception that the board has been changing its legal standards without saying so? Consider the view that the real engine behind *Allentown Mack* is not Part III of the opinion but is really Part IV, where the Court emphasizes its view that the agency was violating the rule of law, by announcing one rule and applying another. Perhaps the Court's opinion can be seen as an effort to ensure more transparency and accountability from the NLRB, by asking it to state its standards clearly and to apply them faithfully. So understood, *Allentown Mack* fits well with Justice Scalia's general interest in clear rules.

For illustrative cases involving the substantial evidence test, see Peabody Coal Co. v. Groves, 277 F.3d 836 (6th Cir. 2002); Echostar Communications Corp. v. FCC, 292 F.3d 749 (D.C. Cir. 2002); Elliott v. Commodity Futures Trading Commission, 202 F.3d 926 (7th Cir. 2000); Hernandez v. NTSB, 15 F.3d 157 (10th Cir. 1994); Earle Industries v. NLRB, 75 F.3d 400 (8th Cir. 1996); Kimm v. Department of Treasury, 61 F.3d 888 (Fed. Cir. 1995); Vemco, Inc. v. NLRB, 79 F.3d 526 (6th Cir. 1996); Sanchet v. Chater, 78 F.3d 305 (7th Cir. 1996). It is important to note that before and after *Allentown Mack*, agency decisions have not uncommonly been invalidated under the substantial evidence test. And in fact, *Allentown Mack* does not appear to have introduced significant changes in judicial application of that test.

5. *The Relevance of Administrative Law Judge Findings*

(a) The difficulties in defining the appropriate scope of judicial review of agency factfinding were exacerbated by the creation of independent hearing examiners, now called administrative law judges. The APA created the office of hearing examiner to receive evidence and make initial findings (subject to review and modification by agency heads) primarily in response to the claims that it was unfair to have all adjudications decided by the agency commissioners themselves; they might be biased in a particular case because they combined policymaking, investigative, prosecutorial, and adjudicatory responsibilities.

Where the agency heads affirm the hearing examiner's factfinding, no special reviewing difficulties are presented. But what is a reviewing court to do when the agency rejects the hearing examiner's findings? If the reviewing court gives no weight to the hearing examiner's conclusions, the agency heads would have little incentive to pay heed to the findings of hearing examiners, who would tend to lose their effectiveness as a check on the possible "bias" of the commissioners. Hearing examiners might become only evidence collectors; the real decision would occur later, with wasteful duplication of effort by private parties and the prosecuting staff of the agency. Of course, commissioners would likely give weight to the opinions of hearing examiners in routine cases, for the commissioners are pressed for time, and, in any event, they know the examiner has "lived with" the case. Yet in important cases they might be tempted to "redecide" the lot.

On the other hand, if courts gave near conclusive weight to the factual conclusions of hearing examiners, some of the special virtues of administrative factfinding could be largely destroyed. The hearing examiner is more limited than the commissioner in the ability to draw inferences from the reviews of agency staff, for commissioners can more readily consult staff experts. More important, it is perfectly proper for agency heads to use individual cases to elaborate on, or to change, agency policy. Since it is not always easy to distinguish discretion to draw specialized inferences of factfinding from discretion to make law or policy, forced reliance on the hearing examiner's factual findings could unduly cabin administrators' policymaking discretion. Finally, the agency heads usually know the hearing examiner and are familiar with his or her biases. They thus may know when one of his or her factual findings are likely to be wrong.

Caught between these competing policies, reviewing courts can follow the course suggested by the Supreme Court in *Universal Camera* — giving the hearing examiner's findings some undefined weight as a relevant part of the record, and setting aside the agency's decision if it does not meet the substantial evidence test. See, e.g., Parker v. Bowen, 788 F.2d 1512, 1520-1521 (11th Cir. 1986). Courts have also sometimes remanded for further proceedings rather than attempt to choose among competing findings by the hearing examiner and the agency heads. They have done so when the agency heads did not explicitly state their reasons for overturning the hearing examiner's decision, and when they overturned the hearing examiner without considering the testimony that he or she had considered.

(b) The problem of what weight to give to hearing examiners' findings that have been reversed by the agency heads is particularly acute where witness credibility is an issue. The hearing examiner has observed the demeanor of witnesses; the agency heads and reviewing court have not. But, as we have already noted, the credibility of testimony is not solely a function of the witness's demeanor but also of that testimony's inherent plausibility. The cases do not clearly delineate the extent to which an agency is free to reject a hearing examiner's factual conclusions, including those of credibility, by relying on the agency's specialized experience with practices in a given field of administration or the hearing examiner's lack of it.

6. *Burdens of Persuasion and Burdens of Production*

(a) The "burden of persuasion" with respect to a factual issue falls on the party who will lose on that issue unless the relevant evidence sufficiently preponderates in his favor to meet a given "standard of proof." The "burden of production" with respect to an issue falls on the party who must bring forward some evidence on that issue to avoid an adverse decision on that issue; but once some evidence has been produced, either he or the other party may have the burden of persuading the trier of fact of the proposition's truth or falsity.

(b) The "standard of proof" that a trier of fact will use to determine whether a "burden of persuasion" has been met is quite a different thing from the "standard of review" used by a court in reviewing the decision of the trier of fact. This is obvious in the typical criminal case. To convict a defendant, the prosecution must persuade the jury of his guilt beyond a reasonable doubt. But, to sustain a guilty verdict, an appellate court need not itself be convinced of guilt beyond a reasonable doubt. It need only be convinced that a jury could have reasonably believed so.

This distinction played an important role in Woodby v. Immigration & Naturalization Service, 385 U.S. 276 (1966). A resident alien, the wife of an American soldier, was ordered deported because she had engaged in prostitution. In reaching this conclusion, the Board of Immigration Appeals had not specifically considered the persuasion burden defining the degree of certainty with which deportability must be established. The Court of Appeals noted that §106(a)4 of the Immigration and Naturalization Act states that a deportation order, "if supported by reasonable, substantial, and probative evidence on the record considered as a whole, shall be conclusive," and §242(b)(4) of the act provides that "no decision of deportability shall be valid unless it is based upon reasonable, substantial, and probative evidence." It concluded that the burden on the government was to establish deportability by "reasonable, substantial and probative evidence on the record as a whole," and that this burden had been satisfied. The Supreme Court, however, decided that "these two statutory provisions are addressed not to the degree of proof required at the administrative level in deportation proceedings, but to a quite different subject — the scope of judicial review." In the absence of a statutory provision defining the burden of persuasion at trial, the Court, noting that the persuasion burden was a question traditionally left to the judiciary to resolve, chose to require that the government prove its allegations by "clear, unequivocal, and convincing evidence." The Court decided that this persuasion burden, which was the same one it had required in denaturalization and expatriation cases, was appropriate because "[t]he immediate hardship of deportation is often greater than that inflicted by denaturalization, which does not, immediately at least, result in expulsion from our shores. And many resident aliens have lived in this country longer and established stronger family, social, and economic ties here than some who have become naturalized citizens." Id. at 276.

In Steadman v. Securities & Exchange Commission, 450 U.S. 91, 102 (1981), the Supreme Court held that §556(d) was intended to establish a "preponderance of the evidence" standard of proof for agency hearings "except as otherwise provided by statute." Cf. Bender v. Clark, 744 F.2d 1424, 1429 (10th Cir. 1984) (preponderance of the evidence standard must also be applied in informal administrative hearings not covered by the APA "unless the type of case and the sanctions or hardship imposed require a higher standard").

(c) APA §556(d) provides, "Except as otherwise provided by statute, the proponent of a rule or order has the burden of proof." It is not clear whether "burden of proof" means burden of persuasion or burden of production. The legislative history is ambiguous. For many years, it was agreed that the burden of proof, within the meaning of the APA, included the burden of production, but there was much dispute about whether it included the burden of persuasion as well. In Director, OWCP v. Greenwich Collieries, 512 U.S. 273 (1994), the Court resolved the controversy. It held that under the APA, the proponent of a rule of order has both burdens. The Court relied on the text of the APA, which, it said, clearly meant to include burden of persuasion. The Court said that it would presume "the phrase to have the meaning generally accepted in the legal community at the time of enactment," a meaning that had been settled, in the Court's view, by 1946, notwithstanding considerable ambiguity before that time. The Court acknowledged that its holding was inconsistent with language in previous decisions.

In so holding, the Court rejected a longstanding practice of the Department of Labor, which had for 31 years applied the so-called true doubt rule in adjudicating benefits claims under the Black Lung Benefits Act (BLBA). While claimants were required to meet the burden of establishing a prima facie case, either by relying on rebuttable presumptions established by statute or regulation or by production of evidence, the true doubt rule essentially shifted the burden of persuasion to the party opposing the benefits claim. When the evidence regarding the cause of the disability was evenly balanced, the benefits claimant would win. The Court rejected this approach.

Outside of the APA, there are possible distinctions between the burden of production and the burden of proof. Consider, for example, cases involving a claim for disability compensation under the Social Security Act. Courts have agreed that the ultimate burden of persuasion on "disability" falls on the claimant. To show disability, a claimant must show not only an inability to continue former work, but also inability to perform *any* type of work. But, recognizing the difficulties that claimants would have in proving a broad negative — that no employment is available to them — some courts have ruled that a claimant need only come forward with evidence that she could not perform her former job; the burden then shifted to the secretary to produce evidence that work existed in the claimant's geographic area that she could perform and for which she would be hired. In 1967,

Congress amended the Social Security Act to ease the burden the courts had placed on the secretary; for example, evidence that a claimant could perform work that existed generally in the *national* economy would be sufficient to defeat the claim for disability. But the courts continued to place the burden of production on this issue on the secretary, despite indications of congressional displeasure with past court rulings. Similarly, courts have held, despite the APA's language, that the burden of proving affirmative defenses rests on an opponent rather than a proponent of an order when this allocation is supported by the basic purposes of a statutory scheme. Moreover, courts that have read the APA to place the burden of persuasion on an order's "proponent" may find that the person who initiates the proceeding is not the "true" proponent. A further source of flexibility in allocating burdens arises out of the APA's exception, "where otherwise provided by statute."

In *Greenwich Collieries*, supra, the Supreme Court has cast significant doubt on this flexible approach to interpreting §556(d), not only because of its general holding, but also because of its conclusion that the BLBA did not "otherwise provide."

(d) The National Labor Relations Act §8(a)(3) makes it an unfair labor practice for an employer "by discrimination in regard to . . . tenure of employment . . . to . . . discourage membership in any labor organization." 29 U.S.C. §518(a)(3). In NLRB v. Transportation Mgmt. Corp., 462 U.S. 393 (1983), the Supreme Court held that the board could interpret the act (the same as that at issue in *Universal Camera*) to forbid "a discharge . . . in any way motivated by a desire to frustrate union activity." In proving a violation, NLRB general counsel need only make out a prima facie case of bad motive by showing, for example, that the employer knew of the worker's union activities and that other circumstances of the discharge suggested the existence of "bad" motive. The Court held that the board can then require the employer to prove it would have fired the worker even without union activity. Compare NLRB v. Eastern Smelting & Refining Corp., 598 F.2d 666 (1st Cir. 1979).

7. *Alternative Standards of Review*

The substantial evidence test is the dominant standard for judicial review of factual determinations by agencies, at least (and this is an important qualification) in proceedings "on the record." It is specified in the APA as the standard of review in cases of formal adjudication and rulemaking, see 5 U.S.C. §706(2)(E), and in many other statutes governing particular agencies. But there are statutes that call for a different test. Most important, in informal proceedings, including notice-and-comment rulemaking, the APA calls for "arbitrary or capricious" review of agency decisions, including decisions involving facts.

In some instances, the statutory standard broadens the scope of judicial review, as in the Commodity Exchange Act, 7 U.S.C. §8, which states that administrative findings shall be conclusive if "supported by the weight of the evidence." Under this standard, the reviewing court supposedly weighs the evidence to determine whether its judgment as to the preponderance of the evidence matches that of the agency. But if courts continue to defer to administrative experience and credibility findings, the end result thus may not differ significantly from the result produced under the substantial evidence test.

The APA also provides that reviewing courts shall determine whether agency findings are "unwarranted by the facts to the extent that the facts are subject to trial de novo by the reviewing court." The drafters of the APA probably intended this standard of review to apply to informal rulemaking and adjudication proceedings that do not generate a trial-type record. But the Supreme Court, in Citizens to Preserve Overton Park v. Volpe, 401 U.S. 402 (1971), rejected such a broad view, stating that de novo review is authorized by the APA only when "the action is adjudicatory in nature and the agency factfinding procedures are inadequate" (a possibility it failed to elaborate) or "when issues that were not before the agency are raised in a proceeding to enforce nonadjudicatory agency action," and indicated that these situations would occur only rarely. This decision reflects a general reluctance by courts to undertake de novo review, which, for reasons developed by Justice Brandeis in his Crowell v. Benson dissent, can make much of the administrative process superfluous.

Some statutes narrow the scope of review of agency factfinding or seek to foreclose it entirely, often through a provision that the findings of an agency shall be "final." The courts, however, have strained against preclusion of judicial review, especially where personal liberties are at stake. Despite such finality language, the judicial revision of finality provisions has been particularly noticeable in immigration and draft cases.

Problems

1. Should a reviewing court reverse the following findings of fact if made by a judge? A jury? An administrative agency?

(a) A workers' compensation proceedings turns on whether the dead man first had a heart attack and then fell from a ladder or whether he first fell and then had a heart attack. The only evidence on this point is that he was found dead of a heart attack at the bottom of the ladder. The factfinder finds that his fall came first, and compensation is awarded.

(b) In the case above, assume that the proceeding is a malpractice claim against a doctor for allowing a patient to return to work too soon. If the heart attack preceded the fall, liability would be found. The factfinder finds that the heart attack came first and awards damages. Does it matter if the agency has the power to revoke the physician's license?

(c) A workers' compensation proceeding turns in part on whether the dead man died as a result of a 300-pound cake of ice falling on him as he unloaded it from a truck on January 15, 1958. The evidence on this point consists of testimony by his wife and doctor that, just before dying of delirium tremens, the dead man told them that the ice fell on him; testimony by fellow workers who were with him all day on January 15 that they saw no cake of ice fall on him; and undisputed testimony by doctors that there were no bruises on his body. The factfinder finds that the ice fell and awards compensation.

2. Reconsider Universal Camera in light of Allentown:

(a) Suppose the NLRB had justified its decision as follows: "Based on our experience in many proceedings and labor relations generally, discharge of employees following employee testimony favorable to the union is almost invariably attributable to the employer's anti-union motives. Testimony by supervisory personnel that the discharge was for other reasons is almost always an effort to disguise its real purpose." Should a reviewing court then have sustained the board's order? Does Allentown have anything to say on that question?

(b) Why should the reviewing court in this case have given any weight to the hearing examiner's findings? How much weight should those findings have?

(c) Might the Universal Camera case have been simplified for the board and for the Court if either had paid more attention to defining appropriate rules for burden of proof and less attention to the question of scope of review? How might such rules have been defined?

(d) Suppose that there are witnesses supporting both sides, and the NLRB accepts the testimony of some but rejects the testimony of others. Is this acceptable? Many cases say that the agency owes a duty of explanation in such cases, and that without explanation, the agency's view will be held unsupported by substantial evidence. See, e.g., Adorno v. Shalal, 40 F.3d 43 (3d Cir. 1994).

8. Immigration, Substantial Evidence, and Act versus Policy

Zhen Li Iao v. Gonzales
400 F.3d 530 (7th Cir. 2005)

POSNER, Circuit Judge.

An immigration judge ordered the petitioner, a citizen of China seeking asylum in the United States, to be removed (deported) from the United States, and the Board of Immigration Appeals affirmed without opinion. The basis of the immigration judge's ruling was that the petitioner is not entitled to asylum because she lacks a well-founded fear of being persecuted by the Chinese government should she return to China.

A woman in her early 20s, Li arrived in the United States in 2000. At the removal hearing she testified through an interpreter that she had begun to practice Falun Gong in China and — the Chinese government having outlawed Falun Gong in 1999 — that police and village officials had learned of her activity (probably through her employer) and decided to investigate. Village officials made repeated visits to the house in which she lived with her parents to tell her to abandon Falun Gong, but she eluded them by residing mainly in her aunt's house. Police visited the parents' home and delivered a summons commanding Li to come to the police station for an interview. She did not comply with the summons. They kept coming back to the home, looking for her, and she fled the country.

Since arriving in the United States, Li has, again according to her testimony, practiced Falun Gong in Chicago (where she lives) and has also participated in street demonstrations against the Chinese government's persecution of the movement. When she arrived in this country she knew the name of the founder of Falun Gong (Li Hongzhi, now in exile in the United States) and had done the physical exercises that are the primary manifestation of adherence to Falun Gong, but she was vague about its doctrines and unfamiliar with its symbol. She has since become more familiar with the movement's doctrines and symbol. At the hearing before the immigration judge she presented letters from her mother in China, and the Chinese man who had introduced her to Falun Gong there, corroborating her testimony.

Falun Gong is an international movement, though primarily Chinese, that is often referred to as a "religion" (or, by its critics, as a "cult"), though it is not a religion in the Western sense. Like other Asian "religions," such as Buddhism and Confucianism — on both of which Falun Gong draws — there is no deity. The emphasis is on spiritual self-perfection through prescribed physical exercises; in this respect the movement has affinities with traditional Chinese medicine. . . .

As Falun Gong is neither theistic nor, so far as appears, political, the ferocious antipathy to it by the Chinese government — that government's determination to eradicate it root and branch — is mysterious, but undeniable. If Li practiced Falun Gong in China, as she testified she did, or if she attempted to practice it upon returning to China, she would face a substantial likelihood of persecution. . . .

The immigration judge gave five reasons for nevertheless denying Li's application for asylum. The first is that she was not persecuted in China. But she does not claim to have been; it is a nonissue. The fifth reason is that her brother, who lives in the United States, is a follower of Falun Gong yet failed to submit an affidavit attesting that his sister is too. The judge misread the record; the brother is not a follower of Falun Gong.

Reasons 2 through 4 overlap. Reason 2 is that Li failed to present persuasive evidence that she is a follower of the movement, because in her testimony she was "quite vague concerning her beliefs." For example, she didn't know that Falun Gong has a symbol (the "Falun Wheel" composed of reverse swastikas, a Buddhist symbol). But the heart of Falun Gong observance is the exercises, which she testified without contradiction that she does.

Reason 3 was that there were inconsistencies in her testimony about the visits of the police to her home. This was not, as the immigration judge thought, an independent reason for denying the application for asylum; rather, it was a reason not to credit her testimony about being a member of Falun Gong. The inconsistencies were trivial, however, and may well have been due to the fact that Li was testifying through an interpreter who appears not to have had a good command of English. When Li testified about the delivery of the summons to her home by the police, the immigration judge asked her whether she had had any prior "confrontations" with the government and she said no, but later explained that although the police didn't start coming to her home until they served the summons, village officials had visited earlier. Were these "confrontations"? She was never at home when they visited. And goodness knows how the translator translated "confrontations" into Chinese.

Reason 4 was that when interviewed by an asylum officer at the time she first applied for asylum, Li testified that after the village officials got wind of her involvement with Falun Gong she "went into hiding at different locations and never went back home." The immigration judge said that she "did not specifically testify in this manner (e.g. that she went into hiding) nor does the rest of the record support this statement." That is not correct. Although Li (more precisely, the translator) did not use the word "hiding," she said she wasn't at home when the police visited and that sometimes she was "at my aunt that I mentioned at her house." Apparently the village officials and police visited her home repeatedly, and since she was never there when they showed up it is a logical inference, supported also by her mother's letter, that she was indeed trying to evade the authorities.

The immigration judge's opinion cannot be regarded as reasoned; and there was no opinion by the Board of Immigration Appeals. So we have to vacate the decision and send the matter back to the immigration service. We do not decide that Li is entitled to asylum; that is a decision for the immigration authorities to make. But she is entitled to a rational analysis of the evidence by them.

The number of followers of Falun Gong in China is estimated to be in the tens of millions, all of them subject to persecution. And among the other billion Chinese there are doubtless many who would prefer to live in the United States than in China. . . . The implications for potential Chinese immigration to the United States may be significant. . . . The United States has every right to control immigration. But Congress has not authorized the immigration service to do so by denying asylum applications in unreasoned decisions.

We close by noting six disturbing features of the handling of this case that bulk large in the immigration cases that we are seeing:

1. A lack of familiarity with relevant foreign cultures. The immigration judge offered no justification for regarding a person's lack of knowledge of Falun Gong doctrines as

evidence of a false profession of faith. Different religions attach different weights to different aspects of the faith. . . .

2. An exaggerated notion of how much religious people know about their religion. Of course a purported Christian who didn't know who Jesus Christ was, or a purported Jew who had never heard of Moses, would be instantly suspect; but many deeply religious people know very little about the origins, doctrines, or even observances of their faith.

3. An exaggerated notion of the availability, especially in poor nations, of documentary evidence of religious membership. An acephalous, illegal religious movement is particularly unlikely to issue membership cards. The immigration judge's zeal for documentation reached almost comical proportions when after Li had testified at length and in considerable detail about locations, including the street in front of the Chinese consulate in Chicago, in which she had participated in demonstrations against the persecution of Falun Gong, he upbraided her for having "failed to submit to the Court any letters or photographs or any other evidence whatsoever to corroborate these claims." Since the demonstrators are mainly Chinese who might one day want or be forced to return to China, they are hardly likely to be taking photos of each other demonstrating, or to be creating other documentary proof of participating in demonstrations of which the Chinese government deeply disapproves.

4. Insensitivity to the possibility of misunderstandings caused by the use of translators of difficult languages such as Chinese, and relatedly, insensitivity to the difficulty of basing a determination of credibility on the demeanor of a person from a culture remote from the American, such as the Chinese. Behaviors that in our culture are considered evidence of unreliability, such as refusing to look a person in the eyes when he is talking to you, are in Asian cultures a sign of respect.

5. Reluctance to make clean determinations of credibility. When an immigration judge says not that he believes the asylum seeker or he disbelieves her but instead that she hasn't carried her burden of proof, the reviewing court is left in the dark as to whether the judge thinks the asylum seeker failed to carry her burden of proof because her testimony was not credible, or for some other reason.

6. Affirmances by the Board of Immigration Appeals either with no opinion or with a very short, unhelpful, boilerplate opinion, even when, as in this case, the immigration judge's opinion contains manifest errors of fact and logic.

We do not offer these points in a spirit of criticism. The cases that we see are not a random sample of all asylum cases, and the problems that the cases raise may not be representative. Even if they are representative, given caseload pressures and, what is the other side of that coin, resource constraints, it is possible that nothing better can realistically be expected than what we are seeing in this and like cases. But we are not authorized to affirm unreasoned decisions even when we understand why they are unreasoned.

The petition for review is granted and the matter returned to the immigration service for further proceedings consistent with this opinion.

Questions

1. Can Judge Posner be charged with second-guessing an administrative agency on issues peculiarly within its specialized expertise? The court's opinion does appear to look fairly close at agency factfinding. Is this because technical issues are not really involved? Consider the claim that the BIA is politically accountable, and that accountability helps explain its behavior in this and similar cases. If so, is the court's opinion strengthened or weakened?

2. Perhaps the court's opinion is quite close to *Allentown Mack*, in the sense that the animating concern is the lack of transparency — the fear that the agency is operating on

the basis of a kind of policy judgment that has not been articulated, but that lies behind its otherwise puzzling factfinding. If this is correct, then what, exactly, is the policy that is animating the BIA here?

3. The most striking part of the opinion is of course the list of six "disturbing" features of the case, features that the court apparently finds to be common. Why did the court find it necessary to make out this list?

4. Conflicts between reviewing courts and the BIA have been frequent in the last decade, and a glance at the cases suggests the possibility that they have intensified since September 11, 2001. Are the terrorist attacks of that day a reason for greater, or less, deference to the BIA? Note that immigration policy is often a means of protecting the nation's security; and it is almost always a way of managing relations with both friendly and unfriendly nations. Suppose that the BIA develops a self-conscious policy — perhaps articulated, perhaps not — of ensuring that its adjudicative decisions (1) help to promote or at least do not compromise security interests, (2) help to manage relations with other nations, emphatically including China, Saudi Arabia, Iraq, Iran, North Korea, and Russia. Suppose that BIA seems to impose a high burden on people who allege persecution in Iraq, because it does not want to compromise our delicate relationship with that country; or suppose that it does the same for Saudi Arabia, because it fears terrorism. Or suppose that its policy in connection with Falun Gong is affected by a concern that Falun Gong members might seek refuge in the United States in huge numbers — or that China might object if we offer Falun Gong members refuge here because of a claimed threat of "persecution." What can the BIA do to accomplish its goals? Can it use factfinding? Must it use something else instead?

B. The "Constitutional Fact" Doctrine: Notes on Ratemaking

1. Introductory Note

Recall the debate in Crowell v. Benson between Chief Justice Hughes & Justice Brandeis about whether there are special "constitutional facts" or "jurisdictional facts" that a litigant can ask a court to redetermine de novo. The Chief Justice concluded that the existence of "navigable waters" was one such question, and he argued that in Ng Fung Ho even Justice Brandeis had conceded the need for special review of findings of fact that led to deportation.

The argument about the proper role of judicial review of "jurisdictional" or "constitutional" fact has been much influenced by the subject matter of the cases that raised the issue. In the 1930s and 1940s, most of these cases involved public utility ratemaking. The legal question was whether prices set by an administrative body (a rate commission) allowed the utility to earn a rate of return high enough to avoid "confiscation." A rate was "confiscatory" if it was so low that it constituted a "taking" of the company's property — a taking made unlawful by the fourteenth amendment's prohibition of deprivation of "property without due process of law." The underlying institutional issue was whether the courts should independently determine whether a particular rate of return was confiscatory or whether they should give weight to an administrative judgment that it was not.

An understanding of ratemaking in this controversy is important for two distinct reasons, First, *cost of service ratemaking.*, used to set electricity rates, is also used almost without exception when the government seeks to set prices in any particular industry. Thus, a student of the administrative process should be familiar with how this system works and with a few of the typical problems that arise when it is applied.

Second, only by understanding the details of how ratemaking works can one assess the comparative competencies of court and agency in determining a fair, proper, or adequate level for rates. And these comparative competencies arguably should play a role in determining the extent of factual review — at least as much of a role as a characterization of an issue as jurisdictional or constitutional.

2. The Natural Monopoly

The classic case for rate regulation is the "natural monopoly." A natural monopoly exists, in the economic sense, when there is a relation between the size of the market and the size of the most efficient firm in that market such that one firm of efficient size can produce all the market can absorb at a remunerative price and can continually expand its capacity at less cost than that of a new firm entering the business. Changing technology, population growth, and the like may either create or eliminate natural monopolies. Developments in transportation over the years eliminated many local monopolies—in effect, local markets were merged into much larger markets. Mass production techniques tend in the direction of monopoly, but often new innovations will reverse the trend. By and large, in highly developed countries like the United States, few industries fall in the natural monopoly category.

The question of what is and what is not a natural monopoly has become increasingly controversial. Local distribution of power, gas, water, telephone, and perhaps cable television service still tend to be considered natural monopolies — though this is not a unanimous view. Scholarly opinion particularly divides about electricity generation and long-distance telephone service. The weight of that opinion suggests that neither electricity generation nor long-distance service are natural monopolies. AT&T's long-distance service is subject to competition from other firms, such as MCI and Sprint. The presence of some competition, however, does not prove the nonexistence of a natural monopoly. If a natural monopolist can (or is required to) charge prices well above its costs, it may provide a "price umbrella," allowing new firms to enter the market even if it would be more efficient for a single firm to meet the entire demand at a lower price. Regardless, when monopoly is the problem, the purpose of government ratemaking is to impose maximum prices to protect the public from monopolistic exploitation. Similarly, a variety of collateral controls over costs and quality of product is usually thought necessary in an endeavor to provide a substitute for the forces of competition.

3. Cost-of-Service Ratemaking

In principle, ratemaking might be thought to have as its object the setting of prices equal to those that the firm would set if it did not have monopoly power; that is, to replicate a "competitive price." In practice, maximum prices are set through a "cost-of-service" method. Whether this method leads to a "competitive" price is for you to judge.

Cost-of-service ratemaking is designed to set prices that will provide the regulated firm with revenues just sufficient to cover its costs (which include a reasonable profit). First, the regulator determines the firm's probable future costs. Ordinarily, the ratemaker determines these costs by looking at historical costs in the last period of operations for which company records are available; this is called the "test period." Costs in the coming period are assumed to equal those in the test period. The ratemaker then sets prices for the coming period designed to yield the revenue requirement. Ordinarily, it is assumed that the quantity sold in the coming period will remain roughly the same as that in the test period, regardless of price.

4. Statutes That Govern Ratemaking

The following provisions, taken from the Natural Gas Act, 15 U.S.C. §§717(c), (d), are typical of both state and federal legislative mandates authorizing agencies to control the maximum prices charged by natural monopolies. The provisions reproduced here give the Federal Power Commission (FPC) the power to set the rates of large interstate gas pipelines.

> Sec. 4. . . . (c) Under such rules and regulations as the Commission may prescribe, every natural-gas company shall file with the Commission . . . schedules showing all rates and charges for any transportation or sale subject to the jurisdiction of the Commission, and the classification, practices, and regulations affecting such rates and charges, together with all contracts which in any manner affect to relate to such rates, charges, classifications, and services.
>
> (d) Unless the Commission otherwise orders, no changes shall be made by any natural-gas company in any such rate, charge, classification, or service, or in any rule, regulation, or contract relating thereto, except after thirty days' notice to the Commission and to the public. . . .
>
> (e) Whenever any such new schedule is filed the Commission shall have authority . . . to enter upon a hearing concerning the lawfulness of such rate, charge, classification, or service; and, pending such hearing and decision thereon, the Commission . . . may suspend the operation of such schedule . . . but not for a longer period than five months beyond the time when it would otherwise go into effect; and after full hearings . . . the Commission may make such orders with reference thereto as would be proper in a proceeding initiated after it had become effective. If the proceeding has not been concluded and an order made at the expiration of the suspension period . . . the proposed change of rate, charge, classification or service shall go into effect. Where increased rates or charges are thus made effective, the Commission may . . . order such natural-gas company to refund, with interest, the portion of such increased rates or charges by its decision found not justified. At any hearing involving a rate or charge sought to be increased, the burden of proof to show that the increased rate or charge is reasonable shall be upon the natural gas company. . . .
>
> Sec. 5. (a) Whenever the Commission . . . shall find that any rate, charge, or classification demanded, observed, charged, or collected by any natural-gas company in connection with any transportation or sale of natural gas, subject to the Commission, or that any rule, regulation, practice, or contract affecting such rate, charge, classification is [unlawful,] the Commission shall determine the just and reasonable rate,

charge, classification, rule, regulation, practice, or contract to be thereafter observed and in force, and shall fix the same by order. . . .

5. Determining the Rate Base: The Role of the Courts and Traditional Methods of Evaluation

The following cases will give you an idea of the controversy that surrounded ratemaking in the first half of the century. Modern courts have abandoned nearly all efforts to control agency ratemaking. But why?

Smyth v. Ames
169 U.S. 466 (1898)

[In 1893 the Nebraska state legislature passed a statute imposing maximum rates for intrastate shipments of goods by railroads operating in the state. These rates averaged 29.5 percent less than the rates that had been charged in the immediately preceding years. Evidence accepted by the lower court indicated that if these rates had been charged during the years 1891-1893, the railroads, except in four instances, would not have recovered their operating expenses on intrastate shipments, let alone obtain a contribution to interest on bonded debt or return to stockholders. The lower court declared that application of the statutory rates in such circumstances was an unconstitutional deprivation of property without due process of law. In affirming, the Supreme Court commented in part as follows.]

Mr. Justice HARLAN delivered the opinion of the Court:

. . . If a railroad corporation has bonded its property for an amount that exceeds its fair value, or if its capitalization is largely fictitious, it may not impose upon the public the burden of such increased rates as may be required for the purpose of realizing profits upon such excessive valuation or fictitious capitalization; and the apparent value of the property and franchises used by the corporation, as represented by its stocks, bonds and obligations, is not alone to be considered when determining the rates that may be reasonably charged. . . .

A corporation maintaining a public highway, although it owns the property it employs for accomplishing public objects, must be held to have accepted its rights, privileges and franchises subject to the condition that the government creating it, or the government within whose limits it conducts its business, may by legislation protect the people against unreasonable charges for the services rendered by it. It cannot be assumed that any railroad corporation, accepting franchises, rights and privileges at the hands of the public, ever supposed that it acquired, or that it was intended to grant to it, the power to construct and maintain a public highway simply for its benefit, without regard to the rights of the public. But it is equally true that the corporation performing such public services and the people financially interested in its business and affairs have rights that may not be invaded by legislative enactment in disregard of the fundamental guarantees for the protection of property. The corporation may not be required to use its property for the benefit of the public without receiving just compensation for the services rendered by it. How such compensation may be ascertained, and what are the necessary elements in such an inquiry, will always be an embarrassing question. . . .

We hold, however, that the basis of all calculations as to the reasonableness of rates to be charged by a corporation maintaining a highway under legislative sanction must be the fair value of the property being used by it for the convenience of the public. And in order to ascertain that value, the original cost of construction, the amount expended in permanent improvements, the amount and market value of its bonds and stock, the present as compared with the original cost of construction, the probable earning capacity of the property under particular rates prescribed by statute, and the sum required to meet operating expenses, are all matters for consideration, and are to be given such weight as may be just and right in each case. We do not say that there may not be other matters to be regarded in estimating the value of the property. What the company is entitled to ask is a fair return upon the value of that which it employs for the public convenience. On the other hand, what the public is entitled to demand is that no more be exacted from it for the use of a public highway than the services rendered by it are reasonably worth. But even upon this basis, and determining the probable effect of the act of 1893 by ascertaining what could have been its effect if it had been in operation during the three years immediately preceding its passage, we perceive no ground on the record for reversing the decree of the Circuit Court. On the contrary, we are of opinion that as to most of the companies in question there would have been, under such rates as were established by the act of 1893, an actual loss in each of the years ending June 30, 1891, 1892, and 1893; and that, in the exceptional cases above stated, when two of the companies would have earned something above operating expenses, in particular years, the receipts or gains, above operating expenses, would have been too small to affect the general conclusion that the act, if enforced would have deprived each of the railroad companies involved in these suits of the just compensation assured to them by the Constitution. Under the evidence there is no ground for saying that the operating expenses of any of the companies were greater than necessary.

The *Ben Avon* Doctrine

In Ohio Valley Water Co. v. Ben Avon Borough, 253 U.S. 287 (1920), the Supreme Court announced (through Justice McReynolds) that the courts must review factual questions related to confiscation "independently." A water company had appealed a commission valuation ruling to state court; the lower court made its own valuation and reversed the ruling; the state supreme court reinstated the commission's order. The U.S. Supreme Court interpreted the state supreme court's decision as having withheld "from the courts power to determine the question of confiscation according to their own independent judgment when the action of the Commission comes to be considered on appeal. [I]f the owner claims confiscation, . . . the State must provide a fair opportunity for submitting that issue to a judicial tribunal for determination upon its own independent judgment as to both law and facts; otherwise the order is void because in conflict with the due process clause, Fourteenth Amendment."

FPC v. Hope Natural Gas Co.

320 U.S. 591 (1944)

[Mr. Justice DOUGLAS delivered the opinion of the Court.]

. . . When we sustained the constitutionality of the Natural Gas Act in the *Natural Gas Pipeline Co.* case, we stated that the "authority of Congress to regulate the prices of commodities in interstate commerce is at least as great under the Fifth Amendment as is that of the States under the Fourteenth to regulate the prices of commodities in intrastate commerce." 315 U.S. at 582. Rate-making is indeed but one species of price-fixing. Munn v. Illinois, 94 U.S. 113, 134. The fixing of prices, like other applications of the police power, may reduce the value of the property which is being regulated. But the fact that the value is reduced does not mean that the regulation is invalid. Block v. Hirsh, 256 U.S. 135, 155-157; Nebbia v. New York, 291 U.S. 502, 523-539 and cases cited. . . . The heart of the matter is that rates cannot be made to depend upon "fair value" when the value of the going enterprise depends on earnings under whatever rates may be anticipated.

We held in Federal Power Commission v. Natural Gas Pipeline Co., that the Commission was not bound to the use of any single formula or combination of formulae in determining rates. Its rate-making function, moreover, involves the making of "pragmatic adjustments." . . . And when the Commission's order is challenged in the courts, the question is whether that order "viewed in its entirety" meets the requirements of the Act. . . . Under the statutory standard of "just and reasonable" it is the result reached not the method employed which is controlling. It is not theory . . . but the impact of the rate order which counts. If the total effect of the rate order cannot be said to be unjust and unreasonable, judicial inquiry under the Act is at an end. The fact that the method employed to reach that result may contain infirmities is not then important. . . .

From the investor or company point of view it is important that there be enough revenue not only for operating expenses but also for the capital costs of the business. These include service on the debt and dividends on the stock. . . . By that standard the return to the equity owner should be commensurate with returns on investments in other enterprises having corresponding risks. That return, moreover, should be sufficient to assure confidence in the financial integrity of the enterprise, so as to maintain its credit and to attract capital. . . .

Note

After *Hope*, federal court review of ratemaking dwindled dramatically. The extent to which the Court, under *Hope*, was willing to accept a commission determination may be indicated by Market St. Ry. v. Railroad Commn., 324 U.S. 548 (1945). The book value of company property was $42 million, its reproduction value $25 million, the face value of its outstanding securities $38 million, and its salvage value $8 million. The commission reduced fares from 7 cents. It claimed that a 6-cent fare would earn the company a return of 6 percent on $8 million — the salvage value. The Supreme Court held this order constitutional, arguing that the firm faced a profitless future under any rate structure; thus the property's only value was as salvage. If the commission was right in believing a fare reduction would lead to a "traffic increase, . . . it would earn [a return] on the salvage value. . . . If expectations of increased traffic were unfounded, it could probably not earn a return from any rate that could be devised." Id. at 568.

6. *Determining the Rate of Return*

The rate of return and the rate base are related in that multiplying them produces a pile of money — profits — that will be distributed to investors. The basic regulatory question is how large that pile is to be. To decide, for administrative reasons, that the rate base will normally equal historical net investment does not by itself determine the rate of return.

The *Hope* case, while dropping the fair value rate base requirement, reiterates the three previously described tests: "[T]he return to the equity owner should be commensurate with returns on investments in other enterprises having corresponding risks. That return, moreover, should be sufficient to assure confidence in the financial integrity of the enterprise, so as to maintain its credit and to attract capital." *Hope*, 320 U.S. at 603.

While these standards remain good law, they do not give commissions a particular method, nor a single, measurable goal, for setting the rate of return. Nor do they tell commissions how to deal with certain policy concerns that may arise independent of constitutional guarantees, such as (1) the need to be fair to investors, (2) the need to attract roughly the amount of investment that competitive market considerations would dictate, and (3) the need for administrative simplicity.

Part of the commissions' problem can be readily solved. Those who have invested in fixed income securities can be paid the coupon rate of interest. Persons buying 8 percent bonds will be paid back 8 percent per year on the dollars they invested; and the utility will be allowed to earn enough profit to pay them, so long as it can do so. Unregulated firms in competitive markets would treat their bondholders no differently; such a payment is fair, it is readily calculable, and it is consistent with valuing the rate base — the plant and equipment that the borrowed money was used to purchase — at historical cost.

The more difficult problem is that of calculating a fair return on equity. That is to say, how large should the profit pool be, over and above the amount needed to pay bondholders? To put the same question differently, what price should the company be allowed to charge so that the return it earns on its total investment (valued at historical cost) after subtracting the amount paid to bondholders (and the amount of book value their investment represents) leaves enough to pay a "fair" or "proper" return to equity-holders on their investment (which should equal the remainder of the firm's book value)?

It is clear that setting a rate of return cannot, even in principle, be reduced to an exact science. To spend hours of hearing time considering elaborate "rate of return" models is of doubtful value; and suggestions of a proper rate — carried out to several decimal places — give an air of precision that must be false. All this is assuming one accepts the standard: "Give the investor just that return she will insist upon to make her investment and no more." Such a standard would equate book and market investment values. Yet suppose regulators met the standard. What incentive would a firm have to become more efficient? Could courts play a constructive role in answering such questions?

C. Review of Questions of Law

1. What Is a Question of Law?

United States v. Fifty-Three Eclectus Parrots

685 F.2d 1131 (9th Cir. 1982)

CANBY, Circuit Judge. Allen appeals from a summary judgment . . . ordering the forfeiture [to customs] of 56 eclectus parrots. We affirm.

Appellant Allen raises and trades birds as a vocation. On his behalf, an importer bought eclectus parrots from a bird dealer in Singapore and imported them into the United States. The birds originated in Indonesia, which has prohibited the export of [certain wildlife, including eclectus parrots] since 1972. Allen did not know of the Indonesian Law; nor, evidently, did U.S. customs authorities when he asked them about the law prior to importation when the birds arrived in the United States. However, customs authorities, apparently having learned of Indonesia's law, seized them, under the authority of 19 U.S.C. §1527 (1976), which states in relevant part, "If the laws . . . of any country . . . restrict the taking, killing, possession, or exportation to the United States, of any wild . . . bird, . . . no such . . . bird . . . shall . . . be imported. . . . Any bird . . . imported . . . in viola-tion of th[is] provision . . . shall be subject to seizure and forefeiture. . . ."

[The circuit court first considered, and rejected, Allen's argument that forfeiture of the parrots was unlawful because he was not "culpable"; he had done all required to find out whether Indonesia protected the birds; he had made an innocent mistake. The court ruled that the statute applies to "innocent" as well as "culpable" efforts to import and that forfeiture was appropriate. The court also rejected the argument that customs had a duty to tell Allen about the Indonesian law.]

Finally, Appellant contends that the eclectus parrots are not "wild" within the meaning of §1527, since breeders have had some limited success in breeding the birds in captivity, and some of the birds show signs of having been so bred. The government main-tains that §1527 applies to any foreign bird whose species is normally found in a wild state if the country of origin protects the species. We adopt the government's definition of "wild." A contrary interpretation would create obvious enforcement difficulties. The inquiry must be directed to the species. Cf. 18 U.S.C. §42(a)(2) (Lacey Act defines "wild" to mean creatures that "normally are found in a wild state"). Since Appellant did not present any evidence that the species is no longer normally found in a wild state, there was no genuine issue of material fact, and the United States was entitled to summary judgment as a matter of law. Summary judgment was therefore proper. See Fed. R. Civ. P. 56(a).

Affirmed.

Notes and Questions

1. Is the argument over the application of the statutory term "wild bird" to these parrots an argument about "fact" or "law"? Allen opposed the government's summary judgment motion in part by stating that (a) numerous lists of endangered species, includ-ing an important international convention that lists 20 species of parrots, make no mention of eclectus parrots; (b) eclectus parrots "are commonly bought and sold in the marketplace in the United States"; (c) zoologists report that captive eclectus parrots are bred around the world, perhaps even in Indonesia; (d) the 60 parrots were "domesticated in the sense that I use the word, in considering the ease with which they settled in their new home." The government submitted an affidavit by a New York zoo bird curator stating that the eclectus parrot is wild because "it has not bred for multiple generations in captivity." Why do these conflicting statements not create an issue of fact?

The government also argued that the term in the statute refers to bird species that are (a) wild and (b) protected in the country of origin. This is a legal argument, isn't it? And, if correct, no relevant facts are in dispute. How did you distinguish the factual from the legal argument? What sorts of expertise might have been relevant to the two different sorts of decision? Was it difficult to distinguish fact from law? Do you believe the views of the customs authorities are entitled to more "respect" by a court in matters of fact or of law?

2. Some people urge that the distinction between questions of law and fact is entirely manipulable. This was a particular theme in the legal realist movement. Several realists argued the judges characterize an issue as one of law when they seek to exercise control, and they characterize an issue as one of fact when they seek to defer (for example, to a jury or an administrative agency). But even if the distinction can be manipulated in practice, is it really manipulable in principle?

Reconsider the *Benzene* case. Was the question in that case — whether the governing statute required the government to show a "significant risk" — a question of law, fact, or both? Evaluate the following hypothesis. The question whether a certain substance "causes cancer" is purely one of fact; legal competence is utterly irrelevant to that question. (Legal competence would be relevant if and only if "causes cancer" were a legal term of art.) The question whether a statute requires the government to show a "significant risk" is purely one of law; it requires an understanding only of law, not one of fact or policy. Finally, the question whether benzene itself causes a "significant risk," if that phrase is a legal term of art, is a mixed question of law and fact, and it is important to disentangle the legal and factual components of that question.

Evaluate the following response. The question whether a statute requires an agency to show a "significant risk" is not really one of law alone; it has important elements of both fact and policy. Whether a statute should be understood in that way depends on an assessment of the *consequences of that understanding* — and hence on fact and policy, not only law. Indeed, a judgment whether a substance "causes cancer" may well have dimensions of policy or even law, at least when the facts are in dispute. These points are worth considering in connection with the *Chevron* case.

3. In O'Leary v. Brown-Pacific-Maxon, Inc., 340 U.S. 504 (1951), a Deputy Commissioner of the Bureau of Employees' Compensation, U.S. Department of Labor, had awarded Longshoremen's and Harbor Workers' Act compensation to the dependent mother of an employee of a U.S. contractor operating in Guam. The employee had been using a company recreation area that was next to a shore area posted as dangerous to swimmers. He heard cries for help from two swimmers in trouble, went to rescue them, and drowned. The deputy commissioner found as a "fact" that the drowning gave rise to compensation because (in the statute's words) the death "arose out of and in the course of employment."

Justice Frankfurter, writing for the Court, upheld the award for three reasons. First, the statutory requirement that an accident arise "out of and in the course of employment" is satisfied if the "'obligations or conditions' of employment create the 'zone of special danger' out of which the injury arose." Second, a rescue attempt might or might not be the product of a "zone of special danger" created by the employment. Whether it was the result of such a "zone" in this case was for the agency to decide. Third, the deputy commissioner's finding that the accident in question was compensable was one of "fact"; thus the appropriate standard of judicial review was the substantial evidence standard of *Universal Camera*. Here the conclusion does not involve a determination of the existence or nonexistence of a "simple, external, physical event" but rather "concerns a combination of happenings and inferences [which] presuppose applicable standards. . . . Yet the standards are not so severable from the experience of industry nor of such nature as to be particularly appropriate for independent judicial ascertainment as 'questions of law.'"

Reviewing the finding as one of "fact," the Court finds it supported by "substantial evidence."

Three dissenters asserted that the undisputed evidence, showing that the employee had voluntarily initiated the rescue attempt and that he was out on his own in the channel when he died, established that the deputy commissioner's finding of a causal connection between employment and death was "false." They accused the majority of finding "facts where there are no facts."

In O'Keeffe v. Smith, Hinchman Grylls Associates, 380 U.S. 359 (1965), the Supreme Court upheld a deputy commissioner's award of similar compensation to an American employee working in Korea who, on a private Sunday recreational outing, filled a rowboat with sand, tried to row across a lake, and drowned when the boat capsized. The employer was an American firm that paid the employee's wages and living expenses. The Court wrote that the deputy commissioner's finding could not be said to be "irrational or without substantial evidence on the record as a whole." In both O'Leary and O'Keeffe, the Supreme Court reversed circuit court holdings reversing the deputy commissioner.

Justice Harlan, in dissent, asserted that courts must ensure that agencies are faithful to the terms and purposes of relevant statutes. But where a statute does not dictate a result one way or another, the agency has the discretion to choose appropriate policy. Under this approach, he found that O'Leary was correctly decided because either a decision that the accidental death was within the scope of employment or a decision that it was not was consistent with the statutory purpose. Hence the agency was free to decide either way. Here, however, Justice Harlan found that the accidental death was in no way related to any special danger created by employment in Korea. The accident — on a weekend away from work — could as easily have happened in the United States. To award compensation in these circumstances would be inconsistent with the statute's purpose of compensating only work-related injuries. Hence, the Court should find the award contrary to the statute.

Justice Frankfurter in O'Leary suggests he is dealing with what Justice Jackson referred to as "mixed findings of law and fact." Dobson v. Commissioner, 320 U.S. 489, 501 (1943). Judge Friendly divides cases in which an agency applies a statutory label to a set of facts into (1) those where the issue is really factual (the meaning of the statute is not really disputed); (2) those where the issue is really legal (the facts are not really disputed); and (3) those where the agency's conclusion rests on disputed matters of both law and fact. NLRB v. Marcus Trucking Co., 286 F.2d 583 (2d Cir. 1961). In Professor Davis's view, this last category presents "mixed" questions, with the courts classifying them as questions of fact or of law on the basis of "practical considerations" not "analysis." See 5 K. Davis, Administrative Law Treatise §§29.9-29.14, §30.10 (1984).

Yet can one not, at least conceptually, separate out the "factual" from the "legal" elements that are in dispute? Can you not do so, even in the two Longshoremen's Act cases? What sort of *factual* argument might you have made to the commissioner for the claimant in the two cases? What sort *of legal* argument?

4. A major question is what sort of standard of review the courts should apply when considering an agency's decision while applying a statutory term to a set of facts that rests in part on an agency's legal interpretation of a statutory term as well as on agency factual findings. Should the court treat the legal part of the findings with the same respect it treats factual findings? Should it review the legal questions involved "independently"? Some courts, finding it particularly difficult to apply separate review standards when the agency itself has not divided the "factual" from the "legal" part of its decision, are tempted to call

the whole case "factual," or to suggest that the case presents matters of fact and of law that are "inextricably mixed"; on this view, a "fact-type" standard of review is appropriate. Consider the analogous problems faced by a court in reviewing a general verdict by a jury in a negligence case where the facts are disputed.

Our immediate problem is the standard of review as to "questions of law." In approaching this question, you should consider (1) whether there is a clear conceptual distinction between questions of law and of fact, and (2) even if there is, should the standard of review differ depending on whether the issue presented is one of law or fact, or should other considerations be controlling?

5. For your information, counsel in the parrot case has said that of 53 parrots seized, all but 18 have died. The good news, however, is that the 18 live parrots have been breeding. Their young, born in captivity in the United States, aren't "wild," are they?

2. *The Basic "Statutory Interpretation" Problem: The Years before Chevron*

> The reviewing court shall decide all relevant questions of law, interpret . . . statutory provisions . . .

Administrative Procedure Act §706 (1946).

The dominant case on judicial review of agency interpretation of law is Chevron v. Natural Resources Defense Council, 467 U.S. 837 (1984). It is difficult, however, to understand *Chevron* without having a sense of what preceded it. In this section we outline pre-*Chevron* law.

Despite the language of the APA instructing courts to decide "all relevant" questions of law, the courts have long said that some questions of law are for some agencies to decide. With respect to those legal questions, the courts will "defer" to the agency's judgment, overturning the agency only if its legal determination is "unreasonable," "impermissible," or "arbitrary." One way to reconcile judicial deference with the language of the APA is to say that under some or perhaps many statutes, a court's decision about the "relevant question of law" is that Congress has given the agency, not the court, the discretion to choose among various different interpretations. In other words, sometimes the law is what the agency says that it is, because Congress has, under the relevant law, given the agency the authority to make that decision. See Monaghan, *Marbury* and the Administrative State, 83 Colum. L. Rev. 1 (1983).

The basic question in this area is: When should a court "defer" or "give weight to" an agency's determination of a legal question? The basic answer might be: When Congress has said so. But often Congress has not spoken with clarity, and courts must reconstruct congressional instructions on the basis of their own assessment of what approach makes best sense. There are competing considerations here. If courts never deferred to agencies and decided all questions of law on their own, the law might lose some of the advantages of agency administration — advantages growing out of the agency's democratic pedigree, its knowledge, and its experience in working with highly detailed statutes, applying them in hosts of different factual circumstances. On the other hand, might it be difficult to justify turning over the authority to decide many, or all, legal questions to administrative agencies? One reason we have courts, after all, is to decide questions of law. Judge Leventhal has urged: "Congress has been willing to delegate its legislative powers broadly — and courts have upheld such delegation — because there is court review to assure that the agency exercises the delegated power within statutory limits." Ethyl Corp. v. EPA, 541 F.2d 1, 68 (D.C. Cir. 1976). How can the court keep the agency within its statutory bounds without itself deciding what the statute means? Isn't a court that simply, and almost automatically, accepts the interpretation of one of the litigants abdicating its judicial responsibility?

In 1976, Judge Friendly, in Pittston Stevedoring Corp. v. Dellaventura, 544 F.2d 35 (2d Cir. 1976), wrote that "there are two lines of cases on this subject which are analytically in conflict." Judge Friendly conceded that the Supreme Court had made clear that agencies have broad legal power to formulate rules that have the effect of law, when Congress delegates that power to the agency. But the matter is more difficult when the legal question at issue consists, for example, of whether the statute properly applies to a particular set of facts. Skeptics about the New Deal's enthusiasm for administrative agencies insisted on independent judicial review of agency interpretations of law, and the great constitutional cases involving the early administrative state were paralled by a number of cases in which courts rejected agency interpretations. But after the New Deal era, a number of leading cases supported the view that great deference must be given to the decision of an administrative agency applying a statute to the facts and that such decisions can be reversed only if without rational basis. See, e.g., Rochester Telephone Corp. v. United States, 307 U.S. 125, 146 (1939); Gray v. Powell, 314 U.S. 402, 411 (1941); and NLRB v. Hearst Publications, 322 U.S. 111 (1944). Later cases were in the same vein. In Ford Motor Co. v. NLRB, 441 U.S. 488 (1979), the Court said that, if the labor board's "construction of the statute is reasonably defensible, it should not be rejected merely because the courts prefer another view of the statute." The Court similarly wrote that the Federal Reserve Board's interpretation of its governing statute will control as long as it is reasonable or not "demonstrably irrational." Ford Motor Credit Co. v. Milhollin, 44 U.S. 555, 565 (1980). It upheld the Federal Election Commission's interpretation of its statute, writing that "the task for the Court of Appeals was not to interpret the statute as it thought best but rather the narrower inquiry into whether the Commission's construction was 'sufficiently reasonable' to be accepted by a reviewing court." FEC v. Democratic Senatorial Campaign Comm., 454 U.S. 27, 39 (1981). See also Udall v. Tallman, 380 U.S. 1, 16 (1965).

On the other hand, the Court sometimes refused to "defer" to an agency interpretation of a statute. When refusing to do so, the Court typically referred to the fact that "courts are the final authorities on issues of statutory construction. They must reject administrative constructions of a statute . . . that are inconsistent with the statutory language or that frustrate the policy that Congress sought to implement." FEC v. Democratic Senatorial Campaign Comm., 454 U.S. 27, 32 (1981). See, e.g., Alcoa v. Central Lincoln People's Util. Dist., 467 U.S. 380, 402 n.3 (1984); NLRB v. Insurance Agents, 361 U.S. 477, 499 (1960); NLRB v. Highland Park Mfg. Co., 341 U.S. 322 (1951); Northeast Marine Terminal Co. v. Caputo, 432 U.S. 249 (1977). Thus there was an impressive body of law sanctioning free substitution of judicial for administrative judgment when the question involves the meaning of a statutory term. Illustrative cases are Office Employees Intl. Union v. NLRB, 353 U.S. 3133 (1957); Davies Warehouse Co. v. Bowles, 321 U.S. 144 (1944); and Morton v. Ruiz, 415 U.S. 199, 237 (1974).

In 1984, the D.C. Circuit reiterated the problem that these different lines of cases created. It complained that the

> case law . . . has not crystallized around a single doctrinal formulation which captures the extent to which courts should defer to agency interpretations of law. Instead two

"opposing platitudes" exert countervailing "gravitational pulls" on the law. At one pole stands the maxim that courts should defer to "reasonable" agency interpretive positions, a maxim increasingly prevalent in recent decisions. Pulling in the other direction is the principle that courts remain the final arbitrators of statutory meaning: that principle, too, is embossed with recent approval.

NRDC v. EPA, 725 F.2d 761, 767 (D.C. Cir. 1984). As the D.C. Circuit also pointed out, there are competing "submaxims" for determining just when "deference" is appropriate. Some might think, for example, that when an agency has followed a particular interpretation for a long period of time, it is entitled to "special" deference. On the other hand, should an agency not be permitted to change an interpretation when it concludes that change is needed "to match the statute's construction to the original congressional intent?" Id. at 765.

In addition, some courts used "functional" considerations in deciding how much "deference" to give. In *Pittston*, for example, Judge Friendly thought that the Benefits Review Board was not entitled to much deference in deciding how Compensation Act amendments applied to certain harbor workers because (1) the board was an "umpiring," not a "policymaking," body; (2) its decision was not carefully considered; (3) its decision was made before it had much experience administering the act; and (4) the interpretation depended, in any event, upon review of legal materials, not experience.

Consider how these considerations bear on the following old but fairly typical case.

NLRB v. Hearst Publications
322 U.S. 111 (1944)

Mr. Justice RUTLEDGE delivered the opinion of the Court.

These cases arise from the refusal of respondents, publishers of four Los Angeles daily newspapers, to bargain collectively with a union representing newsboys who distribute their papers on the streets of that city. Respondents [contend] that they were not required to bargain because the newsboys are not their "employees" within the meaning of that term in the National Labor Relations Act. . . .

[The NLRB, after hearings,] concluded that the regular full-time newsboys selling each paper were employees within the Act [and Hearst was ordered to bargain with them].

[T]he Circuit Court of Appeals, one judge dissenting, set aside the Board's orders. Rejecting the Board's analysis, the court independently examined the question whether the newsboys are employees within the Act, decided that the statute imports common-law standards to determine that question, and held the newsboys are not employees. . . .

I

The principal question is whether the newsboys are "employees." Because Congress did not explicitly define the term, respondents say its meaning must be determined by reference to common-law standards. . . .

. . . Few problems in the law have given greater variety of application and conflict in results than the cases arising in the borderland between what is clearly an employer-employee relationship and what is clearly one of independent, entrepreneurial dealing. . . .

. . . It is enough to point out that, with reference to an identical problem, results may be contrary over a very considerable region of doubt in applying the distinction, depending upon the state or jurisdiction where the determination is made. . . .

Mere reference to these possible variations as characterizing the application of the Wagner Act in the treatment of persons identically situated in the facts surrounding their employment and in the influences tending to disrupt it, would be enough to require pause before accepting a thesis which would introduce them into its administration. . . .

. . . Both the terms and the purposes of the statute, as well as the legislative history, show that Congress had in mind no such patchwork plan for securing freedom of employees' organization and of collective bargaining. . . .

II

Whether, given the intended national uniformity, the term "employee" includes such workers as these newsboys must be answered primarily from the history, terms and purposes of the legislation. . . .

. . . Congress had in mind a wider field than the narrow technical legal relation of "master and servant," as the common law had worked this out in all its variations, and at the same time a narrower one than the entire area of rendering service to others. The question comes down therefore to how much was included of the intermediate region between what is clearly and unequivocally "employment," by an appropriate test, and what is as clearly entrepreneurial enterprise and not employment. . . .

Congress . . . sought to find a broad solution, one that would bring industrial peace by substituting, so far as its power could reach, the rights of workers to self-organization and collective bargaining for the industrial strife which prevails where these rights are not effectively established. . . .

The mischief at which the Act is aimed and the remedies it offers are not confined exclusively to "employees" within the traditional legal distinctions separating them from "independent contractors." Myriad forms of service relationships, with infinite and subtle variations in the terms of employment, blanket the nation's economy. Some are within this Act, others beyond its coverage. Large numbers will fall clearly on one side or on the other, by whatever test may be applied. But intermediate there will be many, the incidents of whose employment partake in part of the one group, in part of the other, in varying proportions of weight, And consequently the legal pendulum, for purposes of applying the statute, may swing one way or the other, depending upon the weight of this balance and its relation to the special purpose at hand. . . .

It is not necessary in this case to make a completely definitive limitation around the term "employee." That task has been assigned primarily to the agency created by Congress to administer the Act. Determination of "where all the conditions of the relation require protection" involves inquiries for the Board charged with this duty. Everyday experience in the administration of the statute gives it familiarity with the circumstances and backgrounds of employment relationships in various industries, with the abilities and needs of the workers for self-organization and collective action, and with the adaptability of collective bargaining for the peaceful settlement of their disputes with their employers. The experience thus acquired must be brought frequently to bear on the question who is an employee under the Act. Resolving that question, like determining whether unfair labor practices have been committed, "belongs to the usual administrative routine" of the Board. Gray v. Powell, 314 U.S. 402, 411 [(1941)].

. . . Undoubtedly questions of statutory interpretation, especially when arising in the first instance in judicial proceedings, are for the courts to resolve, giving appropriate weight to the judgment of those whose special duty is to administer the questioned statute. Norwegian Nitrogen Products Co. v. United States, 288 U.S. 294 [(1933)]. . . . But where the question is one of specific application of a broad statutory term in a proceeding in which the agency administering the statute must determine it initially, the reviewing court's function is limited. Like the commissioner's determination under the Longshoremen's & Harbor Workers' Act, that a man is not a "member of a crew" . . . or that he was injured "in the course of employment" . . . the Board's determination that specified persons are "employees" under this Act is to be accepted if it has "warrant in the record" and a reasonable basis in law.

In this case . . . the Board concluded that the newsboys are employees. The record sustains the Board's findings and there is ample basis in the law for its conclusion. . . .

Does *Hearst* hold that "pure" questions of law should be decided independently by courts, but that applications of law to fact should be reviewed for reasonableness? In Gray v. Powell, 314 U.S. 402, 412 (1941), cited in *Hearst*, the Court sustained an agency's determination that a particular firm's activities were subject to regulation by the Department of the Interior, stating that

> Where, as here, a determination has been left to an administrative body, this delegation will be respected and the administrative conclusion left untouched. Certainly, a finding on congressional reference that an admittedly constitutional act is applicable to a particular situation does not require such further scrutiny. Although we have here no dispute as to the evidentiary facts, that does not permit a court to substitute its judgment for that of the Director. It is not the province of a court to absorb the administrative functions to such an extent that the executive or legislative agencies become mere fact finding bodies deprived of the advantages of prompt and definite action.

After *Hearst* Congress amended the statute to define "employee" so as not to include "an individual having the status of an independent contractor." 29 U.S.C. §152(3). Does this show that *Hearst* misconstrued the statute? Does the possibility of congressional correction of judicial mistakes argue in favor of any particular approach to statutory interpretation? For evidence that Congress does overrule judicial interpretations of which it disapproves, see Eskridge, Overruling Supreme Court Statutory Interpretation Decisions, 101 Yale L.J. 331 (1991).

3. *"Legislative Rules" versus Agency Interpretations*

Skidmore v. Swift & Co.
323 U.S. 134 (1944)

Mr. Justice JACKSON delivered the opinion of the Court.

Seven employees of the Swift and Company packing plant at Fort Worth, Texas, brought an action under the Fair Labor Standards Act to recover overtime, liquidated damages, and attorneys' fees, totaling approximately $77,000. . . .

It is not denied that the daytime employment of these persons was working time within the Act. . . .

Under their oral agreement of employment, however, petitioners undertook to stay in the fire hall on the Company premises, or within hailing distance, three and a half to four nights a week. This involved no task except to answer alarms, either because of fire or because the sprinkler was set off for some other reason. No fires occurred during the period in issue, the alarms were rare, and the time required for their answer rarely exceeded an hour. For each alarm answered the employees were paid in addition to their fixed compensation an agreed amount, fifty cents at first, and later sixty-four cents. The Company provided a brick fire hall equipped with steam heat and air-conditioned rooms. It provided sleeping quarters, a pool table, a domino table, and a radio. The men used their time in sleep or amusement as they saw fit, except that they were required to stay in or close by the fire hall and be ready to respond to alarms. It is stipulated that "they agreed to remain in the fire hall and stay in it or within hailing distance, subject to call, in event of fire or other casualty, but were not required to perform any specific tasks during these periods of time, except in answering alarms." The trial court . . . said as a "conclusion of law" that "the time plantiffs spent in the fire hall subject to call to answer fire alarms does not constitute hours worked, for which overtime compensation is due them under the Fair Labor Standards Act, as interpreted by the Administrator and the Courts," and in its opinion observed, "of course we know pursuing such pleasurable occupations or performing such personal chores, does not constitute work." The Circuit Court of Appeals affirmed.

[N]o principle of law found either in the statute or in Court decisions precludes waiting time from also being working time. We have not attempted to, and we cannot, lay down a legal formula to resolve cases so varied in their facts as are the many situations in which employment involves waiting time. Whether in a concrete case such time falls within or without the Act is a question of fact to be resolved by appropriate findings of the trial court. Walling v. Jacksonville Paper Co., 317 US. 564, 572. This involves scrutiny and construction of the agreements between the particular parties, appraisal of their practical construction of the working agreement by conduct, consideration of the nature of the service, and its relation to the waiting time, and all of the surrounding circumstances. Facts may show that the employee was engaged to wait, or they may show that he waited to be engaged. His compensation may cover both waiting and task, or only performance of the task itself. Living quarters may in some situations be furnished as a facility of the task and in another as a part of its compensation. The law does not impose an arrangement upon the parties. It imposes upon the courts the task of finding what the arrangement was. . . .

Congress did not utilize the services of an administrative agency to find facts and to determine in the first instance whether particular cases fall within or without the Act. Instead, it put this responsibility on the courts. . . . But it did create the office of Administrator, impose upon him a variety of duties, endow him with powers to inform himself of conditions in industries and employments subject to the Act, and put on him the duties of bringing injunction actions to restrain violations. Pursuit of his duties has accumulated a considerable experience in the problems of ascertaining working time in employments involving periods of inactivity and a knowledge of the customs prevailing in reference to their solution. From these he is obliged to reach conclusions as to conduct without the law, so that he should seek injunctions to stop it, and that within the law, so that he has no call to interfere. He has set forth his views of the application of the Act under different circumstances in an interpretative bulletin and in informal rulings. They provide a practical guide to employers and employees as to how the office representing the public interest in its enforcement will seek to apply it. Wage and Hour Division, Interpretative Bulletin No. 13.

The Administrator thinks the problems presented by inactive duty require a flexible solution, rather than the all-in or all-out rules respectively urged by the parties in this case, and his Bulletin endeavors to suggest standards and examples to guide in particular situations. In some occupations, it says, periods of inactivity are not properly counted as working time even though the employee is subject to call. Examples are an operator of a small telephone exchange where the switchboard is in her home and she ordinarily gets several hours of uninterrupted sleep each night; or a pumper of a stripper well or watchman of a lumber camp during the off season, who may be on duty twenty-four hours a day but ordinarily "has a normal night's sleep, has ample time in which to eat his meals, and has a certain amount of time for relaxation and entirely private pursuits." Exclusion of all such hours the Administrator thinks may be justified. In general, the answer depends "upon the degree to which the employee is free to engage in personal activities during periods of idleness when he is subject to call and the number of consecutive hours that the employee is subject to call without being required to perform active work." "Hours worked are not limited to the time spent in active labor but include time given by the employee to the employer. . . ."

The facts of this case do not fall within any of the specific examples given, but the conclusion of the Administrator, as expressed in the brief amicus curiae, is that the general tests which he has suggested point to the exclusion of sleeping and eating time of these employees from the workweek and the inclusion of all other on-call time: although the employees were required to remain on the premises during the entire time, the evidence shows that they were very rarely interrupted in their normal sleeping and eating time, and these are pursuits of a purely private nature which would presumably occupy the employees' time whether they were on duty or not and which apparently could be pursued adequately and comfortably in the required circumstances; the rest of the time is different because there is nothing in the record to suggest that, even though pleasurably spent, it was spent in the ways the men would have chosen had they been free to do so.

There is no statutory provision as to what, if any, deference courts should pay to the Administrator's conclusions. And, while we have given them notice, we have had no occasion to try to prescribe their influence. The rulings of this Administrator are not reached as a result of hearing adversary proceedings in which he finds facts from evidence and reaches conclusions of law from findings of fact. They are not, of course, conclusive, even in the cases with which they directly deal, much less in those to which they apply only by analogy. They do not constitute an interpretation of the Act or a standard for judging factual situations which binds a district court's processes, as an authoritative pronouncement of a higher court might do. But the Administrator's policies are made in pursuance of official duty, based upon more specialized and broader investigations and information than is likely to come to a judge in a particular case. They do determine the policy which will guide applications for enforcement by injunction on behalf of the Government. Good administration of the Act and good judicial administration alike require that the standards of public enforcement and those for determining private rights shall be at variance only where justified by very good reasons. The fact that the Administrator's policies and standards are not reached by trial in adversary form does not mean that they are not entitled to respect. This Court has long given considerable and in some cases decisive weight to Treasury Decisions and to interpretative regulations of the Treasury and of other bodies that were not of adversary origin.

We consider that the rulings, interpretations and opinions of the Administrator under this Act, while not controlling upon the courts by reason of their authority, do constitute a body of experience and informed judgment to which courts and litigants may properly resort for guidance. The weight of such a judgment in a particular case will depend upon the thoroughness evident in its consideration, the validity of its reasoning, its consistency with earlier and later pronouncements, and all those factors which give it power to persuade, if lacking power to control. . . .

Each case must stand on its own facts. But in this case, although the district court referred to the Administrator's Bulletin, its evaluation and inquiry were apparently restricted by its notion that waiting time may not be work, an understanding of the law which we hold to be erroneous.

[Reversed.]

Notes

1. What is the difference between a legislative rule and an interpretative rule, and how does the difference bear on the courts' approach to agency "interpretations of law"? Note that the terminology is a bit misleading, for a legislative rule *may well be an interpretation.* Consider K. Davis, 2 Administrative Law Treatise 36, 51-52 (1979):

> A legislative rule is the product of an exercise of delegated legislative power to make law through rules. An interpretative rule is any rule an agency issues without exercising delegated legislative power to make law through rules. . . .
>
> An administrator who has a discretionary power but no delegated power to make rules may state how he will exercise his discretion, and the result may be interpretative rules to which a court may give the effect of law if the court is persuaded by the rules. But because the legislative body has not delegated legislative power to the administrator, the rules are not binding on the court; the court is free, if it chooses, to substitute its judgment as to the content of the interpretative rules. . . .
>
> An interpretative rule, according to the *Skidmore* opinion, . . . is not "controlling upon the courts" but may have "power to persuade, if lacking power to control." By contrast, a legislative rule, if constitutional, within the granted power, and properly issued, is "law" as if it were a statute, and is "controlling upon courts." . . .

We will deal below with the difference between judicial review of a legislative rule and judicial review of an interpretative rule.

2. Even if the conceptual distinction between "legislative" and "interpretative" rules is fairly clear (is it?), deciding whether Congress has given the agency the power to promulgate rules with the force of law may be difficult. See, e.g., National Nutritional Foods Assn. v. Weinberger, 512 F.2d 688 (2d Cir. 1975).

Judge Stephen Williams sought to synthesize the criteria for distinguishing between interpretative and legislative rules in American Mining Congress v. Mine Safety & Health Administration, 995 F.2d 1106, 1112 (D.C. Cir. 1993):

> [I]nsofar as our cases can be reconciled at all, we think it almost exclusively on the basis of whether the purported interpretive rule has "legal effect" which in turn is best ascertained by asking (1) whether in the absence of the rule there would not be an adequate legislative basis for enforcement action or other agency action to confer benefits or ensure the performance of duties, (2) whether the agency has published the rule in the Code of Federal Regulations, (3) whether the agency has explicitly invoked its general legislative authority, or (4) whether the rule effectively amends a

prior legislative rule. If the answer to any of these questions is affirmative, we have a legislative, not an interpretative rule.

Judge Williams reconsidered the consequences of publication in the C.F.R. in Health Insurance Assn. v. Shalala, 23 F.3d 412, 423 (D.C. Cir. 1994), where he found that publication in the C.F.R., rather than being dispositive, was "a snippet of evidence" of agency intent with respect to a rule. Other effects to formulate the destruction are found in Fertilizer Institute v. EPA, 935 F.2d 1303,1307-1308 (D.C. Cir. 1991) (interpretative rule states what the agency thinks the statute means and reminds affected parties of existing duties, while legislative rules create new law, rights, or duties, and the test is whether agency intended to create new duties, not whether the rule has the effect of creating new duties); Metropolitan School District v. Davila, 969 F.2d 485 (7th Cir. 1992) (starting point is agency's characterization of the rule, then consider whether the rule creates new law, rights, or duties). We will deal with this issue too in greater detail below.

3. *Skidmore* is famous for suggesting a separate and distinct judicial approach to interpretative rules. Such rules seem not to be "binding": they have merely persuasive authority, whose weight depends on the circumstances.

This suggestion raises some broader questions: What determines *how much* "deference" the courts will grant an agency interpretation, legislative or otherwise? In the years before *Chevron*, courts and commentators said that the answer to this question depends on a host of factors. (We shall explore how much of this analysis survives today.) *Skidmore* lists some of these factors: the "thoroughness evident" in the agency's consideration, "the validity of its reasoning, its consistency with earlier and later pronouncements, and all those factors which give it power to persuade, if lacking power to control."

Some factors, often mentioned, seem directly relevant to the likelihood that the agency knows better than the court what Congress actually meant by the statute. These factors include whether the agency's interpretation was made near the time the statute was enacted, whether its interpretation is long-standing, and whether Congress reenacted the same language in the presence of the interpretation.

Other factors seem relevant both to this question and to the question of the likelihood that Congress intended the court to pay special heed to agency views on this subject. These factors include the nature of the agency's specialized experience in relation to the legal question and the practical implications. Is the question one as to which the agencies or the courts are more likely to be "expert"? Does it, on the one hand, draw on common law or constitutional law sources, or, on the other hand, does it primarily involve matters of agency administration? Is the question an "important" one that Congress focused on and likely provided an answer to in the statute? Or is it "interstitial"; is the "correct" (that is, practical, effective) answer likely to emerge out of the knowledge derived from daily administration of the statute? To what extent will the court's answer to the legal question illuminate, clarify, and stabilize a broad area of the law or of the statute's administrative scheme? It may also be relevant to ask whether the court "trusts" the agency; have previous cases led it to fear agency bias or "tunnel vision"? If one focuses on these latter questions as relevant to the weight the court should place on agency legal interpretations, then one will tend to blur the difference in practical effect (but not necessarily the conceptual difference) between "legislative" rules and agency interpretations. We will revisit these issues too after discussing *Chevron*. (The "legislative-interpretative" distinction is important for a different reason, for the APA's "notice and comment" rulemaking provisions make an exception for "interpretative rules," a matter we discuss in Chapter 6.)

4. Commentators have made various attempts to develop unifying explanations of, or theories about, the courts' approach to reviewing agency decisions of law. Professor Davis's view, already described in part, involves a clear distinction between "legislative" rules and agency interpretations, a less clear set of "factors" for determining the proper weight to be given agency interpretations in differing circumstances, and a frank admission that the courts sometimes act inconsistently.

Under one view, a court must also identify and give effect to *Congress's instructions as to what weight the court should give the agency's views when the court interprets the statute.* Where Congress makes it clear that the court should give considerable weight, we have Professor Davis's "legislative rule." But what happens when Congress is silent? One might then turn to the various factors listed above in Note 3 as clues or elements to be considered in determining congressional instructions (or "intent") on that question — knowing that such instructions are being reconstructed on the basis of an understanding of what makes best sense, rather than merely found. See R. Dworkin, Law's Empire (1985).

Accordingly, in interpreting a statute to resolve relevant questions of law, the courts might adopt several different approaches. They might look not only to legislative history, language, structure, history, purpose of the program, and so forth but also to the other factors referred to in Note 3 to determine what attitude Congress intends courts to take toward the agency's views on the meaning of the statute. Alternatively, they might try to develop a single rule about when to "defer"; the *Chevron* case set out after these notes develops such a "simplified" approach. In either case, deference, when it existed, would be based on the view that "what the law is" is, in certain circumstances, what the agency says that it is. See Monaghan, *Marbury* and the Administrative State, 83 Colum. L. Rev. 1 (1983).

5. The analysis developed above identifies two distinct (if operationally overlapping) reasons why a court might defer to an agency's resolution of a question of law. First, the court might conclude that the statute granted the agency discretion to decide the issue one way or another. Second, the court might accept the agency's resolution as a presumptively correct interpretation of the statutory commands to which the court should defer. Which mode of deference the court adopts is likely to have important consequences for the agency's ability later to decide the same question of law in a different way.

If a court has deferred to the agency for the second reason — because of the greater likelihood that the agency's interpretation of the statute is "correct" — then the court will be reluctant to allow the agency to change a long-standing interpretation. (But is such change totally foreclosed?) If, however, the court has deferred to the agency for the first reason — because the decision is in an area where it is reasonable to infer a congressional desire for agency lawmaking discretion — then the court will be less reluctant to allow a change in interpretation. The issue has considerable practical significance. Under the Reagan administration, for example, agencies altered previous views and relaxed or abandoned regulation, placing greater reliance on market competition. In some cases, the courts gave considerable weight to past agency interpretations and disapproved changes. See Western Coal Traffic League v. United States, 691 F.2d 1104 (3d Cir. 1982) (striking down Interstate Commerce Commission (ICC) effort to abandon certain forms of railroad regulation). So too, the Clinton administration often rejected interpretations by the Reagan and Bush administrations. A large question, taken up shortly, is how the *Chevron* case bears on changed interpretations.

D. *Chevron*: Synthesis or Revolution?

Chevron, Inc. v. Natural Resources Defense Council

467 U.S. 837 (1984)

Justice STEVENS delivered the opinion of the Court.

[The case concerns the interpretation of the words "stationary source" in the 1977 Amendments to the Clean Air Act. The statute requires states to develop air pollution plans that "require permits for the construction and operation of new or modified major stationary sources in accordance with section 173," 42 U.S.C. §7502(b)(6). Section 173 governs controls on new sources in "nonattaintnent" areas of the nation that have not yet achieved national air quality standards. It imposes extremely strict requirements. For example, it requires an applicant to certify that all his other sources comply with nonpollution standards. It subjects the "new or modified" source to an elaborate preconstruction review process. It requires the new source to comply with "the most stringent emission limitation which is contained in the implementation plan of any state" (lowest achievable emission rate, or LAER), and to obtain "offsets" (reductions from emissions from existing sources in the region) at least equal to its emission increases.

The Environmental Protection Agency (EPA) promulgated rules that allowed states to define an entire plant, containing many different kinds of pollution-emitting units, as if it were a single "stationary source." Thus, a firm could modify one unit within the plant and increase its emissions, or introduce a new unit, without complying with the various requirements of §173. It could do this as long as pollution from the plant, *considered as a whole*, did not increase, because it reduced equivalent emissions from other, existing units. The EPA said its rule, in effect, allowed the states to treat each plant as if a bubble were placed over it; the owner would remain free to act as he wished *within* the bubble as long as the total emissions coming from the bubble, considered as a single "source," became no worse.

The proponents of this concept argued that it would allow plants to achieve the most cost-effective way of controls between new and existing units, provide industry with incentives to find new ways of cleaning up existing units, and eliminate time-consuming preconstruction review. The opponents claimed it did not force owners to incorporate the most advanced unit technologies in new units and that regulators could force reductions from existing units without relying on "bubble" incentives. The Court of Appeals held that the statute did not permit the EPA to allow a "bubble-like" definition of "stationary source" in nonattainment areas of the country because it would undermine Congress's goal of speedy compliance with national air quality standards.

The statute itself provides the following definitions:

> (j) Except as otherwise expressly provided, the terms "major stationary source" and "major emitting facility" mean any stationary facility or source of air pollutants which directly emits, or has the potential to emit, one hundred tons per year or more of any air pollutant (including any major emitting facility or source of fugitive emission of any such pollutant, as determined by rule by the Administrator). 91 Stat. 770.

In addition, a different part of the statute, §112, not directly applicable here (imposing certain minimum "performance standards" on all new "stationary sources" of pollution regardless of whether they are located in a nonattainment region), said:

(3) The term "stationary source" means any building, structure, facility, or installation which emits or may emit any air pollutant.

During the Carter administration, the EPA had considered adopting a plant-wide definition of "source," thus authorizing the "bubble," but eventually adopted a regulation defining each unit as a "source." The Reagan administration EPA changed the regulation and allowed states to adopt a plant-wide definition of "source."]

II

When a court reviews an agency's construction of the statute which it administers, it is confronted with two questions. First, always, is the question whether Congress has directly spoken to the precise question at issue. If the intent of Congress is clear, that is the end of the matter; for the court, as well as the agency, must give effect to the unambiguously expressed intent of Congress.[1] If, however, the court determines Congress has not directly addressed the precise questions at issue, the court does not simply impose its own construction on the statute,[2] as would be necessary in the absence of an administrative interpretation. Rather, if the statute is silent or ambiguous with respect to the specific issue, the question for the court is whether the agency's answer is based on a permissible construction of the statute.[3]

"The power of an administrative agency to administer a congressionally created . . . program necessarily requires the formulation of policy and the making of rules to fill any gap left, implicitly or explicitly, by Congress." Morton v. Ruiz, 415 U.S. 199, 231 (1974). If Congress has explicitly left a gap for the agency to fill, there is an express delegation of authority to the agency to elucidate a specific provision of the statute by regulation. Such legislative regulations are given controlling weight unless they are arbitrary, capricious, or manifestly contrary to the statute. Sometimes the legislative delegation to an agency on a particular question is implicit rather than explicit. In such a case, a court may not substitute its own construction of a statutory provision for a reasonable interpretation made by the administrator of an agency.

We have long recognized that considerable weight should be accorded to an executive department's construction of a statutory scheme it is entrusted to administer, and the principle of deference to administrative interpretations

> has been consistently followed by this Court whenever decision as to the meaning or reach of a statute has involved reconciling conflicting policies, and a full understanding of the force of the statutory policy in the given situation has depended upon more than ordinary knowledge respecting the matters subjected to agency regulations. . . .
>   . . . If this choice represents a reasonable accommodation of conflicting policies that were committed to the agency's care by the statute, we should not disturb it unless it

---

1. The judiciary is the final authority on issues of statutory construction and must reject administrative constructions that are contrary to clear congressional intent. If a court, employing traditional tools of statutory construction, ascertains that Congress has an intention on the precise question at issue, that intention is the law and must be given effect.

2. See generally R. Pound, The Spirit of Common Law 174-175 (1921).

3. The court need not conclude that the agency construction was the only one it permissibly could have adopted to uphold the construction, or even the reading the court would have reached if the question initially had arisen in a judicial proceeding. . . .

appears from the statute or its legislative history that the accommodation is not one that Congress would have sanctioned. United States v. Shimer, 367 U.S. 374, 382, 383 (1961).

In light of these well-settled principles it is clear that the Court of Appeals misconceived the nature of its role in reviewing the regulations at issue. Once it determined, after its own examination of the legislation, that Congress did not actually have an intent regarding the applicability of the bubble concept to the permit program, the question before it was not whether in its view the concept is "inappropriate" in the general context of a program designed to improve air quality, but whether the Administrator's view that it is appropriate in the context of the particular program is a reasonable one. Based on the examination of the legislation and its history which follows, we agree with the Court of Appeals that Congress did not have a specific intention on the applicability of the bubble concept in these cases, and conclude that the EPA's use of that concept here is a reasonable policy choice for the agency to make. . . .

VII

In this Court respondents . . . contend that the text of the Act requires the EPA to . . . [say that] if either a component of a plant, or the plant as a whole, emits over 100 tons of pollutant, it is a major stationary source. . . .

STATUTORY LANGUAGE

The definition of the term "stationary source" in Section 111(a)(3) refers to "any building, structure, facility, or installation" which emits air pollution. . . . The text of the statute does not make this definition applicable to the [§173] permit program. Petitioners therefore maintain that there is no statutory language even relevant to ascertaining the meaning of stationary source in the permit program aside from Section 3020)(j), which defines the term "major stationary source." . . . We disagree with petitioners on this point.

The definition of Section 302(j) tells us what the word "major" means — a source must emit at least 100 tons of pollution to qualify — but it sheds virtually no light on the meaning of the term "stationary source." It does equate a source with a facility — a "major emitting facility" and a "major stationary source" are synonymous under Section 302(j). The ordinary meaning of the term "facility" is some collection of integrated elements which has been designed and constructed to achieve some purpose. Moreover, it is certainly no affront to common English usage to connote an entire plant as opposed to its constituent parts. Basically, however, the language of Section 302(j) simply does not compel any given interpretation of the term "source."

Respondents recognize that, and hence point to Section 111(a)(3). Although the definition in that section is not literally applicable to the [§173] permit program, it sheds as much light on the meaning of the word "source" as anything in the statute. As respondents point out, use of the words "building, structure, facility, or installation," as the definition of source, could be read to impose the permit conditions on an individual building that is part of a plant.

. . . On the other hand, the . . . language may reasonably be interpreted to impose the requirement on any discrete, but integrated, operation which pollutes. This gives meaning to all of the terms — a single building, not part of a larger operation, would be covered if it emits more than 100 tons of pollution, as would any facility, structure, or installation. Indeed, the language itself implies a "bubble concept" of sorts: each enumerated item would seem to be treated as if it were encased in a bubble. While respondents insist that each of these terms must be given a discrete meaning, they also argue that Section 111(a)(3) defines "source" as that term is used in Section 302(j). The latter section, however, equates a source with a facility, whereas the former defines "source" as a facility, among other items.

We are not persuaded that parsing of general terms in the text of the statute will reveal an actual intent of Congress. . . . To the extent any congressional "intent" can be discerned from this language, it would appear that the listing of overlapping, illustrative terms was intended to enlarge, rather than confine, the scope of the agency's power to regulate particular sources in order to effectuate the policies of the Act.

LEGISLATIVE HISTORY

In addition, respondents urge that the legislative history and policies of the Act foreclose the plantwide definition, and that the EPA's interpretation is not entitled to deference because it represents a sharp break with prior interpretations of the Act.

Based on our examination of the legislative history, we agree with the Court of Appeals that it is unilluminating. . . . We find that the legislative history as a whole is silent on the precise issue before us. It is, however, consistent with the view that the EPA should have broad discretion in implementing the policies of the 1977 Amendments.

More importantly, that history plainly identifies the policy concerns that motivated the enactment; the plantwide definition is fully consistent with one of those concerns — the allowance of reasonable economic growth — and, whether or not we believe it most effectively implements the other [controlling pollution], we must recognize that the EPA has advanced a reasonable explanation for its conclusion that the regulations serve the environmental objectives as well. . . .

Our review of the EPA's varying interpretations of the word "source" — both before and after the 1977 Amendments — convinces us that the agency primarily responsible for administering this important legislation has consistently interpreted it flexibly — not in a sterile textual vacuum, but in the context of implementing policy decisions in a technical and complex arena. The fact that the agency has from time to time changed its interpretation of the term "source" does not, as respondents argue, lead us to conclude that no deference should be accorded the agency interpretation of the statute. An initial agency interpretation is not instantly carved in stone. On the contrary, the agency, to engage in informed rulemaking, must consider varying interpretations.

POLICY

The arguments over policy that are advanced in the parties' briefs create the impression that respondents are now waging in a judicial forum a specific policy battle which they ultimately lost in the agency and in the 32 [state] jurisdictions opting for the "bubble concept," but one which was never waged in the Congress. Such policy arguments are more properly addressed to legislators or administrators, not judges.[4]

In these cases the Administrator's interpretation represents a reasonable accommodation of manifestly competing interests and is entitled to deference: the regulatory scheme is technical and complex, the agency considered the matter in a detailed and reasoned fashion, and the decision involves reconciling conflicting policies. Congress intended to accommodate both [economic and environmental] interests, but did not do so itself on the level of specificity presented by these cases. Perhaps that body consciously desired the Administrator to strike the balance at this level, thinking that those with great expertise and charged with responsibility for administering the provision would be in a better position to do so; perhaps it simply did not consider the question at this level; and perhaps Congress was unable to forge a coalition on either side of the question, and those on each side decided to take their chances with the scheme devised by the agency. For judicial purposes, it matters not which of these things occurred.

Judges are not experts in the field, and are not part of either political branch of the government. Courts must, in some cases, reconcile competing political interests, but not on the basis of the judges' personal policy preferences. In contrast, an agency to which Congress has delegated policymaking responsibilities may, within the limits of that delegation, properly rely upon the incumbent administration's views of wise policy to inform its judgments. While agencies are not directly accountable to the people, the Chief Executive is, and it is entirely appropriate for this political branch of the Government to make such policy choices — resolving the competing interests which Congress itself either inadvertently did not resolve, or intentionally left to be resolved by the agency charged with the administration of the statute in light of everyday realities.

When a challenge to an agency construction of a statutory provision, fairly conceptualized, really centers on the wisdom of the agency's policy, rather than whether it is a reasonable choice within a gap left open by Congress, the challenge must fail. In such a case, federal judges — who have no constituency — have a duty to respect legitimate policy choices made by those who do. The responsibilities for assessing the wisdom of such policy choices and resolving the struggle between competing views of the public interest are not judicial ones; "Our Constitution vests such responsibilities in the political branches." TVA v. Hill, 437 U.S. 153 (1978).

We hold that the EPA's definition of the term "source" is a permissible construction of the statute which seeks to accommodate progress in reducing air pollution with economic growth, "The Regulations which the Administrator has adopted provide what the agency would allowably view as [an] effective reconciliation of these twofold ends. . . ." United States v. Shimer, 367 U.S., at 383.

The judgment of the Court of Appeals is reversed.

---

4. Respondents point out if a brand-new factory that will emit over 100 tons of pollutants is constructed in a non-attainment area, that plant must obtain a permit pursuant to Section 172(b)(6) and in order to do so, it must satisfy the Section 173 conditions, including the LAER requirement. Respondents argue if an old plant containing several large emitting units is to be modernized by the replacement of one or more units emitting over 100 tons of pollutants with a new unit emitting less — but still more than 100 tons — the result should be no different simply because "it happens to be built not at a new site, but with a preexisting plant."

Notes and Questions

1. In a remarkably short period, *Chevron* has become one of the most cited cases in all of American law. Indeed, it may have become the most frequently cited case of all time. As of December 2005, *Chevron* had been cited in federal courts nearly 8000 times — far more than three far better known and much older cases, Brown v. Board of Education (1829 cites), Roe v. Wade (1801 cites), and Marbury v. Madison (1559 cites) — and indeed far more often than the three of them combined! In terms of sheer number of citations, *Chevron* may well qualify as the most influential case in the history of American public law. But there are questions about the extent to which *Chevron* actually produced, is producing, or will produce large-scale shifts in the law, for reasons to be discussed.

2. *Chevron* appears to establish a "two-step" process for judicial review of agency interpretations of law. The first step is to ask whether the statute is clear (or, in other words, if Congress has directly decided the precise question at issue). If so, the case is at an end. The second step is to ask whether, if the statute is ambiguous, the agency interpretation is "permissible" or "reasonable." As of this writing, no Supreme Court decision has invalidated an agency decision under step 2, though several courts of appeals decisions do so.

If *Chevron*'s basic holding is that ambiguous statutory terms should be interpreted by agencies rather than courts, *Chevron* can be seen as a kind of counter-*Marbury* for the administrative state. If so, *what are the foundations* of *Chevron*? What led the Court to this position? Does the case rest on a judgment that Congress has told courts to defer to agency interpretations of law? If so, where has Congress said that? Consider APA §706, which says that "the reviewing *court* shall decide all relevant questions of law" (emphasis added). The prevailing explanation, elaborated below, is that *Chevron* is best understood as reflecting an understanding that Congress, as a general rule, has given administrative agencies authority to resolve ambiguities in statutes. See Smiley v. Citibank (S.D.), N.A., 517 U.S. 735, 740-741 (1996); United States v. Haggar Apparel Co., 526 U.S. 380 (1999). But there are alternative, perhaps overlapping accounts.

In one view, *Chevron* should be taken to rest on the judgment that agencies have comparative advantages over courts in interpreting statutory terms, because political accountability and technical specialization are relevant to interpretation. Perhaps the particular situation in *Chevron* itself supports such a judgment, for the appropriate definition of "source" calls for complex decisions about issues of environmental policy. It is hard to know whether a plant-wide definition of source makes sense without knowing the economic and environmental consequences of that decision; and courts are in a poor position to be able to obtain that knowledge. Indeed, the plant-wide definition is part of a general movement in environmental policy toward "emissions trading" systems, which are designed to ensure least-cost methods of obtaining pollution goals. See the note below; see also P. Menell & R. Stewart, Environmental Law and Policy 377-414 (1992); Hahn & Hester, Where Did All the Markets Go? An Analysis of EPA's Emissions Trading Programs, 16 Yale J. Reg. 109 (1989), for overviews. A court looking at the word "source" is not likely to be in a good position to assess the underlying considerations.

In another view, *Chevron* rests on the judgment that a rule of deference can reduce the disparateness and balkanization of federal administrative law by limiting the number of circuit conflicts. If courts review agency interpretations independently, it is likely that there will be many divisions in the courts of appeals. If courts uphold any reasonable interpretation of ambiguous statutes, it is likely that the courts of appeals will unite around a single view: that of the agency. See below for more details on this theme.

3. In an influential essay, Justice Scalia defends *Chevron* in the following way:

> What, then, is the theoretical justification for allowing reasonable administrative interpretations to govern? The cases, old and new, that accept administrative interpretations, often refer to the "expertise" of the agencies in question, their intense familiarity with the history and purposes of the legislation at issue, their practical knowledge of what will best effectuate those purposes. In other words, they are more likely than the courts to reach the correct result. That is, if true, a good practical reason for accepting the agency's views, but hardly a valid theoretical justification for doing so. If I had been sitting on the Supreme Court when Learned Hand was still alive, it would similarly have been, as a practical matter, desirable for me to accept his views in all of his cases under review, on the basis that he is a lot wiser than I, and more likely to get it right. But that would hardly have been theoretically valid. Even if Hand would have been de facto superior, I would have been ex officio so. So also with judicial acceptance of the agencies' views. If it is, as we have always believed, the constitutional duty of the courts to say what the law is, we must search for something beyond relative competence as a basis for ignoring that principle when agency action is at issue.
>
> One possible validating rationale that has been suggested in some recent articles — and that can perhaps even be derived from some of the language of *Chevron* itself — is that the constitutional principle of separation of powers requires *Chevron*. The argument goes something like this: When, in a statute to be implemented by an executive agency, Congress leaves an ambiguity that cannot be resolved by text or legislative history, the "traditional tools of statutory construction," the resolution of that ambiguity necessarily involves policy judgment. Under our democratic system, policy judgments are not for the courts but for the political branches; Congress having left the policy question open, it must be answered by the Executive.
>
> Now there is no one more fond of our system of separation of powers than I am, but even I cannot agree with this approach. To begin with, it seems to me that the "traditional tools of statutory construction" include not merely text and legislative history but also, quite specifically, the consideration of policy consequences. Indeed, that tool is so traditional that it has been enshrined in Latin: "*Ratio est legis anima; mutata legis ratione mutatur et lex.*" ("The reason for the law is its soul; when the reason for the law changes, the law changes as well.") Surely one of the most frequent justifications courts give for choosing a particular construction is that the alternative interpretation would produce "absurd" results, or results less compatible with the reason or purpose of the statute. This, it seems to me, unquestionably involves judicial consideration and evaluation of competing policies, and for precisely the same purpose for which (in the context we are discussing here) agencies consider and evaluate them — to determine which one will best effectuate the statutory purpose. Policy evaluation is, in other words, part of the traditional judicial tool-kit that is used in applying the first step of *Chevron* — the step that determines, before deferring to agency judgment, whether the law is indeed ambiguous. Only when the court concludes that the policy furthered by neither textually possible interpretation will be clearly "better" (in the sense of achieving what Congress apparently wished to achieve) will it, pursuant to *Chevron*, yield to the agency's choice. But the reason it yields is assuredly not that it has no constitutional competence to consider and evaluate policy.
>
> The separation-of-powers justification can be rejected even more painlessly by asking one simple question: If, in the statute at issue in *Chevron*, Congress had specified that in all suits involving interpretation or application of the Clean Air Act the courts were to give no deference to the agency's views, but were to determine the issue

de novo, would the Supreme Court nonetheless have acquiesced in the agency's views? I think the answer is clearly no, which means that it is not any constitutional impediment to "policy-making" that explains *Chevron*.

In my view, the theoretical justification for *Chevron* is no different from the theoretical justification for those *pre-Chevron* cases that sometimes deferred to agency legal determinations. As the D.C. Circuit, quoting the First Circuit, expressed it: "The extent to which courts should defer to agency interpretations of law is ultimately "a function of Congress' intent on the subject as revealed in the particular statutory scheme at issue." An ambiguity in a statute committed to agency implementation can be attributed to either of two congressional desires: (1) Congress intended a particular result, but was not clear about it; or (2) Congress had no particular intent on the subject, but meant to leave its resolution to the agency. When the former is the case, what we have is genuinely a question of law, properly to be resolved by the courts. When the latter is the case, what we have is the conferral of discretion upon the agency, and the only question of law presented to the courts is whether the agency has acted within the scope of its discretion — i.e., whether its resolution of the ambiguity is reasonable. As I read the history of developments in this field, the pre-Chevron decisions sought to choose between (1) and (2) on a statute-by-statute basis. Hence the relevance of such frequently mentioned factors as the degree of the agency's expertise, the complexity of the question at issue, and the existence of rulemaking authority within the agency. All these factors make an intent to confer discretion upon the agency more likely. *Chevron*, however, if it is to be believed, replaced this statute-by-statute evaluation (which was assuredly a font of uncertainty and litigation) with an across-the-board presumption that, in the case of ambiguity, agency discretion is meant.

It is beyond the scope of these remarks to defend that presumption (I was not on the Court, after all, when *Chevron* was decided). Surely, however, it is a more rational presumption today than it would have been thirty years ago — which explains the change in the law. Broad delegation to the Executive is the hallmark of the modern administrative state; agency rulemaking powers are the rule rather than, as they once were, the exception; and as the sheer number of modern departments and agencies suggests, we are awash in agency "expertise." If the *Chevron* rule is not a 100% accurate estimation of modern congressional intent, the prior case-by-case evaluation was not so either — and was becoming less and less so, as the sheer volume of modern dockets made it less and less possible for the Supreme Court to police diverse application of an ineffable rule. And to tell the truth, the quest for the "genuine" legislative intent is probably a wild-goose chase anyway. In the vast majority of cases I expect that Congress neither (1) intended a single result, nor (2) meant to confer discretion upon the agency, but rather (3) didn't think about the matter at all. If I am correct in that, then any rule adopted in this field represents merely a fictional, presumed intent, and operates principally as a background rule of law against which Congress can legislate.

If that is the principal function to be served, *Chevron* is unquestionably better than what preceded it. Congress now knows that the ambiguities it creates, whether intentionally or unintentionally, will be resolved, within the bounds of permissible interpretation, not by the courts but by a particular agency, whose policy biases will ordinarily be known. The legislative process becomes less of a sporting event when those supporting and opposing a particular disposition do not have to gamble upon whether, if they say nothing about it in the statute, the ultimate answer will be provided by the courts or rather by the Department of Labor.

Scalia, Judicial Deference to Agency Interpretations of Law, 1989 Duke L.J. 511. Note that the Court has increasingly converged on the general claim that Chevron is best understood to suggest that deference is based on an implicit congressional delegation of law-interpreting power. See, e.g., FDA v. Brown & Williamson Tobacco Corp., 529 U.S. 120 (2000), excerpted below. Compare the views in Breyer, Judicial Review of Questions of Law and Policy, 38 Admin. L. Rev. 363 (1986), arguing against the "simple" approach of Chevron and supporting a multifactored approach. We take up these issues in more detail below.

4. Suppose that Justice Scalia is correct to say that *Chevron* is best understood as an interpretation of Congress's interpretive instructions — that is, as a holding that Congress has told courts to defer to reasonable agency interpretations where there is ambiguity. Is there sufficient reason to believe that Congress has in fact said this? Return to the language of APA §706, and consider the fact that the APA was born in a period of distrust of agency discretion, and that it was intended partly as a means of strengthening judicial control of administrators. See *Universal Camera*, supra. Does anything in the text and background of the APA support the view that Congress generally wanted courts to accept reasonable agency interpretations of law, rather than to decide legal questions on their own? Perhaps the key statute is the Clean Air Act, not the APA. But is there anything in the text and background of the Clean Air Act to support this interpretation of Congress's instructions? If the answer is no, is it sufficient for Justice Scalia to refer to the need to decide on the question of deference by rule, rather than on an ad hoc basis?

5. Perhaps the growth in the number of federal appellate judges has something to do with *Chevron*. There are now more than 174 such judges, compared with under 100 thirty years ago. With more and more cases being reviewed, and more and more reviewing panels, and a Supreme Court too busy to iron out all possible conflicts, the federal administrative agencies may fear that conflicting statutory interpretations will hinder their work. If this is a problem, the shift of interpretive power from court to agency could help unify the law, for there is but one agency, while there are many appellate courts. See the discussion of this matter in Strauss, One Hundred Fifty Cases per Year: Some Implications of the Supreme Court's Limited Resources for Judicial Review of Agency Action, 87 Colum. L. Rev. 1093 (1987). But if Congress becomes aware that the federal courts are less closely supervising agency determinations of, for example, the scope of their own legal mandates, will it wish to continue delegating authority through broad statutory language? Would it be better for Congress, in any event, to use more specific language? See Shapiro & Glicksman, Congress, the Supreme Court, and the Quiet Revolution in Administrative Law, 1988 Duke L.J. 819.

Does *Chevron* therefore give Congress good incentives by telling it to be clear, lest an executive agency have power to interpret the law? Compare Manning, Textualism as a Nondelegation Doctrine, 97 Colum. L. Rev. 673 (1997).

6. Consider the view that *Chevron* is, in a sense, an ultimate triumph of legal realism. The legal realists believed that "law" was not autonomous, in the sense that judgments of both policy and principle lie behind any real-world judgment about "what the law is." If the realists were right, perhaps it follows, post-New Deal, that administrative agencies should have a large role in saying what the law is because they are better than courts at the relevant judgments at policy and principle. Their comparative advantages stem from their better democratic pedigree and their immersion in the facts and policies of particular areas of law. See also R. Dworkin, Law's Empire (1985), arguing that to identify "the law," a decisionmaker has to make the "best constructive interpretation" of past legal events. On Dworkin's view, the best constructive interpretation requires a judgment of "fit" (what is the preexisting law?) and "justification" (how can we make best sense out of existing law?). Dworkin applies this view to statutory interpretation as well as to common law and constitutional law. If Dworkin is right, does it follow that agencies should have a

large role in interpreting statutory ambiguities? See also Sunstein, Justice Scalia's Democratic Formalism, 107 Yale L.J. 529 (1997), arguing that agencies should have substantial room to interpret statutes so as to adapt them to particular circumstances.

7. Perhaps the simplest question about *Chevron* is whether it has made a difference. The evidence is quite powerful that is has indeed made a rather large difference. An early study found that, post-*Chevron*, the rate of judicial affirmance of agency decisions went from 71 percent to 81 percent, and that controlling for various factors did not affect this result. See Peter H. Schuck & E. Donald Elliott, To the Chevron Station: An Empirical Study of Federal Administrative Law, 1990 Duke L.J. 984, 1026 (1991). Later studies have, for the most part, reached similar conclusions. See, e.g., Orin S. Kerr, Shedding Light on Chevron: An Empirical Study on the Chevron Doctrine in the U.S. Courts of Appeals, 15 Yale J. on Reg. 1 (1998); Richard Revesz, Environmental Regulation, Ideology, and the D.C. Circuit, 83 Va. L. Rev. 1717 (1997). There is some question about the magnitude of the *Chevron* effect, but not about the existence of the effect.

Why might this be? The simplest hypothesis is that *Chevron* is a signal from the Supreme Court to lower courts, indicating that lower court decisions that overturn agency policies are now more likely to be reversed. The Court's members might be motivated to send this signal by any number of considerations, for example the need to centralize federal administrative law, as discussed in Peter Strauss, supra. Another approach is to trace, in detail, the processes by which *Chevron* has had an effect on agencies and courts. Consider the following, by a former General Counsel of the Environmental Protection Agency:

> The fundamental difference between the role of EPA OGC [Office of General Counsel] (and probably in any other agency as well) pre-*Chevron* and post-*Chevron* is this: pre-*Chevron*, OGC usually gave its legal advice as a point estimate, e.g., "the statute means this. There is only one meaning to the statute. We in OGC are the keepers of what the statute means. The statute speaks to every question, and you must follow what we in OGC tell you is the correct/best interpretation of the statute or you will lose in court." In other words, the pre-*Chevron* conception of a statute was as a prescriptive text having a single meaning, discoverable by specialized legal training and tools. This "single-meaning" conception of statutes created a very powerful role for lawyers and OGC within agencies. The privileged role for lawyers in defining what the statute required on every issue in turn led to a great deal of implicit policy-making by lawyers in OGC. They may have in all good faith believed that they were divining the one true and correct meaning of the statute, but intentionally or unintentionally, they may have smuggled a great deal of their policy preferences into their legal advice. As EPA's General Counsel, I tried to get our lawyers to separate their legal opinions from their policy advice and to differentiate between the two.
>
> Post-*Chevron*, the form of OGC opinions is no longer a simple point estimate of what a statute means. Rather, OGC opinions now attempt to describe a permissible range of agency policy-making discretion that arises out of a statutory ambiguity. Post-*Chevron* statutes no longer possess a single prescriptive meaning on many questions; rather, they describe what I call a "policy space," a range of permissible interpretive discretion, within which a variety of decisions that the agency might make would be legally defensible to varying degrees. So the task of OGC today is to define the boundaries of legal defensibility, and thereby to recognize that often there is more than one possible interpretation of the meaning of key statutory terms and concepts. The agency's policy-makers, not its lawyers, should decide which of several different but legally defensible interpretations to adopt.

Chevron opened up and validated a policy-making dialogue within agencies about what interpretation the agency should adopt for policy reasons, rather than what interpretation the agency must adopt for legal reasons. I believe that this expanded policy dialogue is productive and that it takes place more inside EPA today than it did pre-Chevron, and normatively, that is a good thing. For example, it is good that Chevron has increased the weight given to the views of air pollution experts in the air program office relative to the lawyers in OGC.

A second effect of the Chevron decision is somewhat more subtle. Post-Chevron, lawyers in an agency often have to say that the right answer to a question of agency authority is not "you can or cannot do it," but rather that "it depends." That legal advice usually provokes a rejoinder: "And what does it depend on?" Because of the nature of the "Chevron deference" that courts now give to agencies, the answer is usually that whether an agency's interpretation of its authority will be upheld depends on how strong its reasons are; it depends on what justifications the agency would be able to give for a policy. In other words, whether a court will uphold an agency's interpretation of its authority depends on contingent, consequentialist justifications. It depends on what one can write into a preamble justifying an interpretation in terms of factual support and policy-justifications.

This refocusing of the dialogue inside the agency to the consequences of adopting particular policies is also an extremely good thing. By refocusing the question of legal authority on the strength of an agency's justification for a proposed policy, Chevron displaces the dialogue about whether something is legal in the abstract to a consideration of anticipated consequences in the real world. Chevron moved the debate from a sterile, backward-looking conversation about Congress' nebulous and fictive intent to a forward-looking, instrumental dialogue about what future effects the proposed policy is likely to have. Shifting the focus to questions like which policy choice is actually likely to do a better job of cleaning up the air is a progressive change. This question is ultimately more important than courts imagining what some inexperienced congressional staffer might or might not have intended when writing legislative history.

The effect of Chevron on the internal dynamics of agency decision-making is significant and positive. Chevron is significant for reducing the relative power of lawyers within EPA and other agencies and for increasing the power of other professionals. At the margins, agency decisions after Chevron reflect more weight on policy choices and less on legalistic interpretations.

E. Donald Elliott, Chevron Matters: How the Chevron Doctrine Redefined the Roles of Congress, Courts and Agencies in Environmental Law, 16 Vill. Envtl. L.J. 1 (2005).

Note on Economic Incentives

Chevron involved an effort to create economic incentives for pollution control, by allowing a form of "emission trading." Under the bubble policy, a firm could "trade" an increase in one emitting "source" (under the previous definition of source) by producing a decrease in another emitting "source." If the firm could cheaply reduce pollution in one place, it would thus be permitted to make this trade, and in that way it could produce the least-cost method for obtaining a certain degree of pollution control.

There has been a great deal of recent interest in using economic incentives to achieve regulatory goals. See, e.g., A. Denny Ellerman et al., Markets for Clean Air (2000). This interest came first from economists, who urged that economic incentives could achieve regulatory goals more efficiently. Thus, it is said that requiring all firms to adopt the "best available technology" is a far too costly way of reducing pollution; it would be far better to give firms incentives to reduce pollution in the most efficient manner. It is also said that economic incentives have democratic advantages because they reduce interest-group maneuvering over the "means" of obtaining regulatory goals. Struggles over "means" can be a recipe for interest-group battle. See B. Ackerman & W. Hassler, Clean Coal/Dirty Air (1983). See generally C. Sunstein, Free Markets and Social Justice (1997) ch. 10.

Economic incentives come in various forms. First, government may impose a fee or a tax on harm-producing behavior. For example, firms that use CFCs (which cause stratospheric ozone depletion) or that emit certain pollutants may be allowed to do so if and only if they pay a specified amount per unit of pollution. The fee or tax might be set by government in advance; it might emerge from an auction. The workers' compensation statutes can be seen as a version of an economic incentive, to the extent that they require employers to pay a certain amount per injury or death. There is in fact evidence that workers' compensation statutes have been far more effective than the Occupational Health and Safety Administration (OSHA) in reducing workplace injuries. See W. Kip Viscusi, Reforming Products Liability (1993).

Second, government might not impose a fee or tax at all but instead set an overall ceiling for harm, or harm-producing activity, and give out tradable licenses or permits. Government might, for example, allow companies to have permits to put sulfur dioxide (which causes acid deposition) into the atmosphere; companies might be permitted to buy and sell the resulting permits. As opposed to the "wrongdoers pay" idea, a comparative advantage of this kind of system is that the government need not attempt to determine the per unit "cost" of harm-producing activity. A comparative disadvantage is that the government is required to decide on the aggregate amount of the relevant harm, and that judgment may be extremely difficult to make with any reliability.

Economic incentives have proved controversial, and initiatives in this direction raise many questions. One question, of course, involves the informational demands that they impose on government. See Latin, Ideal Versus Real Regulatory Efficiency, 37 Stan. L. Rev. 1267 (1985). Another question is whether economic incentives might not allow concentration of harm-producing activity in certain geographically limited areas. See S. Breyer, Regulation and Its Reform (1982). Yet another question is whether it is inappropriate to allow people to engage in certain conduct so long as they are willing to pay enough to do so. See S. Kelman, What Price Incentives? (1984).

An important series of administrative initiatives have brought about emissions trading, especially under the Clean Air Act. Under the EPA's policy, a firm that reduces its emissions below legal requirements may obtain "credits" that can be used against higher emissions elsewhere. Through the "off set" policy, which is formally codified in the Clean Air Act, a company may locate in an area not in compliance with national air quality standards if and only if it can offset the new emissions by reducing existing emissions, either from its own sources or from other firms. Through the "banking" policy, firms are permitted to store emission credits for their own future use. Companies may also engage in "netting," by which a firm modifies a source but avoids the most stringent emissions limits that would otherwise be applied to the modification by reducing emissions from another source within the same plant. And through "bubbles," existing sources may place an imaginary bubble over their plants, allowing different emissions levels by each emitting device so long as the total emissions level is in compliance with aggregate requirements.

There is now a good deal of evidence about the emissions trading program. For various reasons, the use of the program has been quite limited. Overall, the program produced, within its first ten years, savings of between $525 million and $12 billion. On balance, moreover, the environmental consequences have been beneficial.

As part of the process for eliminating lead from gasoline — a decision that was, not incidentally, strongly supported by a cost-benefit study — the EPA also permitted emissions trading. Under this policy, a refinery that produced gasoline with lower than required lead levels could earn credits. These could be traded with other refineries or banked for future use. Until the termination of the program in 1987, when the phase-down of lead ended, emissions credits for lead were widely traded, EPA concluded that there had been cost savings of about 20 percent over alternative systems, marking total savings in the hundreds of million of dollars. There have been similar efforts with water pollution and ozone depletion.

Perhaps the most dramatic program of economic incentives can be found in the 1990 amendments to the Clean Air Act. The act now explicitly creates an emissions trading system for the control of acid deposition. In these amendments, Congress made an explicit decision about aggregate emissions level for a pollutant. Whether the particular decision is the correct one may be disputed. But perhaps there are large democratic benefits from ensuring that public attention is focused on that issue, 42 U.S.C. §7651 et seq. The acid deposition program is estimated to have saved $357 million annually in its first five years, and is expected to save $2.28 billion annually in its next fifteen years, for total savings in excess of $29 billion. See Ellerman et al., supra.

Congress has also said that polluters may obtain allowances for emissions avoided through energy conservation and renewable energy. In this way, avoidance of this kind is turned into dollars, in the form of an increased permission to pollute. This provision creates an incentive to shift to conservation and renewable sources, without providing further environmental degradation. Polluters are explicitly permitted to trade their allowances; this is a first in national legislation. In this way, people who are able to reduce their pollution below the specified level receive economic benefits. Again, incentives are created for environmentally beneficial behavior. An especially intriguing provision allows spot and advance sales of sulfur dioxide allowances, to be purchasable at $1500 per ton. Through this route, polluters must — for the first time — pay a fee for their pollution. Even more intriguing is a provision calling for auction sales of specified numbers of sulfur dioxide allowances. Here, the market is permitted to set the price for polluting activity.

Requirements of disclosure, or provision of information, are sometimes described as economic incentives. Mandatory messages about risks from cigarette smoking, first set out in 1965 and modified in 1969 and 1984, are the most familiar example. The Food and Drug Administration (FDA) has long maintained a policy of requiring risk labels for pharmaceutical products. The EPA has done the same for pesticides and asbestos. Congress requires warnings on products with saccharin. There are numerous other illustrations. Indeed, the effort to provide information counts as one of the most striking, if incipient, developments in modern regulatory law. Three recent initiatives are especially striking.

In 1983, OSHA issued a Hazard Communication Standard (HCS), applicable to the manufacturing sector. In 1986, the HCS was made generally applicable. Under the HCS, chemical producers and importers must evaluate the hazards of the chemicals they produce or import; develop technical hazard information for materials' safety data sheets and labels for hazardous substances; and, most important, transmit this information to users of the relevant substances. All employers must adopt a hazard communication program — including individual training — and inform workers of the relevant risks. 29 C.F.R. 1910.1200(g) (1990).

In 1986, Congress enacted an ambitious new statute, the Emergency Planning and Community Right to Know Act (EPCRA). 42 U.S.C. §11,044. Under this statute, firms and individuals must report, to state and local government, the quantities of potentially hazardous chemicals that have been sorted or released into the environment. Users of such chemicals must report to their local fire departments about the location, types, and quantities of stored chemicals. They must also give information about potential adverse health effects. EPCRA has had important beneficial effects, spurring innovative, cost-effective programs from the EPA and from state and local government. For a valuable discussion, see Karkkainen, Information as Environmental Regulation, 89 Georgetown L.J. 257 (2001).

The FDA has also adopted informational strategies. In its most ambitious set of proposals, the FDA has (a) compelled nutritional labeling on nearly all processed foods, including information relating to cholesterol, saturated fat, calories from fat, and fiber; (b) required compliance with government-specified serving sizes; (c) compelled companies to conform to government definitions of standardized terms, including, "reduced," "fresh," "free," and "low"; and (d) allowed health claims only if these (1) are supported by scientific evidence and (2) communicate clear and complete information about such matters as fat and heart disease, fat and cancer, sodium and high blood pressure, and calcium and osteoporosis. 58 Fed. Reg. 2927 (1992).

1. A Chevron *Sampler*

Chevron raises a number of quite concrete questions, which we will take up in sequence. At this point, however, it will be useful to get a general sense of its meaning and reach by exploring a set of post-*Chevron* cases. A pervasive question is whether the Court has consistently deferred to agency interpretations of ambiguous statutory provisions, or whether it has rejected some such interpretations because factors in the particular context suggested that the agency was wrong, even if the statute could plausibly be interpreted in the way the agency sought to do. Merrill, Judicial Deference to Executive Precedent, 101 Yale L.J. 969 (1992), and Merrill, Textualism and the Future of the *Chevron* Doctrine, 72 Wash. U. L.Q. 351 (1994), reach the general conclusion that the Supreme Court has been highly inconsistent in its use of *Chevron*, and that the Court has frequently rejected agency interpretations of ambiguous terms. Do the following cases support that suggestion? We emphasize cases decided between *Chevron* itself and 1990, taking up the more recent cases in the following sections. Note that despite the inconsistent signals given by the Supreme Court, there is some evidence that the most important administrative law court, the D.C. Circuit, is generally applying *Chevron* in a predictable and consistent manner. See Revesz, Environmental Regulation, Ideology, and the DC Circuit, 83 Va. L. Rev. 1717 (1997).

Immigration & Naturalization Service v. Cardoza Fonseca

480 U.S. 421 (1987)

Justice STEVENS delivered the opinion of the Court.

[Section 243(h) of the Immigration Act *forbids* the attorney general to deport an alien "if the Attorney General determines that such alien's life or freedom would be threatened" for reasons such as race, religion, nationality, or political belief. Section 208(a) of the act *permits* the attorney general to grant asylum to an alien who does not wish to return home "because of . . . a well-founded fear of persecution" for similar reasons. The INS had long held, with court approval, that to qualify under the first statute, the alien must show a "clear probability of persecution," that is, that persecution is more likely than not. It had also held that to qualify under the second statute, the alien also must show that persecution is "more likely than not." The question presented is whether the latter interpretation of the second statute (the "permissive" asylum statute) is legally correct.

The INS interpretation of the second statute is wrong. For one thing, the language of the two statutes differs significantly. The first speaks objectively of "life or freedom" that "would be threatened." The second uses the words "well-founded fear," which focus on the individual's subjective beliefs. For another, the legislative history of the latter statute, in part showing that Congress based it on a United Nations Protocol, reveals that Congress intended the latter statute to have a broader scope than the first statute.]

The Government's second principal argument in support of the proposition that the "well-founded fear" and "clear probability" standards are equivalent is that the [agency] so construes the two standards. The Government argues that the [agency] construction of the Refugee Act of 1980 is entitled to substantial deference, even if we conclude that the Court of Appeal's reading of the statutes is more in keeping with Congress' intent. This argument is unpersuasive.

The question whether Congress intended the two standards to be identical is a pure question of statutory construction for the courts to decide. Employing traditional tools of statutory construction, we concluded that Congress did not intend the two standards to be identical. In Chevron U.S.A., Inc. v. Natural Resources Defense Council, 467 U.S. 837 (1984), we explained:

> The judiciary is the final authority on issues of statutory construction and must reject administrative constructions which are contrary to clear congressional intent. If a court, employing traditional tools of statutory construction, ascertains that Congress had an intention on the precise question at issue, that intention is the law and must be given effect.

The narrow legal question whether the two standards are the same is, of course, quite different from the question of interpretation that arises in each case in which the agency is required to apply either or both standards to a particular set of facts. There is obviously some ambiguity in a term like "well-founded fear" which can only be given concrete meaning through a process of case-by-case adjudication. In that process of filling "any gap left, implicitly or explicitly, by Congress," the courts must respect the interpretation of the agency to which Congress had delegated the responsibility for administering the statutory program.

But our task today is much narrower, and is well within the province of the judiciary. We do not attempt to set forth a detailed description of how the well-founded fear test should be applied. Instead, we merely hold that the Immigration Judge and the BIA were incorrect in holding that the two standards are identical.

Justice SCALIA, concurring in the judgment. . . .

I am . . . troubled by the Court's discussion of the question of whether the INS's interpretation of "well-founded fear" is entitled to deference. This Court has consistently interpreted *Chevron* — which has been an extremely important and frequently cited opinion, not only in this Court but in the Courts of Appeals — as holding that courts must give effect to a reasonable agency interpretation of a statute unless that interpretation is inconsistent with a clearly expressed congressional intent. The Court's discussion is flatly inconsistent with this well-established interpretation. The Court first implies that courts may substitute their interpretation of a statute for that of an agency whenever, "[e]mploying traditional tools of statutory construction," they are able to reach a conclusion as to the proper interpretation of the statute. But this approach would make deference a doctrine of desperation, authorizing courts to defer only if they would otherwise be unable to construe the enactment at issue. This is not an interpretation, but an evisceration of *Chevron*.

The Court also implies that courts may substitute their interpretation of a statute for that of an agency whenever they face "a pure question of statutory construction for the courts to decide," rather than a "question of interpretation [in which] the agency is required to apply [a legal standard] to a particular set of facts." No support is adduced for this proposition, which is contradicted by [*Chevron* itself].

YOUNG v. COMMUNITY NUTRITION INSTITUTE, 476 U.S. 974 (1986). The relevant statute said that "when" a "poisonous or deleterious substance" is "required in the production" of food "or cannot be . . . avoided" by good food manufacturing practice, then "the Secretary" of Health and Human Services "shall promulgate regulations limiting the quantity therein or thereon to such extent as he finds necessary for the protection of public health. . . ." The secretary did not promulgate an appropriate regulation limiting the quantity of "aflotoxin," a concededly "deleterious" substance found on wheat. The secretary pointed to a long-standing agency interpretation of the statute to the effect that the words "as he finds necessary . . ." modify the word "shall" (that is, the secretary "shall, as he finds necessary for the protection of human health, promulgate . . ."). Nonetheless, since the statute was "ambiguous," and, given *Chevron*, the Court upheld the agency's interpretation. Justice Stevens, *Chevron*'s author, dissented on the ground that the statute was not ambiguous, and it could not support the agency's interpretation. He found the "intent of Congress" to be clear. He added that "to say that the statute is susceptible of two meanings, . . . is not to say that either is acceptable." Regardless, "the singularly judicial role of marking the boundaries of agency choice is [not] at an end. As Justice Frankfurter reminds us, "[t]he purpose of construction being the ascertainment of meaning, every consideration brought to bear for the solution of that problem must be devoted to that end alone.' . . . The Court, correctly self-conscious of the limits of the judicial role, employs a reasoning so formulaic that it trivializes the art of judging."

MAISLIN INDUSTRIES, U.S. v. PRIMARY STEEL, 497 U.S. 116 (1990). A statute says that a "carrier [such as a trucker] may not charge or receive a different compensation for" a service other "than the rate specified in [its] tariff" filed at the ICC, "whether by returning a part of that rate to a person, giving a person a privilege . . . or another device." The ICC decided that a different statutory provision, one that requires that a carrier's "practices" be "reasonable," authorized it to forbid carriers to charge a shipper a lower rate while telling the shipper that it had filed the low tariff rate with the ICC, and then later to try to collect a higher charge from the shipper by pointing out that it had lied about what it had filed at the ICC and, in fact, it had filed a higher tariff rate at the ICC. The Court held that the first statute forbad the ICC from outlawing this practice, despite an ICC interpretation of the first statute to the contrary. Justice Stevens, dissenting, said he failed to understand how the Court could dismiss *Chevron* "by means of a conclusory assertion that the agency's interpretation is inconsistent with 'the statutory scheme as a whole.'" He noted that the Supreme Court itself had, for many years, interpreted the first statute's language quite strictly. But, he said, all those earlier cases arose at a time when the ICC was interpreting the act the same way. The ICC had changed its mind, in part as a result of new laws that partly deregulated trucking. A "commission," he said, "faced with new developments, or in light of reconsideration of the relevant facts and its mandate may alter its past interpretations and overturn past administrative rulings and practice. [T]his kind of flexibility and adaptability to changing needs and patterns of transportation is an essential part of the office of a regulatory agency." Justice Scalia agreed with the majority on the ground that the language of the statute was clear.

Notes and Questions

1. The analysis in the last paragraph of *Cardoza Fonseca* is reminiscent of the approach in the old *Hearst* case, distinguishing between pure questions of law and applications of law to fact. Would it be better if the Court returned to the pure-mixed distinction, or is it too troublesome, and too irrelevant, to be worthwhile? Consider the view that it is hard to know when a question is "purely" one of law, and the further view that even if a question is purely legal, agencies should prevail in the face of ambiguity.

Interestingly, Justice Stevens, the author *of Chevron*, dissented sharply from the Court's use of *Chevron* in *Community Nutrition Institute*, and subsequently wrote the majority opinion in *Cardoza Fonseca*, which can be understood as an attempt to cabin the reach of *Chevron* itself. But the distinction between "pure" and "mixed" questions has been ignored, and implicitly rejected, in many subsequent cases.

2. Can you construct an opinion using *Chevron* to support exactly the opposite outcome in *Cardoza Fonseca*? Perhaps it is reasonable to think that a person does not have "a well-founded fear of persecution" unless there is at least a 50 percent chance that she will in fact be persecuted. Doesn't the agency interpretation fit with ordinary understandings of the language? This question raises a further one: What is the difference between *Chevron* and *Cardoza Fonseca*? Note that the question how to interpret this provision of the Immigration and Naturalization Act raises delicate issues of policy, involving our nation's relationship with other nations and also strong domestic constituencies. The INS has a degree of political accountability, and its interpretation of such terms as "well-founded fear" triggers political concern; the INS also knows a great deal about the consequences of competing interpretations. Is there enough in the text and background of the act to justify judicial rejection of the INS's conclusion?

3. In Young v. Community Nutrition Institute, the statutory phrase required the administrator to "promulgate regulations limiting the quantity [of a poisonous or deleterious substance] therein or thereon to such extent as he finds necessary for the protection of public health." Isn't this phrase mandatory, and thus notably different from one that would allow the administrator to promulgate regulations if and as he sees fit? Did the Court allow the administrator to rewrite an important and apparently mandatory statute?

2. *The Reach of* Chevron

[handwritten: Step Zero: Should court 259 use Chevron @ All? Congressional Delegation]

To what agency decisions does *Chevron* apply? What is *Chevron*'s scope? Does it apply to interpretative rules? To litigating positions? These are the principal issues discussed in this section. For overviews, see Sunstein, Chevron Step Zero, 92 Va. L. Rev. (2006); Merrill & Hickman, *Chevron's* Domain, 89 Georgetown L.J. 833 (2001). If *Chevron* suggests a "two-step" test for the legality of agency interpretations of law, the inquiry into *Chevron*'s scope might be taken to comprise a "step zero," in the form of an inquiry into "whether courts should turn to the *Chevron* framework at all." Merrill & Hickman, supra, at 836.

[handwritten: Legality test]

Christensen v. Harris County

529 U.S. 576 (2000)

[handwritten: Opinion Letters / Memos not granted same Authority as regulatory Rulemaking.]

Justice THOMAS covered the opinion of the Court.

[The Federal Labor Standards Act] generally provides that hourly employees who work in excess of 40 hours per week must be compensated for the excess hours at a rate not less than 1 1/2 times their regular hourly wage. . . .

Congress acted to mitigate the effects of applying the FLSA to States and their political subdivisions, passing the Fair Labor Standards Amendments. Those amendments permit States and their political subdivisions to compensate employees for overtime by granting them compensatory time at a rate of 1 1/2 hours for every hour worked. To provide this form of compensation, the employer must arrive at an agreement or understanding with employees that compensatory time will be granted instead of cash compensation. . . . The FLSA also caps the number of compensatory time hours that an employee may accrue. After an employee reaches that maximum, the employer must pay cash compensation for additional overtime hours worked. In addition, the FLSA permits the employer at any time to cancel or "cash out" accrued compensatory time hours by paying the employee cash compensation for unused compensatory time. And the FLSA entitles the employee to cash payment for any accrued compensatory time remaining upon the termination of employment.

Petitioners are 127 deputy sheriffs employed by respondents Harris County, Texas, and its sheriff, Tommy B. Thomas (collectively, Harris County). It is undisputed that each of the petitioners individually agreed to accept compensatory time, in lieu of cash, as compensation for overtime.

As petitioners accumulated compensatory time, Harris County became concerned that it lacked the resources to pay monetary compensation to employees who worked overtime after reaching the statutory cap on compensatory time accrual and to employees who left their jobs with sizable reserves of accrued time. As a result, the county began looking for a way to reduce accumulated compensatory time. It wrote to the United States Department of Labor's Wage and Hour Division, asking "whether the Sheriff may schedule non-exempt employees to use or take compensatory time." The Acting Administrator of the Division replied:

[handwritten: Interp of Law]

> [I]t is our position that a public employer may schedule its nonexempt employees to use their accrued FLSA compensatory time as directed if the prior agreement specifically provides such a provision. . . .

Absent such an agreement, it is our position that neither the statute nor the regulations permit an employer to require an employee to use accrued compensatory time.

After receiving the letter, Harris County implemented a policy under which the employees' supervisor sets a maximum number of compensatory hours that may be accumulated. When an employee's stock of hours approaches that maximum, the employee is advised of the maximum and is asked to take steps to reduce accumulated compensatory time. If the employee does not do so voluntarily, a supervisor may order the employee to use his compensatory time at specified times.

Petitioners sued, claiming that the county's policy violates the FLSA because [the relevant section] — which requires that an employer reasonably accommodate employee requests to use compensatory timer — provides the exclusive means of utilizing accrued time in the absence of an agreement or understanding permitting some other method. . . .

In an attempt to avoid the conclusion that the FLSA does not prohibit compelled use of compensatory time, petitioners and the United States contend that we should defer to the Department of Labor's opinion letter, which takes the position that an employer may compel the use of compensatory time only if the employee has agreed in advance to such a practice. Specifically, they argue that the agency opinion letter is entitled to deference under our decision in [Chevron].

Here, however, we confront an interpretation contained in an opinion letter, not one arrived at after, for example, a formal adjudication or notice-and-comment rulemaking. Interpretations such as those in opinion letters — like interpretations contained in policy statements, agency manuals, and enforcement guidelines, all of which lack the force of law — do not warrant Chevron-style deference. . . . Instead, interpretations contained in formats such as opinion letters are "entitled to respect" under our decision in [Skidmore], but only to the extent that those interpretations have the "power to persuade," . . . We find unpersuasive the agency's interpretation of the statute at issue in this case.

Of course, the framework of deference set forth in Chevron does apply to an agency interpretation contained in a regulation. But in this case the Department of Labor's regulation does not address the issue of compelled compensatory time. . . . Nothing in the regulation even arguably requires that an employer's compelled use policy *must* be included in an agreement. Its command is permissive, not mandatory. . . . [The Court went on to hold that the statutory construction announced by the agency in its opinion letter was "unpersuasive."]

Justice SCALIA, concurring in part and concurring in the judgment.

. . . Skidmore deference to authoritative agency views is an anachronism, dating from an era in which we declined to give agency interpretations (including interpretive regulations, as opposed to "legislative rules") authoritative effect. . . . While Chevron in fact involved an interpretive regulation, the rationale of the case was not limited to that context. . . . In my view, therefore, the position that the county's action in this case was unlawful unless permitted by the terms of an agreement with the sheriff's department employees warrants Chevron deference if it represents the authoritative view of the Department of Labor. The fact that it appears in a single opinion letter signed by the Acting Administrator of the Wage and Hour Division might not alone persuade me that it occupies that status. But the Solicitor General of the United States, appearing as an amicus in this action, has filed a brief, cosigned by the Solicitor of Labor, which represents the position set forth in the opinion letter to be the position of the Secretary of

Labor. That alone, even without existence of the opinion letter, would in my view entitle the position to *Chevron* deference. . . .

I nonetheless join the judgment of the Court because [the] Secretary's position does not seem to me a reasonable interpretation of the statute.

Justice BREYER, with whom Justice GINSBURG joins, dissenting.

Justice SCALIA may well be right that the position of the Department of Labor, set forth in both brief and letter, is an "authoritative" agency view that warrants deference under *Chevron*. But I do not object to the majority's citing [*Skidmore*] instead. And I do disagree with Justice Scalia's statement that what he calls "*Skidmore* deference" is "an anachronism[.]"

Skidmore made clear that courts may pay particular attention to the views of an expert agency where they represent "specialized experience," even if they do not constitute an exercise of delegated lawmaking authority. The Court held that the "rulings, interpretations and opinions of" an agency, "while not controlling upon the courts by reason of their authority, do constitute a body of experience and informed judgment to which courts and litigants may properly resort for guidance." . . .

Chevron made no relevant change. It simply focused upon an additional, separate legal reason for deferring to certain agency determinations, namely, that Congress had delegated to the agency the legal authority to make those determinations. And, to the extent there may be circumstances in which *Chevron*-type deference is inapplicable — e.g., where one has doubt that Congress actually intended to delegate interpretive authority to the agency (an "ambiguity" that *Chevron* does not presumptively leave to agency resolution) — I believe that *Skidmore* nonetheless retains legal vitality. If statutes are to serve the human purposes that called them into being, courts will have to continue to pay particular attention in appropriate cases to the experienced-based views of expert agencies.

. . . [T]he Labor Department's position in this matter is eminently reasonable, hence persuasive, whether one views that decision through *Chevron*'s lens, through *Skidmore*'s, or through both.

United States v. Mead Corporation

533 U.S. 218 (2001)

Justice SOUTER delivered the opinion of the Court.

Admin opinions may carry force of Law when Congress Delegation suggests it should.

The question is whether a tariff classification ruling by the United States Customs Service deserves judicial deference. [We hold] that a tariff classification has no claim to judicial deference under *Chevron*, there being no indication that Congress intended such a ruling to carry the force of law, but we hold that under *Skidmore*, the ruling is eligible to claim respect according to its persuasiveness.

I

A

Imports are taxed under the Harmonized Tariff Schedule of the United States (HTSUS), 19 U.S.C. §1202. Title 19 U.S.C. §1500(b) provides that Customs "shall, under rules and regulations prescribed by the Secretary [of the Treasury] . . . fix the final classification and rate of duty applicable to . . . merchandise" under the HTSUS. Section 1502(a) provides that

Rulemaking Authority, But Look @ 264 Bottom.

> the Secretary of the Treasury shall establish and promulgate such rules and regulations not inconsistent with the law (including regulations establishing procedures for the issuance of binding rulings prior to the entry of the merchandise concerned), and may disseminate such information as may be necessary to secure a just, impartial, and uniform appraisement of imported merchandise and the classification and assessment of duties thereon at the various ports of entry.

The Secretary provides for tariff rulings before the entry of goods by regulations authorizing "ruling letters" setting tariff classifications for particular imports. A ruling letter "represents the official position of the Customs Service with respect to the particular transaction or issue described therein. . . ."

After the transaction that gives it birth, a ruling letter is to "be applied only with respect to transactions involving articles identical to the sample submitted with the ruling request or to articles whose description is identical to the description set forth in the ruling letter." §177.9(b)(2). As a general matter, such a letter is "subject to modification or revocation without notice to any person, except the person to whom the letter was addressed," §177.9(c), and the regulations consequently provide that "no other person should rely on the ruling letter or assume that the principles of that ruling will be applied in connection with any transaction other than the one described in the letter," ibid. Since ruling letters respond to transactions of the moment, they are not subject to notice and comment before being issued, may be published but need only be made "available for public inspection," 19 U.S.C. §1625(a), and, at the time this action arose, could be modified without notice and comment under most circumstances. A broader notice-and-comment requirement for modification of prior rulings was added by statute in 1993, and took effect after this case arose.

Any of the 46 port-of-entry Customs offices may issue ruling letters, and so may the Customs Headquarters Office, in providing "advice or guidance as to the interpretation or proper application of the Customs and related laws with respect to a specific Customs transaction [which] may be requested by Customs Service field offices . . . at any time, whether the transaction is prospective, current, or completed," 19 CFR §177.1 1(a) (2000). Most ruling letters contain little or no reasoning, but simply describe goods and state the appropriate category and tariff. A few letters, like the Headquarters ruling at issue here, set out a rationale in some detail.

B

Respondent, the Mead Corporation, imports "day planners," three-ring binders with pages having room for notes of daily schedules and phone numbers and addresses, together with a calendar and suchlike. The tariff schedule on point falls under the HTSUS heading for "registers, account books, notebooks, order books, receipt books, letter pads, memorandum pads, diaries and similar articles," HTSUS subheading 4820.10, which comprises two subcategories. Items in the first, "diaries, notebooks and address books, bound; memorandum pads, letter pads and similar articles," were subject to a tariff of 4.0% at the time in controversy. Objects in the second, covering "other" items, were free of duty.

Between 1989 and 1993, Customs repeatedly treated day planners under the "other" HTSUS subheading. In January 1993, however, Customs changed its position, and issued a Headquarters ruling letter classifying Mead's day planners as "Diaries . . . , bound" subject to tariff under subheading 4820.10.20. That letter was short on explanation, but after Mead's protest, Customs Headquarters issued a new letter, carefully reasoned but never published, reaching the same conclusion. This letter considered two definitions of "diary" from the Oxford English Dictionary, the first covering a daily journal of the past day's events, the second a book including "'printed dates for daily memoranda and jottings; also . . . calendars. . . .'" Id., at 33a-34a (quoting Oxford English Dictionary 321 (Compact ed. 1982)). Customs concluded that "diary" was not confined to the first, in part because the broader definition reflects commercial usage and hence the "commercial identity of these items in the marketplace." As for the definition of "bound," Customs concluded that HTSUS was not referring to "bookbinding," but to a less exact sort of fastening described in the Harmonized Commodity Description and Coding System Explanatory Notes to Heading 4820, which spoke of binding by "'reinforcements or fittings of metal, plastics, etc.'" . . .

We hold that administrative implementation of a particular statutory provision qualifies for *Chevron* deference when it appears that Congress delegated authority to the agency generally to make rules carrying the force of law, and that the agency interpretation claiming deference was promulgated in the exercise of that authority. Delegation of such authority may be shown in a variety of ways, as by an agency's power to engage in adjudication or notice-and-comment rulemaking, or by some other indication of a comparable congressional intent. The Customs ruling at issue here fails to qualify, although the possibility that it deserves some deference under *Skidmore* leads us to vacate and remand.

II

A

[Whether] or not they enjoy any express delegation of authority on a particular question, agencies charged with applying a statute necessarily make all sorts of interpretive choices, and while not all of those choices bind judges to follow them, they certainly may influence courts facing questions the agencies have already answered. The fair measure of deference to an agency administering its own statute has been understood to vary with circumstances, and courts have looked to the degree of the agency's care, its consistency, formality, and relative expertness and to the persuasiveness of the agency's position. . . .

Since 1984, we have identified a category of interpretive choices distinguished by an additional reason for judicial deference. This Court in *Chevron* recognized that Congress not only engages in express delegation of specific interpretive authority, but that "sometimes the legislative delegation to an agency on a particular question is implicit." Congress, that is, may not have expressly delegated authority or responsibility to implement a particular provision or fill a particular gap. Yet it can still be apparent from the agency's generally conferred authority and other statutory circumstances that Congress would expect the agency to be able to speak with the force of law when it addresses ambiguity in the statute or fills a space in the enacted law, even one about which "Congress did not actually have an intent" as to a particular result. When circumstances implying such an expectation exist, a reviewing court has no business rejecting an agency's exercise of its generally conferred authority to resolve a particular statutory ambiguity simply because the agency's chosen resolution seems unwise, but is obliged to accept the agency's position if Congress has not previously spoken to the point at issue and the agency's interpretation is reasonable.

We have recognized a very good indicator of delegation meriting *Chevron* treatment in express congressional authorizations to engage in the process of rulemaking or adjudication that produces regulations or rulings for which deference is claimed. It is fair to assume generally that Congress contemplates administrative action with the effect of law when it provides for a relatively formal administrative procedure tending to foster the fairness and deliberation that should underlie a pronouncement of such force. Thus, the overwhelming number of our cases applying *Chevron* deference have reviewed the fruits of notice-and-comment rulemaking or formal adjudication. That said, and as significant as notice-and-comment is in pointing to *Chevron* authority, the want of that procedure here does not decide the case, for we have sometimes found reasons for *Chevron* deference even when no such administrative formality was required and none was afforded. The fact that the tariff classification here was not a product of such formal process does not alone, therefore, bar the application of *Chevron*.

There are, nonetheless, ample reasons to deny *Chevron* deference here. The authorization for classification rulings, and Customs's practice in making them, present a case far removed not only from notice-and-comment process, but from any other circumstances reasonably suggesting that Congress ever thought of classification rulings as deserving the deference claimed for them here.

B

No matter which angle we choose for viewing the Customs ruling letter in this case, it fails to qualify under *Chevron*. On the face of the statute, to begin with, the terms of the congressional delegation give no indication that Congress meant to delegate authority to Customs to issue classification rulings with the force of law. We are not, of course, here making any global statement about Customs's authority, for it is true that the general rulemaking power conferred on Customs, see 19 U.S.C. §1624, authorizes some regulation with the force of law. . . . It is true as well that Congress had classification rulings in mind when it explicitly authorized, in a parenthetical, the issuance of "regulations establishing procedures for the issuance of binding rulings prior to the entry of the merchandise concerned." The reference to binding classifications does not, however, bespeak the legislative type of activity that would naturally bind more than the parties to the ruling, once the goods classified are admitted into this country. And though the statute's direction to disseminate "information" necessary to "secure" uniformity, 19 U.S.C. §1502(a), seems to assume that a ruling may be precedent in later transactions, precedential value alone does not add up to *Chevron* entitlement; interpretive rules may sometimes function as precedents, and they enjoy no *Chevron* status as a class. . . .

It is difficult, in fact, to see in the agency practice itself any indication that Customs ever set out with a lawmaking pretense in mind when it undertook to make classifications like these. Customs does not generally engage in notice-and-comment practice when issuing them, and their treatment by the agency makes it clear that a letter's binding character as a ruling stops short of third parties. . . .

Indeed, to claim that classifications have legal force is to ignore the reality that 46 different Customs offices issue 10,000 to 15,000 of them each year. Any suggestion that rulings intended to have the force of law are being churned out at a rate of 10,000 a year at an agency's 46 scattered offices is simply self-refuting. Although the circumstances are less startling here, with a Headquarters letter in issue, none of the relevant statutes recognizes this category of rulings as separate or different from others; there is thus no indication that a more potent delegation might have been understood as going to Headquarters even when Headquarters provides developed reasoning, as it did in this instance.

Nor do the amendments to the statute made effective after this case arose disturb our conclusion. The new law requires Customs to provide notice-and-comment procedures only when modifying or revoking a prior classification ruling or modifying the treatment accorded to substantially identical transactions, 19 U.S.C. §1625(c); and under its regulations, Customs sees itself obliged to provide notice-and-comment procedures only when "changing a practice" so as to produce a tariff increase, or in the imposition of a restriction or prohibition, or when Customs Headquarters determines that "the matter is of sufficient importance to involve the interests of domestic industry." The statutory changes reveal no new congressional objective of treating classification decisions generally as rulemaking with force of law, nor do they suggest any intent to create a *Chevron* patchwork of classification rulings, some with force of law, some without.

In sum, classification rulings are best treated like "interpretations contained in policy statements, agency manuals, and enforcement guidelines." *Christensen*, 529 U.S. at 587. They are beyond the *Chevron pale*.

C

Some Deference Afforded. (under Skidmore)

To agree with the Court of Appeals that Customs ruling letters do not fall within *Chevron* is not, however, to place them outside the pale of any deference whatever. *Chevron* did nothing to eliminate *Skidmore*'s holding that an agency's interpretation may merit some deference whatever its form, given the "specialized experience and broader investigations and information" available to the agency, and given the value of uniformity in its administrative and judicial understandings of what a national law requires.

There is room at least to raise a *Skidmore* claim here, where the regulatory scheme is highly detailed, and Customs can bring the benefit of specialized experience to bear on the subtle questions in this case: whether the daily planner with room for brief daily entries falls under "diaries," when diaries are grouped with "notebooks and address books, bound; memorandum pads, letter pads and similar articles," HTSUS subheading 4820.10.20; and whether a planner with a ring binding should qualify as "bound," when a binding may be typified by a book, but also may have "reinforcements or fittings of metal, plastics, etc." A classification ruling in this situation may therefore at least seek a respect proportional to its "power to persuade." Such a ruling may surely claim the merit of its writer's thoroughness, logic and expertness, its fit with prior interpretations, and any other sources of weight.

D

Underlying the position we take here, like the position expressed by Justice Scalia in dissent, is a choice about the best way to deal with an inescapable feature of the body of congressional legislation authorizing administrative action. That feature is the great variety of ways in which the laws invest the Government's administrative arms with discretion, and with procedures for exercising it, in giving meaning to Acts of Congress. Implementation of a statute may occur in formal adjudication or the choice to defend against judicial challenge; it may occur in a central board or office or in dozens of enforcement agencies dotted across the country; its institutional lawmaking may be confined to the resolution of minute detail or extend to legislative rulemaking on matters intentionally left by Congress to be worked out at the agency level.

Although we all accept the position that the Judiciary should defer to at least some of this multifarious administrative action, we have to decide how to take account of the great range of its variety. If the primary objective is to simplify the judicial process of giving or withholding deference, then the diversity of statutes authorizing discretionary administrative action must be declared irrelevant or minimized. If, on the other hand, it is simply implausible that Congress intended such a broad range of statutory authority to produce only two varieties of administrative action, demanding either *Chevron* deference or none at all, then the breadth of the spectrum of possible agency action must be taken into account. Justice Scalia's first priority over the years has been to limit and simplify. The Court's choice has been to tailor deference to variety. This acceptance of the range of statutory variation has led the Court to recognize more than one variety of judicial deference, just as the Court has recognized a variety of indicators that Congress would expect *Chevron* deference.

Our respective choices are repeated today. Justice Scalia would pose the question of deference as an either-or choice. . . . The Court, on the other hand, said nothing in *Chevron* to eliminate *Skidmore*'s recognition of various justifications for deference depending on statutory circumstances and agency action; *Chevron* was simply a case recognizing that even without express authority to fill a specific statutory gap, circumstances pointing to implicit congressional delegation present a particularly insistent call for deference. . . . We think, in sum, that Justice Scalia's efforts to simplify ultimately run afoul of Congress's indications that different statutes present different reasons for considering respect for the exercise of administrative authority or deference to it. Without being at odds with congressional intent much of the time, we believe that judicial responses to administrative action must continue to differentiate between *Chevron* and *Skidmore*. . . .

Since the *Skidmore* assessment called for here ought to be made in the first instance by the Court of Appeals for the Federal Circuit or the Court of International Trade, we go no further than to vacate the judgment and remand the case for further proceedings consistent with this opinion.

It is so ordered.

Justice SCALIA, dissenting.

[handwritten: Scalia wants Deferance or NO — No middle ground.]

Today's opinion makes an avulsive change in judicial review of federal administrative action. Whereas previously a reasonable agency application of an ambiguous statutory provision had to be sustained so long as it represented the agency's authoritative interpretation, henceforth such an application can be set aside unless "it appears that Congress delegated authority to the agency generally to make rules carrying the force of law," as by giving an agency "power to engage in adjudication or notice-and-comment rulemaking, or . . . some other [procedure] indicating comparable congressional intent," and "the agency interpretation claiming deference was promulgated in the exercise of that authority." What was previously a general presumption of authority in agencies to resolve ambiguity in the statutes they have been authorized to enforce has been changed to a presumption of no such authority, which must be overcome by affirmative legislative

[handwritten: Change from previous Assumption of correct.]

intent to the contrary. And whereas previously, when agency authority to resolve ambiguity did not exist the court was free to give the statute what it considered the best interpretation, henceforth the court must supposedly give the agency view some indeterminate amount of so-called *Skidmore* deference. We will be sorting out the consequences of the *Mead* doctrine, which has today replaced the *Chevron* doctrine, for years to come. I would adhere to our established jurisprudence, defer to the reasonable interpretation the Customs Service has given to the statute it is charged with enforcing, and reverse the judgment of the Court of Appeals.

. . . Today the Court collapses [the] doctrine, announcing instead a presumption that agency discretion does not exist unless the statute, expressly or impliedly, says so. . . . Only when agencies act through "adjudication[,] notice-and-comment rulemaking or . . . some other [procedure] indicating comparable congressional intent [whatever that means]" is *Chevron* deference applicable — because these "relatively formal administrative procedures [designed] to foster . . . fairness and deliberation" bespeak (according to the Court) congressional willingness to have the agency, rather than the courts, resolve statutory ambiguities. Once it is determined that *Chevron* deference is not in order, the uncertainty is not at an end — and indeed is just beginning. Litigants cannot then assume that the statutory question is one for the courts to determine, according to traditional interpretive principles and by their own judicial lights. No, the Court now resurrects, in full force, the pre-*Chevron* doctrine *of Skidmore* deference. . . . The Court has largely replaced *Chevron*, in other words, with that test most beloved by a court unwilling to be held to rules (and most feared by litigants who want to know what to expect): th' ol' "totality of the circumstances" test.

The Court's new doctrine is neither sound in principle nor sustainable in practice.

A

As to principle: The doctrine of *Chevron* — that all *authoritative* agency interpretations of statutes they are charged with administering deserve deference — was rooted in a legal presumption of congressional intent, important to the division of powers between the Second and Third Branches. When, *Chevron* said, Congress leaves an ambiguity in a statute that is to be administered by an executive agency, it is presumed that Congress meant to give the agency discretion, within the limits of reasonable interpretation, as to how the ambiguity is to be resolved. By committing enforcement of the statute to an agency rather than the courts, Congress committed its initial and primary interpretation to that branch as well.

There is some question whether *Chevron* was faithful to the text of the Administrative Procedure Act (APA), which it did not even bother to cite. But it was in accord with the origins of federal-court judicial review. . . .

The basis in principle for today's new doctrine can be described as follows: The background rule is that ambiguity in legislative instructions to agencies is to be resolved not by the agencies but by the judges. Specific congressional intent to depart from this rule must be found — and while there is no single touchstone for such intent it can generally be found when Congress has authorized the agency to act through (what the Court says is) relatively formal procedures such as informal rulemaking and formal (and informal?) adjudication, and when the agency in fact employs such procedures. . . . The Court's principal criterion of congressional intent to supplant its background rule seems to me quite implausible. There is no necessary connection between the formality of procedure and the power of the entity administering the procedure to resolve authoritatively questions of law. The most formal of the procedures the Court refers to — formal adjudication — is modeled after the process used in trial courts, which of course are not generally accorded deference on questions of law. The purpose of such a procedure is to produce a closed record for determination and review of the facts — which implies nothing about the power of the agency subjected to the procedure to resolve authoritatively questions of law. . . .

B

As for the practical effects of the new rule:

(1)

The principal effect will be protracted confusion. As noted above, the one test for *Chevron* deference that the Court enunciates is wonderfully imprecise: whether "Congress delegated authority to the agency generally to make rules carrying the force of law, . . . as by . . . adjudication[,] notice-and-comment rulemaking, or . . . some other [procedure] indicating comparable congressional intent." But even this description does not do justice to the utter flabbiness of the Court's criterion, since, in order to maintain the fiction that the new test is really just the old one, applied consistently throughout our case law, the Court must make a virtually open-ended exception to its already imprecise guidance: In the present case, it tells us, the absence of notice-and-comment rulemaking (and "[who knows?] [of] some other [procedure] indicating comparable congressional intent") is not enough to decide the question of *Chevron* deference, "for we have sometimes found reasons for *Chevron* deference even when no such administrative formality was required and none was afforded." . . .

(2)

Another practical effect of today's opinion will be an artificially induced increase in informal rulemaking. . . . As I have described, the Court's safe harbor requires not merely that the agency have been given rulemaking authority, but also that the agency have *employed* rulemaking as the means of resolving the statutory ambiguity. (It is hard to understand why that should be so. Surely the mere *conferral* of rulemaking authority demonstrates — if one accepts the Court's logic — a congressional intent to allow the agency to resolve ambiguities. And given that intent, what difference does it make that the agency chooses instead to use another perfectly permissible means for that purpose?) Moreover, the majority's approach will have a perverse effect on the rules that do emerge, given the principle (which the Court leaves untouched today) that judges must defer to reasonable agency interpretations of their own regulations. Agencies will now have high incentive to rush out barebones, ambiguous rules construing statutory ambiguities, which they can then in turn further clarify through informal rulings entitled to judicial respect.

(3)

Worst of all, the majority's approach will lead to the ossification of large portions of our statutory law. Where *Chevron* applies, statutory ambiguities remain ambiguities subject to the agency's ongoing clarification. They create a space, so to speak, for the exercise of continuing agency discretion. As *Chevron* itself held, the Environmental Protection Agency can interpret "stationary source" to mean a single smokestack, can later replace that interpretation with the "bubble concept" embracing an entire plant, and if that proves undesirable can return again to the original interpretation. For the indeterminately large number of statutes taken out of *Chevron* by today's decision, however, ambiguity (and hence flexibility) will cease with the first judicial resolution. *Skidmore* deference gives the agency's current position some vague and uncertain amount of respect, but it does not, like *Chevron*, *leave* the matter within the control of the Executive Branch for the future. Once the court has spoken, it becomes *unlawful* for the agency to take a contradictory position; the statute now *says* what the court has prescribed. It will be bad enough when this ossification occurs as a result of judicial determination (under today's new principles) that there is no affirmative indication of congressional intent to "delegate"; but it will be positively bizarre when it occurs simply because of an agency's failure to act by rulemaking (rather than informal adjudication) before the issue is presented to the courts. . . .

(4)

And finally, the majority's approach compounds the confusion it creates by breathing new life into the anachronism of *Skidmore*. . . . Justice Jackson's eloquence notwithstanding, the rule *of Skidmore* deference is an empty truism and a trifling statement of the obvious: A judge should take into account the well-considered views of expert observers.

It was possible to live with the indeterminacy *of Skidmore* deference in earlier times. But in an era when federal statutory law administered by federal agencies is pervasive, and when the ambiguities (intended or unintended) that those statutes contain are innumerable, totality-of-the-circumstances *Skidmore* deference is a recipe for uncertainty, unpredictability, and endless litigation. To condemn a vast body of agency action to that regime (all except rulemaking, formal (and informal?) adjudication, and whatever else might now and then be included within today's intentionally vague formulation of affirmative congressional intent to "delegate") is irresponsible.

To decide the present case, I would adhere to the original formulation of *Chevron*. . . . Nothing in the statute at issue here displays an intent to modify the background presumption on which *Chevron* deference is based. The Court points to 28 U.S.C. §2640(a), which provides that, in reviewing the ruling by the Customs Service, the Court of International Trade (CIT) "shall make its determinations upon the basis of the record made before the court." But records are made to determine the facts, not the law. All this provision means is that new evidence may be introduced at the CIT stage; it says nothing about whether the CIT must respect the Customs Service's authoritative interpretation of the law. More significant than §2640(a), insofar as the CIT's obligation to defer to the Customs Service's legal interpretations is concerned, is §2639(a)(1), which requires the CIT to accord a "presum[ption of] correctness" to the Customs Service's decision. Another provision cited by the Court is §2638, which provides that the CIT "by rule, may consider any new ground in support" of the challenge to the Customs Service's ruling. Once again, it is impossible to see how this has any connection to the degree of deference the CIT must accord the Customs Service's interpretation of its statute. Such "new grounds" may be intervening or newly discovered facts, or some intervening law or regulation that might render the Customs Service's ruling unsound.

There is no doubt that the Customs Service's interpretation represents the authoritative view of the agency. . . . No one contends that it is merely a "post hoc rationalization" or an "agency litigating position wholly unsupported by regulations, rulings, or administrative practice." . . . [In a footnote Justice Scalia added:] The Court's parting shot, that "there would have to be something wrong with a standard that accorded the status of substantive law to every one of 10,000 "official customs classifications rulings turned out each year from over 46 offices placed around the country at the Nation's entryways," misses the mark. I do not disagree. The "authoritativeness" of an agency interpretation does not turn upon whether it has been enunciated by someone who is actually employed by the agency. It must represent the judgment of central agency management, approved at the highest levels. I would find that condition to have been satisfied when, a ruling having been attacked in court, the general counsel of the agency has determined that it should be defended. If one thinks that that does not impart sufficient authoritativeness, then surely the line has been crossed when, as here, the General Counsel of the agency and the Solicitor General of the United States have assured this Court that the position represents the agency's authoritative view. . . .

Finally, and least importantly, even were I to accept the Court's revised version of *Chevron* as a correct statement of the law, I would still accord deference to the tariff classification ruling at issue in this case. . . .

For the reasons stated, I respectfully dissent from the Court's judgment. . . . I dissent even more vigorously from the reasoning that produces the Court's judgment, and that makes today's decision one of the most significant opinions ever rendered by the Court dealing with the judicial review of administrative action. Its consequences will be enormous, and almost uniformly bad.

BARNHART v. WALTON, 535 U.S. 212 (2002).   The Court upheld a legislative rule, promulgated through notice-and-comment procedures, but issued dictum stating that *Chevron* deference can apply to interpretive rules promulgated informally, so long as the totality of the circumstances suggest an implicit congressional delegation of law-interpreting authority. Relevant circumstances, according to *Walton*, include "the interstitial nature of the legal question, the related expertise of the Agency, the importance of the question to the administration of the statute, the complexity of that administration, and the careful consideration the Agency has given the question over a long period of time. . . ."

Chevron's Scope: Questions and Puzzles

1. Let us begin with what seems to be common ground, post-*Chevron*. (a) Courts have said that agency "litigating positions" are not entitled to deference, see Bowen v. Georgetown Univ. Hosp., 488 U.S. 204 (1988); Florida Manufactured Hosp. Assn. v. Cisneros, 53 F.3d 1565, 1574 (11th Cir. 1995). (b) Courts have also said that an agency is not entitled to deference insofar as it is acting as prosecutor, see Crandon v. United States, 494 U.S. 152, 158 (1990). (For a provocative argument that *Chevron* should apply to Department of Justice interpretations in the criminal context, see Kahan, Is *Chevron* Relevant to Federal Criminal Law?, 110 Harv. L. Rev. 469 (1996).) (c) Courts have held that *Chevron* applies to legal interpretations adopted by agencies in adjudication, see INS v. Aguirre-Aguirre, 526 U.S. 415 (1999), though *Mead* raises a question about whether all interpretations adopted in adjudication require deference, see Merrill and Hickman, supra, at 842-843. (d) There is also no indication, in any Supreme Court decisions, that agencies

are permitted to interpret the APA. See Metro Stevedore Co. v. Rambo, 521 U.S. 121, 137 n.9 (1997) (no deference to interpretations of APA); Prof'l Reactor Operator Society v. NRC, 939 F.2d 1047, 1051 (D.C. Cir. 1991) (same). (e) An agency does not receive deference if it is interpreting a statute that is enforced by many agencies. See, e.g., DuBois v. United States Dept. of Agric., 102 F.3d 1273, 1285 n.15 (1st Cir. 1996); Reporters Comm. for Freedom of the Press v. United States DOJ, 816 F.2d 730 (D.C. Cir. 1987).

2. On the view suggested by these agreed-upon principles, a predicate for *Chevron* is a delegation of interpretive power to agencies, and there has been no delegation in the cases in which *Chevron* deference is not applied. Justice Scalia accepts this view no less than anyone else. What, then, is he arguing about in *Christenson* and *Mead*? Perhaps he is simply urging that when an agency is issuing an interpretative rule, and it has the authority to do that, it should be presumed to have been given, by Congress, the power to resolve ambiguities. Why does the Court disagree?

3. Consider the possibility that Justice Scalia greatly overstates the effect of *Mead* on the preexisting law. Doesn't *Chevron* apply to the vast range of cases in which agencies issue rules and adjudicate? On the other hand, agencies do much of what they do through less formal channels. How do we know, after *Mead*, whether less formal interpretations get deference?

Some of the latter questions were seemingly clarified, though in dictum, in *Barnhart v. Walton* and other recent cases. See, e.g., Edelman v. Lynchburg College, 535 U.S. 106, 115 (2002) (stating in dictum that "deference under *Chevron* . . . does not necessarily require an agency's exercise of express notice-and-comment rulemaking power"). However, instability resurfaced in Clackamas Gastroenterology Assoc. v. Wells, 538 U.S. 440, 459 (2003) (citing *Christensen* for the proposition that "policy statements, agency manuals and enforcement guidelines" do not receive *Chevron* deference; no discussion of *Mead* or *Walton*).

Obviously the law of "Chevron Step Zero" is currently in flux; seemingly, the Justices are inconsistent, perhaps even confused. In this environment, what are lower courts to do? For an argument that the complexity and instability of the *Mead* framework imposes large decisionmaking burdens on lower courts, see Vermeule, *Mead* in the Trenches, 71 Geo. Wash. L. Rev. 347 (2003).

On this view, *Mead* has made administrative law worse, not better, through a kind of perfectionism. Assume, as the *Mead* Court does, that the ultimate predicate for *Chevron* deference is a congressional intention, or meta-intention, to delegate law-interpreting power to agencies rather than courts, where there is statutory silence or ambiguity. For the *Mead* Court, it followed inevitably that administrative law should "tailor deference to variety" by examining, in particular settings, whether such an intention exists. In some passages, the *Mead* Court seems to talk as though the mere existence of a background goal or justification — here, the idea that deference is a function of congressional intent — entails as a conceptual or logical matter that only an all-things-considered inquiry into that justification is legally permissible.

But that does not follow at all. The judicial inquiry into congressional intentions, where they exist, might be structured either through rules or through standards. Justice Scalia's proposed test, under which any "authoritative" agency pronouncement would receive *Chevron* deference, is relatively rule-like, while the Court's more fine-grained approach is relatively standard-like. Rules and standards are simply different, equally permissible devices for structuring the decisionmaking environment. To evaluate their comparative merits, one must know something about the costs and benefits of each, both in terms of judicial mistakes in determining congressional intentions, and in terms of decisionmaking burdens on judges, agencies, and legislators. Rules might reduce uncertainty for litigants, if they make planning easier; they might reduce decision costs for lower courts, because they reduce the range of facts and questions that are legally relevant.

More surprisingly, rules might sometimes reduce error on the part of lower-court judges, even though rules are overinclusive and underinclusive, relative to the rules' background justifications. If the cognitive load imposed by open-ended standards is large, so that decisionmakers using such standards will frequently (even in good faith) stray widely from the background justification, then even the distortion that rules create might produce greater net accuracy than would a comparable standard. As to all of these points, there are many variables to be considered. Plausibly, the extra complexity and nuance introduced by *Mead*'s standards impose costs, in terms of decisional burdens and legal uncertainty, that are greater than their benefits.

Of course congressional intentions about delegation are sometimes or often fictional, and this makes *Mead* look even worse; a complex, fine-grained inquiry into whether a fictional entity is present or absent in particular cases does not seem very sensible. Nor did the *Mead* Court itself follow through on its preference for standards. Recall that the *Mead* Court, despite its dismissal of Justice Scalia's relatively rule-like alternative test, filters the congressional intent inquiry through rule-like procedural categories designed to make the inquiry more tractable. To the extent that is so, Justice Scalia's alternative cannot be dismissed simply on the ground that courts should "tailor deference to variety"; the *Mead* Court itself only went part way toward that goal, and it is an open question whether it went too far, not far enough, or just the right distance.

4. On the scope *of Chevron*, a number of issues remain open. (a) An agency is deciding on its own jurisdiction. Does it get deference? The lower courts are divided on this question. See, e.g., New York Shipping Assns. v. FMC, 854 F.2d 1338 (D.C. Cir. 1988) (deference inappropriate); Oklahoma Nat'l Gas Co. v. FERC, 28 F.3d 1281,1283-1284 (deference appropriate); United Trans. Union v. STB, 183 F.3d 606 (7th Cir. 1999) (deference inappropriate). See Merrill & Hickman, supra, at 909-914. (b) An agency is saying that its own decisions are not subject to judicial review, or that the plaintiff does not have standing to challenge its decision. The general understanding seems to be that deference is inappropriate in such circumstances. But see Shalala v. Illinois Council on Long-Term Care, 529 U.S. 1, 21 (2000), appearing to give deference to an agency interpretation of a statute governing review of its own actions. (c) An agency denies that a statutory deadline is applicable to it. (d) An agency tries to interpret a statute that makes a cross-reference to general law. Here, there is a conflict among the circuits. See Koch Gateway Pipeline Co. v. FERC, 136 F.3d 810, 815 n.10 (D.C. Cir. 1998). (e) Lower-level agency employees interpret the statute. Here too, there has been lower court uncertainty. See, e.g., Elizabeth Blackwell Health Center for Women v. Knoll, 61 F.3d 170, 181-182 (3d Cir. 1995); Capistrano Unified Sch. Dist. v. Wartenberg, 59 F.3d 884, 894 (9th Cir. 1995). Can you argue that *Mead* resolves this issue unfavorably to the agency employees? For discussion of some of these questions, and others, see Merrill & Hickman, supra.

3. Chevron, *Textualism, Literalism: Problems in Step 1*

We now turn to questions raised by *Chevron* step 1, which requires the Court to ask if the statute is ambiguous or if Congress has directly decided the precise question at issue.

Recall that in a footnote, the *Chevron* Court said that the "traditional tools of statutory interpretation" are to be used in step 1. But what are those tools?

Babbitt v. Sweet Home Chapter of Communities for a Great Oregon

515 U.S. 687 (1995)

Justice STEVENS delivered the opinion of the Court.

The Endangered Species Act of 1973 contains a variety of protections designed to save from extinction species that the Secretary of the Interior designates as endangered or threatened. Section 9 of the Act makes it unlawful for any person to "take" any endangered or threatened species. The Secretary has promulgated a regulation that defines the statute's prohibition on takings to include "significant habitat modification or degradation where it actually kills or injures wildlife." This case presents the question whether the Secretary exceeded his authority under the Act by promulgating that regulation.

I

Section 9(a)(1) of the Endangered Species Act provides the following protection for endangered species:

> Except as provided in sections 1535(g)(2) and 1539 of this title, with respect to any endangered species of fish or wildlife listed pursuant to section 1533 of this title it is unlawful for any person subject to the jurisdiction of the United States to — . . .
>   (B) take any such species within the United States or the territorial sea of the United States[.] 16 U.S.C. §1538(a)(1).

Section 3(19) of the Act defines the statutory term "take":

> The term "take" means to harass, harm, pursue, hunt, shoot, wound, kill, trap, capture, or collect, or to attempt to engage in any such conduct. 16 U.S.C. §1532(19).

The Act does not further define the terms it uses to define "take." The Interior Department regulations that implement the statute, however, define the statutory term "harm":

> Harm in the definition of "take" in the Act means an act which actually kills or injures wildlife. Such act may include significant habitat modification or degradation where it actually kills or injures wildlife by significantly impairing essential behavioral patterns, including breeding, feeding, or sheltering. 50 C.F.R. §17.3 (1994).

This regulation has been in place since 1975.[5]

---

5. The Secretary, through the Director of the Fish and Wildlife Service, originally promulgated the regulation in 1975 and amended it in 1981 to emphasize that actual death or injury of a protected animal is necessary for a violation. See 40 Fed. Reg. 44412, 44416 (1975); 46 Fed. Reg. 54748, 54750 (1981).

A limitation on the §9 "take" prohibition appears in §10(a)(1)(B) of the Act, which Congress added by amendment in 1982. That section authorizes the Secretary to grant a permit for any taking otherwise prohibited by §9(a)(1)(B) "if such taking is incidental to, and not the purpose of, the carrying out of an otherwise lawful activity." 16 U.S.C. §1539(a)(1)(B).

In addition to the prohibition on takings, the Act provides several other protections for endangered species. Section 4, 16 U.S.C. §1533, commands the Secretary to identify species of fish or wildlife that are in danger of extinction and to publish from time to time lists of all species he determines to be endangered or threatened. Section 5, 16 U.S.C. §1534, authorizes the Secretary, in cooperation with the States, see 16 U.S.C. §1535, to acquire land to aid in preserving such species. Section 7 requires federal agencies to ensure that none of their activities, including the granting of licenses and permits, will jeopardize the continued existence of endangered species "or result in the destruction or adverse modification of habitat of such species which is determined by the Secretary . . . to be critical." 16 U.S.C. §1536(a)(2).

Respondents in this action are small landowners, logging companies, and families dependent on the forest products industries in the Pacific Northwest and in the Southeast, and organizations that represent their interests. They brought this declaratory judgment action. . . . Respondents challenged the regulation on its face. Their complaint alleged that application of the "harm" regulation to the red-cockaded woodpecker, an endangered species, and the northern spotted owl, a threatened species, had injured them economically. . . .

II *Reasons Sec.'s interp was reasonable.*

Because this case was decided on motions for summary judgment, we may appropriately make certain factual assumptions in order to frame the legal issue. First, we assume respondents have no desire to harm either the red-cockaded woodpecker or the spotted owl; they merely wish to continue logging activities that would be entirely proper if not prohibited by the ESA. On the other hand, we must assume arguendo that those activities will have the effect, even though unintended, of detrimentally changing the natural habitat of both listed species and that, as a consequence, members of those species will be killed or injured. Under respondents' view of the law, the Secretary's only means of forestalling that grave result — even when the actor knows it is certain to occur — is to use his §5 authority to purchase the lands on which the survival of the species depends. The Secretary, on the other hand, submits that the §9 prohibition on takings, which Congress defined to include "harm," places on respondents a duty to avoid harm that habitat alteration will cause the birds unless respondents first obtain a permit pursuant to §10.

(1) The text of the Act provides three reasons for concluding that the Secretary's interpretation is reasonable. First, an ordinary understanding of the word "harm" supports it. The dictionary definition of the verb form of "harm" is "to cause hurt or damage to: injure." Webster's Third New International Dictionary 1034 (1966). In the context of the ESA, that definition naturally encompasses habitat modification that results in actual injury or death to members of an endangered or threatened species. Respondents argue that the Secretary should have limited the purview of "harm" to direct applications of force against protected species, but the dictionary definition does not include the word "directly" or suggest in any way that only direct or willful action that leads to injury constitutes "harm." Moreover, unless the statutory term "harm" encompasses indirect as well as

direct injuries, the word has no meaning that does not duplicate the meaning of other words that §3 uses to define "take." A reluctance to treat statutory terms as surplusage supports the reasonableness of the Secretary's interpretation.[6]

Second, the broad purpose of the ESA supports the Secretary's decision to extend protection against activities that cause the precise harms Congress enacted the statute to avoid. In TVA v. Hill, 437 U.S. 153 (1978), we described the Act as "the most comprehensive legislation for the preservation of endangered species ever enacted by any nation." Whereas predecessor statutes enacted in 1966 and 1969 had not contained any sweeping prohibition against the taking of endangered species except on federal lands, see id., at 175, the 1973 Act applied to all land in the United States and to the Nation's territorial seas. As stated in §2 of the Act, among its central purposes is "to provide a means whereby the ecosystems upon which endangered species and threatened species depend may be conserved. . . ." 16 U.S.C. §1531(b). . . .

Respondents advance strong arguments that activities that cause minimal or unforeseeable harm will not violate the Act as construed in the "harm" regulation. Respondents, however, present a facial challenge to the regulation. Thus, they ask us to invalidate the Secretary's understanding of "harm" in every circumstance, even when an actor knows that an activity, such as draining a pond, would actually result in the extinction of a listed species by destroying its habitat. Given Congress' clear expression of the ESA's broad purpose to protect endangered and threatened wildlife, the Secretary's definition of "harm" is reasonable.[7]

Third, the fact that Congress in 1982 authorized the Secretary to issue permits for takings that §9(a)(1)(B) would otherwise prohibit, "if such taking is incidental to, and not the purpose of, the carrying out of an otherwise lawful activity," 16 U.S.C. §1539(a)(l)(B), strongly suggests that Congress understood §9(a)(1)(B) to prohibit indirect as well as deliberate takings. . . .

The Court of Appeals made three errors in asserting that "harm" must refer to a direct application of force because the words around it do. First, the court's premise was flawed. Several of the words that accompany "harm" in the §3 definition of "take," especially "harass," "pursue," "wound," and "kill," refer to actions or effects that do not require direct applications of force. Second, to the extent the court read a requirement of intent or purpose into the words used to define "take," it ignored §9's express provision that a "knowing" action is enough to violate the Act. Third, the court employed noscitur a sociis

[handwritten margin note: Why Circ. Court Got it wrong.]

---

6. In contrast, if the statutory term "harm" encompasses such indirect means of killing and injuring wildlife as habitat modification, the other terms listed in §3 — "harass," "pursue," "hunt," "shoot," "wound," "kill," "trap," "capture," and "collect" — generally retain independent meanings. Most of those terms refer to deliberate actions more frequently than does "harm" and they therefore do not duplicate the sense of indirect causation that "harm" adds to the statute. In addition, most of the other words in the definition describe either actions from which habitat modification does not usually result (e.g., "pursue," "harass") or effects to which activities that modify habitat do not usually lead (e.g., "trap," "collect"). To the extent the Secretary's definition of "harm" may have applications that overlap with other words in the definition, that overlap reflects the broad purpose of the Act.

7. The dissent incorrectly asserts that the Secretary's regulation (1) "dispenses with the foreseeability of harm" and (2) "fail[s] to require injury to particular animals." . . . As to the first assertion, the regulation merely implements the statute, and it is therefore subject to the statute's "knowingly violates" language, see 16 U.S.C. §§1540(a)(1), (b)(1), and ordinary requirements of proximate causation and foreseeability. . . . Nothing in the regulation purports to weaken those requirements. To the contrary, the word "actually" in the regulation should be construed to limit the liability about which the dissent appears most concerned, liability under the statute's "otherwise violates" provision. The Secretary did not need to include "actually" to connote "but for" causation, which the other words in the definition obviously require. As to the dissent's second assertion, every term in the regulation's definition of "harm" is subservient to the phrase "an act which actually kills or injures wildlife."

to give "harm" essentially the same function as other words in the definition, thereby denying it independent meaning. The canon, to the contrary, counsels that a word "gathers meaning from the words around it." Jarecki v. G. D. Searle & Co., 367 U.S. 303, 307 (1961). The statutory context of "harm" suggests that Congress meant that term to serve a particular function in the ESA, consistent with but distinct from the functions of the other verbs used to define "take." The Secretary's interpretation of "harm" to include indirectly injuring endangered animals through habitat modification permissibly interprets "harm" to have "a character of its own not to be submerged by its association." Russell Motor Car Co. v. United States, 261 U.S. 514, 519 (1923).

Nor does the Act's inclusion of the §5 land acquisition authority and the §7 directive to federal agencies to avoid destruction or adverse modification of critical habitat alter our conclusion. Respondents' argument that the Government lacks any incentive to purchase land under §5 when it can simply prohibit takings under §9 ignores the practical considerations that attend enforcement of the ESA. Purchasing habitat lands may well cost the Government less in many circumstances than pursuing civil or criminal penalties. In addition, the §5 procedure allows for protection of habitat before the seller's activity has harmed any endangered animal, whereas the Government cannot enforce the §9 prohibition until an animal has actually been killed or injured. The Secretary may also find the §5 authority useful for preventing modification of land that is not yet but may in the future become habitat for an endangered or threatened species. The §7 directive applies only to the Federal Government, whereas the §9 prohibition applies to "any person." Section 7 imposes a broad, affirmative duty to avoid adverse habitat modifications that §9 does not replicate, and §7 does not limit its admonition to habitat modification that "actually kills or injures wildlife." Conversely, §7 contains limitations that §9 does not, applying only to actions "likely to jeopardize the continued existence of any endangered species or threatened species," 16 U.S.C. §1536(a)(2), and to modifications of habitat that has been designated "critical" pursuant to §4, 16 U.S.C. §1533(b)(2). Any overlap that §5 or §7 may have with §9 in particular cases is unexceptional, and simply reflects the broad purpose of the Act set out in §2 and acknowledged in TVA v. Hill.

We need not decide whether the statutory definition of "take" compels the Secretary's interpretation of "harm," because our conclusions that Congress did not unambiguously manifest its intent to adopt respondents' view and that the Secretary's interpretation is reasonable suffice to decide this case. See generally [Chevron]. The latitude the ESA gives the Secretary in enforcing the statute, together with the degree of regulatory expertise necessary to its enforcement, establishes that we owe some degree of deference to the Secretary's reasonable interpretation. See Breyer, Judicial Review of Questions of Law and Policy, 38 Admin. L. Rev. 363, 373 (1986).

III *Legis History Also Supports Secretary.*

Our conclusion that the Secretary's definition of "harm" rests on a permissible construction of the ESA gains further support from the legislative history of the statute. The Committee Reports accompanying the bills that became the ESA do not specifically discuss the meaning of "harm," but they make clear that Congress intended "take" to apply broadly to cover indirect as well as purposeful actions. The Senate Report stressed that " '[t]ake' is defined . . . in the broadest possible manner to include every conceivable way in which a person can " 'take' or attempt to 'take' any fish or wildlife." S. Rep. No. 93-307, p.7 (1973). The House Report stated that "the broadest possible terms" were used to define restrictions on takings. H.R. Rep. No. 93-412, p.15 (1973). The House Report underscored the breadth of the "take" definition by noting that it included "harassment, whether intentional or not." Id., at 11. The Report explained that the definition "would allow, for example, the Secretary to regulate or prohibit the activities of birdwatchers where the effect of those activities might disturb the birds and make it difficult for them to hatch or raise their young." Ibid. These comments, ignored in the dissent's welcome but selective foray into legislative history support the Secretary's interpretation that the term "take" in §9 reached far more than the deliberate actions of hunters and trappers. . . .

IV   *Power Delegation supports Sec.*

When it enacted the ESA, Congress delegated broad administrative and interpretive power to the Secretary. See 16 U.S.C. §§1533, 1540(f). The task of defining and listing endangered and threatened species requires an expertise and attention to detail that exceeds the normal province of Congress. Fashioning appropriate standards for issuing permits under §10 for takings that would otherwise violate §9 necessarily requires the exercise of broad discretion. The proper interpretation of a term such as "harm" involves a complex policy choice. When Congress has entrusted the Secretary with broad discretion, we are especially reluctant to substitute our views of wise policy for his. See *Chevron*, 467 U.S., at 865-866. In this case, the reluctance accords with our conclusion, based on the text, structure, and legislative history of the ESA, that the Secretary reasonably construed the intent of Congress when he defined "harm" to include "significant habitat modification or degradation that actually kills or injures wildlife."

In the elaboration and enforcement of the ESA, the Secretary and all persons who must comply with the law will confront difficult questions of proximity and degree; for, as all recognize, the Act encompasses a vast range of economic and social enterprises and endeavors. These questions must be addressed in the usual course of the law, through case-by-case resolution and adjudication.

The judgment of the Court of Appeals is reversed.

Justice O'CONNOR, concurring.

My agreement with the Court is founded on two understandings. First, the challenged regulation is limited to significant habitat modification that causes actual, as opposed to hypothetical or speculative, death or injury to identifiable protected animals. Second, even setting aside difficult questions of scienter, the regulation's application is limited by ordinary principles of proximate causation, which introduce notions of foreseeability. . . .

Does Not Buy Proximate Causation issue.

Justice SCALIA, with whom The Chief Justice and Justice THOMAS join, dissenting.

I think it unmistakably clear that the legislation at issue here (1) forbade the hunting and killing of endangered animals, and (2) provided federal lands and federal funds *for the acquisition of private lands*, to preserve the habitat of endangered animals. The Court's holding that the hunting and killing prohibition incidentally preserves habitat on private lands imposes unfairness to the point of financial ruin — not just upon the rich, but upon the simplest farmer who finds his land conscripted to national zoological use. I respectfully dissent. . . .

The regulation has three features which, for reasons I shall discuss at length below, do not comport with the statute. First, it interprets the statute to prohibit habitat modification

— No Causality Proof

that is no more than the cause-in-fact of death or injury to wildlife. Any "significant habitat modification" that in fact produces that result by "impairing essential behavioral patterns" is made unlawful, regardless of whether that result is intended or even foreseeable, and no matter how long the chain of causality between modification and injury.

Second, the regulation does not require an "act": the Secretary's officially stated position is that an omission will do. The previous version of the regulation made this explicit. See 40 Fed. Reg. 44412, 44416 (1975) ("'Harm' in the definition of 'take' in the Act means an act or omission which actually kills or injures wildlife. . . ."). When the regulation was modified in 1981 the phrase "or omission" was taken out, but only because (as the final publication of the rule advised) "the [Fish and Wildlife] Service feels that 'act' is inclusive of either commissions or omissions which would be prohibited by section [1538(a)(1)(B)]." 46 Fed. Reg. 54748, 54750 (1981). In its brief here the Government agrees that the regulation covers omissions, see Brief for Petitioners 47 (although it argues that "[a]n 'omission' constitutes an 'act' . . . only if there is a legal duty to act"), ibid.

The third and most important unlawful feature of the regulation is that it encompasses injury inflicted, not only upon individual animals, but upon populations of the protected species. "Injury" in the regulation includes "significantly impairing essential behavioral patterns, including breeding," 50 CFR §17.3 (1994). Impairment of breeding does not "injure" living creatures; it prevents them from propagating, thus "injuring" a population of animals which would otherwise have maintained or increased its numbers. What the face of the regulation shows, the Secretary's official pronouncements confirm. The Final Redefinition of "Harm" accompanying publication of the regulation said that "harm" is not limited to "direct physical injury to an individual member of the wildlife species," 46 Fed. Reg. 54748 (1981), and refers to "injury to a *population*," id., at 54749 (emphasis added).

None of these three features of the regulation can be found in the statutory provisions supposed to authorize it. The term "harm" in §1532(19) has no legal force of its own. An indictment or civil complaint that charged the defendant with "harming" an animal protected under the Act would be dismissed as defective, for the only operative term in the statute is to "take." If "take" were not elsewhere defined in the Act, none could dispute what it means, for the term is as old as the law itself. To "take," when applied to wild animals, means to reduce those animals, by killing or capturing, to human control. See, e.g., 11 Oxford English Dictionary (1933) ("Take . . . To catch, capture (a wild beast, bird, fish, etc.)"); Webster's New International Dictionary of the English Language (2d ed. 1949) (take defined as "to catch or capture by trapping, snaring, etc., or as prey"). [The] taking prohibition, in other words, is only part of the regulatory plan of §1538(a)(1), which covers all the stages of the process by which protected wildlife is reduced to man's dominion and made the object of profit. It is obvious that "take" in this sense — a term of art deeply embedded in the statutory and common law concerning wildlife — describes a class of acts (not omissions) done directly and intentionally (not indirectly and by accident) to particular animals (not populations of animals). . . .

The verb "harm" has a range of meaning: "to cause injury" at its broadest, "to do hurt or damage" in a narrower and more direct sense. See, e.g., 1 N. Webster, An American Dictionary of the English Language (1828) ("Harm, v.t. To hurt; to injure; to damage; *to impair soundness of body, either animal* or vegetable") (emphasis added); American College Dictionary 551 (1970) ("harm . . . n. injury; damage; hurt: *to do him bodily harm*"). In fact the more directed sense of "harm" is a somewhat more common and preferred usage; "harm has in it a little of the idea of specially focused hurt or injury, as if a personal injury has been anticipated and intended." J. Opdycke, Mark My Words: A Guide to Modern Usage and Expression 330 (1949). See also American Heritage Dictionary of the English Language (1981) ("Injure has the widest range. . . . Harm and hurt refer principally to what causes physical or mental distress to living things"). To define "harm" as an act or omission that, however remotely, "actually kills or injures" a population of wildlife through habitat modification, is to choose a meaning that makes nonsense of the word that "harm" defines — requiring us to accept that a farmer who tills his field and causes erosion that makes silt run into a nearby river which depletes oxygen and thereby "impairs [the] breeding" of protected fish, has "taken" or "attempted to take" the fish. It should take the strongest evidence to make us believe that Congress has defined a term in a manner repugnant to its ordinary and traditional sense.

Here the evidence shows the opposite. "Harm" is merely one of 10 prohibitory words in §1532(19), and the other 9 fit the ordinary meaning of "take" perfectly. To "harass, pursue, hunt, shoot, wound, kill, trap, capture, or collect" are all affirmative acts (the provision itself describes them as "conduct," see §1532(19)) which are directed immediately and intentionally against a particular animal — not acts or omissions that indirectly and accidentally cause injury to a population of animals. The Court points out that several of the words ("harass," "pursue," "wound," and "kill") "refer to actions or effects that do not require direct *applications of force*." . . . That is true enough, but force is not the point. Even "taking" activities in the narrowest sense, activities traditionally engaged in by hunters and trappers, do not all consist of direct applications of force; pursuit and harassment are part of the business of "taking" the prey even before it has been touched. What the nine other words in §1532(19) have in common — and share with the narrower meaning of "harm" described above, but not with the Secretary's ruthless dilation of the word — is the sense of affirmative conduct intentionally directed against a particular animal or animals. . . .

[T]he Court's contention that "harm" in the narrow sense adds nothing to the other words underestimates the ingenuity of our own species in a way that Congress did not. To feed an animal poison, to spray it with mace, to chop down the very tree in which it is nesting, or even to destroy its entire habitat in order to take it (as by draining a pond to get at a turtle), might neither injure nor kill, but would directly and intentionally harm.

The penalty provisions of the Act counsel this interpretation as well. Any person who "knowingly" violates §1538(a)(1)(B) is subject to criminal penalties under §1540(b)(1) and civil penalties under §1540(a)(1); moreover, under the latter section, any person "who otherwise violates" the taking prohibition (i.e., violates it unknowingly) may be assessed a civil penalty of $500 for each violation, with the stricture that "[e]ach such violation shall be a separate offense." This last provision should be clear warning that the regulation is in error, for when combined with the regulation it produces a result that no legislature could reasonably be thought to have intended: A large number of routine private activities — farming, for example, ranching, roadbuilding, construction and logging — are subjected to strict-liability penalties when they fortuitously injure protected wildlife, no matter how remote the chain of causation and no matter how difficult to foresee (or to disprove) the "injury" may be (e.g., an "impairment" of breeding). The Court says that "[the strict-liability provision] is potentially sweeping, but it would be so with or without the Secretary's 'harm' regulation." . . . That is not correct. Without the regulation, the routine "habitat modifying" activities that people conduct to make a daily living would not carry exposure to strict penalties; only acts directed at animals, like those described by the other words in §1532(19), would risk liability.

The Court says that "[to] read a requirement of intent or purpose into the words used to define 'take' . . . ignore[s] [§1540's] express provision that a 'knowing' action is enough to violate the Act." . . . This presumably means that because the reading of §1532(19) advanced here ascribes an element of purposeful injury to the prohibited acts, it makes superfluous (or inexplicable) the more severe penalties provided for a "knowing" viola- tion. That conclusion does not follow, for it is quite possible to take protected wildlife purposefully without doing so knowingly. A requirement that a violation be "knowing" means that the defendant must "know the facts that make his conduct illegal," Staples v. United States, 511 U.S. 600 (1994). The hunter who shoots an elk in the mistaken belief that it is a mule deer has not knowingly violated §1538(a)(1)(B) — not because he does not know that elk are legally protected (that would be knowledge of the law, which is not a requirement . . .), but because he does not know what sort of animal he is shooting. The hunter has nonetheless committed a purposeful taking of protected wildlife, and would therefore be subject to the (lower) strict-liability penalties for the violation. . . .

[T]he Court seeks support from a provision which was added to the Act in 1982, the year after the Secretary promulgated the current regulation. The provision states:

> [T]he Secretary may permit, under such terms and conditions as he shall prescribe — . . .
> "any taking otherwise prohibited by section 1538(a)(1)(B) . . . if such taking is inciden-
> tal to, and not the purpose of, the carrying out of an otherwise lawful activity."
> 16U.S.C. §1539(a)(1)(B).

This provision does not, of course, implicate our doctrine that reenactment of a statutory provision ratifies an extant judicial or administrative interpretation, for neither the taking prohibition in §1538(a)(1)(B) nor the definition in §1532(19) was reenacted. See Central Bank of Denver, N.A. v. First Interstate Bank of Denver, N.A., 511 U.S. 164 (1994). The Court claims, however, that the provision "strongly suggests that Congress understood [§1538(a)(1)(B)] to prohibit indirect as well as deliberate takings." . . . That would be a valid inference if habitat modification were the only substantial "otherwise lawful activity" that might incidentally and nonpurposefully cause a prohibited "taking." Of course it is not. This provision applies to the many otherwise lawful takings that inci- dentally take a protected species — as when fishing for unprotected salmon also takes an endangered species of salmon, see Pacific Northwest Generating Cooperative v. Brown, 38 F.3d 1058, 1067 (CA9 1994). Congress has referred to such "incidental takings" in other statutes as well — for example, a statute referring to "the incidental taking of . . . sea turtles in the course of . . . harvesting [shrimp]" and to the "rate of incidental taking of sea turtles by United States vessels in the course of such harvesting," 103 Stat. 1038, §609(b)(2), note following 16 U.S.C. §1537 (1988 ed., Supp. V); and a statute referring to "the incidental taking of marine mammals in the course of commercial fishing opera- tions," 108 Stat. 546, §118(a). The Court shows that it misunderstands the question when it says that "[n]o one could seriously request an 'incidental' take permit to avert . . . liability for direct, deliberate action *against a member of an endangered or threatened species.*" . . . That is not an incidental take at all. . . .

[T]he Court and the concurrence suggest that the regulation should be read to contain a requirement of proximate causation or foreseeability, principally *because the statute does* — and "[n]othing in the regulation purports to weaken those requirements [of the statute]." . . . I quite agree that the statute contains such a limitation, because the verbs of purpose in §1538(a)(1)(B) denote action directed at animals. *But the Court has rejected that reading.* The critical premise on which it has upheld the regulation is that, despite the weight of the other words in §1538(a)(1)(B), "the statutory term 'harm' encompasses indirect as well as direct injuries." . . . Consequently, unless there is some strange category of causation that is indirect and yet also proximate, the Court has already rejected its own basis for finding a proximate-cause limitation in the regulation. In fact "proximate" causation simply means "direct" causation. See, e.g., Black's Law Dictionary 1103 (5th ed. 1979) (defining "[p]roximate" as "Immediate; nearest; *direct*") (emphasis added); Webster's New International Dictionary of the English Language 1995 (2d ed. 1949) ("proximate cause. A cause which *directly*, or with no mediate agency, produces an effect") (emphasis added).

The only other reason given for finding a proximate-cause limitation in the regulation is that "by use of the word 'actually,' the regulation clearly rejects speculative or conjectural effects, and thus itself invokes principles of proximate causation." . . . Non sequitur, of course. That the injury must be "actual" as opposed to "potential" simply says nothing at all about the length or foreseeability of the causal chain between the habitat modification and the "actual" injury. It is thus true and irrelevant that "the Secretary did not need to include 'actually' to connote 'but for' causation"; "actually" defines the requisite *injury*, not the requisite *causality*.

The regulation says (it is worth repeating) that "harm" means (1) an act which (2) actually kills or injures wildlife. If that does not dispense with a proximate-cause requirement, I do not know what language would. And changing the regulation by judicial invention, even to achieve compliance with the statute, is not permissible. . . .

But since the Court is reading the regulation and the statute incorrectly in other respects, it may as well introduce this novelty as well — law a la carte. As I understand the regulation that the Court has created and held consistent with the statute that it has also created, habitat modification can constitute a "taking," but only if it results in the killing or harming of *individual* animals, and only if that consequence is the direct result of the modification. This means that the destruction of privately owned habitat that is essential, not for the feeding or nesting, but for the breeding, of butterflies, would not violate the Act, since it would not harm or kill any living butterfly. I, too, think it would not violate the Act — not for the utterly unsupported reason that habitat modifications fall outside the regulation if they happen not to kill or injure a living animal, but for the textual reason that only action directed at living animals constitutes a "take."

MCI Telecommunications Corp. v. American Telephone & Telegraph Co.

512 U.S. 218 (1994)

Justice SCALIA delivered the opinion of the Court.

[The 1934 Communications Act, 49 U.S.C. §203, requires long-distance telephone carriers to file tariffs for services and rates with the Federal Communications Commission (FCC) and charge customers only in accordance with filed tariffs. The Act, §203(b), authorizes the commission to "modify" these requirements. By rule, the FCC provided that only AT&T — historically the "dominant" long-distance carrier — was required to file tariffs, and that other new long-distance carriers, such as MCI, need not file tariffs.]

The dispute between the parties turns on the meaning of the phrase "modify any requirement" in §203(b)(2). Petitioners argue that it gives the Commission authority to make even basic and fundamental changes in the scheme created by that section. We disagree. The word "modify" — like a number of other English words employing the root "mod-" (deriving from the Latin word for "measure"), such as "moderate," "modulate," "modest," and "modicum" — has a connotation of increment or limitation. Virtually every dictionary we are aware of says that "to modify" means to change moderately or in minor fashion. See, e.g., Random House Dictionary of the English Language 1236 (2d ed. 1987) ("to change somewhat the form or qualities of; alter partially; amend"); Webster's Third New International Dictionary 1452 (1976) ("to make minor changes in the form or structure of; alter without transforming"); 9 Oxford English Dictionary 952 (2d ed. 1989) ("[t]o make partial changes in; to change (an object) in respect of some of its qualities; to alter or vary without radical transformation"); Black's Law Dictionary 1004 (6th ed. 1990) ("[t]o alter; to change in incidental or subordinate features; enlarge; extend; amend; limit; reduce").

In support of their position, petitioners cite dictionary definitions contained in or derived from a single source, Webster's Third New International Dictionary 1452 (1976) ("Webster's Third"), which includes among the meanings of "modify," "to make a basic or important change in." Petitioners contend that this establishes sufficient ambiguity to entitle the Commission to deference in its acceptance of the broader meaning, which in turn requires approval of its permissive detariffing policy [citing *Chevron*]. In short, they contend that the courts must defer to the agency's choice among available dictionary definitions. . . .

Most cases of verbal ambiguity in statutes involve . . . a selection between accepted alternative meanings shown as each by many dictionaries. One can envision (though a court case does not immediately come to mind) having to choose between accepted alternative meanings, one of which is so newly accepted that it has only been recorded by a single lexicographer. (Some dictionary must have been the very first to record the widespread use of "projection," for example, to mean "forecast.") But what petitioners demand that we accept as creating an ambiguity here is a rarity even rarer than that: a meaning set forth in a single dictionary (and, as we say, its progeny) which not only supplements the meaning contained in all other dictionaries, but contradicts one of the meanings contained in virtually all other dictionaries. Indeed, contradicts one of the alternative meanings contained in the out-of-step dictionary itself — for as we have observed, Webster's Third itself defines "modify" to connote both (specifically) major change and (specifically) minor change. It is hard to see how that can be. When the word "modify" has come to mean both "to change in some respects" and "to change fundamentally" it will in fact mean neither of those things. It will simply mean "to change," and some adverb will have to be called into service to indicate the great or small degree of the change.

If that is what the peculiar Webster's Third definition means to suggest has happened — and what petitioners suggest by appealing to Webster's Third — we simply disagree. "Modify," in our view, connotes moderate change. It might be good English to say that the French Revolution "modified" the status of the French nobility — but only because there is a figure of speech called understatement and a literary device known as sarcasm. And it might be unsurprising to discover a 1972 White House press release saying that "the Administration is modifying its position with regard to prosecution of the war in Vietnam" — but only because press agents tend to impart what is nowadays called "spin." Such intentional distortions, or simply careless or ignorant misuse, must have formed the basis for the usage that Webster's Third, and Webster's Third alone, reported.

It is perhaps gilding the lily to add this: In 1934, when the Communications Act became law — the most relevant time for determining a statutory term's meaning — Webster's Third was not yet even contemplated. To our knowledge all English dictionaries provided the narrow definition of "modify," including those published by G.&C. Merriam Company. See Webster's New International Dictionary 1577 (2d ed. 1934); Webster's Collegiate Dictionary 628 (4th ed. 1934). We have not the slightest doubt that is the meaning the statute intended.

Since an agency's interpretation of a statute is not entitled to deference when it goes beyond the meaning that the statute can bear . . . (the Commission's permissive detariffing policy can be justified only if it makes a less than radical or fundamental change in the Act's tariff-filing requirement.

Rate filings are, in fact, the essential characteristic of a rate-regulated industry. It is highly unlikely that Congress would leave the determination of whether an industry will be entirely, or even substantially, rate-regulated to agency discretion — and even more unlikely that it would achieve that through such a subtle device as permission to "modify" rate-filing requirements.

Bearing in mind, then, the enormous importance to the statutory scheme of the tariff-filing provision, we turn to whether what has occurred here can be considered a mere "modification." The Commission stresses that its detariffing policy applies only to nondominant carriers, so that the rates charged to over half of all consumers in the long-distance market are on file with the Commission. It is not clear to us that the proportion of customers affected, rather than the proportion of carriers affected, is the proper measure of the extent of the exemption (of course all carriers in the long-distance market are exempted, except AT&T). But even assuming it is, we think an elimination of the crucial provision of the statute for 40% of a major sector of the industry is much too extensive to be considered a "modification." "What we have here, in reality, is a fundamental revision of the statute, changing it from a scheme of rate regulation in long-distance common-carrier communications to a scheme of rate regulation only where effective competition does not exist. That may be a good idea, but it was not the idea Congress enacted into law in 1934,

[Justice O'Connor did not participate in the decision.]

[Justice STEVENS entered a dissenting opinion, joined by Justices BLACKMUN and SOUTER.]

The communications industry has an unusually dynamic character. In 1934, Congress authorized the Federal Communications Commission (FCC) to regulate "a field of enterprise the dominant characteristic of which was the rapid pace of its unfolding." National Broadcasting Co. v. United States, 319 U.S. 190, 219 (1943).

In response to new conditions in the communications industry, including stirrings of competition in the long-distance telephone market, the FCC in 1979 began reexamining its regulatory scheme. . . .

. . . The Commission plausibly concluded that any slight enforcement benefits a tariff-filing requirement might offer were outweighed by the burdens it would put on new entrants and consumers. . . .

According to the Court, the term "modify," as explicated in all but the most unreliable dictionaries, rules out the Commission's claimed authority to relieve nondominant carriers of the basic obligation to file tariffs. Dictionaries can be useful aids in statutory interpretation, but they are not substitute for close analysis of what words mean as used in a particular statutory context. Even if the sole possible meaning of "modify" were to make "minor" changes, further elaboration is needed to show why the detariffing policy should fail. The Commission came to its present policy through a series of rulings that gradually relaxed the filing requirements for nondominant carriers. Whether the current policy should count as a cataclysmic or merely an incremental departure from the §203(a) base-line depends on whether one focuses on particular carriers' obligations to file (in which case the Commission's policy arguably works a major shift) or on the statutory policies behind the tariff-filing requirement (which remain satisfied because market constraints on nondominant carriers obviate the need for rate-filing). . . .

The Court seizes upon a particular sense of the word "modify" at the expense of another, long-established meaning that fully supports the Commission's position. That word is first defined in Webster's Collegiate Dictionary 628 (4th ed. 1934) as meaning "to limit or reduce in extent or degree." The Commission's permissive detariffing policy fits comfortably within this common understanding of the term. The FCC has in effect adopted a general rule stating that "if you are dominant you must file, but if you are nondominant you need not." The Commission's partial detariffing policy — which excuses nondominant carriers from filing on condition that they remain nondominant — is simply a relaxation of a costly regulatory requirement that recent developments had rendered pointless and counterproductive in a certain class of cases. . . .

Whatever the best reading of §203(b)(2), the Commission's reading cannot in my view be termed unreasonable. It is informed (as ours is not) by a practical understanding of the role (or lack thereof) that filed tariffs play in the modern regulatory climate and in the telecommunications industry. . . .

Public Citizen v. Young

831 F.2d 1108 (D.C. Cir. 1987)

De Minimis & Admin Rulemaking [handwritten]

[The issue in this case was whether the FDA could allow an exemption to the literal language of the Delaney Clause, quoted below, for trivial or "de minimis" risks.]

WILLIAMS, Circuit Judge:

. . . Assuming that the quantitative risk assessments are accurate, as we do for these purposes, it seems altogether correct to characterize these risks as trivial. For example, CTFA notes that a consumer would run a one-in-a-million lifetime risk of cancer if he or she ate one peanut with the FDA-permitted level of aflatoxins once every 250 days (liver cancer). Another activity posing a one-in-a-million lifetime risk is spending 1,000 minutes (less than 17 hours) every year in the city of Denver — with its high elevation and cosmic radiation levels — rather than in the District of Columbia. Most of us would not regard these as high-risk activities. Those who indulge in them can hardly be thought of as living dangerously. Indeed, they are risks taken without a second thought by persons whose economic position allows them a broad range of choice.

According to the risk assessments here, the riskier dye poses one ninth as much risk as the peanut or Colorado hypothetical; the less risky one poses only one 19,000th as much. It may help put the one-in-a-million lifetime risk in perspective to compare it with a concededly dangerous activity, in which millions nonetheless engage, cigarette smoking. Each one-in-a-million risk amounts to less than one 200,000th the lifetime risk incurred by the average male smoker. Thus, a person would have to be exposed to more than 2,000 chemicals bearing the one-in-a-million lifetime risk, at the rates assumed in the risk assessment, in order to reach 100th the risk involved in smoking. To reach that level of risk with chemicals equivalent to the less risky dye (Orange No. 17), he would have to be exposed to more than 40 million such chemicals.

The Delaney Clause of the Color Additive Amendments provides as follows:

> a color additive . . . (ii) shall be deemed unsafe, and shall not be listed, for any use which will not result in ingestion of any part of such additive, if, after tests which are appropriate for the evaluation of the safety of additives for such use, or after other relevant exposure of man or animal to such additive, it is found by the Secretary to induce cancer in man or animal. . . .

21 U.S.C. §376(b)(5)(B).

The natural — almost inescapable — reading of this language is that if the Secretary finds the additive to "induce" cancer in animals, he must deny listing. Here, of course, the agency made precisely the finding that Orange No. 17 and Red No. 19 "induce[] cancer when tested in laboratory animals." . . .

Courts (and agencies) are not, of course, helpless slaves to literalism. One escape hatch, invoked by the government and CTFA here, is the de minimis doctrine, shorthand for *de minimis non curat lex* ("the law does not concern itself with trifles"). The doctrine — articulated in recent times in a series of decisions by Judge Leventhal — serves a number of purposes. One is to spare agency resources for more important matters. But that is a goal of dubious relevance here. The finding of trivial risk necessarily followed not only the elaborate animal testing, but also the quantitative risk assessment process itself; indeed, application of the doctrine required additional expenditure of agency resources.

More relevant is the concept that "notwithstanding the 'plain meaning' of a statute, a court must look beyond the words to the purpose of the act where its literal terms lead to 'absurd or futile results.'" Imposition of pointless burdens on regulated entities is obviously to be avoided if possible, especially as burdens on them almost invariably entail losses for their customers: here, obviously, loss of access to the colors made possible by a broad range of dyes.

. . . Assuming as always the validity of the risk assessments, we believe that the risks posed by the two dyes would have to be characterized as "acceptable." Accordingly, if the statute were to permit a de minimis exception, this would appear to be a case for its application.

Moreover, failure to employ a de minimis doctrine may lead to regulation that not only is "absurd or futile" in some general cost-benefit sense but also is directly contrary to the *primary* legislative goal. . . . In a certain sense, precisely that may be the effect here. The primary goal of the Act is human safety, but literal application of the Delaney Clause may in some instances increase risk. No one contends that the Color Additive Amendments impose a zero-risk standard for non-carcinogenic substances; if they did, the number of dyes passing muster might prove miniscule. As a result, makers of drugs and cosmetics who are barred from using a carcinogenic dye carrying a one-in-20-million lifetime risk may use instead a noncarcinogenic, but toxic, dye carrying, say, a one-in-10-million lifetime risk. The substitution appears to be a clear loss for safety.

Judge Leventhal articulated the standard for application of de minimis as virtually a presumption in its favor: "Unless Congress has been extraordinarily rigid, there is likely a basis for an implication of de minimis authority to provide [an] exemption when the burdens of regulation yield a gain of trivial or no value." But the doctrine obviously is not available to thwart a statutory command; it must be interpreted with a view to "implementing the legislative design." Nor is an agency to apply it on a finding merely that regulatory costs exceed regulatory benefits.

Here, we cannot find that exemption of exceedingly small (but measurable) risks tends to implement the legislative design of the color additive Delaney Clause. The language itself is rigid; the context — an alternative design admitting administrative discretion for all risks other than carcinogens tends to confirm that rigidity. . . .

[The court then examined the legislative history of the 1960 Color Additive Amendments, searching for indications that Congress might not have intended the Delaney Clause to be applied literally in all cases.]

Like all legislative history, this is hardly conclusive. But short of an explicit declaration in the statute barring use of a de minimis exception, this is perhaps as strong as it is likely to get. Facing the explicit claim that the Clause was "extraordinarily rigid," a claim well supported by the Clause's language in contrast with the bill's grants of discretion elsewhere, Congress persevered.

Moreover, our reading of the legislative history suggests some possible explanations for Congress's apparent rigidity. One is that Congress, and the nation in general (at least as perceived by Congress), appear to have been truly alarmed about the risks of cancer. This concern resulted in a close focus on substances increasing cancer threats and a willingness to take extreme steps to lessen even small risks. Congress hoped to reduce the incidence of cancer by banning carcinogenic dyes, and may also have hoped to lessen public fears by demonstrating strong resolve.

A second possible explanation for Congress's failure to authorize greater administrative discretion is that it perceived color additives as lacking any great value. . . . It is true that the legislation as a whole implicitly recognizes that color additives are of value, since one of its purposes was to allow tolerances for certain dyes — harmful but not carcinogenic — that would have been banned under the former law. . . . Nevertheless, there is evidence that Congress thought the public could get along without carcinogenic colors, especially in view of the existence of safer substitutes. Thus the legislators may have estimated the costs of an overly protective rule as trivial.

So far as we can determine, no one drew the legislators' attention to the way in which the Delaney Clause, interacting with the flexible standard for determining safety of non-carcinogens, might cause manufacturers to substitute more dangerous toxic chemicals for less dangerous carcinogens. But the obviously more stringent standard for carcinogens may rest on a view that cancer deaths are in some way more to be feared than others.

Finally, as we have already noted, the House committee (or its amanuenses) considered the possibility that its no-threshold assumption might prove false and contemplated a solution: renewed consideration by Congress.

Considering these circumstances — great concern over a specific health risk, the apparently low cost of protection, and the possibility of remedying any mistakes — Congress's enactment of an absolute rule seems less surprising.

Apart from their contentions on legislative history, the FDA and CTFA assert two grounds for a de minimis exception: an analysis of two cases applying de minimis concepts in the food and drug regulation context, and contentions that, because of scientific advances since enactment, the disallowance of de minimis authority would have preposterous results in related areas of food and drug law. . . .

Monsanto Co. v. Kennedy, [613 F.2d 947 (D.C. Cir. 1979)], considered whether acrylonitrile in beverage containers was a "food additive" within the meaning of the Food, Drug and Cosmetic Act's definition of that term. . . .

By operation of the second law of thermodynamics, any substance, obviously including acrylonitrile, will migrate in minute amounts from a bottle into a beverage within the bottle. Questions had been raised about its safety. The court found the FDA's decision to ban its use insufficiently well considered. In remanding the case for reconsideration, the court emphasized the FDA Commissioner's discretion to exclude a chemical from the statutory definition of food additives if "the level of migration into food . . . is so negligible as to present no public health or safety concerns." The opinion makes no suggestion that anyone supposed acrylonitrile to be carcinogenic, or that the Delaney Clause governing food additives was in any way implicated. Thus the case cannot support a view that the food additive Delaney Clause (or, obviously, the color additive one) admits of a de minimis exception.

Scott v. Food and Drug Administration, [728 F.2d 322 (6th Cir. 1989)], involves the color additive Delaney Clause, but is nonetheless distinguishable. . . . Application of a de minimis exception for *constituents* of a color additive, however, seems to us materially different from use of such a doctrine for the color additive itself. As the Scott court noted, the FDA's action was completely consistent with the plain language of the statute, as there was no finding that the dye caused cancer in animals. Here, as we have observed, application of a de minimis exception requires putting a gloss on the statute qualifying its literal terms.

Monsanto and *Scott* demonstrate that the de minimis doctrine is alive and well in the food and drug context, even on the periphery of the Delaney Clauses. But no case has applied it to limit the apparent meaning of any of those Clauses in their core operation.

The CTFA also argues that in a number of respects scientific advance has rendered obsolete any inference of congressional insistence on rigidity. . . . If the color additive Delaney Clause has no de minimis exception, it follows (they suggest) that the food additive one must be equally rigid. The upshot would be to deny the American people access to a healthy food supply.

As a historical matter, the argument is overdrawn: the House committee was clearly on notice that certain common foods and nutrients were suspected carcinogens. Beyond that, it is not clear that an interpretation of the food additive Delaney Clause identical with our interpretation of the color additive clause would entail the feared consequences. The food additive *definition* contains an exception for substances "generally recognized" as safe (known as the "GRAS" exception), an exception that has no parallel in the color additive definition, 21 U.S.C. §321(t)(1). That definition may permit a de minimis exception at a stage that logically precedes the FDA's ever reaching the food additive Delaney Clause. Indeed, *Monsanto* so holds — though, as we have noted, in a case not trenching upon the food additive Delaney Clause. Moreover, the GRAS exception itself builds in special protection for substances used in food prior to January 1, 1958, which may be shown to be safe "through either scientific procedures or experience based on common use in food." Indeed, the Kistiakowsky Report, filed with the [1960] House committee, stated that the grandfathering provision of the food additives Delaney Clause "considerably narrows [its] effect . . . on industry and the public."

The relationship of the GRAS exception and the food additive Delaney Clause clearly poses a problem: if the food additive definition allows the FDA to classify as GRAS substances carrying trivial risks . . . but the food additive Delaney Clause is absolute, then

Congress has adopted inconsistent provisions. . . . On the other hand, if (1) the GRAS exception does not encompass substances with trivial carcinogenic effect (especially if its special provision for substances used before 1958 does not do so for long-established substances), and (2) the food additive Delaney Clause is as rigid as we find the color additive clause to be, conceivably the consequences identified by the CTFA, or some of them, may follow. All these are difficult questions, but they are neither before us nor is their answer foreordained by our decision here.

Moreover, we deal here only with the color additive Delaney Clause, not the one for food additives. Although the clauses have almost identical wording, the context is clearly different. Without having canvassed the legislative history of the food additive Delaney Clause, we may safely say that its proponents could not have regarded as trivial the social cost of banning those parts of the American diet that CTFA argues are at risk.

Finally, even a court decision construing the food additive provisions to require a ban on dietary essentials would not, in fact, bring about such a ban. As Secretary Flemming noted, in words selected by the House Report for quotation, the FDA could bring critical new discoveries to Congress's attention. If the present law would lead to the consequences predicted, we suppose that the FDA would do so, and that Congress would respond.

After Public Citizen initiated the litigation, the FDA published a notice embellishing the preamble to its initial safety determinations. These notices effectively apply quantitative risk assessment at the stage of determining whether a substance "induce[s] cancer in man or animal." They assert that even where a substance does cause cancer in animals in the conventional sense of the term, the FDA may find that it does not "induce cancer in man or animal" within the meaning of 21 U.S.C. §376(b)(5)(B). It is not crystal clear whether such a negative finding would flow simply from a quantitative risk assessment finding the risk to be trivial for humans under conditions of intended use, or whether it would require a projection back to the laboratory animals: i.e., an assessment that the risk would be trivial for animals exposed to the substance in quantities proportional to the exposure hypothesized for human risk assessment purposes. (Perhaps the distinction is without a difference.) . . .

The notices acknowledged that the words "to induce cancer" had not been "rigorously and unambiguously" so limited in the previous notices. This is a considerable understatement. The original determinations were quite unambiguous in concluding that the colors induced cancer in animals in valid tests. . . .

The plain language of the Delaney Clause covers all animals exposed to color additives, including laboratory animals exposed to high doses. It would be surprising if it did not. High-dose exposures are standard testing procedure, today just as in 1960; such high doses are justified to offset practical limitations on such tests: compared to expected exposure of millions of humans over long periods, the time periods are short and the animals few. Many references in the legislative history reflect awareness of reliance on animal testing, and at least the more sophisticated participants must have been aware that this meant high-dose testing. A few so specified.

All this indicates to us that Congress did not intend the FDA to be able to take a finding that a substance causes only trivial risk in humans and work back from that to a finding that the substance does not "induce cancer in . . . animals." This is simply the basic question — is the operation of the clause automatic once the FDA makes a finding of carcinogenicity in animals? — in a new guise. The only new argument offered in the notices is that, without the new interpretation, only "primitive techniques" could be used.

In fact, of course, the agency is clearly free to incorporate the latest breakthroughs in animal testing; indeed, here it touted the most recent animal tests as "state of the art." The limitation on techniques is only that the agency may not, once a color additive is found to induce cancer in test animals in the conventional sense of the term, undercut the statutory consequence. As we find the FDA's construction "contrary to clear congressional intent," we need not defer to it.

In sum, we hold that the Delaney Clause of the Color Additive Amendments does not contain an implicit de minimis exception for carcinogenic dyes with trivial risks to humans. We based this decision on our understanding that Congress adopted an "extraordinarily rigid" position, denying the FDA authority to list a dye once it found it to "induce cancer in . . . animals" in the conventional sense of the term. We believe that, in the color additive context, Congress intended that if this rule produced unexpected or undesirable consequences, the agency should come to it for relief. That moment may well have arrived, but we cannot provide the desired escape.

Food and Drug Administration v. Brown & Williamson Tobacco Corporation

529 U.S. 120 (2000)

Justice O'CONNOR delivered the opinion of the Court.

This case involves one of the most troubling public health problems facing our Nation today: the thousands of premature deaths that occur each year because of tobacco use. In 1996, the Food and Drug Administration (FDA), after having expressly disavowed any such authority since its inception, asserted jurisdiction to regulate tobacco products. The FDA concluded that nicotine is a "drug" within the meaning of the Food, Drug, and Cosmetic Act (FDCA or Act), as amended, 21 U.S.C. §301 et seq., and that cigarettes and smokeless tobacco are "combination products" that deliver nicotine to the body. Pursuant to this authority, it promulgated regulations intended to reduce tobacco consumption among children and adolescents. The agency believed that, because most tobacco consumers begin their use before reaching the age of 18, curbing tobacco use by minors could substantially reduce the prevalence of addiction in future generations and thus the incidence of tobacco-related death and disease.

[In] this case, we believe that Congress has clearly precluded the FDA from asserting jurisdiction to regulate tobacco products. Such authority is inconsistent with the intent that Congress has expressed in the FDCA's overall regulatory scheme and in the tobacco-specific legislation that it has enacted subsequent to the FDCA. In light of this clear intent, the FDA's assertion of jurisdiction is impermissible.

I

The FDCA grants the FDA, as the designee of the Secretary of Health and Human Services, the authority to regulate, among other items, "drugs" and "devices." The Act defines "drug" to include "articles (other than food) intended to affect the structure or any function of the body." 21 U.S.C. §321(g)(l)(C). It defines "device," in part, as "an instrument, apparatus, implement, machine, contrivance, . . . or other similar or related article, including any component, part, or accessory, which is . . . intended to affect the structure or any function of the body." §321(h). The Act also grants the FDA the authority to regulate so-called "combination products," which "constitute a combination of a drug, device, or biologic product." §353(g)(1). The FDA has construed this provision as giving it the discretion to regulate combination products as drugs, as devices, or as both.

On August 28, 1996, the FDA issued a final rule entitled "Regulations Restricting the Sale and Distribution of Cigarettes and Smokeless Tobacco to Protect Children and Adolescents." The FDA determined that nicotine is a "drug" and that cigarettes and smokeless tobacco are "drug delivery devices," and therefore it had jurisdiction under the FDCA to regulate tobacco products as customarily marketed — that is, without manufacturer claims of therapeutic benefit. First, the FDA found that tobacco products "'affect the structure or any function of the body'" because nicotine "has significant pharmacological effects." Specifically, nicotine "exerts psychoactive, or mood-altering, effects on the brain" that cause and sustain addiction, have both tranquilizing and stimulating effects, and control weight. Second, the FDA determined that these effects were "intended" under the FDCA because they "are so widely known and foreseeable that [they] may be deemed to have been intended by the manufacturers"; consumers use tobacco products "predominantly or nearly exclusively" to obtain these effects; and the statements, research, and actions of manufacturers revealed that they "have 'designed' cigarettes to provide pharmacologically active doses of nicotine to consumers." Finally, the agency concluded that cigarettes and smokeless tobacco are "combination products" because, in addition to containing nicotine, they include device components that deliver a controlled amount of nicotine to the body.

Having resolved the jurisdictional question, the FDA next explained the policy justifications for its regulations, detailing the deleterious health effects associated with tobacco use. It found that tobacco consumption was "the single leading cause of preventable death in the United States." According to the FDA, "more than 400,000 people die each year from tobacco-related illnesses, such as cancer, respiratory illnesses, and heart disease." The agency also determined that the only way to reduce the amount of tobacco-related illness and mortality was to reduce the level of addiction, a goal that could be accomplished only by preventing children and adolescents from starting to use tobacco. . . .

Based on these findings, the FDA promulgated regulations concerning tobacco products' promotion, labeling, and accessibility to children and adolescents. The access regulations prohibit the sale of cigarettes or smokeless tobacco to persons younger than 18; require retailers to verify through photo identification the age of all purchasers younger than 27; prohibit the sale of cigarettes in quantities smaller than 20; prohibit the distribution of free samples; and prohibit sales through self-service displays and vending machines except in adult-only locations. The promotion regulations require that any print advertising appear in a black-and-white, text-only format unless the publication in which it appears is read almost exclusively by adults; prohibit outdoor advertising within 1,000 feet of any public playground or school; prohibit the distribution of any promotional items, such as T-shirts or hats, bearing the manufacturer's brand name; and prohibit a manufacturer from sponsoring any athletic, musical, artistic, or other social or cultural event using its brand name. The labeling regulation requires that the statement, "A Nicotine-Delivery Device for Persons 18 or Older," appear on all tobacco product packages.

The FDA promulgated these regulations pursuant to its authority to regulate "restricted devices." See 21 U.S.C. §360j(e). The FDA construed §353(g)(1) as giving it the discretion to regulate "combination products" using the Act's drug authorities, device authorities, or bgth, depending on "how the public health goals of the act can be best accomplished." Given the greater flexibility in the FDCA for the regulation of devices, the FDA determined that "the device authorities provide the most appropriate basis for regulating cigarettes and smokeless tobacco." Under 21 U.S.C. §360j(e), the agency may "require that a device be restricted to sale, distribution, or use . . . upon such other conditions as [the FDA] may prescribe in such regulation, if, because of its potentiality for harmful effect or the collateral measures necessary to its use, [the FDA] determines that there cannot otherwise be reasonable assurance of its safety and effectiveness." The FDA reasoned that its regulations fell within the authority granted by §360j(e) because they related to the sale or distribution of tobacco products and were necessary for providing a reasonable assurance of safety.

II

The FDA's assertion of jurisdiction to regulate tobacco products is founded on its conclusions that nicotine is a "drug" and that cigarettes and smokeless tobacco are "drug delivery devices." . . . [A]ssuming, *arguendo*, that a product can be "intended to affect the structure or any function of the body" absent claims of therapeutic or medical benefit, the FDA's claim to jurisdiction contravenes the clear intent of Congress.

. . . Under *Chevron*, a reviewing court must first ask "whether Congress has directly spoken to the precise question at issue." If Congress has done so, the inquiry is at an end; the court "must give effect to the unambiguously expressed intent of Congress." [In] determining whether Congress has specifically addressed the question at issue, a reviewing court should not confine itself to examining a particular statutory provision in isolation. The meaning — or ambiguity — of certain words or phrases may only become evident when placed in context. [We] find that Congress has directly spoken to the issue here and precluded the FDA's jurisdiction to regulate tobacco products.

A

Viewing the FDCA as a whole, it is evident that one of the Act's core objectives is to ensure that any product regulated by the FDA is "safe" and "effective" for its intended use. This essential purpose pervades the FDCA. . . . [T]here must be a "reasonable assurance of the safety and effectiveness of the device." Even the "restricted device" provision pursuant to which the FDA promulgated the regulations at issue here authorizes the agency to place conditions on the sale or distribution of a device specifically when "there cannot otherwise be reasonable assurance of its safety and effectiveness." 21 U.S.C. §360j(e). Thus, the Act generally requires the FDA to prevent the marketing of any drug or device where the "potential for inflicting death or physical injury is not offset by the possibility of therapeutic benefit."

In its rulemaking proceeding, the FDA quite exhaustively documented that "tobacco products are unsafe," "dangerous," and "cause great pain and suffering from illness.["] . . . These findings logically imply that, if tobacco products were "devices" under the FDCA, the FDA would be required to remove them from the market. Consider, first, the FDCA's provisions concerning the misbranding of drugs or devices. The Act prohibits "the introduction or delivery for introduction into interstate commerce of any food, drug, device, or cosmetic that is adultered or misbranded." 21 U.S.C. §331(a). In light of the FDA's findings, two distinct FDCA provisions would render cigarettes and smokeless tobacco misbranded devices. First, §352(j) deems a drug or device misbranded "if it is dangerous to health when used in the dosage or manner, or with the frequency or duration prescribed, recommended, or suggested in the labeling thereof." The FDA's findings make clear that tobacco products are "dangerous to health" when used in the manner prescribed. Second, a drug or device is misbranded under the Act "unless its labeling bears . . . adequate directions for use . . . in such manner and form, as are necessary for the protection of users," except where such directions are "not necessary for the protection of the public health." §352(f)(1). Given the FDA's conclusions concerning the health consequences of tobacco use, there are no directions that could adequately protect consumers. That is, there are no directions that could make tobacco products safe for obtaining their intended effects. Thus, were tobacco products within the FDA's jurisdiction, the Act would deem them misbranded devices that could not be introduced into interstate commerce. . . .

Second, the FDCA requires the FDA to place all devices that it regulates into one of three classifications. The agency relies on a device's classification in determining the degree of control and regulation necessary to ensure that there is "a reasonable assurance of safety and effectiveness." The FDA has yet to classify tobacco products. Instead, the regulations at issue here represent so-called "general controls," which the Act entitles the agency to impose in advance of classification. Although the FDCA prescribes no deadline for device classification, the FDA has stated that it will classify tobacco products "in a future rulemaking" as required by the Act. Given the FDA's findings regarding the health consequences of tobacco use, the agency would have to place cigarettes and smokeless tobacco in Class III because, even after the application of the Act's available controls, they would "present a potential unreasonable risk of illness or injury." As Class III devices, tobacco products would be subject to the FDCA's premarket approval process. Under these provisions, the FDA would be prohibited from approving an application for premarket approval without "a showing of reasonable assurance that such device is safe under the conditions of use prescribed, recommended, or suggested on the labeling thereof." 21 U.S.C. §360e(d)(2)(A). In view of the FDA's conclusions regarding the health effects of tobacco use, the agency would have no basis for finding any such reasonable assurance of safety. Thus, once the FDA fulfilled its statutory obligation to classify tobacco products, it could not allow them to be marketed.

The FDCA's misbranding and device classification provisions therefore make evident that were the FDA to regulate cigarettes and smokeless tobacco, the Act would require the agency to ban them. . . . Congress, however, has foreclosed the removal of tobacco products from the market. A provision of the United States Code currently in force states that "the marketing of tobacco constitutes one of the greatest basic industries of the United States with ramifying activities which directly affect interstate and foreign commerce at every point, and stable conditions therein are necessary to the general welfare." 7 U.S.C. §1311(a). More importantly, Congress has directly addressed the problem of tobacco and health through legislation on six occasions since 1965. When Congress enacted these statutes, the adverse health consequences of tobacco use were well known, as were nicotine's pharmacological effects. . . . Congress' decisions to regulate labeling and advertising and to adopt the express policy of protecting "commerce and the national economy . . . to the maximum extent" reveal its intent that tobacco products remain on the market. . . .

The FDA apparently recognized this dilemma and concluded, somewhat ironically, that tobacco products are actually "safe" within the meaning of the FDCA. In promulgating its regulations, the agency conceded that "tobacco products are unsafe, as that term is conventionally understood." Nonetheless, the FDA reasoned that, in determining whether a device is safe under the Act, it must consider "not only the risks presented by a product but also any of the countervailing effects of use of that product, including the consequences of not permitting the product to be marketed." Applying this standard, the FDA found that, because of the high level of addiction among tobacco users, a ban would likely be "dangerous." . . . The FDA therefore concluded that, "while taking cigarettes and smokeless tobacco off the market could prevent some people from becoming addicted and reduce death and disease for others, the record does not establish that such a ban is the appropriate public health response under the act."

It may well be, as the FDA asserts, that "these factors must be considered when developing a regulatory scheme that achieves the best public health result for these products." But the FDA's judgment that leaving tobacco products on the market "is more effective in achieving public health goals than a ban," is no substitute for the specific safety determinations required by the FDCA's various operative provisions. Several provisions in the Act require the FDA to determine that the *product itself* is safe as used by consumers. That is, the product's probable therapeutic benefits must outweigh its risk of harm. In contrast, the FDA's conception of safety would allow the agency, with respect to each provision of the FDCA that requires the agency to determine a product's "safety" or "dangerousness," to compare the aggregate health effects of alternative administrative actions. This is a qualitatively different inquiry. Thus, although the FDA has concluded that a ban would be "dangerous," it has *not* concluded that tobacco products are "safe" as that term is used throughout the Act.

Considering the FDCA as a whole, it is clear that Congress intended to exclude tobacco products from the FDA's jurisdiction. A fundamental precept of the FDCA is that any product regulated by the FDA — but not banned — must be safe for its intended use. Various provisions of the Act make clear that this refers to the safety of using the product to obtain its intended effects, not the public health ramifications of alternative administrative actions by the FDA. That is, the FDA must determine that there is a reasonable assurance that the product's therapeutic benefits outweigh the risk of harm to the consumer. According to this standard, the FDA has concluded that, although tobacco products might be effective in delivering certain pharmacological effects, they are "unsafe" and "dangerous" when used for these purposes. Consequently, if tobacco products were within the FDA's jurisdiction, the Act would require the FDA to remove them from the market entirely. But a ban would contradict Congress' clear intent as expressed in its more recent, tobacco-specific legislation. The inescapable conclusion is that there is no room for tobacco products within the FDCA's regulatory scheme. If they cannot be used safely for any therapeutic purpose, and yet they cannot be banned, they simply do not fit.

B

In determining whether Congress has spoken directly to the FDA's authority to regulate tobacco, we must also consider in greater detail the tobacco-specific legislation that Congress has enacted over the past 35 years. . . .

Congress has enacted six separate pieces of legislation since 1965 addressing the problem of tobacco use and human health. Those statutes, among other things, require that health warnings appear on all packaging and in all print and outdoor advertisements;

prohibit the advertisement of tobacco products through "any medium of electronic communication" subject to regulation by the Federal Communications Commission (FCC); require the Secretary of Health and Human Services (HHS) to report every three years to Congress on research findings concerning "the addictive property of tobacco," 42 U.S.C. §290aa-2(b)(2); and make States' receipt of certain federal block grants contingent on their making it unlawful "for any manufacturer, retailer, or distributor of tobacco products to sell or distribute any such product to any individual under the age of 18," §300x-26(a)(1).

In adopting each statute, Congress has acted against the backdrop of the FDA's consistent and repeated statements that it lacked authority under the FDCA to regulate tobacco absent claims of therapeutic benefit by the manufacturer. In fact, on several occasions over this period, and after the health consequences of tobacco use and nicotine's pharmacological effects had become well known, Congress considered and rejected bills that would have granted the FDA such jurisdiction. Under these circumstances, it is evident that Congress' tobacco-specific statutes have effectively ratified the FDA's long-held position that it lacks jurisdiction under the FDCA to regulate tobacco products. Congress has created a distinct regulatory scheme to address the problem of tobacco and health, and that scheme, as presently constructed, precludes any role for the FDA.

. . . As the FDA concedes, it never asserted authority to regulate tobacco products as customarily marketed until it promulgated the regulations at issue here. . . . The FDA's position was also consistent with Congress' specific intent when it enacted the FDCA. Before the Act's adoption in 1938, the FDA's predecessor agency, the Bureau of Chemistry, announced that it lacked authority to regulate tobacco products under the Pure Food and Drug Act of 1906, unless they were marketed with therapeutic claims. . . .

Moreover, before enacting the FCLAA in 1965, Congress considered and rejected several proposals to give the FDA the authority to regulate tobacco. . . .

Not only did Congress reject the proposals to grant the FDA jurisdiction, but it explicitly preempted any other regulation of cigarette labeling: "No statement relating to smoking and health, other than the statement required by . . . this Act, shall be required on any cigarette package." Id., §5(a), 79 Stat. 283. The regulation of product labeling, however, is an integral aspect of the FDCA, both as it existed in 1965 and today. The labeling requirements currently imposed by the FDCA, which are essentially identical to those in force in 1965, require the FDA to regulate the labeling of drugs and devices to protect the safety of consumers. . . . Further, the FCLAA evidences Congress' intent to preclude *any* administrative agency from exercising significant policymaking authority on the subject of smoking and health. In addition to prohibiting any additional requirements for cigarette labeling, the FCLAA provided that "no statement relating to smoking and health shall be required in the advertising of any cigarettes the packages of which are labeled in conformity with the provisions of this Act." Thus, in reaction to the FTC's attempt to regulate cigarette labeling and advertising, Congress enacted a statute reserving exclusive control over both subjects to itself. Subsequent tobacco-specific legislation followed a similar pattern. . . .

Taken together, these actions by Congress over the past 35 years preclude an interpretation of the FDCA that grants the FDA jurisdiction to regulate tobacco products. We do not rely on Congress' failure to act — its consideration and rejection of bills that would have given the FDA this authority — in reaching this conclusion. Indeed, this is not a case of simple inaction by Congress that purportedly represents its acquiescence in an agency's position. To the contrary, Congress has enacted several statutes addressing the

particular subject of tobacco and health, creating a distinct regulatory scheme for cigarettes and smokeless tobacco. . . . Under these circumstances, it is clear that Congress'
tobacco-specific legislation has effectively ratified the FDA's previous position that it lacks
jurisdiction to regulate tobacco. . . .

Although the dissent takes issue with our discussion of the FDA's change in position,
our conclusion does not rely on the fact that the FDA's assertion of jurisdiction represents
a sharp break with its prior interpretation of the FDCA. Certainly, an agency's initial interpretation of a statute that it is charged with administering is not "carved in stone." [The]
consistency of the FDA's prior position is significant in this case for a different reason: it
provides important context to Congress' enactment of its tobacco-specific legislation. . . .
Although not crucial, the consistency of the FDA's prior position bolsters the conclusion
that when Congress created a distinct regulatory scheme addressing the subject of tobacco
and health, it understood that the FDA is without jurisdiction to regulate tobacco products
and ratified that position. . . .

C

Finally, our inquiry into whether Congress has directly spoken to the precise question at issue is shaped, at least in some measure, by the nature of the question presented.
Deference under *Chevron* to an agency's construction of a statute that it administers is
premised on the theory that a statute's ambiguity constitutes an implicit delegation from
Congress to the agency to fill in the statutory gaps. In extraordinary cases, however, there
may be reason to hesitate before concluding that Congress has intended such an implicit
delegation. Cf. Breyer, Judicial Review of Questions of Law and Policy, 38 Admin.
L. Rev. 363, 370 (1986) ("A court may also ask whether the legal question is an important one. Congress is more likely to have focused upon, and answered, major questions,
while leaving interstitial matters to answer themselves in the course of the statute's daily
administration.").

This is hardly an ordinary case. Contrary to its representations to Congress since
1914, the FDA has now asserted jurisdiction to regulate an industry constituting a significant portion of the American economy. . . . Given this history and the breadth of the
authority that the FDA has asserted, we are obliged to defer not to the agency's expansive
construction of the statute, but to Congress' consistent judgment to deny the FDA this
power.

. . . As in *MCI*, we are confident that Congress could not have intended to delegate
a decision of such economic and political significance to an agency in so cryptic a
fashion. . . . [Reading] the FDCA as a whole, as well as in conjunction with Congress'
subsequent tobacco-specific legislation, it is plain that Congress has not given the FDA
the authority that it seeks to exercise here. For these reasons, the judgment of the Court of
Appeals for the Fourth Circuit is affirmed.

It is so ordered.

Justice BREYER, with whom Justice STEVENS, Justice SOUTER, and Justice GINSBURG
join, dissenting.

[In] its own interpretation, the majority nowhere denies the following two salient
points. First, tobacco products (including cigarettes) fall within the scope of this statutory
definition, read literally. Cigarettes achieve their mood-stabilizing effects through the
interaction of the chemical nicotine and the cells of the central nervous system. Both

cigarette manufacturers and smokers alike know of, and desire, that chemically induced result. Hence, cigarettes are "intended to affect" the body's "structure" and "function," in the literal sense of these words.

Second, the statute's basic purpose — the protection of public health — supports the inclusion of cigarettes within its scope. . . .

Despite the FDCA's literal language and general purpose (both of which support the FDA's finding that cigarettes come within its statutory authority), the majority nonetheless reads the statute as *excluding* tobacco products for two basic reasons:

(1) The FDCA does not "fit" the case of tobacco because the statute requires the FDA to prohibit dangerous drugs or devices (like cigarettes) outright, and the agency concedes that simply banning the sale of cigarettes is not a proper remedy; and

(2) Congress has enacted other statutes, which, when viewed in light of the FDA's long history of denying tobacco-related jurisdiction and considered together with Congress' failure explicitly to grant the agency tobacco-specific authority, demonstrate that Congress did not intend for the FDA to exercise jurisdiction over tobacco.

In my view, neither of these propositions is valid. . . .

The majority nonetheless reaches the "inescapable conclusion" that the language and structure of the FDCA as a whole "simply do not fit" the kind of public health problem that tobacco creates. That is because, in the majority's view, the FDCA requires the FDA to ban outright "dangerous" drugs or devices (such as cigarettes); yet, the FDA concedes that an immediate and total cigarette-sale ban is inappropriate.

This argument is curious because it leads with similarly "inescapable" force to precisely the opposite conclusion, namely, that the FDA *does* have jurisdiction but that it must ban cigarettes. More importantly, the argument fails to take into account the fact that a statute interpreted as requiring the FDA to pick a more dangerous over a less dangerous remedy would be a perverse statute, *causing*, rather than preventing, unnecessary harm whenever a total ban is likely the more dangerous response. . . .

[T]he statute's language does not restrict the FDA's remedial powers in this way. The FDCA permits the FDA to regulate a "combination product" — i.e., a "device" (such as a cigratte) that contains a "drug" (such as nicotine) — under its "device" provisions. 21 U.S.C. §353(g)(1). And the FDCA's "device" provisions explicitly grant the FDA wide remedial discretion. For example, where the FDA cannot "otherwise" obtain "reasonable assurance" of a device's "safety and effectiveness," the agency may restrict by regulation a product's "sale, distribution, or use" upon "*such . . . conditions as the Secretary may prescribe.* §360j(e)(1) (emphasis added). And the statutory section that most clearly addresses the FDA's power to ban (entitled "Banned devices") says that, where a device presents "an unreasonable and substantial risk of illness or injury," the Secretary "*may*" — not *must* — "initiate a proceeding . . . to make such device a banned device." §360(f)(a) (emphasis added).

The statute's language, then permits the agency to choose remedies consistent with its basic purpose — the overall protection of public health.

The second reason the FDCA does not require the FDA to select the more dangerous remedy is that, despite the majority's assertions to the contrary, the statute does not distinguish among the kinds of health effects that the agency may take into account when assessing safety. . . . [T]he FDCA expressly *permits* the FDA to take account of comparative safety in precisely this manner. See, e.g., 21 U.S.C. §360h(2)(B)(i)(II) (no device recall if "risk or recall" presents "a greater health risk than" no recall); §360h(a) (notification "unless" notification "would present a greater danger" than "no such notification"). . . .

In my view, where linguistically permissible, we should interpret the FDCA in light of Congress' overall desire to protect health. That purpose requires a flexible interpretation that both permits the FDA to take into account the realities of human behavior and allows it, in appropriate cases, to choose from its arsenal of statutory remedies. A statute so interpreted easily "fits" this, and other, drug- and device-related health problems.

In the majority's view, laws enacted since 1965 require us to deny jurisdiction, whatever the FDCA might mean in their absence. But why? Do those laws contain language barring FDA jurisdiction? The majority must concede that they do not. Do they contain provisions that are inconsistent with the FDA's exercise of jurisdiction? With one exception, the majority points to no such provision. Do they somehow repeal the principles of law that otherwise would lead to the conclusion that the FDA has jurisdiction in this area? The companies themselves deny making any such claim.

. . . [W]hatever individual Members of Congress after 1964 may have assumed about the FDA's jurisdiction, the laws they enacted did not embody any such "no jurisdiction" assumption. And one cannot automatically *infer* an antijurisdiction intent, as the majority does, for the later statutes are both (and similarly) consistent with quite a different congressional desire, namely, the intent to proceed without interfering with whatever authority the FDA otherwise may have possessed. . . .

Until the early 1990's, the FDA expressly maintained that the 1938 statute did not give it the power that it now seeks to assert. It then changed its mind. The majority agrees with me that the FDA's change of positions does not make a significant legal difference. Nevertheless, it labels those denials "important context" for drawing an inference about Congress' intent. In my view, the FDA's change of policy, like the subsequent statutes themselves, does nothing to advance the majority's position.

When it denied jurisdiction to regulate cigarettes, the FDA consistently stated *why* that was so. In 1963, for example, FDA administrators wrote that cigarettes did not satisfy the relevant FDCA definitions — in particular, the "intent" requirement — because cigarette makers did not sell their product with accompanying "therapeutic claims." . . .

What changed? For one thing, the FDA obtained evidence sufficient to prove the necessary "intent" despite the absence of specific "claims." This evidence, which first became available in the early 1990's, permitted the agency to demonstrate that the tobacco companies *knew* nicotine achieved appetite-suppressing, mood-stabilizing, and habituating effects through chemical (not psychological) means, even at a time when the companies were publicly denying such knowledge.

Moreover, scientific evidence of adverse health effects mounted, until, in the late 1980's, a consensus on the seriousness of the matter became firm. . . . Finally, administration policy changed. Earlier administrations may have hesitated to assert jurisdiction for the reasons prior Commissioners expressed. Commissioners of the current administration simply took a different regulatory attitude.

Nothing in the law prevents the FDA from changing its policy for such reasons. . . .

[O]ne might claim that courts, when interpreting statutes, should assume in close cases that a decision with "enormous social consequences," 1994 Hearings 69, should be made by democratically elected Members of Congress rather than by unelected agency administrators. If there is such a background cannon of interpretation, however, I do not believe it controls the outcome here.

Insofar as the decision to regulate tobacco reflects the policy of an administration, it is a decision for which that administration, and those politically elected officials who support it, must (and will) take responsibility. And the very importance of the decision taken there, as well as its attendant publicity, means that the public is likely to be aware of it and to hold those officials politically accountable. Presidents, just like Members of Congress, are elected by the public. Indeed, the President and Vice President are the *only* public officials whom the entire Nation elects. I do not believe that an administrative agency decision of this magnitude — one that is important, conspicuous, and controversial — can escape the kind of public scrutiny that is essential in any democracy. And such a review will take place whether it is the Congress or the Executive Branch that makes the relevant decision. . . .

Consequently, I dissent.

Notes on *Chevron*, Literalism, and Statutory Text

1. The key issue raised by the preceding cases involves *Chevron* step 1. A pervasive question is whether an agency is bound by what the Court sees as the "literal" or "ordinary" meaning of the statutory term, or whether the agency may use its specialized knowledge and democratic accountability to "bend" a term in the direction that makes best sense, all things considered. Can the results in these cases be reconciled with one another?

There appears to be a post-1990 trend in favor of less deference and toward greater reliance on the "plain meaning" of statutory terms. In addition to *MCI* and *Brown & Williamson*, see, e.g., Metropolitan Stevedore Co. v. Rambo, 521 U.S. 121 (1995); Brown v. Gardner, 513 U.S. 115 (1994); NLRB v. Health Care & Retirement Corp., 511 U.S. 571 (1994); Pierce, The Supreme Court's New Hypertextualism: A Prescription for Cacophony and Incoherence in the Administrative State, 95 Colum. L. Rev. 749 (1995). More generally, there has been a discernible movement toward the use of dictionaries in statutory interpretation. See Eskridge, The New Textualism, 37 UCLA L. Rev. 621 (1990); Note, Looking It Up, 107 Harv. L. Rev. 1437 (1995). The movement toward the use of dictionary definitions seems motivated by the idea that statutes should be interpreted in accordance with ordinary usage, partly for rule-of-law reasons; the dictionary might be seen as a good guide to ordinary usage. But should the dictionary really have such authority, in the face of an agency interpretation the other way? See generally the argument for "dynamic statutory construction" in W. Eskridge, Dynamic Statutory Construction (1996). But consider the rule-of-law values that might be served by an ordinary meaning, dictionary-based approach, and cf. I. Mueller, Hitler's Justice (1995), suggesting that in Nazi Germany, a primary technique for legal change was judicial reliance on the "purposes" of the law, rather than the text, and showing that a major strategy of the Allies after the war was to encourage German judges to refer to the "plain meaning" of legal texts.

2. There are, however, some contrary indications, in cases in which courts seem to bend statutory text to allow agencies to make sense rather than nonsense of the law. Consider, for example, the EPA's approach to lead contamination in water. The Safe Drinking Water Act requires the EPA to produce maximum contaminant level goals (MCLG) for water contaminants. 42 U.S.C. §300g-1(b). These goals are required to "be set at the level at which no known or anticipated adverse effects on the health of persons occur," with an adequate margin of safety. For lead, the EPA's MCLG was zero, because no safe threshold had been established. Once an MCLG is established, EPA is required to set a maximum contaminant level (MCL), to be set "as close to the maximum contaminant level goal as is feasible." The EPA is authorized not to set a maximum contaminant level, and to require "the use of a treatment technique in lieu of establishing" that level, if

it finds "that it is not economically or technologically feasible to ascertain the level of the contaminant." 42 U.S.C. §300g-1(b)(6)(D).

At first glance, this set of provisions has a familiar structure. The EPA is required to set a standard of performance, and not to require a "technique" for achieving the desired performance, unless it is not feasible to monitor water quality. For lead, then, we would expect EPA to set its MCL as close as "feasible" (economically and technologically) to the MCLG of zero, except if it was not "feasible" to ascertain the level of lead contamination. But this is not what EPA did, because of some distinctive features of the lead problem. Source water is basically lead-free; the real problem comes from corrosion of service lines and plumbing materials. With this point in mind, EPA refused to set any MCL for lead, on the ground that an MCL would require public water systems to use extremely aggressive corrosion control techniques, which, while economically and technologically "feasible," would be counterproductive, because they would increase the level of other contaminants in the water. What appeared to be the legally mandated solution would make the water less safe, not more so. The EPA therefore chose a more modest approach. Instead of issuing an MCL, it required all large water systems to institute certain corrosion control treatment, and required smaller systems to do so if and only if representative sampling found significant lead contamination.

Did the EPA violate the Safe Water Drinking Act? At first glance, it seems clear that it did. The EPA did not contend that an MCL was not "feasible" to implement, nor did it argue that it was not "feasible," in the economic or technological sense, to monitor lead levels in water. Nonetheless, the court upheld the agency's decision. American Water Works v. EPA, 40 F.3d 1266, 1271 (D.C. Cir. 1994). The court accepted the EPA's suggestion that the word "feasible" could be construed to mean "capable of being accomplished in a manner consistent with the Act." The court said that "case law is replete with examples of statutes the ordinary meaning of which is not necessarily what the Congress intended," and it added that "where a literal meaning of a statutory term would lead to absurd results," that term "has no plain meaning." Because an MCL would itself lead to more contamination, "it could lead to a result squarely at odds with the purpose of the Safe Drinking Water Act." The court therefore accepted EPA's view "that requiring public water systems to design and implement custom corrosion control plans for lead will result in optimal treatment of drinking water overall, i.e., treatment that deals adequately with lead without causing public water systems to violate drinking water regulations for other contaminants."

Consider the suggestion that this analysis is in considerable tension with some of the principal cases, because it amounts to a decision to allow agencies to disregard the text in the interest of rationality. Note also that in a series of cases, the D.C. Circuit has developed a principle authorizing agencies to make de minimis exceptions to regulatory requirements. The initial case was Monsanto Co. v. Kennedy, 613 F.2d 947 (D.C. Cir. 1979). There, the agency banned acrylonitrile on the ground that it counts as a "food additive," migrating in small amounts from bottles into drinks within bottles. The FDA concluded that the ban was justified on safety grounds, a conclusion that the court found inadequately justified. But what is more important in the case is the general language with which the court remanded the case to the FDA. The court stressed that the agency had discretion to exclude a chemical from the statutory definition of food additives if "the level of migration into food . . . is so negligible as to present no public health or safety concerns."

A related case presented the question whether the EPA was permitted to make categorical exemptions under the Prevention of Significant Deterioration program of the Clean Air Act. *Alabama Power Co. v. Costle*, 636 F.2d 323 (D.C. Cir. 1979). Here, the court spoke in more ambitious terms, showing considerable enthusiasm for de minimis exemptions. It announced that "[c]ategorical exemptions may be permissible as an exercise of agency power, inherent in most statutory schemes, to overlook circumstances that in context may fairly be considered de minimis. It is commonplace, of course, that the law does not concern itself with trifling matters, and this principle has often found application in the administrative context. Courts should be reluctant to apply the literal terms of a statute to mandate pointless expenditures." In fact the court expressly connected this principle with the idea that the court should "look beyond the words to the purpose of the act" to avoid "absurd or futile results." Thus the court concluded, in its broadest statement on the point, that "most regulatory statutes, including the Clean Air Act, permit" de minimis exemptions upon an adequate factual showing. There are many cases in the same vein. See, e.g., *Sierra Club v. EPA*, 992 F.2d 337, 343-345 (D.C. Cir. 1993); *EDF v. EPA*, 82 F.3d 451 (D.C. Cir. 1996); *Public Citizen v. FTC*, 869 F.2d 1541, 1556-1557 (D.C. Cir. 1989); *Ohio v. EPA*, 997 F.2d 1520,1535 (D.C. Cir. 1993) (suggesting that "the literal meaning of a statute need not be followed where the precise terms lead to absurd or futile results, or where failure to allow a de minimis exemption is contrary to the primary legislative goal").

Consider also *State of Michigan v. EPA*, 213 F.3d 663 (2000). At issue there was an EPA decision to approve a state implementation plan (SIP) for the regulation of ozone. The statutory term provided that SIPs must contain provisions adequately prohibiting "any source or other type of emissions activity within the state from emitting any air pollutants in amounts which will . . . contribute significantly to nonattainment in, or interfere with maintenance by, any other State with respect to any such national primary or secondary ambient air quality standard." 42 U.S.C. §7410(a)(2)(D)(I)(I). At first glance, this provision might well be read as a kind of absolute ban on "significantly contributing" pollutants. But the EPA did not understand it that way. Instead, the EPA reached a more subtle conclusion. It would adopt a low threshold for deciding whether a contribution was "significant." But the "significant contributors" would be required to reduce their ozone only by the amount achievable via "highly cost-effective controls," meaning those that could produce large reductions relatively cheaply. In states with high control costs, then, relatively low reductions would be required.

Challenging the EPA's interpretation, environmental groups urged that the statute banned any consideration of costs at all. In their view, "contribute significantly" made no room for an inquiry into the costs of compliance. The court rejected the argument, finding no "clear congressional intent to preclude consideration of costs." But the court obviously had a difficult time with the statutory terms "contribute significantly," which seem to refer to environmental damage, not to environmental damage measured in light of cost. In upholding the EPA's decision, the court insisted that significance should not "be measured in only one dimension," that of "health alone." In fact, in some settings, the term "begs a consideration of costs." In the court's view, EPA would be unable to determine "'significance' if it may consider only health," especially in light of the fact that ozone causes adverse health effects at any level. If adverse effects exist on all levels, the court asked, how can EPA possibly choose a standard without giving some weight to cost? This line of analysis might also be taken to suggest a willingness to allow agencies to depart from the literal text, if they are attempting to promote sense and rationality in the law. For general discussion of these issues, see Sunstein, Cost-Benefit Default Principles, 99 Mich. L. Rev. 1651 (2001).

3. Do *MCI* and *Brown & Williamson* create a general exception to *Chevron*? Do they suggest that "large" public policy issues cannot be resolved by agencies, but must be resolved by Congress? Perhaps such an exception could be justified on nondelegation grounds. Cf. Sunstein, Nondelegation Canons, 67 U. Chi. L. Rev. 315 (2000). Would such an exception be consistent with the basic point of *Chevron*? Consider Justice Breyer's objection that "large" public policy issues are subject to presidential control.

4. There are several possible "readings" of the majority opinion in *Sweet Home*. (1) The statute was ambiguous, and therefore *Chevron* deference was appropriate. (2) The statute, literally interpreted, strongly supported the government, and it is likely (though not certain) that any administration would be required, by the literal text, to reject Justice Scalia's position. (3) The statute, literally interpreted, did not support the government's interpretation, but courts properly allow the government some flexibility to adapt the "literal" text to facts and values as the Interior Department, accountable and specialized as it is, sees them.

If reading (3) is correct, is *Sweet Home* inconsistent with *MCI*, *Public Citizen*, and *American Mining Company*? If it is, are the latter cases wrong? Why should courts use the dictionary, or (what is not the same thing) ordinary understandings of statutory terms, to prevent agencies from adjusting the law to their own view of facts and values? Return to Justice Stevens's dissenting opinion in the *MCI* case; does it make sense to constrain agency interpretations in this way?

Do you read Justice Scalia's dissenting opinion in *Sweet Home* to say (1) the statute should be construed narrowly, so as to prevent arguably unconstitutional takings of private property, (2) the statute should be read in accordance with the long-standing and specifically legal understanding of what a "taking" of an animal is, or (3) the ordinary understanding of the statutory terms is what controls, and that ordinary understanding defeats the agency's view? On (1), consider the materials below on the relation between *Chevron* and the canons of construction. On (2), why should statutory terms, written by Congress for novel regulatory programs, be read in accordance with long-standing understandings based on old common law notions? Consider the possibility of defending Justice Scalia's approach by reference to the kind of jurisprudential thinking defended by Edmund Burke — a kind of thinking that values traditions and incremental developments, and that sees the law as a kind of organic whole, consistent over time and across different areas of concern. On (3), just what is the ordinary understanding of the statutory terms?

5. Suppose that OSHA decided to interpret its governing statute so as to require cost-benefit analysis. Should such an interpretation survive under *Chevron*? Note in this regard that there is an old principle of statutory interpretation to the effect that statutes will not be construed so as to create absurdity. Thus, courts sometimes interpret statutes more expansively than their text suggests, and also less expansively than their text suggests. See Riggs v. Palmer, 22 N.E. 188 (N.Y. 1889) (refusing to allow a nephew who murdered his uncle to inherit under his uncle's will, notwithstanding the apparently plain and contrary text of the inheritance statute); Church of the Holy Trinity v. United States, 143 U.S. 457 (1892) (allowing a church to pay for the importation of a rector into the United States, notwithstanding the apparently plain text of a broad statutory ban on employer payment for importation of employees). (For a challenge to the *Holy Trinity* decision, see Scalia, A Matter of Interpretation (1996).)

Might it be possible to argue that in the modern era, administrative agencies are, effectively, our common law courts, and that in view of their specialized competence and democratic pedigree, they should have greater latitude for adjusting text than the common law judges did? Compare Scalia, Judicial Deference to Agency Interpretations of Law, 1989 Duke L.J. 511 (arguing in favor of judicial insistence on text against agency interpretations), with Sunstein, Justice Scalia's Democratic Formalism, 102 Yale L.J. 529 (1997) (arguing for administrative flexibility to adapt statutory text, including literal text, to circumstances and values).

Why isn't Public Citizen v. Young a strong case for judicial deference to an administrative effort to prevent absurdity? Consider the agency's plight in the case. The Delaney Clause was written to promote human health by decreasing the risk of cancer; in the 1950s, carcinogens were hard to detect, and a detectable carcinogen was likely to be highly carcinogenic. In the 1990s, carcinogens are easy to detect, and some detectable carcinogens pose tiny risks. Many observers believe that in such circumstances, a "literal" reading of the Delaney Clause actually increases risks to human health by eliminating from the market substances that pose lower risks than those that are now in use (and that were tested with cruder techniques and that may well pose higher risks of, for example, heart disease).

In these circumstances, the agency sought to interpret the Delaney Clause so as to improve human health. If the factual record supported its conclusion, could it not be said that the agency was faithfully interpreting the statute under changed circumstances? See Lessig, Understanding Changed Readings: Fidelity and Translation, 47 Stan. L. Rev. 395 (1995).

Note that Congress largely repealed the Delaney Clause in 1996, so as to require exemptions of insignificant risks and to mandate a form of "reasonableness" balancing in the regulation of carcinogenic substances. Does this repeal support or undermine the outcome in Public Citizen v. Young?

Note on the Regulation of Carcinogens[10]

To understand several of these cases, it helps to consider some of the practical problems that OSHA, the FDA, and other safety agencies face when dealing with potential cancer-causing substances.

What is safety? Agencies obviously seek to make the workplace (or food additives or drugs) safe, or safer. But safety comes in degrees, not absolutes, and there is no widespread agreement about how safe. Consider, for example, the EPA's deliberations about whether to reduce permissible levels of arsenic in drinking water under the Safe Drinking Water Act. For many years, the maximum permissible level was 50 parts per billion (ppb). In response to fear of harm at lower levels, EPA considered reducing the permissible level to 3 ppb, 5 ppb, 10 ppb, and 20 ppb. The EPA estimated that as compared with the 50 ppb maximum, the 3 ppb maximum would avoid between 57 and 138 cancer cases; a 5 ppb maximum would avoid between 51 and 100 such cases; a 10 ppb limit would avoid between 37 and 56 such cases; and a 20 ppb limit between 19 and 20 such cases. See 66 Fed. Reg. at 7009 (2001). Is 3 ppb safe? Is 20 ppb? If the question of safety is unanswerable, what questions should agencies ask, when deciding what level to require? OSHA calls for removal of "significant risks." But how do we know which risks are significant? The Safe Drinking Water Act allows a form of cost-benefit balancing, which raises issues taken up below.

---

10. For the source of some of the facts contained in this Note, see S. Breyer, Regulation and Its Reform ch. 7 (1982).

Regulatory objectives. There is not even agreement about the precise objectives of safety regulation. Some proponents of regulation argue that consumers or workers do not have adequate information to evaluate risks; the regulator should supply information that the market does not offer. Others claim that wage rates or product prices do not reflect the cost of disease or accidents that accompany the related work or product; regulators should correct for this adverse "spillover." It is also asserted, for example, that workers, even when fully informed, lack the power to bargain for the safe workplaces they need. (But note that in such circumstances regulation may make workers worse off, by banning them from making their preferred "deal," and in the process giving them more safety but less in the way of wages.) And still others may seek safety regulation on the paternalistic ground that workers or buyers are not the best judges of their long-term interest and tend, even when informed, to choose an unduly dangerous workplace or product. This argument might be fortified by reference to the problems people have in dealing with low-probability events. See R. Thaler, Quasi-Rational Economics (1993); Tversky & Kahneman, Judgment Under Uncertainty: Heuristics and Biases, 185 Science 1124 (1978); Tversky & Kahneman, Rational Choice and the Framing of Decisions, 59 J. Bus. 251 (1986).

Disagreement about the underlying rationale can be covered up for a while by agreement that the objective is "safety." But differences reemerge as soon as one asks "How much safety?" No one believes it is possible to eliminate all risk. But one's view of the "proper rationale" for safety regulation might well affect one's view of how much, or what sort, of risk is tolerable.

Practical problems. Several practical difficulties surrounding regulation of carcinogens make uncertainty and disagreement all too likely once an agency attempts to make particular judgments. In the case of arsenic, for example, the EPA did not have direct information about cancer risks between 3 ppb and 50 ppb. It had to extrapolate from existing epidemiological data, involving much higher exposure levels, and mostly coming from Taiwan. To come up with specific numbers, it had to make some controversial judgments. Consider just two.

- It rejected the claim that the evidence from Taiwan was unreliable, even though some people urged that the health and diet of the Taiwanese population led to an overstatement of the risk faced by Americans.
- It assumed a "linear" dose-response curve, meaning that as exposure to arsenic is decreased, the incidence of cancer falls by a straight line, rather than falling more rapidly at low levels than at high levels. This was especially controversial, because the National Research Council, on which EPA generally relied, urged that a sublinear curve was more likely. Federal agencies generally assume a linear curve, though many scientists claim that this is a policy choice, not a scientifically defensible one. A pervasive issue, referred to below, is the choice of dose-response curves; they come in many shapes, and often we lack reliable data for the carcinogenic that concerns us. See Sunstein, The Arithmetic of Arsenic, available at www.aei.brookings.org/publications/abstract.asp?pID=157.

Testing for risk. There are over 63,000 chemicals in common use in the United States. Human beings are generally exposed to such chemicals in small amounts over a long period of time, producing a very small cumulative individual risk. The problem is to find practical tests that will identify the different levels of risk posed by different chemicals. There are a few inexpensive tests (such as the Ames salmonella test) that can narrow the field of suspects (by showing, for example, whether a chemical can alter DNA). But these tests are crude. Safety agencies must rely on far more expensive "epidemiological" tests (as in the arsenic case) or "animal" tests, which require increased amounts of both time and money. The National Cancer Institute has noted that to test each substance typically involves several years, several hundred test animals, and several hundred thousand dollars. And the tests all too often yield results that are ambiguous.

For example, the most accurate type of test, in principle, is a prospective epidemiologic test on a human population. One group receives the substance; a carefully selected control group does not. The test is "double blind," in that neither administrator nor recipient knows who receives which substance. Results are matched to see whether the exposed group is more likely to contract the disease.

While such a test might work for a large, immediate risk, it is impractical in the case of a small, delayed risk, because the number of controls needed is too great and the time of observation too lengthy. To obtain a rough idea of the magnitude of the problem, imagine that the risk of a person in the population at large getting bladder cancer is 1 in 6000. If one wishes to test a substance that in reality doubles the risk of bladder cancer, a test group of 6000 and a control group of 6000 are far too small. One could not be certain whether a result showing that two exposed persons and one control person developed bladder cancer was not just chance — like heads on a coin flip coming up twice in a row. To know that there are fewer than 5 chances out of 100 that this result is due to chance alone (which statisticians call the 95 percent confidence level), one would need close to 50,000 exposed persons and 50,000 controls. To follow so large a group for 20 years or more would be impossible.

The epidemiologist may seek to avoid this practical problem by observing groups in the society at large. He may observe a large, naturally exposed selected group — say, those who use saccharin — and match them against others who do not use saccharin. Yet if the groups are not artificially selected, he will not know whether saccharin is the cause of any small increase in bladder cancer observed among the exposed. The higher cancer rate could be caused by obesity or any of hundreds of other factors correlated with saccharin use. The test groups would have been "selected" by nature not man, so they need not have been selected at random.

For these practical reasons, epidemiologists prefer to use retrospective testing. The epidemiologist will take a group of people with disease and match them against identical controls without disease; he will then note whether those in the first group have used more of the suspect ingredient than those in the second. If he takes a group of 200 persons with bladder cancer and a matched group of 200 without, and if in fact saccharin doubles the risk of getting bladder cancer, he will find that far more people in the first group use saccharin than in the second.

But one still faces the problem of selecting the groups — a problem that is formidable when small risks and unknown biological causes (as in some types of cancer) are at issue. Has the cancer group been properly selected? Are those interviewed to be found in hospitals? Are they better educated? Perhaps saccharin is used more by educated people. Are controls well matched? Or have they come from a particular geographic area or social, economic, or cultural group that is less likely to use saccharin? Are those who use saccharin more likely to be overweight? To smoke? To drink coffee? Are there other factors more closely related to the problem? Designing a study with controls that can take into account smoking, occupation, coffee drinking, medical history, social status, type of water supply, and other factors is extremely difficult — particularly when the mystery of cancer means that the epidemiologist does not know what all those factors are. Moreover, the most serious cancer cases may die quickly, making access to case histories difficult. Others may be incorrectly diagnosed. Controls may not accurately report saccharin use, particularly in the form of diet soft drinks, over a period of 20 years or more. Cancer victims, on the other hand, may remember the use of any suspect substance more vividly, for they tend to mull over possible causes of their disease. Mail questionnaires are plagued with poor response rates, selective returns, and differences in interpreting questions. Yet personal interviews run the risk that interviewers may unconsciously project personal biases. Finally, one can never be certain whether cases and controls together constitute a special group such that the relationship between them does not apply elsewhere. Thus, a saccharin-cancer relationship, established in Japan where everyone eats fish containing iodine, may not exist in Mexico where the people do not eat much fish. All these problems can be serious when the relation between a substance and disease is weak, when long time periods are involved, when the biology is not well understood, and when many confounding factors are at work.

The result is that epidemiologic tests may well leave the regulator in the dark. In the case of arsenic, there has been a great deal of epidemiologic testing. But as we have seen, there are large issues about how to apply data in Taiwan, for example, to populations in the United States.

Given the difficulties of epidemiologic testing, most tests for small risks are carried out on animals and the results extrapolated to human beings. But the statistical need for large test populations still raises practical difficulties. A leading group of scientists stated that "if one wanted to test for an incidence of, say, less than one tumor per 500,000 test animals . . . with 0.999 confidence [it] would require negative results in over 3,000,000 test animals."

Because of this practical problem, scientists typically use fewer animals but feed them higher doses of the test substance. Positive results are then extrapolated backward to determine a safe low-dose level for a human being. But what is the proper way to extrapolate from a high animal dose to a lower human dose? First, how are smaller doses likely to affect rats? Second, how are rat effects likely to compare with human effects?

There are several mathematical models that extrapolate effects from high to low doses. One assumes a simple linear relation between dose and response: If a 5 percent saccharin diet causes tumors in 30 percent of all rats, a .5 percent diet presumably would affect 3 percent and a .0005 percent diet would affect .003 percent. Another model uses a different mathematical curve relating dose and response such that lower doses adversely affect slightly more than a proportional percentage of the population. Still another model presumes a dose threshold below which the substance causes no adverse effect.

Each of these models is mathematical, not scientific, biological, or medical. The model used depends on the user's view of the scientific nature of the disease and the substance at issue. Suppose the user believes that cancer occurs when a susceptible person comes into contact with a carcinogen. Suppose, further, he or she believes that susceptibility is a matter of sensitivity to a particular substance and that it is distributed in the population normally and at random. Such a user might believe that the first model accurately depicts the effects of small saccharin doses. Another user might, for a variety of reasons, have a different view about the distribution of susceptibility in society, which would make the second model appropriate. A third might believe in the existence of a threshold exposure below which the additive has no deleterious effect. After all, sugar when fed to rats in high doses (say, 25 grams for each kilogram of body weight) can kill through dehydration; yet low doses are helpful, not harmful, to human beings. Indeed, iodine, which kills both man and animals in high doses, is not merely harmless, but *necessary* for life, in low doses.

Thus, proper extrapolation from high dose to low requires a knowledge of the etiology of the disease and the chemical and biological effects of the substance. When this knowledge is uncertain — as in the case of cancer and several other diseases — one cannot be certain of the validity of the extrapolation.

To extrapolate from animal to human is equally difficult. Obviously, chemicals and diseases follow different courses in animals, but beyond that obvious point, how should one take into account the weight differences between humans and animals? A human weighs about 140 times as much as a rat. Does this mean that the same dose in a human is 1/140 of a rat dose? Humans also live about 35 times as long. Does this mean that the same dose in a human is 35 times 1/140, or 1/4, the rat dose? Much depends on whether one expects saccharin's effects to depend on weight, body area, or accumulation. That, in turn, depends on the biological causes and characteristics of cancer. Further, to what extent should one consider the fact that laboratory animals are genetically homogeneous? Or the fact that humans are exposed to many more carcinogens than laboratory animals?

For these and similar reasons, the National Academy of Sciences concluded that the "question of scaling from animals to humans . . . has never been fully resolved." The uncertainty surrounding the extrapolation of animal test results is not mere scientific hedging. Rather, it is fundamental, leaving the conscientious regulator genuinely uncertain about the result.

The use of experts. The regulator, faced with a difficult scientific issue and without any simple testing method to determine risk, may well seek to rely on a panel of experts to decide what to do. The regulator may well feel that, at worst, the uncertainty of the expert is a more informed uncertainty than that of the lawyer, politician, or bureaucrat who will otherwise make the regulatory decision. But the use of such panels is beset with enough difficulties to shake one's confidence in the objectivity of their decisions.

First, selecting members of the expert panel is difficult. The agency tries to avoid obvious conflicts of interest. This results in drug or food additive panels consisting of academic scientists rather than those directly connected with industry. However, detailed firsthand expertise may well reside in industry; there may be no academic scientists with firsthand experience of the health aspects of adipic acid, rennet, arsenic, papain. Moreover, the make-up of the panel creates bias. If industry experts are included, their views may reflect the interest of their firms. But if they are not, a reverse bias may be created. Finally, panel members must devote a great deal of time and effort to the panel's task. Hence, recruiting can be difficult. The basic literature searches and evaluations are thus done by the panel's professional staff. And, if the panel is not conscientious, much of the value of turning the problem over to the experts is lost.

Second, the experts may find little information available and what they find may be limited, or difficult to digest. As a result, panel members may consult informally, "inquiring of those currently active or productive in the field" for information about the substance. Such inquiry limits the effectiveness of conflict-of-interest criteria that govern panel composition. More important, the unavailability of good information increases the likelihood that the subjective point of view of individual panel members, rather than objective analysis, will influence the result. That is to say, if academics tend to distrust practitioners, the less information there is available the more that distrust is likely to affect the panel's decision.

Third, expert scientific panels may reach only very limited conclusions, particularly if they know that their conclusions will be made public. Good scientific work tends to hold constant a broad range of variables and to investigate very carefully the effect of X on Y. The merit of the work often lies in the care and thoroughness with which the narrow, specific investigation is done. A lawyer or policymaker does a poor job when he leaves out some relevant factor; a scientist does a poor job when she fails to analyze thoroughly those factors within her study. A lawyer is expected to recommend a result; a scientist need not say more than that the evidence is inconclusive. In the case of arsenic, the National Research Council showed a great deal of tentativeness, whereas the EPA attempted to produce specific numbers, reflecting the expected number of cancers avoided. It is not at all clear that the specific numbers could be defended from the scientific point of view.

Fourth, expert panel members, while restrained by their professional discipline from going beyond the scientific evidence, may be aware of what the regulator is likely to do, and they may therefore seek to write their ultimate policy views into the report "between the lines." Thus, the tone of the report may reflect the subjective views of panel members, rather than the objective evidence.

The problem is not the panel's use of subjective judgment, but the indirect, disguised way in which the subjective element is communicated to the regulator. He does not know whether it reflects a judgment of the science, to which he should defer, or a philosophical view, with which he might disagree. Judgments about how to allocate the burden of uncertainty are not solely scientific in nature.

Notes on Cost-Benefit Analysis, with Particular Reference to Carcinogens

In Chapter 3, we discussed the general idea of cost-benefit analysis (CBA). Many people favor CBA on economic grounds; they want regulation to be efficient, and they think that CBA can ensure efficiency. See W. Kip Viscusi, Fatal Tradeoffs (1992). Other people suppose CBA is a way of informing officials and citizens about the consequences of competing courses of action. In this view, CBA is simply a decision procedure, one that is "useful" and "should be routinely used by agencies. CBA is superior to rival method-ologies in enabling agencies to evaluate projects according to the extent to which they contribute to overall well-being." See Adler & Posner, Rethinking Cost-Benefit Analysis, 109 Yale L.J. 165, 245 (1999). For Adler and Posner, CBA "enables agencies to weigh the advantages and disadvantages of projects in a clear and systematic way." Id. In this view, CBA might even have democratic advantages. Still others argue that CBA can be defended on cognitive grounds, as a way of overcoming people's errors in thinking about risks. See Sunstein, Cognition and Cost-Benefit Analysis, 29 J. Legal Stud. 913 (2000).

In this view, CBA places the actual effects of regulation "on screen," thus ensuring that people's decisions will not be rooted in confusion. For an important decision appearing to create a principle allowing agencies to consider costs unless Congress has explicitly held that they may not do so, see Michigan v. EPA, 213 F.3d 1161 (D.C. Cir. 2000).

As noted, there are two possible problems with CBA. The first problem is that it is incompletely specified. To be workable, much needs to be done to say how the relevant variables should be valued. Is a life worth $500,000, $1 million, $10 million, or $50 million? By itself, the idea of CBA does not say. The second problem is that once specified, CBA may depend on a conception of value that is controversial or wrong. If, for example, health values are assessed in terms of private "willingness to pay," see W. Kip Viscusi, Fatal Tradeoffs (1992), many citizens will object.

Many agencies have come to use CBA explicitly or implicitly when regulating risks. Under the executive orders described in Chapter 2, cost-benefit is generally required and indeed has become quite routine. See T. McGarrity, Reinventing Rationality (1985). With respect to statistical lives, consider the following table (borrowed from Matthew Adler and Eric Posner, Implementing Cost-Benefit Analysis When Preferences Are Distorted, in Cost-Benefit Analysis (Matthew Adler and Eric Posner eds. 2001):

Valuations of Life

Agency	Regulation	Citation	Value ($ mil.)
Department of Transportation — Federal Aviation Administration	Proposed Establishment of the Harlingen Airport Radar Service Area, TX	55 F.R. 32064 August 6, 1990	1.5
Department of Agriculture — Food Safety and Inspection Service	Pathogen Reduction: Hazard Analysis and Critical Control Point Systems	61 F.R. 38806 July 25, 1996	1.6
Department of Health and Human Services — Food and Drug Administration	Regulations Restricting the Sale and Distribution of Cigarettes and Smokeless Tobacco to Protect Children and Adolescents	61 F.R. 44396 August 28, 1996	2.5
Department of Transportation — Federal Aviation Administration	Aircraft Flight Simulator Use in Pilot Training, Testing, and Checking and at Training Centers	61 F.R. 34508 July 2, 1996	2.7
Environmental Protection Agency	Protection of Stratospheric Ozone	53 F.R. 30566 August 12, 1988	3
Department of Health and Human Services — Food and Drug Administration	Proposed Rules to Amend the Food Labeling Regulations	56 F.R. 60856 November 27, 1991	3
Department of Transportation — Federal Aviation Administration	Financial Responsibility Requirements for Licensed Launch Activities	61 F.R. 38992 July 25, 1996	3

Agency	Title	F.R. Citation	
Department of Agriculture — Food and Nutrition Service	Proposed National School Lunch Program and School Breakfast Program	59 F.R. 30218 June 10, 1994	1.5, 3.0
Environmental Protection Agency	National Ambient Air Quality Standards for Particulate Matter	62 F.R. 38652 July 18, 1997	4.8
Environmental Protection Agency	National Ambient Air Quality Standards for Ozone	62 F.R. 38856 July 18, 1996	4.8
Department of Health and Human Services — Food and Drug Administration	Medical Devices: Current Good Manufacturing Practice	61 F.R. 52602 October 7, 1996	5
Department of Health and Human Services — Public Health Service, Food and Drug Administration	Quality Mammography Standards	62 F.R. 55852 October 28, 1997	5
Environmental Protection Agency	Requirements for Lead-Based Paint Activities in Target Housing and Child-Occupied Facilities	61 F.R. 45778 August 29, 1996	5.5
Environmental Protection Agency	National Primary Drinking Water Regulations: Disinfectants and Disinfection Byproducts	63 F.R. 69390 December 16, 1998	5.6
Environmental Protection Agency	Radon in Drinking Water Health Risk Reduction and Cost Analysis	64 F.R. 9560 February 26, 1999	5.8

A careful analysis of the impact of CBA is Economic Analyses at EPA (R. Morgenstern ed. 1997), finding, broadly speaking, that CBA has produced good results, often by suggesting alternative ways to accomplish regulatory goals. Note too that CBA encouraged aggressive regulation in the context of the control of both lead and stratospheric ozone depletion. The Morgenstern book is worth careful consultation by those interested in seeing how CBA generally works in practice. We raise a few of the underlying issues here. See also G. Tolley et al., Valuing Health for Policy (1995).

1. *Calculating and monetizing multiple effects.* To produce reasonable results when considering risk regulation, agencies are often driven to consider, either formally or informally, the benefits of the substance they might ban and thus the costs of any ban. Any agency that decides to examine the benefit and costs of the ban must first determine which benefits and costs to consider and then decide how to measure them. Suppose, for example, that the government is considering whether to ban saccharin. What are the relevant effects of such a ban, and how should they be calculated?

To answer this question, the regulator has to make some predictions about public behavior if saccharin is banned. Will some, many, or all former consumers turn to other, riskier products? Might former saccharin users eat more sweets? A reasonably thorough study would require a risk analysis of any major substitute for the item banned. To fail to do so can lead to tragic results. Those who promulgated regulatory rules designed to make children's sleepwear less flammable did not consider that the manufacturing process for doing so involved the use of TRIS, a flame-retardant chemical that turned out to be seriously carcinogenic. Thus, an effort to consider health benefits will involve the very difficulties that plague the determination of health risks, but multiplied across all possible risky alternatives to the banned substance. This question raises the general problem of substitute risks, or "health-health tradeoffs," taken up in more detail below.

In addition, many health benefits are intangible or difficult to measure. Consider, for example, the various benefits of increased physical vitality of the population, better eating habits, lower-cost food, and animal drugs that lower farming costs (while perhaps leaving small-risk residues in the food). How are these potential health benefits to be estimated, and how should they be monetized? If a cheap pesticide (which turns out to be carcinogenic) used on apples is banned, perhaps the costs of producing apples will increase, and perhaps fewer people will eat apples. If apple consumption goes down, might the health costs of the ban outweigh the health benefits? Eating fruits and vegetables appears to be a possible way to combat cancer; maybe a ban on the cheap pesticide will actually increase the total number of lives lost from cancer.

To see how these questions might be answered in practice, consider a recent analysis by EPA, in connection with regulation of ozone and particulates:

Health Endpoint	Mean WTP Value per Incident (1990 $)
Mortality	
Life saved	$4.8 million
Life year extended	$120,000
Hospital Admissions:	
All Respiratory Illnesses, all ages	$12,700
Pneumonia, age >65+	$13,400

Health Endpoint	Mean WTP Value per Incident (1990 $)
COPD, age >65+	$15,900
Ischemic Heart Disease, age >65+	$20,600
Congestive Heart Failure, age >65+	$16,600
Emergency Visits for Asthma	$9,000
Chronic Bronchitis	$260,000
Upper Respiratory Symptoms	$19
Lower Respiratory Symptoms	$12
Acute Respiratory Symptoms (any of 19)	$18
Asthma	$32
Shortness of Breath	$5.30
Sinusitis and Hay Fever	not monetized
Work Loss Days	$83
Restricted Activity Days (RAD)	
Minor RAD	$38
Respiratory RAD	not monetized
Worker Productivity	$1 per worker per 10% change in ozone
Visibility: residential	$14 per unit decrease in deciview per household
Recreational	Range of $7.30 to $11 per unit decrease in deciview pet household
Household Soiling Damage	$2.50 per household per $\cdot g/m^3$

2. *Markets for nonhealth effects.* Is it easier to monetize nonhealth benefits and costs? Many such benefits and costs might be reflected in the amount of money users would pay for the product. (But is this any different from health effects, where markets also develop for smoke alarms, safer cars, and so forth?) The practice of cost-benefit analysis was developed in the context of evaluating government dams and irrigation projects, and its practitioners developed methods of placing rough values on benefits for which there might be a market, such as irrigation, navigation, flood control, and municipal and industrial water supplies. Market information can help place a rough value on the benefits of items designed to be sold.

3. *Commensurability.* A difficult problem for the regulator is making various sorts of risks and benefits commensurable so that some sort of global estimate of each can be reached, allowing them to be weighed against one another. Economists tend to reduce each to dollar equivalents, because monetization is virtually the only way to arrive at common, comparable terms for summation of various kinds of benefits and summation of various kinds of costs. Yet monetization as an effort to produce commensurability faces some difficulties. Perhaps we lose sight of qualitative differences among social goods when we align them all along the single metric of dollars. In this view, cost-benefit analysis is obtuse, since it elides the qualitative differences among the various effects of regulation. See E. Anderson, Value in Ethics and Economics (1993); Sunstein, Incommensurability and Valuation in Law, 92 Mich. L. Rev. 779, 782-785 (1994). Part of the problem lies in the qualitative differences among (for example) increased prices, greater unemployment,

cleaner beaches, greater visibility, and lower cancer risks. Part of the problem is that one cannot easily make benefits (or risks) commensurable when they are distributed differently among groups of people.

Even if the single metric of dollars has problems, it is necessary to make tradeoffs among conflicting goods — almost no one denies that — and this point suggests that some form of cost-benefit balancing is indispensable. Perhaps dollars can be used as the metric of choice, but with an understanding that the dollar figures do not capture everything that is at stake.

4. *Distributional questions.* Many economists tend to favor actions that yield a net increase in benefits — the gainers might compensate the losers and have added benefits to spare. This is the criterion of "potential Pareto superiority." But one might hesitate to allow decisions that impose serious risks to health on one group while helping another or that involve benefits (or risks) that are very large in amount and very badly distributed, when the compensating transaction is never actually made. Such problems are compounded when one considers actions that may have serious, irreversibly harmful effects on future generations. Could such problems be solved by giving certain "distributional weights" to particular outcomes? Would it make sense to give particular weights to risks that are disproportionately faced by poor people, African-Americans, or women?

Return here to EPA's regulation of arsenic in drinking water. For a reduction in the maximum level from 50 ppb to 10 ppb, most families would pay less than $40 annually in increased water bills, but some families would pay over $300 annually. Does it matter if those families are rich or poor? Consider President Clinton's Executive Order 12,898, which is designed to address problems of "environmental justice," which are said to arise when environmental problems are especially severe in low-income or minority communities.

5. *Willingness to pay and willingness to accept.* Many studies have found a difference between how much people are "willing to pay" to obtain a certain benefit, and how much they are "willing to accept" to give up a certain benefit. See generally R. Thaler, Quasi-Rational Economics (1993). People are willing to pay far less to get a good — environmental quality, improved statistical risk — than they must be paid to give up the equivalent good. Thus, the aggregated willingness to pay to protect beaches from degradation or to protect visibility in a certain region may be far lower than the aggregated willingness to accept to prevent beach degradation or decreased visibility.

The disparity creates a problem for regulators. Suppose, for example, that most people would be willing to pay $200 to reduce a risk from .002 to .001, but also that they would be willing to accept no less than $1000 to allow a risk to increase from .001 to .002. How much should a risk reduction be valued?

6. *Weighing and weighting (and waiting).* A regulator must consider how to weigh risks to human life against economic or nonhealth benefits. In the case of arsenic, for example, the reduction to 10 ppb was projected to cost $210 million annually, whereas the monetized benefits would be between $140 million and $198 million. EPA concluded that the reduction was worthwhile, because the reduction would also produce "potential nonquantified benefits," in the form of health benefits that were too speculative to be quantified. What do you think of this form of weighing benefits and costs?

It is sometimes argued that such a weighing is improper — that no amount of money is too great to save a human life. This argument seems less convincing, however, as soon as one considers risks to life, instead of certainty of death, and when large amounts of money become involved. Though ethical principles may require spending vast sums to save an identified individual facing death — a trapped coal miner or astronaut — those principles do not dictate expenditures of 10 percent of the gross national product to fence in the Grand Canyon or to wrap all machines in soft plastic. Indeed, to spend huge amounts of money to lower statistical risk and thereby save a single human life (say, by putting foam rubber under the Empire State Building) would waste lives, for the same money would buy far more safety when spent elsewhere.

How, then, should dollars be weighed against lives? Some have tried to measure the value of a life as the discounted value of the earnings forgone. Yet this approach makes the value of the individual depend on how well he or she is paid. How strong an objection is this? Might it make sense to value all goods, including risks, in terms of how much people are willing to pay for them, or for their elimination? This is a more popular approach within the agencies, producing numbers, as we have seen, of between $1 million and $6.1 million per life saved. (According to one of the most prominent economists, the number should be between $5 million and $7 million per statistical life saved. See W. Kip Viscusi, Fatal Tradeoffs (1992).) Under the most common approach, it is necessary to ask not what persons would pay to save their lives, but rather what they would pay to lower the risk of death (or, in the case of illness or injury, morbidity effects). This approach focuses on what agencies actually seek when they screen out substances: the lowering of statistical risk of sickness, injury, or death.

Still, how is one to measure this willingness to pay? There are hard issues of measurement. It is disputed whether a decision to take a risky job, to buy a smoke alarm, or to pay extra for a safer car reflects a usable "risk premium." The prevailing answer is that careful analysis of the market shows that $5 million to $7 million is around the middle of what the good studies tend to show. See EPA, Guidelines for Preparing Economic Analyses 89 (2000). Those studies do come up with some disparate numbers — from as low $1 million to as high as $16 million. Is it sensible to take the midpoint of (say) twenty reputable studies? If not, what should be done instead?

Perhaps some people's willingness to pay is affected by ignorance of the facts or wishful thinking. Perhaps people do not want to think that the risks that they face are high, and hence they discount those risks unduly. See J. Elster, Sour Grapes (1983). (Whether this is so is an empirical question, one that is hard to test.) Or perhaps regulators should attempt not to aggregate private preferences as measured by private willingness to pay (the market model of regulation), but ask instead what informed people, in their capacity as citizens deliberating with one another, think to be the best course. See M. Sagoff, The Economy of the Earth (1989).

7. *Qualitative differences among risks.* The problem of valuing lowered risk is intensified by the fact that individuals ordinarily do not know how to react to changes in very small risk. Moreover, an individual's reaction — and society's view of a proper response — to a particular degree of risk varies with the individual, the type of risk, and the substance at issue. Regardless of countervailing benefits, people are less concerned with risks that they voluntarily assume than with those forced on them, and they may be more concerned with food purity than with safety in the workplace. Some of the factors that affect the value of a particular degree of lowered risk include:

Factor	*Countervailing Factor*
Risk assumed voluntarily	Risk borne involuntarily
Effect immediate	Effect delayed
No alternative available	Many alternatives available

Factor	*Countervailing Factor*
Risk known with certainty	Risk not known
Exposure is an essential	Exposure is a luxury
Encountered occupationally	Encountered nonoccupationally
Common hazard	Dread hazard
Affects average people	Affects especially sensitive people
Will be used as intended	Likely to be misused
Consequences reversible	Consequences irreversible

W. Lawrence, Of Acceptable Risk (1976).

See also H. Margolis, Dealing with Risk (1996), for an outline and discussion of psychological evidence; Pildes & Sunstein, Reinventing the Regulatory State, 62 U. Chi. L. Rev. 1 (1995). Ideally, the use of private willingness to pay could take account of these considerations because people would be willing to pay more to avoid risks having the characteristics on the right-hand side. But market measures may not be available. There is also a serious controversy over the use of this factor-countervailing factor approach. Is it really true, for example, that some risks are voluntarily incurred, and some risks involuntarily incurred? Mightn't this be a continuum, with the real issue being the costs of risk avoidance? See H. Margolis, supra. How much of a difference is there, in principle, between risks falling in the two different "categories"? See Sunstein, Bad Deaths, 14 J. Risk & Uncertainty 235 (1997).

One way to avoid the difficulties of reducing risk and benefits to a dollar value is for the regulator to resort to a subjective weighing of the relevant factors. First, the regulator compiles several lists containing different varieties of risks and benefits. He then arranges the risk and benefits under alternative courses of action available to him. Finally, he chooses the best action on the basis of his subjective valuation and weighing of each alternative.

The virtue of this approach is that it makes explicit the subjectivity and uncertainty involved in efforts to monetize and to compare apparently incommensurable elements. Its major vice is that it explicitly grants a great deal of discretion to the regulator.

Yet the alternatives have problems of their own. Using controversial formulas to place dollar values on the relevant elements may prevent the regulator from using common sense. Refusing to consider certain effects may lead to equally bad results, such as health or safety rules that end up killing more people than they save. In fact, a decision must be made that inevitably implies some tradeoffs among them.

8. *The discount rate.* An enormous question involves the treatment of future costs and benefits. It is generally agreed that a dollar today is worth more than a dollar in ten years, and hence that a "discount rate" is properly applied to monetary costs and benefits. But what if someone would have cancer twenty years from now, rather than now? What if future generations would be hurt? The cost-benefit analysis might essentially turn on the choice of discount rate. We will return to this question. See Revesz, Environmental Regulation, Cost-Benefit Analysis, and the Discounting of Human Lives, 99 Colo. L. Rev. 941 (1999).

9. *Bottom lines.* Some skeptics might be tempted to conclude from this discussion that agencies should simply ban many, most, or all substances that pose any risk whatever of causing cancer — without regard to benefits. But wouldn't doing so deprive us of many desired, useful, and safer substances? Coffee? Tea? Gasoline? Should we ban plastic drink

bottles (a few molecules of material may migrate into the food; in high doses plastic may cause cancer in some test animals)? Would manufacturers then switch to glass bottles, which can injure thousands? Or consider the view, embodied in OSHA as now interpreted, that agencies should regulate "significant risks" to the extent "feasible." Is this better than cost-benefit balancing?

Many agencies have attempted to respond to these problems by adopting a benchmark value for various goods. We have noted that a statistical life, for example, is often valued between $1 million and $7 million. This number also tends to be toward the median of agency regulations on the "cost-effectiveness" charts. Should Congress enact benchmark values for regulatory benefits, including life, and require agencies to explain departures? Notably, congressional enthusiasm for cost-benefit analysis has been unaccompanied by specification of how agencies are to value the relevant goods. Does this mean that cost-benefit analysis is mostly procedural? Before answering "yes," note that the case studies in Morgenstern, supra, suggest that cost-benefit analysis has often proved highly illuminating to the EPA, suggesting better alternatives and pointing out the reasonableness, and unreasonableness, of various initiatives.

A Further Note on Regulating Risk

The problem of regulating risk reoccurs throughout the many governmental programs regulating health, safety, and the environment. As these regulatory programs have become more important and more expensive, the need to coordinate "risk-related" regulatory activities has increased, as has the difficulty for the courts in interpreting statutes apparently written without many of the difficulties in mind. Consider the following.

OFFICE OF MANAGEMENT AND BUDGET, REGULATORY PROGRAM OF THE UNITED STATES GOVERNMENT, April 1, 1986-March 31,1987, pp. xx-xxi. The goal in managing risks is to provide the greatest net benefits to the general public. To do this, regulators must have a way to compare the effectiveness of different approaches for reducing various risks to society. Without such a comparative, quantitative procedure, the government could spend society's resources on efforts that do not reduce risks efficiently. This procedure is often divided into two parts — "risk assessment" and "risk management." Risk assessment is a purely scientific process that measures the riskiness of various activities. For example, a risk assessment could tell the mountain climber that his chance of dying on a 2-day climb is greater than 1 in 1,000. And it could tell the automobile user that his risk of dying is 2 in 10,000 each year. What risk assessment cannot tell these people is what they should do about these risks. That is where risk management comes in. Risk management takes the scientific risk assessment and combines it with other information such as the cost and feasibility of reducing risks, to determine how far to reduce risks efficiently. While individuals often make risk management decisions spontaneously without consciously analyzing the tradeoffs, policymakers must carefully and expressly balance costs and risk reduction benefits to make risk management decisions that will result in net benefits to society.

Table 4-1 presents the annual fatality risk per million persons engaged in each of 15 activities. The extent of risk varies greatly for these 15 different activities — ranging from

TABLE 4-1
Annual Fatality Risk for Selected Activities

Activity or cause	Annual fatality risk for every 1 million exposed individuals
1. Smoking (all causes)	3,000
2. Motor vehicle accidents	243
3. Work (all industries)	113
4. Alcohol	50
5. Using unvented space heater*	27
6. Working with ethylene oxide*	26
7. Swimming	22
8. Servicing single-piece wheel rims*	14
9. Aflatoxin (corn)	9
10. Football	6
11. Saccharin	5
12. Fuel system in automobiles*	5
13. Lightning	0.5
14. DES in cattlefeed*	0.3
15. Uranium mill tailings (active sites)*	0.02
From all causes in U.S.	8,695
From cancer in U.S.	1,833

*Indicates that the risk was regulated by the Federal government in the last 10 years. For these activities or causes, the risks in the table are estimates of risk prior to Federal regulation.

3,000 fatalities per million for smoking to 0.02 fatalities per million people for exposure to radon from uranium mill tailings [about 2 million people die in the United States each year; about 400,000 of them die of cancer].

The risks of certain activities may be surprising to some people because some risks that we encounter — and accept — daily are larger than some risks that we fear greatly. The six activities marked with an asterisk in Table 4-1 were the subject of federal regulatory actions between 1975 and 1984. Obviously, the level of a risk from an activity was not the sole basis for determining whether to regulate it. For example, exposure to the natural contaminant aflatoxin poses a risk of nine fatalities per million and exposure to the additive saccharin poses a risk of five fatalities per million. Both of these risks are significantly greater than the 0.3 per million risk of DES in cattlefeed or 0.02 per million risk posed by radon in uranium mill tailings, but the latter were recently regulated while the former have not been.

Although it may seem logical to try and reduce the largest risks first, this would not result necessarily in the most efficient reduction in risks because our ability to reduce risks is not constant; that is, it costs more to reduce some risks than others. Some risks can be reduced at low costs to society; reducing other risks can be very expensive. For example, motor vehicle accidents (the second largest cause of death in Table 4-1) could be eliminated if driving were prohibited, but, of course, no risk manager could ever ban driving because the cost to society — both economic and noneconomic — would be unacceptable. Clearly, the magnitude of risk based on a risk assessment alone does not

TABLE 4-2
Risk-Cost Tradeoffs for Selected Regulations

Regulation	Agency	Year issued	Cost per statistical life saved ($ millions)
1. Unvented space heaters	CPSC	1980	$0.07
2. Servicing wheel rims	OSHA	1984	0.25
3. Fuel system integrity	NHTSA	1975	0.29
4. Uranium mill tailings (active)	EPA	1983	53.00
5. Ethylene oxide	OSHA	1984	60.00
6. DES ban in cattlefeed	FDA	1979	132.00

provide enough information for a risk manager to make an appropriate decision. In deciding whether — or how much — to regulate, a regulatory official must look not only at total risks but also at the risk reduction that could be achieved and the cost of doing so. Balancing these factors is the challenge of risk management.

To measure and compare the costs and risk reduction associated with different strategies for controlling risks in a meaningful way, risk managers must use a common yardstick. Regulators and academics often use the term "cost-effectiveness" of different strategies to mean the costs of reducing a unit of risk. This is usually stated as the "cost per case avoided" or "cost per life saved." The "cases" or "lives saved" used in these cost-effectiveness statistics are statistical cases of illness, injury, or death, based on estimates of probabilities that a series of events will occur. In other words, as used in these measures, a life saved does not represent the avoided death of a specific person, but a reduced probability of death, say by one chance in a million, for a million people.

For each of the six regulations issued by the Federal agencies in Table 4-1, Table 4-2 presents the average annual cost per case avoided. We calculated these figures by dividing the expected annual reduction in risk. The cost and risk reduction data are based on published estimates developed by the agencies that issued the regulations or by academicians assessing the effects of these regulations.

Comparison of Tables 4-1 and 4-2 demonstrates again that a more cost-effective regulation is not necessarily one that addresses the greater risk. For example, the National Highway Traffic Safety Administration's (NHTSA's) fuel system integrity regulation has a far lower cost per case avoided ($290,000) than OSHA's ethylene oxide regulation ($60 million), even though the risk addressed by the OSHA regulation (26 deaths per million people) is greater than the risk addressed by the NHTSA regulation (5 deaths per million). To reduce the probability of death by 5 chances in a million per year, or, in other words, to save 5 statistical deaths per year per million persons, the NHTSA regulation would cost $1.5 million and the OSHA regulation would cost $300 million.

We also note that there is a very great range in the cost per case avoided for different regulations. Table 4-2 shows that the cost per life saved is over 1,800 times greater for banning the use of DES (a growth stimulant in cattlefeed) than for regulating unvented space heaters.

This large difference in cost-effectiveness for different regulations indicates that we might have provided greater risk reduction at the same or lower total costs by regulating other, more cost-effective risks. Similarly, some activities probably should be regulated more stringently than they are now, and others less. For example, imagine that there are two types of activities that can be regulated — activity A that costs $25 million per statistical life saved and activity B that costs $250,000 per statistical life saved. Spending $100 million less on activity A would increase predicted risk by 4 deaths. Applying that $100 million to activity B would reduce risk by 400 deaths. Consequently, with no change in total outlays for risk reduction, 396 more lives could be saved.

Some would argue that we need not make these tradeoffs at all, but should pursue all opportunities to reduce risk. Of course, it would be desirable to eliminate all risks that technically could be eliminated. Such a policy, however, would quickly run into resource constraints. For example, if all 400,000 cancer deaths per year could be eliminated at a cost per expected life saved equal to the cost of reducing the risk of cancer death from occupational exposure to ethylene oxide, the annual costs to society would be almost $24 trillion ($60,000,000 × 400,000) — a figure about 6 times the Gross National Product.

ZECKHAUSER & VISCUSI, RISK WITHIN REASON, 248 Science 559 (1990).   The authors explain some of the common problems that arise in determining the amount of risk and its significance, and ask several important questions. (a) Human beings tend to overestimate the likelihood of low probability events (death by tornado) and underestimate the probability of high probability events (heart disease or stroke). Public estimates change radically in the face of a well-publicized risky event (Three Mile Island). These facts create political pressures for regulation (or sometimes tolerate inadequate regulation) in potentially irrational ways. (b) The public may consistently choose riskier courses of action (taking a baby in a car during a ten-minute errand) over less risky courses of action (leaving the baby sleeping at home alone for ten minutes) for reasons that are not necessarily irrational but difficult to determine. (c) How is one to estimate risks when faced with only a single instance, the consequences of which are difficult to predict? What did the presence of cyanide traces in two grapes from Chile signify? Did it warrant banning all Chilean grape imports? (d) Some advocate simply "informing the public" about risks without removing risky substances from the market, but how can that be done? Can a reader interpret a label that says there is a 1 in 100,000 chance of cancer? What about a risk of 1 in 7 million? (California has recently passed a law requiring labeling of any product more dangerous than the 1 in 7 million threshold.) (e) Others advocate just being "conservative" and banning anything with any risk of, say, cancer. But would such a ban not deprive us of important benefits? Indeed, sustained economic development (rather than banning of dangerous substances) would seem the primary factor in explaining improved mortality rates (for example, in Japan from 1955 to 1975 mortality rates for men fell by nearly one-third). (f) The basic problem is institutional. What governmental arrangements will most likely diminish risk appropriately, bringing about greater safety but avoiding waste of safety dollars? For a good description of the government's efforts to deal with these and other problems related to risk regulation, see J. Cohrssen & V. Covello, Risk Analysis: A Guide to Principles and Methods for Analyzing Health and Environmental Risks (Council on Environmental Quality 1989).

Note on Priority-Setting

Does the regulatory state set priorities in a sufficiently thoughtful way? Many people believe that it does not, and that new institutions should be considered to improve priority-setting. See generally S. Breyer, Breaking the Vicious Circle (1993).

As much as $500 billion may be spent each year on regulation, Thomas D. Hopkins, The Costs of Federal Regulation, 2 J. Reg. & Soc. Costs 5, 25 table 2 (1992) (estimate of $400 million), and of this amount, more than $130 billion is spent on environmental protection. See Portney & Stavins, Regulatory Review of Environmental Policy, 8 J. Risk & Uncertainty 111, 119 n.1 (1995). With respect to good priority-setting, a general study suggests that better allocations of existing health expenditures could save an additional 60,000 lives at no increased cost — and that with better allocations, we could save the same number of lives we now save with $31 billion in annual savings. Tengs et al., Five Hundred Life-Saving Interventions and Their Cost-Effectiveness, 15 Risk Analysis 369 (1995).

There are also serious and apparently unjustified asymmetries in life-saving expenditures (see Table 4-1 p. 316). Consider the fact that for transportation, there is a median expenditure per life year saved of $56,000; for occupational regulation, the number is $346,000; for environmental regulation, it is $4,207,000. Tengs et al., supra. There are enormous variations within each group as well. Annual lives saved are highly variable. See Table 3-1 on pages 151-152, from W. Kip Viscusi, Fatal Tradeoffs 264 (1992). Consider OSHA's hazard communication regulation, saving 200 lives per year; the CPSC's unvented space heaters regulation, saving over 60 lives per year; the FAA's seat cushion flammability regulation, saving 37 lives per year; OSHA's oil and gas well service regulation, saving 50 lives per year; OSHA's grain dust regulation, saving 4 lives per year; EPA's asbestos regulation, saving 10 lives per year; OSHA's formaldehyde regulation, saving 0.010 lives per year; EPA's land disposal regulation, saving 2.5 lives per year; and the NHTSA's passive restraints/belts regulation, saving no fewer than 1,850 lives per year.

Of course calculations of costs and benefits are somewhat speculative, and the numbers are of uncertain reliability; they also depend on contentious assumptions. See Heinzerling, Regulatory Costs of Mythic Proportions, 107 Yale L.J. 1981 (1998). But with better allocations, many people think that much could be done to make things better. Breyer, supra, suggests that modern regulation faces three fundamental problems of "tunnel vision" (a focus on "the last 10 percent," where the costs of further improvements may be very high in comparison to the benefits), "random agenda selection," and "inconsistency." He lays special stress on the fact that expert judgments about the seriousness of risks are very different from public judgments. Consider the evidence rating health risks in Table 4-3. See S. Breyer, Breaking the Vicious Circle at 24, and citing as source Frederick Allen, U.S. EPA, based on EPA report "Unfinished Business: A Comparative Assessment of Environmental Problems" (1987) and national public opinion polls by the Roper Organization in December 1987 and January 1988.

In Breyer's view, the lack of sensible priority-setting is partly attributable to public pressure that is inadequately informed by scientific knowledge or by an appreciation of the full set of problems faced by government. "Agency priorities and agendas may more closely reflect public rankings, politics, history, or even chance than the kind of priority list that environmental experts would deliberately create." Id. at 20.

This possibility raises a large question: When should expert views be preferred to those of the public? Sometimes public views are based on mistaken understandings of facts. But sometimes they are rooted in the qualitative factors, as the public considers risks to be especially serious if they are involuntarily incurred, potentially catastrophic, unusually dreaded, new, ill-understood, and unfairly distributed. In any case Breyer argues that a "vicious circle" of public perceptions, congressional reaction, and uncertainties in the regulatory process help produce a system in which priorities are not adequately set.

TABLE 4-3
Health Risks

Public	EPA experts
1. Hazardous waste sites	Medium-to-low
2. Exposure to worksite chemicals	High
3. Industrial pollution of waterways	Low
4. Nuclear accident radiation	Not ranked
5. Radioactive waste	Not ranked
6. Chemical leaks from underground storage tanks	Medium-to-low
7. Pesticides	High
8. Pollution from industrial accidents	Medium-to-low
9. Water pollution from farm runoff	Medium
10. Tap water contamination	High
11. Industrial air pollution	High
12. Ozone layer destruction	High
13. Coastal water contamination	Low
14. Sewage-plant water pollution	Medium-to-low
15. Vehicle exhaust	High
16. Oil spills	Medium-to-low
17. Acid raid	High
18. Water pollution from urban runoff	Medium
19. Damaged wetlands	Low
20. Genetic alteration	Low
21. Nonhazardous waste sites	Medium-to-low
22. Greenhouse effect	Low
23. Indoor air pollution	High
24. X-ray radiation	Not ranked
25. Indoor radon	High
26. Microwave oven radiation	Not ranked

The goal of achieving sensible priority-setting is further undermined by the fact that agencies have quite different standards for deciding when risks are large enough to require any regulation at all. Sadowitz & Graham, A Survey of Permitted Residual Cancer Risks, 6 Risk 17 (1995). The International Commission on Radiological Protection recommends that environmental factors should not be allowed to cause an incremental cancer risk, for those exposed over a lifetime, of about 3 in 1000. American agencies do not follow this recommendation, and their own practices are highly variable. The NRC sees 1 in 1000 as acceptable; the EPA's acceptable range varies from 1 in 10,000 to 1 in 1 million. The FDA has tried to use a standard of 1 in 1 million, but under the Delaney Clause, courts have required a standard of essentially 0. Public Citizen v. Young, 831 F.2d 1108 (D.C. Cir. 1987). OSHA's understanding of the "significant risk" requirement means a risk of 1 in 1000; labor groups have sought an increase to 1 in 1 million. In the face of these variations, good priority-setting is unlikely.

What institutions might be created to respond to the problem of poor priority-setting? Breyer, supra, suggests that consideration might be given to the establishment of a new career path for people trained in various disciplines and empowered to ensure that limited resources are devoted to the most serious problems. "The group I have in mind, composed of civil servants who are following the proposed career path, would draw strength from its ability to harness several virtues inherent in many administrative systems: rationalization, expertise, insulation, and authority." Breyer, supra. For critical discussion, see Pildes & Sunstein, Reinventing the Regulatory State, 62 U. Chi. L. Rev. 1 (1995). How would you compare this proposal to those of the 104th Congress discussed in Chapter 2, section D2?

Note on Health-Health Tradeoffs

In the area of risk regulation, a particular problem arises from "health-health" trade-offs (sometimes described as "risk-risk" tradeoffs), which occur when government control of one health risk actually increases another health risk. It is important to ensure that risk regulation does not actually increase risks on balance. Suppose, for example, that elimination of asbestos — a carcinogenic substance — makes cars less safe, because asbestos is the best substance to use in making brake linings. Cf. Corrosion Proof Fittings v. EPA, 947 F.2d 1201 (5th Cir. 1991). Or suppose that a regulatory requirement designed to encourage the use of electric cars — and thus to reduce air pollution from motor vehicles — turns out to increase other environmental problems, because the production of electric cars increases hazardous waste problems. It is pervasively true that controls on one risk may increase another risk. See J. Graham & J. Wiener, Risk-Risk Tradeoffs (1995), for an overview; see also Symposium, 8 J. Risk & Uncertainty 5 (1994); A. Wildavsky, Searching for Safety (1987). Unfortunately, risk regulation is not designed with this problem in mind. See Sunstein, Health-Health Tradeoffs, 63 U. Chi. L. Rev. 1533 (1996).

There is also an incipient literature suggesting that regulatory expenditures can actually cost lives, because regulatory expenditures can produce greater unemployment and hence poverty, and because poor people do not live as long as people who are not poor. One study attempted to develop a model to quantify the view that "richer is safer." Keeney, Mortality Risks Induced by Economic Expenditures, 10 Risk Analysis 147 (1990). According to Keeney, a single fatality might result from an expenditure of from $3 million to $7.5 million. In a concurring opinion in a case involving occupational safety and health regulation, Judge Williams invoked this evidence to suggest that OSHA's refusal to engage in cost-benefit analysis might not be beneficial for workers. See International Union, U.A.W. v. OSHA, 938 F.2d 1310 (D.C. Cir. 1991). Judge Williams reasoned that if a fatality results from an expenditure of $7.5 million, some regulations might produce more fatalities than they prevent. Many regulations, of course, cost more than $7.5 million per life saved. In Judge Williams's view, an agency that fails to measure costs against benefits might be failing to measure mortality gains against mortality losses. See R. Hahn et al., Do Federal Regulations Decrease Mortality (2001), for a recent discussion.

Suppose that regulatory requirements can impose health risks, because "richer is safer" or because controls of one health problem can increase another health problem. How might this problem be handled by regulatory agencies? Should courts follow Judge Williams's lead and inquire into the question on judicial review? Might legislative changes be necessary or appropriate?

Recent cases suggest an emerging principle of interpretation, in the form of a strong presumption in favor of permitting (and even requiring) agencies to take account of substitute risks, and hence to undertake health-health tradeoffs. In *American Trucking Association*, 175 F.3d at 1051, for example, it was argued that while ground-level ozone creates certain health risks, it also produces certain health benefits, above all because it provides protection against skin cancer and cataracts. The EPA responded that it lacked authority to consider the risks created by regulation or (to put the point slightly differently) the health benefits of an air pollutant. In a passage that suggests a strong presumption in favor of health-health tradeoffs, the court said that the statute was unambiguous, and that "EPA's interpretation fails even the reasonableness standard . . . ; it seems bizarre that a statute intended to improve human health would . . . lock the agency into looking at only one half of a substance's health effects in determining the maximum level for that substance." What is most striking about this suggestion is that the court seems to have gone beyond the view that the agency is permitted to engage in health-health tradeoffs if it chooses, and to require the EPA to do so even if it would choose otherwise.

Or consider Competitive Enterprise Institute v. NHTSA, 956 F.2d 321 (D.C. Cir. 1992), where the plaintiffs challenged fuel economy standards precisely on the ground that the agency had failed to take account of the adverse effects of such standards on automobile safety. In the face of an ambiguous statute, the court insisted that a full explanation was required for a decision that, in the abstract, would seem to create serious substitute risks. Id. at 324. As a result of this decision, it is now the law that NHTSA must take into account any evidence of adverse safety effects in the process of setting fuel economy standards. On remand, NHTSA confronted the evidence and concluded that the alleged effect could not be demonstrated — a conclusion that the court upheld on appeal, Competitive Enterprise Institute v. NHTSA, 45 F.3d 481, 484-486 (D.C. Cir. 1995). What is important for present purposes is the clear holding that the agency is permitted and even obliged to consider health-health tradeoffs in setting fuel economy standards.

4. Chevron, *Agency Discretion, and "Canons" of Construction*

Kent v. Dulles
357 U.S. 116 (1958)

Mr. Justice DOUGLAS delivered the opinion of the Court.

This case concerns two applications for passports, denied by the Secretary of State. One was by Rockwell Kent, who desired to visit England and attend a meeting of an organization known as the "World Council of Peace" in Helsinki, Finland. The Director of the Passport Office informed Kent that issuance of a passport was precluded by §51.135 of the Regulations promulgated by the Secretary of State on two grounds: (1) that he was a Communist and (2) that he had had "a consistent and prolonged adherence to the Communist Party line." The letter of denial specified in some detail the facts on which those conclusions were based. . . .

A passport not only is of great value — indeed necessary — abroad; it is also an aid in establishing citizenship for purposes of re-entry into the United States. . . . But throughout most of our history — until indeed quite recently — a passport, though a great convenience in foreign travel, was not a legal requirement for leaving or entering the United States. Apart from minor exceptions . . . it was first made a requirement by §215 of the Act of June 27, 1952, which states that, after a prescribed proclamation by the President, it is "unlawful for any citizen of the United States to depart from or enter, or attempt to depart from or enter, the United States unless he bears a valid passport." And the Proclamation necessary to make the restrictions of this Act applicable and in force has been made.

Prior to 1952 there were numerous laws enacted by Congress regulating passports and many decisions, rulings, and regulations by the Executive Department concerning them. [I]n 1856 Congress enacted what remains today as our basic passport statute. [In 1926 Congress codified it; it reads:] "The Secretary of State may grant and issue passports . . . under such rules as the President shall designate and prescribe for and on behalf of the United States, and no other person shall grant, issue, or verify such passports."

[F]or most of our history a passport was not a condition to entry or exit.

It is true that, at intervals, a passport has been required for travel. [Restrictions were] imposed during the War of 1812 and during the Civil War. A . . . restriction, which was the forerunner of that contained in the 1952 Act, was imposed by Congress in 1918.

The 1918 Act was effective only in wartime. It was amended in 1941 so that it could be invoked in the then-existing emergency. It was invoked by Presidential Proclamation No. 2523, November 14, 1941. That emergency continued until April 28, 1952. Congress extended the statutory provisions until April 1, 1953. [The President also renewed the Proclamation of Emergency.] It was during this extension period that the Secretary of State issued the Regulations here complained of.

Under the 1926 Act and its predecessor a large body of precedents grew up which repeat over and again that the issuance of passports is "a discretionary act" on the part of the Secretary of State. The scholars, the courts, the Chief Executive, and the Attorneys General, all so said. This long-continued executive construction should be enough, it is said, to warrant the inference that Congress had adopted it. . . . But the key to that problem, as we shall see, is in the manner in which the Secretary's discretion was exercised, not in the bare fact that he had discretion.

The right to travel is a part of the "liberty" of which the citizen cannot be deprived without due process of law under the Fifth Amendment. . . . Freedom of movement across frontiers in either direction, and inside frontiers as well, was a part of our heritage. Travel abroad, like travel within the country, may be necessary for a livelihood. It may be as close to the heart of the individual as the choice of what he eats, or wears, or reads. Freedom of movement is basic in our scheme of values. . . .

Freedom to travel is, indeed, an important aspect of the citizen's "liberty." We need not decide the extent to which it can be curtailed. We are first concerned with the extent, if any, to which Congress has authorized its curtailment.

The difficulty is that while the power of the Secretary of State over the issuance of passports is expressed in broad terms, it was apparently long exercised quite narrowly. So far as material here, the cases of refusal of passports generally fell into two categories. First, questions pertinent to the citizenship of the applicant and his allegiance to the United States had to be resolved by the Secretary, for the command of Congress was that "no passport shall be granted or issued to or verified for any other persons than those owing allegiance, whether citizens or not, to the United States." 32 Stat. 386, 22 U.S.C. §212. Second, was the question whether the applicant was participating in illegal conduct, trying to escape the toils of the law, promoting passport frauds, or otherwise engaging in conduct which would violate the laws of the United States. . . .

The grounds for refusal asserted here do not relate to citizenship or allegiance on the one hand or to criminal or unlawful conduct on the other. Yet, so far as relevant here, those two are the only ones which it could fairly be argued were adopted by Congress in light of prior administrative practice. One can find in the records of the State Department rulings of subordinates covering a wider range of activities than the two indicated. But as respects Communists these were scattered rulings and not consistently of one pattern. We can say with assurance that whatever may have been the practice after 1926, at the time the Act of July 3, 1926 was adopted, the administrative practice, so far as relevant here, had jelled only around the two categories mentioned. We, therefore, hesitate to impute to Congress, when in 1952 it made a passport necessary for foreign travel and left its issuance to the discretion of the Secretary of State, a purpose to give him unbridled discretion to grant or withhold a passport from a citizen for any substantive reason he may choose.

More restrictive regulations were applied in 1918 and in 1941 as war measures. We are not compelled to equate this present problem of statutory construction with problems that may arise under the war power.

Since we start with an exercise by an American citizen of an activity included in constitutional protection we will not readily infer that Congress gave the Secretary of State unbridled discretion to grant or withhold it. If we were dealing with political questions entrusted to the Chief Executive by the Constitution we would have a different case. But there is more involved here. [A]s we have seen, the right of exit is a personal right included within the word "liberty" as used in the Fifth Amendment. If that "liberty" is to be regulated, it must be pursuant to the law-making functions of the Congress. Youngstown Sheet & Tube Co. v. Sawyer, 343 U.S. 579 (1952). And if that power is delegated, the standards must be adequate to pass scrutiny by the accepted tests. Where activities or enjoyment, natural and often necessary to the well-being of an American citizen, such as travel, are involved, we will construe narrowly all delegated powers that curtail or dilute them. . . .

Thus we do not reach the question of constitutionality. We only conclude that §1185 [Act of 1952] and §21la [Act of 1856] do not delegate . . . the . . . authority exercised here. Reversed.

[Mr. Justice Clark, with whom Mr. Justice Burton, Mr. Justice Harlan, and Mr. Justice Whittaker concurred, dissented on the grounds that past practices showed that the secretary had withheld passports "for reasons of national security," both during wartime and in times of "national emergency," such as the present.]

Questions on *Kent v. Dulles* and "Clear Statement" Principles

1. Kent v. Dulles is one of a large number of cases reading agency authority narrowly so as to avoid a serious constitutional question. The basic idea is that Congress must provide a "clear statement" for courts to allow certain results to be reached.

There are two different formulations of this clear statement principle. (1) Sometimes, courts interpret statutes narrowly so as to avoid *invalidity*. (2) Sometimes, courts interpret statutes narrowly so as to avoid *ruling on a serious constitutional issue*. The second formulation allows far more judicial "bending" of statutes because it allows statutes to be construed away from the domain of constitutional doubt even if they would not be found unconstitutional if the court reached the constitutional issue. Can the second formulation be justified? Might it not create a kind of "penumbral Constitution," in which the courts press statutes in particular directions, and legislative inertia is such that the judicial interpretation is usually final?

Consider the possibility that the clear statement principle, in this second form, is a more modest and targeted version of the nondelegation principle. The idea is that Congress, not agencies, must make particular decisions when constitutionally sensitive interests are at stake; courts will not allow agencies to make such decisions when Congress has not thought about the issue with particularity. See J. Ely, Democracy and Distrust

131-133 (1980). Consider too the possibility that the second formulation is a response to the fact that some constitutional norms are "underenforced." See Sager, Fair Measure: The Legal Status of Underenforced Constitutional Norms, 91 Harv. L. Rev. 1222 (1978). On this view, courts are aware of their institutional limits and hence do not enforce the Constitution to its full extent. The clear statement principle does not result in invalidity and hence reflects some modesty on the part of the courts; but it signals the existence of a constitutional norm that Congress, at least, must take into account. On this view, the clear statement principle can be understood as a kind of "nondelegation canon," barring agencies from deciding certain sensitive issues on their own. See Sunstein, Nondelegation Canons, 67 U. Chi. L. Rev. 315 (2000).

2. But how can the Court possibly read such a broad grant of authority — "under such rules as the President shall designate and prescribe" — as limiting the secretary's power to deny the issuance of passports to cases of disloyalty or illegality? Is the Court claiming that, despite the broad language of the statute, Congress intended to grant a much narrower discretion?

3. Is the Court's position rather that Congress's "intent," or the ordinary meaning of the statutory terms, is irrelevant, because the executive's consistent exercise of the passport power in specified ways has operated to circumscribe the power delegated? Why should administrative practice redefine the extent of a delegated power? Is this a kind of "adverse possession" rule for statutory interpretation? Might it be an effort to discipline administrative authority by invoking principles of stare decisis, akin to those used by courts?

4. Why didn't the Court invalidate the entire passport statute as an unconstitutional delegation of legislative power due to lack of any standards? Why might the approach actually taken in *Kent* be preferable to total invalidation?

5. Given the widespread criticism of agency "failure," should all delegations of authority to administrators be narrowly construed? Courts have sometimes stretched legislative grants of authority to enable agencies to deal with all related aspects of a regulatory problem. Would narrow construction be a better way of limiting agency discretion than attempting to force greater legislative specificity through use of the nondelegation doctrine?

6. Should the principle of clear statement extend to interests that do not enjoy constitutional status? Consider, for example, Judge Leventhal's conclusion that the statute in *Amalgamated Meatcutters*, did not authorize wage and price controls that were unfair or inequitable. Is this not an application of clear statement principles to economic regulation?

Beyond the problem of identifying those interests to which clear statement principles apply is the problem of deciding when Congress has spoken with sufficient explicitness to satisfy the requirement of clear statement. Does the degree of explicitness required depend on the constitutional importance of the interest involved?

Chevron vs. Canons of Construction?

1. What happens when clear statement principles conflict with *Chevron* deference? Would or should Kent v. Dulles come out the other way after *Chevron*? Many cases suggest that the principle of clear statement takes precedence over *Chevron* — that an agency may not interpret an ambiguous statute so as to raise a serious constitutional

question. See, e.g., Solid Waste Agency v. U.S. Army Corps of Engineers, 121 S. Ct. 675, 683 (2001); DeBartolo Corp. v. Florida Gulf Coast, 485 U.S. 568 (1988) (construing NLRA narrowly so as to avoid potential first amendment problem); see also Bowen v. Georgetown Univ. Hospital, 488 U.S. 204 (1988) (construing statute narrowly so as to avoid retroactivity, thus trumping *Chevron*); California State Bd. v. FTC, 910 F.2d 976 (D.C. Cir. 1990) (invalidating Federal Trade Commission (FTC) rule despite *Chevron* because of federalism-related canons).

Consider in this regard the following important case. The Public Health Service Act provides for federal funding for public and nonprofit family planning projects. It provides that no such funds "shall be used in programs where abortion is a method of family planning." In 1988, the secretary of Health and Human Services (HHS), reversing a long-standing contrary policy, issued regulations providing that no federally funded project could inform clients about abortion as a means of terminating pregnancy or refer them to abortion services. In Rust v. Sullivan, 500 U.S. 173 (1991), the Court upheld the validity of the regulations. It found the statutory language and history ambiguous on the question whether abortion counseling and referrals were proscribed. *Chevron* deference was therefore appropriate. "The Secretary's construction should not be disturbed as an abuse of discretion if it reflects a plausible construction of the statute and does not otherwise conflict with Congress' intent."

Finding that the regulations satisfied this test, the Court (again citing *Chevron*) also rejected contentions that deference was inappropriate because they represented a reversal of the agency's prior position.

This Court has rejected the argument that an agency's interpretation "is not entitled to deference because it represents a sharp break with prior interpretations" of the statute in question. *Chevron*, 467 U.S. at 862. In *Chevron*, we held that a revised interpretation deserves deference because "[a]n initial agency interpretation is not instantly carved in stone" and "the agency, to engage in informed rulemaking, must consider varying interpretations and the wisdom of its policy on a continuing basis." An agency is not required to "establish rules of conduct to last forever," but rather "must be given ample latitude to 'adapt [its] rules and policies to the demands of changing circumstances.'"

We find that the Secretary amply justified his change of interpretation with a "reasoned analysis." The Secretary explained that the regulations are a result of his determination, in the wake of the critical reports of the General Accounting Office (GAO) and the Office of the Inspector General (OIG), that prior policy failed to implement properly the statute and that it was necessary to provide "clear and operational guidance to grantees to preserve the distinction between Title X programs and abortion as a method of family planning." 53 Fed. Reg. 2923-2924 (1988). He also determined that the new regulations are more in keeping with the original intent of the statute, are justified by client experience under the prior policy, and are supported by shift in attitude against the "elimination of unborn children by abortion." We believe that these justifications are sufficient to support the Secretary's revised approach. Having concluded that the plain language and legislative history are ambiguous as to Congress' intent in enacting Title X, we must defer to the Secretary's permissible construction of the statute.

Moreover, and most relevant for present purposes, the statute should not be interpreted to invalidate the regulations to avoid constitutional issues. The regulations did not present "the sort of 'grave and doubtful constitutional questions' . . . that would lead us to assume that Congress did not intend to authorize their issuance." Then the Court emphasized that *Chevron* deference would be withdrawn if and only if the constituted issue were "grave." The Court proceeded to reject claims that the regulations violated first amendment free speech rights and a woman's right to choose abortion. Three dissenting justices would have required a clearer statement of Congress's intent to authorize regulations raising these constitutional issues.

> [W]here an otherwise acceptable construction of a statute would raise serious constitutional problems, "the Court will construe the statute to avoid such problems unless such construction is plainly contrary to the intent of Congress." Edward J. DeBartolo Corp. v. Florida Gulf Coast Building & Construction Trades Council, 485 U.S. 568, 575 (1988). . . . In these cases, we need only tell the Secretary that his regulations are not a reasonable interpretation of the statute; we need not tell Congress that it cannot pass such legislation. If we rule solely on statutory grounds, Congress retains the power to force the constitutional question by legislating more explicitly. It may instead choose to do nothing. That decision should be left to Congress; we should not tell Congress what it cannot do before it has chosen to do it. It is enough in this case to conclude that neither the language nor the history of §1008 compels the Secretary's interpretation, and that the interpretation raises serious First Amendment concerns. On this basis alone, I would . . . invalidate the challenged regulations.

2. The principle that statutes will be construed so as to avoid serious constitutional doubts is hardly the only clear statement principle. Courts have said, for example, that implied repeals are disfavored; that ambiguous statutes will be construed so as to apply only within the territory of the United States; that statutes will be construed favorably to Native Americans; that statutes will not likely be taken to intrude on the traditional power of the president; that there is a presumption against preemption of state law; that judicial review will be presumed. For an extensive catalog, see W. Eskridge, Dynamic Statutory Construction 323-328 (1995).

What is the relationship between these various principles or canons and *Chevron*? If an agency interprets a statute so as to apply outside the United States or so as to interfere with the sovereignty of Native Americans, what happens? Consider the view that when a principle is designed to elicit the meaning of legislative instructions, it trumps *Chevron*; that when a principle is intended to ensure legislative deliberation on some issue, it trumps *Chevron*; but that all other principles are trumped by *Chevron*. What might this view miss? In several cases, the Court has held that canons of construction trump *Chevron*. INS v. St. Cyr, 533 U.S. 289 (2001), says that statutes are normally understood to be prospective only, and hence that under *Chevron* step 1, there is no ambiguity to trigger deference. See also Bowen v. Georgetown University Hospital, 488 U.S. 204, 208-209, 212-213 (1988) (holding anti-retroactivity canon trumps *Chevron*). For a holding that the agency interpretation does not trump the canon against extraterritorial application of federal law, see EEOC v. Arabian Am. Oil Co., 499 U.S. 244 (1991). For general discussion, see Merrill & Hickman, supra; Sunstein, Nondelegation Canons, supra; Sunstein, Law and Administration After *Chevron*, 90 Colum. L. Rev. 2013 (1990).

5. Chevron *Step 2*

We have been focusing thus far on *Chevron* step 1 — on how to tell whether a statute is ambiguous and about the role of canons of construction in answering that question.

Recall that under *Chevron* step 2, agency decisions about the meaning of ambiguous provisions are to be upheld if they are "permissible" or "reasonable." There is a great deal of confusion about what step 2 specifically entails.

How, exactly, does step 2 differ from step 1? At first glance, it might seem that a decision would be impermissible or unreasonable only if it ran up against a clear expression of congressional will (and thus violated step 1). See, e.g., Toledo Hosp. v. Shalala, 104 F.3d 791 (6th Cir. 1997). This view would have the unfortunate consequence of collapsing step 2 and step 1. At second glance, it might seem that step 2 is not an inquiry into congressional instructions, but instead an assessment of whether the agency's decision survives judicial scrutiny of whether it is "reasonable" on the merits. In that view, for example, the policy in *Chevron* would fail under step 2 if the definition of source compromised both economic and environmental goals, or badly compromised environmental goals while producing little economic gain. This interpretation of step 2 — which appears to be the prevailing one — would make it very close to judicial review of agency policy choices for arbitrariness under the hard look doctrine. Recent cases, including suggestions from the Supreme Court, point clearly in this direction. See, e.g., Verizon Communications v. FCC, 535 U.S. 467 (2002) (upholding FCC regulations as "within the zone of reasonable interpretation subject to deference under *Chevron*" because the FCC had explained its approach in a reasoned fashion); Consumer Fedn. of Am. v. DHHS, 83 F.3d 1497 (D.C. Cir. 1996); Florida Manufactured Housing Assn. v. Cisneros, 53 F.3d 1565 (11th Cir. 1995); Consumer Madison Gas & Elec. Co. v. EPA, 25 F.3d 526 (7th Cir. 1994).

Some courts have, however, appeared or tried to distinguish between *Chevron* step 2 and review of agency decisions for arbitrariness. See, e.g., Republican National Comm. v. Federal Election Comm., 76 F.3d 400, 407 (D.C. Cir. 1996); Continental Air Lines v. Department of Transp., 843 F.2d 1444 (D.C. Cir. 1988). In this view, *Chevron* step 2 is focused on the reasonableness of the agency's interpretation of law, whereas review for arbitrariness is focused on the reasonableness of the agency's policy choice.

Consider Arent v. Shalala, 70 F.3d 610 (D.C. Cir. 1995), where the court divided on the proper analysis. The majority said that the two forms of review "overlap in some circumstances" but that *Chevron* applies to the question of statutory authority, whereas arbitrariness review applies to the question whether the policy judgment was reasonable. Judge Wald saw things somewhat differently:

> The second step [of *Chevron*] . . . entrusts agencies with authority to interpret statutory ambiguities, provided they do so in a manner that is reasonable and consistent with the statute. By contrast, garden-variety APA review . . . focuses more heavily on the agency's decisionmaking process. . . . Given these differences in the central concerns behind the two analytic frameworks, there are certainly situations where a challenge to an agency's regulation will fall squarely within one rubric, rather than another. For example, we might invalidate an agency's decision under *Chevron* as inconsistent with its statutory mandate, even though we do not believe that the decision reflects an arbitrary policy choice. Such a result might occur when we believe the agency's course of action to be the most appropriate and effective means of achieving a goal, but determine that Congress has selected a different — albeit, in our eyes, less propitious — path. Conversely, we might determine that although not barred by statute, an agency's action is arbitrary and capricious because the agency has not considered certain relevant factors or articulated any rationale for its choice. Or, along similar lines, we might find a regulation arbitrary and capricious, while

deciding that *Chevron* is inapplicable because Congress' delegation to the agency is so broad as to be virtually unreviewable.

Do you agree with Judge Wald? Notice the differences between *Chevron* step 1 and *Chevron* step 2 in the following case.

Ohio v. Department of Interior

880 F.2d 432 (D.C. Cir. 1989)

[Various environmental groups, states, and industry groups sought judicial review of the natural resource damage assessment regulations promulgated by the Interior Department (DOI), challenging different parts of the regulations. The portions of the opinion excerpted below deal with issues relating to the valuation of damages. Part III of the opinion was written by Judge Wald, Part VI was written by Judge Mikva, and Part XIII by Judge Robinson.]

III. THE "LESSER-OF" RULE

The most significant issue in this case concerns the validity of the regulation providing that damages for despoilment of natural resources shall be "the *lesser of*: restoration or replacement costs; or diminution of use values." 43 C.F.R. §11.35(b)(2)(1987) (emphasis added).

State and Environmental Petitioners challenge Interior's "lesser of" rule, insisting that CERCLA requires damages to be at least sufficient to pay the cost in every case of restoring, replacing or acquiring the equivalent of the damaged resource (hereinafter referred to shorthandedly as "restoration"). Because in some — probably a majority of — cases lost-use-value will be lower than the cost of restoration, Interior's rule will result in damages awards too small to pay for the costs or restoration.

. . . A hypothetical example will illustrate the point: imagine a hazardous substance spill that kills a rookery of fur seals and destroys a habitat for seabirds at a sealife reserve. The lost use value of the seals and seabird habitat would be measured by the market value of the fur seals' pelts (which would be approximately $15 each) plus the selling price per acre of land comparable in value to that on which the spoiled bird habitat was located. Even if, as likely, that use value turns out to be far less than the cost of restoring the rookery and seabird habitat, it would nonetheless be the only measure of damages eligible for the presumption of recoverability under the Interior rule.

After examining the language and purpose of CERCLA, as well as its legislative history, we conclude that Interior's "lessor of" rule is directly contrary to the expressed intent of Congress. The precise question here is . . . whether DOI is entitled to treat use value and restoration cost as having equal presumptive legitimacy as measure of damages.

Interior's "lessor of" rule operates on the premise that, as the cost of a restoration project goes up relative to the value of the injured resource, at some point it becomes wasteful to require responsible parties to pay the full cost of restoration. . . . The logic behind the rule is the same logic that prevents an individual from paying $8,000 to repair a collision-damaged car that was worth only $5,000 before the collision. . . . What is significant about Interior's rule is the point at which it deems restoration "inefficient." Interior chose to draw the line not at the point where restoration becomes practically impossible, nor at the point where the cost of restoration becomes grossly disproportionate to the use value of the resource, but rather at the point where restoration cost exceeds — by any amount, however small — the use value of the resource. . . .

Interior's "lessor of" rule squarely rejects the concept of any clearly expressed congressional preference for recovering the full cost of restoration from responsible parties. The challenged regulation treats the two alternative measures of damages, restoration cost and use value, as though the choice between them were a matter of complete indifference from the statutory point of view: thus, in any given case, the rule makes damages turn solely on whichever is less expensive.

The strongest linguistic evidence of Congress' intent to establish a distinct preference for restoration costs as the measure of damages is contained in §107(f)(1) of CERCLA. That section states that natural resource damages recovered by a government trustee are "for use only to restore, replace, or acquire the equivalent of such natural resources." . . . It goes on to state: "The measure of damage in any action under [§107(a)(C)] shall not be limited by sums which can be used to restore or replace such resources."

By mandating the use of all damages to restore the injured resources, Congress underscored in §107(f)(1) its paramount restorative purpose for imposing damages. . . .

Interior justifies the "lessor of" rule as being economically efficient. Under DOI's economic efficiency view, making restoration cost the measure of damages would be a waste of money whenever restoration would cost more than the use value of the resource.

The fatal flaw of Interior's approach, however, is that it assumes that natural resources are fungible goods, just like any other, and that the value to society generated by a particular resource can be accurately measured in every case — assumptions that Congress apparently rejected. As the forgoing examination of CERCLA's text, structure and legislative history illustrates, Congress saw restoration as the presumptively correct remedy for injury to natural resources. To say that Congress placed a thumb on the scales in favor of restoration is not to say that it forswore the goal of efficiency. "Efficiency," standing alone, simply means that the chosen policy will dictate the result that achieves the greatest value to society. Whether a particular choice is efficient depends on *how the various alternatives are valued.*

Our reading of CERCLA does not attribute to Congress an irrational dislike of "efficiency"; rather, it suggests that Congress was skeptical of the ability of human beings to measure the true "value" of a natural resource. Indeed, even the common law recognizes that restoration is the proper remedy for injury to property where measurement of damages by some other method will fail to compensate fully for the injury.[11]

Congress' refusal to view use value and restoration cost as having equal presumptive legitimacy merely recognizes that natural resources have value that is not readily measured by traditional means.

Our reading of the complex of relevant provisions concerning damages under CERCLA convinces us that Congress established a distinct preference for restoration cost as the measure of recovery in natural resource damage cases. This is not to say that DOI may not establish some class of cases where other considerations — i.e., infeasibility of restoration or grossly disproportionate cost to use value — warrant a different standard.

---

11. See, e.g., Trinity Church v. John Hancock Mut. Life Ins. Co., 399 Mass. 43, 502 N.E.2d 532, 536 (1987) (restoration cost is proper measure where diminution in market value is unsatisfactory or unavailable as a measure of damages, as in the case of structural damage to a church). . . .

We hold the "lesser of" rule based on comparing costs alone, however, to be an invalid determinant of whether or not to deviate from Congress' preference.

VI. THE HIERARCHY OF ASSESSMENT METHODS

The regulations establish a rigid hierarchy of permissible methods for determining "use values," limiting recovery to the price commanded by the resource on the open market, unless the trustee finds that "the market for the resource is not reasonably competitive." . . . If the trustee makes such a finding, it may "appraise" that market value in accordance with the relevant sections of the "Uniform Appraisal Standards for Federal Land Acquisition.". . . . Only when neither the market value nor the appraisal method is "appropriate" can other methods of determining use value be employed. . . .

Environmental petitioners maintain that Interior's emphasis on market value is an unreasonable interpretation of the statute, under the so-called "second prong" of *Chevron U.S.A., Inc. v. Natural Resources Defense Council, Inc.*, 467 U.S. 837, 845 . . . (1984), and we agree. While it is not irrational to look to market price as *one* factor in determining the use value of a resource, it is unreasonable to view market price as the exclusive factor, or even the predominant one. From the bald eagle to the blue whale and snail darter, natural resources have values that are not fully captured by the market system. . . .

As we have previously noted in the context of the "lessor of" rule, see supra . . . , market prices are not acceptable as primary measures of the use values of natural resources. . . . We find that DOI erred by establishing "a strong presumption in favor of market price and appraisal methodologies." 51 Fed. Reg. 27,720 (1986).

We are not satisfied that the problem is solved by the provision in section 11.83(c)(1) [of the regulations] permitting nonmarket methodologies to be used when the market for the resource is not "reasonably competitive." There are many resources whose components may be traded in "reasonably competitive markets,["] but whose total use values are not fully reflected in the prices they command in those markets. Interior itself provides ample proof of the inadequacy of the "reasonably competitive market" caveat. For example, DOI has noted that "the hierarchy established in the type B regulation" would dictate a use value for fur seals of $15 per seal, corresponding to the market price for the seal's pelt. . . . Another example of DOI's erroneous equation of market price with use value is its insistence that the sum of the fees charged by the government for the use of a resource, say, for admission to a national park, constitutes "the value to the public of recreational or other public uses of the resource" [b]ecause "these fees are what the government has determined to represent the value of the natural resource and represent an offer by a willing seller." . . . This is quite obviously and totally fallacious; there is no necessary connection between the total value to the public of a park and the fees charged as admission, which typically are set not to maximize profits but rather to encourage the public to visit the park, see 16 U.S.C. §§460-k-3, 4601-6a. In fact, the decision to set entrance fees far below what the traffic would bear is evidence of Congress's strong conviction that parks are priceless national treasures and that access to them ought to be as wide as possible, and not, as DOI would have it, a sign that parks are really not so valuable after all.

Neither the statute nor its legislative history evinces any congressional intent to limit use values to market prices. On the contrary, Congress intended the damage assessment Regulations to capture fully all aspects of loss. CERCLA section 301(c)(2) commands Interior to "identify the best available procedures to determine [natural resource] damages, including both direct and indirect injury, destruction or loss." . . .

On remand, DOI should consider a rule that would permit trustees to derive use values for natural resources by summing up all reliably calculated use values, however measured, so long as the trustee does not double count. Market valuation can of course serve as one factor to be considered, but by itself it will necessarily be incomplete. In this vein, we instruct DOI that its decision to limit the role of non-consumptive values, such as option and existence values, in the calculation of use values rests on an erroneous construction of the statute. The regulations provide that "[e]stimation of option and existence values shall be used only if the authorized official determines that no use values can be determined." . . .

DOI has erroneously construed the statute. First, section 301(c)(2) requires Interior to "take into consideration factors including, *but not limited to* . . . use value." . . . The statute's command is expressly not limited to use value; if anything, the language implies that DOI is to include in its regulations other factors in addition to use value. Second, even under its reading of section 301(c), DOI has failed to explain why option and existence values should be excluded from the category of recognized use values. . . . Option and existence values may represent "passive" use, but they nonetheless reflect utility derived by humans from a resource, and thus, prima facie, ought to be included in a damage assessment. See Cross, Natural Resource Damage Valuation, 42 Vand. L. Rev. 269, 285-89 (1989) (noting that surveys reveal that the opinion and existence value of national parks may be quite large). DOI is entitled to rank methodologies according to its view of their reliability, but it cannot base its complete exclusion of option and existence values on an incorrect reading of the statute.

We hold that the hierarchy of use values is not a reasonable interpretation of statute.

[Part VII of the opinion upheld DOI's use of a 10 percent discount rate, based on an OMB circular, to discount future year costs and benefits in determining damages and making decisions about restoration plans. Environmentalists had challenged the 10 percent figure as unduly high, resulting in undervaluation of the long-range benefits of resource restoration.]

XIII. CONTINGENT VALUATION

A. THE REGULATORY BACKGROUND

DOI's natural resource damage assessment regulations define "use value" as:

> the value to the public of recreational or other public uses of the resource, as measured by changes in consumer surplus, any fees or other payments collectable by the government or Indian tribe for a private party's use of the natural resource, and any economic rent accruing to a private party because the government or Indian tribe does not charge a fee or price for the use of the resource.

The regulations provide several approaches to use valuation. When the injured resource is traded in a market, the lost use value is the diminution in market price. When that is not precisely the case, but similar resources are traded in a market, an appraisal technique may be utilized to determine damages. When, however, neither of these two situations obtains, non-marketed resource methodologies are available. One of these is "contingent valuation" (CV), the subject of controversy here.

The CV process "includes all techniques that set up hypothetical markets to elicit an individual's economic valuation of a natural resource." CV involves a series of interviews with individuals for the purpose of ascertaining the values they respectively attach to particular changes in particular resources. Among the several formats available to an interviewer in developing the hypothetical scenario embodied in a CV survey are direct questioning, by which the interviewer learns how much the interviewee is willing to pay for the resource; bidding formats, for example, the interviewee is asked whether he or she would pay a given amount for a resource and, depending upon the response, the bid is set higher or lower until a final price is derived; and a "take or leave it" format, in which the interviewee decides whether or not he or she is willing to pay a designated amount of money for the resource. CV methodology thus enables ascertainment of individually-expressed values for different levels of quality of resources, and dollar values of individuals' changes in well-being. The regulations also sanction resort to CV methodology in determining "option"[12] and "existence"[13] values.

Industry Petitioners' complaint is limited to DOI's inclusion of CV in its assessment methodology. They claim fatal departures from CERCLA on grounds that CV methodology is inharmonious with common law damage assessment principles, and is considerably less than a "best available procedure." These petitioners further charge the DOI's extension of CERCLA's rebuttable presumption to CV assessments is arbitrary and capricious, and violation of the due process rights of a potentially responsible party. We find none of these challenges persuasive.

B. CONSISTENCY WITH CERCLA

Industry Petitioners point out that at common law there can be no recovery for speculative injuries, and they contend that CV methodology is at odds with that principle. CV methodology, they say, is rife with speculation, amounting to no more than ordinary public opinion polling.

We have already noted our disagreement with the proposition that the strictures of the common law apply to CERCLA. . . . CERCLA does, however, require utilization of the "best available procedures" for determinations of damages flowing from destruction of or injury to natural resources, and Industry Petitioners insist that CV methodology is too flawed to qualify as such. In their eyes, the CV process is imprecise, is untested, and has a built-in bias and a propensity to produce overestimation.

It cannot be gainsaid that DOI's decision to adopt CV was made intelligently and cautiously. DOI scrutinized a vast array of position papers and discussions addressing the use of CV. It recognized and acknowledged that CV needs to be "properly structured and professionally applied." . . . We find DOI's promulgation of CV methodology reasonable and consistent with congressional intent, and therefore worthy of deference.

---

12. Option value is the dollar amount an individual is willing to pay although he or she is not currently using a resource but wishes to reserve the option to use that resource in a certain state of being in the future. Final Rule, supra note 70, 51 Fed. Reg. at 27,692, 27,721. For example, an individual who does not plan to use a beach or visit the Grand Canyon may nevertheless place some value on preservation of the resource in its natural state for personal enjoyment in the event of a later change of mind.

13. Existence value is the dollar amount an individual is willing to pay although he or she does not plan to use the resource, either at present or in the future. The payment is the knowledge that the resource will continue to exist in a given state of being. Final Rule, supra note 70, 51 Fed. Reg. at 27,692, 27,721. Though lacking any interest in personally enjoying the resource, an individual may attach some value to it because he or she may wish to have the resource available for others to enjoy.

The primary argument of Industry Petitioners is that the possibility of bias is inherent in CV methodology, and disqualifies it as a "best available procedure." In evaluating the utility of CV methodology in assessing damages for impairment of natural resources, DOI surveyed a number of studies which analyzed the methodology, addressed the shortcomings of various questionnaires, and recommended steps needed to fashion reliable CV assessments. For example, an early study by the Water Resources Council advised that questions in CV surveys be "carefully designed and pretested." . . .

Industry Petitioners urge, however, that even assuming that questions are artfully drafted and carefully circumscribed, there is such a high degree of variation in size of the groups surveyed, and such a concomitant fluctuation in aggregations of damages, that CV methodology cannot be considered a "best available procedure."[14] We think this attack on CV methodology is insufficient in a facial challenge to invalidate CV as an available assessment technique. The extent of damage to natural resources from releases of oil and hazardous substances varies greatly, and though the impact may be widespread and severe, it is in the mission of CERCLA to assess the public loss. . . . The argument of Industry Petitioners strikes at CERCLA, not CV's implementation, and can appropriately be considered only by Congress.

Similarly, we find wanting Industry Petitioners' protest that CV does not rise to the status of a "best available procedure" because willingness-to-pay — a factor prominent in CV methodology — can lead to overestimates by survey respondents. The premise of this argument is that respondents do not actually pay money, and likely will overstate their willingness-to-pay. One study relied upon by Industry Petitioners hypothesizes that respondents may "respond in ways that are more indicative of what they would like to see done than how they would behave in an actual market." . . . The simple and obvious safeguard against overstatement, however, is more sophisticated questioning. Even as matters now stand, the risk of overestimation has not been shown to produce such egregious results as to justify judicial over-ruling of DOI's careful estimate of the caliber and worth of CV methodology.

We sustain DOI in its conclusion that CV methodology is a "best available procedure." As such, its conclusion in the Natural Resource Damage Assessment regulations was entirely proper.

Note on Valuing Regulatory Benefits

The Ohio case raises, in an especially dramatic setting, the problem of how to value regulatory benefits that are not traded on markets. Should such benefits be valued in accordance with their use value? Some such benefits, as the court emphasizes, are valued not merely for use, and their value (in exactly what sense?) appears to be greater than their use value. But does this make an agency's emphasis on use value unreasonable under *Chevron* step 1?

---

14. Industry Petitioners cite a study estimating the combined option and existence values to Texas residents of whooping cranes at $109,000,000 (13.9 million Texas residents ±ml $7.13). The estimate rested upon responses to a survey eliciting the amount an individual would pay for a permit to visit the National Wildlife Refuse where the whooping crane winters. Had the survey been nationwide in scope, the estimate would have been $1.58 billion. Brief for Industry Petitioners at 14 n.24 (referring to J. Stoll & L. Johnson, Concepts of Value, Non-market Valuation, and the Case of the Whooping Crane (National Resources Working Paper Series, National Resource Workgroup, Dep't of Agricultural Economics, Texas A & M Univ.) (1984) at 23-24, J.A. 2828-2829).

The goal of contingent valuation method is to decide how much to value goods that are not traded on markets. Some people think that valuation might be ascertained by looking at how people value goods that are in fact treaded on markets. See W. Kip Viscusi, Fatal Tradeoffs (1992). But judgments about how much to spend to reduce statistical risks are highly contextual, and it is not clear that a decision to purchase a smoke alarm tells us a great deal about how much people are willing to reduce (for example) a risk of death from excessive levels of sulfur dioxide. The use of contingent valuation methods in inspired by a desire to obtain more specific, contextual assessments. Rather than looking at actual choices, these methods ask people hypothetical questions about how much they would be willing to pay to avoid certain harms or conditions. See G. Tolley et al., Valuing Health for Policy 290-294 (1995); Symposium, Contingent Valuation, 8 J. Econ. Persp. 3 (1994). Much recent work with contingent valuation techniques has sought to elicit values for different states of health. In such studies, for example, people purport to be willing to pay a much greater amount to avert cancer deaths (from $1.5 million to $9.5 million) than to avert unforeseen instant death (from $1 million to $5 million). Tolley, supra, at 290-294. More generally, this work generates statistics like the following, see Tolley, supra, at 294:

Mortality Values by Cause of Death

Category *(per statistical life)*	Value estimates, in million $, low, medium, and high		
unforeseen instant death	1	2	5
asthma/bronchitis	1.3	2.5	5.5
heart disease	1.25	2.75	6
emphysema	1.4	3.5	9
lung cancer	1.5	4	9.5

Similarly, these survey techniques purport to show that people value days of illness — from coughing spells, headaches, nausea, sinus congestion, and so forth — in diverse amounts.

Despite their apparent promise, contingent valuation methods have serious limitations, related to the difficulty of mapping normative judgments into dollars and the problems created by framing effects. A special problem is that of "indifference to quantity," reflected in the fact that people will give the same dollar number to save 2000, 20,000, and 200,000 birds — or the same number to save one, two, or three wilderness areas. See Diamond and Hausman, Contingent Valuation, 8 J. Econ. Persp. 45 (1994); Kahneman & Ritov, Determinants of Stated Willingness to Pay for Public Goods, 9 J. Risk & Uncertainty 5 (1994). Consider the finding that Toronto residents are willing to pay almost as much to maintain fishing by cleaning up the lakes in a small area of Ontario as they are willing to pay to maintain fishing in all Ontario lakes. Kahneman & Knetch, Valuing Public Goods, 22 J. Envtl. Econ. & Mgt. 57 (1992). Thus a similar willingness to pay was found to preserve 110 or 10,000 acres of wetland in New Jersey. Desvousges et al., Measuring Non-Use Damages Using Contingent Valuation, Research Triangle Monograph 92-1. Relatedly, the valuation of a resource is much affected by whether it is offered alone or with other goods. Willingness to pay for spotted owls drops significantly when the spotted owl is asked to be valued with and in comparison to other species. It is pertinent in this connection that the order and number of questions seems crucial in determining valuation. When asked for their willingness to pay to preserve visibility in the Grand Canyon, people offer a number five times higher when this is the first question than when it is the third question. See id. A general conclusion is that "[i]n contrast to everyday purchases, where customers normally insist on fairly detailed information about the goods they buy, contributors to good causes are usually content with the general knowledge that something will be done." Kahneman & Ritov, supra.

What lessons emerge from these findings? It is very possible that people are not "purchasing a good" but instead are contributing to the solution of a problem. See Schkade & Payne, How People Respond to Contingent Valuation Questions: A Verbal Protocol Analysis of Willingness to Pay for an Environmental Regulation, 26 J. Envtl. Econ. & Mgt. 88 (1994). In other words, subjects in contingent valuation studies do not understand themselves as buying something in return for cash; they instead understand themselves as donors. What they are reflecting with their answer is an attitude of some kind, not a willingness to pay as understood in market behavior.

Do these points support or undermine the court's unwillingness to invalidate the Department of Interior's use of contingent valuation?

6. *More* Chevron *Puzzles*

Chevron has raised a host of additional issues. We outline some of the principal ones here.

1. *The place of legislative history.* Suppose that the text of the statute is ambiguous, but that there is legislative history arguing against the agency's view. The legislative history may appear, for example, in the House and Senate Committee reports. This question asks whether the Court means (1) the first ("clear and unambiguous") step of *Chevron* is satisfied only when the statute on its face is clear and unambiguous, or (2) the first step is satisfied when the statute is clear and unambiguous using legislative history as one of the traditional tools of statutory construction. The first of these possibilities suggests a rather revolutionary change. It would take a considerable amount of legal work away from the courts and give it to the agencies. One might view the first possibility as an administratively simple way of making sure that courts carry out Congress's desire to delegate a degree of lawmaking authority to agencies. Indeed, "textualism" — the emphasis on text as opposed to legislative history — has been defended as a way of preventing Congress from delegating lawmaking authority to its own committees and subcommittees; this idea would press in the direction of (1). See Manning, Textualism as a Nondelegation Doctrine, 97 Colum. L. Rev. 673 (1997).

As the law now stands, courts seem to use legislative history as part of *Chevron* step 1, and hence agencies will likely lose if the history counts strongly against them. See, e.g., Immigration & Naturalization Service v. Cardoza Fonseca. But to evaluate this idea, it is necessary to assess the role of legislative history in administrative law. Justice Scalia has sharply criticized judicial reliance on legislative history.

> My view that the objective indication of the words, rather than the intent of the legislature, is what constitutes the law leads me . . . to the conclusion that legislative history should not be used as an authoritative indication of a statute's meaning. This was the traditional English, and the traditional American, practice. . . . What is most exasperating about the use of legislative history, however, is that it does not even make sense for

those who accept legislative intent as the criterion. It is much more likely to produce a false or contrived legislative intent than a genuine one. The first and most obvious reason for this is that, with respect to 99.99 percent of the issues of construction reaching the courts, there is no legislative intent, so that any clues provided by the legislative history are bound to be false. The issues almost invariably involve points of relative detail, compared with the major sweep of the statute in question. . . . But assuming, contrary to all reality, that the search for "legislative intent" is a search for something that exists, that something is not likely to be found in the archives of legislative history. In earlier days, when Congress has a small staff and enacted less legislation, it might have been possible to believe that a significant number of senators or representatives were present for the floor debate, or read the committee reports, and actually voted on the basis of what they heard or read. Those days, if they existed, are long gone.

Antonin Scalia, A Matter of Interpretation 29-32 (1996). To these points it is sometimes added that legislative history often reflects the will of powerful private groups unable to get their full agenda through Congress as a whole, and that isolated factions in Congress sometimes use legislative history when they cannot use text.

An alternative position is urged in Breyer, On the Uses of Legislative History in Interpreting Statutes, 65 S. Cal. L. Rev. 845 (1992):

Congress is no longer (was it ever?) made up of part-time citizen-legislators, extemporaneous orators, who burn the midnight oil as they themselves draft the laws needed to resolve the social and political problems revealed during the day's interchange of spontaneous debate. Rather, Congress is a bureaucratic organization with twenty thousand employees, working full-time, generating legislation through complicated, but organized, processes of interaction with other institutions and groups, including executive branch departments, labor unions, business organizations, and public interest groups. These other institutions and groups (including interest groups) through their representatives (including lobbyists) often initiate legislation; they typically make clear to congressional staff just what they are trying to achieve, and why; they may suggest content and text, not only for statutes, but also for reports or floor statements; they review proposed changes; and they negotiate and compromise with staff, with legislators and with each other. The staff, working with these groups, the legislators, and other staff members, will do the same.

When this process works properly, staff members for each legislator carefully review statutory language, report language, and significant proposed language for floor statements (of the staff member's own, and of other legislators), checking for consistency with the legislator's own objectives and positions, suggesting changes, and negotiating compromises. The staff member flags matters of significant substantive or political controversy, brings them to the legislator's attention, discusses them with the legislator, and obtains instructions from the legislator about how to proceed. On important matters, staff members for legislators who are directly involved will examine with care each word and proposed change, often with representatives of affected interest groups or institutions not only in the language of the statute, but also in each committee report and the many floor statements. Significant matters will again be brought to the attention of the legislators for development of their individual positions, and for them to discuss and resolve with other legislators. The process involves continuous interaction among legislators, staff members, and representatives of those institutions or groups most likely to be affected be the proposed legislation. This process requires each legislator to rely upon staff, in the first instance, to separate the matters that are significant from those that are not; it requires each legislator to make decisions about, and to resolve with other legislators, each significant matter; and it requires each legislator further to rely upon drafters and negotiators to carry out the legislator's decisions.

The process I have just described is an institutional one, in which the legislator relies in part upon the work of staff. In this process, no legislator reads every word of every report or floor statement or proposed statute, which may consist of hundreds of pages of text. However, in this process those words are carefully reviewed by those whom they will likely affect and by the legislator's own employees. Moreover, in this process the legislator makes the significant decisions and takes responsibility for the outcome.

This institutional process, in which the legislator serves as a kind of manager, should seem familiar to those who manage other large institutions such as businesses, labor unions, and government departments. No one expects the top officials in such institutions to have read every document they generate. Yet those top officials typically are held responsible for those documents, and the outside world typically treats those documents as genuine reflections of the institution's position, whether or not the top officials actually read them. Many, if not most, institutions work through downward delegation, with responsibility flowing upward. . . . Why should the fairly public congressional legislative process, which involves checking with those whom the legislation will most likely affect, and then perhaps publicly adopting and explaining their related points of view, diminish the legitimacy of the resulting legislative history? . . .

Consider the implications of a rule that forbids the court from examining a statute's history. . . . First, how would our court have answered the interpretive question [in a case involving transit workers] without its history? Viewed from the perspective of those who worked on the law in 1964, might our answer not seem random? And would a different answer not have had at least one objectionable aspect, namely that it would frustrate the reasonable expectations of those (on both sides) who created the law in Congress?

Second, what would the effect on Congress be if it knew that courts would not consider legislative history? Suppose, in 1964, that the employers, unions, and states had thought that committee testimony, report language, floor statements, and the like could not influence a later judicial interpretation of the law's text. How would the states and employers have obtained the preemption assurance that they sought and that the unions were willing to give? They might have tried to write a statutory provision that embodied appropriate "preemption" language. But, one can easily imagine that time, the complexity and length of the overall bill, and the difficulty of foreseeing future circumstances (including how courts would interpret "anti-preemption" language) might have made it impossible for the groups to agree on statutory language. It was easier, however, for them to agree about floor statements or report language about an "intent." This language is more general in form, and would not bind courts in cases where it would make no sense to do so.

It is possible, then, that if the relevant groups, institutions, and individuals involved in the process did not believe courts would look to legislative history, they might not have agreed on the legislation. Without agreement, perhaps Congress would have enacted no "labor protection" at all, or perhaps it would have failed to pass the Urban Mass Transportation Act. An institutional device that facilitates compromise and helps develop the consensus needed to pass important legislation has at least that much to be said in its favor.

In sum, [there are five] different circumstances in which courts might turn to legislative history for help in interpreting a statute: (1) avoiding an absurd result; (2) preventing the law from turning on a drafting error; (3) understanding the meaning of specialized terms; (4) understanding the "reasonable purpose" a provision might serve; and (5) choosing among several possible "reasonable purposes" for language in a politically controversial law. The first three are not very controversial. The last two are controversial. The last two examples suggest, however, how in certain contexts reference to legislative history can promote interpretations that more closely correspond to the expectations of those who helped create the law (and whom the law will likely affect). To that extent, its use seems likely to promote fair and workable results.

Do you agree with Justice Scalia or Justice Breyer? Are there empirical disagreements between the two that might illuminate their debate?

2. *Long-standing and consistent interpretations.* Before *Chevron*, courts held that long-standing and consistent agency interpretations were entitled to special deference; a showing that agencies had been inconsistent would reduce or eliminate deference to an agency interpretation of law. Does this idea survive *Chevron*? It would be possible to argue that the whole point of *Chevron* is to enable the executive branch to resolve the "policy" questions raised whenever a statute is ambiguous. In this view, *Chevron* deference applies whether or not an agency interpretation is long-standing and consistent. See Florida Manufacturers Association v. Cisneros, 53 F.3d 1565 (11th Cir. 1995), upholding some agency interpretations, but invalidating one as reflecting an unexplained change in position. See generally Comment, *Chevron*, Take Two: Deference to Revised Agency Interpretation of Statutes, 64 U. Chi. L. Rev. 681 (1997). Some Supreme Court decisions support this view. See Rust v. Sullivan, 500 U.S. 173, 186-187 (1991) (upholding agency shift to ban funding place where abortion counseling is provided). There are some indications in Supreme Court opinions, however, suggesting that it continues to matter whether the interpretation is longstanding and consistent. See Immigration & Naturalization Service v. Cardoza Fonseca, 480 U.S. 421 (1987); Pauley v. Beth-Energy Mines, 501 U.S. 680, 698 (1991) (saying that "the case for judicial deference is less compelling with respect to agency interpretations that are inconsistent with previously held views").

In Good Samaritan Hospital v. Shalala, 500 U.S. 402 (1993), the Court, in upholding HHS Medicare reimbursement regulations observed that

> it is true that over the years the agency has embraced a variety of approaches to the statute. . . . The Secretary is not estopped from changing a view she believes to have been grounded upon a mistaken legal interpretation. Indeed, an administrative agency is not disqualified from changing its mind; and when it does, the courts still sit in review of the administrative decision and should not approach the statutory construction issue de novo and without regard to the administrative understanding of the statutes. On the other hand, the consistency of an agency's position is a factor in assessing the weight that position is due. . . . In the circumstances of this case, where the agency's interpretation of a statute is at least as plausible as competing ones, there is little, if any, reason not to defer to its construction.

Compare Malcomb v. Island Creek Coal Co., 15 F.3d 364, 369 (4th Cir. 1994), holding that deference was not due to the agency's interpretation of its rules because that interpretation was, without explanation, "shockingly inconsistent with its prior and subsequent interpretations"; Hanover v. Reich, 82 F.3d 1304 (4th Cir. 1996) (normal *Chevron* deference is not due to a new interpretation or statute by agency).

3. *Deference to whom?* Exactly which agency under *Chevron* is entitled to deference? Even where "deference" is appropriate, it is not always clear just to whom the courts should "defer." The OSH Act, for example, gives to the secretary of labor the power to

promulgate regulations and to enforce them. The secretary, in enforcing the law, must bring a proceeding against an employer before an independent commission, called the Occupational Safety and Health Review Commission (OSHRC). To whose opinion about the meaning of an OSHA regulation should the courts give weight, the secretary of labor's or OSHRC's? Several circuits, noting that the secretary is the "policymaking" expert, while OSHRC's "expertise" typically concerns factual adjudications, have deferred to the secretary. See, e.g., Donovan v. A. Amorello & Sons, 761 F.2d 61 (1st Cir. 1986). But other circuits have deferred to OSHRC. See, e.g., Brock v. Bechtel Power Co., 803 F.2d 999 (9th Cir. 1986). In Martin v. OSHRC, 499 U.S. 144 (1991), the Court held that deference was owed the secretary, finding that the power to render authoritative interpretations of OSH Act regulations is a "necessary adjunct" of the secretary's power to promulgate and enforce those regulations.

4. *Rules and case-by-case judgments.* Pauley v. Beth-Energy Mines, 501 U.S. 680, 698 (1991), involved a statute transferring administration of the federal "Black Lung" program for compensating mine workers disabled by pneumoconiosis from the HHS to the Department of Labor. HHS had promulgated regulations providing that if claimants presented certain medical evidence and work history they gained a presumption that they were "totally disabled due to pneumoconiosis" and hence entitled to compensation. Employers could rebut the presumption by showing that claimants were doing usual coal mine work or its equivalent or were capable of such work. Labor issued revised regulations providing that employers could also rebut the presumption by showing that a claimant's disability was not due to coal mine employment or that the claimant did not in fact have pneumoconiosis. The statute provided that the Department of Labor's eligibility regulations "shall not be more restrictive" than those of HHS. Labor defended its regulations on the ground that they were consistent with the basic purpose of the HHS regulations and the statute, to ensure that benefits are paid only to those disabled by pneumoconiosis resulting from mine employment. The Court upheld the validity of the Labor Department's regulations. The statute and the HHS regulations were ambiguous, and the eligibility issues involved "require significant expertise, and entail the exercise of judgment grounded in policy concerns." Hence *Chevron* deference to the Labor Department was appropriate. Justice Scalia, dissenting, found no ambiguity in the "no more restrictive" provision in the statute, nor did he find ambiguity in the HHS regulations, although they were "Byzantine." In any event, *Chevron* did not entitle one agency to deference in interpreting another's regulations, a conclusion confirmed by Martin v. OSHRC.

In this light, one might ask just how the "clear-ambiguous statutory language" distinction would help separate those instances in which Congress wished to delegate this power from those instances in which it did not. Why would one tend to think the two distinctions work in tandem? Consider, for example, a social security disability compensation statute that liberalized mental disability requirements, ordered judges to send currently pending cases back to HHS, and said that the "Secretary shall notify [individual members of certain class action suits] about reopened proceedings." The judge in one of the pending class actions thought the secretary's notification to members of that class was "gobbledegook" and rewrote it. Does the statute permit the judge to do so? The statute says nothing about a judge's power; in that respect it is ambiguous. Should the court have deferred to the secretary's legal judgment about the meaning of the statute? Certainly not. Congress would not have wanted to give the secretary the authority to second-guess the judge in this minor procedural matter relating to a pending class action. But we know this because we know about class actions, about judges' authority in class actions, about how Congress would expect judges to behave, and about what Congress was thinking in writing the statute, not because of any message, open or hidden, in the statute's language. See Avery v. Secretary of Health & Human Servs., 762 F.2d 158 (1st Cir. 1985).

A possible conclusion is that there may be a host of different reasons, indeed, different kinds of reasons, differing radically among the many thousands of various statutes and regulatory schemes, that in particular circumstances would, or would not, lead a court to conclude that Congress wanted to delegate a degree of ("legislative" or "interpretive") legal power in respect to a particular statutory question. Perhaps that is why cases following *Chevron* have often used the "traditional tools of statutory interpretation" test to invalidate agency decisions. But to what extent, you should ask, does this test make *Chevron* the revolutionary decision that it has so often been thought? Does that test not suggest that courts will defer, or not defer, on legal matters depending on what "makes sense" in the individual circumstance?

5. *Procedure and affirmative grants.* Does the type of procedure through which an agency announces its interpretation of a statute affect the degree of judicial deference accorded? *Chevron* involved regulations adopted through notice-and-comment rule-making. It is now accepted that the same level of deference applies to interpretations invoked by an agency to decide adjudications. Bowen v. Georgetown Univ. Hosp., however, states that deference is not due to interpretation and accompanying rationales offered for the first time by agency counsel in briefs defending the agency's action on review. What about other circumstances? See Motor Vehicle Mfrs. Assn. v. New York State Dept. of Envtl. Conservation, 17 F.3d 521, 535 (2d Cir. 1994) (rejecting EPA's claim that its position advanced in an amicus brief was entitled to deference under *Chevron*); Skandalis v. Rowe, 14 F.3d 173 (2d Cir. 1994) (court applied *Chevron* deference to statutory interpretation urged during litigation in agency's amicus brief because agency was not party to action, agency filed amicus brief at court's request, and agency advanced a position that it had held and implemented consistently over time); Kelley v. E. I. Du Pont de Nemours & Co., 17 F.3d 836 (6th Cir. 1994) (*Chevron* deference not due an agency's interpretation of a statute adopted in a policy statement, although such interpretations are entitled to limited and contingent deference); Koray v. Sizer, 21 F.3d 558, 562 (3d Cir. 1994) (*Chevron* deference not due a statutory interpretation contained in agency's unpublished internal guidelines); In re Appletree Markets, 19 F.3d 969 (5th Cir. 1994) (*Chevron* deference not due agency's proposed rule). See also National R.R. Passenger Corp. v. Boston & Maine Corp., 503 U.S. 407 (1992) (deferring to an interpretation that was not articulated by ICC but was a "necessary presupposition" of its decision).

What is the interplay between *Chevron* and stare decisis? Lechmere v. NLRB, 502 U.S. 527 (1992), held that *Chevron* deference was not due an NLRB interpretation of the NLRA, which was contrary to the interpretation reached by the Court in a 1956 decision that did not discuss the issue of deference to the board's contrary view. But in NLRB v. Viola Indus.-Elevator Div., 979 F.2d 1384 (10th Cir. 1992) (en banc) the court held that it should defer to the agency's new interpretation, even though the agency's prior contrary interpretation had been judicially sustained. The court noted that, although courts had found the NLRB's former interpretation of the act defensible, these opinions did not represent independent or conclusive interpretations of the statute that would bar the board from changing its mind. Because the new interpretation of the statute was also defensible, it too was upheld, contrary existing precedent notwithstanding.

Should the scope of deference be greater when Congress affirmatively grants broad lawmaking power to an agency, as compared to a situation, as in *Chevron*, where a statutory term is general or vague? The remedial provisions of the National Labor Relations Act authorize the NLRB "to take such affirmative action including reinstatement of employees with or without back pay, as will effectuate the policies of the Act." ABF Freight System v. NLRB, 510 U.S. 317 (1994), upheld the board's reinstatement of a discharged worker notwithstanding that the worker had lied in sworn testimony before the board. The Court stated: "When Congress expressly delegates to an administrative agency the authority to make specific policy determinations, [its] views warrant the greatest deference." In the case of a rule, should the scope of *Chevron* deference vary depending on whether the agency's interpretation is embodied in a "legislative" as opposed to an "interpretive" rule?

6. *Effects*. What have been the real-world effects of *Chevron*? An interesting empirical study of administrative law cases found that *Chevron* made a considerable short-term difference, raising affirmance rates from 71 percent (in the pre-*Chevron* year of 1984) to 81 percent (in the post-*Chevron* year of 1985). Overall, "affirmance" rates have increased dramatically since the mid-1960s and mid-1970s. In 1965, of all administrative appeals decided on the merits, 43 percent were reversed or remanded; by 1975 that number had fallen to 39 percent; by 1985, it had fallen to 17 percent. One can speculate about possible causes. (To what extent does this reflect a different mix of cases or an increase in the appellate court caseload leading to higher affirmance rates overall, or other factors?) Still, the number is interesting, for it suggests that in the vast majority of cases the agency's decision is ultimately controlling. See Schuck and Elliot, To the *Chevron* Station: An Empirical Study of Federal Administrative Law, 42 Duke L.J. 984 (1989).

Empirical studies by Thomas Merrill reach a different conclusion, finding that the Supreme Court, at least, is far from consistent in its use of *Chevron*. See Merrill, Judicial Deference to Executive Precedent, 101 Yale L.J. 969 (1992); Merrill, Textualism and the Future of the *Chevron* Doctrine, 72 Wash. U. L.Q. 351 (1994).

Does it matter whether judges applying *Chevron* are inclined to agree, or not to agree, with the agency? For some striking and perhaps somewhat alarming sets of findings, see Richard Revesz, Environmental Regulation, Ideology, and the D.C. Circuit, 83 Va. L. Rev. 1717 (1997). Cross & Tiller, Judicial Partisanship and Obedience to Legal Doctrine: Whistleblowing on the Federal Courts of Appeals, 107 Yale L.J. 2155 (1998). Revesz finds that a panel of three Republican appointees is far more likely than a panel of two Republican appointees and one Democrat to reverse an environmental decision at the behest of industry challengers.

7. *Readings*. It is a gross understatement to say that many articles have been written about *Chevron*. In addition to those cited above, you might want to look at one or more of the following. Anthony, Which Agency Interpretations Should Bind the Courts?, 7 Yale J. Reg. 1 (1990); Breyer, Judicial Review of Questions of Law and Policy, 38 Admin. L. Rev. 363 (1986); Byse, Judicial Review of Administrative Interpretation of Statutes: An Analysis of *Chevron*'s Step Two, 2 Admin. L.J. 255 (1988); Pierce, *Chevron* and Its Aftermath: Judicial Review of Agency Interpretations of Statutory Provisions, 41 Vand. L. Rev. 301 (1988); Starr, Judicial Review in the Post-*Chevron* Era, 3 Yale J. Reg. 283 (1986).

7. Chevron *Summary: A Broad Version and Four Narrowing Techniques*

It may be helpful, as an overview and organizational device, to think first of the broadest (or perhaps strongest) possible version of *Chevron*, and then of some ways in which the broad version can and has been narrowed or weakened.

At one extreme lies Justice Scalia's view of *Chevron*'s scope: *Chevron* deference is triggered whenever an agency makes an "authoritative" pronouncement. *Chevron* deference then applies to all determinations of law that the agency makes, even those about the scope of the agency's own "jurisdiction." This view creates a useful baseline, not because it is necessarily correct, but because it is rather simple and sweeping. Of course, much depends on what counts as "authoritative," and Justice Scalia would admit many of the exceptions to *Chevron*'s scope we have discussed supra, such as the principle that *Chevron* does not apply when multiple agencies are charged with administering the same statute.

Given this baseline, we might then organize the *Chevron* framework around four different ways of narrowing or weakening this relatively broad version:

(1) *No deference on "pure" questions of law.* This was the tack attempted by *Chevron*'s author, Justice Stevens, in *Cardoza-Fonseca*, supra. It has implicitly been rejected many times, and shows no signs of reviving. It remains of interest, however, as a possible indicator that Justice Stevens favors a relatively narrow version of *Chevron*; consider his opinion in Sweet Home v. Babbitt, excerpted above and discussed in (4) below.

(2) Chevron *Step Zero.* We have seen that, in *Christensen, Mead*, and subsequent decisions, a decisive coalition of Justices — including Breyer, Stevens, and Souter — have introduced a rather elaborate series of preconditions for applying *Chevron* at all. *Mead*'s central innovation is to switch the default rule from the one Justice Scalia would apply: rather than presuming that statutory silence or ambiguity entails an implicit delegation of law-interpreting authority to agencies, this line of cases stipulates that such a delegation must be affirmatively shown in each case (although *Mead*'s procedural proxies may make this showing easy where the agency has acted formally). On a historical view, Justice Breyer rather than Justice Stevens may be the moving force here; we may see the evolution of an elaborate "Step Zero" inquiry as implementing his view that deference should rest on a case-by-case determination of legislative intentions. See Sunstein, *Chevron* Step Zero, supra.

(3) Chevron *and the canons.* We have also seen that, increasingly, the courts are willing to trump *Chevron* with canons of construction, such as the canon that statutes be construed to avoid serious constitutional questions. In this connection, consider especially the idea that statutes should be construed to avoid constitutional questions arising under the nondelegation doctrine, discussed in Chapter 2. The *MCI* opinion suggests, and the *Brown & Williamson* opinion explicitly states, that Congress will have to speak clearly to assign questions of "great economic and political" significance to agencies; we may see this as an application of the constitutional avoidance canon, with the unexpressed premise that real nondelegation questions arise when agencies are given charge of such decisions.

A nondelegation canon strikes at the heart of *Chevron*, which is after all premised on the view that Congress intends, or for institutional reasons should be taken to intend, to delegate law-interpreting power to agencies. Suppose that the relevant statutes at issue in *Brown & Williamson* had been indisputably clear in favor of the dissent's view that the FDA has jurisdiction to prohibit tobacco. Would there be a plausible claim that the nondelegation doctrine had been violated? Does anything in the modern nondelegation case law suggest that serious nondelegation questions would arise when decisions of great economic and political significance are vested in agencies? (How about the FCC's authority to regulate telecommunications in "the public interest" — is this not of great significance?) Would it be too simple to say that after the Whitman v. American Trucking case, excerpted in Chapter 2, all such challenges are extremely unlikely to succeed?

If this is so, perhaps *Brown & Williamson*'s nondelegation canon cannot, after all, be justified as an application of the constitutional avoidance canon. Could we defend the nondelegation canon on precisely the opposite ground — that nondelegation is an "underenforced constitutional norm"? On this view, an interpretive canon is necessary precisely because no serious constitutional question is posed by nondelegation challenges, in turn because the constitutional nondelegation doctrine is moribund.

But if both such rationales are available, doesn't it mean that an argument for trumping *Chevron* is always available, whether or not there is an underlying constitutional problem? Is this a sort of Potemkin *Chevron*?

(4) *Weightless* Chevron. Trumping *Chevron* with the canons is a special case of a more general technique for diminishing *Chevron*'s importance. On this general approach, evident in Sweet Home and Brown & Williamson, *Chevron* "applies" in a nominal sense, but a broad range of other sources — canons, legislative history, other statutes, common law background, and considerations of policy — do all the heavy lifting. Deference is a consideration with little or no weight; at best it acts as a tiebreaker where all other sources are in equipoise. Consider the remarkable majority and dissenting opinions in *Sweet Home*. In neither opinion was *Chevron* a prominent theme; the majority opinion, which might have relied on *Chevron* to uphold the agency regulation, does not mention it until a brief concluding passage, and then only for the idea that, in the circumstances at hand, the Court owes "some degree of deference" to the secretary's reasonable interpretation. *Sweet Home*, supra (citing Breyer, Judicial Review of Questions of Law and Policy, 38 Admin. L. Rev. 363, 373 (1986)). In such cases, it looks as though the judges do statutory interpretation exactly as they would do it were there no agency in the picture.

8. Chevron *at War*?

In response to the terrorist attacks of September 11, 2001, Congress passed a resolution authorizing the President to "use all necessary and appropriate force against those nations, organizations, or persons he determines planned, authorized, committed, or aided the terrorist attacks" or "harbored such organizations or persons, in order to prevent any future acts of international terrorism against the United States by such nations, organizations or persons." Authorization for Use of Military Force ("the AUMF"), 115 Stat. 224. Presidential determinations and actions under this and similar statutes are typically treated under the rubric of constitutional law, foreign affairs law, or national security law. Is it helpful, additionally or instead, to see them as ordinary administrative law questions?

The question has many ramifications; two are especially important. The first, addressed here, is whether legal determinations by the President under statutes touching on war, emergency, and foreign affairs might be viewed through the lens of *Chevron* when those determinations are subject to judicial review. The second, addressed in Chapter 8, is whether and when Presidential determinations under such statutes — determinations of "fact" as well as "law" — are reviewable at all.

Is *Chevron* the right framework, or a valid framework, for judicial deference to presidential determination of legal questions? For discussion, see Sunstein, Administrative Law Goes to War, 118 Harv. L. Rev. 2663 (2005); Bradley, Chevron Deference and Foreign Affairs, 86 Va. L. Rev. 649 (2000).

Consider the relevance of the following two cases. The APA authorizes judicial review only of "agency" actions. Franklin v. Massachusetts, 505 U.S. 788 (1992), held that the 1990 census, which was statutorily required to be submitted by the president to the Congress as the basis for apportioning representation in the Congress, could not be reviewed on claims that it was arbitrary and capricious because (1) the Census Act does not provide for judicial review, and (2) the president is not an "agency" for APA purposes and hence review could not be based on the APA. With respect to the application of the APA to the president, Justice O'Connor wrote:

> The APA defines "agency" as "each authority of the Government of the United States, whether or not it is within or subject to review by another agency, but does not include — (A) the Congress; (B) the courts of the United States; (C) the governments of the territories or possessions of the United States; (D) the government of the District of Columbia." 5 U.S.C. §§701(b)(1), 551(1). The President is not explicitly excluded from the APA's purview, but he is not explicitly included, either. Out of respect for the separation of powers and the unique constitutional position of the President, we find that textual silence is not enough to subject the President to the provisions of the APA. We would require an express statement by Congress before assuming it intended the President's performance of his statutory duties to be reviewed for abuse of discretion.

Franklin was followed and extended in Dalton v. Spector, 511 U.S. 462 (1994), where plaintiffs challenged various actions taken to close military bases under the Defense Base Closure and Realignment Act of 1990. Under the Act, the Base Closing Commission would recommend the closing of specified bases, and then the president would submit to Congress his certification of approval of the Commission's report. The five-justice majority held that the recommendation by the Commission is not reviewable because it is not "final agency action" — and that the president's submission to Congress of his approval is unreviewable because the president is not an agency. For a pertinent qualification, see Chamber of Commerce v. Reich, 74 F.3d 1322 (D.C. Cir. 1996), where the court held that unless the governing statute precludes review of presidential action, acts of the president are subject to nonstatutory review if the plaintiff alleges that (a) those acts are ultra vires and (b) those acts violate a specific statutory provision or deprive an individual of a right explicitly or implicitly granted by the statute.

Some questions:

(1) If the President is not an "agency" within the meaning of the Administrative Procedure Act, what follows for *Chevron*? Consider this possible answer: Nothing follows, because *Chevron* is not based upon a reading of the Administrative Procedure Act. *Chevron* rests on either or both of two bases: (1) a judicial determination that, where statutes are silent or ambiguous, Congress can in some circumstances be taken to have an implicit intention that courts should defer to relevant administrators — emphatically including the President; (2) a judicial determination, on institutional grounds, that where statutes permit, legal policy will be improved if judges defer to administrative policymakers who are expert and politically accountable — emphatically including the President. On either reading of *Chevron*, it would be irrelevant that the president is not an "agency."

(2) Suppose that presidential determinations under a statute like the AUMF, described above, are not made through rulemaking or APA-style adjudication; rather they are made through informal processes. Does the *Mead* decision then suggest that no *Chevron* deference is due the president? For a negative answer to this question, see Sunstein, Administrative Law Goes to War, supra.

(3) As we have seen, with increasing frequency the Court "trumps" *Chevron* deference with other interpretive canons. What canons might be taken to trump *Chevron*

deference to the president? Consider whether and to what extent it would be sensible to apply any of the following canons, all with support in case law, to a presidential determination that a person seized in a foreign combat zone, such as Afghanistan, counts as an "enemy combatant" for purposes of international or domestic law: (a) statutes should be construed not to apply extraterritorially, unless Congress clearly indicated the contrary; (b) statutes should be construed to incorporate traditional principles of international law and foreign affairs law, unless the statute clearly rejects those principles; (c) statutes involving "core functions" of the executive should be construed to authorize executive action, if it is fairly possible to do so; (d) statutes will be construed, if fairly possible, not to infringe constitutionally protected liberty interests or otherwise to raise serious constitutional questions. For more on the "enemy combatant" problem in connection with reviewability, see the Note on Reviewability at War in Chapter 8.

9. Agency Interpretations of Agency Regulations

Should courts defer to agency interpretations of agency regulations? The usual answer is that when regulations are ambiguous, agencies get to interpret them.

Note that the interpretation by an agency of its own regulations presents a different question from those raised by agency interpretation of a statute. In such a case, traditional doctrine has it that the court has a strong obligation to "look to the administrative construction of the regulation if the meaning of the words is in doubt." Thus, the leading case says that "the ultimate criterion is the administrative interpretation, which becomes of controlling weight unless it is plainly erroneous or inconsistent with the regulation." Bowles v. Seminole Rock Co., 325 U.S. 410, 413-414 (1945). This view was reaffirmed in Auer v. Robbins, 519 U.S. 79 (1997). The Court said that an agency interpretation of an agency rule is "controlling unless plainly erroneous or inconsistent with the regulation." It said this even though the interpretation appeared in a mere brief. In the Court's view, a "rule requiring the Secretary to construe his own regulations narrowly would make little sense, since he is free to write the regulations as broadly as he wishes, subject only to the limits imposed in the statute." For rejection of an agency interpretation of an agency rule, see Director, OWCP v. Greenwich Collieries, 512 U.S. 267 (1994); Jicarilla Apache Tribe v. FERC, 578 F.2d 289, 292-293 (10th Cir. 1978). But there is some uncertainty in the law. Indeed, there has been some rethinking of the *Seminole Rock* principle.

Shalala v. Guernsey Memorial Hospital, 514 U.S. 89 (1995), involved denial by HHS of certain medicare reimbursement claims by a hospital for accounting losses ("defeasance cost") associated with refinancing of the hospital's bonded debt. The hospital contended that all of this cost should be recognized in the year of refinancing; HHS contended that it should be amortized over the life of the old bonds. The Medicare statute authorizes HHS to promulgate regulations "establishing the method or methods to be used" in determining cost reimbursement, and directs HHS in doing so to "consider, among other things, the principles applied by national organizations" in computing reimbursement amounts. HHS issued cost reimbursement regulations providing: "The principles of cost reimbursement require that providers maintain sufficient financial records and statistical data for proper determination of costs payable under the [Medicare] program. Standardized definitions, accounting statistics and reporting practices that are widely accepted in the hospital and related fields are followed."

The hospital claimed that the reference in the reimbursement regulations to "standardized definitions, accounting statistics, and reporting practices" were the equivalent of the generally accepted accounting principles (GAAP) recognized by the accounting profession, and that under GAAP, the entire amount of defeasance cost was reimbursable in the year of financing. HHS rejected this claim, asserting that the regulations' reference to standardized methods only governed how hospital records should be kept, not the substantive principles governing reimbursement. Instead, it relied on informal HHS guidelines that provided that defeasance losses should be amortized over the life of the old bonds.

Without citing *Chevron*, the Court upheld the position of HHS, finding that its regulations were clearly authorized by the Medicare statute and that HHS's interpretation of its regulations was "reasonable." The Court quoted prior decisions that "because applying an agency's regulation to complex or changing circumstances calls upon the agency's unique expertise and policymaking prerogatives, we presume that the power authoritatively to interpret its own regulations is a component of the agency's delegated lawmaking powers," and that an "agency's construction of its own regulations is entitled to substantial deference." The Court also held that HHS was not required to adopt its interpretation of the defeasance cost issue through notice-and-comment rulemaking.

Four justices, dissenting, concluded that the regulations incorporated GAAP, and that HHS could not in any event rely on the interpretation in its informal guidance because the Medicare statute requires that all policies regarding cost reimbursement be incorporated in regulations adopted after notice and opportunity for comment.

Manning, Constitutional Structure and Judicial Deference to Agency Interpretations of Agency Rules, 96 Colum. L. Rev. 612 (1996), attacks the *Seminole Rock* principle at the same time it defends *Chevron*. Part of Manning's argument is that if agencies are entitled to interpret their own regulations as they see fit, they will be given less of an incentive to provide clear guidance before the fact and will be tempted instead to issue ambiguous regulations, secure in the knowledge that the regulations can be interpreted as they wish. In this respect, Manning argues that the *Seminole Rock* principle is far more fragile than the *Chevron* principle.

E. The "Arbitrary and Capricious" Standard and the Hard Look Doctrine

Under the APA, courts are instructed to set aside agency action that is "arbitrary, capricious, or an abuse of discretion." What does this mean?

1. The Road to Overton Park and the Origins of "Hard Look" Review

There are many puzzles about the original meaning of judicial review under the "arbitrary and capricious" standard. Often, agency processes would not produce a "record" at all under the APA as it was originally written. (Review of a record would be for "substantial evidence," as discussed at the beginning of this chapter.) Moreover, the legislative history of the APA explains the arbitrary and capricious standard by reference to Supreme Court decisions under the due process clause reviewing government decisions for "rationality." Hence, it would be possible to think that judicial review under that standard was supposed to be highly deferential. Some early cases suggested that it was enough for the agency to show a minimally plausible connection between a statutory goal and the choice actually made. Under this approach, almost all of the cases to be discussed here would come out the same way: The agency would win.

But there are countervailing considerations. In some cases, the APA appears to call for de novo review, in which district courts actually engage in independent factfinding. See APA §706. Perhaps the drafters of the APA contemplated de novo review of agency action for which there was no record. See Nathanson, Probing the Mind of the Administrator, 75 Colum. L. Rev. 721 (1975). (The *Overton Park* case reads the de novo review provision very narrowly.) Moreover, the due process cases cited in the legislative history of the APA were decided during the *Lochner* era, in which the Supreme Court was quite aggressive. Finally, a prime goal of the APA was to strengthen judicial review of agency decisions, and at least in an era in which much of agency policymaking takes place via informal rulemaking (and hence subject to the arbitrary and capricious standard), it might seem odd to say that courts should uphold agency decisions whenever they are minimally rational.

In the 1960s, courts were under considerable pressure to strengthen judicial review of agency rulemaking. Agencies were frequently said to be "captured" by one or another side. (See Chapter 3.) At the same time, agencies were increasingly using informal rulemaking as the procedural vehicle of choice, thus making substantial evidence review unavailable. In these circumstances, courts gave birth to the "hard look doctrine." At first, this meant that courts would ensure that agencies themselves took a "hard look" at the problem. Thus, courts required agencies to consider in their proceedings and opinions all of the relevant policies and factors bearing on discretionary policy choices. But soon thereafter courts began to take a "hard look" on their own. Thus, sometimes courts closely scrutinized the logical and factual bases for the choices made. In an influential essay, this approach was explained by Judge Leventhal of the District of Columbia Circuit Court of Appeals, who asserted that reviewing courts must determine whether the agency both has taken a "hard look" at the relevant evidence and policy alternatives, and has made a reasoned exercise of its discretion in a given case. See Leventhal, Environmental Decisionmaking and the Role of the Courts, 122 U. Pa. L. Rev. 509, 511 (1974). That "hard look" approach requires agencies to develop an evidentiary record reflecting the factual and analytical basis for their decisions, to explain in considerable detail their reasoning, and to give "adequate consideration" to the evidence and analysis submitted by private parties.

This approach to judicial review of discretion emphasizes process. The agency ultimately employs discretion to choose among relevant alternatives not foreclosed by statute. But it must develop relevant information about the effects of the alternatives, and it must explain the considerations involved in choosing among them. We may describe as the "procedural hard look" the idea that agencies must consider alternatives, respond to counterarguments, listen to affected interests, and offer detailed explanations of their conclusions. This process approach may be contrasted with a "substantive" version of arbitrary and capricious review, under which the court judges the alternative chosen by the agency to be so irrational that it must be ruled out. Thus, the "substantive hard look" entails close judicial control of the merits.

Under the "hard look" or "adequate consideration" approach, the court usually does not condemn the agency's policy choice as irremediably faulty, but simply concludes that the agency has not adequately justified its choice. The normal remedy is a remand for further proceedings in which the agency may attempt to buttress its original policy choice with more extensive analysis and explanation. The court may find the decision to be "arbitrary and capricious" because it is not adequately explained or justified, but the agency remains free to try again.

The "hard look" or "adequate consideration" approach has its roots in SEC v. Chenery Corp., 318 U.S. 80 (1943), examined in Chapter 5, which required that an agency provide a sustainable explanation for an exercise of this discretion. But the real development of this approach occurred during the late 1960s and early 1970s, considerably encouraged by the Supreme Court's *Overton Park* decision; although stating that the ultimate substantive standard of review under the "arbitrary and capricious" standard is narrow, the Court emphasized that courts reviewing agency discretion should engage in a "searching and careful inquiry" into the agency's "consideration of the relevant factors" and the factual foundations of its policy choice. Consider the following cases.

Scenic Hudson Preservation Conference v. FPC (I)

354 F.2d 608 (2d Cir. 1965)

HAYS, Circuit Judge: . . .

[Consolidated Edison wished to build a pumped storage hydroelectric project on the west side of the Hudson River at Storm King Mountain. The project consisted of a water reservoir, a power house, and power lines. It was estimated to cost $162 million. Conservationists opposed its construction.

Consolidated Edison needed a license for the project from the FPC (now the Federal Energy Regulatory Commission (FERC)). After elaborate hearings the FPC granted the license. It noted that under the relevant statute, it had to consider all relevant factors (including recreational and scenic factors), it had to make certain that there was no alternative to the Storm King plan that would be "better adapted to the development of the Hudson River for all beneficial uses, including scenic beauty," but, if it determined that the Storm King plan was (in the statute's words) "best adapted to a comprehensive plan for improving or developing a waterway," then it should grant the license.

The Court of Appeals found that the commission had failed adequately to consider several factors, the most important of which consisted of testimony by Mr. Alexander Lurkis, a former chief engineer of the New York City Bureau of Gas and Electric, in which he presented "a detailed proposal for using gas turbines" as an alternative, a proposal that he claimed would save consumers $132 million. The record contained only a "scanty," less than ten-page discussion seeking to explain why the gas turbine alternative would not work. Although Mr. Lurkis did not present his plan until two months after the FPC granted the license and four months after final oral argument, a statute permits a court to require the FPC to consider "additional evidence" if it is "material" and there were "reasonable grounds for failure to adduce" it earlier.]

Especially in a case of this type, where public interest and concern is so great, the Commission's refusal to receive the Lurkis testimony, as well as proffered information on fish protection devices and underground transmission facilities, exhibits a disregard of the statute and of judicial mandates instructing the Commission to probe all feasible alternatives. . . . As Commissioner Ross said in his dissent:

> I do feel the public is entitled to know on the record that no stone has been left unturned. . . . A regulatory commission can insure continuing confidence in its decisions only when it has used its staff and its own expertise in a manner not possible for the uninformed and poorly financed public. [I]t should be possible to resolve all doubts as to alternative sources. This may have been done but the record doesn't speak. . . .

The Commission has an affirmative duty to inquire into and consider all relevant facts. . . . The Commission should reexamine all questions on which we have found the record insufficient and all related matters [including danger to fish, power pooling, and the use of underground transmission wires]. The Commission's renewed proceedings must include as a basic concern the preservation of natural beauty and of national historic shrines, keeping in mind that, in our affluent society, the cost of a project is only one of several factors to be considered. The record as it comes to us fails markedly to make out a case for the Storm King project on, among other matters, costs, public convenience and necessity, and absence of reasonable alternatives. [The case is] remanded for further proceedings.

Scenic Hudson Preservation Conference v. FPC (II)

453 F.2d 463 (2d Cir. 1971), rehearing en banc denied by equally divided court, id. at 494, cert. denied, 407 U.S. 926 (1972)

HAYS, Circuit Judge.

[This case reached the court five years after the court's remand in *Scenic Hudson I*. In the meantime the Commission had held an additional hearing involving 100 hearing days, 675 exhibits, and a record of 19,000 pages. In its new opinion] the Commission reviewed the power needs of the area served . . . and considered several possible alternatives to the Storm King project in terms of reliability, cost, air and noise pollution, and overall environmental impact. Concluding that there was no satisfactory alternative, the Commission evaluated the environmental effects of the project itself. It concluded that the scenic impact would be minimal, that no historic site would be adversely affected, that the fish would be adequately protected and the proposed park and scenic overlook would enhance recreational facilities. [It found that] further undergrounding of transmission lines would result in unreliability . . . and would be too costly. [The Commission issued a license, again approving the project, but as modified to put the powerhouse entirely underground (instead of just 80 percent underground), to include fish-protection devices, to reroute certain transmission lines, and to include a park and other recreational facilities.]

Where the Commission has considered all relevant factors, and where the challenged findings, based on such full considerations are supported . . . , we will not allow our personal views as to the desirability of the result reached . . . to influence us. [T]he proceedings of the Commission and its report meet the objections upon the basis of which we remanded the earlier determination . . . and . . . the evidence supporting the

Commission's conclusions amply meets the statutory requirement. . . . We do not consider the five years of additional investigation which followed our remand were spent in vain. [T]he Commission has reevaluated the entire project [and made some modifications]. Whether the project as it now stands represents a perfect balance of these needs is not for this court to decide. . . .

Questions

1. What law gives the court the power to remand in *Scenic Hudson I? Scenic Hudson I* involved a special statute calling for "substantial evidence" review; would the court have found the agency decision to have been arbitrary or capricious?

2. Why should the commission not have been able to reject the gas turbine testimony on the basis of its own expertise?

3. Was the remand "in vain"? After all, the commission reached the same result. But wait: The five-year delay meant mounting costs, a deterioration in Consolidated Edison's financial position, and changing power needs, *with the consequence that the Storm King project was never built.* Can the court fairly say, then, that the litigation was not "in vain"? From whose point of view? Of course, the object is not to stop the project but to produce a better decisionmaking process and hence a better outcome. Would you say that the litigation exemplifies that better process? Or was the plaintiff's object simply to stop the project?

Judicial remands may have a range of different consequences. One possibility, exemplified by the case, is a set of delays that ultimately prevents a rule or project from going forward. Another possibility is a significant change in the agency's position; this happened after the Supreme Court remanded the Reagan administration's repeal of its passive restraint rule. And often remanded cases will simply lead to a reaffirmation of the original decision, which then takes effect. In Independent U.S. Tanker Owners v. Dole, 809 F.2d 847 (D.C. Cir. 1987), for example, the court considered a statute that grants shipbuilders a subsidy but simultaneously specifies that a ship built with a subsidy may not enter the domestic coastal trade where it would compete with unsubsidized ships. The Department of Transportation permitted subsidized ships to enter the domestic coastal trade after the ship owner repaid to the government any ship-construction subsidy that had been received. The court held that the decision was arbitrary because the Department of Transportation had placed considerable weight on certain factors (the need for competition in the coastal trade) that the statute did not mention, while failing to discuss factors that the statute did mention. The case went back to the agency and returned to the court, 884 F.2d 587 (1989). This time the court upheld the same decision because the secretary of transportation had discussed the statute's factors and found that they justified the same result.

It would be extremely valuable to have a careful empirical study of the consequences of judicial remands under hard look review. Do you have intuitions about what such a study would show? J. Mashaw & D. Harfst, The Struggle for Auto Safety (1990), is an important argument that in the context of automobile safety, hard look review has moved the government away from informal rulemaking and toward regulation by recalling defective cars — in the authors' view, a perverse outcome. In fact, Mashaw and Harfst argue that hard look review has resulted in many lost lives and serious injuries, as the National Highway Traffic and Safety Administration (NHTSA), fearful of losing in court, has abandoned rulemaking almost entirely. The book is worth careful study.

Note on Environmental Regulation

Many traditional agencies with missions other than environmental quality have been required by statutes and reviewing courts to give increased attention to environmental concerns. Why are government measures to protect environmental quality needed? In one view, associated with the economist A. C. Pigou, the answer lies in the "spillover" quality of environmental harms. A factory polluting a stream or a motorist polluting the air imposes harms — health, aesthetic, economic — on others. The fact that part of the costs of such activities are not borne by the actor (which economists term a problem of external costs) encourages the actor to engage in more pollution than if he or she had to bear all the costs of pollution. In a standard view, the presence of spillover harms creates a form of "market failure" resulting in a higher level of pollution than would be the case if the costs of all spillover harms were internalized to those generating them.

In a second view, associated with Nobel Prize winner Ronald Coase, environmental problems are more productively seen as involving transactions costs rather than spillovers. Those who are injured by pollution could take steps to prevent the injury, for example, by moving elsewhere or taking precautions against dirty water. In this view, the problem of environmental degradation arises because people who produce pollution cannot easily bargain with people who suffer from pollution. See Coase, The Problem of Social Cost, in R. H. Coase, The Firm, the Market, and the Law ch. 5 (1988).

Conceivably, the problem of environmental degradation might be handled through private litigation in the courts. Excessive pollution could be curtailed indirectly by the threat of damage awards to victims of pollution or directly through the award of injunctions. In practice, however, court litigation has not proved adequate to deal with environmental degradation in a modern society. The underlying technical issues are extremely complex. The requirement of establishing causation is very difficult to satisfy when plaintiff's injury (for example, cancer) could have many causes other than defendant's emissions. The inadequacies of judicial machinery are accentuated where the harm suffered by any given individuals is small or consists of a low risk that they will suffer some future harm (as in the case of latent health injury), or where the harm (such as smog in Los Angeles) is caused by many actors. Courts are not democratically elected, and perhaps choices about the optimal level of environmental degradation should be made democratically, not judicially. To provide remedies that are prophylactic and operate on a more comprehensive scale, legislatures have empowered administrative agencies to issue regulations and orders requiring pollution sources to adopt controls or prohibiting certain forms of environmental degradation by private actors. (As previously noted, many people have criticized command-and-control regulation and argued for economic incentives instead.)

Thus, one of the most dramatic trends of regulation since the 1960s has involved the creation of new national statutes designed to deal with environmental issues. Consider, for example, the Clean Air Act (1963, 1967, 1970, 1977, 1990); the National Environmental Policy Act (1969); the Federal Insecticide, Fungicide, and Rodenticide Act (1972); the Marine Mammal Protection Act (1972); the Federal Water Pollution Control Act (1972); the Safe Drinking Water Act (1974); the Toxic Substances Control Act (1976); the National Ocean Pollution Planning Act (1978); the Fish and Wildlife Conservation Act (1980); the Comprehensive Environmental Response, Compensation, and Liability Act (1980); the Emergency Planning and Community Right-to-Know Act (1986); the Shore Protection Act (1988); the Pollution Prevention Act (1990).

Government actions can also cause "spillovers" that impair environmental quality. For example, government construction of a highway through a park not only destroys some parkland but also lessens the aesthetic appeal of the remaining parkland. Spillovers may also be generated by government research and development promotion of new technologies (such as the "breeder" nuclear reactor) that generate environmental hazards (such as highly radioactive nuclear wastes). Government development of natural resources owned by it (such as timber in national forests or oil in outer continental shelf lands) may also cause environmental harms. Environmental protection is replete with "risk-risk tradeoffs," that is, with environmental policies that reduce certain risks while creating other risks, as discussed below.

One view of environmental protection holds that the government should carefully weigh the environmental costs of any proposed action and balance them against the expected benefits before going ahead. See W. Kip Viscusi, Fatal Tradeoffs (1992). Another view calls for a form of democratic deliberation in which private preferences are not taken as given but are a subject of reflection and debate. See E. Anderson, Value in Ethics and Economics (1993); M. Sagoff, The Economy of the Earth (1990). Whatever the governing ideal, there are many problems in practice.

Congress sometimes legislates with unrealistic precision, requiring the EPA and affected agencies to do specific things by specific times; it is most unclear whether Congress has the information to make appropriate choices, and it is very clear that legislative specificity is sometimes a product of the exercise of political power of well-organized private groups, using environmental legislation to obtain benefits for themselves. See B. Ackerman & W. Hassler, Clean Coal/Dirty Air (1983), for a classic discussion. And sometimes Congress delegates great discretion over such decisions to administrative agencies whose influences and mission may lead them (1) to favor well-organized private groups; (2) to downplay the social costs of environmental protection, including the environmental costs of some forms of environmental protection; or (3) to overestimate the benefits of proposed action and disregard and downplay the environmental costs involved.

For example, the basic mission of the Highway Bureau was to build highways at lowest cost, while the basic mission of the Atomic Energy Commission (AEC) was to promote the development of nuclear power. The mission orientation of such agencies — which may be accentuated by constant lobbying from industry and other organized client interests with a major stake in the agency's promotion of its mission — leads to a form of "bureaucratic externality" in which the agency tends to ignore or discount the adverse effects of its choices on values or goals that are not central to its mission.

Bureaucratic tunnel vision is by no means limited to agencies with developmental missions. Agencies whose prime mission is to protect the environment or health — such as the EPA and the OSHA — often tend to downplay or disregard the economic (and environmental) costs that protective regulations impose on industry and consumers. As noted below, costly regulations may increase unemployment and poverty, and increased unemployment and poverty are likely to produce adverse health effects.

On occasion, concern with environmental quality has created strong pressures on traditional doctrines of judicial review of administrative action. Industry and others subject to administrative controls to protect health and the environment claim that controls are unreasonable or excessively costly, and have called on the courts to scrutinize closely decisions by environmental regulatory agencies. At the same time, environmental advocates have objected to what they see as the disregard of environmental spillovers by government agencies with developmental missions, and have asked courts to abandon traditional principles of deference to force such agencies to adopt policies more favorable to environmental concerns. Frequently, environmental groups claim that "government failure" mimics "market failure": the problem of transaction costs barriers, especially in the form of collective action problems faced by beneficiaries of regulatory programs, is said to call for aggressive judicial review. Should courts respond to "government failure" if it is a predictable consequence of organizational difficulties faced by one side or another? What problems do you see in a judicial role of this sort?

Note on Ethyl Corp. v. EPA

A general question involves the competence of the courts to apply a hard look or adequate consideration approach to review agency policy choices involving complex technical issues. The problem was discussed many decades ago in influential concurring opinions filed by Chief Judge Bazelon and Judge Leventhal in Ethyl Corp. v. EPA, 541 F.2d 1 (D.C. Cir. 1976) (en banc), cert. denied, 426 U.S. 941 (1976). The EPA is authorized to prohibit the use of additives in motor vehicle fuel if it determines that their use "will endanger the public health or welfare." The EPA adopted regulations substantially eliminating the use in gasoline of lead additives (designed to increase octane ratings and improve engine efficiency), asserting that clinical tests and epidemiological data on the health of persons exposed to different lead levels in everyday living established that airborne lead attributable to emissions from automobiles using leaded gas was a health hazard. The scientific and medical evidence was voluminous, often conflicting, and hardly clear-cut.

A panel of the court of appeals initially set aside the EPA's action for want of adequate proof that lead additives caused illness. On reconsideration en banc, the EPA's action was sustained by a five-to-four vote. The majority opinion by Judge Wright emphasized that the determination whether the evidence established a health hazard was in considerable degree a "legislative-type policy judgment," but the majority opinion also reviewed the relevant medical and scientific evidence in great detail, as did the principal dissenting opinion. It is worth glancing at the opinions, which total some 118 pages in the *Federal Reporter*, in order to appreciate the extent and detail of their examination of medical, chemical, statistical, and other technical issues.

Concurring in the majority opinion, Chief Judge Bazelon (joined by Judge McGowan) expressed these views:

> I agree with the court's construction of that statute that the Administrator is called upon to make "essentially legislative policy judgments" in assessing risks to public health. But I cannot agree that this automatically relieves the Administrator's decision from the "procedural . . . rigor proper for questions of fact." Quite the contrary, this case strengthens my view that ". . . in cases of great technological complexity, the best way for courts to guard against unreasonable or erroneous administrative decisions is not for the judges themselves to scrutinize the technical merits of each decision. Rather, it is to establish a decision-making process that assures a reasoned decision that can be held up to the scrutiny of the scientific community and the public."
>
> This record provides vivid demonstration of the dangers implicit in the contrary view, ably espoused by Judge Leventhal, which would have judges "steeping" themselves in technical matters to determine whether the agency "has

exercised a reasoned discretion." It is one thing for judges to scrutinize FCC judgments concerning diversification of media ownership to determine if they are rational. But I doubt judges contribute much to improving the quality of the difficult decisions which must be made in highly technical areas when they take it upon themselves to decide, as did the panel in this case, that "in assessing the scientific and medical data the Administrator made clear errors of judgment." The process of making a de novo evaluation of the scientific evidence invites judges of opposing views to make plausible-sounding, but simplistic, judgments of the relative weight to be afforded various pieces of technical data.

. . . But this is a temptation which, if not resisted, will not only impose severe strains upon the energies and resources of the court but also compound the error of the panel in making legislative policy determinations alien to its true function. . . .

Because substantive review of mathematical and scientific evidence by technically illiterate judges is dangerously unreliable, I continue to believe we will do more to improve administrative decision-making by concentrating our efforts on strengthening administrative procedures.

541 F.2d at 66-67.

Judge Leventhal replied as follows:

[Judge Bazelon's] opinion — if I read it right — advocates engaging in no substantive review at all, whenever the substantive issues at stake involve technical matters that the judges involved consider beyond their individual technical competence. . . .

Taking the opinion in its fair implication, as a signal to judges to abstain from any substantive review, it is my view while giving up is the easier course, it is not legitimately open to us at present. In the case of legislative enactments, the sole responsibility of the courts is constitutional due process review. In the case of agency decision-making the courts have an additional responsibility set by Congress. Congress has been willing to delegate its legislative powers broadly — and courts have upheld such delegation — because there is court review to assure that the agency exercises the delegated power within statutory limits, and that it fleshes out objectives within those limits by an administration that is not irrational or discriminatory. Nor is that envisioned judicial role ephemeral, as *Overton Park* makes clear.

Our present system of reviewing assumes judges will acquire whatever technical knowledge is necessary as background for decision of the legal questions. It may be that some judges are not initially equipped for this role, just as they may not be technically equipped initially to decide issues of obviousness and infringement in patent cases. If technical difficulties loom large, Congress may push to establish specialized courts. Thus far, it has proceeded on the assumption that we can both have the important values secured by generalist judges and rely on them to acquire whatever technical background is necessary.

The aim of the judges is not to exercise expertise or decide technical questions, but simply to gain sufficient background orientation. Our obligation is not to be jettisoned because our initial technical understanding may be meager when compared to our initial grasp of FCC or freedom of speech questions. When called upon to make de novo decisions, individual judges have had to acquire the learning pertinent to complex technical questions in such fields as economics, science, technology and psychology. Our role is not as demanding when we are engaged in review of agency decisions, where we exercise restraint, and affirm even if we would have decided otherwise so long as the agency's decisionmaking is not irrational or discriminatory.

The substantive review of administrative action is modest, but it cannot be carried out in a vacuum of understanding. Better no judicial review at all than a charade that gives the imprimatur without the substance of judicial confirmation that the agency is not acting unreasonably. Once the presumption of regularity in agency action is challenged with a factual submission, and even to determine whether such a challenge has been made, the agency's record and reasoning has to be looked at. If there is some factual support for the challenge, there must be either evidence or judicial notice available explicating the agency's result, or a remand to supply the gap. . . .

On issues of substantive review, on conformance to statutory standards and requirements of rationality, the judges must act with restraint. Restraint, yes, abdication, no.

541 F.2d at 68-69.

The difficulties faced by courts in reviewing engineering and economic issues remain serious. Nonetheless, judges brave voluminous records and dauntingly difficult technical issues to enforce hard look review, relying on the arguments of counsel, their law clerks, and their own study and pluck. In concluding her voluminous opinion in Sierra Club v. Costle, 657 F.2d 298, 410 (D.C. Cir. 1981), Judge Wald summed up the contemporary enterprise of judging in this way:

> Since the issues in [these] proceedings were joined in 1973 . . . we have had several lawsuits, almost four years of substantive and procedural maneuvering before the EPA, and now this extended court challenge. In the interim, Congress has amended the Clean Air Act once and may be ready to do so again. The standard we uphold has already been in effect for almost two years, and could be revised within another two years.
>
> We reach our decision after interminable record searching (and considerable soul searching). We have read the record with as hard a look as mortal judges can probably give its thousands of pages. We have adopted a simple and straight-forward standard of review, probed the agency's rationale, studied its references (and those of appellants), endeavored to understand them where they were intelligible (parts were simply impenetrable), and on close questions given the agency the benefit of the doubt out of deference for the terrible complexity of its job. We are not engineers, computer modelers, economists or statisticians, although many of the documents in this record require such expertise — and more.
>
> Cases like this highlight the critical responsibilities Congress has entrusted to the courts in proceedings of such length, complexity and disorder. Conflicting interests play fiercely for enormous stakes, advocates are prolific and agile, obfuscation runs high, common sense correspondingly low, the public interest is often obscured.
>
> We cannot redo the agency's job; Congress has told us, at least in proceedings under this Act, that it will not brook reversal for small procedural errors; *Vermont Yankee* [Nuclear Power Corp. v. Natural Resources Defense Council] reinforces the admonition. So in the end we can only make our best effort to understand, to see if the result makes sense, and to assure that nothing unlawful or irrational has taken place. In this case, we have taken a long while to come to a short conclusion: the rule is reasonable.
>
> Affirmed.

Notes and Questions

1. What is the *point* of hard look review, according to Judges Bazelon and Leventhal? A possible answer is that courts are trying to improve the democratic character of the administrative process. As a substitute for the nondelegation doctrine, perhaps courts are

attempting to make the administrative process more open to affected groups. The requirement of "adequate consideration" — of alternatives, of objections from affected groups — might be seen as an effort to ensure a form of "interest representation" at the agency level. Interest representation is associated with "interest group pluralism" — the idea that a well-functioning democracy allows all affected groups to press their preferences on government, in an effort to ensure some kind of aggregation of interests and preferences. See Stewart, The Reformation of American Administrative Law, 88 Harv. L. Rev. 1667 (1975). Alternatively, the requirement might be seen as part of a judicial effort to ensure a process of democratic deliberation at the agency level; in that process of deliberation, reason-giving is crucial, and preferences need not be taken as "given."

Ideas of this kind suggest a political conception of administration; that is, they suggest that administrative judgments are fundamentally political in character, and the point of judicial review is to make sure that the political process works well, in the sense that it is not subject to domination or capture by narrow interests. We have seen cases where the political character of administration is said to argue for a deferential judicial role. See, e.g., Chevron v. Natural Resources Defense Council. Judge Bazelon seems to be suggesting that an aggressive judicial role can work in the service of a well-functioning democratic process. But is it realistic to think that hard look review will actually have good effects? Might it not instead empower interest groups to move the administrative process in their preferred directions, lead to judicial judgments rather than political ones, produce delay, and thus entrench the status quo?

2. Some people favor a technocratic rather than political conception of administration; they emphasize the role of expertise in producing good decisions. Does Judge Leventhal endorse this view? If so, what does he see as the point of hard look review? Perhaps hard look review can be defended as a means of preventing serious errors of analysis and also the distortion of expertise by narrow political interests; in this view, courts help ensure the healthy application of specialization and serve to insulate experts from greedy political forces. This idea suggests an inversion of the New Deal enthusiasm for administrative autonomy as an institutional response to the need for expertise in governance. Under what assumptions does it make sense?

2. The Overton Park Synthesis

Citizens to Preserve Overton Park, Inc. v. Volpe
401 U.S. 402 (1971)

Opinion of the Court by Mr. Justice Marshall, announced by Mr. Justice STEWART.

The growing public concern about the quality of our natural environment has prompted Congress in recent years to enact legislation designed to curb the accelerating destruction of our country's natural beauty. We are concerned in this case with §4(f) of the Department of Transportation Act of 1966, as amended, and §18(a) of the Federal-Aid-to-Highways Act of 1968, 82 Stat. 823, 23 U.S.C. §138 (1964 ed. Supp. V) (hereafter, §138). These statutes prohibit the Secretary of Transportation from authorizing the use of federal funds to finance the construction of highways through public parks if a "feasible and prudent" alternative route exists. If no such route is available, the statutes allow him to approve construction through parks only if there has been "all possible planning to minimize harm" to the park.

Petitioners, private citizens as well as local and national conservation organizations, contend that the Secretary has violated these statutes by authorizing the expenditure of federal funds for the construction of a six-lane interstate highway through a public park in Memphis, Tennessee. Their claim was rejected by the District Court, which granted the Secretary's motion for summary judgment, and the Court of Appeals for the Sixth Circuit affirmed. After oral argument, this Court granted a stay that halted construction and, treating the application for the stay as a petition for certiorari, granted review. 400 U.S. 939. We now reverse the judgment below and remand for further proceedings in the District Court.

Overton Park is a 342-acre city park located near the center of Memphis. The park contains a zoo, a nine-hole municipal golf course, an outdoor theater, nature trails, a bridle path, an art academy, picnic areas, and 170 acres of forest. The proposed highway, which is to be a six-lane, high-speed, expressway, will sever the zoo from the rest of the park. Although the roadway will be depressed below ground level except where it crosses a small creek, 26 acres of the park will be destroyed. The highway is to be a segment of Interstate Highway I-40, part of the National System of Interstate and Defense Highways. I-40 will provide Memphis with a major east-west expressway which will allow easier access to downtown Memphis from the residential areas on the eastern edge of the city.

Although the route through the park was approved by the Bureau of Public Roads in 1956 and by the Federal Highway Administrator in 1966, the enactment of §4(f) of the Department of Transportation Act prevented distribution of federal funds for the section of the highway designated to go through Overton Park until the Secretary of Transportation determined whether the requirements of §4(f) had been met. Federal funding for the rest of the project was, however, available; and the state acquired a right-of-way on both sides of the park. In April 1968, the Secretary announced that he concurred in the judgment of local officials that I-40 should be built through the park. And in September 1969 the state acquired the right-of-way inside Overton Park from the city. Final approval for the project — the route as well as the design — was not announced until November 1969, after Congress had reiterated in §138 of the Federal-Aid-to-Highways Act that highway construction through public parks was to be restricted. Neither announcement approving the route and design of I-40 was accompanied by a statement of the Secretary's factual findings. He did not indicate why he believed there were no feasible and prudent alternative routes or why design changes could not be made to reduce the harm to the park.

Petitioners contend that the Secretary's action is invalid without such formal findings and that the Secretary did not make an independent determination but merely relied on the judgment of the Memphis City Council. They also contend that it would be "feasible and prudent" to route I-40 around Overton Park either to the north or to the south. And they argue that if these alternative routes are not "feasible and prudent," the present plan does not include "all possible" methods for reducing harm to the park. Petitioners claim that I-40 could be built under the park by using either of two possible tunneling methods, and they claim that, at a minimum, by using advanced drainage techniques the expressway could be depressed below ground level along the entire route through the park including the section that crosses the small creek.

Respondents argue that it was unnecessary for the Secretary to make formal findings, and that he did, in fact, exercise his own independent judgment which was supported by the facts. In the District Court, respondents introduced affidavits, prepared specifically for this litigation, which indicated that the Secretary had made the decision and that the decision was supportable. These affidavits were contradicted by affidavits introduced by petitioners, who also sought to take the deposition of a former Federal Highway Administrator who had participated in the decision to route I-40 through Overton Park.

We agree [with the lower courts] that formal findings were not required. But we do not believe that in this case judicial review based solely on litigation affidavits was adequate.

A threshold question — whether petitioners are entitled to any judicial review — is easily answered. Section 701 of the Administrative Procedure Act, 5 U.S.C. §701 (1964 ed. Supp. V), provides that the action of "each authority of the government of the United States," which includes the Department of Transportation, is subject to judicial review except where there is a statutory prohibition on review or where "agency action is committed to agency discretion by law." In this case, there is no indication that Congress sought to prohibit judicial review and there is most certainly no "showing of 'clear and convincing evidence' of a . . . legislative intent" to restrict access to judicial review. Abbott Laboratories v. Gardner, 387 U.S. 136, 141 (1967). . . .

Similarly, the Secretary's decision here does not fall within the exception for action "committed to agency discretion." This is a very narrow exception. The legislative history of the Administrative Procedure Act indicates that it is applicable in those rare instances where "statutes are drawn in such broad terms that in a given case there is no law to apply." S. Rep. No. 752, 79th Cong., 1st Sess., 26 (1945).

Section 4(f) of the Department of Transportation Act and §138 of the Federal-Aid-to-Highways Act are clear and specific directives. Both the Department of Transportation Act and the Federal-Aid-to-Highways Act provide that the Secretary "shall not approve any program or project" that requires the use of any public parkland "unless (1) there is no feasible and prudent alternative to the use of such land, and (2) such program includes all possible planning to minimize harm to such park. . . ." This language is a plain and explicit bar to the use of federal funds for construction of highways through parks — only the most unusual situations are exempted.

Despite the clarity of the statutory language, respondents argue that the Secretary has wide discretion. They recognize that the requirement that there be no "feasible" alternative route admits of little administrative discretion. For this exemption to apply the Secretary must find that as a matter of sound engineering it would not be feasible to build the highway along any other route. Respondents argue, however, that the requirement that there be no other "prudent" route requires the Secretary to engage in a wide-range balancing of competing interests. They contend that the Secretary should weigh the detriment resulting from the destruction of parkland against the cost of other routes, safety considerations, and other factors, and determine on the basis of the importance that he attaches to these other factors whether, on balance, alternative feasible routes would be "prudent."

But no such wide-ranging endeavor was intended. It is obvious that in most cases considerations of cost, directness of route, and community disruption will indicate that parkland should be used for highway construction whenever possible. Although it may be necessary to transfer funds from one jurisdiction to another, there will always be a smaller outlay required from the public purse when parkland is used since the public already owns the land and there will be no need to pay for right-of-way. And since people do not live or work in parks, if a highway is built on parkland no one will have to leave his home or give up his business. Such factors are common to substantially all highway construction. Thus, if Congress intended these factors to be on an equal footing with preservations of parkland there would have been no need for the statutes.

Congress clearly did not intend that cost and disruption of the community were to be ignored by the Secretary. But the very existence of the statutes indicates that protection of parkland was to be given paramount importance. The few green havens that are public parks were not to be lost unless there were truly unusual factors present in a particular case or the cost or community disruption resulting from alternative routes reached extraordinary magnitudes. If the statutes are to have any meaning, the Secretary cannot approve the destruction of parkland unless he finds that alternative routes present unique problems.

Plainly, there is "law to apply" and thus the exemption for action "committed to agency discretion" is inapplicable. But the existence of judicial review is only the start: the standard for review must also be determined. For that we must look to §706 of the Administrative Procedure Act, 5 U.S.C. §706. . . . "[A] reviewing court shall . . . hold unlawful and set aside agency action, findings, and conclusions found" not to meet six separate standards. In all cases agency action must be set aside if the action was "arbitrary, capricious, an abuse of discretion, or otherwise not in accordance with law" or if the action failed to meet statutory, procedural, or constitutional requirements. . . . In certain narrow, specifically limited situations, the agency action is to be set aside if the action was not supported by "substantial evidence." And in other equally narrow circumstances the reviewing court is to engage in a de novo review of the action and set it aside if it was "unwarranted by the facts." . . .

Petitioners argue that the Secretary's approval of the construction of I-40 through Overton Park is subject to one or the other of these latter two standards of limited applicability. First, they contend that the "substantial evidence" standard of §706(2)(E) must be applied. In the alternative, they claim that §706(2)(F) applies and that there must be a de novo review to determine if the Secretary's action was "unwarranted by the facts." Neither of these standards is, however, applicable.

Review under the substantial-evidence test is authorized only when the agency action is taken pursuant to a rulemaking provision of the Administrative Procedure Act itself, 5 U.S.C. §553 . . . or when the agency action is based on a public adjudicatory hearing. See 5 U.S.C. §§556, 557. . . . The Secretary's decision to allow the expenditure of federal funds to build I-40 through Overton Park was plainly not an exercise of a rule-making function. . . . And the only hearing that is required by either the Administrative Procedure Act or the statutes regulating the distribution of federal funds for highway construction is a public hearing conducted by local officials for the purpose of informing the community about the proposed project and eliciting community views on the design and route. 23 U.S.C. §128. . . . The hearing is nonadjudicatory, quasi-legislative in nature. It is not designed to produce a record that is to be the basis of agency action — the basic requirement for substantial-evidence review. . . .

Petitioner's alternative argument also fails. De novo review of whether the Secretary's decision was "unwarranted by the facts" is authorized by §706(2)(F) in only two circumstances. First, such de novo review is authorized when the action is adjudicatory in nature and the agency factfinding procedures are inadequate. And, there may be independent judicial factfinding when issues that were not before the agency are raised in a proceeding to enforce nonadjudicatory agency action. H.R. Rep. No. 1980, 79th Cong., 2d Sess. Neither situation exists here.

Even though there is no de novo review in this case and the Secretary's approval of the route of I-40 does not have ultimately to meet the substantial-evidence test, the generally applicable standards of §706 require the reviewing court to engage in a substantial inquiry. Certainly, the Secretary's decision is entitled to a presumption of regularity. . . . But that presumption is not to shield his action from a thorough, probing, in-depth review.

The court is first required to decide whether the Secretary acted within the scope of his authority. . . . This determination naturally begins with a delineation of the scope of the Secretary's authority and discretion. L. Jaffe, Judicial Control of Administrative Action 359 (1965). As has been shown, Congress has specified only a small range of choices that the Secretary can make. Also involved in this initial inquiry is a determination of whether on the facts the Secretary's decision can reasonably be said to be within that range. The reviewing court must consider whether the Secretary properly construed his authority to approve the use of parkland as limited to situations where there are no feasible alternative routes or where feasible alternative routes involve uniquely difficult problems. And the reviewing court must be able to find that the Secretary could have reasonably believed that in this case there are no feasible alternatives or that alternatives do involve unique problems.

Scrutiny of the facts does not end, however, with the determination that the Secretary has acted within the scope of his statutory authority. Section 706(2)(A) requires a finding that the actual choice made was not "arbitrary, capricious, an abuse of discretion, or otherwise not in accordance with law." . . . To make this finding the court must consider whether the decision was based on a consideration of the relevant factors and whether there has been a clear error of judgment. . . . Although this inquiry into the facts is to be searching and careful, the ultimate standard of review is a narrow one. The court is not empowered to substitute its judgment for that of the agency.

The final inquiry is whether the Secretary's action followed the necessary procedural requirements. Here the only procedural error alleged is the failure of the Secretary to make formal findings and state his reason for allowing the highway to be built through the park.

Undoubtedly, review of the Secretary's action is hampered by his failure to make such findings, but the absence of formal findings does not necessarily require that the case be remanded to the Secretary. Neither the Department of Transportation Act nor the Federal-Aid-to-Highways Act requires such formal findings. Moreover, the Administrative Procedure Act requirements that there be formal findings in certain rulemaking and adjudicatory proceedings do not apply to the Secretary's action here. See 5 U.S.C. §§553(a)(2), 554(a). . . . And, although formal findings may be required in some cases in the absence of statutory directives when the nature of the agency action is ambiguous, those situations are rare. . . . Plainly, there is no ambiguity here; the Secretary has approved the construction of I-40 through Overton Park and has approved a specific design for the project. . . .

That administrative record is not, however, before us. The lower courts based their review on the litigation affidavits that were presented. These affidavits were merely "post hoc" rationalizations . . . which have traditionally been found to be an inadequate basis for review. . . . SEC v. Chenery Corp., 318 U.S. 80, 87 (1943). And they clearly do not constitute the "whole record" compiled by the agency: the basis for review required by §706 of the Administrative Procedure Act. . . .

Thus it is necessary to remand this case to the District Court for plenary review of the Secretary's decision. That review is to be based on the full administrative record that was before the Secretary at the time he made his decision. But since the bare record may not disclose the factors that were considered or the Secretary's construction of the evidence it may be necessary for the District Court to require some explanation in order to determine if the Secretary acted within the scope of his authority and if the Secretary's action was justifiable under the applicable standard.

The court may require the administrative officials who participated in the decision to give testimony explaining their action. Of course, such inquiry into the mental processes of administrative decisionmakers is usually to be avoided. United States v. Morgan, 313 U.S. 409, 422 (1941). And where there are administrative findings that were made at the same time as the decision, as was the case in *Morgan,* there must be a strong showing of bad faith or improper behavior before such inquiry may be made. But here there are no such formal findings and it may be that the only way there can be effective judicial review is by examining the decisionmakers themselves.

The District Court is not, however, required to make such an inquiry. It may be that the Secretary can prepare formal findings . . . that will provide an adequate explanation for his action. Such an explanation will, to some extent, be a "post hoc rationalization" and thus must be viewed critically. If the District Court decides that additional explanation is necessary, that court should consider which method will prove the most expeditious so that full review may be had as soon as possible.

Reversed and remanded.

[On remand, the district court decided to make a "thorough, probing, in-depth review" of the secretary's decision rather than remanding to the secretary for fresh proceedings and administrative findings. On the basis of extensive hearings, including submission of personal affidavits of the secretary, testimony by some of his assistants, and numerous documentary exhibits, the court concluded that the secretary had not given serious consideration to alternative routes, as required by the Supreme Court's decision. However, the court concluded, on the basis of extensive factual evidence, that the secretary could reasonably decide either way on the question whether there was a feasible and prudent alternative available "without his decisions being arbitrary or capricious or without committing a clear error of judgment," and that if he chose to select the park routing, the statutory requirement of "all possible planning to minimize harm to such park" would be satisfied. Accordingly, the case was remanded to the secretary for an exercise of his discretion to choose among alternative routings. Citizens to Preserve Overton Park, Inc. v. Volpe, 335 F. Supp. 873 (W.D. Tenn. 1972). Subsequently, the secretary disapproved the Overton Park route without identifying a "prudent and feasible" alternative. This action was invalidated by the district court at the behest of state highway officials contending that the secretary could not disapprove a given route without specifying alternatives, 357 F. Supp. 846 (W.D. Tenn. 1973), but on appeal the secretary's action was sustained, 494 F.2d 1212 (6th Cir. 1974).]

Notes and Questions

1. The Supreme Court's *Overton Park* opinion addresses several important questions, including the availability of judicial review of administrative decisions that are informal and discretionary; the means for developing a record for review of informal administrative action in the absence of trial-type hearing requirements; the construction of relevant statutes; and the scope of judicial review of the agency's exercise of the discretion conferred by the statute. We are concerned only with the latter questions here: The availability of judicial review and the problem of a record will be discussed in subsequent chapters. It should be noted, however, that *Overton's* application of a presumption of

reviewability to informal administrative action effectively converted what had been thought to be exclusively political and administrative matters into legal ones as well as represented a significant innovation that substantially expanded the reach of administrative law over the workings of government. See Strauss, Revisiting *Overton Park*: Political and Judicial Controls over Administrative Actions Affecting the Community, 39 UCLA L. Rev. 1251 (1992).

2. Note that *Overton Park* structures judicial review of questions of law as a multi-step process. First, the Court construes the relevant statute to determine the scope and terms of the agency's authority to determine whether the agency is acting within the authority conferred (note that the Court's subsequent *Chevron* decision recognizes a significant role for the agency in this initial step of statutory construction). The determination of the scope and terms of the agency's authority determines the extent of the agency's discretion (if any). Second, if the agency has discretion to choose among two or more courses of action, the court next decides whether the agency exercised its discretion based on a consideration of relevant factors. Third, even if the agency has discretion and based its decision on relevant factors, the Court will consider whether the agency's weighing of the relevant factors and the particular course chosen were "arbitrary, capricious, and abuse of discretion, or otherwise not in accordance with law." What is the distinction between these two inquiries? Does the Court's position imply that statutes may authorize arbitrary and capricious action by administrators? It might be best to take these passages as a bit of a mess, and to see them as setting the stage for the clearer, three-step approach of current law: *Chevron* step 1; *Chevron* step 2; arbitrariness review.

3. In discussing the scope of the secretary's authority, the Supreme Court laid down a rule narrowly restricting his power to approve highway routings through parks to a few cases where "truly unusual factors" were present or "the cost or community disruption resulting from alternative routes reached extraordinary magnitudes." Otherwise, the Court found the statutory language to be "a plain and explicit bar to the use of federal funds for construction of highways through parks." Is this a sound construction of the statute? The legislative history shows that the statutory provisions in question were regarded as far more of a compromise between pro-highway and anti-highway forces than the Court's opinion admits. Might the Court's construction of the statute be justified on the ground that the text deserves priority, and the more ambiguous legislative history is entitled to little weight in light of the plain "ordinary meaning" of the words? Recall the earlier discussion of text and history.

Alternatively, might the Court's "tilt" in favor of parks have been justified to provide a counterweight to the apparent biases of highway agencies? To protect "underrepresented" environmental interests?

In what ways does the technique used in *Overton Park* to control agency discretion resemble and differ from the techniques used in the OSHA cases? Does *Overton Park* survive *Chevron*? Make an argument that on the statutory issue, it does not.

4. One reading of *Overton Park* — a now conventional reading — is that the Court was attempting to ensure that the Department of Transportation, with its obvious, pro-highway mission orientation, would not ignore underrepresented environmental interests. Thus, the decision can be seen as one of a large number of administrative law cases attempting to vindicate interests that were able to obtain statutory protection but that were at great risk in the administrative process. In this account, courts and Congress work together to protect certain groups against narrow-minded administrators.

An important and extremely interesting revisionist view suggests that the actual story of *Overton Park* was much more complicated. See Strauss, Revisiting *Overton Park*, 39 UCLA L. Rev. 1251 (1992). Professor Strauss offers two principal points. First, the statute construed in *Overton Park* was a complex compromise among affected interests, not an unambiguous assertion of the priority of parks over highways. In that compromise, environmental interests received a sympathetic hearing, but Congress saw that other interests were at stake. On this view, the Court was wrong to see the statute as a clear protection of parks at the expense of development. Second, the judgment about what to do with the park in Memphis involved a wide range of interests and problems, including socioeconomic variables and questions of race, and the solution sought by the Citizens to Preserve Overton Park would have compromised other legitimate interests. "A fuller appreciation for the *Overton Park* controversy, whether viewed from Washington, D.C. or Memphis, Tennessee shows wide and effective engagement of a variety of political actors in the controversy. The effect of the Court's action in surrogate politics was to empower one of those actors to an extent that had not been contemplated, and that is not sustainable on any general political view." Thus Professor Strauss finds that the failures of the pro-park interests "were failures of persuasion, not the result of either institutional barriers to being heard or politicians insensitive to the importance of the values being promoted."

Suppose that what Professor Strauss says is true. Does it show that *Overton Park* was wrongly decided? If so, is the lesson limited to that case, or is it (as Professor Strauss himself urges) more general because courts do not see the role of political forces in persuading administrators?

Do you care what Overton Park is like now, or what its role is in the area? A recent description offers the following: "This is the home of the Memphis Brooks Museum of Art, the Memphis College of Art, and the Overton Park Municipal Golf Course, but the park is a lovely place to visit for its own sake. There are trails for hiking and biking, tennis courts, a playground, picnic area, and huge, shady trees to relax under. The rainbow-painted amphitheater, once the location of concerts by Elvis Presley and ZZ Top, is now seldom used, but still a good place to sit and ponder the glories of music gone by."

5. *Overton Park* says that a court may set aside an agency's "policy choice" when that choice is "arbitrary, capricious, an abuse of discretion." It adds, "To make this finding the Court must consider whether the decision was based on a consideration of the relevant factors and whether there has been a clear error of judgment." The court's inquiry must be "searching and careful," but the "ultimate standard of review is a narrow one." What kind of signal is sent by these words? In fact, lower courts took *Overton Park* to be an important endorsement of hard look review.

3. The "Relevant Factors"

The governing statute, as interpreted by the court, normally determines the factors that are "relevant." Under *Chevron*, the agency will have a degree of leeway in interpreting a statute to determine which factors are relevant. But if a court finds the agency erred in concluding that a given factor was relevant or irrelevant, the court will require the agency to make the decision over again based on consideration of the relevant factors. That fact does not necessarily mean the agency will reach a different result. Consider the following cases.

PENSION BENEFIT GUARANTY CORP. v. LTV CORP., 496 U.S. 633 (1990). The Pension Benefit Guaranty Corp. (PBGC) is a federal agency that "guarantees" workers they will be paid benefits under private pension plans, including those that employers terminate because, say, of bankruptcy. The PBGC, after negotiations with LTV, permitted LTV to terminate certain plans, and it worked out revised LTV pension obligations. But when LTV's fortunes began to revive, PBGC insisted that LTV "restore" the old pension plans. The Second Circuit held that the PBGC's decision was "arbitrary" because it had not considered all relevant factors. In particular, it said, "because ERISA [the federal pension guaranty law], bankruptcy, and labor law are all involved in the case at hand, there must be a showing on the administrative record that PBGC, before reaching its decision considered all of these areas of law, and to the extent possible, honored the policies underlying them."

The Supreme Court reversed. For one thing, the statute (Title IV of ERISA) authorized PBGC to restore a plan where "appropriate and consistent with its duties *under this title*." For another, as a matter of administrative law, "if agency action may be disturbed whenever a reviewing court is able to point to an arguably relevant statutory policy that was not explicitly considered, then [given the large number of federal statutes and policies] a very large number of agency decisions might be open to judicial invalidation." Further, since PBGC can claim no expertise in these other fields of law, "it may be ill-equipped to undertake the difficult task of discerning and applying the 'policies and goals' of those fields." *Question:* Do these circumstances argue for greater presidential control of agency decisionmaking to ensure consistency among related policies for which different agencies are responsible?

NATIONAL COALITION AGAINST MISUSE OF PESTICIDES v. THOMAS, 809 F.2d 875 (D.C. Cir. 1987), and 828 F.2d 42 (D.C. Cir. 1987). EPA set a "zero tolerance level" for ethylene dibromide in imported mangoes. It then changed the tolerance level, permitting concentrations of up to 30 parts per billion. Its chief reason for doing so was that the zero tolerance level would have a highly adverse impact on the economies of less developed nations that export mangoes to the United States. The D.C. Circuit pointed out that the relevant statute gave EPA the authority to promulgate pesticide tolerance levels "to the extent necessary to protect the public health." The statute also listed several specific factors the EPA should consider "among other relevant factors." It did not list the economic welfare of foreign nations. Hence, the court concluded, EPA had relied primarily on a factor that the statute did not intend EPA to take into account. EPA's rationale for the change was "wholly inadequate." EPA did not make any change in its new tolerance level; it kept the tolerance level at 30 parts per billion. It did change its rationale. It wrote that implementation of a zero tolerance level "at this point could damage cooperative efforts that have characterized relations among the U.S. and various food-exporting nations. Since effective enforcement of food safety laws depends upon such cooperation, a ban might increase the risk that fruit and vegetables would enter the U.S. treated with unsafe levels of pesticides or infested with pests or disease." The EPA's action was again challenged in court, but this time the D.C. Circuit found the rationale adequate.

4. A "Clear Error of Judgment"

The *Overton Park* Court says that an agency's decision is unlawful if it reflects a "clear error of judgment." This view has been criticized as identical to the "clearly erroneous" standard used by appellate courts in reviewing district court findings of fact; on the conventional view, reviewing courts should be more deferential to agency policy decisions than to findings of fact by a lower court. On the other hand, it is possible to question the conventional view (can you see how?), and in any case it is not clear that there is a material difference between the "clear error" idea and a purportedly more deferential understanding of the arbitrary or capricious test.

Litigants attempting to persuade a reviewing court that the balance struck by an agency among relevant factors is "arbitrary and capricious" must be prepared to persuade the court that the agency's decision has no reasonable basis. Given the artfulness of agency opinion writers, the skills of government lawyers, and the plausibility of agency claims of "expertise," this is a difficult burden to carry. But sometimes it has been carried, as we will see below.

COMMUNITY NUTRITION INSTITUTE v. BERGLAND, 493 F. Supp. 488 (D.D.C. 1989).   Federal legislation directed the secretary of agriculture to adopt regulations identifying nutritious foods to be provided to schoolchildren under federally assisted school lunch programs, and to specify competing non-nutritious foods whose sale at schools receiving federal assistance would be barred. A nonprofit nutrition organization challenged the secretary's adoption of regulations authorizing competing sale of certain otherwise non-nutritious foods if they were fortified with nutrient additives. Judge Gesell wrote: "Congress expected and intended that new affirmative steps would be taken to restrict access by school children to foods of low nutritional value. The legislative debates convey an unmistakable concern that 'junk foods,' notably various types of candy bars, chewing gum and soft drinks, not be allowed to compete in participating schools." Judge Gesell found that, on the whole, the challenged regulations reflected thorough inquiry and analysis, and were well considered. Nonetheless, he invalidated the regulations' authorization of sale of otherwise non-nutritious foods that had been fortified.

"The regulation prohibits sale of soda water or carbonated beverages, water ices, chewing gum, and certain candies in competition with school meals on the ground that they lack minimal nutritional value. However, the Secretary expressly authorizes fortification of these prohibited foods. . . . A recommended daily allowance for eight designated nutrients is stated, and by adding one such nutrient in the specified amount and filing a petition, an otherwise nonacceptable food in the classes indicated can be sold."

The Secretary in his general statement concludes that fortified snack foods should not be encouraged. He specifically discusses the risks associated with inappropriate fortification, including nutritional imbalance, toxicity, and confusion or deception among consumers. . . . The Food and Drug Administration ("FDA"), recognizing these problems and others, has promulgated guidelines which strongly discourage fortification of snack foods such as candies and carbonated beverages. . . . Several Congressmen adverted in highly critical terms to the prospect of fortified snack foods being available in schools. E.g., 123 Cong. Rec. 21765 (Sen. McGovern); 21779 (Sen. Dole). The health risks associated with fortification are particularly acute when linked to the availability of soft drinks artificially sweetened with saccharin, a potential carcinogen in humans.

"Given the stated intent of the Secretary, the overwhelming weight of the evidence presented, and the expressions of congressional concern, permitting otherwise non-nutritious foods in the restricted categories to be fortified can only be viewed as irrational and arbitrary."

MICROCOMPUTER TECHNOLOGY INSTITUTE v. RILEY, 139 F.2d 1044 (5th Cir. 1998). The agency adopted a new interpretation of an old regulation, which the court deemed to be reasonable. The agency also decided to apply the interpretation retroactively. The court held that the retroactive application was arbitrary and capricious. The court examined "the extent of the agency's departure from previous interpretation and the reasonableness of the aggrieved party's reliance, on one side of the balance, and the statutory or regulatory interest in retroactivity, on the other." *Chevron* was inapplicable because retroactivity "involves no policy considerations, but concerns only the application of settled policy under particular circumstances. It does not call any agency expertise into play; rather, it is a legal concept involving settled principles of law and is no more subject to deference than is an agency's interpretation of, say, a statute of limitations." Weighing the various factors, the court invalidated the agency's decision.

U.S. AIR TOUR ASSN. v. F.A.A., 298 F.3d 997 (D.C. Cir. 2002). The FAA issued a rule to reduce aircraft noise in the Grand Canyon National Park. In so doing, the agency considered only the noise produced by air tour operators. The Grand Canyon Trust challenged the rule on the ground that it did not reflect consideration of the noise from other aircraft that fly over the Grand Canyon. According to the Trust, the rule arbitrarily overstated how quiet the Park really is, and hence was less stringent than it ought to have been. The court agreed. In its view, "the FAA cannot dispute that whether or not non-tour aircraft are regulated, natural quiet does not exist when the sound they make is audible."

Questions

1. Environmentalists have often argued that the tradition of judicial deference should be abandoned in environmental cases. See, for an early statement, Sive, Some Thoughts of an Environmental Lawyer in the Wilderness of Administrative Law, 70 Colum. L. Rev. 612 (1970). Sive asserts that a litigant attempting to show that administrative decisions lack a "rational basis" or "substantial evidence" to support them "has a difficult task," a task exacerbated by the limited resources available to environmental litigants who are typically in the position of "a David challenging a Goliath." This situation, Sive argues, leaves promotion-oriented government agencies substantially free to pursue policies that seriously degrade the environment. Accordingly, the traditional deference to agency discretion should be altered in favor of more aggressive review to "neutralize the effluents of affluence," prevent "the asphalt jungle from supplanting most of the still green part of our one earth," and "enable courts to decree in judgments the basic ecological principle that one community's toilet is another's faucet."

What do you think of this argument? Does it apply in the domain of communications? If so, does it call for stringent judicial review of deregulation — or stringent judicial review of regulation?

2. With prominent exceptions, some of them mentioned both above and below, courts have generally been reluctant to use the "arbitrary and capricious" standard aggressively. But why? Why shouldn't a judge substitute his or her judgment for that of an agency on an ad hoc issue of policy when the judge believes that the agency's choice is palpably unwise? Who is better qualified to evaluate competing social values — a relatively disinterested, but uninformed, generalist judiciary, or a specialized administrative agency with possible "tunnel vision"? We shall explore this issue in considerable detail

below, not least with reference to the risk that stringent judicial review will simply freeze the status quo.

3. If a more intrusive, less deferential version of the arbitrary and capricious standard (or substantial evidence standard, applied to policy choices) were adopted, should it be employed across the board in all cases, or should it be limited to certain types of administrative decisions or to the protection of certain classes of interests affected by agency decisions? For example, can the arguments for more searching judicial review be limited to cases where government projects such as highways threaten the environment? What of administrative decisions touching on health and safety or the interests of consumers or the poor? What of pollution control regulations claimed by industry to be unjustifiably rigorous and costly?

Note that the intensity of judicial review unquestionably varies in practice. Courts look more searchingly at decisions by agencies that they think least competent or most biased, and they are most deferential to those agencies having a reputation for competence and impartiality.

Thus, the notion of arbitrary or capricious review embodies a range of standards; it is not applied uniformly. At times in American history, for example, courts seem to have looked askance at the decisions of the National Labor Relations Board and the Immigration and Naturalization Service; the Nuclear Regulatory Commission and the Environmental Protection Agency have also been subject to occasionally close scrutiny.

5. The Hard Look Now (?)

Motor Vehicle Manufacturers' Association v. State Farm Mutual Automobile Insurance Co.
463 U.S. 29 (1983)

Justice WHITE delivered the opinion of the Court. . . .

[T]he National Traffic and Motor Vehicle Safety Act of 1966 directs the Secretary of Transportation or his delegate to issue motor vehicle safety standards that "shall be practicable, shall meet the need for motor vehicle safety, and shall be stated in objective terms." 15 U.S.C. §1392(a). . . . We review today whether NHTSA acted arbitrarily and capriciously in revoking the requirement in Motor Vehicle Safety Standard 208 that new motor vehicles produced after September 1982 be equipped with passive restraints to protect the safety of the occupants of the vehicle in the event of a collision. Briefly summarized, we hold that the agency failed to present an adequate basis and explanation for rescinding the passive restraint requirement and that the agency must either consider the matter further or adhere to or amend Standard 208 along lines which its analysis supports.

The regulation whose rescission is at issue bears a complex and convoluted history. Over the course of approximately 60 rulemaking notices, the requirement has been imposed, amended, rescinded, reimposed, and now rescinded again.

As originally issued by the Department of Transportation in 1967, Standard 208 simply required the installation of seatbelts in all automobiles. . . . In 1969, the Department formally proposed a standard requiring the installation of passive restraints, . . . and in 1972, the agency amended that standard to require full passive protection for all front seat occupants of vehicles manufactured after August 15, 1975. [The standard would require either seat belts attached to the door which automatically surround the driver and passenger or airbags which inflate automatically in a crash, cushioning those in the front seat.] In the interim, vehicles built between August 1973 and August 1975 were to carry either passive restraints or lap and shoulder belts coupled with an "ignition interlock" that would prevent starting the vehicle if the belts were not connected. . . .

In preparing for the upcoming model year, most car makers chose the "ignition interlock" option, a decision which was highly unpopular, and led Congress to amend the Act to prohibit a motor vehicle safety standard from requiring or permitting compliance by means of an ignition interlock or a continuous buzzer designed to indicate that safety belts were not in use. Motor Vehicle and Schoolbus Safety Amendments of 1974. . . . In June 1976, Secretary of Transportation William Coleman initiated a new rulemaking on the issue. . . . Although he found passive restraints technologically and economically feasible, the Secretary expect[ed] that there would be widespread public resistance to the new systems. He instead proposed a demonstration project involving up to 500,000 cars installed with passive restraints, in order to smooth the way for public acceptance of mandatory passive restraints at a later date.

Coleman's successor as Secretary of Transportation [Brock Adams] disagreed. He issued a new mandatory passive restraint regulation [which] mandated the phasing in of passive restraints, beginning with large cars in model year 1982 and extending to all cars by model year 1984. The two principal systems that would satisfy the standard were airbags and passive belts; the choice of which system to install was left to the manufacturers. . . . In February 1981, however, Secretary of Transportation Andrew Lewis reopened the rulemaking due to changed economic circumstances and, in particular, the difficulties of the automobile industry. . . . After receiving written comments and holding public hearings, NHTSA issued a final rule (Notice 25) that rescinded the passive restraint requirement contained in Modified Standard 208.

II

In a statement explaining the rescission, NHTSA maintained that it was no longer able to find, as it had in 1977, that the automatic restraint requirement would produce significant safety benefits. . . . This judgment reflected not a change of opinion on the effectiveness of the technology, but a change in plans by the automobile industry. In 1977, the agency had assumed that airbags would be installed in 60% of all new cars and automatic seatbelts in 40%. By 1981 it became apparent that automobile manufacturers planned to install the automatic seatbelts in approximately 99% of the new cars. For this reason, the life-saving potential of airbags would not be realized. Moreover, it now appeared that the overwhelming majority of passive belts planned to be installed by manufacturers could be detached easily and left that way permanently. Passive belts, once detached, then required "the same type of affirmative action that is the stumbling block to obtaining high usage levels of manual belts." . . . For this reason, the agency concluded that there was no longer a basis for reliably predicting that the standard would lead to any significant increased usage of restraints at all.

In view of the possibly minimal safety benefits, the automatic restraint requirement no longer was reasonable or practicable in the agency's view. The requirement would require $1 billion to implement and the agency did not believe it would be reasonable to impose such substantial costs on manufacturers and consumers without more adequate assurance that sufficient safety benefits would accrue. In addition, NHTSA concluded that automatic restraints might have an adverse effect on the public's attitude toward safety. Given the high expense and limited benefits of detachable belts, NHTSA feared that many consumers would regard the standard as an instance of ineffective regulation, adversely affecting the public's view of safety regulation and, in particular, "poisoning popular sentiment toward efforts to improve occupant restraint systems in the future." . . .

III

Unlike the Court of Appeals, we do not find the appropriate scope of judicial review to be the "most troublesome question" in the case. Both the Motor Vehicle Safety Act and the 1974 Amendments concerning occupant crash protection standards indicate that motor vehicle standards are to be promulgated under the informal rule-making procedures of §553 of the Administrative Procedure Act, 5 U.S.C. §553 (1976). The agency's action in promulgating such standards therefore may be set aside if found to be "arbitrary, capricious, an abuse of discretion, or otherwise not in accordance with law." 5 U.S.C. §706(2)(A). Citizens to Preserve Overton Park v. Volpe, 401 U.S. 402, 414 (1971); Bowman Transportation, Inc. v. Arkansas-Best Freight System, Inc., 419 U.S. 281 (1974). We believe that the rescission or modification of an occupant protection standard is subject to the same test. [T]he revocation of an extant regulation is substantially different than a failure to act. Revocation constitutes a reversal of the agency's former views as to the proper course. A "settled course of behavior embodies the agency's informed judgment that, by pursuing that course, it will carry out the policies committed to it by Congress. There is, then, at least a presumption that those policies will be carried out best if the settled rule is adhered to." Atchison, T. & S.F.R. Co. v. Wichita Bd. of Trade, 412 U.S. 800, 807-808 (1973). Accordingly, an agency changing its course by rescinding a rule is obligated to supply a reasoned analysis for the change beyond that which may be required when an agency does not act in the first instance.

In so holding, we fully recognize that "regulatory agencies do not establish rules of conduct to last forever," American Trucking Assoc., Inc. v. Atchison, T. & S.F.R. Co., 387 U.S. 397, 416 (1967), and that an agency must be given ample latitude to "adapt their rules and policies to the demands of changing circumstances." Permian Basin Area Rate Cases, 390 U.S. 747, 784 (1968). But the forces of change do not always or necessarily point in the direction of deregulation. . . .

The Department of Transportation accepts the applicability of the "arbitrary and capricious" standard. It argues that under this standard, a reviewing court may not set aside an agency rule that is rational, based on consideration of the relevant factors and within the scope of the authority delegated to the agency by the statute. We do not disagree with this formulation. The scope of review under the "arbitrary and capricious" standard is narrow and a court is not to substitute its judgment for that of the agency. Nevertheless, the agency must examine the relevant data and articulate a satisfactory explanation for its action including a "rational connection between the facts found and the choice made." Burlington Truck Lines v. United States, 371 U.S. 156, 168 (1962). In reviewing that explanation, we must "consider whether the decision was based on a consideration of the relevant factors and whether there has been a clear error of judgment." Bowman Transp. Inc. v. Arkansas-Best Freight System, supra, at 285; Citizens to

Preserve Overton Park v. Volpe, supra, at 416. Normally, an agency rule would be arbitrary and capricious if the agency has relied on factors which Congress has not intended it to consider, entirely failed to consider an important aspect of the problem, offered an explanation for its decision that runs counter to the evidence before the agency, or is so implausible that it could not be ascribed to a difference in view or the product of agency expertise. The reviewing court should not attempt itself to make up for such deficiencies: "We may not supply a reasoned basis for the agency's action that the agency itself has not given." SEC v. Chenery Corp., 322 U.S. 194, 196 (1947). We will, however, uphold a decision of less than ideal clarity if the agency's path may reasonably be discerned. Bowman Transp. Inc. v. Arkansas-Best Freight Systems, supra, at 286. . . . For purposes of this case, it is also relevant that Congress required a record of the rulemaking proceedings to be compiled and submitted to a reviewing court, 15 U.S.C. §1394, and intended that agency findings under the Motor Vehicle Safety Act would be supported by "substantial evidence on the record considered as a whole." S. Rep. No. 1301, 89th Cong., 2d Sess., p.8 (1966); H.R. Rep. No. 1776, 89th Cong,, 2d Sess. p.21 (1966). . . .

V

The ultimate question before us is whether NHTSA's rescission of the passive restraint requirement of Standard 208 was arbitrary and capricious. We conclude, as did the Court of Appeals, that it was. . . .

A

The first and most obvious reason for finding the rescission arbitrary and capricious is that NHTSA apparently gave no consideration whatever to modifying the Standard to require that airbag technology be utilized. Standard 208 sought to achieve automatic crash protection by requiring automobile manufacturers to install either of two passive restraint devices: airbags or automatic seatbelts. There was no suggestion in the long rulemaking process that led to Standard 208 that if only one of these options were feasible, no passive restraint standard should be promulgated. . . . Although it was then foreseen that 60% of the new cars would contain airbags and 40% would have automatic seatbelts, the ratio between the two was not significant as long as the passive belt would also assure greater passenger safety.

The agency has now determined that the detachable automatic belts will not attain anticipated safety benefits because so many individuals will detach the mechanism. . . . Given the effectiveness ascribed to airbag technology by the agency, the mandate of the Safety Act to achieve traffic safety would suggest that the logical response to the faults of detachable seatbelts would be to require the installation of airbags. At the very least this alternative way of achieving the objectives of the Act should have been addressed and adequate reasons given for its abandonment. But the agency not only did not require compliance through airbags, it did not even consider the possibility in its 1981 rulemaking. Not one sentence of its rulemaking statement discusses the airbags-only option. . . . We have frequently reiterated that an agency must cogently explain why it has exercised its discretion in a given manner, Atchison, T & S.F.R. Co. v. Wichita Bd. of Trade, 412 U.S. 800, 806 (1973); and we reaffirm this principle again today.

The automobile industry has opted for the passive belt over the airbag, but surely it is not enough that the regulated industry has eschewed a given safety device. . . .

[P]etitioners recite a number of difficulties that they believe would be posed by a mandatory airbag standard. These range from questions concerning the installation of airbags in small cars to that of adverse public reaction. But these are not the agency's reasons for rejecting a mandatory airbag standard. Not having discussed the possibility, the agency submitted no reasons at all. The short — and sufficient — answer to petitioner's submission is that the courts may not accept appellate counsel's post hoc rationalizations for agency action. Burlington Truck Lines v. United States, supra, at 168. It is well-established that an agency's action must be upheld, if at all, on the basis articulated by the agency itself. Ibid.; Chenery v. SEC, 332 U.S. 194, 196 (1945); American Textile Manufacturers Inst. v. Donovan, 452 U.S. 490, 539 (1981).[15]

Petitioners also invoke our decision in Vermont Yankee Nuclear Power Corp. v. NRDC, 435 U.S. 519 (1977). . . . It is true that a rulemaking "cannot be found wanting simply because the agency failed to include every alternative device and thought conceivable by the mind of man . . . regardless of how uncommon or unknown that alternative may have been. . . . " 435 U.S., at 551. But the airbag is more than a policy alternative to the passive restraint standard; it is a technological alternative within the ambit of the existing standard. We hold only that given the judgment made in 1977 that airbags are an effective and cost-beneficial life-saving technology, the mandatory passive-restraint rule may not be abandoned without any consideration whatsoever of an airbags-only requirement.

B

Although the issue is closer, we also find that the agency was too quick to dismiss the safety benefits of automatic seatbelts. NHTSA's critical finding was that, in light of the industry's plans to install readily detachable passive belts, it could not reliably predict "even a 5 percentage point increase as the minimum level of expected usage increase." . . . The Court of Appeals rejected this finding because there is "not one iota" of evidence that Modified Standard 208 will fail to increase nationwide seatbelt use by at least 13 percentage points, the level of increased usage necessary for the standard to justify its cost. . . .

. . . We agree with petitioners that just as an agency reasonably may decline to issue a safety standard if it is uncertain about its efficacy, an agency may also revoke a standard on the basis of serious uncertainties if supported by the record and reasonably explained. . . . Recognizing that policymaking in a complex society must account for uncertainty, however, does not imply that it is sufficient for an agency to merely recite the terms "substantial uncertainty" as a justification for its actions. The agency must explain the evidence which is available, and must offer a "rational connection between the facts found and the choice made." Burlington Truck Lines, Inc. v. United States, supra, at 168.

15. The Department of Transportation expresses concern that adoption of an airbags-only requirement would have required a new notice of proposed rulemaking. Even if this were so, and we need not decide the question, it would not constitute sufficient cause to rescind the passive restraint requirement. The Department also asserts that it was reasonable to withdraw the requirement as written to avoid forcing manufacturers to spend resources to comply with an ineffective safety initiative. We think that it would have been permissible for the agency to temporarily suspend the passive restraint requirement or to delay its implementation date while an airbags mandate was studied. But, as we explain in text, the option had to be considered before the passive restraint requirement could be revoked.

. . . We start with the accepted ground that if used, seatbelts unquestionably would save many thousands of lives and would prevent tens of thousands of crippling injuries. Unlike recent regulatory decisions we have reviewed, Industrial Union Department v. American Petroleum Institute, 448 U.S. 607 (1980); American Textile Manufacturers Inst., Inc. v. Donovan, 452 U.S. 490 (1981), the safety benefits of wearing seatbelts are not in doubt and it is not challenged that were those benefits to accrue, the monetary costs of implementing the standard would be easily justified. We move next to the fact that there is no direct evidence in support of the agency's finding that detachable automatic belts cannot be predicted to yield a substantial increase in usage. The empirical evidence on the record, consisting of surveys of drivers of automobiles equipped with passive belts, reveals more than a doubling of the usage rate experienced with manual belts.[16] Much of the agency's rulemaking statement — and much of the controversy in this case — centers on the conclusions that should be drawn from these studies. The agency maintained that the doubling of seatbelt usage in these studies could not be extrapolated to an across-the-board mandatory standard because the passive seatbelts were guarded by ignition inter-locks and purchasers of the tested cars are somewhat atypical.[17] Respondents insist these studies demonstrate that Modified Standard 208 will substantially increase seatbelt usage. We believe that it is within the agency's discretion to pass upon the generalizability of these field studies. This is precisely the type of issue which rests within the expertise of NHTSA, and upon which a reviewing court must be most hesitant to intrude.

But accepting the agency's view of the field tests on passive restraints indicates only that there is no reliable real-world experience that usage rates will substantially increase. To be sure, NHTSA opines that "it cannot reliably predict even a 5 percentage point increase as the minimum level of increased usage." . . . But this and other statements that passive belts will not yield substantial increases in seatbelt usage apparently take no account of the critical difference between detachable automatic belts and current manual belts. A detached passive belt does require an affirmative act to reconnect it, but — unlike a manual seatbelt — the passive belt, once reattached, will continue to function automat-ically unless again disconnected. Thus, inertia — a factor which the agency's own studies have found significant in explaining the current low usage rates for seatbelts — works in *favor of* not *against*, use of the protective device. Since 20 to 50% of motorists currently wear seatbelts on some occasions, there would seem to be grounds to believe that seatbelt use by occasional users will be substantially increased by the detachable passive belts. Whether this is in fact the case is a matter for the agency to decide, but it must bring its expertise to bear on the question. . . .

The agency also failed to articulate a basis for not requiring nondetachable belts under Standard 208. It is argued that the concern of the agency with the easy detachability of the currently favored design would be readily solved by a continuous passive belt, which

16. Between 1975 and 1980, Volkswagen sold approximately 350,000 Rabbits equipped with detachable passive seatbelts that were guarded by an ignition interlock. General Motors sold 8,000 1978 and 1979 Chevettes with a similar system, but eliminated the ignition interlock on the 13,000 Chevettes sold in 1980. NHTSA found that belt usage in the Rabbits averaged 34% for manual belts and 84% for passive belts. Regulatory Impact Analysis (RIA) at IV-52, App. 108. For the 1978-1979 Chevettes, NHTSA calculated 34% usage for manual belts and 71% for passive belts. On 1980 Chevettes, the agency found these figures to be 31% for manual belts and 70% for passive belts.

17. "NHTSA believes that the usage of automobile belts in Rabbits and Chevettes would have been substantially lower if the automatic belts in those cases were not equipped with a use-included device inhibiting detachment." Notice 25, 46 Fed. Reg. at 53,422.

allows the occupant to "spool out" the belt and create the necessary slack for easy extrication from the vehicle. The agency did not separately consider the continuous belt option, but treated it together with the ignition interlock device in a category it titled "option of use-compelling features." . . . The agency was concerned that use-compelling devices would "complicate extrication of [a]n occupant from his or her car. . . . To require that passive belts contain use-compelling features," the agency observed, "could be counterproductive [given] widespread, latent and irrational fear in many members of the public that they could be trapped by the seat belt after a crash." In addition, based on the experience with the ignition interlock, the agency feared that use-compelling features might trigger adverse public reaction.

By failing to analyze the continuous seatbelts in its own right, the agency has failed to offer the rational connection between facts and judgment required to pass muster under the arbitrary and capricious standard. [In 1978] NHTSA was satisfied that this belt design assured easy extricability: "the agency does not believe that the use of [such] release mechanisms will cause serious occupant egress problems. . . ." While the agency is entitled to change its view on the acceptability of continuous passive belts, it is obligated to explain its reasons for doing so.

The agency also failed to offer any explanation why a continuous passive belt would engender the same adverse public reaction as the ignition interlock. . . . We see no basis for equating the two devices: the continuous belt, unlike the ignition interlock, does not interfere with the operation of the vehicle. More importantly, it is the agency's responsibility, not this Court's to explain its decision.

VI

"An agency's view of what is in the public interest may change, either with or without a change in circumstances. But an agency changing its course must supply a reasoned analysis. . . ." Greater Boston Television Corp. v. FCC, 444 F.2d 841, 852 (CADC), cert. denied, 403 U.S. 923 (1971). Accordingly, we vacate the judgment of the Court of Appeals and remand the case to that court with directions to remand the matter to the NHTSA for further consideration consistent with this opinion.

Justice Rehnquist, joined by the Chief Justice, Justice Powell, and Justice O'Connor, found that NHTSA's view of detachable automatic seatbelts was not arbitrary and capricious, and therefore dissented from part V.B of the Court's opinion. In a widely cited passage, Justice Rehnquist considered the agency's view that automatic seatbelts might not work a reasonable view and one not disproved by the study cited in the majority opinion. He added:

> The agency's changed view of the standard seems to be related to the election of a new President of a different political party. It is readily apparent that the responsible members of one administration may consider public resistance and uncertainties to be more important than do their counterparts in a previous administration. A change in administration brought about by the people casting their votes is a perfectly reasonable basis for an executive agency's reappraisal of the costs and benefits of its programs and regulations. As long as the agency remains within the bounds established by Congress, it is entitled to assess administrative records and evaluate priorities in light of the philosophy of the administration.

Note on Regulatory Standard-Setting

The long delays and argument surrounding "passive restraints" are all too typical of many major standards that NHTSA has promulgated (governing, for example, head restraints, brakes, bumpers, and tires) and of standards set by other agencies as well. The sources of this delay and controversy are multiple. See J. Mashaw & D. Harfst, The Struggle for Auto Safety (1990), for general discussion. The task of setting a new major standard in any area of regulation is far more difficult than most people realize. When first created, agencies like the NHTSA simply copied already existing standards developed by, for example, states, the ICC, the General Services Administration (which has standards for purchasing cars), the post office, the Society of Automotive Engineers, foreign countries, and so forth. NHTSA in this way was able to promulgate about 20 major standards in the first year or so of operation — between 1966 and 1968. This approach gives an impression of great activity and a false impression of efficacy.

To proceed further to create entirely new standards is far more difficult. First and foremost, the agency must obtain accurate information. But where can it find the information? From *industry*? Is it a biased source? From *independent experts*? Who are they? *Professors*? Will they have sufficiently detailed information? Did they obtain it from industry? *Consumer groups*? Where do they get their information? Do they suffer anti-industry bias? Should the agency develop the information *in-house*? Will it then seek to replicate a second General Motors, inside NHTSA? Consider the information source problem in light of a typical agency need: Should tires be tested for wear after 5000 miles or after 10,000 miles (which might favor certain firms whose tires wear out proportionately more slowly)? Who has unbiased information on this very minor, but critical, question necessary to the promulgation of a tire standard?

Second, the agency must consider a host of questions related to the type of standard it wishes to promulgate. Should the standard aim directly at the evil targeted by the regulatory program (for example, ecological harm to aquatic life caused by water pollution) or at a surrogate (for example, a "biological oxygen demand" measure of pollution that correlates very roughly with ecological harm)? How specific should the standard be? Should it try to "force" technological development by requiring the industry to meet a standard that it does not yet have the technical ability to meet? Technology-forcing may be desirable if an industry is able to develop new technologies relatively cheaply but does not do so because it has not been required to internalize the social costs of its actions. But technology-forcing may well be a stab in the dark by government. How does government know the precise point to which it is appropriate to force technology?

Should there be a "performance standard" or a "design standard"? Performance standards that state their obligations in terms of ultimate outputs (for example, a standard limiting permitted pollution discharges to a certain amount) permit flexibility and change; they do not freeze existing technology. Many people are increasingly enthusiastic about performance standards on the ground that they allow companies to choose the least expensive means of achieving regulatory goals. With performance standards, means are chosen by the market, not by the state, and hence the Reagan, Bush, and Clinton administrations have expressed a general enthusiasm for performance standards. Yet design standards that require, for example, the use of a specific end-of-pipe pollution caution technology may be far easier to enforce; they avoid arguments about complex testing procedures necessary to see if the performance standard has been satisfied.

Third, the agency must modify or shape the standard in light of enforcement needs. Developing a fair but replicable testing system is often very difficult; indeed NHTSA was told by one court of appeals that imprecise specifications for dummies used to test passive restraints made the rule "irrational." (NHTSA lacked the information necessary to describe a "dummy's neck" in a way that would make it just like a human neck.) See Chrysler Corp. v. Department of Transp., 472 F.2d 659 (6th Cir. 1972). This decision had a significant impact on NHTSA, making it fear that any rule might be vulnerable on some ground that could be made persuasive to a court of appeals. In any case, the cost of testing and enforcing standards must be taken into account. And the agency may well decide to simplify or to weaken its standards considerably to increase the likelihood of voluntary compliance.

Fourth, the agency should take account of various "competitive" concerns. How will a new standard affect competition among existing firms? Will it unnecessarily favor some firms over others? Will it favor all existing firms over new firms by unnecessarily making entry into the industry more difficult? (The "new" firms, by definition, are not yet around to argue their case to the agency.) Will a new standard "freeze" technology, inhibiting research and development of a better, or a safer, product?

Fifth, the agency may have to "negotiate" a final standard. It finds before it different parties — the industry, suppliers, consumer groups, members of Congress, its own staff — each with importantly or slightly different objectives. At the very least, each party may see different aspects of the problem as more important. Industry groups, for example, may emphasize cost; suppliers, competitive fairness; consumer groups, lifesaving; staff, ease of administration and enforcement. And each group has a different weapon: The staff can recommend stricter or less strict standards. The industry and suppliers possess critical information that they can make available more — or less — readily. They can also threaten court action or political action by, say, emphasizing the potential job loss. Consumer groups can also threaten court action or political action by appealing to Congress or to the public through the press. A wise agency may recognize the various powers that the parties wield, and it may shape the standard to minimize opposition, thereby increasing the likelihood of voluntary compliance and diminishing the likelihood of court delays. Regardless, the final outcome is likely to reflect to some degree a "compromise" among these interests.

Sixth, the agency must survive judicial review — a potentially lengthy process with serious delays. It must create a solution to a "polycentric" problem — one with many potential tradeoffs among various factors — within the legal confines of "back and forth" notice-and-comment rulemaking. The agency suggests a solution; the parties discuss it; they cannot readily meet informally, making various suggestions until agreement is reached or until all considerations are out in the open. The agency must show its decision is "rational." Thus, it must keep records (though the records are likely kept by agency lawyers, not its engineers); and it risks reversal if it follows the engineer's "inspired guess" (such as the decision to require development of soft, nonmetallic bumpers). Given the uncertainties and complexities described above, a decision might strike an agency as rational but appear arbitrary, illogical, or inconsistent to a judge. A judge may not have the information or insight to understand, in a particular case, the agency's need to make decisions under conditions of uncertainty, to consider ease of administration and enforcement, or to secure a compromise.

Regulatory agencies will have an easier time in court if they set standards in areas where documentation with hard facts is readily available. But is there any reason to believe that these are the areas where the most lives can be saved?

How well NHTSA has managed to overcome these problems and to set effective safety standards is a matter of considerable debate. NHTSA, for example, claimed in its early years that federal safety programs "have combined to reduce the fatality rates (number of deaths per 100 million vehicle miles driven) by 39 percent." U.S. Dept. of Transportation, Motor Vehicle Safety, 1980 p. iii. Indeed, the number of total traffic deaths declined from 53,000 annually in 1966 (and from a high of nearly 56,000 in 1969) to 46,000 in 1975, creeping back up to about 52,000 in 1979. The fatality *rate* (which takes account of the fact that there are more cars, more drivers, and more miles driven) fell, as NHTSA has pointed out, from 5.7 in 1966 to 3.40 in 1979. Critics have noted, however, that the fatality rate has fallen steadily and almost consistently each year since 1947, when it stood at 8.82. (It fell from 3.82 to 5.70 during the 1947-1966 period when there was no regulation.) The critics also pointed to such factors as the oil embargo, the 55 mph speed limit, and the aging population, not NHTSA, as responsible for the continued decline.

Similar ambiguities emerge from the recent data. NHTSA found that the 1996 fatality rate per million drivers was 1.7 percent, equal to its historic low in 1993, half of the rate in 1979. NHTSA attributes the decrease to a reduction of the role of alcohol in fatal crashes (to 40.9 percent) and 68 percent safety belt use nationwide (a number perhaps spurred indirectly by *State Farm*, through NHTSA's decision, on remand, to go forward with the regulation unless a majority of states enacted seatbelt legislation; though a majority of states fail to require seatbelt use, a number of them did so). The total number of persons killed in motor vehicle crashes in 1996 was 35,579, an increase over the recent low of 32,880 in 1992, but a substantial decrease from the numbers between 1986 and 1989, which ranged from 38,000 to 39,000. About 3.3 million people were injured in accidents, up from the recent historic low of 2.9 million in 1992, and indeed higher than in 1988 and 1989. Consider Table 4-4 below.

Query: If fatalities and injuries are mostly a product of speeding, drunk driving, and failure to use safety belts, what would a sensible regulatory program look like, if its goal is substantially to decrease deaths and injuries from motor vehicle accidents?

TABLE 4-4
Persons Killed and Injured and Fatality and Injury Rates, 1986-1996

				Killed	
Year	Fatalities	Resident population (thousands)	Fatality rate per 100,000 population	Licensed drivers (thousands)	Fatality rate per 100,000 licensed drivers
1986	46,087	240,133	19.19	159,487	28.90
1987	46,390	242,289	19.15	161,818	28.67
1988	47,087	244,499	19.26	162,853	28.91
1989	45,582	246,819	18.47	165,555	27.53
1990	44,599	249,403	17.88	167,015	26.70
1991	41,508	252,138	16.46	168,995	24.56
1992	39,250	255,039	15.39	173,125	22.67
1993	40,150	257,800	15.57	173,149	23.19
1994	40,716	260,350	15.64	175,403	23.21
1995	41,817	262,755	15.91	176,628	23.68
1996	41,907	265,284	15.80	*	*

		Resident population (thousands)	Injury rate per 100,000 population	Injured	
Year	Injuries			Licensed drivers (thousands)	Injury rate per 100,000 licensed drivers
1988	3,416,000	244,499	1,397	162,853	2,098
1989	3,284,000	246,819	1,331	165,555	1,984
1990	3,231,000	249,403	1,295	167,015	1,934
1991	3,097,000	252,138	1,228	168,995	1,833
1992	3,070,000	255,039	1,204	173,125	1,773
1993	3,149,000	257,800	1,221	173,149	1,819
1994	3,265,000	260,350	1,254	175,403	1,861
1995	3,465,000	262,755	1,319	176,628	1,953
1996	3,511,000	265,284	1,323	*	*

*Data not available.
Note: Injury data for the years 1993-1995 have been revised by NHTSA.
Source: NHTSA.

Changing the Substance of Regulatory Law

To what extent are agencies permitted to change their minds? This is a pervasive question, of special importance in any period of presidential transition, but likely to arise frequently in practice. We have already investigated a similar question in the *Chevron* context, where courts have struggled with the question whether *Chevron* deference should be reduced if an agency is departing from a previous interpretation. Here we examine whether shifts in position raise questions of arbitrariness.

State Farm is the dominant decision here. Does the Supreme Court's approach "freeze" existing standards, inhibiting agency flexibility? The Second Circuit in New York Council, Assn. of Civilian Technicians v. Federal Labor Relations Auth., 757 F.2d 502 (1985), upholding an agency change of position, interpreted *State Farm* as follows:

> Although there is not a "heightened standard of scrutiny, ["] . . . the agency must explain why the original reasons for adopting the rule or policy are no longer dispositive. Brae Corp. v. United States, 740 F.2d 1023, 1038 (D.C. Cir. 1984) [emphasis added by the court]. Even in the absence of cumulative experience, changed circumstances or judicial criticism, an agency is free to change course after reweighing the competing statutory policies. But such a flip-flop must be accompanied by a reasoned explanation of why the new rule effectuates the statute as well as or better than the old rule.

Many decisions emphasize the need to explain a change in position. See, e.g., Williston Basin Interstate Pipeline Co. v. FERC, 165 F.3d 54 (D.C. Cir. 1999); City of Fort Morgan v. FERC, 181 F.3d 1155 (10th Cir. 1999). The Supreme Court has recently stressed the point: "Though the agency's discretion is unfettered at the outset, if it announces and follows — by rule or by settled course of adjudication — a general policy by which its exercise of discretion will be governed, an irrational departure from that policy (as opposed to an avowed alteration of it) could constitute action that must be overturned as 'arbitrary, capricious, [or] an abuse of discretion. . . .'" INS v. Yang, 519 U.S. 26

(1996). But this sentence leaves the hard questions open. It does not say, for example, whether the Bush Administration could repeal a Clinton Administration rule requiring television broadcasters to provide three hours of children's educational programming per week. It is worthwhile to keep this general issue — when an agency can change position — in mind as you read the materials to follow.

Notes and Questions

1. In 1981, NHTSA confronted an existing standard (FMVSS 208) that required (effective 1984) passive restraints but allowed manufacturers a choice among alternative types, including passive detachable seat belts and airbags. Once it learned that nearly all manufacturers would comply by using detachable seatbelts, it repealed the standard as ineffective. Consider the rationality of this action as seen by NHTSA, as well as by the Supreme Court.

(a) Was it "arbitrary and capricious" to believe the existing standard would prove ineffective? The Court accepted NHTSA's view that to be worth the cost, the standard would have to increase average seatbelt use 13 percentage points, from an average use of 11 percent to an average use of 24 percent — an increase by a factor of 2.2. The Court apparently assumed that this might happen. It pointed to a study in the record that compares use of manual and passive belts in Volkswagen Rabbits and GM Chevettes. The use of passive belts in Volkswagen Rabbits was 2.5 times the use of manual belts (84 compared to 34 percent); the factor for 1978-1979 Chevettes was 2.1 (71 compared to 34 percent); and for 1980 Chevettes it was 2.3 (70 compared to 31 percent). In NHTSA's view, however, these data were not greatly significant because (1) Volkswagen (and all small car) owners are known to use seatbelts much more than the average anyway; (2) the passive belts had forms of "interlocks" that made detaching them unusually difficult or unpleasant; and (3) the owners of passive belts in these cars for the most part had *voluntarily* paid more money to buy passive systems; they were not compelled by law to do so. What may be more surprising, then, is not the high passive belt use rate in the studies, but the fact that 30 percent or so of those who *voluntarily* bought passive systems ended up detaching them. Does the Court deal with the study satisfactorily? Can it still find this aspect of NHTSA's decision arbitrary and capricious?

(b) Was it "arbitrary and capricious" not to investigate the "continuous spool nondetachable" belt alternative before repealing FMVSS 208? NHTSA argued that (1) there was little safety or use information about these belts, and use of an untested system might itself violate the Safety Act as there was no evidence it would "meet the need for motor vehicle safety"; (2) the legislative repeal of the interlock showed congressional hostility to "use-compelling" devices; (3) although the use of belts made loss of consciousness less likely in an accident, nondetachable belts might make more difficult rescue of those who do lose consciousness; and (4) public fears of entrapment and dislike of belts might lead many car owners to cut out the belt entirely, thereby stopping even occasional (highway) belt use and making cars still less safe. Does the Court deal adequately with these arguments in your view? Why might it still consider NHTSA's decision (in this respect) "arbitrary"?

(c) Was it "arbitrary and capricious" not to investigate the "airbag only" alternative before repealing FMVSS 208? Why should NHTSA not have done so? (1) The rule before NHTSA was essentially a "seatbelt rule"; although auto manufacturers might in theory use airbags to comply, almost all were going to comply by using seatbelts. (2) NHTSA has always considered airbags as one, but not the *only*, way to comply with a passive restraint standard. When it first promulgated a standard in 1970, NHTSA stated that it in no way "'favored' or expected the introduction of airbag systems to meet [the FMVSS 208] requirements"; the notice added that there were "equally acceptable" ways to meet it; and from February 1972 onwards NHTSA had very clearly emphasized these alternatives; thus "airbags only" is a very new and different idea. (3) The major argument against airbags is, of course, cost. The Court of Appeals mentioned estimated costs, if *all* cars were equipped, of $200 to $330 per car and, if only some cars (say 10,000 per year) were equipped, of $1200 per car. Whether all car buyers should be forced to pay these costs (amounting to several billion dollars annually) becomes a difficult question (even if doing so would save 9000 lives a year) once one realizes that exactly the same result can be achieved at a fraction of the price by buckling up a seatbelt. (4) The Safety Act mandates performance standards, not design standards. (5) To explore the implications of "airbags only" is time consuming; manufacturers must know what to do *now*. They will gear up for passive belts unless we repeal FMVSS 208. How convincing do you find these arguments when compared with the Court's analysis? What is the relevance of the fact that they were not made in the decision repealing FMVSS 208 and could therefore have been raised for the first time by NHTSA only in its brief on appeal?

(d) Many foreign nations have simply required by law, under penalty of severe fines, that front seat passengers "buckle up." This method has the virtues of low cost and perhaps effectiveness. "Prosecutorial discretion" can forgive the unbuckled belt on a five-minute trip to the grocery store but can deal harshly with the interstate highway driver. (Drivers may find belts most annoying and unnecessary on short local trips.) But Congress has not passed such a law, nor have most states. At the same time driver rebellion led Congress to pass a law canceling the "interlock," a device that forces drivers to buckle up by making an irritating noise. Should NHTSA then "force" them to buckle up anyway with a nondetachable belt? Should it instead force them to pay several hundred dollars extra when they buy a car, adding between $3 and $12 billion dollars to the annual cost of driving? Should it let 9000 persons more die each year? What is the "reasonable" solution? Can it be that there is *no* "reasonable" course of agency behavior? What was "arbitrary and capricious" about NHTSA's decision? Its factual findings and predictions? Its decision's analytic approach? Its policy preferences?

2. Where does the Court's remand leave FMVSS 208? What options are available to NHTSA following the remand? NHTSA adopted a rule requiring installation of automatic passive restraints in all new cars made after 1989, unless mandatory laws to require "'buckling up" were enacted in sufficient states to total two-thirds of the American population. 49 Fed. Reg. 28,962 (July 17, 1984). The requisite number of states was never reached. Consequently in mid-1989 the "passive restraint" rule took effect. Did *State Farm* require NHTSA to take this action?

3. Consider the fact that the National Traffic and Motor Vehicle Safety Act was enacted by Democrats in 1966 at the beginning of the consumer and environmental movements and a time when the U.S. auto industry was the envy of the world. The repeal of FMVSS 208 was accomplished by the Reagan administration, elected in considerable part by a growing antiregulation movement and a concern about the sharply declining position of key U.S. industries, including the auto industry. The repeal of FMVSS 208 was part of a larger package of "regulatory relief" for the automobile industry adopted by the Reagan administration. See G. Eads & M. Fix: Relief or Reform?: Reagan's Regulatory Dilemma 125-133 (1984). The act grants considerable regulatory discretion to the Transportation Department. Does it include discretion to scale back regulatory

requirements based not on the interests of automobile consumers and users but on the interests of the domestic auto industry?

Recall Justice Rehnquist's suggestion that NHTSA's "changed view . . . seems to be related to the election of a new President. . . . As long as the agency remains within the bounds established by Congress, it is entitled to assess administrative records and evaluate priorities in light of the philosophy of the administration." To what extent do you agree or disagree with this statement?

It is possible to infer that the majority thought that the case involved a problem of agency capture — situation in which NHTSA (run by a new administration insistent on deregulation) was abandoning a well-considered rule simply because industry chose an ineffective means of compliance. Perhaps NHTSA, with its various predictions and references to numbers, was disguising a more straightforwardly political judgment, to the effect that the interest in private autonomy was sufficient to rule out a governmental role in this setting. If NHTSA said something like this on remand, should its decision be upheld? See generally Sunstein, Deregulation and the Hard-Look Doctrine, 1983 Sup. Ct. Rev. 471. Suppose that NHTSA had explicitly justified its position on the ground that President Reagan had been elected in large part because he had attacked the Carter administration for overregulation that imposed excessive burdens on the economy and unduly limited individual freedom of choice, and that the repeal of FMVSS 208 was based on this shift in regulatory policy, which had been overwhelmingly endorsed by the electorate? Or suppose it had justified its action not by attempting to attack the efficacy of the standard, but by concluding that the costs for consumers and burdens on domestic manufacturers and their workers that it would impose were greater than the safety benefits that the standard would achieve, in light of the alternative of achieving those benefits by requiring that passengers use the manual seat belts already installed in cars? How far should courts impede deregulation initiatives by the executive branch that respond to current political and economic concerns but that are arguably contrary to the purposes of regulatory statutes enacted in earlier eras? For discussion, see Edwards, Judicial Review of Deregulation, 11 N. Ky. L. Rev. 229 (1984). See also Garland, Deregulation and Judicial Review, 98 Harv. L. Rev. 505 (1988); Mikva, The Changing Role of Judicial Review, 68 Admin. L. Rev. 115 (1986). More generally, how far should courts strive to turn politically driven administration into a "rational" and "scientific" exercise? Does such an approach promote or impede democratic accountability and legitimacy? See C. Edley, Administrative Law: Rethinking Judicial Control of Bureaucracy 63-65 (1990).

4. *State Farm* also stresses the need for the agency to consider reasonable alternatives. The D.C. Circuit, referring to *State Farm*, has written that it

> is well settled that an agency has "a duty to consider responsible alternatives and to give a reasoned explanation for its rejection of such alternatives." . . . Of course, . . . this duty extends only to "significant and viable alternatives," . . . not to "every alternative device thought conceivable by the mind of man . . . regardless of how uncommon or unknown that alternative may have been." . . . But with that sensible caveat, the fact remains that "the failure of an agency to consider obvious alternatives has led uniformly to reversal."

City of Brookings Municipal Tel. Co. v. FCC, 822 F.2d 1153 (D.C. Cir. 1987).

This standard leaves open the question of when an alternative is a "reasonable" one that the agency ought to have considered. What made the airbags alternative "reasonable"?

The fact that it was within the "technological ambit" of the existing standard? Consider the possibility that whether an alternative is reasonable depends, in part, on (a) the likelihood that it will prove attractive, (b) the cost of investigating it, (c) its proximity to the action under discussion, and (d) the legal authority of the agency to implement it.

Does *State Farm* leave the agency free simply to repromulgate the rule after considering the previously unconsidered alternative? If so, is the decision futile? Or does it raise the spectre of "paralysis by analysis"?

Consider the following discussion and criticism of the practical effect of these approaches to view:

> Strict judicial review creates one incentive that from a substantive perspective may be perverse. The stricter the review and the more clearly and convincingly the agency must explain the need for change, the more reluctant the agency will be to change the status quo. Consider, for example, the D.C. Circuit's recent review of the Federal Highway Administration's efforts to simplify the 30-year-old truck driver "logging" and reporting requirements, designed to help the agency enforce a different rule that limits the number of consecutive hours a truck driver may drive. International Brotherhood of Teamsters v. United States, 735 F.2d 1525 (D.C. Cir. 1984). The major question before the agency was whether to allow the industry to use nonstandardized forms, a change that one consultant estimated would save about $160 million per year. The agency decision came after its notice of the proposed change, its receipt of 1,300 comments, and its modifications of its initial proposal. About two years elapsed from the time of public notice until the conclusion of court review. The court allowed the agency to simplify much of its standardized form, but the court set aside two changes the agency wished to make.
>
> FHA had decided that drivers still had to use a standardized grid showing hours driven and also to include on the form: date, total miles driven today, truck number, carrier name, signature, starting time, office address, and remarks. It said, however, that they could omit the name of any co-driver, total mileage today, home terminal address, total hours, shipping document number or name of shipper, or origin and destination points. The agency believed many of these items were redundant or "unnecessary" and that deletion would "reduce driver preparations by approximately 50 percent without affecting the enforcement capability." The court held to the contrary, concluding that the added items seemed useful. It would help an enforcement agency, for example, to check with a co-driver or shipper to see if a log was accurate. In any event, the court said FHA had not adequately explained the omissions.
>
> The agency also had decided to expand the scope of an exemption from its "log rules," an exemption that originally applied to "pick up and delivery" drivers, defined as those who drive within a radius of 50 miles and whose driving takes place within a 15-hour period each day. In 1980, perhaps recognizing that pick-up and delivery now often extends beyond 50 miles, the FHA changed the definition to 100 miles, but reduced the hour period to 12. In 1982 it increased the hour period to 15. The court concluded that the agency had not adequately explained why it made these changes; it should have further investigated an "alternative," namely having two exemptions, one for "50 miles/15 hours" and another for "100 miles/12 hours."
>
> One cannot tell from the opinion whether the court or agency is correct about the wisdom of the agency's new policies. Yet, it is easy to imagine how the head of an agency might react to the court's strict review of the policy merits of what seem to be rather trivial changes in reporting and examination rules. The head might say,
>
> > Why bother? Why should I try to simplify paperwork? A decision about what specific items to include on a log, or the exact point to draw an exemption line

must, within broad limits, be arbitrary. I suppose I could do cost-benefit analyses, and hire experts to "field-test" every possible change, but I haven't the money. I can't respond in depth to every argument made in 1,300 comments about every minor point in this record-keeping proposal. And, if I'm not even allowed to wait and see, as to these very minor matters, what a challenger says in a court brief, and then respond in my court brief, let's forget the whole thing. I'll keep whatever rules I've inherited and not try to make any minor improvements.

The reason agencies do not explore all arguments or consider all alternatives is one of practical limits of time and resources. Yet, to have to explain and to prove all this to a reviewing court risks imposing much of the very burden that not considering alternatives aims to escape. Of course, the reviewing courts may respond that only *important* alternatives and arguments must be considered. But what counts as "important"? District courts often find that parties, having barely mentioned a legal point at the trial level, suddenly make it the heart of their case on appeal, emphasizing its (sudden but) supreme importance. Appellate courts typically consider such arguments as long as they have been at least mentioned in the district court. But district courts, unlike agencies dealing with policy change, do not face, say, 10,000 comments challenging different aspects of complex policies. And, when appellate courts "answer" an argument, they write a few words or paragraphs, perhaps citing a case or two. A satisfactory answer in the agency context may mean factfinding, empirical research, or detailed investigation. Accordingly, one result of strict judicial review of policy decisions is a strong conservative pressure in favor of the status quo.[18]

When, then, is an agency's refusal to consider an alternative arbitrary or capricious? Remote and speculative alternatives need not be considered; alternatives that appear promising, and which might be investigated at very low cost, probably must be considered. Can these ideas be developed into a general test for deciding which alternatives must be considered?

5. Hard look review is necessarily highly contextualized, based on the framework established by the relevant statute or statutes, the agency's program and policies, past and present, the issues in the particular cast, the record, and the contentions advanced by those opposing the agency's action. These variations, along with the inherently open-textured character of "hard look" review, give courts considerable latitude in the intensity of their "supervision" of agency exercise of discretion.

State Farm is regarded as having endorsed a relatively intensive version of "hard look" review, of the type pioneered by the D.C. Circuit (why do you suppose that the D.C. Circuit was the pioneer?). But in the very same term in which it decided *State Farm*, the Court embraced a far more deferential stance. See Baltimore Gas & Electric Co. v. NRDC, 462 U.S. 976 (1983), upholding NRC's assumption, in connection with licensing new nuclear power plants, that permanent storage of the nuclear waste that they would generate would have no adverse environmental effects. Some lower court decisions continue to reflect considerable deference, despite *State Farm*. Judge Leon Higgenbotham, in dissent in Grant v. Shalala, 989 F.2d 1332, 1345, 1359 (3d Cir. 1993), complained that the majority had abandoned hard look review in favor of a "quick glance" doctrine. Other decisions adopt a far more rigorous stance.

18. Breyer, Judicial Review of Questions of Law and Policy, 38 Admin. L. Rev. 363 (1986). Reprinted with permission from the Administrative Law Review, published by the section of Administrative Law, American Bar Associations.

See also the striking decision in *Allentown*, supra, suggesting a willingness to look quite carefully at both the NLRB's factual findings and policy judgments. We can even take *Allentown* to be the Court's latest "hard look" case, going well beyond *State Farm* itself. To be sure, *Allentown* involved the substantial evidence test, whereas most hard look cases involve the arbitrary and capricious test. But it is increasingly thought that the two tests are the same. Indeed, the statute in *State Farm* itself called for a substantial evidence test, which the Court ignored in invoking the arbitrariness standard. And other cases specifically say that there is no difference between the two tests. See, e.g., Bangor Hydro-Electric Co. v. FERC, 78 F.3d 659, 663 n.3 (D.C. Cir. 1996).

There are several underlying issues here:

First, what factors should a court take into account in deciding whether to scrutinize the agency's exercise of discretion more or less closely, depending on the particular case? Above are listed a variety of factors that might guide a court in determining the degree of deference to be given to an agency's statutory interpretation. Should the same or different factors shape judicial deference to agency exercise of discretion? Judge Leventhal, in his pioneering decision in Greater Boston Television v. FCC, 444 F.2d 841, 852-853 (D.C. Cir. 1970), suggested that searching review is especially appropriate if the court finds "danger signals" that the agency has "not genuinely engaged in reasoned decision-making." What examples of "danger signals" occur to you?

Second, should the overall judicial tendency be toward a less deferential or more deferential approach to hard look review?

Syracuse Peace Council v. FCC

867 F.2d 654 (D.C. Cir. 1989)

WILLIAMS, Circuit Judge:

Under the "fairness doctrine," the Federal Communications Commission has, as its 1985 Fairness Report explains, required broadcast media licensees (1) "to provide coverage of vitally important controversial issues of interest in the community served by the licensees" and (2) "to provide a reasonable opportunity for the presentation of contrasting viewpoints on such issues." Report Concerning General Fairness Doctrine Obligations of Broadcast Licensees, 102 F.C.C.2d 143, 146 (1985). In adjudication of a complaint against Meredith Corporation, licensee of station WTVH in Syracuse, New York, the Commission concluded that the doctrine did not serve the public interest and was unconstitutional. Accordingly it refused to enforce the doctrine against Meredith. Although the Commission somewhat entangled its public interest and constitutional findings, we find that the Commission's public interest determination was an independent basis for its decision and was supported by the record. We uphold that determination without reaching the constitutional issue. . . .

At no time during the long and intricate proceedings in this case has any party suggested that the fairness doctrine is constitutionally compelled. Nor can it be claimed here, in view of this court's TRAC decision, that the doctrine is statutorily mandated. Accordingly, the Commission has the authority to reject the doctrine if it concludes, without being arbitrary or capricious, that it no longer serves the public interest. . . .

The FCC's decision that the fairness doctrine no longer serves the public interest is a policy judgment. There is no real dispute that fostering fair, balanced and diverse coverage of controversial issues is a good thing. Nor, so far as we can tell from the record or

briefs, is there any question that discouraging any coverage at all, having government officials second-guess editorial judgments, or allowing incumbents an opportunity for abuse
of power are things to be avoided, all other things being equal. The Commission's
problem was to make predictive and normative judgments about the tendency of the fairness doctrine to produce each of these things, about how bad the bad effects were and
how good the good ones, and ultimately about whether bad effects outweighed good. . . .

The Commission's factual judgments here are almost entirely predictive — statements about the overall effects of a policy on licensees and others. The Supreme Court
has observed that "In such cases complete factual support for the Commission's ultimate
conclusions is not required since 'a forecast of the direction in which the future public
interest lies necessarily involves deductions based on the expert knowledge of the agency.'"
FCC v. WNCN Listeners Guild, 450 U.S. at 594-95 (internal quotations omitted). . . .

Of course, an agency can act arbitrarily or capriciously in the exercise of a policy
judgment, and we must assure ourselves that that did not happen here. The challengers'
primary claims are that the supporting evidence was insufficient, that the Commission
failed to consider the whole record or to consider alternative solutions adequately, and
that its decision in the present case was an arbitrary departure from its 1985 decision to
retain the doctrine.

Before addressing those specific attacks, we must describe two core findings of the
1985 Report — that the fairness doctrine often operated to chill broadcaster speech on
controversial issues and that recent increases in broadcasting outlets undercut the need
for the doctrine — on which the Commission relied heavily in the present decision. It
found that the doctrine produced chilling effects by placing burdens on stations which
chose to air numerous programs on controversial issues — including the fear of denial of
license renewal due to fairness doctrine violations, the cost of defending fairness doctrine
attacks and of providing free air time to opposing views if a fairness violation is found, and
the reputational harm resulting from even a frivolous fairness challenge. While the FCC
recognized that to a degree the first prong of the fairness doctrine offset this effect by
requiring broadcasters to present some controversial issues, it nonetheless found that
broadcasters were encouraged

> to air only the minimal amount of controversial issue programming sufficient to
> comply with the first prong. By restricting the amount and type of controversial
> programming aired, a broadcaster minimizes the potentially substantial burdens asso-
> ciated with the second prong of the doctrine while remaining in compliance with the
> strict letter of its regulatory obligations. Therefore, despite the first prong obligation,
> in net effect the fairness doctrine often discourages the presentation of controversial
> issue programming.

The 1985 Fairness Report also noted that paradoxically the chilling effect often fell
on the expression of unorthodox or "fringe" views on controversial issues. Since the
doctrine compelled coverage only of "major" or "significant" opinions, the FCC claimed
that in assessing fairness doctrine compliance, the Commission was called upon to evaluate broadcasters' decisions concerning the importance of given viewpoints. The Report
expressed its fear that the fairness doctrine thus had the potential "to interject the government, even unintentionally, into the position of favoring one type of opinion over
another."

In assessing whether any need for the doctrine persisted, the 1985 Report found a
dramatic increase in broadcasting outlets since the 1974 Fairness Report. This expansion

in broadcasting capacity was found to have been spread widely across American society. The FCC found that by 1984 96% of television households received five or more over-the-air (non-cable) television signals, compared with 83% in 1972. Those receiving nine or more signals had tripled, from 21% of TV households in 1972 to 64% in 1984. Id. Of course some signals may for one reason or another be unable to function as serious alternative sources. But the new signals are plainly not trivial in the aggregate, as they have driven the networks' audience share down from 90% in 1982 to 76% in 1984.

The Commission also found significant growth in radio outlets since the 1974 Fairness Report. The number of radio stations grew by 30% between 1974 and 1985. The subset of FM service increased during the same period by 60%, leading the FCC to proclaim that "there has also been a fundamental change in the structure of the radio market. Once predominantly an AM only service, radio is now composed of two very competitive services." Id. at 203. The Commission noted that radio expansion impacted smaller communities as well as larger urban areas; "the number of radio voices available in each local market has grown." Id.

Looking at substitute electronic media such as low power television, video cassette recorders, satellite master antenna systems, and so forth, the Commission found that the gains in radio and television accessibility and diversity actually understated the true development of broadcast media available to the viewing public. The Report also noted that print media coverage of controversial issues offered Americans exposure to the type of information which the fairness doctrine was designed to foster.

We now turn to the specific objections to the Commission's conclusions. . . .

Several parties [have] attacked the evidence of broadcaster chill and what they contend is the Commission's failure to respond adequately to the attacks.

In its present decision the Commission said that the record compiled for the 1985 Report contained "over 60 reported instances in which the fairness doctrine inhibited broadcasters' coverage of controversial issues." 2 F.C.C. Rcd. at 5050. It appears that numerically the main body of evidence comes from the comments submitted to the Commission by the National Association of Broadcasters, which presented 45 broadcaster accounts of the effects of the fairness doctrine on their industry and policies. It is clear, however, that the FCC also relied on important additional sources, including submissions by some proponents of the fairness doctrine. For example, it pointed to evidence from Public Media Center that after it had warned broadcasters that it would demand free response time from stations that accepted advertising on a specific controversy, more than two-thirds of those contacted had refused to sell advertising on the subject at all.

The 1985 Report responded substantially to the BCFM and MAP/TRAC attacks made on the NAB study. The FCC defenses took several forms. First, critics argued that the NAB examples should be heavily discounted because the participating broadcasters were "self-interested." The FCC noted that because "chill" is a subjective perception, broadcasters' comments provided the best evidence of its existence: "This evidence is more probative than the statements of persons who, by necessity, have to second-guess the broadcasters' state of mind." The Commission also labeled broadcasters' claims of chilling effect "admission[s] against interest," as such confessions could expose broadcasters to potential fairness doctrine attacks. Finally, the Commission argued that the critics' argument proved too much: "The identical charge could be leveled against every statement of every commenting party. We have never held that the evidence of interested parties lack probity; indeed, were we to adopt such a rule it would be virtually impossible for us to come to any conclusion about any issue raised in this proceeding." We are persuaded that the self-interested character of the broadcasters' evidence did not bar the Commission from giving it substantial weight. . . .

Finally, UCC attacks any reliance on the NAB study on the ground that it was "not based on a statistically valid sample of broadcasters' experiences, but rather, was merely a series of anecdotal accounts." The comment is quite valid, but in the absence of either any statistically valid evidence on the other side, or even a suggestion of how the Commission could have constructed a statistically valid study, we are perplexed as to what the Commission was supposed to have done. Editorial decisions are obviously driven by many factors. Isolation of causes in any scientific way seems virtually impossible. The fairness doctrine has been applicable in one form or another from 1949 until the present decision, so the Commission could not compare stations' practices under the rule with their conduct free of the rule. (Comparison to practice in other nations would encounter the usual cross-cultural difficulties.) . . .

UCC also charges that the Commission ignored or discounted evidence of the benefits derived from the fairness doctrine. We think part of the problem here arises out of UCC's apparent assumption that the Commission believed that the fairness doctrine rarely (or never) increased diversity of expression. Indeed, the Commission only purported to find that "the overall net effect of the doctrine is to reduce the coverage of controversial issues of public importance," a finding clearly consistent with a belief that the doctrine frequently produced its intended effects. We do not read the Commission's focus on the negative aspects as manifesting a blindness to unwelcome evidence but rather as a focus on what it viewed as novel or surprising. To say that a rule has often produced its intended effects is to tell a dog-bites-man story — not front-page stuff. The Commission was naturally more struck by evidence of unintended consequences — hardly in the man-bites-dog class, but closer. . . .

Some parties complain that the present decision represents an unexplained abandonment of the Commission's 1985 decision to persist in enforcement of the doctrine, Cf. Motor Vehicle Mfrs. Ass'n v. State Farm Mutual Automobile Ins. Co., 463 U.S. 29, 41-44 (1983) (agency changing course required to supply reasoned analysis for the change); Center for Auto Safety v. Peck, 751 F.2d 1336, 1343 (D.C. Cir. 1985).

The 1985 Fairness Report had found that the doctrine disserved the public interest, but had refrained from dropping the doctrine on policy grounds only because of concern that perhaps it was statutorily mandated, and because of the intense congressional interest then brewing over the fairness doctrine. This court's TRAC decision removed the first obstacle (except insofar as the Supreme Court might find otherwise); a successful presidential veto of Congress's attempt to mandate the fairness doctrine clearly diminished the second. Though we find no explicit reference to these reasons in the decision under review, they appear so obvious and compelling that a remand to extract the magic words from the Commission would be pure waste.

Several parties attack the Commission's repeal of the so-called "first prong" of the fairness doctrine — the requirement that broadcasters provide coverage of important controversial issues of interest to the community they serve. . . .

In explaining its rejection of the first prong, the Commission has argued that the doctrine is a unified whole, so that, once it rejected the second requirement on policy and constitutional grounds, it would be inappropriate to preserve the first. We regard this as a statement of a conclusion, not a reason, so that if it stood alone we would be compelled to reverse this aspect of the Commission's action. The Commission analogizes its action to that of a court that has held part of a statute unconstitutional and must then consider whether to sever other parts. Reconsideration Order. The analogy only underscores the deficiency of the Commission's "unified doctrine" declaration. In making a severability decision a court essentially inquires what the legislature would have done had it been aware of the infirmity of one part. Here, the Commission was acting both as adjudicator and legislative body, and was thus perfectly free to decide what it wanted. Moreover, even a court making a severability decision tries to explain why it believes the legislature would prefer the valid portions of the statute to fall or survive.

In other portions of its decision, however, the Commission went on to supply reasons for terminating the first prong. The Commission's vigor in expressing these reasons leaves us no serious doubt that it would have proceeded to end the first prong even if it had recognized that its "unified doctrine" statement was a mere conclusion.

First, removal of the fairness doctrine's second requirement would reduce the need for the coverage requirement. With the chilling effects of the second requirement ended, the Commission expected that "coverage of controversial issues will be forthcoming naturally, without the need for continued enforcement of the first prong." It viewed the first prong as having originated in part as a "backstop[ ]" to the second prong, so that removal of the latter removed much of the reason for the former.

Second, it viewed the coverage requirement as in significant part duplicative of its independent requirement that broadcasters cover issues "of importance" to their communities. While the FCC acknowledged on reconsideration that the two programming requirements were not identical, it saw sufficient similarity to believe that the community issues rule would fill any material regulatory gap.

Third, in its discussion of the fairness doctrine as a whole the Commission relied heavily on its view that government involvement in the editorial process was offensive. That judgment of course applies to the editorial decisions required for enforcement of the first prong, and the Commission made the point expressly: "The doctrine requires the government to second-guess broadcasters' judgment on such sensitive and subjective matters as the 'controversiality' and 'public importance' of a particular issue. . . ." It also alluded to the offensive character of government first-prong decisions in distinguishing that part of the doctrine from the community issues requirement:

> While enforcement of the doctrine's first prong requires the government to judge, on a case-by-case basis, whether a specific issue is both controversial and of vital importance to mandate coverage by the broadcaster, enforcement of the issue responsive obligation requires a different level of government intervention in determining, at renewal time, whether broadcasters' overall programming covered the needs and interests of its community.

We believe that these reasons, particularly in light of the Commission's background findings on the increased diversity of outlets and programming, adequately support its removal of the first prong.

We conclude that the FCC's decision that the fairness doctrine no longer served the public interest was neither arbitrary, capricious nor an abuse of discretion, and are convinced that it would have acted on the finding to terminate the doctrine even in the absence of its belief that the doctrine was no longer constitutional. Accordingly we uphold the Commission without reaching the constitutional issues. The petition for review is denied.

WALD, Chief Judge, concurring in part and dissenting in part:

. . . I dissent, . . . from Part V, which sustains the Commission's decision to eliminate the fairness doctrine's first prong, an FCC rule requiring broadcasters to "provide coverage of vitally important controversial issues of interest in the community served by the licensees." I believe that this aspect of the Commission's decision is not supported by the record. . . .

. . . The FCC has offered three arguments in support of the elimination of the first prong. First, analogizing to principles concerning the severability of statutes, the Commission argued that the fairness doctrine was a unified whole and that one part therefore could not be severed from the rest. Second, the Commission concluded that the obligations imposed by the first prong were comparable to those imposed by the existing duty of broadcasters to cover issues of importance to their communities, and that "retaining both obligations would be duplicative." Syracuse Peace Council, 2 F.C.C. Rcd. 5043, 5048 (1987). Finally, the Commission argued that enforcement of the first prong would no longer be necessary: with the chilling effect of the second prong removed, broadcasters would of their own volition cover controversial issues.

The Commission's first two arguments appear flatly contradictory. The agency is arguing both that the first prong makes no sense without the second and that it will in essence continue to enforce the first prong under a different authority. If the first prong is desirable only as an adjunct to the second, and if the community issues requirement is substantially equivalent to the first prong, then it is not at all clear why the agency bothers to keep the community issues rule on the books at all. Leaving this incongruity aside, however, the Commission's three arguments do not, in my view, meet the threshold of reasonableness.

The Commission's analogy to the severability of statutes is misguided. In deciding whether to sever the defective part of a statute, a court inquires into legislative intent: would the enacting body have wished to let the rest of the statute stand without the offensive part? Since the Commission functions as both an adjudicative and rulemaking body, it need not inquire into what some other entity would have decided: it can make the choice for itself. The agency's purported reliance on severability principles is thus merely a reaffirmation of its basic decision not to retain the first prong. It has made no case that it could not, if it wished, enforce one prong without the other.

Neither can the Commission's action be justified by reference to the overlap between first prong obligations and the duty to cover issues of importance to the community. While a substantial overlap does exist, the requirements are by no means duplicative. The community issues requirement obliges broadcasters to devote reasonable air time to the coverage of issues important to the local community. The first prong of the fairness doctrine focuses on the broadcaster's obligation to cover controversial issues. It seems entirely foreseeable that some broadcasters might provide abundant coverage of community issues generally but might — perhaps from fear of incurring the displeasure of the public or of advertisers — steer clear of issues of a controversial nature. In another proceeding, in fact, the FCC has emphasized the distinction between the two obligations. The community issues requirements, in short, imposes obligations which are related to but distinct from the broadcaster's duties under the first prong. The continued viability of the community issues requirement is therefore an insufficient justification for the abrogation of the first prong.

Finally, I am unconvinced by the agency's assertion that the demise of the first prong is justified because, in the absence of the chill produced by the second prong's requirements, broadcasters can be expected to cover controversial issues voluntarily. Certainly the Commission might reasonably conclude that the first prong would become a less significant regulatory tool once the second prong had been eliminated. But the FCC has made no argument that, once the second prong is eliminated, the first prong will be counterproductive. The FCC's position is in essence that, after the demise of the second prong, most broadcasters will not need the incentive provided by the first prong. This seems to me to be plainly insufficient to justify repeal.

Clearly an agency could not justify the promulgation of a new regulation by arguing merely that the rule would not do much harm. The FCC appears, however, to defend the converse of this position: the agency asserts that the first prong may be eliminated simply because, after the second prong's elimination, the first prong is likely to do little good. The agency's position in this case seems to rest on an implicit distinction between the initiation and the abrogation of rules. That distinction, however, has been flatly rejected by the Supreme Court. "Revocation constitutes a reversal of the agency's former views as to the proper course. . . . In the abstract, there is no more reason to presume that changing circumstances require the rescission of prior action, instead of a revision in or even the extension of current regulation. If Congress established a presumption from which judicial review should start, that presumption . . . is not against . . . regulation, but against changes in current policy that are not justified by the rulemaking record." Motor Vehicle Manufacturers Association v. State Farm Mutual Automobile Insurance Co., 463 U.S. 29, 41, 42 (1983). It was therefore incumbent upon the Commission to establish some plausible basis for believing that the world would somehow be better if the first prong were eliminated. The agency made no attempt whatsoever to articulate such a basis.

Of course, in one respect the decision to deregulate may legitimately involve a different calculus from that required for the promulgation of a new rule. An agency making regulatory decisions may take administrative costs into account; consequently, an agency might sometimes justify the abrogation of a rule on the ground that its beneficial effects are small and that these benefits will be outweighed by the costs of its administration. In the present case, however, the Commission neither referred to nor presented evidence of the costs of administering the first prong as a justification for the agency's decision.

The real-world effects of the first prong's demise are difficult to predict. It might be that, with the removal of the second prong, the first prong would have been reduced in significance. On the other hand, the Commission may have overestimated the extent to which market forces will foster programming on controversial issues. This is a predictive judgment on which courts would ordinarily defer to agency discretion. Here, however, the uncertainty concerns only the size of the benefit which the first prong would produce; the agency has failed to identify any costs.

Moreover, I do not believe that the FCC's obligation to identify the costs of an unwanted regulation could be satisfied by a bare showing that the rule would impinge on broadcasters' editorial freedom, I believe it is still the law that, in the regulation of electronic media, "it is the right of the viewers and listeners, not the right of the broadcasters, which is paramount." Red Lion Broadcasting Co. v. FCC, 395 U.S. 367, 390 (1969). I therefore believe that it was incumbent on the Commission to identify some plausible chain of events through which a given restriction on editorial discretion could be expected to lead to a reduction in the range or quality of programming available to the public. In explaining its decision to eliminate the fairness doctrine's second prong, the FCC did not emphasize the hardships suffered by broadcasters. Rather, the agency quite properly focused on the ways in which enforcement of the rule might chill controversial speech and thereby adversely affect the range of available programming. But the

Commission has made no effort whatsoever to explain how continued enforcement of the doctrine's first prong could induce broadcasters to alter their programming decisions in ways which would ultimately disserve the public interest.

I dissent from the Commission's eradication of prong one because the agency's actions appear to me the very model of arbitrary and capricious decisionmaking. . . . Moreover, the agency has provided absolutely no evidence — indeed, it has not even asserted — that the net effect of continued enforcement would be harmful. In fact, the agency has failed to identify any deleterious effects whatsoever of continued first prong enforcement. In eliminating prong one along with prong two of the fairness doctrine, the FCC appears to have been motivated primarily by a morbid fear that it might be accused of doing things halfway. This is deregulation running riot.

Corrosion Proof Fittings v. U.S.E.P.A.

947 F.2d 1201 (5th Cir. 1991)

JERRY E. SMITH, Circuit Judge:

The Environmental Protection Agency (EPA) issued a final rule under section 6 of the Toxic Substances Control Act (TSCA) to prohibit the future manufacture, importation, processing, and distribution of asbestos in almost all products. Petitioners claim that the EPA's rulemaking procedure was flawed and that the rule was not promulgated on the basis of substantial evidence. . . . Because the EPA failed to muster substantial evidence to support its rule, we remand this matter to the EPA for further consideration in light of this opinion.

I. FACTS AND PROCEDURAL HISTORY

Asbestos is naturally occurring fibrous material that resists fire and most solvents. Its major uses include heat-resistant insulators, cements, building materials, fireproof gloves and clothing, and motor vehicle brake linings. Asbestos is a toxic material, and occupational exposure to asbestos dust can result in mesothelioma, asbestosis, and lung cancer.

The EPA began these proceedings in 1979.

An EPA-appointed panel reviewed over one hundred studies of asbestos and conducted several public meetings. Based upon its studies and the public comments, the EPA concluded that asbestos is potential carcinogen at all levels of exposure, regardless of the type of asbestos or size of the fiber. The EPA concluded in 1986 that exposure to asbestos "poses an unreasonable risk to human health" and thus proposed at least four regulatory options for prohibiting or restricting the use of asbestos, including a mixed ban and phase-out of asbestos over ten years; a two-stage ban of asbestos, depending upon product usage; a three-stage ban on all asbestos products leading to a total ban in ten years; and labeling of all products containing asbestos.

Over the next two years, the EPA updated its data, received further comments, and allowed cross-examination on the updated documents. In 1989, the EPA issued a final rule prohibiting the manufacture, importation, processing, and distribution in commerce of most asbestos-containing products. Finding that asbestos constituted an unreasonable risk to health and the environment, the EPA promulgated a staged ban on most commercial uses of asbestos. The EPA estimates that this rule will save either 202 or 148 lives, depending upon whether the benefits are discounted, at a cost of approximately $450-800 million, depending upon the price substitutes.

The rule is to take effect in three stages, depending upon the EPA's assessment of how toxic each substance is and how soon adequate substitutes will be available.[19]

IV. THE LANGUAGE OF TSCA

A. STANDARD OF REVIEW

Our inquiry into the legitimacy of the EPA rulemaking begins with a discussion of the standard of review governing this case. EPA's phase-out ban of most commercial uses of asbestos is a TSCA §6(a) rulemaking. TSCA provides that a reviewing court "shall hold unlawful and set aside" a final rule promulgated under §6(a) "if the court finds that the rule is not supported by substantial evidence in the rulemaking record . . . taken as a whole." 15 U.S.C. §2618(c)(1)(B)(i). . . .

B. THE EPA'S BURDEN UNDER TSCA

TSCA provides, a pertinent part, as follows:

> (a) Scope of regulation — If the Administrator finds that there is a *reasonable basis* to conclude that the manufacture, processing, distribution in commerce, use, or disposal of a chemical substance or mixture, or that any combination of such activities, presents or will present an *unreasonable risk of injury* to health or the environment, the Administrator shall by rule apply one or more of the following requirements to such substance or mixture to the extent necessary *to protect adequately* against such risk using the *least burdensome requirement*.

Id. (emphasis added). As the highlighted language shows, Congress did not enact TSCA as a zero-risk statute. The EPA, rather, was required to consider both alternatives to a ban and the costs of any proposed actions and to "carry out this chapter in a reasonable and prudent manner [after considering] the environment, economic, and social impact of any action." 15 U.S.C. §2601(c).

1. Least Burdensome and Reasonable

TSCA requires that the EPA use the least burdensome regulation to achieve its goal of minimum reasonable risk. This statutory requirement can create problems in evaluating just what is a "reasonable risk." Congress's rejection of a no-risk policy, however, also means that in certain cases, the least burdensome yet still adequate solution may entail somewhat more risk than would other, known regulations that are far more burdensome on the industry and the economy. The very language of TSCA requires that the EPA, once

---

19. The main products covered by each ban stage are as follows:
(1)   Stage 1: August 27, 1990: ban on asbestos-containing floor materials, clothing, roofing felt, corrugated and flat sheet materials, pipeline wrap, and new asbestos uses;
(2)   Stage 2: August 25, 1993: ban on asbestos-containing "friction products" and certain automotive products or uses;
(3)   Stage 3: August 26, 1996: ban on other asbestos-containing automotive products or uses, asbestos-containing building materials including non-roof and roof coatings, and asbestos cement shingles.
See 54 Fed. Reg. at 29,461-62.

it has determined what an acceptable level of non-zero risk is, choose the least burden-some method of reaching that level.

In this case, the EPA banned, for all practical purposes, all present and future uses of asbestos — a position the petitioner's characterize as the "death penalty alternative," as this is the most burdensome of all possible alternatives listed as open to the EPA under TSCA. TSCA not only provides the EPA with a list of alternative actions, but also provides those alternatives in order of how burdensome they are. The regulations thus provide for EPA regulation ranging from labeling the least toxic chemicals to limiting the total amount of chemicals an industry may use. Total bans head the list as the most burden-some regulatory option.

By choosing the harshest remedy given to it under TSCA, the EPA assigned to itself the toughest burden in satisfying TSCA's requirement that its alternative be the least burdensome of all those offered to it. Since, both by definition and by the terms of TSCA, the complete ban of manufacturing is the most burdensome alternative — for even strin-gent regulation at least allows a manufacturer the chance to invest and meet the new, higher standard — the EPA's regulation cannot stand if there is any other regulation that would achieve an acceptable level of risk as mandated by TSCA. . . .

The EPA considered, and rejected, such options as labeling asbestos products, thereby warning users and workers involved in the manufacture of asbestos-containing products of the chemical's dangers, and stricter workplace rules. EPA also rejected controlled use of asbestos in the workplace and deferral to other government agencies charged with worker and consumer exposure to industrial and product hazards, such as OSHA, the CPSC, and the MSHA. The EPA determined that deferral to these other agencies was inappropriate because no one other authority could address all the risks posed "throughout the life cycle" by asbestos, and any action by one or more of the other agencies still would leave an unacceptable residual risk.

Much of the EPA's analysis is correct, and the EPA's basic decision to use TSCA as a comprehensive statute designed to fight a multi-industry problem was a proper one that we uphold today on review. What concerns us, however, is the manner in which the EPA conducted some of its analysis. TSCA requires the EPA to consider, along with the effects of toxic substances on human health and the environment, "the benefits of such substance[s] or mixture[s] for various uses and the availability of substitutes for such uses," as well as "the reasonably ascertainable economic consequences of the rule, after consid-eration for the effect on the national economy, small business, technological innovation, the environment, and public health." Id. §2605(c)(1)(C-D).

The EPA presented two comparisons in the record: a world with no further regula-tion under TSCA, and a world in which no manufacture of asbestos takes place. The EPA rejected calculating how many lives a less burdensome regulation would save, and at what cost. Furthermore the EPA, when calculating the benefits of its ban, explicitly refused to compare it to an improved workplace in which currently available control tech-nology is utilized. See 54 Fed. Reg. at 29,474. This decision artificially inflated the purported benefits of the rule by using a baseline comparison substantially lower than what currently available technology could yield.

Under TSCA, the EPA was required to evaluate, rather than ignore, less burden-some regulatory alternatives. TSCA imposes a least-to-most-burdensome hierarchy. In order to impose a regulation at the top of the hierarchy — a total ban of asbestos — the EPA must show not only that its proposed action reduces the risk of the product to an adequate level, but also that the actions Congress identified as less burdensome also would not do the job. The failure of the EPA to do this constitutes a failure to meet its burden of showing that its actions not only reduce the risk but do so in the Congressionally-mandated least burdensome fashion.

2. The EPA's Calculations

Furthermore, we are concerned about some of the methodology employed by the EPA in making various of the calculations that it did perform. In order to aid the EPA's reconsideration of this and other cases, we present our concerns here.

First, we note that there was some dispute in the record regarding the appropriateness of discounting the perceived benefits of the EPA's rule. In choosing between the calculated costs and benefits, the EPA presented variations in which it discounted only the costs, and counter-variation in which it discounted both the costs and the benefits, measured in both monetary and human injury terms. As between these two variations, we choose to evaluate the EPA's work using its discounted benefits calculations.

Although various commentators dispute whether it ever is appropriate to discount benefits when they are measured in human lives, we note that it would skew the results to discount only costs without according similar treatment to the benefits side of the equation. Adopting the position of the commentators who advocate not discounting benefits would force the EPA similarly not to calculate costs in present discounted real terms, making comparisons difficult. Furthermore, in evaluating situations in which different options incur costs at varying time intervals, the EPA would not be able to take into account that soon-to-be-incurred costs are more harmful than postponable costs. Because the EPA must discount costs to perform its evaluation properly, the EPA also should discount benefits to preserve an apples-to-apples comparison, even if this entails discounting benefits of a non-monetary nature. See What Price Posterity?, The Economist, March 23, 1991 at 73 (explaining use of discount rates for non-monetary goods).

When the EPA does discount costs or benefits, however, it cannot choose an unreasonable time upon which to base its discount calculation. Instead of using the time of injury as the appropriate time from which to discount, as one might expect, the EPA instead used the time of exposure.

The difficulties inherent in the EPA's approach can be illustrated by an example. Suppose two workers will be exposed to asbestos in 1995, with worker X subjected to a tiny amount of asbestos that will have no adverse health effects, and worker Y exposed to massive amounts of asbestos that quickly will lead to an asbestos-related disease. Under the EPA's approach, which takes into account only the time of exposure rather than the time at which any injury manifests itself, both examples would be treated the same. The EPA's approach implicitly assumes that the day on which the risk of injury occurs is the same day the injury actually occurs. Such an approach might be proper when the exposure and injury are one and the same, such as when a person is exposed to an immediately fatal poison, but is inappropriate for discounting toxins in which exposure often is followed by a substantial lag time before manifestation of injuries.[20]

---

20. We also note that the EPA chose to use a real discount rate of 3%. Because historically the real rate of interest has tended to vary between 2% and 4%, this figure was not inaccurate. The EPA also did not err by calculating that the price of substitute goods is likely to decline at a rate of 1% per year, resulting from economies of scale and increasing manufacturing prowess. Because the EPA properly limited the scope of these declines in its models so that the cost of substitutes would not decline so far as to make the price of the substitutes less than the cost of the asbestos they were forced to replace, this was not an unreasonable real rate of price decline to adopt.

Of more concern to us is the failure of the EPA to compute the costs and benefits of its proposed rule past the year 2000, and its double-counting of the costs of asbestos use. In performing its calculus, the EPA only included the number of lives saved over the next thirteen years, and counted any additional lives saved as simply "unqualified benefits." 54 Fed. Reg. at 29,486. The EPA and intervenors now seek to use these unqualified lives saved to justify calculations as to which the benefits seem far outweighed by the astronomical costs. For example, the EPA plans to save about three lives with its ban of asbestos pipe, at a cost of $128-227 million (i.e., approximately $43-76 million per life saved). Although the EPA admits that the price tag is high, it claims that the lives saved past the year 2000 justify the price. See generally id. at 29,473 (explaining use of unquantified benefits).

Such calculations not only lessen the value of the EPA's cost analysis, but also make any meaningful judicial review impossible. While TSCA contemplates a useful place for unquantified benefits beyond the EPA's calculation, unquantified benefits never were intended as a trump card allowing the EPA to justify any cost calculus, no matter how high.

The concept of unquantified benefits, rather, is intended to allow the EPA to provide a rightful place for any remaining benefits that are impossible to quantify after the EPA's best attempt, but which still are of some concern. But the allowance for unquantified costs is not intended to allow the EPA to perform its calculations over an arbitrarily short period so as to preserve a large unquantified portion.

Unquantified benefits can, at times, permissibly tip the balance in close cases. They cannot, however, be used to effect a wholesale shift on the balance beam. Such a use makes a mockery of the requirements of TSCA that the EPA weigh the costs of its actions before it chooses the least burdensome alternatives.[21]

We do not today determine what an appropriate period for the EPA's calculations would be, as this [is] a matter better left for agency discretion. See Motor Vehicle Mfrs. Ass'n, 463 U.S. at 53. We do note, however, that the choice of a thirteen-year period is so short as to make the unqualified period so unreasonably large that any EPA reliance upon it must be displaced.

Under the EPA's calculations, a twenty-year-old worker entering employment today still would be at risk from workplace dangers for more than thirty years after the EPA's analysis period had ended. The true benefits of regulating asbestos under such calculations remain unknown. The EPA cannot choose to leave these benefits high and then use the high unknown benefits as a major factor justifying EPA action.

We also note that the EPA appears to place too great a reliance upon the concept of population exposure. While a high population exposure certainly is a factor that the EPA

---

21. We thus reject the arguments made by the Natural Resources Defense Council, Inc., and the Environmental Defense Fund, Inc., that the EPA's decision can be justified because the EPA "relied on many serious risks that were understated or not quantified in the final rule," presented figures in which the "benefits are calculated only for a limited time period," and undercounted the risks to the general population from low-level asbestos exposure. In addition, the interveners argue that the EPA rejected using upper estimates, see 54 Fed. Reg. at 29,473, and that this court now should use the rejected limits as evidence to support the EPA. They thus would have us reject the upper limit concerns when they are not needed, but use them if necessary. We agree that these all are valid concerns that the EPA legitimately should take into account when considering regulatory action. What we disagree with, however, is the manner in which the EPA incorporated these concerns. By not using such concerns in its quantitative analysis, even where doing so was not difficult, and reserving them as additional factors to buttress the ban, the EPA improperly transformed permissible considerations into determinative factors.

must consider in making its calculations, the agency cannot count such problems more than once. For example, in the case of asbestos brake products, the EPA used factors such as risk and exposure to calculate the probable harm of the brakes, and then used, as an additional reason to ban the products, the fact that the exposure levels were high. Considering that calculation of the probable harm level, when reduced to basics, simply are a calculation of population risk multiplied by population exposure, the EPA's redundant use of population exposure to justify its actions cannot stand.

3. Reasonable Basis

In addition to showing that its regulation is the least burdensome one necessary to protect the environment adequately, the EPA also must show that it has a reasonable basis for the regulation. 15 U.S.C. §2605(a). To some extent, our inquiry in this area mirrors that used above, for many of the methodological problems we have noted also indicate that the EPA did not have a reasonable basis. We here take the opportunity to highlight some areas of additional concern.

Most problematic to us is the EPA's ban of products for which no substitutes presently are available. In these cases, the EPA bears a tough burden indeed to show that under TSCA a ban is the least burdensome alternative, as TSCA explicitly instructs the EPA to consider "the benefits of such substance or mixture for various uses and the availability of substitutes for such uses." Id. §2605(c)(1)(C). These words are particularly appropriate where the EPA actually has decided to ban a product, rather than simply restrict its use, for it is in these cases that the lack of an adequate substitute is most troubling under TSCA.

As the EPA itself states, "[w]hen no information is available for a product indicating that cost-effective substitutes exist, the estimated cost of a product ban is very high." 54 Fed. Reg. at 29,468. Because of this, the EPA did not ban certain uses of asbestos, such as its use in rocket engines and battery separators. The EPA, however, in several other instances, ignores its own arguments and attempts to justify its ban by stating that the ban itself will cause the development of low-cost, adequate substitute products.

As a general matter, we agree with the EPA that a product ban can lead to great innovation, and it is true that an agency under TSCA, as under other regulatory statutes, "is empowered to issue safety standards which require improvements in existing technology or which require the development of new technology." Chrysler Corp. v. Department of Transp., 472 F.2d 659, 673 (6th Cir. 1972). As even the EPA acknowledges, however, when no adequate substitutes currently exist, the EPA cannot fail to consider this lack when formulating its own guidelines. Under TSCA, therefore, the EPA must present a stronger case to justify the ban, as opposed to regulation, of products with no substitutes.

We note that the EPA does provide a waiver provision for industries where the hoped-for substitutes fail to materialize in time. See 54 Fed. Reg. at 29,464. Under this provision, if no adequate substitutes develop, the EPA temporarily may extend the planned phase-out.

The EPA uses this provision to argue that it can ban any product, regardless of whether it has an adequate substitute, because inventive companies soon will develop good substitutes. The EPA contends that if they do not, the waiver provision will allow the continued use of asbestos in these areas, just as if the ban had not occurred at all.

The EPA errs, however, in asserting that the waiver provision will allow a continuation of the status quo in those cases in which no substitutes materialize. By its own terms, the exemption shifts the burden onto the waiver proponent to convince the EPA that the waiver is justified. See id. As even the EPA acknowledges, the waiver only "may be granted by [the] EPA in very limited circumstances." Id. at 29,460.

The EPA thus cannot use the waiver provision to lessen its burden when justifying banning products without existing substitutes. While TSCA gives the EPA the power to ban such products, the EPA must bear its heavier burden of justifying its total ban in the face of inadequate substitutes. Thus, the agency cannot use its waiver provision to argue that the ban of products with no substitutes should be treated the same as the ban of those for which adequate substitutes are available now.

We also are concerned with the EPA's evaluation even in those instances in which the record shows that they are available. The EPA explicitly rejects considering the harm that may flow from the increased use of products designed to substitute for asbestos, even when the probable substitutes themselves are known carcinogens. Id. at 29,481-83. The EPA justifies this by stating that it has "more concern about the continued use and exposure to asbestos than it has for the future replacement of asbestos in the products subject to this rule with other fibrous substitutes." Id. at 29,481. The agency thus concludes that any "[r]egulatory decisions about asbestos which pose well-recognized, serious risks should not be delayed until the risk of all replacement materials are fully quantified." Id. at 29,483.

This presents two problems. First, TSCA instructs the EPA to consider the relative merits of its ban, as compared to the economics effects of its action. The EPA cannot make this calculation if it fails to consider the effects that alternative substitutes will pose after a ban.

Second, the EPA cannot say with any assurance that its regulation will increase workplace safety when it refuses to evaluate the harm that will result from the increased use of substitute products.

While EPA may be correct in its conclusion that the alternate materials pose less risk than asbestos, we cannot say with any more assurance that that flowing from an educated guess that this conclusion is true.

Considering that many of the substitutes that the EPA itself concedes will be used in the place of asbestos have known carcinogenic effects, the EPA not only cannot assure this court that it has taken the least burdensome alternative, but cannot even prove that its regulations will increase workplace safety. Eager to douse the dangers of asbestos, the agency inadvertently actually may increase the risk of injury Americans face. The EPA's explicit failure to consider the toxicity of likely substitutes thus deprives its order of a reasonable basis. Cf. American Petroleum Inst. v. OSHA, 581 F.2d 493, 504 (5th Cir. 1978) (An agency is required to "regulate on the basis of knowledge rather than the unknown.") . . .

4. Unreasonable Risk of Injury

The final requirement the EPA must satisfy before engaging in any TSCA rulemaking is that it only takes steps designed to prevent "unreasonable" risks. In evaluating what is "unreasonable," the EPA is required to consider the costs of any proposed actions to "carry out this chapter in a reasonable and prudent manner [after considering] the environmental, economic, and social impact of any action." 15 U.S.C. §2601(c).

As the District of Columbia Circuit stated when evaluating similar language governing the Federal Hazardous Substances Act, "[t]he requirement that the risk be 'unreasonable' necessarily involves a balancing test like that familiar in tort law: The regulation may issue if the severity of the injury that may result from the product, factored by the likelihood of the injury, offsets the harm the regulation itself imposes upon manufacturers and consumers." Forester v. CPSC, 559 F.2d 774, 789 (D.C. Cir. 1977). We have quoted this language approvingly when evaluating other statutes using similar language. See, e.g., *Aqua Side*, 569 F.2d at 839.

That the EPA must balance the costs of its regulation against their benefits further is reinforced by the requirement that it seek the least burdensome regulation. While Congress did not dictate that the EPA engage in an exhaustive, full-scale cost-benefit analysis, it did require the EPA to consider both sides of the regulatory equation, and it rejected the notion that the EPA should pursue the reduction of workplace risk at any cost. See American Textile Mfrs. Inst., 452 U.S. at 510 n.30 ("unreasonable risk" statutes require "a generalized balancing of costs and benefits" (citing *Aqua Slide*, 569 F.2d at 839)). Thus, "Congress also plainly intended the EPA to consider the economic impact of any actions taken by it under . . . TSCA." *Chemical Mfrs. Ass'n*, 899 F.2d at 348.

Even taking all of the EPA's figures as true, and evaluating them in the light most favorable to the agency's decision (non-discounted benefits, discounted costs, analogous exposure estimates included), the agency's analysis results in figures as high as $74 million per life saved. For example, the EPA states that its ban of asbestos pipe will save three lives over the next thirteen years, at a cost of $128-277 million ($43-76 million per life saved), depending upon the price of substitutes; that its ban of asbestos shingles will cost $23-34 million to save 0.32 statistical lives ($72-106 million per life saved); that its ban of asbestos coatings will cost $46-181 million to save 3.33 lives ($14-54 million per life saved); and that its ban of asbestos paper products will save 0.60 lives at cost of $4-5 million ($7-8 million per life saved). See 54 Fed. Reg. at 29,48-85. Were the analogous exposure estimates not included, the cancer risks from substitutes such as ductile iron pipe factored in, and the benefits of a ban appropriately discounted from the time of the manifestation of an injury rather than the time of exposure, the costs would shift even more sharply against the EPA's position.

While we do sit as a regulatory agency that must make the difficult decision as to what an appropriate expenditure is to prevent someone from incurring the risk of an asbestos-related death, we do note that the EPA, in its zeal to ban any and all asbestos products, basically ignored the cost side of the TSCA equation. The EPA would have this court believe that Congress, when it enacted its requirement that the EPA consider the economic impacts of its regulations, thought that spending $200-300 million to save approximately seven lives (approximately $30-40 million per life) over thirteen years is reasonable.

As we stated in the OSHA context, until an agency "can provide substantial evidence that the benefits to be achieved by [a regulation] bear a reasonable relationship to the costs imposed by the reduction, it cannot show that the standard is reasonably necessary to provide safe or healthful workplaces." *American Petroleum Inst.*, 581 F.2d at 504. Although the OSHA statute differs in major respects from TSCA, the statute does require substantial evidence to support the EPA's contention that its regulations both have a reasonable basis and are the least burdensome means to a reasonably safe workplace.

The EPA's willingness to argue that spending $23.7 million to save less than one-third of a life reveals that its economic review of its regulations, as required by TSCA, was meaningless. As the petitioners' brief and our review of EPA caselaw reveals, such high costs are rarely, if ever, used to support a safety regulation. If we were to allow such cavalier treatment of the EPA's duty to consider the economic effects of its decision, we would have to excise entire sections and phrases from the language of TSCA. Because we are judges, not surgeons, we decline to do so. . . .

Notes and Questions

1. Can *Syracuse Peace Council* be reconciled with *State Farm*? Aren't both cases ones in which deregulation was produced, in part, by an agency's willingness to give a great deal of weight to information, and influence, from the affected industry? Consider the question whether the fairness doctrine made sense as a matter of policy. In a world with so many communications options, why isn't the doctrine a clear anachronism? If so, wasn't *Syracuse Peace Council* an easy case? Now ask about a current policy of the FCC, requiring television broadcasters to provide three hours of educational programming for children each week. Assume that no statute explicitly calls for that requirement. Should the educational programming policy fail hard look review? What would the FCC have to show to defend the policy? Now suppose that a new administration — the Bush Administration? — revokes the three-hour-per-week rule, saying that it is unnecessary in a period in which nearly 70 percent of households have cable, where educational programming for children is pervasive. Would the revocation be arbitrary? If it might be, what else would you urge the FCC to say, and show, in revoking the rule?

2. *Corrosion Proof Fittings* may in some respects represent the wave of the future of administrative law. Congress has shown considerable enthusiasm for cost-benefit balancing, and in recent years legislation that would embody a cost-benefit "supermandate," amending all and almost all existing legislation, has attracted considerable support. Smaller cost-benefit mandates can be found not only in the Toxic Substances Control Act, but also in the Safe Drinking Water Act and the Fungicide, Pesticide, and Rodenticide Act.

Does the outcome *in Corrosion Proof Fittings* argue for or against such a cost-benefit requirement? In one view, the outcome raises some serious problems, because it suggests the possibility that good lawyers will be able to attack agency decisions, whatever they may be. The complexities in cost-benefit balancing should make it more than possible for a skillful lawyer to attack agency action. Note in this regard that the executive orders that call for cost-benefit balancing are not subject to judicial review. Evidently presidents seeking such balancing feared that judicial supervision would make things worse rather than better. Does *Corrosion Proof Fittings* support or undermine this fear?

Consider the suggestion that all agencies ought to be required to show that what they are proposing will cause "more good than harm." See H. Margolis, Dealing With Risk (1996). Does this simple idea support *Corrosion Proof Fittings*? Would it help give general content to the notion of review for arbitrary or capricious action? Or should any "more good than harm" principle be administered only by the executive branch, not by the courts?

3. There has been a great deal of recent concern with the alleged "ossification" of rulemaking. See McGarity, Some Thoughts on "Deossifying" the Rulemaking Process, 1992 Duke L.J. 1385. The notion of ossification is intended to refer to the extraordinarily time-consuming nature of any effort to produce a rule. Ossification is often said to result from

costly procedural requirements imposed on agencies by all three branches of government — Congress, courts, and the president (recall the Executive Orders discussed in Chapter 2). The asbestos rule invalidated in *Corrosion Proof Fittings*, took about ten years to produce. Do you think that the EPA will be likely to take much action in the future under the Toxic Substances Control Act (TSCA)? In fact *Corrosion Proof Fittings* seems to have been the death knell for TSCA. Under that statute, the EPA has issued *no* major rules in the last decade.

4. A pervasive problem faced by agencies is how best to force companies to come up with innovative technologies that produce less harm than existing technologies. Often, economic incentives — a fee or tax for harm-producing activities — are said to be the preferred route. (Do you see why? Return to the note on economic incentives, p.252 supra.) But the Toxic Substances Control Act does not permit fees or taxes. In these circumstances, why was it arbitrary for the EPA to require companies to come up with safe substitutes for asbestos, but to allow a waiver if it could be shown that safe substitutes could not be developed? Consider the view that this was a quite reasonable kind of balancing judgment — one that avoided the problems that would arise with a flat ban on asbestos (problems that include the possibility that no safe substitutes could be developed). Why was that judgment arbitrary?

5. Agencies are frequently asked to make health-health or risk-risk tradeoffs, which arise when regulation designed to reduce one health risk simultaneously gives rise to another health risk. Does *Corrosion Proof Fittings* suggest that in general, it is unlawful, because arbitrary, for an agency to fail to consider health-health tradeoffs? Why shouldn't agencies generally be asked to show that they have considered any health problem that they might be creating? See also Competitive Enterprise Institute v. NHTSA, 956 F.2d 321 (D.C. Cir. 1992), striking down fuel economy standards on the ground that the agency failed to take account of the safety risks that might be provided if such standards result in smaller and more dangerous cars.

6. The *Corrosion Proof Fittings* court thought that the cost-benefit judgments were, in some applications, unreasonable, and hence unlawful. Would it be unlawful for an agency to value a statistical life at $200,000, $1 million, $5 million, $10 million, $20 million, $40 million, of $60 million? What criteria can a court invoke to say that one or another of these numbers is too high — or too low? Agencies have now conversed on a range, for a value of a statistical life, of between $5 million and $6 million. See Sunstein, Valuing Life: A Plea for Disaggregation, 54 Duke L.J. 385 (2004). This number grows out of studies of market behavior, in which workers and consumers are said to be "compensated," in real dollars, for statistical risks (usually ranging from 1/10,000 to 1/100,000; for further discussion, see p.334). Hence agencies are not really assigning a value to a "statistical life"; instead they are assigning values to statistical risks. But current practice is controversial for many reasons. See id. Should courts scrutinize agency judgments carefully, to make sure that they are based on a sound foundation in actual behavior, or to ensure that they are not grounded in implausible moral judgments?

Should Congress give guidance about issues of valuation in statutes like the Toxic Substances Control Act?

Some people think that an agency should look not to number of lives saved but to number of life-years saved. On this view, it is better to save a child (with, say, a probability of 70 future years of life) than to save an elderly person (with, say, a probability of 3 future years of life). Would you favor a focus on life-years rather than lives?

Discounting Lives and Health

One of the largest issues raised in *Corrosion Proof Fittings* involves the appropriate "discount rate" for benefits in terms of life and health. Government agencies have often been reluctant to apply the same discount rate to future mortality and morbidity "savings" as they apply to financial costs and benefits. This is an especially important issue, because the outcome of cost-benefit analysis will often depend on the choice of discount rate. See Heinzerling, Regulatory Costs of Mythic Proportions, 107 Yale L.J. 1981 (1998), for a demonstration. (There was a large struggle between OMB and EPA on this issue in *Corrosion Proof Fittings*. Note the court's emphasis on the need for an "apples-to-apples" comparison, one that uses the same discount rate for money as for mortality and morbidity savings.) To understand the underlying issues, some background is in order.

In terms of ultimate outcomes, the decisions matter a great deal. If an agency chooses not to discount the benefits calculation will shift dramatically from what it would be if the agency chose a discount rate of, for example, 10 percent. If a human life is valued at $8 million, and no discount rate is applied, a life saved 100 years from now is worth the same expenditure as a life saved now: $8 million. But at a discount rate of 10 percent, the same life would justify a modern expenditure of only $581. For regulation whose effects would be felt centuries from now, any reasonable discount rate will reduce apparently substantial benefits to close to nothing. The Office of Management and Budget now suggests that agencies should prepare analyses using rates of both 3 percent and 7 percent, departing from its suggested 10 percent rate in the 1980s. But these numbers remain controversial. Consider the fact that the midpoint figure — 5 percent — would ensure that if a human life is valued at $8 million, one hundred deaths in one hundred years would be worth only $6.25 million.

Monetary costs and benefits are often "discounted," on two theories. First, a dollar today is worth more than a dollar a year from today, simply because it can be invested and be allowed to grow. Second, people have a "time preference" for current income, that is, they would prefer a dollar today over a dollar tomorrow. For these reasons, most people agree that it is appropriate to apply some kind of discount rate to financial costs and benefits. Many economists, and economically inspired students of regulation, think that all future gains should be discounted too; the court of appeals in *Corrosion Proof Fittings* seems to believe this, with its skepticism about an "applies-to-oranges" comparison.

But a moment's reflection should show that it is not obvious that future benefits in terms of lives saved and illnesses averted should be discounted. Why is a life saved twenty years from now worth less than a life saved now? Why are recreational and aesthetic benefits worth less in 2020 than in 1999? It is inadequate to say that a life saved now can be "invested" so as to produce more later. And it is not clear whether the "time preference" for money is identical to the time preference for health savings. To be sure, an immediate saving might save more "life years," and if government is interested in life years rather than lives, this is an important consideration. But a shift to "life years" does not, strictly speaking, have anything to do with the discount rate at all. It is also true that medical and technological advances may mean that anticipated harms will be far less than we expect. But this too is not a point about the discount rate; it simply suggests that what we are "discounting" may well turn out to be less serious because of scientific advances. See T. Cowen & D. Parfit, Against the Social Discount Rate, in Justice Between Age Groups and Generations 144, 148 (P. Laslett & J. S. Fishkin eds., 1992).

For an extremely helpful discussion, see Revesz, Environmental Regulation, Cost-Benefit Analysis, and the Discounting of Human Lives, 99 Colo. L. Rev. 941 (1999).

Revesz makes a useful distinction between (a) discounting lives of members of future generations and (b) discounting future savings for people now living. In his view, it is wrong to discount the life of someone not yet born. Revesz urges that a person saved in 2030 should not count less than a person saved in 2005. But in his view, it is right to discount a future benefit for someone now living. Thus, for example, a saving of Jones in 2030 should count less than a saving of Jones in 2010. But Revesz objects to the idea that the discount rate for mortality and morbidity gains should be the *same* as the discount rate for money. After all, such gains cannot be invested, and hence one of the key arguments for discounting money does not apply.

Consider these rejoinders. First, government's use of a discount rate does not really mean that the government is discounting mortality and morbidity gains. What the government is discounting is the money that people are willing to pay to avoid statistical risks — and so there is no discounting of risks at all (any more than there is when the government discounts any other money, such as the money that might be spent on education or medical care). Second, a refusal to discount risks faced by members of future generations ignores the fact that we could invest the money that we spend on those risks — and watch it grow. Indeed, a refusal to discount may be harmful to future generations. (a) It may be harmful if we end up taking regulatory action at great expense, simply because that expense will make future generations poorer. (b) It may be harmful if, as many have argued, a decision to discount costs but not lives leads to a delay of life-saving programs. The basic argument here is that if regulators are indifferent as between lives saved now and lives saved in the future, but discount costs at some positive rate, then it makes sense for them to delay life-saving expenditures indefinitely, simply because the cost-benefit ratio will (always) be better in the future. "[T]he discounting of costs but not benefits . . . has a paralyzing effect on a decisionmaker. . . . For any attractive program, there is always a superior delayed program which should be funded first. The result is that no program with a finite starting date can be selected." Keeler & Cretin, Discounting of Life-Saving and Other Nonmonetary Effects, 29 Management Science 300, 303 (1983).

These claims obviously raise many complex issues, which Revesz and others have explored. See Discounting and Intergenerational Equity (P. R. Portney & J. P. Weyant eds., 1999). In view of the underlying complexities, would it be wrong to say that courts should defer to any minimally plausible approach from agencies? If so, was the *Corrosion Proof Fittings* court wrong to insist on an "apples-to-apples" comparison, by urging the same discount rate for mortality and morbidity gains as for dollars?

6. Telecommunications Controversies

FOX TELEVISION STATIONS, INC. v. FCC, 280 F.3d 1027 (D.C. Cir. 2002).   A section of the Telecommunications Act instructs the FCC to review each of its "ownership" rules — designing to prevent monopolies and near-monopolies in the telecommunications industry — every two years. The FCC refused to repeal the National Television Station Ownership (NTSO) rule, which bans any entity from controlling television stations whose potential audience reach exceeds 35 percent of the television households in the United States. The court struck down the refusal to repeal on the ground that it was arbitrary and capricious. The court acknowledged that the FCC could attempt to promote diversity, but it did not find an adequate explanation of why the rule was necessary to promote that goal. "In sum, we agree with the networks that the Commission has adduced not a single valid reason to believe that the NTSO rule is necessary in the public interest, either to safeguard diversity or to enhance competition."

SINCLAIR BROADCASTING GROUP, INC. v. FCC, 284 F.3d 148 (D.C. Cir. 2002). The FCC refused to alter its local television ownership rule, which allows common ownership of two television stations in the same local market only if two conditions are met: one of the stations is not among the four highest ranked stations in the market and eight independently owned, full-power television stations remain in the market after the merger. The agency justified these conditions as an effort to ensure a large number of independent voices in any given local market; it feared that undue concentration would produce excessive uniformity in the relevant voices.

The court struck down the agency's rule on the ground that its definition of "voices" was arbitrary. In deciding what counted as a "voice," the FCC looked only at broadcast stations, without looking at cable television, and newspapers as other sources of information. If those sources were included, perhaps the requirement of eight independently owned stations would be impossible to justify. The court noted that the FCC had adopted a broader definition of voices for other regulations, and hence the exclusion of "all media sources except broadcast television" seemed questionable. The FCC did argue that broadcast television remains the primary source of news and information for most Americans, but the evidentiary support for this argument was thin. The FCC questioned whether nonbroadcast alternatives are widely available and provide meaningful substitutes, but it appeared to conclude that they were both available and meaningful for purposes of other rules. Hence the court found the agency's decision to be arbitrary. *Query:* Is there anything that the agency could say, or prove, to overcome the court's objection? (For further developments, see Prometheus Radio Project v. FCC, 373 F.3d 372 (3d Cir. 2004), striking down many of the FCC's changes in its ownership rules, on the ground that it was arbitrary to retain some of those rules and also arbitrary to modify others.)

As these cases suggest, along with *Syracuse Peace Council*, there has been a great deal of important litigation over federal regulation of the communications market. The litigation has been spurred by rapidly changing development in that market, including the rise of cable television and the Internet, ensuring that consumers have many more available options. Both regulation and deregulation are easily subjected to "hard look" attack, especially because any step will depend on contentious assumptions. One consequence of hard look review, here as elsewhere, is to freeze the status quo and to disable the agency — as reflected in the cases just mentioned, which invalidate both the agency's failure to deregulate and its decision to deregulate. Would it be possible to conclude that in light of the rapidly changing nature of the market, and the evidence relevance of political judgments, courts should take a soft look? Notice that the FCC assumed a much more deregulatory posture under President Bush than under President Clinton.

Concluding Note

Might a foreigner read cases in Section C of this chapter, particularly *Chevron*, and then compare the cases in Section D, particularly *State Farm* and *Corrosion Proof Fittings*, and exclaim: "How odd. The American courts defer to agencies on questions of law, where courts are expert, but they conduct 'in-depth' reviews of policy, where agencies are expert. They seem to have it backwards."

To what extent are courts likely to bring about better substantive policies by giving agency decisions a closer look? Appellate judges base their decisions on a record. This record typically reflects a trial, a hearing, or some other procedure under which lawyers present evidence and make arguments. This system aspires to be fair (at least if the contesting parties have roughly equivalent resources), for the parties have a roughly equivalent chance to present their own side of the story and to contest that of their opponents. It may also be reasonably accurate in cases of typically adjudicative matters, such as who did what to whom and when. But are these courtroom procedures reliable in hotly contested, uncertain matters of legislative policy? Is carnauba wax really dangerous? What about saccharin? Arsenic in drinking water? A record on these subjects made at length by paid advocates reflects what they choose to put in it. Such a record, once made, is not readily changed; the judge who reviews the record cannot use the telephone to clarify obscurity or to discover, by calling different experts, the present state of scientific knowledge. When, from society's point of view, what really counts is that a matter be decided in accordance with norms of procedural fairness, court-type procedure and judicial review may help. If society, however, is vitally interested in the accuracy of the result and if legislative facts are at issue, can more extensive court review help?

Conceivably the function of quality control over discretionary agency policies could be transferred from courts to a nonjudicial body, such as the Congressional Office of Technology Assessment or an executive branch authority independent of the agencies subject to review. Consider a proposal to create a Policy Review Board in the executive branch that would consist of scientists, economists, engineers, systems analysts, and other specialists, and would review the technical soundness and breadth of major administrative decisions. Such a body could bring technically informed judgments to bear in scrutinizing administrative choices. An alternative model is provided by European systems that rely on tribunals (such as the French Conseil d'Etat or the Italian Cosiglio di Stato) located within the administrative branch and composed of senior civil servants, to exercise a supervisory, "quality control" function. What advantages and drawbacks can you foresee in the French or Italian approach? Why is the United States unique in relying so heavily on the general-purpose judiciary to control administrative officials? Can you imagine an empirical study that would reveal whether this reliance is worthwhile?

"Common Law" Requirements: Clarity, Consistency, "Fairness"

We have seen how courts impose certain limits on the agency's ability to make and to apply policy. Nonetheless, those limits offer the agency vast scope to make and apply "reasonable" policies within the broad authority delegated by constitutional, highly general, statutory language. In their effort to prevent agencies from using this broad authority unfairly, courts have developed certain "common law" principles. Agencies must articulate their reasons for reaching policy judgments. They must explain why they are applying those policies to particular individuals. They must apply those policies similarly to similar individuals; and, when changing policies, they must take reasonable account of the individual expectations that their previous policies created.

In this chapter, we explore several of these basic principles of fair agency behavior. We begin by focusing on the extent to which insistence on the creation of explicit agency rules and standards helps to promote consistent, and thus "fair," treatment of individuals. We do so to underscore two basic, and conflicting, notions of "fairness" in administrative law, as elsewhere in the law: (1) treating like persons alike, a principle that argues for "rules," or for "law"; and (2) treating different persons differently, a principle that some-times argues for "exceptions" from a rule, or "equity." We go on to consider the need for consistent explanations, for explanations of changes in policy, for an agency to follow its own rules, and for exceptions from new policies because of "estoppel" or "res judicata."

A. Does the Constitution Require Agencies to Make Rules?

Boyce Motor Lines v. United States

342 U.S. 337 (1952)

Mr. Justice CLARK delivered the opinion of the Court.

The petitioner is charged with the violation of a regulation promulgated by the Interstate Commerce Commission under 18 U.S.C. §835 [which says, "The Interstate Commerce Commission shall formulate regulations for the safe transportation within the limits of the United States of explosives and other dangerous articles. . . . Such regulations shall be in accord with the best-known practicable means for securing safety in transit. . . ."]. The Regulation provides:

> Drivers of motor vehicles transporting any explosive, inflammable liquid, inflammable compressed gas, or poisonous gas shall avoid, so far as practicable, and, where feasible, by prearrangement of routes, driving into or through congested thoroughfares, places where crowds are assembled, street car tracks, tunnels, viaducts, and dangerous crossings.

The statute directs that "[w]hoever knowingly violates" the Regulation shall be subject to fine or imprisonment or both.

The indictment, in counts 1, 3, and 5, charges that petitioner on three separate occasions sent one of its trucks carrying carbon bisulphide, a dangerous and inflammable liquid, through the Holland Tunnel, a congested thoroughfare. . . . On the third of these trips the load of carbon bisulphide exploded in the tunnel and about sixty persons were injured. The indictment further states that "there were other available and more practicable routes for the transportation of said shipment, and . . . the [petitioner] well knew that the transportation of the shipment of carbon bisulphide . . . into the . . . Holland Tunnel was in violation of the regulations promulgated . . . by the Interstate Commerce Commission. . . ." There is no allegation as to the feasibility of prearrangement of routes, and petitioner is not charged with any omission in that respect.

The District Court dismissed those counts of the indictment which were based upon the Regulation in question, holding it to be invalid on the ground that the words "so far as practicable, and, where feasible" are "so vague and indefinite as to make the standard of guilt conjectural." 90 F. Supp. 996, 998. The Court of Appeals for the Third Circuit reversed. . . .

A criminal statute must be sufficiently definite to give notice of the required conduct to one who would avoid its penalties, and to guide the judge in its application and the lawyer in defending one charged with its violation. But few words possess the precision of mathematical symbols, most statutes must deal with untold and unforeseen variations in factual situations, and the practical necessities of discharging the business of government inevitably limit the specificity with which legislators can spell out prohibitions. Consequently, no more than a reasonable degree of certainty can be demanded. Nor is it unfair to require that one who deliberately goes perilously close to an area of proscribed conduct shall take the risk that he may cross the line. . . .

The Regulation challenged here is the product of a long history of regulation of the transportation of explosives and inflammables. Congress recognized the need for protecting the public against the hazards involved in transporting explosives as early as 1866. The inadequacy of the legislation then enacted led to the passage, in 1908, of the Transportation of Explosives Act, which was later extended to cover inflammables. In accordance with that Act, the Commission in the same year issued regulations applicable to railroads. In 1934 the Commission exercised its authority under the Act to promulgate regulations governing motor trucks, including the Regulation here in question. In 1940 this Regulation was amended to substantially its present terminology. That terminology was adopted only after more than three years of study and a number of drafts. The trucking industry participated extensively in this process, making suggestions relating to drafts submitted to carriers and their organizations, and taking part in several hearings. The Regulation's history indicates the careful consideration which was given to the difficulties involved in framing a regulation which would deal practically with this aspect of the problem presented by the necessary transportation of dangerous explosives on the highways.

The statute punishes only those who knowingly violate the Regulation. This requirement of the presence of culpable intent as a necessary element of the offense does much to destroy any force in the argument that application of the Regulation would be so unfair that it must be held invalid. That is evident from a consideration of the effect of the requirement in this case. To sustain a conviction, the Government not only must prove that petitioner could have taken another route which was both commercially practicable and appreciably safer (in its avoidance of crowded thoroughfares, etc.) than the one it did follow. It must also be shown that petitioner knew that there was such a practicable, safer route and yet deliberately took the more dangerous route through the tunnel, or that petitioner willfully neglected to exercise its duty under the Regulation to inquire into the availability of such an alternative route.

In an effort to give point to its argument, petitioner asserts that there was no practicable route its trucks might have followed which did not pass through places they were required to avoid. If it is true that in the congestion surrounding the lower Hudson there was no practicable way of crossing the River which would have avoided such points of danger to a substantially greater extent than the route taken, then petitioner has not violated the Regulation. But that is plainly a matter for proof at the trial. We are not so conversant with all the routes in that area that we may, with no facts in the record before us, assume the allegations of the indictment to be false. We will not thus distort the judicial notice concept to strike down a regulation adopted only after much consultation with those affected and penalizing only those who knowingly violate its prohibition.

We therefore affirm the judgment of the Court of Appeals remanding the cause to the District Court with directions to reinstate counts 1, 3, and 5 of the indictment.

Affirmed.

Mr. Justice JACKSON, with whom Mr. Justice BLACK and Mr. Justice FRANKFURTER join, dissenting.

Congress apparently found the comprehensive regulation needed for the transportation of explosives and inflammables too intricate and detailed for its own processes. It delegated the task of framing regulations to the Interstate Commerce Commission and made a knowing violation of them criminal. Where the federal crime-making power is delegated to such a body, we are justified in requiring considerable precision in its exercise. Kraus & Bros. v. United States, 327 U.S. 614, 621-622.

This regulation does not prohibit carriage of explosives. It presupposes that they must be transported, and, therefore, attempts to lay down a rule for choice of routings. Petitioner was admonished to avoid congested thoroughfares, places where crowds are assembled, streetcar tracks, tunnels, viaducts and dangerous crossings. Nobody suggests that it was possible to avoid all of these in carrying this shipment from its origin to its destination. Nor does the regulation require that all or any of them be avoided except "so far as practicable." I do not disagree with the opinion of Chief Justice Hughes and the Court in Sproles v. Binford, 286 U.S. 374, that, in the context in which it was used, "'shortest practicable route' is not an expression too vague to be understood." A basic standard was prescribed with definiteness — distance. That ordinarily was to prevail, and, if departed from, the trucker was to be prepared to offer practical justifications.

But the regulation before us contains no such definite standard from which one can start in the calculation of his duty. It leaves all routes equally open and all equally closed.

The carrier must choose what is "practicable," not, as in the Sproles case, by weighing distance against obstacles to passage. We may, of course, take judicial notice of geography. Delivery of these goods was impossible except by passing through many congested thoroughfares and either tunnels, viaducts or bridges. An explosion would have been equally dangerous and equally incriminating in any of them. What guidance can be gleaned from this regulation as to how one could with reasonable certainty make a choice of routes that would comply with its requirements?

It is said, however, that definiteness may be achieved on the trial because expert testimony will advise the jury as to what routes are preferable. Defects in that solution are twofold: first, there is no standard by which to direct, confine and test the expert opinion testimony and, second, none to guide a jury in choosing between conflicting expert opinions.

It is further suggested that a defendant is protected against indefiniteness because conviction is authorized only for knowing violations. The argument seems to be that the jury can find that defendant knowingly violated the regulation only if it finds that it knew the meaning of the regulation he was accused of violating. With the exception of Screws v. United States, 325 U.S. 91, which rests on a very particularized basis, the knowledge requisite to knowing violation of a statute is factual knowledge as distinguished from knowledge of the law. I do not suppose the Court intends to suggest that if petitioner knew nothing of the existence of such a regulation its ignorance would constitute a defense. . . .

This question is before this Court on the indictment only. In some circumstances we might feel it better that a case should proceed to trial and our decision be reserved until a review of the conviction, if one results. But a trial can give us no better information than we have now as to whether this regulation contains sufficiently definite standards and definition of the crime. An acquittal or disagreement would leave this unworkable, indefinite regulation standing as the only guide in a matter that badly needs intelligible and rather tight regulation. It would remain, at least to some extent, as an incoherent barrier against state enactment or enforcement of local regulations of the same subject. Would it not be in the public interest as well as in the interest of justice to this petitioner to pronounce this vague regulation invalid, so that those who are responsible for the supervision of this dangerous traffic can go about the business of framing a regulation that will specify intelligible standards of conduct?

Notes and Questions

1. Note that the commission has been authorized to promulgate regulations, the violation of which is made by statute a criminal offense. The constitutionality of this arrangement is well established. See, e.g., United States v. Grimaud, 220 U.S. 506 (1911). However, it is accepted that agencies themselves may not be delegated authority to determine whether violation of their regulations is a crime; only the legislature may authorize criminal sanctions. This rule was reaffirmed by Loving v. United States, 517 U.S. 748 (1996) (upholding congressional delegation to the executive of the authority to define elements of aggravating factors in death penalty cases under the Uniform Code of Military Justice). Once Congress had decided that the violation of the regulation would be a crime, the president could fill in the details.

Why did Congress not lay down a standard of liability itself? Why did it delegate this power to an agency?

2. Did Congress intend the ICC to enact a regulation that does little more than reiterate the language of the statute? What alternative methods of dealing with the dangerous cargo problem were open to the ICC?

3. The majority opinion seems to assume that the only relevant function of specific rules and standards is to give "fair warning" to those subject to sanctions. It is persuaded that specific standards to provide fair warning are not required in this case because the statute requires a finding of "knowing" violation of the regulations before sanctions may be imposed. Does this argument persuade you?

Suppose you are counsel to a trucking concern that asks you what steps it should take to avoid criminal liability under this statute. What advice do you give?

What critique of the regulation would Ralph Nader make?

4. If the dissent's approach were followed, how would reviewing courts determine whether the standards or regulations adopted by an agency were sufficiently specific?

5. The Departments of Natural Resources in Minnesota and Wisconsin have adopted identical regulations governing the speed of motorboats on lakes and rivers. The regulations require in the Lower Saint Croix River, "motorboats shall not proceed at a rate 'in excess of a slow speed.'" In other designated zones, motorboats are forbidden to be operated at a rate "in excess of a slow-no wake speed." "Slow-no wake" is defined to mean "operation of a motor boat at the slowest possible speed necessary to maintain steerage," while "slow speed" is defined to mean operation "at a leisurely speed, less than planing speed, whereby the wake or wash created by the motorboat is minimal." These regulations are challenged as providing insufficient guidance to motorboat operators. What result? St. Croix Waterway Assn. v. Meyer, 178 F.3d 515 (8th Cir. 1999) (upholding speed regulations).

Forsyth County, Georgia v. The Movement

505 U.S. 123 (1992)

Justice BLACKMUN delivered the opinion of the Court.

In this case, with its emotional overtones, we must decide whether the free speech guarantees of the First and Fourteenth Amendments are violated by an assembly and parade ordinance that permits a government administrator to vary the fee for assembling or parading to reflect the estimated cost of maintaining public order.

I

Petitioner Forsyth County is a primarily rural Georgia county approximately 30 miles northeast of Atlanta. It has had a troubled racial history. In 1912, in one month, its entire African-American population, over 1,000 citizens, was driven systematically from the county in the wake of the rape and murder of a white woman and the lynching of her accused assailant. Seventy-five years later, in 1987, the county population remained 99% white.

Spurred by this history, Hosea Williams, an Atlanta city councilman and civil rights personality, proposed a Forsyth County "March Against Fear and Intimidation" for January 17, 1987. Approximately 90 civil rights demonstrators attempted to parade in Cumming, the county seat. The marchers were met by members of the Forsyth County Defense League (an independent affiliate of respondent, The Nationalist Movement), of the Ku Klux Klan, and other Cumming residents. In all, some 400 counterdemonstrators lined the parade route, shouting racial slurs. Eventually, the counterdemonstrators, dramatically outnumbering police officers, forced the parade to a premature halt by throwing rocks and beer bottles.

Williams planned a return march the following weekend. It developed into the largest civil rights demonstration in the South since the 1960's. On January 24, approximately

20,000 marchers joined civil rights leaders, United States Senators, Presidential candidates, and an Assistant United States Attorney General in a parade and rally. The 1,000 counter-demonstrators on the parade route were contained by more than 3,000 state and local police and National Guardsmen. Although there was sporadic rock throwing and 60 counter-demonstrators were arrested, the parade was not interrupted. The demonstration cost over $670,000 in police protection, of which Forsyth County apparently paid a small portion. . . .

"As a direct result" of these two demonstrations, the Forsyth County Board of Commissioners enacted Ordinance 34 on January 27, 1987. . . . The ordinance recites that it is "to provide for the issuance of permits for parades. . . . The ordinance required the permit applicant to defray these costs by paying a fee, the amount of which was to be fixed "from time to time" by the Board. . . .

Ordinance 34 was amended on June 8, 1987, to provide that every permit applicant "'shall pay in advance for such permit, for the use of the County, a sum not more than $1,000.00 for each day such parade, procession, or open air public meeting shall take place.'". . . In addition, the county administrator was empowered to "'adjust the amount to be paid in order to meet the expense incident to the administration of the Ordinance and to the maintenance of public order in the matter licensed.'" . . .

In January 1989, respondent The Nationalist Movement proposed to demonstrate in opposition to the federal holiday commemorating the birthday of Martin Luther King, Jr. In Forsyth County, the Movement sought to "conduct a rally and speeches for one and a half to two hours" on the courthouse steps on a Saturday afternoon. The county imposed a $100 fee. The fee did not include any calculation for expenses incurred by law enforcement authorities. . . .

The Movement did not pay the fee and did not hold the rally. Instead, it . . . request[ed] a temporary restraining order and permanent injunction prohibiting Forsyth County from interfering with the Movement's plans. . . .

II

Respondent mounts a facial challenge to the Forsyth County ordinance. It is well established that in the area of freedom of expression an overbroad regulation may be subject to facial review and invalidation, even though its application in the case under consideration may be constitutionally unobjectionable. . . . Thus, the Court has permitted a party to challenge an ordinance under the overbreadth doctrine in cases where every application creates an impermissible risk of suppression of ideas, such as an ordinance that delegates overly broad discretion to the decisionmaker. . . .

The Forsyth County ordinance requiring a permit and a fee before authorizing public speaking, parades, or assemblies in "the archetype of a traditional public forum," is a prior restraint on speech. Although there is a "heavy presumption" against the validity of a prior restraint, the Court has recognized that government, in order to regulate the competing uses of public forums, may impose a permit requirement on those wishing to hold a march, parade, or rally. Such a scheme, however, must meet certain constitutional requirements. It may not delegate overly broad licensing discretion to a government official. . . .

A

Respondent contends that the county ordinance is facially invalid because it does not prescribe adequate standards for the administrator to apply when he sets a permit fee.

A government regulation that allows arbitrary application is "inherently inconsistent with a valid time, place, and manner regulation because such discretion has the potential for becoming a means of suppressing a particular point of view." Heffron v. International Society for Krishna Consciousness, Inc., 452 U.S. 640, 649 (1981). To curtail that risk, "a law subjecting the exercise of First Amendment freedoms to the prior restraint of a license" must contain "narrow, objective, and definite standards to guide the licensing authority." . . . The reasoning is simple: If the permit scheme "involves appraisal of facts, the exercise of judgment, and the formation of an opinion," . . . by the licensing authority, "the danger of censorship and of abridgment of our precious First Amendment freedoms is too great" to be permitted. . . .

In the present litigation, the . . . ordinance can apply to any activity on public property — from parades, to street corner speeches, to bike races — and the fee assessed may reflect the county's police and administrative costs. Whether or not, in any given instance, the fee would include any or all of the county's administrative and security expenses is decided by the county administrator. . . .

Based on the county's implementation and construction of the ordinance, it simply cannot be said that there are any "narrowly drawn, reasonable and definite standards," guiding the hand of the Forsyth County administrator. The decision how much to charge for police protection or administrative time — or even whether to charge at all — is left to the whim of the administrator. There are no articulated standards either in the ordinance or in the county's established practice. The administrator is not required to rely on any objective factors. He need not provide any explanation for his decision, and that decision is unreviewable. Nothing in the law or its application prevents the official from encouraging some views and discouraging others through the arbitrary application of fees. The First Amendment prohibits the vesting of such unbridled discretion in a government official. . . .

B

The Forsyth County ordinance contains more than the possibility of censorship through uncontrolled discretion. As construed by the county, the ordinance often requires that the fee be based on the content of the speech.

The county envisions that the administrator, in appropriate instances, will assess a fee to cover "the cost of necessary and reasonable protection of persons participating in or observing said . . . activity." . . . In order to assess accurately the cost of security for parade participants, the administrator " 'must necessarily examine the content of the message that is conveyed,' " estimate the response of others to that content, and judge the number of police necessary to meet that response. The fee assessed will depend on the administrator's measure of the amount of hostility likely to be created by the speech based on its content. Those wishing to express views unpopular with bottle throwers, for example, may have to pay more for their permit. . . .

Petitioner insists that its ordinance cannot be unconstitutionally content based because it contains much of the same language as did the state statute upheld in Cox v. New Hampshire, 312 U.S. 569 (1941). Although the Supreme Court of New Hampshire had interpreted the statute at issue in Cox to authorize the municipality to charge a permit fee for the "maintenance of public order," no fee was actually assessed. See id., at 577. Nothing in this Court's opinion suggests that the statute, as interpreted by the New Hampshire Supreme Court, called for charging a premium in the case of a controversial political message delivered before a hostile audience. In light of the Court's subsequent First Amendment jurisprudence, we do not read Cox to permit such a premium.

C

Petitioner, as well as the Court of Appeals and the District Court, all rely on the maximum allowable fee as the touchstone of constitutionality. Petitioner contends that the $1,000 cap on the fee ensures that the ordinance will not result in content-based discrimination. . . . Neither the $1,000 cap on the fee charged, nor even some lower nominal cap, could save the ordinance because in this context, the level of the fee is irrelevant. A tax based on the content of speech does not become more constitutional because it is a small tax. . . .

The judgment of the Court of Appeals is affirmed.

[Justice Rehnquist dissented, suggesting that the case should be remanded to gather a record on the way in which a parade permit ordinance was actually administered.]

Notes and Questions

1. As *Forsyth County* suggests, courts are more likely to demand that administrative discretion be controlled if first amendment rights are at stake. The Court argues that the risk that administrative discretion can be used to affect the content of public discourse, to discriminate against certain points of view, and to aid favored viewpoints provides a set of special reasons for restraining administrators. Do you agree?

2. Consider the following:

(a) Plaintiff tattooed a small cross between her thumb and index finger. She claims to have done this as an act of religious expression. Subsequently, her high school instituted a regulation stating that "gang-related activities such as display of 'colors,' symbols, signals, signs, etc., will not be tolerated on school grounds. Students in violation will be suspended from school and/or recommended to the Board for expulsion." School officials examined the tattoo, concluded that it was gang-related, suspended plaintiff, and threatened permanently to exclude plaintiff from school if she failed to have the tattoo removed. Plaintiff sues, claiming the school regulation is too vague. What result? See Stephenson v. Davenport Community Sch. Dist, 110 F.3d 1303 (8th Cir. 1997) (finding unconstitutional a school regulation).

(b) Members of "Families Achieving Independence and Respect" (FAIR), a grassroots welfare rights organization, sought to post materials, distribute materials, and speak with welfare recipients in the lobby of the state Department of Social Services (DSS) office. The DSS administers various welfare and benefits programs for residents of the state but does not formulate policy. To reduce congestion in the office's waiting areas, the administrator enforced an *unwritten* policy that (1) excluded all advocacy groups, regardless of whether or not the department agreed with the messages, and (2) gave access only to groups that provided a "direct benefit" associated with the "basic needs of the welfare recipients." Only four groups — one providing income tax assistance, one providing nutrition information, one registering children in preschool classes, and one registering people in "English as a Second Language" courses — had been allowed access under the policy. When FAIR was excluded from the waiting area, it sued, claiming the policy was too vague. What result? See Families Achieving Independence & Respect v. Nebraska Dept. of Social Servs., 111 F.3d 1408 (8th Cir. 1997) (en banc) (finding policy sufficiently specific and certain).

(c) A city ordinance controlled the size and appearance of newsracks. Newsracks were required to be a certain make and model, or "equivalent." The ordinance further defined "equivalent" newsracks to be those of "the same size, dimensions and style of the specified newsrack." A new newspaper put nonconforming newsracks on the streets and, when the newsracks were confiscated by the city, complained that the ordinance was too vague and left too much discretion in the hands of city officials. See Gold Coast Publications v. Corrigan, 42 F.3d 1336 (11th Cir. 1994), *cert. denied*, 516 U.S. 931 (1995) (finding ordinance sufficiently specific); but see City of Lakewood v. Plain Dealer Publishing Co., 486 U.S. 750 (1988) (finding that a newsrack licensing ordinance vested unbridled and hence unconstitutional discretion in government officials because the challenged ordinance allowed the mayor to approve or reject applications for annual newsrack permits, and to condition approval on "any 'other terms and conditions deemed necessary and reasonable by the Mayor'" 486 U.S. at 753-754, as long as he provided reasons for any rejections); Miami Herald Publishing Co. v. City of Hallandale, 734 F.2d 666 (11th Cir. 1984) (holding a licensing tax on vending machines unconstitutional because it "vest[ed] city officials with untoward discretion to deny licenses, and furnish[ed] inadequate safeguards to ensure against abuse of that discretion." 734 F.2d at 676.).

3. Some recent cases have found ways to distinguish *Forsyth County*. In Northeast Ohio Coalition for the Homeless v. Cleveland, 105 F.3d 1107 (6th Cir. 1997), the court upheld a fifty-dollar fee for all peddlers within Cleveland because there was no discretion to vary the fee for different peddlers and because the fifty dollars helped defray the city's cost of preventing fraud. In MacDonald v. Ohio, 243 F.3d 1021 (7th Cir. 2001), the court rejected an attack on a municipal ordinance requiring the police commissioner to find that the police had enough officers to control hazards before a parade permit could issue. The court distinguished *Forsyth County* because the commissioner was to consider only traffic hazards unrelated to the parade messages and because the commissioner had to issue a permit for a different day and/or place if the permit originally sought was denied. See also Grider v. Abramson, 180 F.3d 739 (6th Cir. 1999) (rejecting attack on complete ban on oratory within police buffer zone at a rally and demonstration because restrictions were necessary and narrowly drafted); Morascini v. Commisioner of Public Safety, 675 A.2d 1340 (D. Conn. 1996) (upholding statute requiring nightclub owner to pay for police services because no fee for protection from hostile audience and because police officials had limited amounts of discretion).

K. Davis, 1 Administrative Law Treatise (2d ed.) (1978)

208-209, 211-212, 213-214

(a) The basic purpose of the traditional non-delegation doctrine is unsatisfactory and should be changed. It should no longer be either to prevent delegation of legislative power or to require meaningful statutory standards. The purpose should be to do what can be done through such a doctrine to *protect private parties against injustice on account of unnecessary and uncontrolled discretionary power.*

Instead of saying that delegations are unlawful or that delegations are unlawful unless accompanied by meaningful standards, the courts should affirmatively assert that delegations are lawful and desirable, as long as the broad legislative purpose is discernible and as long as protections against arbitrary power are provided. Courts should assert that congressional formulation and enactment of the content of the Code of Federal Regulations would mean worse government, not better government, because Congress is and should be geared to major policies and main outlines, and administrators are better qualified to legislate the relative details, often including even major policy determinations. The courts should recognize that administrative legislation through the superb rulemaking procedure that is rapidly developing usually provides better protection to private interests than congressional enactment of detail.

The change in the basic purpose is essential because the underlying problem is broader than control of delegation; the problem is to provide effective protection against administrative arbitrariness. Solving that problem requires protection not only against delegated power but also against undelegated power, especially the enormous undelegated power of selective and sometimes discriminatory enforcement, an undelegated power which is typically exercised without either statutory or administrative standards, without procedural safeguards prescribed by statutes or by administrative rules or by reviewing courts, and without judicial review.

(b) Safeguards are usually more important than standards, although both may be important. The criterion for determining the validity of a delegation should be the totality of the protection against arbitrariness, not just the one strand having to do with statutory standards.

For instance, a delegation *without standards* of power to make rules in accordance with proper rulemaking procedure and a delegation *without standards* of power to work out policy through case-to-case adjudication based on trial-type hearings should normally be sustained, whenever the general legislative purpose is discernible. The risk of arbitrary or unjust action is much greater than informal discretionary action, but even there the protection from safeguards is likely to be more effective than protection from standards. For instance, if one administrator in exercising discretionary power without hearings use[d] a system of open findings, open reasons, and open precedents, but another who is also acting without hearings never states findings or reasons and never uses precedents as a guide, the delegation to the first administrator is much more deserving of judicial support than the delegation to the second. . . .

(c) The crucial consideration is not what the statute says but what the administrators do. The safeguards that count are the ones the administrators use, not the ones mentioned in the statute. The standards that matter are the ones that guide the administrative determination, not merely the ones stated by the legislative body. The test should accordingly be *administrative* safeguards and standards, not *statutory* safeguards and standards.

The alteration in the nondelegation doctrine in this respect can be a rather small one: The courts should continue their requirement of meaningful standards, except that when the legislative body fails to prescribe the required standards for discretionary action in particular cases, the administrators should be allowed to satisfy the requirement by prescribing them within a reasonable time.

When an administrator is making a discretionary determination affecting a private party, standards which have been adopted through administrative rulemaking are just as effective in confining and guiding the discretionary determination as would be standards stated in the statute. They are not only as effective but in one important aspect they are better. The weakness of a judicial requirement of statutory standards is that legislators are often unable or unwilling to supply them. The strength of a judicial requirement of administrative standards is that, with the right kind of judicial prodding, the administrators can be expected to supply them. To the extent that the objective is to require standards to guide discretionary determinations in cases affecting particular parties, that objective can be better attained through judicial insistence that administrators create the standards through rulemaking than by judicial insistence upon statutory standards.

Legislative bodies should clarify their purposes to the extent that they are able and willing to do so, but when they choose to delegate without standards, the courts should uphold the delegation whenever the needed standards to guide particular determinations have been supplied through administrative rules or policy statements. . . .

(d) Another strength in the idea that the courts should require administrative standards whenever statutory standards are inadequate is that the idea opens the way for courts to give more attention to the manner in which administrators confine and structure their discretionary power. The requirement of administrative standards will and should naturally grow into a somewhat larger requirement — that administrators must do what they reasonably can do to develop and make known the needed confinements of their discretionary power through not only standards but also principles and rules. In other words, the nondelegation doctrine will evolve into a broad spectrum of judicial protection against unnecessary and uncontrolled discretionary power.

When standards are lacking to guide the exercise of discretionary power in individual cases, courts should in appropriate circumstances require administrative rulemaking to provide the standards, the guides, the rules, the limits, and the procedures. . . .

Notes and Questions

1. As a doctrinal matter, Professor Davis's proposal had some success at first, followed by total rejection. The success came in *Amalgamated Meat Cutters*, Chapter 2 supra, which seemed to suggest that administrators could vitiate a nondelegation challenge by promulgating standards to constrain their own discretion. The rejection occurred in *American Trucking*, Chapter 2 supra, which said that self-imposed limitations on agency discretion are irrelevant to the nondelegation issue, which is just whether Congress itself has provided an "intelligible principle" to govern the agency's exercise of its statutory authority.

2. As a normative matter, is Professor Davis's proposal appealing? Substituting a requirement of administrative standards for the nondelegation doctrine as a means of limiting administrative discretion would avoid serious political confrontations like that provoked by the *Schechter* decision (see Chapter 2, section C2). Courts have traditionally exercised an important role in controlling administrative officials, and requiring administrators to crystallize their discretion in standards would be consonant with judicial traditions of promoting predictability and impartiality in the application of governmental sanctions.

But how much certainty and predictability is either feasible or desirable in the context of administrative action? Recall that one of the reasons for creation of administrative agencies was the perceived need for self-starting, prophylactic initiatives to deal with rapidly changing economic and social problems. To the extent that administrators are charged with management of given sectors of the economy, isn't a business model of decisionmaking more appropriate than a judicial one? Consider also that highly specific rules might invite circumvention and evasion through creation of "loopholes," and that political constraints and disagreements, both within and without the agency, may prevent it from reaching a firm position on controversial issues of policy.

Professor Davis acknowledges the need for flexibility and asserts that in differing contexts it will be appropriate to develop rules of varying degrees of specificity "to locate the optimum degree of structuring in each respect for each discretionary power." K. Davis, Discretionary Justice: A Preliminary Inquiry 99 (1969). But how well equipped are reviewing courts to identify this "optimum" in the face of agency claims in given contexts that specific rules are not feasible or desirable? Consider Professor Davis's proposal in light of the *Boyce* decision. See also Stewart, The Reformation of American Administrative Law, 88 Harv. L. Rev. 1667, 1698-1702 (1975), which asserts that Professor Davis's proposal contains many of the drawbacks of the nondelegation doctrine it is designed to replace because it requires courts to second-guess the judgments of frontline decisionmakers as to how far it is wise and feasible to develop more specific policies in a given field of government, and whether it is politically possible to achieve agreement on any specific policy.

3. Professor Davis seems to believe that the use of more precise standards will lead to "fairer" decisions. Is this true? How should administrators deal with the need for exceptions and for tempering the rigors of "law" with "equity"? Consider in this regard the following five cases.

SOGLIN v. KAUFFMAN, 418 F.2d 163 (7th Cir. 1969).   The University of Wisconsin brought disciplinary proceedings against members of Students for a Democratic Society. The university charged them with "misconduct" consisting of physical obstruction of university buildings to prevent representatives of Dow Chemical Company from conducting interviews. The students brought an action in federal court, claiming that disciplinary proceedings for "misconduct" violate the due process clause of the fourteenth amendment. The court wrote: "[Defendants] argue that 'misconduct' represents the inherent power of the University to discipline students and that this power may be exercised without the necessity of relying on a specific rule of conduct. This rationale would justify the ad hoc imposition of discipline without reference to any preexisting standards of conduct so long as the objectionable behavior could be called misconduct at some later date. . . . The use of 'misconduct' as a standard in imposing the penalties threatened here must . . . fall for vagueness. The inadequacy of the rule is apparent on its face. It contains no clues which could assist a student, an administrator or a reviewing judge in determining whether conduct not transgressing statutes is susceptible to punishment by the University as 'misconduct.'

". . . We only hold that expulsion and prolonged suspension may not be imposed on students by a university simply on the basis of allegations of 'misconduct' without reference to any preexisting rule which supplies an adequate guide. The possibility of the sweeping application of the standard of 'misconduct' to protected activities does not comport with the guarantees of the First and Fourteenth Amendments. The desired end must be more narrowly achieved."

HORNSBY v. ALLEN, 326 F.2d 605 (5th Cir. 1964).   "Appellant Mrs. Hornsby is an unsuccessful applicant for a license to operate a retail liquor store in Atlanta, Georgia. She brings this action under [42 U.S.C. §1983] to redress an alleged deprivation of civil rights. The Mayor, the City Clerk, and the Aldermen of Atlanta are defendants. In her complaint, Mrs. Hornsby alleges that although she met all the requirements and qualifications, as to moral character of the applicant and proposed location of the store, prescribed for the holder of a retail liquor dealer's license, her application was denied 'without a reason therefor' by the Mayor and Board of Aldermen. This action is characterized as 'arbitrary, unreasonable, unjust, capricious, discriminatory' and in contravention of the due process and equal protection clauses of the 14th Amendment. The complaint also charges that a system of ward courtesy was followed in the issuance of liquor licenses; under this system licenses allegedly would be granted only upon the approval of one or both of the aldermen of the ward in which the store was to be located. This too is said to constitute a violation of the 14th Amendment. . . .

"We find in this case that Mrs. Hornsby's allegations, if borne out by the evidence, are sufficient to show a violation of her 14th Amendment rights. If her application was actually denied because the delegation from her ward decided, from their own knowledge of the circumstances, that Mrs. Hornsby should not be issued a liquor license, then she was deprived of the hearing which due process requires, since she could not discover the claims of those opposing her and subject their evidence to cross-examination. In addition, Mrs. Hornsby was not afforded an opportunity to know, through reasonable regulations promulgated by the board, of the objective standards which had to be met to obtain a license.

". . . We are of the opinion that the complaint alleged sufficient facts to show that the denial of appellant's application for a license did not meet [federal constitutional] standards, and, since done under color of state statute, constituted a violation of 42 U.S.C. §1983.

"It follows that the trial court must entertain the suit and determine the truth of the allegations. If it develops that no ascertainable standards have been established by the Board of Aldermen by which an applicant can intelligently seek to qualify for a license, then the court must enjoin the denial of licenses under the prevailing system and until a legal standard is established and procedural due process provided in the liquor store licensing field.

"The judgment is reversed."

HOLMES v. NEW YORK CITY HOUSING AUTHORITY, 398 F.2d 262 (2d Cir. 1968). Applicants for low-rent apartments administered by the New York City Housing Authority sued the authority claiming that its selection procedures violated the federal Constitution.

"Each year the Authority receives approximately 90,000 applications out of which it is able to select an average of only 10,000 families for admission to its public housing projects. In doing so the Authority gives preference to certain specified classes of candidates, e.g., 'site residents,' families in 'emergency need of housing,' 'split families,' 'doubled up and overcrowded families.' . . .

"In the complaint the named plaintiffs allege that although they have filed with the Authority a total of 51 applications for admission to its housing facilities, 36 in 1965 or earlier, and some as long ago as 1961, none has been advised in writing at any time of his eligibility, or ineligibility, for public housing.

"The complaint [says that applications] received by the Authority are not processed chronologically, or in accordance with ascertainable standards, or in any other reasonable and systematic manner. All applications, whether or not considered and acted upon by the Authority, expire automatically at the end of two years. A renewed application is given no credit for time passed, or precedence over a first application of the same date. There is no waiting list or other device by which an applicant can gauge the progress of his case and the Authority refuses to divulge a candidate's status on request. Many applications are never considered by the Authority. If and when a determination of ineligibility is made (on any ground other than excessive income level), however, the candidate is not informed of the Authority's decision, or of the reasons therefor.

"The complaint charges that these procedural defects increase the likelihood of favoritism, partiality, and arbitrariness on the part of the Authority, and deprive the plaintiffs of a fair opportunity to petition for admission to public housing, and to obtain review of any action taken by the Authority. The deficiencies are alleged to deprive applicants of due process of law in violation of the Fourteenth Amendment to the Federal Constitution.

"Clearly there is sufficient [*sic*] in the complaint to state a claim for relief under §1983 and the due process clause. . . . It hardly need be said that the existence of an absolute and uncontrolled discretion in an agency of government vested with the administration of a vast program, such as public housing, would be an intolerable invitation to abuse. See Hornsby v. Allen, 326 F.2d 605, 609-610 (5th Cir. 1964). For this reason alone due process requires that selections among applicants be made in accordance with 'ascertainable standards,' id. at 612, and, in cases where many candidates are equally qualified under these standards, that further selections be made in some reasonable manner such as 'by lot or on the basis of the chronological order of application.' Hornsby v. Allen, 330 F.2d 55, 56 (5th Cir. 1964) (on petition for rehearing)." . . .

FOOK HONG MAK v. IMMIGRATION & NATURALIZATION SERVICE, 435 F.2d 728 (2d Cir. 1970).   Fook Hong Mak entered the United States on a "transit authorization." He was traveling from Hong Kong to South America. His authorization permitted him to stay for eight days. He stayed illegally for six months. The INS found him and tried to deport him. He asked the INS to change his status to that of "lawfully admitted" alien. The relevant statute, §245 of the act, says the attorney general "may . . . in his discretion" make this change. The attorney general refused to change Fook Hong Mak's status because of a regulation that said that a "transit authorization" was granted on the condition "that the alien will not apply for . . . adjustment of status under §245 of the Act." 8 C.F.R. §214.2(c). Fook Hong Mak argued that the attorney general had to consider his case individually; he could not deny an adjustment solely on the basis of the rule. Judge Friendly wrote for the court:

"We are unable to understand why there should be any general principle forbidding an administrator, vested with discretionary power, to determine by appropriate rulemaking that he will not use it in favor of a particular class on a case-by-case basis, if his determination is founded on considerations rationally related to the statute he is administering. The legislature's grant of discretion to accord a privilege does not imply a mandate that this must inevitably be done by examining each case rather than by identifying groups. The administrator also exercises the discretion accorded him when, after appropriate deliberation, he determines certain conduct to be so inimical to the statutory scheme that all persons who have engaged in it shall be ineligible for favorable consideration, regardless of other factors that otherwise might tend in their favor. He has then decided that one element is of such determinative negative force that no possible combination of others could justify an affirmative result. By the same token he could select one characteristic as entitling a group to favorable treatment despite minor variables. Nothing in this offends the basic concept that like cases should be treated similarly and unlike ones differently. The administrator has simply determined that the one paramount element creates such 'likeness' that other elements cannot be so legally significant as to warrant difference in treatment. This may be an even 'juster justice' than to accord different treatment because of trivial differences of fact; at least it is competent for the administrator to think so. The leading student of the problem has recently counseled: 'When legislative bodies delegate discretionary power without meaningful standards, administrators should develop standards at the earliest feasible time, and then, as circumstances permit, should further confine their own discretion through principles and rules.' Davis, Discretionary Justice: A Preliminary Inquiry 55 (1969). . . .

"We know of no rule which requires a case by case approach; the Attorney General certainly may proceed by regulation. . . . It was reasonable for the Attorney General to conclude that aliens admitted [as transits without visas] were not within the spirit of §245 and thus could not deserve favorable exercise of his discretion, even if they came within the letter. He could properly have thought also that to entertain such applications in any case would encourage aliens to obtain admission under the pretense that they were in 'immediate and continuous transit' and then stay for years, as Fook Hong Mak has managed to do, thereby upsetting the balance of benefit and burden that Congress had envisioned."

ASIMAKOPOULOS v. IMMIGRATION & NATURALIZATION SERVICE, 445 F.2d 1362 (9th Cir. 1971). The petitioners, a husband and wife, came to the United States with visas that gave them a "protected status," as visitors and students. They stayed illegally for several years and had children; the INS caught them, and it tried to deport them. They asked the attorney general to "suspend deportation" under a statute that said he "may, in his discretion" do so if the illegal alien had lived here for seven years, was of good character, and would suffer extreme hardship because of deportation, 8 U.S.C. §1254(a)(1). The attorney general refused to suspend deportation. He relied on an earlier INS case, Matter of Lee (B.I.A. 1966), 11 I & N Dec. 649, which held that he could exercise his discretion in favor of an alien who had been in this country in a "protected status" only if the equities were "particularly strong." The court held the attorney general could not rely on this rule. Judge Hufstedler wrote:

"We overturn Lee and the decision of the Board in this case on an additional ground. Although eligibility for suspension does not compel the granting of the requested relief . . . eligibility does trigger the exercise of discretion. . . . The standard announced in Matter of Lee effectively precludes the exercise of discretion in many cases in which the applicant would otherwise qualify for relief. The Board's failure to exercise discretion is reversible error. . . . Accordingly, reliance on a test that prevents the exercise of discretion is also reversible in error. . . . We do not express any opinion about the manner in which the Attorney General or his delegates should exercise the discretion committed to him."

Notes and Questions

1. Note that in Soglin, Hornsby, and Holmes federal courts are reviewing the validity of state administrative action. In cases such as Boyce, involving federal agencies, federal courts may find that the administrator's conduct (including the failure to adopt more specific standards) violates the statute creating the agency or the provisions of the Administrative Procedures Act (APA). (Would any provisions in the APA require the administrative adoption of standards had Holmes, Hornsby, or Soglin involved federal agencies?) But where state administrative action is involved, federal courts are bound, under the principle of Erie R.R. v. Tompkins, 304 U.S. 64 (1938), by state court interpretations of state law, including the agency's conformance with state statutes. Unless there is an overriding federal statute governing the action of state officials (such as federal statutory requirements regarding the disposition by states of federal grants-in-aid), the only federal claims normally available for challenging state administrative action are those based on the federal Constitution. Accordingly, challenges to state administrative action in federal court often assume a constitutional form and are often procedural in character — typically, a claim that state officials transgressed the due process clause of the fourteenth amendment and 42 U.S.C. §1983.

2. Why does the Constitution require state (or federal) agencies to develop and adhere to standards when neither criminal sanctions (as in *Boyce*) nor civil sanctions (such as a fine or forfeiture) are involved? *Soglin* is perhaps explicable as involving a form of "punishment" directed at activities with first amendment overtones. But *Hornsby* and *Holmes* involved government allocation of scarce benefits or opportunities. Why does the federal Constitution require that this allocation be accomplished through judicial models of standards and reasoned decision? Are standards required by principles of equal protection? Cf. *Yick Wo v. Hopkins*, 118 U.S. 356 (1886) (systemic exercise of laundry-licensing authority to discriminate against persons of Asian extraction violates equal protection). Can *Boyce* be reconciled with *Hornsby* and *Holmes*? Of what relevance is the doctrine against delegation of legislative power?

3. Suppose that in *Holmes* and *Hornsby* the state had argued that, in the state's judgment, the key to liquor licensing or allocating scarce public housing tenancies is the character and fitness of the applicant, and that these qualifications can only be ascertained through essentially subjective personal judgments by state administrators? If standards are required, what standards might these agencies adopt?

4. The judicial requirement that agencies formulate standards can be viewed as an example of an appealing theory of institutional roles. Courts are experts at procedure, not substantive policy; by imposing a procedural requirement of standard-setting the court exercises its procedural competence, leaving it to the agency to exercise its substantive competence. See, e.g., *City of Santa Clara v. Kleppe*, 418 F. Supp. 1243 (N.D. Cal. 1976).

This rationale is most persuasive in cases, such as *Holmes* and *Hornsby*, where the agency has failed to establish any standards at all (although even here the question put in Note 3 should raise doubts). But what should courts do when an agency has established some standards but they are attacked as insufficiently specific? For example, are public housing regulations that provide, without further elaboration, for "just cause" for eviction adequately specific? See *Bogan v. New London Housing Auth.*, 366 F. Supp. 861 (D. Conn. 1973) (upholding constitutionality of such a regulation where tenants were to be evicted because they persisted in keeping a dog in violation of their lease). *Hornsby* talks of "reasonable regulations." How can a court judge whether administrative regulations are "reasonable" or adequately specific for due process purposes without making substantive judgments about policy?

5. Can an agency meet the requirements of *Holmes* and *Hornsby* by developing (or promising to develop) standards through case-by-case adjudication?

6. Another potential distinction between *Boyce*, *Hornsby*, and *Holmes* is offered by Professors Gellhorn & Robinson, Perspectives on Administrative Law, 75 Colum. L. Rev. 771, 792-793 (1975). They argue that procedural requirements — such as agency adoption of specific rules or standards — can only be understood and justified as a means of securing underlying substantive rights. In their view, the *Hornsby* and *Holmes* rulings are based on an implicit underlying right to a fair and evenhanded system for allocation of scarce government benefits. They argue that decisions such as *Holmes* are not authority for requiring specific rules in other areas of administration where no substantive entitlement exists.

7. We shall explore the relation between substantive entitlements and procedural rights in greater detail in Chapter 6. As we show there, the Supreme Court has during the past 25 years created constitutional doctrines giving a right to some form of administrative hearing to persons claiming, as against the agency, a well-defined entitlement created by federal statute or state law. But the Court has made it rather clear that no hearing is required when the agency has discretion to act one way or another. These hearing

decisions seem to imply that there is likewise no due process right, in the absence of a relevant substantive entitlement, that administrators adopt standards to confine or structure their discretion. For if there were general obligations to develop standards, these standards would in turn create entitlements triggering a right to hearing in every case — a result arguably inconsistent with Court decisions denying hearing in cases where statutes confer broad discretion on administrators. A number of lower federal courts continue to follow *Holmes* and *Hornsby*. For example, in the 1970s and 1980s courts required agencies to adopt standards to structure administrative discretion in issuing licenses, Jensen v. Administrator of FAA, 641 F.2d 797 (9th Cir. 1981) (pilot's license), *vacated*, 680 F.2d 593 (9th Cir. 1982); allocating low cost housing, Ressler v. Pierce, 692 F.2d 1212 (9th Cir. 1982) (Department of Housing and Urban Development must adopt regulations limiting tenant-selection criteria of federally subsidized housing project owners); but see Eidson v. Pierce, 745 F.2d 453, 460 (7th Cir. 1984) (criticizing Ressler v. Pierce); granting parole, Franklin v. Shields, 569 F.2d 784 (4th Cir. 1977); and distributing general assistance payments, Carey v. Quern, 588 F.2d 230 (7th Cir. 1978); White v. Roughton, 530 F.2d 750 (7th Cir. 1976); Baker-Chaput v. Cammett, 406 F. Supp. 1134 (D.N.H. 1976). In some instances, courts have sought to square holdings requiring standards with the entitlement logic of the Supreme Court hearing cases by asserting that statutory *eligibility* for assistance or other benefits itself creates an *entitlement* to the availability of benefits and that standards are necessary to provide procedural protection for the entitlement. See, e.g., Baker-Chaput v. Cammett, supra; Curry v. Block, 738 F.2d 1556 (11th Cir. 1984).

A few cases continued to follow this approach in the 1990s. Burke v. United States, 968 F. Supp. 672, 680 (M.D. Ala. 1997) (finding Drug Enforcement Administration violated due process guarantees by reversing earlier recognition of security interest in seized truck in absence of written guidelines for doing so); Ginaitt v. City of Warwick, 806 F. Supp. 311 (R.I. 1992) (finding that city violated due process by terminating firefighter's disability benefits without written standards, and without "procedures, policies, ordinances, or practices" providing for appeals of decisions). For example, in Martinez v. Iberia, 759 F. Supp. 664 (D. Colo. 1991), Colorado administered a program that provided an alternative to Medicaid. For seriously ill patients who would qualify for Medicaid support for institutional treatment, Colorado provided "Colorado Home and Community Based Care," which supplied money for in-home care. When Colorado added a second, additional screening process — called "Most In Need Screen" or "MINS" — through which applicants had to pass prior to getting any support, patients sued, claiming lack of due process. The district court found a violation and wrote:

> Having established the importance of the medical review, I find fault with the appeal process described in the MIN regulation. First, the review procedure is never articulated in clear, written standards. In White v. Roughton, 530 F.2d 750 (7th Cir. 1976), a case where public assistance was denied, the court required of the municipality, "Fair and consistent application of . . . written standard and regulations." Id., at 754. The court was leery of the official's "unfettered discretion." Such discretion violates due process. Plaintiffs cite several documents and A.L.J. opinions produced after CFMC review. The materials differ on the relative importance of factors like dependency on Medicaid services and the availability of family members as alternate care providers. The defendant failed to call attention to any significant regulation guiding the CFMC panels in their review.

759 F. Supp. at 667.

But in the majority of recent cases, the courts reject the claim of due process violation, regardless of whether a sanction or a benefit is involved. See, e.g., *Barna Tomato Co. v. U.S. Dept. of Agriculture*, 112 F.3d 1542 (11th Cir. 1997) (refusing vagueness-based due process challenge to USDA regulations); *Albuquerque v. Browner*, 97 F.3d 415 (10th Cir. 1996) (upholding Native American tribe's water quality regulations against vagueness challenge); *Hill v. Jackson*, 64 F.3d 163 (4th Cir. 1995) (refusing to find any liberty or property interest in parole because of a lack of guidelines controlling discretion, and consequently refusing to reach the due process claim of a right to a parole hearing); *Orkin v. SEC*, 31 F.3d 1056 (11th Cir. 1994) (upholding disciplinary sanctions by the National Association of Securities Dealers against broker for violation of "markup" rules); *Sweeton v. Brown*, 27 F.3d 1162 (6th Cir. 1994) (rejecting claim of due process in parole hearings where state law has not guaranteed process); *Throckmorton v. National Transp. Safety Bd.*, 963 F.2d 441 (D.C. Cir. 1992); *San Filippo, Jr. v. Bongiovanni*, 961 F.2d 1125 (3d Cir. 1992) (allowing revocation of tenure and dismissal of professor under standard of "gross neglect of established University obligations appropriate to the appointment"); *Shawgo v. Spradlin*, 701 F.2d 470 (5th Cir. 1983) (denying due process challenge to police officers' suspensions despite admittedly egregious process violations).

8. Who has the more persuasive position, Judge Friendly in *Fook Hong Mak* or Judge Hufstedler in *Asimakopoulos*?

The immigration statutes typically emphasize the discretionary nature of the authority granted to the INS, in part to avoid the impression of granting any "rights" to aliens and to limit accordingly the scope of judicial review. Ironically, this feature of the statutes was relied on in *Asimakopoulos* to sustain the alien's position.

9. *Asimakopoulos* and *Fook Hong Mak* reflect a more general conflict in administrative law and practice between consistent treatment, which would be promoted through categorical rules and individuation of agency decisions by tailoring them to the particular circumstances of each case. Is the procedural ruling in *Asimakopoulos* based on an implicit underlying right to individual consideration?

10. Once an agency adopts general rules to decide cases, may it depart from them in individual cases where they might be inappropriate?

11. Would it surprise you to learn that none of the cases finding a *constitutional* requirement, of either rulemaking or individualized decisionmaking, is much followed? Why or why not?

B. Requiring Consistent Explanation: The *Chenery* Litigation

Note: The Public Utility Holding Company Act

The Public Utility Holding Company Act of 1935, 15 U.S.C. §§79 et seq., gave the Securities and Exchange Commission (SEC) sweeping authority to reorganize and simplify the complex corporate structure typical of many of the public utility empires assembled by financial entrepreneurs in the 1920s.

The Act requires public utility holding companies to register with the SEC, which is empowered to impose reorganization terms on registered companies. However, voluntary reorganizations, subject to SEC approval, are also provided for and encouraged. Section 7 of the act authorizes the SEC to approve the issuance of new securities pursuant to a voluntary reorganization unless the commission finds that "the terms and conditions of the issue or scale of the security are detrimental to the public interest or the interest of investor; or consumers." Section 11 authorizes the submission of voluntary reorganization plans "[i]n accordance with such rules and regulations or orders as the Commission may deem necessary or appropriate in the public interest or for the protection of investors or consumers," and authorizes the commission to approve such a plan if it finds the plan to be "fair and equitable to the person affected by such plan."

SEC v. Chenery Corp. (I)

318 U.S. 80 (1943)

Mr. Justice FRANKFURTER delivered the opinion of the Court.

[Respondents Chenerys were officers, directors, and controlling shareholders of Federal Water Service Corporation (Federal), a public utility holding company (whose assets consisted of controlling shares in a variety of public utility corporations) subject to reorganization under the Public Utility Holding Company Act. From 1937 to 1940 respondents negotiated with the SEC over the terms of a proposed voluntary reorganization that called for the merger of Federal and certain affiliated corporations into a single new corporation with one class of common stock. The Chenerys were unsuccessful in persuading the SEC to authorize holders of class B common stock of Federal (a controlling but junior class of shares owned by the Chenerys) to exchange these shares for the common of the reorganized company. Participation was limited to holders of the Federal's preferred stock and class A common, with the preferred shareholders being allocated 94.7 percent of the common in the reorganized company. During the period 1937-1940, while the reorganization plan was being negotiated, the Chenerys purchased from brokers in the over-the-counter market 12,407 shares of Federal's preferred stock. Had the Chenerys been permitted to participate in the reorganization by exchanging these shares for common stock in the reorganized company, they would have been entitled to more than 10 percent of the reorganized company's common, representing a controlling block of shares. The price at which the Chenerys purchased the preferred was substantially less than the book value of the equivalent common of the reorganized company. The Chenerys purchased the preferred in part for the purpose of continuing their management of the enterprise.]

In ascertaining whether the terms of issuance of the new common stock were "fair and equitable" or "detrimental to the interests of investors" within §7 of the Act, the Commission found that it could not approve the proposal plan so long as the preferred stock acquired by the respondents would be permitted to share on a parity with other preferred stock. The Commission did not find fraud or lack of disclosure, but it concluded that the respondents, as Federal's managers, were fiduciaries and hence under a "duty of fair dealing" not to trade in the securities of the corporation while plans for its reorganization were before the Commission. . . .

Accordingly, the plan was thereafter amended to provide that the preferred stock acquired by the respondents, unlike the preferred stock held by others, would not be converted into stock of the reorganized company, but could only be surrendered at cost plus 4 percent interest. The Commission, over the respondents' objections, approved the plan as amended, and it is this order which is now under review. . . .

The Commission did not find that the respondents as managers of Federal acted covertly or trade[d] on inside knowledge, or that their position as reorganization managers enabled them to purchase the preferred stock at prices lower than they would otherwise have had to pay, or that their acquisition of the stock in any way prejudiced the interests of the corporation or its stockholders. To be sure, the new stock into which the respondents' preferred stock would be converted under the plan of reorganization would have a book value — which may or may not represent market value — considerably greater than the prices paid for the preferred stock. But it would equally be true of purchases of preferred stock made by other investors. The respondents, the Commission tells us, acquired their stock as the outside world did, and upon no better terms. . . .

Applying by analogy the restrictions imposed on trustees in trafficking in property held by them in trust for others, Michoud v. Girod, 4 How. 503, 557, the Commission ruled that even though the management does not hold the stock of the corporation in trust for the stockholders, nevertheless the "duty of fair dealing" which the management owes to the stockholders is violated if those in control of the corporation purchase its stock, even at a fair price, openly and without fraud. The Commission concluded that "honesty, full disclosure, and purchase at a fair price do not take the case outside the rule."

In reaching this result the Commission stated that it was merely applying "the broad equitable principles enunciated in the cases heretofore cited," namely, Pepper v. Litton, 308 U.S. 295; Michoud v. Girod, 4 How. 503, 557; Magruder v. Drury, 235 U.S. 106, 119-20; and Meinhard v. Salmon, 249 N.Y. 458, 164 N.E. 545. Its opinion plainly shows that the Commission purported to be acting only as it assumed a court of equity would have acted in a similar case. Since the decision of the Commission was explicitly based upon the applicability of principles of equity announced by courts, its validity must likewise be judged on that basis. The grounds upon which an administrative order must be judged are those upon which the record discloses that its action was based.

In confining our review to a judgment upon the validity of the grounds upon which the Commission itself based its action, we do not disturb the settled rule that, in reviewing the decision of a lower court, it must be affirmed if the result is correct "although the lower court relied upon a wrong ground or gave a wrong reason." Helvering v. Gowran, 302 U.S. 238, 245. The reason for this rule is obvious. It would be wasteful to send a case back to a lower court to reinstate a decision which it had already made but which the appellate court concluded should properly be based on another ground within the power of the appellate court to formulate. But it is also familiar appellate procedure that where the correctness of the lower court's decision depends upon a determination of [facts] which only a jury could make but which has not been made, the appellate court cannot take the place of the jury. Like considerations govern review of administrative orders. If an order is valid only as a determination of policy or judgment which the agency alone is authorized to make and which it has not made, a judicial judgment cannot be made to do service for an administrative judgment. For purposes of affirming no less than reversing its orders, an appellate court cannot intrude upon the domain which Congress has exclusively entrusted to an administrative agency.

If, therefore, the rule applied by the Commission is to be judged solely on the basis of its adherence to principles of equity derived from judicial decisions, its order plainly cannot stand.

[After reviewing the judicial precedent relied on by the SEC, the Court found that such precedent did not prohibit reorganization purchases in the circumstances presented here, and accordingly did not support the SEC's prohibition of the Chenerys' participation in the reorganization.]

Determination of what is "fair and equitable" called for the application of ethical standards to particular sets of facts. But these standards are not static. In evolving standards of fairness and equity, the Commission is not bound by settled judicial precedents. Congress certainly did not mean to preclude the formation by the Commission of standards expressing a more sensitive regard for what is right and what is wrong than those prevalent at the time the Public Utility Holding Company Act of 1935 became law. But the Commission did not in this case proffer new standards reflecting the experience gained by it in effectuating the legislative policy. On the contrary, it explicitly disavowed any purpose of going beyond those which the courts had theretofore recognized. Since the Commission professed to decide the case before it according to settled judicial doctrines, its action must be judged by the standards which the Commission itself invoked. . . .

But the Commission urges here that the order should nevertheless be sustained because "the effect of trading by management is not measured by the fairness of individual transactions between buyer and seller, but by its relation to the timing and dynamics of the reorganization which the management itself initiates and so largely controls." Its argument lays stress upon the "strategic position enjoyed by the management in this type of reorganization proceeding and the vesting in it of statutory powers available to no other representative of security holders." It contends that these considerations warrant the stem rule applied in this case since the Commission "has dealt extensively with corporate reorganization, both under the Act, and other statutes entrusted to it," and "has, in addition, exhaustively studied protective and reorganization committees," and that the situation was therefore "peculiarly within the Commission's special administrative competence." . . .

But the difficulty remains that the considerations urged here in support of the Commission's order were not those upon which its action was based. The Commission did not rely upon "its special administrative competence"; it formulated no judgment upon the requirements of the "public interest or the interest of investors or consumers" in the situation before it. Through its preoccupation with the special problems of utility reorganizations the Commission accumulates an experience and insight denied to others. Had the Commission, acting upon its experience and peculiar competence, promulgated a general rule of which its order here was a particular application, the problem for our consideration would be very different. Whether and to what extent directors or officers should be prohibited from buying or selling stock of the corporation during its reorganization, presents problems of policy for the judgment of Congress or of the body to which it has delegated power to deal with the matter. Abuse of corporate position, influence, and access to information may raise questions so subtle that the law can deal with them effectively only by prohibitions not concerned with the fairness of a particular transaction. But before transactions otherwise legal can be outlawed or denied their usual business consequences, they must fall under the ban of some standards of conduct prescribed by an agency of government authorized to prescribe such standards — either the courts or Congress or an agency to which Congress has delegated its authority. Congress itself did not proscribe the respondents' purchases of preferred stock in Federal. Established judicial doctrines do not condemn these transactions. Nor has the Commission, acting under the rule making powers delegated to it by §11(e), promulgated new general standards of conduct. It purported merely to be applying an existing judge-made rule of equity. The Commission's determination can stand, therefore, only if it found that the specific transactions under scrutiny showed misuse by the respondents of their position as reorganization managers, in that as such managers they took advantage of the corporation or the other stockholders or the investing public. The record is utterly barren of any such showing. Indeed, such a claim against the respondents was explicitly disavowed by the Commission. . . .

Judged, therefore, as a determination based upon judge-made rules of equity, the Commission's order cannot be upheld. Its action must be measured by what the Commission did, not by what it might have done. It is not for us to determine independently what is "detrimental to the public interest or the interest of investors or consumers" or "fair or equitable" within the meaning of §§5, 7 and 11 of the Public Utility Holding Company Act of 1935. The Commission's action cannot be upheld merely because findings might have been made and considerations disclosed which would justify its order as an appropriate safeguard for the interests protected by the Act. There must be such a responsible finding. . . . There is no such finding here.

Congress has seen fit to subject to judicial review such orders of the Securities and Exchange Commission as the one before us. That the scope of such review is narrowly circumscribed is beside the point. For the courts cannot exercise their duty of review unless they are advised of the considerations underlying the action under review. If the action rests upon an administrative determination — an exercise of judgment in an area which Congress has entrusted to the agency — of course it must not be set aside because the reviewing court might have made a different determination were it empowered to do so. But if the action is based upon a determination of law as to which the reviewing authority of the courts does come into play, an order may not stand if the agency has misconceived the law. In either event the orderly functioning of the process of review requires that the grounds upon which the administrative agency acted be clearly disclosed and adequately sustained. "The administrative process will best be vindicated by clarity in its exercise." Phelps Dodge Corp. v. Labor Board, 313 U.S. 177, 197. What was said in that case is equally applicable here: "We do not intend to enter the province that belongs to the Board, nor do we do so. All we ask of the Board is to give clear indication that it has exercised the discretion with which Congress has empowered it. This is to affirm most emphatically the authority of the Board." Ibid.

In finding that the Commission's order cannot be sustained, we are not imposing any trammels on its powers. We are not enforcing formal requirements. We are not suggesting that the Commission must justify its exercise of administrative discretion in any particular manner or with artistic refinement. We are not sticking in the bark of words. We merely hold that an administrative order cannot be upheld unless the grounds upon which the agency acted in exercising its powers were those upon which its action can be sustained.

The cause should therefore be remanded to the Court of Appeals with directions to remand to the Commission for such further proceedings, not inconsistent with this opinion, as may be appropriate.

So ordered.

Mr. Justice DOUGLAS took no part in the consideration and decision of this case.

Mr. Justice BLACK, with whom Mr. Justice REED and Mr. Justice MURPHY concur, dissenting.

. . . The conclusions of the Court with which I disagree are those in which it holds that while the Securities and Exchange Commission has abundant power to meet the situation presented by the activities of these respondents, it has not done so. This conclusion is apparently based on the premise that the Commission has relied upon the common law rather than on "new standards reflecting the experience gained by it in effectuating legislative policy," and that the common law does not support its conclusion; that the Commission could have promulgated "a general rule of which its order here was a particular application," but instead made merely an ad hoc judgment; and that the Commission made no finding that these practices would prejudice anyone.

The Commission's actual finding was that "The plan of reorganization herein considered, like the previous plans filed with us over the past several years, was formulated by the management of Federal, and discussions concerning the reorganization of this corporation have taken place between the management and the staff of the Commission over the past several years"; that C. T. Chenery purchased 8,618 shares of preferred stock during this period; that other officers and directors of the concerns involved acquired 3,789 shares during the same period; that for this stock these respondent fiduciaries paid $328,346.89 and then submitted their latest reorganization plan, under which this purchased stock would have a book value in the reorganization company of $1,162,431.90. In the light of these and other facts the Commission concluded that the new plan would be "unfair, inequitable, and detrimental, so long as the preferred stock purchased by the management at low prices is to be permitted to share on a parity with other preferred stock." The Commission declined to give "effectiveness" to the proposed plan and entered "adverse findings" against it under §§7(d)(1) and 7(d)(2) of the controlling Act, resting its refusal to approve on this statement: "We find that the provisions for participation by the preferred stock held by the management result in the terms of issuance of the new securities being detrimental to the interests of investors and the plan being unfair and inequitable."

The grounds upon which the Commission made its findings seem clear enough to me. . . .

While I consider that the cases on which the Commission relied give full support to the conclusion it reached, I do not suppose, as the Court does, that the Commission's rule is not fully based on Commission experience. The Commission did not "explicitly disavow" any reliance on what its members had learned in their years of experience, and of course they, as trade experts, made their findings that respondent's practice was "detrimental to the interests of investors" in the light of their knowledge. That they did not unduly parade fact data across the pages of their reports is a commendable saving of effort since they meant merely to announce for their own jurisdiction an obvious rule of honest dealing closely related to common law standards. Of course, the Commission can now change the form of its decision to comply with the Court's order. The Court can require the Commission to use more words; but it seems difficult to imagine how more words or different words could further illuminate its purpose or its determination. A judicial requirement of circumstantially detailed findings as the price of court approval can bog the administrative power in a quagmire of minutiae. Hypercritical exactions as to findings can provide a handy but an almost invisible glideway enabling courts to pass "from the narrow confines of law into the more spacious domain of policy." Phelps Dodge Corp. v. Labor Board, 313 U.S. 177, 194.

That the Commission has chosen to proceed case by case rather than by a general pronouncement does not appear to me to merit criticism. The intimation is that the Commission can act only through general formulae rigidly adhered to. In the first place, the rule of the single case is obviously a general advertisement to the trade, and in the second place the briefs before us indicate that this is but one of a number of cases in which the Commission is moving to an identical result on a broad front. But aside from these considerations the Act gives the Commission wide powers to evolve policy standards, and this may well be done case by case. . .

Federal Water Service Corp. (The SEC Decision on Remand)

18 S.E.C. 231 (1945)

. . . If in any case we had proof that reorganization managers had actually purchased future control at bargain prices *intentionally* created or maintained by their own acts, plainly we would be unable to find fair and equitable a plan of reorganization which embodied provisions allowing them to reap the benefits.

But even where proof of intentional wrongdoing is lacking, should the answer be substantially different? We think not. Where the management embarks upon a stock purchase program during a reorganization, it places its personal interests actively at odds with the interests of other stockholders it represents in the reorganization. Where that occurs, and the management thereafter submits a plan by which it would realize substantial benefits through stock acquired during its purchase program, it asks us to make what in effect is a positive finding that its realization of such benefits is fair and equitable to all persons affected by the plan. In such circumstances we do not believe the statute limits our power and duty to withhold approval solely to cases in which someone is able to establish by affirmative evidence that actual misconduct accompanied such a conflict of interests. It is the responsibility of the proponents of the plan to satisfy us that the plan is fair and equitable under Section 11(e). An affirmative determination of that kind cannot appropriately be left to rest upon conjecture. . . .

The problem before us is, therefore, one of temptations combined with powers of accomplishment. Since the achieving of personal gain through the use of fiduciary power is unfair, we believe the incentive to misuse such power must be removed so that the potentialities of harm to investors and the public will to that extent be eliminated. For the reasons we have already given, we deem it impossible to do less. . . .

The intervenors urge that we have no alternative but to act first by general rule or published statement of policy if we are to act at all in a matter of this kind. The Supreme Court indicated the advisability of promulgating a general rule, though we do not understand its opinion to hold that the absence of a preexisting rule is fatal to the decision we have reached. Now that we have had the question sharply focused in this and other cases before us, and have had an extensive period in which to consider the problems involved, we may well decide that a general rule, with adequately flexible provisions, would be both practicable and desirable; but we do not see how the promulgation of such a rule now or later would affect our duty to act by order in this case in deciding whether this plan is fair and equitable and meets the other standards of the Act. We therefore reserve for further consideration the question whether or not a rule should be adopted.

SEC v. Chenery Corp. (II)

332 U.S. 194 (1947)

Mr. Justice MURPHY delivered the opinion of the Court.

The latest order of the Commission definitely avoids the fatal error of relying on judicial precedents which do not sustain it. This time, after a thorough reexamination of the problem in light of the purposes and standards of the Holding Company Act, the Commission has concluded that the proposed transaction is inconsistent with the standards of §§7 and 11 of the Act. It has drawn heavily upon its accumulated experience in dealing with utility reorganizations. And it has expressed its reasons with a clarity and thoroughness that admit of no doubt as to the underlying basis of its order.

The argument is pressed upon us, however, that the Commission was foreclosed from taking such a step following our prior decision. It is said that, in the absence of findings of conscious wrongdoing on the part of Federal's management, the Commission could not determine by an order in this particular case that it was inconsistent with the statutory standards to permit Federal's management to realize a profit through the reorganization purchases. All that it could do was to enter an order allowing an amendment to the plan so that the proposed transactions could be consummated. Under this view, the Commission would be free only to promulgate a general rule outlawing such profits in future utility reorganizations; but such a rule would have to be prospective in nature and have no retroactive effect upon the instant situation.

We reject this contention, for it grows out of a misapprehension of our prior decision and of the Commission's statutory duties. We held no more and no less than that the Commission's first order was unsupportable for the reasons supplied by that agency. But when the case left this Court, the problem whether Federal's management should be treated equally with other preferred stockholders still lacked a final and complete answer. It was clear that the Commission could not give a negative answer by resort to prior judicial declarations. And it was also clear that the Commission was not bound by settled judicial precedents in a situation of this nature. 318 U.S. at 80. Still unsettled, however, was the answer the Commission might give were it to bring to bear on the facts the proper administrative and statutory considerations, a function which belongs exclusively to the Commission in the first instance. The administrative process had taken an erroneous rather than a final turn. Hence we carefully refrained from expressing any view as to the propriety of an order rooted in the proper and relevant considerations. . . .

It is true that our prior decision explicitly recognized the possibility that the Commission might have promulgated a general rule dealing with this problem under its statutory rulemaking powers, in which case the issue for our consideration would have been entirely different from that which did confront us. 318 U.S. 92-93. But we did not mean to imply thereby that the failure of the Commission to anticipate this problem and to promulgate a general rule withdrew all power from that agency to perform its statutory duty in this case. To hold that the Commission had no alternative in this proceeding but to approve the proposed transaction, while formulating any general rules it might desire for use in future cases of this nature, would be to stultify the administrative process. That we refuse to do.

Since the Commission, unlike a court, does have the ability to make new law prospectively through the exercise of its rule-making powers, it has less reason to rely upon ad hoc adjudication to formulate new standards of conduct within the framework of the Holding Company Act. The function of filling in the interstices of the Act should be performed, as much as possible, through this quasi-legislative promulgation of rules to be applied in the future. But any rigid requirement to that effect would make the administrative process inflexible and incapable of dealing with many of the specialized problems which arise. See Report of the Attorney General's Committee on Administrative Procedure in Government Agencies, S. Doc. No. 8, 77th Cong., 1st Sess., p. 29. Not every principle essential to the effective administration of a statute can or should be cast immediately into the mold of a general rule. Some principles must await their own development, while others must be adjusted to meet particular, unforeseeable situations. In performing its important functions in these respects, therefore, an administrative agency must be equipped to act either by general rule or by individual order. To insist upon one form of action to the exclusion of the other is to exalt form over necessity.

In other words, problems may arise in a case which the administrative agency could not reasonably foresee, problems which must be solved despite the absence of a relevant general rule. Or the agency may not have had sufficient experience with a particular problem to warrant rigidifying its tentative judgment into a hard and fast rule. Or the problem may be so specialized and varying in nature as to be impossible to capture within the boundaries of a general rule. In those situations, the agency, must retain power to deal with the problems on a case-to-case basis if the administrative process is to be effective. There is thus a very definite place for the case-by-case evolution of statutory standards. And the choice made between proceeding by general rule or by individual, ad hoc litigation is one that lies primarily in the informed discretion of the administrative agency. See Columbia Broadcasting System v. United States, 316 U.S. 407, 421.

Hence we refuse to say that the Commission, which had not previously been confronted with the problem of management trading during reorganization, was forbidden from utilizing this particular proceeding for announcing and applying a new standard of conduct. That such action might have a retroactive effect was not necessarily fatal to its validity. Every case of first impression has a retroactive effect, whether the new principle is announced by a court or by an administrative agency. But such retroactivity must be balanced against the mischief of producing a result which is contrary to a statutory design or to legal and equitable principles. If that mischief is greater than the ill effect of the retroactive application of a new standard, it is not the type of retroactivity which is condemned by law.

[The Court then summarized the reasons given by the Commission for its decision on remand.]

We are unable to say in this case that the Commission erred in reaching the result it did. The facts being undisputed, we are free to disturb the Commission's conclusion only if it lacks any rational and statutory foundation. In that connection, the Commission has made a thorough examination of the problem, utilizing statutory standards and its own accumulated experience with reorganization matters. In essence, it has made what we indicated in our prior opinion would be an informed, expert judgment on the problem.

. . . The "fair and equitable" rule of §11(e) and the standard of what is "detrimental to the public interest or the interest of investors or consumers" under §7(d)(6) and §7(e) were inserted by the framers of the Act in order that the Commission might have broad powers to protect the various interests at stake. 318 U.S. at 90-91. The application of those criteria, whether in the form of a particular order or a general regulation, necessarily requires the use of informed discretion by the Commission. The very breadth of the statutory language precludes a reversal of the Commission's judgment save where it has plainly abused its discretion in these matters. . . . Such an abuse is not present in this case.

[The Court reversed the judgment of the Court of Appeals, which had set aside the Commission's denial of the Chenerys' application for amendment of the reorganization plan. Justice Burton concurred in the result, and Chief Justice Vinson and Justice Douglas did not participate in the decision.]

Mr. Justice JACKSON, dissenting.

The Court by this present decision sustains the identical administrative order which only recently it held invalid. SEC v. Chenery Corp., 318 U.S. 80. As the Court correctly notes, the Commission has only "recast its rationale and reached the same result". . . . There being no change in the order, no additional evidence in the record and no amendment of relevant legislation, it is clear that there has been a shift in attitude between that of the controlling membership of the Court when the case was first here and that of those who have the power of decision on this second review.[1]

I feel constrained to disagree with the reasoning offered to rationalize this shift. It makes judicial review of administrative orders a hopeless formality for the litigant, even where granted to him by Congress. It reduces the judicial process in such cases to a mere feint. While the opinion does not have the adherence of a majority of the full Court, if its pronouncements should become governing principles they would, in practice, put most administrative orders over and above the law.

The essential facts are few and are not in dispute. This corporation filed with the Securities and Exchange Commission a voluntary plan of reorganization. While the reorganization proceedings were pending sixteen officers and directors bought on the open market about 7% of the corporation's preferred stock. Both the Commission and the court admit that these purchases were not forbidden by any law, judicial precedent, regulation or rule of the Commission. Nevertheless, the Commission has ordered these individuals to surrender their shares to the corporation at cost, plus 4% interest, and the Court now approves that order.

It is helpful, before considering whether this order is authorized by law, to reflect on what it is and what it is not. It is not conceivably a discharge of the Commission's duty to determine whether a proposed plan of reorganization would be "fair and equitable." It has nothing to do with the corporate structure, or the classes and amounts of stock, or voting rights or dividend preferences. It does not remotely affect the impersonal financial or legal factors of the plan. It is a personal deprivation denying particular persons the right to continue to own their stock and to exercise its privileges. Other persons who bought at the same time and price in the open market would be allowed to keep and convert their stock. Thus, the order is in no sense an exercise of the function of control over the terms and relations of the corporate securities.

Neither is the order one merely to regulate the future of property. It literally takes valuable property away from its lawful owners for the benefit of other private parties without full compensation and the Court expressly approves the taking. . . . Admittedly, the value above cost, and interest on it, simply is taken from the owners, without compensation. No such power has ever been confirmed in any administrative body.

It should also be noted that neither the Court nor the Commission purports to adjudge a forfeiture of this property as a consequence of sharp dealing or breach of trust. The Court says, "The Commission admitted that the good faith and personal integrity of this management were not in question. . . ." And again, "It was frankly admitted that the management's purpose in buying the preferred stock was to protect its interest in the new company. It was also plain that there was no fraud or lack of disclosure in making these purchases." . . .

---

1. Between *Chenery I* and *Chenery II*, Justice Roberts and Chief Justice Stone left the Court, and three new Justices — Vinson, Burton, and Rutledge — joined it. The two departing Justices had both joined in the majority opinion in *Chenery I*; of the three new Justices, one (Rutledge) joined the new plurality (with Murphy, Black, and Reed, the three dissenters in *Chenery I*), one (Vinson) did not participate in *Chenery II*, and another (Burton) concurred in the result. — EDS.

As there admittedly is no law or regulation to support this order, we peruse the Court's opinion diligently to find on what grounds it is now held that the Court of Appeals, on pain of being reserved for error, was required to stamp this order with its approval. We find but one. That is the principle of judicial deference to administrative experience. That argument is five times stressed in as many different contexts. . . .

What are we to make of this reiterated deference to "administrative experience" when in another context the Court says, "Hence we refuse to say that the Commission, *which had not previously been confronted with the problem of management trading during reorganization*, was forbidden from utilizing this particular proceeding for announcing and applying a new standard of conduct"? (Emphasis supplied.)

The Court's reasoning adds up to this: The Commission must be sustained because of its accumulated experience in solving a problem with which it had never before been confronted!

Of course, thus to uphold the Commission by professing to find that it has enunciated a "new standard of conduct" brings the Court squarely against the invalidity of retroactive law-making. But the Court does not falter. "That such action might have a retroactive effect was not necessarily fatal to its validity." . . . "But such retroactivity must be balanced against the mischief of producing a result which is contrary to a statutory design or to legal and equitable principles." Of course, if what these parties did really was condemned by "statutory design" or "legal and equitable principles," it could be stopped without resort to a new rule and there would be no retroactivity to condone. But if it had been the Court's view that some law already prohibited the purchases, it would hardly have been necessary three sentences earlier to hold that the Commission was not prohibited "from utilizing this particular proceeding for announcing and applying a *new standard of conduct*." . . . (Emphasis supplied.)

I give up. Now I realize what Mark Twain meant when he said, "The more you explain it, the more I don't understand it." . . .

The truth is that in this decision the Court approves the Commission's assertion of power to govern the matter *without* law, power to force surrender of stock so purchased whenever it will, and power also to overlook such acquisitions if it so chooses. The reasons which will lead it to take one course as against the other remain locked in its own breast, and it has not and apparently does not intend to commit them to any rule or regulation. This administrative authoritarianism, this power to decide without law, is what the Court seems to approve in so many words: "The absence of a general rule or regulation governing management trading during reorganization did not affect the Commission's duties. . . ." This seems to me to undervalue and to belittle the place of law, even in the system of administrative justice. It calls to mind Mr. Justice Cardozo's statement that "Law as a guide to conduct is reduced to the level of mere futility if it is unknown and unknowable."

Mr. Justice FRANKFURTER joins in this opinion.

Notes and Questions: *Chenery* and Consistent Explanations

1. The *Chenery* cases raise three interrelated issues:

   a. The requirement that agencies explain their decisions, and the associated principle of consistent explanations;

    b. The extent, if any, to which courts will bar agencies from adopting and enforcing new or changed policies in ways that violate expectation interests or are otherwise unfairly "retroactive" in effect; and

    c. The extent, if any, to which courts will limit agencies' discretion to choose between case-by-case adjudication and rulemaking to develop policy.

We examine the first issue here. The latter two are developed later.

    2. Did the SEC, in its decision on remand from the Supreme Court's first *Chenery* decision, adequately explain its result? Review the controlling provisions of the act, and consider the various potential grounds that might justify the commission in denying the Chenerys' participation in the reorganized company. Consider also Justice Jackson's dissent. If the SEC on remand failed adequately to justify its action, why didn't the Supreme Court in its second *Chenery* decision remand again?

    3. As noted in Chapter 4, the *Chenery* requirement that agencies explain their exercise of discretion is an important foundation of the "hard look" approach to review that reigns today. But would the SEC's opinion on remand pass muster on "hard look" review? Is it relevant that the SEC was just beginning to implement the act?

    4. What is the impact of the *Chenery* requirement that agencies explain their decisions (or suffer a remand for further proceedings) on the quality of agency deliberations and decisions? This is an empirical question. Judge Friendly believes that it has made important contributions. He expresses this view in *Chenery* Revisited: Reflections on Reversal and Remand of Administrative Orders, 1959 Duke LJ. 199, 209-210:

> Thus the *Chenery* Court was saying to the SEC: "Here, instead of doing something traditional, as you wrongly believed, you are venturing into terra incognita. Principles of equity do not compel the ruling you made, although the statute permits you to make it. Have you given enough thought to your choice? Are you entirely sure the evil calls for any remedy, let alone the drastic one you have chosen? Would compulsory disclosure of dealings be a preferable alternative to forfeiture of profits? Have you sufficiently considered the propriety of applying the rule to parties who acted without knowledge that you would impose it, as against using your rule-making authority? These were questions worth asking. Even if the *Chenery* Court had scant doubt how they would be answered in the instant case, such a declaration to the agencies, indicating that decisions based on a wrong reason generally cannot be expected to stand even though a reviewing court can discern the possibility of a right one, should improve the administrative process in general.

Judge Friendly goes on to discuss cases in which he believes that remands for more adequate agency explanations have significantly improved administrative decisionmaking. Such cases, he believes, refute the view that remands simply invite "the mechanical regurgitation of 'canned' findings. . . ."

    Others have followed Justice Black to take a less favorable view of the impact of judicial attention to detailed agency statements and explanations, concluding that in most instances it merely forces agencies to rationalize decisions reached on other grounds and leads to time-consuming remand proceedings that accomplish little or nothing except to satisfy judicial instincts for tidiness and order. Chapter 4 presents some evidence on this question.

    5. The entire *Chenery* episode continues to be cited with approval by the Court. See FEC v. Akins, 524 U.S. 11, 25 (1998); Allentown Mack Sales and Services, 522 U.S. 359, 374 (1998).

C. Consistency in Applying Regulations: "An Agency Must Follow Its Own Rules"

We have already examined the problem of consistency in agency adjudication. Here we explore the question of consistency where an agency elects to develop policy through rulemaking, The *Arizona Grocery* case, which follows, is famous for its enunciation of a basic principle of administrative law, namely, that an agency must follow its own rules. The case also embodies a classical problem of ratemaking: how rates are to be structured so that each customer pays an appropriate share of fixed costs or overhead. We shall consider both aspects of the case here. As shall become apparent, an appreciation of the substantive regulatory issue helps to determine the proper disposition of the procedural issue. We shall then consider other contexts in which the problems of consistency in applying regulations have arisen.

1. Rate Structures: Economic Background

Recall the discussion of cost-of-service ratemaking at page 262. There we considered how the regulator determined the firm's "revenue requirement," that is, how much money it would need to cover its costs, including a reasonable profit. Here we shall consider one of the problems that arises when the regulator sets prices designed to yield revenues that equal that requirement. One obvious problem is determining how the prices that one sets affect demand for the product. Clearly, the revenues generated by a price increase depend on the extent to which the increase leads to a fall in sales. Yet accurate information about this relationship — demand elasticity — is notoriously difficult for the agency to develop.

A further set of problems can be grouped under the heading "rate structure." These problems concern the relationship among the various prices the regulated firm charges for its various products sold to different customers, sold at different places, or sold at different times. Typical of such problems are those concerning joint costs (which include fixed or overhead costs) incurred in providing a number of different products. For example, the cost of constructing and maintaining the roadbed is a joint cost of all services performed by railroads in transporting passengers and various commodities. The problem of joint costs is especially acute in an industry, such as the railroad industry, with relatively high fixed overhead costs (land, terminal facilities, and track) and relatively low incremental costs.

In such an industry, prices set equal to the incremental cost of increasing production or services by another unit will not earn enough revenue to cover fixed overhead costs, including the payment of return to investors for the use of their money to purchase land, track, and other fixed-cost items. A long-run policy of incremental or marginal cost pricing will therefore not be possible in such an industry.

Here one might ask two preliminary but important questions. First, why should prices be set equal to incremental cost? To answer this question in detail, with appropriate qualifications, would require a lengthy essay on welfare economics. Briefly, when prices throughout the economy equal incremental costs (as is the case in most competitive industries), consumers face a relative set of prices that tells them the true cost to the economy of consuming a bit more of A or a bit less of B — a factor that tends to make buying and selling choices economically efficient. Where the prices of some commodities are set equal to incremental costs and the prices of other commodities are not, consumers are given a misleading set of price signals that can lead to consumption and production decisions that are economically inefficient. Suppose that the price ($1) of one product (A) is far in excess of its incremental cost ($.50), while the price of other products (B and C) is equal to their incremental cost ($.75), which is somewhat higher than that of A. Consumers would compare the price of A with that of B and C and choose relatively more of B and C, even though (1) they would prefer relatively more of A if its price were set equal to incremental cost, and (2) it would cost society less in terms of resources expended to produce relatively more A, and less B and C. Whether one ought always to price at incremental costs — particularly in a world where differences between cost and price may vary among industries — is much debated. But the ability of such prices to inform the public about the true economic cost of buying a bit more or less of the regulated product — and thus direct buying decisions toward the cheapest way to satisfy preferences — is a strong point in their favor.

Second, one might ask, if fixed investment is very high and incremental costs are low, should we regulate, or should we nationalize, the firm? This question is worth considering for the light it sheds on a proper rate structure. Consider a famous example: A bridge costs, say, $10 million to build, but will last forever. Assume the resource cost of one person's crossing — the wear and tear on the bridge — is 5 cents. To charge more than 5 cents will prevent some potential users from crossing, leading them to spend their money on less preferred alternatives that cost society more to produce. Yet, if the bridge owner charges only 5 cents, how is he to pay back the investors who put up $10 million to build the bridge? The answer, the argument goes, is nationalization. If the government invests $10 million, needed bridges will be built, while as long as it charges a toll of only 5 cents once the bridge is built, no one will be unnecessarily discouraged from using it. Nationalization, however, has problems of its own. Consider two common ones related to allocation and efficiency:

(a) How is the government to know where to build bridges? Unless bridge users are prepared to pay not only 5 cents but also enough additional money to pay the investment cost, it is wasteful to build the bridge. The investment funds should be spent on other projects that the public wants more. A private investor will build bridges only where users can, and will, pay enough to cover investment costs. The government can try to replicate (or improve on) the private investor's decision by asking the civil service to work out a cost-benefit calculus related to each project and invest only in those that show an adequate social return. But will such studies produce results as accurate as those flowing from the discipline imposed on investors by the knowledge that users must in fact pay sufficient tolls if the investment is to be recovered? (Critics of the work of the Army Corps of Engineers typically argue not.)

(b) Are nationalized industries less efficiently operated than those run by private firms? Do they run the risk of undue political interference? Ambrose Bierce defined a lighthouse as a building near a seashore containing a large lantern and a friend of a politician.

The point to be noted here is that regulation, a step short of nationalization, will not, and is not designed to, yield prices that equal incremental costs. Even when regulation works perfectly, it cannot cure the "inefficiency" caused by a private firm's need to cover average costs when (because of large fixed costs) they are greater than incremental costs. Rather, regulation must aim to set prices that allow fixed investment — investment in rights-of-way or railway beds, representing unrepeatable expenditure — to be paid for or recovered. Doing so will lead to a certain amount of allocative waste compared to the ideal.

Now let us turn to the regulator's "rate structure" problem. Suppose that our hypo-thetical bridge is built by private enterprise. Suppose further that, to provide investors a return on the capital invested to build the bridge, an extra $1 million must be raised annu-ally, over and above the revenues generated by a 5-cent toll to cover incremental operat-ing expenses. How should tolls be set to raise the needed extra revenue?

At first one might think "charge everyone the same," for each obtains the same service from the bridge, namely one crossing. Yet to charge each crosser equally (say, 10 cents) can have several pernicious effects. For one thing, some potential crossers, willing to pay, say, 8 cents but not 10 cents for bridge crossing, will stay at home — a pity, in that the economy could give them what they value at 8 cents, for an economic expen-diture of only 5 cents' worth of additional resources. For another thing, they might buy something else for 8 cents, say, a ride in a ferryboat, and thereby require the economy to use 8 cents' worth of resources giving them less satisfaction than might have been given them (through bridge crossing) with an economic expenditure of only 5 cents' worth of extra resources. And one can imagine the waste involved if a host of 8-cent-cost ferryboats appear, attracting passengers from the 5-cents bridge because of its 10-cent price.

To minimize this waste, economists have sometimes advocated charging prices that reflect an allocation of fixed costs in inverse relation to elasticity of demand. That is to say, those to whom bridge use is worth more will be charged a higher proportion of fixed costs; those to whom it is worth less will be charged less and, as a result, are less likely to stop using the bridge or switch to a ferryboat. The resulting pattern of resource use makes it more likely to resemble what it would have been if prices were set equal to incremental cost. The now defunct ICC, for example, traditionally had railroads charge more for ship-ping valuable items than for shipping inexpensive ones, presumably because a small extra charge is less likely to affect the shipping behavior of those who send expensive items.

Aside from a theoretical point — that this type of pricing does not always minimize economic waste — this effort to minimize waste when allocating fixed costs often founders on administrative obstacles. As previously mentioned, to measure demand elas-ticities is extremely difficult. But this difficulty is compounded by efforts to classify customers or services into administerable categories that correspond, even roughly, to demand elasticities. Thus, for example, the ICC's old system of varying rates according to the value of the product shipped bore only a distant relation to the "inverse demand elas-ticity" it is supposed to represent. Do shippers of diamonds, in fact, care less about trans-portation cost per pound than shippers of salt? Perhaps so, for transportation is a smaller proportion of final selling price. But their willingness to do so may also depend in large part, not on the proportion of transportation costs in final value, but on the state of competition in the diamond market and the availability of alternative transport. If diamond selling is fiercely competitive, to the point where sellers look for any and every cost-saving device, and if equally good truck transport is readily available, even a small increase in rail prices will lead diamond sellers to use trucks, while a monopolistic salt industry that does not have alternative modes of transport readily available to it may be willing to pay quite high rail prices before it would use other modes of transport.

A simplified example will help to explain the form in which this problem arises in the *Arizona Grocery* case, which we consider below. Assume that a railroad builds a track connecting A, B, and C (Fig. 5-1). Assume that the track costs $5 million. Assume further that, once the track is built, it costs an additional $2 million to buy special cars for carrying oil from A through B to C. Suppose that points A and C are connected by a river, plied by barge lines. The incremental cost of carrying the oil by rail from A to C is $2 million — the amount needed for cars and upkeep, and the amount that the railroad would save by refusing to carry oil from A to C. The fully allocated cost of carrying the oil by rail from A to C, however, includes a "fair" portion of the overhead necessary to supply any rail transport between A and C whatsoever. In particular, it includes a proportionate share of the cost of the railbed — a sunk cost that need never be incurred again. Let us assume that that "fair share" of the overhead is $1 million. In that case, the fully allocated cost of carrying oil between A and C for the railroad is $3 million, and the incremental cost is $2 million.

Suppose that a barge can carry oil from point A to point C at a cost of $2.5 million. Should the railroad be allowed to cut its price for carrying oil from A to C, let us say, to $2.2 million — a price near incremental cost? Or should the ICC insist that it keep its price in the range of $3 million?

The major economic arguments for allowing the railroad to cut its price are the following: First, unless the railroad cuts its price, all oil will be carried by barge. That means that the portion of fixed costs previously borne by the A to C oil shippers will no longer be borne by them; the fares the railroad charges other shippers will therefore have to rise to recover the additional amount of fixed cost. In our example, if the railroad cut its prices to $2.2 million, the oil shippers will still contribute $200,000 to overhead. If these shippers are lost to the barge lines because the railroad is not allowed to cut its prices, this $200,000 will have to be made up by other railroad customers. Second, since the railroad fixed costs are in place — the roadbed will never have to be built again — the extra resources that the economy must put forth to carry the oil from A to C by rail amount to $2 million worth of resources. To carry that same amount from A to C by barge, however, requires an extra $2.5 million worth of resources. Thus we can do the same job and have $500,000 worth of resources left over if the shipper sends his oil by rail.

These economic arguments are well known and widely accepted. Other economic arguments, however, suggest that in some circumstances the government should not allow the railroad to cut price to incremental cost. First, suppose that the barge line's cost of $2.5 million includes a fee of $1 million that the barge line must pay to the government to cover the cost of initially improving the river or digging a canal. If those costs are nonrepeatable, that fee of $1 million also represents payment for a fixed cost, and the true incremental cost for barge line carriage is $1.5 million — in other words, the barge line's incremental costs are lower than the railroad's, but it may not be legally possible for the barge line to lower its prices to its own incremental costs. In such a situation, it may be economically sensible to prevent the railroads from charging a fee equal to the railroad's incremental cost — when that cost is greater than the barge line's incremental cost but less than the barge line's fully allocated cost. Second, transport by barge may serve some other social purpose; for example, it may help provide for national defense, add to the scenic beauty of the countryside, or help people in some other way not reflected in

FIGURE 5-1

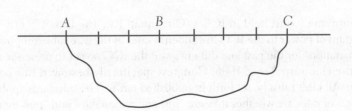

FIGURE 5-2

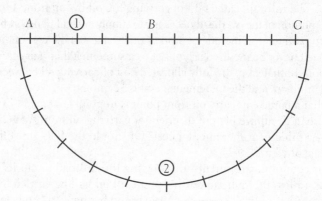

the price charged for the service. To serve this other social goal, the government may want to impose a rate structure to ensure that the goods move by barge rather than by rail.

Finally, one should consider the plight of an oil-using widget producer located at *B* in competition with a similar oil-using widget producer located at *C*. If the railroad is allowed to cut its price for oil transport to *C* due to riverboat competition, the *B* producer will often end up paying a higher price for oil than the *C* producer (though incremental costs of shipment are lower), and widget producers will tend to locate at *C*, not *B*. The source of this discrimination is that fixed costs must be collected from someone, and we often must ask *B* to make a larger contribution than *C* to prevent a rail-barge shipping misallocation; in doing so, we create a *B-C* producer-location misallocation. It may be some comfort to you (but not to *B*) to realize that even if the regulator keeps the *C* rail prices high, *B* is not helped. Oil will then go by barge to *C* and so will the oil-using widget makers.

Does the situation change any if, instead of a barge, another rail line runs between *A* and *C* (Fig. 5-2)? In this case, allowing rail line #1 to lower its *A-C* price to incremental costs not only hurts *B*, but also seems unnecessary. It is unlikely that the incremental costs for the *A-C* oil on line #2 will be much below line #1; indeed, they are likely to be higher. Moreover, the regulator can control the prices of each. Thus, a refusal to let #1 lower its *A-C* price and raise its *A-B* price is unlikely to end up with oil shippers using a higher incremental cost mode of transport. The discriminatory harm to *B* is not counterbalanced by so clear an allocative good.

2. *Arizona Grocery*

Note: The ICC's Ratemaking Powers

The Supreme Court held in ICC v. Cincinnati Ry., 167 U.S. 479 (1897), that the 1887 act's grant of power to the ICC to condemn rates as unreasonable empowered it only to award reparations for the past and did not grant the ICC power to prescribe rates for the future. In the Hepburn Act of 1906, Congress specifically bestowed this power on the commission: All rates must be set forth in published tariffs. The standards applied to judge the lawfulness of rates are whether they are "just and reasonable" and "nondiscriminatory."

In the Transportation Act of 1920, the ICC was empowered to prescribe minimum as well as maximum rates; this power was granted to enable the ICC to prevent "destructive" or predatory competition through low rates that might drive competing carriers out of business. The commission's rate regulation authority was subsequently extended to motor carriers and water carriers (barges).

There were four basic types of relief that the commission could provide through its rate regulation authority:

(1) Shippers could challenge an existing rate as unreasonably high and seek reparations (damages) equal to the difference between the rate they have been charged and a "reasonable" rate, as determined by the commission.

(2) Shippers could challenge an existing rate as unreasonably high and ask the commission to establish a lower rate for the future. (Shippers will usually join a request for this remedy, which is similar to that provided by §4 of the National Gas Act, with a demand for reparations.)

(3) Most rates would be reviewed when the carrier filed a tariff seeking to change a rate (for a given commodity between given points). A competing carrier or a shipper could then ask the ICC to suspend the proposed rate (which it could do for seven months) while it determined its lawfulness. If the proceeding was not completed within seven months, the rate took effect subject to a refund obligation if it was later found to have been too high (similar to §5 of the Natural Gas Act).

(4) The ICC in one proceeding could (at the behest of carriers, shippers, or on its own motion) investigate the costs or revenues of all railroads in a region, or in the whole country, and make a blanket adjustment in all rates to increase (or limit) the total revenue carriers received.

Congress has enacted laws effectively "deregulating" rail rates where railroads effectively compete with each other. The commission now can set rail rates only where a carrier has "market dominance." See Staggers Rail Act of 1980, 94 Stat. 1895, codified at 49 U.S.C. §10101a and elsewhere.

The ICC's Decision in *Arizona Grocery*

In 1920, railroads maintained a rate of $1.045 per 100 pounds on sugar from California points to Phoenix, Arizona. Shippers contended that the rates were unreasonably high; the ICC awarded reparations based on a rate of 96.5 cents and directed the railroads to charge a rate no higher than 96.5 cents in the future. The railroads subsequently established rates at or below 96.5 cents. In 1922, Phoenix merchants challenged the then-existing San Francisco rates as unreasonable and sought reparations. In 1925, the ICC ordered that the rate from San Francisco to Phoenix be reduced to 73 cents, seemingly because the railroads had lowered the rate from San Francisco to Chicago to 84 cents. The commission also awarded reparation on San Francisco-to-Phoenix shipments on or after July 1, 1922; the amount of reparations was based on the difference between the rates charged by the railroads and 73 cents. In Traffic Bureau of Phoenix Chamber of Commerce v. Atchison, Topeka & Santa Fe Ry., 95 I.C.C. 244, 248 (1925), a dissenting commissioner argued:

> Some of these complainants came before us in June, 1920, attacking the rates on sugar, in carloads, from California refineries to Phoenix and asking for reparation, just as they do here. . . . We found the rate unreasonable to the extent that it exceeded 96.5 cents, which we then prescribed for the future. . . . They now come by

complaint filed November 3, 1922, and allege that a rate on the same traffic of 96 cents, 0.5 cent lower than that so prescribed, has been unreasonable since February 17, 1921, four months prior to our former decision, and again ask reparation. Meantime, on July 26, 1922, we had found not unreasonable a rate of 96.5 cents, minimum 60,000 pounds, from California refining points to destinations in Nevada and Utah for hauls ranging from 419 to 823 miles, as compared with the hauls here considered ranging from 489 to 800 miles over the Santa Fe, and 451 to 921 miles over the Southern Pacific. Nevada Public Commission v. S.P. Co., 73 I.C.C. 240. That rate also was reduced by the carriers to 96 cents. The general 10 per cent reduction of July 1, 1922, brought this reasonable rate down to 86.5 cents and later, in the general sugar readjustment, the carriers established to Phoenix a rate of 84 cents, minimum 60,000 pounds. All of these were lower than what we had found reasonable and prescribed.

The majority do not reverse those decisions. They do not show change in circumstances and conditions. . . . And yet they find unreasonable rates lower than the rate prescribed [in the commission's earlier decision establishing a 96.5 cent rate on sugar from California to Phoenix.]

The rate of 84 cents [on shipments of sugar from San Francisco to Chicago] established January 11, 1924, as a result of our findings in Sugar Cases of 1922, 81 I.C.C. 448, is necessary if California sugar, concededly far exceeding the local demands, is to find a market in the Middle West in competition with sugar from refineries on the Atlantic seaboard and Gulf of Mexico.

Arizona Grocery Co. v. Atchison, Topeka & Santa Fe Railway

284 U.S. 370 (1932)

Mr. Justice ROBERTS delivered the opinion of the Court.

This case turns upon the power of the Interstate Commerce Commission to award reparations with respect to shipments which moved under rates approved or prescribed by it.

[The Court recited the history of the proceedings before the ICC.]

The respondents objected that they should not be required to pay reparations on shipments which moved under rates approved or prescribed by the Commission as reasonable. To this that body replied, "We reserve the right, upon a more comprehensive record, to modify our previous findings, upon matters directly in issue before us as to which it clearly appears that our previous findings would not accord substantial justice under the laws which we administer. We have such a case here. For the first time the record before us is comprehensive in the evidence which it contains upon the reasonableness of the rates assailed. Upon this record we reach the conclusion that the rate prescribed in the first Phoenix case, during the period embraced in these complaints, was unreasonable and that a lower rate would have been reasonable during that period. If we are within our authority in finding that a lower rate would have been reasonable, then it must follow that shippers who paid the freight charges at the higher rate paid charges which were unreasonable, and are entitled to reparation. . . ."

The carriers having failed to pay the amount awarded, the petitioner sued therefor in the District Court, and recovered judgment. The Circuit Court of Appeals reversed. . . .

The exaction of unreasonable rates by a public carrier was forbidden by the common law. Interstate Commerce Comm. v. Baltimore & Ohio R. Co., 145 U.S. 263, 275. The public policy which underlay this rule could, however, be vindicated only in an action brought by him who paid the excessive charge, to recover damages thus sustained. Rates, fares, and charges were fixed by the carrier, which took its chances that in an action by the shipper these might be adjudged unreasonable and reparation be awarded.

But we are here specially concerned with the Interstate Commerce Act of 1887 and with some of the changes or supplements adopted since its original enactment. That Act did not take from the carriers their power to initiate rates — that is, the power in the first instance to fix rates, or to increase or to reduce them. . . . In order to render rates definite and certain and to prevent discrimination and other abuses, the statute required the filing and publishing of tariffs specifying the rates adopted by the carrier, and made these the legal rates, that is, those which must be charged to all shippers alike. Any deviation from the published rate was declared a criminal offense, and also a civil wrong giving rise to an action for damages by the injured shipper. Although the Act thus created a legal rate, it did not abrogate, but expressly affirmed, the common-law duty to charge no more than a reasonable rate, and left upon the carrier the burden of conforming its charges to that standard. In other words, the legal rate was not made by the statute a lawful rate — it was lawful only if it was reasonable. Under §6 the shipper was bound to pay the legal rate; but if he could show that it was unreasonable he might recover reparation.

The Act altered the common law by lodging in the Commission the power theretofore exercised by courts, of determining the reasonableness of a published rate. If the finding on this question was against the carrier, reparation was to be awarded the shipper, and only the enforcement of the award was relegated to the courts. In passing upon the issue of fact, the function of the Commission was judicial in character; its action affected only the past, so far as any remedy of the shipper was concerned and adjudged for the present merely that the rate was then unreasonable; no authority was granted to prescribe rates to be charged in the future. Indeed, after a finding that an existing rate was unreasonable, the carrier might put into effect a new and slightly different rate and compel the shipper to resort to a new proceeding to have this declared unreasonable. Since the carrier had complete liberty of action in making the rate, it necessarily followed that upon a finding of unreasonableness, an award of reparation should be measured by the excess paid, subject only to statutory limitation of time. . . .

The Hepburn Act and the Transportation Act [of 1920] evince an enlarged and different policy on the part of Congress. The first granted the commission power to fix the maximum reasonable rate; the second extended its authority to the prescription of a named rate, or the maximum or minimum reasonable rate, or the maximum and minimum limits within which the carriers' published rate must come. When under this mandate the Commission declares a specific rate to be reasonable and lawful rate for the future, it speaks as the legislature, and its pronouncement has the force of a statute. . . .

But it is suggested that the mere setting of limits by Commission order leaves the carrier free to name any rate within those limits, and, as to common law, it must at its peril publish a reasonable rate within the boundaries set by the order; that as it has the initiative it must take the burden, notwithstanding the Commission's order, of maintaining the rate at a reasonable level, and will be answerable in damages if it fails so to do. This argument overlooks the fact that in declaring a maximum rate the Commission is exercising a delegated power legislative in character; that it may act only within the scope of the delegation; that its authority is to fix a maximum or minimum reasonable rate; for it is precluded by the statute from fixing one which is unreasonable, which by the statute is declared unlawful. If it were avowedly to attempt to set an unreasonably high maximum its order would be a nullity.

The report and order of 1921 involved in the present case declared in terms that 96.5 cents was, and for the future would be, a reasonable rate. There can be no question that when the carriers, pursuant to that finding, published a rate of 96 cents, the legal rate thus established, to which they and the shipper were bound to conform, became by virtue of the Commission's order also a lawful — that is, a reasonable — rate.

Specific rates prescribed for the future take the place of the legal tariff rates theretofore in force by the voluntary action of the carriers, and themselves become the legal rates. As to such rates there is therefore no difference between the legal or published tariff rate and the lawful rate. The carrier cannot change a rate so prescribed and take its chances of an adjudication that the substituted rate will be found reasonable. It is bound to conform to the order of the Commission. If that body sets too low a rate, the carrier has no redress save a new hearing and the fixing of a more adequate rate for the future. It cannot have reparation from the shippers for a rate collected under the order upon the ground that it was unreasonably low. This is true because the Commission, in naming the rate, speaks in its quasi-legislative capacity. The prescription of a maximum rate, or maximum and minimum rates, is as legislative in quality as the fixing of a specified rate. . . .

As respects its future conduct the carrier is entitled to rely upon the declaration as to what will be a lawful, that is, a reasonable rate; and if the order merely sets limits it is entitled to protection if it fixes a rate which falls within them. Where, as in this case, the Commission has made an order having a dual aspect, it may not in a subsequent proceeding, acting in its quasi-judicial capacity, ignore its own pronouncement promulgated in its quasi-legislative capacity and retroactively repeal its own enactment as to the reasonableness of the rate it has prescribed. . . .

It could repeal the order as it affected future action, and substitute a new rule of conduct as often as occasion might require, but this was obviously the limit of its power, as of that of the legislature itself.

The argument is pressed that this conclusion will work serious inconvenience in the administration of the Act; will require the Commission constantly to reexamine the fairness of rates prescribed, and will put an unbearable burden upon that body. If this is so, it results from the new policy declared by the Congress, which, in effect, vests in the Commission the power to legislate in specific cases as to the future conduct of the carrier. But it is also to be observed that so long as the Act continues in its present form, the great mass of rates will be carrier-made rates, as to which the Commission need take no action except of its own volition or upon complaint, and may in such case award reparation by reason of the charges made to shippers under the theretofore existing rate.

Where the Commission has, upon complaint and after hearing, declared what is the maximum reasonable rate to be charged by a carrier, it may not at a later time, and upon the same or additional evidence as to the fact situation existing when its previous order was promulgated, by declaring its own finding as to reasonableness erroneous, subject a carrier which conformed thereto to the payment of reparation measured by what the Commission now holds it should have decided in the earlier proceeding to be a reasonable rate.

The judgment is affirmed.

Mr. Justice HOLMES and Mr. Justice BRANDEIS think that the judgment should be reversed for the reasons stated by Judge Hutcheson in the concurring opinion in Eagle Cotton Oil Co. v. Southern Ry. Co., 51 F.2d 443, 445.

[In that opinion, Judge Hutcheson asserted that the ICC should not be precluded from awarding reparations under a rate it had previously approved or promulgated, and that this approach was consonant with the basic spirit of the Interstate Commerce Act, which allowed carriers considerable flexibility in adjusting rates, subject to limited intervention by the ICC. Judge Hutcheson contrasted the federal act with many state systems of railroad rate regulation (some of which require all rates to be approved by the relevant regulatory commission), which preclude shipper reparations under commission-approved rates, leaving shippers the sole remedy of "a seasonable application for a change of rate before any damage had been suffered."]

Notes and Questions

1. *Arizona Grocery* is normally cited for the proposition that an agency must follow its own rules (until they are properly changed). Was that point disputed in the case? What was the argument between the majority and the dissenters about?

2. Why *should* agencies be required to follow their own regulations unless and until those regulations are changed or withdrawn? Why shouldn't an agency be free to depart from a regulation in individual cases to exercise the sort of flexibility that agencies enjoy in case-by-case adjudication?

What is the legal basis for the idea that agencies must follow their own rules? Under *Vermont Yankee*, courts cannot impose on agencies procedural requirements that are not in positive law. Consider the following views: (a) The APA's definition of rule requires agencies to comply with rules while they are on the books; (b) Sometimes agencies that violate their own rules thereby violate the due process clause; (c) It is arbitrary and capricious for an agency not to follow its own rules. Return to the question after the *Caceres* case.

As we pointed out above, the railroad industry has been effectively "deregulated." The ICC will regulate rates only where the railroad enjoys "market dominance," that is to say, where there is no effective competition. Why did the deregulation occur? Is it sufficient to say that there is no longer any problem of monopoly, in light of the range of transportation options? Nonetheless, the "rate structure" principles applicable to railroads before deregulation still apply in some regulated industries, such as electricity, and in partially deregulated industries such as local telecommunications. They also continue to apply, to a lesser degree, to continued regulation of trucking, and even to railroads (where still regulated). For typical discussions of their applications in those areas, see Union Elec. Co. v. FERC, 890 F.2d 1193, 1198-1201 (D.C. Cir. 1989) (Williams, J.); Breyer, Antitrust, Deregulation, and the Newly Liberated Marketplace, 75 Cal. L. Rev. 1005, 1027-1031 (1987).

3. *Subsequent History of the* Arizona Grocery *Procedural Principle*

There are numerous cases reaffirming the general proposition on which *Arizona Grocery* has been thought to stand: that "an administrative ruling until changed binds both the outside world and the agency," and that an agency is obliged to adhere to its existing regulations when adjudicating and may not make ad hoc exceptions or departures. In fact, a public interest plaintiff obtained a ruling from a District of Columbia court that the firing of Archibald Cox in the famous "Saturday night massacre" was unlawful. The Department of Justice had promulgated regulations that restricted the government's power to fire Mr. Cox. Although the president, or the attorney general, might have withdrawn or modified those regulations, neither had done so. Hence they were legally binding. See Nader v. Boric, 366 F. Supp. 104 (D.D.C. 1973). The Supreme Court is occasionally quite emphatic about the *Arizona Grocery* principle, saying for example that a procedurally valid formal rule with the force of law trumps even "allegedly longstanding agency practice" to the contrary. Central Laborers' Pension Fund v. Heinz, 124 S. Ct. 2230 (2004).

Is the consistency requirement limited to formal regulations? Gardner v. FCC, 530 F.2d 1086 (D.C. Cir. 1976), invalidated the commission's failure to adhere to long-established procedures even though they had not been formalized in regulations. Moreover, in Massachusetts Fair Share v. Law Enforcement Assistance Admin., 758 F.2d 708 (D.C. Cir. 1985), the court considered a statement in a Department of Justice guideline manual that said the heads of the Law Enforcement Assistance Administration (LEAA) and the Agency per Voluntary Service (AVS) would jointly award grants for an urban crime prevention program. Massachusetts Fair Share's application for an urban crime prevention program was granted provisionally; the head of LEAA then rejected the application without the participation of the head of AVS. The court found that the manual established the procedures for administering the program, that those procedures meant that the head of a single agency, acting alone, could not withdraw a provisionally accepted grant, and that the agency must follow its own procedures as indicated in the manual.

Massachusetts Fair Share has not, in general, been followed. See Chiu v. United States, 948 F.2d 711 (Fed. Cir. 1991); Cooper v. United States R.R. Retirement Bd., 306 U.S. App. D.C. 306, 24 F.3d 1414 (D.C. Cir. 1994); but see Montilla v. INS, 926 F.2d 162 (2d Cir. 1991) (reversing the Immigration and Naturalization Service for failing to follow their own published procedures).

On the other hand, exceptions to the general rule have sometimes been permitted where the regulations in question concern internal agency procedures or where a rule is waived to afford more lenient treatment of a person. What objections could there be to allowing an agency to waive a regulation to treat a particular individual more leniently? There are also cases suggesting that interpretive rules and informal guidelines are not binding, see Sullivan v. United States, 348 U.S. 170 (1954); United States v. Fitch Oil Co., 676 F.2d 673 (Temp. Emer. Ct. App. 1982); Caterpillar Tractor Co. v. United States, 589 F.2d 1040, 1043 (Ct. Cl. 1978). *Caterpillar* has been followed by other courts, e.g., Hamlet v. United States, 63 F.3d 1097 (Fed. Cir. 1995). See also the discussion of "intentions to be good" in Chapter 7.

In the following case, the Supreme Court further restricted the application of the *Arizona Grocery* principle and raised important questions of judicial authority to enforce that principle on agencies.

United States v. Caceres
440 U.S. 741 (1979)

[The Court held that a defendant in a criminal prosecution may not exclude evidence obtained in violation of Internal Revenue Service (IRS) regulations requiring Justice Department approval before electronic surveillance of meetings between taxpayers and IRS agents was undertaken. The surveillance did not violate any constitutional or statutory requirement. In sustaining the conviction, Justice Stevens's opinion for the Court stated as follows:]

[This is not] a case in which the Due Process Clause is implicated because an individual has reasonably relied on agency regulations promulgated for his guidance or benefit. . . . Agency violations of their own regulations, whether or not also in violation of the Constitution, may well be inconsistent with the standards of agency action which the APA directs the courts to enforce. Indeed, some of our most important decisions holding agencies bound by their regulations have been in cases originally brought under the APA.

But this is not an APA case, and the remedy sought is not invalidation of the agency action. Rather, we are dealing with a criminal prosecution in which respondent seeks judicial enforcement of the agency regulations by means of the exclusionary rule. . . . [W]e decline to adopt any rigid rule requiring federal courts to exclude any evidence obtained as a result of a violation of these rules. . . . [W]e cannot ignore the possibility that a rigid application of an exclusionary rule to every regulatory violation could have a serious deterrent impact on the formulation of additional standards to govern prosecutorial and police procedures. Here, the Executive itself has provided for internal sanctions in cases of knowing violations of the electronic-surveillance regulations. To go beyond that, and require exclusion in every case, would take away from the Executive Department the primary responsibility for fashioning the appropriate remedy for the violation of its regulations. But since the content, and indeed the existence, of the regulations would remain within the Executive's sole authority, the result might well be fewer and less protective regulations. In the long run, it is far better to have rules like those contained in the IRS Manual, and to tolerate occasional erroneous administration of the kind displayed by this record, than either to have no rules except those mandated by statute, or to have them framed in a mere precatory form. . . .

Reversed.

Mr. Justice MARSHALL, with whom Mr. Justice BRENNAN joins, dissenting. . . .

In a long line of cases beginning with Bridges v. Wixon, 326 U.S. 135, 152-153 (1945), this Court has held that "one under investigation . . . is legally entitled to insist upon the observance of rules" promulgated by an executive or legislative body for his protection. See Morton v. Ruiz, 415 U.S. 199, 235 (1974); Vitarelli v. Seaton, 359 U.S. 535 (1959); Service v. Dulles, 354 U.S. 363 (1957); United States ex rel. Accardi v. Shaughnessy, 347 U.S. 260 (1954). Underlying these decisions is a judgment, central to our concept of due process, that government officials no less than private citizens are bound by rules of law. Where individual interests are implicated, the Due Process Clause requires that an executive agency adhere to the standards by which it professes its action to be judged. . . .

This Court has consistently demanded governmental compliance with regulations designed to safeguard individual interests even when the rules were not mandated by the Constitution or federal statute. In United States ex rel. Accardi v. Shaughnessy, supra, the court granted a writ of habeas corpus where the Attorney General had disregarded applicable procedures for the Board of Immigration Appeals' suspension of deportation orders. Although the Attorney General had final power to deport the petitioner and had no statutory or constitutional obligation to provide for intermediate action by the Board, this Court held that while suspension procedures were in effect, "the Attorney General denies himself the right to sidestep the Board or dictate its decision." 347 U.S., at 267. On similar reasoning, the Court in Service v. Dulles vacated a Foreign Service officer's national security discharge. While acknowledging that the Secretary of State was not obligated to adopt "rigorous substantive and procedural safeguards," the Court nonetheless held that "having done so he could not, so long as the Regulations remained unchanged, proceed without regard to them." 354 U.S., at 388. Similarly, in Vitarelli v. Seaton we demanded adherence to Department of the Interior employee-discharge procedures that were "generous beyond the requirements that bind [the] agency." 359 U.S., at 547. . . . And most recently, in Morton v. Ruiz, we declined to permit the Bureau of Indian Affairs to depart from internal rules for establishing assistance-eligibility requirements although the procedures were "more rigorous than otherwise would be required." 415 U.S., at 235. . . .

To make subjective reliance controlling in due process analysis deflects inquiry from the relevant constitutional issue, [which is] the legitimacy of government conduct. . . .

Implicit in these decisions, and in the Due Process Clause itself, is the premise that regulations bind with equal force whether or not they are outcome determinative. As its very terms make manifest, the Due Process Clause is first and foremost a guarantor of process. It embodies a commitment to procedural regularity independent of result. . . .

Finally, the Court declines to order suppression because "a rigid application of an exclusionary rule to every regulatory violation could have a serious deterrent impact on the formulation of additional standards to govern prosecutorial and police procedures." No support is offered for that speculation. . . . Under today's decision, regulations largely unenforced by the IRS will be unenforceable by the courts.

Notes and Questions

1. Why should the requirement that agencies follow their own regulations be enforced only in cases falling under the APA? Recall that the APA was not in existence when *Arizona Grocery* was decided. Or does *Caceres* suggest that *Arizona Grocery* was wrongly decided? Consider whether the APA or the due process clause justifies courts in requiring agencies to follow their own rules.

2. Does due process require that agencies follow their own regulations? If Justice Marshall's position were accepted, would federal courts be required to hear and resolve claims that state administrators had not followed state regulations? Would such "federalization" of state administrative law be desirable? Consider the view that a litigant should at least be required to show that he or she relied on agency regulations and was prejudiced by their violation to obtain relief on due process grounds.

3. The Federal Aviation Administration (FAA) publishes an enforcement manual, used by its employees, called "Compliance and Enforcement Program Handbook." The Handbook tells FAA enforcement employees that "suspension of a pilot's certificate may be used as a punishment when the nature of the pilot's violation so warrants." In §205b, it sets forth six criteria that FAA prosecutors "should consider" in deciding whether to ask the National Transportation Safety Board (NTSB) to impose suspension, or some lesser penalty, as a sanction. Among them are "hardship to the pilot," and "ability to pay a civil monetary fine instead."

The FAA recently asked the NTSB to suspend the license of John Capuano for a period of 45 days. The board did so. Capuano seeks judicial review. He concedes that he had an opportunity to make all relevant arguments before the board. He says that the FAA prosecutor, however, did not consider the personal hardship the request for suspension would cause. (The government agrees that the prosecutor argued only the serious nature of the offense and that suspension would deter others.)

What result?

4. The Environmental Protection Agency (EPA) has a rule that says that, in certain geographical areas, a company that builds a "new unit" (for example, a new boiler) must obtain a permit if the new unit will emit more pollutants than the old unit. The EPA decides this by measuring the capacity of the new unit to emit, compared with the *actual* amount the old unit emitted. PR Cement Co. wants to modify one of its cement-making kilns so that it will become more efficient. The old kiln emitted 200 tons of sulfur dioxide last year. The modified kiln will emit 100 tons if PR Cement uses it to produce the same amount of cement as last year, but it has the capacity to emit 300 tons if operated to full capacity.

PR Cement does not want to go through the long, time-consuming permit process. EPA has refused to issue it a document called a "non-applicability determination" (a "NAD"), which would allow it to avoid the permitting process. PR Cement appeals this refusal to a reviewing court.

PR Cement argues that EPA's permit rule does not apply to the *modification* of an existing facility, at least not to a modification that does no more than make the production process more efficient, creating less pollution for any given level of production. PR Cement concedes that several official internal EPA documents support EPA's interpretation of the rule. It points to other documents, however, that are ambiguous. And it has found one NAD letter, issued by a regional office, that grants a NAD on the very theory that PR Cement advocates.

The EPA responds as follows: "No large agency can guarantee that all of its administrators will react similarly, or interpret regulations identically, throughout the United States. The purpose of the consistency doctrine does not warrant setting aside the EPA's determination here."

What result?

5. Suppose that an executive order requiring use of cost-benefit analysis (described above) contains the following provision:

> Section 9. *Judicial Review.* This Order is intended only to improve the internal management of the Federal government, and is not intended to create any right or benefit, substantive or procedural, enforceable at law by a party against the United States, its agencies, its officers or any person.

Suppose that a federal agency adopts a regulation without following the cost-benefit analysis required by the order. A firm subject to the regulation brings suit to set it aside, alleging that the regulation would not have been adopted at all or would have been less rigorous if the cost-benefit analysis had been performed and considered.

What result?

Note

Consider the various ways in which agencies might adopt and then change their policies, and the potential responses by courts to claims that any such changes were arbitrary or unfair because they destroyed important expectation interests.

First, an agency may adopt a policy through adjudication and then adopt and enforce a change in that policy in a second adjudication. As we saw earlier in this chapter in the materials dealing with adjudicatory consistency, courts in some limited circumstances invalidate such changes as arbitrary; the general rule is that an agency may change its policies through adjudication if those policies were originally made via adjudication.

Second, an agency might initially adopt a policy through rulemaking and then adopt and enforce a change in that rule through adjudication. *Arizona Grocery* holds that such changes are per se invalid. What is the justification for such a sharp distinction in judicial treatment of adjudication-adjudication changes and rulemaking-adjudication changes?

Third, an agency may adopt a policy through rulemaking and then change that policy through a second rulemaking proceeding. Should courts ever restrict an agency's change of policy by this route? We shall consider this problem later, in the context of retroactive application of a new policy.

D. Estoppel and Res Judicata

1. Estoppel

The law governing estoppel of the government has undergone many twists and turns. In the recent past, the rule has gone from hardly any estoppel, to some estoppel, back to hardly any estoppel.

In the first edition of his Administrative Law Treatise (1958), Professor Davis wrote:

> Although the courts have developed a doctrine of equitable estoppel, under which one who makes a representation to another who reasonably relies to his detriment is estopped to deny the truth of the representation or to gain by taking a position inconsistent with the representation, the courts usually hold that the doctrine of equitable estoppel does not apply to the government.

Id. at 491. Indeed, in 1947 the District of Columbia wrote of the "well settled doctrine that res judicata and equitable estoppel do not ordinarily apply to decisions of administrative tribunals." Churchill Tabernacle v. FCC, 160 F.2d 244, 246 (D.C. Cir. 1947). Professor Davis traced the origin of this doctrine back to sovereign immunity and the notion that "the King cannot be estopped for it cannot be presumed the King would do wrong to any person." He argued strongly that the doctrine was outmoded and was gradually being replaced by decisions that estopped government agencies.

In Federal Crop Ins. Corp. v. Merrill, 332 U.S. 380 (1947), the Supreme Court refused to estop the government under the following circumstances: (1) Plaintiffs applied for crop insurance, told the government's county committee that their wheat was "reseeded," were told the wheat was insurable, and paid the premium. (2) Unbeknownst to plaintiffs and to the local government agents, an agency regulation prohibited insuring reseeded wheat. The Court held that the government did *not* have to pay when the crop failed.

Professor Davis contrasted *Merrill* with Moser v. United States, 341 U.S. 41 (1951). A statute provided that an alien who sought exemption from the draft could never become a U.S. citizen. Moser (a Swiss citizen living in the United States) wanted a draft exemption. He asked the Swiss legation if the exemption would bar him from becoming a U.S. citizen. The Swiss legation told him it would not. The legation presumably relied on misinformation from the State Department. Moser relied on this representation, asked for and received the exemption. He later applied for citizenship; a decision denying him citizenship was overturned by the Supreme Court, which held that he had not "knowingly and intentionally waived his rights."

Moser did not mention estoppel directly, and it involved citizenship, perhaps a special area. But by the time of Professor Davis's 1970 supplement, he could find many lower court cases holding the government estopped. The Court of Claims held a government contracting officer's delay in contesting an "adjustment" made by a private contractor "constituted a waiver" by the government to claims that the work could have been done in another manner, resulting in savings to the government. The court wrote: "[W]hen the government is acting in its proprietary capacity, it may be estopped by an act of waiver in the same manner as a private contractor." Roberts v. United States, 357 F.2d 938, 946-947 (Ct. Cl. 1966). The courts had also held the commissioner of Internal Revenue estopped in tax cases where denial of the estoppel would have been particularly unfair.

By 1976, Professor Davis wrote of the traditional "nonestoppel" doctrine: "The opposite . . . now has almost uniform [case] support. . . . The doctrine of equitable estoppel does apply to the government." Administrative Law of the Seventies 399 (1976). Thus, the courts estopped the government from claiming land that formed part of a national forest because it had (wrongly) told plaintiff the land was outside the forest and plaintiff had invested $350,000 in managing it. United States v. Georgia-Pacific Co., 421 F.2d 92 (9th Cir. 1970). And the government was not allowed to recover soil bank money paid to plaintiffs (in violation of regulations) because a government officer had helped plaintiffs draw up their leaseholds so they would qualify. United States v. Lazy FC Ranch, 481 F.2d 985 (9th Cir. 1973).

On the other hand, in other cases courts refused to estop the government. In Montilla v. United States, 457 F.2d 978 (Ct. Cl. 1972), for example, Montilla retired from the army, having been led to believe by a superior officer that he qualified for retirement pay. He did not, and despite his statement that he had been misled and would have remained in the army to qualify, the Court of Claims held that *Merrill* controls. Then, in 1981, the Supreme Court decided the following case, which started the process back toward a rule of rare, or no, estoppel of the government.

Schweiker v. Hansen
450 U.S. 785 (1981)

Per Curiam. On June 12, 1974, respondent met for about 15 minutes with Don Connelly, a field representative of the Social Security Administration (SSA), and orally inquired of him whether she was eligible for "mothers insurance benefits" under §202(g) of the Social Security Act (Act). . . . Connelly erroneously told her that she was not, and she left the SSA office without having filed a written application. By the Act's terms, such benefits are available only to one who, among other qualifications, "has filed application." 42 U.S.C. §402(g)(1)(D). By a regulation promulgated pursuant to the Act, only written applications satisfy the "filed application" requirement. 20 CFR §404.601 (1974). The SSA's Claims Manual, an internal Administration handbook, instructs field representatives to advise applicants of the advantages of filing written applications and to recommend to applicants who are uncertain about their eligibility that they file written applications. Connelly, however, did not recommend to respondent that she file a written application; nor did he advise her of the advantages of doing so. [Respondent eventually filed a written application and began receiving benefits in 1975.] The question is whether Connelly's erroneous statement and neglect of the Claims Manual estop petitioner, the Secretary of

Health and Human Services, from denying retroactive benefits to respondent for a period in which she was eligible for benefits but had not filed a written application. . . .

A divided panel of the Court of Appeals for the Second Circuit . . . considered the written-application requirement a mere "procedural requirement" of lesser import than the fact that respondent in June 1974 had been "substantively eligible" for the benefits. In such circumstances, the majority held, "misinformation provided by a Government official combined with a showing of misconduct (even if it does not rise to the level of a violation of a legally binding rule) should be sufficient to require estoppel." . . .

Judge Friendly dissented.

We agree with the dissent. . . .

This Court has never decided what type of conduct by a government employee will estop the Government from insisting upon compliance with valid regulations governing the distribution of welfare benefits. . . . This Court has recognized, however, "the duty of all courts to observe the conditions defined by Congress for charging the public Treasury." [Citing *Merrill*. Connelly's conduct did not amount to "affirmative misconduct."]

Connelly erred in telling respondent that she was ineligible for the benefit she sought. . . . But at worst, Connelly's conduct did not cause respondent to take action, cf. Federal Crop Insurance Corp. v. Merrill, supra, or fail to take action, cf. Montana v. Kennedy, supra, that respondent could not correct at any time.

Similarly, there is no doubt that Connelly failed to follow the Claims Manual in neglecting to recommend that respondent file a written application and in neglecting to advise her of the advantages of a written application. But the Claims Manual is not a regulation. It has no legal force, and it does not bind the SSA. Rather, it is a 13-volume handbook for internal use by thousands of SSA employees, including the hundreds of employees who receive untold numbers of oral inquiries like respondent's each year. If Connelly's minor breach of such a manual suffices to estop petitioner, then the Government is put "at risk that every alleged failure by an agent to follow instructions to the last detail in one of a thousand cases will deprive it of the benefit of the written application requirement which experience has taught to be essential to the honest and effective administration of the Social Security Laws." 619 F.2d at 956 (Friendly, J., dissenting). See United States v. Caceres, 440 U.S. 741, 755-756 (1979). . . .

[Mr. Justice MARSHALL, joined by Mr. Justice BRENNAN, dissented.]

Notes and Questions

1. Was *Schweiker* an estoppel case at all? Consider the view that Hansen was not seeking to estop the government, because she was not trying to prevent the government from denying the truth of the matter asserted. She was claiming that she relied to her detriment on a misrepresentation, to be sure, but she was not claiming that an official could bind the government in a way that violated existing regulations or statutes. Might this fact argue on Hansen's behalf? A possible problem with estopping the government is that estoppel allows bureaucrats to alter the substance of enacted law; was this a problem in *Schweiker*?

2. In defining the question of what constitutes the "affirmative misconduct" element of an estoppel against the government, two post-*Schweiker* cases are instructive. In Mukherjee v. Immigration & Naturalization Service, 793 F.2d 1006 (9th Cir. 1986), the court held that a vice-counsel's statement that an alien would not be subject to an INS regulation requiring him to reside in the country of his nationality following his medical

training in the United States to become a resident alien was negligent but was not a deliberate lie or pattern of false promises and therefore did not rise to the level of affirmative misconduct necessary to estop the government. In Fano v. O'Neill, 806 F.2d 1262 (5th Cir. 1987), the court reversed the district court's grant of summary judgment against a plaintiff whose claim for resident status was delayed in violation of an INS operations manual guideline and who therefore became statutorily ineligible for such status. The court held that plaintiffs claim that the INS had willfully delayed processing his application, singling him out for unjust discrimination, would, if proven, establish affirmative misconduct warranting estoppel.

3. The D.C. Circuit has suggested that estoppel may vary depending on the importance of enforcement of the congressional policy in question. Boulez v. Commissioner of Internal Revenue, 810 F.2d 209, 218 (D.C. Cir. 1987) ("when a compromise of tax liability is at issue, the need for rigorous compliance with pertinent regulations may be at its greatest, for not only the integrity of the public fisc but also public faith in the equitable enforcement of the tax laws hangs in the balance").

4. Compare the following cases:

a. A person is told that she is not eligible for certain financial benefits, when in fact she is, under the governing statute. She relies to her detriment on this misinformation. (This is the situation of Schweiker v. Hansen.)

b. A person is told that she is eligible for certain financial benefits, when in fact she is not, under the governing statute. She relies to her detriment on this misinformation.

c., d. Same as a and b above, but the relevant law can be found in a regulation, not a statute.

e. A person is told that he has a right to land held by the government, when he does not, under the governing statute.

f. Same as e, but the law is embodied in a regulation, not a statute.

Might these cases be different? Is case b strongest for the government? Consider the following case.

Office of Personnel Management v. Richmond

496 U.S. 414 (1990)

Justice KENNEDY delivered the opinion of the Court. . . .

Respondent was a welder at the Navy Public Works Center in San Diego, California. He left this position in 1981 after petitioner, the Office of Personnel Management (OPM), approved his application for a disability retirement. OPM determined that respondent's impaired eyesight prevented him from performing his job and made him eligible for a disability annuity under 5 U.S.C. Sec. 8337(a). Section 8337(a) provides this benefit for disabled federal employees who have completed five years of service. The statute directs, however, that the entitlement to disability payments will end if the retired employee is "restored to an earning capacity fairly comparable to the current rate of pay of the position occupied at the time of retirement." 5 U.S.C. Sec. 8337(d). . . .

Prior to 1982, an individual was deemed restored to earning capacity, and so rendered ineligible for a disability annuity, if "in *each of 2 succeeding calendar* years the income of the annuitant from wages or self-employment . . . equals at least 80 percent of the current rate of pay of the position occupied immediately before retirement."

The provision was amended in 1982 . . . to change the measuring period for restoration of earning capacity from two years to one. . . .

After taking disability retirement for his vision impairment, respondent undertook part-time employment as a school bus driver. From 1982-1985, respondent earned an average of $12,494 in this job, leaving him under the 80% limit for entitlement to continued annuity payments. In 1986, however, he had an opportunity to earn extra money by working overtime. Respondent asked an Employee Relations Specialist at the Navy Public Works Center's Civilian Personnel Department for information about how much he could earn without exceeding the 80% eligibility limit. Relying upon the terms of the repealed pre-1982 statute, under which respondent could retain the annuity unless his income exceeded the 80% limit in two consecutive years, the specialist gave incorrect advice. The specialist also gave respondent a copy of Attachment 4 to Federal Personnel Manual Letter 831-64, published by petitioner OPM, which also stated the former 2-year eligibility rule. The OPM form was correct when written in 1981; but when given to respondent, the form was out of date and therefore inaccurate. Respondent returned to the Navy in January 1987, and again was advised in error that eligibility would be determined under the old 2-year rule.

After receiving the erroneous information, respondent concluded that he could take on the extra work as a school bus driver in 1986 while still receiving full disability benefits for impaired vision so long as he kept his income for the previous and following years below the statutory eligibility limit. OPM discontinued respondent's disability annuity on June 30, 1987. The annuity was restored on January 1, 1988, since respondent did not earn more than allowed by the statute in 1987. Respondent thus lost his disability payments for a 6-month period, for a total amount of $3,993. . . . The Court of Appeals [ordered the government to pay this money. The] majority decided that "[b]ased on the Supreme Court's acknowledgment that the estoppel against the government is not foreclosed and based on court of appeals rulings applying estoppel against the government, our view is that estoppel is properly applied against the government in the present case." . . .

II

[We reverse.] From our earliest cases, we have recognized that equitable estoppel will not lie against the Government as against private litigants. . . .

The principles of these and many other cases were reiterated in Federal Crop Insurance Corporation v. Merrill, 332 U.S. 390 (1947), the leading case in our modern line of estoppel decisions. . . .

Despite the clarity of these earlier decisions, dicta in our more recent cases have suggested the possibility that there might be some situation in which estoppel against the Government could be appropriate. . . .

Since [then], federal courts have continued to accept estoppel claims under a variety of rationales and analyses. In sum, courts of appeals have taken our statements as an invitation to search for an appropriate case in which to apply estoppel against the Government, yet we have reversed every finding of estoppel that we have reviewed. . . . But it remains true that we need not embrace a rule that no estoppel will be against the Government in any case in order to decide this case. We leave for another day whether an estoppel claim could ever succeed against the Government. A narrower ground of decision is sufficient to address the type of suit presented here, a claim for payment of money from the Public Treasury contrary to a statutory appropriation.

III

The Appropriations Clause of the Constitution, Art. I, Sec. 9, cl. 7, provides that: "No Money shall be drawn from the Treasury, but in Consequence of Appropriations made by Law." For the particular type of claim at issue here, a claim for money from the Federal Treasury, the Clause provides an explicit rule of decision. Money may be paid out only through an appropriation made by law, in other words, the payment of money from the Treasury must be authorized by a statute. All parties here agree that the award respondent seeks would be in direct contravention of the federal statute upon which his ultimate claim to the funds must rest, 5 U.S.C. Sec. 8337. . . .

Our cases underscore the straightforward and explicit command of the Appropriations Clause. "It means simply that no money can be paid out of the Treasury unless it has been appropriated by an act of Congress." Cincinnati Soap Co. v. United States, 301 U.S. 308, 321 (1937) (citing Reeside v. Walker, 11 How. 272, 291 (1861)). . . .

Just as the pardon power cannot override the command of the Appropriations Clause, so too judicial use of the equitable doctrine of estoppel cannot grant respondent a money remedy that Congress has not authorized. See INS v. Pangilianan, 486 U.S. 875, 883 (1988) ("'Courts of equity can no more disregard statutory and constitutional requirements than can courts of law'").

We have not had occasion in past cases presenting claims of estoppel against the Government to discuss the Appropriations Clause, for reasons that are apparent. Given the strict rule against estoppel applied as early as 1813 in Lee v. Munroe & Thornton, 7 Cranch 366 (1813), claims of estoppel could be dismissed on that ground without more. . . .

The obvious practical consideration . . . for adherence to the requirement of the Clause is the necessity, existing now as much as at the time the Constitution was ratified, of preventing fraud and corruption. . . . But the Clause has a more fundamental and comprehensive purpose of direct relevance to the case before us. It is to assure that public funds will be spent according to the letter of the difficult judgments reached by Congress as to the common good, and not according to the individual favor of Government agents or the individual pleas of litigants.

Extended to its logical conclusion, operation of estoppel against the Government in the context of payment of money from the Treasury could in fact render the Appropriations Clause a nullity. If agents of the Executive were able, by their unauthorized oral or written statements to citizens, to obligate the Treasury for the payment of funds, the control over public funds that the Clause reposes in Congress in effect could be transferred to the Executive. . . .

The whole history and practice with respect to claims against the United States reveals the impossibility of an estoppel claim for money in violation of a statute. Congress' early practice was to adjudicate each individual money claim against the United States, on the ground that the Appropriations Clause forbade even a delegation of individual adjudicatory functions where payment of funds from the treasury was involved. See W. Cowen, P. Nichols, & M. Bennett, The United States Court of Claims, A History, 216 Ct. Cl. 1, 5 (1978). As the business of the federal legislature has grown, Congress has placed the individual adjudication of claims based on the Constitution, statutes, or contracts, or on specific authorizations of suit against the Government, with the Judiciary. See, e.g., the Tucker Act, 28 U.S.C. Sections 1346, 1491. But Congress has always reserved to itself the power to address claims of the very type presented by respondent, those founded not on any statutory authority, but upon the claim that "the equities and circumstances of a case create a moral obligation on the part of the Government to extend relief to an individual." Subcommittee on Administrative Law and Governmental Relations of the House Committee on the Judiciary, Supplemental Rules of Procedure for Private Claims Bills, 101st Cong., 1st Sess., 2 (Comm. Print 1989).

In so-called "congressional reference" cases, Congress refers proposed private bills to the United States Claims Court for an initial determination of the merits of the claim, but retains final authority over the ultimate appropriation. See 28 U.S.C. Sections 1492, 2509(c). Congress continues to employ private legislation to provide remedies in individual cases of hardship. . . .

Even short of collusion by individual officers or improper Executive attempts to frustrate legislative policy, acceptance of estoppel claims for Government funds could have pernicious effects. It ignores reality to expect that the Government will be able to "secure perfect performance from its hundreds of thousands of employees scattered throughout the continent." Hansen v. Harris, 619 F.2d 943, 954 (CA2 1980) (Friendly, J., dissenting), rev'd sub nom. Schweiker v. Hansen, 450 U.S. 785 (1981). To open the door to estoppel claims would only invite endless litigation over both real and imagined claims of misinformation by disgruntled citizens, imposing an unpredictable drain on the public fisc. Even if most claims were rejected in the end, the burden of defending such estoppel claims would itself be substantial.

Also questionable is the suggestion that if the Government is not bound by its agents' statements, then citizens will not trust them, and will instead seek private advice from lawyers, accountants, and others, creating wasteful expenses. Although mistakes occur, we may assume with confidence that Government agents attempt conscientious performance of their duties, and in most cases provide free and valuable information to those who seek advice about Government programs. A rule of estoppel might create not more reliable advice, but less advice. See Hansen, supra, at 788-789, and n.5. The natural consequence of a rule that made the Government liable for the statements of its agents would be a decision to cut back and impose strict controls upon Government provision of information in order to limit liability. Not only would valuable informational programs be lost to the public, but the greatest impact of this loss would fall on those of limited means, who can least afford the alternative of private advice. . . .

Whether there are any extreme circumstances that might support estoppel in a case not involving payment from the Treasury is a matter we need not address. As for monetary claims, it is enough to say that this Court has never upheld an assertion of estoppel against the Government by a claimant seeking public funds. In this context there can be no estoppel, for courts cannot estop the Constitution. The judgment of the Court of Appeals is reversed.

Justice STEVENS, concurring in the judgment:
Although I join the Court's judgment, I cannot accept its reasoning. The Appropriations Clause of the Constitution has nothing to do with this case. Payments of pension benefits to retired and disabled federal servants are made "in Consequence of Appropriations made by Law" even if in particular cases they are the product of a mistaken interpretation of a statute or regulation. The Constitution contemplates appropriations that cover programs — not individual appropriations for individual payments. The Court's creative reliance on constitutional text is nothing but a red herring.

The dispute in this case is not about whether an appropriation has been made; it is instead about what rules govern administration of an appropriation that has been made. Once the issue is appropriately framed, it quickly becomes obvious that the Court's resolution of it is untenable. Three hypothetical changes in the facts of this case will illustrate the error in the Court's approach. Assume, first, that the forfeiture involved a permanent and total loss of pension benefits rather than a 6-month hiatus. Suppose also that respondent was a disabled serviceman, totally incapable of productive work, who was promised that his benefits would be unaffected if he enlisted in the reserve forces to show his continuing commitment to his country. Finally, assume that respondent was activated briefly for the sole purpose of enhancing his earnings, thereby depriving him of his pension permanently. Would the Court apply the harsh rule against estoppel that it announces today? I think not. Unless it found in the statute some unambiguous abrogation of estoppel principles, the Court would apply them to nullify the forfeiture. In doing so, the Court would construe the statute in a way consistent with congressional intent, and would ensure that the Executive administered the funds appropriated in a manner consistent with the terms of the appropriation.

This case, however, does not involve such extreme facts. Respondent's loss of benefits was serious but temporary, and, even if we assume that respondent was not adequately compensated for the stress of his increased workload, his additional earnings certainly mitigated the shortfall of benefits. I agree with Justice Marshall that there are strong equities favoring respondent's position, but I am persuaded that unless the 5-to-4 decision in Federal Crop Ins. Corp. v. Merrill, 322 U.S. 380 (1947), is repudiated by Congress or this Court, this kind of maladministration must be tolerated. . . .

[The dissenting Justices agreeing with Justice STEVENS about the Appropriations Clause, also concluded that the facts merited estoppel.]

Notes, Questions, Problems

1. Imagine that government postal employees assure a jeweler that the jewels in his package are "semiprecious" and he therefore can purchase $25,000 worth of postal insurance. They make this assurance after consulting postal manuals with photographs showing identical jewels categorized as "semiprecious." The jeweler buys insurance, ships the jewels, and the jewels are lost. It then turns out that the photographs, manuals, and employees were all mistaken. The jewels, according to more authoritative postal regulations, are "precious," not "semiprecious," and the postal statutes do not authorize insurance for "precious" stones.

a. Assume this case arose prior to OPM v. Richmond. Is it the special kind of case where the government should be estopped? Would Justice Stevens find estoppel? The ordinary factors that govern estoppel against private parties include (1) actions by the defendant, (2) that lead plaintiff to rely, (3) reasonably, (4) to his detriment. What other special factors are at stake when the government is the defendant? Compare San Pedro v. United States, 79 F.3d 1065 (11th Cir. 1996) (finding estoppel in a deportation case) with Kowalczyk v. INS, 245 F.3d 1143 (10th Cir. 2001) (estoppel against the government is especially disfavored in immigration settings); see United States v. Marine State Processors, 81 F.3d 1329 (5th Cir. 1996) (refusing to find estoppel in hazardous substance case).

b. Assume the district court writes the following: "The government is estopped. The court is estopped. The court is aware of OPM v. Richmond, but that case is not to the contrary. Here, the government is simply estopped from denying that the jewels in question are semiprecious. Since Congress authorized insurance for semiprecious stones, the Appropriations Clause of the Constitution poses no problem." What should the court of appeals say about this statement?

2. The Tucker Act authorizes the claims court to award compensation where property is "taken" by the federal government in violation of the fifth amendment's due process clause. Congress has appropriated money to pay such judgments. Could Richmond have argued that to deprive him of his benefits under these circumstances amounts to a deprivation of "property without due process of law"? (We shall discuss the due process clause later in this casebook.) If he had argued this successfully, would he then have recovered?

3. How can it be that the government is bound by its own rules, but not subject to estoppel? Is it incongruous to say that rules are binding (because they create legitimate expectations) whereas representations are not (even though they may create extremely strong expectations)? Consider the view that agencies are bound by their own rules because those rules are the governing law, and not bound by representations because and to the extent that those representations do not represent and indeed violate the governing law.

4. What are the differences between cases holding the government estopped and those that we discussed in the preceding section holding that agencies may not, through adjudication, engage in certain retroactive changes in law or policy?

5. Should Congress enact a statute saying that government will be estopped when the ordinary requirements for estoppel are met? Might not such a statute lead to an optimal level of advice-giving, including more accurate advice? How forceful is it to say that estopping the government would diminish the amount of total advice? Isn't there a sufficient public demand for advice to overcome this concern? What is wrong with the view that the principal effect of an estoppel rule would be to get agency officials to speak accurately about the law?

6. After *Schweicker* and *Richmond*, there appears to be precious little space for successful estoppel claims. However, the Supreme Court and lower courts have found room to maneuver, partly by relying on other doctrines in cases that resemble estoppel claims, and partly by finding the facts of a case so exceptional that estoppel is warranted. The most famous case in the first category is undoubtedly United States v. Winstar, 518 U.S. 839 (1996), which grew out of the attempt to stave off disaster in the savings and loan industry. During the 1980s, many savings and loans became insolvent, and the Federal Savings and Loan Insurance Corporation encouraged healthy savings and loans to acquire the insolvent ones. Because FSLIC did not have enough cash to pour into the transactions to make them rational for the acquiring firms, FSLIC had to offer some other inducement. (Note that without some inducement it would be financial madness to take over a savings and loan with liabilities greatly in excess of assets.) To persuade healthy savings and loans to acquire the insolvent ones, FSLIC and the healthy savings and loans reached understandings, memorialized in letters, according to which the savings and loans would be allowed to use accounting principles that differed greatly from generally accepted accounting principles. In particular, the savings and loans were allowed to put "goodwill" assets onto the books where no goodwill really existed, effectively lowering the capital reserve requirement for the new savings and loan. This was a very risky strategy, and raised the risk of much larger defaults. In 1989, Congress passed the Financial Institutions Reform, Recovery, and Enforcement Act, which outlawed the accounting practices to which FSLIC and the savings and loans had agreed. When FSLIC enforced FIRREA, many savings and loans became insolvent, and some of them sued. The Supreme Court held that the letters of understanding between FSLIC and the savings

and loans constituted contracts, and that the change in regulatory treatment constituted a breach, necessitating damages. Of course, because the regulatory treatment was promised in letters of agreement that asked for consideration, *Winstar* is fundamentally different from the typical regulatory case involving orders or rules.

Another case finding a court using another legal doctrine to decide an estoppel case is Socop-Gonzales v. INS, 272 F.3d 1176 (9th Cir. 2001) (en banc). Although the plaintiff's reasonable reliance on an INS officer's mistaken advice could not form the basis of a successful estoppel claim, the court found that the INS had to allow equitable tolling of a filing period. Compare Jordan Hospital v. Shalala, 276 F.3d 72 (1st Cir. 2002) (equitable tolling not available where the statute states the deadline in an "unusually emphatic" way and tolling would create administrative problems).

If the facts of a particular case are sufficiently appealing, a court may still find that equitable estoppel applies. In Bailey v. West, 160 F.3d 1360 (Fed. Cir. 1998) (en banc) a veteran filed a claim for benefits with the Veterans Administration, claiming that his lung condition was connected to his service in the armed forces. The VA rejected his claim, the Board of Veterans Appeals upheld the denial, and the VA sent Bailey a notice setting out his rights to appeal to the Court of Veterans Appeals within 120 days of the BVA's decision. Bailey went to the local VA office and, with the assistance of a Veterans Benefits Counselor, filled out a notice of appeal within the 120-day period. The Benefits Counselor told Bailey that she would mail it for him, but then mistakenly attached it to his file instead, so the notice was not sent within the 120-day period. In addition, giving the written notice to the VA did *not* count as notice of appeal to the Court of Veterans Appeals. When Bailey attempted to press his appeal with Court of Veterans Appeals, the VA objected, saying the appeal was barred. The Federal Circuit set out the issues: "[Precedent] leaves us with two remaining questions: would equitable tolling be available between private litigants in Bailey's situation, and did Congress provide otherwise[?] . . . Is there good reason to believe that Congress did not want the equitable tolling doctrine to apply in a suit against the United States?" The Federal Circuit, sitting en banc, decided that this fact pattern, including a "paternalistic relationship" between veterans and the VA, would provide for equitable tolling of the filing deadline in a suit between private parties. Because there was insufficient evidence that Congress wanted equitable tolling to be unavailable in veterans appeals, the six-judge majority of the court applied equitable tolling. A four-judge dissent argued that the timing of appeals was jurisdictional and hence could not be altered through equitable doctrines.

Of course, no list of egregious governmental conduct would be complete without a case from the Internal Revenue Service. In Fredericks v. Commissioner of Internal Revenue, 126 F.3d 433 (3rd Cir. 1997) the IRS assessed additional tax and penalties on the taxpayer regarding a 1977 tax shelter. During the investigation, the IRS persuaded the taxpayer to sign several extensions of the statute of limitations. One of these, Form 872-A, was to remain in effect until revoked.

> [T]he IRS committed the following misconduct in connection with the forms [the taxpayer] and the IRS executed to extend the statute of limitations. First, the IRS misrepresented in 1981 that it never received a Form 872-A (Special Consent to Extend the Time to Assess Taxes), which Fredericks had signed to authorize an indefinite extension of the statute of limitations. Second, the IRS confirmed this misrepresentation in 1981, 1982 and 1983, by soliciting and executing three separate Forms 872, which extend the statute of limitations for one year. Third, the IRS discovered that it possessed the Form 872-A sometime before June 30, 1984, the date the last

one-year extension expired, decided to rely on that form in continuing its investigation of Fredericks' tax return and failed to notify the taxpayer of its changed course of action. Fourth, the IRS used the Form 872-A to assess a deficiency in 1992, 11 years after informing the taxpayer that the Form 872-A did not exist, and eight years after the final one-year extension expired. Finally, the IRS imposed interest penalties totaling over five times the amount of the tax and covering the entire duration of its protracted investigation of the tax shelter. . . .

We conclude that this taxpayer has met his burden of proving the traditional elements of equitable estoppel, and has mounted the high hurdle of establishing other special factors applicable to estoppel claims against the government.

Of course, in most circumstances the courts will still refuse to find equitable estoppel; the recent trend has been emphatically against estoppel. See, for example, Schism v. United States, 316 F.3d 1259 (Fed. Cir. 2002) (en banc) (government not estopped to honor promises made by military recruiters about health care benefits for those who serve at least 20 years); Brice v. Secretary of Health and Human Services, 240 F.3d 1367 (Fed. Cir. 2001) (refusing to toll a deadline for filing claims under the National Childhood Vaccine Injury Act of 1986); Smith v. VA, 13 Vet. App. 525 (Ct. Vet. Cl. 2000) (refusing to equitably toll a deadline for a veteran's claim); Bonneville Associates v. Barram, 165 F.3d 1360 (Fed. Cir. 1999) (refusing to equitably toll an appeal of a contract officer's finding of liability to the government arising out of government contract); Former Employees of Siemens Information Communication Networks v. Secretary of Department of Labor, 120 F. Supp. 2d 1107 (2000) (refusing to equitably toll a claim by workers for assistance under the Trade Act of 1974); and Brookville Mining Equipment v. Selective Insurance Co. of America, 74 F. Supp. 2d 477 (W.D. Pa. 1999) (refusing to apply equitable estoppel to a flood insurance contract where plaintiff missed a 60-day deadline for proving loss).

7. John Best, an Irish citizen, worked for many years as a civilian employee of the Department of the Air Force. Because he was an alien, a regulation of the air force placed him in the "excepted," not the "competitive," service. In 1984 he became a citizen. The air force employment officer told him he was eligible to be in the "competitive" service and that the air force would transfer him. Best checked with the personnel office three times between 1984 and 1986. On each occasion, the officer in charge looked at the computer files and told him he had been placed in the competitive service. In 1989 the air force dismissed employees as part of a "reduction in force." Its rules require dismissal of "excepted" employees first. It told Best that he was dismissed, for the air force, in fact, had never transferred him to the competitive service. It pointed to a regulation that said aliens who became citizens had to take an examination to become members of the "competitive" service. The air force conceded that this regulation was part of a set of regulations disqualifying aliens from civil service eligibility, which regulations the Supreme Court had held unconstitutional. Best says the government is estopped from denying that he is a member of the competitive service.

What result?

2. Res Judicata

Consider the following basic principles as put by the American Law Institute, Restatement of Judgments.

1. Personal Judgments

Where a reasonable opportunity has been afforded to the parties to litigate a claim before a court which has jurisdiction over the parties and the cause of action, and the court has finally decided the controversy, the interests of the State and of the parties require that the validity of the claim and any issue actually litigated in the action shall not be litigated again by them.

27. Issue Preclusion — General Rule

When an issue of fact or law is actually litigated and determined by a valid and final judgment, and the determination is essential to the judgment, the determination is conclusive in a subsequent action between the parties, whether on the same or a different claim.

28. Exceptions to the General Rule of Issue Preclusion

[Relitigation is not precluded in several circumstances including the following:]

(2) The issue is one of law and (a) the two actions involve claims that are substantially unrelated, or (b) a new determination is warranted in order to take account of an intervening change in the applicable legal context or otherwise to avoid inequitable administration of the laws; or . . .

(5) There is a clear and convincing need for a new determination of the issue (a) because of the potential adverse impact of the determination on the public interest or the interests of persons not themselves parties in the initial action. . . .

83. Adjudicative Determination by Administrative Tribunal

[A valid] and final adjudicative determination by an administrative tribunal has the same effects under the rules of res judicata, subject to the same exceptions and qualifications, as a judgment of a court [but only if] the proceeding resulting in the determination entailed the essential elements of adjudication [and not] if the scheme of remedies permits assertion of the second claim notwithstanding the adjudication of the first claim [and also not] if according preclusive effect to determination of the issue would be incompatible with a legislative policy that:

(a) The determination of the tribunal adjudicating the issue is not to be accorded conclusive effect in subsequent proceedings; or

(b) The tribunal in which the issue subsequently arises be free to make an independent determination of the issue in question.

Note how the courts have decided the following cases:

(a) A Maryland Board of County Commissioners, sitting as the zoning board, changed the zoning status of a 47-acre parcel of land in 1964 from "restricted to detached one family houses" to "suitable for garden apartments." The owners of the land had twice previously sought changes in the zoning and after having been turned down a second time by the board in 1961 (on a proposal similar to this one) had unsuccessfully appealed to the courts.

Those protesting the latest decision appealed to the courts, which overturned the board's decision on grounds of res judicata. The facts had not changed sufficiently since the last application to warrant rezoning, reasoned the court; hence the board's decision is arbitrary and capricious. The board acts as an adjudicatory agency exercising power delegated by the legislature and therefore cannot act arbitrarily.

A dissent argued that res judicata did not apply because the rezoning action was "legislative" and not "judicial." It noted that even without res judicata, Maryland's "mistake/change" rule (which allowed piecemeal zoning changes only on strong evidence for an original mistake or substantial change in conditions) might apply, but either these were sufficient changes or the rule was too strict for such legislative decision-making. Woodlawn Area Citizen Assn. v. Board of County Commrs., 241 Md. 187, 216 A.2d 149 (1966).

(b) In 1929 the Federal Trade Commission (FTC) found Raladam guilty of an unfair trade practice in misrepresenting the weight-reducing properties of his product "Mermola." The Supreme Court set aside the finding on the ground that the evidence did not show that Raladam's competitors were injured (a statutory prerequisite at that time). The FTC began the case again, introduced evidence of harm to competitors, found Raladam guilty, and rejected a claim of res judicata. The Supreme Court affirmed. FTC v. Raladam Co., 316 U.S. 149 (1942).

(c) An administrative hearing was held to determine whether to dismiss a policeman for accepting money from a gambler. At a first hearing, the gambler would not testify, and the commissioner held that the charges were unproved. Then, the gambler decided to testify, and a new hearing was held. The courts held that res judicata did not bar the new hearing. Evans v. Monaghan, 306 N.Y. 312, 118 N.E.2d 452 (1954).

(d) Plaintiff owned a chain of retail liquor stores. He also had a wholesaler's license, and he sold considerable liquor at wholesale to his own retail stores. A statute said that a wholesale license should be revoked unless the wholesaler carried on a bona fide wholesale business and "sale by a wholesale licensee to himself as a retail licensee" is not bona fide.

In the 1950s the licensing board decided not to revoke plaintiff's license because plaintiff bought large quantities of liquor, had made substantial investment, and had relied on a prior administrative construction suggesting this was adequate to keep the license. The board warned, however, that it might change its view if there were a future showing that the holding of the license presents "a situation which is contrary to the public welfare and morals and detrimental to the public interest."

In the early 1960s the board revoked plaintiff's wholesale license because plaintiff sold only to himself. The court rejected plaintiff's claim of res judicata. It reasoned that only collateral estoppel might apply and it did not because "factors, i.e., public interest and effect upon third parties, strongly indicate that the prior determination of the board should not preclude" reexamination of the statute and applying the correct interpretation to plaintiff. Louis Stores, Inc. v. Department of Alcoholic Beverage Controls, 22 Cal. Rptr. 14, 371 P.2d 758 (1962).

(e) The Patent Office rejected an application by plaintiff on the ground of "obviousness." The plaintiff applied again and submitted new evidence. The new evidence overcame the objection but the Patent Office still denied on grounds of res judicata. The courts overturned the Patent Office decision. Application of Herr, 377 F.2d 610 (C.C.P.A. 1967).

(f) In proceedings to certify a collective bargaining unit, the National Labor Relations Board (NLRB) ruled that certain employees were within the bargaining unit. In subsequent unfair labor practice proceedings involving the same unit, the board invoked res judicata in refusing to reconsider the appropriateness of classifying them as members of the unit. Held, the board must reconsider the question; the evidentiary record in the first proceeding was defective (in part due to the employer's counsel), while that in the second proceeding was more complete. Burns Electronic Security Servs. v. NLRB, 624 F.2d 403

(2d Cir. 1980). But see Mosher Steel Co. v. NLRB, 568 F.2d 436 (5th Cir. 1978) (board may not, at urging of union, reopen, in second related proceeding, finding of employee misconduct in first proceeding in which union had full opportunity to litigate issue).

(g) In Labelle Processing Co. v. Swarrow, 72 F.3d 308 (3d Cir. 1995), plaintiff first applied for benefits under the Black Lung Benefits Act and was denied. Some time later, plaintiff submitted a new claim and submitted new medical evidence. The ALJ awarded disability benefits to the plaintiff because there was a material change in conditions. The employer appealed, claiming that the award to plaintiff violated principles of res judicata. The Third Circuit rejected the employer's attack, pointing out that pneumoconiosis is a progressive disease, so the evidence naturally changes as time passes.

Which of the above seven cases do you believe were correctly decided? Why? For an extraordinary underlying set of facts, see Olson v. Morris, 188 F.3d 1083 (D.C. Cir. 1999), involving a challenge to a decision of the Arizona Board of Psychologist Examiners to revoke Olson's license to practice psychology. Two child protective services had referred a child to Olson for psychological evaluation and counseling. Olson, who was also a minister, performed an exercism on the child, who had been a victim of satanic ritual abuse. The Board of Examiners held that this was unprofessional conduct and revoked Olson's license. Instead of appealing to the Arizona state courts, as was his right, Olson brought suit in federal District Court, suing everyone in sight. The District Court held, and the D.C. Circuit affirmed, that Olson's claims were barred by res judicata.

United States v. Mendoza
464 U.S. 154 (1984)

Justice REHNQUIST delivered the opinion for a unanimous Court.

[Mendoza, a Filipino national, challenged the government's asserted failure to adequately implement a law facilitating nationalization of aliens who had served in the United States armed forces in World War II. In a previous case, 68 Filipinos had prevailed on the same claims in a district court decision that the government ultimately decided not to appeal.] Under the judicially developed doctrine of collateral estoppel, once a court has decided an issue of fact or law necessary to its judgment, that decision is conclusive in a subsequent suit based on a different cause of action involving a party to the prior litigation. . . . Collateral estoppel [goes] beyond its common-law limits . . . by abandoning the requirement of mutuality of parties, Blonder-Tongue Laboratories, Inc. v. University of Illinois Foundation, 402 U.S. 313 (1971), and by conditionally approving the "offensive" use of collateral estoppel by a nonparty to a prior lawsuit. Parklane Hosiery Co., Inc. v. Shore, 439 U.S. 322 (1979).

In Standefer v. United States, 447 U.S. 10, 24 (1980), however, we emphasized the fact that *Blonder-Tongue* and *Parklane Hosiery* involved disputes over private rights between private litigants. . . .

We have long recognized that "the Government is not in a position identical to that of a private litigant, . . . both because of the geographic breadth of Government litigation and also, most importantly, because of the nature of the issues the Government litigates. It is not open to serious dispute that the Government is a party to a far greater number of cases on a nationwide basis than even the most litigious private entity; in 1982, the United States was a party to more than 75,000 of 206,193 filings in the United States District Courts. . . .

A rule allowing nonmutual collateral estoppel against the government in such cases would substantially thwart the development of important questions of law by freezing the first final decision rendered on a particular legal issue. Allowing only one final adjudication would deprive this Court of the benefit it receives from permitting several courts of appeals to explore a difficult question before this Court grants certiorari. . . .

The Solicitor General's policy for determining when to appeal an adverse decision would also require substantial revision. The Court of Appeals faulted the Government in this case for failing to appeal a decision that it now contends is erroneous. . . . But the Government's litigation conduct in a case is apt to differ from that of a private litigant. Unlike a private litigant who generally does not forgo an appeal if he believes that he can prevail, the Solicitor General considers a variety of factors, such as the limited resources of the Government and the crowded dockets of the courts, before authorizing an appeal. . . . The application of nonmutual estoppel against the Government would force the Solicitor General to abandon those prudential concerns and to appeal every adverse decision in order to avoid foreclosing further review.

In addition . . . the panoply of important public issues raised in governmental litigation may quite properly lead successive administrations of the Executive Branch to take differing positions with respect to the resolution of a particular issue. . . .

For example, in recommending to the Solicitor General in 1977 that the Government's appeal in *68 Filipinos* be withdrawn, newly appointed INS Commissioner Castillo commented that such a course "would be in keeping with the policy of the [new] Administration," described as "a course of compassion and amnesty." . . . But for the very reason that such policy choices are made by one administration, and often reevaluated by another administration, courts should be careful when they seek to apply expanding rules of collateral estoppel to Government litigation. The Government of course may not now undo the consequences of its decision not to appeal the District Court judgment in the *68 Filipinos* case; it is bound by that judgment under the principles of res judicata. But we now hold that it is not further bound in a case involving a litigant who was not a party to the earlier litigation.

Problems

1. The Van Kirkland Underwriting Company agreed to underwrite a security issued by the Edsel Vacuum Cleaner Co. The underwriting agreement between Van Kirkland and Edsel contained a clause releasing Van Kirkland from its obligation if at the time scheduled for issuance of the security any lawsuit was pending challenging the issue's legality. Such a lawsuit was filed, and Van Kirkland refused to proceed. Believing that Van Kirkland may have procured the suit to be instituted to avoid its obligations, the SEC began an investigation and asked certain attorneys for Van Kirkland to appear and testify. The attorneys refused, on the basis of the lawyer-client privilege, and the SEC brought an action in a federal district court to compel their appearance. After considering the SEC's investigative record, the court dismissed the complaint, holding that no prima facie showing of fraud had been made out that would justify overriding the attorney-client privilege. Several months later, the SEC instituted an administrative proceeding to consider whether Van Kirkland's broker-dealer registration should be suspended or revoked, and whether the company should be expelled or suspended from membership in the National Association of Securities Dealers because of alleged fraud in connection with the Edsel matter. Van Kirkland, alleging that the SEC had no evidence that was not presented to

the court in the prior action, sued in federal court to enjoin the commission from reexamining the question of fraud.

On the commission's motion to dismiss for failure to state a claim, what result?

2. In Parklane Hosiery Co. v. Shore, 439 U.S. 322 (1979), the Court held that the seventh amendment right to jury trial was not violated when (1) the SEC sued a corporation and its controlling shareholders, directors, and officers in federal district court for violation of the securities laws, and obtained an injunction following a nonjury trial; and (2) other shareholders of the corporation, who did not participate in the SEC proceeding, brought suit against the same defendants for damages, and successfully invoked the SEC's judgment "offensively" as collateral estoppel on the question of violation.

Suppose that the first proceeding had been an administrative proceeding before the SEC rather than a court suit. Would the seventh amendment ruling have been the same? Cf. Bowen v. United States, 570 F.2d 1311 (7th Cir. 1978). See Note, The Collateral Estoppel Effect of Administrative Agency Actions in Federal Civil Litigation, 46 Geo. Wash. L. Rev. 65 (1977).

3. The *Mendoza* case obviously bears on a general problem sometimes described as one of "nonacquiescence." That problem arises when the government refuses to acquiesce in a court's decision, by complying in the particular case, but refusing to follow the decision in other cases not before the court. Under President Reagan, for example, the executive branch sometimes complied with a court of appeals ruling by awarding disability benefits in the particular case before the court, but at the same time refused to follow the rule announced by the court of appeals in other, identical cases. Is nonacquiescence an attack on Marbury v. Madison, or is it merely a sensible recognition that the government cannot appeal every adverse decision and is allowed to behave strategically in deciding what to do before a Supreme Court appeal, and when to make such an appeal? The answer might be thought to depend on why the government refuses to "acquiesce." See Estreicher & Revesz, Nonacquiescence by Federal Agencies, 98 Yale L.J. 679 (1989). Lower courts, however, have embraced the nonacquiescence principle of *Mendoza*, typically saying that a nonacquiescence rule is necessary to generate circuit disagreements that will eventually produce a clarifying resolution from the Supreme Court. See Holland v. National Mining Ass'n, 309 F.3d 808 (D.C. Cir. 2002); Virginia Society for Human Life v. FEC, 263 F.3d 379 (4th Cir. 2001).

Might the ability of the federal government to appeal only the cases it wants, and to refuse to acquiesce in the others, have systematic effects on the development of the law? Consider the following argument: When the government gets an adverse decision from one of the courts of appeal, its decision about whether to appeal to the Supreme Court is affected by the ability to nonacquiesce. If the federal government does not appeal, it must comply with that holding but may refuse to comply with the rule in other cases. If the government appeals to the Supreme Court and wins, it need not comply in the instant case, and all the other cases where it was going to refuse to acquiesce if it had not appealed. But if the government loses its appeal at the Supreme Court, it must comply everywhere, for the Court will have authoritatively declared "the law of the land." Thus, there are large risks to the government from appealing losses in the courts of appeals. The only time it will make sense for the federal government to appeal is when it is quite certain of victory. Private litigants, in contrast, will not be subject to the same pressures because of nonacquiescence. Thus, the federal government should win a higher percentage of the cases decided by the Supreme Court than it would otherwise win, and the path of the law may be biased, thereby, in favor of the federal government. For evidence tending to confirm this hypothesis, see Cohen & Spitzer, The Government Litigant Advantage: Implications for the Law, 28 Fla. St. U.L. Rev. 391 (2000).

E. Requiring Consistency to Safeguard Expectations — Problems of Retroactivity

1. Adjudication

In this section we shall explore a "procedural principle," the principle forbidding unexplained inconsistency. We shall first consider the issue in the setting of adjudication and then turn to rulemaking.

a. Inconsistent Decisions

Suppose an agency has enunciated in a case, or developed through precedent, a particular policy. The agency surely can change that policy later on. Common law courts change policies through the process of distinguishing earlier decisions. Agencies should have at least as much leeway to do the same. Nonetheless, the agency must explain its change. Why? Consider this judicial statement of the reasons:

> The law that governs an agency's significant departure from its own prior precedent is clear. The agency cannot do so without explicitly recognizing that it is doing so and explaining why. As Professor Davis has pointed out, "[t]he dominant law clearly is that an agency must either follow its own precedents or explain why it departs from them. "2 K. Davis, Administrative Law Treatise Sec. 8:9 at 198 (1979). The agency has a duty to explain its departure from prior norms. The agency may flatly repudiate those norms, deciding, for example, that changed circumstances mean that they are no longer required in order to effectuate congressional policy. Or it may narrow the zone in which some rule will be applied, because it appears that a more discriminating invocation of the rule will best serve congressional policy. Or it may find that, although the rule in general serves useful purposes, peculiarities of the case before it suggest that the rule not be applied in that case. *Whatever the ground for departure from prior norms, however, it must be clearly set forth so that the reviewing court may understand the basis of the agency's action and so may judge the consistency of that action with the agency's mandate. . . .*
>
> [If] the agency distinguishes earlier cases, [it must] assert [] distinctions that, when fairly and sympathetically read in the context of the entire opinion of the agency, reveal the policies it is pursuing. Atchison, Topeka & Santa Fe Railway Co. v. Wichita Board of Trade, 412 U.S. 800, 808-809. . . .
>
> It is, of course, true that the Board is free to adopt new rules or decisions and that the new rules of law can be given retroactive application. Nevertheless the Board may not depart sub silentio, from its usual rules of decision to reach a different, unexplained result in a single case. [T]here may not be a rule for Monday, another for Tuesday, a rule for general application, but denied outright in a specific case. [A]n inadequately explained departure solely for purposes of a particular case, or the creation of conflicting lines of precedent governing the identical situation, is not be tolerated.

NLRB v. International Union of Operating Engineers, Local 925, 460 F.2d 589, 604 (5th Cir. 1972) (citations omitted). See also WLSO T.V. v. FCC. 932 F.2d 993, 998 (D.C. Cir. 1991) (vacating and remanding FCC decision denying station's request to acquire another station and operate it as a "satellite" because "[t]he Commission failed to explain or even recognize its departure from agency precedent").

Brennan v. Gilles & Cotting, Inc.

504 F.2d 1255 (4th Cir. 1974)

[This case arose from the administrative imposition of a fine on a general contractor where a subcontractor on the job had used unsafe equipment in violation of Occupational Safety and Health Administration (OSHA) regulations. The OSHA Review Commission (an agency in the Labor Department) overturned the fine on the ground that no employees of the general contractor had been shown to be *present* at the part of the job site where the unsafe equipment was used. The commission failed to mention or discuss prior decisions holding that potential access by general contractor employees to the unsafe equipment was sufficient to impose liability. On appeal the court reversed and remanded on the ground that the commission decision was "an unexplained departure from the rule of decision" followed in other decisions by the same agency. It added:]

[W]hile administrative agencies change previously announced policies, . . . and can fashion exceptions and qualifications, they must explain departures from agency policies or rules apparently dispositive of a case. . . .

Notes and Questions

1. The requirements of consistency imposed in *Gilles & Cotting* reflect the judicial insistence that agencies explain decisional inconsistencies. But these decisions involve cases where the agency failed to make any explanation at all. Suppose the agency does offer some explanation, for example, that on reconsideration it has concluded that the factors underlying the previous decision were erroneously weighed and that the prior decision should therefore be overruled?

2. What if there are conflicting agency precedents in a given area? May the agency, without further explanation, simply follow the most recent precedent? See NLRB v. Sunnyland Packing Co., 557 F.2d 1157 (5th Cir. 1977) (upholding such a practice). If not, doesn't the nominally "procedural" requirement of "consistency" impose substantive limits on the agency's discretion?

3. Should an agency be permitted to defend inconsistencies of the sort revealed in *Gilles & Cotting* on the ground that there had been intervening changes in the agency's membership? Changes in judicial doctrines are often explained by changes in a court's membership. May such changes be justified by the new membership?

b. Retroactivity

Agency evolution of policy through case-by-case adjudication creates a danger that the governing legal rules will be altered after the relevant events occurred, creating potentially harsh and inequitable defeat of expectations generated by the preexisting law.

However, the automatic assumption that every instance of change in legal rules through adjudication is unfairly "retroactive" is not warranted. The change may have been foreseeable; the magnitude of the reliance interest may be negligible; and so forth. One must in each case consider the nature, extent, and legitimacy of the expectation interests claimed to have been defeated by an adjudicatory change in the law. Consider, for example, the *Chenery* litigation. Did the SEC's decisions represent harsh "retroactive" lawmaking, as claimed by the Chenerys and Justice Jackson?

When case-by-case evolution of policy does work unforeseen changes in the law that defeat substantial and legitimate expectation interests, should the courts prohibit agencies from enforcing such changes? Where would reviewing courts derive the power to preclude "retroactive" agency lawmaking in adjudication? (Courts themselves, of course, have long been engaged in "retroactive" adjudicatory lawmaking.)

Even if courts do have authority to preclude agencies from changing the law through adjudication when important expectation interests would be defeated, on what occasions should such authority be exercised? What about the need for flexibility and change in agency policies?

Should courts attempt to evaluate and balance the justifications for an adjudicatory policy change against the harm to expectation interests that it would cause? *Chenery II* suggests that such a balancing approach is appropriate. But how well equipped is the court to undertake such a task? How does it measure the justifications for policy change? The extent of harm to expectations? Doesn't "balancing" involve the sort of discretionary weighing of relevant statutory factors that is normally done by the agency? Such balancing must also include considerations of administrative procedure and management. If agencies are barred from using adjudication to change policy, they will have to resort to rulemaking or attempt some form of prospective overruling.

In some cases, the courts have invalidated the practice of "retroactive" adjudication (thereby requiring an agency to use rulemaking or some other "prospective" method to change policy). In other cases, they have sustained it. Consider, in addition to *Chenery II*, the following decisions. Do they show that courts are engaged in an essentially subjective balancing process, or do consistent principles emerge? Consider in particular whether:

1. (a) the challenged agency decision was a case of first impression or a clarification of an issue where the prior law was unclear, or (b) the decision overrules a prior and different agency position (even here, one might ask whether the overruling has been prefigured in intervening decisions);

2. the change is one in the substantive standard of conduct required of those regulated or is in the availability or severity of remedies for substantive violations;

3. the relief afforded is prospective or consists of damages or a penalty imposed by reason of past conduct.

Following your review of the cases, test your views through the problems that follow them. (Note that the NLRB has statutory authority to make law by issuing regulations as well as by adjudicating particular cases.) The Supreme Court has not spoken to the issue since *Chenery*, and these relatively old cases continue to capture the current learning.

NLRB v. GUY F. ATKINSON CO., 195 F.2d 141 (9th Cir. 1952). This case involved an action brought by the NLRB to enforce an order declaring the respondent company guilty of an unfair labor practice for discharging one of its employees, Herves, for not paying union dues. The lawfulness of his discharge therefore hinged on the validity of a closed shop agreement between the Atkinson Co. and the AFL Building Trades

Department. The board held that the agreement was invalid, relying on two changes in policy adopted in board decisions handed down after Herves's discharge. First, the board had held that a union chosen by a majority of employees and recognized by the employer at a time when employment was small could not continue as the exclusive bargaining representative when employment had greatly expanded (in the absence of a new election or evidence of support by a majority of the new workforce). This ruling was applied to Atkinson and the AFL, Atkinson's workforce having greatly expanded since its initial recognition of the AFL. Second, at the time of the Atkinson-AFL agreement and Herves's discharge, the NLRB was following a decisional policy of not exercising jurisdiction over the building and construction trades. This policy was reversed in subsequent decisions, and the board applied the new policy in the instant case. The court set aside the board's order, requiring Herves's reinstatement with back pay.

"We think it apparent that the practical operation of the Board's change of policy, when incorporated in the order now before us, is to work hardship upon respondent altogether out of proportion to the public ends to be accomplished. The inequity of such an impact of retroactive policy making upon a respondent innocent of any conscious violation of the [Wagner] act, and who was unable to know, when it acted, that it was guilty of any conduct of which the Board would take cognizance, is manifest. It is the sort of thing our system of law abhors." 195 F.2d at 149.

NLRB v. LOCAL 176, UNITED BROTHERHOOD OF CARPENTERS, 276 F.2d 583 (1st Cir. 1960). The court sustained a board adjudicatory change of policy that outlawed previously permitted union hiring hall arrangements tending to favor union members, but refused to enforce an order, based on the changed policy, against the union requiring it to refund dues paid by members. The court noted that the union's conduct "was recognized as unlawful only after it had occurred," and that "a disgorgement order would seem to be an ex post facto penalty." 276 F.2d at 586.

NLRB v. E & B BREWING CO., 276 F.2d 594 (6th Cir. 1960), *cert. denied*, 366 U.S. 908 (1961). The NLRB ordered reinstated, with back pay, one of E & B's employees who had been terminated, at the insistence of the union, on the grounds that he had been hired in violation of the hiring hall provisions of the union's labor contract with E & B. The NLRB's disapproval of such hiring hall provisions as per se unfair labor practices overruled a line of earlier board decisions, which tolerated them. Held, the NLRB's new policy was impermissibly retroactive in that it "work[ed] hardship . . . altogether out of proportion to the public ends to be accomplished." 276 F.2d at 600, citing NLRB v. Guy F. Atkinson Co., 195 F.2d 141, 149 (9th Cir. 1952).

LEEDOM v. IBEW, 278 F.2d 237 (D.C. Cir. 1960). In a 1953 decision, the NLRB adopted a rule that "during the life of any bargaining agreement with a term up to five years, no representation proceedings could be instituted by a labor organization not a party to that contract, provided a substantial part of the industry involved was covered by contracts of a similar term." In a 1958 case, the board shortened its "contract bar" rule to two years and required a representation election at the behest of a competing union even though a three-year-contract between the existing union and the employer had ten months to run. The board's action was sustained.

"The Board does not deny that the [respondent] union may have relied upon the [original bar rule then in effect] when negotiating the contract. Nor does it gainsay that retroactive application of the new bar may work a hardship upon the Union. Rather it points out that periodic adjustments in the contract bar rules are necessary to [achieve statutory objectives]. It further contends that immediate application of its revised rule was necessary to prevent 'an administrative monstrosity.' . . . In weighing these opposing claims, we think the balance falls in favor of the Board." 278 F.2d at 241-242.

NLRB v. APW PRODUCTS, 316 F.2d 899 (2d Cir. 1963). The board in a prior adjudication had adopted a "tolling rule." Under this rule, if a trial examiner refused to reinstate an employee who had brought charges of discrimination against his or her employer, and if the board reversed the trial examiner, the employee would not be entitled to back pay for the period between the trial examiner's decision and the board's decision. In this case, the board, reversing its hearing examiner, ordered reinstatement and also revoked its tolling rule, awarding back pay for the entire period since discharge.

The NLRB's action was upheld by the court, although the court noted, "It is not apparent why in the ten months that the Examiner's report was before it, the Board could not have found means to inform the parties — and other interested persons — that overruling of its tolling rule was being considered and to give them some opportunity to express their views." 316 F.2d at 906.

NLRB v. MAJESTIC WEAVING CO., 355 F.2d 854 (2d Cir. 1966). Majestic negotiated with the union before a majority of its employees had affiliated themselves with it. The board found this to be "unlawful assistance to a union" in violation of 29 U.S.C. §158(a)(2), overruling a prior long-standing decision. The court ruled against the board on the grounds that Majestic was not adequately notified before the hearing of the substantive claims to be advanced by the board.

In dictum, the court (noting that the NLRB had required the employer to refund to employees dues paid to the union) added, "Although courts have not generally balked at allowing administrative agencies to apply a rule newly fashioned in an adjudicative proceeding to past conduct, a decision branding as 'unfair' conduct stamped 'fair' at the time the party acted, raises judicial hackles considerably more than a determination that merely brings within the agency's jurisdiction an employer previously left without, . . . or shortens the period in which a collective bargaining agreement may bar a new election . . . or imposes a more severe remedy for conduct already prohibited. . . ." 355 F.2d at 860.

H. & F. BINCH CO. PLANT OF NATIVE LACES & TEXTILE DIVISION OF INDIAN HEAD, INC. v. NLRB, 456 F.2d 357 (2d Cir. 1972). The court upheld a board order directing reinstatement with back pay of strikers who had unconditionally applied for reinstatement on departure of those hired during the strike to replace them. Following decisions in other circuits, it rejected the employer's argument that the NLRB's decision requiring that strikers be rehired reflected a change of policy that should not be "retroactively" enforced through a back pay award. While noting that "it is indeed surprising that the Board should so consistently have refused to utilize its rule-making powers," the court found that the decision "was hardly a great surprise" in view of other decisions eroding employers' freedom in refusing to rehire strikers. The court found it appropriate to "weigh the hardship" in imposing liability on the employer for conduct that had not previously been proscribed against denial to employees of "important rights that are now recognized to have been properly theirs," concluding that it would "await a stronger case before we refuse to give retroactive force to a Board order because it was founded on a decision enunciating a stricter rule of conduct for employers or unions than the Board had previously imposed."

Problems

1. William Budd, an employee of the Vendetta Co., was subpoenaed by the NLRB in 1969 to testify in an unfair labor practice proceeding against the company. Shortly after giving his testimony, Budd was discharged by the company without any explanation. An unfair labor practice complaint was filed against the company under §8(a)(4) of the National Labor Relations Act (NLRA), which prohibits discharge of an employee because "he has filed charges or given testimony under this Act." As authorized by statute, the board has adopted (through adjudication) jurisdictional requirements limiting the cases in which it would hear charges of unfair labor practices to those involving firms whose revenues exceed a given amount. In 1970, while this proceeding was pending, the NLRB in a series of adjudicatory decisions (which did not involve Vendetta and concerned allegations of unfair labor practices other than §8(a)(4) violations) and press releases adopted new and stricter jurisdictional requirements under which Vendetta's annual volume (from 1965 to 1970 large enough to exceed the board's dollar minimum then in effect) became too small to fall within the board's general jurisdictional boundaries. On this basis, the board decided to dismiss the proceeding against Vendetta without reaching the merits of the case. Budd seeks judicial review of the board's decision.

What result?

2. Acting pursuant to its authority under §9 of the NLRA, the NLRB directed an election among the employees of the A company. There were two competing unions, B and C, and the company manifested its support of B by threatening to close down if C won the election and by threatening to fire those employees who supported C. (These acts are plainly unfair labor practices under §8 and therefore subject to the board's remedial powers.) The election was held; B won; and C filed objections on the ground that A's preelection conduct prevented a fair election from being held. While these objections were pending, A entered into a collective bargaining agreement with B. (If the first election was subject to invalidation because of A's conduct and a second election warranted, A's entry into a contract with B would constitute unlawful assistance of a labor organization under §8.) Fourteen months after the election, the objections were still pending, and the board in another case overruled the following two long-standing policies: (1) that a union was deemed to have waived any objections to an employer's preelection conduct if it passed up an opportunity to file objections to that conduct prior to the election; and (2) that the board would not rule on the merits of any objections to an election, no matter when they were filed, if more than a year had lapsed since that election. Several additional months have passed, and a new NLRB proceeding has been instituted against A seeking to have its contract with B declared to constitute unlawful assistance under §8. The questions now before the board are whether it should apply its newly announced policies so as (1) to declare that A's recognition of B is an unfair labor practice and to enjoin continued recognition, and (2) to set aside the election and order a new one.

How should the board rule on these questions? If it does apply the new policies, what should a reviewing court do? Consider APA §706.

2. Rulemaking

Suppose that an agency adopts a new policy by promulgating a rule or regulation. May it lawfully apply that new policy to prior, unchangeable behavior? The court in Daughters of Miriam Center for the Aged v. Mathews, 590 F.2d 1250 (3d Cir. 1978), invalidated an item change in policy regarding use of accelerated depreciation by nursing homes in determining the amount of Medicare reimbursement In 1967, the Department of Health, Education, and Welfare (HEW) adopted regulations allowing nursing homes a choice between straight-line and accelerated depreciation. HEW belatedly realized that the regulation would create a loophole by allowing homes to recoup the bulk of their investment from Medicare by using accelerated depreciation in the early years of operation, and then make high profits by leaving the Medicare program and serving commercial patients during later years. In 1970, HEW modified the regulations to eliminate accelerated depreciation for new homes or new assets, and to provide for recapture by HEW of any post-1970 excess of accelerated over straight-line depreciation if a home left the Medicare program, or if its number of Medicare patients dropped by a specified percentage. In 1972, HEW's Provider Reimbursement Manual, which interprets and elaborates on Medicare regulations, was modified to provide for recapture of excess pre-1970 depreciation enjoyed by homes that leave the program or experience a drop in Medicare patients. HEW applied this new guideline to recapture excess pre-1970 depreciation from the Daughters of Miriam Center, which had experienced a substantial decline in the percentage of its patients on Medicare as a result of new HEW regulations tightening Medicare eligibility requirements. The court set aside HEW's action. The court reasoned that pre-1970 application of the recapture policy might be justified in the case of a home that voluntarily left the Medicare program, but that it could not be justified in the case of a home, like Miriam Center, that continued in the program and suffered an involuntary drop in its Medicare patient percentage because of changed HEW eligibility regulations. The court also stated:

> In a retroactivity challenge, such as the present one, a critical question is how the challenger's conduct, or the conduct of others in its class, would have differed if the rule in issue had applied from the start. In the Center's case, that question may be answered with a degree of certainty. Had the Center been apprised in 1967, when it first joined the Medicare program, that upon choosing to depreciate its capital assets on an accelerated basis it also assumed the risk that should its utilization by Medicare patients substantially decrease in the future it would be vulnerable to recapture of the excess depreciation already taken, the Center undoubtedly would have opted for the straight-line method. . . . When the "rules of the game" were suddenly modified, HEW claimed that the Center owed the Medicare program over $148,000. This severe impact upon the Center's finances, overturning its settled expectations, outweighs the negligible public interest in applying the new provision retroactively to it.

See Natural Gas Pipeline Co. of America v. FERC, 590 F.2d 664 (7th Cir. 1979), and Standard Oil Co. v. Department of Energy, 596 F.2d 1029 (Temp. Emer. Ct. App. 1978), invalidating changes in energy price regulations that were applied to conduct occurring before the changes. See also General Tel. Co. of Southwest v. United States, 449 F.2d 846 (5th Cir. 1971) (sustaining retroactive rule); National Assn. of Indep. TV Producers v. FCC, 502 F.2d 249, 255 (2d Cir. 1974).

Bowen v. Georgetown University Hospital

488 U.S. 204 (1988)

[Health and Human Services (HHS) sets limits on the amount of money Medicare will reimburse hospitals. It uses indices of average wages in calculating the limits. In 1981, it promulgated a rule saying it would not look at federally owned hospitals' wages when calculating these indices. In 1983, the D.C. Circuit invalidated the 1981 rule on procedural grounds. In 1984, HHS held new, procedurally proper rulemaking proceedings, and it reissued the 1981 rule with retroactive effect. Because Congress had changed the law in the meantime, however, the 1984 rule applied only to cost reimbursement for 1981 and 1982. Several hospitals that had benefited from the invalidation of the 1981 rule sought judicial review of the 1984 rule, claiming it was unlawfully retroactive.]

Justice KENNEDY delivered the opinion of the Court.

Under the Medicare program, health care providers are reimbursed by the Government for expenses incurred in providing medical services to Medicare beneficiaries. See Title XVIII of the Social Security Act, 79 Stat. 291, as amended, 42 U.S.C. Sec. 1395 et seq. (the Medicare Act). Congress had authorized the Secretary of Health and Human Services to promulgate regulations setting limits on the levels of Medicare costs that will be reimbursed. The question presented here is whether the Secretary may exercise this rulemaking authority to promulgate cost limits that are retroactive.

It is axiomatic that an administrative agency's power to promulgate legislative regulations is limited to the authority delegated by Congress. In determining the validity of the Secretary's retroactive cost-limit rule, the threshold question is whether the Medicare Act authorizes retroactive rulemaking.

Retroactivity is not favored in the law. Thus, congressional enactments and administrative rules will not be construed to have retroactive effect unless their language requires this result. By the same principle, a statutory grant of legislative rulemaking authority will not, as a general matter, be understood to encompass the power to promulgate the retroactive rules unless that power is conveyed by Congress in express terms.

The Secretary contends that the Medicare Act provides the necessary authority to promulgate retroactive cost-limit rules in the unusual circumstances of this case. He [invokes first] the specific grant of authority to promulgate regulations to "provide for the making of suitable retroactive corrective adjustments," 42 U.S.C. Sec. 1395x(v)(1)(A)(ii) [and second the] authority to promulgate cost reimbursement regulations [which] is set forth in Sec. 1395x(v)(A). That subparagraph also provides that:

> Such regulations shall . . . (ii) provide for the making of suitable retroactive corrective adjustments where, for a provider of services for any fiscal period, the aggregate reimbursement produced by the methods of determining costs proves to be either inadequate or excessive.

This provision on its face permits some form of retroactive action. We cannot accept the Secretary's argument, however, that it provides authority for the retroactive promulgation of cost-limit rules. To the contrary, we agree with the Court of Appeals that clause (ii) directs the Secretary to establish a procedure for making case-by-case adjustments to reimbursement payments where the regulations prescribing computation methods do not reach the correct result in individual cases. The structure and language of the statute require the conclusion that the retroactivity provision applies only to case-by-case adjudication, not to rulemaking. . . .

The statutory provisions establishing the Secretary's general rulemaking power contain no express authorization of retroactive rulemaking. Any light that might be shed on this matter by suggestions of legislative intent also indicates that no such authority was contemplated. In the first place, where Congress intended to grant the Secretary the authority to act retroactively, it made that intent explicit. As discussed above, Sec. 1395s(v)(1)(A)(ii) directs the Secretary to establish procedures for making retroactive corrective adjustments; in view of this indication that Congress considered the need for retroactive agency action, the absence of any express authorization for retroactive cost-limit rules weighs heavily against the Secretary's position.

The legislative history of the cost-limit provision directly addresses the issue of retroactivity. In discussing the authority granted by Sec. 223(b) of the 1973 amendments, the House and Senate Committee Reports expressed a desire to forbid retroactive cost-limit rules: . . . "The proposed new authority to set limits on costs . . . would be exercised on a prospective, rather than retrospective, basis so that the provider would know in advance the limits to Government recognition of incurred costs and have the opportunity to act to 'avoid having costs that are not reimbursable.'" H.R. Rep. No. 92-231, p.83 (1971); see S. Rep. No. 92-1230, p.188 (1972), U.S. Code Cong. & Admin. News 1972, pp.4989, 5070, sub. (b)(2), (8) (1980).

The Secretary nonetheless suggests that, whatever the limits on his power to promulgate retroactive regulations in the normal course of events, judicial invalidation of that prospective rule is a unique occurrence that creates a heightened need, and thus a justification, for retroactive curative rulemaking. The Secretary warns that congressional intent and important administrative goals may be frustrated unless an invalidated rule can be cured of its defect and made applicable to past time periods. The argument is further advanced that the countervailing reliance interests are less compelling than in the usual case of retroactive rulemaking, because the original invalidated rule provided at least some notice to the individuals and entities subject to its provisions.

Whatever weight the Secretary's contentions might have in other contexts, they need not be addressed here. The case before us is resolved by the particular statutory scheme in question. Our interpretation of the Medicare Act compels the conclusion that the Secretary has no authority to promulgate retroactive cost-limit rules.

Justice SCALIA, concurring. . . .

I agree with the District of Columbia Circuit that the APA independently confirms the judgment we have reached.

The first part of the APA's definition of "rule" states that a rule "means the whole or a part of an agency statement of general or particular applicability *and future effect* designed to implement, interpret, or prescribe law or policy or describing the organization, procedure, or practice requirements of an agency. . . ." 5 U.S.C. Sec. 551(4) (emphasis added).

The only plausible reading of the italicized phrase is that rules have legal consequences only for the future. It could not possibly mean that merely some of their legal consequences must be for the future, though they may also have legal consequences for the past, since that description would not enable rules to be distinguished from "orders," see 5 U.S.C. Sec. 551(6), and would thus destroy the entire dichotomy upon which the most significant portions of the APA are based. Adjudication — the process for formulating orders, see Sec. 551(7) — has future as well as past legal consequences, since the principles announced in an adjudication cannot be departed from in future adjudications without reason. [T]here is really no alternative except the obvious meaning, that a rule is a statement that has legal consequences only for the future. If the first part of the definition left any doubt of this, however, it is surely eliminated by the second part (which the Acting Solicitor General's brief regrettably submerges in ellipsis). After the portion set forth above, the definition continues that a rule

> includes the approval or prescription for the future of rates, wages, corporate or financial structures or reorganizations thereof, prices, facilities, appliances, services or allowances therefor or of valuations, costs, or accounting, or practices bearing on any of the foregoing. 3 U.S.C. Sec. 551(4).

It seems to me clear that the phrase "for the future" — which even more obviously refers to future operation rather than a future effective date — is not meant to add a requirement to those contained in the earlier part of the definition, but rather to repeat, in a more particularized context, the prior requirement "of future effect." And even if one thought otherwise it would not matter for purposes of the present case, since the HEW "cost-limit" rules governing reimbursement are a "prescription" of "practices bearing on" "allowances" for "services."

The position the Government takes in this litigation is out of accord with its own most authoritative interpretation of the APA, the 1947 Attorney General's Manual on the Administrative Procedure Act (AG's Manual).

> Of particular importance is the fact that "rule" includes agency statements not only of general applicability applying either to a class or to a single person. In either case, they must be of future effect, implementing or prescribing future law.
>
> [T]he entire Act is based upon a dichotomy between rule making and adjudication. . . . Rule making is agency action which regulates the future conduct of either groups of persons or a single person; it is essentially legislative in nature, not only because it operates in the future but also because it is primarily concerned with policy considerations. . . . Conversely, adjudication is concerned with the determination of past and present rights and liabilities.

Id. at 13-14.

These statements cannot conceivably be reconciled with the Government's position here that a rule has future effect merely because it is made effective in the future. Moreover, the clarity of these statements cannot be disregarded on the basis of the single sentence elsewhere in the Manual, that "[n]othing in the Act precludes the issuance of retroactive rules when otherwise legal and accompanied by the finding required by section 4(c)." Id. at 37. What that statement means [is] that "[t]he phrase 'future effect' does not preclude agencies from considering and, so far as legally-authorized, dealing with past transactions in prescribing rules for the future." Ibid. The Treasury Department might prescribe, for example, that for purposes of assessing future income tax liability, income from certain trusts that has previously been considered nontaxable will be taxable — whether those trusts were established before or after the effective date of the regulation. That is not retroactivity in the sense at issue here, i.e., in the sense of altering the past legal consequences of past actions. Rather, it is what has been characterized as "secondary" retroactivity, see McNulty, Corporations and the Intertemporal Conflict of Laws, 55 Cal. L. Rev. 12, 58-60 (1967). A rule with exclusively future effect (taxation of future trust incomes) can unquestionably affect past transactions (rendering the previously established trusts less desirable in the future), but it does not for that reason cease to be a rule under the APA. Thus, with respect to the present matter, there is no question that the Secretary could have applied her new wage-index formulas to respondents in the future, even though respondents may have been operating under long-term labor and supply contracts negotiated in reliance upon the pre-existing rule. But when the Secretary prescribed such a formula for costs reimbursable while the prior rule was in effect, she changed the law retroactively, a function not performable by rule under the APA.

A rule that has unreasonable secondary retroactivity — for example, altering future regulation in a manner that makes worthless substantial past investment incurred in reliance upon the prior rule — may for that reason be "arbitrary or capricious," see 5 U.S.C. Sec. 706, and thus invalid. . . . It is erroneous, however, to extend this "reasonableness" inquiry to purported rules that not merely affect past transactions but change what was the law in the past. Quite simply, a rule is an agency statement "of future effect," not "of future effect and/or reasonable past effect." . . .

The dire consequences that the Government predicts will ensue from reading the APA as it is written (and as the Justice Department originally interpreted it) are not credible. From the more than 40 years of jurisprudence since the APA has been in effect, the Government cites only one holding and one alternate holding (set forth in a footnote) sustaining retroactive regulations. See Citizens to Save Spencer County v. EPA, 195 U.S. App. D.C. 30, 669 F.2d 844 (1979); National Helium Corp. v. FEA, 569 F.2d 1137, 1145 n.18 (Temp. Emerg. Ct. App. 1977). They are evidently not a device indispensable to efficient government. . . . It makes no difference. The issue is not whether retroactive rulemaking is fair; it undoubtedly may be, just as may prospective adjudication. The issue is whether it is a permissible form of agency action under the particular structure established by the APA. The Government provides nothing that can bring it within that structure.

Questions

1. What is the difference between "primary" and "secondary" retroactivity? What is the difference between the circumstances of *Miriam Center* and *Georgetown Hospital*? Why does the HHS Georgetown Hospital 1984 rule change the "law" retroactively while the HHS Miriam Center rule changes only future legal effects of past transactions?

2. It is certainly true that statutes, rules, and laws ordinarily apply only prospectively, but must they always do so? Why? What is wrong with applying rules retroactively where (1) there are good policy reasons for doing so, and (2) no unfairness is involved? Since the hospitals must have thought that the 1981 rule might well be upheld, what "unfairness" is there in applying the identical 1984 rule to the 1981-1982 period?

3. Does it do violence to the APA or to the attorney general's manual to read their definition of "rule" as applying in the ordinary, or normal, situation, but not as precluding the retroactive application of a rule in special circumstances? Are there special circumstances in *Georgetown Hospital*? Is Justice Scalia's approach a sensible reading of the "plain meaning" of the statute, or does he add to the statute a meaning that simply is not there?

4. "If it is unfair, or unjustified, to apply a new policy retroactively, the courts should hold that application arbitrary, capricious, an abuse of discretion whether the policy is

promulgated in a rulemaking or an adjudicatory proceeding; otherwise they should uphold it." Discuss this proposition.

5. Despite the ringing denunciation of retroactivity in Bowen v. Georgetown University Hospital, subsequent cases have varied in their acceptance of retroactivity. Consider, as an example of extreme tolerance toward retroactivity, United States v. Carlton, 512 U.S. 26 (1994), unanimously upholding an obvious and admittedly retroactive tax as a rational means of furthering a legitimate legislative purpose — raising revenue. Perhaps a perception that Congress was closing a loop-hole affected the opinion.

In Landgraf v. USI Film Products, 511 U.S. 244 (1994), a female worker was sexually harassed by another employee. She quit her job and filed a complaint at the Equal Employment Opportunity Commission (EEOC), which denied her claim, finding that although she had been sexually harassed, the employer had responded sufficiently to remedy the problem. She filed suit in the District Court, and lost because the harassment had not been severe enough to justify quitting (and so ordering reinstatement was not possible), and there was no other relief, such as damages, available under statute. While the District Court's decision was on appeal, Congress passed a statute creating a damages remedy for this sort of sexual harassment cause of action, and giving plaintiffs a right to a jury trial. Both the Court of Appeals and the Supreme Court affirmed the District Court, in part on the ground that the congressional act should not be interpreted to give rights retroactively. The Supreme Court addressed tensions between two canons of statutory construction:

> It is not uncommon to find "apparent tension" between different canons of statutory construction. As Professor Llewellyn famously illustrated, many of the traditional canons have equal opposites. The first is the rule that "a court is to apply the law in effect at the time it renders its decision," *Bradley*, 416 U.S. at 711. The second is the axiom that "retroactivity is not favored in the law," and its interpretive corollary that "congressional enactments and administrative rules will not be construed to have retroactive effect unless their language requires this result." *Bowen*, 488 U.S. at 208. . . .
>
> As Justice SCALIA has demonstrated, the presumption against retroactive legislation is deeply rooted in our jurisprudence, and embodies a legal doctrine centuries older than our Republic. Elementary considerations of fairness dictate that individuals should have an opportunity to know what the law is and to conform their conduct accordingly; settled expectations should not be lightly disrupted. For that reason, the "principle that the legal effect of conduct should ordinarily be assessed under the law that existed when the conduct took place has timeless and universal appeal." *Kaiser*, 494 U.S. at 855 (Scalia, J., concurring). In a free, dynamic society, creativity in both commercial and artistic endeavors is fostered by a rule of law that gives people confidence about the legal consequences of their actions.
>
> It is therefore not surprising that the antiretroactivity [sic] principle finds expression in several provisions of our Constitution. . . .
>
> These provisions demonstrate that retroactive statutes raise particular concerns. The Legislature's unmatched powers allow it to sweep away settled expectations suddenly and without individualized consideration. Its responsivity to political pressures poses a risk that it may be tempted to use retroactive legislation as a means of retribution against unpopular groups or individuals.
>
> The Constitution's restrictions, of course, are of limited scope. Absent a violation of one of those specific provisions, the potential unfairness of retroactive civil legislation is not a sufficient reason for a court to fail to give a statute its intended scope. Retroactivity provisions often serve entirely benign and legitimate purposes, whether

to respond to emergencies, to correct mistakes, to prevent circumvention of a new statute in the interval immediately preceding its passage, or simply to give comprehensive effect to a new law Congress considers salutary. However, a requirement that Congress first make its intention clear helps ensure that Congress itself has determined that the benefits of retroactivity outweigh the potential for disruption or unfairness.

The largest category of cases in which we have applied the presumption against statutory retroactivity has involved new provisions affecting contractual or property rights, matters in which predictability and stability are of prime importance. The presumption has not, however, been limited to such cases.

Our statement in *Bowen* that "congressional enactments and administrative rules will not be construed to have retroactive effect unless their language requires this result," was in step with this long line of cases. *Bowen* itself was a paradigmatic case of retroactivity in which a federal agency sought to recoup, under cost limit regulations issued in 1984, funds that had been paid to hospitals for services rendered earlier; our search for clear congressional intent authorizing retroactivity was consistent with the approach taken in decisions spanning two centuries. . . .

Although we have long embraced a presumption against statutory retroactivity, for just as long we have recognized that, in many situations, a court should "apply the law in effect at the time it renders its decision," even though that law was enacted after the events that gave rise to the suit. There is, of course, no conflict between that principle and a presumption against retroactivity when the statute in question is unambiguous. . . .

Changes in procedural rules may often be applied in suits arising before their enactment without raising concerns about retroactivity. We note the diminished reliance interests in matters of procedure. Because rules of procedure regulate secondary rather than primary conduct, the fact that a new procedural rule was instituted after the conduct giving rise to the suit does not make application of the rule at trial retroactive. . . .

When a case implicates a federal statute enacted after the events in suit, the court's first task is to determine whether Congress has expressly prescribed the statute's proper reach. If Congress has done so, of course, there is no need to resort to judicial default rules. When, however, the statute contains no such express command, the court must determine whether the new statute would have retroactive effect, i.e., whether it would impair rights a party possessed when he acted, increase a party's liability for past conduct, or impose new duties with respect to transactions already completed. If the statute would operate retroactively, our traditional presumption teaches that it does not govern absent clear congressional intent favoring such a result.[2]

Does this discussion conflict with *Bowen*? Reread the final paragraph. Does the Court's approach remind you of the *Chevron* two-step? Do you expect such an approach to increase the predictability of outcomes?

In Smiley v. Citibank, 517 U.S. 735 (1996), a plaintiff sued the bank that issued his credit cards for improperly charging late fees. Such fees were illegal in California, the plaintiff's state of residence, but legal in South Dakota, the location of Citibank. If the late charges were "interest," then 12 U.S.C. §85 controlled the case. Under that statute, national banks can charge whatever interest is legal in the state in which they are located, and contrary state law is preempted. While the case was wending its way through the courts, the Comptroller of the Currency issued an interpretation of "interest" to include

___

2. 511 U.S. 263-280.

late fees. The Supreme Court gave deference to this interpretation, and applied it to the facts of *Smiley*, which preceded the Comptroller's interpretation. In response to *Smiley*'s claim that applying the Comptroller's interpretation to her case would be impermissibly retroactive under *Bowen*, the Court issued footnote 3:

> In a four-line footnote on the last page of her reply brief, and unpursued in oral argument, petitioner raised the point that deferring to the regulation in this case involving antecedent transactions would make the regulation retroactive, in violation of *Bowen v. Georgetown Univ. Hospital*. There might be substance to this point if the regulation replaced a prior agency interpretation — which, as we have discussed, it did not. Where, however, a court is addressing transactions that occurred at a time when there was no clear agency guidance, it would be absurd to ignore the agency's current authoritative pronouncement of what the statute means.

Would the *Bowen* court have been equally dismissive of *Smiley*'s claim?

In the wake of *Bowen* and *Landgraf*, the cases are complex, fact-specific and not clearly consistent. See, for example, Regions Hospital v. Shalala, 522 U.S. 448 (1998) (upholding the reauditing of a medical school's costs and reduction in the teaching hospital's reimbursement, pursuant to a new rule implementing an amendment to the Medicare Act, because the rule was merely applying correct general principles that were in effect at the time of the first audit, and because the audit period was a full three years under the regulatory statute, allowing for reaudits); FDA v. Brown and Williamson Tobacco, 529 U.S. 120 (2000) (dissent would have upheld FDA's assertion of jurisdiction over tobacco products and would have turned away a retroactivity challenge in the process of doing so); Disabled Americans v. Secretary of Veterans Affairs, 327 F.3d 1339 (Fed. Cir. 2003) (upholding Veterans' Administration application of a new evidentiary rule to pending cases); Stone v. Hamilton, 308 F.3d 751 (7th Cir. 2002) (states may not retroactively apply new rules for recoupment of overpayments of food stamps); Covey v. Hollydale Mobilhome Estates, 125 F.3d 1281 (9th Cir. 1997) (refusing to retroactively apply Housing and Urban Development regulations giving exemptions to mobile home operators for familial status discrimination); and Service Employees International Union v. County of San Diego, 60 F.3d 1346 (9th Cir. 1995) (giving retroactive effect to a DOL rule).

6

Procedural Requirements in Agency Decisionmaking: Rulemaking and Adjudication

In this chapter, we examine the two basic procedural modes that agencies use when they make general policy and apply that policy in particula r contexts, namely, rulemaking and adjudication. This procedural dichotomy is well established in the constitutional doctrine, in the Administrative Procedure Act (APA), and in case law generally. The procedural requirements that an agency must follow have five basic sources:

1. The organic statute creating an agency or vesting it with powers often specifies applicable procedures.
2. The agency may have adopted procedural regulations, which it must follow in accordance with the *Arizona Grocery* principle.
3. The APA provides procedural requirements of general applicability.
4. The courts, as will be shown, have created "federal common law," imposing procedural requirements on agencies; these requirements, based neither on specific statutory provisions nor the Constitution, are designed to facilitate judicial review. (The requirement, developed in *Chenery* and subsequent cases, that agencies articulate a sustainable justification for discretionary decisions, is an example.)
5. Judicially defined constitutional requirements of due process may also be applicable.

In any particular case, you should carefully consider the applicability of each of these sources of procedural law. You should also take care to examine the particular type of procedures that might be required. Beware of oversimplified labels like the term *hearing*. A "verbal coat of many colors," the term *hearing* is used by courts and commentators to refer to a wide variety of procedural requirements, ranging from "legislative" hearings where interested persons are invited to express views orally to a decisionmaker and respond to questions, to informal appearances by a party before a decisionmaker, to full trial-type procedures with oral testimony and formal presentation of documentary evidence, cross-examination by counsel, and decision on the basis of a formal record. Using the term *hearing* is often unavoidable because of its convenience, but you should always identify the particular type of "hearing" in question.

Last, you should consider why insistence on procedural formalities has always played such an important role in American administrative law. (In Britain, as well as other industrial democracies, far less emphasis has been placed on procedural formalities as a means of controlling agency action.) Consider the several goals that procedural formalities might serve: promoting accuracy in agency factfinding; securing agency conformance to statutory directives; enhancing the quality of agency policy judgments; permitting persons affected by decisions to have their say; facilitating judicial review. Are there other purposes that might be relevant? To what extent could procedural requirements be viewed as a functional substitute for detailed legislative specification of policy choices? As a reflection of courts' reluctance to enforce their substantive judgments in reviewing agency decisions?

A. Rulemaking and Adjudication: The Constitutional Distinction

Londoner v. Denver
210 U.S. 373 (1908)

[Plaintiffs, owners of property in Denver, challenged the assessment of a tax against them to cover the costs of paving a public street on which their property fronted. Relevant Colorado statutes provided that the Board of Public Works might, after notice and opportunity for hearing, order the paving of a street on petition of a majority of the owners of property fronting thereon. However, before taking effect, this order had to be approved and implemented through adoption, by the Denver City Council, of an ordinance authorizing the paving. Following completion of the paving, the board was directed to determine the total cost of the work and apportion it among the properties fronting on the street. This assessment was again required to be approved by the city council by adoption of an implementing ordinance. The statutes provided that, before taking such action, the council must provide notice and opportunity to file written objections. The statutes also provided that the determinations by the council of the propriety of the improvement and assessment orders should be conclusive and binding on the Colorado courts.

In the instant case, after the paving had been ordered by the board, approved by the council, and completed, and after the board had recommended assessments but before action by the city council, plaintiffs filed with the council written objections to the proposed assessment, contending, among other matters, (1) that the authorization of the improvement was invalid because a petition by a majority of affected property owners had not been filed, and the council had not afforded a hearing on that issue; (2) the paving had not been properly completed; (3) the apportionment of costs was improper and not in proportion to the benefits afforded by the paving to the respective property owners; (4) the hearing procedures afforded by the council with respect to the assessment were inadequate. The city council then approved the proposed assessment without affording any further opportunity for plaintiffs to be heard.

After the Colorado courts rejected their challenge to the council's action, the Supreme Court entertained plaintiffs' claims that the council's action violated the due process clause of the fourteenth amendment. The Court, in an opinion by Justice Moody, rejected all of the plaintiffs' challenges to the merits of the council's actions and to its authority under Colorado law, and addressed the procedural validity of the council's actions. The Court first considered whether the council's action in authorizing the improvements without notice and opportunity for hearing violated due process.]

. . . We think it does not. The proceedings, from the beginning up to and including the passage of the ordinance authorizing the work, did not include any assessment or necessitate any assessment, although they laid the foundation for an assessment, which might or might not subsequently be made. Clearly all this might validly be done without hearing to the landowners, provided a hearing upon the assessment itself is afforded.

[The Court next considered whether the council's approval of the assessments without opportunity for an oral hearing was constitutional.]

[W]here the legislature of a State, instead of fixing the tax itself, commits to some subordinate body the duty of determining whether, in what amount, and upon whom it shall be levied, and of making its assessment and apportionment, due process of law requires that at some stage of the proceedings before the tax becomes irrevocably fixed, the taxpayer shall have an opportunity to be heard, of which he must have notice, either personal, by publication, or by a law fixing the time and place of the hearing. . . . It must be remembered that the law of Colorado denies the landowner the right to object in the courts to the assessment, upon the ground that the objections are cognizable only by the [city council].

If it is enough that, under such circumstances, an opportunity is given to submit in writing all objections to and complaints of the tax to the [council], then there was a hearing afforded in the case at bar. But we think that something more than that, even in proceedings for taxation, is required by due process of law. Many requirements essential in strictly judicial proceedings may be dispensed with in proceedings of this nature. But even here a hearing in its very essence demands that he who is entitled to it shall have the right to support his allegations by argument however brief, and, if need be, by proof, however informal. . . .

It is apparent that such a hearing was denied to the plaintiffs in error. . . . The assessment was therefore void, and the plaintiffs in error were entitled to a decree discharging their lands from a lien on account of it. . . .

Judgment reversed.

The Chief Justice and Mr. Justice HOLMES dissent.

Questions

1. Why does the fourteenth amendment require notice and opportunity for hearing when an administrative arm of the state assesses a tax? The Court implicitly concedes that no such procedural requirement would apply if the state legislature had directly assessed the tax. Why should there be any federal constitutional limitations on the discretion of a state legislature to delegate certain of its responsibilities to administrative agencies unencumbered by procedural requirements not applicable to the legislature itself?

2. Why·is oral presentation of evidence and argument before a state administrative decisionmaker required by the federal Constitution? Why was the opportunity to make written submissions, which was afforded, inadequate?

Bi-Metallic Investment Co. v. State Board of Equalization

239 U.S. 441 (1915)

Mr. Justice HOLMES delivered the opinion of the Court.

This is a suit to enjoin the State Board of Equalization and the Colorado Tax Commission from putting in force, and the defendant Pitcher as assessor of Denver from obeying, an order of the boards increasing the valuation of all taxable property in Denver forty percent. The order was sustained and the suit directed to be dismissed by the Supreme Court of the State. . . . The plaintiff is the owner of real estate in Denver and brings the case here on the ground that it was given no opportunity to be heard and that therefore its property will be taken without due process of law, contrary to the Fourteenth Amendment of the Constitution of the United States. That is the only question with which we have to deal. There are suggestions on the one side that the construction of the state constitution and laws was an unwarranted surprise and on the other that the decision might have been placed, although it was not, on the ground that there was an adequate remedy at law. With these suggestions we have nothing to do. They are matters purely of state law. . . .

For the purposes of decision we assume that the constitutional question is presented in the baldest way that neither the plaintiff nor the assessor of Denver, who presents a brief on the plaintiff's side, nor any representative of the city and county, was given an opportunity to be heard, other than such as they may have had by reason of the fact that the time of meeting of the boards is fixed by law. On this assumption it is obvious that injustice may be suffered if some property in the county already has been valued at its full worth. But if certain property has been valued at a rate different from that generally prevailing in the county the owner has had his opportunity to protest and appeal as usual in our system of taxation, Hagar v. Reclamation District, 111 U.S. 701, 709, 710, so that it might be assumed that the property owners in the county all stand alike. The question then is whether all individuals have a constitutional right to be heard before a matter can be decided in which all are equally concerned here, for instance, before a superior board decides that the local taxing officers have adopted a system of undervaluation throughout a county, as notoriously often has been the case. . . .

Where a rule of conduct applies to more than a few people it is impracticable that every one should have a direct voice in its adoption. The Constitution does not require all public acts to be done in town meeting or an assembly of the whole. General statutes within the state power are passed that affect the person or property of individuals, sometimes to the point of ruin, without giving them a chance to be heard. Their rights are protected in the only way that they can be in a complex society, by their power, immediate or remote, over those who make the rule. If the result in this case had been reached as it might have been by the State's doubling the rate of taxation, no one would suggest that the Fourteenth Amendment was violated unless every person affected had been allowed an opportunity to raise his voice against it before the body entrusted by the state constitution with the power. In considering this case in this court we must assume that the proper state machinery has been used, and the question is whether, if the state constitution had declared that Denver had been under-valued as compared with the rest of the State and had decreed that for the current year the valuation should be forty percent higher, the objection now urged could prevail. It appears to us that to put the question is to answer it. There must be a limit to individual argument in such matters if government is to go on. In Londoner v. Denver, 210 U.S. 373, 385, a local board had to determine whether, in what amount, and upon whom a tax for paving a street should be levied for special benefits. A relatively small number of persons was concerned, who were exceptionally affected, in each case upon individual grounds, and it was held that they had a right to a hearing. But that decision is far from reaching a general determination dealing only with the principle upon which all the assessments in a county had been laid.

Judgment affirmed.

Notes and Questions

1. Note the grounds on which Justice Holmes seeks to distinguish Londoner v. Denver. Are they persuasive? Would the result in *Bi-Metallic* have been different if a class action procedure had been available to streamline the representation of large numbers of persons in agency proceedings?

2. Professor Davis has asserted that the key to determining whether a trial-type hearing is required is whether the controversy turns on "adjudicative facts" or "legislative facts." Professor Davis explains the distinction as follows:

> Adjudicative facts are the facts about the parties and their activities, businesses, and properties. Adjudicative facts usually answer the question of who did what, where, when, how, why, with what motive or intent; adjudicative facts are roughly the kind of facts that go to a jury in a jury case. Legislative facts do not usually concern the immediate parties but are general facts which help the tribunal decide questions of law and policy and discretion.
>
> Facts pertaining to the parties and their businesses and activities, that is, adjudicative facts, are intrinsically the kind of facts that ordinarily ought not to be determined without giving the parties a chance to know and to meet any evidence that may be unfavorable to them, that is, without providing the parties an opportunity for trial. The reason is that the parties know more about the facts concerning themselves and their activities than anyone else is likely to know, and the parties are therefore in an especially good position to rebut or explain evidence that bears upon adjudicative facts. Yet people are not necessarily parties, frequently the agencies and their staffs, may often be the masters of legislative facts. Because the parties may often have little or nothing to contribute to the development of legislative facts, the method of trial often is not required for the determination of disputed issues about legislative facts.

K. Davis, 1 Administrative Law Treatise §7.02 (1958).

Does Professor Davis's distinction explain the difference in result between *Londoner* and *Bi-Metallic*? Even if "legislative" facts are involved, why shouldn't the affected parties be entitled to some type of hearing to put in evidence concerning these facts? You should consider the utility and predictive value of Professor Davis's distinction throughout the materials that follow, including those dealing with statutory and judge-made "common law," requirements as well as requirements of constitutional due process.

3. Note that in *Londoner*, statutes precluded review of the agency's decision in the state courts, whereas in *Bi-Metallic* a taxpayer could challenge the validity of any tax eventually imposed in the courts. Does this explain the difference in result?

4. The principle that the Constitution does not impose any procedural requirements when either legislatures or administrative agencies adopt general laws or rules is recognized in many decisions. For example, McMurtray v. Holladay, 11 F.3d 499 (5th Cir. 1993), addressed a Mississippi state law that suspended for one year the job protection afforded certain state agency employees. The plaintiffs were former state agency employees who had lost their tenured jobs during the period of suspension; they claimed that they had been deprived of property without due process of law. The Fifth Circuit found that the legislature, which had created the property interest in the plaintiffs' tenured jobs, could also take it away, and that, when a legislature extinguishes a property right by way of legislation that affects a general class of people, the legislative process provides all the

process that is due. In Interport Pilots Agency v. Sammis, 14 F.3d 133 (2d Cir. 1994), the Second Circuit held that a New York agency's issuance of a "policy statement" revoking certain preexisting rights of ship pilots licensed by Connecticut was not subject to due process requirements, because the agency action was legislative rather than adjudicative. Compare Coniston Corp. v. Village of Hoffman Estates, 844 F.2d 461 (7th Cir. 1988), in which a "small" class of land owners challenged as violative of due process the procedures followed by the Village Board of Trustees (its governing body) in denying their application for a site plan for land development. The board operated under no stated criteria, reached its decision in executive session, and gave no reasons. Judge Posner rejected their claims on the ground that the decision was not adjudicative in nature. "The decision whether and what kind of land use to permit does not have the form of a judicial decision. The potential criteria and considerations are too open-ended and ill-defined."

What justifies or explains this principle? A group of college professors argued that the first amendment requires Minnesota's state college administrators to give them some kind of forum to present their views to those administrators when they formulate policy about labor relations matters related to college teaching. The Supreme Court rejected their claim. Minnesota Bd. for Community Colleges v. Knight, 465 U.S. 271 (1984). Justice O'Connor wrote the following for the Court:

> The Constitution does not grant to members of the public generally a right to be heard by public bodies making decisions of policy. . . .
>
> Not least among the reasons for refusing to recognize such a right is the impossibility of its judicial definition and enforcement. Both federalism and separation-of-powers concerns would be implicated in the massive intrusion into state and federal policymaking that recognition of the claimed right would entail. Moreover, the pragmatic considerations identified by Justice Holmes in Bi-Metallic Investment Co. v. State Board of Equalization, supra, are as weighty today as they were in 1915. Government makes so many policy decisions affecting so many people that it would likely grind to a halt were policymaking constrained by constitutional requirements on whose voices must be heard. . . . Absent statutory restrictions, the State must be free to consult or not to consult whomever it pleases.
>
> However wise or practicable various levels of public participation in various kinds of policy decisions may be, this Court has never held, and nothing in the Constitution suggests it should hold, that government must provide for such participation. In Bi-Metallic the Court rejected due process as a source of an obligation to listen. Nothing in the First Amendment or in this Court's case law interpreting it suggests that the rights to speak, associate, and petition require government policymakers to listen or respond to individuals' communications on public issues. Indeed, in Smith v. Arkansas State Highway Employees, 441 U.S. 463, 464-466 (1979), the Court rejected the suggestion. No other constitutional provision has been advanced as a source of such a requirement. Nor, finally, can the structure of government established and approved by the Constitution provide the source. It is inherent in a republican form of government that direct public participation in government policymaking is limited. See The Federalist No. 10 (J. Madison). Disagreement with public policy and disapproval of officials' responsiveness, as Justice Holmes suggested in Bi-Metallic, supra, is to be registered principally at the polls.

Given the vast delegations by legislatures of discretionary rulemaking authority to agencies, how realistic is Knight's invocation of elections as a mechanism for control and accountability of administrative decisionmaking?

Southern Railway v. Virginia

290 U.S. 190 (1933)

Mr. Justice MCREYNOLDS delivered the opinion of the Court.

This appeal questions the validity of Ch. 62, Acts General Assembly of Virginia, 1930; Michie's Code 1930, §3974a. Pertinent portions are in the margin.[1] The claim is that enforcement of the Act as construed by the State Supreme Court, would deprive appellant of property without due process of law and thus violate the XIV Amendment.

Purporting to proceed under the challenged chapter, the Highway Commissioner, without prior notice, advised appellant that in his opinion public safety and convenience required elimination of the grade crossing near Antlers; also, he directed construction there of an overhead passage according to accompanying plans and specifications. Replying, the Company questioned the Commissioner's conclusion upon the facts, denied the validity of the Act, and refused to undertake the work. . . . The Commission . . . directed the Railway to construct the overhead. The Supreme Court construed the statute and approved this action.

As authoritatively interpreted the challenged Act permits the Highway Commissioner — an executive officer — without notice or hearing to command a railway company to abolish any designated grade crossing and construct an overhead when, in his opinion, necessary for public safety and convenience. His opinion is final upon the fundamental question whether public convenience and necessity require the elimination, unless what the [Virginia] Supreme Court denominates "arbitrary" exercise of the granted power can be shown. Upon petition, filed within sixty days, the Corporation Commission may consider the proposed plans and approve or modify them, but nothing more. That statute makes no provision for review by any court. But the Supreme Court has declared that a court of equity may give relief under an original bill where "arbitrary" action can be established.

As construed and applied, we think the statute conflicts with the XIV Amendment.

Certainly, to require abolition of an established grade crossing and the outlay of money necessary to construct an overhead would take the railway's property in a very real sense. This seems plain enough both upon reason and authority. . . .

If we assume that by proper legislation a State may impose upon railways the duty of eliminating grade crossings, when deemed necessary for public safety and convenience, the question here is whether the challenged statute meets the requirements of due process of law. Undoubtedly, it attempts to give an administrative officer power to make final determination in respect of facts — the character of a crossing and what is necessary for the public safety and convenience — without notice, without hearing, without evidence; and upon this ex-parte finding, not subject to general review, to ordain that expenditures

---

1. ". . . Whenever the elimination of an existing crossing at grade of a State road by a railroad, or a railroad by a State road, and the substitution therefor of an overhead . . . crossing becomes, in the opinion of the state highway commissioner, necessary for public safety and convenience, . . . the state highway commissioner shall notify in writing the railroad company . . . upon which the existing crossing at grade . . . is, . . . stating particularly the point at which . . . the existing grade is to be eliminated . . . and that the public safety or convenience requires that the crossing be made . . . above . . . the tracks of said railroad, or that the existing grade crossing should be eliminated or abolished, and a crossing constructed above . . . the tracks of said railroad, . . . and shall submit to said railroad company plans and specifications of the proposed work. . . . It shall thereupon be the duty of the railroad company to provide all equipment and materials and construct the overhead . . . crossing, . . . in accordance with the plans and specifications submitted by the state highway commissioner. . . ."

shall be made for erecting a new structure. The thing so authorized is no mere police regulation.

In Interstate Commerce Commn. v. Louisville & N.R. Co., 227 U.S. 88, 91, replying to the claim that a Commission's order made without substantial supporting evidence was conclusive, this Court declared:

> A finding without evidence is arbitrary and baseless. And if the Government's contention is correct, it would mean that the Commission had a power possessed by no other officer, administrative body, or tribunal under our Government. It would mean that where rights depended upon facts, the Commission could disregard all rules of evidence, and capriciously make findings by administrative fiat. Such authority, however beneficently exercised in one case, could be injuriously exerted in another; is inconsistent with rational justice, and comes under the Constitution's condemnation of all arbitrary exercise of power. . . .

. . . Counsel submit that the Legislature, without giving notice or opportunity to be heard, by direct order might have required elimination of the crossing. Consequently, they conclude the same end may be accomplished in any manner which it deems advisable, without violating the Federal Constitution. But if we assume that a state legislature may determine what public welfare demands and by direct command require a railway to act accordingly, it by no means follows that an administrative officer may be empowered, without notice or hearing, to act with finality upon his own opinion and ordain the taking of private property. There is an obvious difference between legislative determination and the finding of an administrative official not supported by evidence. In theory, at least, the legislature acts upon adequate knowledge after full consideration and through members who represent the entire public.

Chapter 62 undertakes to empower the Highway Commissioner to take railway property if and when he deems it necessary for public safety and convenience. It make[s] no provision for a hearing, and grants no opportunity for a review in any court. This, we think, amounts to the delegation of purely arbitrary and unconstitutional power unless the indefinite right of resort to a court of equity referred to by the court below affords adequate protection. . . .

This Court often recognized the power of a State, acting through an executive officer or body, to order the removal of grade crossings; but in all these cases there was the right to a hearing and review by some court. . . .

After affirming appellant's obligation to comply with the Commissioner's order, the court below said: "The railroad is not without remedy. Should the power vested in the Highway Commissioner be arbitrarily exercised, equity's long arm will stay his hand." But, by sanctioning the order directing the Railway to proceed, it, in effect, approved action taken without hearing, without evidence, without opportunity to know the basis therefor. This was to rule that such action was not necessarily "arbitrary." There is nothing to indicate what that court would deem arbitrary action or how this could be established in the absence of evidence or hearing. In circumstances like those here disclosed no contestant could have fair opportunity for relief in a court of equity. There would be nothing to show the grounds upon which the Commissioner based his conclusion. He alone would be cognizant of the mental processes which begot his urgent opinion.

The infirmities of the enactment are not relieved by an indefinite right of review in respect of some action spoken of as arbitrary. Before its property can be taken under the edict of an administrative officer the appellant is entitled to a fair hearing upon the fundamental facts. This has not been accorded. The judgment below must be reversed. The cause will be remanded for further proceedings not inconsistent with this opinion.

Reversed.

THE CHIEF JUSTICE, Mr. Justice STONE and Mr. Justice CARDOZO dissent upon the ground that there has been a lawful delegation to the State Highway Commissioner of the power to declare the need for the abatement of a nuisance through the elimination of grade crossings dangerous to life and limb; that this power may be exercised without notice or a hearing . . . provided adequate opportunity is afforded for review in the event that the power is perverted or abused; and that such opportunity has been given by the statutes of Virginia as construed by its highest court.

Notes and Questions

1. What if the highway commissioner had been given statutory authority to issue regulations to implement the act, had promulgated a regulation requiring elimination of grade crossings at all locations at which an accident had occurred during the past year, and had then applied the regulation to require elimination of a particular grade crossing at which several accidents had concededly occurred during the past year? Would a hearing be constitutionally required at any point?

2. As procedures for summary judgment illustrate, see Fed. R. Civ. Proc. 56, even in court adjudication a trial-type evidentiary hearing need not be held if the relevant facts are not in dispute. The same principle applies to administrative adjudication. Would a trial-type hearing have been required if it were undisputed that several accidents had occurred at the crossing in question during the past year, and the commissioner justified his action by asserting that the public convenience and necessity required elimination of a grade crossing at any site at which an accident had occurred during the previous year?

3. Can *Bi-Metallic, Londoner,* and *Southern Railway* all be reconciled under the principle that a hearing (either before an agency or a court) is required in adjudication but not in rulemaking? Does it follow that an administrative hearing would not be required before adoption by a railroad commission of maximum rates? Would it matter if the rates regulated were that of only one as opposed to several carriers?

4. What purposes does *Southern Railway* assume might be served by a hearing? Should a hearing be constitutionally required in cases where the administrator's decision is purely a discretionary one?[2]

5. Justice Holmes in *Bi-Metallic* argues that an agency need not hold a hearing because the legislature would not be required to do so in taking similar action, while

---

2. See Jackson County Pub. Water Supply Dist. No. 1 v. State Highway Commn., 365 S.W.2d 553 (Mo. 1963), where the State Highway Commission directed certain highway improvements necessitating relocation of the Water District's mains and required the District to bear the costs of relocation despite the latter's claim that it could not afford to do so. The court found that the allocation of costs was a matter committed by statute to the Commission's discretion, and that therefore the District was not entitled to a trial-type hearing on the issue of relocation cost allocation under a state administrative procedure act providing for such a hearing where "legal rights, duties or privileges are at stake." Cf. State v. Weinstein, 322 S.W.2d 778 (Mo. 1959), where a water company challenged the State Highway Commission's order directing relocation of its pipelines on the ground that relocation was not necessitated by the Commission's building plans. Asserting that the case turned on "adjudicative facts," the court held that a trial-type hearing was required pursuant to the state administrative procedure act. Is *Jackson County* therefore to be explained on the ground that only "legislative" facts were involved there, or is there another basis for distinction?

Justice McReynolds in *Southern Railway* rejects the legislative analogy. Which position is the more persuasive? Are they inconsistent?

6. The majority in *Southern Railway* seems to concede that a hearing before the agency might not be required if more extensive review of the merits of the commissioner's decision were available in the state courts. If the agency fails to hold a hearing and generates no record of the relevant evidence, how can the court review agency factfinding? In what ways might judicial review serve as a substitute for an agency hearing? Is it a completely adequate substitute?

B. The Procedural Requirements of the APA and the Interplay between Rulemaking and Adjudication

1. Introductory Note on the Procedural Provisions of the APA

While the APA's procedural requirements may be (and often are) supplemented or overridden by specific provisions in particular statutes, they have, since 1946, provided the basic structure of procedures for federal administrative agencies. (You should review the definition of "agency" in APA §551(1) to determine which federal government authorities are subject to the APA's procedural requirements.)

The APA requirements are geared to the fundamental distinction between rulemaking and adjudication. Another fundamental distinction is whether the organic statute establishing the administrative function in question requires that the agency act on the basis of a "record" after opportunity for an agency "hearing."

These two sets of distinction (together with the corresponding APA procedural provisions) generate a matrix defining four basic categories of administrative procedures.

	Organic Statute Requirement of Decision on "Record" After Opportunity for "Hearing"	
	Yes	*No*
Rulemaking	Formal rulemaking §§553(c), 556-557	Notice-and-comment rulemaking §553
Adjudication	Formal adjudication §§554, 556-557	Informal adjudication (no APA procedures)

The paragraphs that follow provide an overview of the content and background of these various procedures. We shall then discuss more thoroughly the development of the procedural requirements for informal notice-and-comment rulemaking, which has become the primary engine of law and policymaking in the contemporary administrative state.

The distinction between rulemaking and adjudication for APA purposes is similar in some respects but different in others from the rulemaking-adjudication distinction in due process constitutional analysis that we have already examined. You should review carefully the definitions in APA §551(5)-(9) to determine what constitutes rulemaking and adjudication for purposes of the APA.

Note the broad, residual character of the definition of "adjudication" in §551(6), (7) to include the "whole or part of a final disposition . . . of an agency in a matter other than rulemaking but including licensing." This definition sweeps into the category of "adjudication" almost every variety of administrative decision other than issuance of rules and regulations. Adjudication includes the resolution of specific litigation controversies between adversary parties — such as an agency's denial of an individual's claims for benefits, the administrative imposition of penalties on a firm, or the revocation of a license. But it also includes a broad array of other administrative decisions in particular matters, including agency decisions to spend or not to spend money on a given project, to grant a lease to private parties to cut timber on public lands, to authorize a branch bank, to enter into or rescind contracts with suppliers, and so on. Thus, *Overton Park* held that the expenditure of federal funds to build a highway through a park "was plainly not an exercise of the rulemaking function," 401 U.S. at 414, but rather was an instance of adjudication for APA purposes. Thus, adjudication under the APA includes many management and administrative functions that would not be regarded as adjudication in a conventional sense, or involve any due process entitlement to procedural requirements. Recall, however, that the APA grants a right to a trial-type hearing in adjudication only where a relevant statute provides for decision on the record after opportunity for agency hearing.

How would you classify, for APA purposes, termination by the Indian Health Services of funding for a program of clinical services for handicapped Indian children? Rulemaking or adjudication? See Lincoln v. Virgil, 508 U.S. 182 (1993), where the recipients claimed that the action was rulemaking subject to notice and comment procedures, which the service had not followed. The Supreme Court managed to avoid deciding the question, holding that even if the decision amounted to rulemaking, it was not subject to notice-and-comment procedures because of exceptions to notice-and-comment requirements set forth in §553.

We now summarize the procedures provided by the APA for the four categories of agency decisionmaking that it establishes, discussing them in descending order of the extent of procedures required: formal on-the-record adjudication, formal on-the-record rulemaking, informal notice-and-comment rulemaking, and informal adjudication.

a. Formal On-the-Record Adjudication

If the statute governing the agency's action in an adjudication requires that the decision be made on the record after opportunity for agency hearing, the requirements in §554 apply (with stated exceptions listed in §554(a)). Section 554(c)(2) in turn invokes the requirements of §§556 and 557. Sections 554, 556, and 557 together establish a set of trial-type procedures for formal adjudication. How does a court determine whether the relevant statute provides for decision "on the record" after "opportunity for agency hearing" and therefore triggers these formal adjudication procedures? In many cases, the statute authorizing the agency's action contains the quoted language or its equivalent. But even where the relevant statute lacks such explicit language, courts tend to interpret the statute as providing for a hearing on the record in cases where the agency is imposing a sanction or liability on a party; such interpretations reflect the background constitutional understanding, reflected in *Londoner*, that some form of hearing is constitutionally required in such cases.

In Seacoast Anti-Pollution League v. Costle, 572 F.2d 872, *cert. denied*, 439 U.S. 824 (1978), the court held that the APA's formal adjudication procedures applied to an initial licensing of a power plant. The Clean Water Act provided for decision "after opportunity for a public hearing" but did not specify that the agency's decision to grant or withhold a license be "on the record." The court held that the requirements of §§554, 556, and 557 were applicable. "Only the rights of the specific applicant will be affected" by the decision. The Environmental Protection Agency (EPA) "must make specific factual findings about the effects of discharges" from a specific facility. "That is exactly the kind of quasi-judicial proceeding for which the adjudicatory procedures of the APA were intended." The court added: "Our holding does not render the opening phrases of §554 of the APA meaningless. We are persuaded that their purpose was to exclude 'governmental functions, such as the administration of loan programs, which traditionally have never been exercised through other than business procedures.' Attorney General's Manual on the Administrative Procedure Act 40 (1947). [O]ne of the Senate documents explained the opening phrases of §554 as follows: 'Limiting application of the sections to those cases in which statutes require a hearing is particularly significant, because thereby are excluded the great mass of administrative routine as well as pensions, claims, and a variety of similar matters in which Congress has usually intentionally or traditionally refrained from requiring an administrative hearing. Senate Comparative Print of June 1945, p.7 (Sen. Doc. P. 22).'"

The influence of constitutional due process norms became explicit in Wong Yang Sung v. McGrath, 339 U.S. 33 (1950), in which the Court concluded that due process required an adjudicatory hearing in deportation of an alien; it accordingly read a hearing requirement into the immigration statutes and held that the trial-type procedures of §§554-557 were triggered.

Agencies, however, increasingly seek to avoid the burdens of trial-type hearings, and courts often (but not always) agree with the contentions. For example, in Chemical Waste Management, Inc. v. U.S.E.P.A., 873 F.2d 1477 (D.C. Cir. 1989), the court agreed with the EPA that a formal adjudicatory hearing need not be held on issuance by EPA of orders to specific parties requiring cleanups of hazardous wastes. In doing so, it upheld EPA regulations specifying procedures to be followed in connection with issuance of "corrective action" orders under the Resource Conservation and Recovery Act (RCRA), requiring licensed hazardous waste facilities to investigate and take interim measures to clean up hazardous wastes located on a facility. RCRA requires a "public hearing" on the issuance of such orders. The EPA regulations provided for submission of evidence in written form and oral argument at a public hearing. Testimony and cross examination of witnesses was not allowed. The presiding officer may be "an attorney employed by [the EPA], who has had no prior connection with the case, including performance of any investigative or prosecuting functions." The court gave *Chevron* deference to the regulations and held that the formal adjudicatory requirements of APA §§554, 556, and 557 did not apply to any EPA order requiring interim corrective action. *Questions:* If these requirements were applicable, how would the EPA's procedures violate them? Was it appropriate to give *Chevron* deference to EPA's regulations? Note that the EPA regulations provide for full APA §§554, 556, and 557 adjudicatory procedures in cases where EPA seeks to impose penalties or revoke a license in connection with corrective action orders.

The Federal Aviation Administration also avoided adjudicatory hearing requirements in Penobscot Air Services Ltd. v. FAA, 164 F.3d 713 (1st Cir. 1999), which provides another example of the interplay between the APA, the provisions of the specific statute authorizing the agency's action, agency regulations, and background constitutional norms in determining whether a formal adjudicatory hearing is required. Penobscot filed a complaint and supporting documentation with the FAA, asserting that respondent local airport authority had violated federal requirements by according preferential treatment to a competitor. Without affording Penobscot an oral hearing, the FAA dismissed the claim as lacking in merit. The Federal Aviation Act provides that the FAA "may dismiss a complaint without hearing when the agency is of the opinion that the compliant does not state facts that warrant an investigation or action," but that "if the agency finds in an investigation . . . that a person is violating [the Act], after notice and opportunity for a hearing . . . the agency shall issue an order to compel compliance." The FAA's regulations required a complainant to supply all supporting documentation upon which it relies. They further provided that "in rendering an initial determination, the FAA may rely entirely on the complaint and the responsive pleadings," and that a hearing is required only if the FAA's "initial determination finds the respondent to be in noncompliance and proposes the issuance of a compliance order." The court rejected Penobscot's claim that it was entitled to a hearing because its complaint stated a prima facie case of violation. In so ruling, the court accorded *Chevron* deference to and relied upon the agency's regulations. On what evidentiary basis will the court review the merits of the FAA's determination that the complainant is not entitled to relief? Under the court's interpretation, is a complaining party ever entitled to a hearing? Do only parties in the position of defendants have a right to a hearing? Does this unduly neglect the interests of parties in the position of plaintiffs? Do constitutional due process hearing requirements apply to claims by a specific party (such as Penobscot) that is not seeking to avoid the coercive imposition by government of liabilities or requirements (as in *Londoner* and *Southern Rwy.*), but rather seeking affirmative government regulatory protection or remedy against third parties? See Brock v. Roadway Express, p. 666, infra.

Are agency decisions about the sort of hearing required by statute entitled to *Chevron* deference? In Citizens Awareness Network v. United States, 391 F.3d 338 (2004), the First Circuit hinted they might be. The court followed *Seacoast*, but suggested that its "vitality in the post-*Chevron* era" deserves reconsideration: "[W]hile the type of hearing required by a statute turns [upon] congressional intent, *Chevron* adds a new dimension, requiring that the agency's reasonable interpretation be accorded deference if there is any ambiguity as to that intent. To what extent (if at all) this reality erodes *Seacoast*'s rationale is a question we leave for another day." 391 F.3d 349 n.4 (internal citations omitted).

What procedures must be followed in a case subject to formal on-the-record adjudication? You should carefully review the provisions of §§554, 556, and 557. They establish an administrative approximation of a civil trial. These provisions provide for submission of testimony and documentary evidence at a hearing before a hearing officer, although, as we have seen, the rules of evidence applicable to a trial in court do not apply.[3] The agency must notify the party or parties of the time, place, and nature of the hearing, the legal authority under which it is held, and the matters of fact and law asserted — usually in the form of a

---

3. In cases where the agency is determining claims for money or benefits or applications for initial licenses, §556(d) authorizes documentary presentation of evidence when parties will not be prejudiced thereby. See NRDC v. EPA, 859 F.2d 156 (D.C. Cir. 1988) (EPA free to limit oral testimony and cross-examination in initial licensing procedures). But see Seacoast Anti-Pollution League v. Costle, supra, holding that although the APA, §556(d), might permit the submission of evidence in documentary form in an initial licensing under the Clean Water Act, the Act's provision for a "public hearing" precluded such a procedure. This decision illustrates how provisions in particular statutes may supplement or modify the procedures imposed by the APA.

written complaint or the equivalent. §554(b)(3). Although the APA does not provide for pretrial discovery against the agency, such discovery is often available pursuant to agency regulations or the Freedom of Information Act, discussed below at pages 681-690. Other parties may be entitled to intervene in the proceeding. The hearing itself is generally conducted by an administrative law judge (ALJ), although the APA authorizes an agency head or heads to preside. Section 556(b) parties are entitled to, and often are, represented by counsel. As we have seen in Chapter 4, the APA imposes an internal separation of administrative functions in formal adjudication where the agency is a party, walling off the agency officials responsible for prosecuting the agency's case from the administrative decisionmakers. In some cases, such as workers' compensation cases, it may be that the only parties to the proceeding are private parties. A record is kept of the hearing, in the form of a recording or stenographic transcript plus documents submitted as evidence; this record constitutes the "exclusive record for decision." §556(e). The APA adjudicatory hearing provisions impose certain prohibitions against ex parte contacts with the decisionmaker that are designed to protect the integrity of the hearing record. Normally, the ALJ prepares an initial decision, which then may be appealed to the agency head or heads or delegate, based on the record and submission at the hearing. The decisionmaker must provide a "statement of . . . findings and conclusions, and the reasons or basis therefor, on all the material issues of fact, law, or discretion presented on the record." §557(c). See Armstrong v. Commodity Futures Trading Commission, 12 F.3d 401 (3d Cir. 1993), holding that this requirement was not satisfied where the commission affirmed the administrative law judge's opinion as "substantially correct" without indicating what part of the ALJ's opinion might be incorrect. Section 706(2)(E) provides for judicial review of agency factfinding under the substantial evidence standard based on the record as a whole in proceedings governed by §§556-557 or where a specific statute requires an on-the-record decision.

b. Formal On-the-Record Rulemaking

In cases where a relevant statute provides that "rules . . . be made on the record after opportunity for an agency hearing," §553(c) requires that an agency engaged in rulemaking use the procedures of §§556 and 557. The traditional understanding — as a matter of statutory construction but not of constitutional due process — was that formal rulemaking was generally required in setting rates and similar requirements that determined the revenues and profits of regulated firms. But in the *Florida East Coast* decision (p. 514, infra), the Supreme Court, concerned about the delays and other dysfunctions attributed to formal rulemaking requirements, severely restricted the coverage of the APA's formal rulemaking procedures by insisting that the relevant statute explicitly provide for a "hearing" "on the record." The §§556-557 procedures — called "formal" or "on-the-record" rulemaking — in contradistinction to "informal" or "notice-and-comment" rulemaking under §553, normally include the taking of evidence by an ALJ or other agency hearing officer through adversary trial-type proceedings involving testimony and cross-examination, an initial or recommended decision by that officer based on the evidence presented, followed by opportunity for an appeal procedure before the agency head or heads or their delegate on the basis of the record compiled by the hearing officer. However, §556(d) provides that in such rulemaking "an agency may, when a party will not be prejudiced thereby, adopt procedures for the submission of all or part of the evidence in written form." Section 706(2)(E) provides for court review of the formal rulemaking under the substantial evidence standard.

c. Notice-and-Comment Rulemaking

In a case of rulemaking where the applicable statute does not provide for a "hearing" "on the record," the basic procedure for rulemaking is the notice-and-comment procedure provided in §553. Its ingredients are as follows:

(1) general notice of proposed rulemaking in the *Federal Register*, specifying the time and place of the rulemaking proceedings, the legal authority relied on for their issuance, and the content or subject matter of the proposed rules;

(2) opportunity for "interested persons" to comment on the proposed rules by written submissions and, at the option of the agency, opportunity for oral argument;

(3) issuance, when rules are finally promulgated, of "a concise general statement of their basis and purpose";

(4) provision, in the case of "substantive" rules, that they shall not be effective in less than 30 days after promulgation.

In framing notice-and-comment procedures, the intent of the APA drafters was to emulate the model of legislative hearings. The purpose of the procedure is to enlighten the decisionmaker by exposure to the viewpoints of interested persons, and to enable them to have a say. Following the analogy to legislative practice, the courts traditionally assumed that an agency is not required to base its final decision on the written comments submitted or whatever materials might be included in the notice of proposed rulemaking. Rather, it was thought that the agency could base its decision on "information available in its own files," and on its general "knowledge and expertise." Notice-and-comment rulemaking, in contrast to formal rulemaking, was thus not "on the record," and the "substantial evidence" standard of review in §706(2)(E) did not apply.[4] Since agencies engaged in rulemaking have, in the absence of specific requirements in statutes or agency regulations, traditionally been free to base their decisions on whatever knowledge or material they deem relevant, without presenting the same as evidence or disclosing it to those submitting comments, it is difficult to understand how a substantial evidence standard of judicial review could be applied to notice-and-comment rulemaking.

Section 553 contains many exceptions allowing agencies to avoid the basic notice-and-comment requirements.

Under §553(a), military and foreign affairs functions[5] and rules relating to "agency management or personnel or to public property, loans, grants, benefits or contracts" are

---

4. California Citizens Band Assn. v. United States, 375 F.2d 43, 54 (9th Cir.), *cert. denied*, 389 U.S. 844 (1967). Notice-and-comment rulemaking traditionally was not "on the record," since it did not generate an exclusive set of evidentiary materials upon which the decision is based, any more than the oral hearings of a congressional committee and the letters that it receives constitute the exclusive basis for its recommendations. See Auerbach, Informal Rule Making: A Proposed Relationship Between Administrative Procedures and Judicial Review, 72 Nw. U.L. Rev. 15, 23-24 (1977).

5. International Brotherhood of Teamsters v. Pena, 17 F.3d 1478, 1486 (D.C. Cir. 1994), involved a rule issued by the Federal Highway Administration to implement a memorandum of understanding between the United States and Mexico in which each country agreed to recognize each other's commercial drivers' licenses. The court held that the rule was exempt from the APA's notice-and-comment procedures because it involved a foreign relations function of the United States within the meaning of APA §553(a)(1). Because the rule did no more than implement an agreement between the United States and Mexico, the United States would have been reneging on international obligations if the agency had not issued the rule.

excluded altogether from the requirements of §553. The latter exception, which includes many highly important functions of modern government (such as management of public lands, the award of government contracts, and the administration of welfare, disability, educational, and other grants and loans) has been sharply attacked, and its repeal was urged by the Administrative Conference of the United States. Many agencies have adopted regulations providing for use of notice-and-comment procedures for issuing certain types of rules relating to these subjects.

Under §553(b)(A) and (B), the requirements of notice in the *Federal Register* (and the corresponding §553(c) requirements of opportunity for notice and comment) do not apply (except when notice or hearing is required by relevant statute) to "interpretative rules, general statements of policy, or rules of agency organization, procedure, or practice," or when the agency for "good cause" finds that notice-and-comment procedure is impracticable, unnecessary, or contrary to the public interest. Agency determinations of "good cause" are judicially reviewable for abuse of discretion.

In cases of informal rulemaking not subject to §553 notice and comment, the APA does not provide any applicable procedures.

Over the past 25 years, agencies have increasingly turned from adjudication to rulemaking in order to decide basic issues of regulatory policy. This development, coupled with the restrictive *Florida East Coast* view of formal rulemaking requirements and the modest character of traditional notice-and-comment procedures, threatened to leave much important agency decisionmaking free of procedural requirements that would allow effective input from outside parties and generate a record on which judicial review could be had. In response, the lower federal courts, as we shall shortly see, expanded notice-and-comment requirements to fashion a new "paper hearing" procedure that creates a record for judicial review but is procedurally less demanding than formal rulemaking or adjudication.

d. Informal Adjudication

In instances where a relevant statute does not require that adjudicatory decisions be made "on the record after opportunity for agency hearing," the APA as such provides no procedures that must be followed. The lack of APA procedures for "informal adjudication" is quite significant when one recalls that §551(6), (7) defines "adjudication" broadly to include "the whole or a part of a final disposition . . . of an agency in a matter other than rulemaking but including licensing." Because "adjudication" is a very broad residual category that encompasses all agency dispositions other than rulemaking, it includes a vast number and variety of agency decisions. How, then, are courts to determine the legality of an informal agency adjudication when it is challenged by a litigant in the absence of any procedures? In *Overton Park* (Chapter 4), the Court stated that review should be based on the administrative "record" — the relevant documents in the agency's files. If the "record" is inadequate for review, courts should either conduct discovery of agency decisionmakers or remand for development of a more adequate record. In practice, courts follow the latter course. *Overton Park* also held that agency factfinding in informal adjudication should be reviewed under an "arbitrary and capricious" standard.

2. *The Scope of Agency Rulemaking Authority and the Choice of Rulemaking versus Adjudication as a Means for Developing Agency Policy*

a. Agency Rulemaking Authority

In this subsection, we shall examine the agency's choice of either rulemaking or adjudicative procedures for setting agency policy. Should the agency, procedurally speaking, act like a "little legislature" or a "little court"?

Many administrative agencies are statutorily empowered to decide particular cases through adjudication and also to engage in rulemaking. Prior to the 1970s, most federal regulatory agencies relied primarily or exclusively on adjudication to make law and policy. Thus, the Federal Trade Commission (FTC) developed the law of "unfair competition" through case-by-case issuance of orders against particular firms, requiring them to cease and desist from unfair methods of competition. The Federal Communications Commission (FCC) fleshed out what the "public interest and convenience" requires in broadcast regulation through individual licensing decisions. The National Labor Relations Board (NLRB) developed the law of unfair labor practices through case-by-case adjudication of particular labor controversies. These adjudicatory decisions were typically required by statute to be conducted on the record after opportunity for hearing, and were accordingly subject to the trial-type hearing procedures provided in APA for formal adjudication.

In recent decades, however, most federal agencies have increasingly turned from case-by-case adjudication to rulemaking in developing law and policy. (Some agencies, such as the NLRB and the National Highway Traffic Safety Administration (NHTSA) still rely predominantly on adjudication to make law and policy. And, where agencies rely on rulemaking to make basic law and policy, they must still use adjudication to enforce and apply their rules in particular cases.) In many cases, this shift has raised questions about the exact nature and scope of the rulemaking authority that an agency has. The nature and scope of statutory provisions granting rulemaking authority vary widely. For example, the agency may be authorized to prescribe standards of conduct, and sanctions are provided for the violation of agency regulations. In some instances, portions of the statutory scheme cannot become operative until after the agency has issued such regulations. In many environmental regulatory statutes, Congress has mandated agency use of rulemaking to implement the statute. In other instances, the agency may be given rulemaking authority to "interpret" the statute. In still other instances, the organic statute contains a catchall provision authorizing the agency to issue such regulations as may be necessary to carry out the purposes of the statute, creating debate about whether the agency has been authorized to prescribe substantive standards of conduct or whether its power to issue regulations is limited to interpretations, policy statements, and matters of internal administration and procedure. The following case involves this question.

National Petroleum Refiners Association v. FTC

482 F.2d 672 (D.C. Cir. 1973)

WRIGHT, Circuit Judge.

This case presents an important question . . . whether the Federal Trade Commission, under its governing statute, 15 U.S.C.A. §41 et seq., is empowered to promulgate substantive rules of business conduct or, as it terms them, "Trade Regulation Rules." The effect of these rules would be to give greater specificity and clarity to the broad standard of illegality — "unfair methods of competition in commerce, and unfair or deceptive acts or practices in commerce" — which the agency is empowered to prevent. Once promulgated, the rules would be used by the agency in adjudicatory proceedings aimed at producing cease and desist orders against violations of the statutory standard. The central question in such adjudicatory proceedings would be whether the particular defendant's conduct violated the rule in question.

The case is here on appeal from a District Court ruling that the Commission lacks authority under its governing statute to issue rules of this sort. . . . Specifically at issue in the District Court was the Commission's rule declaring that failure to post octane rating numbers on gasoline pumps at service stations was an unfair method of competition and an unfair or deceptive act or practice. . . .

As always, we must begin with the words of the statute creating the Commission and delineating its powers. Section 5 directs the Commission to "prevent persons, partnerships, or corporations . . . from using unfair methods of competition in commerce and unfair or deceptive acts or practices in commerce." Section 5(b) of the Trade Commission Act specifies that the Commission is to accomplish this goal by means of issuance of a complaint, a hearing, findings as to the facts, and issuance of a cease and desist order. . . .

. . . Section 6(g) of the Act, 15 U.S.C.A. §46(g), states that the Commission may "[f]rom time to time . . . classify corporations and . . . make rules and regulations for the purpose of carrying out the provisions of section 41 to 46 and 47 to 58 of this title."

According to appellees, however, this rule-making power is limited to specifying the details of the Commission's non-adjudicatory, investigative and informative functions spelled out in the other provisions of Section 6 and should not be read to encompass substantive rule-making in implementation of Section 5 adjudication. . . .

[After an analysis of the act's statutory language, legislative history, and court decisions, the court sustained the FTC's claim to "substantive" rulemaking power, discounting earlier statements by FTC commissioners (concurred in by most commentators) that it did not enjoy such power.]

Thus there is little question that the availability of substantive rulemaking gives any agency an invaluable resources-saving flexibility in carrying out its task of regulating parties subject to its statutory mandate. More than merely expediting the agency's job, use of substantive rulemaking is increasingly felt to yield significant benefits to those the agency regulates. Increasingly, courts are recognizing that use of rule-making to make innovations in agency policy may actually be fairer to regulated parties than total reliance on case-by-case adjudication.

[U]tilizing rule-making procedures opens up the process of agency policy innovation to a broad range of criticism, advice and data that is ordinarily less likely to be forthcoming in adjudication. Moreover, the availability of notice before promulgation and wide public participation in rule-making avoids the problem of singling out a single defendant among a group of competitors for initial imposition of a new and inevitably costly legal obligation. . . .

Such benefits are especially obvious in cases involving initiation of rules of the sort the FTC has promulgated here. [A] vast amount of data had to be compiled and analyzed, and the Commission, armed with these data, had to weigh the conflicting policies of increasingly knowledgeable consumer decision-making against alleged costs to gasoline dealers which might be passed on to the consumer. True, the decision to impose a bright-line standard of behavior might have been evolved by the Commission in a single or a succession of adjudicatory proceedings, much as the Supreme Court has imposed per se rules of business behavior in antitrust cases. See, e.g., United States v. Topco Associates, Inc., 405 U.S. 596 (1972) (horizontal territorial restraints); United States v. Socony-Vacuum Oil Co., 310 U.S. 150 (1940) (price fixing). But evolution of bright-line rules is often a slow process and may involve the distinct disadvantage of acting without the broad range of data and argument from all those potentially affected that may be flushed out through use of legislative-type rule-making procedures. And utilizing rule-making in advance of adjudication here minimizes the unfairness of using a purely case-by-case approach requiring "compliance by one manufacturer while his competitors [engaging in similar practices] remain free to violate the Act." Weinberger v. Bentex Pharmaceuticals, Inc., . . . 412 U.S. at 653. . . .

[Problems of delay and inefficiency] have plagued the Trade Commission down to the present. . . . There is little disagreement that the Commission will be able to proceed more expeditiously, give greater certainty to businesses subject to the Act, and deploy its internal resources more efficiently with a mixed system of rule-making and adjudication than with adjudication alone. With the issues in Section 5 proceedings reduced by the existence of a rule delineating what is a violation of the statute . . . proceedings will be speeded up. For example, in an adjudication alone based on a violation of the octane rating rule at issue here, the central question to be decided will be whether or not pumps owned by a given refiner are properly marked. Without the rule, the Commission might well be obliged to prove and argue that the absence of the rating markers in each particular case was likely to have injurious and unfair effects on consumers or competition. Since the laborious process might well have to be repeated every time the Commission chose to proceed subsequently against another defendant on the same ground, the difference in administrative efficiency between the two kinds of proceedings is obvious. Furthermore, rules, as contrasted with the holdings reached by case-by-case adjudication, are more specific as to their scope, and industry compliance is more likely simply because each company is on clearer notice whether or not specific rules apply to it.

Moreover, when delay in agency proceedings is minimized by using rules, those violating the statutory standard lose an opportunity to turn litigation into a profitable and lengthy game of postponing the effect of the rule on the current practice.

Any fears that the agency could successfully use rule-making power as a means of oppressive or unreasonable regulation seem exaggerated in view of courts' general practice in reviewing rules to scrutinize their statement of basis and purpose to see whether the major issues of policy pro and con raised in the submissions to the agency were given sufficient consideration. . . . We hold that under the terms of its governing statute, and under Section 6(g) . . . in particular, the Federal Trade Commission is authorized to promulgate rules defining the meaning of the statutory standards of the illegality the Commission is empowered to prevent.

Notes and Questions

1. Why was the commission in National Petroleum Refiners so anxious to establish that it had authority to issue "substantive" "legislative" regulations, infractions of which

would per se constitute "unfair competition" in violation of the act?[6] Why couldn't the commission, in the context of a particular adjudicatory proceeding against gasoline distributors, adopt a per se decisional rule that failure to post octane ratings is an instance of "unfair competition," and apply that rule in subsequent adjudications? Or why couldn't the FTC espouse a rule in an interpretive rule or statement of policy, a press release, or a speech by the chairperson, or an advisory opinion to a firm subject to its jurisdiction and simply follow that rule in all subsequent formal cases? How might the strategic position of the FTC and of regulated firms differ under such approaches in comparison to rulemaking?

One important consideration in answering these questions is that when an agency adopts "legislative" rules, those rules are binding on both the agency and private parties until and unless the regulations are changed. Thus, in a subsequent enforcement action, the respondent (as well as the agency) will be precluded from arguing that a different rule should be applied. But where the agency's position is set forth in interpretive rules or statements of policy, the respondent is free to advocate and litigate for a different position in a subsequent case. But what of the possibility of establishing per se rules through adjudication, like the per se rules that the Supreme Court has developed in antitrust cases?

Another consideration may be found in the Chapter 4 discussion of judicial review, which indicates that courts have given greater deference to agency decisions on questions of law when such decisions are made by "legislative" as opposed to "interpretative" regulations or simple case-by-case adjudication. But what is the effect of *Chevron* and *Mead Corp.*

2. As previously noted, many federal agencies — particularly the "independent" regulatory commissions — traditionally placed preponderant reliance on case-by-case adjudication to develop administrative policy. This practice was subjected to sharp criticism by distinguished commentators, who urged much greater reliance on rulemaking.[7] The main grounds of criticism were that reliance on case-by-case adjudication creates uncertainty and inconsistency; that rulemaking procedures are superior for formulating policy of general applicability because they facilitate input to the decision by all those affected; and that rulemaking encourages agencies to make clear choices among alternative policies, promoting both the efficacy and political accountability of the agency. A study conducted by the General Accounting Office in 1994 lends credence to those views. In a review of adjudicative resolutions of Medicare disputes in several different regions of the country, the GAO found widely inconsistent rates in the granting or denial

---

6. If the FTC's statutory rulemaking power had been held not to include substantive rulemaking authority, what would it include? The court's analysis of the relevant legislative history and precedent on the questions of the FTC's "substantive" rulemaking power is lengthy and has therefore been omitted. It is fair to conclude that when Congress adopted the Federal Trade Commission Act in 1914, it did not anticipate that the FTC would wield "substantive" rulemaking powers. Given the more established place of agencies today and the exigencies of modern administration, should the act nonetheless be construed as granting such power, based on a contemporary judgment that it is desirable or necessary for accomplishment of the commission's mission? In the Federal Trade Commission Improvement Act of 1974 (Magnuson-Moss Act), 15 U.S.C. §57(a), Congress explicitly granted the commission authority to specify acts or practices that are "unfair or deceptive" and therefore proscribed, and to assess civil penalties rather than merely issue cease-and-desist orders for their violation. The act, however, imposed a number of burdensome procedural requirements, beyond the standard APA notice-and-comment requirements, on the rulemaking authority granted.

7. See K. Davis, Discretionary Justice: A Preliminary Inquiry 52-96 (1969); H. Friendly, The Federal Administrative Agencies: The Need for Better Definition of Standards (1962); Wright, book review of Discretionary Justice. A Preliminary Inquiry by Kenneth Culp Davis (1971), 81 Yale L.J. 575 (1972).

of reimbursement for many of the most utilized and costly services offered by the Medicare program.[8] But see Robinson, The Making of Administrative Policy: Another Look at Rulemaking and Adjudication and Administrative Procedure Reform, 118 U. Pa. L. Rev. 485, 529-539 (1970), asserting that the choice between rulemaking and adjudication is a factor of minor significance in the agencies' failure to articulate clear, sound policies, citing as evidence frequent instances of agency "failure" by the FCC despite its recent reliance on rulemaking in many aspects of its administration.

3. Contrast with *National Petroleum Refiners*, Amalgamated Transit Union v. Skinner, 894 F.2d 1362 (D.C. Cir. 1990), which found that the authority of the Urban Mass Transit Authority (UMTA) to specify, by regulation, "terms and conditions" on its grants and loans did not authorize UMTA to adopt a rule requiring local mass transit agencies receiving federal funds to prescribe random drug testing for their employees. The court found that another statutory provision, authorizing UMTA authority to investigate safety problems at local mass transit agencies, and to withhold funds if a local agency does not deal adequately with safety problems (a form of adjudication), was the sole means authorized for dealing with drug-related safety problems.

b. Agency Choice Between Rulemaking and Adjudication

During the past three decades, there was a dramatic shift toward greater use of rulemaking by many agencies. As reflected in the materials that follow, this shift was primarily due to changing calculations of agency self-interest in the face of procedural requirements and to congressional directives. What are the comparative advantages of rulemaking and adjudication from the viewpoint of administrators considering how to implement a new regulatory program? Suppose you were SEC staff counsel at the time of the *Chenery* reorganization proceedings and had been asked by the commission to make a recommendation as to whether the SEC should deal with the problem of management stock purchases pending reorganization through case-by-case decisions of reorganization applications or by general regulations. What factors would you consider, and what would you recommend?

The following may serve as a preliminary outline of relevant considerations.

Procedures. As developed more fully in this chapter, there are important differences between the procedures employed in formal adjudication by regulatory agencies and those governing rulemaking. Adjudication to enforce regulatory controls frequently (but not necessarily in initial licensing) involves the use of trial-type proceedings involving an ALJ, oral testimony, cross-examination, and decisions exclusively on the basis of the hearing record. Rulemaking typically involves less formal notice-and-comment procedures in which the agency publishes proposed regulations in the *Federal Register,* and any member of the public may submit written comments on the proposal. Consider the differences in the "databases" likely to be generated by trial-type adjudication as opposed to notice-and-comment rulemaking. Consider also the burdens on the agency of the two types of procedure.

---

8. Davis & Pierce, 2000 Cumulative Supplement, Administrative Law Treatise 212 (3d ed. 2000), citing Inconsistent Denial Rates for Medical Necessity Across Six Carriers. Testimony of Eleanor Chelimsky Before the Sub-Committee on Regulation, Business Opportunities, and Technology, of the House Committee on Small Business (Mar. 29, 1994).

The degree of agency commitment to new policies. Despite Professor Davis's insistence that the content of regulations can be as flexible and open-ended as adjudicatory rationales, the promulgation of regulations of general applicability has traditionally been viewed as committing an agency more specifically and more permanently to a given policy than case-by-case adjudication. Why might administrators wish to avoid such commitments? On the other hand, might use of detailed regulations make for greater effectiveness in the agency's discharge of its responsibilities? Recall again the *Boyce* case (Chapter 5).

Retroactivity/prospectivity. Bearing in mind all of the caveats discussed in Chapter 5, accomplishing changes in legal rules through rulemaking rather than adjudication is likely to interfere less with expectation interests. Why might any agency nonetheless prefer use of adjudication in a situation such as that presented in the *Chenery* decisions? Consider the issues presented in *Bell Aerospace* and related cases (Chapter 5).

Scope of judicial review. What differences might there be in the scope of judicial review when an agency announces a new rule through generally applicable regulations promulgated without a trial-type record that includes witness cross-examination as compared to its adoption in a particular adjudication with specific facts revealed in the record?

Consistency and uniformity vs. individuation. Policy formulations through rulemaking could be expected to promote more consistent and evenhanded treatment of similarly situated individuals than case-by-case development of policy through adjudication. Consider also that case-by-case "fine tuning" of, for example, the pollution controls applicable to a given industry will increase decisionmaking costs and arguably lead to competitive inequalities. But uniform rules may ignore relevant differences among persons and produce undue bureaucratic rigidity. Recall the debate on standards vs. individuation, Chapter 5.

Clarity and publicity. Professor David Shapiro has argued that rulemaking affords administrators less scope to "hide the ball" through an often murky path of case-by-case adjudication whose direction and net significance can be understood, if at all, only by specialist lawyers who closely monitor the agency in question. See Shapiro, The Choice of Rulemaking or Adjudication in the Development of Administrative Policy, 78 Harv. L. Rev. 921 (1965). By contrast, rulemaking encourages the agency to articulate policy in a more crystallized fashion that can be more readily understood and evaluated by a broader segment of the public. But, again, consider the *Boyce* case.

Fairness to parties in adjudicative proceedings. The FTC Trade Regulation Rule on cigarette advertising, 29 Fed. Reg. 8324, 8367 (1964), notes: "If the tribunal in an adjudicative proceeding is too intent upon fashioning rules for future guidance, the task of rendering a fair result on the record before it may be slighted. Since the task of assessing individual liability on the basis of past practices and the task of fashioning rules of general application for future guidance are different, it has been argued that a tribunal that seeks to lay down broad rules in deciding individual cases may frequently fail to do complete justice to the parties before it." This problem has been found to exist in NLRB adjudications. See Peck, The Atrophied Rule-Making Powers of the National Labor Relations Board, 70 Yale L.J. 729, 758-759 (1961). Might an agency nonetheless wish to single out a particular firm in an industry through adjudication to develop new policy? For an expanded discussion about when courts should reject an agency's decision to proceed by adjudication because of fairness concerns, see William D. Araiza, Agency Adjudication, The Importance of Facts, and the Limitations of Labels, 57 Wash. & Lee L. Rev. 351 (2000).

Planning. If adjudication is relied on as a vehicle for policy formulation, agencies may have less control over the content and evolution of their policies, since policies will only be announced when cases are brought that can serve as vehicles for them. However, as Professor Shapiro points out: "But many agencies, like the FTC, have the power to initiate cases as well as to decide them, and these agencies can exercise virtually the same degree of planning in the commencement of adjudicatory proceedings as they can in rulemaking." 78 Harvard L. Rev. at 932. In addition, reliance on adjudication may encourage administrators to "muddle through" on a case-by-case basis, focusing on the special facts of each proceeding, and to neglect a more global "planning" approach to the problems faced by the agency that rulemaking may encourage. On the other hand, lack of knowledge, disagreements within the agency, or political constraints may make case-by-case "muddling through" the only feasible course.

The considerations sketched above may indicate why most agencies have shifted increasingly to rulemaking to carry out expanding regulatory obligations. For a game-theory analysis of agency choices among alternative lawmaking techniques, taking into account the likely responses of reviewing courts, see Emerson H. Tiller and Pablo T. Spiller, Strategic Instruments: Legal Structure and Political Games in Administrative Law, 15 J. L. Econ. & Org. (July 1999). In addition, Congress in many cases has mandated agency use of regulations to implement environmental and other regulatory programs.

See, e.g., the Clean Air Act, 42 U.S.C. §§7401 et seq. Such mandates reflect congressional belief that use of rulemaking will better ensure that regulatory programs are implemented speedily, consistently, and effectively.

Before he became a justice, Antonin Scalia argued that agencies may find it advantageous to return to policymaking by adjudication, in part because of the growth of procedural formalities in hitherto "informal" rulemaking (a development we examine in detail below) and the rise of "hard look" review of rules. Consider the following excerpt from Scalia, Back to Basics: Making Law Without Making Rules, Regulations 25, 26-27 (July/Aug. 1981):

> Some of the advantages [of rulemaking] have been found to have their darker side: If the prospective nature of rulemaking renders agency action fairer, it also encourages expansive interpretation of statutory commands. The public might protest, and the courts balk at, the determination that a long-standing and generally-accepted business practice has always been "unfair or deceptive" under the Federal Trade Commission Act, so that persons employing the practice are subject to the liabilities or at least the obloquy that violation of the law entails. The case seems different, however (though the same solipsistic assessment of unfairness and deception is involved), when the agency merely says the practice will be unlawful in the future. The ability of everyone to participate means that organizations with substantial public constituencies (such as the Sierra Club or the Chamber of Commerce) can more readily and directly inject political calculations into even those agency decisions that should be made on a technical basis. And if rulemaking helps the agency to set its own agenda and permits joint consideration of related issues, by the same token it fosters decisionmaking in the abstract, outside the context of a concrete, detailed situation that may serve to clarify both the facts and the equities relevant to decision.
>
> In addition, some of the comparative advantages of rulemaking have eroded in recent years. The modern practice of the courts has taught us that it is quite possible to announce prospective prescription in adjudication, and to allow liberal intervention and *amicus* briefing by nonparties. The Federal Register and the Code of Federal Regulations are not the concise reference books they were once thought to be; and commercial services increasingly render agency case law more accessible. But most important of all, the procedural advantages of rulemaking for the agency itself are headed for extinction.

The courts have attached many procedural requirements not explicit in the APA. These include the requirements that the agency publish and permit the public to comment on all data and studies on which it intends significantly to rely, and that the agency justify the rule in detail and respond to all substantial objections raised by the public comments. The "arbitrary and capricious" standard for judicial review has evolved from a lick-and-a-promise to a "hard look" by appellate courts.

Congress has also roughened the procedural road, by requiring certain agencies to use adjudication-type procedures (including cross examination), by prescribing for many rules the more rigorous "substantial evidence" test of judicial review, and by imposing on some rules a procedural burden beyond anything applicable to adjudication — the requirement that they be submitted to Congress for possible legislative veto.

Even the White House has helped to take the bloom off the rule-making rose, by establishing a demanding and time-consuming process of regulatory analysis and Office of Management and Budget (OMB) clearance, applicable not only to new rules but, though a periodic review process, to old rules as well.

See also J. Mashaw & D. Harfst, The Struggle for Auto Safety (1990) (finding that the National Highway Safety Transportation Administration has largely shifted to adjudication, in the form of auto safety recall orders, to advance auto safety because of the burdens and impediments associated with the adoption of safety standards through rulemaking).

As discussed below, pages 568-570, there is considerable concern today that the rulemaking process has become "ossified" as a result of unduly elaborate procedures that create enormous administrative records (often running to hundreds of thousands or millions of pages) and create delay (five to ten years to produce a major rule). "Ossification" has led agencies to make policy through adjudication, but also through other even more informal methods of making law and policy, including policy statements and internal agency guidance documents that are exempt from §553 notice-and-comment rulemaking procedures. We discuss below the debate over the extent of the ossification problem, its causes, and its potential cures. For an overview and evaluation of the advantages and disadvantages of rulemaking as a lawmaking instrument, see Sunstein, Problems with Rules, 83 Cal. L. Rev. 953 (1995).

c. Judicial Control of Agency Choice of Procedures

To what extent may or should reviewing courts limit or control agencies' choices between rulemaking and adjudication to develop law and policy? Reread those portions of the *Chenery* decisions by the Supreme Court and the SEC (Chapter 4), that discuss whether the Commission should deal with the problem of management stock purchases during reorganization by rulemaking or by adjudication. Then consider the following questions in light of the preceding comparison of the respective advantages and disadvantages of the two modes of procedure.

Why did the SEC elect to deal with the management purchase problem through adjudication rather than rulemaking?

Is it true, as urged in Justice Jackson's *Chenery II* dissent, that *Chenery I* required the SEC to utilize rulemaking if it wished to go beyond judicial precedent prohibiting management stock purchases pending reorganization? If Justice Jackson is correct, why didn't the Court in *Chenery I* dismiss the case rather than remanding?

Did the Commission on remand from *Chenery I* give any meaningful reasons for its reliance on adjudication rather than rulemaking to deal with the problem of management stock purchases? If not, doesn't *Chenery I* require a second remand requiring the Commission to explain its choice?

What justification does the Court advance in *Chenery II* for refusing to disturb the SEC's choice of adjudication rather than rulemaking? Note that the Court (following the SEC's opinion on this point) discusses the problem of retroactive effect with the claim that "Every case of first impression has a retroactive effect, whether the new principle is announced by a court or an administrative agency" (p. 430 supra). How relevant is this assertion in the context of administrative proceedings in which the agency, unlike a court, has the option of making changes in the law through rulemaking?

Does *Chenery II* mean that agencies enjoy complete discretion in choosing to develop policy through adjudication or rulemaking? Given that most commentators urge greater use of rulemaking as fairer and more likely to yield sound policies, why shouldn't courts exercise greater control over agencies' use of one procedure or another? What would be the source of the courts' authority to do so?

Note: The APA and Judicial Review of Agency Choice Between Rulemaking and Adjudication

Two parts of the APA have potential application to an agency's choice between rulemaking and adjudication.

Section 706 of the Act requires reviewing courts to set aside agency action that is contrary to statute or is "arbitrary, capricious, an abuse of discretion." Conceivably, there might be cases in which an agency had been given general authority to proceed by rulemaking or adjudication, but the statute explicitly or implicitly requires the agency to determine certain matters by one procedure or the other.[9] Normally, however, the relevant statute will provide no guidance on the choice, and review must be had under the "arbitrary and capricious" standard. As indicated by the *Bell Aerospace* decision reproduced below, courts have generally refused to utilize this standard to control agency choice of procedures, continuing the pre-APA deference to agency discretion reflected in *Chenery II*.

However, in some cases (discussed in Chapter 5), courts have set aside agency efforts to change policy through adjudication where such changes are judged unfairly "retroactive." (Most such cases involve a change in a standard of conduct previously established by the agency, and the ex post facto imposition of a penalty for conduct that occurred before change and conformed to the previous standard.) These rulings may be understood as holding the agency's adjudicatory change of policy "arbitrary and capricious" because it violates important expectations and basic principles of fairness. Such rulings may force the agency to use rulemaking if it wants to change established policy.

Another limit on the agency's choice of procedures may arise from other sections of the APA that specifically define "rulemaking" and "adjudication" for APA purposes, and specify the procedures to be utilized in the two forms of lawmaking. For definitions, review §551(4)-(9).

This system of classification raises the question whether certain forms of lawmaking are, as a matter of APA definition, exclusively "rulemaking" or exclusively "adjudication" that can only be accomplished through the corresponding APA procedures. If so, the combination of APA definitions and procedural specifications might constrain agency

---

9. After reading Morton v. Ruiz, p. 509, supra, consider whether it might be based on a requirement in the Snyder Act that BIA limitations of eligibility be accomplished only through rulemaking.

choices between alternative procedures quite independently of "arbitrary and capricious" review. This question is presented in the decision which follows.

NLRB v. Wyman-Gordon Co.

394 U.S. 759 (1969)

Mr. Justice FORTAS announced the judgment of the Court and delivered an opinion in which THE CHIEF JUSTICE, Mr. Justice STEWART, and Mr. Justice WHITE join.

[The NLRB ordered Wyman-Gordon to provide a list of the names and addresses of its employees to unions seeking to organize their employees. The Board based its order on an earlier Board decision, Excelsior Underwear Inc., 156 N.L.R.B. 1236 (1966), which enunciated a general requirement that employment lists be furnished to unions. *Excelsior* was an adjudicatory proceeding brought by the Board against two employers who had failed to furnish lists. The Board, before deciding *Excelsior,* invited various employer and union groups to brief and argue the list issue. In deciding the case, it concluded that a list requirement was appropriate but that it would be unfair to apply this new requirement to the two employers. It announced that the requirement would only apply to future elections occurring after 30 days from the date of its decision.

The First Circuit set aside the Board's order against Wyman-Gordon, finding (1) that the requirement announced in *Excelsior* was procedurally invalid because the requirement was a "rule" which must be adopted through rulemaking procedures rather than adjudication; (2) that the order against Wyman-Gordon was invalid because it was based on the procedurally invalid *Excelsior* "rule." The plurality opinion by Justice FORTAS agreed with ruling (1) but rejected (2).]

The rule-making provisions of that Act, which the Board would avoid, were designed to assure fairness and mature consideration of rules of general application. See H.R. Rep. No. 1980, 79th Cong., 2d Sess., 21-26 (1946); S. Rep. No. 752, 79th Cong., 1st Sess., 13-16 (1945). They may not be avoided by the process of making rules in the course of adjudicatory proceedings. There is no warrant in law for the Board to replace the statutory scheme with a rule-making procedure of its own invention. . . . The "rule" created in *Excelsior* was not published in the Federal Register, which is the statutory and accepted means of giving notice of a rule as adopted; only selected organizations were given notice of the "hearing," whereas notice in the Federal Register would have been general in character; under the Administrative Procedure Act, the terms of substance of the rule would have to be stated in the notice of hearing, and all interested parties would have an opportunity to participate in the rulemaking. . . .[10]

There is no questions that, in an adjudicatory hearing, the Board could validly decide the issue whether the employer must furnish a list of employees to the union. But that is not what the Board did in *Excelsior.* The Board did not even apply the rule it made to the parties in the adjudicatory proceeding the only entities that could properly be subject to the order in that case. Instead, the Board purported to make a rule: i.e., to exercise its quasi-legislative power.

In the present case, however, the respondent itself was specifically directed by the Board to submit a list of the names and addresses of its employees for use by the unions in

---

10. Ed. Note: The Board had never utilized the Act's rulemaking procedures. It has been criticized for contravening the Act in this manner. See, e.g., 1 K. Davis, Administrative Law Treatise §6.13 (Supp. 1965); Peck, The Atrophied Rule-Making Powers of the National Labor Relations Board, 70 Yale L.J. 729 (1961).

connection with the election. This direction, which was part of the order directing that an election be held, is unquestionably valid. See, e.g., NLRB v. Waterman S.S. Co., 309 U.S. 206, 226 (1940). Even through the direction to furnish the list was followed by citation to "Excelsior Underwear Inc., 156 N.L.R.B. No. 111," it is an order in the present case that the respondent was required to obey.

Because the Board in an adjudicatory proceeding directed the respondent itself to furnish the list, the decision of the Court of Appeals for the First Circuit must be reversed.[11]

II

The respondent also argues that it need not obey the Board's order because the requirement of disclosure of employees' names and addresses is substantively invalid. This argument lacks merit. . . .

Mr. Justice BLACK, with whom Mr. Justice BRENNAN and Mr. Justice MARSHALL join, concurring in the result.

I agree with [Part II] of the prevailing opinion of Mr. Justice Fortas, holding that the *Excelsior* requirement that an employer supply the union with the names and addresses of its employees prior to an election is valid on it merits. . . . But I cannot subscribe to the criticism in that opinion of the procedure followed by the Board in adopting that requirement in the *Excelsior* case, 156 N.L.R.B. 1236 (1966). Nor can I accept the novel theory by which the opinion manages to uphold enforcement of the *Excelsior* practice in spite of what it considers to be statutory violations present in the procedure by which the requirement was adopted. Although the opinion is apparently intended to rebuke the Board and encourage it to follow the plurality's conception of proper administrative practice, the result instead is to free the Board from all judicial control whatsoever regarding compliance with procedures specifically required by applicable federal statues. . . . Apparently, under the prevailing opinion, courts must enforce any requirement announced in a purported "adjudication" even if it clearly was not adopted as an incident to the decision of a case before the agency, and must enforce "rules" adopted in a purported "rule making" even if the agency materially violated the specific requirements that Congress has directed for such proceedings in the Administrative Procedure Act. I for one would not give judicial sanction to any such illegal agency action.

In the present case, however, I am convinced that the *Excelsior* practice was adopted by the Board as a legitimate incident to the adjudication of a specific case before it, and for that reason I would hold that the Board properly followed the procedures applicable to "adjudication" rather than "rule making."

In the present case there is no dispute that all the procedural safeguards required for "adjudication" were fully satisfied in connection with the Board's *Excelsior* decision, and it seems plain to me that that decision did constitute "adjudication" within the meaning of the Administrative Procedure Act, even though the requirement was to be prospectively applied. . . .

11. Mr. Justice Harlan's dissent argues that because the Board improperly relied upon the Excelsior "rule" in issuing its order, we are obliged to remand. He relies on SEC v. Chenery Corp., 318 U.S. 80 (1943). To remand would be an idle and useless formality. *Chenery* does not require that we convert judicial review of agency action into a ping-pong game. In *Chenery*, the Commission had applied the wrong standards to the adjudication of a complex factual situation, and the Court held that it would not undertake to decide whether the Commission's result might have been justified on some other basis. Here, by contrast, the substance of the Board's command is not seriously contestable. There is not the slightest uncertainty as to the outcome of a proceeding before the Board, whether the Board acted through a rule or an order. It would be meaningless to remand.

The prevailing opinion seems to hold that the *Excelsior* requirement cannot be considered the result of adjudication because the Board did not apply it to the parties in the *Excelsior* case itself, but rather announced that it would be applied only to elections called 30 days after the date of the *Excelsior* decision. But the *Excelsior* order was nonetheless an inseparable part of the adjudicatory process. . . . [T]he Board did not feel that it should upset the Excelsior Company's justified reliance on previous refusals to compel disclosure by setting aside this particular election.

Apart from the act that the decisions whether to accept a "new" requirement urged by one party and, if so, whether to apply it retroactively to the other party are inherent parts of the adjudicatory process, I think the opposing theory accepted by the Court of Appeals and by the prevailing opinion today is a highly impractical one. In effect, it would require an agency like the Labor Board to proceed by adjudication only when it could decide, *prior* to adjudicating a particular case, that any new practice to be adopted would be applied retroactively. Obviously, this decision cannot properly be made until all the issues relevant to adoption of the practice are fully considered in connection with the final decision of that case. If the Board were to decide, after careful evaluation of all the arguments presented to it in the adjudicatory proceeding, that it might be fairer to apply the practice only prospectively, it would be faced with the unpleasant choice of either starting all over again to evaluate the merits of the question, this time in a "rule-making" proceeding, or overriding the consideration of fairness and applying its order retroactively anyway, in order to preserve the validity of the new practice of avoid duplication of effort. I see no good reason to impose any such inflexible requirement on the administrative agencies.

For all of the foregoing reasons I would hold that the Board acted well within its discretion in choosing to proceed as it did, and I would reverse the judgment of the Court of Appeals on this basis.

Mr. Justice DOUGLAS, dissenting. . . .

I am willing to assume that, if the Board decided to treat each case on its special facts and perform its adjudicatory function in the conventional way, we should have no difficulty in affirming its action. The difficulty is that it chose a different course in the *Excelsior* case and, having done so, it should be bound to follow the procedures prescribed in the Act as my Brother Harlan has outlined them. When we hold otherwise, we let the Board "have its cake and eat it too." [I]t is no answer to say that the order under review was "adjudicatory." For as my Brother Harlan says, an agency is not adjudicating when it is making a rule to fit future cases. A rule like the one in *Excelsior* is designed to fit all cases at all times. It is not particularized to special facts. It is a statement of far-reaching policy covering all future representation elections.

It should therefore have been put down for the public hearing prescribed by the Act.

The rule-making procedure performs important functions. It gives notice to an entire segment of society of those controls or regimentation that is forthcoming. It gives an opportunity for persons affected to be heard.

This is a healthy process that helps make a society viable. The multiplication of agencies and their growing power make them more and more remote from the people affected by what they do and make more likely the arbitrary exercise of the powers. . . .

It has been stated that "the survival of a questionable rule seems somewhat more likely when it is submerged in the facts of a given case" than when rule making is used. See Shapiro, The Choice of Rulemaking or Adjudication in the Development of Administrative Policy, 78 Harv. L. Rev. 921, 946-947 (1965). Moreover, "agencies appear to be freer to disregard their own prior decisions than they are to depart from their regulations." Id., at 947. Failure to make full use of rulemaking power is attributable at least in part to "administrative inertia and reluctance to take a clear stand." Id., at 972.

Rule making is no cure-all; but it does force important issues into full public display and in that sense makes for more responsible administrative action.

I would hold the agencies governed by the rule-making procedure strictly to its requirements and not allow them to play fast and loose as the National Labor Relations Board apparently like to do. . . .

Mr. Justice HARLAN, dissenting.

The language of the Administrative Procedure Act does not support the Government's claim that an agency is "adjudicating" when it announces a rule which it refuses to apply in the dispute before it. The Act makes it clear that an agency "adjudicates" only when its procedures result in the "formulation of an *order.*" 5 U.S.C. §551(7). (Emphasis supplied.) An "order" is defined to include "the whole or a *part* of a final disposition . . . of an agency *in a matter other than rule making.* . . ." 5 U.S.C. §551(6). (Emphasis supplied.) This definition makes it apparent that an agency is not adjudicating when it is making a rule, which the Act defines as "an agency statement of general or particular applicability and *future effect.* . . ." 5 U.S.C. §551(4). (Emphasis supplied.) Since the Labor Board's *Excelsior* rule was to be effective only 30 days after its promulgation, it clearly falls within the rule-making requirements of the Act.

Nor can I agree that the natural interpretation of the statute should be rejected because it requires the agency to choose between giving its rules immediate effect or initiating a separate rule-making proceeding. An agency chooses to apply a rule prospectively only because it represents such a departure from pre-existing understandings that it would be unfair to impose the rule upon the parties in pending matters. But it is precisely in these situations, in which established patterns of conduct are revolutionized, that rule-making procedures perform the vital functions that my Brother Douglas describes so well in a dissenting opinion with which I basically agree.

Given the fact that the Labor Board has promulgated a rule in violation of the governing statute, I believe that there is no alternative but to affirm the judgment of the Court of Appeals in this case. If, as the plurality opinion suggests, the NLRB may properly enforce an invalid rule in subsequent adjudications, the rule-making provisions of the Administrative Procedure Act are completely trivialized. . . .

[Justice Harlan also argued that *Chenery I* required denial of the subpoena because the Board, in issuing it, had relied solely on the *Excelsior* decision.]

Since the major reason the Board has given in support if its order is invalid, *Chenery* requires remand. . . . The prevailing opinion explains its departure from our leading decisions in this area on the ground that: "There is not the slightest uncertainty as to the outcome of [this] proceeding" on remand. [Note 11, p. 505 supra.] I can perceive no justification whatever for this assertion. Since the *Excelsior* rule was invalidly promulgated, it is clear that, at a minimum, the Board is obliged on remand to recanvass all of the competing considerations before it may properly announce its decision in this case.[12] We cannot know what the outcome of such a reappraisal will be. . . .

I would affirm the judgment of the Court of Appeals.

---

12. . . . I would go further and require the Board to initiate a new rule-making proceeding where, as here, it has previously recognized that the proposed new rule so departs from prior practices that it cannot fairly be applied retroactively. In the absence of such a proceeding, the administrative agency must be obliged to follow its earlier decisions which did not require employers to furnish Excelsior lists to unions during organizing campaigns.

Notes and Questions

1. Consider first the plurality opinion by Justice Fortas, which finds that the Board engaged in APA "rulemaking" in *Excelsior* without following the appropriate procedures, yet sustains a subsequent Board order based on the *Excelsior* rule, on the ground that the subsequent order can be independently sustained as a valid adjudication. Is this rationale consistent with *Chenery I*? What deterrent is there against future Board evasions of APA rulemaking requirements by repeating the *Excelsior/Wyman-Gordon* strategy?

2. Consider now Justice Black's concurring opinion, which denies that the Board in *Excelsior* was engaged in "rulemaking" for APA purposes. Who has the better of the statutory analysis on this point, Justice Black or Justice Harlan? How persuasive are the considerations of administrative convenience raised by Justice Black, at least in the case of the NLRB, which has shunned rulemaking and deliberately used adjudication to enunciate general requirements of law?

3. Courts now engage in prospective overruling.[13] Agencies, or course, often have the alternative of making law prospectively through rulemaking. Does this alternative cut for or against the use of agencies of prospective overruling in adjudication?

4. Why is *Excelsior* analyzed as if it were enunciating a rule? Why can't it be given some weight purely as a precedent? Its prospective nature? The fact that it is of general applicability?[14] Just why is the NLRB so anxious to avoid rulemaking and to utilize adjudication as a vehicle of policy change? Do any of the various *Wyman-Gordon* opinions suggest any limits on this practice so long as the Board applies the new policy adopted to the case before it?

5. In order to obtain information on sales and industrial concentration in various product markets, the FTC served identical Line of Business (LB) reporting orders on 450

---

13. For discussion of prospective overruling in the context of judicial adjudication, see Mishkin, The High Court, The Great Writ, and the Due Process of Time and Law, 79 Harv. L. Rev. 56 (1965); Schwartz, Retroactivity, Reliability, and Due Process: A Reply to Professor Mishkin, 33 U. Chi. L. Rev. 719 (1966).

14. If the Board hadn't cited Excelsior, would its decision be set aside for failure to give adequate reasons? Suppose the Board simply reiterated the rationale of Excelsior without mentioning that decision by name? See Robinson, The Making of Administrative Policy: Another Look at Rulemaking and Adjudication in Administrative Procedure Reform, 118 U. Pa. L. Rev. 485, 512 (1970):

> Wyman-Gordon can and should be analyzed and understood primarily with reference to the particular practice of the NLRB involved. The vice of the practice lies not in the fact that the Board has used adjudication to develop labor relations policy; nor in the fact that in particular cases principles have developed which go beyond the immediate case and must in some sense be "obeyed" by other parties. The real trouble, rather, lies in the fact that the Board has not even purported to develop its policy rules as an incident to its litigation of cases, but has virtually singled out individual cases as vehicles in which to consider and promulgate general policy rules which are largely independent of the facts and issues of the particular case. In some instances, it may not be unfair to say that individual cases have been manipulated or at least distorted for the ulterior ends of rulemaking.

See also Retail, Wholesale and Dept. Store Union v. NLRB, 466 F.2d 380 (D.C. Cir. 1972) (*Wyman-Gordon* does not preclude "prospective overruling" by the Board in adjudication so long as the changed rule is applied to the case in which it is announced).

For a useful discussion of the problems involved in the NLRB's adjudicative approach to policy formulation, see Bernstein, The NLRB's Adjudication-Rulemaking Dilemma Under the Administrative Procedure Act, 79 Yale L.J. 571 (1970); K. Kahn, The NLRB and Higher Education: The Failure of Policymaking Through Adjudication in the Development of Administrative Policy, 78 Harv. L. Rev. 921, 944-957 (1965).

For a defense of the Board's reliance on adjudication to develop policy, see Note, NLRB Rulemaking: Political Reality Versus Procedural Fairness, 89 Yale L.J. 982 (1980).

corporations and identical Corporate Patterns (CP) reporting orders on 1100 corporations. The Commission acted pursuant to §6(b) of the Federal Trade Commission Act, empowering the FTC to require businesses to file informational reports concerning their "business, conduct [and] practices." In Appeal of FTC Line of Business Report Litigation, 595 F.2d 685 (D.C. Cir. 1978), *cert. denied*, 439 U.S. 958 (1979), the court held that this was not rulemaking subject to §553.

The court, drawing on the legislative history of the APA, concluded that the APA distinguishes three forms of agency activity: rulemaking, adjudication, and investigation. It held that because the issuance of investigative orders is addressed by §555(c), the FTC was not required to follow the rulemaking procedures of §553(c) before instituting the LB and CP reporting programs. The court was evidently concerned that a contrary ruling might unduly hamper an agency's ability to gather information. But should §555(c) be read as excluding compliance with other requirements of the APA? Why shouldn't the FTC have complied with notice and comment procedures in instituting new, broad-scale reporting requirements whose compliance costs are substantial and whose value is disputed? May an agency avoid rulemaking procedures by initiating simultaneously a number of adjudicatory proceedings seeking identical relief? See American Trucking Assn., Inc. v. United States, 688 F.2d 1337 (11th Cir. 1982) (simultaneous ICC revocation of all "special permission authorities" to institute rate changes immediately is a "rule" for purposes of APA that must be accomplished through notice-and-comment rulemaking), *reversed and remanded*, 104 S. Ct. 2458 (1984).

6. Although the NLRB prevailed in *Wyman-Gordon*, would you advise an agency that it can safely engage in prospective overruling in adjudication? If not, won't agencies be forced to use rulemaking to change policies in cases where it would be unfairly "retroactive" to make such a change in adjudication?[15] Is this foreclosure of an agency's choice of procedure consistent with *Chenery I*?

Morton v. Ruiz

415 U.S. 199 (1974)

[Ruiz, a full-blooded Papago Indian living 15 miles from a reservation, was denied general assistance benefits under the Snyder Act by the Bureau of Indian Affairs (BIA). The BIA contended that the Snyder Act and appropriations under it had limited benefits to Indians living on reservations. Alternatively, BIA relied upon a provision in the BIA Manual (a collection of internal agency management directives not published in a form available to the general public), stating that "Eligibility for general assistance is limited to Indians living on reservations. . . ." BIA referred to this provision in its letter to Ruiz denying benefits.

The Court, in an unanimous opinion by Justice Blackmun, initially rejected BIA's statutory argument, concluding, in the light of the legislative history, that Congress had authorized assistance for Indians such as Ruiz who lived "near" reservations as well as those living on the reservations. However, the Court concluded that the BIA might enjoy

---

15. Suppose that an agency in an adjudication adopts a changed policy and applies it to the party before it. On review a court sets aside the order as unfairly retroactive. May the agency follow the changed policy in future adjudications without conducting a rulemaking proceeding?

some residual discretion in defining the class of eligible recipients, particularly if appropriations were not sufficient to provide adequate benefits to all those potentially eligible under the statute. The Court then considered whether this discretion had been validly exercised by BIA to limit eligibility to those living on reservations.]

Assuming, arguendo, that the Secretary rationally could limit the "on or near" appropriation to include only the smaller class of Indians who lived directly "on" the reservation . . . the question that remains is whether this has been validly accomplished. The power of an administrative agency to administer a congressionally created and funded program necessarily requires the formulation of policy and the making of rules to fill any gap left, implicitly or explicitly, by Congress. In the area of Indian affairs, the Executive has long been empowered to promulgate rules and policies,[16] and the power has been given explicitly to the Secretary and his delegates at the BIA.[17] This agency power to make rules that affect substantial individual rights and obligations carries with it the responsibility not only to remain consistent with the governing legislation, but also to employ procedures that conform to the law. No matter how rational or consistent with congressional intent a particular decision might be, the determination of eligibility cannot be made on an ad hoc basis by the dispenser of the funds.

The Administrative Procedure Act was adopted to provide, inter alia, that administrative policies affecting individual rights and obligations be promulgated pursuant to certain stated procedures so as to avoid the inherently arbitrary nature of unpublished ad hoc determinations. That Act states in pertinent part:

> Each Agency shall separately state and currently publish in the Federal Register for the guidance of the public — . . .
>
> (D) substantive rules of general applicability adopted as authorized by law, and statements of general policy or interpretations of general applicability formulated and adopted by the agency. [5 U.S.C. §552(a)(1)]

The sanction added in 1967 by Pub. L. 90-23, 81 Stat. 54, provides

> Except to the extent that a person has actual and timely notice of the terms thereof, a person may not in any manner be required to resort to, or be adversely affected by, a matter required to be published in the Federal Register and not so published. . . .

In the instant case the BIA itself has recognized the necessity of formally publishing its substantive policies and has placed itself under the structure of the APA procedures. The 1968 introduction to the Manual reads:

> *Code of Federal Regulations:* Directives which relate to the public, including Indians, are published in the Federal Register and codified in 25 Code of Federal Regulations (25 CFR). These directives inform the public of privileges and benefits available; eligibility qualifications, requirements and procedures; and of appeal rights and procedures. . . .

---

16. "The President may prescribe such regulations as he may think fit for carrying into effect the various provisions of any act relating to Indian affairs." 25 U.S.C. §9. This provision relates back to the Act of June 30, 1834, §17, 4 State. 738.

17. "The Commissioner of Indian Affairs shall, under the direction of the Secretary of the Interior, and agreeably to such regulations as the President may prescribe, have the management of all Indian affairs and of all matters arising out of Indian relations." 25 U.S.C. §2.

Unlike numerous other programs authorized by the Snyder Act and funded by the annual appropriations, the BIA has chosen not to publish its eligibility requirements for general assistance in the Federal Register or in the CFR. This continues to the present time. The only official manifestation of this alleged policy of restricting general assistance to those directly on the reservations is the material in the Manual which is, by BIA's own admission, solely an internal-operations brochure intended to cover policies that "do not relate to the public." Indeed, at oral argument the Government conceded that for this to be a "real legislative rule," itself endowed with the force of law, it should be published in the Federal Register. . . .

Where the rights of individuals are affected, it is incumbent upon agencies to follow their own procedures. This is so even where the internal procedures are possibly more rigorous than otherwise would be required. . . . The BIA, by its Manual, has declared that all directives that "inform the public of privileges and benefits available" and of "eligibility requirements" are among those to be published. The requirement that, in order to receive general assistance, an Indian must reside directly "on" a reservation is clearly an important substantive policy that fits within this class of directives. Before the BIA may extinguish the entitlement of these otherwise eligible beneficiaries, it must comply, at a minimum, with its own internal procedures.

The overriding duty of our Federal Government to deal fairly with Indians wherever located has been recognized by this Court on many occasions. See, e.g., Seminole Nation v. United States, 316 U.S. 286, 296 (1942); Board of County Commrs. v. Seber, 318 U.S. 705 (1943). [I]t is essential that the legitimate expectation of these needy Indians not be extinguished by what amounts to an unpublished ad hoc determination of the agency that was not promulgated in accordance with its own procedures, to say nothing of those of the Administrative Procedure Act. The denial of benefits to these respondents under such circumstances is inconsistent with "the distinctive obligation of trust incumbent upon the Government in its dealings with these dependent and sometimes exploited people." Seminole Nation v. United States, 316 U.S., at 296; see Squire v. Capoeman, 351 U.S. 1 (1956). Before benefits may be denied to these otherwise entitled Indians, the BIA must first promulgate eligibility requirements according to established procedures.

Questions

1. Does the Court hold that BIA limitations on eligibility for general assistance must be accomplished through rulemaking rather than adjudication? If so, is the decision consistent with *Chenery II*? Is the Court simply announcing a special rule for Indians?

2. Alternatively, does the Court leave open the possibility that BIA might have dealt with the eligibility problem on a case-by-case basis, holding only that (a) BIA had elected to deal with the issue through general regulations and had invoked these regulations to deny assistance to Ruiz, and (b) that accordingly BIA was required to follow APA requirements and the policy stated in its manual[18] of publishing such regulations in the Federal

---

18. We examined, in Chapter 4, the principle that agencies must follow their own regulations. Why should BIA be required to follow the statement in the introduction to its manual that directives relating to eligibility would be published in the *Federal Register* and codified in CFR, when the manual itself has not been made publicly available?

Does *Ruiz* rest on an implicit substantive requirement of a fair general system for the allocation of limited government benefits? Cf. *Hornsby* and *Holmes*, Chapter 4.

Register and CFR? Does this mean that all internal agency directives and guidelines must be published in the Federal Register?

3. Even if the BIA violated the APA by not publishing the regulation, why isn't its denial of assistance to Ruiz sustainable under *Wyman-Gordon*?[19]

NLRB v. Bell Aerospace Co.

416 U.S. 267 (1974)

[The NLRB had consistently held in prior adjudications that buyers who determine specifications, prices, and the selection of suppliers for their employers are "managerial employees" not subject to the protections of the Labor Act. Among the questions in this case was whether the NLRB, in the context of an unfair labor practice adjudication involving Bell Aerospace, could overrule that precedent, classify Bell Aerospace buyers as "nonmanagerial employees," and compel Bell Aerospace to bargain with a union selected by the employees. The Court of Appeals held that it would be unfairly retroactive to accomplish such change through adjudication. It must be done through rulemaking. The Supreme Court unanimously rejected this holding. The Court quoted at length from *Chenery II*'s language dealing with agency discretion to proceed either by rulemaking or adjudication; the Court noted that *Chenery II* did not involve the APA, but asserted it "is nevertheless analogous."]

The view expressed in *Chenery II* and *Wyman-Gordon* make plain that the Board is not precluded from announcing new principles in an adjudicative proceeding and that the choice between rulemaking and adjudication lies in the first instance within the Board's discretion. Although there may be situations where the Board's reliance on adjudication would amount to an abuse of discretion or a violation of the Act, nothing in the present case would justify such a conclusion. Indeed, there is ample indication that adjudication is especially appropriate in the instant context. As the Court of Appeals noted, "[t]here must be tens of thousands of manufacturing, wholesale and retail units which employ buyers, and hundreds of thousands of the latter." 475 F.2d, at 496. Moreover, duties of buyers vary widely depending on the company or industry. It is doubtful whether any generalized standard could be framed which would have more than marginal utility. The board thus has reason to proceed with caution, developing its standards in a case-by-case manner with attention to the specific character of the buyers' authority and duties in each company. The Board's judgment that adjudication best serves this purpose is entitled to great weight.

The possible reliance of industry on the Board's past decisions with respect to buyers does not require a different result. It has not been shown that the adverse consequences ensuing from such reliance are so substantial that the Board should be precluded from reconsidering the issue in an adjudicative proceeding. Furthermore, this is not a case in which some new liability is sought to be imposed on individuals for past actions which were taken in good-faith reliance on Board pronouncements. Nor are fines or damages involved here. In any event, concern about such consequences is largely speculative, for the Board has not yet finally determined whether these buyers are "managerial."

---

19. For a broadside attack on the Morton v. Ruiz decision, see Davis, Administrative Law Surprises in the *Ruiz* Case, 75 Colum. L. Rev. 823 (1975).

It is true, of course, that rulemaking would provide the Board with a forum for soliciting the informed views of those affected in industry and labor before embarking on a new course. But surely the Board has discretion to decide that the adjudicative procedures in this case may also produce the relevant information necessary to mature and fair consideration of the issues. Those most immediately affected, the buyers and the company in the particular case, are accorded a full opportunity to be heard before the Board makes its determination.

Notes and Questions

1. Does *Bell Aerospace* give agencies complete discretion to utilize adjudication rather than rulemaking in formulating and changing policy (at least so long as the agency eschews prospective overruling of the *Wyman-Gordon* type)? Is Morton v. Ruiz still good law?[20]

2. Despite the broad reaffirmation of agency procedural discretion in *Bell Aerospace*, lower courts have sometimes ruled that certain policy changes must be accomplished through rulemaking, even where there is no question of unfair "retroactivity." For example, Ford Motor Co. v. FTC, 673 F.2d 1008 (9th Cir. 1981), *cert. denied*, 459 U.S. 999 (1982), held that the FTC might not, through an adjudicatory cease-and-desist order, impose new restrictions on secured creditor practices when (1) it intended to impose the new restrictions on the entire industry and (2) the practices in question were the subject of a pending rulemaking proceeding.

3. Jean v. Nelson, 711 F. 2d 1455 (11th Cir. 1983), invalidated a general policy shift in the treatment of undocumented aliens apprehended by the Immigration and Naturalization Service. In response to a massive influx of Haitian refugees, the prior policy of generally granting parole to such aliens was shifted in favor of administrative detention pending disposition of their cases. The shift was not embodied in any formal regulation or directive, and INS officers retained considerable discretion in individual cases. Thereafter, most Haitian refugees were held in detention centers pending exclusion hearings. The court held that the policy change must either be an APA "rule" or "order," that because it was prospective and general it must be a "rule," and that it must therefore be accomplished by notice-and-comment rulemaking procedures. The government was required to grant parole in accordance with prior policy. (*Query:* Can this ruling be understood as a cousin of the *Holmes* and *Hornsby* principle, Chapter 4, that in some special areas the government must adopt and follow specific rules and standards?)

---

20. Consider Chisholm v. FCC, 538 F. 2d 349 (D.C. Cir. 1976), *cert. denied*, 429 U.S. 890 (1976), in which the FCC utilized an adjudicatory proceeding to overturn prior decisions and substantially expand the "bona fide news events" exemption from the "equal time" requirement imposed on broadcasters with respect to coverage of political candidates. Relying on *Bell Aerospace*, a majority of the court rejected the contention of petitioners that the change must be accomplished by rulemaking, noting that petitioners had been afforded ample opportunity in the Commission's adjudicatory proceedings to submit their view.

Judge Wright dissented, contending (1) that *Bell Aerospace* involved a situation where (as the Supreme Court pointed out) rulemaking was inappropriate because of the many different conditions of buyers' employment, whereas here the FCC has established a uniform new general "rule" for which rulemaking was appropriate; (2) that rulemaking might encourage a broader submission of views; and (3) that the legislative history of the Communications Act indicated that Congress had expected the Commission to utilize rulemaking to define the scope of the equal time requirement.

See also the decision in *Citizens Communications Center II*, Chapter 4, permitting the FCC to develop license renewal criteria through adjudication rather than rulemaking.

4. While most cases involve claims that agencies improperly used adjudication rather than rulemaking to make new policy, agencies have also been attacked, generally without success, for employing rulemaking procedures when the proceeding is assertedly adjudicatory in character. For example, Hercules Inc. v. EPA, 598 F.2d 91 (D.C. Cir. 1978), upheld the EPA's authority to adopt pollution control requirements through rulemaking, even though the resulting rules apply to only a single plant.

3. *Formal On-the-Record Rulemaking*

United States v. Florida East Coast Railway
410 U.S. 224 (1973)

Mr. Justice REHNQUIST delivered the opinion of the Court.

Appellees, two railroad companies, brought this action in the District Court for the Middle District of Florida to set aside the incentive per diem rates established by appellant Interstate Commerce Commission in a rulemaking proceeding. . . . The District Court held that the language of §1(14)(a)[21] of the Interstate Commerce Act required the Commission in a proceeding such as this to act in accordance with the Administrative Procedure Act, 5 U.S.C. §556(d) ["formal rulemaking"], and that the Commission's determination to receive submissions from the appellees only in written form was a violation of that section because the appellees were "prejudiced" by that determination within the meaning of that section.

. . . We here decide that the Commission's proceeding was governed only by §553 of that Act, and that appellees received the "hearing" required by §1(14)(a) of the Interstate Commerce Act. We, therefore, reverse the judgment of the District Court. . . .

I. Background of Chronic Freight Car Shortages

This case arises from the factual background of a chronic freight-car shortage on the Nation's railroads. . . . Congressional concern for the problem was manifested in the enactment in 1966 of an amendment to §1(14)(a) of the Interstate Commerce Act, enlarging the Commission's authority to prescribe per diem charges for the use by one railroad of freight cars owned by another. . . .

---

21. Section 1(14)(a) provides:

The Commission may, after hearing, on a complaint or upon its own initiative without complaint, establish reasonable rules, regulations, and practices with respect to car service by common carriers by railroad subject to this chapter, including the compensation to be paid and other terms of any contract, agreement, or arrangement for the use of any locomotive, car, or other vehicle not owned by the carrier using it (and whether or not owned by another carrier), and the penalties or other sanctions for nonobservance of such rules, regulations, or practices. In fixing such compensation to be paid for the use of any type of freight car, the Commission shall give consideration to the national level of ownership of such type of freight car and to other factors affecting the adequacy of the national freight car supply, and shall, on the basis of such consideration, determine whether compensation should be computed solely on the basis of elements of ownership expense involved in owning and maintaining such type of freight car, including a fair return in value, or whether such compensation should be increased by [an] incentive element. . . .

[The commission instituted rulemaking proceedings with the expectation that a formal §556 evidentiary hearing would be required. However, a Senate subcommittee held oversight hearings in which the ICC's delay in implementing the 1966 Amendments was sharply criticized.]

Judge Friendly, describing the same event in Long Island R. Co. v. United States [318 F. Supp. 490 (E.D.N.Y. 1970),] said: "To say that the presentation was not received with enthusiasm would be a considerable understatement. Senators voiced displeasure at the Commission's long delay at taking action under the 1966 amendment, engaged in some merriment over what was regarded as an unintelligible discussion of methodology . . . and expressed doubt about the need for a hearing. . . . But the Commission's general counsel insisted that a hearing was needed . . . and the Chairman of the Commission agreed. . . ." 318 F. Supp., at 494.

The Commission, now apparently imbued with a new sense of mission, issued in December 1969 an interim report. . . . The Commission concluded . . . that in view of the 1966 amendment it could impose additional "incentive" per diem charges [above the level needed to provide boxcar owners with an adequate return on investment] to spur prompt return of existing cars and to make acquisition of new cars financially attractive to the railroads. It did so by means of a proposed schedule that established such charges on an across-the-board basis. . . . Embodied in the report was a proposed rule adopting the Commission's tentative conclusions and a notice to the railroads to file statements of position within 60 days. . . .

Both appellee railroads filed statements objecting to the Commission's proposal and requesting an oral hearing, as did numerous other railroads. In April 1970, the Commission, without having held further "hearings," issued a supplemental report making some modifications in the tentative conclusions earlier reached, but overruling in toto the requests of appellees.

The District Court held that in so doing the Commission violated §556(d). . . .

II. Applicability of Administrative Procedure Act

In United States v. Allegheny-Ludlum Steel Corp., supra, we held that the language of §1(14)(a) of the Interstate Commerce Act authorizing the Commission to act "after hearing" was not the equivalent of a requirement that a rule be made "on the record after opportunity for an agency hearing" as the latter term is used in §553(c) of the Administrative Procedure Act. Since the 1966 amendment to §1(14)(a), under which the Commission was here proceeding, does not by its terms add to the hearing requirement contained in the earlier language, the same result should obtain here unless that amendment contains language that is tantamount to such a requirement. Appellees contend that such language is found in the provisions of that Act requiring that: "[T]he Commission shall give consideration to the national level of ownership of such type of freight car and to other factors affecting the adequacy of the national freight car supply, and shall, on the basis of such consideration, determine whether compensation should be computed. . . ." While this language is undoubtedly a mandate to the Commission to consider the factors there set forth in reaching any conclusions as to imposition of per diem incentive charges, it adds to the hearing requirements of the section neither expressly nor by implication. . . .

[The court in the Long Island R. Co. case, which also found formal rulemaking procedures applicable] felt that because §1(14)(a) of the Interstate Commerce Act had required a "hearing," and because that section was originally enacted in 1917, Congress was probably thinking in terms of a "hearing" such as that described in the opinion of this Court in the roughly contemporaneous case of ICC v. Louisville & Nashville R. Co., 227 U.S. 88, 93 (1913). The ingredients of the "hearing" were there said to be that "[a]ll parties must be fully apprised of the evidence submitted or to be considered, and must be given opportunity to cross-examine witnesses, to inspect documents and to offer evidence in explanation or rebuttal." . . .

Insofar as this conclusion is grounded on the belief that the language "after hearing" of §1(14)(a), without more, would trigger the applicability of §§556 and 557, it, too, is contrary to our decision in Allegheny-Ludlum, supra. The District Court observed that it was "rather hard to believe that the last sentence of §553(c) was directed only to the few legislative sports where the words "on the record' or their equivalent had found their way into the statute book." 318 F. Supp., at 496. This is, however, the language which Congress used, and since there are statutes on the books that do use these very words, see, e.g., the Fulbright Amendment to the Walsh-Healey Act, 41 U.S.C. §43a, and 21 U.S.C. §371(e)(3), the regulations provision of the Food and Drug Act, adherence to that language cannot be said to render the provision nugatory or ineffectual. We recognized in Allegheny-Ludlum that the actual words "on the record" and "after . . . hearing" used in §553 were not words of art, and that other statutory language having the same meaning could trigger the provisions of §§556 and 557 in rulemaking proceedings. But we adhere to our conclusion, expressed in that case, that the phrase "after hearing" in §1(14)(a) of the Interstate Commerce Act does not have such an effect.

III. "Hearing" Requirement of §1(14)(a) of the Interstate Commerce Act

[The Court indicated that even if the language of §1(14)(a) did not trigger the formal rulemaking requirements of §§556 and 557 of the APA, it might by its own force require greater procedural formalities than the ICC had provided.]

The term "hearing" in its legal context undoubtedly has a host of meanings. Its meaning undoubtedly will vary, depending on whether it is used in the context of a rulemaking-type proceeding or in the context of a proceeding devoted to the adjudication of particular disputed facts. It is by no means apparent what the drafters of . . . the first part of §1(14)(a) of the Interstate Commerce Act, meant by the term.

[The Court discounted statements made at the time of the 1966 amendments to §1(14)(a) that the commission could only exercise its authority after a "hearing," because the speakers did not specify that the contemplated "hearing" must include oral testimony, cross-examination, and oral argument. The Court also referred to the documentary procedures authorized in APA §556(d) as an indication that the term "hearing" need not include these ingredients.

The Court noted that the railroads had not claimed that the precedent afforded by the ICC violated due process. It then sought to distinguish ICC v. Louisville & Nashville R. Co., 227 U.S. 88 (1913):]

. . . The type of proceeding there, in which the Commission adjudicated a complaint by a shipper that specified rates set by a carrier were unreasonable, was sufficiently different from the nationwide incentive payments ordered to be made by all railroads in this proceeding so as to make the Louisville & Nashville opinion inapplicable in the case presently before us.

The basic distinction between rulemaking and adjudication is illustrated by this Court's [decisions in Londoner v. Denver and Bi-Metallic Investment Co. v. State Board of Equalization].

Here, the incentive payments proposed by the Commission in its tentative order, and later adopted in its final order, were applicable across the board to all of the common carriers by railroad subject to the Interstate Commerce Act. No effort was made to single out any particular railroad for special consideration based on its own peculiar circumstances. Indeed, one of the objections of appellee Florida East Coast was that it and other terminating carriers should have been treated differently from the generality of the railroads. But the fact that the order may in its effects have been thought more disadvantageous by some railroads than by others does not change its generalized nature. Though the Commission obviously relied on factual inferences as a basis for its order, [they] were used in the formulation of a basically legislative-type judgment, for prospective application only, rather than in adjudicating a particular set of disputed facts.

[The decision of the district court was reversed.]

Mr. Justice DOUGLAS, with whom Mr. Justice STEWART concurs, dissenting.

The present decision makes a sharp break with traditional concepts of procedural due process. The Commission order under attack is tantamount to a rate order. Charges are fixed that nonowning railroads must pay owning railroads for boxcars of the latter that are on the tracks of the former. This is the imposition on carriers by administrative fiat of new financial liability. I do not believe it is within our traditional concepts of due process to allow an administrative agency to saddle anyone with a new rate, charge, or fee without a full hearing that includes the right to present oral testimony, cross-examine witnesses, and present oral argument. That is required by the Administrative Procedure Act, 5 U.S.C. §556(d). . . .

. . . A hearing under §1(14)(a) of the Interstate Commerce Act fixing rates, charges, or fees is certainly adjudicatory, not legislative in the customary sense.

The question is whether the Interstate Commerce Commission procedures used in this rate case "for the submission of . . . evidence in written form" avoided prejudice to the appellees so as to comport with the requirements of the Administrative Procedure Act [citing §556(d)].

. . . [Appellee] Seaboard argued that it had been damaged by what it alleged to be the Commission's sudden change in emphasis from specialty to unequipped boxcars and that it would lose some $1.8 million as the result of the Commission's allegedly hasty and experimental action. Florida East Coast raised significant challenges to the statistical validity of the Commission's data[22] and also contended that its status as a terminating railroad left it with a surfeit of standard boxcars which should exempt it from the requirements to pay incentive charges. . . .

. . . I believe that "prejudice" was shown when it was claimed that the very basis on which the Commission rested its finding was vulnerable because it lacked statistical validity or other reasoned basis. At least in that narrow group of cases, prejudice for lack of a proper hearing has been shown. . . .

---

22. Florida East Coast argues, for example, that the Commission's finding of a boxcar shortage may be attributable to a variety of sampling or definitional errors, asserting that it is unrealistic to define boxcar deficiencies in such a manner as "to show as a 'deficiency' the failure to supply a car on the day requested by the shipper no matter when the request was received." . . .

Accordingly, I would hold that appellees were not afforded the hearing guaranteed by §1(14)(a) of the Interstate Commerce Act and 5 U.S.C. §§553, 556 and 557, and would affirm the decision of the District Court.

Notes and Questions

1. The Supreme Court's decision must be understood against the background of two developments not mentioned in the opinion.

First is the pronounced increase in the use of rulemaking procedures, particularly by regulatory agencies that had formerly relied extensively or principally on case-by-case adjudication to develop policy. Probably the most important factor in this shift from the viewpoint of the agencies themselves was the desire to escape the long delays and resource burdens involved in formulating policy through formal adjudication. Moreover, in adopting new "social regulation" programs through environmental, health, safety, and civil rights statutes beginning in the 1960s Congress began to require the use of rulemaking to implement these statutes.

Second, developing experience with the use of formal, on-the-record procedures in rulemaking persuaded many observers that such formalities were inordinately cumbersome and time-consuming, and offered few advantages over more informal, notice-and-comment rulemaking procedures. Special notoriety attached to the requirements in the Food, Drug and Cosmetic Act §371(e) that the Food and Drug Administration (FDA) use "on-the-record" rulemaking procedures in establishing standards of identity for foods, requirements for labeling of foods for special dietary purposes, and other specified requirements. Of 16 such proceedings during the 1960s, not one was completed in less than two years, and the average elapsed time between first proposal and final order was four years. Two proceedings lasted more than ten years. In one of the two, the main issue was whether it would "promote honesty and fair dealing in the interest of consumers" to require that peanut butter contain at least 90 percent peanuts (as proposed by the FDA) or 87 percent peanuts (as proposed by the industry). The proceedings were prolix, and their utility doubtful. For example, the first government witness consumed an entire day in presenting a survey of cookbook and patent peanut butter formulations and in being cross-examined on missing recipes as well as on his personal preferences in peanut butter. The other mammoth hearing, Foods for Special Dietary Uses, considered whether the diet of the average American is reasonably adequate in vitamins and minerals; it took 247 days of testimony to produce 32,405 pages of transcript.

Against this background, the Supreme Court would have been understandably reluctant to saddle the increasing use by agencies of rulemaking with the trial-type procedures seemingly discredited by studies of the FDA and other agencies.

2. Even if formal rulemaking procedures are often counterproductive, did the Supreme Court give too much weight to "functional" considerations in construing the "after hearing" language of §1(14)(a)? Judge Friendly, in his opinion in Long Island R. Co. v. United States, 318 F. Supp. 490 (E.D.N.Y. 1970) (which reviewed the same ICC action at issue in *Florida East Coast*), and in his article, "Some Kind of Hearing," 123 U. Pa. L. Rev. 1267, 1305-1315 (1975), argued powerfully that when Congress enacted the "after hearing" language in 1917 it contemplated use of a trial-type evidentiary hearing of the sort that the Supreme Court had recently described in ICC v. Louisville & Nashville R.R., 227 U.S. 88 (1913). To what extent should the understanding of Congress in 1917 be disregarded in light of current attitudes toward administrative procedures and the slow

pace of the ICC in implementing the 1966 amendment to §1(14)a? Should we ignore the intent of Congress in 1917? Should the Court give less weight to Congress's often nebulous procedural expectations than to its clear purpose, in amending the substantive provisions of the Interstate Commerce Act, to eliminate freight car shortages expeditiously?

3. Even if "functional" considerations are entitled to considerable weight, it is not clear that they justify the decision in *Florida East Coast*. Sections 556 and 557 allow for substantial streamlining of on-the-record proceedings to accommodate flexibility and a need for expedition. Recall that §556(d) permits agencies engaged in rulemaking to require documentary submission of evidence when the parties will not be prejudiced thereby, and §557 permits the agency to omit the time-consuming practice of an initial or recommended decision by the hearing officer. Additional possibilities for expedition are suggested in §556(e), which contemplates agency use of an official notice procedure, subject to a party's opportunity for rebuttal. It would thus appear that on-the-record rulemaking could be streamlined to the following essentials unless a party carries the burden of showing prejudice: all evidence, rulings, and decisions must be included in a documentary record that must be made available to the parties, who must be afforded the opportunity to submit documentary evidence and to argument and object to a tentative decision issued by the agency. On the other hand, one may well ask why agencies, such as the FDA, that are clearly subject to formal rulemaking requirements in carrying out certain regulatory programs have not used the streamlining possibilities suggested above. May not agencies legitimately fear that any departures from the trial-type norm — in particular, denial of the right to cross-examine — may be successfully attacked as prejudicial on judicial review?

4. After *Florida East Coast*, do §§556 and 557 apply only where the relevant statute repeats the talismanic §554(c) phrase "on the record after opportunity for an agency hearing"? The Court's opinion leaves open the possibility that "other statutory language having the same meaning could trigger the provisions of §§556 and 557," but lower courts have understood *Florida East Coast* as making the terms *on the record* and *hearing* "virtually . . . a touchstone test" of formal rulemaking requirements. Mobil Oil Corp. v. FPC, 483 F.2d 1238 (D.C. Cir. 1973). Explicit statutory provision for formal rulemaking is rare. In the last several decades, Congress has not enacted any such provisions and has amended the Food, Drug and Cosmetic Act to eliminate a number of existing formal rulemaking requirements. Nutritional Labeling and Education Act of 1990, 104 Stat. 2353.

5. Note that *Florida East Coast* discusses potential constitutional objections to its interpretation of the Interstate Commerce Act by referring to the *Londoner/Bi-Metallic* distinction between rulemaking and adjudicating. Does this mean that there can never be a constitutional right to some form of trial-type procedure in rulemaking? Suppose the ICC's regulations, while drafted in general terms, happened to apply to only one carrier or turned on sharply focused and disputed facts, such as the cost of new boxcars. Would due process require trial-type procedures in such a case? Consider in this respect the position espoused by Justice Douglas in dissent. Does it introduce too much procedural uncertainty in comparison to the formal distinction between rulemaking and adjudication?

6. Why should there be any government regulation of boxcar rates at all? Why not leave the matter to contract among railroads?

7. Some courts have been less willing to follow the restrictive approach adopted by *Florida East Coast* in the context of *rulemaking* in determining whether proceedings involving *adjudication* where an agency imposes regulatory controls or sanctions on a single party, and have held APA formal adjudicatory hearing requirements applicable

even though the relevant agency statute does not provide for a "hearing" "on the record." See, e.g., Seacoast Anti-Pollution League v. Costle (APA formal adjudication procedures required in initial licensing under the Clean Water Act, which provides for a decision "after opportunity for a public hearing" but does not provide for decision "on the record"). Why are some courts more willing to imply trial-type procedural formalities in adjudication than in rulemaking? Undoubtedly, tradition and black-letter constitutional law, which ordinarily requires a trial-type hearing in tax or regulatory adjudication that involves imposition of controls or liabilities on specific parties but not in rulemaking, exert a powerful influence. Courts may also believe that trial-type procedures pose a lesser threat to efficient administration in adjudication than in rulemaking, which often involves more parties and a wider range of issues.

Nonetheless, courts as well as agencies are beginning to display concern that automatic insistence on trial-type formalities in regulatory adjudication can seriously impede effective administration. See Costle v. Pacific Legal Found., 445 U.S. 198 (1980) (upholding EPA regulations requiring parties to show relevant "material issues of fact" to obtain a formal adjudicatory hearing in initial licensing under the Clean Water Act); Chemical Waste Mgmt. Inc. v. U.S.E.P.A., page 490, supra (deferring to EPA regulations denying formal adjudicatory hearing on corrective action orders). Courts have evoked concern that broadly defined hearing rights could cripple the implementation of environmental programs that involve the issuance of tens of thousands of permits. Courts have also stated that the interest of a license applicant is less than that of a person subject to coercive impositions by government, and have expressed doubt whether the scientific, economic, and engineering issues often involved in such licensing are appropriately resolved through trial-type hearings. Recall, however, that the EPA regulations at issue in *Chemical Waste Management* provided for full trial-type hearings in cases involving imposition of penalties or license revocation.

4. Notice-and-Comment Rulemaking Procedures

a. Implications of Increasing Agency Use of Rulemaking

Florida East Coast encouraged the agency shift from adjudication to rulemaking to develop law and policy, for it largely eliminated earlier fears that rulemaking could only be carried out through cumbersome trial-type procedures like those used in the FDA peanut butter case. The shift to rulemaking, however, threatened to deprive litigants and reviewing courts of any evidentiary record at all. Because trial-type hearings have been the norm in regulatory adjudication, the traditional use by regulatory agencies of adjudication to make and implement policy produced an extensive evidentiary record that could be used to scrutinize the agency's action. As a result of *Florida East Coast*, much rulemaking is now notice and comment. Recall that the traditional understanding of notice-and-comment rulemaking was that it did not produce an evidentiary record and that an agency in adopting a rule could rely on whatever material it deemed relevant without disclosing such materials. In these circumstances, judicial review of the validity of an agency rule was necessarily quite modest; a rule would be sustained if it did not transgress relevant statutory directives, was not irrational on its face, and was supportable by some set of facts that the agency might plausibly allege to exist. E.g., Superior Oil Co. v. FPC, 22 F.2d 601, 619 (9th Cir. 1963), *cert. denied*, 377 U.S. 922 (1964). In earlier decisions, courts had analogized judicial review of agency regulations to that of legislative statutes, concluding that the agency was no more required to support its measures by evidence of record than was the legislature. E.g., Assigned Car Cases, 274 U.S. 564 (1927). Lacking the opportunity to ferret out and challenge the evidence supposedly supporting the agency's action, the position of a litigant attacking a rule adopted after notice and comment was not an enviable one.

Further, recall that at the same time agencies were shifting to rulemaking (beginning in the late 1960s), public distrust of agency performance was increasing, and courts were developing a "hard look" approach to review of agency discretion. Hard look review is impossible without an evidentiary record, for it requires the court to closely examine the agency's findings, reasoning, and decisions in light of the evidentiary facts and analysis generated by the agency and outside parties. The agencies' increasing use of rulemaking thus threatened to make an "end run" around developing efforts by litigants and courts to impose tighter controls on agency discretion. For example, to avoid the delays involved in case-by-case adjudicatory determination of safety issues in the context of individual licensing hearings for nuclear generating plants, the Atomic Energy Commission (AEC), and its successor, the Nuclear Regulatory Commission (NRC), shifted to notice-and-comment rulemaking to resolve issues such as reactor safety or fuel recycling. However, this shift deprived environmental groups of opportunities for cross-examination to probe and test the assumptions and data behind nuclear safety decisions. See the *Vermont Yankee* litigation, pp. 338-344, infra.

In this and the following subsection, we examine two possible responses to this "end run" threat. The first, which the courts refused to adopt, is to allow persons regulated to challenge the factual underpinnings of a regulation when the regulation is applied to a particular person through an enforcement proceeding. An enforcement order is an adjudication to which trial-type hearing requirements would normally apply. Litigants argued, unsuccessfully, that the enforcement hearing should cover not only the question of the regulation's applicability to a given party but also the underlying validity of the regulation itself.

The second possible response to the rulemaking "end run" is to transform notice-and-comment rulemaking into new "paper hearing" procedures — more demanding than traditional notice and comment but less demanding than trial-type formal rulemaking — that generate a documentary record for "hard look" judicial review of rules. This was the response ultimately taken by the courts and Congress.

b. The Impact of Rulemaking on Adjudicatory Hearing Rights

FPC v. Texaco, Inc.
377 U.S. 33 (1964)

Mr. Justice DOUGLAS delivered the opinion of the Court.

The Federal Power Commission through notice and comment rulemaking, adopted regulations governing the terms of contracts between independent natural gas producers and pipelines to whom they supplied gas. The regulations prohibited "escalator" clauses adjusting the contract price for gas to future (higher) prices for newly delivered gas. . . . No oral argument was had but an opportunity was afforded for all interested parties to submit their views in writing; and the two respondents in this case — Texaco and Pan American — along with others, did so.

Later, each respondent submitted an application for a certificate of public convenience and necessity under §7 of the Natural Gas Act, to supply natural gas to a pipeline company. Section 7 provides, with exceptions not presently material, that the Commission "shall set" such an application "for hearing." Since, however, the applications disclosed price clauses that are not "permissible" under the regulations, the Commission without a hearing rejected the applications. . . .

The main issue in the case is whether the "hearing" granted under [APA §553] is adequate, so far as the price clauses are concerned, for purposes of §7 of the Natural Gas Act. We think the Court of Appeals erred . . . and that the statutory requirement for a hearing under §7 does not preclude the Commission from particularizing statutory standards through the rule-making process and barring at the threshold those who neither measure up to them nor show reasons why in the public interest the rule should be waived. . . .

[T]here is a procedure provided in the regulations whereby an applicant can ask for a waiver of the rule complained of.[23] Facts might conceivably be alleged sufficient on their face to provide a basis for waiver of the price-clause rules and for a hearing on the matter. But no such attempt was made here. . . .

To require the Commission to proceed only on a case-by-case basis would require it, so long as its policy outlawed indefinite price-changing provisions, to repeat in hearing after hearing its conclusions that condemn all of them. There would be a vast proliferation of hearings. . . . We see no reason why under this statutory scheme the processes of regulation need be so prolonged and so crippled. . . .

Notes and Questions

1. The APA defines "adjudication" to encompass all agency dispositions other than rulemaking, and specifically to include licensing. The FPC's denial of the particular applications tendered by Texaco was certainly not rulemaking; it was plainly the denial of the licenses sought by the applicants and therefore "adjudication" for APA purposes.

Should the Court therefore have held that the Natural Gas Act triggered the formal adjudicatory requirements of §§554, 556, and 557? Even if these requirements applied (did they?), a hearing was not needed because of the absence of material disputed facts. An agency, no less than a court, should be permitted to use "summary judgment" procedures and dispense with an evidentiary hearing when there are no material facts in dispute and the matter can be disposed of on the law alone. In *Texaco*, there was no dispute that the FPC's regulations required the FPC to deny the producers' applications. Since the sole issue was the legal validity of the pricing provisions, administrative summary judgment was proper. See Weinberger v. Hynson, Wercott & Dunning, Inc., 412 U.S. 609 (1973) (no hearing required on FDA order for withdrawal from market where manufacturer could not produce "adequate and well controlled clinical studies" of its safety and efficacy, as required by FDA regulations).

2. Justice Stewart dissented on the ground that the absence of a hearing interfered with judicial review of the rule. He thought that the producers should be given an

---

23. Regulation §1.7(b), 18 C.F.R. (Cum. Supp. 1963), §1.7(b), provides in relevant part:

A petition for the issuance, amendment, waiver, or repeal of a rule by the Commission shall set forth clearly and concisely petitioner's interest in the subject matter, the specific rule, amendment, waiver, or repeal requested, and cite by appropriate reference the statutory provision or other authority therefor. . . .

opportunity to test the factual bases for the commission's rule. But if each producer were entitled to a trial-type evidentiary hearing whenever a general regulation was applied to it, the advantages of rulemaking could be considerably weakened. Yet, the question remains, on what basis is a court to review the factual and analytic underpinnings of a rule adopted through §553 procedures?

3. To what extent was or should the Court's ruling be based on the FPC's provisions for waiver of its regulation in individual cases? What would an applicant have to establish to obtain a waiver? See Aman, Administrative Equity: An Analysis of Exceptions to Administrative Rules, 1982 Duke L.J. 277.

4. American Airlines v. Civil Aeronautics Board, 359 F.2d 624 (D.C. Cir. 1966) (en banc), applied the logic of *Texaco* to sustain a CAB regulation, adopted pursuant to notice-and-comment rulemaking, restricting authority to sell "blocked space" for air cargo carriage ("wholesale" sales for carriage of a specified quantity of cargo carriage in advance of specific shipments) to all-cargo airlines. Prior to adoption of the regulations, "combination" airlines carrying passengers as well as cargo could also sell blocked space. The board justified the regulation on the need to strengthen the position of all-cargo carriers. The combination carriers contended that the regulation amounted to an amendment of their existing board certificates to engage in air transport and that accordingly a trial-type adjudicatory hearing was required, pursuant to Civil Aeronautics Act provisions requiring such a hearing where the board modified existing certificates. In rejecting this contention, Judge Leventhal wrote for the court:

> [R]ulemaking is a vital part of the administrative process, particularly adapted to and needful for sound evolution of policy in guiding the future development of industries subject to intensive administrative regulation in the public interest, and . . . rulemaking is not to be shackled, in the absence of clear and specific Congressional requirement, by importation of formalities developed for the adjudicatory process and basically unsuited for policy rule making. . . .
>
> The proceeding before us is rulemaking both in form and effect. There is no individual action here masquerading as a general rule. . . .

See also Air Line Pilots Assn. v. Quesada, 276 F.2d 892 (2d Cir. 1960) (sustaining an FAA regulation lowering the maximum flying age of pilots on scheduled airlines to age 60, in effect amending pilots' existing licenses).

By what procedure might the combination carriers challenge the appropriateness of the rule if experience contradicted the board's assumptions in enacting it? See APA §553(e).

Heckler v. Campbell
461 U.S. 458 (1983)

Justice POWELL delivered the opinion of the Court.

The Social Security Act defines "disability" in terms of the effect a physical or mental impairment has on a person's ability to function in the workplace. It provides disability benefits only to persons who are unable "to engage in any substantial gainful activity by reason of any medically determinable physical or mental impairment." . . . And it specifies that a person must "not only [be] unable to do his previous work but [must be unable], considering his age, education, and work experience, [to] engage in any other kind of substantial gainful work which exists in the national economy, regardless of whether such work exists in the immediate area in which he lives, or whether a specific job vacancy exists for him, or whether he would be hired if he applied for work." [The Act provides that an applicant denied disability benefits is entitled to a trial-type adjudicatory hearing before an ALJ.]

In 1978, the Secretary of Health and Human Services promulgated regulations [providing] that certain impairments are so severe that they prevent a person from pursuing any gainful work. . . . A claimant who establishes that he suffers from one of these impairments will be considered disabled without further inquiry. . . . If a claimant suffers from a less severe impairment, the Secretary must determine whether the claimant retains the ability to perform either his former work or some less demanding employment. If a claimant can pursue his former occupation, he is not entitled to disability benefits. . . . If he cannot, the Secretary must determine whether the claimant retains the capacity to pursue less demanding work.

The regulations divide this last inquiry into two stages. First, the Secretary must assess each claimant's present job qualifications. The regulations direct the Secretary to consider the factors Congress has identified as relevant: physical ability, age, education, and work experience. [This determination is based on an individual inquiry into each claimant's characteristics.] Second, she must consider whether jobs exist in the national economy that a person having the claimant's qualifications could perform.

Prior to 1978, the Secretary relied on vocational experts to establish the existence of suitable jobs in the national economy. After a claimant's limitations and abilities had been determined at a hearing, a vocational expert ordinarily would testify whether work existed that the claimant could perform. Although this testimony often was based on standardized guides, . . . vocational experts frequently were criticized for their inconsistent treatment of similarly situated claimants. . . .[24]

[The regulations adopted by HHS included medical-vocational guidelines that] relieve the Secretary of the need to rely on vocational experts by establishing through rulemaking the types and numbers of jobs that exist in the national economy. They consist of a matrix of the four factors identified by Congress — physical ability, age, education, and work experience[25] — and set forth rules that identify whether jobs requiring specific combinations of these factors exist in significant numbers in the national economy.[26] Where a claimant's qualifications correspond to the job requirements identified by a rule,[27] the guidelines direct a conclusion as to whether work exists that the claimant could perform. If such work exists, the claimant is not considered disabled.

24. The Social Security hearing system is "probably the largest adjudicative agency in the western world." J. Mashaw, C. Goetz, F. Goodman, W. Schwartz, P. Verkuil & M. Carrow, Social Security Hearings and Appeals xi (1978). Approximately 2.3 million claims for disability benefits were filed in fiscal year 1981. Department of Health and Human Services, Social Security Annual Report to the Congress for Fiscal Year 1981, pp. 32, 35 (1982). More than a quarter of a million of these claims required a hearing before an administrative law judge. Id., at 38. The need for efficiency is self-evident.

25. Each of these four factors is divided into defined categories. A person's ability to perform physical tasks, for example, is categorized according to the physical exertion requirements necessary to perform varying classes of jobs — i.e., whether a claimant can perform sedentary, light, medium, heavy, or very heavy work. . . . Each of these work categories is defined in terms of the physical demands it places on a worker, such as the weight of objects he must lift and whether extensive movement or use of arm and leg controls is required.

26. For example, Rule 202.10 provides that a significant number of jobs exist for a person who can perform light work, is closely approaching advanced age, has a limited education but who is literate and can communicate in English, and whose previous work has been unskilled.

27. . . . If an individual's capabilities are not described accurately by a rule, the regulations make clear that the individual's particular limitations must be considered. . . . Additionally, the regulations declare that the administrative law judge will not apply the age categories "mechanically in a borderline situation," . . . and recognize that some claimants may possess limitations that are not factored into the guidelines. . . . Thus, the regulations provide that the rules will be applied only when they describe a claimant's abilities and limitations accurately.

In 1979, Carmen Campbell applied for disability benefits because a back condition
. . . prevented her from continuing her work as a hotel maid. After her application was
denied, she requested a hearing de novo before an Administrative Law Judge. He determined that her back problem was not severe enough to find her disabled without further
inquiry, and accordingly considered whether she retained the ability to perform either
her past work or some less strenuous job. . . . He concluded that even though Campbell's
back condition prevented her from returning to her work as a maid, she retained the physical capacity to do light work. . . . In accordance with the regulations, he found that
Campbell was 52 years old, that her previous employment consisted of unskilled jobs,
and that she had a limited education. . . . He noted that Campbell, who had been born in
Panama, experienced difficulty in speaking and writing English. She was able, however,
to understand and read English fairly well. . . . Relying on the medical-vocational guidelines, the Administrative Law Judge found that a significant number of jobs existed that a
person of Campbell's qualifications could perform. Accordingly, he concluded that she
was not disabled.

[The court of appeals held that the Social Security Administration (SSA) was
required to include in the administrative record more specific evidence, beyond the
guidelines, of available jobs in the national economy that claimant was capable of
performing. It held that the failure to provide such evidence deprived the claimant of a
meaningful adjudicatory hearing. It set aside the SSA's finding that the claimant was
disabled as unsupported by substantial evidence.]

[The court of appeals'] requirement that additional evidence be introduced . . .
prevents the Secretary from putting the guidelines to their intended use and implicitly
calls their validity into question.

The Social Security Act directs the Secretary to "adopt reasonable and proper rules
and regulations to regulate and provide for the nature and extent of the proofs and evidence
and the method of taking and furnishing the same" in disability cases. 42 U.S.C. §405(a).

We do not think that the Secretary's reliance on medical-vocational guidelines is
inconsistent with the Social Security Act. It is true that the statutory scheme contemplates
that disability hearings will be individualized determinations based on evidence adduced
at a hearing. See 42 U.S.C. §423(d)(2)(A) (specifying consideration of each individual's
condition); 42 U.S.C. §405(b) (1976 ed., Supp. V) (disability determination to be based
on evidence adduced at hearing). But this does not bar the Secretary from relying on
rulemaking to resolve certain classes of issues. The Court has recognized that even where
an agency's enabling statute expressly requires it to hold a hearing, the agency may rely
on its rulemaking authority to determine issues that do not require case-by-case consideration. See FPC v. Texaco Inc.

[The determination whether jobs exist in the national economy for a person with
a claimant's characteristics] is not unique to each claimant. This type of general
factual issue may be resolved as fairly through rulemaking as by introducing the
testimony of vocational experts at each disability hearing. See American Airlines,
Inc. v. CAB. . . .

As the Secretary has argued, the use of published guidelines brings with it a uniformity that previously had been perceived as lacking. To require the Secretary to relitigate
the existence of jobs in the national economy at each hearing would hinder needlessly an
already overburdened agency. We conclude that the Secretary's use of medical-vocational
guidelines does not conflict with the statute, nor can we say on the record before us that
they are arbitrary and capricious.

Notes and Questions

1. The HHS medical-vocational guidelines have been referred to as "grid" regulations because they specify parameters that automatically determine an applicant's capacity for work in the national economy once the applicant's age, work experience, education, and physical condition are determined. How can claimants challenge the factual and other assumptions underlying the SSA "grid" regulations? As a legal matter? As a practical matter? How realistic is the opportunity, referred to in note 15 to the Court's opinion, that a claimant can obtain an individualized hearing on her claim that her particular capabilities are not properly captured by the rule, and the provision that the "grid" regulations should not be applied "mechanically in borderline cases"? We consider further the social security disability programs, and the role of adjudicatory hearings in their implementation below.

2. Heckler v. Campbell was followed in Bowen v. Yackert, 482 U.S. 137 (1987), upholding SSA regulations similar to those presented in *Campbell,* and in American Hospital Assn. v. NLRB, 499 U.S. 606 (1991), upholding the NLRB's denial of an adjudicatory hearing on the appropriate bargaining unit for hospital workers on the basis of a board rule defining units of eight employees as appropriate in acute-care hospital facilities, notwithstanding statutory requirement of hearing "in each case." But Sullivan v. Zerbly, 493 U.S. 606 (1990), overturned SSA's reliance on children's disability regulations to deny, without an adjudicatory hearing, benefits to a child claimant under a Supplemental Security Income (SSI) program providing benefits to children suffering from an impairment of "comparable severity" to those that would render an adult unable to engage in gainful employment. SSA's adult disability regulations specify 125 different medical conditions; an adult possessing one of these conditions would be deemed unemployable at the threshold. Only if a claimant did not have one of these conditions would SSA go on to consider the four claimant-specific factors (physical ability, age, education, work experience) challenged in the "grid" regulations at issue in Heckler v. Campbell. The children's disability regulations incorporated these 125 conditions plus an additional 57 conditions particular to children. A child would be deemed disabled only if the child had a listed condition. The Court set aside the regulations and the denial of benefits based thereon. First, the regulations did not include some conditions or combinations thereof that would disable a child from normal activity; while they allowed a child claimant to qualify on a showing that his condition was similar in type and severity to a listed condition, this option was restrictively defined. Second, the regulations did not provide for a second-stage inquiry of an individual child's functional capacity, comparable to the inquiry into the capacity of an adult claimant to engage in gainful employment; SSA claimed that it was not feasible to develop a test of functional capacity for children comparable to the "grid" for adults. The Court held that the regulations accordingly failed to implement fully disabled children's entitlement to SSI. It rejected as unrealistically burdensome the dissent's suggestion that if the regulations were underinclusive by failing to include some instances of disability, a claimant could establish such disability through a submission of proof that she was in fact disabled and, if necessary, obtain judicial review of a denial of benefits.

Problem

The FTC issues trade regulation rules. It states:

> Where a trade regulation rule is relevant to any issue involved in an adjudicative proceeding thereafter instituted, the commission may rely upon the rule to resolve

such issue provided that the respondent shall have been given fair hearing on the legality and propriety of applying the rule to the particular case.

After notice and comment procedures, the FTC in 1997 promulgated the following rule:

[I]n connection with the sale, offering for sale, or distribution in commerce . . . of cigars it is an unfair or deceptive act or practice within the meaning of section 5 of the Federal Trade Commission Act . . . to fail to disclose, clearly and prominently, in all advertising and on every pack, box, carton or other container in which cigars are sold to the consuming public that cigar smoking is dangerous to health and may cause death from cancer and other diseases.

In 1998, the U.S. Cigar Company was organized and began to market Mellow cigars. It claimed in its advertising to have the lowest tar and nicotine content of any cigar containing tobacco, and failed to place any health warning in either its advertising or its labeling. The FTC brought a §5 proceeding against this company, claiming that it had failed to include the required warnings and that the name of the brand was deceptive. The FTC Act requires a trial-type adjudicatory hearing in §5 proceedings. The Commission introduced evidence showing that U.S. Cigar violated the rule and demands summary judgment on both claims. What procedural claims might U.S. Cigar make in response? What result?

c. Judicial Transformation of §553 Notice-and-Comment Procedures

The decisions in the previous subsection reflect judicial sensitivity to the practical implications of allowing those regulated to challenge, through trial-type hearings, the underlying evidentiary validity of regulations in every adjudicatory proceeding to enforce those regulations. Even were such a practice allowed, it would not solve the problem of how to create a record for preenforcement review when the validity of regulations is challenged in court immediately after they have been adopted and before they have been enforced against anyone. As we shall develop in Chapter 8, such "preenforcement" review is now widely available and widely used.

The drafters of the APA apparently contemplated that courts reviewing agency rules adopted through notice and comment or other less formal procedures would themselves hear evidence and develop a factual record to judge the validity of the rule. See Williams, "Hybrid Rulemaking" under the Administrative Procedure Act: A Legal and Empirical Analysis, 42 U. Chi. L. Rev. 401, 418-424 (1975). But there are many difficulties in this approach. Relevant statutes often provide for judicial review in a court of appeals, which has no regular evidence-gathering machinery. Postdecision assembly of a record invites post hoc rationalization by the agency. Moreover, the function of procedural safeguards is not only to provide a record for judicial review, but to enlighten and shape the agency's exercise of its discretion by ensuring input of evidence and views by interested persons. This latter function would be greatly attenuated if procedures for submission of evidence and argument were postponed to the stage of judicial review; moreover, practicalities dictate that in many cases there will be no judicial review.

As the materials that follow show, in lieu of developing the relevant facts independently, courts required agencies to develop an evidentiary base for their regulations through "paper hearing" or "hybrid" rulemaking procedures that are less formal than a full-fledged trial-type hearing but more substantial than traditional notice-and-comment requirements.

United States v. Nova Scotia Food Products Corp.

568 F.2d 240 (2d Cir. 1977)

[Pursuant to the Food, Drug, and Cosmetic Act, the FDA conducted §553 notice-and-comment rulemaking proceedings to promulgate safety regulations for the smoking of fish to safeguard against botulism poisoning. It sued to enjoin Nova Scotia Food Products Corp. and its officers from processing hot-smoked whitefish in violation of the regulations. The district court granted an injunction against Nova Scotia.]

GURFEIN, Circuit Judge. . . .

II

[Nova Scotia and others] contend that there is an inadequate administrative record upon which to predicate judicial review, and that the failure to disclose to interested parties the factual material upon which the agency was relying vitiates the element of fairness which is essential to any kind of administrative action. Moreover, they argue that the "concise general statement of . . . basis and purpose" by the Commissioner was inadequate. 5 U.S.C. §553.

. . . The extent of an administrative record required for judicial review of informal rulemaking is largely a function of the scope of judicial review. Even when the standard of judicial review is whether the promulgation of the rule was "arbitrary, capricious, an abuse of discretion, or otherwise not in accordance with law," as specified in 5 U.S.C. §706(2)(A), judicial review must nevertheless be based on the "whole record" (id.). . . .

This raises several questions regarding the informal rulemaking procedure followed here: (1) What record does a reviewing court look to? (2) How much of what the agency relied on should have been disclosed to interested parties? (3) To what extent must the agency respond to criticism that is material?

A

No contemporaneous record was made or certified. When, during the enforcement action, the basis for the regulation was sought through pretrial discovery, the record was created by searching the files of the FDA and the memories of those who participated in the process of rulemaking. [The "record" thus generated consisted of the comments received from outside parties during the notice-and-comment period, and previously undisclosed scientific data on which the commissioner relied.]

B

The key issues were (1) whether, in the light of the rather scant history of botulism in whitefish, that species should have been considered separately rather than included in a general regulation which failed to distinguish species from species; (2) whether the application of the proposed [time-temperature-salinity or T-T-S] requirements to smoked whitefish made whitefish commercially unsaleable; and (3) whether the agency recognized that prospect, but nevertheless decided that the public health needs should prevail even if that meant commercial death for the whitefish industry. The procedural issues were whether, in the light of these key questions, the agency procedure was inadequate because (i) it failed to disclose the scientific data and the methodology upon which it relied; and (ii) because it failed utterly to address itself to the pertinent question of commercial feasibility.

[The court briefly reviewed evidence from the record showing that botulism in hot-smoked whitefish has been extremely rare.]

The Scientific Data

Interested parties were not informed of the scientific data, or at least of a selection of such data deemed important by the agency, so that comments could be addressed to the data. Appellants argue that unless the scientific data relied upon by the agency are spread upon the public records, criticism of the methodology used or the meaning to be inferred from the data is rendered impossible. [The court agreed with appellants' claim.]

Though a reviewing court will not match submission against counter-submission to decide whether the agency was correct in its conclusion on scientific matters (unless that conclusion is arbitrary), it will consider whether the agency has taken account of all "relevant factors and whether there has been a clear error of judgment." *Overton Park*, 401 U.S. at 415.

If the failure to notify interested persons of the scientific research upon which the agency was relying actually prevented the presentation of relevant comment, the agency may be held not to have considered all "the relevant factors." . . . To suppress meaningful comment by failure to disclose the basic data relied upon is akin to rejecting comment altogether. For unless there is common ground, the comments are unlikely to be of a quality that might impress a careful agency. The inadequacy of comment in turn leads in the direction of arbitrary decision-making.

C.

[The FDA provided only cursory responses to suggestions by the Bureau of Commercial Fisheries that regulations should be set on a species-by-species basis and by appellants that "heating of certain types of fish to high temperatures will completely destroy the product." The FDA also failed to respond to comments by the Bureau of Commercial Fisheries that nitrite and salt as additives would make smoking at lower temperatures safer. Nor did the FDA answer claims made by the Association of Smoked Fish Processors, Inc., that the proposed regulations were not based on adequate scientific evidence concerning the variety of smoked products to be included under the regulations.]

Appellants additionally attack the "concise general statement" required by APA, 5 U.S.C. §553, as inadequate. We think that, in the circumstances, it was less than adequate. It is not in keeping with the rational process to leave vital questions, raised by comments which are of cogent materiality, completely unanswered. The agencies certainly have a good deal of discretion in expressing the basis of a rule, but the agencies do not have quite the prerogative of obscurantism reserved to legislatures. "Congress did not purport to transfer its legislative power to the unbounded discretion of the regulatory body." FCC v. RCA Communications, Inc., 346 U.S. 86, 90. . . .

The Secretary was squarely faced with the question whether it was necessary to formulate a rule with specific parameters that applied to all species of fish, and particularly whether lower temperatures with the addition of nitrite and salt would not be sufficient [to deal with the risk of botulism in whitefish]. Though this alternative was suggested by an agency of the federal government, its suggestion, though acknowledged, was never answered.

Moreover, the comment that to apply the proposed T-T-S requirements to whitefish would destroy the commercial product was neither discussed nor answered. We think that to sanction silence in the face of such vital questions would be to make the statutory requirement of a "concise general statement" less than an adequate safeguard against arbitrary decision-making.

One may recognize that even commercial infeasibility cannot stand in the way of an overwhelming public interest. Yet the administrative process should disclose, at least, whether the proposed regulation is considered to be commercially feasible, or whether other considerations prevail even if commercial infeasibility is acknowledged.

In the light of the history of smoked whitefish to which we have referred, we find no articulate balancing here sufficient to make the procedure followed less than arbitrary.

[The court reversed the lower court's grant of an injunction and dismissed the complaint.]

[Note that *Nova Scotia* allows the respondent in an enforcement action to contest the validity of the regulations being enforced. Is this consistent with *Texaco*?]

Note: The Judicial Development of "Paper Hearing" Procedures

Nova Scotia provides a good illustration of how federal appeals courts built on the opportunity for comment and "concise general statement" requirements of §553 to transform notice-and-comment procedures into a more elaborate "paper hearing" process that generates a documentary record and a full agency opinion (in the form of a "preamble" that is published in the *Federal Register* along with the final rule) as the basis for "hard look" judicial review. While *Nova Scotia* involved the FDA, many other key court decisions in this evolutionary process involved the efforts of the EPA to implement a variety of important and controversial environmental regulatory programs.

A fundamental element in the transformation of notice-and-comment rulemaking was the requirement that agencies disclose the evidentiary and analytical documentation relied on in proposing a rule to permit informed and effective comment. While agencies might be tempted to disclose only those materials supporting their position, courts required that all relevant material be disclosed.[28] Moreover, all relevant internal agency documents would generally be subject to eventual public discovery under the Freedom of Information Act, 5 U.S.C. §552.

---

28. See Kent County, Delaware Levy Court v. EPA, 963 F.2d 391, 396 (D.C. Cir. 1992), which involved a challenge to EPA's listing of a site on the National Priorities List under the Comprehensive Environmental Response, Compensation and Liability Act (CERCLA or "Superfund"). In making the listing decision, EPA had relied on a memorandum developed under a different statutory program — the Resource Conservation and Recovery Act — to conclude that it should use only unfiltered groundwater samples in determining a site's waste characteristics, but had deliberately or negligently failed to locate relevant EPA regional CERCLA files on this issue; these files turned out to contain documents that contradicted its conclusion. The court found that EPA's failure to examine the regional CERCLA files for documents discussing the issue was arbitrary and capricious, and ordered the administrative record supplemented with the relevant documents. The court went on to find that, in light of the conflicting EPA memoranda, EPA's decision to use only unfiltered samples was arbitrary and capricious.

In addition to requiring full agency disclosure of documents, courts required EPA and other agencies to explain, in the preamble statement accompanying a final rule, their grounds for decision, including in particular their reasons for rejecting adverse outside comments on proposed regulations and the agency data and analysis disclosed in agency documents. Where such explanations were inadequate, courts would either find a procedural violation of §553 or conclude that the failure to provide adequate explanation was arbitrary and capricious under §706. This development can be seen as the rulemaking analogue of the "adequate consideration" requirement in adjudication pioneered in *Scenic Hudson.*

As a practical matter, the requirement that an agency respond to adverse comments, data, and analysis often means that an agency must, after receiving initial comments, develop further data and analysis before issuing a final regulation because the comments show flaws in the initial proposal and supporting materials too serious to survive "hard look" review. After the agency has generated new data and analysis (and perhaps modified its proposals), a second round of opportunity for comment may be required. If the second round of comments again shows serious flaws in the agency's proposal, further rounds of comment and agency response may be required. In the process, the agency's original proposed rule may be so drastically reshaped that a new notice must be issued with a new proposed rule and opportunity for comment thereon.

As a result of these developments, notice-and-comment rulemaking has been transformed, especially as regards controversial proposals, into a rather elaborate "paper hearing" procedure that generates as the basis for judicial review a full documentary record and an elaborate agency opinion that attempts to justify the agency rule and respond to evidentiary, analytical, and policy criticisms of the rule and its supporting material. These procedural transformations have enabled courts to implement (and are an integral part of) the "hard look" approach to review of discretion examined in Chapter 4. At the same time, as discussed further below, these changes have, in the case of major, controversial rulemakings, prolonged the notice-and-comment process and made it more burdensome for agencies. The rulemaking record can run to millions of pages.

Weyerhauser Co. v. Costle

590 F.2d 1011 (D.C. Cir. 1978)

[Pulp and paper manufacturers challenged the EPA's adoption, pursuant to the Clean Water Act, of regulations limiting effluent discharges from pulp, paper, and paperboard mills.]

McGOWAN, Circuit Judge:

[I]n the informal rulemaking context involved herein, this inquiry asks whether the agency gave "interested parties an opportunity to participate in the rulemaking through submission of written [or other] data" and whether it "incorporate[d] in the rule adopted a concise general statement of their basis and purpose."[29] . . .

---

29. . . . In the case of highly technical regulations, and especially regulations calling for refined scientific judgments, the reviewing court should be careful to insure that the procedures used as a vehicle for promulgation are ample enough to support their substantive cargo. . . . Moreover, the use in Section 553 of the dyad "basis and purpose" suggests that the explanatory statement should discuss both the factual premises, if any, and the policy considerations underlying the administrative action. . . .

The one procedural inadequacy attributed to EPA in this case . . . concerns EPA's derivation of one effluent limitation (out of three in all) for one subdivision of the industry (out of 66 in all): the BOD (biochemical oxygen demand) limitation for acetate grade dissolving sulfite mills. [The challenge] revolves around EPA's computation of the "secondary waste load"[30] that must be treated by typical acetate grade dissolving sulfite mills using Best Practicable Control Technology Currently Available. . . .

EPA originally computed the secondary waste load for these mills at 487 pounds of waste to be treated per ton of product (lbs./ton), a figure to which the industry did not object. Between the publication of the Interim Final Limitations and the Final Limitations, however, the Agency apparently secured new data and recalculated the waste load as lower, i.e., 404 lbs./ton. EPA purportedly arrived at the latter figure after it (1) studied two other factors that it realized would require adjusting the figure upwards and downwards respectively, but then (2) decided to disregard the two factors on the assumption that they cancelled each other out. We say "purportedly" because the record includes no mention of the two factors, much less their mode of being considered. Finally, in making its cost calculation, EPA took the 404 lbs./ton figure and reduced it to 314 lbs./ton on a further assumption that it now admits is erroneous. . . .

. . . Most obviously, the defect stems from the inadequacy of the Agency's final published explanation. That explanation includes, and we presume the Agency relied upon, computations now admitted to be erroneous. Further, it deletes mention of a phantom set of not-quite-offsetting adjustments that Agency attorneys now deem crucial to the viability of EPA's cost determination.

Absent a coherent discussion — in the record — of the factual "basis" and legislative "purpose" underlying EPA's conclusion, we are unable to rely on our usual assumption that the Agency, when relying on supportable facts and permissible policy concerns and when obligated to explain itself, will rationally exercise the duties delegated to it by Congress. It is for this reason that we take no solace in the fact that the Agency's counsel, after the fact, may be able convincingly to rationalize the Agency's decision.

Moreover, the Agency's procedures in this limited instance improperly denied petitioners the opportunity to comment on a significant part of the Agency's decision-making process as required by Section 553. . . .

Our conclusion does not imply any dissatisfaction with the rule that the Agency need not subject every incremental change in its conclusions after each round of notice and comment to further public scrutiny before final action. But in this case, the Agency's final conclusions are far from the "logical outgrowth" of the preceding notice and comment process. . . .

For all of the foregoing reasons, therefore, we must remand the regulation setting forth the BOD limitation for acetate grade dissolving sulfite mills. . . .

Notes and Questions

1. You should now review the *State Farm Mutual* (airbags) case (Chapter 4) which can be read as endorsement by the Supreme Court of the approach to review developed in *Nova Scotia* and *Weyerhauser*. The agency must support its decision to adopt a given

30. "Raw waste load" is the total amount of waste generated by the mill before treatment. After this waste goes through primary treatment (i.e., after being pumped into a sedimentary tank where solid waste settles out), the remaining pollution, called "secondary waste load," is subjected to secondary treatment (breakdown of bacteria) in order to cut down BOD. Accordingly, the amount of secondary waste load determines the amount and cost of secondary treatment sufficient to meet the BOD limitation.

rule with specific findings and explanations (set forth in the rule preamble) that respond adequately to evidence and arguments submitted in comments and find adequate support in the "paper hearing" record of the rulemaking. Note the *Weyerhauser* court's refusal to defer to agency judgment if these requirements are not met and its insistence that adequate, well-supported explanations be provided by the agency at the time that it adopts a rule, not by counsel in subsequent litigation. This approach reaffirms *Chenery*.

2. How logical or wise is the court's suggestion in *Weyerhauser* (fn.17) that more elaborate procedural requirements are especially appropriate when the agency's decision involves highly complex and technical engineering, economic, and scientific issues? Recall the debate between Judge Leventhal and Judge Bazelon in *Ethyl* about procedural formalities and "hard look" review (Chapter 4). Can the suggestion be defended on the ground that judges are experts in procedure if not in substance?

3. What is the source of the courts' authority to invalidate the regulations success-fully challenged in *Nova Scotia* and *Weyerhauser*? Are the defects in the agencies' deci-sions "procedural," as the *Weyerhauser* opinion indicates?

4. Suppose that an agency gives notice containing a proposed rule, receives comments, and decides, in light of those comments, to change its proposal. Must the agency give a new notice with the proposed change and receive a new round of comments? Not if the change is a "logical outgrowth" of the original proposal. "The task is essentially one of balancing the advantages of additional comment — improvement in the quality of rules, fairness for affected parties, and facilitation of judicial review — against the burden on 'the public interest in expedition and finality.'" Action Alliance of Senior Citizens v. Bowen, 846 F.2d 1449 (D.C. Cir. 1988).

American Medical Assn. v. United States, 887 F.2d 760 (7th Cir. 1989), summarized the relevant case law as follows:

> The adequacy of notice in any case must be determined by a close examination of the facts of the particular proceeding which produced a challenged rule. However, without reciting in detail the facts of other cases, we note that courts have upheld final rules which differed from proposals in the following significant respects: outright rever-sal of the agency's initial position; elimination of compliance options contained in an NPR; collapsing, or further subdividing, distinct categories of regulated entities estab-lished in a proposed rule; exempting certain entities from the coverage of final rules; or altering the method of calculating or measuring a quantity relevant to a party's obli-gations under the rule.
>
> On the other hand, a rule will be invalidated if no notice was given of an issue addressed by the final rules. Moreover, courts have held on numerous occasions that notice is inadequate where an issue was only addressed in the most general terms in the initial proposal, or where a final rule changes a pre-existing agency practice which was only mentioned in an NPR in order to place unrelated changes in the overall regulatory scheme into their proper context.
>
> The crucial issue, then, is whether parties affected by a final rule were put on notice that "their interests [were] 'at stake'"; in other words, the relevant inquiry is whether or not potential commentators would have known that an issue in which they were interested was "on the table" and was to be addressed by a final rule. From this perspective it is irrelevant whether the proposal contained in the NPR was favorable to a particular party's interests; the obligation to comment is not limited to those adversely affected by a proposal. [I]f interested parties favor a particular regulatory proposal, they should intervene in the rulemaking to support the approach an agency has tentatively advanced.

American Medical found that the American Medical Association, which had not filed comments on a proposed rule, had had adequate notice that its interests were "at stake." But see Horsehead Resource Dev. Co. v. Browner, 16 F.3d 1246 (D.C. Cir.), *cert. denied*, 513 U.S. 816 (1994), in which the D.C. Circuit invalidated an EPA rule that regulated the burning of hazardous waste as fuel pursuant to the Resource Conservation and Recovery Act. Although EPA had given notice with respect to individual components of the final rule, the notice was held inadequate because the agency did not give notice of the combination of components in the final rule, thereby precluding meaningful participation in the rulemaking process by the regulated community. 16 F.3d at 1267-1268.[31]

As part of the notice requirement, the agency must identify and make available technical studies and data that it employed in reaching the decision to propose particular rules in time to allow for meaningful commentary. Solite Corp. v. EPA, 952 F.2d 473, 484 (D.C. Cir. 1991).

5. In a notice-and-comment rulemaking proceeding, the agency maintains a file of all the relevant documents in its public records room. The file will contain *Federal Register* publications relating to the rulemaking, including the notice of proposed rulemaking; the internal and other documents relied on by the agency in developing the rule; written comments received from outside the agency; and the final published rule and preamble. Special rules apply to comments received from the Office of Management and Budget (OMB) in connection with its review of rules pursuant to executive order (see Chapter 3). The issue of off-the-record oral communications is discussed below. Suppose a litigant challenging a regulation asserts that a rulemaking record omits certain relevant material adverse to the agency. May the litigant introduce such material on judicial review and have it considered by the courts on the merits to have the regulation set aside? Reviewing courts generally decline this invitation, ruling that if the record is incomplete the appropriate remedy is a remand for the development by the agency of a more adequate record. The court in *Nova Scotia* so ruled in a portion of its opinion not included in our excerpt.

This solution, implied by *Chenery*, gives the agency an opportunity to respond to the omitted material before the court is required to decide its significance on the merits. But the courts cannot avoid some appraisal of omitted documents in ruling whether the delay and expense of a remand to reopen the record is warranted. Omission of potentially relevant material is inevitable because of what might be called the "dribble over" phenomenon. A major controversial rulemaking, such as that in *Weyerhauser*, will generate many studies and analyses, both inside and outside the agency. At some point, the agency must call a halt to public comments, close the record, and decide the case. But considerable time elapses between the closing of the rulemaking record and the agency's actual decision. Additional time elapses before the court hears the case. In the interim, additional studies in progress will have been completed, and litigants will contend that these studies

---

31. When an agency has failed to comply with the notice and comment requirements because a final rule is not the "logical outgrowth" of the proposed rule, a party challenging the final rule is not required to show that they would have submitted new arguments to invalidate the rules if they had been given an opportunity to comment, unless the agency offers persuasive evidence that all possible objections to its final rules had already been given sufficient consideration. Shell Oil Co. v. EPA, 950 F.2d 741, 752 (D.C. Cir. 1991).

Also, when the agency has failed to provide notice of a provision in a final rule, the agency cannot invoke comments on the proposed rule that also addressed matters contained in the final rule to excuse the failure to give adequate notice. Fertilizer Inst. v. EPA, 935 F.2d 1303, 1312 (D.C. Cir. 1991). The fact that comments on a proposed rule indicate an awareness of the potential contours of the final rule, however, can serve as evidence of the adequacy of notice. Shell Oil Co. v. EPA, 950 F.2d 741, 757 (D.C. Cir. 1991).

must be included in the record and an opportunity to comment on them be provided. For an example of judicial efforts to deal with such claims, see Sierra Club v. Costle, 657 F.2d 298 (D.C. Cir. 1981), involving claims that an EPA notice-and-comment rulemaking proceeding had been rendered defective by the appearance, after the period for public comment had ended, of some 300 studies and documents. EPA decided to include the documents in the public file. (If it had refused to do so, would it have been vulnerable to a charge of relying on ex parte communications never made public?) Environmental Defense Fund (EDF) complained that it had been deprived of the opportunity to comment on the studies. The court, however, found that EDF had in no way been prejudiced because many of the materials were cumulative and EDF could subsequently have submitted counterdocumentation.

6. Section 553(c) requires an agency, on adopting a rule, to "incorporate in the rules adopted a concise general statement of their basis and purpose." As a result of such decisions as *Nova Scotia* and *State Farm*, the rule preambles that accompany rules published in the *Federal Register* are often neither "concise" nor "general." In major contested rulemakings, the rule preamble runs to dozens of pages of fine double-column print in the *Federal Register*; in some cases, they run to more than 100 pages. The preamble will discuss in detail the agency's justification for its rule, the reasons why it did not adopt alternatives to the rule adopted, the criticisms advanced by opponents of the rule, and the record evidence pro and con. This practice reflects the response, possibly over-cautious, of agency lawyers to rulings such as *Nova Scotia*, *Weyerhauser*, and *State Farm*. The D.C. Circuit has cautioned against "an overly literal reading of the terms 'concise' and 'general' [which must be] accommodated to the realities of judicial scrutiny." Independent U.S. Tanker Owners Comm. v. Dole, 809 F.2d 847, *cert. denied*, 484 U.S. 819 (1987), quoting Automotive Parts & Accessories Assn. v. Boyd, 407 F.2d 330, 338 (D.C. Cir. 1968). In *Tanker*, the court invalidated a rule, adopted by the secretary of transportation under the Merchant Marine Act, allowing U.S. tankers engaged in foreign commerce (which receive federal subsidies) to compete with tankers engaged in U.S. domestic traffic (which are unsubsidized), provided that they repay to the government a portion of their subsidies. Some domestic tankers, which the navy thought valuable for national security purposes, would be forced out of business as a result. The secretary sought to justify the rule by invoking "economic efficiency," "use of underemployed resources," "increased competition," and the like. The court found that the secretary had failed to link these highly general considerations to the objectives of the Merchant Marine Act in a fashion that justified the rule adopted or to discuss adequately alternatives to the proposed rule.

Suppose a reviewing court sets aside an agency rule because the agency's explanation for its adoption is inadequate. On remand, may the agency simply rewrite its explanation, or must it start the entire notice-and-comment process all over again? See Action on Smoking & Health v. CAB, 699 F.2d 1209 (D.C. Cir. 1983) (requiring new notice-and-comment proceeding). Compare the post-remand history of *State Farm*.

7. Might one, borrowing the old refrain about the Grand Old Duke of York, conclude that *Florida East Coast* marched the agencies down the hill of formal rulemaking only to have the courts of appeals march them up (or almost all the way up) again? The "paper hearing" procedures that have emerged from judicial transformation of §553 do not seem very different from a streamlined version of §§556-557 outlined at p. 519, supra. Was *Florida East Coast* wrongly decided? Does it matter by what route the "paper hearing" norm is achieved?

General reviews of the evolution of notice-and-comment rulemaking and associated issues of judicial review are found in DeLong, Informal Rulemaking and the Integration of Law and Policy, 65 Va. L. Rev. 257 (1979); Diver, Policymaking Paradigms in Administrative Law, 95 Harv. L. Rev. 393 (1981).

Note on Decisions Requiring Procedural Formalities in Rulemaking beyond "Paper Hearing"

During the initial judicial development of expanded notice-and-comment procedures, occasional court decisions went beyond the requirements of detailed explanation and a "paper hearing" to require, on a largely ad hoc basis, that the EPA grant a limited trial-type hearing on specified issues in notice-and-comment rulemaking. For example, in International Harvester Co. v. Ruckelshaus, 478 F.2d 615 (D.C. Cir. 1973), the Court of Appeals for the District of Columbia Circuit set aside the EPA's refusal to grant an extension of the 1975 deadlines for achievement of certain automotive emission limitations, relying on inadequacies in EPA's response to manufacturer criticisms of EPA methodologies for handling relevant data. In remanding the case, the court indicated that limited cross-examination would be an appropriate means of dealing with disputed technical issues. Similarly, in Appalachian Power Co. v. Ruckelshaus, 477 F.2d 495 (4th Cir. 1973), the court stated that limited cross-examination should be afforded on certain types of technical and economic issues at some point before air pollution control requirements became effective. As we will shortly see, the Supreme Court in its *Vermont Yankee* decision called a halt to this judicial development of further procedural requirements going beyond "paper hearing" rulemaking.

Note on Statutory Requirements for Hybrid Procedures in Rulemaking

The "common law" development by reviewing courts of hybrid rulemaking procedures has been endorsed by Congress. Several of the regulatory statutes enacted by Congress during the 1970s explicitly grant rulemaking power to administrators, but hedge its exercise with specific procedural requirements that go beyond §553 notice-and-comment procedures without requiring trial-type evidentiary hearings in every case.

For example, the 1977 Clean Air Act Amendments, 42 U.S.C. §60(d) (1977), codify the "paper hearing" requirements imposed on EPA by courts. They provide for agency maintenance of a public file that includes all relevant agency documents as well as outside comments, and full agency explanation of its decision, including a discussion of adverse data, analysis, and comment. However, additional procedures such as cross-examination are generally not required.

The Federal Trade Commission Improvement Act of 1974 (Magnuson-Moss Act), 15 U.S.C. §57(a), provides a more complex set of "hybrid" rulemaking procedures. It confirms the result in National Petroleum Refiners Assn. v. FTC by explicitly granting the commission rulemaking authority to define with specificity acts or practices that are "unfair or deceptive" and also authorizes the commission to assess civil penalties for their violation. In promulgating such regulations, the FTC is directed to use notice-and-comment procedures, subject to additional, statutorily defined "informal hearing" practices under which the FTC must provide for the conduct of proceedings by "hearing officers"; an "interested person is entitled . . . to present his position orally or by documentary submission (or both)." If "the Commission determines that there are disputed issues of material fact it is necessary to resolve," it must afford parties the opportunity to file "rebuttal submissions," and "such cross-examination of persons as the Commission determines (i) to be appropriate, and (ii) to be required for a full and true disclosure with respect to such issues." However, the commission is authorized to impose time limitations on oral presentations, to itself conduct the cross-examination on behalf of parties, or to require that persons having common interests appoint one representative for purposes of cross-examination. 15 U.S.C. §57(a). Transcripts of oral presentations and cross-examination, as well as all written submissions, together with the rule, the commission's decision, "and any other information which the commission considers relevant to such rule," constitute the record on review, and the court is directed to use a "substantial evidence" standard of review of facts.

The FTC's experience under the act was unhappy. The rulemaking proceedings that it initiated in the late 1970s took many years; a majority were eventually withdrawn or abandoned, and a number of the survivors were invalidated by the courts. See B. Boyer, Report on the Trade Regulation Rulemaking Procedures of the FTC (1979), in U.S. Administrative Conference: Recommendations and Reports 41 (1980). Many commentators viewed the act's "hybrid" procedures as difficult to implement, producing expense and delay with little benefit to the decisionmaking process. Yet there were other confounding factors in the FTC's troubles with rulemaking, including acute political controversy stirred by the commission's rulemaking initiatives (launched during the Carter administration by liberal Democrat Chairman Mike Perschuck) against vocational schools, funeral homes, used car dealers, and hearing aid sales. These triggered congressional legislation in the form of the Federal Trade Commission Improvements Act of 1980 — which limited the commission's powers and imposed a one-house legislative veto. The latter was invalidated in the wake of the *Chadha* decision (Chapter 2). See Consumers Union v. FTC, 691 F.2d 575 (D.C. Cir. 1982), aff'd, 463 U.S. 1216 (1983). In any event, congressional interest in hybrid rulemaking has waned. Congress has not subsequent to the 1970s adopted procedures like those in Magnuson-Moss for any major regulatory function.

Other rulemaking formalities beyond notice and opportunity for comment required by statutes include consultation with specific officials or organizations,[32] creation of and consultation with advisory committees,[33] and shared responsibility with other agencies for promulgating rules.[34]

The question whether an organic statute may *implicitly* require special hybrid rulemaking procedures beyond the "paper hearing" procedures developed under §553 was addressed in Mobil Oil Corp. v. FPC, 483 F.2d 1238 (D.C. Cir. 1973), involving FPC

---

32. See Air Pollution Prevention and Control Act of 1977, 42 U.S.C. §§7401, 7421 (state and local authorities or advisory groups and federal agencies); Federal Coal Mine Health and Safety Act Amendments of 1977, 30 U.S.C. §§801, 812 (federal and state agencies and representatives of coal mine operators and miners).

33. Contract Work Hours and Safety Standard Act, 40 U.S.C. §333 (1970) (advisory committee of building trade employee representatives, contractors); Color Additive Amendments of 1960, 21 U.S.C. §376(b)(5)(D); Federal Coal Mine Health and Safety Act Amendments of 1977, 30 U.S.C. §§801, 812 (regulatory agency must consult other federal and state agencies and representatives of coal mine operators and miners).

34. Federal Coal Mine Health and Safety Act (HEW and Interior); Comprehensive Drug Abuse Prevention and Control Act (HEW and Department of Justice). See generally Hamilton, Procedures for the Adoption of Rules of General Applicability: The Need for Procedural Innovation in Administrative Rulemaking, 60 Calif. L. Rev. 1276 (1972).

natural gas pipeline rate regulations. Because the Natural Gas Act does not require that FPC regulations be issued after a "hearing" or made on the basis of a "record," the court invoked *Florida East Coast* and held the formal rulemaking procedures of APA §§556-557 inapplicable. The act, however, provides for judicial review of regulation under a "substantial evidence" standard. This, the court reasoned, was a "term of art" in administrative law, which (following *Universal Camera*) requires a record developed through adversary procedures in order to permit judicial review of factual issues on the whole record, including materials adverse to as well as those supporting the position of the agency. At least in cases like the present one, involving sharply contested factual issues, some mechanism beyond notice and comment for adversary testing of such issues was accordingly required:

> Compliance with this standard could conceivably be achieved in a number of ways. There must, however, be some mechanism whereby adverse parties can test, criticize and illuminate the flaws in the evidentiary basis being advanced regarding a particular point. The traditional method of doing this is cross-examination, but the Commission may find it appropriate to limit or even eliminate altogether oral cross-examination and rely upon written questions and responses. In proceedings involving numerous parties, the Commission might find it expedient to screen the written interrogatories. . . .

The statute in *Mobil Oil* is itself something of a hybrid, imposing a "substantial evidence" standard of review without explicitly requiring its natural corollary, an "on-the-record" agency hearing procedure. Such anomalies occur not infrequently because of last-minute congressional compromise or sheer inadvertence.[35] To what extent does the adoption, in particular of regulatory statutes of additional, "hybrid" procedural requirements that go beyond those required by the APA, reflect efforts by political opponents of regulatory programs to hobble procedurally the agency's ability to implement the program when they have failed to block or limit Congress's grant of substantive regulatory authority to the agency? See McNollgast, Structure and Process, Politics and Policy: Administrative Arrangements and the Political Control of Agencies, 75 Va. L. Rev. 431 (1989).

d. Halting Judicial Transformation: The *Vermont Yankee* Litigation

For decades, the federal government has grappled unsuccessfully with the daunting problem of arranging for safe permanent disposal of radioactive high-level nuclear wastes. Most wastes are military, but wastes from civilian sources, especially nuclear power plants, have also been a highly contentious political, regulatory, and legal issue. Opponents of nuclear power have argued that no new nuclear plants should be built

---

35. For example, in enacting the Occupational Health and Safety Act, Congress provided for notice-and-comment rulemaking supplemented by informal legislative-type oral hearings but also provided for "substantial evidence" review. This structure was the result of a compromise in conference; the judicial review provision was drawn from the House bill, which had also provided for formal rulemaking, while the procedural provisions were drawn from the Senate version, which had been silent on the standard of review. See Note, Judicial Review Under the Occupational Safety and Health Act: The Substantial Evidence Test as Applied to Informal Rulemaking, 1974 Duke L.J. 459. Judge McGowan, in discussing the legally anomalous statute that resulted, complained of the "additional burdens" on the judiciary "deriving from the illogic of legislative compromise," Industrial Union Dept., AFL-CIO v. Hodgson, 499 F.2d 467, 469 (D.C. Cir. 1974). In a related context, Judge Friendly has remarked of congressional drafting that "one would almost think there had been a conscious effort never to use the same phraseology twice." Associated Indus. of New York, Inc. v. Department of Labor, 487 F.2d 342, 345 n.2 (2d Cir. 1973).

until the problem of disposing of their spent fuel has been solved. During the early 1970s, the Atomic Energy Commission (AEC), whose nuclear regulatory responsibilities have since been transferred to the Nuclear Regulatory Commission (NRC), was forced to confront this issue in licensing new nuclear power plants. The AEC concluded, as a matter of substantive policy, that the waste disposal problem should not preclude licensing of new nuclear plants; the NRC has followed the same policy. Opponents of nuclear power and environmental groups have challenged this policy in regulatory proceedings and the courts. It had been widely assumed, until the Carter administration later decided otherwise, that most spent fuel would be reprocessed into plutonium. But the AEC in adopting its policy did not simply rely on the reprocessing option; it also considered permanent storage. The most promising option seems to be burial in stable geologic formations such as salt beds.

In dealing with the spent fuel disposal question in licensing new nuclear plants, the AEC decided as a procedural matter not to deal with the issue on a case-by-case basis through the adjudicatory hearing procedures for new plant licensing. Instead, it instituted a generic notice-and-comment rulemaking proceeding to specify the spent fuel hazards associated with a hypothetical "typical" plant. The results of the rulemaking would then be factored into adjudicatory decisions whether to license specific plants (decisions required by statute to be made through on-the-record adjudicatory hearings) without affording further proceedings on spent fuel hazards issues, following the logic of FPC v. Texaco.

In the generic rulemaking, interested persons were given opportunity to submit written comments and opportunity for oral argument before an AEC hearing panel. There were no relevant statutory provisions suggesting that anything other than §553 notice-and-comment procedures were required. Demands by environmental groups that they be afforded additional procedural rights, including the right to cross-examine AEC staff and probe the factual basis for staff documents and statements with respect to spent fuel disposal, were denied.

In AEC's notice-and-comment rulemaking proceedings, Dr. Frank Pittman of the commission staff submitted a 20-page statement describing in general terms the problems in devising a secure method of storing radioactive wastes and the types of storage facilities (aboveground and underground) that might be developed. He provided some engineering details concerning a proposed aboveground storage facility. Two pages of his statement were devoted to the permanent storage problem, asserting that substantial progress on underground disposition of wastes was being made, and that the problem would probably be resolved in the relatively near future. At the oral hearing, the panel asked a few general questions about the proposed surface storage facility. The commission, relying heavily on Dr. Pittman's submission, concluded that the environmental hazards associated with spent nuclear fuel were negligible, judging that "under normal conditions" no radioactivity would be released and that the possibility of a serious accident was "incredible." It incorporated this "zero release" conclusion in a rule containing a table specifying numerical values for various environmental hazards that would be posed by construction of a nuclear plant. Based on the environmental conclusions incorporated in the rule, it granted an operating license for a new nuclear plant (Vermont Yankee) on the basis of these conclusions without affording any hearing rights on the waste disposal issue in the Vermont Yankee licensing adjudication.

Environmental groups sought review of the license grant and the "zero release" rule. In an opinion by Chief Judge Bazelon, the D.C. Circuit reversed both. National Resources Defense Council v. NRC, 547 F.2d 633 (D.C. Cir. 1976). It found that the rulemaking proceeding was defective because the commission had failed to expose and permit adequate adversary probing of waste disposal issues. It stated:

> Many procedural devices for creating a genuine dialogue on these issues were available to the agency — including informal conferences between intervenors and staff, document discovery, interrogatories, technical advisory committees comprised of outside experts with differing perspectives, limited cross-examination, funding independent research by intervenors, detailed annotation of technical reports, surveys of existing literature, memoranda explaining methodology. We do not presume to intrude on the agency's province by dictating to it which, if any, of these devices it must adopt to flesh out the record.
>
> Since the rule was procedurally invalid, the adjudicatory license grant to Vermont Yankee, which was based on the rule, was also held invalid.

Judge Tamm, concurring in the result, agreed that the record in the rulemaking proceedings did not provide adequate data or analysis to support the commission's conclusion that spent fuel hazards were negligible, and concluded that the commission's decision that such hazards were insignificant was therefore "arbitrary and capricious." However, he took issue with the majority opinion's emphasis on additional procedures, stating that the appropriate remedy was a remand to enable the commission to provide additional and stronger documentation to support its zero-release assumption.

Judge Tamm's concurrence provoked a separate opinion from Judge Bazelon alone:

> I reject the implication that any techniques beyond rudimentary notice and comment are needless "over-formalization" of informal rulemaking. . . .
>
> Decisions in areas touching the environment or medicine affect the lives and health of all. These interests, like the First Amendment, have "always had a special claim to judicial protection." . . .
>
> . . . I am convinced that in highly technical areas, where judges are institutionally incompetent to weigh evidence for themselves, a focus on agency procedures will prove less intrusive, and more likely to improve the quality of decisionmaking, than judges "steeping" themselves "in technical matters to determine whether the agency has exercised a reasoned discretion." See Ethyl Corp. v. EPA (Bazelon, C.J., concurring). . . .

Vermont Yankee Nuclear Power Corp. v. Natural Resources Defense Council

435 U.S. 519 (1978)

Mr. Justice REHNQUIST delivered the opinion of the Court.

In 1946, Congress enacted the Administrative Procedure Act, which as we have noted elsewhere was not only "a new, basic and comprehensive regulation of procedures in many agencies," Wong Yang Sung v. McGrath, 339 U.S. 33 (1950), but was also a legislative enactment which settled "long-continued and hard-fought contentions, and enacts a formula upon which opposing social and political forces have come to rest." Id., at 40. Interpreting [§553] of the Act in United States v. Allegheny-Ludlum Steel Corp., 406 U.S. 742 (1972), and United States v. Florida East Coast Railroad Co., 410 U.S. 224 (1973), we held that generally speaking this section of the Act established the maximum procedural requirements which Congress was willing to have the courts impose upon agencies in conducting rulemaking procedures.[36] Agencies are free to grant additional procedural rights in the exercise of their discretion, but reviewing courts are generally not free to impose them if the agencies have not chosen to grant them. This is not to say necessarily that there are no circumstances which would ever justify a court in overturning agency action because of a failure to employ procedures beyond those required by the statute. But such circumstances, if they exist, are extremely rare.

Even apart from the Administrative Procedure Act this Court has for more than four decades emphasized that the formulation of procedures was basically to be left within the discretion of the agencies to which Congress had confided the responsibility for substantive judgments. In FCC v. Schreiber, 381 U.S. 279, 290 (1965), the Court explicated this principle, describing it as "an outgrowth of the congressional determination that administrative agencies and administrators will be familiar with the industries which they regulate and will be in a better position than federal courts or Congress itself to design procedural rules adapted to the peculiarities of the industry and the tasks of the agency involved." . . .

[The Court found that the court of appeals majority had invalidated the commission's rulemaking because the procedures that it had employed were inadequate, and not just because the administrative record did not provide adequate support for its zero-release assumption.]

. . . Absent constitutional constraints or extremely compelling circumstances, "the administrative agencies 'should be free to fashion their own rules of procedure and to pursue methods of inquiry capable of permitting them to discharge their multitudinous duties.'" Federal Communications Commn. v. Schreiber, 381 U.S. 279, 290 (1965). . . .

There are compelling reasons for construing [§553] in this manner. In the first place, if courts continually review agency proceedings to determine whether the agency employed procedures which were, in the court's opinion, perfectly tailored to reach what the court perceives to be the "best" or "correct" result, judicial review would be totally unpredictable. And the agencies, operating under this vague injunction to employ the "best" procedures and facing the threat of reversal if they did not, would undoubtedly adopt full adjudicatory procedures in every instance. [A]ll the inherent advantages of informal rulemaking would be totally lost. . . .

Finally, and perhaps most importantly, this sort of review fundamentally misconceives the nature of the standard for judicial review of an agency rule. The court below uncritically assumed that additional procedures will automatically result in a more adequate record because it will give interested parties more of an opportunity to participate and contribute to the proceedings. But informal rulemaking need not be based solely on the transcript of a hearing held before an agency. Indeed, the agency need not even hold a formal hearing. See 5 U.S.C. §553(c) (1976 ed.). Thus, the adequacy of the "record" in this type of proceeding is not correlated directly to the type of procedural devices employed, but rather turns on whether the agency has followed the statutory mandate of the Administrative Procedure Act or other relevant statutes.

There remains, of course, the question of whether the challenged rule finds sufficient justification in the administrative proceedings that it should be upheld by the

---

36. While there was division in this Court in United States v. Florida East Coast Railroad Co., supra, with respect to the constitutionality of such an interpretation in a case involving ratemaking, which Mr. Justice Douglas and Mr. Justice Stewart felt was "adjudicatory" within the terms of the Act, the cases in the Court of Appeals for the District of Columbia Circuit which we review here involve rulemaking procedures in their most pristine sense.

reviewing court. Judge Tamm, concurring in the result reached by the majority of the Court of Appeals, thought that it did not. There are also intimations in the majority opinion which suggest that the judges who joined it likewise may have thought the administrative proceedings an insufficient basis upon which to predicate the rule in question. We accordingly remand so that the Court of Appeals may review the rule as the Administrative Procedure Act provides. . . . The court should engage in this kind of review and not stray beyond the judicial province to explore the procedural format or to impose upon the agency its own notion of which procedures are "best" or most likely to further some vague, undefined public good.

. . . Nuclear energy may some day be a cheap, safe source of power or it may not. But Congress has made a choice to at least try nuclear energy, establishing a reasonable review process in which courts are to play only a limited role. The fundamental policy questions appropriately resolved in Congress and in the state legislatures are not subject to reexamination in the federal courts under the guise of judicial review of agency action. Time may prove wrong the decision to develop nuclear energy, but it is Congress or the States within their appropriate agencies which must eventually make that judgment. In the meantime courts should perform their appointed function. . . . It is to insure a fully informed and well-considered decision, not necessarily a decision the judges of the Court of Appeals or of this Court would have reached had they been members of the decision-making unit of the agency. Administrative decisions should be set aside in this context, as in every other, only for substantial procedural or substantive reasons as mandated by statute, . . . not simply because the court is unhappy with the result reached. . . .

Reversed and remanded.

Notes and Questions

1. The Supreme Court's *Vermont Yankee* opinion reads the APA to preclude, absent unspecified exceptional circumstances, judicial requirements that agencies use additional procedures beyond those specified in the 1946 APA or other relevant statutes. Is this reading persuasive or wise? Should we rely entirely on Congress or agencies themselves to adopt procedural innovations to resolve the problems generated, including the problems posed for reviewing courts, by increased administrative use of rulemaking to devise and implement policy? Have the courts nothing useful to contribute?[37]

2. While relying on the assertedly preclusive intent of the APA, the Court's Vermont Yankee opinion raises two additional objections to judicial imposition of procedural requirements beyond those imposed by statutes: First, agencies will be uncertain as to what procedures reviewing courts may find necessary; as a defensive response to the uncertainty, they will adopt an elaborate panoply of formal procedures that will cripple the administrative process. Second, courts will manipulate procedural requirements to control, indirectly, policy decisions that should properly be made by agencies. How

---

37. For debate over the respective role of courts, agencies, and Congress in devising new procedures in response to changing patterns of administrative decisionmaking, compare Stewart, *Vermont Yankee* and the Evolution of Administrative Procedure, 91 Harv. L. Rev. 1805 (1978), with Byse, *Vermont Yankee* and the Evolution of Administrative Procedure: A Somewhat Different View, 91 Harv. L. Rev. 1823 (1978). For a history of the legislative battles and legal and political controversies that led up to the adoption of the APA as enacting "a formula upon which opposing social and political forces have come to rest," see Shepherd, Fierce Compromise: The Administrative Procedure Act Emerges from New Deal Politics, 90 Nw. U. L. Rev. 1557 (1996).

weighty are these objections? Do they apply with equal force to *any* effort by courts to control agencies' exercise of discretion? Or does judicial imposition of procedural formalities beyond those required by statute involve special drawbacks not presented by other judicial techniques, such as "hard look" review, for controlling agency discretion?[38]

3. The Supreme Court's *Vermont Yankee* opinion castigates the court of appeals majority for imposing procedures not required by statute. However, following the rationale expressed in Judge Tamm's concurring opinion, it acknowledges that courts should scrutinize the adequacy of the administrative "record" developed in notice-and-comment rulemaking, and may remand for further proceedings if the record is not adequate to permit a court to review and sustain the agency's decision on the merits. Are these two aspects of the Court's decision consistent? The APA does not require agencies to create an evidentiary "record" in notice-and-comment rulemaking.[39] Nor does it authorize reviewing courts to remand for additional proceedings when they judge the record inadequate even though an agency has fully complied with the procedural requirements of §553. By endorsing a requirement of an "adequate record" in notice-and-comment rulemaking, has the Court violated its own ban on procedural innovation by courts?[40] Is the "adequate record" requirement subject to the very same objections that the Supreme Court levied on Judge Bazelon's approach: uncertainty in the content of the requirement and danger that it will be manipulated by reviewing courts to influence substantive policy outcomes?

Is *Vermont Yankee* logically inconsistent with the "hard look" approach to judicial control of agency discretion and the Court's *State Farm* decision in Chapter 4?

Most courts have read *Vermont Yankee* as imposing strict limits on their ability to impose new or additional procedural requirements beyond those required by the APA and the particular statute governing the agency's action.

4. Lower courts have invoked *Vermont Yankee* to reject demands for trial-type procedures, such as cross-examination, in notice-and-comment rulemaking or informal adjudication. In Wisconsin Gas v. FERC, 770 F.2d 1144 (D.C. Cir. 1985), the court held "to the extent that it imposes procedural requirements not required by the Natural Gas Act or the APA [*Mobil Oil*] cannot survive *Vermont Yankee*. [The] 'substantial evidence' provision in the Natural Gas Act does not affect the procedure the Commission is required to follow." However, some courts, when blocked by *Vermont Yankee* from imposing procedural requirements under the APA, have interpreted the specific statute under which an

38. Consider the further history of *Vermont Yankee*. On remand, the court of appeals again struck down the zero-release provision in NRC's rule. It did not rule on procedural grounds (in the interim NRC has supplemented the rulemaking record), but held the rule arbitrary and inconsistent with the National Environmental Policy Act by foreclosing consideration of the uncertainties in the zero-release assumption in individual licensing decisions, finding that these uncertainties might in some cases tip the balance against granting a license to a new nuclear plant. NRDC v. NRC, 685 F.2d 459 (D.C. Cir. 1982). Again the Supreme Court reversed, finding that the NRC had considered relevant factors and presented a reasoned basis for the way in which it had balanced these factors; the courts should not second-guess the balance struck. Baltimore Gas & Elec. Co. v. NRDC, 462 U.S. 87 (1983).

39. As previously explained, the notice-and-comment provisions of §553 contemplate a "legislative" model of decision that does not involve creation of a "record" forming a basis for review. See Auerbach, Informal Rulemaking: A Proposed Relationship Between Administrative Procedures and Judicial Review, 72 Nw.U.L. Rev. 15, 25 & n.51 (1977), quoting from the legislative history of the APA: "Congressman Walter, who guided passage of the APA on the floor of the House explained: 'Where there is no statutory administrative hearing to which review is confined, the facts pertinent to any relevant question of law must of course be tried and determined de novo by the reviewing court.' Cong. Rec., May 24, 1946."

40. The Court has also ruled that agencies, to facilitate judicial review of the merits, may be required to create an "adequate record" in informal adjudication, even though no such requirement is imposed by the APA. See pages 659-660.

agency has acted to impose such requirements; for example, one court used this technique to ban off-the-record communications between the agency and outside parties in the context of notice-and-comment rulemaking.[41]

For an overview of the history of rulemaking procedures, see Strauss, From Expertise to Politics: The Transformation of American Rulemaking, 31 Wake Forest L. Rev. 745 (1996).

5. *Notice-and-Comment Rulemaking: The Exceptions*

As previously noted, the §553 requirement of an opportunity for notice and comment does not apply to "(1) interpretative rules, (2) general statements of policy, or (3) rules of agency organization, procedure, or practice." Section 553(b) also authorizes an agency to dispense with notice and comment when it "for good cause finds" it to be "impracticable, unnecessary, or contrary to the public interest." Courts have often found it difficult to determine just when these exceptions apply, as the materials below attest.[42] The issue is of increasing practical importance; as courts have transformed notice-and-comment rulemaking into a more formal and time-consuming process, agencies have increasingly sought to avoid the burdens of that process by adopting policy through rules claimed to be exempt from notice-and-comment requirements. A study of the *Federal Register* for the first six months of 1987, for example, found that 40 percent of the rules published had been adopted without notice-and-comment rulemaking by agencies invoking one or more of the above exemptions.[43] Agencies also increasingly formulate and apply policy through "guidance" documents or other internal memoranda that may direct decisions by lower-level agency personnel as effectively as formal regulations.

Following an introductory overview, we address in turn the exemptions for "general statements of policy," "interpretative" or interpretive rules, and rules of agency organization, procedure or practice. We then consider the "good cause" exemption.

a. Overview

American Hospital Association v. Bowen

834 F.2d 1037 (D.C. Cir. 1987)

WALD, C.J. [Congress enacted legislation requiring the creation of Peer Review Organizations (PROs) to oversee the expenditure of Medicare money by doctors and

---

41. See, e.g., United States Lines, Inc. v. FMC, 584 F.2d 519 (D.C. Cir. 1978).

42. As noted above, §553(a) excepts rules relating to a variety of subject matters, including rules related to "agency management or personnel or to public property, loans, grants, benefits or contracts." These exceptions have occasioned much less litigation over their interpretation than the four identified in the text above. Many federal agencies, such as the Department of Health and Human Services (HHS) and the Department of Housing and Urban Development (HUD) that oversee important benefit programs, have adopted regulations providing for notice-and-comment procedures for the adoption of rules otherwise subject to these exceptions. See, e.g., 24 C.F.R. Pt. 10 (HUD).

43. Juan Lavilla, The Good Cause Exemption to Notice and Comment Rulemaking Requirements Under the Administrative Procedure Act, 3 Admin. L.J. 317 (1989).

hospitals. These PROs would contract with the Department of Health and Human Services (HHS), conduct the review that these contracts required them to carry out, and determine whether the hospitals and doctors were performing in accordance with certain standards. If they were not doing so, HHS would not pay them certain Medicare reimbursement funds, or it might impose other sanctions. HHS promulgated a host of regulations concerning the organization of PROs, their activities, and their enforcement powers. HHS also placed standard terms in PROs contracts that required them to see that hospitals would meet (or, at least, try to meet) certain specific costs and efficiency standards. HHS did not follow notice-and-comment procedures in taking any of these steps. The court of appeals held that these rules and regulations were procedural in nature, for they simply constituted the PROs, which, in effect, were agents of HHS; they imposed no direct substantive obligations on the hospitals. The court also held that the terms in the contracts, requiring the PROs to see that the hospitals met certain substantive standards, were "rules" or "regulations" but that they merely set goals rather than imposing definite standards; hence, they were simply "statements of policy." In reaching these conclusions, the court described the three §553(c) exceptions as follows:]

The reading of the §553 exemptions that seems most consonant with Congress' purpose in adopting the APA is to construe them as an attempt to preserve agency flexibility in dealing with limited situations where substantive rights are not at stake. [They] "accommodate situations where the policies promoted by public participation in rule-making are outweighed by the countervailing considerations of effectiveness, efficiency, expedition and reduction in expense." . . .

The function of §553's first exemption, that for "interpretive rules," is to allow agencies to explain ambiguous terms in legislative enactments without having to undertake cumbersome proceedings. As we explained long ago in Gibson Wine Co. v. Snyder, 194 F.2d 329, 331 (D.C. Cir. 1952), ". . . 'substantive rules,' or 'legislative rules' are those which create law . . . whereas interpretive rules are statements as to what an administrative officer thinks the statute or regulation means."

. . . Substantive rules are ones which "grant rights, impose obligations, or produce other significant effects on private interests," or which "effect a change in existing law or policy." . . . Interpretive rules, by contrast, "are those which merely clarify or explain existing law or regulations," are "essentially hortatory and instructional," . . . and "do not have the full force and effect of a substantive rule but [are] in the form of an explanation of particular terms" [citing precedent].

Determining whether a given agency action is interpretive or legislative is an extraordinarily case-specific endeavor. . . . Nevertheless, recent cases shed some light on the scope of the §553 interpretive rules exemption. In Cabais v. Egger, 690 F.2d 234 (D.C. Cir. 1982), we upheld as interpretive of the Federal Unemployment Tax Act directives from the Secretary of Agriculture recommending to state agencies that they pass legislation conforming their unemployment income plans to a federal scheme as they were required to do under a federal statute. Cabais thus stands for the important proposition that where an agency activity merely reminds parties of existing duties . . . it is interpretive, not legislative. [I]n American Postal Workers Union v. United States Postal Service, 707 F.2d 548 (D.C. Cir. 1983), ... [We held that the] Postal Service's new method of calculating the civil service retirement benefits of part-time postal workers constituted an interpretive rule. [The method in question changed a prior system of calculating annuity eligibility for substitute workers on the basis of the time they were available for work; the new method calculated annuities only on the basis of time actually worked and pay actually received. The change reduced the expected annuity payments of 113,000 substitute workers.] We concluded this method was exempt from notice and comment because it turned solely on the agency's construction of the statutory term, "average pay." . . .

American Postal Workers thus demonstrates that the mere fact that a rule may have a substantial impact "does not transform it into a legislative rule." . . . By contrast, the classic example of an agency rule held not to be interpretive — and thus requiring notice and comment as a prerequisite to validity — was the use by a parole board of guidelines establishing specific factors for determining parole eligibility that were "calculated to have a substantial effect on ultimate parole decisions." See Pickus v. United States Board of Parole, 507 F.2d 1107, 1112-1113 (D.C. Cir. 1974).

The function of the second §553 exemption, for "general policy statements," is to allow agencies to announce their "tentative intentions for the future," . . . without binding themselves. We have previously contrasted "a properly adopted substantive rule" with a "general statement of policy," observing that while a substantive rule "establishes a standard of conduct which has the force of law" in subsequent proceedings,

> [A] general statement of policy, on the other hand, does not establish a "binding norm." It is not finally determinative of the issues or rights to which it is addressed. The agency cannot apply or rely upon a general statement of policy as law because a general statement of policy only announces what the agency seeks to establish as policy.

[Citing Pacific Gas & Elec. Co. v. FPC, 506 F.2d 33, 38 (D.C. Cir. 1974).]

The perimeters of the exemption for general statements of policy, like those for interpretive pronouncements, are fuzzy. . . . Nevertheless, our prior cases, in seeking to discern the line between these two types of agency pronouncements, have provided considerable guidance. One useful formulation is the two-criteria test set forth by Judge McGowan in American Bus Association v. United States:

> First, courts have said that, unless a pronouncement acts prospectively, it is a binding norm. Thus . . . a statement of policy may not have a present effect: a "general statement of policy" is one that does not impose any rights and obligations . . . The second criterion is whether a purported policy statement genuinely leaves the agency and its decision makers free to exercise direction.

627 F.2d 525, 529 (D.C. Cir. 1980). . . . In applying these two criteria, we have observed that an agency's characterization of its own action, while not decisive, is a factor that we do consider. . . .

. . . We offer here several telling examples of cases upholding agency pronouncements as constituting mere statements of policy, not subject to notice and comment requirements. [I]n *Pacific Gas* we held that a Federal Power Commission order setting forth the Commission's view of the proper priority schedule to be followed in curtailing supplies of natural gas to certain customers in the hypothetical event of a natural gas shortage was nonbinding and hence a mere policy statement. [I]n Brock v. Cathedral Bluffs Shale Oil Co., 796 F.2d 533 (D.C. Cir. 1986), we upheld as a mere general statement of policy the Secretary of Labor's "guidelines" on when to cite independent contractors for violating safety standards, placing heavy emphasis on the agency's frequent assertion in the past that the Secretary retained discretion to supersede these guidelines in particular cases. By contrast, we found no such retained discretion in *Batterton* [v. Marshall, 648 F.2d 694

(D.C. Cir. 1980)], where we held that the Department of Labor's statistical methodology for calculating unemployment statistics triggering an emergency job program was binding and hence not a mere general statement, or in *Community Nutrition* [v. Young, 818 F.2d 943 (D.C. Cir. 1987) (excerpted at pp. 549-551)], where we held that the Food and Drug Administration's determination of "action levels" that told food producers the allowable limits of certain contaminants in food was also a binding norm requiring the agency to undertake notice and comment procedures.

The distinctive purpose of §553's third exemption, for "rules of agency organization, procedure or practice," is to ensure "that agencies retain latitude in organizing their internal operations." *Batterton*, 648 F.2d at 707.

> A useful articulation of the exemption's critical feature is that it covers agency actions that do not themselves alter the rights or interests of parties, although it may alter the manner in which parties present themselves or their viewpoints to the agency.

Id. (citation omitted).

Over time, our Circuit in applying the §553 exemption for procedural rules has gradually shifted focus from asking whether a given procedure has a "substantial impact" on parties . . . to inquiring more broadly whether the agency action also encodes a substantive value judgment or puts a stamp of approval or disapproval on a given type of behavior. The gradual move away from looking solely into the substantiality of the impact reflects a candid recognition that even unambiguously procedural measures affect parties to some degree.

. . . In Neighborhood TV Co. Inc. v. FCC, 742 F.2d 629 (D.C. Cir. 1984), we held that a FCC decision to freeze applications for television licenses on some frequencies affected an applicant's interest "only incidentally," id. at 637, and thus was procedural. In *Guardian Federal Savings & Loan Association*, we held that a directive specifying that requisite audits be performed by nonagency accountants was exempt as a procedural measure. And in United States Department of Labor v. Kast Metals Corp., 755 F.2d 1145 (5th Cir. 1984) [the court] held that the agency's rules governing the selection of employers for workplace safety investigations was a procedural rule. By contrast, we have struck down as nonprocedural an agency rule foreclosing home health agencies from the right to deal with the Secretary of HHS in order to gain reimbursement for Medicare, see *National Association of Home Health Agencies*, [690 F.2d 832], and, as noted earlier, we have held that a parole board's selection of parole eligibility guidelines had the intent and effect of changing substantive outcomes.

APPALACHIAN POWER CO. v. EPA, 208 F.3d 1015 (D.C. Cir. 2000). The federal Clean Air Act establishes a regulatory program under which states issue permits for stationary sources of air pollution. Permits must incorporate relevant federal and state emissions standards and the emissions-monitoring requirements specified in those standards. State-issued permits are subject to review and veto by EPA for compliance with federal requirements. Following notice and comment, EPA issued regulations providing that where an applicable federal or state emissions standard does not require "periodic testing or instrumental or non-instrumental monitoring," states must include in permits requirements for "periodic monitoring . . . sufficient to yield reliable data from the relevant time period that are representative of the source's compliance with the permit." EPA thereafter issued, without notice and comment, a document entitled "Periodic Monitoring Guidance" that it posted on its web site. The Guidance provides that, regardless of whether an emission standard provides for "periodic testing," or includes other monitoring requirements, additional monitoring requirements "may be necessary" in a permit if the monitoring required by the standard "does not provide the necessary assurance of compliance." The Guidance provides that states must assess the sufficiency of the existing monitoring requirements in federal and state emissions standards, and include additional monitoring requirements in permits if necessary to assure a source's compliance with a standard. The court held that the Guidance was a final, binding determination that amended the 1992 regulations by requiring states to include in permits additional monitoring requirements, even where a standard already provides for "periodic testing or instrumental or non-instrumental monitoring." It rejected EPA's argument (set forth in the Guidance) that the 1992 rule implicitly included such a requirement. It accordingly set aside the Guidance. In so ruling, the court observed:

> The phenomenon we see in this case is familiar. Congress passes a broadly worded statute. The agency follows with regulations containing broad language, open-ended phrases, ambiguous standards and the like. Then as years pass, the agency issues circulars or guidance or memoranda, explaining, interpreting, defining and often expanding the commands in the regulations. One guidance document may yield another and then another and so on. Several words in a regulation may spawn hundreds of pages of text as the agency offers more and more detail regarding what its regulations demand of regulated entities. Law is made, without notice and comment, without public participation, and without publication in the *Federal Register* or the *Code of Federal Regulations*. With the advent of the Internet, the agency does not need these official publications to ensure widespread circulation; it can inform those affected simply by posting its new guidance or memoranda or policy statement on its web site. An agency operating in this way gains a large advantage. "It can issue or amend its real rules, i.e., its interpretative rules and policy statements, quickly and inexpensively without following any statutorily prescribed procedures." Richard J. Pierce, Jr., Seven Ways to Deossify Agency Rulemaking, 47 L.R. 59, 85 (1995). The agency may also think there is another advantage: immunizing its lawmaking from judicial review.

EPA argued that the Guidance was not subject to judicial review or to notice-and-comment rulemaking because it was neither final nor binding. In rejecting this position, the court stated:

> If an agency acts as if a document issued at headquarters is controlling in the field, if it treats the document in the same manner as it treats a legislative rule, if it bases enforcement actions on the policies or interpretations formulated in the document, if it leads private parties or state permitting authorities to believe that it will declare permits invalid unless they comply with the terms of the document, then the agency document is for all practical purposes "binding." . . .
>
> . . . EPA points to the concluding paragraph of the document, which contains a disclaimer: "The policies set forth in this paper are intended solely as guidance, do not represent final Agency action, and cannot be relied upon to create any rights enforceable by any party." . . . This language is boilerplate, since 1991 EPA has been placing it at the end of all its guidance documents. See . . . Peter L. Strauss, Comment, The Rulemaking Continuum, 41 Duke L.J. 1463, 1485 (1992) (referring to EPA's notice as "a charade, intended to keep the proceduralizing courts at bay"). Insofar as the "policies" mentioned in the disclaimer consist of requiring State permitting authorities to search for deficiencies in existing monitoring regulations and replace them through terms and conditions of a permit, "rights" may not be created but "obligations" certainly are — obligations on the part of the State regulators and those they regulate. At any rate, the entire Guidance, from beginning to end — except the last

paragraph — reads like a ukase. It commands, it requires, it orders, it dictates. Through the Guidance, EPA has given the States their "marching orders" and EPA expects the States to fall in line, as all have done, save perhaps Florida and Texas.

b. Rules That Represent "General Statements of Policy"

Community Nutrition Institute v. Young

818 F.2d 943 (D.C. Cir. 1987)

PER CURIAM: [The FDA may bring a court action to condemn any interstate shipment of food that is "adulterated." In any such action, the FDA must prove the fact of adulteration to the court. The FDA established through a regulation, adopted without notice and comment, "action levels," informing food producers of the maximum amount of unavoidable contaminants that it would permit. It said, for example, that it would permit no more than 20 parts per billion of a carcinogen called "aflatoxin" that occurs unavoidably and naturally in corn. The FDA expected to initiate enforcement actions to condemn corn that contained any aflatoxin level higher than its "action levels."]

... FDA ... argues that notice-and-comment requirements do not apply by virtue of subsection (b)(3)(A) of section 553, which carves out an exception for "interpretative rules [and] general statements of policy." According to the FDA, action levels represent nothing more than nonbinding statements of agency enforcement policy. CNI, on the other hand, argues that the action levels restrict enforcement discretion to such a degree as to constitute legislative rules. . . .

[The court cited the two-criteria test formulated by Judge McGowan in *American Bus Association*, quoted in *American Hospital*, p. 546]

First. The language employed by FDA in creating and describing action levels suggests that those levels both have a present effect and are binding. Specifically, the agency's regulations on action levels explain an action level in the following way:

[A]n action level for an added poisonous or deleterious substance . . . may be established to define the level of contamination at which food *will be deemed to be adulterated*. An action level may *prohibit any detectable amount of substance in food*. . . .

Second. This view of action levels — as having a present, binding effect — is confirmed by the fact that FDA considers it necessary for food producers to secure exceptions to the action levels. . . .

Third. On several occasions, in authorizing blending of adulterated with unadulterated corn, the FDA has made statements indicating that action levels establish a binding norm. For example, in a telegram to the Commissioner of the South Carolina Department of Agriculture, in which it indicated its approval of a blending plan, the FDA stated that "[a]ny shipments made independent of this plan would, if found to exceed the 20 ppb level, be considered adulterated and subject to condemnation." . . .

. . . Our holding today in no way indicates that agencies develop written guidelines to aid their exercise of discretion only at the peril of having a court transmogrify those guidelines into binding norms. We recognize that such guidelines have the not inconsiderable benefits of apprising the regulated community of the agency's intentions as well as informing the exercise of discretion by agents and officers in the field. . . .

We conclude that in the circumstances of this case, FDA by virtue of its own course of conduct has chosen to limit its discretion and promulgated action levels which it gives a present, binding effect. Having accorded such substantive significance to action levels, FDA is compelled by the APA to utilize notice-and-comment procedures in promulgating them. . . .

STARR, Circuit Judge, dissenting in part:

The abiding characteristic of a legislative rule is that it is law. It defines a standard of conduct that regulated individuals or entities ignore at their peril, in the face of possible enforcement action. Significantly, the only issue in any such proceeding is whether the rule applies to the facts at hand. . . .

In the modern administrative state, many "laws" emanate not from Congress but from administrative agencies, inasmuch as Congress has seen fit to vest broad rulemaking power in the executive branch, including independent agencies. . . . Congress has also provided in the APA for certain procedural protections before that which achieves the lofty status of "law" is promulgated by an agency acting in its congressionally authorized lawmaking capacity. Chief among these protections are the notice-and-comment requirements laid down in the familiar provision of 5 U.S.C. §553. In a sense, notice-and-comment procedures serve as a congressionally mandated proxy for the procedures which Congress itself employs in fashioning its "rules," as it were, thereby insuring that agency "rules" are also carefully crafted (with democratic values served by public participation) and developed only after assessment of relevant considerations. It is thus, in theory, important for APA procedures to be followed before an agency pronouncement is deemed a binding legislative rule not merely because the APA says so, but because in saying so the APA is protecting a free people from the danger of coercive state power undergirding pronouncements that lack the essential attributes of deliberativeness present in statutes. . . .

[T]he APA excepts, as the panel opinion recounts, interpretative rules and general statements of policy from the general notice-and-comment requirements. While it is no doubt true, and indeed is frequently recognized, that such agency pronouncements may have a direct effect on the regulated community, and may even be judicially reviewable, . . . these pronouncements still lack the dignity of "law." Before that status can be achieved, the agency must run its policies through the notice-and-comment gauntlet. Perhaps in part because the agency here has avoided testing its pronouncements in this way, it must in any future proceeding defend and justify its chosen standard in the face of a challenge to that standard. . . .

. . . If the pronouncement has the force of law in future proceedings, it is a legislative rule. Unless that critical feature is present, however, the agency statement should be considered to be a lower form of pronouncement, a "non-law" as it were, or in APA terms as "interpretative rule" or "general statement of policy." The correct measure of a pronouncement's force in subsequent proceedings is a practical one: must the agency merely show that the pronouncement has been violated or must the agency, if its hand is called, show that the pronouncement itself is justified in light of the underlying statute and the facts.

Application of this test can readily be illustrated by the case at hand. Action levels offer guidance to the regulated community with respect to what products FDA deems adulterated within the meaning of the FDC Act. But in an enforcement proceeding in which FDA seeks to impose sanctions for shipment of an adulterated product or to enjoin shipment of an adulterated product, the agency must prove the product is "adulterated."

That is, FDA cannot merely show that the product at issue fails to comply with the action level. . . . Rather, FDA must offer scientific or other probative evidence to support its contention that the product is adulterated. Thus, the action level does not have the force of law in the subsequent proceeding. Indeed, it has no "force" at all. . . .

While I [disagree with the majority's approach], I recognize a potential danger lurking in the [approach that I endorse]. Agencies may yield to temptation and seek to shield their regulations from the scrutiny occasioned by notice-and-comment procedures, choosing instead to cast would-be regulations as interpretative rules. The rule would still, of course, be subject to scrutiny in a subsequent proceeding, but this fact may be of little comfort to prospective commentors, given the deference accorded agency views in any such proceedings. See generally Chevron U.S.A. Inc. v. NRDC, 467 U.S. 837 (1984). But upon analysis, the danger is more theoretical than real. . . .

PROFESSIONALS & PATIENTS FOR CUSTOMIZED CARE v. SHALALA, 56 F.3d 592 (5th Cir. 1995).   Retail pharmacies have traditionally engaged in "compounding" — combining drugs, pursuant to physician prescription — on a case-by-case basis to create medications, not commercially available from pharmaceutical companies, tailored to the special needs of individual patients. The FDA became concerned that certain pharmacies were engaging in compounding on a wholesale basis, effectively creating and marketing new drugs in circumvention of FDA regulatory requirements. FDA issued, without notice and comment, "CPG" regulations describing when the FDA would initiate enforcement actions against such practices. The CPG regulation identified nine "factors that the FDA 'will consider' in determining whether to initiate an enforcement action, but explains that the 'list of factors is not intended to be exhaustive and other factors may be appropriate for consideration in a particular case.'" FDA classified the CPG as a "statement of policy" and "advisory opinion" designed to guide agency enforcement personnel but not establishing a "legal requirement." The court stated: "[Petitioner] relies on numerous informal agency communications as evidence that the FDA has treated [CPG] as establishing a binding norm. . . . (1) the FDA has used the nine factors listed in CPG when inspecting pharmacies, and has relied on those factors to determine whether federal enforcement actions were warranted; (2) in numerous letters the FDA has warned pharmacists that they were engaged in drug manufacturing, rather than traditional compounding, because they were conducting some, or all, of the activities listed in CPG, and (3) the FDA has furnished copies of CPG to pharmacists who inquired about the legal restrictions on drug compounding." The court held that these circumstances did not establish that CPG was a "legislative" rule. CPG did not "draw 'a line in the sand' that, once crossed, removes all discretion" from the agency and its enforcement personnel.

UNITED STATES TELEPHONE ASSOCIATION v. FCC, 28 F.3d 1232 (D.C. Cir. 1994).   The Federal Communications Act authorizes the FCC to impose administrative penalties for violations of the act and regulations thereunder. The FCC decided to abandon its case-by-case approach to assessing penalties; it adopted, without notice and comment, an "order" to "adopt more specific standards" for assessing penalties. The order specified base penalties for different types of violations, expressed as percentages of statutory maxima, and also specified aggravating and mitigating factors to be used in adjusting the base amount up or down. The court, in an opinion by Judge Silberman, rejected the commission's argument that the regulations were a "general statement of policy" and therefore exempt from APA notice-and-comment requirements.

"The Commission labeled the standards as a policy statement and reiterated 12 times that it retained discretion to depart from the standards in specific applications. The difficulty we see in the Commission's position is that [its order] sets forth a detailed schedule of penalties applicable to specific infractions as well as the appropriate adjustments for particular situations. It is rather hard to imagine an agency wishing to publish such an exhaustive framework for sanctions if it did not intend to use that framework to cabin its discretion. Indeed, no agency to our knowledge has ever claimed that such a schedule of fines was a policy statement. It simply does not fit the paradigm of a policy statement, namely, an indication of an agency's current position on a particular regulatory issues."

". . . The schedule of fines has been employed in over 300 cases and only in 8 does the Commission even claim that it departed from the schedule." [The court found that 7 of the 8 cases involved no departure and that the remaining case was doubtful.] "If there were any doubt as to the nature of the standards — and we do not think there is — the Commission's own Common Carrier Bureau in David L. Hollingsworth, 7 F.C.C.R. 6640 (Com. Car. Bur. 1992) [refused] to consider a claim that the fine set forth in the schedule was inequitable as applied to a particular respondent. The Bureau responded to this challenge to the substance of the policy statement by asserting that the argument 'should have been raised in a petition by [respondent] for reconsideration of the Policy Statement.' Id. That certainly indicates that the Bureau thought the 'Policy Statement' was a rule in masquerade."

". . . It seems that the Commissioner has sought to accomplish the agency hat trick — avoid defense of its policy at any stage."

c. Rules That Are "Interpretative"

AMERICAN MINING CONGRESS v. U.S. DEPARTMENT OF LABOR, 995 F.2d 1106 (D.C. Cir. 1993).   The Federal Mine Safety and Health Act requires mine operators to submit reports and information as the Secretary of Labor "may reasonably require." The secretary exercised his general rulemaking authority to adopt, through notice-and-comment procedures, regulations requiring reporting of specified occupational illnesses within ten days after they are "diagnosed." The Labor Department's Mine Safety and Health Administration (MSHA) issued Program Policy Letters (PPLs) to mine operators stating that chest X-rays of miners that "scored" above a certain opacity ("darkness") scale would be considered a "diagnosis" that the employee had one of the illnesses specified in the regulations; such illnesses could give rise to employer liability for disability. MSHA did not use notice-and-comment rulemaking in adopting the PPLs and did not publish them in the *Federal Register* or Code of Federal Regulations. Judge Williams, in his opinion for the court, held that the PPLs were interpretive and not subject to notice-and-comment requirements.

Evidently frustrated with past judicial efforts to distinguish legislative and interpretive rules, he formulated the following test: "[I]nsofar as our cases can be reconciled at all, we think it almost exclusively on the basis of whether the purported interpretive rule has 'legal effect,' which in turn is best ascertained by asking (1) whether in the absence of the rule there would not be an adequate legislative basis for enforcement action or other agency action to confer benefits or ensure the performance of duties, (2) whether the agency has published the rule in the Code of Federal Regulations, (3) whether the agency has explicitly invoked its general legislative authority, or (4) whether the rule effectively amends a prior legislative rule. If the answer to any of these questions is affirmative, we have a legislative, not an interpretive rule." These tests were not met. The existing MSHA regulations required reporting of the specified illnesses in question; hence, "there is no legislative gap" that required issuance of PPLs "as a predicate to enforcement/action." MSHA had not published the PPLs in the Code of Federal Regulations or invoked legislative rulemaking authority. Judge Williams also concluded that the PPLs were not a "de facto amendment" of the general reporting regulations: "A rule does not, in this inquiry, become an amendment merely because it supplies crisper and more detailed lines than the authority being interpreted. If that were so, no rule could pass as an interpretation of a legislative rule unless it were confined to parroting the rule or replacing the original vagueness with another."

Judge Williams added: "We stress that deciding whether an interpretation is an amendment of a legislative rule is different from deciding the substantive validity of that interpretation. An interpretive rule may be sufficiently within the language of a legislative rule to be a genuine interpretation and not an amendment, while at the same time being an incorrect interpretation of the agency's statutory authority." He further cautioned: "A non-legislative rule's capacity to have a binding effect is limited in practice by the fact that agency personnel at every level act under the shadow of judicial review. If they believe that courts may fault them for brushing aside the arguments of persons who contest the rule or statement, they are obviously far more likely to entertain those arguments. And, as failure to provide notice-and-comment rulemaking will usually mean that affected parties have had no prior formal opportunity to present their contentions, judicial review for want of reasoned decisionmaking is likely, in effect, to take place in review of specific agency actions implementing the rule. Similarly, where the agency must defend its view as an application of *Chevron* 'prong two' (i.e., where Congress has not 'clearly' decided for or against the agency interpretation), so that only reasonableness is at issue, agency disregard of significant policy arguments will clearly count against it. As Donald Elliott has said, agency attentiveness to parties' arguments must come sooner or later. 'As in the television commercial in which the automobile repairman intones ominously "pay me now, or pay me later," the agency has a choice. . . .' E. Donald Elliott, Reinventing Rulemaking, 41 Duke L.J. 1490, 1491 (1992)."

Judge Williams's effort to develop bright-line categorical tests for distinguishing "legislative" from "interpretive" and "policy" rules reflects a judicial trend away from an earlier approach that sought to make review turn on whether the rule in question has a significant practical impact on those affected. See Mayton, A Concept of a Rule and the "Substantial Impact" Test in Rulemaking, 33 Emory L.J. 889 (1984). The result of this trend has been to expand the availability of the exceptions to notice-and-comment requirements.

Note: An Agency's "Interpretation" of Its Prior Regulations

One situation that arises with some frequency is where an agency first adopts a rule through notice-and-comment rulemaking, and subsequently issues an "interpretation" of the rule. Is a notice-and-comment rulemaking required on the ground that the new interpretation amends the prior rule? Note that 5 U.S.C. §551(5) defines rulemaking to include agency process for "amending" a rule.

This issue was addressed in National Family Planning & Reproductive Health Assn. v. Sullivan, 979 F.2d 227 (D.C. Cir. 1992). HHS in 1988 adopted, after notice and comment, a so-called gag rule prohibiting physicians and other health care personnel in certain federally funded health care programs from abortion counseling or referral for pregnant women. This rule was upheld against constitutional and statutory attack in Rust v. Sullivan, 500 U.S. 173 (1991). Thereafter, President Bush directed HHS not to apply the rule in a fashion that interfered with the doctor-patient relationship. HHS issued instructions to regional HHS administrators telling them not to enforce the rule in a way that would contravene the president's directive. Petitioner organizations, who sought outright repeal of the rule and accordingly thought that the president's directive did not go far enough, challenged it as violative of APA notice-and-comment requirements. The court agreed with petitioners, stating:

> When an agency promulgates a legislative regulation by notice and comment directly affecting the conduct of both agency personnel and members of the public, whose meaning the agency announces as clear and definitive to the public . . . , it may not subsequently repudiate that announced meaning and substitute for it a totally different meaning without proceeding through the notice and comment rulemaking normally required for amendments of a rule. To sanction any other course would render the requirements of §553 basically superfluous in legislative rulemaking by permitting agencies to alter their requirements for affected public members at will through the ingenious device of "reinterpreting" their own rule. . . .

On the other hand, in Shalala v. Guernsey Memorial Hospital, 514 U.S. 87 (1995), the Court held that HHS "reimbursement guidelines" regarding accounting for expenses claimed by health care providers under the Medicare program did not modify its prior issued regulations on the subject; the guidelines were accordingly interpretive and hence not subject to notice-and-comment requirements. Petitioners claimed that prior HHS regulations, adopted after notice and comment, required use of generally accepted accounting principles (GAAP); that the guidelines were inconsistent with the regulations; and that notice and comment was therefore required. The court stated: "We can agree that APA rulemaking would . . . be required if [the guidelines] adopted a new position inconsistent with any of the Secretary's existing regulations." But, it found that the prior HHS regulations did not incorporate GAAP. Hence, the guidelines did not make a substantive change in existing regulations.

As *Guersey* illustrates, courts must interpret the agency's prior regulation in order to determine whether the agency's more recent interpretation constitutes a change. See also Appalachian Power Co. v. EPA, 208 F.3d 1015 (D.C. Cir. 2000), summarized below, where the court concluded that the position taken by EPA in a Guidance document was a change in the position taken by EPA in a prior adopted regulation, rejecting EPA's claim that the Guidance was consistent with the regulations, properly interpreted; Carvio v. Blockbuster, 193 F.3d 730 (3d Cir. 1999) (rejecting agency claim that its subsequent interpretation of regulation did not change but merely confirmed its original meaning).

Also consider the following decisions:

JERRI'S CERAMIC ARTS v. CONSUMER PRODUCT SAFETY COMMISSION, 874 F.2d 205 (4th Cir. 1989).   The Federal Hazardous Substances Act, 15 U.S.C. §1261, authorizes the CPSC to promulgate regulations that identify hazardous substances and prohibit their introduction into interstate commerce. The commission, in 1978, properly promulgated a legislative rule that identified certain objects as "dangerously small": those that fit into a cylinder of a certain size. The regulation excluded "paper, fabric, yarn, fuzz, elastic, and string," along with "pieces" of those materials. In 1987, the commission decided that the exclusion applied only to "pieces" that might become detached from another object; thus, small objects that themselves were made out of, say, paper, would be included. The commission announced this "interpretation" of its rule without any prior notice or comment. The appeals court held that the "interpretation" was not an "interpretative rule." It said that the change "has the clear intent of eliminating a former exemption and of providing the Commission with power to enforce violations of a new rule. For example, the statement gives the Commission authority to impose the full range of civil and criminal penalties provided by Congress. [It] imposes new duties that have the force of law and that it can proceed to enforce. [T]he Commission's contention that the rule does not 'command performance' is simply incredible. . . . Moreover, the new interpretation does not 'remind [anyone of]' existing duties, [but it radically changes a previous] longstanding position. [Finally,] the new rule directly impacts on an enormous range of children's products industries, including toys, apparel, furniture and furnishings, the latter of which, because of the fabric exemption, were formerly excluded from the rule. As a result, the statement would, for the first time, have the effect of bringing within the sweep of the regulation entirely new classes of business."

NEW YORK CITY EMPLOYEES' RETIREMENT SYSTEM v. SEC, 45 F.3d 7 (2d Cir. 1994).   The New York City Employees' Retirement System (NYCERS) acquired shares in Cracker Barrel Old Country Store, Inc., which had discharged several gay employees. NYCERS submitted a proxy proposal for Cracker Barrel's annual meeting calling on its board of directors to prohibit discrimination on the basis of employee sexual orientation. Cracker Barrel refused to include the proposal in management proxy materials on the ground that under SEC Rule 14a-8 (adopted after notice and comment), it related to "ordinary business operations" and therefore, as provided by the rule, was not required to be included. In 1976, the SEC proposed notice and comment revisions to Rule 14a-8 to narrow this exemption. Following comment, the SEC published a notice in the *Federal Register* stating that it would retain the "ordinary business operations" exemption but would interpret it to exclude shareholder proposals regarding "matters which have significant policy, economic, or other implications in them." Cracker Barrel had written to the SEC's Corporate Finance Division inquiring whether the NYCERS's proposal was within the "ordinary business operations" exemption. NYCERS wrote the division claiming that the exemption was inapplicable. Thereafter the division wrote a no action letter to Cracker Barrel, stating that it would not bring an enforcement action if it omitted the proposal and further stating: "[The] Division has determined that the fact that a shareholder proposal concerning a company's employment policies and practices for the general workforce is tied to a social issue will no longer be viewed as removing the proposal from the realm of ordinary business operations of the registrant. Rather, determinations with respect to any such proposals are properly governed by the employment-based nature of the proposal." The SEC affirmed the division's action on NYCER's protest. Held: The division's no action letter while "not a garden variety no action letter," is "interpretive." It is not "binding" on the parties or the courts and is subject to reconsideration by the SEC. It therefore did not and could not amend the commission's "legislative" Rule 14a-8.

HOCTOR v. U.S. DEPARTMENT OF AGRICULTURE, 82 F.3d 165 (7th Cir. 1996) (Posner, C.J.).   The Animal Welfare Act, designed to assure humane treatment of animals, authorizes the Secretary of Agriculture to "promulgate such rules . . . as he may deem necessary" to carry out the act's purposes. Following notice-and-comment procedures, the secretary adopted a rule requiring housing for animals that is "structurally sound" in order "to protect the animals from injury and to contain the animals." Hoctor, who kept "Big Cats" (lions, tigers, etc.) in pens on his farm in Indiana, built (at the suggestion of an Agriculture Department inspector) a six-foot fence around the pens. Thereafter, the department issued an internal memorandum to its inspectors, stating that in the case of "dangerous animals" (including lions, tigers, etc.) the perimeter fence must be at least eight feet high. Thereafter Hoctor was cited on several occasions by Agriculture Department inspectors for failure to have an eight-foot perimeter fence. The department claimed that the eight-foot provision was "interpretive." The court noted that: "Notice and comment rulemaking is time-consuming, facilitates the marshaling of opposition to a proposed rule, and may result in the creation of a very long record that may in turn provide a basis for a judicial challenge to the rule if the agency decides to promulgate it. . . . Every governmental agency that enforces a less than crystalline statute must interpret the statute, and it does the public a favor if it announces the interpretation in advance of enforcement, whether the announcement takes the form of a rule or of a policy statement, which the Administrative Procedure Act assimilates to an inter- pretive rule. It would be no favor to the public to discourage the announcement of agencies' interpretations by burdening the interpretive process with cumbersome formalities."

Nonetheless, the court concluded that the eight-foot provision could not be adopted without notice and comment. It was not an interpretation of any specific statutory provi- sion. Nor, without more explanation from the department, could it be defended as an interpretation of the "structurally sound" regulation because the eight-foot specification was essentially arbitrary in relation to the general objective of "back-up" containment of "Big Cats" who were kept in pens. Specifying an eight-foot fence, "as opposed to a seven- and-a-half foot or nine-foot fence" could not "be derived from the regulation by a process reasonably described as interpretation."

The court continued: "There are thousands of animal dealers, and some unknown fraction of these face the prospect of having to tear down their existing fences and build new, higher ones at great cost. The concerns of these dealers are legitimate and since, as we are stressing, the rule could well be otherwise, the agency was obliged to listen to them before settling on a final rule. . . ."

Query: Why couldn't Hoctor's objections to the eight-foot provision be raised by way of defense to an enforcement proceeding?

Notes and Questions

1. In Dismas Charities v. United States Department of Justice, 401 F.3d 666 (6th Cir. 2005), Judge Rogers offered a rationale for exempting interpretive rules from notice- and-comment procedures. "The distinction [between legislative and interpretive rules] reflects the primary purpose of Congress in imposing notice and comment requirements for rulemaking — to get public input so as to the wisest rules. That purpose is not served when the agency's inquiry is not 'what is the wisest rule,' but 'what is the rule.' The inter- pretative rule exception reflects the idea that public input will not help an agency make a legal determination of what the law already is." Id. at 681. Query whether the two situa- tions identified by Judge Rogers can or should be entirely distinguished in practice.

2. What if an agency adopts a regulation through notice-and-comment rulemaking, then adopts one interpretation of the regulation in the course of implementing it, and thereafter adopts a different interpretation? Assuming that neither interpretation is compelled by the regulation itself, must the changed interpretation be accomplished through notice-and-comment rulemaking? According to the test enunciated by Judge Williams in *American Mining Congress*, pp. 552-553, the answer is clearly no. But

some recent decisions say yes. See Alaska Professional Hunters Association v. FAA, 177 F.3d 1030 (D.C. Cir. 1999) (emphasizing reliance interest of regulated community on prior interpretation); Shell Offshore Co. v. Babbitt, 238 F.3d 622 (5th Cir. 2001). This new direction in the law has drawn opposition from several commentators. See Richard J. Pierce, Distinguishing Legislative Rules from Interpretive Rules, 52 Admin. L. Rev. 547 (2000); Michael Asimov and Robert A. Anthony, A Second Opinion? Inconsistent Interpretive Rules, 25 Admin. & Reg. L. News 16 (2000).

d. Rules of "Procedure"

Air Transport Association of America v. Department of Transportation

900 F.2d 369 (D.C. Cir. 1990), vacated, 111 S. Ct. 944 (1991)

HARRY T. EDWARDS, Circuit Judge:

The issue in this case is whether respondent governmental agencies (collectively "Federal Aviation Administration" or "FAA") were obliged to engage in notice and comment procedures before promulgating a body of regulations governing the adjudication of administrative civil penalty actions. . . .

[Congress amended the Federal Aviation Act to authorize the FAA to establish a program of administrative penalties for violation of the act's requirements. The FAA issued its "Penalty Rules" implementing the program without notice and opportunity for comment.]

. . . Effective immediately upon their issuance, the Penalty Rules established a schedule of civil penalties, including fines of up to $10,000 for violation of the safety standards of the Federal Aviation Act and related regulations. . . . The Penalty Rules also established a comprehensive adjudicatory scheme providing for formal notice, settlement procedures, discovery, an adversary hearing before an ALJ and an administrative appeal. . . .

The FAA argues that the Penalty Rules are exempt as "rules of agency organization, procedure, or practice" because they establish "procedures" for adjudicating civil penalty actions. According to the FAA, it would have been obliged to permit public participation in the rulemaking process only if the Penalty Rules affected aviators' "substantive" obligations under the Federal Aviation Act. We find this analysis unpersuasive.

Our cases construing section 553(b)(A) have long emphasized that a rule does not fall within the scope of the exception merely because it is capable of bearing the label "procedural." . . .

Rather than focus on whether a particular rule is "procedural" or "substantive," these decisions employ a functional analysis. . . . Where nominally "procedural" rules "encode[] a substantial value judgment" or "substantially alter the rights or interest of regulated" parties, however, the rules must be preceded by notice and comment. [Citations omitted.]

The Penalty Rules fall outside the scope of section 553(b)(A) because they substantially affect a civil penalty defendant's *right to an administrative adjudication*. Under both the due process clause . . . and the APA . . . a party has a right to notice and a hearing before being forced to pay a monetary penalty. Congress expressly directed the FAA to incorporate these rights into its civil penalty program. . . . In implementing this mandate, the FAA made discretionary — indeed, in many cases, highly contentious — choices concerning what process civil penalty defendants are due. Each one of these choices "encode[d] a substantive value judgment," on the appropriate balance between a defendant's rights to adjudicatory procedures and the agency's interest in efficient prosecution. The FAA was no less obliged to engage in notice and comment before taking action affecting these adjudicatory rights than it would have been had it taken action affecting aviators' "substantive" obligation under the Federal Aviation Act. . . .

. . . In using the term "rules of agency organization, procedure and practice," Congress intended to distinguish not between rules affecting different *classes of rights* — "substantive" and "procedural" — but rather to distinguish between rules affecting different *subject matters* — the rights or interest of regulated parties and agencies' "internal operations." Because the Penalty Rules substantially affect civil penalty defendants' "right to avail [themselves] of an administrative adjudication," members of the aviation community had a legitimate interest in participating in the rulemaking process. . . .

SILBERMAN, Circuit Judge, dissenting: . . .

If we assume a spectrum of rules running from the most substantive to the most procedural, I would describe the former as those that regulate "primary conduct" . . . and the latter are those furthest away from primary conduct. In other words, if a given regulation purports to direct, control, or condition the behavior of those institutions or individuals subject to regulation by the authorizing statute it is not procedural, it is substantive. At the other end of the spectrum are those rules, such as the ones before us in this case, which deal with enforcement or adjudication of claims of violations of the substantive norm but which do not purport to affect the substantive norm. These kinds of rules are, in my view, clearly procedural. Rules are no less procedural because they are thought to be important or affect outcomes. Congress did not state, when it passed the APA, that all but insignificant rules must be out for notice and comment. And to say, as does the majority, that the rules are covered by section 553's notice and comment requirement because they "substantially affect a civil defendant's *right to an administrative adjudication*" (emphasis in original), is, I respectfully submit, circular reasoning. It assumes the conclusion by describing petitioner's interest in the agency's adjudicatory procedures as if it were a substantive right. . . .

Of course, procedure impacts on outcomes and thus can virtually always be described as affecting substance, but to pursue that line of analysis results in the obliteration of the distinction that Congress demanded. . . .

It might be thought that there is something vaguely underhanded about an agency publishing important rules without an opportunity for those affected to comment. And lawyers and judges tend to prefer, on the margin, added procedure. But . . . we have been admonished somewhat dramatically by *Vermont Yankee* to not add more procedure to the APA than Congress required. I am afraid the majority opinion by obliterating the distinction between substance and procedure in section 553 does just that.

Compare National Whistleblower Center v. NRC, 208 F.3d 256 (D.C. Circuit 2000): The Nuclear Regulatory Commission changed its standard for granting requests for filing extensions of the time for filing interventions in nuclear power plant license renewal proceedings from "good cause" to one of "unavoidable and extreme circumstances" as part of its goal to adopt "a streamlined schedule" for license renewals. The court held that the NRC was free to adopt the new standard without resort to notice-and-comment rulemaking; rules that prescribe a timetable for asserting substantive right are procedural. The Center had adequate time (85 days) to intervene in the renewal proceeding at issue.

CHAMBER OF COMMERCE v. DEPARTMENT OF LABOR, 174 F.3d 206 (D.C. Cir. 1999). The Occupational Safety and Health Administration issued a "Directive" announcing the adoption of a "Cooperative Compliance Program" instituting a new cooperative approach to the problem of worker safety at some 12,500 relatively dangerous workplaces. The Directive placed these sites on a "primary inspection list" that subjected them to a comprehensive inspection by OSHA before the end of 1999. The designated workplaces would be removed from the inspection list if the employer enrolled in the Cooperative Compliance Program (CCP). The program required, among other things, that employers implement a safety and health program that goes beyond the requirements of the OSH Act by complying, for example, with applicable "voluntary standards, industry practices, and suppliers' safety recommendations." Basically, the Cooperative Compliance Program sought to induce employers with a particularly poor history of worker safety to take steps beyond those required by law. The Agency conceded that the Directive was a "rule" but argued that notice-and-comment rulemaking was not required for its adoption because the directive fell into the §553 exception for agency rules of procedure and general statements of policy.

The Court rejected OSHA's arguments that the Directive was "procedural" because it was merely an inspection plan and because any substantive impact on employer conduct was voluntary. Initially, Judge Ginsburg's opinion for the court distinguished procedural rules, which do not by themselves "alter the rights or interests of the parties" from substantive rules that have a "substantive impact" on private parties and "puts a stamp of agency approval or disapproval" on a given type of behavior; he noted, however, that the distinction is difficult to apply because "even a purely procedural rule can affect the substantive outcome of an agency proceeding." The court then stated that "if the function of the CCP were simply to provide each employer with the option of substituting self-inspection for an equivalent inspection conducted by the OSHA, then the agency could make a creditable argument that the Directive does not represent the kind of normative judgment characteristic of a substantive rule." But, it stated, that at least to the extent that participation in the CCP requires more than adherence to existing law, "the directive has a substantive element. The Directive is intended to, and no doubt will, affect the safety practices of thousands of employers." The court also discounted the absence of legal sanctions if an employer failed to enlist in the program. The court stated that "we examine how the rule affects not only the 'rights' of aggrieved parties but their 'interests' as well." Here, the leverage of the inspection power meant that, "in practical terms," the Directive would have the same impact on employer interests as a substantive rule directly mandating Program requirements.

The Court also rejected OSHA's attempt to avoid notice-and-comment rulemaking by characterizing the Directive as a general statement of policy. Policy statements do not bind the agency but leave "agency decisionmakers free to exercise their informed discretion in individual cases." Here, the Directive mandated both inspection of facilities on the list and removal from the list of facilities that agreed to the program. Accordingly, the Directive could not be "shoehorned into the exception for policy statements."

As discussed below, notice-and-comment rulemaking, especially on controversial issues, often takes years to complete. Does the court's decision unduly hobble desirable flexibility and innovation in regulatory strategies?

In Public Citizen v. Department of State, 276 F.3d 634 (D.C. Cir. 2002), the court applied the "encoding a substantive value judgment" criterion for substantive rules and supplied a contrasting criterion for at least some procedural rules. The State Department processed Freedom of Information Act requests according to rules promulgated without notice and comment. These rules specified that the date of the request, as opposed to the date when the document search is performed, would be the cut off date for documents released pursuant to a given request. The court found that these rules fell under the exception for procedural rules (though they went on to reject them as unreasonable both in general and as applied). In doing so, it noted that its prior decisions had "gradually shifted focus from asking whether a given procedure has a substantial impact on parties to inquiring more broadly whether the agency action encodes a substantive value judgment." But it also noted that it had been forced to clarify the new inquiry: "[I]n referring to 'value judgments' . . . we had not intended to include judgments about what mechanics and processes are most efficient because to do so would threaten to swallow the procedural exception to notice and comment." 276 F.3d at 641 (internal quotation marks and citation omitted).

Query: Is the question of whether a rule "encodes" a substantive value judgment or a judgment about procedural efficiency any clearer than the question of whether a rule is substantive or procedural? When does a rule encode a substantive value judgment? Must the agency actually have based the rule on a value judgment for it to encode that judgment?

e. The "Good Cause" Exception

APA §553(b)(B) authorizes an agency to dispense with notice and comment "[w]hen the agency for good cause finds (and incorporates the finding and a brief statement of reasons therefore in the rules issued) that notice and public procedure thereon are impracticable, unnecessary, or contrary to the public interest." One situation where the "good cause" exception is successfully invoked is where the agency is imposing new requirements that might be evaded if advance notice thereof were provided. See DeRieux v. Five Smiths, 499 F.2d 1321 (Temp. Emer. Ct. App.), *cert. denied*, 419 U.S. 896 (1974) (general notice of a proposed rule that would freeze prices was found impracticable on the assumption that there would have been a massive rush to raise prices before the freeze deadline). In these circumstances, notice and the delay associated with comment may be "impracticable" and "contrary to the public interest" by defeating the purpose of the administrative program and the rules adopted to implement it. Another recurring situation is where the agency must act pursuant to a statutory deadline, and the agency seeks to excuse notice and comment on account of the delay involved. Compare Clay Broadcasting Corp. v. United States, 464 F.2d 1313 (5th Cir. 1971) (upholding FCC revised schedule of fees published without notice, on the ground that the agency was acting under a congressional directive to cover as much of the current fiscal year as possible), with New Jersey v. United States EPA, 626 F.2d 1038, 1049-1050 (D.C. Cir. 1980) (EPA's approval of state plans for compliance with Clean Air Act required public comment, despite time pressure created by statutory deadline). See generally Jordan, The Administrative Procedure Act's "Good Cause" Exception, 36 Admin. L. Rev. 113 (1984); Lavilla, the Good Cause Exception to Notice and Comment Rulemaking Requirements under the Administrative Procedure Act, 8 Admin. L.J. 317 (1989).

Agencies often invoke the "unnecessary" exception in the case of "technical" amendments to existing regulations; controversy over such amendments is rare. However, sometimes even technical amendments necessitated by clerical error may trigger notice-and-comment requirements. In Utility Solid Waste Activities Group v. EPA, 236 F.3d 749 (D.C. Cir. 2001), EPA, after notice and comment, adopted a rule regulating the use of porous surfaces contaminated by PCBs. The rule contained mistaken PCB concentration levels due to an erroneous use of the WordPerfect find/replace command, which had the effect of changing the intended stringency of the rule. EPA reissued the rule, correcting the errors, without notice and comment; it claimed "inherent power" to correct "technical errors" without going through §553 procedures. The court held that notice and comment was required. It conceded that courts have inherent authority to correct clerical errors in their judgments without giving notice to the parties, and that administrative agencies have similar authority in cases of adjudication. But, in rulemaking, EPA's action is legislative in nature. Congress corrects technical errors in statutes, but does so through new legislation. The court indicated that EPA in this case might have been able to invoke successfully the good cause exception from notice and comment, but had not sought to do so. The court rejected the position taken in Chlorine Institute, Inc. v. Occupational Safety and Health Administration, 613 F.2d 120 (5th Cir. 1980), upholding agency power to make technical changes in rules without notice and comment, even though the substance of the rule was materially altered as a result.

Notes and Questions on the Exemptions from Notice and Comment

1. During the 1970s, reviewing courts tended to disregard various labels and to find that a rule fell within §553(c)'s notice-and-comment requirements on the basis of "functional" considerations. Is the rule important enough, does it sufficiently interest those affected to warrant notice-and-comment safeguards?[44] In Batterton v. Marshall, 648 F.2d 694 (D.C. Cir. 1980), for example, the court considered a new methodology adopted by the Department of Labor (DOL) for computing unemployment statistics. The statistics, in turn, would determine the allocation of federal job training funds among the states. The court held that DOL had to follow notice-and-comment procedures before promulgating the new methodology. The methodology was not "interpretive" because the statute gave DOL wide discretion to select methodologies and they determined the allocation of federal funds. The methodology was not a "general statement of policy" because it had a present effect. It was not "procedural" because it "trenches on substantive private rights and interests." Do you believe that the courts would reach the same result today? Would Judge Starr? Would Judge Wald?[45] To what extent are the tests currently used by the

44. See, e.g., Roadway v. Department of Agriculture, 514 F.2d 809 (D.C. Cir. 1975); Warren, Notice Requirements in Administrative Rulemaking: An Analysis of Legislative and Interpretive Rules, 29 Admin. L. Rev. 367 (1976).

45. Consider, for example, Madaluna v. Fitzpatrick, 813 F.2d 1006 (9th Cir. 1987). The Immigration and Naturalization Service (INS) promulgated an "Operating Instruction" that told the INS district directors that, at their discretion, they may recommend to the INS that it defer action on deporting an individual (which recommendation would inevitably have meant that the illegal alien could remain in the United States). The "Operating Instruction" then listed various criteria to use in making that decision. Despite the practical likelihood that the regulation would have an important impact upon illegal aliens, the court held that it fell within the notice-and-comment exception for general statements of policy. The court noted that the Attorney General's manual described such statements as "statements issued by an agency to advise the public prospectively of the manner in which the agency proposes to exercise a discretionary power." The court added that, besides "informing the public concerning the agency's future plans and priorities for exercising its discretionary power, they serve to 'educate' and provide direction to the agency's personnel in the field, who are required to implement its policies and exercise its discretionary power in specific cases. . . . To the extent that the directive merely provides guidance to agency officials in exercising their discretionary power while preserving their flexibility and their opportunity to make 'individualized determinations,' it constitutes a general statement of policy."

courts to determine the applicability of notice-and-comment requirements "formal" rather than "functional" in character? Which is the better approach?

2. Under Judge Starr's view of the law, would the "interpretations" at issue in *Jerri's Ceramic Arts* and *Appalachian Power* require notice and comment? Are they "interpretive" or "legislative" rules? Just what is the practical difference? Under the tests proposed by the courts, is it, in effect, up to the agency to classify a rule as "legislative" or "interpretive" simply by calling it one or the other and using, or not using, notice and comment?

3. Who do you think is right in *Air Transport Association?* Why?

4. "The courts have it backwards. The courts, when reviewing a rule and when deciding the degree of deference to give it, should look to see if the agency has followed notice-and-comment procedures. The procedure followed should determine the classification (and the consequent amount of deference) rather than the other way around." Support or oppose this statement.

In formulating your position, consider Judge Starr's discussion of *Chevron* and the significance in this context of the Court's decision in United States v. Mead Corp., 533 U.S. 218 (2001), involving Customs Service letter rulings that had been adopted without use of notice and comment or other procedural formalities. See Chapter 4. The Court stated that "a very good indicator of delegation meriting *Chevron* deference is express congressional authorizations to engage in the process of rulemaking or adjudication that produces regulations or rulings for which deference is claimed." The Court also stated that "Congress contemplates administrative action with the effect of law" — entitled to *Chevron* deference — "when it provides for a relatively formal administrative procedure tending to underlie a pronouncement of such force. . . . Thus, the overwhelming number of our cases applying *Chevron* deference have reviewed the fruits of notice and comment rulemaking or formal adjudication [citing cases]. That said, and as significant as notice-and-comment is in pointing to *Chevron* authority, the want of that procedure does not decide [this case], for we have sometimes found reasons for *Chevron* deference even when no such administrative formality was required and none was afforded. The fact that the tariff classification here at issue was not a product of such formal process does not alone, therefore, bar the application of *Chevron*." The Court concluded, however, that the letter ruling in issue was not, for a number of other reasons, entitled to *Chevron* deference, although indicating that it might still enjoy a lesser degree of judicial deference. See also Christensen v. Harris County, 529 U.S. 576 (2000), where the Court ruled that an interpretation contained in an agency opinion letter was not entitled to *Chevron* defense. Rather, the Court stated that "an interpretation contained in an opinion letter, not one arrived at by notice and comment, is entitled to respect but only to the extent that those interpretations in light of the agency experience and expertise ha[ve] the power to persuade."

For discussion of the exceptions to notice-and-comment requirements, see Anthony, Interpretive Rules, Policy Statements, Guidance Manuals, and the Like — Should Federal Agencies Use Them to Bind the Public? 41 Duke L.J. 1311 (1992); Asimow, Nonlegislative Rulemaking and Regulatory Reform, 1985 Duke L.J. 381; Saunders, Interpretive Rules and Legislative Effect: An Analysis and a Proposal for Public Participation, 1986 Duke L.J. 346.

Problems

1. On January 22, 1993, President Clinton ordered HHS to suspend the "gag" rule at issue in National Family Planning and conduct rulemaking to overturn it. On February 5,

1993, the Secretary of HHS suspended the gag rule and noticed proposed substitute regulations for public comment. The secretary found that initiative of the rulemaking to repeal the gag rule provided "good cause" for suspending it without notice and comment. Pro-life groups challenge the suspension, claiming that it requires notice-and-comment rulemaking. What result?

2. The Resource Conservation and Recovery Act gives the EPA the power to promulgate regulations defining "hazardous wastes." Firms must follow very burdensome rules in disposing of any such waste. In 1986, EPA announced to the public that it would use a model, called the VHS model, to predict how quickly and how far certain types of sludge would spread from the place they were buried in order to determine whether they are "hazardous." The EPA did not follow notice-and-comment procedures. It said that it "will use" the model in the future to predict levels of toxic seepage, but that the model was simply "one of many tools" that it would use, that it was only "one factor" involved in the decision, and that the EPA "retained discretion" to deviate from the model. It added that, even if it used the model and consequently listed a particular sludge, buried at a particular place, as "hazardous," a firm could always apply for "delisting," and it could persuade the EPA to take many nonmodel factors into account "provided that it made a compelling case for doing so." More recently, EPA has admitted that, in only 4 instances out of 100 had it delisted wastes that the model would have classified as "hazardous."

McLouth Steel produces "sludge x" as an unwanted by-product. The VHS model indicated that "sludge x" is "hazardous." McLouth applied for "delisting," which the EPA denied. McLouth argues, on review, that the EPA should have followed notice-and-comment procedures in promulgating the model. What arguments will counsel for both sides make? Who will win? See McLouth Steel Products Corp. v. Thomas, 838 F.2d 1317 (D.C. Cir. 1988). Compare American Mining Congress v. Marshall, 671 F.2d 1251 (10th Cir. 1982) (a DOL "strategy" consisting of guidelines for placing dust sampling devices in coal mines and a list of potential dust-generating sources is only a general policy statement because it does not bind mine owners, for the owners can challenge the policy embodied in the "strategy" if DOL seeks to enforce against them the legal requirement that they monitor breatheable dust levels and relies on the "strategy" to show a violation).

3. The National Park Service, after notice and comment, issued a regulation that says that a permit given to demonstrators, camped on Lafayette Park just outside the White House, shall impose a condition that they cannot have with them "more personal property than is reasonably required for a twenty-four hour demonstration." The same regulation says that "[a] permit may contain additional reasonable conditions consistent with this section." The Park Service then decided that all Lafayette Park permits would contain a condition that defined the property a person might have with him to include such matters as a "coat, thermos, and a small quantity of literature," but that the person could not have with him any "construction materials, such as lumber or paint" and that "food, bedding, and luggage may not be stored in the park at all." The adoption by the Park Service of these additional policies was not preceded by notice and comment.

Concepcion Picciotto has engaged in a 24-hour vigil (to warn the public about nuclear war) in Lafayette Park for many months. He has recently been arrested because he had with him a bedroll, paint, and lumber. He challenges the lawfulness of the regulation. What result? See United States v. Picciotto, 875 F.2d 345 (D.C. Cir. 1989).

Note: The Record for Judicial Review of Rules Within §553 Exceptions to Notice and Comment

A person adversely affected by one of the "excepted" rules may challenge its legal validity. The court, in reviewing the lawfulness of such a rule, presumably will look at the "administrative record." If, however, a rule is excepted from notice-and-comment requirements, the APA provides no procedures that must be followed in adopting it. In such a case, where and how is the "administrative record" to be found? This same problem arises in informal adjudication, where the APA likewise provides no procedures. Under *Overton Park*, review in cases of informal adjudication is generally based on whatever documents the agency may have in its files regarding the matter. If these materials are not adequate to permit review, the court generally remands to the agency to prepare a more adequate record. The same procedure is followed for excepted rules. The alternative, also endorsed by *Overton Park*, of judicial discovery of agency officials to determine the basis for their decision is rarely followed.

Even if rules, regulations, or policy statements fall within one of the exceptions to §553's notice-and-comment requirement, the APA requires agencies to keep the public informed about many of them. Section 552(a) says that each "agency shall separately state and currently publish in the *Federal Register* . . . substantive rules of general applicability adopted as authorized by law *and statements of general policy or interpretations of general applicability* formulated and adopted by the agency. . . ." (Emphasis added.) It also requires each agency, in accordance with published rules, to "make available for public inspection and copying . . . those statements of policy and interpretations which have been adopted by the agency and are not published in the *Federal Register*, and . . . administrative staff manuals and instructions to staff that affect a member of the public."

6. *The Standard for Judicial Review of Agency Factfinding in Informal Rulemaking*

What standard should courts apply in reviewing agency factual determinations in the case of rules adopted through notice-and-comment procedures or excepted rules? As we have seen, in formal rulemaking, the "substantial evidence" standard applies by virtue of APA §706(2)(E). But this standard was regarded as not applicable to notice-and-comment rulemaking because, as traditionally understood, it did not generate a "record." Now that courts have developed a "paper hearing" requirement in notice-and-comment rulemaking, which does generate an exclusive documentary record as the basis for the rule, should the substantial evidence standard apply in judicial review of such rules? What standard should apply to rulemakings that are excepted from §553 notice-and-comment requirements?

As we will shortly see, similar problems arise in the case of judicial review of factfinding in informal adjudication. The drafters of the APA anticipated that review of both informal rulemaking and informal adjudication would be infrequent, and that in such cases courts would, in the absence of an administrative record, determine the facts de novo, as provided by §706(2)(F). In its 1971 *Overton Park* decision (Chapter 4) involving a case of informal adjudication, the Court, however, rejected this approach and instead adopted the "arbitrary and capricious" standard for review of agency policymaking discretion in §706(2)(A) as the standard that should also be used for reviewing an agency's factual determinations in informal adjudication. The same arbitrary and capricious standard for review of agency factfinding has also been adopted by courts as the applicable APA standard for review of facts in challenges to rules adopted through notice and comment as well as those adopted without notice and comment. Certain specific statutes, however, provide for "substantial evidence" review of factual elements in rules adopted through notice-and-comment rulemaking, including, for example, the Occupational Safety and Health Act and the Toxic Substance Control Act. What difference does it make if a notice-and-comment rule is reviewed under an "arbitrary and capricious" or a "substantial evidence" standard? Some courts and most academic commenters have concluded that the tests are the same in practice.

7. Consequences of the Transformation of Notice-and-Comment Rulemaking

a. Some Practical Consequences

The increased procedural requirements that the courts have imposed on informal notice-and-comment rulemaking have probably created a fairer system, a system that will lead to rules based on information contained in a public record, and a system that permits courts to review the rationality of the resulting rules. At the same time, they have created a more cumbersome and legalistic system, which tends to give agency lawyers considerable authority within the agency, and which means delay. The EPA, for example, administers seven major laws affecting major areas of pollution, water, air, waste disposal, and so forth. To administer those laws, the EPA must develop regulations. The EPA says that, at any one time, its staff is at work on between 200 and 250 rules and regulations. Of those, 10 to 20 percent are what the EPA would call "major rules." The EPA estimates that 85 percent of those major rules will be challenged in court by industry, environmental groups, states, and so on. A third or more of the rules challenged will be found defective by reviewing courts, often leading to further rule-making proceedings.

Virtually all these rules, including the major rules, require notice-and-comment procedures. The EPA generally develops initial proposals on its own, though in doing so, its staff usually meets individually with representatives of many different interest groups. In some instances EPA will publish an Advanced Notice of Proposed Rulemaking (ANPR) in the *Federal Register*, stating that it is considering the initiation of rulemaking on a given subject and inviting the submission of views as to whether and how it should proceed. In the case of a major rule, this initial preparation of a proposal takes 18 to 20 months on average. The EPA then publishes the proposal in the *Federal Register* and receives comment over the next three to six months. It often receives hundreds of adverse public comments. It must analyze each of them, and respond to the most important comments in the preamble to the final rule. It may revise its proposed rule. It may even ask for another round of comments. On average, it takes the EPA 16 months from the time of notice to the promulgation of a final, major rule. And, as we have said, there is an 85 percent chance of subsequent court litigation.

The total time involved in the creation and promulgation of a major rule (excluding "court review" time) typically is about three and a half years. The EPA has prepared a time chart, which looks like this:

Average Timeline for Issuance of a Major Rule

18-20 months	*6 months*	*16 months*
EPA internal preparation of proposal	public comment	analysis of public comment — final rule

b. A Framework for Analysis

Bearing in mind the practical consequences discussed above, reconsider the cases and materials that you have just read. And consider the following.

1. Begin with *Florida East Coast*. That case, perhaps in reaction to the FDA's time-consuming efforts to regulate peanut butter via formal rulemaking procedures, created a rule for reading federal statutes narrowly so that very few of them imposed formal rule-making requirements. The result is that informal notice-and-comment procedures apply instead to vast numbers of potential rules, of very different kinds, applicable to many different kinds of subject matter.

2. If the courts had read the notice-and-comment requirements of §553 literally and in light of Congress's expectations in 1946, consistent with pre-1970 court interpretations, the "informal rulemaking" procedural requirements would have been limited. The 1970s, however, saw an enormous growth in the number of federal "social" and other regulatory programs created by statute. Often, statutes would give a single administrator, or a small group of commissioners, the authority to promulgate rules and regulations, many of which would have vast impact on the public, greater than the impact of many laws passed by Congress. To control, to regularize, to oversee the power that those statutes thereby granted administrators (exercised without the "political" checks applicable to individual members of Congress), the courts began to read the language specifying the procedural content of notice and comment rulemaking as imposing fairly strict procedural requirements. Eventually, *Vermont Yankee* called a halt to this development, but it left "paper hearing" rules in place, along with "hard look" review.

3. The added procedural requirements themselves threatened to create "peanut butter" problems, such as problems of delay. More importantly, the "informal rulemaking" box contained within it not only very important rules, but also many rules of lesser importance, rules where elaborate "paper hearing" requirements might seem pointless or overkill.

4. The courts, responding to this latter problem, have begun to read the §553 notice-and-comment exceptions more broadly, thereby reserving the now-elaborate notice-and-comment procedures for more important, "legislative" rules, but leaving other lesser rules without any significant procedural protections.

There are difficulties with this analysis. For one thing, if you return to subpart (3) and review the "exceptions," you will find that they are not limited to less-important rules. To the contrary, the distinction between legislative rules, on the one hand, and interpretive rules, general policy statements, and procedural rules, on the other, does not track the distinction between "more important" and "less important" rules. For another thing, a broad reading of the exceptions means that all of the rules to which they apply are not subject to any APA procedural requirements. (This is not quite true, since they still must be published in the *Federal Register* or made available for public inspection, see §552.)

Nonetheless, one can view the development of rulemaking's procedural law as an effort by courts to find appropriate procedural controls for agencies where (1) "appropriateness" must be judged in terms of accountability, fairness, and efficiency, and (2) the courts must generally carry out this task by interpreting a single statute, the APA, while (3) the rules and adjudications to which that statute applies involve many different statutes, different subject matters, and different kinds of circumstance. Is it surprising that one cannot easily find a single, or even a handful, of procedures that will achieve our objectives?

Consider two possible alternatives. First, what might have happened if *Florida East Coast* had been decided differently? Suppose statutes were interpreted "liberally" to conclude that Congress intended formal rulemaking "on a record." Suppose further that courts had interpreted broadly §556(d)'s authorization to streamline formal rulemaking by dispensing with oral procedures. And suppose courts had given a "bare-bones," traditional interpretation of §553 notice-and-comment procedures, not requiring a "paper record" and elaborate preamble explanations. Suppose, finally, that §553's "exceptions" were interpreted narrowly. Would the result have been better? Would the "fit" between rulemaking procedure and need — a fit judged according to standards of "control of discretion," "fairness," and "efficiency" — have been better?

Second, what about leaving up to Congress the job of tailoring particular procedures, agency by agency, statute by statute? What reason is there for thinking the results would be better? For thinking they would be worse?

c. Assessments of Current Arrangements and Possible Alternatives

Assessments of the current state of procedural requirements for rulemaking vary widely. Some commenters believe that "paper hearing" requirements and associated "hard look" review have, for example, contributed to the improvement of EPA decisionmaking because the agency must be prepared to expose the factual and methodological bases for its decision and face judicial review on a record that encompasses the contentions and evidence of the agency and its opponents, including responses by the agency to criticisms of its decision. These procedures promote the flow of information and, arguably, the democratic accountability of agency decisionmaking. See Pedersen, Formal Records and Informal Rulemaking. 85 Yale L.J. 38, 59-60 (1975).

Others are skeptical, stressing the delays and costs involved in more formalized rulemaking procedures, which may make it difficult for a given four-year presidential administration to carry a policy initiative through to a judicially sustainable end. In addition to the APA rulemaking requirements, as construed and elaborated by the courts, critics note that a variety of other statutes and a number of executive orders impose additional requirements on rulemaking. The Rulemaking Committee of the ABA Section on Administrative Law and Regulatory Procedure has identified 20 different statutes and executive orders that impose a patchwork of varying requirements on agency rulemaking, including the APA, the Negotiated Rulemaking Act of 1990, the Regulatory Flexibility Act, the Small Business Regulatory Enforcement Fairness Act, legislation providing for congressional review of agency rulemaking, the Unfunded Mandates Reform Act, the Paperwork Reduction Act, the Federal Advisory Committee Act, and the National Environmental Policy Act. It compiled a table summarizing these requirements. See Mark Seidenfeld, A Table of Requirements for Federal Administrative Rulemaking, 27 Fla. St. Univ. L. Rev. 533 (2000). Seidenfeld notes the concern of many scholars that such requirements will result in "paralysis by analysis." He also notes that the patchwork of different requirements has created a "confusing labyrinth" that agencies must negotiate. The table is designed to provide a roadmap to the labyrinth. The skeptics also doubt whether these procedures have done much to "improve" agency decisions or do more than create work for lawyers who seek to mask "political" decisions by agency officials with elaborate legal and technical boilerplate. (Consider, in this respect, the history of the passive restraints policy in State Farm Mutual.) Consider also Elliott, Reinvesting Rulemaking, 41 Duke L.J. 1490, 1492-1493 (1992):

> No administrator in Washington turns to full-scale notice-and-comment rulemaking when she is genuinely interested in obtaining input from interested parties. Notice-and-comment rulemaking is to public participation as Japanese Kabuke theater is to human passions — a highly stylized process for displaying in a formal way the essence of something which in real life takes place in other venues. To secure the genuine reality, rather than a formal show, of public participation, a variety of techniques is available — from informal meetings with trade associations and other constituency groups, to roundtables, to floating "trial balloons" in speeches or leaks to the trade press, to the more formal techniques of advisory committees and negotiated rulemaking.

Several scholars have decried an "ossification" of the rulemaking process.[46] In addition to generating delay and transaction costs, commenters have found that the rulemaking gauntlet has caused agencies to switch from rulemaking to adjudicatory techniques that are less effective in furthering regulatory goals,[47] and impeded needed changes in existing regulatory policy,[48] as well as new regulatory initiatives. OSHA, for example, has experienced severe difficulties in adopting regulations to control the multitude of toxic chemicals found in various workplaces. In the first two decades after its creation, it had adopted only 24 substance-specific and 3 generic regulations. It thereupon initiated a mammoth rulemaking to adopt permissible exposure limits (PELs) for 428 toxic substances. In AFL v. OSHA, 965 F.2d 962 (11th Cir. 1992), the court set aside these regulations notwithstanding OSHA's claim that its "wholesale" approach to rulemaking was "the only practical way" of "making major strides towards improving worker health and safety." The agency's explanations for its regulations was "virtually devoid of reasons for setting individual standards. In most cases OSHA cited a few studies and then established a PEL without explaining why the studies mandated the particular PEL chosen."

The "ossification" thesis has been challenged. See William S. Jordan III, Ossification Revisited: Does Arbitrary and Capricious Review Significantly Interfere with Agency Ability to Achieve Regulatory Goals through Informal Rulemaking? 94 Nw. U.L. Rev. 393 (2000). Yet there is substantial evidence that the burdens associated with notice-and-comment rulemaking have led agencies to make policy through "interpretive" rules, policy statements, guidelines, and other informal arrangements that are not subject

---

46. See, e.g., McGarity, Some Thoughts on "Deossifying" the Rulemaking Process, 1992 Duke L.J. 1385; Pierce, Seven Ways to Deossify Agency Rulemaking, 47 Admin. L. Rev. 59 (1995).

47. J. Mashaw and D. Harfst, The Struggle for Auto Safety (1990).

48. Pierce, The Unintended Effects of Judicial Review of Agency Rules: How Federal Courts Have Contributed to the Electricity Crisis of the 1990s, 43 Admin. L. Rev. 7 (1991); Rossi, Redeeming Judicial Review: The Hard Look Doctrine and Federal Regulatory Efforts to Restructure the Electric Utility Industry, 1994 Wis. L. Rev. 763.

to notice and comment,[49] thereby arguably diminishing public input and accountability, transparency, and fair notice.[50]

One suggestion for dealing with these problems is to relax the rigor of "hard look" review and the accompanying demand for extensive records and elaborate agency explanations in rulemaking, reversing *State Farm* (or at least the portion thereof dealing with seat belts rather than airbags). For example, Thomas McGarity has suggested that judges should apply the requirement of reasoned decisionmaking the way that a professor might grade, on a pass-fail basis, an examination in a complicated subject about which the professor knows little.[51] Defenders of the existing approach believe, however, that its contributions outweigh its drawbacks, and that critics have overstated the extent to which judges have caused undue "ossification."[52] Indeed, some not only oppose relaxing "paper hearing" procedures and "hard look" judicial review of rules, but believe that they should be extended to informal agency statements of policy and "guidance."[53]

Other suggested steps to deal with ossification include eliminating the ability of litigants to challenge a rule immediately on its adoption, postponing judicial review to the enforcement stage and thereby generating pressure on regulated firms and others to compromise their differences with the agency rather than resort to litigation;[54] referral of major rules to Congress for adoption through "fast track" legislation, bypassing judicial review in favor of direct political control;[55] and greater reliance on executive oversight and control of rulemaking, perhaps through a new institution similar to the French *Conseil d'Etat*.[56] A further possibility is adoption of rules through regulatory negotiation, discussed in the following subsection.

Agencies have developed a number of innovations in rulemaking to deal with the "ossification" problem. One initiative, recommended by the Administrative Conference of the United States, a federal research entity since abolished, is the use of direct final rulemaking for those rules that the agency expects to be uncontroversial. Under this procedure, the agency publishes a rule with a statement of its basis and purpose, a statement that the agency expects the rule to be noncontroversial, and a procedure for the

49. See R. S. Melnick, Regulation and the Courts: The Case of the Clean Air Act 190-192 (1983).

50. See R. A. Anthony, "Well, You Want the Permit, Don't You?" Agency Efforts to Make Nonlegislative Documents Bind the Public, 44 Admin. L. Rev. 31 (1992) (describing agency use of policy statements and guidelines that are not binding in form but are in practice).

51. See McGarity, supra note 46 at 1453. See also Pierce, supra note 48. Seidenfeld, Demystifying Deossification: Rethinking Recent Proposals to Modify Judicial Review of Notice and Comment Rulemaking, 75 Tex. L. Rev. 483 (1997) (stressing impact of uncertainty in application of judicial review standards generally rather than "hard look" judicial demands for detailed explanations).

52. See Jordan, Ossification Revisited: Does Arbitrary and Capricious Review Significantly Interfere with Agency Ability to Achieve Regulatory Goals Through Informal Rulemaking? 94 Nw. U.L. Rev. 393 (2000). Jordan studied rulemaking remands under the arbitrary and capricious standard decided in the D.C. Circuit between 1985 and 1995. He concludes that the hard look standard did not significantly impede agencies in the pursuit of their policy goals during the decade under review.

Courts have sought to limit "ossification" in some cases involving rules that lack adequate agency justification by remanding but not vacating the rule, leaving it in effect while the agency attempts to provide an adequate justification, e.g., Allied Signal, Inc. v. NRC, 988 F.2d 146 (D.C. Cir. 1993), or by allowing an agency (under the "good cause" exception) to adopt without notice and comment a similar interim rule while it attempts to repair the original rule, e.g., Mid-Tex Elec. Coop. v. FERC, 822 F.2d 1123 (D.C. Cir. 1987). Thus, a court finding that a rule is "arbitrary and capricious" does not automatically result in its being set aside.

53. See Anthony & Codevilla, Pro-Ossification: A Harder Look at Agency Policy Statements, 31 Wake Forest L. Rev. 667 (1996).

54. See Mashaw, Improving the Environment of Agency Rulemaking: An Essay on Management, Games, and Accountability, 57 Law & Contemp. Probs. 195 (1994).

55. See Verkuil, Comment: Rulemaking Ossification — A Modest Proposal, 47 Admin. L. Rev. 453 (1995).

56. See S. Breyer, Breaking the Vicious Circle (1993) (executive "superagency" for risk regulation).

rule to become effective within a relatively short time, such as 60 or 90 days, unless significant adverse comments are received, in which case the agency will initiate full-fledged notice-and-comment procedures. A number of agencies, including EPA and FDA have used this procedure. Over a recent four-year period, federal agencies issued over 1000 direct final rules, of which 62 elicited significant adverse comment. See Lars Noah, Doubts About Direct Final Rulemaking, 51 Admin. L. Rev. 401, 410 (1999). For varying assessments of the legality and desirability of this innovation, see id.; Ronald M. Levin, Direct Final Rulemaking, 64 Geo. Wash. L. Rev. 1 (1995).

Another initiative, also recommended by the Administrative Conference, is interim final rulemaking, which involves a different procedure. Agencies that wish to make a rule immediately effective in order to act expeditiously while believing it desirable to obtain and, if appropriate, respond to comment on it issue a rule in final form, generally relying on the "good cause" exception to notice-and-comment requirements. At the same time, they invite public comment on the rule and commit to review comments and, if appropriate, modify or withdraw the rule in light of the comments. It has been estimated that hundreds of interim final rules are issued by federal agencies annually. This procedure is an alternative to simply issuing a rule in final form by invoking the good cause exception and leaving it to private parties to petition the agency for modification or repeal. See Michael Asimow, Interim-Final Rules: Making Haste Slowly, 51 Admin. L. Rev. 703 (1999).

d. Negotiated Rulemaking

Some federal agencies have tried to develop rules through a process of negotiation. The agency selects a facilitator to convene meetings of interested parties. They will meet with staff to propose rules, to discuss their own proposals, and to try to come up with a final, agreed-on rule, including the rule's specific language. At that point, the agency proposes the rule and goes through the §553 notice-and-comment process. The agency may promise during the negotiations to adopt the consensus proposal, at least if subsequent notice and comment do not reveal serious flaws. See generally Harter, Regulatory Negotiation: A Cure for Malaise, 71 Geo. L.J. 1 (1981).

The EPA is fairly enthusiastic about the possibilities of negotiated rulemaking. It has found that it takes about seven months to develop a proposal to the point where negotiations can begin, that negotiations take about six months, that subsequent public "notice-and-comment" process takes three more months, and that the analysis of the comments takes an additional ten months. The total time necessary for the rulemaking process has been reduced from about three and a half years to about two and one-quarter years in cases involving successful negotiation of a major rule. Moreover, the likelihood of subsequent court challenges seems far lower than the more than 75 percent likelihood in the case of major rules adopted through traditional rulemaking processes. The EPA's "negotiated rulemaking" timeline looks like this:

3 months	4.5 months	6 months	3 months	10 months
Initial work	Evaluation	Negotiations	Public comment	Analysis/ promulgation

Negotiated rulemaking, however, has been tried with only a comparatively small number of major rules. It seems to work best when each party involved has the power to influence the outcome of a pending decision, when the number of parties is fairly small, when the issues are in a focused form fit for decision, when the parties are under pressure to decide, when each party has something to gain from negotiation, when tradeoffs are possible, when the issues do not easily admit of an "objective" solution, and when decisions of the group can be fairly easily implemented. Of course, negotiation can harm the interests of those who are not present at the negotiating table; insuring adequate representation of all affected interests is a potential problem. OSHA has experimented with negotiated rulemaking, but apparently with less success than the EPA. Some of the factors that may promote or impede the success of regulatory negotiation are examined in Perritt, Negotiated Rulemaking Before Federal Agencies: Evaluation of Recommendations by the Administrative Conference of the United States, 74 Geo. L.J. 1625 (1986) (examining experience at OSHA and the Department of Transportation). Even where negotiation does not produce full consensus, it may narrow the range of disagreement.

Several analysts have challenged the feasibility or desirability of negotiated rules. For example, Professor William Funk, a participant in the regulatory negotiation of the EPA's air pollution emission standards for wood stoves, found that the rule in question was a "multipart compromise" designed to accommodate each of the interests represented in the negotiation: EPA, national environmental groups, several states, wood stove manufacturers and trade associations, manufacturers of emission control equipment, and a consumer organization. He found, however, that important elements of the rule exceeded the EPA's regulatory authority or were otherwise inconsistent with the Clean Air Act. While the parties to the negotiation were happy with the result, the proposed rule that emerged bore "scant resemblance to what was contemplated by the statute." The public notice-and-comment process was perfunctory. The EPA adopted the proposed rule without change. No one sought judicial review. Professor Funk concludes that regulatory negotiation distorts the proper role and responsibility of an agency, "first by reducing the agency to the level of a mere participant in the formulation of the rule, and second, by essentially denying that the agency has any responsibility beyond giving effect to the consensus achieved by the group." Funk, When Smoke Gets in Your Eyes: Regulation Negotiation and the Public Interest — EPA's Woodstove Standards, 18 Envtl. L. 55 (1987). Cf. Fiss, Against Settlement, 93 Yale L.J. 1073 (1984). Consider also whether regulatory negotiation is consistent with the purpose and process of OMB review of agency regulation pursuant to executive order. Will the prospect of such review make it more difficult to achieve consensus in negotiations? Should OMB be a participant? For a recent review of experience with negotiated rulemaking that is generally skeptical of its performance, see Coglianese, Assessing Consensus: The Promise and Performance of Negotiated Rulemaking, 46 Duke L.J. 55 (1997). See also David B. Spence & Lekha Gopalakrishnan, Bargaining Theory and Regulatory Reform: The Political Logic of Inefficient Regulation, 53 Vand. L. Rev. 599 (2000), offering a strategic explanation for why bargaining participants in regulation negotiations might forgo changes in the status quo that are net-beneficial for all participants by using their power to veto such changes in order to extract further policy concession from other stakeholders.

Defenders of regulated negotiation have disputed these criticisms. See Philip J. Harter, Assessing the Assessors: The Actual Performance of Negotiated Rulemaking, 9 N.Y.U. Envtl. L.J. 32 (2000); Hody Feeman & Laura I. Langbein, Regulatory Negotiation and the Legitimacy Benefit, 9 N.Y.U. Envtl. L.J. 60 (2000). The Administrative Conference of the

United States strongly recommended that agencies use negotiated rulemaking as well as providing recommendations as to how they should go about doing so. See Administrative Conference Recommendations 82-4, 85-5, and its Negotiated Rulemaking Sourcebook (1990). In 1990, Congress passed the Negotiated Rulemaking Act, P.L. 101-648, 104 Stat. 4969, codified at 5 U.S.C. §§561-570. It authorizes an agency to employ negotiated rule-making when it determines, based on consideration of enumerated factors, that such a procedure is in the "public interest"; authorizes agency employment of an outside "convenor" of the negotiation; requires agency publication of the subject of the proposed rule and the procedures for applying for representation on the negotiating committee (which includes a representative of the agency); provides for agency conduct of the negotia-tion with the assistance of a "facilitator," nominated by the agency, from either within or without the federal government; and authorizes the agency to pay compensation and expenses of committee members where their presence is needed to ensure representation of relevant interests and where they would otherwise lack financial ability to participate. The agency must either publish for notice and comment rules adopted by consensus of the nego-tiating committee or explain its refusal to do so. Agency action regarding the existence and function of a committee is not subject to judicial review. Consensus rules adopted after notice and comment are fully subject to judicial review. The Act provides that "[a] rule which is the product of negotiated rulemaking and is subject to judicial review shall not be accorded any greater deference by a court than a rule which is the product of other rule-making procedures." In addition to the Negotiated Rulemaking Act, Congress in 1990 also enacted the Administrative Dispute Resolution Act, 5 U.S.C. §§571-583, which authorizes agencies, under certain circumstances, to employ techniques such as mediation, arbitra-tion, and minitrials. An overview of the role of negotiation and mediation in resolving controversies over public policy is provided in L. Susskind and J. Cruikshank, Breaking the Impasse: Consensual Approaches to Resolving Public Policy Disputes (1987).

What should be the proper role of appellate courts in reviewing rules created through negotiation? Phillip Harter argues that after an agency has promulgated a final rule supported by all interested parties, judicial review should be very limited:

> [T]he directly affected parties are in a far better position than the agency or a review-ing court to determine what the "relevant factors" are and the weight to be accorded each. . . . That the rule reflects a consensus of the affected parties therefore goes a long way towards meeting the goals of *Overton Park* and ensures that the rule is neither arbitrary nor capricious.

See Harter, The Role of Courts in Regulatory Negotiation — A Response to Judge Wald, 11 Colum. J. Envtl. L. 51, 65 (1986). Harter also asserts that courts should not, absent special circumstances, allow interested parties who decline to participate in negotiations later to challenge the final rule in court. Rather, the main role of courts in reviewing nego-tiated rules should be (1) to ensure that the rule is within the agency's statutory authority, (2) to prevent unprincipled logrolling, and (3) to prevent sell-outs in which a party or the agency agrees to something short of what it should obtain under the governing law.

Judge Patricia Wald questioned the wisdom of this approach. See Wald, Negotiation of Environmental Disputes: A New Role for the Courts? 10 Colum. J. Envtl. L. 1 (1985). She believes that courts must still look beyond consensus to determine if the agency's choice of rule reflects rational decisionmaking. She also opposed stringent limits on the availability of judicial review for those not participating in the negotiations, which some negotiated rulemaking advocates have claimed is necessary to prevent circumvention of the negotiation process:

> I have trouble, however, seeing the justice or efficiency of a rule that requires every party potentially affected by a negotiation to either demand personal representation or take his chances on whether the designated interest group representative will truly represent his interest. This sort of standing rule might well encourage unnecessary challenges to the original committee if it became necessary to preserve an opportunity for later, substantive appeals.

Wald also questions the interest group model of administrative law on which Harter's view of negotiated rulemaking rests:

> Harter's proposal for limiting judicial review of negotiated regulations has its roots in a theory of administrative law that rejects both the expertise and non-delegation doctrines as meaningful ways to govern the relationship between agencies and courts. This tradition views the regulatory process in essentially political terms and grounds the legitimacy of agency action, indeed of all government action, on the ability of the government to reconcile conflicting political and practical interests as expressed by interest group representatives. . . .
>
> By suggesting that affected parties play a direct role in the development of regulations from day one, it rejects the notion that regulatory dilemmas can be solved through technological rationality or enlightened expertise. . . .
>
> Historically, however, the attempt to model the regulatory process on the political process has been troubled by three thorny problems. For any particular agency action, interest group pluralists have to determine which interest groups should be represented before the agency, what kind of participation is appropriate, and what sort of procedural rules will govern the ironing out of a consensus among those conflicting group interests. These are essentially the same problems that linger in Harter's proposed standard for judicial review of negotiated regulations.

Harter has responded by proposing that all groups who represent parties that would be significantly affected by the rule should be able to participate, that all should have "equal access to the table," and that "a workable definition of 'consensus' is that each interest represented at the table concurs in the result and that each representative signs the document." See Harter, supra. Is such a process feasible or desirable? See also Robert Choo, Judicial Review of Negotiated Rulemaking: Should *Chevron* Apply? 52 Rutgers Univ. L. Rev. 1069 (2000) (arguing against *Chevron* deference to negotiated rules).

The debate about the proper judicial role in reviewing negotiated rules may be of greater theoretical than practical importance, for such rules have rarely been challenged in court. For example, no one, whether or not a party to the negotiations, challenged the EPA woodstove regulation that troubled Professor Funk. But what if an agency refuses to adopt the negotiated consensus? Consider the following.

USA GROUP LOAN SERVICES v. U.S. DEPARTMENT OF EDUCATION, 83 F.3d 708 (7th Cir. 1996).   Pursuant to the Higher Education Act, which establishes federal guaranteed loan programs, the Department of Education adopted regulations imposing unlimited liability on "servicers" (private organizations who act as agents for educational institutions, lenders, and guarantors in connection with student loans) for violations of laws that result in losses to the programs that the department is unable to recoup from the servicers' clients. A

1992 amendment to the Act required the department to submit draft regulations to a process of negotiated rulemaking; the department conducted the negotiation pursuant to the Negotiated Rulemaking Act. Servicers unsuccessfully challenged the rule, contending, among other matters, that the department had negotiated in bad faith. Chief Judge Posner wrote for the court: "During the negotiations, an official of the Department of Education promised the servicers that the Department would abide by any consensus reached by them unless there were compelling reasons to depart. The propriety of such a promise may be questioned. It sounds like an abdication of regulatory authority to the regulated, the full burgeoning of the interest-group state, and the final confirmation of the 'capture' theory of administrative regulation. At all events, although the servicers reached a firm consensus that they should not be liable for their mistakes the Department refused to abide by its official's promise. What is more, the draft regulations that the Department submitted to the negotiating process capped the servicers' liability at the amount of the fees they received from their customers, yet when it came time to propose a regulation as the basis for the notice and comment rulemaking the Department abandoned the cap. The breach of the promise to abide by consensus in the absence of compelling reasons not here suggested, and the unexplained withdrawal of the Department's proposal to cap the servicers' liability, form the basis for the claim that the Department negotiated in bad faith." Judge Posner concluded as follows: "We have doubts about the propriety of the official's promise to abide by a consensus of the regulated industry, but we have no doubt that the Negotiated Rulemaking Act did not make the promise enforceable. The practical effect of enforcing it would be to make the Act extinguish notice and comment rulemaking in all cases in which it was preceded by negotiated rulemaking; the comments would be irrelevant if the agency were already bound by promises that it had made to the industry. There is no textual or other clue that the Act meant to do this. Unlike collective bargaining negotiations, to which the servicers compare negotiated rulemaking, the Act does not envisage that the negotiations will end in a binding contract. The Act simply creates a consultative process in advance of the more formal arms' length procedure of notice and comment rulemaking." The court also rejected petitioners' request for factual discovery of the department to buttress their claim of bad faith: "A contrary conclusion would stretch out such judicial proceedings unconscionably. The Act's purpose — to reduce judicial challenges to regulations by encouraging the parties to narrow their differences in advance of the formal rulemaking proceeding — would be poorly served if the negotiations became a source and focus of litigation."[57]

C. The Scope of the Right to Decision on the Record

1. The Need for Facts to Be Found in the Record and the Official Notice Problem

One of the most basic rules of adversary jurisprudence is that the evidentiary facts on which a decision rests must be found in a record constituting the exclusive basis for

---

57. See also NRDC v. EPA, 859 F.2d 156 (D.C. Cir. 1988) (EPA commitment to propose negotiated consensus rule for public notice and comment did not preclude EPA from ultimately adopting a different rule even though no public comments adverse to the consensus rule were received).

decision. Without this rule, hearings could be rendered meaningless, and judicial review might be totally frustrated. Section 7(d) of the APA, 5 U.S.C. §556(e), makes "the transcript of testimony and exhibits, together with all papers and requests filed in the proceeding . . . the exclusive record for decision." This provision (which applies to formal, on-the-record adjudication and rulemaking) prevents agencies from relying on secret reports to decide cases or from questioning witnesses off the record.

Even in the court system, however, the requirement to spread all the relevant facts out on the record is not taken literally. Through the device of judicial notice, courts have always dispensed with the necessity of proving those facts that are obvious and notorious. Dean Wigmore contended that trial courts should assume all facts that are unlikely to be challenged, as well as those considered indisputable. This approach gives the trier of fact some flexibility in controlling the trial and avoids the time-consuming proof of every proposition.[58] Another school of thought, led by Professor Morgan, seems less concerned with judicial administration and would limit the scope of judicial notice to matters that are indisputable.[59] Still a third position is that of Judge Weinstein: "Much more formality is required in jury trials — particularly in criminal trials — than in bench trials. In the former, the Morgan approach should be applied with some precision. In the latter, the [Wigmore] view seems sound; . . .[60] Rule 201 of the Federal Rules of Evidence defines a judicially noticed fact as one "not subject to reasonable dispute in that it is either (1) generally known within the territorial jurisdiction of the trial court or (2) capable of accurate and ready determination by resort to sources whose accuracy cannot reasonably be questioned."

A more difficult problem is raised when appellate courts resort to the use of extra-record facts. Such courts have lawmaking and policy-setting functions, particularly in the public law context, and may arguably resort to judicial notice of "legislative" facts in order to carry out these functions. When essentially private disputes are appealed, it can be argued that the appellate courts have a stronger duty to resolve the dispute based on the record before them. But problems arise in a public law case when a litigant does not properly develop the record and prove some essential fact.[61]

In administrative decisionmaking, the administrative law judge and the agency heads (together with their staff) are familiar with technical issues and equipped to draw specialized inferences based on their experience. Should they have broader discretion to notice facts in the area of their expertise than a trial judge or appellate court? Professor Davis has long advocated broad latitude in the concept of official notice — the counterpart in administrative proceedings to the principle of judicial notice. He argues that agencies are more properly concerned with developing good public policies than doing justice between private parties, and that requiring all of the factual bases for technical or policy judgments by agencies to be spread on the record would unduly hobble the administrative process.[62]

---

58. 9 Wigmore, Evidence, §§2569-2583 (3d ed. 1940).

59. E. Morgan, Basic Problems of Evidence 9 (1962); see McNaughton, Judicial Notice — Excerpts Relating to the Morgan-Wimore Controversy, 14 Vand. L. Rev. 779 (1961).

60. I. J. Weinstein & M. Berger, Weinstein's Evidence 201-228 (1976).

61. Should the court remand for further hearings, thereby consuming precious judicial resources, or should it utilize a relatively loose concept of judicial notice to decide the case? In Daniel v. Paul, 395 U.S. 298 (1969), a civil rights case turning on the question of whether a segregated establishment served interstate travelers, the Supreme Court's finding of fact ("it would be unrealistic to assume that none of the 100,000 patrons actually served by the Club each season was an interstate traveler") was directly contrary to the findings of both lower courts. As Justice Black pointed out in dissent, "There is not a word of evidence that such an interstate traveler was ever there. . . ." 395 U.S. at 310.

62. K. Davis, Administrative Law Treatise, §15.01 (1958).

If the scope of official notice is to be broad, one must then inquire as to precisely what information may be noticed. What about previous decisions of the agency? What about the records in those cases and the facts proven therein? Must both parties have been involved in the previous case? One? What if neither party was involved? What about data concerning the financial condition of a regulated firm or industry, or the scientific or technical state of the art in a given discipline? If the agency notices any of this material, is it obligated to notify the parties and give them an adequate opportunity to respond? If we require agencies to follow strict adversary hearing standards, will they be tempted to rely on extra-record facts sub silentio and never notify anyone of such reliance?

The APA provides a partial answer to the problem of official notice in the "on record" proceedings governed by 5 U.S.C. §556(e), which provides that "[w]hen an agency decision rests on official notice of a material fact not appearing in the evidence in the record, a party is entitled, on timely request, to an opportunity to show the contrary." Section 706 is also critical to an understanding of the APA approach. "In making the foregoing determinations, the court shall review the whole record or those parts of it cited by a party, and due account shall be taken of the rule of prejudicial error." So long as parties must be notified of agency reliance on facts officially noticed, one could argue that there is no reason to limit the technique of official notice.

Does it follow that the APA permits an agency to officially notice its entire case, thereby shifting to the respondent the entire burden of coming forward with evidence? On the other hand, does APA §556(e) require an opportunity to rebut indisputable facts? If not, what is the hearing examiner to do when an argument arises as to whether a fact is indeed indisputable?[63]

Perhaps a tripartite classification along the following lines would prove workable in practice and sufficiently responsive to the due process concerns of the parties:

1. facts that an agency may officially notice and that are not subject to rebuttal
2. facts that an agency may officially notice and that are subject to rebuttal
3. facts that an agency must put into the record

The Supreme Court cases that follow were all decided before the APA was enacted, but they give a good sense of how judges have tried to reconcile adversary norms and the administrative process.

United States v. Abilene & Southern Ry.

265 U.S. 274 (1924)

[This decision set aside an ICC order that granted a new division of joint rates on traffic interchanged between the Kansas City, Mexico and Orient Railway Company

---

63. Professor Davis believes that the appropriate approach depends on whether the facts in question are legislative or adjudicative, not how subject to dispute they are. K. Davis, Administrative Law Treatise, §15.12 (1958). Cf. K. Davis, Administrative Law of the Seventies, §15 (1976). Most of the major federal agencies now have some provision concerning official notice in their rules of practice. The NLRB, for instance, merely copies the APA provision. 29 C.F.R. §101.10(b)(3) (1976). By way of contrast, the SEC declares that it may officially notice any material fact that might be noticed by a district court, any matter in the public records of the Commission, or any matter peculiarly within the knowledge of the SEC as an expert body. 17 C.F.R. §201.14(d) (1976).

(Orient), which was then in receivership, and 40 other railroads. The trial examiner, acting pursuant to ICC rules, made use of the annual reports of the 40 respondent railroads in order to determine the impact of various divisions on carrier revenues and profits. The Court, in an opinion by Justice Brandeis, held that the ICC had failed to develop sufficient evidence of record to justify the particular divisions ordered, and that its decision must therefore be set aside. It also considered procedural objections:]

... The plaintiffs contend that the order is void because it rests upon evidence not legally before the Commission. It is conceded that the finding rests in part, upon data taken from the annual reports filed with the Commission by the plaintiff carriers pursuant to law; that these reports were not formally put in evidence; that the parts containing the data relied upon were not put in evidence through excerpts; that attention was not otherwise specifically called to them; and that objection to the use of the reports, under these circumstances, was seasonably made by the carriers and was insisted upon. . . . The contention of the Commission is that, because its able examiner gave notice that "no doubt it will be necessary to refer to the annual reports of all these carriers," its Rules of Practice permitted matter in the reports to be used as freely as if the data had been formally introduced in evidence.

... A finding without evidence is beyond the power of the Commission. Papers in the Commission's files are not always evidence in a case. . . . Nothing can be treated as evidence which is not introduced as such. . . . Every proceeding is adversary, in substance, if it may result in an order in favor of one carrier as against another. Nor was the proceeding under review any the less an adversary one, because the primary purpose of the Commision was to protect the public interest through making possible the continued operation of the Orient system.

It is sought to justify the procedure followed by the clause in Rule XIII which declares that the "Commission will take notice of items in tariffs and annual or other periodical reports of carriers properly on file." But this clause does not purport to relieve the Commission from introducing, by specific reference, such parts of the reports as it wishes to treat as evidence. It means that as to these items there is no occasion for the parties to serve copies. The objection to the use of the data contained in the annual reports is not lack of authenticity or untrustworthiness. It is that the carriers were left without notice of the evidence with which they were, in fact, confronted, as later disclosed by the finding made. The requirement that in an adversary proceeding specific reference be made is essential to the preservation of the substantial rights of the parties.

Questions

1. Should litigants be permitted to challenge the factual accuracy of official reports submitted by them? Some courts have not permitted such challenge.[64] How likely is a litigant to succeed in attacking the accuracy of its own data? For what purposes other than challenging the accuracy of the underlying data might a litigant wish to be notified of the particular reports and records relied on by an agency?

2. How literally should we take Justice Brandeis's statement: "Nothing can be treated as evidence which is not introduced as such"? The Commission might not be in a position to decide which of its official records were relevant until it is engaged in the process of decision, long after the hearing of evidence and submission of briefs. In such a case,

64. See Wisconsin v. FPC, 201 F.2d 183 (D.C. Cir. 1952), *cert. denied*, 345 U.S. 934 (1953); Riss & Co. v. United States, 717 F. Supp. 296 (W.D. Mo.), *aff'd per curiam*, 346 U.S. 890 (1953).

why isn't it sufficient that the Commission specify in its decision the record relied upon, and provide the parties with the opportunity to petition for rehearing if they wish to challenge its use of such records?

Ohio Bell Tel. Co. v. Public Utilities Commn.
301 U.S. 292 (1937)

[Employing traditional principles of utility ratesetting, the Commission held extensive hearings and accepted volumes of evidence bearing on the value of the Company's investment. After eight years, the Commission had enough evidence to enable it to fix the value of the Company's property as of the year 1925. It then adjusted the property value for each of the years 1926 to 1933 by taking official notice of price trends, and set rates for these years at levels requiring substantial refunds by the Company to its customers.

The price trends, which were not placed in the record and which the Company had no opportunity to rebut, were gleaned from examinations of (1) the tax values in communities where the Company had its largest real estate holdings, (2) price indexes in a construction industry magazine, and (3) the findings of an Illinois federal court in a case involving Western Electric, an affiliated corporation. There was no way for Ohio Bell to identify items (1) or (2) or learn their precise content. Mr. Justice Cardozo wrote for the Court:]

. . . The fundamentals of a trial were denied to the appellant when rates previously collected were ordered to be refunded upon the strength of evidential facts not spread upon the record.

. . . Without warning or even the hint of warning that the case would be considered or determined upon any other basis than the evidence submitted, the Commission cut down the values for the years after the date certain upon the strength of information secretly collected and never yet disclosed. . . . This is not the fair hearing essential to due process. It is condemnation without trial.

. . . From the standpoint of due process — the protection of the individual against arbitrary action — a deeper vice is this, that even now we do not know the particular or evidential facts of which the Commission took judicial notice and on which it rested its conclusion. Not only are the facts unknown; there is no way to find them out.

. . . The Commission contents itself with saying that in gathering them it went to journals and tax lists, as if a judge were to tell us, "I looked at the statistics in the Library of Congress, and they teach me thus and so." This will never do if hearings and appeals are to be more than empty forms. . . .

. . . To put the problem more concretely: how was it possible for the appellate court to review the law and the facts and intelligently decide that the findings of the Commission were supported by the evidence when the evidence that is approved was unknown and unknowable? . . .

Market Street Ry. v. Railroad Commn.
324 U.S. 548 (1945)

[The Market Street Railway Company operated a public transportation system in San Francisco. On its own motion, the Railroad Commission began an inquiry into the

Company's rates and reduced its fare from seven to six cents, finding that lowering fares would stimulate demand sufficiently to provide adequate revenues to cover its expenses and a return on capital. Justice Jackson, for a unanimous Court, rejected the Company's contention that it had been denied procedural due process:]

. . . It also is urged that the order is invalid under the due process clause because it is based on matters outside the record. The decision of the Commission stated that "In the eight months' period, January to August, inclusive, of 1943 the operating revenues of the company amounted to $5,689,775," and compared this with the operating revenues for the same period of 1942 and found an increase of 20 percent. On this basis it estimated the total for the full year of 1943 under the prevailing seven-cent fare. Challenged upon the ground that the operating revenues from January to August of 1943 were not in the record, the Commission admitted that these figures were taken from the appellant's monthly reports filed with the Commission. . . . No contention is made here that the information was erroneous or was misunderstood by the Commission, and no contention is made that the Company could have disproved it or explained away its effect for the purpose for which the Commission used it. The most that can be said is that the Commission in making its predictive findings went outside of the record to verify its judgement by reference to actual traffic figures that became available only after the hearings closed. It does not appear that the Company was in any way prejudice[d] thereby, and it makes no showing that, if a rehearing were held to introduce its own reports, it would gain much by cross-examination, rebuttal, or impeachment of its own auditors or the reports they had filed. Due process, of course, requires that Commission proceed upon matters in evidence and that parties have opportunity to subject evidence to the test of cross-examination and rebuttal. But due process deals with matters of substance and is not to be trivialized by formal objections that have no substantial bearing on the ultimate rights of parties. . . .

Boston Edison Co. v. FERC
885 F.2d 962, 966-967 (1st Cir. 1989)

The Commission made a second adjustment applicable to the rate of return for the period after March 25, 1988. The Commission believed that because interest rates had fallen and stock prices had risen between 1985 and 1988, the rate of return based upon dividend yields (and other factors) in 1984-85 overstated the cost of equity capital. It therefore adjusted the rate of return downwards as follows: (a) It took the interest rate paid by Government 10-year bonds during the six-month period ending in April 1985 (the period the staff had used to calculate the rate of return); it noted that the rate was 11.54 percent. (b) It took the return that the same bonds yielded in the most recent six-month period (September 1987 to March 1988); that rate was 8.95 percent. (c) It subtracted the second figure from the first, which resulted in a difference of 2.59 points. (d) It subtracted the 2.59 points from the rate of return it had calculated based upon its adjusted 1985 figures (13.73 percent), leaving 11.14 percent. (If one assumes that the returns utility investors would insist upon declined just as did treasury bond returns, then the cost of utility equity capital would also have declined by 2.59 points.) (e) It pointed out that the resulting figure (11.14 percent) was lower tha[n] the lower bound of the "zone of reasonableness." So, it picked the lower bound of that zone, 13.08 percent (the result of the staff's "discounted cash flow" calculation, as adjusted by using six months of 1984-85 data instead of a year's worth of data). And, it held that it would consider that 13.08 percent figure as the cost of equity capital for rate setting purposes after March 25, 1985.

Boston Edison first argues that the Commission's decision to use the treasury bond data violates the Administrative Procedure Act's requirement that

> [W]hen an agency decision rests on official notice of a material fact not appearing in the evidence in the record, a party is entitled, on timely request, to an opportunity to show the contrary.

5 U.S.C. §556(e). Boston Edison does not dispute the accuracy of the "material fact" in question, however, namely the relevant treasury bond interest rates. Moreover, the Commission gave Boston Edison an adequate opportunity to argue against the adjustment or any other factual matter in its petition for rehearing. . . .

Boston Edison next argues that it is unreasonable for the Commission to adjust the rate of return for changes in interest rates: it says utility investors do not react in precisely the same way as treasury bond holders; thus a fall in treasury rates does not automatically mean that required utility equity returns have fallen similarly. (And, Boston Edison included in its brief to the Commission, as it has included here, some cost data suggesting differences.) The Commission, however, "frequently adjusts the return [on equity] . . . when warranted by changing circumstances in the financial markets after the close of the record since such information is not typically subject to dispute." . . . And we can find nothing unreasonable about making such an adjustment. The short answer to Boston Edison's claim that utility investors do not react precisely the same way as investors in treasury bonds, is that the drop in interest rates here was substantial (nearly 23 percent) but the Commission adjusted its rate of return downward by only 0.65 points (less than 5 percent), certainly not an unreasonably large downward adjustment. Boston Edison has not explained how the material it submitted to the Commission showed that some significant downward adjustment to reflect lower interest rates was inappropriate. And, even if we assume, for the sake of argument, that changes in reasonable utility share returns do not exactly track changes in bond interest rates, the Supreme Court has made clear that "infirmities" in Commission methodology are "not . . . important," provided that the "result reached," the "impact of the rate order," cannot "be said to be unjust and unreasonable." Federal Power Commission v. Hope Natural Gas Company, 320 U.S. at 602, . . . In our view, some downward adjustment in light of the significant change in interest rates was perfectly reasonable.

Union Elec. Co. v. FERC
890 F.2d 1193, 1201-1204 (D.C. Cir. 1990)

Here the Commission addressed a problem created by the two-year lag between the AJL's development of a record, which ended August 15, 1985, see *Initial Decision*, 35 FERC at 65,237, and the issuance of the Commission's own decision on July 20, 1987. During this period, the yield on 10-year Treasury bonds fell 4.09 percent from 11.42 percent (averaged from December 1984 to May 1985) to 7.33 percent (averaged from November 1986 to April 1987). On this basis, the Commission reduced the AJL's figure for the equity rate of return by the same amount. Later, in response to Union's arguments in its petition for rehearing that the Commission could and should have taken into account two later months, making the updated Treasury rate 7.77 percent (rather than 7.33 percent), the Commission reduced the adjustment from 4.09 percent to 3.65 percent. Order on Rehearing, 42 FERC at 61,923-27. Thus, it ultimately approved a rate of 12.15 percent, rather than the 15.08 percent rate recommended by the staff and found reasonable by the ALJ. . . .

Union argues that the Commission's refusal here to let it challenge the use of the Treasury bond data violated its rights under the Administrative Procedure Act, specifically 5 U.S.C. §556(e) (1988), and under the due process clause of the Fourteenth Amendment. We agree that the Commission's extension of its earlier approach violated the APA. We do not reach the constitutional claim.

Section 556(e) provides:

> When an agency decision rests on official notice of a material fact not appearing in the evidence in the record, a party is entitled, on the request, to all opportunity to show the contrary.

The section must be interpreted in light of pre-APA challenges to official notice, most notably Ohio Bell Telephone Co. v. Public Utilities Commission of Ohio. . . .

We read *Ohio Bell* as establishing two prerequisites for use of official evidence. First, the information noticed must be appropriate for official notice. Second, the agency must follow proper procedures in using the information, disclosing it to the parties and affording them a suitable opportunity to contradict it or "parry its effect."

We have no difficulty with FERC's taking notice of a change in the rate on 10-year Treasury bonds. It is true that *judicial* notice is generally limited to "matters of common knowledge." Id. at 301 . . . but official notice is broader, allowing an agency in addition to notice "technical or scientific facts that are within the agency's area of expertise." McLeod v. INS, 802 F.2d 89, 93 n.4 (3d Cir. 1986). The logic behind this expanded scope of official notice is that since "administrative agencies necessarily acquire special knowledges in their sphere of activity," certain highly technical facts "may become to the administrators, as obvious and notorious 'facts' as facts susceptible of judicial notice are to judges." Administrative Procedure in Government Agencies: Report of the Committee on Administrative Procedure, Appointed by the Attorney General 71 (1946) ("*Attorney General's Report*"). As the FERC decisions mentioned above reflect, the Commission has long taken notice of the interest rates on Treasury bonds for ratemaking purposes. . . . FERC's taking official notice of such interest rates is not troubling because "such information is not typically subject to dispute." . . .

The Commission's procedures in using the Treasury interest rates for inferences on the cost of equity, however, did not adequately protect Union's right to "parry [their] effect," i.e., to challenge the Commission's inference. In *Ohio Bell*, the Court had no difficulty with the Ohio commission's taking notice of the Great Depression, but invalidated its use of that fact (plus undisclosed additional material) for inferences about the value of Ohio Bell's assets. Because of variations from industry to industry, the Commission could not draw such inferences automatically. Ohio Bell was entitled to an opportunity to raise objections and attempt to "parry [the] effect" of the data relied on. Here we have precisely the same problem: the Commission apparently assumed a linear relationship between the trend for 10-year Treasury bond rates and that for Union's cost of equity capital. Union raised substantial objection to the official notice and was therefore entitled to an opportunity to dispute the Commission's findings. See Market Street Railway Co. v. Railroad Commission of California, 324 U.S. 548, 562. . . .

Section 556(e)'s assurance that parties must have "an opportunity to show the contrary" encompasses a chance not only to dispute the facts noticed but also to "parry [their] effect," i.e., to offer evidence or analysis contesting the Commission's inferences. The Attorney General's Report on the APA confirms this reading, saying that the section entitles parties "not only to refute but, what in this situation is usually more important, to supplement, explain and give different perspectives to the facts upon which the agency relies." *Attorney General's Report* at 72. . . .

Here, as we have seen, Union was allowed a partial opportunity "to show the contrary." Union contended that two later months should be used in calculating the yield on Treasury bonds, with a resulting reduction in the adjustment from 4.09 percent to 3.65 percent. The Commission agreed and adopted Union's data. By hearing Union's complaint and responding to it reasonably, the Commission satisfied §556(e) on this point.

The Commission did not, however, seriously address Union's broader attack on its use of the Treasury bond rates. In its request for rehearing Union submitted an affidavit asserting that there was "no generally accepted financial theory which supports the Commission's assumption that a Company's cost of common equity capital varies linearly with the yield on ten-year U.S. Treasury bonds."

Union did not rely merely on the general truism of company-to-company variation. It offered an analysis suggesting that in the same period there had been a marked increase in its stock's "beta," a commonly used measure of volatility (and therefore risk). Given Union's showing that the variation among companies was of potential importance in this case, its right to an opportunity to "parry [the] effect" of the noticed treasury rates encompassed a right to have its proof either accepted or appropriately refuted. Instead of responding to Union on the merits, the Commission dismissed its claim out of hand saying that "Union should have been aware based upon past precedent that the Commission might consider updating the return on common equity under the circumstances present in order to determine just and reasonable rates to be charged on a prospective basis." *Order on Rehearing*, 41 FERC at 61,926. [This response was inadequate.] . . .

The effect of our decision is quite limited. It does not draw in question the Commission's past practice of making posthearing adjustments within a range of reasonableness previously determined on the record. The First Circuit has recently approved such an adjustment, *Boston Edison Co.*, 885 F.2d at 966-69 (reduction in allowed rates only one-fifth the fall in Treasury bond rates), and we do not disagree. If there should be any sign of the Commission's artificially stretching the range of reasonableness for these purposes, however, courts would obviously respond with careful monitoring.

Note on Official Notice in Immigration Asylum Cases

The issue of official notice has arisen frequently in the context of immigration hearings on political asylum claims involving changes in politicial regimes in Nicaragua. In de la Llana-Castellon v. INS, 16 F.3d 1093 (10th Cir. 1994), Castellon sought asylum in the United States based on a claim that if he were forced back to Nicaragua, he would be persecuted by the Sandinistas. The Board of Immigration Appeals (BIA), overturning an immigration judge ruling in his favor, took notice that (1) the Sandinistas lost the 1990 election in Nicaragua, (2) the Sandinistas no longer controlled Nicaragua, and (3) Castellon accordingly no longer had a well founded fear of persecution by the Sandinistas. The BIA gave no notice of these determinations to Castellon or an opportunity to rebut them. The Tenth Circuit rejected the second and third findings; it stated that neither was indisputable, reasoning that the Sandinistas might still retain considerable power. It concluded that the matters were outside the scope of proper official notice, and that accordingly the INS had denied Castellon due process. *Castilla-Villarga v. INS*, 972 F.2d 1017 (9th Cir. 1992), reached the same result on similar facts in another Nicaraguan asylum case. Contrast *Gonzalez v. INS*, 77 F.3d 1015 (7th Cir. 1996), where the court upheld BIA's denial of asylum. In that case, the immigration judge had taken official notice of the changed political condition in Nicaragua but had provided the asylum claimant an opportunity to submit rebuttal evidence.

One commentator has argued that the *de la Llana-Castellon* decision was improper in requiring courts to receive evidence on the subject of who is in control of a nation. Such a requirement may lead to "massive delay and interdecisional inconsistency." A better solution would allow the agency to rule on such a situation once and rely on that resolution unless the applicant tenders significant rebuttal evidence. R. Pierce, Administrative Law Treatise, §10.6 (3d ed., 2000 Cumulative Supplement).[65] Suppose the BIA had held that, as a matter of law, asylum based on claims of political persecution would be granted only where the asserted persecutors hold government office?

Questions

1. Can *Market Street Ry.* be reconciled with *Ohio Bell* and *Abilene & Southern*? If not, which is the correct approach?

2. Why did the circuit courts reach different, and opposite, results in *Boston Edison* and *Union Electric*? Does the difference between the cases consist of lack of opportunity for presentation of argument and evidence or failure of the agency adequately to explain its conclusions?

3. Judge Posner has pointed to considerable authority "that the non-judicial decision maker — the agency or its hearing officer . . . 'should state the reasons for his determination and indicate the evidence he relied on.' This is a backup safeguard, designed to make sure . . . that the hearing . . . is a meaningful one, as it would not be if the decision-maker based his decision on material outside the record . . . other than such extra-record materials as the agency could properly take official notice of." *Hameetman v. City of Chicago*, 776 F.2d 636 (7th Cir. 1985). A judge might sometimes write in an opinion, in respect to rather trivial arguments, something like, "We find the remaining arguments without merit." Can an agency do the same? Why not?

4. To what extent can the decisions summarized above be explained by the Supreme Court's statement in a recent decision that "[i]t is well established that as long as a party has an opportunity to respond, an administrative agency may take official notice of such legislative facts within its special knowledge and is not confined to the evidence in their record in reaching its expert judgment." *City of Erie, et al. v. Pap's A.M.*, 529 U.S. 277, 298 (2000).

5. Professor Davis believes that the appropriate approach depends on whether the facts in question are legislative or adjudicative, not how subject to dispute they are. K. Davis, Administrative Law Treatise §15.12 (1958). Cf. K. Davis, Administrative Law of the Seventies §15 (1976). To what extent can the decided cases be explained by this

---

65. For additional commentary, see Standgurg, Official Notice of Changed Country Conditions in Asylum Adjudication: Lessons From International Refugee Law, 11 Georgetown Immigration L.J. 45 (1996); Roonery, Note, Administrative Notice, Due Process, and the Adjudication of Asylum Claims in the United States, 17 Fordham Intl. L.J. 955 (1994).

distinction? Is it an appropriate and workable approach to resolving questions of official notice? Were the facts at issue in the asylum cases "legislative" or "adjudicative"?

6. Colgate Co. advertises that its shaving cream is so good that it shaves sandpaper. Colgate produces a television advertisement in which an actor shaves some sandpaper. The ad uses a "mock-up," however, in which the sand is "special" and has been previously detached from the paper. The Federal Trade Commission brings a charge of false advertising against Colgate. Colgate argues that its shaving cream really will shave sandpaper. It says it loosened the grain on the paper, and used "special" paper because, for technical reasons, real sandpaper looks odd on television; only special sandpaper, with loosened grains, looks like real sandpaper.

The FTC holds against Colgate. It writes, "We accept as true Colgate's claim about its shaving cream and about the technical limitations of television. Nonetheless, a viewer, after watching the ad, would believe that he has seen sandpaper shaved with his own eyes. That proposition is false, for he saw only a mock-up. We also believe that this false proposition is material, for it may well lead such viewers to buy Colgate's shaving cream."

Can the Commission reason in this way — can it adopt the last mentioned proposition about consumer buying behavior — without introducing evidence on the point? Argue both sides of this equation. Consider: (a) In a proceeding for renewal of a television license, can an FCC hearing examiner take into account the fact that he himself has seen the programs broadcast and they are terrible? (b) The NLRB has a basic rule that an employer can prohibit union solicitation on his premises only if the harm the solicitation would cause the employer outweighs the harm that a ban would cause the union. Can the Board based on its "general experience," adopt a presumption that such a ban always causes the union some harm? How does it know?

2. The Problem of Off-the-Record Communications

We deal here with communications outside the record between agency decisionmakers and persons outside the agency. The problem of off-the-record communications between agency decisionmakers and other personnel within the same agency is dealt with in Chapter 7.

a. "On-the-Record" Proceedings

It has traditionally been understood that in adjudicatory or rulemaking proceedings required to be conducted "on the record" through trial-type hearing procedures like those specified in the APA §§554, 556-557, it would be improper for interested parties to communicate evidence or argument off-the-record to agency decisionmakers during the course of the proceedings. (Why?) Because formulation and implementation of regulatory policy require agencies to work closely with the affected industries and interest groups, however, it is also recognized that it would be unwise to forbid all meetings between agency decisionmakers and interested private parties. The competing objectives involved — fostering public confidence in agency decisionmaking, providing decision-makers access to relevant information, encouraging flexibility and cooperation between regulatory bodies and affected parties — are important in understanding the development and evolution of procedural limitations on ex parte communications.

There are difficulties in transferring ex parte communications principles developed in judicial proceedings to the context of a bureaucratic agency where formal proceedings are simply one element in a continuous, often informal, process of policy choice and implementation. An example is the practice by the Civil Aeronautics Board in the early 1970s, when it adopted a policy of refusing to allow airlines to fly new routes — the "route moratorium." This policy was implemented through delay or denial of individual carrier applications for new routes that were required by statute to be resolved through "on-the-record" proceedings. But the "route moratorium," which protected existing carriers, was never explicitly adopted through any formal procedures and was conceived and implemented against a background of continuous informal contact and discussion between Board members and carrier representatives. The Senate Subcommittee on Administrative Practice and Procedure found, for example, that 769 such meetings occurred in 1974. The Subcommittee's report[66] stated:

> Large numbers of private meetings — while not necessarily improper on an individual basis — raise a problem of public confidence in the agency. Whether or not a Commission member can maintain perfect objectivity (and constant exposure to the industry viewpoint makes objectivity more difficult), the public is uncertain whether, in fact, decisions of major importance have been made on the merits for reasons set out in the public record. This concern is multiplied when private meetings with major members of the industry are followed by speeches that espouse that point of view into formal Board policy, all without benefit of hearing or court review as occurred in the case of the route moratorium.
>
> The problem is difficult, however, for it seems unwise to forbid all meetings between members of the industry and the Board. To do so risks enclosing Board members in an "ivory tower" from which the isolated Board members may find it more difficult to obtain important, relevant information. It is also probably desirable for Board members to meet major industry figures personally, in order to have some idea what the people who run the airlines are like.

Member West articulated this tension very well:

> I am aware that the appearance of a fair hearing and a fair opportunity and fair treatment is oftentimes as important as the fact that you oftentimes receive fair treatment, and I am not at all arguing that there is not a basis for concern about kind of a persuasive influence.
>
> "But I am a bit disturbed that there may be some rules that almost require you to live in a vacuum to prevent you from — now, I have been accused of not being an expert in the field and I plead guilty, but I am not sure how, if we are restricted to almost a vacuum-like atmosphere, that we would be able to even determine what the questions are, let alone the solutions, and there is a problem in my own mind about how to conduct myself.
>
> In some respects, we are held to the same rigid standards that a court is held, with regard to making decisions, and yet, we are determining policy in which all sorts of inputs should be received before you can make very much of a quality decision, and where I can obtain that is a bit of a problem without some contact with the industry.

66. Report of the Subcommittee on Admin. Prac. & Proc. of the Civil Aeronautics Board, 94th Cong., 1st Sess. (1975), at 91-93.

The legal treatment of this problem developed over several decades. Prompted by congressional studies of industry "influence peddling" in regulatory agencies (including, in particular, efforts to influence FCC license awards),[67] the U.S. Administrative Conference recommended in 1962 that ex parte communications be banned in proceedings required to be held on the record.[68] Most of the major federal agencies adopted these recommendations in whole or in large part. In an effort to return public confidence in government after Watergate, Congress in 1976 enacted the Government in the Sunshine Act, the relevant provisions of which are contained in the APA in §§551(14) and 557(d), and in the fourth sentence of §556(d), which you should now carefully review. Note in particular that these provisions are limited to formal "on-the-record" proceedings governed by §§556-557.

Professional Air Traffic Controllers Org. v. Federal Labor Relations Auth.

685 F.2d 547 (D.C. Cir. 1982)

EDWARDS, J.

[The Professional Air Traffic Controllers Organization (PATCO), the certified exclusive bargaining representative for air traffic controllers employed by the Federal Aviation Administration (FAA), called a strike in 1981. The FAA promptly applied to the Federal Labor Relations Authority (FLRA) to have PATCO's certification revoked under §7120(f) of the Civil Service Reform Act.[69]

The FLRA granted revocation and PATCO immediately sought judicial review. Just prior to oral argument before the D.C. Circuit, however, the Department of Justice raised allegations that FLRA's consideration of the case was marred by ex parte communications. The court invoked a special procedure for the FLRA to hold, with the aid of a specially appointed ALJ, an evidentiary hearing to determine the nature, extent, and effect of the alleged improprieties. The evidentiary hearing uncovered numerous communications with FLRA members that were at least arguably related to the FLRA's consideration of the PATCO case. However, the ALJ concluded that there was no evidence indicating that the final decision had been actually affected by these communications. While the D.C. Circuit court found the majority of the contacts with FLRA members to be unobjectionable, the court considered two occurrences to be "somewhat more troubling": one involving telephone calls placed by Department of Transportation Secretary Andrew L. Lewis, Jr. to FLRA members, and the other a dinner conversation between an FLRA member and Albert Shanker, president of the American Federation of Teachers.]

---

67. See investigation of Regulatory Commissions and Agencies, Hearings Before a Subcommittee of the House Commerce Committee, 85th Cong., 2d Sess. (1958). Concern by lawyers and administrators with the ex parte communication problem is reflected in, e.g., Peck, Regulation and Control of Ex Parte Communications with Administrative Agencies, 76 Harv. L. Rev. 233 (1962).

68. Recommendation No. 16, S. Doc. No. 24, 88th Cong., 1st Sess. 6 (1963).

69. Federal law prohibits a person who "participates in a strike . . . against the government of the United States" from accepting or holding a position in the federal government, 5 U.S.C. §7311(2) (1976). Section 7120(f) of Title VII of the Civil Service Reform Act (1978) provides that the FLRA shall "revoke the exclusive recognition status of a registered union," or "take any other appropriate disciplinary action" against any labor organization, where it is found that the union has called, participated in, or condoned a strike, work stoppage or slow-down against a federal agency in a labor-management dispute.

Three features of the prohibition on ex parte communications in agency adjudications are particularly relevant to the contacts here at issue. First, by its terms, section 557(d) applies only to ex parte communication to or from "interested persons." Congress did not intend, however, that the prohibition on ex parte communications would therefore have only a limited application. A House Report explained:

> The term "interested person" is intended to be a wide, inclusive term covering any individual or other person with an interest in the agency proceeding that is greater than the general interest the public as a whole may have. The interest need not be monetary, nor need a person . . . be a party to, or intervenor in, the agency proceeding to come under this section. The term includes, but is not limited to, parties, competitors, public officials, and nonprofit or public interest organizations and associates with a special interest in the matter regulated. The term does not include a member of the public at large who makes a casual or general expression of opinion about a pending proceeding.

Second, the Government in the Sunshine Act defines an "ex parte communication" as "an oral or written communication not on the public record to which reasonable prior notice to all parties is not given, but . . . not includ[ing] requests for status reports on any matter or proceeding." . . . 5 U.S.C. §551(4) (1976). Requests for status reports are thus allowed under the statute. Nevertheless, the legislative history of the Act cautions:

> A request for a status report or a background discussion may in effect amount to an indirect or subtle effort to influence substantive outcome of the proceedings. The judgment will have to be made whether a particular communication could affect the agency's decision on the merits. In doubtful cases the agency officials should treat the communication as ex parte so as to protect the integrity of the decision making process.

S. Rep. No. 354, 94th Cong. 1st Sess., 1975.

Third, and in direct contrast to status reports, §557(d) explicitly prohibits communications "relevant to the merits of the proceeding." Congressional reports state that the phrase should "be construed broadly and . . . include more than the phrase 'fact in issue' currently used in (§554(d)(1)) of the Administrative Procedure Act." S. Rep. No. 354 supra, at 36. The disclosure of ex parte communications serves two distinct interests. Disclosure is important in its own right to prevent the appearance of impropriety from secret communications in a proceeding that is required to be decided on the record. Disclosure is also important as an instrument of fair decisionmaking; only if a party knows the arguments presented to a decision-maker can the party respond effectively and ensure that its position is fairly considered. If, however, the communication is truly not relevant to the merits of an adjudication and, therefore, does not threaten the interests of openness and effective response, disclosure is unnecessary.

Under the case law in this Circuit, improper ex parte communications, even when undisclosed during agency proceedings, do not necessarily void an agency decision. Rather, agency proceedings that have been blemished by ex parte communications have been held to be voidable.

In enforcing this standard, a court must consider whether, as a result of improper ex parte communications, the agency's decisionmaking process was irrevocably tainted so as to make the ultimate judgment of the agency unfair, either to an innocent party or to the public interest that the agency was obliged to protect. In making this determination, a number of considerations may be relevant: the gravity of the ex parte communications; whether the contacts may have influenced the agency's ultimate decision; whether the party making the improper contacts benefited from the agency's ultimate decision; whether the contents of the communications were unknown to opposing parties, who therefore had no opportunity to respond; and whether vacation of the agency's decision and remand for new proceedings would serve a useful purpose.

[Department of Transportation Secretary Andrew L. Lewis, Jr. telephoned FLRA member Frazier on August 13, 1981, to inform him that, contrary to some news reports, no meaningful efforts to settle the strike were under way. Secretary Lewis stated that the purpose of the call was not to discuss the substance of the PATCO proceeding but to urge the FLRA to expedite handling of the case. Secretary Lewis later placed a similar call to member Applewhaite.]

Transportation Secretary Lewis was undoubtedly an "interested person" within the meaning of §557(d) and the FLRA Rules when he called Members Frazier and Applewhaite on August 13. Secretary Lewis' call clearly would have been an improper ex parte communication if he had sought to discuss the merits of the PATCO case. The Secretary explicitly avoided the merits, however, and mentioned only his view on the possibility of settlement and his desire for a speedy decision. Although Secretary Lewis did not in fact discuss the merits of the case, even a procedural inquiry may be a subtle effort to influence an agency decision.

We need not decide, however, whether Secretary Lewis' contacts were in fact improper. Even if they were, the contacts did not taint the proceedings or prejudice PATCO. Secretary Lewis' central concern in his conversations with Member Frazier and Member Applewhaite was that the case be handled expeditiously.

[The court then considered the meeting between Shanker and member Applewhaite. The two men, who had maintained professional and social ties for many years, spent most of the hour-and-a-half dinner discussing events unrelated to the PATCO proceedings. Toward the end of the dinner, however, they discussed various approaches to public employee strikes at the state and federal level. Mr. Shanker expressed his view that punishment of a striking union should fit the crime and that revocation of certification as a punishment for an illegal strike was tantamount to "killing a union." There were no threats made, and Member Applewhaite did not reveal his position regarding the PATCO case.]

We believe that Mr. Shanker falls within the intended scope of the term "interested person." Mr. Shanker was (and is) the President of a major or public-sector labor union. As such, he has a special and well-known interest in the union movement and the developing law of labor relations in the public sector. The PATCO strike, of course, was the subject of extensive media coverage and public comment. Some union leaders undoubtedly felt that the hard line taken against PATCO by the Administration might have an adverse effect on other unions, both in the Federal and in state and local government sectors. Mr. Shanker apparently shared this concern. From August 3, 1981, to September 21, 1981, Mr. Shanker and his union made a series of widely publicized statements in support of PATCO. Mr. Shanker urged repeatedly in public statements that disproportionately severe punishment not be inflicted on PATCO. Thus, Mr. Shanker's actions, as well as his union office, belie his implicit claim that he had no greater interest in the case than a member of the general public.

Even if we were to adopt Mr. Shanker's position that he was not an interested person, we are astonished at his claim that he did nothing wrong. Mr. Shanker frankly concedes that he "desired to have dinner with Member Applewhaite because he felt strongly about the PATCO case and he wished to communicate directly to Member Applewhaite sentiments he had previously expressed in public."

In case any doubt still lingers, we take the opportunity to make one thing clear: It is simply unacceptable behavior for any person directly to attempt to influence the decision of a judicial officer in a pending case outside of the formal, public proceedings. This is true for the general public, for "interested persons," and for the formal parties to the case.

We do not hold, however, that Member Applewhaite committed an impropriety when he accepted Mr. Shanker's dinner invitation. Member Applewhaite and Mr. Shanker were professional and social friends. We recognize, of course, that a judge "must have neighbors, friends and acquaintances, business and social relations, and be a part of his day and generation."

The majority of the dinner conversation was unrelated to the PATCO case. [A]s the conversation turned to the discipline appropriate for a striking union like PATCO, Member Applewhaite should have promptly terminated the discussion. Had Mr. Shanker persisted in discussing his views of the PATCO case, Member Applewhaite should have informed him in no uncertain terms that such behavior was inappropriate. Unfortunately, he did not do so.

This indiscretion, this failure to steer the conversation away from the PATCO case, eventually led to the special evidentiary hearing in this case. . . . We now know that Mr. Shanker did not in any way threaten Member Applewhaite during the dinner. Mr. Shanker did not tell Member Applewhaite that if he voted to decertify PATCO he would be unable to get cases as an arbitrator if and when he left the FLRA. Mr. Shanker did not say that he was speaking "for top AFL-CIO officials" or that Member Applewhaite would need labor support to secure reappointment. Moreover, Mr. Shanker did not make any promises of any kind to Member Applewhaite, and Member Applewhaite did not reveal how he intended to vote in the PATCO case.

In these circumstances, we do not believe that it is necessary to vacate the FLRA decision and remand the case. First, no threats or promises were made. . . .

Second, A.L.J. Vittone found that the Applewhaite/Shanker dinner had no effect on the ultimate decision of Member Applewhaite or of the FLRA as a whole in the PATCO case. . . .

Third, no party benefited from the improper contact. The ultimate decision was adverse to PATCO, the party whose interests were most closely aligned with Mr. Shanker's position. . . .

Finally, we cannot say that the parties were unfairly deprived of an opportunity to refute the arguments propounded in the ex parte communication. PATCO has not identified any manner in which it was denied a reasonable opportunity to respond or any new arguments, which it would present to the FLRA if given an opportunity.

[The court upheld FLRA's action on the merits.]

Notes and Questions

1. Does the court's interpretation of "interested party" under §557(d)(l) prohibit all communications arguably relevant to the merits of a proceeding by any person, whether or not a party? While it is clear that the term "interested party" is not limited to parties to the proceeding; does the court's interpretation ignore the requirement that the communicator be "interested"?

2. Why should requests for status reports (widely used by members of Congress to show their interest in a proceeding involving a constituent or supporter) not be included in the record?

3. Does the court's "harmless error" standard deprive the Act of adequate deterrent effect? Consider that a high proportion of whatever ex parte communications occur probably

go undetected. Compare with PATCO the decision in Press Broadcasting Co. v. FCC, 59 F.3d 1365 (D.C. Cir. 1995). One of the parties to a contested licensing proceeding before the FCC's Mass Media Bureau engaged in ex parte contacts with Bureau officials, in violation of FCC regulations, and thereby succeeded in obtaining the license. Upon discovery of the contacts, the Bureau immediately recused itself from further participation and referred the case to the full FCC. The full FCC engaged in de novo review of the case and decided in favor of the party who had engaged in the ex parte contact. The court decided that the contacts with the Bureau did not irreparably taint the decisionmaking process by the full FCC because there was not a "nexus" between the improper communications and the ultimate decision. The court, however, set aside the Commission's failure adequately to justify its refusal to sanction the winning party for its violation of the rules, rejecting as plainly erroneous the Commission's conclusion that the violations had been unintentional. The court found that the party had been told many times that the licensing dispute was subject to ex parte rules. It accordingly remanded the issue of sanctions to the Commission for further consideration. What sanctions might or should the Commission impose?

4. What if the ex parte communications had occurred prior to the initiation of formal proceedings against PATCO? Agency members must presumably be free to discuss informally with outsiders general issues of administrative policy that are not yet the subject of any proposed proceedings. Yet if the prohibition against ex parte communications did not become operative until after formal proceedings were commenced, there is a danger that the agency's ultimate position would already have been significantly influenced by off-record communications. How does the Sunshine Act resolve this timing problem?

5. It is important to remember that not all private communications that may have some relevance to a pending adjudication are necessarily improper. At issue in Louisiana Assn. of Indep. Producers v. FERC was a high-stakes adjudication in which FERC authorized construction of a $1 billion gas pipeline from Canada to the United States. 958 F.2d 1101 (D.C. Cir. 1992). Opponents of the project sought to invalidate the certification on the basis that the applicant had met several times in private with the Commissioners prior to the decision to allow construction. The record before the court indicated that the meetings focused upon general problems within the energy industry, the impact that certain other cases pending before the Commission might have on the project, and procedural aspects of the contested application. The court upheld the Commission, stating that:

> [B]ecause the record reveals at best subtle and indirect attempts to influence Commission officials, no disinterested observer would infer that those officials had in any measure prejudged the applications. It is expected through experience with recurring issues. Such expertise should not be lightly tossed aside. In short, while there were meetings between agency officials and Iroquois and other industry officials, the record supports the Commission's conclusion that there was nothing improper about those meetings. Agency officials may meet with members of the industry both to facilitate settlement and to maintain the agency's knowledge of the industry it regulates. As this court has noted before, "such informal contacts between agencies and the public are the 'bread and butter' of the process of administration and are completely appropriate so long as they do not frustrate judicial review or raise serious questions of fairness" [citing Home Box Office]. Because we find no evidence in the record indicating that judicial review has been frustrated or that any serious questions of fairness have been presented, we sustain the Commission's finding that "the integrity of the decisionmaking process has been fully maintained."

One comment on the decision concluded that it would be "absurdly inefficient and counterproductive to engage in informal communications concerning the basic characteristics of the industry and its product or of the broad implications of a billion dollar international project." Kenneth Davis & Richard J. Pierce, Administrative Law Treatise, §8.4 (3d ed. 1994). Is the decision consistent with *PATCO*?

b. Informal Agency Decisions

Ex parte Comm. Ass-isn 22.

The traditional understanding regarding ex parte communications sharply distinguished "on-the-record" proceedings in which such communications were banned, and informal proceedings, such as notice-and-comment rulemaking or informal adjudication, in which they were not. The distinction was logical; notice-and-comment rulemaking and other informal proceedings were traditionally not required to be decided on the basis of an exclusive "record" and left the agency free to consult informally, in "legislative" fashion, with interested outsiders and to investigate sources of data. In such informal processes of decision, the very notion of an "off the record" "ex parte" communication is inappropriate. Recall also that the Sunshine Act's prohibitions against ex parte communications do not apply to notice-and-comment rulemaking or informal adjudication.

However, rulemaking may in some cases resolve the competing claims of private parties in ways that resemble traditional adjudication, calling adversary norms into play. In addition, the shift of agency policymaking from formal adjudication to notice-and-comment rulemaking has raised fears that the regulated industry will use off-the-record communication of data and views to exert undue influence over the agency. The related development of "paper hearing" rulemaking procedures has created a documentary record in notice-and-comment rulemaking: Off-the-record communications, whether oral or written, are arguably inconsistent with these new procedures.

Sangamon Valley Television Corp. v. United States

269 F.2d 221 (D.C. Cir. 1959)

EDGERTON, C.J.

[In 1956, the FCC conducted notice-and-comment rulemaking proceedings to determine whether to switch the location of a VHF station license from Springfield, Illinois, to St. Louis, Missouri. The switch was favored by Signal Hill, which would likely be awarded the license if the station were moved, and opposed by Sangamon, which was the leading Springfield contender.

While the proceeding was pending before the Commission, Signal Hill's president, Tenenbaum, repeatedly spoke to FCC Commissioners in their offices about the need to switch the station to St. Louis. In addition, he took each of the Commissioners out to lunch and sent them turkeys for Thanksgiving. He urged members of Congress to intervene with the Commission in favor of St. Louis. More than seven weeks after the deadlines for filing comments with the Commissioner had passed, Tenenbaum also submitted to each Commissioner a letter that asserted and sought to document the claim that the station would reach more viewers in Illinois if it were located in St. Louis than in Springfield. The letter was not placed in the public file of the proceeding. Thereafter, the Commissioners decided to move the station to St. Louis. Supporters of Springfield had also contacted the Commissioners informally.]

. . . Interested attempts "to influence any member of the Commission . . . except by the recognized and public processes" go to the very core of the Commission's quasi-judicial powers. . . . Massachusetts Bay Telecasters, Inc. v. Federal Communications Commission, 261 F.2d 55, 66, 67. That case involved licensing not rulemaking. Ordinarily allocation of TV channels among communities is a matter of rule-making governed by [APA §553], rather than adjudication governed by [§554]. The Commission and the intervenor contend that because the proceeding now on review was "rule-making," ex parte attempts to influence the Commissioners did not invalidate it. The Department of Justice disagrees. On behalf of the United States, the Department urges that whatever the proceeding may be called it involved not only allocation of TV channels [to] communities but also resolution of conflicting private claims to a valuable privilege, and that basic fairness requires such a proceeding to be carried on in the open. We agree with the Department of Justice. Accordingly the private approaches to the members of the commission vitiated its action and the proceeding must be reopened.

[The court also held that Tenenbaum's submission of the letter violated Commission regulations establishing a cut-off point for filing comments. It remanded the case to the FCC. After an investigation, the FCC concluded that ordinarily ex parte communications are proper in rule-making proceedings but where an individual has a strong self-interest such communications are improper. Eventually, the whole case was begun again, and in 1962 the Commission came to the same conclusion it had reached in 1957: It assigned Channel 2 to St. Louis.]

Home Box Office, Inc. v. FCC

567 F.2d 9 (D.C. Cir. 1977), cert. denied, 434 U.S. 829, reh'g denied, 434 U.S. 988 (1977)

Before Wright and MacKinnon, Circuit Judges and Weigel, District Judge.

[After notice-and-comment rulemaking proceedings, the FCC adopted general regulations limiting the type of programming that could be offered by cable television services and subscription broadcast television stations, which sought judicial review of the Commission's actions. The Commission had specified a deadline for filling written comments on its proposed rules, and therefore afforded oral argument to various industry and public interest representatives. The regulations adopted by the FCC made it difficult or impossible for "pay cable" companies to originate certain popular sports events or certain feature films. The argument of the Commission and of traditional television broadcasters in support of the rules was that "pay cable" would "siphon" such popular programs from "free" TV and the viewer would end up paying directly for the same programs he now sees for "free."

Whether such "siphoning" was actually likely to occur or whether the "antisiphoning rules" simply represented an effort by existing broadcasters to prevent potential pay cable competitors from getting started was hotly disputed before the Commission.

The court, in a per curiam opinion held the FCC's rules invalid, for reasons related to the FCC's jurisdictional authority and to the First Amendment. It also dealt with the question of ex parte communications.]

It is apparently uncontested that a number of participants before the Commission sought out individual commissioners or Commission employees for the purpose of discussing ex parte and in confidence the merits of the rules under review here. . . . In an attempt to clarify the facts this court sua sponte ordered the Commission to provide "a list of all of the ex parte presentations together with the details of each, made to it, or to any of its members or representatives, during the rulemaking proceedings." In response to this order the Commission filed a document over 60 pages long which revealed, albeit imprecisely widespread ex parte communications involving virtually every party before this court. [These included representatives of broadcasters, cable companies, and pay TV companies. Off-the-record communications were also held between commissioners and staff and members of congress, members of the press, and representatives of various performing arts groups.] . . . It is important to note that many contacts occurred in the crucial period between the close of oral argument on October 25, 1974, and the adoption of the first Report and Order on March 20, 1975, when the rulemaking record should have been closed while the Commission was deciding what rules to promulgate. The information submitted to this court by the Commission indicates that during this period broadcast interests met some 18 times with Commission personnel, cable interests nine times, motion picture and sports interests five times each, and "public interest" intervenors not at all.

Although it is impossible to draw any firm conclusions about the effect of ex parte presentations upon the ultimate shape of the pay cable rules, the evidence is certainly consistent with often-voiced claims of undue industry influence over Commission proceedings, and we are particularly concerned that the final shaping of the rules we are reviewing here may have been by compromise among the contending industry forces, rather than by exercise of the independent discretion in the public interest the Communications Act vests in individual commissioners. . . . Our concern is heightened by the submission of the Commission's Broadcast Bureau to this court which states that in December 1974 broadcast representatives "described the kind of pay cable regulation that, in their view broadcasters 'could live with.' ". . . If actual positions were not revealed in public comments, as this statement would suggest, and, further, if the Commission relied on these apparently more candid private discussions in framing the final pay cable rules, then the elaborate public discussion in these dockets has been reduced to a sham.

Even the possibility that there is here one administrative record for the public and this court and another for the Commission and those "in the know" is intolerable. Whatever the law may have been in the past,[70] there can now be no doubt that implicit in the decision to treat the promulgation of rules as a "final" event in an ongoing process of administration is an assumption that an act of reasoned judgement has occurred, an assumption which further contemplates the existence of a body of material — documents, comments, transcripts, and statements in various forms declaring agency expertise or policy — with reference to which

---

70. The legislative history of the Administrative Procedure Act has been read to imply that there is no such thing as an administrative record in informal rulemaking. See, e.g., U.S. Dept. of Justice, Attorney General's Manual on The Administrative Procedure Act 31 (1947) ("Section 4(b) does not require the formulation of rules upon the exclusive basis on any 'record' made in informal rule making proceedings"). Professor Nathanson has similarly concluded. . . .

> Section 553's notice-and-comment provisions were [originally] conceived of as instruments for the education of the administrator, especially on questions of policy; there is not the slightest indication that the purpose of the notice-and-comment proceedings was to develop a record by which a reviewing court could test the validity of the rule which the Administrator finally adopted. Apparently, an underlying assumption of the APA draftsmen was that any factual issues which became pertinent in a challenge to the validity of a Section 553 rule would be resolved in the first instance in judicial proceedings — either in enforcement proceedings or in suits to enjoin enforcement. . . .

Nathanson, Probing the Mind of the Administrator: Hearing Variations and Standards of Judicial Review Under the Administrative Procedure Act and Other Federal Statutes, 75 Colum. L. Rev. 721, 745-755 (1975). . . . See also Verkuil, Judicial Review of Informal Rule Making, 60 Va. L. Rev. 185, 202-205 (1974).

such judgement was exercised. Against this material, "the full administrative record that was before [an agency official] at the time he made his decision," Citizens to Preserve Overton Park, Inc. v. Volpe, . . . it is the obligation of this court to test the actions of the Commission for arbitrariness or inconsistency with delegated authority. Yet here agency secrecy stands between us and fulfillment of our obligation. As a practical matter, *Overton Park's* mandate means that the public record must reflect what representations were made to an agency so that relevant information supporting or refuting those representations may be brought to the attention of the reviewing courts by persons participating in agency proceedings. This course is obviously foreclosed if communications are made to the agency in secret and the agency itself does not disclose the information presented. Moreover, where, as here, an agency justifies its actions by reference only to information in the public file while failing to disclose the substance of other relevant information that has been presented to it, a reviewing court cannot presume that the agency has acted properly, . . . but must treat the agency's justifications as a fictional account of the actual decision-making process and must perforce find its actions arbitrary. . . .

The failure of the public record in this proceeding to disclose all the information made available to the Commission is not the only inadequacy we find here. Even if the Commission had disclosed to this Court the substance of what was said to it ex parte, it would still be difficult to judge the truth of what the Commission asserted it knew about the television industry because we would not have the benefit of an adversarial discussion among the parties. The importance of such discussion to the proper functioning of the agency decisionmaking and judicial review process is evident [in] our cases. . . . From what has been said above, it should be clear that information gathered ex parte from the public which becomes relevant to a rulemaking will have to be disclosed at some time. On the other hand, we recognize that informal contacts between agencies and the public are the "bread and butter" of the process of administration and are completely appropriate so long as they do not frustrate judicial review or raise serious questions of fairness. Reconciliation of these considerations in a manner which will reduce procedural uncertainty leads us to conclude that communications which are received prior to issuance of a formal notice of rulemaking do not, in general, have to be put in a public file. Of course, if the information contained in such a communication forms the basis for agency action, then under well-established principles, that information must be disclosed to the public in some form. Once a notice of proposed rulemaking has been issued, however, any agency official or employee who is or may reasonably be expected to be involved in the decisional process of the rulemaking proceeding, [should refuse to discuss matters relating to the disposition of the rulemaking with any interested party].

Action for Children's Television v. FCC
564 F.2d 458 (D.C. Cir. 1977)

Before TAMM, MACKINNON and WILKEY, Circuit Judges.
TAMM, Circuit Judge:
[Action for Children's Television (ACT), a nonprofit public interest organization, petitioned the FCC to adopt regulations prohibiting commercials in or sponsorship of children's televisions programs and mandating a minimum amount of programming suitable for children of various age groups. The FCC instituted a notice-and-comment rulemaking

proceeding on ACT's proposal; numerous written comments were received, most strongly supporting ACT's basic goals. The Commission also heard oral argument and panel discussions on the proposal.

In response to ACT's proposals, the broadcast industry took some initial steps toward self-regulation of children's program content and advertising. Following a private meeting between officials of the National Association of Broadcasters (NAB) and the Commission Chairman, the NAB amended its Television Code to limit the amount and content of advertising on children's programs. Thereafter, the FCC concluded the rulemaking proceeding by an opinion in which it enunciated certain broad principles, which it believed should govern advertising on children's programs but declined to adopt ACT's proposal or issue-specific regulations on the ground that the broadcast industry was implementing these principles through self-regulation. The Commission stated that it would monitor the industry's efforts and take further steps if necessary.

ACT claimed that the private meeting between the Commission Chairman and NAB officials invalidated the proceeding. The court held that it would consider ACT's claims of improper ex parte contacts, even though ACT had not raised it before the Commission. It also held that the possibility that the FCC might ultimately rely on industry self-regulation was clearly foreseeable to ACT, and that the Commission's failure to mention that possibility in its initial *Federal Register* notice or to issue a second notice specifically proposing self-regulation as a solution after the negotiations with the NAB did not violate 5 U.S.C. §553(b)(3), which requires that such notice describe "either the terms or substance of the proposed rule or a description of the subjects and issues involved."]

. . . The Commission substantially met [the requirements of §553] by permitting a lengthy period for the submission of written comments and by holding six days of informal panel discussions and formal oral arguments . . . . While the agency must consider, analyze and rely on those factual materials which are in the public domain, the agency may draw upon its own expertise in interpreting the facts or upon broader policy considerations not present in the record. We believe that the Commission operated within this framework in this case.

. . . [T]he commission did explain the reason for its decision to rely for the time being on self-regulation rather than specific rules. This explanation is contained in the record now before us, and it furnishes a basis for effective judicial review.

In holding that ACT's position was not prejudiced by the manner in which the commission pursued . . . these proceedings, we wish to emphasize that we are not insensitive to ACT's disenchantment with what it considers to be the agency's undue deference to the interests of those it was created to regulate. Meaningful public participation is always to be encouraged. . . . Nevertheless, while it may have been impolitic for the Commission not to invite further comment on the NAB's proposals, especially in view of the fact that there was no necessity for deciding these difficult issues quickly, we still cannot say that the Commission abused its discretion in deciding not to. . . .[71]

---

71. . . . If we were to accept the proposition implicit in petitioner's argument — that the FCC may never resort to discussion with members of the industry in a general effort to have its regulatees conform to their public service obligations — the Commission would have little choice but to abandon any reasonable expectation of salutary self-regulation and to affirmatively regulate throughout the areas of children's programming and advertising. The problem, of course, is necessarily a matter of degree, and an agency may well be found to have abused its authority were it to employ overbearing "jawboning" or "arm-twisting" tactics. . . .

At least in the case now before us, however, we are satisfied that the Commission did not coerce the industry into accepting agency-decreed policies of standards negotiated at closed-door meetings. . . .

In so concluding, we necessarily are confronted with the recent decision of this court in Home Box Office, Inc. v. FCC. . . . [Judge Tamm quotes portions of the last paragraph of the court's *Home Box Office* opinion, p.594, supra.]

For the reasons set forth below, we [find] that the above-quoted rule should not apply — as the opinion clearly would have it — to every case of informal rulemaking. [The Court stated that the rulings in *Home Box Office* and *Sangamon* should not apply to all instances of notice-and-comment rulemaking but only to those involving "conflicting private claims to a valuable privilege." The rulemaking proceedings here instead involved "the possible formulation of programming policy revisions of general applicability."]

On the other hand, though, we have Citizens to Preserve Overton Park, Inc. v. Volpe, 401 U.S. 402 (1971) — a somewhat Delphic opinion concerning informal administrative action rather than informal rulemaking — which we believe as a practical matter should not be read as mandating that the public record upon which our review is based reflect every informational input that may have entered into the decisionmaker's deliberative process. . . .

If we go as far as *Home Box Office* does in its ex parte ruling in ensuring a "whole record" for our review, why not go further to require the decisionmaker to summarize and make available for public comment every status inquiry from a Congressman or any germane material that he or she reads or their evening-hour ruminations? In the end, why not administer a lie-detector test to ascertain whether the required summary is an accurate and complete one? The problem is obviously a matter of degree, and the appropriate line must be drawn somewhere. [W]e would draw that line at the point where the rulemaking proceedings involve "competing claims to a valuable privilege."

It is at that point where the potential for unfair advantage outweighs the practical burdens, which we imagine would not be insubstantial, that [a rule prohibiting any off-the-record communications in informal rule-making] would place upon administrators.

Questions

1. On what authority do the courts in *Sangamon* and *Home Box Office* prohibit agency reliance on off-the-record communications? Are the rulings based on due process? The APA? See Electric Power Supply Assoc. v. FERC, 391 F.3d 1255, 1267 (D.C. Circuit 2005). Have these decisions been effectively overruled by the subsequent decision of the Supreme Court in *Vermont Yankee*, p.540, supra. In light of *Vermont Yankee*, the D.C. Circuit, while not overruling *Home Box Office*, has expressly limited it to its facts. See, e.g.. Iowa State Commerce Commission v. Office of Federal Inspector, 730 F.2d 1566 (D.C. Circuit 1984).

2. Which is more persuasive, *Home Box Office* or *Action for Children's Television* (ACT)? *ACT* would limit the prohibition against ex parte communications in informal rule-making to cases involving "competing private claims to a valuable privilege." Why? Can *ACT* be successfully distinguished from *Home Box Office* in terms of this standard?[72]

3. If *Home Box Office* were followed, should its requirements apply to all informal rulemaking? To informal adjudication? Suppose that in *Overton Park* the secretary had, in the course of his deliberations, consulted informally with proponents of the park route without disclosing the substance of the communications to opponents? Are there other alternatives? What about the practice, followed by some high government officials, of

72. Concurring in *Home Box Office*, Judge MacKinnon suggested that the standard should be whether the proceeding is "in effect an adjudication." (Justice Douglas' dissenting opinion in *Florida East Coast*, p.517, supra, suggests a similar test.) Is this test more appropriate or workable than the "competing claims" test?

keeping a publicly available diary that records all meetings or calls with outsiders and a brief summary of the subject discussed? Should the APA be amended in order to resolve these issues, and if so, how?

4. Does *ACT* frustrate the efforts of courts to monitor agency discretion exercised though rulemaking? For example, how can a reviewing court determine whether an agency has taken a "hard look" at all relevant considerations if the agency is free to rely on materials and communications never disclosed to the court or to litigants challenging the agency's decision?

5. Members of the FCC concede that all major rules governing CATV systems were worked out in part through negotiation with industry representatives at private meetings. If asked why these private meetings were necessary, they might respond as follows:

Why Private Mtgs. Misnt Be important.

Without privacy, negotiation will prove impossible, yet negotiation is important for several reasons. First, at issue are a set of rules that will allow a new set of competitors to enter the field and injure, or perhaps destroy, an existing major industry with billions of dollars of investment. We cannot determine, through studies of independent experts, the extent to which any given set of rules will hurt the broadcasters, for the studies conflict and information is imperfect. If the broadcasters agree or come close to agreeing that a given set of rules is acceptable, at least we know we are unlikely to destroy them, and if the cable owners agree, they must be getting something that will facilitate their entry.

Second, if we promulgate rules that are too threatening to the broadcasters, they will obtain legislation that will permanently block cable. Senator Blank, the Chairman of the Communication Subcommittee, has phoned three of us several times and made it perfectly clear he does not want to see, as he puts it, the "Industry destroyed." Unless we can negotiate a solution, informally, the industry will simply maintain total opposition and the Commission will retain very restrictive anti-cable rules.

Now, one might ask, why should the Commission listen to Senator Blank? Why should it not simply do what it thinks is right and let Congress, if it wishes, pass legislation nullifying the action? To take this attitude overlooks a sincere desire on the part of the Commissioner to achieve in the world a concrete result that they believe good for communications. It also overlooks the power of Senator Blank, who can not only seek legislation, but can also hold oversight hearings designed to embarrass us personally, cut our appropriation, or make certain we obtain no other jobs in the government ever. Moreover, if he is prevented from telling us his views by phone, he will do so in other ways. A negotiated solution satisfies him, the broadcasters, and the cable interests as well. It is most unlikely that any such solution here would injure the public.

Third, a negotiated solution will minimize the possibility of court challenge. We have worked on these rules for many years. To have a solution delayed for an additional four or five while a court reviews (and possibly remands) is undesirable.

Can it be possible that negotiated solutions are never permissible or desirable? They take place every day of the week within the legislature. Why then should the courts not allow agencies to use similar approaches — at least some of the time?

What do you think of this hypothetical argument?

Problem

The Federal Trade Commission has brought an action charging Happy Grocery Store with failing to mark prices individually on each can of goods, which the FTC claims is "unfair" or "deceptive."

The Commission has also issued a press release stating that it is considering whether to institute rulemaking proceedings concerning the marking of prices on food items in supermarkets. In particular, it is considering a rule requiring that each individual item be marked in "arabic numerals, regardless of whether it is marked in computer code or some other way."

The National Association of Grocery Retailers fears that such a rule would prevent computer code pricing. Such pricing consists of bars marked on the food cans by the manufacturer. A "reading machine" at the checkout counter automatically "reads" the price, thus saving time and eliminating mistakes. The store manager can tell the machine each day to "translate" any given set of bars into any given price. Thus, he retains control of each pricing decision. Prices in arabic numerals would be noted on the shelf but not on the can, saving the labor costs involved in marking each can and reordering the price of each item, at the checkout counter, by hand.

The President of the Association and several directors (none of whom is connected with Happy Grocery Store) seek a private meeting with the Chairman of the FTC, and one or two other members, in order to make their own views known "at the policymaking level." They are anxious to keep the meeting private in order to discuss what they believe to be the true basis of opposition to the "automated checkout" system — fear that the system will put some retail grocery employees out of work.

(a) At this point you, as counsel to the Association, are asked if the meeting should be held as planned. Should you join in it? What problems do you foresee? How would you avoid or minimize them?

(b) Assume you are FTC General Counsel advising the FTC chairman. Should the chairman hold such a meeting? If so, what conditions should he stipulate?

c. Off-the-Record Communications by Agencies with Other Federal Government Officials

The considerations relating to the propriety of communications off the record are different when agency officials communicate not with interested private persons but with other government officials — members of Congress or their staff, representatives of the White House, officials of executive or "independent" agencies. Congress has broad powers over agencies. The president's constitutional duty to take care that the laws be faithfully executed implies a coordinating and directing power exercised through White House staff and the Office of Management and Budget (OMB). The various line agencies have overlapping jurisdiction; conflicts over turf must be resolved, and some effort made to coordinate government policies. These important processes would be greatly impeded if all communications had to be matters of public record. The First Circuit has stated, "In our tripartite system of government, inter-branch communication and cooperation are not terrible diseases, to be avoided at all costs, but, rather, are a tested means of improving the health of the body politic. Thus, evidence that such a rapport exists without more does not cast doubt on the validity of agency action." Strickland v. Commissioner, Maine Dept. of Human Services, 48 F.3d 12, 25 (1st Cir. 1995). Moreover, it may be argued that the need for public transparency (and attendant adversary testing) is less where communications come from government officials who are (presumptively) pursuing some conception of the general welfare rather than a private interest.

However, there are countervailing arguments. Government officials, including members of Congress and the White House staff, may have far more influence over agency decisions than outsiders. Hence, it may be thought especially important to expose their views to adversary interests. Moreover, it is often claimed that such officials represent private interests, or at least conceptions of a general interest contrary to that deciding agency and its statutory mission.

Efforts by the executive branch to review and coordinate regulatory policy have aroused fears that the president and his staff exert too much influence over regulatory agency decisions. Under executive orders issued by Presidents Reagan and Clinton, agencies are required to prepare regulatory import analysis, including cost-budget analysis for major new rules; these analysis and the rules are subject to review by OMB. See Chapter 2. Environmentalists and consumer advocates have charged that the White House and OMB have used the review process to impose off-the-record "pressures" on EPA to relax regulatory stringency. They also charge that the regulatory review process has been used as a covert backdoor conduit for industry arguments that are never publicly disclosed and subjected to adversary testing. These critics believe that public disclosure of all communications between OMB and agencies, and between outside interests and OMB, should be made public. Compare, e.g., Morrison, OMB Interference with Agency Rulemaking; The Wrong Way to Write a Regulation, 99 Harv. L. Rev. 1059 (1986), with Eisenberg, White House Review of Agency Rulemaking, 99 Harv. L. Rev. 1075 (1986).

This procedural criticism raises an important structural question. What is the conceptually appropriate unit of administrative decisionmaking? Should it be the agency with direct statutory responsibility for a program — an agency like EPA or OSHA, likely to show a mission-oriented bias? Or should it be the executive branch as a whole, allowing the president to curb the mission-orientation of particular agencies in the pursuit of broader national goals (or perhaps, short-term political objectives). The critics argue for the former model, contending that it is substantively improper for the White House to interfere with a particular agency's exercise of statutory discretion as well as procedurally improper to do so off the record. But why should the appropriate level of aggregation be as large as the agency? Why not require communications among officials within the same agency to be on the record? (We explore this question in Chapter 7.)

Sierra Club v. Costle
657 F.2d 298 (D.C. Cir. 1981)

[Some of the legal issues presented by White House review of regulation were addressed in Sierra Club v. Costle, 657 F.2d 298 (D.C. Cir. 1981). The EPA adopted emission control requirements for new coal-fired electric power plants that were less stringent than some environmental groups had sought and that favored high-sulfur eastern coal in comparison to low-sulfur western coal. The procedures followed by the EPA consisted of "paper hearing" procedures mandated by §307(d) of the Clean Air Act, adopted in 1977. The procedures, based in large part on the analysis and recommendations in Peterson, Formal Records and Informal Rulemaking, 85 Yale L.J. 38 (1975), require the EPA to maintain a public docket file of all documents relevant to the rulemaking.[73]

---

73. Section 307(d) requires the public docket file to include "[a]ll data, information and documents . . . on which [a] proposed rule relies," "all written comments and documentary information on the proposed rule received from any person for inclusion in the docket during the comment period," all written materials submitted by the EPA to the OMB for interagency review of proposed and final rules, and "all written comments thereon by other agencies."

The Environmental Defense Fund (EDF) complained that the standards that ultimately emerged were the result of an "ex parte blitz" by eastern coal interests, senators, and White House officials. In particular, the EDF challenged nine off-the-record, post-comment-period meetings that involved high administration officials and, in two cases, Senator Byrd of West Virginia, Senate Majority Leader and a strong defender of eastern coal interests. Seven of the meetings were summarized in memoranda placed in the public docket file at the EPA. The failure to prepare and docket a summary of one of the remaining meetings was found by the court to be an oversight that did not prejudice the EDF. The other remaining meeting involved the President.

The court found that §307(d) did not prohibit such off-the-record meetings, and that *Vermont Yankee* precluded the court from imposing its own rule to that effect.]

Under our system of government, the very legitimacy of general policymaking performed by unelected administrators depends in no small part upon the openness, accessibility and amenability of these officials to the needs and ideas of the public from whom their ultimate authority derives and upon whom their commands must fall. As judges we are insulated from these pressures because of the nature of the judicial process in which we participate; but we must refrain from the easy temptation to look askance at all face-to-face lobbying efforts, regardless of the forum in which they occur, merely because we see them as inappropriate in the judicial context. Furthermore, the importance to effective regulation of continuing contact with a regulated industry, other affected groups, and the public can not be underestimated. Informal contacts may enable the agency to win needed support for its program, reduce future enforcement requirements by helping those regulated to anticipate and shape their plans for the future and spur the provision of information which the agency needs. The possibility of course exists that in permitting ex parte communications with rulemakers we create the danger of "one administrative record for the public and this court and another for the Commission." Under the Clean Air Act procedures, however, "[t]he promulgated rule may not be based (in part or whole) on any information or data which has not been placed in the docket. . . ."[74] Thus EPA must justify its rulemaking solely on the basis of the record it compiles and makes public.

Regardless of this court's views on the need to restrict all post-comment contacts in the informal rulemaking context, however, it is clear to us that Congress has decided not to do so.

[The court noted that Congress, in enacting the Sunshine Act, declined to extend to §553 notice-and-comment rulemaking the ban on ex parte communications it imposed on formal proceedings subject to §§556-557.]

Lacking a statutory basis for its position, EDF would have us extend our decision in Home Box Office, Inc. v. FCC to cover all meetings with individuals outside EPA during the post-comment period. Later decisions of this court, however, have declined to apply *Home Box Office* to informal rulemaking of the general policymaking sort involved here,[75] and there is no precedent for applying it to the procedures found in the Clean Air Act Amendments of 1977.

[The court, however, held that it was a "fair inference" from §307(d)(4)(B)(i) of the Act, requiring that all documents of "central relevance" to the rulemaking be included in

---

74. 42 U.S.C. §7607(d)(6)(C).
75. See [*Action for Children's Television*].

the public docket, that summaries of comparably important oral communications be prepared and included in the docket.]

This is so because unless oral communications of central relevance to the rulemaking are also docketed in some fashion or other, information central to the justification of the rule could be obtained without ever appearing on the docket, simply by communicating it by voice rather than by pen, thereby frustrating the command of section 307 that the final rule not be "based (in part or in whole) on any information or data which has not been placed in the docket. . . ."

EDF is understandabl[y] wary of a rule which permits the agency to decide for itself when oral communications are of such central relevance that a docket entry for them is required. Yet the statute itself vests EPA with the discretion to decide whether "documents" are of central relevance and therefore must be placed in the docket; surely EPA can be given no less discretion in docketing oral communications, concerning which the statu[t]e has no explicit requirements whatsoever. . . . A judicially imposed blanket requirement that all post-comment period oral communications be docketed would . . . contravene our limited powers of review [citing *Vermont Yankee*], would stifle desirable experimentation in the area by Congress and the agencies, and is unnecessary for achieving the goal of an established, procedure-defined docket, viz., to enable reviewing courts to fully evaluate the stated justification given by the agency for its final rule.

[The court then considered whether in the particular circumstances of this case a summary of the meeting involving the president should be prepared and docketed:]

The court recognizes the basic need to the President and his White House staff to monitor the consistency of executive agency regulations with Administration policy. He and his White House advisers surely must be briefed fully and frequently about rules in the making, and their contributions to policy-making considered. The executive power under our Constitution, after all, is not shared — it rests exclusively with the President. . . . To ensure the President's control and supervision over the Executive Branch, the Constitution — and its judicial gloss — vests him with the powers of appointment and removal, the power to demand written opinions from executive officers, and the right to invoke executive privilege to protect consultative privacy. . . .

[T]he desirability of such control is demonstrable from the particular realities of administrative rulemaking. Regulations such as those involved here demand a careful weighing of cost, environmental, and energy considerations. They also have broad implications for national economic policy. Our form of government simply could not function effectively or rationally if key executive policymakers were isolated from each other and from the Chief Executive. Single mission agencies do not always have the answers to complex regulatory problems. An over-worked administrator exposed on a 24-hour basis to a dedicated but zealous staff needs to know the arguments and ideas of policy-makers in other agencies as well as in the White House.

. . . We recognize, however, that there may be instances where the docketing of conversations between the President or his staff and other Executive Branch officers or rulemakers may be necessary to ensure due process. This may be true, for example, where such conversations directly concern the outcome of adjudications or quasi-adjudicatory proceedings; there is no inherent executive power to control the rights of individuals in such settings. Docketing may also be necessary in some circumstances where a statute like this one specifically requires that essential "information or data" upon which a rule is based be docketed. But in the absence of any further congressional requirements, we hold that it was not unlawful in this case for EPA not to docket a face-to-face policy session involving the President and EPA officials during the post-comment period, since EPA makes no effort to base the rule on any "information or data" arising from that meeting. Where the President himself is directly involved in oral communications with Executive Branch officials, Article II considerations — combined with the strictures of *Vermont Yankee* — require that courts tread with extraordinary caution in mandating disclosure beyond that already required by statute.

Of course, it is always possible that undisclosed presidential prodding may direct an outcome that is factually based on the record, but different from the outcome that would have obtained in the absence of presidential involvement. In such a case, it would be true that the political process did affect the outcome in a way the courts could not police. But we do not believe that Congress intended that the courts convert informal rulemaking into a rarified technocratic process, unaffected by political considerations or the presence of political power.

[The court also rejected the EDF's claims that the meetings with Senator Byrd represented improper congressional pressure, distinguishing D.C. Federation of Civic Associations v. Volpe, 259 F.2d 1231 (D.C. Cir. 1971), *cert. denied*, 405 U.S. 1030 (1972), which set aside the Transportation Department's approval of a bridge (the Three Sisters Bridge) across a scenic area of the Potomac River because a powerful member of Congress threatened to withhold funding for the D.C. subway system unless the bridge was built. The court noted that protection of eastern coal producers was, given the legislative background of the Clean Air Act, a statutorily legitimate consideration in the agency's decision, unlike the subway funding in *D.C. Federation*.

Compare EDF v. Blum, 458 F. Supp. 650 (D.D.C. 1978), where off-the-record communications led the court to set aside the EPA's grant, through notice and comment rulemaking, of permission to use the pesticide ferriamicide to deal with fire ants. While the court found that the EDF had an opportunity to discover and rebut, some of the off-the-record communications fell outside the "harmless error" category because they were made just before the EPA's decision and had a material impact upon it.]

Notice-and-Comment Rulemaking and Congress

Radio Assn. v. Department of Transportation, 47 F.3d 794 (6th Cir. 1995), involved claims of undue congressional pressure on the exercise by the Federal Highway Administration (FHWA) of its authority to issue regulations pertaining to the safe operation of trucks. In May 1988, a group of safety organizations along with police agencies and representatives of the insurance industry filed a petition for rulemaking to ban the use of radar detectors in commercial vehicles (CMV). The FHWA declined to promulgate such a rule, finding that states could effectively deal with the problem. Four years later, Congress passed legislation that required the FHWA to publish a notice of proposed rulemaking prohibiting the use of radar detectors in CMVs. The FHWA did so and received thousands of responses with widely varying viewpoints. It found no direct link between radar detector use and CMV accidents and took no final action on the rulemaking. A year later, the Senate Appropriations Committee directed the FHWA to conduct further research about the causal link between radar detectors and accidents. It also stated, "The Committee is displeased that the FHWA has not moved forward with the rulemaking that would ban radar detectors." It called for the Highway Administration to inform the Committee as soon as possible on the future direction that the agency would pursue regarding this matter. Two months later, the FHWA issued a final rule banning the devices. The preamble of the rule stated that it was predicated on findings that the rule would result in a reduction of speed in trucks and a decline in the severity of accidents. The FHWA performed a cost-benefit analysis and found a benefit of $68 million.

Opponents of the rule sought to overturn it on the ground that the agency was improperly influenced by congressional pressure. The opponents argued that the order to publish a notice of proposed rulemaking in effect constituted a direct order to adopt the rule. Opponents also complained that the Senate Appropriations Committee comments improperly placed pressure on the FHWA to adopt the rule. The court rejected these arguments. It held that congressional pressure must be "egregious" before it will be considered problematic. The court found that the notice of proposed rulemaking was no more than a mechanism for soliciting testimony regarding a potential ban on radar detectors. Furthermore, it stated that the Senate Committee comments "merely expressed its displeasure that the agency had not taken action in the 18 months following the release of the rule proposal." Id. at 808. The court cited the statement in Sierra Club v. Costle that elected representatives must be allowed to voice their grievances on such policy matters. Finally, the court noted that the FHWA stated in its preamble that the basis of the rule was grounded in the safety issues presented in the comments it received and other studies.

Compare D.C. Federation of Civic Associations v. Volpe, 259 F.2d 1231 (D.C. Cir. 1971), *cert. denied*, 405 U.S. 1030 (1972), discussed in Sierra Club v. Costle, where the court invalidated the Department of Transportation's decision to build a highway bridge across the Potomac River from Virginia to the District of Columbia as a result of pressure from a powerful member of Congress who threatened to cut off funding for the D.C. subway system if the bridge was not built. The court set aside the Department of Transportation's decision on the grounds that it had acted contrary to its statutory authority in approving the bridge on the basis of subway funding because the latter was not, under the federal highway statutes, one of the factors that the Department of Transportation may lawfully consider in deciding on highway construction.

Off-the-Record White House Communications in Formal Adjudicatory Proceedings

In Portland Audubon Socy. v. Endangered Species Committee, 984 F.2d 1543 (9th Cir. 1993), the Ninth Circuit held that off-the-record communications from White House officials to decisionmakers in a formal adjudicatory hearing are unlawful, rejecting the government's reliance on Sierra Club v. Costle. The Endangered Species Act (ESA) creates an Endangered Species Committee (popularly known as the "God Squad") and empowers it to grant case-by-case exemptions from the Act's ban on federal projects and activities that threaten harm to endangered or threatened species. The Committee is composed of cabinet secretaries and other high federal political officials as well as representatives of affected states. The Act sets forth several standards governing the committee's decision. Exemption decisions must be made on the basis of the record developed in a formal hearing pursuant to APA §§556-557. In *Portland Audubon*, several environmental groups claimed that a committee-approved exemption of Interior Department timber sales on public lands was improperly granted because of ex parte communications between committee members and high White House staff including the president. Two press reports claimed that three or more Committee members had been summoned to the White House and pressured to vote for the exemption. Evidence also suggested that at least one Committee vote may have been altered because of White House contacts.

The court found that the Committee's proceedings were a form of formal adjudication, and thus governed by the ban on ex parte communications in Section 557(d)(1) of the APA, which bars off-the-record communications between a "member of the body comprising the agency" or relevant agency employee and any "interested party outside the agency." The court held that communications between White House officials and federal committee members were not subject to this prohibition because all were members of the executive branch, and that a contrary ruling would offend separation of powers within the meaning of 557(d)(1).

The court emphasized the importance of maintaining a system that demanded all Committee decisions be made in a public manner:

> The public's right to attend all Committee meetings, participate in all Committee hearings, and have access to all Committee records would be effectively nullified if the Committee were permitted to base its decisions on the private conversations and secret talking points and arguments to which the public and the participating parties have no access. If ex parte communications with Committee members were permissible, it would render futile the efforts contained in the remainder of the regulations to make the Committee's deliberative process open to the public . . . ex parte contacts are antithetical to the very concept of an administrative court reaching impartial decision through formal adjudication.

The Court held that the ruling in Sierra Club v. Costle did not apply, noting that it was explicitly based on the circumstance that the proceedings at issue there were notice-and-comment rulemaking, which is not subject to the prohibitions set forth in 557(d)(1). The Court's ruling is discussed and criticized in Michael A. Bosh, Note, The "God Squad" Proves Mortal: Ex Parte Contacts and the White House After Portland Audubon Society, 51 Wash. & Lee L. Rev. 1029 (1994).

Notes and Questions

1. The opinion in Sierra Club v. Costle has had substantial influence beyond the limited question decided: whether an off-the-record communication between the president and the head of an "executive" agency was allowed by §307(d) of the Clean Air Act. The greatest influence of the opinion may be in conceptualizing a distinction between "hard" data and analysis, on the one hand, which must (whatever its origin and mode of transmission, oral or written) be placed on the record whenever a "paper hearing" is required (whether by organic statute or judicial revamping of APA §553), and "soft" arguments of policy and politics, on the other hand, which need not be placed on the record. Prevailing agency practice in major rulemaking proceedings reflects this fact. Hard data and analysis are placed in the public record, but agencies generally feel free, so long as the public comment file is open, to discuss policy considerations off the record with outside private parties as well as other governmental officials. Once the public record is closed and the agency begins to produce a decision, such communications are generally limited to other government officials. Is this a satisfactory resolution of the problem of off-the-record communications in informal rulemaking? Does it meet Judge Wright's concern — that courts cannot engage in effective "hard look" review unless they know the *real* basis for an agency's decision? But can courts ever know the real basis for an agency decision without cross-examining (and perhaps psychoanalyzing) most of the administrative officials involved and then applying a powerful (and yet to be invented) theory of organizational

decisionmaking and bureaucratic politics? Should hard look review have the more modest role of ensuring that agencies' explanations for their decisions are consistent with relevant factual and analytical materials? Does this give agencies too much leeway to rationalize decisions made on "political" grounds? Reconsider *State Farm Mutual*, Chapter 4.

2. President Clinton's Executive Order 12866, retained at least through the first eleven months of the Bush Administration, attempts to control the problem of off-the-record communications between persons outside the government and OIRA. It does so, first, by requiring that only the Administrator of OIRA (or a specified designee) may receive oral communications from people outside the executive branch and second, by saying that no meeting with outsiders can occur without inviting a representative of the agency whose rule is involved. In addition, information about these contacts and communications must be disclosed to the public. Further, written (but not oral) communications between OMB and the rulemaking agency (which often occur after the close of the public comment period) must be made public *after* the agency's promulgation of a rule. See Chapter 2. How far do these provisions go beyond what the APA requires? Why did the Clinton Administration take these steps, if not required by law? How well do these provisions meet the concern, voiced by environmental and public interest representatives, that the OMB review process can be used as a system of covert "backdoor" White House influence by industry to weaken regulation? That it can be used by OMB to pressure agencies to relax proposed regulations without adequate opportunity for the public to know and counter OMB's views? How well do the current procedures for the conduct of the review process balance the competing interests in transparency and the need for frank and full dialogue within the executive branch on policy issues?

D. Due Process Hearing Rights and the "New Property"

1. *The Traditional Learning*

Under the traditional model of administrative law, law was understood as a mechanism for preventing government officials from trespassing on private interests when such incursions had not been authorized by the legislature. The sphere of private interests protected against unauthorized intrusion was defined by the common law. When a government official seizes a person's property to satisfy a tax claim, or imprisons him for failure to obey a government directive, the official has committed a common law tort that would be actionable unless that action had been authorized by the legislature. The official's actions would thus constitute an intrusion on the person's interest in common law "property" or "liberty," protected by the due process clauses of the Fifth and Fourteenth Amendments. See Stewart, The Reformation of American Administrative Law, 88 Harv. L. Rev. 1669, 1717 n.235 (1975) (cases asserting congruence of interests protected by common law and interests protected by due process clause). In these circumstances, a trial-type hearing traditionally was required to establish the officer's authority to impose regulatory requirements or liabilities backed by the coercive enforcement powers of the state. See Londoner v. Denver, p.480, supra; Southern Railway v. Virginia, p.485, supra.

This traditional model, however, affords no redress when a government official causes injury by withholding or terminating benefits and opportunities not legally protected by the common law. If a private person fails to give me a gratuity, or refuses me employment, or denies me a supply contract, the common law ordinarily affords me no redress. Similarly, when a government official refuses me welfare benefits, or terminates my at-will government employment, or declines to purchase my goods, that official has not infringed on any of my protected "liberty" or "property" interests that are protected by common law, and accordingly need not show legislative warrant for his or her action. Even if he or she has assertedly transgressed legislative commands, it is *damnum absque injuria* as far as the traditional model is concerned. Because no legally recognized right of the plaintiff has been infringed, there is no occasion for a hearing to decide whether the officer complied with applicable statutes. Due process requires no hearing, because the plaintiff has no constitutionally protected "liberty" or "property" at stake.

This conceptual model, keyed to the protection of personal interests at common law, perhaps worked tolerably well up until the New Deal. The basic functions of government were comparatively limited and primarily consisted of taxation and economic regulation enforced by sanctions that would invade common-law-protected interests and would trigger the procedural protections of the traditional model (notable exceptions included military pensions and the allocation of the public lands). Most of the decisions reviewed earlier in this chapter involved controls of this sort. However, the traditional model has serious limitations in the context of the modern welfare and service state. Government today engages in a wide variety of activities that powerfully affect individual welfare. It disburses an array of disability, old age, unemployment, and other assistance payments and grants. Government is a major source of employment and supply contracts. It provides education at all levels. It provides housing, medical care, and other services. Through licensing schemes, it authorizes individuals and firms to engage in a variety of useful or profitable activities, such as driving automobiles or selling liquor. In short, government provides a wide variety of important benefits and advantageous opportunities. See Reich, The New Property, 73 Yale L.J. 733 (1964). Although deprivation of these advantages may have consequences to those affected equal to or greater than the exercise of traditional coercive sanctions, the common law would generally afford no redress for denial or withdrawal of such advantages by a private person, and therefore the traditional model of administrative law likewise provided no protection when the government refused or withdrew such advantages. Due process required no hearing, because such government action did not trench on common-law-protected "liberty" or "property." This concept was encapsulated in the notion that licenses, grants, or government employment and other government benefits were "privileges," not procedurally protected "rights."

This section chronicles the gradual demise of the "right-privilege" distinction and the expansion of due process procedural safeguards to include a variety of advantageous opportunities conferred by government. This "due process explosion" has also carried over into administrative and custodial "enclaves," such as hospitals, prisons, and the military, which traditionally were largely immune from judicial control. After examining applications of the earlier "right-privilege" doctrine, we will examine, in turn, two aspects of the extension of due process safeguards: first, the expanding definition of interests entitled to due process protection; and, second, judicial determination of what types of procedures are required by due process to protect such interests in a variety of circumstances. In the past two decades, the Supreme Court has imposed various restrictions on the expansion of due process protections, in part out of concern to avoid excessive burdens on the federal courts and intrusions on the autonomy of state administrative practices. In reviewing this process of expansion and restriction, you should again consider what various purposes procedural safeguards might serve, and you should critically examine the doctrinal evolution in light of those purposes.

It will also be helpful to keep in mind the particular type of governmental functions involved. Consider the utility of the following classifications:

1. regulation (including licensing) and taxation (in the case of regulation, consider the interests of consumers or other members of the public whom regulation is designed to protect, as well as the interests of those subject to regulatory requirements)
2. government insurance and assistance benefits, whether in the form of cash or "in kind" benefits (food stamps, public housing)
3. "proprietary" functions of government: employment, contracting, management of government-owned enterprises and resources
4. custodial "enclaves": schools, prisons, mental hospitals

a. The Right-Privilege Distinction

This part illustrates traditional applications of the right-privilege notion in a number of subject areas. Subsequent Supreme Court decisions, such as Goldberg v. Kelly, 397 U.S. 254 (1970), rejected or undermined the right-privilege distinction, but the earlier cases furnish essential background and arguably have some continuing vitality. This part seeks to convey the flavor of some of the decisions and the conceptual untidiness of many of the distinctions that they reflect. For additional discussion, see Van Alstyne, The Demise of the Right-Privilege Distinction in Constitutional Law, 81 Harv. L. Rev. 1439 (1968); compare Smolla, The Reemergence of the Right-Privilege Distinction in Constitutional Law, 35 Stan. L. Rev. 69 (1982).

Licensing. Courts had long held that government may revoke at will licenses and other forms of official permission. As recently as 1969 the Iowa Supreme Court affirmed the state's power to revoke a liquor license without notice or hearing, relying on precedent that reasoned that:

> [A] license to [sell liquor] is a privilege granted by the state and is in no sense a property right. Such a license does not constitute a contract with the state. . . . When the licensee takes this privilege he does so subject to the provisions of the statutes under which it is granted; and if these statutes say or fairly imply that he is entitled to no notice or hearing before revocation, he cannot be heard to complain if he is given none.

This "privilege" rationale was widely used by courts to deny due process claims to a hearing in licensing cases.[76] However, this "privilege" rationale was not applied to all

---

76. E.g., Smith v. Iowa Liquor Control Commn., 169 N.W.2d 803 (Iowa 1969), *appeal dismissed*, 400 U.S. 885 (1970); Darling Apartment Co. v. Springer, 25 D. Ch. 420, 22 A.2d 397, 401 (Del. 1941) (Summary revocation of liquor license sustained because the "right of a licensee can rise no higher than the terms of the law under which the license is issued; and the licensee accepts the privilege subject to such conditions, including the cause and manner of revocation or suspension."). Similar logic was used to uphold summary revocation of licenses: to exhibit motion pictures, Thayer Amusement Corp. v. Moulton, 64 R.I. 182, 7 A.2d 682 (1939); to operate a motor vehicle, Nulter v. State Road Commn., 119 W. Va. 312, 193 S.E. 549 (1937); Lee v. State, 187 Kan. 566, 358 P.2d 765 (1961); to conduct a pocket billiards business, Commonwealth v. Kinsley, 133 Mass. 578 (1882); or to race horses, Fink v. Cole, 1 N.Y.2d 48, 133 N.E.2d 691, 150 N.Y.S.2d 175 (1956). To what extent might the denial of a hearing in these cases reflect a judgment that the licensing decision turns primarily on the character and reputation of the licensee, factors that might not be illumined through trial-type processes?

cases of licensing. In some instances, courts drew a distinction between activities (such as the sale of liquor) that the state could prohibit entirely, and those activities that it could only regulate. Where a state could prohibit absolutely, it was reasoned, the privilege of conducting such activities could be conditioned on whatever terms the state might please. But where the state could only regulate, and where it used a system of licensing to abet its regulatory ends, the citizen maintained a property or liberty interest and was entitled to due process protection. This distinction was used to require hearings prior to revocation of a license to drive a taxi, operate a school of cosmetology, or practice medicine. Hecht v. Monaghan, 307 N.Y. 461, 121 N.E.2d 421 (1954); Gilchrist v. Bierring, 14 N.W.2d 724 (Iowa 1944); Smith v. State Bd. of Medical Examiners, 140 Iowa 66, 117 N.W. 1116 (1908). The grounds of classification were often obscure; a Texas court found that a license to sell cigarettes was "somewhere in between" a "right" and a "privilege," and had difficulty determining whether it was more analogous to a liquor license ("privilege") or to a license to sell dental services ("property right"). The court finally concluded that a hearing was required. House of Tobacco, Inc. v. Calvert, 394 S.W.2d 654 (Tex. 1965). An activity might be labeled a "right" in one state and a "privilege" in another. Note, 44 Tex. L. Rev. 1360 (1966).

In applying the right/privilege distinction in the licensing context, courts have displayed a special solicitude in extending procedural safeguards to protect licensed professionals. As early as 1873, the Supreme Court held that a lawyer might not be disbarred without notice and opportunity for hearing, asserting that procedural safeguards are as necessary in proceedings "to deprive him of his right to practice his profession as when they are taken to reach his real or personal property." Willner v. Committee on Character and Fitness, 373 U.S. 96 (1963), required an evidentiary hearing when an applicant for admission to a state bar was denied admission because of alleged character deficiencies. The requirement of a hearing on applications for professional licensure has been extended to insurance brokers, beauticians, and pharmacists. Do these decisions simply reflect judges' solicitude for lawyers and the extension of that solicitude to other professions? Or do they reflect a residue of substantive due process hostility to state regulation of private labor, coupled with a healthy suspicion that professional licensing is often used to restrict competition or practice various forms of discrimination? See M. Friedman, Capitalism and Freedom 149-159 (1962); Kessel, The A.M.A. and the Supply of Physicians, 35 Law & Contemp. Probs. 267 (1970); Note, Due Process Limitations on Occupational Licensing, 59 Va. L. Rev. 1097 (1973).

Aliens. It has long been held that aliens may be excluded from the United States without notice or hearing. See The Chinese Exclusion Case (Chae Chan Ping v. United States), 130 U.S. 581 (1889). In United States ex rel. Knauff v. Shaughnessy, 338 U.S. 537 (1950), the Court upheld the exclusion, without hearing, of the alien wife of an American citizen who sought admission under the War Brides Act. Finding that Congress had authorized exclusion without hearing, the Court reasoned that "[a]dmission of aliens is a privilege granted by the sovereign United States Government . . . upon such terms as the United States shall prescribe," and that, accordingly, "[w]hatever the procedure authorized by Congress is, it is due process so far as an alien denied entry is concerned." See also Shaughnessy v. United States ex rel. Mezei, 345 U.S. 206 (1953), sustaining the government's refusal to readmit an alien, resident in the United States for 25 years, who had sought readmission following a 19-month visit with relatives in Europe. Because of the refusal of any other nation to accept him, Mezei had been detained in limbo at Ellis Island for 23 months at the time of the Court's decision.

By contrast, an alien resident in the United States may not be deported without a hearing, at which the government must establish that the alien is subject to deportation under the relevant statutes and regulations. The Japanese Immigrant Case (Yamataya v. Fisher), 189 U.S. 86 (1903); Wong Yang Sung v. McGrath, 339 U.S. 33 (1950). The Court also recently rejected the notion that *Mezei* stands for the proposition that alien status can justify indefinite detention. Zadvydas v. Davis, 121 S. Ct. 2491 (2001), dealt with immigration statutes that provide that an alien found to be unlawfully present in and subject to a final order of removal from the United States may be held in custody for 90 days pending removal and "may" be detained beyond the 90-day period. The Court interpreted the statute to require release of an alien after 90 days unless the government shows that continued detention is necessary to secure the alien's removal (e.g., by preventing the alien from becoming a fugitive). The Court stated that "a statute permitting indefinite detention of an alien would raise a serious constitutional problem" and thus the statute was interpreted to avoid such an issue. But in Jay v. Boyd, 351 U.S. 345 (1956), the Court held that an alien is not entitled to a hearing on the immigration authorities' refusal to exercise discretionary authority (conferred by statute) to suspend the deportation of an otherwise deportable alien meeting specified hardship, good character, and residence requirements, reasoning that the relief, like probation or suspension of a criminal sentence "comes as an act of grace" and "cannot be demanded as a right." (*Query*: Under the "privilege" rationale, why couldn't Congress admit an alien on the condition that he might be subject to deportation without hearing?)

Education. While not presenting procedural issues, Hamilton v. Regents of the Univ. of Calif., 293 U.S. 245 (1934), illustrates the application of the right-privilege notion to public education. A college student was suspended for failure to attend a mandatory military training course because of religious scruples. While acknowledging that the student might have a constitutionally protected interest in avoiding mandatory military training, the Court ruled that the university might impose conditions on the "privilege" of attendance, and, since the student could refuse to attend, no deprivation of his liberty was involved. Steier v. New York State Educ. Comm., 271 F.2d 13 (2d Cir. 1959), ruled that due process did not require a hearing prior to expulsion of a student from Brooklyn College for public criticism of the college president, while Bluett v. University of Illinois, 10 Ill. App. 2d 207, 134 N.E.2d 635 (1956), followed many earlier cases in sustaining a college student's expulsion, without hearing, for alleged cheating.

The contemporary extension of due process safeguards to students was foreshadowed in Dixon v. Alabama State Bd. of Educ., 294 F.2d 150 (5th Cir.), *cert. denied*, 368 U.S. 930 (1961), requiring that students at a state college be accorded rudimentary notice and hearing prior to expulsion for asserted misconduct (here, participation in sit-in demonstrations protesting lunch-counter segregation). (In the rest of this chapter, you should consider the extent to which an exceptionally sympathetic fact situation, as in this case, has triggered major changes in due process doctrine.)

Other subjects. Right-privilege thinking was evident in many other areas where courts traditionally refused to afford procedural rights or other legal protection to those denied advantageous opportunities by government, including public employment, draft exemptions, government contracts, parole, and government pensions. See Laba v. Newark Bd. of Educ., 23 N.J. 364, 129 A.2d 273 (1957) (public employment; hearing not required on discharge); Pickus v. Board of Educ., 9 Ill. 2d 599, 138 N.E.2d 532 (1956) (same); United States v. Nugent, 346 U.S. 1 (1953) (confrontation and cross-examination by applicant of adverse witnesses not required in denial of conscientious objector exemption from draft); Hiatt v. Compagna, 178 F.2d 42 (5th Cir. 1949), *aff'd*, 340 U.S. 880

(1950) (hearing not required in revocation of parole); Perkins v. Lukens Steel Co., 310 U.S. 113 (1940) (no judicial review of government contractor's challenge to contract terms as contrary to statute); Reaves v. Ainsworth, 219 U.S. 296 (1911) (no judicial review of government rejection of pension claim).

Bailey v. Richardson

182 F.2d 46 (D.C. Cir. 1950), aff'd by an equally divided Court, 341 U.S. 918 (1951)

PRETTYMAN, Circuit Judge.

[Plaintiff Bailey had been rehired by the federal government in 1948, subject to removal within 18 months by the Civil Service Commission (CSC) if investigation disclosed disqualification. The commission's regulations listed as a disqualification: "On all the evidence, reasonable grounds exist for belief that the person involved is disloyal to the Government of the United States."

Miss Bailey received interrogatories from the Regional Loyalty Board of the Commission stating that it had received information that she was a member of the Communist Party, had attended meetings, and had associated with members.]

Miss Bailey answered the interrogatories directly and specifically, denying each item of information recited therein as having been received by the Commission, except that she admitted past membership for a short time in the American League for Peace and Democracy. She vigorously asserted her loyalty to the United States. She requested an administrative hearing. A hearing was held before the Regional Board. She appeared and testified and presented other witnesses and numerous affidavits. No person other than those presented by her testified.

On the same day, a letter was sent by the Board to Miss Bailey, reading in part:

> [I]t has been found that, on all the evidence, reasonable grounds exist for belief that you are disloyal to the Government of the United States.

[Bailey was dismissed from her government employment and barred from Civil Service employment for three years. She filed suit, challenging the validity of the board's action and seeking reinstatement. The court first rejected Bailey's argument that the board's procedures violated the executive order establishing the loyalty program, which provides for removal if "evidence" shows disloyalty. Bailey argued that "evidence" was a term of art that does not include information received by a tribunal in secret with no opportunity for adversary testing. The court held that in this context "evidence" merely meant "information" because other parts of the order clearly required that the identities of confidential informers remain confidential. It also held that courts should follow an administrative interpretation of an administrative order unless it is clearly erroneous.

The court then held that the board's order banning Bailey from civil service employment for three years was "punishment" which, under the sixth amendment, could only be imposed through a criminal prosecution. The court invoked United States v. Lovett, 328 U.S. 303 (1946), which had held a similar ban to be an unconstitutional bill of attainder.

However, it also ruled that her dismissal from government service was not "punishment" and was not subject to the safeguards required in criminal prosecutions by the sixth amendment.]

FIFTH AMENDMENT

It is next said on behalf of appellant that the due process clause of the Fifth Amendment requires that she be afforded a hearing of the quasi-judicial type before being dismissed. The due process clause provides: "No person shall . . . be deprived of life, liberty, or property, without the due process of law; . . ." It has been held repeatedly and consistently that Government employ is not "property" and that in this particular it is not a contract. We are unable to perceive how it could be held to be "liberty." Certainly, it is not "life." So much that is clear would seem to dispose of the point. In terms the due process clause does not apply to the holding of a Government office.

Other considerations lead to the same conclusion. Never in our history has a Government administrative employee been entitled to a hearing of the quasi-judicial type upon his dismissal from Government service. That record of a hundred and sixty years of Government administration is the sort of history which speaks with great force. It is pertinent to repeat in this connection that the Lloyd-La Follette Act,[77] sponsored and enacted by advocates of a merit classified government service, expressly denies the right to such a hearing. Moreover, in the acute and sometimes bitter historic hundred-year contest over the wholesale summary dismissal of Government employees, there seems never to have been a claim that, absent congressional limitation, the President was without constitutional power to dismiss without notice, hearing or evidence, except for the question as to officials appointed with the advice and consent of the Senate. . . .

Constitutionally, the criterion for retention or removal of subordinate employees is the confidence of superior executive officials. Confidence is not controllable by process. What may be required by acts of the Congress is another matter, but there is no requirement in the Constitution that the executive branch rely upon the services of persons in whom it lacks confidence. The opinion in the *Myers* case [272 U.S. 52 (1926)] makes this proposition amply clear. . . .

But it is said that the public does not distinguish, that she has been stigmatized and her chance of making a living seriously impaired. . . . On behalf of the individual, our sense of justice rebels, but the counter-balancing essentials of effective government lead us to assent without equivocation to the rules of immunity.

[The court also rejected Bailey's contention that her discharge was a sanction for her entertaining certain political views and therefore violated the first amendment. Judge Edgerton dissented, arguing that the executive order required the government to present evidence to sustain its charges and afford cross-examination and that dismissal for "disloyalty" is "punishment" and requires all the safeguards of a judicial trial.]

Questions

1. In the celebrated case of McAuliffe v. Mayor of City of New Bedford, 155 Mass. 216, 29 N.E. 517 (1892), Justice Holmes sustained the dismissal of a city policeman for engaging in political activities in violation of a city regulation with the curt observation that "[t]he petitioner may have a constitutional right to talk politics, but he has no constitutional

---

77. The Lloyd-La Follette Act, enacted in 1913 and codified in 5 U.S.C. §§7501-7504, requires "cause" for dismissal of certain government civil service employees, but does not provide for a trial-type hearing on such dismissal. Its provisions are discussed in Arnett v. Kennedy, p.634, infra. — EDS.

right to be a policeman," and that, accordingly, he could not complain "as he takes the employment on the terms which are offered him." Is *Bailey* founded on this same conceptualism — here, that government employment may be conditioned on liability to discharge without a trial-type hearing? Or is the decision based on the practical implications of recognizing government employment as a species of "liberty" or "property" protected by due process? If government employment were constitutionally protected, would a hearing be required for demotion? Transfer? Failure to hire? Failure to promote? Would the grounds for personnel decisions be reduced to those that could be established in a courtroom? Is *Bailey* explained by the court's fear of hard cases making bad law?

2. Note the majority's treatment of Bailey's claim to a hearing based on the injury to her reputation. Why shouldn't Bailey be entitled to a hearing to clear her name without being entitled to reinstatement? Could the stigma problem be avoided by making the sole ground of discharge "for the good of the service"?

b. Nonconstitutional Avenues to Procedural Protection

Greene v. McElroy
360 U.S. 474 (1959)

[Greene, a defense contractor executive, had his security clearance revoked by the Defense Department because of alleged associations with communists. At a hearing Green and other witnesses testified in refutation of the charges. The government produced no witnesses and relied on secret reports by confidential informers to cross-examine Greene and his witnesses. As a result of revocation of his security clearance, Greene was discharged from his $18,000 per year position and forced to find employment as an architectural draftsman at a salary of $4700 per year.

The Court did not decide whether the Constitution permitted this procedure, nor did it decide whether the president had inherent constitutional authority to use this procedure to protect secrets because, in its view, the Defense Department claimed to be acting under a delegation of authority from Congress, and Congress, said the Court, had not delegated the power to use so unfair a procedure.

Chief Justice Warren wrote for the Court:]

Certain principles have remained relatively immutable in our jurisprudence. One of these is that where governmental action seriously injures an individual, and the reasonableness of the action depends on fact findings, the evidence used to prove the Government's case must be disclosed to the individual so that he has an opportunity to show that it is untrue. While this is important in the case of documentary evidence, it is even more important where the evidence consists of the testimony of individuals whose memory might be faulty or who, in fact, might be perjurers or persons motivated by malice, vindictiveness, intolerance, prejudice, or jealousy. We have formalized these protections in the requirements of confrontation and cross-examination. They have ancient roots.

[The Court then reviewed various presidential directives and statutes relating to government security clearances. It concluded:]

If acquiescence or implied ratification were enough to show delegation of authority to take actions within the area of questionable constitutionality, we might agree with respondents that delegation has been shown here. [But decisions by the president or

Congress to delegate authority to administrators to use unfair procedures] cannot be assumed by acquiescence or non-action. Kent v. Dulles, 357 U.S. 116. . . . They must be made explicitly not only to assure that individuals are not deprived of cherished rights under procedures not actually authorized . . . but also because explicit action, especially in areas of doubtful constitutionality, requires careful and purposeful consideration by those responsible for enacting and implementing our laws. Without explicit action by lawmakers, decisions of great constitutional import and effect would be relegated by default to administrators who, under our system of government, are not endowed with authority to decide them.

[The Court reversed the decision of the court of appeals sustaining the government's action.]

Notes and Questions

1. To what extent is the result in *Greene* dictated by Kent v. Dulles, Chapter 4? Why wasn't the same approach used in Bailey v. Richardson?

2. During the 1950s, the Court was assiduous in overturning employee discharges and revocations of security clearances without reaching the constitutional issues raised by plaintiffs.[78] During the 1960s, nonconstitutional rulings were used by lower courts to invalidate adverse governmental actions taken without opportunity for hearing in matters other than employment and security clearance. For example, Gonzalez v. Freeman, 334 F.2d 570 (D.C. Cir. 1964), set aside the debarment by the Department of Agriculture, without hearing, of government contractors for violation of regulations. The court held that the department's debarment practices must be codified in regulations, and the failure to do so violated APA §552(a)(1)(B), requiring *Federal Register* publication of "statements of the general course and method by which its functions are channelled and determined, including the nature and requirements of all formal and informal procedures available." Debarment could not be "left to administrative improvisation on a case-by-case basis."

Cafeteria Workers v. McElroy
367 U.S. 886 (1961)

Mr. Justice STEWART delivered the opinion of the Court.

In 1956 the petitioner Rachel Brawner was a short-order cook at a cafeteria operated by her employer, M & M Restaurants, Inc., on the premises of the Naval Gun Factory in the city of Washington. She had worked there for more than six years, and from her employer's point of view her record was entirely satisfactory.

[The contract between the Gun Factory and M & M Restaurants required the restaurant's employees to meet naval security requirements. Brawner's clearance to work at the

---

78. Cole v. Young, 351 U.S. 536 (1956), found insufficient congressional authority for application of a loyalty program to a food and drug inspector in the FDA whose work was not closely related to national security. In Peters v. Hobby, 349 U.S. 331 (1955), the dismissal of a government employee as a security risk was set aside because the Court found no authority in applicable statutes or regulations for the Loyalty Review Board's sua sponte reversal of a judgment by a trial board favorable to the employee. In Service v. Dulles, 354 U.S. 363 (1957), and in Vitarelli v. Seaton, 359 U.S. 535 (1959), the Court found that employee discharges without hearings violated the relevant agencies' own procedural regulations despite quite plausible claims by the agencies that the regulations were inapplicable to dismissals because of suspected disloyalty or security risks.

base was revoked by navy officials for failure to meet base security requirements. Her requests for a hearing or further explanation were denied.]

Since the day her identification badge was withdrawn Mrs. Brawner has not been permitted to enter the Gun Factory. M & M offered to employ her in another restaurant which the company operated in the suburban Washington area, but she refused on the ground that the location was inconvenient. . . .

As the case comes here, two basic questions are presented. Was the commanding officer of the Gun Factory authorized to deny Rachel Brawner access to the installation in the way he did? If he was so authorized, did his action in excluding her operate to deprive her of any rights secured to her by the Constitution? . . .

I

The control of access to a military base is clearly within the constitutional powers granted to both Congress and the President. . . .

Congress has provided that the Secretary of the Navy "shall administer the Department of the Navy" and shall have "custody and charge of all . . . property of the Department." 10 U.S.C. §5031(a) and (c). In administering his Department, the Secretary has been given statutory power to "prescribe regulations, not inconsistent with law, for the government of his department, . . . and the custody, use, and preservation of the . . . property appertaining to it." 5 U.S.C. §22. [The secretary had issued regulations giving commanding officers plenary authority over bases.] The law explicitly requires that United States Navy Regulations shall be approved by the President, 10 U.S.C. §6011, and the pertinent regulations in effect when Rachel Brawner's identification badge was revoked had, in fact, been expressly approved by President Truman on August 9, 1948.

[The Court concluded that Congress and the president had sufficiently authorized the navy's action in this case.]

II

The question remains whether Admiral Tyree's action in summarily denying Rachel Brawner access to the site of her former employment violated the requirements of the Due Process Clause of the Fifth Amendment. This question cannot be answered by easy assertion that, because she had no constitutional right to be there in the first place, she was not deprived of liberty or property by the Superintendent's action. "One may not have a constitutional right to go to Baghdad, but the Government may not prohibit one from going there unless by means consonant with due process of law." Homer v. Richmond, 110 U.S. App. D.C. 226, 229, 292 F.2d 719, 722. It is the petitioners' claim that due process in this case required that Rachel Brawner be advised of the specific grounds for her exclusion and be accorded a hearing at which she might refute them. We are satisfied, however, that under the circumstances of this case such a procedure was not constitutionally required.

The Fifth Amendment does not require a trial-type hearing in every conceivable case of government impairment of private interest. . . . The very nature of due process negates any concept of inflexible procedures universally applicable to every imaginable situation. " '[D]ue process,' unlike some legal rules, is not a technical conception with a fixed content unrelated to time, place and circumstances." It is "compounded of history, reason, the past course of decisions. . . ." Joint Anti-Fascist Comm. v. McGrath, 341 U.S. 123, 162-163 (concurring opinion).

[C]onsideration of what procedures due process may require under any given set of circumstances must begin with a determination of the precise nature of the government function involved as well as of the private interest that has been affected by governmental action. Where it has been possible to characterize that private interest (perhaps in over-simplification) as a mere privilege subject to the Executive's plenary power, it has traditionally been held that notice and hearing are not constitutionally required. . . .

What, then, was the private interest affected by Admiral Tyree's action in the present case? It most assuredly was not the right to follow a chosen trade or profession. . . . Rachel Brawner remained entirely free to obtain employment as a short-order cook or to get any other job, either with M & M or with any other employer. All that was denied her was the opportunity to work at one isolated and specific military installation.

Moreover, the governmental function operating here was not the power to regulate or license, as lawmaker, an entire trade or profession, or to control an entire branch of private business, but rather, as proprietor, to manage the internal operation of an important federal military establishment. . . . In that proprietary military capacity, the Federal Government, as has been pointed out, has traditionally exercised unfettered control.

. . . This case, like Perkins v. Lukens Steel Co., 310 U.S. 113, involves the Federal Government's dispatch of its own internal affairs. The Court has consistently recognized that an interest closely analogous to Rachel Brawner's, the interest of a government employee in retaining his job, can be summarily denied. It has become a settled principle that government employment, in the absence of legislation, can be revoked at the will of the appointing officer. . . . We may assume that Rachel Brawner could not constitutionally have been excluded from the Gun Factory if the announced grounds for her exclusion had been patently arbitrary or discriminatory — that she could not have been kept out because she was a Democrat or a Methodist. It does not follow, however, that she was entitled to notice and a hearing when the reason advanced for her exclusion was, as here, entirely rational and in accord with the contract with M & M.

Finally, it is to be noted that this is not a case where government action has operated to bestow a badge of disloyalty or infamy, with an attendant foreclosure from other employment opportunity. . . . All this record shows is that, in the opinion of the security officer of the Gun Factory, concurred in by the Superintendent, Rachel Brawner failed to meet the particular security requirements of that specific military installation. There is nothing to indicate that this determination would in any way impair Rachel Brawner's employment opportunities anywhere else. . . . For all that appears, the Security Officer and the Superintendent may have simply thought that Rachel Brawner was garrulous, or careless with her identification badge.

For these reasons, we conclude that the Due Process Clause of the Fifth Amendment was not violated in this case.

Affirmed.

Mr. Justice BRENNAN, with whom THE CHIEF JUSTICE, Mr. Justice BLACK and Mr. Justice DOUGLAS join, dissenting.

I have grave doubts whether the removal of petitioner's identification badge for "security reasons" without notice of charges or opportunity to refute them was authorized by statute or executive order. See Greene v. McElroy, 360 U.S. 474 (1959). But under compulsion of the Court's determination that there was authority, I pass to a consideration of the more important constitutional issue, whether petitioner has been deprived of liberty or property without due process of law in violation of the Fifth Amendment.

I read the Court's opinion to acknowledge that petitioner's status as an employee at the Gun Factory was an interest of sufficient definiteness to be protected by the Federal Constitution from some kinds of governmental injury. . . . In other words, if petitioner Brawner's badge had been lifted avowedly on grounds of her race, religion, or political opinions, the Court would concede that some constitutionally protected interest — whether "liberty" or "property" it is unnecessary to state — had been injured. But, as the Court says there has been no such open discrimination here. The expressed ground of exclusion was the obscuring formulation that petitioner failed to meet the "security requirements" of the naval installation where she worked. I assume for present purposes that separation as a "security risk," if the charge is properly established, is not unconstitutional. But the Court goes beyond that. It holds that the mere assertion by government that exclusion is for a valid reason forecloses further inquiry. That is, unless, the government official is foolish enough to admit what he is doing — and few will be so foolish after today's decision — he may employ "security requirements" as a blind behind which to dismiss at will for the most discriminatory of causes.

Such a result in effect nullifies the substantive right — not to be arbitrarily injured by Government — which the Court purports to recognize. What sort of right is it which enjoys absolutely no procedural protection? . . . She may be the victim of the basest calumny, perhaps even the caprice of the government officials in whose power her status rested completely. In such a case, I cannot believe that she is not entitled to some procedures. . . .

[T]he Court holds that petitioner has a right not to have her identification badge taken away for an "arbitrary" reason, but no right to be told in detail what the reason is, or to defend her own innocence, in order to show, perhaps, that the true reason for deprivation was one forbidden by the Constitution. That is an internal contradiction to which I cannot subscribe.

One further circumstance makes this particularly a case where procedural requirements of fairness are essential. Petitioner was not simply excluded from the base summarily, without a notice and chance to defend herself. She was excluded as a "security risk," that designation most odious in our times. [The Court] ought not to affix a "badge of infamy" . . . to a person without some statement of charges, and some opportunity to speak in reply.

Questions

1. Why didn't the Court in *Cafeteria Workers* follow Greene v. McElroy? Is the Court more solicitous of corporate executives than short-order cooks?

2. Note that the Court adopts a "balancing" approach to due process. Does its approach repudiate the right-privilege distinction, or does it serve to preserve the distinction in a new guise? What are the ingredients in such a balancing process, and how are they to be weighed?

3. Why does the majority concede that Brawner could not be discharged because of her race, religion, or political affiliation? If government employment, a security badge, or any other advantageous opportunity conferred by government is merely a "privilege," why may not it be denied or withdrawn on any ground whatsoever? Is the Court's concession compelled by its "balancing" test? What other justifications might there be for such a concession?

4. If the government may not deny employment, security clearance, or other benefits for certain reasons, then isn't Justice Brennan correct in concluding that administrators should provide an explanation for their action, which could be tested in an administrative hearing? Or is it sufficient that a person allegedly discriminated against could bring a lawsuit in court to protest the government's action and secure a judicial

hearing on the reasons for it? Cf. Nickey v. Mississippi, 292 U.S. 393 (1934), sustaining the denial of an administrative hearing on a tax assessment because of the availability of de novo judicial review. See also the discussion of Southern Ry. v. Virginia, p.487, supra.

5. Even if there is no automatic right to an administrative hearing, should there not at least be a requirement in cases like *Cafeteria Workers* that administrators provide a reason for their actions?

c. Summary Administrative Action: The Timing of and Forum for a Hearing

North American Cold Storage Co. v. Chicago
211 U.S. 306 (1908)

[A Chicago ordinance prohibited cold storage houses from storing food unfit for human consumption, and authorized summary seizure and destruction by city health officers of unfit food so stored. Defendants, Chicago health officials, ordered complainant storage warehouse to deliver up for destruction assertedly putrid poultry. On refusal of the warehouse to comply, defendants threatened summary destruction of stored goods deemed by them to be unfit and prohibited further deliveries to the warehouse. The warehouse applied for an injunction prohibiting the stoppage of deliveries and the threatened destruction. The lower federal court dismissed for want of jurisdiction.]

Mr. Justice PECKHAM . . . delivered the opinion of the court. . . .

The general power of the State to legislate upon the subject embraced in the above ordinance of the city of Chicago, counsel does not deny. . . . Nor does he deny the right to seize and destroy unwholesome or putrid food, provided that notice and opportunity to be heard be given the owner or custodian of the property before it is destroyed. We are of opinion, however, that provision for a hearing before seizure and condemnation and destruction of food which is unwholesome and unfit for use, is not necessary. . . . The right to so seize and destroy is, of course, based upon the fact that the food is not fit to be eaten. Food that is in such a condition, if kept for sale or in danger of being sold, is in itself a nuisance, and a nuisance of the most dangerous kind, involving, as it does, the health, if not the lives, of persons who may eat it. A determination on the part of the seizing officers that food is in an unfit condition to be eaten is not a decision which concludes the owner. The ex parte finding of the health officers as to the fact is not in any way binding upon those who own or claim the right to sell the food. If a party cannot get his hearing in advance of the seizure and destruction he has the right to have it afterward, which right may be claimed upon the trial in an action brought for the destruction of his property, and in that action those who destroyed it can only successfully defend if the jury shall find the fact of unwholesomeness as claimed by them. . . .

Complainant, however, contends that there was no emergency requiring speedy action for the destruction of the poultry in order to protect the public health from danger resulting from consumption of such poultry. It is said that the food was in cold storage, and that it would continue in the same condition it then was for three months, if properly stored, and that, therefore, the defendants had ample time in which to give notice to complainant or the owner and have a hearing of the question as to the condition of the poultry, and as the ordinance provided for no hearing, it was void. But we think this is not required. . . . We think when the question is one regarding the destruction of food which is not fit for human use the emergency must be one which would fairly appeal to the reasonable discretion of the legislature as to the necessity for a prior hearing, and in that case its decision would not be a subject for review by the courts. As the owner of the food or its custodian is amply protected against the party seizing the food, who must in a subsequent action against him show as a fact that it was within the statute, we think that due process of law is not denied the owner or custodian. . . .

Notes and Questions

1. Why wouldn't impoundment of the food pending an administrative hearing on the issue of contamination adequately protect the government's interest here? More generally, how can a court evaluate the government's interest in summary action and weigh it against the hearing interests of persons threatened with summary action?

2. Note that the Court suggests that the availability of a subsequent tort action against the individual officials who seized its food adequately protects the owner. Does it? What would the test of liability be? What are plaintiff's chances of collecting any judgment that it might win? What tort remedy, if any, might be available against the city?

3. In Bowles v. Willingham, 321 U.S. 503 (1944), the Court considered a World War II order, issued by price control administrative officials to Willingham without affording her a hearing, reducing the rent Willingham could charge for premises that she owned from $137.50 per month to $90.00 per month. Justice Douglas wrote for the Court:

> Congress has provided for judicial review of the Administrator's action. To be sure, that review comes after the order has been promulgated; and no provision for a stay is made. But . . . that review satisfies the requirements of due process. As stated by Mr. Justice Brandeis for a unanimous Court in Phillips v. Commissioner, 283 U.S. 589, 596-597 [(1931)]: "Where only property rights are involved, mere postponement of the judicial inquiry is not a denial of due process, if the opportunity given for the ultimate judicial determination of the liability is adequate. . . . Delay in the judicial determination of property rights is not uncommon where it is essential that governmental needs be immediately satisfied." . . . Congress was dealing here with the exigencies of wartime conditions and the insistent demands of inflation control. . . .
>
> . . . To require hearings for thousands of landlords before any rent control order could be made effective might have defeated the program of price control. Or Congress might well have thought so. National security might not be able to afford the luxuries of litigation and the long delays which preliminary hearings traditionally have entailed.

Suppose a court later determined that the rent fixed by the Office of Price Administration (OPA) was unreasonably low. Could Willingham later recover the rent that she lost by reason of the OPA's order? From whom?

4. The federal taxing authorities have long exercised the authority, without prior notice and hearing to the taxpayer, to demand instant payment by a taxpayer of deficiency assessments on an administrative determination that collection is in immediate jeopardy (because the taxpayer may convey away his assets, flee with them), and summarily seize and sell the taxpayer's property if payment is not made at once. This procedure was sustained against due process challenge in Phillips v. Commissioner, 283 U.S. 589 (1931) (relied on in *Willingham*), on the grounds that the practice was long established and that the taxpayer could challenge the propriety of the assessment in subsequent judicial proceedings.

5. Courts have upheld summary administrative action in a wide variety of regulatory contexts. Some examples follow. Consider in each of these cases whether the availability

of subsequent judicial remedies would provide an adequate remedy if the agency's action were unlawful:

Fahey v. Mallonee, 332 U.S. 245 (1947), sustained the action, taken without notice and hearing, of the Federal Home Loan Administration in appointing a conservator to assume control of a savings and loan association that was assertedly being managed in an "unlawful, unauthorized, and unsafe manner." The Court stressed that summary measures of this sort were traditional in control of banking, "one of the longest regulated and most closely supervised of public callings."

Ewing v. Mytinger & Casselberry, 339 U.S. 594 (1950), dealt with the FDA's statutory authority to seize, without hearing, articles that it finds probable cause to believe to be "misbranded" and dangerous to health, fraudulent, or misleading to consumers. Following seizure, the articles must be brought before a federal court for condemnation, at which point the manufacturer or owner is entitled to a full hearing. In this case, the FDA had simultaneously and in different areas of the country made ten seizures (and threatened additional seizures) of a "Nutrilite Food Supplement" distributed by Mytinger & Casselberry; the FDA did not claim that the product was harmful to health, but asserted that its labeling claims for the product were misleading and that the product was therefore "misbranded." Mytinger & Casselberry asserted that the seizures would destroy its business before opportunity for trial. A three-judge district court, finding that there was no emergency justifying immediate action to protect the public, held that before seizures could be instituted Mytinger & Casselberry was entitled to an administrative hearing on whether there was probable cause to believe that the product was misbranded. The Supreme Court reversed, analogizing the FDA's seizure actions to the initiation of a criminal prosecution by a prosecutor or grand jury, which can also cause severe harm to reputation or business pending a judicial determination of the merits. The Court also held that Congress might extend the remedy of summary seizure traditional in the protection of public health to instances of misleading labeling. Justices Frankfurter and Jackson dissented, asserting that the district court should review whether the FDA had abused its discretion by instituting multiple seizures. In addition to denying Mytinger & Casselberry the right to a preseizure administrative hearing, the Court held that the FDA's institution of seizures was not subject to judicial review. After studying Chapter 8, you should consider whether this holding is still good law.

Catanzaro v. Weiden, 188 F.3d 56 (2d Cir. 1998): A car crashed into the first floor of a building in Middletown, New York, owned by plaintiffs. City officials, finding one-inch cracks in the building, had it immediately destroyed, fearing that it would collapse and injure adjacent buildings. Plaintiffs brought a Section 1983 action against the city and city officials, claiming that no emergency warranting summary demolition existed because only the building facade had been damaged, and that the failure to afford them a prior hearing on the demolition violated due process. The court affirmed summary judgment for defendants, finding that plaintiffs could establish a due process violation only if they showed the city officials had acted arbitrarily or abused their discretion in determining that an emergency warranting immediate demolition existed, and that they had failed to make such a showing.

d. Pre-*Goldberg* Due Process Decisions by the Supreme Court

In the two decades prior to its 1970 decision in Goldberg v. Kelly, 397 U.S. 254 (requiring hearings prior to state termination of welfare payments to assertedly ineligible recipients), the Supreme Court issued a number of decisions imposing constitutional restrictions on states' withdrawal or withholding of advantageous opportunities tradition-ally characterized as "privileges." For example, Wieman v. Updegraff, 344 U.S. 183 (1952), invalidated exclusion from employment in state colleges because of membership in specified "subversive" organizations, regardless of the member's knowledge of or commitment to the organization's goals. Slochower v. Board of Higher Educ., 350 U.S. 551 (1956), prohibited summary dismissal of a state college professor for invocation of the privilege against self-incrimination in connection with testimony unrelated to his employ-ment. Sherbert v. Verner, 374 U.S. 398 (1963), invalidated state denial of unemployment benefits because of the recipient's refusal, for religious reasons, to seek employment on a Saturday. But these and similar rulings involved an independent constitutional limitation on governmental action — first amendment protections of speech and religious freedom, and the constitutional privilege against self-incrimination — rather than recognition of employment or other government benefits as "liberty" or "property" in themselves.

2. The Evolution of the New Due Process: The Definition of Interests Entitled to Procedural Protection

In the remaining portions of this section, we examine the development of proce-dural due process protections in the decades following the Supreme Court's decision in Goldberg v. Kelly, 397 U.S. 254 (1970), which unambiguously extended constitutional safeguards to advantageous relations with government ("privileges") and ordered a government welfare agency to provide welfare recipients with extensive administrative hearing rights prior to termination of benefits on grounds of ineligibility. In this subsec-tion, we examine, through a series of Supreme Court decisions, the expanding (and contracting) definition of the interests entitled to claim due process protection. In the two subsequent subsections, we review the determination by the federal courts of what types of procedural safeguards are required by due process and the use of alternatives to formal hearing procedures. Throughout the materials that follow, you should again ask yourself what purposes are potentially served by procedural safeguards and how emphasis on one purpose, as opposed to another, might influence the definition of protected interests or the choice among alternative procedural requirements. You should also consider the rele-vance of the different governmental functions in question.

Goldberg v. Kelly
397 U.S. 254 (1970)

Mr. Justice BRENNAN delivered the opinion of the Court.
. . . This action was brought in the District Court for the Southern District of New York by residents of New York City receiving financial aid under the federally assisted program of Aid to Families with Dependent Children (AFDC) or under New York State's general Home Relief program. Their complaint alleged that the New York State and New York City officials administering these programs terminated, or were about to terminate, such aid without prior notice and hearing, thereby denying them due process of law.
[At the time of the Court's decision, state law (amended in an attempt to settle this suit and in response to revised federal regulations) provided for the following procedures

for termination of assistance payments:] A caseworker who has doubts about the recipient's continued eligibility must first discuss them with the recipient. If the caseworker
concludes that the recipient is no longer eligible, he recommends termination of aid to a
unit supervisor. If the latter concurs, he sends the recipient a letter stating the reasons for
proposing to terminate aid and notifying him that within seven days he may request that a
higher official review the record, and may support the request with a written statement
prepared personally or with the aid of an attorney or other person. If the reviewing official
affirms the determination of ineligibility, aid is stopped immediately and the recipient is
informed by letter of the reasons for the action. Appellees' challenge to this procedure
emphasizes the absence of any provisions for the personal appearance of the recipient
before the reviewing official, for oral presentation of evidence, and for confrontation and
cross-examination of adverse witnesses. However, the letter does inform the recipient that
he may request a post-termination "fair hearing." This is a proceeding before an independent state hearing officer at which the recipient may appear personally, offer oral
evidence, confront and cross-examine the witnesses against him, and have a record made
of the hearing. If the recipient prevails at the "fair hearing" he is paid all funds erroneously withheld. A recipient whose aid is not restored by a "fair hearing" decision may
have judicial review. The recipient is so notified.

I

The constitutional issue to be decided, therefore, is the narrow one whether the Due
Process Clause requires that the recipient be afforded an evidentiary hearing *before* the
termination of benefits. The District Court held that only a pre-termination evidentiary
hearing would satisfy the constitutional command, and rejected the argument of the state
and city officials that the combination of the post-termination "fair hearing" with the informal pre-termination review disposed of all due process claims. The court said: "While
post-termination review is relevant, there is one overpowering fact which controls here. By
hypothesis, a welfare recipient is destitute, without funds or assets. . . . Suffice it to say that
to cut off a welfare recipient in the face of . . . 'brutal need' without a prior hearing of some
sort is unconscionable, unless overwhelming considerations justify it." . . .

Appellant does not contend that procedural due process is not applicable to the
termination of welfare benefits. Such benefits are a matter of statutory entitlement for
persons qualified to receive them.[79] Their termination involves state action that adjudi-

---

79. It may be realistic today to regard welfare entitlements as more like "property" than a "gratuity." Much
of the existing wealth in this country takes the form of rights that do not fall within traditional common-law
concepts of property. It has been aptly noted that:

> [S]ociety today is built around entitlement. The automobile dealer has his franchise, the doctor
> and lawyer their professional licenses, the worker his union membership, contract, and pension
> rights, the executive his contract and stock options; all are devices to aid security and indepen-
> dence. Many of the most important of these entitlements now flow from government: subsidies
> to farmers and businessmen; routes for airlines and channels for television stations; long term
> contracts for defense, space, and education; social security pensions for individuals. Such sources
> of security, whether private or public, are no longer regarded as luxuries or gratuities; to the recip-
> ients they are essentials, fully deserved, and in no sense a form of charity. It is only the poor whose
> entitlements, although recognized by public policy, have not been effectively enforced.

Reich, Individual Rights and Social Welfare: The Emerging Local Issues, 74 Yale L.J. 1245, 1255 (1965).
See also Reich, The New Property, 73 Yale L.J. 733 (1964).

cates important rights. The constitutional challenge cannot be answered by an argument that public assistance benefits are "a 'privilege' and not a 'right.'" . . . Relevant constitutional restraints apply as much to the withdrawal of public assistance benefits as to disqualification for unemployment compensation, Sherbert v. Verner, 374 U.S. 398 (1963); or to denial of a tax exemption, Speiser v. Randall, 357 U.S. 513 (1958); or to discharge from public employment, Slochower v. Board of Higher Education, 350 U.S. 551 (1956).[80] The extent to which procedural due process must be afforded the recipient is influenced by the extent to which he may be "condemned to suffer grievous loss," Joint Anti-Fascist Refugee Committee v. McGrath, 341 U.S. 123, 168 (1951) (Frankfurter, J., concurring), and depends upon whether the recipient's interest in avoiding that loss outweighs the governmental interest in summary adjudication. Accordingly, as we said in Cafeteria & Restaurant Workers Union v. McElroy, 367 U.S. 886, 895 (1961), "consideration of what procedures due process may require under any given set of circumstances must begin with a determination of the precise nature of the government function involved as well as of the private interest that has been affected by governmental action." . . .

[The remainder of the Court's opinion, which follows, deals with the question of what procedures are constitutionally required. While you will want to read it, we postpone discussion of it until the next section of this chapter dealing with the determination of what due process safeguards are required in various situations once it has been determined that the interests of the person seeking them are constitutionally protected.]

It is true, of course, that some governmental benefits may be administratively terminated without affording the recipient a pre-termination evidentiary hearing.[81] But we agree with the District Court that when welfare is discontinued, only a pre-termination evidentiary hearing provides the recipient with procedural due process. Cf. Sniadach v. Family Finance Corp., 395 U.S. 337 (1969). For qualified recipients, welfare provides the means to obtain essential food, clothing, housing, and medical care. . . . Thus the crucial factor in this context — a factor not present in the case of the blacklisted government contractor, the discharged government employee, the taxpayer denied a tax exemption, or virtually anyone else whose governmental entitlements are ended — is that termination of aid pending resolution of a controversy over eligibility may deprive an eligible recipient of the very means by which to live while he waits. Since he lacks independent resources, his situation becomes immediately desperate. His need to concentrate upon finding the means for daily subsistence, in turn, adversely affects his ability to seek redress from the welfare bureaucracy.

Moreover, important governmental interests are promoted by affording recipients a pre-termination evidentiary hearing. From its founding the Nation's basic commitment has been to foster the dignity and well-being of all persons within its borders. We have come to recognize that forces not within the control of the poor contribute to their poverty. This perception, against the background of our traditions, has significantly influ-

80. See also Goldsmith v. United States Board of Tax Appeals, 270 U.S. 117 (1926) (right of a certified public accountant to practice before the Board of Tax Appeals); Hornsby v. Allen, 326 F.2d 605 (5th Cir. 1964) (right to obtain a retail liquor store license); Dixon v. Alabama State Board of Education, 294 F.2d 150 (C.A. 5th Cir.), cert. denied, 368 U.S. 930 (1961) (right to attend a public college).

81. One court of appeals has stated: "In a wide variety of situations, it has long been recognized that where harm to the public is threatened, and the private interest infringed is reasonably deemed to be of less importance, an official body can take summary action pending a later hearing." R. A. Holman & Co. v. SEC, 299 F.2d 127, 131, cert. denied, 370 U.S. 911 (1962) (suspension of exemption from stock registration requirement). See also, for example, Ewing v. Mytinger & Casselberry, Inc., 339 U.S. 594 (1950) (seizure of mislabeled vitamin product); North American Cold Storage Co. v. Chicago, 211 U.S. 306 (1908) (seizure of food not fit for human use); Yakus v. United States, 321 U.S. 414 (1944) (adoption of wartime price regulations). . . .

enced the development of the contemporary public assistance system. Welfare, by meeting the basic demands of subsistence, can help bring within the reach of the poor the same opportunities that are available to others to participate meaningfully in the life of the community. At the same time, welfare guards against the societal malaise that may flow from a widespread sense of unjustified frustration and insecurity. Public assistance, then, is not mere charity, but a means to "promote the general Welfare, and secure the Blessings of Liberty to ourselves and our Posterity." The same governmental interests that counsel the provision of welfare, counsel as well its uninterrupted provision to those eligible to receive it; pre-termination evidentiary hearings are indispensable to that end.

Appellant does not challenge the force of these considerations but argues that they are outweighed by countervailing governmental interests in conserving fiscal and administrative resources. These interests, the argument goes, justify the delay of an evidentiary hearing until after discontinuance of the grants. Summary adjudication protects the public fisc by stopping payments promptly upon discovery of reason to believe that a recipient is no longer eligible. Since most terminations are accepted without challenge, summary adjudication also conserves both the fiscal and administrative time and energy by reducing the number of evidentiary hearings actually held.

We agree with the District Court, however, that these governmental interests are not overriding in the welfare context. The requirements of a prior hearing doubtless involve some greater expense, and the benefits paid to ineligible recipients pending decision at the hearing probably cannot be recouped, since these recipients are likely to be judgment-proof. But the State is not without weapons to minimize these increased costs. Much of the drain on fiscal and administrative resources can be reduced by developing procedures for prompt pre-termination hearings and by skillful use of personnel and facilities. Indeed, the very provision for a post-termination evidentiary hearing in New York's Home Relief program is itself cogent evidence that the State recognizes the primacy of the public interest in correct eligibility determinations and therefore in the provision of procedural safeguards. Thus, the interest of the eligible recipient in uninterrupted receipt of public assistance, coupled with the State's interest that his payments not be erroneously terminated, clearly outweighs the State's competing concern to prevent any increase in its fiscal and administrative burdens. . . .

II

We also agree with the District Court, however, that the pre-termination hearing need not take the form of a judicial or quasi-judicial trial. We bear in mind that the statutory "fair hearing" will provide the recipient with a full administrative review. Accordingly, the pre-termination hearing has one function only: to produce an initial determination of the validity of the welfare department's grounds for discontinuance of payments in order to protect a recipient against an erroneous termination of his benefits. . . . Thus, a complete record and a comprehensive opinion, which would serve primarily to facilitate judicial review and to guide future decisions, need not be provided at the pre-termination stage. We recognize, too, that both welfare authorities and recipients have an interest in relatively speedy resolution of questions of eligibility, that they are used to dealing with one another informally, and that some welfare departments have very burdensome caseloads. These considerations justify the limitation of the pre-termination hearing to minimum procedural safeguards, adapted to the particular characteristics of welfare recipients, and to the limited nature of the controversies to be resolved. We wish to add that we, no less than the dissenters, recognize the importance of not imposing upon the States or the Federal Government in this developing field of law any procedural requirements beyond those demanded by rudimentary due process. . . . In the present context these principles require that a recipient have timely and adequate notice detailing the reasons for a proposed termination, and an effective opportunity to defend by confronting any adverse witnesses and by presenting his own arguments and evidence orally. These rights are important in cases such as those before us, where recipients have challenged proposed terminations as resting on incorrect or misleading factual premises or on misapplication of rules or policies to the facts of particular cases.[82]

[The Court found New York procedures for notifying recipients of proposed terminations to be adequate.]

The city's procedures presently do not permit recipients to appear personally with or without counsel before the official who finally determines continued eligibility. Thus a recipient is not permitted to present evidence to that official orally, or to confront or cross-examine adverse witnesses. These omissions are fatal to the constitutional adequacy of the procedures.

The opportunity to be heard must be tailored to the capacities and circumstances of those who are to be heard. It is not enough that a welfare recipient may present his position to the decision maker in writing or secondhand through his caseworker. Written submissions are an unrealistic option for most recipients, who lack the educational attainment necessary to write effectively and who cannot obtain professional assistance. . . .

In almost every setting where important decisions turn on questions of fact, due process requires an opportunity to confront and cross-examine adverse witnesses [citing Greene v. McElroy]. Welfare recipients must therefore be given an opportunity to confront and cross-examine the witnesses relied on by the department.

. . . We do not say that counsel must be provided at the pre-termination hearing, but only that the recipient must be allowed to retain an attorney if he so desires. Counsel can help delineate the issues, present the factual contentions in an orderly manner, conduct cross-examination, and generally safeguard the interests of the recipient. We do not anticipate that this assistance will unduly prolong or otherwise encumber the hearing. . . .

Finally, the decisionmaker's conclusion as to a recipient's eligibility must rest solely on the legal rules and evidence adduced at the hearing. Ohio Bell Tel. Co. v. PUC, 301 U.S. 292 (1937); United States v. Abilene & S.R. Co., 265 U.S. 274, 288-289 (1924). To demonstrate compliance with this elementary requirement, the decisionmaker should state the reasons for his determination and indicate the evidence he relied on, . . . though his statement need not amount to a full opinion or even formal findings of fact and conclusions of law. And, of course, an impartial decisionmaker is essential. . . . We agree with the District Court that prior involvement in some aspects of a case will not necessarily bar a welfare official from acting as a decisionmaker. He should not, however, have participated in making the determination under review.

Affirmed.

Mr. Justice BLACK, dissenting.

In the last half century the United States, along with many, perhaps most, other nations of the world, has moved far toward becoming a welfare state, that is, a nation that for one reason or another taxes its most affluent people to help support, feed, clothe, and shelter its less fortunate citizens. . . .

---

82. This case presents no question requiring our determination whether due process requires only an opportunity for written submission, or an opportunity both for written submission and oral argument, where there are no factual issues in dispute or where the application of the rule of law is not intertwined with factual issues. . . .

The more than a million names on the relief rolls in New York, and the more than nine million names on the rolls of all the 50 States were not put there at random. The names are there because state welfare officials believed that those people were eligible for assistance. Probably in the officials' haste to make out the lists many names were put there erroneously in order to alleviate immediate suffering, and undoubtedly some people are drawing relief who are not entitled under the law to do so. Doubtless some draw relief checks from time to time who know they are not eligible, either because they are not actually in need or for some other reason. Many of those who thus draw underserved gratuities are without sufficient property to enable the government to collect back from them any money they wrongfully receive. But the Court today holds that it would violate the Due Process Clause of the Fourteenth Amendment to stop paying those people weekly or monthly allowances unless the government first affords them a full "evidentiary hearing" even though welfare officials are persuaded that the recipients are not rightfully entitled to receive a penny under the law. In other words, although some recipients might be on the lists for payment wholly because of deliberate fraud on their part, the Court holds that the government is helpless and must continue, until after an evidentiary hearing, to pay money that it does not owe, never has owed, and never could owe. I do not believe there is any provision in our Constitution that should thus paralyze the government's efforts to protect itself against making payments to people who are not entitled to them. . . .

I would have little, if any, objection to the majority's decision in this case if it were written as the report of the House Committee on Education and Labor, but as an opinion ostensibly resting on the language of the Constitution I find it woefully deficient. Once the verbiage is pared away it is obvious that this Court today adopts the views of the District Court "that to cut off a welfare recipient in the face of . . . 'brutal need' without a prior hearing of some sort is unconscionable," and therefore, says the Court, unconstitutional. . . . Today's balancing act requires a "pre-termination evidentiary hearing" yet there is nothing that indicates what tomorrow's balance will be. Although the majority attempts to bolster its decision with limited quotations from prior cases, it is obvious that today's result does not depend on the language of the Constitution itself or the principles of other decisions, but solely on the collective judgment of the majority as to what would be a fair and humane procedure in this case.

. . . Had the drafters of the Due Process Clause meant to leave judges such ambulatory power to declare laws unconstitutional, the chief value of a written constitution, as the Founders saw it, would have been lost. . . .

The Court apparently feels that this decision will benefit the poor and needy. In my judgment the eventual result will be just the opposite. . . . In the next case the welfare recipients are bound to argue that cutting off benefits before judicial review of the agency's decision is also a denial of due process. Since, by hypothesis, termination of aid at that point may still "deprive an *eligible* recipient of the very means by which to live while he waits," . . . I would be surprised if the weighing process did not compel the conclusion that termination without full judicial review would be unconscionable. [I]t is difficult to believe that the same reasoning process would not require the appointment of counsel, for otherwise the right to counsel is a meaningless one since these people are too poor to hire their own advocates. Cf. Gideon v. Wainwright, 372 U.S. 335, 344 (1963). Thus the end result of today's decision may well be that the government, once it decides to give welfare benefits, cannot reverse that decision until the recipient has had the benefits of full administrative and judicial review, including, of course, the opportunity to present his case to this Court. Since this process will usually entail a delay of several years, the inevitable result of such a constitutionally imposed burden will be that the government will not put a claimant on the rolls initially until it has made an exhaustive investigation to determine his eligibility. While this Court will perhaps have insured that no needy person will be taken off the rolls without a full "due process" proceeding, it will also have insured that many will never get on the rolls, or at least that they will remain destitute during the lengthy proceedings followed to determine initial eligibility.

For the foregoing reasons I dissent from the Court's holding. The operation of a welfare state is a new experiment for our Nation. For this reason, among others, I feel that new experiments in carrying out a welfare program should not be frozen into our constitutional structure. They should be left, as are other legislative determinations, to the Congress and the legislatures that the people elect to make our laws.

Notes and Questions

1. Note that the Court's opinion first addresses, as a threshold issue, whether due process applies at all to welfare benefit termination. It then considers what process is due: whether a predetermination hearing must be afforded, whether cross-examination is required, and so on. This two-step approach to due process protection — which should be contrasted with that taken in *Cafeteria Workers* — has been followed ever since.

2. On what basis does the Court decide that plaintiffs' interests in continued receipt of assistance payments are entitled to due process protection? Is it plaintiffs' "brutal need" that triggers constitutional safeguards? Or is it the fact that plaintiffs are entitled by statute to receive benefits if they meet "statutory criteria" of eligibility? Is it a question of balancing the interests of the government and the recipient? Does the precedent cited by Justice Brennan support his conclusions? Given that the state conceded the applicability of due process, did the Court even need to decide this question?

3. What is the constitutional relevance of the fact that there is a statutory entitlement to benefits? The statutory entitlement rationale was vigorously asserted by Charles Reich in his celebrated article, The New Property, 73 Yale L.J. 733 (1964), cited supra in note 79 (footnote 8 in the original) to the Court's opinion. Reich's basic argument is that in the modern society much wealth consists of advantageous opportunities conferred by government. Reich further argues that where statutes provide that government benefits, such as assistance payments, shall be afforded to individuals meeting certain criteria of entitlement, those individuals should be recognized as having a property right in such benefits, whose deprivation should be protected by procedural safeguards similar to those utilized to protect "old" property, such as land, from governmental deprivation. What difficulties might there be in extending procedural safeguards in this fashion? Should substantive as well as procedural constitutional protection be extended to the "new property"? For example, should congressional abolition of certain welfare benefits be held an unconstitutional "taking" of property?

Board of Regents of State College v. Roth

408 U.S. 564 (1972)

Mr. Justice STEWART delivered the opinion of the Court.

[David Roth was hired for a one-year term as assistant professor at the Wisconsin State University, Oshkosh, from September 1968 through June 1969. At the end of his term he was not rehired; no reason was given by the university for the failure to rehire him. Under

Wisconsin statutory law, a state university teacher acquires tenure only after four consecutive years of employment; the decision whether to rehire a one-year appointee is committed to the unfettered discretion of university officials. Roth brought suit against relevant university officials in federal district court under the 1871 Civil Rights Act, 42 U.S.C. §1983, contending that the failure to rehire him violated his fourteenth amendment rights. First, Roth asserted that the failure to rehire was constitutional retribution for his exercise of his free speech rights in issuing statements critical of the university administration. Second, he contended that in any event the university's failure to give him reasons or opportunity for hearing on the rehiring decision violated procedural due process. The district court denied plaintiff's summary judgment on the free speech claim, finding disputed factual issues regarding the university's reasons for not rehiring Roth. However, the district court granted summary judgment for Roth on the procedural due process issue. The court of appeals affirmed that judgment, and the Supreme Court granted certiorari. Since there had been no final resolution in the district court on the free speech claim, it was not subject to appeal and therefore was not before the Supreme Court.]

I

The requirements of procedural due process apply only to the deprivation of interests encompassed by the Fourteenth Amendment's protection of liberty and property. When protected interests are implicated, the right to some kind of prior hearing is paramount. But the range of interests protected by procedural due process is not infinite.

The District Court decided that procedural due process guarantees apply in this case by assessing and balancing the weights of the particular interests involved. It concluded that the respondent's interest in re-employment . . . outweighed the University's interest in denying him re-employment summarily. . . . Undeniably, the respondent's re-employment prospects were of major concern to him — concern that we surely cannot say was insignificant. And a weighing process has long been a part of any determination of the *form* of hearing required in particular situations by procedural due process. But, to determine whether due process requirements apply in the first place, we must look not to the "weight" but to the nature of the interest at stake. . . . We must look to see if the interest is within the Fourteenth Amendment's protection of liberty and property.

"Liberty" and "property" are broad and majestic terms. They are among the "[g]reat [constitutional] concepts . . . purposely left to gather meaning from experience. [T]hey relate to the whole domain of social and economic fact, and the statesmen who founded this Nation knew too well that only a stagnant society remains unchanged." National Ins. Co. v. Tidewater Co., 337 U.S. 582, 646 (Frankfurter, J., dissenting). For that reason, the Court has fully and finally rejected the wooden distinction between "rights" and "privileges" that once seemed to govern the applicability of procedural due process rights.[83] The Court has also made clear that the property interests protected by procedural due process extend well beyond actual ownership of real estate, chattels, or money. By the same token, the Court has required due process protection for deprivations of liberty beyond the sort of formal constraints imposed by the criminal process.

---

83. In a leading case decided many years ago, the Court of Appeals for the District of Columbia Circuit held that public employment in general was a "privilege," not a "right," and that procedural due process guarantees therefore were inapplicable. Bailey v. Richardson, 86 U.S. App. D.C. 248, 182 F.2d 46, *aff'd by an equally divided Court*, 341 U.S. 918. The basis of this holding has been thoroughly undermined in the ensuing years. . . .

Yet, while the Court has eschewed rigid or formalistic limitations on the protection of procedural due process, it has at the same time observed certain boundaries. For the words "liberty" and "property" in the Due Process Clause of the Fourteenth Amendment must be given some meaning.

II

"While this Court has not attempted to define with exactness the liberty . . . guaranteed [by the fourteenth amendment], the term has received much consideration and some of the included things have been definitely stated. Without doubt, it denotes not merely freedom from bodily restraint but also the right of the individual to contract, to engage in any of the common occupations of life, to acquire useful knowledge, to marry, establish a home and bring up children, to worship God according to the dictates of his own conscience, and generally to enjoy those privileges long recognized . . . as essential to the orderly pursuit of happiness by free men." Meyer v. Nebraska, 262 U.S. 390, 399. In a Constitution for a free people, there can be no doubt that the meaning of "liberty" must be broad indeed. . . .

There might be cases in which a state refused to re-employ a person under such circumstances that interests in liberty would be implicated. But this is not such a case.

The State, in declining to rehire the respondent, did not make any charge against him that might seriously damage his standing and associations in his community. It did not base the nonrenewal of his contract on a charge, for example, that he had been guilty of dishonesty, or immorality. Had it done so, this would be a different case. For "[w]here a person's good name, reputation, honor, or integrity is at stake because of what the government is doing to him, notice and an opportunity to be heard are essential." Wisconsin v. Constantineau, 400 U.S. 433, 437. . . . See Cafeteria Workers v. McElroy, 367 U.S. 886, 898. In such a case, due process would accord an opportunity to refute the charge before University officials. In the present case, however, there is no suggestion whatever that the respondent's "good name, reputation, honor, or integrity" is at stake.

Similarly, there is no suggestion that the State, in declining to reemploy the respondent, imposed on him a stigma or other disability that foreclosed his freedom to take advantage of other employment opportunities. . . .[84]

To be sure, the respondent has alleged that the nonrenewal of his contract was based on his exercise of his right to freedom of speech. But this allegation is not now before us. . . .[85]

---

84. The District Court made an *assumption* "that non-retention by one university or college creates concrete and practical difficulties for a professor in his subsequent academic career." 310 F. Supp., at 979. And the Court of Appeals based its affirmance of the summary judgment largely on the premise that "the substantial adverse effect non-retention is likely to have upon the career interests of an individual professor" amounts to a limitation on future employment opportunities sufficient to invoke procedural due process guarantees. 446 F.2d, at 809. But even assuming, arguendo, that such a "substantial adverse effect" under these circumstances would constitute a state-imposed restriction on liberty, the record contains no support for these assumptions. . . .

85. . . . The Court of Appeals, nonetheless, argued that opportunity for a hearing and a statement of reasons were required here "as a *prophylactic* against non-retention decisions improperly motivated by exercise of protected rights." 446 F.2d, at 810 (emphasis supplied). . . . When a State would directly impinge upon interests in free speech or free press, this Court has on occasion held that opportunity for a fair adversary hearing must precede the action, whether or not the speech or press interest is clearly protected under substantive First Amendment standards. Thus, we have required fair notice and opportunity for an adversary hearing before an injunction is issued against the holding of rallies and public meetings. Carroll v. Princess Anne, 393 U.S. 175. . . . In the respondent's case, however, the State has not directly impinged upon interests in free speech or free press in any way comparable to a seizure of books or an injunction against meetings. Whatever may be a teacher's rights of free speech, the interest in holding a teaching job at a state university, simpliciter, is not itself a free speech interest.

Hence, on the record before us, all that clearly appears is that the respondent was not rehired for one year at one university. It stretches the concept too far to suggest that a person is deprived of "liberty" when he simply is not rehired in one job but remains as free as before to seek another. Cafeteria Workers v. McElroy, supra. . . .

III

The Fourteenth Amendment's procedural protection of property is a safeguard of the security of interests that a person has already acquired in specific benefits. These interests — property interests — may take many forms.

Thus, the Court has held that a person receiving welfare benefits under statutory and administrative standards defining eligibility for them has an interest in continued receipt of those benefits that is safeguarded by procedural due process. Goldberg v. Kelly, 397 U.S. 254. . . .

. . . To have a property interest in a benefit, a person clearly must have more than an abstract need or desire for it. He must have more than a unilateral expectation of it. He must, instead, have a legitimate claim of entitlement to it. It is a purpose of the ancient institution of property to protect those claims upon which people rely in their daily lives, reliance that must not be arbitrarily undermined. It is a purpose of the constitutional right to a hearing to provide an opportunity for a person to vindicate those claims.

Property interests, of course, are not created by the Constitution. Rather, they are created and their dimensions are defined by existing rules or understandings that stem from an independent source such as state law — rules or understandings that secure certain benefits and that support claims of entitlement to those benefits. Thus, the welfare recipients in Goldberg v. Kelly, supra, had a claim of entitlement to welfare payments that was grounded in the statute defining eligibility for them. The recipients had not yet shown that they were, in fact, within the statutory terms of eligibility. But we held that they had a right to a hearing at which they might attempt to do so.

Just as the welfare recipients' "property" interest in welfare payments was created and defined by statutory terms, so the respondent's "property" interest in employment at Wisconsin State University-Oshkosh was created and defined by the terms of his appointment. Those terms secured his interest in employment up to June 30, 1969. But the important fact in this case is that they specifically provided that the respondent's employment was to terminate on June 30. They did not provide for contract renewal absent "sufficient cause." Indeed, they made no provision for renewal whatsoever.

Thus, the terms of the respondent's appointment secured absolutely no interest in re-employment for the next year. They supported absolutely no possible claim of entitlement to re-employment. Nor, significantly, was there any state statute or University rule of policy that secured his interest in re-employment or that created any legitimate claim to it.[86] In these circumstances, the respondent surely had an abstract concern in being rehired, but he did not have a property interest sufficient to require the University authorities to give him a hearing when they declined to renew his contract of employment.

___

86. To be sure, the respondent does suggest that most teachers hired on a year-to-year basis by Wisconsin State University-Oshkosh are, in fact, rehired. But the District Court has not found that there is anything approaching a "common law" of re-employment, . . . so strong as to require University officials to give the respondent a statement of reasons and a hearing on their decision not to rehire him.

IV

. . . We must conclude that the summary judgment for the respondent should not have been granted, since the respondent has not shown that he was deprived of liberty or property protected by the Fourteenth Amendment. . . .

Mr. Justice MARSHALL, dissenting.

. . . In my view, every citizen who applies for a government job is entitled to it unless the government can establish some reason for denying the employment. This is the "property" right that I believe is protected by the Fourteenth Amendment and that cannot be denied "without due process of law." And it is also liberty — liberty to work — which is the "very essence of the personal freedom and opportunity" secured by the Fourteenth Amendment. . . .

Employment is one of the greatest, if not the greatest, benefits that governments offer in modern-day life. When something as valuable as the opportunity to work is at stake, the government may not reward some citizens and not others without demonstrating that its actions are fair and equitable. And it is procedural due process that is our fundamental guarantee of fairness, our protection against arbitrary, capricious, and unreasonable government action. . . .

[I]t is not burdensome to give reasons when reasons exist. . . .

[P]roper procedures will surely eliminate some of the arbitrariness that results, not from malice, but from innocent error. . . . When the government knows it may have to justify its decisions with sound reasons, its conduct is likely to be more cautious, careful, and correct. . . .

Perry v. Sindermann
408 U.S. 593 (1972)

[A companion case to *Roth*, Perry v. Sindermann involved a teacher who had been employed in the Texas state college system for ten years, most recently at Odessa Junior College, under a series of one-year contracts. The college had no formal tenure system. After his embroilment in public controversy with the college's board of regents, the board voted not to offer him a contract for the following year. No hearing or statement of reasons was provided. Sindermann brought suit in federal district court under 42 U.S.C. §1983, asserting that the board's action was in retaliation for his exercise of first amendment rights to free speech. The district court granted summary judgment for the board; the court of appeals reversed and remanded for a trial on the merits. The Supreme Court affirmed in an opinion by Mr. Justice Stewart.

First, the Court held that if the board's failure to renew Sindermann's contract was in retaliation for Sindermann's exercise of first amendment rights, that action would be an unlawful infringement of constitutionally protected "liberty" regardless of the fact that Sindermann lacked tenure or a contractual right to renewal. The opinion asserted that "even though a person has no 'right' to a valuable government benefit and even though the government may deny him the benefit for any number of reasons, there are some reasons upon which the government may not rely. It may not deny a benefit to a person on a basis that infringes his constitutionally protected interests — especially, his interest in freedom of speech." Accordingly, Sindermann was entitled to an opportunity at a hearing on remand before the district court to prove his allegations that the failure to renew was based on his exercise of free speech.

Second, the Court considered Sindermann's claim that, despite the absence of a formal tenure system at the college, there was an informal system of tenure that gave him a "property" interest in continued employment, independent of his free speech claim, protected by due process, requiring that he be given an administrative hearing before a board decision not to renew his contract.]

. . . He claimed that he and others legitimately relied upon an unusual provision that had been in the college's official Faculty Guide for many years:

> *Teacher Tenure:* Odessa College has no tenure system. The Administration of the College wishes the faculty member to feel that he has permanent tenure as long as his teaching services are satisfactory and as long as he displays a cooperative attitude toward his co-workers and his superiors, and as long as he is happy in his work.

Moreover, the respondent claimed legitimate reliance upon guidelines promulgated by the Coordinating Board of the Texas College and University System that provided that a person, like himself, who had been employed as a teacher in the state college and university system for seven years or more has some form of job tenure. . . .

We have made clear in *Roth* . . . that "property" interests subject to procedural due process protection are not limited by a few rigid, technical forms. Rather, "property" denotes a broad range of interests that are secured by "existing rules or understandings." . . . A person's interest in a benefit is a "property" interest for due process purposes if there are such rules or mutually explicit understandings that support his claim of entitlement to the benefit and that he may invoke at a hearing.

[T]here may be an unwritten "common law" in a particular university that certain employees shall have the equivalent of tenure. . . .[87]

In this case, the respondent has alleged the existence of rules and understandings, promulgated and fostered by state officials, that may justify his legitimate claim of entitlement to continued employment absent "sufficient cause." We disagree with the Court of Appeals insofar as it held that a mere subjective "expectancy" is protected by procedural due process, but we agree that the respondent must be given an opportunity to prove the legitimacy of his claim of such entitlement in light of "the policies and practices of the institution." . . . Proof of such property interest would not, of course, entitle him to reinstatement. But such proof would obligate college officials to grant a hearing at his request, where he could be informed of the grounds for his nonretention and challenge their sufficiency.

Therefore, while we do not wholly agree with the opinion of the Court of Appeals, its judgment remanding this case to the District Court is affirmed.

---

87. We do not now hold that the respondent has any such legitimate claim of entitlement to job tenure. For "[p]roperty interests . . . are not created by the Constitution. Rather, they are created and their dimensions are defined by existing rules or understandings that stem from an independent source such as state law. . . ." Board of Regents v. Roth, supra. . . . If it is the law of Texas that a teacher in the respondent's position has no contractual or other claim to job tenure, the respondent's claim would be defeated.

Notes and Questions: *Roth* and *Sindermann*

1. Note that the Court in these opinions restates in quite emphatic terms the two-stage approach used in *Goldberg*. The threshold test of whether an interest is protected by liberty or property is a "category" rather than a "balancing test": An interest must be of a certain type (rather than weight) to qualify for due process protection. The second step of determining what process is due to protected interests is defined in balancing terms. What justifications does the Court provide for this structure? Is it consistent with the approach taken in *Cafeteria Workers*?

2. Note also that the Court, in developing the first-stage threshold test, distinguishes two categories of interests protected by due process: "liberty" interests and "property" interests. What is the difference between the two categories? What justification does the Court give for this structure?

3. How is "liberty" defined by the Court? By Justice Marshall? Does a person have a protected "liberty" interest only to the extent that the U.S. Constitution grants a substantive entitlement to that person (such as the right not to be discharged from government employment for exercising free speech)? What purpose would be served by defining "liberty" more broadly for procedural due process purposes, to encompass interests that do not enjoy substantive constitutional protection? In such cases, wouldn't the government be free to decide against a person regardless of what facts were developed at a hearing?

Does or should the Constitution impose substantive limits on the state's refusal to renew Roth's employment when such refusal would hurt his reputation and career? If not, should his interest in reemployment nonetheless be recognized as "liberty" protected by procedural due process? What purpose would a hearing serve?

4. How is "property" defined by the Court? By Justice Marshall? When state governmental action is involved, what are the respective roles of the federal and state courts in determining whether a plaintiff's interest constitutes a "property" entitlement protected by federal due process? Suppose the Texas courts had ruled that practices and understandings invoked by Sindermann as creating reasonable expectations of tenure did not, as a matter of Texas law, impose any restraints whatsoever on the board's discretion whether or not to renew a teaching contract. Would a federal court still be free to find that the practices and understandings created "property" for purposes of federal due process and that Sindermann should accordingly be given notice and opportunity for hearing? If so, would the board remain entirely free to refuse renewal of Sindermann's contract, even if the facts developed at a hearing showed him to be an exemplary scholar and teacher? What then would have been accomplished by requiring an administrative hearing?

5. How does one distinguish between "liberty" interests, which the Constitution requires states to respect, and "property" interests, which states are free to modify or abolish? Although decided in the context of a takings claim rather than a due process claim, Schneider v. California Dept. of Corrections, 151 F.3d 1194 (9th Cir. 1998), emphasizes that there are limits on states' authority to eliminate or redefine property rights so as to eliminate constitutional protections. The court upheld a claim by inmates that a California statute that provided that no interest would be paid on prisoner earnings deposited in inmate trust accounts (ITA) amounted to an unconstitutional taking of their property, concluding that entitlement to interest on principal is a core traditional property right that may not be taken by the state without payment of compensation. The court

rejected the state's reliance on *Roth* as establishing "plenary control over the definition and recognition of . . . property interests":

> The Roth Court's recognition of the unremarkable proposition that state law may affirmatively create constitutionally protected "new property" interests in no way implies that a State may, by statute or regulation, roll back or eliminate traditional old property rights. Rather there is we think a core notion of constitutionally protected property into which state regulations simply may not intrude without prompting Takings Clause scrutiny. The States' power vis-à-vis property thus operates as a one-way ratchet of sorts: States may, under certain circumstances, confer "new property" status on interests located outside the core of constitutionally protected property, but they may not encroach upon traditional old property interests found within the core.

6. Does a person have a procedurally protected "property" entitlement whenever, as a matter of state or federal statutory law, he has a legal remedy or cause of action against the government? For example, *Overton Park* holds that the environmental plaintiffs in that case had a legal right (1) to enjoin the secretary of transportation from locating a highway through a park when to do so would exceed his statutory authority and (2) to require that the secretary exercise his statutory discretion in a reasonable, nonarbitrary way. Does it follow that the plaintiffs have an entitlement with respect to highway locations that is "property" for due process purposes, and that the courts must therefore make an independent determination of the adequacy of the administrative procedures afforded to vindicate that entitlement? Can administrative regulations create "property" entitlements by virtue of *Arizona Grocery*?

Note: §1983 Due Process Litigation

The plaintiffs in *Roth* and *Sindermann* brought suit against the relevant state officials under the Civil Rights Act of 1871, now codified as 42 U.S.C. §1983. The act provides for damage awards and equitable redress against persons, typically government officials, who "under color of" state law, deprive any person of "any rights, privileges, or immunities secured by the Constitution and laws" of the United States. These "rights, privileges, and immunities," of course, include procedural rights protected by the fourteenth amendment's due process clause. Jurisdiction for §1983 actions in the federal courts is provided, without regard to amount in controversy, by 28 U.S.C. §1343(3). We discuss in greater detail in Chapter 8 the scope of §1983 and remedies under it (including doctrines of official immunity that limit the liability in damages of individual officials). We also discuss the analogous development by the federal courts of damage remedies against federal government officials for constitutional violations.

The expansion by the Supreme Court of federal due process protections has led to a rapid growth in §1983 actions seeking redress for asserted violations. Widespread invocation of §1983 by litigants in turn led to concern, particularly within the Supreme Court, that broad construction of §1983 and of the rights it protects would lead to significant intrusions by the federal judiciary on state government. For an empirical analysis of the growth of §1983 actions generally and a skeptical assessment of claims that they are overburdening the federal courts with cases that should enjoy low priority, see Eisenberg, Section 1983: Doctrinal Foundations and an Empirical Study, 67 Cornell L. Rev. 482 (1982). The exposure of state officials to damage awards for mistaken judgments about procedural rights makes decisional uncertainty in the applicability and content of due process safeguards particularly troubling.

See the discussion of §1983 actions in Chapter 8. These concerns are reflected in the subsequent development of the Court's due process jurisprudence, set forth below.

Arnett v. Kennedy

416 U.S. 134 (1974)

Mr. Justice REHNQUIST announced the judgment of the Court in an opinion in which The Chief Justice and Mr. Justice Stewart join.

[Wayne Kennedy, a federal civil service employee in the Office of Economic Opportunity (OEO), was discharged by his superior, Wendell Verduin, on charges that Kennedy had falsely and recklessly accused Verduin of attempted bribery in connection with Verduin's official duties. Kennedy was informed by Verduin of the charges and afforded an opportunity to respond to the charges orally and in writing, and to submit affidavits. Kennedy did not respond to the substance of the charges against him, but instead asserted that the proceedings were unlawful because he had a right to a pretermination trial-type hearing before an impartial hearing officer before he could be removed from his employment. The relevant provisions of the Lloyd-Lafollette Act, governing federal civil service employment, provide that "[a]n individual in the competitive service may be removed or suspended without pay only for such cause as will promote the efficiency of the service." Section 7501(b) establishes the administrative procedures by which an employee's rights under subsection (a) are to be determined, providing that an employee is entitled to notice of the action sought and the reasons therefor, including any charges preferred against him; a reasonable time for filing a written answer to the charges, with affidavits; and a written decision on the answer at the earliest practicable date. Section 7501(b) further provides that "Examination of witnesses, trial, or hearing is not required but may be provided in the discretion of the individual directing the removal or suspension without pay. . . ."]

. . . Here appellee did have a statutory expectancy that he not be removed other than for "such cause as will promote the efficiency of [the] service." But the very section of the statute which granted him that right, a right which had previously existed only by virtue of administrative regulation, expressly provided also for the procedure by which "cause" was to be determined, and expressly omitted the procedural guarantees which appellee insists are mandated by the Constitution. Only by bifurcating the very sentence of the Act of Congress which conferred upon appellee the right not to be removed save for cause could it be said that he had an expectancy of that substantive right without the procedural limitations which Congress attached to it. In the area of federal regulation of government employees, where in the absence of statutory limitation the government employer has had virtually uncontrolled latitude in decisions as to hiring and firing, Cafeteria Workers v. McElroy, 367 U.S. 886, 896-897 (1961), we do not believe that a statutory enactment such as the Lloyd-La Follette Act may be parsed as discretely as appellee urges. Congress was obviously intent on according a measure of statutory job security to governmental employees which they had not previously enjoyed, but was likewise intent on excluding more elaborate procedural requirements which it felt would make the operation of the new scheme unnecessarily burdensome in practice. Where the focus of legislation was thus strongly on the procedural mechanism for enforcing the substantive right which was simultaneously conferred, we decline to conclude that the substantive right may be viewed wholly apart from the procedure provided for its enforcement.

The employee's statutorily defined right is not a guarantee against removal without cause in the abstract, but such a guarantee as enforced by the procedures which Congress has designated for the determination of cause.

[W]here the grant of substantive right is inextricably intertwined with the limitations on the procedures which are to be employed in determining that right, a litigant in the position of appellee must take the bitter with the sweet. . . .

Appellee also contends in this Court that because of the nature of the charges on which his dismissal was based, he was in effect accused of dishonesty, and that therefore a hearing was required before he could be deprived of this element of his "liberty" protected by the Fifth Amendment against deprivation without due process. . . . But that liberty is not offended by dismissal from employment itself, but instead by dismissal based upon an unsupported charge which could wrongfully injure the reputation of an employee. Since the purpose of the hearing in such a case is to provide the person "an opportunity to clear his name," a hearing afforded by administrative appeal procedures after the actual dismissal is a sufficient compliance with the requirements of the Due Process Clause. . . .

Reversed and remanded.

Mr. Justice POWELL, with whom Mr. Justice BLACKMUN joins, concurring in part and concurring in the result in part.

Application of [*Roth* and *Sindermann*] to the instant case makes plain that appellee is entitled to invoke the constitutional guarantee of procedural due process. Appellee was a nonprobationary federal employee, and as such he could be discharged only for "cause." 5 U.S.C. §7501(a). The federal statute guaranteeing appellee continued employment absent "cause" for discharge conferred on him a legitimate claim of entitlement which constituted a "property" interest under the Fifth Amendment. Thus termination of his employment requires notice and a hearing.

The plurality opinion evidently reasons that the nature of appellee's interest in continued federal employment is necessarily defined and limited by the statutory procedures for discharge and that the constitutional guarantee of procedural due process accords to appellee no procedural protections against arbitrary or erroneous discharge other than those expressly provided in the statute. The plurality would thus conclude that the statute governing federal employment determines not only the nature of appellee's property interest, but also the extent of the procedural protections to which he may lay claim. It seems to me that this approach is incompatible with the principles laid down in *Roth* and *Sindermann*. Indeed, it would lead directly to the conclusion that whatever the nature of an individual's statutorily created property interest, deprivation of that interest could be accomplished without notice or a hearing at any time. This view misconceives the origin of the right to procedural due process. That right is conferred, not by legislative grace, but by constitutional guarantee. While the legislature may elect not to confer a property interest in federal employment, it may not constitutionally authorize the deprivation of such an interest, once conferred, without appropriate procedural safeguards. As our cases have consistently recognized, the adequacy of statutory procedures for deprivation of a statutorily created property interest must be analyzed in constitutional terms.

[Justice Powell agreed with the majority's result, however, because] on balance, I would conclude that a prior evidentiary hearing is not required and that the present statute and regulation comport with due process by providing a reasonable accommodation of the competing interests.

Mr. Justice White concluded that due process required an impartial pretermination decisionmaker and that this requirement had been violated in Kennedy's case.]

Mr. Justice Marshall, with whom Mr. Justice Douglas and Mr. Justice Brennan concur, dissenting.

[A] majority of the Court rejects Mr. Justice Rehnquist's argument that because appellee's entitlement arose from statute, it could be conditioned on a statutory limitation of procedural due process protections, an approach which would render such protection inapplicable to the deprivation of any statutory benefit — any "privilege" extended by Government — where a statute prescribed a termination procedure, no matter how arbitrary or unfair. It would amount to nothing less than a return, albeit in somewhat different verbal garb, to the thoroughly discredited distinction between rights and privileges which once seemed to govern the applicability of procedural due process. . . . [Justice Marshall found the government's interest in avoiding a pretermination hearing was far less substantial than Kennedy's interest in obtaining one. He concluded that the Constitution required a pretermination hearing.]

Questions

1. Justice Rehnquist's "bitter with the sweet" position with respect to "property" rights seems to follow quite logically from the logic of *Roth* and *Sindermann*. Nonetheless, a majority of the Justices in *Arnett* reject this position. Where is the logical flaw in Justice Rehnquist's argument? If it were accepted, would legislatures be free to redefine "old" property and liberty as well, and provide that one's right to own land or right to be free from arrest would be redefined as entitlements whose substance would be determined only through certain procedures specified by the legislature?

2. Consider the following variations on the statute involved in *Arnett*. Suppose Congress had passed a statute:

(a) Directing supervisory officials to dismiss government employees only for "cause" but providing that "nothing in this statute shall be deemed to create any legal entitlement or cause of action in any employee."

(b) Providing dismissal only for "cause" but stating that "the determination of what constitutes cause for discharge shall be determined solely in the discretion of the supervisory official and shall not be reviewed or examined in any court."

(c) Providing that employees may only be terminated for "cause" but that terms of employment shall only be for one year and that the decision whether to rehire for another year shall be solely in the discretion of the supervisory employees.

In which (if any) of these cases would the employee's interest in continued employment be protected by due process and require an independent judicial determination of the adequacy of the procedures afforded?

3. The basic premise of the Justices who reject Justice Rehnquist's "bitter with the sweet" argument seems to be that procedure and substance are different, and that while legislatures are free to define the substantive content of property entitlements, the due process clause gives the judiciary an independent and final say on the adequacy of the procedures for determining and vindicating those entitlements. But this is more in the nature of a conclusion or assertion than an argument. What considerations might justify

such a position? For a sample of attempts to provide such arguments, see Michelman, Formal and Associated Aims in Procedural Due Process, in Nomos: Due Process (Penncock & Chapmen eds. 1977); Stewart & Sunstein, Public Programs and Private Rights, 95 Harv. L. Rev. 1193, 1258-1263 (1982); Tribe, Structural Due Process, 10 Harv. C.R.-C.L.L. Rev. 269 (1975). For criticism, see Easterbrook, Substance and Due Process, 1982 Sup. Ct. Rev. 85. Can procedure be so neatly divorced from substance?

4. If a state creates entitlements to certain state-created benefits and state officials conclude that an individual does not qualify for such benefits, is a person denied those benefits entitled to federal court review, not only of the adequacy of the state's procedures in making the determination but also of whether the evidence adequately supported the state's determination to deny the benefits?

Subsequent Judicial Evolution of "Property" and "Liberty"

GOSS v. LOPEZ, 419 U.S. 565 (1975).   The Court held, 5-4, that a school district must provide high school students with a hearing before suspending them for less than ten days for disorderly behavior. State law grants a free education to all residents between 5 and 21 years old. State statutes also permit suspensions for up to ten days, but each school has rules specifying grounds for suspension; no school could suspend "without any ground whatsoever." Accordingly, the Court held, "Ohio may not withdraw" the right to an education "on ground of misconduct, absent fundamentally fair procedures to determine whether the misconduct has occurred." Because of the potentially prohibitive costs involved in imposing elaborate hearing requirements in school suspension cases, and the risk of hobbling suspension as a disciplinary part of the teaching process, due process requires only that the student have oral or written notice of the charge, an explanation of the evidence that the school had, and an opportunity to present his side of the story.

Justice Powell, dissenting, concluded that the Ohio statute, permitting brief suspensions without any hearing, effectively qualifies, and thereby eliminates, whatever "property" or "liberty" entitlement that state law would otherwise confer. Moreover, when "an immature student merits censure for his conduct, he is rendered a disservice if appropriate actions are not applied or if procedures for their application are so formalized as to invite a challenge to the teachers' authority — an invitation which rebellious or even merely spirited teenagers are likely to accept. . . . Maintaining order and reasonable decorum in school buildings and classrooms is a major educational problem. [T]he Court ignores the commonality of interest of the State and pupils in the public school system. Rather, it thinks in traditional judicial terms of an adversary situation." Finally, he asked, once the courts enter this "thicket," where is the stopping place? What about grades, promotions, subject matter requirements, athletics? Is "due process" required before a school can deprive a student of any, or all, of them?

BISHOP v. WOOD, 426 U.S. 341 (1976).   The Court, 5-4, held that the town of Marion, North Carolina, could discharge a policeman without giving him a pretermination hearing. The policeman was a "permanent employee." A city ordinance said that if such an employee "fails to perform work up to the standard of the classification" and continues to be negligent, inefficient, or unfit to perform his duties, he may be dismissed by the city manager, who must give him "written notice . . . and reasons for his discharge." The Court, after pointing out that a "property interest in employment can . . . be created by ordinance or by an implied contract," added that the "sufficiency of the claim of entitlement must be decided by state law." The U.S. district judge, who "sits in North Carolina and practiced law there for many years," concluded that, notwithstanding the ordinance requirements for notice and reasons and its other provisions, the policeman "held his position at the will and pleasure of the city." Under that interpretation of the state law, the "City's Manager's determination of the adequacy of the ground for discharge is not subject to judicial review; the employee is merely given certain procedural rights which the District Court found not to have been violated in this case. Under that view of the law, petitioner's discharge did not deprive him of a property interest protected by the Fourteenth Amendment." Justice Brennan, dissenting, said that there is "certainly a federal dimension to the definition of 'property' in the Federal Constitution. [T]he relevant inquiry is whether it was objectively reasonable for the employee to believe he could rely on continued employment."

PAUL v. DAVIS, 424 U.S. 693 (1976). The county police had circulated material that included the plaintiff's name and picture in a section called "active shoplifters." The court of appeals had held that their doing so without "due process," infringed a "liberty" interest of plaintiff in his reputation, relying on Wisconsin v. Constantineau, 400 U.S. 433 (1971) (posting notice in liquor stores identifying plaintiff as an habitual drunkard requires "due process" giving plaintiff opportunity to dispute the charge). The Supreme Court reversed, 5-3, in an opinion by Justice Rehnquist. It found *Constantineau* involved more than simply injury to reputation, for the posting of the "habitual drunkard" notice deprived the plaintiff of his preexisting right to buy alcohol. It said that in every past case where the Court had held the Constitution protects an interest in "reputation," an independent "right or status previously recognized by state law was distinctly altered or extinguished." There was always an injury to reputation *plus* an additional deprivation of status. The "interest in reputation is simply one of a number which the State may protect against injury by virtue of its tort law," but "any harm or injury to that interest, even where inflicted . . . by an officer of the State, does not result in the deprivation of any 'liberty' or 'property' recognized by state or federal law." The Court's opinion feared that an expansive definition of "liberty" and "property" would enable plaintiffs to transform a vast range of state law claims into federal constitutional claims, which the federal courts must hear by virtue of §1983.

CLEVELAND BOARD OF EDUCATION v. LOUDERMILL, 470 U.S. 532 (1985). The plaintiff, a security guard, was dismissed because he had lied on his initial job application. Under Ohio law, he was a "classified civil service employee" entitled to hold his job "during good behavior and efficient service" and was dismissable only for "misfeasance, malfeasance, or nonfeasance in office." The statute provided minimal procedural protections, which the state complied with. The Court considered the argument that the "property" was "conditioned" by the statute's procedures, and it squarely rejected that argument. With Chief Justice Rehnquist alone dissenting, the Court wrote that the *Arnett* plurality's "bitter with the sweet" theory "was specifically rejected by the other six Justices." The Court pointed to other cases in which it rejected that theory. It added that, "in light of these holdings, it is settled that the 'bitter with the sweet' approach misconceives the constitutional guarantee. If a clearer holding is needed, we provide it today. The point is straightforward: the Due Process Clause provides that certain substantive rights — life, liberty, and property — cannot be deprived except pursuant to constitutionally adequate procedures. The categories of substance and procedure are distinct. Were the rule otherwise, the Clause would be reduced to a mere tautology. 'Property' cannot be defined by the procedures provided for its deprivation any more than can life or liberty. The right to due process 'is conferred, not by legislative grace, but by constitutional guarantee.' While the legislature may elect not to confer a property interest in [public] employment, it may not constitutionally authorize the deprivation of such an interest, once conferred, without appropriate procedural safeguards. . . . In short, once it is determined that the Due Process Clause applies, 'the question remains what process is due.' . . . The answer to that question is not to be found in the Ohio statute."

MEACHUM v. FANO, 427 U.S. 215 (1976). Plaintiffs, Fano and others, prisoners in Massachusetts state prisons, were transferred from a medium-security prison to a maximum-security prison following a hearing on their responsibility for incidents of arson at the former institution. While they were permitted to testify at the hearings and submit supporting evidence, they were not permitted to confront and cross-examine adverse witnesses, including Meachum, the prison superintendent. The Court, per Justice White, stated: ". . . We reject at the outset the notion that *any* grievous loss visited upon a person by the State is sufficient to invoke the procedural protections of the Due Process Clause. [Citing *Roth*.] We there held that the determining factor is the nature of the interest involved rather than its weight. . . . The Due Process Clause by its own force forbids the State from convicting any person of crime and depriving him of his liberty without complying fully with the requirements of the Clause. But given a valid conviction, the criminal defendant has been constitutionally deprived of his liberty to the extent that the State may confine him to the rules of its prison system so long as the conditions of confinement do not otherwise violate the Constitution. . . . The conviction has sufficiently extinguished the defendant's liberty interest to empower the State to confine him in *any* of its prisons. . . . That life in one prison is much more disagreeable than in another does not in itself signify that a Fourteenth Amendment liberty interest is implicated when a prisoner is transferred to the institution with the more severe rules. . . . Wolff v. McDonnell, on which the Court of Appeals heavily relied, is not to the contrary. Under that case, the Due Process Clause entitles a state prisoner to certain procedural protections when he is deprived of good-time credits because of serious misconduct. But the liberty interest there identified did not originate in the Constitution, which 'itself does not guarantee good-time credit for satisfactory behavior while in prison.' 418 U.S., at 557. The State itself, not the Constitution, had 'not only provided a statutory right to good time but also specifies that it is to be forfeited only for serious misbehavior.' . . . Here, Massachusetts law conferred no right on the prisoner to remain in the prison to which he was initially assigned, defeasible only upon proof of specific acts of misconduct. Insofar as we are advised, transfers between Massachusetts prisons are not conditioned upon the occurrence of specified events. On the contrary, transfer in a wide variety of circumstances is vested in prison officials. . . . Whatever expectation the prisoner may have in remaining at a particular prison so long as he behaves himself, it is too ephemeral and insubstantial to trigger procedural due process protections as long as prison officials have discretion to transfer him for whatever reason or for no reason at all. . . . Holding that arrangements like this are within reach of the procedural protections of the Due Process Clause would place the Clause astride the day-to-day functioning of state prisons and involve the judiciary in issues and discretionary decisions that are not the business of federal judges. We decline to so interpret and apply the Due Process Clause. The federal courts do not sit to supervise state prisons, the administration of which is of acute interest to the States. . . ." Justice Stevens, joined by Justices Brennan and Marshall, dissented, stating that liberty interests are rooted in the Constitution, not created by state law, and that the prison transfer in this case was a sufficiently serious deprivation of the liberty interests that a prisoner retains even after conviction to warrant due process hearing safeguards.

VITEK v. JONES, 445 U.S. 480 (1980).   State prison officials transferred a prisoner from a prison to a mental hospital. The relevant statute permitted such a transfer if a doctor determined that the prisoner "suffers from a mental disease or defect" that "cannot be given proper treatment in prison." The Court held that this language gave the prisoner a constitutionally protected "entitlement," and that a trial-type hearing was required prior to ordering transfer. The Court also said that a transfer from a prison to a mental hospital was "qualitatively different" from a transfer among different prisons, as, for example, the mental hospital could require the prisoner to use behavior-modifying drugs. Thus, the transfer meant a significant additional loss of "liberty."

BOARD OF PARDONS v. ALLEN, 482 U.S. 369 (1987).   The Court considered a Montana parole statute that said the parole "board shall release on parole . . . any person confined . . . when in its opinion there is reasonable probability that the prisoner can be released without detriment to the prisoner or to the community." The statute added that a "parole shall be ordered only for the best interests of society. . . ." The Court, 6-3, held that this statute created a constitutionally protected "liberty" interest for the prisoner. It did so, first, because the statute uses the word "shall," and the word "creates a presumption that parole release will be granted." Second, the "substantive predicates in the statute — delegating significant discretion to the decisionmaker — do 'not deprive the prisoner of the liberty interest' the rest of the statute creates."

KENTUCKY DEPARTMENT OF CORRECTIONS v. THOMPSON, 490 U.S. 454 (1989).   The Court, 6-3, held that a prisoner did not have a protected "liberty" interest in receiving visits at the prison (from, say, relatives). Prison rules said: "Although administrative staff reserves the right to allow or disallow visits, it is the policy of the Kentucky State Reformatory to respect the right of inmates to have visits in the spirit of the Court decisions and the Consent Decree, while insuring the safety and security of the institution. . . . A visitor may be denied a visit at any time if . . . the visitor's presence in the institution would constitute a clear and probable danger to the safety and security of the institution or could interfere with the orderly operation of the institution [as evidenced by such circumstances as] a past record of disruptive conduct, . . . drugs, [refusal to submit to a search, and so forth]." Justice Blackmun, for the Court, concluded that while prisoners certainly retain constitutionally protected "liberty" interests following conviction, the right to receive visitors was not among them. Nor did Kentucky's prison rules create an entitlement to visits; they lacked the "mandatory" language required to trigger due process protection.

SANDIN v. CONNER, 515 U.S. 472 (1995).   Conner, a prisoner in a maximum security Hawaii prison, was found guilty of misconduct in obstructing an intrusive strip search of his person and sentenced to 30 days' solitary confinement after a disciplinary hearing. He was denied the opportunity to call prison staff as witnesses. A prison regulation provided that the disciplinary committee "shall" find guilt where a misconduct charge is supported by "substantial evidence." Relying on *Thompson*, the court of appeals found that the regulation created a liberty interest by creating an entitlement on the part of inmates not to be sanctioned without substantial proof of misconduct, and that the district court (which had granted summary judgment for the state) should proceed to determine whether the hearing afforded was adequate. The Court, in an opinion by Chief Justice Rehnquist, held (5-4) that Conner had no protected liberty interest. The Court held that claimed inmate entitlements based on regulations constraining the disciplinary discretion of prison officials should no longer be recognized as creating a constitutionally protected liberty interest. It acknowledged that administrative regulations might create due process–protected interests in civilians, citing *Ingraham*. But it stated that it is not "sensible" to construe prison regulations as creating such entitlements. First, such a practice would discourage states from codifying prison management procedures. Second, it invites the federal courts to involve themselves in the detailed "day-to-day management of prisons, often squandering judicial resources with little offsetting benefit to anyone." Third, the "mandatory" language test of *Thompson* had proved difficult to apply. Nor does the fact that the purpose of the action was to punish an inmate trigger due process protection: "Discipline by prison officials in response to a wide range of misconduct falls within the expected parameters of [an inmate's] sentence." There might be certain types of "atypical significant deprivation" that would infringe a convict's residual "liberty" interest, such as involuntary commitment to a mental hospital as in Vitek v. Jones, but Conner's deprivation was not of that sort. In dissent, Justice Ginsberg, joined by Justice Stevens, agreed that the existence of a constitutionally protected interest should not turn on the nature of the prison regulations in question, but found that Conner's deprivation was sufficiently severe to infringe his constitutional liberty. Justice Breyer, joined by Justice Souter, advocated a three-part test. Some deprivations, as in *Vitek*, are so severe that they infringe a liberty interest regardless of whether prison officials' authority to impose such deprivations is constrained by state law. At the other extreme, some deprivations are so minor that they would not implicate a liberty interest, even if applicable law constrains administrative discretion in imposing them. The intermediate category — which includes Conner's case — presents line-drawing problems that can appropriately be resolved by looking to applicable local law. If the law cabins the discretion of officials to impose such middle-range deprivations, the law is evidence that the deprivation is significant, and that judicial intervention through procedural safeguards would not unduly undermine administrative discretion. Because the Hawaii regulations did restrict officials' discretion in imposing 30 days' solitary confinement, Conner should therefore be held to have a protected liberty interest.

AMERICAN MANUFACTURERS v. SULLIVAN, 526 U.S. 40 (1999).   Under Pennsylvania workers' compensation law, an employer or its insurer must pay for "reasonable and necessary" medical benefits for work-related injuries. As a cost-control measure, the law was amended in 1993 to provide, on request by an insurer, for review of the reasonableness and necessity of medical treatments by a private "utilization review organization" (URO) in accordance with procedures and criteria established by the state. Claimants are not entitled to any opportunity to be heard before a URO, which must make its determination within 30 days. If the URO decides against payment, the claimant may appeal for a de novo determination before a workers' compensation judge. If the URO decides that payment is required, the insurer must pay the charges plus interest and the cost of the URO review. Plaintiff workers and organizations representing them challenged the absence of any hearing before a URO as a violation of due process.

The Court rejected plaintiffs' challenge on two grounds. First, it held that decisions by UROs on payments did not constitute state action subject to constitutional requirements of due process. The fact that UROs operated pursuant to state requirements and procedures in connection with a statutory workers' compensation scheme was insufficient to implicate constitutional requirements applicable to the state. Second, the Court stated that plaintiffs failed to establish that they had a constitutionally protected property right in payment within 30 days of medical expense claims, noting that state law "limits an employee's entitlement to 'reasonable' and 'necessary' medical treatment and requires that disputes over the reasonableness and necessity of particular treatment must be resolved *before* an employer's obligation to pay" (emphasis in original). While plaintiffs had established their "initial eligibility" for medical treatment because of a job-related injury, "they have yet to make good on their claim that the particular medical treatment they received was reasonable and necessary. Only then does the employee's interest parallel that of the beneficiary of welfare assistance in *Goldberg* and the recipient of disability benefits in *Mathews*."

The Court's first ruling is significant in light of the increasing trend towards privatizing the implementation of government functions. The second ruling, arguably dicta in light of the first ruling, has puzzled commentators and lower courts. Read literally, the Court's opinion seems to embrace a variant of the "bitter with the sweet" concept advanced by Justice Rehnquist in *Arnett*, that would seemingly allow states to eviscerate due process rights through statutes providing that a person does not have any entitlement to specified benefits until after a process established by the statute determines that she in fact has such an entitlement. Concurring opinions in *American Manufacturing*, however, indicated that at least three justices believe that claims for medical benefits like those of plaintiffs are entitled to due process protection, at least in certain circumstances. For contrasting interpretations of *American Manufacture*, see Vazquez, Sovereign Immunity, Due Process, and The Alden Trilogy, 109 Yale Law Journal 1927, 1968 (2000); Wright, Unconstitutional or Impossible: The Irreconcilable Gap Between Managed Care and Due Process in Medicaid and Medicare, 17 J. Contemp. Health L. & Poly. 135, 160-163 (2000). At least two courts have held that employee liability claims are a species of property protected by due process. See Koskela v. Willamette Industries, Inc., 15 P.3d 548 (Or. 2000); Morris v. New York City Employees' Retirement System, 129 F. Supp. 2d 599 (S.D.N.Y. 2001).

Notes and Questions

1. What do you think of *Goss*? What about decisions by a school (a) to suspend a star athlete (with a chance of winning a college scholarship) from participation in athletics; (b) to require graduating seniors to pass a literacy test, a requirement imposed only two weeks before graduation; (c) to refuse to promote a student; (d) to move a student to a lesser academic "track"? Do those decisions involve a constitutionally protected "property" or "liberty" interest? Any of these decisions may be far more important to the individual than, say, a short suspension. How does *Goss* suggest we should answer the "protected interest" question? If the matter is solely one of the extent to which the teacher or administrator applies standards, isn't the result odd? After all, any of these matters may, or may not, involve standards that limit discretion a lot or a little.

2. What do you think of Justice Brennan's dissent in *Bishop*? Could federal courts decide when an "at will" or a "probationary" employee has, in fact, through custom or practice, an "objectively reasonable" expectation of keeping his job? Suppose a state court holds that no tenure right exists under state law notwithstanding the employee's contrary (and perhaps reasonable) expectations?

3. In 1988, the state of Massachusetts hired John Smith as a probationary security guard. Six months later it made him a permanent guard, under a statute that permits his dismissal only "for cause." Subsequently, the state finds that it had the legal right, under state law, to hire Smith permanently only if it advertised the position according to certain "affirmative action" requirements. It also discovers that Smith lied in 1988 when he said on his job application that he had no previous felony convictions, for he had served time in prison for bank robbery. The state dismisses Smith. It gives him no hearing. It says that, since he was not lawfully hired, he did not acquire any constitutionally protected "property" in the first place. What result?

4. Can you find a consistent view of the meaning of "property"? See Stewart & Sunstein, Public Program and Private Rights, 95 Harv. L. Rev. 1193 (1982).

5. *Paul* says an injury to reputation alone does not implicate the Constitution. It creates a rule of "defamation plus" loss of some independent right. What would you say the "plus" consists of? Can you think of some examples? Does the "defamation plus" test make any sense? What would be the implications of holding that a state official's defamation of an individual infringed a constitutionally protected interest? What procedures would be appropriate for protecting such an interest?

6. Does *Sandin* solve the problems created by the Court's earlier prison discipline jurisprudence? How is the line to be drawn between infringements that are sufficiently serious to implicate a liberty interest and those that are not? Does Justice Breyer provide an appropriate solution to this problem?

Why shouldn't prison regulations limiting official discretion in punishment create a protected "property" interest on the behalf of inmates, even if the sanction is not significantly serious to trigger a "liberty" deprivation under *Sandin*? What reasons does Chief Justice Rehnquist give for rejecting such a position? Are they sound? Aren't his reasons equally applicable to other institutional contexts, including schools and public housing?

7. What factors — aside from the changing composition of the Court — explain the contraction in the definitions of "liberty" and "property" advanced by the Court in recent decisions? Is it a fear that imposing increased procedural requirements on agencies will interfere with the effective discharge of their basic missions? Review Justice Black's dissent in *Goldberg*. Certainly, the factor mentioned by Justice Rehnquist in *Paul* — the fear of "federalization" of state tort law via 42 U.S.C. §1983 — is significant. To what extent are those federalization concerns compounded by the fear that constitutional review by federal judges of state agency procedures will inevitably slide into review of their substantive policies as well? Should federal judges apply due process differently in cases challenging federal administrative procedures than in cases challenging state procedures?

Professor Davis explained the Court's post-*Goldberg* decisions as an attempted antidote to "overreaction" and excessive procedural zeal by the lower federal courts, citing decisions such as Muscare v. Quinn, 520 F.2d 1212 (7th Cir. 1975) (hearing required on suspension of fireman because his goatee violated departmental hair regulations); Greenhill v. Bailey, 519 F.2d 5 (8th Cir. 1975) (informal hearing required on suspension, because of poor academic performance, of medical student who ranked near bottom of class and had failed two courses); Fox v. Morton, 505 F.2d 254 (9th Cir. 1974) (evidentiary hearing on nonrenewal of work-assistance program for Native Americans because of insufficient funds). See K. Davis, Administrative Law of the Seventies 272-276 (1976).

8. Does the doctrinal evolution from *Goldberg* through the most recent cases show that *Roth*'s two-stage analysis and its property-liberty division of protected interests are unsound? Should the Court have adhered to the open-ended balancing test used in *Cafeteria Workers*? Are there any other alternatives? Evaluate the following suggestions by two critics of the Court's decisions:

> a. [I]s it plausible to treat freedom from arbitrary adjudicative procedures as a substantive element of one's liberty as well — a freedom whose abridgment government must sustain the burden of justifying, even as it must do when it seeks to subordinate other freedoms, such as those of speech and privacy? I believe that it is plausible to so regard the matter, and that the ideas of liberty and substantive due process may easily accommodate a view that government may not adjudicate the claims of individuals by unreliable means.
>
> Nor does the idea of a liberty-immunity from unwarranted procedural grossness lack . . . flexibility. . . . [T]he processing of a social security application will always require different procedural protections than will a criminal trial. It is perfectly familiar learning that when due process applies, its particular dimensions are nevertheless the function of many contextual considerations.

Van Alstyne, Cracks in "The New Property": Adjudicative Due Process in the Administrative State, 62 Cornell L. Rev. 445, 487-489 (1977). The idea that procedural rights exist as independent entitlements that need not be justified by the extent to which they protect other entitlements will be discussed below.

> b. The major alternative to *Meachum*'s entitlement view . . . may be called an impact view of due process. Unlike the *Meachum* view, impact analysis does not presume that any single variable is absolutely essential before due process becomes operative. Rather, it considers all of the adverse impacts or effects of a state disciplinary action on an inmate. The key principle animating the impact view is that if "grievous" harm would ensue from a disciplinary deprivation, then procedural protections under the Fourteenth Amendment are warranted. The operation of this principle requires a practical assessment of the desirability of procedural safeguards in each individual case. It differs from a narrow entitlement analysis in that it does not require the existence of an independently grounded legal rule under which a claim of right may be advanced.

Note, Two Views of a Prisoner's Right to Due Process: *Meachum v. Fano*, 12 Harv. C.R.-C.L.L. Rev. 405, 421 (1977).

Note that both these passages suggest that the Court, in effect, recognize all interests (or at least all interests passing a threshold level of "weight" or grievousness of harm) as protected against the state by the Due Process Clause. The question of what process is due for any particular interest would be resolved by a balancing test. Would the approach be preferable to *Roth*'s adoption of a threshold "entitlement"? Note, as developed in the materials that follow, that under the *Roth* approach the Court must in any event engage in a balancing test to determine what process is due if a constitutionally protected entitlement is found.

Compare Farina, Conceiving Due Process, 3 Yale J.L. & Feminism 189 (1991) (criticizing "liberal-legalist drive towards determinancy, predictability, and universality" and arguing for a highly contextualized approach addressed to disparities in power and relations of dependency).

9. Professor Van Alstyne summarizes the post-*Goldberg* trends in terms of the following Mick Jagger lyric:

> You Can't Always Get What You Want
> You Can't Always Get What You Want
> You Can't Always Get What You Want
>   But if you try sometime,
> . . . you just might find you get what you need![88]

Is this assessment accurate? Was *Goldberg* a sui generis case explicable solely in terms of the special situation of terminated welfare beneficiaries?

10. Do Supreme Court decisions such as *Bishop*, *Paul*, and *Meachum* mean that Bailey v. Richardson is still (or again) good law?[89]

Note on the Procedural Implications of Changes in Federal Welfare Law

Many federal welfare and assistance programs, such as the AFDC program at issue in *Goldberg*, are administered by the states. Until recently, federal statutes creating these programs contained detailed provisions regarding who is eligible for benefits and the amount of benefits they are to receive, thereby creating "property" entitlements for those eligible. These entitlements in turn provided the basis for due process claims against state officials administering the federal programs, as in *Goldberg*. Recent federal legislation, such as the Personal Responsibility and Work Opportunity Act of 1996, abolish or limit the extent of detailed individual entitlements in favor of block grants to the states, which enjoy substantial discretion in how they are spent.

This shift has been justified on ground of flexibility, state experimentation, and innovation, encouraging new programs to reduce or end welfare dependency and promote entry into the workforce. Opponents claim that this shift is a means of rolling back benefits. If states use their discretion to create individual entitlements by adopting specific eligibility requirements, those eligible can use such entitlements as a predicate for due process claims. At least some states, however, have given administrators substantial discretion in administering benefits. In Illinois, for example, caseworkers have a wide range of discretion in overseeing how mothers with dependent children spend money and in approving and policing a "personal plan for achieving employment" that each welfare recipient must prepare. It is doubtful whether such arrangements provide a basis for due process claims. Are *Goldberg*-type procedures needed to control the enhanced power of caseworkers and other state administrators as a result of these changes? Or would such formalities impede achievement of laudable welfare reform goals? For discussion, see Rebecca Zietlow, Two Wrongs Don't Add Up to Rights: The Importance of Preserving Due Process in Light of Recent Welfare Reform Measures, 45 Am. U.L. Rev. 1111 (1996); Todd Cosenza, Preserving Procedural Due Process for Legal Immigrants Receiving Food Stamps in Light of the Personal Responsibility Act of 1996, 65 Ford. L. Rev. 2065 (1997). Analogous issues are raised by the shift in federal medical care programs towards

---

88. M. Jagger & K. Richard, You Can't Always Get What You Want (1969, Abkco. Music, Inc.), quoted in Van Alstyne, Cracks in "The New Property": Adjudicative Due Process in the Administrative State, 62 Cornell L. Rev. 445, 470 (1977).

89. See Smolla, The Reemergence of the Right-Privilege Distinction in Constitutional Law: The Price of Protesting Too Much, 35 Stan. L. Rev. 69 (1982).

capitated care through HMO programs. See Eleanor D. Kinney, Procedural Protections for Patients in Capitated Health Plans, 22 Am. J.L. & Med. 301 (1996).

Problem

Under Georgia law, the Georgia Department of Human Resources has the authority to assume custody of "abandoned" children and the responsibility of finding temporary foster parents and permanent adoptive parents for infants in state custody. In a lengthy process, potential adoptive families, including not only parents but also grandparents, uncles, aunts, and cousins, are exhaustively evaluated for suitability. The goal of this process, according to the Department of Human Resources' Adoption Services Manual, is to "seek . . . parents who are emotionally and physically capable of assuming the responsibility of parenthood and who are flexible enough to accept [adopted children] for their intrinsic worth."

While this selection process is going on, children are, if possible, placed in foster homes. Under the statutory scheme, foster homes are considered temporary way-stations on the way to permanent adoption.

Department officials assumed custody of a one-month-old child named Timmy who had been left with an elderly neighbor by his mother before taking a trip to California with a friend. After two weeks, the neighbor, unable to continue to care for the child, had called the department. Two weeks later, Timmy was placed for temporary care in the home of a Mr. and Mrs. Drummond while the department conducted a search for adoptive parents. After a year, no adoptive parents had been found, but the Drummonds had become sufficiently attached to Timmy to request permission to adopt him themselves. Although the Drummonds had been rated as excellent foster parents, the department considered it unwise to allow their relationship with Timmy to ripen into a permanent adoptive one, and decided to reassume custody of Timmy. The reason for this decision seems to have been the fact that Timmy was a "mixed race" child, while the Drummonds were white. The agency believed that adoptions by parents of the same race as the child were more likely to be successful than were interracial adoptions. (Although Timmy's mother was white and his father black, his characteristics were found by the agency to be more closely "black" than "white.") The Drummonds were not present during the sessions at which this decision was reached. The Adoption Services Manual, mentioned above, asserts that "[a] permanent home or plan is the right of every child."

a. What claims for deprivation of procedural due process might be asserted in a §1983 suit against department officials on behalf of Timmy's mother? Mr. and Mrs. Drummond? Timmy himself? How should the court dispose of the respective claims? Drummond v. Fulton County Dept. of Family & Children's Servs., 563 F.2d 1200 (5th Cir. 1977), *cert. denied*, 437 U.S. 910 (1978); Duchesne v. Sugarman, 566 F.2d 817 (2d Cir. 1977). In Smith v. Organization of Foster Families for Equality & Reform, 431 U.S. 816 (1977), plaintiff foster parents brought suit to prevent transfer of their foster child back to his natural parents. The Court failed to decide whether a protected interest existed, ruling that even if an entitlement existed, the plaintiffs received all the process they were due. Justice Stevens, concurring, asserted that the Court should have reached the protected interest question, and decided it against the plaintiffs.

b. What if the department had taken Timmy from the Drummonds' custody to place him with the Kings, foster or adoptive parents whom it considered to be better qualified? How, if at all, would the Drummonds' due process claims be affected?

3. *Determining What Process Is Due*

a. Introduction

Recall that *Roth* and subsequent decisions divide issues of procedural due process into a two-step inquiry. First, what interests are entitled to due process protection? Second, what procedures must be afforded to protected interests? In this section, we examine the latter question. These materials should give you a sense of the perplexities encountered in extending notions of procedural due process developed in the context of criminal or civil litigation or coercive regulation of private economic activity to the variegated activities of the modern welfare state. It should also lead you to consider critically what purposes are or should be served by procedural formalities in this context, and to reexamine the wisdom of *Roth*'s two-step division of due process issues into an "entitlement" threshold and a "what process is due" balancing approach.

Judges characteristically approach the question of how much process is due in terms of the extent to which an administrative proceeding must adopt the panoply of procedural formalities that are found in court trials. Judge Friendly, in his very useful article, Some Kind of Hearing, 123 U. Pa. L. Rev. 1267 (1975),[90] listed the following ingredients of judicial due process: (1) an unbiased tribunal; (2) notice of the proposed action and the grounds asserted for it; (3) opportunity to present reasons why the proposed action should not be taken; (4) the right to present evidence, including the right to call witnesses; (5) the right to know opposing evidence; (6) the right to cross-examine adverse witnesses; (7) decision based exclusively on the evidence presented; (8) right to counsel; (9) requirement that the tribunal prepare a record of the evidence presented; and (10) requirement that the tribunal prepare written findings of fact and reasons for its decision.

How should courts decide which of these measures are required by due process in a given instance of administrative decision? Does it depend on the severity of the deprivation imposed by the government? If so, how should severity be measured? Should it be assessed case by case, or by broad categories? Should it depend on the extent of the affected individual's expectation interests? On whether benefits regularly granted in the past are terminated or a new claim for benefits denied? What interests of the government are relevant? The expense of added formalities? The delay that they may involve? Their impact on substantive policies? The possibility that adversary procedures may generate adversary relations that make effective and cooperative governance impossible? Should it depend on the nature of the issues presented? To what extent do they involve specific controverted issues of "adjudicatory" fact — who did what, when, and where? To what extent do they present issues of judgmental discretion of policy? Technical or other specialized issues requiring expert judgment? What of the interest of third persons, such as other beneficiaries who may have benefits reduced if scarce funds are expended for procedural formalities? Consider also the nature of the issues involved. Are procedural formalities required when the central facts are not disputed, and only questions of policy are at issue? Should the extent of hearing rights afforded depend on whether the relevant evidence consists of witness's testimony, or documentary records?

How should these various factors be weighed in deciding which procedures, alone or in combination, should be required? Judge Friendly's article advances some shrewd and

---

90. The title is a somewhat jocular quotation of Justice White's generalization that "some kind of hearing is required at some time before a person is finally deprived of his property interests." Wolff v. McDonnell, 418 U.S. 539, 557-558 (1974).

useful suggestions, including the principle of functional substitution: Satisfaction on one basic requirement (such as an impartial decisionmaker) may advance due process objectives as much as several alternative requirements (such as requiring a formal hearing, record, and findings when the decisionmaker is not impartial).

It seems fair to conclude that no consistent framework for deciding what process is due has emerged from the decisional law, although you will wish to draw your own conclusions from the materials set forth below. Is it indeed possible to develop a consistent set of procedural guidelines under an interest-balancing approach to due process, or must decisions necessarily be ad hoc and, to a considerable degree, subjective? Should there be three or four standard packages of procedures of differing formality? Should the procedures required be matched to the particular administrative function in question, with different packages of procedures for different functions?

Notes and Questions

1. The Court in *Goldberg*, p.623, supra stated that the pretermination hearing it required "need not take the form of a judicial or quasi-judicial trial." But reread the opinion and consider whether "a judicial or quasi-judicial hearing" isn't exactly what the Court ordered. The following are the pretermination safeguards required by *Goldberg*: an impartial decisionmaker; right to present argument orally; right to present evidence orally; right to confront and cross-examine adverse witnesses; right to be accompanied by counsel; decision based solely on the evidence adduced at the hearing; statement by the decisionmaker of the reasons for decisions and of the hearing evidence relied on. In addition, *Goldberg* required adequate notice to the claimant of the proposed action and the grounds for it, but found that this requirement had been satisfied.

Is this not an extraordinary set of measures to impose on a state agency (the New York City Human Resources Administration) that processes over 2000 contested cases monthly? What justifies such an imposition? Is it:

— the circumstance that claimants have a well-defined statutory entitlement to benefits if in fact they meet eligibility requirements?
— the claimants' "brutal need"?
— the susceptibility of the state agency in question to insistent political pressures to trim the welfare rolls?
— the likely presence of factual issues most appropriately resolved by oral, trial-type hearing procedures?

In *Goldberg*'s application of a balancing approach, the private interest side of the balance is fairly clear here, as it often is in other contexts: The individual has a strong interest in not having welfare payments cut off unjustifiably. But the treatment of the government's interest is more complex. The government concededly has an interest in conserving its fiscal resources, and this interest counterbalances the individual's interest in not having payments cut off. Use of funds to provide hearings may also reduce the amount of benefits available to other claimants. And, if it is too difficult to terminate claimants, the result may be systematic abuse of the system and (as Justice Black suggested) government cutbacks on the availability of benefits in response. But *Goldberg* emphasizes that the government also has an interest in preventing the "social malaise" that would result from unjustified terminations. 397 U.S. at 265. This governmental interest would seem to tip the balance in the direction of more procedural safeguards. Similar points are made by the Court in Morrissey v. Brewer, 408 U.S. 471, 484 (1972) (society has interest in preventing unjustified revocation of parole), and in Memphis Light, Gas, & Water Div. v. Craft, 436 U.S. 1 (1978) (municipal utility has interest in maintaining public confidence by not terminating utility services unjustifiably). Is this a valid way of implementing the what-process-is-due balancing test? Since the legislature did not impose additional procedural safeguards initially, isn't it fair to presume that the asserted governmental "interest" really doesn't exist? Is it reasonable to impute to the government an "interest" it denies having?

2. *Goldberg* and many of the other decisions examined in this chapter involve "mass justice" processing of large numbers of benefit claims, where the amount at stake is relatively modest in comparison to many regulatory controversies, but is of great concern to the claimant. For example, the Social Security Administration (SSA) processes millions of claims a year; the average amount at stake in disability claims is $30,000. In many other contexts the dollar amount at stake is far less. Other decisions examined in this chapter involve the use of hearing rights to control the conduct of institutions that enjoy considerable operational autonomy — schools, prisons, mental hospitals, and so on. Below we examine in more detail the problems in using judicial hearing procedures to control these different types of bureaucracies. For now you should bear in mind the following questions as you examine the materials in this section:

(a) Will hearing rights be of any use unless the person given such a right has a lawyer? Should society provide a lawyer in every case? (Note that *Goldberg* did not require that a lawyer be provided.)

(b) Is a lower standard of due process inevitable in the case of "new property"? How would you respond to the following question from Jones, The Rule of Law and the Welfare State, 58 Colum. L. Rev. 143, 155-156 (1958)?

> Mass produced goods rarely have the quality of goods made in far smaller quantity by traditional hand craftsmanship; an analogous problem challenges the welfare state. In an era when rights are mass produced, can the quality of their protection against arbitrary official action be as high as the quality of protection afforded in the past to traditional legal rights less numerous and less widely dispersed among the members of society?

(c) How can judges know what procedures to require without an intimate understanding of the operational realities of every institution whose procedures are challenged? Can the judges shift the burden of devising more adequate procedures onto the administrators themselves? How can they do so without abdicating their responsibility to ensure that constitutional rights are vindicated?

b. The Mathews v. Eldridge Balancing Test

Mathews v. Eldridge
424 U.S. 319 (1976)

Mr. Justice POWELL delivered the opinion of the Court.

The issue in this case is whether the Due Process Clause of the Fifth Amendment requires that prior to the termination of Social Security disability benefit payments the recipient be afforded an opportunity for an evidentiary hearing. . . .

Cash benefits are provided to workers during periods in which they are completely disabled under the disability insurance benefits program created by [the Social Security Act.][91] Respondent Eldridge was first awarded benefits in June 1968. [In May 1972, the Social Security Administration (SSA) made a final determination that he was no longer eligible to receive disability benefits.]

Instead of requesting reconsideration Eldridge commenced this action challenging the constitutional validity of the administrative procedures established by the Secretary of Health, Education, and Welfare for assessing whether there exists a continuing disability. . . .

[The secretary had conceded that social security disability benefits were statutory entitlements representing "property" protected by due process. The Court then considered what process was due.]

. . . In only one case, Goldberg v. Kelly, 397 U.S. 254, 266-271 (1970), has the Court held that a hearing closely approximating a judicial trial is necessary. . . .

[O]ur prior decisions indicate that identification of the specific dictates of due process generally requires consideration of three distinct factors: first, the private interest that will be affected by the official action; second, the risk of an erroneous deprivation of such interest through the procedures used, and the probable value, if any, of additional or substitute procedural safeguards; and finally, the government's interest, including the function involved and the fiscal and administrative burdens that the additional or substitute procedural requirement would entail. . . .

The disability insurance program is administered jointly by state and federal agencies. . . . The principal reasons for benefits terminations are that the worker is no longer disabled or has returned to work. . . .

The continuing eligibility investigation is made by a state agency [that] periodically communicates with the disabled worker, usually by mail — in which case he is sent a detailed questionnaire — or by telephone, and requests information concerning his present condition, including current medical restrictions and sources of treatment, and any additional information that he considers relevant to his continued entitlement to benefits. . . .

Information regarding the recipient's current condition is also obtained from his sources of medical treatment. . . . If there is a conflict between the information provided by the beneficiary and that obtained from medical sources such as his physician, or between two sources of treatment, the agency may arrange for an examination by an independent consulting physician. . . . Whenever the agency's tentative assessment of the beneficiary's condition differs from his own assessment, the beneficiary is informed that benefits may be terminated, provided a summary of the evidence upon which the proposed determination to terminate is based, and afforded an opportunity to review the medical reports and other evidence in his case file. He also may respond in writing and submit additional evidence. . . .

The state agency then makes its final determination, which is reviewed by an examiner in the SSA Bureau of Disability Insurance. . . . If, as is usually the case, the SSA accepts the agency determination it notifies the recipient in writing, informing him of the reasons for the decision, and of his right to seek de novo reconsiderations by the state agency. . . . Upon acceptance by the SSA, benefits are terminated effective two months after the month in which medical recovery is found to have occurred. . . .

---

91. In fiscal 1974 approximately 3,700,000 persons received assistance under the program. Social Security Administration, The Year in Review 21 (1974).

If the recipient seeks reconsideration by the state agency and the determination is adverse, the SSA reviews the reconsideration determination and notifies the recipient of the decision. He then has a right to an evidentiary hearing before an SSA administrative law judge. . . . The hearing is nonadversary, and the SSA is not represented by counsel. As at all prior and subsequent stages of the administrative process, however, the claimant may be represented by counsel or other spokesmen. . . . If this hearing results in an adverse decision, the claimant is entitled to request discretionary review by the SSA Appeals Council, . . . and finally may obtain judicial review. . . .

Should it be determined at any point after termination of benefits, that the claimant's disability extended beyond the date of cessation initially established, the worker is entitled to retroactive payments. . . .

If, on the other hand, a beneficiary receives any payments to which he is later determined not to be entitled, the statute authorizes the Secretary to attempt to recoup these funds in specific circumstances.

Despite the elaborate character of the administrative procedures provided by the Secretary, the courts below held them to be constitutionally inadequate, concluding that due process requires an evidentiary hearing prior to termination. In light of the private and governmental interests at stake here and the nature of the existing procedures, we think this was error.

Since a recipient whose benefits are terminated is awarded full retroactive relief if he ultimately prevails, his sole interest is in the uninterrupted receipt of this source of income pending final administrative decision on his claim. . . .

Eligibility for disability benefits [in contrast to the benefits at issue in *Goldberg*] is not based upon financial need. Indeed, it is wholly unrelated to the worker's income or support from many other sources. . . .

In view of the torpidity of this administrative review process . . . and the typically modest resources of the family unit of the physically disabled worker, the hardship imposed upon the erroneously terminated disability recipient may be significant. Still, the disabled worker's need is likely to be less than that of a welfare recipient. . . . In view of [other] potential sources of temporary income, there is less reason here than in *Goldberg* to depart from the ordinary principle, established by our decisions, that something less than an evidentiary hearing is sufficient prior to adverse administrative action.

An additional factor to be considered here is the fairness and reliability of the existing pretermination procedures, and the probable value, if any, of additional procedural safeguards. Central to the evaluation of an administrative process is the nature of the relevant inquiry. . . . In order to remain eligible for benefits, . . . a medical assessment of the worker's physical or mental condition is required. This is a more sharply focused and easily documented decision than the typical determination of welfare entitlement. . . .

[T]he decision whether to discontinue disability benefits will turn, in most cases, upon "routine, standard, and unbiased medical reports by physician specialists," Richardson v. Perales, 402 U.S., at 404, concerning a subject whom they have personally examined. . . .

To be sure, credibility and veracity may be a factor in the ultimate disability assessment in some cases. But procedural due process rules are shaped by the risk of error inherent in the truthfinding process as applied to the generality of cases, not the rare exceptions. The potential value of an evidentiary hearing, or even oral presentation to the decisionmaker, is substantially less in this context than in *Goldberg*.

The decision in *Goldberg* also was based on the Court's conclusion that written submissions were an inadequate substitute for oral presentation because they did not provide an effective means for the recipient to communicate his case to the decision-maker. . . .

[Here] the information critical to the entitlement decision usually is derived from medical sources, such as the treating physician. Such sources are likely to be able to communicate more effectively through written documents than are welfare recipients or the lay witnesses supporting their cause. The conclusions of physicians often are supported by X-rays and the results of clinical or laboratory tests, information typically more amenable to written than to oral presentation. . . .

A further safeguard against mistake is the policy of allowing the disability recipient or his representative full access to all information relied upon by the state agency. . . .

In striking the appropriate due process balance the final factor to be assessed is the public interest. This includes the administrative burden and other societal costs that would be associated with requiring, as a matter of constitutional right, an evidentiary hearing upon demand in all cases prior to the termination of disability benefits. The most visible burden would be the incremental cost resulting from the increased number of hearings and the expense of providing benefits to ineligible recipients, pending decision. No one can predict the extent of the increase, but the fact that full benefits would continue until after such hearings would assure the exhaustion in most cases of this attractive option. Nor would the theoretical right of the Secretary to recover undeserved benefits result, as a practical matter, in any substantial offset to the added outlay of public funds. The parties submit widely varying estimates of the probable additional financial cost. We only need say that experience with the constitutionalizing of government procedures suggests that the ultimate additional cost in terms of money and administrative burden would not be insubstantial.

. . . At some point the benefit of an additional safeguard to the individual affected by the administrative action and to society in terms of increased assurance that the action is just, may be outweighed by the cost. Significantly, the cost of protecting those whom the preliminary administrative process has identified as likely to be found undeserving may in the end come out of the pockets of the deserving since resources available for any particular program of social welfare are not unlimited.

. . . We reiterate the wise admonishment of Mr. Justice Frankfurter that differences in the origin and function of administrative agencies "preclude wholesale transplantation of the rules of procedure, trial, and review which have evolved from the history and experience of the courts." FCC v. Pottsville Broadcasting Co., 309 U.S. 134, 143 (1940). The judicial model of an evidentiary hearing is neither a required, nor even the most effective, method of decisionmaking in all circumstances. . . .

We conclude that an evidentiary hearing is not required prior to the termination of disability benefits and that the present administrative procedures fully comport with due process.

[Justice Brennan, dissenting, joined by Justice Marshall, argued that even a temporary deprivation of benefits could cause serious harm and that a trial-type hearing must be afforded prior to termination of benefits.]

GOSS v. LOPEZ, 419 U.S. 565 (1975).   In this pre-*Eldridge* case, the Supreme Court held that, before it could suspend a student for less than ten days, the school must provide the student with the rudiments of due process. These include "oral or written notice of the charges against him and, if he denies them, an explanation of the evidence the authorities have and an opportunity to present his side of the story." The Court added, "Longer suspensions or expulsions for the remainder of the school term may require more formal procedures."

UNIVERSITY OF MISSOURI v. HOROWITZ, 435 U.S. 78 (1978).   Horowitz was dismissed from medical school as a student because her "performance" in her clinical work "was below that of her peers," her attendance was erratic, and she showed disregard for cleanliness and hygiene. The dean informed her, orally and in writing, about her deficiencies. She was given a chance to improve. She had an opportunity to present her views to the dean and to other school officials. She did not have a chance to appear before the faculty coordinating committee or the student-faculty council, which evaluated her work. The Court found these procedures constitutionally sufficient, writing (per Justice Rehnquist) that "academic evaluations of a student, in contrast to disciplinary determinations, bear little resemblance to the judicial and administrative factfinding proceedings to which we have traditionally attached a full hearing requirement. . . . The decision to dismiss respondent . . . rested on the academic judgment of school officials. . . . Such a judgment is by its nature more subjective and evaluative than the typical factual questions presented in the average disciplinary decision. [It] requires expert evaluation . . . and is not readily adapted to the procedural tools of judicial or administrative decisionmaking. . . . We decline to further enlarge the judicial presence in the academic community." See also University of Michigan v. Ewing, 474 U.S. 214 (1985); Ford & Stroup, Judicial Responses to Adverse Academic Decisions Affecting Public Postsecondary Institution Students Since *Horowitz* and *Ewing*, 110 Ed. L. Rep. 517 (1996) (reviewing recent lower court decisions and finding substantial judicial deference to educational institutions' procedures).

SCHWEIKER v. McCLURE, 456 U.S. 188 (1982).   Part B of the federal Medicare program concerns reimbursement for doctors' services and diagnostic tests. HHS contracts with private insurance carriers to administer the Part B program. Those carriers (such as Blue Shield) process hundreds of millions of claims. The doctor (or sometimes the patient) sends a bill to the carrier. The carrier decides whether the charge was reasonable, medically necessary, and otherwise fulfills Part B's requirements. If the claimant disagrees with the carrier's denial of a claim, the claimant will receive a "review determination," which amounts to a review of the written record by a *different* employee of the carrier from the one who made the initial decision denying the claim. If that employee also denies the claim, and the claim is *for more than $100*, the claimant is entitled to an oral hearing. A hearing officer is chosen by the carrier. The hearing officer (who has not been involved in the case previously) receives "evidence and hear[s] arguments." The officer will render a written decision based on the record. There is no further administrative review. The Supreme Court held these procedures sufficient to satisfy due process. It found no need to provide a *government employee* to act as a hearing officer. It focused on the second *Eldridge* factor "that considers the risk of erroneous decision and the probable value, if any, of the additional procedure." Since the statute required that the carrier-selected hearing officer be "qualified" and also "have a thorough knowledge of the Medicare program," the extra value of having a government decisionmaker is not great.

GRAY PANTHERS v. SCHWEIKER, 652 F.2d 146 (D.C. Cir. 1980).   The D.C. Circuit considered the process given to those claimants with Medicare Part B claims worth *less than $100*. The Medicare Act specifically provides that a hearing "shall not be available" if the amount in controversy is less than $100. Nonetheless, the statute does not prohibit the secretary from providing informal procedures. The court held that the statute, read in light of the Constitution's due process clause, requires some kind of further oral procedure. An "oral hearing provides a way to ensure accuracy where facts are in dispute, particularly if credibility is an issue. . . . Caseworkers, auditors, parole officers and other initial decisionmakers, if required to meet personally with those whose lives they are touching, and justify, however briefly, their decisions to those who are dissatisfied, are faced with a powerful disincentive to arbitrary action. . . . An oral hearing requirement thus serves to ensure that decisionmakers recognize that their decisions affect the lives of human beings, a fact that is often obscured by a number of papers and depersonalized identification numbers. . . . A third and perhaps most important reason for generally insisting upon a hearing is that no other procedure so effectively fosters a belief that one has been dealt with fairly, even if there remains a disagreement with the result. . . . We believe, at a minimum, the claimant should be informed or have access to the evidence on which the carrier relied in reaching its initial decision to deny the claim and, within a reasonable time thereafter, an opportunity to present evidence (in oral or written form) in support of his or her position. . . . At some point after the hearing, the claimant should receive a meaningful explanation of the reasons for whatever action is taken on the claim. . . ." Eventually, after remand and a new appeal, the D.C. Circuit upheld the validity of a "toll-free telephone" hearing system, under which the claimants could call a number (although 40 percent would get an initial busy signal) and talk to a hearing officer. See Gray Panthers v. Schweiker, 716 F.2d 23 (D.C. Cir. 1983).

CLEVELAND BOARD OF EDUCATION v. LOUDERMILL, 470 U.S. 532 (1985). In 1979, the board hired Loudermill as a security guard. Under Ohio law it could dismiss him only "for cause." In 1980, it sent him a letter dismissing him because of dishonesty in filling out his job application. Loudermill had not told the board that he had been convicted of grand larceny in 1968. About two months after Loudermill's dismissal, the Cleveland Civil Service Commission provided him a hearing. Loudermill said that he had thought his prior conviction was for a misdemeanor, not for a felony; hence, he thought he did not have to mention it. The hearing examiner recommended reinstatement; the full commission upheld Loudermill's dismissal. The Court found Ohio's procedure constitutionally deficient. Due process requires " 'some kind of hearing' prior to the discharge of an employee who has a constitutionally protected property interest in his employment." The Court balanced the *Eldridge* interests as follows: "First, the significance of the private interest in retaining employment cannot be gainsaid. . . . Second, some opportunity for the employee to present his side of the case is recurringly of obvious value in reaching an accurate decision. . . . Even where the facts are clear, the appropriateness or necessity of the discharge may not be; in such a case the only meaningful opportunity to invoke the discretion of the decisionmaker is likely to be before the termination takes effect. . . ." In a footnote the Court added, "[T]his is not to say that where state conduct is entirely discretionary the Due Process Cause is brought into play. . . . Nor is it to say that a person can insist on a hearing in order to argue that the decisionmaker should be lenient and depart from legal requirements. . . ." The court also stated that: "[A]ffording the employee an opportunity to respond prior to termination would impose neither a significant administrative burden nor intolerable delays. Furthermore the employer shares the employee's interest in avoiding disruption and erroneous decisions; and until the matter is settled, the employer would continue to receive the benefit of the employee's labors. It is preferable to keep a qualified employee than to train a new one. A governmental employee also has an interest in keeping citizens usefully employed rather than taking the possibly erroneous and counter-productive step of forcing its employees onto welfare rolls. Finally, in those situations where the employer perceives a significant hazard in keeping an employee on the job, it can avoid the problem by suspending with pay."

With respect to the process due, the Court stated: " '[T]he pretermination-hearing,' though necessary, need not be elaborate. [R]espondents were later entitled to a full administrative hearing and judicial review. . . . In only one case, Goldberg v. Kelly, has the Court required a full adversarial evidentiary hearing prior to adverse governmental action. . . . Here the pretermination hearing need not definitively resolve the propriety of the discharge. It should be an initial check against mistaken decisions — essentially a determination of whether there are reasonable grounds to believe that the charges against the employee are true and support the proposed action. . . . The tenured public employee is entitled to oral or written notice of the charges against him, an explanation of the employer's evidence, and an opportunity to present his side of the story. To require more than this prior to termination would intrude to an unwarranted extent on the government's interest in quickly removing an unsatisfactory employee." Compare *Arnett*, p.634, supra.

WINEGAR v. DES MOINES INDEPENDENT COMMUNITY SCHOOL DISTRICT, 20 F.3d 895 (8th Cir. 1994). A public high school teacher became engaged in an altercation with a student. The student hit the teacher and knocked him down. The teacher then kicked and slapped the student. The teacher was allowed to represent his version of what happened orally to school authorities, who also collected written statements from the teacher, the student in question, and other students and received written reports from a private investigator that it hired. The school found that the teacher had abused the student; it suspended him for four days and ordered him transferred to another school. The court found that the injury to the teacher's reputation, in conjunction with the suspension and transfer, implicated "liberty" interests. The court held that the teacher should have been afforded an opportunity for an oral evidentiary hearing, including presentation and cross-examination of witnesses, either before or after the school's decision to suspend. The court distinguished *Goss*, which required far less in the way of procedures, on the basis of a school district's need to maintain student discipline, and also found that the teacher's interests were more significant than those implicated by a short-duration student suspension.

GILBERT v. HOMAR, 117 S. Ct. 1807 (1997). Plaintiff, a state university police officer, was temporarily suspended without pay after he was arrested and charged by police with drug offenses. The Court rejected his claim that due process required some form of hearing before he was suspended without pay. *Loudermill* was distinguished on the ground that it involved termination, not suspension. Moreover, plaintiff's arrest and charge provided an objective, reasonable basis for suspension. However, due process requires a prompt postsuspension hearing.

WALTERS v. NATIONAL ASSOCIATION OF RADIATION SURVIVORS, 473 U.S. 305 (1985). The federal government, through its veterans benefits program, pays veterans pensions and also compensation for "service-connected" disabilities or death. A veteran claiming compensation files a form with a local veterans' agency. A "rating board," consisting of a medical specialist, a legal specialist, and an occupational specialist, reviews the claim form at the Veterans Administration regional office. The claimant may appear before the board. No one appears in opposition. The board will help the claimant develop facts. It can obtain service records and order medical exams. The issue before it typically is the extent of the claimant's medical disability and whether it is service-connected. In deciding such questions, the board must "resolve all reasonable doubts" in the claimant's favor. If the board decides against the claimant, it must provide him or her with a "statement of the case," a written description of the facts and applicable law. The claimant may appeal to the Board of Veterans Appeals. The hearing before that board is also informal, with only the claimant's side presented, and without formal questioning, cross-examination, or rules of evidence. Various veterans' organizations across the country will provide any claimant with a "trained service agent," who will act as the claimant's representative before the regional board or the Board of Veterans Appeals, free of charge. A free representative is available for anyone who requests one. Using this system, the Veterans Administration processed about 800,000 claims in 1978. About half were for service-connected death or disability; the other half were pension claims. About half of the 800,000 claims were allowed; 370,000 were denied; 66,000 of the denials were contested at the regional level; 36,000 were appealed to the Board of Veterans Appeals, where about 4500 of the claimants prevailed.

The Court considered the constitutionality of an 1862 statute that limited the fee to be paid to an "agent or attorney" for claims "for monetary benefits" to $10. The Court, 6-3, held in an opinion by Chief Justice Rehnquist that this limitation was constitutional. Although "property" entitlements were at issue, the statute was consistent with due process. "Congress desired that the proceedings be as informal and nonadversarial as possible. The regular introduction of lawyers into the proceedings would be quite unlikely to further this goal. . . . The appearance of counsel for the citizen is likely to lead the Government to provide one — or at least to cause the Government's representative to act like one. The result may be to turn what might have been a short conference leading to an amicable result into a protracted controversy. . . . These problems concerning counsel and confrontation inevitably bring up the question whether we would not do better to abandon the adversary system in certain areas of mass justice. . . . [A]dditional complexity will undoubtedly engender greater administrative costs, with the end result being that less Government money reaches its intended beneficiaries. . . . The flexibility of our approach in due process cases is intended in part to allow room for other forms of dispute resolution. . . . It would take an extraordinarily strong showing of probability of error under the present system and the probability that the presence of attorneys would sharply diminish that possibility to warrant a holding that the fee limitation denies claimants due process of law. [Since figures in the record show that the percentage of cases that claimants win on appeal when they are represented by an attorney is not much greater than when they are not] no such showing was made out on the record before the District Court. . . ." The Court conceded that attorneys might be helpful in "complex" matters involving only a tiny percentage of the total claims for veterans' benefits but that this consideration was insufficient to invalidate the statute. *Question:* Does due process require that the fee limitation be invalidated in the case of a complex claim?

Justice Stevens, dissenting, stated that administrative efficiency did not warrant a total bar on representation by counsel. He added: "The fundamental error in the Court's analysis is its assumption that the individual's right to employ counsel of his choice in a contest with his sovereign is a kind of second-class interest that can be assigned a material value and balanced on a utilitarian scale of costs and benefits. [W]e are not considering a procedural right that would involve any cost to the Government. We are concerned with the individual's right to spend his own money to obtain the advice and assistance of independent counsel in advancing his claim against the Government. [R]egardless of the nature of the dispute between the sovereign and the citizen . . . the citizen's right to consult an independent lawyer and to retain that lawyer to speak on his or her behalf is an aspect of liberty that is priceless. It should not be bargained away on the notion that a totalitarian appraisal of the mass of claims processed by the Veterans Administration does not identify an especially high probability of error. . . ."

In 1988 Congress enacted legislation altering the procedures and institutions for deciding veterans' benefits claims and authorized claimants to retain and be represented by lawyers in the appeals phases of the process; fees must be "reasonable" and may not exceed 20 percent of recoveries for past benefits. Veterans' Judicial Review Act, 38 U.S.C. §5904.

PENOBSCOT v. FEDERAL AVIATION ADMINISTRATION, 164 F.3d 713 (1st Cir. 1999). Applying an *Eldridge* analysis, the court rejected a due process claim by an airplane service operator that the FAA was required to hold an evidentiary hearing before dismissing its complaint against an airport for giving a competitor lower rents and allowing it to provide more services, assuredly in violation of federal requirements. The plaintiff's interest in higher profits and the public's interest in competition were to be given some but not great weight. The risk of error in the FAA's existing procedures for hearing such claims, which allowed the complaining party to submit its case in documentary form, was small, and the gains in accuracy from an evidentiary hearing slight. The administrative burdens of providing an evidentiary hearing for every compliant who demanded one would be large.

Notes and Questions

1. Justice Powell in *Eldridge* assumes that the sole function of due process procedural requirements is to promote accurate decisionmaking. Does he adduce any justifications for this premise? Is it compelled by the *Roth* framework?

2. The opinion suggests a calculus under which additional procedural safeguards are warranted so long as:

$$\begin{matrix} \text{increased accuracy from additional procedures} \end{matrix} \quad \times \quad \begin{matrix} \text{interest of claimant} \end{matrix} \quad > \quad \begin{matrix} \text{increased burden on government} \end{matrix}$$

a. Is the sort of "interest balancing" represented by this calculus an intellectually coherent or operationally feasible enterprise? Can all of the elements in the calculus be reduced to a common denominator? Suppose that it costs $500 to give each claimant a hearing, that hearings increase accuracy and result in a 2 percent increase in claimant victories, and that the average claim is $20,000. Since 2% of $20,000 = $400, does the government win? If the cost of a hearing is only $300, does the claimant win? How do we compare the marginal utility of money to the claimant and to the government (consider that the money spent on hearings might otherwise go to other claimants)? What about intangible factors?

b. Assuming that various interests can be measured and balanced against one another, did the Court do a satisfactory job with the balancing calculus in Mathews v. Eldridge? Did the Court inquire at all into (1) the average financial need of disability payments recipients compared to the average financial need of welfare recipients; (2) the number of disability payments to recipients whose need is comparable to that of welfare recipients; (3) the number of cases where decisions whether to discontinue benefits turn on "routine, standard and unbiased medical reports by physician specialists"; or (4) the cost to the government of a hearing? The Court's application of its balancing test in *Eldridge* is strongly criticized in Mashaw, The Supreme Court's Due Process Calculus for Administrative Adjudication in Mathews v. Eldridge: Three Factors in Search of a Theory of Value, 44 U. Chi. L. Rev. 28 (1976).

c. Is "accuracy" an apt criterion for assessing decisions such as those in *Eldridge*? Professor Mashaw argues persuasively that disability is not a simple "fact" that can be determined with greater or lesser accuracy by different procedures, but is a conclusion based on a judgmental assessment of the claimant's condition, education, work history, employment attitudes, employment opportunities, and a variety of policy considerations. See J. Mashaw, Bureaucratic Justice (1983). In support of his view that "accuracy" is a questionable basis for assessing disability claim procedures, Mashaw points to a General Accounting Office (GAO) study that indicates the difficulties in ensuring consistency in deciding such claims. GAO collected the files of 221 disability claims that had been decided by a state agency, and transmitted them to ten other state agencies and to federal social security officials to determine how they would decide the same cases. In only 32 percent of the cases was there complete agreement on the disposition of the claim. In only about two-thirds of the cases did a majority of the state agencies agree on the disposition of the claim, and in 95 percent of these cases the majority states disagreed on the rationale for deciding the claim. The federal officials agreed with the majority of the states' dispositions in less than half of these cases. Mashaw, 44 U. Chi. L. Rev. 28 (1976). We consider his argument and its implications in greater detail on pp. 673, 680-681, infra.

A number of commentators have suggested that, even in those cases where the Supreme Court purports to follow *Eldridge*, its analysis is not consistent with a cost-benefit approach and that instead the Court uses implicit models and categories of types of decisions and appropriate corresponding procedures. See Mashaw, Conflict and Compromise between Models of Administrative Justice, 1981 Duke L.J. 181; Note, Due Process, Due Politics and Due Respect: Three Models of Legitimate School Government, 94 Harv. L. Rev. 1106 (1981). Mashaw suggests that these models may be generalized as one of "bureaucratic rationality" focusing on "error costs," one stressing the "therapeutic" and "clinical" values inherent in the relationship between service professionals and their clients, and one of "fairness" and "justice" based on the ideal of trial-type judicial proceedings.

d. Should the courts' specification of what process is due be performed on a "whole-sale" basis for various general categories of disputes, or on a "retail" basis taking into account the particular characteristics of each case? Mathews v. Eldridge seems to embrace the "wholesale" approach, determining what procedures should be required for SSD cases as a whole, as does *Walters*: "[P]rocedural due process rules are shaped by the risk of error inherent in the truthfinding process as applied to the generality of cases, not the rare exceptions," 424 U.S. 319, at 344 (1976). Compare this to the Court's approach in Lassiter v. Department of Social Services, 452 U.S. 18 (1981), a case involving an indigent parent's right to counsel in proceedings in which a state seeks to take custody of a child on grounds of parental neglect. The majority, using the Mathews v. Eldridge balancing test, held that counsel need not be appointed because the issues involved in *Lassiter* were not complex. However, when the issues are complicated, the parent may have a right to counsel. The decision must be made on a case-by-case basis because each case is different and precise guidelines are impossible to set. Justice Blackmun (in a dissent joined by Justices Brennan and Marshall) asserted, among other matters, that the case-by-case approach was inconsistent with *Mathews*, and that there should be a right to counsel in all custody cases. Justice Stevens wrote a separate dissent, arguing that there is a special class of liberty interests (including child custody) that should not be subject to a *Mathews*-type balancing test:

> Without so stating explicitly, the Court appears to treat this case as though it merely involved the deprivation of an interest in property that is less worthy of protection than a person's liberty. . . .
>
> In my opinion the reasons supporting the conclusion that the Due Process Clause of the Fourteenth Amendment entitles the defendant in a criminal case to representation by counsel apply with equal force to a case of this kind. The issue is one of fundamental fairness, not of weighing the pecuniary costs against the societal benefits. Accordingly, even if the costs to the State were not relatively insignificant but rather were just as great as the costs of providing prosecutors, judges, and defense counsel to ensure the fairness of criminal proceedings, I would reach the same result in this category of cases. For the value of protecting our liberty from deprivation by the State without due process of law is priceless.

Implicit support for Justice Stevens's approach may be found in Vitek v. Jones, summarized at p.640, supra, where the Court required full trial-type hearings and appointed counsel before a prisoner could be transferred to a mental hospital. The Court did not invoke *Mathews* or articulate a balancing approach. Does this suggest that the balancing approach for determining what process is due for "property" entitlements does not or should not apply to "liberty" entitlements?

e. Consider the typology for determining the process due for different administrative functions developed in Rubin, Due Process and the Administrative State, 72 Cal. L. Rev. 1044 (1984): (1) allocating government benefits, distinguishing between nondiscretionary and discretionary benefits; (2) discharging public employees; and (3) operating custodial institutions such as schools and prisons, distinguishing between routine determinations and unusual disciplinary actions. Professor Rubin attacks the *Roth/Eldridge* framework as an ill-advised effort to develop a special model for due process in administrative law, based on the premise that the sole function of procedures is to vindicate preexisting entitlements. He argues that instead administrative hearing procedures should be developed by analogy to procedures in civil and criminal adjudication, such that adjudicatory decisions can only be made on the basis of general principles or rules applied through fair procedures.

Does traditional due process doctrine governing "old property" permit the sort of utilitarian balancing embraced by Justice Powell? Generally, the amount of due process enjoyed by a taxpayer or a regulated firm does not depend on the dollar amount at stake. Is there a "double standard" in due process — one for "old property" and one for "new property"? (On the other hand, some "old property" cases, such as those allowing summary execution of tax or regulatory impositions in cases of "emergency," see pp. 617-619, supra, also seem to involve balancing.)

Justice Stevens's dissent in *Lassiter* can be seen as building a bridge between "old" property and liberty and "new" liberty and property, asserting that some fundamental interests should be protected by full adversary procedures regardless of a balancing test. How would one determine what interests should be included in this category?

3. What goals or purposes other than accuracy should appropriately be considered in determining what process is due? Some commentators have contrasted the "instrumental" analysis of formal procedures as a means to securing given outcomes, with intrinsic "process" values that serve expressive functions. See Michelman, Formal and Associational Aims in Procedural Due Process, in Nomos: Due Process 126 (J. Pennock and J. Chapman eds. 1977). For a useful discussion of the instrumental view of due process as securing entitlements, see Note, Two Views of a Prisoner's Right to Due Process: Meachum v. Fano, 12 Harv. C.R.-C.L.L. Rev. 405, 411-414 (1977). For example, the approach taken in Mathews v. Eldridge is "instrumental" because procedures are viewed purely as a means for securing accuracy in dispensing statutory entitlements. Another conceivable instrumental goal of due process procedural requirements is to secure adoption of disability policies more favorable to claimants by increasing their ability to impose costly delays on the agency and thus increasing their bargaining leverage. Is alteration of the existing institutional and political balance of power in the policies and practices of the welfare state a proper goal for due process? By contrast, under a "process" approach, affording a disability claimant an oral hearing can be justified on the ground that it affirms her worth and dignity as an individual by enabling her to participate in government decisions seriously affecting her welfare. See Michelman, supra; Tribe, Structural Due Process, 10 Harv. C.R.-C.L.L. Rev. 269 (1975).

Alternatively, procedural formalities can be evaluated in terms of how well they satisfy and affirm traditional community standards of fair play. Thibaut, Walker, LaTour & Houlden, Procedural Justice as Fairness, 26 Stan. L. Rev. 1271 (1974), reports the results of an experiment that seems to demonstrate that people strongly prefer adversarial procedures to procedures that provide them with less participation in the adjudicative process. Should such perceptions matter in assessing what process is due? Consider the following frequently quoted statement from Justice Frankfurter's concurrence in Joint Anti-Fascist Refugee Committee v. McGrath: "No better instrument has been devised for arriving at the truth than to give a person in jeopardy of serious loss notice of the case against him and an opportunity to meet it. Nor has a better way been found for generating *the feeling, so important to a popular government that justice has been done.*" 341 U.S. 123, 171-172 (1951) (emphasis added). For discussion of the importance of designing procedures to reflect community norms of fair treatment and related cultural values including tradition, dignity, equality, and consistency, see Koch, A Community of Interest in the Due Process Calculus, 37 Houston L. Rev. 635 (2000).

How should courts take these differing conceptions and goals into account in determining what process is due?

4. Can you distinguish the post-*Eldridge* case of *Horowitz* from the pre-*Eldridge* case of *Goss*? Does *Eldridge* make the difference? If not, what does?

5. Can the problems of devising fair "mass justice" procedures be solved by electronic communications technologies? Are you convinced by the *Gray Panthers* case in the D.C. Circuit? How expensive are telephone hearings? Do they do any good? Can

older people understand telephone conversations very well? How long will claimants have to wait when they hear a busy signal or someone puts them on hold? Would you say that telephone hearings will leave claimants feeling they have been fairly treated? Will they satisfy the other goals of "due process"? See Toubman, McArdle & Rogers-Tower, Due Process Implications: The Case for an Individualized Approach to Scheduling Telephone Hearings, 29 U. Mich. J.L. Ref. 407 (1995-1996) (finding that in telephone hearings in unemployment compensation cases claimants are less likely to submit evidence through witnesses and documents than in oral hearings and suggesting improvements in telephone hearing procedures); Salkin, Current Developments in Maryland: Video Hearings, 21 Admin. & Reg. L. News 1 (Spring 1996) (summarizing successful experiences with video hearings). What about a web site for processing claims, with a client room and other electronic resources for claimants?

c. Postdeprivation Remedies as a Substitute for Predeprivation Agency Hearings

We have already examined several cases, including *Goldberg* and *Eldridge*, assessing the adequacy of lesser predeprivation procedural safeguards (ex ante procedures) when a full administrative hearing or other procedures are available after the agency acts (ex post procedures). These cases attempt to identify and balance the risk of error in the ex ante as compared to the ex post procedures, the gravity of the interim harm a claimant will suffer before a full hearing is available ex post, and the government's interest in speed and minimizing cost. (But consider again whether the differences in result reflect or can be justified on the basis of any such calculus.)

In some contexts states have been able to avoid a full predeprivation hearing by (a) granting a full postdeprivation hearing and (b) restricting the issues for decision at the pretermination hearing to a few that can be resolved more or less summarily with low risk of error. Thus in Dixon v. Love, 431 U.S. 105 (1977), the Court upheld an Illinois procedure for automatic administrative revocation of a driver's license where records showed that the license had been suspended three times in ten years. A full postsuspension hearing was available. The Court found that the rate of error was likely to be low and stressed the state's interest in highway safety. See also Mackey v. Montrym, 443 U.S. 1 (1979); Gilbert v. Homar, p. 655, supra.

Thus far we have been examining the choice between predeprivation and postdeprivation *administrative* procedures. But there is a third alternative: a postdeprivation *judicial* remedy. A person denied a benefit or suffering a deprivation may go to court to challenge the legality of the agency's action. If, after hearing and determining the facts, the court finds the agency's action unlawful it may seek, through injunctive or restitutionary relief, to undo the illegal action. (For example, it may require a discharged employee to be reinstated with back pay.) Where the illegality cannot be undone or interim harm has been suffered, it may award damages.

Recall that, in the regulatory context, several decisions indicated that an ex post judicial remedy might be a constitutionally adequate substitute for an ex ante administrative hearing. See *North American Cold Storage*, p. 617, supra, *Southern Railway*, p.485, supra. Might the same be true in the case of "new property" hearing requirements? The Supreme Court first explicitly confronted this question in the following case.

Ingraham v. Wright
430 U.S. 651 (1977)

Mr. Justice POWELL delivered the opinion of the Court.

[Plaintiffs had been paddled by public school officials for alleged disciplinary violations while junior high school students in Dade County, Florida, without notice or opportunity for a prior hearing on the disciplinary charges. The paddling of one student resulted in injuries requiring medical treatment and incapacitating him for several days. Another student was struck in the arm, depriving him of its full use for a week. They brought a class action suit against school officials in federal court under 42 U.S.C. §1983, asserting that the paddling constituted cruel and unusual punishment in violation of the eighth amendment, and that the failure to afford a hearing prior to paddling violated due process.

The Supreme Court found no violation of the eighth amendment. However, the Court found that the actions by state officials in physically restraining students and administering corporal punishment for asserted misconduct invaded "liberty" interests in freedom from restraint protected by due process. It then considered what process was due in the circumstances, invoking the three-part balancing calculus formulated in Mathews v. Eldridge.]

. . . The concept that reasonable corporal punishment in school is justifiable continues to be recognized in the laws of most States. . . .

Florida has continued to recognize, and indeed has strengthened by statute, the common law right of a child not to be subjected to excessive corporal punishment in school. . . . If the punishment inflicted is later found to have been excessive — not reasonably believed at the time to be necessary for the child's discipline or training — the school authorities inflicting it may be held liable in damages to the child and, if malice is shown, they may be subject to criminal penalties.

. . . Moreover, because paddlings are usually inflicted in response to conduct directly observed by teachers in their presence, the risk that a child will be paddled without cause is typically insignificant. . . .

In those cases where severe punishment is contemplated, the available civil and criminal sanctions for abuse — considered in light of the openness of the school environment — afford significant protection against unjustified corporal punishment. . . .

But even if the need for advance procedural safeguards were clear, the question would remain whether the incremental benefit could justify the cost. . . . Given the impracticability of formulating a rule of procedural due process that varies with the severity of the particular imposition, the prior hearing petitioners seek would have to precede *any* paddling, however moderate or trivial.

Such a universal constitutional requirement would significantly burden the use of corporal punishment as a disciplinary measure. . . . Teachers, properly concerned with maintaining authority in the classroom, may well prefer to rely on other disciplinary measures — which they may view as less effective — rather than confront the possible disruption that prior notice and a hearing may entail. Paradoxically, such an alteration of disciplinary policy is most likely to occur in the ordinary case where the contemplated punishment is well within the common law privilege.[92]

---

92. The effect of interposing prior procedural safeguards may well be to make the punishment more severe by increasing the anxiety of the child. For this reason, the school authorities in Dade County found it desirable that the punishment be inflicted as soon as possible after the infraction. . . .

. . . We conclude that the Due Process Clause does not require notice and a hearing prior to the imposition of corporal punishment in the public schools, as that practice is authorized and limited by the common law.

[Four Justices dissented in an opinion by Justice White, who asserted that a damages remedy was inadequate because it was unavailable against a teacher who acted in "good faith" even on the basis of mistaken facts, and because damages later did not fully compensate for the unjustified infliction of physical pain.] The logic of [the Court's theory] would permit a State that punished speeding with a one-day jail sentence to make a driver serve his sentence first without a trial and then sue to recover damages for wrongful imprisonment. . . . There is no authority for this theory, nor does the majority purport to find any, in the procedural due process decisions of this Court. . . .

LUJAN v. G&G FIRE SPRINKLERS, INC., 532 U.S. 189 (2001). The California Labor Code authorizes the State to order withholding of payments due a contractor on a public works project if a subcontractor on the project fails to comply with Code requirements; permits the contractor, in turn, to withhold similar sums from the subcontractor; and permits the contractor, or his assignee (i.e., subcontractor) to challenge the noncompliance determination of the awarding body by an action for breach of contract to recover the wages or penalties withheld. A state body determined that G&G Sprinklers, a subcontractor on state projects, violated the Code and issued a directive to the awarding agencies to withhold payment from the contractors who in turn withheld payment from G&G. The Ninth Circuit held that the failure to provide G&G with any notice or form of hearing prior to the issuance of a payment withholding directive violated due process.

The Court reversed and upheld the statute. It stated: "Because we believe that California law affords respondent sufficient opportunity to pursue that claim in state court, we conclude that the California statutory scheme does not deprive G&G of its claim for payment. G&G has not been deprived of any present entitlement. It has been deprived of payment that it contends it is owed under a contract, based on the State's determination that it failed to comply with the contract's terms. That property interest can be fully protected by an ordinary breach of contract suit. . . . The Labor Code, by allowing assignment, provides a means by which a subcontractor may bring a claim for breach of contract to recover wages and penalties withheld. Even if respondent could not obtain assignment of the right to sue the awarding body under the contract, it appears that a suit for breach of contract against the contractor remains available under California common law. That damages may not be awarded until the suit's conclusion does not deprive G&G of its claim."

CLUB MISTY v. LASKI, 208 F.3d 615 (7th Cir.), *cert. denied*, 531 U.S. 1011 (2000). An Illinois statute provides that liquor licenses may be revoked or renewal denied only for good cause. Other provisions in the statute (1) allow a majority of the voters in a precinct to prohibit any sale of liquor in the precinct (local option), (2) allow a majority of precinct voters to prohibit sales of liquor at a particular address; if an establishment at that address holds a liquor license, it becomes void 30 days after the vote. A Chicago precinct typically has about 400 registered voters. The Seventh Circuit, which had previously upheld the local option provision, invalidated the second provision as a violation of due process in a suit brought by two Chicago taverns who had been voted out of business in precinct votes. Chief Judge Posner's opinion for the court held that, under Illinois law, liquor licensees enjoy a constitutionally protected property interest in retaining a license absent a showing of good cause for revocation. The process of local precinct vote violates due process because it lacks any standards or safeguards to ensure protection of this entitlement. "A vote by neighbors to decide whether a particular person or firm is a bad apple exemplifies 'popular justice,' the mode by which an Athenian jury, without deliberation, without instruction or control by professional judges, without possibility of correction on appeal, and without assistance of lawyers, condemned Socrates to death. [The notion] that the democratic process should be left completely unhindered by law . . . is not the theory of our Constitution. An individual's life, liberty, and property are not held or enjoyed at the sufferance of the electorate." A dissent by Judge Bauer made a strong plea for neighborhood democracy: "The process of democratic government does not rely on stern lectures from the highly educated. The least of us has the right to express himself at the ballot box without deference to the ruling classes."

Notes and Questions

1. Recall Paul v. Davis, where plaintiff was branded as a shoplifter (p. 638, supra). The Court held that there was no protected interest; it noted that the defamation in question might be actionable as a tort claim under state law. Why didn't state tort law create a "property" entitlement in that case? If it did so, shouldn't the Court have reviewed the procedural adequacy of the state's tort remedies?

Note that Ingraham doesn't address this "property" issue. It only considers whether state tort law can be a procedurally adequate remedy for a "liberty" entitlement created by the federal Constitution. Should state tort law be recognized as creating protected "property" entitlements (as well as providing a potential remedy for their violation)? An affirmative answer would seemingly turn all questions of state procedural and remedial law in tort, contract, and property into federal constitutional questions. But can a negative answer be squared with Roth and Sindermann? In what respects does the Court's equation of "property" with entitlements created by state law potentially broaden, rather than restrict, the coverage of federal due process?

2. Under the Ingraham approach, how does a court determine whether an ex post damage remedy is a constitutionally adequate substitute for an ex ante administrative hearing?

a. Is the test the relative ability of the two remedies to prevent erroneous deprivations? How does a court find out the percentage of erroneous deprivations deterred by the availability of a tort remedy and the percentage that would be prevented by an ex ante hearing?

b. Even if a tort remedy deters no erroneous deprivations, is due process satisfied on the premise that damages make the plaintiff whole?

c. An ex ante administrative hearing allows a claimant an opportunity to participate in the decisional process and influence the agency's exercise of discretion. This opportunity is lost when the only remedy is an ex post damage remedy. Does this loss count for anything in the due process calculus? If so, how much?

How satisfactorily does the Mathews v. Eldridge balancing test answer these questions? Should some other approach be used for determining when an ex post judicial remedy is a constitutionally adequate substitute for an ex ante administrative remedy? Is the administrative practicality of providing a predeprivation hearing relevant?

3. Consider the foregoing questions in light of the following decisions:

a. Memphis Light, Gas, & Water Div. v. Craft, 436 U.S. 1 (1978). Plaintiff's electricity service had been terminated by a municipally owned utility for nonpayment of a disputed bill. After ruling that under Tennessee law there exists an entitlement to uninterrupted service where a customer has refused to pay a bill that is the object of a bona fide dispute, and that this entitlement represents a "property" interest protected by due process, the Court found existing pretermination hearing procedures inadequate. It rejected arguments that the available judicial remedies of a pretermination injunction, a posttermination suit for damages, and postpayment action for a refund were adequate substitutes. In many cases, the amount in dispute was too small to justify and customers too poor to undertake the expense of a lawsuit. The procedural obstacles and delays in obtaining injunctive relief made it a doubtful pretermination remedy. The interim loss caused by an interruption of service could be serious.

b. Parratt v. Taylor, 451 U.S. 527 (1981). A package of materials mailed to a state prisoner was lost due to asserted negligence by the prison administration. The Court held that the prisoner had been deprived of a constitutionally protected interest, but that a state tort law remedy satisfied due process. A prior administrative hearing was not feasible in cases of unintentional deprivations. The Court rejected plaintiff's claim that since there had already been a deprivation, the appropriate form of damage remedy was a §1983 action (unlike most state tort law, §1983 authorizes recovery by successful plaintiffs of attorneys' fees). To accept this argument would "federalize" all state tort law. Since the state tort law remedy was adequate, the state's procedures did not violate due process, and therefore there was no §1983 violation. Justice Powell, concurring in the result, asserted that only intentional deprivations could violate due process.

c. Daniels v. Williams, 474 U.S. 327 (1986). The plaintiff was a prison inmate who slipped on a pillow that he claimed was negligently left on the stairs by defendant correctional officer. The plaintiff filed suit under §1983, claiming a deprivation of his liberty interest in freedom from bodily injury. The Court dismissed the suit. Rejecting the logic of *Parratt*, the Court held that negligent acts of an official causing unintended loss of or injury to life, liberty, or property do not constitute deprivations under the due process clause. The Court reasoned that both the language and history underlying the word "deprive" in the due process clause implied some sort of official abuse of power rather than a mere negligent harm caused by a state actor. In a companion case, Davidson v. Cannon, 474 U.S. 344 (1986), the Court reaffirmed this holding even though the state sovereign immunity statute left the plaintiff in question with no postdeprivation tort remedy at all.

d. Hudson v. Palmer, 468 U.S. 517 (1984). Palmer, a prison inmate, charged that during a prison shakedown a correctional officer intentionally destroyed some of his personal property. He filed a §1983 action claiming deprivation of his property without due process. The Court upheld state postdeprivation remedies (an action for damages against the officer) as sufficient to satisfy due process. Although the deprivation was caused by an intentional act of a state official, the act was random and unauthorized. A predeprivation hearing in such a circumstance is impractical.

e. Zinermon v. Burch, 494 U.S. 113 (1990). Plaintiff filed a §1983 action against state mental hospital officials, claiming that they failed properly to apply state procedures for voluntary commitment and as a result improperly institutionalized him during a period when he was not competent to give consent. The Court held that the claim could proceed notwithstanding the availability of state tort actions against the officials. Four dissenting justices argued that the case involved isolated misapplication of adequate state procedures and was controlled by *Parratt* and *Hudson*.

f. Vail v. Board of Educ. of Paris Union School Dist. No. 95, 706 F.2d 1435 (7th Cir. 1983), *aff'd by an equally divided Court*, 466 U.S. 377 (1984). Plaintiff, a school football coach, was fired halfway through his two-year employment contract; he was given no hearing or explanation with respect to his discharge. The court of appeals upheld a §1983 damage award for denial of procedural rights. It cited *Sindermann* for the proposition that contract rights are "property" for purposes of due process. It rejected the claim that a damage action in state court was an adequate remedy for due process purposes, distinguishing *Parratt* on the ground that in that case it was not feasible to provide a predeprivation hearing, whereas in this case it was. Judge Posner entered a strong dissent, asserting:

> If this logic is applied unflinchingly, any time a school board or any other local government body breaks a contract without first holding a hearing, the contractor — who need not be an employee, who could be a supplier of paper clips — can get damages in federal court. . . .
>
> . . . There is no federal interest in this case, unless the Fourteenth Amendment is thought to invest with federal significance all state action, however unthreatening to the rights we deem fundamental. Vail was not fired because he exercised his freedom of speech or some other liberty protected by the Constitution, or because of his race (in which event he would have a claim under the equal protection clause of the Fourteenth Amendment), or for any other reason in which the federal courts as tribunals for enforcing the Constitution — viewed as a charter of liberty rather than an invitation to the federal courts to bring the whole business of the states under their wing — have an interest. . . .

Judge Posner argued (1) that plaintiff's interest in the remaining year of his contract was a contract interest as opposed to "property," distinguishing *Sindermann* on the ground that it involved a claim of permanent tenure, a form of "property"; (2) that since under Illinois contract law plaintiff would not have a right to specific performance of his employment contract but only to damages, and such a damage remedy was available, there had been no "deprivation" of property under §1983 and the fourteenth amendment; (3) that even if there had been a "deprivation" of "property," a state law damage action was adequate process due under *Parratt* (and, one might add, *Ingraham*).

4. Does *G&G Fire Sprinklers* effectively overrule the Court's holdings in *Loudermill* (p. 654, supra) and *Winegar* (p.655, supra) requiring hearings prior to termination or suspension of government employees? Does it overrule *Memphis Light*?

5. Consider the decision in *Club Misty*. Does the due process clause prohibit a role for direct democracy in implementing the regulatory state? Suppose that, following the repeal of Prohibition, the new liquor laws adopted by Illinois had provided that liquor licensees could retain their licenses indefinitely once issued unless (1) the licensing authority showed good cause for revocation; (2) a majority of the precinct voters voted for revocation. Would such an arrangement violate due process? If not, why can't Illinois amend a statute that provides for condition (1) by adding condition (2)? Is the court's decision in *Club Misty* consistent with its decision upholding the local option provision in the Illinois liquor laws?

d. The Regulatory Context

Brock v. Roadway Express, Inc.
481 U.S. 252 (1987)

Justice MARSHALL announced the judgment of the Court and delivered an opinion in which Justice Blackmun, Justice Powell, and Justice O'Connor join.

[The Surface Transportation Assistance Act of 1982 has a "whistleblower" protection provision, which takes effect when a transportation industry employee complains to

OSHA that he was discharged because he was a whistleblower. OSHA then investigates. If it finds "reasonable cause" to believe the employee, it must issue an order directing the employer to reinstate the employee immediately. The employer may then request an evidentiary hearing and final decision, but, in the meantime, he must keep the employee at work. The question presented was whether this requirement — to keep the employee at work unless and until OSHA, after hearing, finds that he was not discharged for whistle-blowing — unconstitutionally deprives the employer of procedural due process.

Roadway Express discharged a driver, Hufstetler, for asserted misconduct. The driver claimed that he was discharged for reporting company safety violations. Following an OSHA investigation in which Roadway could present evidence but not obtain evidence presented to OSHA, OSHA ordered the driver's temporary reinstatement; a full hearing was held 19 months later.]

The property right of which Roadway asserts it has been deprived without due process . . . is the right to discharge an employee for cause. . . .

We begin by accepting as substantial the Government's interests in promoting highway safety and protecting employees from retaliatory discharge. . . . We also agree . . . that Roadway's interest in controlling the makeup of its workforce is substantial. . . . In assessing the competing interests, however, the District Court failed to consider another private interest affected by the Secretary's decision: Hufstetler's interest in not being discharged for having complained about the allegedly unsafe condition of Roadway's trucks. . . . In light of the injurious effect a retaliatory discharge can have on an employee's financial status and prospects for alternative interim employment, the employee's substantial interest in retaining the job must be considered. . . . [The plurality opinion concluded that when the employee's interest was added to the calculus, OSHA's general practices and procedures for temporary reinstatement were constitutionally adequate. It held, however, that the preliminary reinstatement order was unconstitutionally imposed in this case because Roadway was not informed of the relevant evidence supporting Hufstetler's complaint and therefore was deprived of an opportunity to prepare a meaningful response. But Roadway was not entitled to a full hearing or opportunity to cross-examine witnesses prior to the entry of the order.]

[Justice Brennan concluded that OSHA's delays in providing a full hearing later meant that it could not compensate for inadequacies in the prereinstatement procedures, and that accordingly "the Secretary may not order preliminary reinstatement without first providing the employer with a chance to confront its accuser, to cross-examine witnesses, and to present its own testimony. . . ."

Justice Stevens reached the same conclusion, stating:] It is wrong to approach the due process analysis in each case by asking anew what procedures seem worthwhile and not too costly. Unless a case falls within a recognized exception, we should adhere to the strongest presumption that the Government may not take away life, liberty or property before making a meaningful hearing available. . . .

Cross-examination is a critical element in the truth determining process. . . . Even if there were merit in the plurality's novel view that the possibility of delay outweighs the value of confrontation, this reasoning does not justify the Department's refusal to provide the parties with a list of the witnesses and a summary of each witness' testimony, which would at least enable the parties to make oral or written arguments about why the investigator should not credit the witness' testimony. This would certainly not cause any intolerable delay.

[Justice White, joined by Chief Justice Rehnquist and Justice Scalia, concluded that OSHA was not required to disclose its witnesses' names and statements prior to ordering temporary reinstatement or to afford the other procedures sought by Roadway Express.]

Notes and Questions

1. In O'Bannon v. Town Court Nursing Center, 446 U.S. 773 (1980), the Supreme Court considered a government action "decertifying" Town Court Nursing Center as eligible for Medicaid reimbursement. Without this reimbursement, Town Court would have to close, and the patients receiving Medicaid assistance there would have to move to another facility. The patients sued, asking for an evidentiary hearing before decertification. The Court held that they had no right to such a hearing. It wrote that the Medicaid statute

> gives recipients [such as the patients] the right to choose among a range of *qualified* providers without government interference. By implication, it also confers an absolute right to be free from government interference with the choice to remain in a home that continues to be qualified. But it clearly does not confer a right on a recipient to enter an unqualified home and demand a hearing to certify it, nor does it confer a right on a recipient to continue to receive benefits for care in a home that has been decertified. Second, although the regulations do protect patients by limiting the circumstances under which a home may transfer or discharge a Medicaid recipient, they do not purport to limit the Government's right to make a transfer necessary by decertifying a facility. Finally, since decertification does not reduce or terminate a patient's financial assistance, but merely requires him to use it for care at a different facility, regulations granting recipients the right to a hearing prior to a reduction in financial benefits are irrelevant. . . .
>
> The simple distinction between government action that directly affects the citizen's legal rights, or imposes a direct restraint on his liberty, and action that is directed against a third party and affects the citizen only indirectly or incidentally, provides sufficient answer to all of the cases on which the patients rely in this Court. . . .

Would the plurality opinion in *Roadway Express* overrule *Town Court*? Does *Town Court*'s result simply reflect the fact that decertification is, with respect to patients, "rulemaking," not "adjudication"?

2. To what extent does the "deprivation" by the government in *Roadway Express* resemble the deprivation in, say, *Loudermill*? In the latter, the government, an interested party, takes a job from an individual. In the former, the government, acting as a regulatory "umpire," deprives a regulated company of its right to dismiss an individual. Are these situations similar for "due process" purposes? Should the basic "due process" analysis be the same? If not, how should it differ?

3. Is the *Roadway Express* analysis limited to cases where a member of the class intended to be benefited by a regulatory program has an entitlement to regulatory protection? If so, how does a court determine whether such an entitlement exists?

4. How is this additional element — the interests of a beneficiary of a regulatory program — to be weighed in the *Eldridge* calculus? Does the addition make the "calculus" more ad hoc and unpredictable than ever? Or does its inclusion more fairly safeguard the interests of those affected by government action? See Rakoff, *Brock v. Roadway Express, Inc.*, and the New Law of Regulatory Due Process, 1988 Sup. Ct. Rev. 157.

5. In Deshaney v. Winnebago County Dept. of Social Servs., 489 U.S. 189 (1989), a child who had been repeatedly and severely beaten by his father, and suffered permanent brain damage, brought a §1983 action against the county and several of its employees, contending that their failure to intervene and protect him despite ample notice of the

father's behavior violated his due process rights. Affirming dismissal for failure to state a claim, the Court in an opinion by Chief Justice Rehnquist held that there was no general constitutional right to affirmative protection from the government, and distinguished prior cases recognizing a constitutional right to "reasonable safety" and medical care on the part of prisoners and others involuntarily committed to state custody. If, as claimed, the state had fallen down on its voluntary undertaking to protect children in plaintiff's circumstances, the appropriate remedy was a tort claim under state law. Justices Brennan, Marshall, and Blackmun dissented. *Query*: Is there any issue of procedural due process presented by this case?

Problems

1. Section 2057 of a state traffic code authorizes the state police to tow any vehicles illegally parked on state roads. Owners of towed vehicles can reclaim their cars by (1) paying the traffic ticket plus towing and storage charges, or (2) requesting a hearing at which the question of whether the car was in fact illegally parked will be litigated. Because of congested dockets, it takes several months to get a hearing. If the owner of the car chooses to pay the money and retrieve his or her car immediately, and if he or she requests a subsequent hearing at which it is established that the car was not in fact illegally parked, then the money is returned.

Dr. Leslie Smith's car was towed while parked in front of a fire hydrant. Instead of either requesting a hearing or ransoming her car, Dr. Smith filed a suit in federal district court under 42 U.S.C. §1983, alleging that when her car was towed, she was making an emergency medical call. Traffic Code §2133 exempts from all parking regulations doctors making such calls. Dr. Smith claimed that the towing of the car deprived her of property without due process of law. She also claimed that the loss of her car has impaired her ability to make housecalls and has thereby resulted in losses to her of some $10,000 in professional fees. What due process claims might she assert in a §1983 lawsuit, and how should they be decided?

2. To receive a White House press pass, accredited reporters must undergo a secret service security check. An accredited reporter is denied a White House press pass. The secret service refuses to give any reason for the denial. What relief can the reporter obtain in court?

3. Raphael Claret is a 14-year-old student in a junior high school in Los Angeles. After a period of more than a year of behavioral difficulties, Claret was suspended from school by the principal for misconduct after a skeletal *Goss* hearing. The case was promptly referred to the district superintendent, who notified Claret's parents, asking them to appear three days later at a "guidance conference." The parents consulted an attorney, who requested that at the conference Claret be allowed the right to be represented by counsel; the right to confront and cross-examine; written findings; a written record; and an impartial decisionmaker. When this request was denied, Claret and his parents brought a §1983 action seeking to enjoin further proceedings and reinstate Claret in school until the requested procedures were afforded.

Under state law, persons between the ages of seven and sixteen are required to attend school. A student may, however, be suspended for being "insubordinate or disorderly" as well as on other grounds. Such a suspension may be a "principal suspension" (for not more than five days) or an "administrative suspension," which remains in effect pending a further decision by the district superintendent. The latter suspension was imposed in Claret's case, and pursuant to the board's procedural regulations, the parents were notified of a guidance conference and invited to attend along with the child. The regulations provide that the parents may bring an interpreter if they do not speak English but may not bring an attorney. (Mr. and Mrs. Claret do not speak English.) The conference is attended by the principal, the school guidance counselor, the district superintendent, and a "school-court coordinator," who takes notes of the conference. (No statements made at the conference, however, are admissible in any subsequent family court or criminal proceeding.)

At this conference, the school personnel discuss the case and then the parents and the child are asked what they think should be done. Sometimes, a social worker who knows the family may also take part. The following actions can be taken as a result of this conference.

(a) The suspended child may be reinstated in the same school.
(b) The suspended child may be transferred to another school of the same level.
(c) The suspended child may be transferred to a special day school for maladjusted children (the "600" schools) or a "residential institution," provided that the parents consent. If the parents refuse to consent, they may be prosecuted for dereliction of parental duties and for violation of the compulsory education laws. In such a proceeding, the full panoply of procedural rights are available to both the parents and the child in family court.

Should the injunction sought by the Clarets be granted? If so, on what conditions should the guidance conference be permitted to proceed?

4. Section 10 of the disciplinary regulations issued by the Rhode Island Department of Corrections pursuant to statutory authority specifies some 25 disciplinary offenses, including disobeying an order of a staff member, "willful refusal to perform work," "tampering with windows or locks," "setting fires," "engaging in unauthorized sexual acts with others," and so forth. Section 10.25 prohibits "any conduct which disrupts or interferes with the security or orderly functioning of the institution." Section 11 of the regulations specifies the sanctions that may be imposed for violations: loss of good-time credits, solitary confinement, loss of visiting privileges, extra work assignments, or reprimand.

William Wayward is an inmate at the Rhode Island Correctional Institute for Men. About half the inmates at the institute (not including Wayward) engage in a work strike to protest poor food and inadequate medical services. Wayward and two other nonstriking inmates are selected by the strikers to present a formal list of grievances to the warden and seek to negotiate a settlement. The warden agrees to delay any action to terminate the strike for 24 hours to receive and consider the list of grievances. Wayward and his colleagues report to the warden that they are unable to agree on a list of grievances. After once extending the 24-hour deadline, the warden is convinced that Wayward is deliberately stalling. The warden disbands the Wayward group and takes action to break the strike.

The next day the warden initiates a disciplinary proceeding against Wayward, charging that his actions during the strike violated §10.25. A hearing is held before a board consisting of two guards and one social worker, all of whom are employed by the institute. The warden testifies that Wayward was deliberately stalling to prolong the strike. Wayward, who is ably represented by a law student, is allowed to question the warden and testify himself but is not permitted to call witnesses. The board finds Wayward guilty as charged and sentences him to 45 days in solitary confinement. The same day, the warden issues an order that after Wayward's sentence is served, he will not be allowed to return to the minimum security portion of the institute where he was formerly assigned, but will be transferred to cellblock 7, a maximum security wing with close and continued surveillance and tightly restricted privileges for the remaining three years of his sentence.

Wayward brings a §1983 action seeking to enjoin his confinement to solitary and his transfer to cellblock 7. What result?

5. The Comprehensive Environmental Response, Compensation and Liability Act (CERCLA), popularly known as "Superfund," authorizes EPA to issue unilateral administrative orders (UAOs) to a wide range of parties with some connection to hazardous wastes at a given site, requiring them to undertake waste cleanup activities in accordance with EPA specifications. UAOs typically run to dozens of pages. CERCLA provides that UAOs are to be issued only in cases of "imminent and substantial endangerment to the public health or welfare." EPA has interpreted this provision to authorize issuance of UAOs in virtually any situation where some hazardous substance is present in the environment; the courts have agreed, holding that EPA need not show that there is a threat of immediate, serious harm. CERCLA provides a notice-and-comment procedure for the selection by EPA of the basic cleanup remedy in a Record of Decision (ROD). UAOs, however, go beyond the ROD by specifying in detail the specific measures to be undertaken by the UAO recipient in accordance with a detailed timetable. Cleanups often take up to ten years to implement. The average remedy costs around $30 million, but can run to hundreds of millions of dollars. If a recipient fails to implement a UAO, EPA may sue it to compel enforcement and obtain penalties for non-compliance and/or complete the cleanup itself and recover four times the amount of cleanup costs from the recipient. CERCLA does not provide for any hearing on UAOs either before or after their issuance. A UAO recipient is precluded from obtaining judicial review of a UAO on its issuance. CERCLA provides only two routes by which a recipient can obtain judicial review of an order's validity. First, if EPA brings an action for enforcement and/or cost reimbursement, the recipient can defend on the ground that the order is invalid. There is no provision which requires EPA to bring such actions at any particular time. Penalties for non-compliance are $27,500 for each day of non-compliance. Thus, if EPA chooses not to bring an immediate enforcement action, large penalties can accumulate quickly. If EPA decides to undertake the remedy itself, quadruple liabilities for cleanup costs can also mount rapidly. A non-compliant recipient thus runs the risk of potentially incurring very large liabilities if EPA delays bringing an enforcement or cost-recovery action. CERCLA provides that a UAO recipient can avoid penalties if it establishes "sufficient cause" for non-compliance. The contours of this defense are unclear. The other route for obtaining judicial review is available only after a UAO recipient has fully implemented the remedy required by a UAO. At that point, the recipient can petition EPA to reimburse its cleanup costs (plus interest) out of the Superfund if it carries the burden of showing that the UAO was arbitrary and capricious or otherwise contrary to law. The petitioner can obtain judicial review of EPA's denial of its petition. Do these provisions satisfy due process?

4. The Impact of Due Process Hearings and Alternative Systems of Bureaucratic Control

The due process explosion that followed *Goldberg* was bound to create problems. The judiciary began requiring procedural safeguards in settings where none had existed (for example, school suspensions) and more extensive procedures where the existing ones were judged inadequate (for example, *Goldberg*). Even aside from the initial burden of adapting agency practice to these new requirements, experience in many areas has suggested that judicial-style hearings are often ill-suited as a method of control and accountability for bureaucracies such as mass justice welfare agencies or prisons and hospitals. Where intensive procedural formalities have been implemented, they have consumed considerable resources, but it is questionable how far they have promoted accuracy in decisionmaking or other goals such as responsiveness to individual situations. In some contexts, such as mass justice welfare administration, hearing rights when exercised may tend to change outcomes in claimants' favor, although even this effect is disputed. What is more clear is that limitations in claimants' knowledge of their rights, or the unavailability of lawyers, means that in most contexts these rights are typically exercised in only a small percentage of cases.

The federal courts have sometimes encountered severe burdens in overseeing the implementation of new procedural requirements. For example, Judge Pettine of the U.S. District Court for Rhode Island approved a consent decree giving inmates procedural rights in prison disciplinary cases consisting of notice of charges, representation by an institutional counselor, an opportunity to present evidence (though not necessarily the opportunity to call or cross-examine witnesses), and an administrative review procedure. Morris v. Travisono, 310 F. Supp. 857 (D.R.I. 1970). Thereafter, Judge Pettine was required to set aside the second and fourth Friday of each month to hear inmate complaints. It is not clear what was achieved by these judicial efforts. A study by the Harvard Center for Criminal Justice found that implementation of the decree's procedural safeguards was often slipshod or nonexistent; that prison staff, which had not been involved in formulating the decree, resented the court's intrusion; and that prisoners continued to be found guilty as charged in all but a handful of cases. However, there was some evidence indicating that punishments were lightened, and that prisoners viewed the court's intervention favorably because it forced officials to acknowledge that prisoners had rights. See Harvard Center for Criminal Justice, Judicial Intervention in Prison Discipline, 63 J. Crim L.C. & P.S. 200 (1972).

At the same time, states and agencies have undertaken a variety of defensive measures to ward off due process requirements. These have included the removal of statutory restrictions on the discretion of prison administrators and other officials to eliminate "property" entitlement claims, and, as with the SSD "grid," the development of rules for benefit administration that permit individual cases to be decided on the basis of readily verifiable facts, avoiding the need for adjudicatory hearings. The Supreme Court has upheld these steps and through other decisions has sought to limit the applicability and extent of due process safeguards.

This history may reflect a familiar pendulum of reform and reaction. But it also suggests that one should examine the potential for means other than adversary hearings and judicial review to provide incentives for better administrative decisionmaking.

a. The Impact of Hearing Requirements

The Social Security disability benefits program (SSD) provides money for employed persons who have subsequently become permanently and totally disabled and therefore unable to engage in any substantial gainful work in the *national* economy. The claims application procedure begins with the initial claim evaluation. These claims are made in written form and evaluated at the state level. By the early 1980s, an average of 1.25 million claims were filed each year. Of those rejected, approximately 250,000 were submitted for a "reconsideration," also done at the state level and again without the benefit of personal appearance by the claimant. Denials at the reconsideration level resulted in about 150,000 requests each year for hearings before an administrative law judge (ALJ) — over 625 ALJs handle these appeals. The ALJ hearing marks the beginning of the federal government's involvement in the claim dispute. It is also the first opportunity for the claimant to appear in person at the time that the claim is being considered. On rejection by the ALJ, 25,000 claimants brought their final administrative appeal before the Appeals Council. Of those, 10,000 sought judicial review in federal district court. J. Mashaw, Bureaucratic Justice 18 (1983).

In the early 1980s, ALJ hearings and court review proceedings mushroomed as a result of administration efforts (spurred in part by congressional budget concerns) to trim from the rolls persons who are receiving SSD payments but are assertedly not disabled, either because they were erroneously classified as disabled in the first place or because they have since lost or overcome their disability. A key legal issue was whether, as the SSA contended, recipients have the burden of showing continuing disability or, as most courts have held, the burden is on SSA to show a change in circumstances that is sufficient to reverse the initial determination of disability. Because the SSA refused to acquiesce in these rulings, recipients had to seek ALJ or court review to stay on the rolls. As a result, ALJ hearings requests swelled to over 320,000 annually, and some 48,000 cases were pending in the federal courts. The system of hearings and appeals approached breakdown.

Recall Justice Black's warning in *Goldberg* that a requirement of burdensome hearings before termination of benefits would encourage agencies to carefully screen applicants, possibly delaying, or foreclosing altogether, the delivery of benefits to the truly needy. The magnitude of this effect is obviously difficult to measure, but it seems reasonable to infer that it is appreciable. A similar problem stemming from the cost of hearings is that as more of an agency's budget is spent on hearings, the pool of money available for the program's beneficiaries may be diminished.

Other aspects of the effort to impose formal hearings on mass justice administration are explored by Professor Jerry Mashaw in an important study of the SSD program, Bureaucratic Justice (1984). Mashaw found that those claimants who sought ALJ hearings or, if unsuccessful there, judicial review, were far more likely to end up being awarded benefits than those who did not. ALJs and district judges reversed benefit denials in about half the cases that they heard. Given these statistics, why do only a relatively small percentage of claimants appeal? The main factors seem to be availability of legal representation and socioeconomic background. Those appealing were more likely to be white, better educated, and have a history of higher incomes — factors that suggest that they were more knowledgeable and better able to deal with a bureaucratic system. Mashaw asserts that this difference in treatment between those who appeal and those who do not is inequitable, particularly in a program that aims at evenhanded distribution of limited benefits. But he is equally clear that society should not provide a lawyer and guarantee an ALJ hearing and judicial review in every case. According to a study of the AFCD program in Wisconsin, however, overall client success actually decreased with the advent of *Goldberg*-type hearings because most recipients were inadequately informed and ill equipped for formal hearings. Note, Procedural Due Process and the Welfare Recipient: A Statistical Study of AFDC Fair Hearings in Wisconsin, 1978 Wis. L. Rev. 145, 217.

Perhaps an appeal process that is disproportionately used by more advantaged claimants would be tolerable if it produced more accurate decisions or otherwise improved the functioning of the system as a whole. But Mashaw's study argues persuasively that neither is the case. The determination that a person is too disabled to work is not one of objective fact, but involves a weighing of several factors, including the person's age, education, and employment history, personal characteristics and attitude toward work, and the state of the local and national economy. Also inescapably relevant are the extent of funds available for benefits, the potential availability of other forms of assistance, and the number and nature of other claims for SSD benefits. The agency, which can maintain a perspective on the caseload as a whole, attempts to develop criteria that match claims granted with available resources and seeks to maintain consistency in the treatment of the many cases in the large gray area between those involving persons clearly too disabled to work and those involving persons clearly able to work.

The ALJ or the federal judge, however, only hears individual claims on a case-by-case basis without much sense of the larger pattern. The ALJ or judge is more inclined to be generous than the SSA, in part because any claimant in the gray area can show some hardship, and in part because the ALJ or judge doesn't have to balance the strength of any one claim against others or be responsible for the overall solvency of the system. Moreover, because the disposition of cases on ALJ or district court appeal is ad hoc, such appeals do not affect the administrative disposition of the great bulk of cases, which are not appealed. Mashaw concludes that hearings and judicial review are "impertinent" and "irrelevant." Other observers have feared that hearing requirements in other contexts may have a substantial negative effect on the administrative system to which they are applied. For example, Justice Powell's dissent in *Goss* made much of the fact that adversary proceedings can be damaging to the purposes of schools; trial-type procedures, however informal, may encourage confrontation on the students' part and undermine the cooperative atmosphere necessary for the day-to-day operation of the educational process. One commentator found that the intrusion of due process hearing requirements may heighten the "impersonality of superior-subordinate relations," cutting off the informal feedback needed to deal with the underlying causes of tension and dissatisfaction in the school. Thus, legalization and distrust feed off one another. See Yudof, Legalization of Dispute Resolution, Distrust of Authority, and Organizational Theory: Implementing Due Process for Students in the Public Schools, 1981 Wis. L. Rev. 891. The atmosphere of learning may become stifled by an air of impersonality and an "us against them" attitude.

This problem is not confined to the educational setting. A Wisconsin study revealed that AFDC caseworkers, who tend to see their role as that of "moral supervisor," are alienated by an adversary system. After elaborate hearing procedures were required, AFDC was no longer viewed as a means of rehabilitation, rather it became an "entitlement." This tended to produce an adversary relation between caseworkers and claimants. The positions of the parties hardened at an earlier stage, reducing the likelihood of compromise. The adversary hearing became the only means for resolution of the dispute. The morale of caseworkers and their concern for recipients declined. See Note, Procedural Due Process and the Welfare Recipient: A Statistical Study of AFDC Fair Hearings in Wisconsin, 1978 Wis. L. Rev. 145.

In the SSD program, hearing requirements led SSA to formulate "grid" regulations (see *Campbell*, p. 523, supra) that seek to "mechanize" benefit determinations by giving readily verifiable facts (such as age and work experience) controlling significance. As a result, consideration of individual circumstances is largely excluded.

This suggests that recipients both gain and lose by making benefits into entitlements. On the one hand, the shift enables claimants who can effectively assert their rights to obtain benefits as a matter of right and to overcome official paternalism or indifference. On the other hand, it may make the administration of benefit programs more mechanical and bureaucratic, more unresponsive to the needs and concerns of particular individuals and special circumstances. Whether this yields a net gain depends on one's assessment of the tradeoff, examined in Chapter 5, between clear standards and individualized determinations. See also Note on the Procedural Implications of Changes in Federal Welfare Law, pp. 645-646, supra.

b. The Goals of Due Process: Hearings and Alternatives

The foregoing analyses of the effects of adversary hearings suggest that the alternative mechanisms of control, incentive, or response might be more appropriate than trials and judicial appeals. But more appropriate to what end? We here sketch some potential goals of due process. In the following subsection, we examine various alternatives that might better meet these goals.

Accuracy. Accuracy has been the Court's stated concern in the new due process cases. An accurate decisionmaking process is one that ensures that those who are entitled to X receive X, and that those who are not entitled to X don't.

Consistency. A consistent system guarantees that like cases are treated alike. A consistent system is not necessarily accurate; a whole category of deserving individuals might be consistently denied benefits owing to inaccurate implementation of the program.

Individual responsiveness. An equitable system should respond to individual circumstances and avoid mechanical application of inflexible rules.

Efficiency. A system for distributing benefits should conserve scarce resources and avoid delay.

Conduciveness to an atmosphere of cooperation. The institution should be able to maintain a nonadversarial relationship with the clients or other constituents of the administrative program.

Promotion of dignity and participation values. The recipient population should believe that the decisional system gives them an opportunity to be heard. The larger objective is for the claimant to feel that her interests have been recognized and respected and that justice has been done.

Agency effectiveness and accountability. The agency or institution should have both the incentives and the latitude to operate in ways that advance the overall social goal of a program.

It should be obvious that there are conflicts or tradeoffs among these criteria. Efforts to promote consistency, for example, may undermine individual responsiveness. Different decisionmaking structures and procedures will perform better in meeting different criteria. Also consider that a grant of hearing rights to advance "process" values like participation is bound to have an impact on the substantive results that emerge.

c. Alternative to Hearings

(1) Objective Rules

Suppose that the legislature were able to establish clear, readily verifiable, objective criteria for eligibility for an entitlement. Under such a scheme, there might seldom be any need for due process mandated hearings. Alternatively, agencies granted broad statutory discretion might try to establish mechanical decisional criteria through notice-and-comment rulemaking. (Recall the AEC's strategy in *Vermont Yankee*, pp. 538-543, supra.)

Consider the problem faced by SSA in determining the employment opportunities available to SSD claimants with varying degrees of physical and mental disability and different ages and educational and employment histories. Litigating such issues on a case-by-case basis in hundreds of thousands of individual ALJ hearings required extensive and expensive use of vocational experts to testify at such hearings. The SSA responded to this problem by instituting notice-and-comment rulemaking procedures to make the employ-ability determination more routinized. The result was a regulation adopting a "grid" matrix that incorporated four factors: age, education, prior work experience (for example, unskilled, semiskilled), and residual functional capacity (RFC) or physical work capability (for example, sedentary work, light work) based on the extent of disability.[93] The grid was based on data concerning general employment opportunities. Once the four variables are ascertained, the grid mechanically determines whether the person in question is "disabled" or "not disabled." By its nature, the grid must use cutoff points that may seem arbitrary. A 50-year-old man may be deemed disabled, while a 49-year-old man with the same educa-tion, prior work experience, and RFC might be deemed employable and denied benefits.

A chief advantage of the grid system is efficiency. There is no longer any need for a vocational expert to testify at every ALJ hearing. The grid makes it possible to dismiss many claims without the burden of an extended hearing.

Another advantage to the grid is its apparent consistency. By zeroing in on objective criteria, the grid ensures that like cases will be treated alike. Two claimants with the same four "factors" will be treated alike, and that alone may be a major improvement over the prior case-by-case system. Under the old system, the outcome of particular cases tended to depend more on the hearing officer than on the facts of the case. See Capowski, Accuracy and Consistency in Categorical Decisionmaking: A Study of Social Security's Medical-Vocational Guidelines — Two Birds with One Stone or Pigeon-Holing Claimants? 42 Md. L. Rev. 329 (1983). But do these four factors tell the whole story? Do they leave out important informa-tion relevant to determining disability? If so, consistency may be purchased at the price of accuracy and other values. But consider Mashaw's argument that "accuracy" is an elusive and inapt goal in the SSD context because determining a person's readiness, ability, and opportu-nity to engage in work involves a complex of judgmental factors and social policies.

Nevertheless, if "accurate" decisions are impossible in the large percentage of cases in the gray area, then perhaps a case-by-case approach that attempts to respond to the individ-ual circumstances of each case is appropriate. Such an approach would promote personal response and allow for a large measure of claimant participation, potentially promoting "dignitary" values. This alternative, which would require elimination of the grid, would also seriously undermine efficiency by requiring hearings in every doubtful case. Mashaw's analysis also indicates that it would not secure consistency. Sensitive to at least some of these factors, the Supreme Court sustained the validity of the grid regulations against arguments that their use impermissibly deprived claimants of an adjudicatory hearing on their individ-ual claims, in violation of the SSD statute and due process. Heckler v. Campbell, p. 523, supra. See also Atkins v. Parker, 472 U.S. 115 (1985) (state officials not required to give notice to food stamp beneficiaries of unfavorable changes in federal eligibility rules; due process "concern[s] the procedural fairness of individual determinations").

---

93. Because RFC depends on a particularized assessment of an individual's condition, it is the one element in the grid that cannot be routinely determined. But Mathews v. Eldridge goes a long way in permitting SSA to make the determination of medical condition on the basis of documentary records, thereby avoiding a trial-type hearing. For discussion, see Goldhammer, The Effect of New Vocational Regulations on Social Security and Supplementary Security Income Disability Claims, 32 Admin. L. Rev. 501, 509 (1980).

Another important criterion is "agency accountability." When an agency adopts specific rules for the decision of claims, the basis for its decisions is more easily discernible and is more subject to public and congressional review than when it decides each case individually. The existence of such rules also facilitates judicial review of agency decisions. If we trust the rulemaking process, the grid approach can thus enhance accountability. On the other hand, the opportunity to participate in a rulemaking proceeding is probably of little practical significance to most benefit recipients; a switch to rulemaking may thus reduce their effective influence on agency policies. For a more comprehensive examination of the potential shortcomings of the grid system, see Capowski, supra.

(2) Informal Processes

An alternative that offers promise in contexts where an ongoing cooperative relationship is sought is the use of informal negotiations, conferences, or grievance procedures. The decisionmaker would assume a more inquisitorial role, while the individual would be allowed to offer his or her own input. The success of such a procedure depends in part on how legitimate it seems to the affected individual. This perception depends in turn on the orientation and qualifications of the decisionmaker, underlying trust relationships, and initial satisfaction with the substantive results of the procedure. This approach may face an initial negative presumption owing to the American public's greater faith in the legal system that they are most accustomed to, the adversary system. See Thibaut & Walker, A Theory of Procedure, 66 Cal. L. Rev. 541 (1978).

Informal, nonadversary procedures may be more appropriate in those situations where objective decisions are difficult, where an answer cannot be reached by simply applying a specific rule, and where many of the issues are subjective and value-laden and best left to the judgment of knowledgeable and responsible officials. Consider, for example, the decision on educational programs for handicapped children. In this context, it would be difficult to enforce specific rules for the purposes of consistency or accuracy. When skillfully and responsibly administered, informal procedures can create the feeling that an individual is being dealt with as an individual. If the individuals affected generally have confidence in the procedures and their administration, conferences, investigations, and other informal methods may also be more efficient than formal hearings, especially if appeals are reduced. See Kirp, Proceduralism and Bureaucracy: Due Process in the School Setting, 28 Stan. L. Rev. 841, 869. Informal processes may serve other values than efficiency, client satisfaction, and promotion of cooperative norms. Decisions about tenure for teachers, for example, are largely judgmental and would become stilted by the application of purely objective standards; ". . . the discretion that due process checks may well be the handmaiden of arbitrariness; it may equally well be prerequisite to the maintenance of institutional excellence." Id. at 874.

Professor Mashaw believes that there may be promise in the use of physician review panels to decide the medical issues in SSD cases. Individuals would be examined by a team of doctors not directly employed by SSA; in addition to disposing of medical aspects of the SSD claim, they might channel claimants into treatment and rehabilitation opportunities. Professional judgment, Mashaw believes, may be superior to either hearings or bureaucratic rules for disposing of at least some of the issues in SSD cases. But he is worried about consistency, and the danger that physician panels largely unconcerned about budget constraints might tend to be unduly generous. J. Mashaw, Bureaucratic Justice 36-37 (1983).

Mashaw also suggests as another alternative the use of "lay advocates" trained to facilitate a claimant's presentation of his or her case in the context of an informal agency process of decision. Such advocates could be made more widely available than lawyers, and their use would not lead to formal procedures and judicial review. But if they were agency employees, doubt might arise concerning their zeal and loyalty to claimants. Compare the problems involved in implementing a system of informal negotiation in regulation. Other proposals to modify the SSD procedures are discussed in Milton M. Carrow: A Tortuous Road to Bureaucratic Fairness: Righting the Social Security Disability Claims Process, 46 Admin. L. Rev. 297 (1994).

In the context of prisoner grievances, dissatisfaction with the costs, burdens, and frequent inappropriateness of formal hearings and judicial review in dealing with many aspects of prison administration[94] has prompted interest in establishing prisoner grievance procedures. Although grievance mechanisms in prisons are not constitutionally mandated, they are becoming extensively used. Such grievance mechanisms may give inmates the satisfaction of having some voice in prison administration. They may also contribute to the penological objectives of prison administrators. One commonly recognized correctional goal is that of rehabilitation. Some riots occur because inmates believe they have no other method of gaining public attention to their conditions. Having complaints reach decisionmaking sources through established channels, which ensure that valid grievances will be considered, may lessen inmate tensions. Grievance procedures may increase the flow of information about trouble spots to prison administrators. Lastly, federal court suits, however futile, challenging prison practices might decline if fair, accessible, alternative methods of dispute resolution were available.

Perhaps the greatest problem with these various alternatives is that they fail to provide judicially verifiable and enforceable controls on agency power. Given the limitations in using formal hearing requirements to control bureaucracies, these alternatives may in many cases be more effective in advancing the various goals of due process. But how can a court — which must take ultimate responsibility for ensuring that due process is afforded but which lacks investigational resources and social science skills — ascertain their efficacy? Moreover, these alternatives may not work well if judicial review of particular grievances is readily available. Accordingly, it may be difficult to reconcile greater use of these alternatives with traditional notions of judicially enforced due process.

(3) Nonjudicial Reviewing Bodies

Judicial review of administrative action brings in its train the expense and adversary culture associated with lawyers and relatively formal administrative decisionmaking procedures to produce a reviewable record. Furthermore, general-purpose judges often lack an understanding of the technical and administrative dimensions of an agency's job.

---

94. Chief Justice Burger noted with dismay a prisoner who engaged the attention of "one district Judge twice, three circuit judges on appeal, and six others in a secondary sense — to say nothing of lawyers, court clerks, bailiffs, court reporters and all the rest" in an effort to recover seven packs of cigarettes assertedly taken unlawfully by a guard. Burger, Report on the Federal Judicial Branch, 59 A.B.A.J. 1128-1129 (1973). The case referred to is Russell v. Bodner, 478 F.2d 1399 (3d Cir. 1973). See also Judge Kaufman's remarks: "A judge is far removed from the atmosphere of the maximum security prison and his sole personal contact with the hard tensions of the prison comes in the form of avid, though able, adversarial debate within the secure walls of a courthouse. He simply does not have the precise sense for the nuances or even the sweat of prison life." Kaufman, Prison: The Judge's Dilemma, 41 Fordham L. Rev. 495, 510 (1973).

These problems suggest the possibility of using bodies other than courts to review, check, and potentially improve agency decisions.

One approach, pioneered in Scandinavia and copied in many diverse contexts, would be an independent ombudsman office that could be established separately for each agency or program or on a more general basis. The officials in such an office would investigate client complaints of maladministration, attempt to secure corrective action where warranted, and recommend changes in procedures to prevent recurrences. But there are important limitations in the use of the ombudsman device. Ombudsman offices in other countries generally do not consider claims that agency action is illegal; such claims are the province of the courts. In the United States, the role of the courts in hearing claims of substantive and procedural illegality is much greater than in, say, Britain, leaving far less scope for the ombudsman office. To "delegalize" administration through this approach, U.S. courts would have to relinquish much of the reviewing power that they have built up over the past 30 years. There is also great doubt how far members of Congress, who profit politically by doing massive administrative "casework" for their constituents, would give power to an ombudsman office that would compete with them for casework. Questions also arise, within the fragmented American political process, whether an ombudsman can be given effective power to secure changes in particular agency decisions or general procedures.

Specialized reviewing bodies are another possibility. Many different federal agencies, such as the SSA, already provide for review by internal administrative appeal bodies. Such review procedures generally represent further steps in the decision process, adding to rather than substituting for initial agency hearings, ALJ hearings, and judicial review. The question is whether the principle of specialized administrative review could be developed as a substitute for ALJ and judicial review of particular cases, leaving the courts with responsibility to decide only general questions of law or procedure. In the regulatory context, we earlier adverted to the possibility of developing specialized executive or administrative reviewing bodies (such as the Office of Management and Budget or the National Academy of Sciences) as a partial substitute for judicial review. In Britain, for example, there is a highly developed system of nonjudicial tribunals to review the determinations of the Public Health Service, the various authorities dispensing grants or benefits to individuals, and other agencies of the welfare state. These tribunals often function in a relatively informal, non-legalistic manner. In many cases, the members of these tribunals are composed in part of private citizens, whose participation is designed to lend a nonbureaucratic perspective to the review function. Judicial review of decisions of such tribunals is generally narrowly limited. Other forms of alternative dispute resolution, including nonbinding arbitration, are another alternative. See Dauber, The Ties That Do Not Bind: Nonbinding Arbitration in Federal Administrative Agencies, 9 Admin. L.J. Am. U. 165 (1995).

There are obvious advantages to such systems in terms of cost, speed, and specialization. But these are countered by potential problems that could limit their acceptability, particularly in the United States. There is fear that a specialized administrative review tribunal would not be sufficiently independent of the agency whose decisions it was reviewing, even if located "outside" the agency on an organizational chart. Specialization may breed tunnel vision and mission-oriented bias. Staffing such tribunals with competent persons is also a potential problem. In the United States, review by independent judges on the basis of adversary hearing procedures has acquired a legitimating power that cannot readily be transferred to administrative or other non-judicial bodies.

(4) "Bureaucratic Rationality"

Professor Mashaw argues that improvements in administration are most likely to be generated by strengthening the internal capacities and control mechanisms of the "line" administrative agencies directly responsible for carrying out given programs. He believes that formal hearing procedures and judicial review tend to foster a case-by-case "moral judgment" approach that is inappropriate or ineffective in cases of mass justice administration or other bureaucratic systems. J. Mashaw, Bureaucratic Justice (1983). For an assessment of Mashaw's position, see Liebman & Stewart, Bureaucratic Vision (Book Review), 96 Harv. L. Rev. 1952 (1983). See also Mashaw, Due Process in the Administrative State (1985). Others have also thought that the proliferation of external control mechanisms dilutes responsibility and undermines accountability.

Professor Mashaw advocates an ideal of "bureaucratic rationality" in which organizational intelligence and incentives are used to ensure the effective and evenhanded implementation of broad social goals. This implies the greater professionalization of agency management, the use of audits and other error identification techniques, and attention to organizational incentives for reducing various types of errors. For example, federal assistance and insurance programs implemented through grants to state agencies typically penalize states (by reducing grants) when the percentage of ineligible recipients on their rolls exceeds a certain figure. But no comparable penalty is generally imposed when the percentage of eligible recipients erroneously denied assistance exceeds a certain amount. Adjusting such incentives may do more to cure administrative errors and promote consistency than an array of formal hearing rights. Mashaw also believes that efforts to rationalize bureaucratic processes are also likely to be superior to a "professional judgment" model that could delegate decision to panels of medical and vocational experts. As noted above, however, he would consider the use of lay advocates to provide claimants with effective informal hearings within the bureaucratic process.

Professor Mashaw would also promote bureaucratic rationality by establishing, at the top of the federal administrative structure, a "superbureau" resembling the French *Conseil d'Etat*. It would perform most of the review of particular agency regulations or decisions now performed by courts. But it would also contrive to study and improve the structure, process, and incentives in administrative decisionmaking. Mashaw hopes that this superbureau would become a model for and tutor of the various "line" agencies and redirect attention from our current "external conception of justice and the rule of law" to "the internal functioning and structure" of agencies and their efficacy in advancing social goals.

Mashaw's ideal must, however, confront the Jacksonian tradition in American government administration, a tradition that is hostile to the model of an elite civil service, which plays such a large role in other industrial democracies such as Japan, France, and the U.K. The top tier of federal administrators in our system are political appointees whose time in office averages about two years. Consider also whether the bureaucratic autonomy posited by Mashaw is compatible with a congressional form of government in which parliamentary discipline is lacking and members' careers are built in large measure on influence over and oversight of particular agencies' programs. Consider also that Americans tend to regard — indeed, have been encouraged by government to regard — social security and disability payments, food stamps, and other benefits as moral and legal entitlements. In our culture, it has been assumed that such entitlements are judicially enforceable. The notion of courts as checks on administrative power has deep and powerful roots. These conceptions will not easily give way to an ideal of bureaucratic rationality. How many of us would trust this ideal to the extent of willingly forgoing the right to hearing or judicial review in an administrative matter of large consequences to us? (But consider, as in the case of expensive medical procedures, that what may be rational from the perspective of an individual's choice may not be socially desirable from a broader societal perspective.)

A final problem is the question of the incentives for legislators and executives to adopt alternatives to formal hearings. With the exception of agency "casework" by legislators on behalf of particular constituents, there do not appear to be large political rewards from improving administration. It may be that the federal courts have taken on such a large role in controlling agencies because the other branches of the federal government and the states have done little and cannot be expected to do more without judicial intervention. Such intervention — often under the banner of due process — could goad the other branches or the states into creative institutional initiatives if alternatives to judicial hearings and review could pass constitutional muster. But here we return to a recurrent problem: How can courts judge and assure the efficacy and adequacy of such alternatives?

E. Public Disclosure of Agency Information and Decisionmaking

1. The Freedom of Information Act

The Freedom of Information Act (FOIA), codified in portions of §552 of the APA, requires federal agencies, on application, to make "promptly" available to "any person" any written information in their possession unless the information is within one of nine exceptions from compelled disclosure. A requester need not establish any particular standing or interest in the material requested in order to obtain disclosure. Any requested "record" (which has been interpreted to include e-mails and other electronic data as well as documents) in the agency's possession must be furnished to the requester unless it falls within nine categories of exempt materials set forth in FOIA. Applicants denied disclosure are entitled to have their complaints heard de novo by a federal district court, and "the burden is on the agency to sustain its action." Noncompliance with court orders for disclosure is punishable as contempt.

FOIA was first enacted in 1966. It was significantly amended and strengthened in 1974 in response to problems including excessive delays by agencies in responding to disclosure requests; agency requirements that requesters identify with precision the specific documents requested when requesters had little or no knowledge regarding such documents; agency requirements that requesters pay excessive document search and copying fees; and the costs and delay of litigation to force disclosure. The amended act provides for the indexing of certain documents, sets administrative time limits within which an agency must respond to requests for information, and subjects government officials who act arbitrarily or capriciously in withholding information to disciplinary proceedings conducted by the Civil Service Commission. In addition, the amendments permit in camera judicial inspection of classified documents at the discretion of the district court; require that the government serve an answer to a FOIA complaint within 30 days (unless the court otherwise directs for good cause shown); require courts to give priority to FOIA cases over others on their dockets; require annual agency FOIA reports to Congress; revise the wording of two exemptions; and permit the awarding of attorneys' fees to plaintiffs who are forced to litigate to secure documents and who substantially prevail in the court suit. Uniform agency fees for search and duplication, limited to direct costs, are also mandated. The fees may be waived or reduced if "furnishing the information can be considered as primarily benefiting the general public."

In 1996 FOIA was expanded again through The Electronic FOIA Amendments. These amendments were passed to ensure that the information of federal agencies in electronic format is available to citizens on the same basis as is information on paper; and to make the process of obtaining agency records, including those in electronic form, faster and easier. The Amendments use technology to ensure that government will be more accessible and accountable to citizens in the future. The Act also hopes to speed the problem of delay associated with FOIA. Commentators have expressed concerns that the changes may greatly expand information dissemination in ways that threaten privacy concerns. See O'Reilly, Expanding the Purpose of Federal Records Access: New Private Entitlement or New Threat to Privacy? 50 Admin. L. Rev. 371 (1998).

FOIA, 5 U.S.C. §552(a)(4)(B), empowers federal courts to enjoin an "agency from withholding agency records and to order the production of any agency records improperly withheld." In Kissinger v. Reporters' Committee for Freedom of the Press, 445 U.S. 136 (1980), the Supreme Court held that FOIA does not require agencies to obtain and disclose records no longer in their possession.[95] FOIA does not obligate agencies to create or maintain records; that is a function of the Federal Records Act or specific statutes. Consistent with precedent under the other provisions of the APA, the president and his advisors have been held not to be an "agency" for purposes of FOIA. See Rushforth v. Council of Economic Advisers, 762 F.2d 1038 (D.C. Cir. 1985). But note that Congress adopted a special definition of "agency" for FOIA purposes, §552(f), that is broader than the general definition of "agency" for APA purposes, §551(1).

If identified records are within an agency's possession, they must be disclosed unless they fall within the nine exemptions set forth in 5 U.S.C. §552(b). If requested records fall within one of the exemptions, the agency is authorized but not required to withhold it. Thus, FOIA leaves an agency free, if it wishes, to disclose records that fall within one of the exemptions. We discuss below the rights of third parties, such as persons who submitted to the government the information in question or whose privacy might be violated as a result of disclosure, to enjoin agency disclosure on the ground that disclosure would violate a statute other than FOIA, such as the Trade Secrets Act or the Privacy Act.

In litigation challenging agency nondisclosure, the agency has the burden of showing that the records requested fall within one of the statutory exemptions. To what extent should the courts take into account the particular requester's specific interest in disclosure and balance it against the policies underlying the exemption invoked by the agency in deciding whether to require disclosure? In a number of decisions, the Supreme Court has consistently held that the specific interests of the requester in disclosure should not be considered; the "only relevant public interest in the FOIA balancing test is the extent to which disclosure of

---

95. Although FOIA does not generally apply to records held outside of an agency, it has been extended to grant recipients doing federally funded research. In 1998, Congress passed a two-sentence requirement for the Office of Management and Budget to revise its circular on federal grants so that hospitals, universities, and other nonprofit entities receiving federal grants would be subject to FOIA access for all records produced under an award. The procedures used for FOIA access to agency records would be applied to public requests for access to the grantee records. T. O'Reilly, Federal Information Disclosure §4.10 (3d ed. 2000).

the information sought would 'shed light on the government's performance of its statutory duties' or otherwise let citizens know 'what their government is up to.'" Department of Defense v. FLRA, 510 U.S. 487, 494 (1994). All members of the public are equally entitled to obtain disclosure. Thus, in U.S. Dept. of Justice v. Tax Analysts, 492 U.S. 136 (1989), the circumstance that the requester, Tax Analysts, a commercial tax law publication, was requesting copies of all opinions and orders in court cases received by the Tax Division of the Justice Department in order to save the expense of collecting the materials directly from the courts was irrelevant; disclosure was required. In *Department of Defense*, unions seeking to organize government workers sought their addresses from government agencies; the Court held that the unions' interests in promoting collective bargaining should not be considered and denied disclosure. Similarly, in Bibles v. Oregon Natural Desert Association, 519 U.S. 355 (1997), the Court held that the interest of the environmental group requester in communicating with recipients of a Bureau of Land Management's (BLM) newsletter in order to counter the BLM's land management policy views should not be considered; the group's request for the names and addresses of the newsletter recipients was denied.

a. The Exemptions from Disclosure

(1) *The National Security Exemption*

This exemption excepts from disclosure matters specifically authorized under criteria established by executive order to be kept secret in the interests of national defense or foreign policy and in fact properly classified. In theory, this provision, together with the provision for in camera judicial review of withheld records, would permit de novo court review of national security classifications by the executive branch. In practice, however, courts may be reluctant to inspect classified documents in camera or to second-guess executive decisions in national security classifications.

(2) *The Internal Personnel Rules and Practices Exemption*

Section 552(b)(2) exempts from disclosure documents that are "related solely to the internal personnel rules and practices of an agency."

Two primary purposes might arguably underlie exemption two: the protection of employee personal privacy (although this matter is specifically addressed in exemption six) and the protection of agencies from harassment. Although its language could be interpreted in an extremely broad fashion, the usefulness of exemption two to agencies as a means of withholding information from the public was substantially limited by the Supreme Court in Department of the Air Force v. Rose, 425 U.S. 353 (1976), which held that student editors of the NYU Law Review doing research on student discipline in the military service academies could obtain disclosure of case summaries of air force academy discipline proceedings with personal references and other identifying information deleted. The Court concluded that the case summaries, edited to preserve anonymity, did not fall within exemption two. The Court also concluded that they fell outside of the "privacy" exemption — exemption six — because the privacy interests of the cadets could be adequately protected by in camera court examination of the summaries to determine whether further editing was required.

The limits of exemption two have been tested in a number of cases involving requests for enforcement manuals employed by federal law enforcement agencies. Such information certainly is used by the agencies to instruct their personnel in the "practices of [the] agency," and thus falls within the rubric of the exemption. For members of the public, however, these manuals arguably resemble the "secret law" that FOIA was designed to open to public scrutiny; information concerning enforcement practices can inform the public of the effective limits of the law by revealing the way the law will be enforced. None of the courts of appeals, however, have allowed these manuals to be released. See Crooker v. Bureau of Alcohol, Tobacco & Firearms, 670 F.2d 1051 (D.C. Cir. 1981) (en banc).

(3) The Exemption for Documents Governed by Statutes That Specifically Direct Nondisclosure

As originally enacted in 1966, exemption three stated that nondisclosure is permissible if the matter is "specifically exempted from disclosure by statute." In FAA Administrator v. Robertson, 422 U.S. 255 (1975), the Supreme Court interpreted this provision to authorize withholding when a relevant statute gave an agency discretion whether to disclose the records in question. In response, Congress amended FOIA in 1976 to restrict significantly the scope of exemption three by limiting it to situations where a statute mandates nondisclosure or establishes criteria or categories for particular types of records to be withheld. Courts uphold agency withholding of records pursuant to such statutes. See Baldridge v. Shapiro, 455 U.S. 345 (1982) (confidentiality provision of Census Act justifies agency refusal to disclose census records).

(4) The Confidential Business Information Exemption

Exemption four of the act, 5 U.S.C. §552(b)(4), provides that "trade secrets or commercial and financial information obtained from a person and privileged or confidential need not be disclosed to the public." The exemption reflects the primary purpose of FOIA to ensure citizen scrutiny of the federal government rather than to open private businesses to public scrutiny.

What constitutes a "trade secret" exempt from disclosure? Public Citizen Health Research Group v. FDA, 704 F.2d 1280 (D.C. Cir. 1983), upholding a request for disclosure of drug manufacturers' clinical studies of drug safety and efficacy, restricted trade secrets to information produced by innovation or substantial effort and directly used in the manufacture or production of commodities.

In Public Citizen Research Group v. FDA, 185 F.3d 898 (D.C. Cir. 1999), a consumer organization challenged refusal by the Food and Drug Administration to disclose documents relating to new drug approval applications that had been abandoned for health or safety reasons. Petitioners argue that disclosure would prevent other drug companies from repeating mistakes, thereby avoiding risk to human health. Consistent with the Supreme Court decisions on the issue, discussed above, the court held that the interest in avoiding health harms to other patients should not be considered, stating that "the Congress has already determined the relevant public interest: if through disclosure the public would learn something directly about the workings of the Government then the information should be disclosed unless it comes within specific exemption." Balancing the general public interest in disclosure of the workings of government against the trade secrecy claims advanced by FDA, the court upheld one claim of disclosure exemption, denied another, and remanded four other claims for a determination by the district court whether nonconfidential information could be segregated and disclosed.

National Parks & Conservation Assn. v. Morton, 498 F.2d 765, 770 (D.C. Cir. 1974), held that information is "confidential" and thus within exemption four if its disclosure would be likely to "cause substantial harm to the competitive position" of the person who submitted it, or if disclosure is likely to "impair the Government's ability to obtain necessary information in the future." Commentators have criticized *National Parks* for construing the exemption too narrowly and have argued, relying on the legislative history, for a broader exemption, including all information "which would not be released to the public by the person from whom it was obtained."[96]

(5) *The Exemptions for Privileged Agency Materials*

Exemption five, 5 U.S.C. §552(b)(5), provides that agencies may withhold "inter-agency or intra-agency memorandums or letters which would not be available by law to a party other than an agency in litigation with the agency." It was intended to incorporate the privilege of the government from discovery in litigation generally. Thus, cases dealing with concepts of privilege in non-FOIA litigation involving the government are relevant to the scope of this exemption. These include the attorney-client and attorney work-product privileges. They also include a "deliberative process" privilege, unique to government, to shield from disclosure records pertaining to or reflecting the process of internal government decisionmaking. The purpose of this privilege is to preserve free and frank discussions within government, which would be hindered if opinions and recommendations advanced during the deliberative process could be obtained by the public. Defining the precise contours of this privilege, including distinguishing "predecisional" materials from those that reflect the substance of a decision made, has not always been easy. See, e.g., U.S. Dept. of Justice v. Julian, 486 U.S. 1 (1988), allowing a person convicted of a federal crime and awaiting sentencing to obtain presentencing reports prepared by the department.

In Department of Interior v. Kalamath Water Users Protective Assn., 532 U.S. 1 (2001), the Court held that records of consultations by the Department's Bureau of Indian Affairs (BIA) with several tribes regarding what position the BIA should take on behalf of the tribes in the state proceedings concerning water allocation rights were not covered by exemption five. The records were sought by parties adverse to the tribes in the proceedings. The Court emphasized that the exemption was limited to "inter-agency or intra-agency" materials. Although the Court acknowledged previous decisions that held that exemption five extends to communications between Government agencies and outside consultants hired by them, it noted that in those cases "the consultant does not represent an interest of its own, or the interest of any other client when it advises the agency that hires it. Its only obligations are to truth and its sense of what good judgment calls for, and in those respects the consultant functions just as an employee would be expected to do." Unlike consultants, the tribes "are self advocates at the expense of others seeking benefits [water rights] inadequate to satisfy everyone." Thus, the Court rejected

96. S. Rep. No. 813, 89th Cong., 1st Sess. 9 (1965).

the exemption and also rejected a government request to recognize an "Indian trust" exception.

(6) The Personal Privacy Exemption

Exemption six protects "personnel and medical files and similar files the disclosure of which would constitute a clearly unwarranted invasion of personal privacy." The basic approach of the federal Privacy Act of 1974 is to prohibit the disclosure of any kind of retrievable information (retrieved by use of the subject's name or identifying number) about an individual without his or her consent. Although the Privacy Act contains an exemption for disclosures mandated by FOIA and was supposed to have no effect on the FOIA, agencies face a potential dilemma because interpretations of the two statutes may differ. For example, if they release records containing information about an individual in response to a FOIA request, they may be later sued by the individual claiming that her rights under the Privacy Act have been violated and that the records were exempt from disclosure under FOIA exemption six. If, on the other hand, agencies refuse disclosure, they may be successfully sued by the requester under FOIA. In Department of the Air Force v. Rose, 425 U.S. 353 (1976), discussed above in connection with exemption two, the Court sought to resolve this tension by holding that summaries of disciplinary proceedings must be disclosed provided that the records were redacted to remove information permitting identification of the individuals subject to discipline.

(7) The Investigatory Records Exemption

FOIA §552(b)(7) permits records to be withheld if their disclosure would (a) interfere with enforcement proceedings, (b) deprive a person of a fair trial or an impartial adjudication, (c) create an unwarranted invasion of personal privacy, or disclose the identity of a confidential source, or (d) disclose investigative techniques and procedures or endanger the life or safety of law enforcement personnel. Because the consequences of an erroneous decision not to withhold in an exemption seven case could be extremely serious, courts are likely to continue to display reluctance to overturn an agency decision not to disclose despite the greater specificity of the exemption as amended in 1974. See NLRB v. Robbins Tire & Rubber Co., 437 U.S. 214 (1978), denying respondents in an unfair labor practice proceeding discovery of witness statements taken by board staff; the Court expressed fear that such discovery would lead to intimidation of employee witnesses by employers. In U.S. Dept. of Justice v. Reporters' Committee for Freedom of the Press, 489 U.S. 749 (1989), the Court upheld the department's refusal to disclose to news organizations the "rap sheet" of an organized crime figure containing otherwise publicly available information about his arrests, indictments, acquittals, convictions, and sentences on the ground that it fell within §552(b)(7)(C). It stated that although this information was otherwise publicly available from court records, it would be difficult as a practical matter for a person to retrieve all this information and that the government had invoked a legitimate privacy interest in maintaining the "practical obscurity" of the information. Is this decision consistent with the Court's earlier decision in Tax Analysts, supra?

Although the courts will often respect an agency decision to withhold information, there is still a procedural threshold that agencies must display to satisfy judges.

For example, in order to establish that information would reveal the identity of a confidential source, the government must do more than merely claim that the document is of a type the agency would normally treat as confidential. Rather they must establish with specific evidence that the source spoke with an understanding that the communication would remain confidential. For example, in Billington v. United States Dept. of Justice, 233 F.3d 581 (D.C. Cir. 2000), the Department claimed that "[i]t is obvious from the released information that these sources warrant confidentiality," and that "the manner in which the FBI actually obtains information from these sources is demonstrative of the express promise of confidentiality." The court held these arguments insufficient to justify nondisclosure, stating: "The government's declarations do not sufficiently detail certain express assurances of confidentiality and do not adequately explain implied assurances of confidentiality for information received." The court remanded to allow the Department to present additional evidence in support of its exemption claim.

(8) The Financial Institution Exemption

Section 552(b)(8) permits nondisclosure of reports prepared by federal agencies, such as the Federal Reserve Board or Federal House Loan Banks Board, about the operations of banks and financial institutions. The purpose of the exemption is to insure the stability of financial institutions, although it has been suggested that the amendment is superfluous because exemption four (confidential commercial and financial information) would appear adequate to cover this situation.

(9) The Geological Exploration Exemption

Exemption nine, §552(b)(9), is perhaps the least explained of the exemptions. It exempts "geological and geophysical information and data, including maps concerning wells . . . ," although again the confidential commercial information protection of exemption four probably would suffice to protect this type of information.

Notes and Questions: FOIA Procedures and Policies

FOIA litigation is a voluminous if technical branch of federal administrative law. These materials can only serve to provide an overview and raise some basic questions. FOIA can be viewed as a mechanism for correcting agency "failure" by providing broader public knowledge and scrutiny of administrative practices and providing another court-enforced procedural mechanism for citizen involvement in government. Substantial FOIA litigation has been brought by public interest groups to expose the workings of government or scrutinize the implementation and enforcement of statutes. The press and media have also used the FOIA. But the FOIA is most frequently used to obtain information that an agency has required third parties to file with it. In most such instances, the requesting party is a business firm seeking to discover a rival's trade secrets or other competitively sensitive information. Finally, FOIA is used extensively as a discovery device by those engaged in litigation against the government. Of the 48,000 FOIA requests made to the FDA in 1993, 82 percent came from industry, commercial FOIA services, and lawyers; 9 percent from the press; and 1 percent from public interest groups.

FDA, Activities Annual Report 1993. In theory, the interest of the requester in disclosure is supposed to be irrelevant, but it is likely to influence agency decisions and perhaps court decisions as well.

FOIA attempts to minimize agency discretion by mandating disclosure in all cases unless the agency establishes that the records requested fall within one of nine categorical exemptions. Yet the statutory exemptions, as the foregoing materials suggest, are not crystal clear, and their application in given cases often requires program-specific factual knowledge and policy judgment. In most other administrative law contexts, these circumstances normally lead a court to attach a presumption of correctness to an agency decision that it is called on to review. The agency has been given initial responsibility to implement a given statute, and normally has specialized experience that the court cannot match. But FOIA is a statute reflecting distrust and suspicion of agencies who will, for bureaucratic reasons, tend to resist disclosure unless forced to disclose information by the court. FOIA itself departs from the normal principles of judicial deference and the general standards of review contained in APA §706 by providing that courts should review disclosure issues de novo. And in FLRA v. United States Dept. of Defense, 984 F.2d 370, 373-374 (10th Cir. 1993), the court stated that agencies are not entitled to *Chevron* deference with regard to their interpretations of the Privacy Act and FOIA because these statutes are not within the area of an agency's expertise. Review of agency interpretations of these statutes is, therefore, de novo. FOIA experts that are members of an ABA Administrative Law and Regulatory Procedure Section project to develop a Statement of Administrative Law have recently concluded, however, that the courts have "seemingly abdicated" their duty under FOIA to place the burden of proof on the government and apply a de novo review standard. According to one member, in most cases the government files boilerplate pleadings, avoids discovery, and quickly obtains judgment. Courts now rarely ask to see documents at issue. Consequently the success rate of requesters has fallen, by one estimate, from 40 percent to 5-7 percent. The courts' crowded dockets may contribute to the reduced level of scrutiny. See William S. Morrow, APA Project Progresses with Panel on FOIA, 25 Admin. & Reg. L. News, 3, 4 (Spring 2000).

Notwithstanding, the courts in many respects are ill equipped to discharge the role of enforcing FOIA. In the first place, it is obviously difficult for a court to review agency claims to exemption without examining the documents in question. But since disclosure to the requester for purposes of litigation would often hand him a victory, such examination must proceed in camera. Although FOIA authorizes this procedure and it is now a common practice, in camera inspections pose serious problems. The requester is fenced out, and the district court is deprived of the benefits of the full adversary process. Thorough in camera review thus places unfamiliar burdens on judges ill equipped by tradition, professional orientation, and institutional capacity to assume an inquisitorial role. On appeal, an appellate court must either defer almost completely to the district judge or itself use uncongenial in camera procedures.

Second, even if the documents are available to the court, it is often ill equipped to assess the justifications for exemption asserted by the agency. Does national security justify secret classification of given documents? Will public disclosure seriously hamper the government's ability to acquire given types of information from private firms?

To avoid these ultimate difficulties, reviewing courts in FOIA cases have, as in other administrative contexts, sought to develop procedural requirements to control agency decisions. For example, in Vaughn v. Rosen, 484 F.2d 820 (D.C. Cir. 1973), *cert. denied,* 415 U.S. 977 (1974), the court required the agency (which has resisted disclosure with sweeping claims of exemption) to prepare an index of the documents covered by the request; to set forth detailed justifications for its claims of exemption; to cross-index documents and justifications; and also to explain why it was not feasible to separate out and disclose information in the requested documents that did not fall within the exemptions. These requirements are now routinely imposed by federal reviewing courts. However, it and similar procedural requirements can only go part way toward resolving the problems that the FOIA poses for reviewing courts.

b. Reverse-FOIA Litigation

The prevalence of requests by competitors (and, on occasion, by public interest groups) for information submitted to agencies by business firms has given rise to reverse-FOIA suits in which a plaintiff seeks to enjoin agency disclosure to third-person requesters of information that the plaintiff was requested or compelled to disclose to an agency. Congress did not legislate an affirmative right of action to protect confidential submissions. Moreover, as discussed previously, agencies may choose to disclose records even if they fall within one of the nine exemptions. Thus, the fact that the records fall within an exemption does not give the person who submitted the information in question the right to enjoin disclosure. Nonetheless, the courts have recognized a right by submitters to enjoin disclosure where disclosure is prohibited by a statute other than FOIA. Thus, in Chrysler Corp. v. Brown, 441 U.S. 281 (1979), the court upheld Chrysler's right to bring a federal district court action under the APA to enjoin the disclosure by the Defense Department to third-party requesters of information which Chrysler, a defense contractor, was required to file with the department; Chrysler contended that the disclosure violated the Trade Secrets Act. The Court found that although the Trade Secrets Act did not itself confer a private right of action on Chrysler to enjoin its violation, violation of its prohibitions by an agency would be reviewable under the APA.

An example of a successful reverse-FOIA litigation built around privacy concerns is Family Farms v. Glickman, 200 F.3d 1180 (8th Cir. 2000). A federal statute authorizes the Department of Agriculture to impose an assessment against pork producers and importers to fund activities by state pork producer associations and the National Pork Producers Council to conduct advertising and promotional campaigns to increase pork production. The law provides that if 15 percent or more of those assessed file a petition requesting it, the department shall conduct a referendum on continuation of the assessment program in which all those subject to assessments may vote by secret ballot. More than 15 percent of those assessed filed a petition requesting such a referendum. The Council filed a FOIA request with the department seeking copies of the petition and the addresses of those signing. The department concluded that it would disclose the requested information, finding that it did not fall within exemption six (personal privacy), and that disclosure was warranted under a department regulation providing that it may release information exempt from mandatory disclosure under FOIA whenever it determines that disclosure would be in the public interest. The regulation provides that "disclosure is considered to be in the public interest if the benefit to the public in releasing the document outweighs any harm likely to result." Plaintiffs, petition signers, and an organization representing such signers sued to enjoin disclosure and obtained a preliminary injunction from the district court. The court of appeals ruled in favor of the plaintiffs and ordered entry of a permanent injunction. It found that disclosure of the petition signers' names and addresses would be a serious invasion of their privacy interests: "To make public such an unequivocal statement of their position [i.e., their signature on the petition] on the referendum would effectively vitiate [plaintiffs'] privacy interest in a secret ballot." Accordingly, the petition was exempt from disclosure under exemption six. The petition was thus not required by FOIA to be disclosed. The department nonetheless had discretion to disclose it, so long as its decision to do so was not arbitrary and capricious. The court concluded however, that given the importance of plaintiffs' privacy interests and the relatively insubstantial interest in disclosure, disclosure would violate the department's regulation, and the department's decision to disclose was arbitrary and capricious.

A practical problem in asserting reverse-FOIA remedies is notice. If an agency does not notify the submitter that someone is requesting information submitted by him, he will probably not have a chance to present his case to the agency or seek a reverse-FOIA injunction prior to disclosure. It has been suggested that a major reason that there have not been more reverse-FOIA suits is the present general lack of any requirement for agencies to notify submitters of requests for information. Does due process require such notice? Even though Congress did not pass proposed legislation guaranteeing submitters uniform rights of notice and causes of action to resist disclosure, many agencies themselves have created various forms of submitter rights.

2. The Government in the Sunshine Act

Requirements that administrative agencies deliberate in public were first developed at the state level. By 1962, 26 states had passed laws requiring open meetings by administrative boards, commissions, and similar bodies, and at present every state and the District of Columbia has an open meeting law or constitutional provision.

In 1976, an overwhelming majority of Congress passed the Government in the Sunshine Act, whose open-meeting provisions are codified in 5 U.S.C. §552b. For the first time, meetings of multimember federal agencies[97] must be open to the public. The act requires that every part of every meeting must be open to the public unless it falls within one of ten specific exemptions. "Meeting" is defined by the act to include the deliberations of at least a quorum of members where the deliberations determine or result in the conduct of agency business — indicating that some degree of formality is required before a gathering is considered to be a meeting. The Supreme Court stated that "this statutory language contemplates discussions that effectively predetermine official actions. Such discussions must be sufficiently focused on discrete proposals or issues as to cause or be likely to cause the individual participating members to form reasonably firm positions regarding matters pending or likely to arise before the agency." FCC v. ITT World Communications, Inc., 466 U.S. 463 (1984).

No meeting may be closed unless a majority of the membership votes to take that action. At least one week in advance, the members must identify the proposed agenda and compare it with the act's ten provisions exempting described meeting subjects from the open meeting requirement. The chief legal officer of the agency must prepare and file a

---

97. The act covers all agencies, as defined in 5 U.S.C. §552(e), headed by a collegial body of two or more members, a majority of whom are appointed by the president with the advice and consent of the Senate. 5 U.S.C. §552b(a)(1).

statement certifying and giving reasons why the meeting may be closed. A copy of each vote on closing a meeting must be made available to the public to inform the public as to the voting record of agency members on open meetings. The agency must announce the time and place of a closed meeting, announce that it is closed, make available a statement of the reasons for the closing, and make public a list of all nonmembers who will attend.

If the majority votes to close the meeting, a full verbatim transcript or electronic recording of the meeting is required. Any portion of the transcript or recording that does not fit within one of the exemptions must be promptly released to the public. This requirement, which goes beyond state open-meeting legislation, was one of the most controversial provisions in the act, and several exceptions to the full transcript requirement were included in its final version.

Seven of the ten exemptions from the act's open meetings requirement parallel exemptions of the FOIA. Under these seven exemptions, a meeting may be closed if it will involve matters that (1) are vital to the national defense or foreign policy; (2) are concerned with the internal personnel rules and practices of the agency; (3) are specifically exempted from disclosure by another statute; (4) concern trade secrets and confidential commercial or financial information; (5) would constitute a clearly unwarranted invasion of personal privacy; (6) would disclose investigatory records compiled for law enforcement purposes under certain limited circumstances; or (7) relate to bank or financial institution examination reports. Three exemptions that do not closely parallel FOIA exemptions permit the closing of meetings if matters will be discussed that (1) involve accusing any person of a crime, or formally censuring any person; (2) would frustrate implementation of a proposed agency action if prematurely known; or (3) concern the agency's participation in formal rulemaking or litigation.

When a meeting is announced to be closed and a person wishes to attend, the act creates a cause of action to enjoin the closing. The court may enjoin the meeting pendente lite, and the burden of proof to support the closing is on the agency. Within 60 days after a closed meeting, the agency may be sued for equitable relief and for access to the transcript of the closed meeting. Any person may sue to enforce the act's requirements. Unlike FOIA, the Sunshine Act authorizes injunctions barring future violations of the act. In ruling on whether an agency has justifiably invoked one of the exemptions, a court may review portions of the meeting transcript that have not been publicly released.

Several court decisions have increased the ability of agencies to make certain kinds of decisions free of public disclosure by narrowly defining what constitutes an "agency" and what constitutes a "meeting." For example, Amerp Corp. v. FTC, 768 F.2d 1171 (10th Cir. 1985), rejected a challenge to issuance of an FTC cease-and-desist order that asserted a new standard of "deception"; the order had been individually reviewed and approved by each commissioner. The court rejected Amerp's contention that the FTC was required to hold an open meeting to adopt the new standard. In Rushforth v. Council of Economic Advisers, 762 F.2d 1038 (D.C. Cir. 1985), the court held that the council (CEA) did not need to promulgate regulations implementing FOIA or the Sunshine Act since, as an adviser to the president, it was not an "agency" within the meaning of either act.

A study made in the mid-1980s for the Administrative Conference of the United States found that open-meeting laws had changed the behavior of those subject to it. A survey of several hundred relevant individuals led the authors to conclude that "public access to information has been enlarged." On the other hand, commissioners tended to make up their minds about issues before meetings, they were reluctant to engage in meaningful negotiation and debate at meetings, and they hesitated to discuss sensitive issues in public. The result is that "the focus of decisionmaking activity has shifted toward the offices of individual members and to the staff level. . . ." Staff members debate and negotiate with each other, they discuss matters with individual commissioners (different staff members acting as agents for different commissioners), and individual commissioners may talk privately one-on-one in their offices. Collegiality suffers, negotiation becomes more difficult, the risk of making decisions without full information or adequate canvassing of consideration increases. "Taken as a group, respondents to the survey were equally divided whether the costs or benefits of the act were greater; as might be expected members of the public were the most enthusiastic — finding a net benefit twice as often as net cost — and officials who had served both before and after the Act's passage, the least so." Welborn, Lyon & Thomas, Implementation and Effects of the Federal Government in the Sunshine Act (1984).

7

Agency Decisionmaking Structure

Any government agency, bureau, or department is a complex bureaucratic structure, organizing civil servants, who perform many different tasks, within an overall administrative unit. Members of that unit may develop loyalties, one to the other, that threaten the legitimacy, efficiency, or fairness of the action the agency takes in relation to members of the public. In this chapter, we examine several legal doctrines that have arisen in an effort to secure better and unbiased decisionmaking while taking account of the agency's practical administrative need to make, and enforce, substantive policy. The chapter also presents materials that ask a more general, more speculative, question: Is it possible to improve the performance of an agency by changing its decisionmaking structure?

A. The Combination of Functions within a Single Agency

In considering the material that follows, it may help to have in mind the organization, structure, and mission of a particular agency. We have chosen as an example the Federal Trade Commission (FTC).

The FTC was born in a spirit of reform in 1914. Its origins can be traced to the progressive movement and the business "trust" issue over which the parties fought in the election of 1912. Essentially, it represented a legislative compromise between those, such as Louis Brandeis, who wanted a strong, new antitrust law making unlawful a specific list of business practices, those who wanted a "sunshine commission" capable only of turning the spotlight of publicity onto undesirable business behavior, and business interests who hoped that the commission would provide relief from the uncertain hazards of the antitrust laws and develop realistic guidelines for fair competitive conduct. The compromise abandoned the "specific list" in favor of a general standard, making unlawful "unfair" methods of competition. It placed enforcement in the hands of a commission with the power to prohibit unlawful behavior. Initially, some commissioners considered their major function to be one of advising industry. Louis Brandeis, however, convinced them that they were to develop and to apply rules of law through adversary procedures, rather like courts of law.

693

The commission has described its structure, organization, and mission as follows.

The Federal Trade Commission

1995/1996 U.S. Government Manual 574-580

The objective of the Federal Trade Commission is to maintain competitive enterprise as the keystone of the American economic system, and to prevent the free enterprise system from being fettered by monopoly or restraints on trade or corrupted by unfair or deceptive trade practices. The Commission is charged with keeping competition both free and fair.

The purpose of the Federal Trade Commission is expressed in the Federal Trade Commission Act (15 U.S.C. 41-58) and the Clayton Act (15 U.S.C. 12), both passed in 1914 and both successively amended in the years that have followed. The Federal Trade Commission Act prohibits the use in or affecting commerce of "unfair methods of competition" and "unfair or deceptive acts or practices." The Clayton Act outlaws specific practices recognized as instruments of monopoly. As an administrative agency, acting quasi-judicially and quasi-legislatively, the Commission was established to deal with trade practices on a continuing and corrective basis. It has no authority to punish; its function is to prevent, through cease-and-desist orders and other means, those practices condemned by the law of Federal trade regulation. However, court-ordered civil penalties up to $10,000 may be obtained for each violation of a Commission order or trade regulation rule.

The Federal Trade Commission was organized as an independent administrative agency in 1914 pursuant to the Federal Trade Commission Act. Related duties subsequently were delegated to the Commission by various statutes, including; the Wheeler-Lea Act, the Trans-Alaska Pipeline Authorization Act, the Clayton Act, the Export Trade Act, the Wool Products Labeling Act, the Fur Products Labeling Act, the Textile Fiber Products Identification Act, the Fair Packaging and Labeling Act, the Lanham Trade-Mark Act of 1946, the Consumer Credit Protection Act, the Robinson-Patman Act, the Hobby Protection Act, the Magnuson-Moss Warranty-Federal Trade Commission Improvement Act, the Federal Trade Commission Improvement Act of 1980, the Smokeless Tobacco Health Education Act of 1986, the Telephone Disclosure and Dispute Resolution Act, the Federal Trade Commission Improvement Act of 1994, the International Antitrust Enforcement Assistance Act of 1994, the Telemarketing and Consumer Fraud and Abuse Prevention Act, and the Federal Trade Commission Act Amendments of 1994.

The Commission is composed of five members. Each member is appointed by the President, with the advice and consent of the Senate, for a team of 7 years. Not more than three of the Commissioners may be members of the same political party. One Commissioner is designated by the President as Chairman of the Commission and is responsible for its administrative management.

ACTIVITIES

The Commission's principal functions are to:

- promote competition in or affecting commerce through the prevention of general trade restraints such as price-fixing agreements, boycotts, illegal combinations of competitors, and other unfair methods of competition;
- safeguard the public by preventing the dissemination of false or deceptive advertisements of consumer products and services generally, and food, drug, cosmet-

ics, and therapeutic devices, particularly, as well as other unfair or deceptive practices;

— prevent pricing discrimination; exclusive-dealing and tying arrangements; corporate mergers, acquisitions, or joint ventures, when such practices or arrangements may substantially lessen competition or tend to create a monopoly; interlocking directorates or officers' positions that may restrain competition; the payment or receipt of illegal brokerage; and discrimination among competing customers in the furnishing of or the payment for services or facilities used to promote the resale of a product;

— enjoin various fraudulent telemarketing schemes;

— bring about truthful labeling of textile, wool, and fur products;

— regulate packaging and labeling of certain consumer commodities within the purview of the Fair Packaging and Labeling Act so as to prevent consumer deception and to facilitate value comparisons;

— supervise the registration and operation of associations of American exporters engaged in export trade;

— achieve accurate credit cost disclosure by consumer creditors (retailers, finance companies, non-Federal credit unions, and other creditors not specifically regulated by another Government agency) as called for in the Truth in Lending Act to ensure a meaningful basis for informed credit decisions, and to regulate the issuance of and liability for the use of credit cards so as to prohibit their fraudulent use in or affecting commerce;

— protect consumers against circulation of inaccurate or obsolete credit reports and ensure that consumer reporting agencies exercise their responsibilities in a manner that is fair and equitable and in conformity with the Fair Credit Reporting Act, the Fair Credit Billing Act, the Equal Credit Opportunity Act, and the Fair Debt Collection Practices Act; and

— gather and make available to the Congress, the President, and the public, factual data concerning economic and business conditions.

ENFORCEMENT

The Commission's law enforcement work falls into two general categories: actions to foster voluntary compliance with the law, and formal administrative litigation leading to mandatory orders against offenders.

For the most part, compliance with the law is obtained through voluntary and cooperative action by way of staff level advice, which is not binding on the Commission; advisory opinions by the Commission; and through issuance of guides and policy statements delineating legal requirements as to particular business practices.

The formal litigation is similar to that in Federal courts. Cases are instituted either by issuance of an administrative complaint charging or by filing a Federal district court complaint charging the person, partnership, or corporation with violating one or more of the statutes administered by the Commission. Cases may be settled by consent orders. If the charges in an administrative matter are not contested, or if the charges are found to be true after an administrative hearing in a contested case, a cease-and-desist order may be issued requiring discontinuance of the unlawful practices and may include other related requirements. Federal district court charges are resolved through either settlements or court-ordered injunctive or other equitable relief.

LEGAL CASE WORK

Cases before the Commission may originate through complaint by a consumer or a competitor; the Congress; or from Federal, State, or municipal agencies. Also, the Commission itself may initiate an investigation into possible violation of the laws it administers. No formality is required in submitting a complaint. A letter giving the facts in detail, accompanied by all supporting evidence in possession of the complaining party, is sufficient. It is the general policy of the Commission not to disclose the identity of any complainant, except as permitted by law or Commission rules.

Upon receipt of a complaint, various criteria are applied in determining whether the particular matter should be investigated. Within the limits of available resources, investigations are initiated that are considered to best support the Commission's goals of maintaining competition and protecting consumers.

The Commission's investigations commonly include requests for voluntary production of relevant information and materials. The Commission also has the authority to issue compulsory process in the form of subpoenas, civil investigative demands, or orders to file reports. The Commission may bring suit in a United States district court to enforce its compulsory process. Also, the Commission often cooperates with other law enforcement agencies, both domestic and, to the extent permitted by U.S. law, foreign and international.

On completion of an investigation, staff will recommend Commission action. The staff may recommend that the matter be closed. If that recommendation is approved, a closing letter is usually sent to the individual or company that was the subject of the investigation. The staff may instead recommend that the Commission approve the settlement of a case, usually by acceptance of an agreement containing a consent order to cease and desist. Such consent orders frequently provide that the respondent does not admit any violation of the law, but agrees to be bound by an order requiring the discontinuance of the challenged practices, and, in some cases, other corrective action.

If the Commission determines that some action other than closing the investigation is appropriate, but no consent agreement can be negotiated, the Commission may issue a formal complaint alleging that the respondent has violated one or more of the laws administered by the Commission. The respondent is then served with a copy of the complaint, often accompanied by a proposed cease-and-desist order to be used if the allegations of law violations are proved. The Commission's counsel supporting the complaint and respondents may negotiate a consent agreement after the issuance of the formal complaint. Otherwise, the case is heard by an administrative law judge, who conducts a trial that is open to the public, and issues an initial decision.

The initial decision becomes the decision of the Commission at the end of 30 days unless the respondent or the counsel supporting the complaint appeals the decision to the Commission, or the Commission by order stays the effective date or places the case on its own docket for review. In the Commission's decision on such an appeal or review, the initial decision may be sustained, modified, or reversed. If the complaint is sustained or modified, a cease-and-desist order is issued. If an initial decision dismissing a complaint is sustained, no cease-and-desist order is issued.

Under the Federal Trade Commission Act, an order to cease and desist or to take other corrective action — such as affirmative disclosure, divestiture, or restitution — becomes final 60 days after date of service upon the respondent, unless within that period the respondent petitions an appropriate United States court of appeals to review the order, and also petitions the Commission to stay the order pending review. If the Commission does not stay the order, the respondent may seek a stay from the reviewing appeals court. The appeals court has the power to affirm, modify, or set the order aside. If the appeals court upholds the Commission's order, the respondent may seek certiorari to the Supreme Court and ask that the appeals court or the Supreme Court continue to stay the order. Provisions requiring divestiture are automatically stayed until any judicial review is complete. Violations of a cease-and-desist order, after it becomes effective, subject the offender to suit by the Government in a United States district court for the recovery of a civil penalty of not more than $10,000 for each violation and, where the violation continues, each day of its continuance is a separate violation.

In addition to, or in lieu of, the administrative proceeding initiated by a formal complaint, the Commission may, in some cases, request that a United States district court issue a preliminary or permanent injunction to halt the use of allegedly unfair or deceptive practices, to prevent an anticompetitive merger from taking place, or to prevent violations of any other statutory obligations enforced by the Commission.

The Commission also has specific authority to ask the United States district court to enjoin the dissemination of advertisements of food, drugs, cosmetics, and devices intended for use in the diagnosis, prevention, or treatment of disease, whenever it has reason to believe that such a proceeding would be in the public interest. Preliminary injunctions remain in effect until a cease-and-desist order is issued and becomes final, or until the complaint is dismissed by the Commission or the order is set aside by the court on review.

Further, the dissemination of a false advertisement of a food, drug, device, or cosmetic, where the use of the commodity advertised may be injurious to health or where there is intent to defraud or mislead, constitutes a misdemeanor. Conviction subjects the offender to a fine of not more than $5,000, or imprisonment of not more than 6 months, or both. Succeeding convictions may result in a fine of not more than $10,000, or imprisonment for not more than 1 year, or both. The statute provides that the Commission shall certify this type of case to the Attorney General for institution of appropriate court proceedings.

COMPLIANCE ACTIVITIES

Through systematic and continuous review, the Commission obtains and maintains compliance with its cease-and-desist orders. All respondents against whom such orders have been issued are required to file reports with the Commission to substantiate their compliance. In the event compliance is not obtained, or if the order is subsequently violated, civil penalty proceedings may be instituted.

TRADE REGULATION RULES

The Commission is authorized to issue trade regulation rules specifically defining acts or practices that are unfair or deceptive. A rule may also specify steps to prevent such practices from occurring. Such rules may be limited to certain industries or be applicable to all businesses within the Commission's jurisdiction. Rules are promulgated under specific procedures providing for participation of interested parties, including oral hearings and comments. The Commission's decision to issue a rule may be appealed to a United States court of appeals. In most cases, once a rule has become final, the Commission can seek the institution of a civil proceeding in a United States district court for knowing violations of the rule and seek civil penalties of up to $10,000 per violation and consumer redress.

COOPERATIVE PROCEDURES

In carrying out the statutory directive to "prevent" the use in or affecting commerce of unfair practices, the Commission makes extensive use of voluntary and cooperative procedures. Through these procedures business and industry may obtain authoritative guidance and a substantial measure of certainty as to what they may do under the laws administered by the Commission.

Whenever it is practicable, the Commission will furnish a formal advisory opinion as to whether a proposed course of conduct, if pursued, would be likely to result in further action by the Commission. An advisory opinion is binding upon the Commission with respect to the person or group to whom the opinion is issued with regard to the acts, practices, or conduct described in the request, where all relevant facts were completely and accurately presented to the Commission, until the advice has been rescinded or revoked and notice has been given to the requester. No enforcement action will be initiated by the Commission concerning any conduct undertaken by the requester in good faith reliance upon the advice of the Commission where such conduct is discontinued promptly upon notification of rescission or revocation of the Commission's approval.

Industry guides are administrative interpretations in laymen's language of laws administered by the Commission for the guidance of the public in conducting its affairs in conformity with legal requirements. They provide the basis for voluntary and simultaneous abandonment of unlawful practices by members of a particular industry or industry in general. Failure to comply with the guides may result in corrective action by the Commission under applicable statutory provisions.

CONSUMER PROTECTION

Consumer protection is one of the two main missions of the Commission. The Commission works to increase the usefulness of advertising by ensuring it is truthful and not misleading; reduce instances of fraudulent, deceptive, or uniform marketing practices; and prevent creditors from using unlawful practices when granting credit, maintaining credit information, collecting debts, and operating credit systems. Consumer protection initiates investigations in many areas of concern to consumers, including health claims in food advertising; environmental advertising and labeling; general advertising issues; health care fraud; telemarketing business opportunity, and franchise and investment fraud; mortgage lending and discrimination; enforcement of Commission orders; and enforcement of credit statutes and trade rules.

The Commission has issued and enforces many trade rules important to consumers. The Used Car Rule requires that dealers display a buyers guide containing warranty information on the window of each vehicle offered for sale to consumers. The Mail Order Rule requires companies to ship merchandise that consumers order by mail or telephone within a certain time, and sets out requirements for notifying consumers about delays and offering them the option of agreeing to the delays or cancelling their orders. The Funeral Rule requires that price and other specific information regarding funeral arrangements be made available to consumers to help them make informed choices and pay only for services they select. The Franchise Rule requires the seller to provide each prospective franchisee with a basic disclosure document containing detailed information about the nature of its business and terms of the proposed franchise relationship. The R-Value Rule requires manufacturers to disclose the R-value (a measure of resistance to heat flow) of their home-insulation products. Under the Cooling-Off Rule, consumers can cancel purchases of $25 or more made door-to-door, or at places other than the seller's usual place of business, within 3 business days of purchase.

Under the Consumer Protection mission, the Commission also enforces a number of specific laws that help consumers. One such law is the Consumer Credit Protection Act, which establishes, among other things, rules for the use of credit cards, the disclosure of the terms on which open- and closed-end credit is granted, and the disclosure of the reasons a business uses in determining not to grant credit.

The Truth in Lending Act is one part of the Consumer Credit Protection Act. Its purpose is to ensure that every customer who has need for consumer credit is given meaningful information with respect to the cost of that credit. In most cases the credit cost must be expressed in the dollar amount of finance charges, and as an annual percentage rate computed on the unpaid balance of the amount financed. The Truth in Lending Act was amended in October 1970 to regulate the issuance, holder's liability, and the fraudulent use of credit cards.

The Fair Credit Reporting Act, another part of the Consumer Credit Protection Act, represents the first Federal regulation of the vast consumer reporting industry, covering all credit bureaus, investigative reporting companies, detective and collection agencies, lenders' exchanges, and computerized information reporting companies. The purpose of this act is to ensure that consumer reporting activities are conducted in a manner that is fair and equitable, upholding the consumer's right to privacy as against the informational demands of others.

MAINTAINING COMPETITION (ANTITRUST)

The second major mission of the Commission is to encourage competitive forces in the American economy. Under the Federal Trade Commission Act, the Commission seeks to prevent unfair practices that may keep one company from competing with others. Under the Federal Trade Commission Act and the Clayton Act, the Commission attempts to prevent mergers of companies if the result may be to lessen competition. Under some circumstances, companies planning to merge must first give notice to the Commission and the Department of Justice's Antitrust Division and provide certain information concerning the operations of the companies involved.

The Commission also enforces the provisions of the Robinson-Patman Act, a part of the Clayton Act prohibiting companies from discriminating among other companies that are its customers in terms of price or other services provided.

ECONOMIC FACTFINDING

The Commission makes economic studies of conditions and problems affecting competition in the economy. Reports of this nature may be used to inform legislative proposals, part of a rulemaking record, in response to requests of the Congress and statutory directions, or for the information and guidance of the Commission and the executive branch of the Government as well as the public. The reports have provided the basis for significant legislation and, by spotlighting poor economic or regulatory performance, they have also led to voluntary changes in the conduct of business, with resulting benefits to the public.

COMPETITION AND CONSUMER ADVOCACY

To promote competition, consumer protection, and the efficient allocation of resources, the Commission has an active program designed to advocate the consumer interest in a competitive marketplace by encouraging courts, legislatures, and government administrative bodies to consider efficiency and consumer welfare as important elements in their deliberations.

The Commission uses these opportunities to support procompetitive means of regulating the Nation's economy, including the elimination of anticompetitive regulations that reduce the welfare of consumers and the implementation of regulatory programs that protect the public and preserve as much as possible the discipline of competitive markets. The competition and consumer advocacy program relies on persuasion rather than coercion.

On page 000 is an organization chart of the FTC. It will help you to keep in mind what an agency "looks like." Note on the chart that the FTC is headed by a body of five commissioners. Each is appointed for a term of seven years by the president, with the advice and consent of the Senate. The terms are staggered such that no more than one expires in any given year. Not more than three of the five commissioners may be members of the same political party. Before 1950, the commission elected its chairman. Now the president appoints the chairman, who makes staff appointments with the full commission's approval 15 U.S.C. §41 sets forth the basic procedure for appointment of FTC commissioners.

The chief staff members include the general counsel, who represents the FTC in court, advises the commission on questions of law and policy, works with state and local officials, and coordinates all liaison activities with Congress. He or she is also responsible for preparing advisory opinions for companies and individuals who want to check the legality of proposed actions.

The executive assistant is the chief operating officer and exercises administrative supervision over all FTC offices, bureaus, and staff members. Under the executive assistant are the three major bureaus. The Bureau of Consumer Protection investigates and litigates matters involving unfair or deceptive acts or practices, as well as some product safety. The Bureau of Competition enforces the basic antitrust law, primarily the FTCA and the Clayton Act. The Bureau of Economics advises the commission on the economic aspects of its activities and assists the other two bureaus in their investigations and trial work. (For FTC organization generally, see 16 C.F.R. §§0.1-0.19.)

Consider next the procedure that the FTC follows when it exercises its policing function. The commission receives complaints from the public or other sources, which agency personnel then investigate. If the investigation discloses sufficient information to constitute a prima facie case, the commission itself issues a complaint. Commission attorneys present the commission's case in an adjudicatory hearing conducted by one of the commission's administrative law judges, whose decision may be appealed either by the respondent or by the complaint counsel to the full commission, which definitively decides the case and often establishes new policy in its decision. Thus, the FTC formulates policies, as does the Congress. It investigates and prosecutes, as does the executive branch. It adjudicates, as does the judiciary. The FTC combines the functions of prosecutor, judge, and manager.

The combination of these functions within a single organization creates conflicts between objectives of fairness and objectives of efficiency. Legal doctrines and compromises

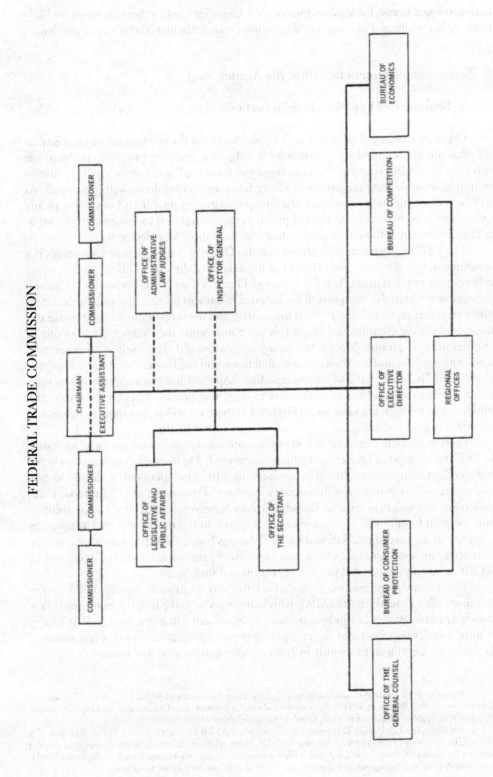

have developed to ease the tensions thus created. Consider whether these doctrines are likely to create fair results and whether they themselves create particular administrative problems.

1. Separation of Functions within the Agency Staff

a. Separation of Functions in Adjudication

One major source of potential unfairness arises from the fact that the same organization that initiates a complaint against a party judges the resulting case. This problem has two aspects: unfairness arising from the vesting of these conflicting powers in the commissioners themselves, and unfairness resulting from conflicting duties within the staff. As will be seen in the next subsection, the first problem is quite difficult to resolve in any satisfactory way; however, the second problem can be relieved to some extent by intra-agency separation of those who prosecute a case from those who decide it.

The FTC organization table shows that the Office of Administrative Law Judges is a separate entity not under direct control of the executive director. This separation alone relieves part of the tension. Yet, the Office of General Counsel is under direct control; prosecutions within the commission are handled by bureau lawyers (the general counsel's office primarily represents the FTC in the courts); and the prosecutors and judges are still responsible to the commission. Might this not compromise the independence of one or another of these groups? Moreover, the agency staff might view itself as members of a team with loyalties and an esprit de corps that transcend the barriers on an organizational chart. Can "isolated" parts of an organization hope to function neutrally when their members ride the same bus to work, work in adjoining offices, share coffee breaks and lunches, and move in the same social circles? Do these criticisms also apply to judges and members of the local bar?

Plans to separate functions at both commission and staff levels have been proposed. In 1937, for example, a blue-ribbon panel recommended to the president that each of the independent commissions should be replaced by a truly independent "judicial" section and an executive-controlled "administrative" section.[1] Proponents soon found that it was difficult or impossible to separate the adjudicatory functions from related responsibilities, and the plan foundered. Another possible response to the problem is that adopted by Congress in the case of the National Labor Relations Board (NLRB) — near total separation of the general counsel (who issues complaints) from the rest of the agency. The NLRB is the only agency that has this organizational structure.[2]

The uneasy compromise that carried the day politically is embodied in the Administrative Procedure Act (APA), which attempts to make hearing examiners (now known as administrative law judges, or ALJs) independent within the agency. The history behind this development and the competing policy justifications for this separation of functions are developed more fully by Justice Jackson in the case that follows.

---

1. Report of the President's Committee on Administrative Management 40-42, 223 (1937). The second Hoover Commission Report in 1955 made a somewhat similar proposal. See Commission on Organizations of the Executive Branch of the Government, Legal Services and Procedure 87-88 (1955).

2. See Klaus, the Taft-Hartley Experiment in Separation of NLRB Functions, 11 Ind. & Lab. Rel. Rev. 371 (1958). The "experiment" did not work out very well. Ms. Klaus relates in harrowing terms the constant sniping between the General Counsel and the Board, which occasionally broke out into open warfare. Repeated legislative attempts to reform the agency into a more conventional structure have come to naught.

Wong Yang Sung v. McGrath
339 U.S. 33 (1950)

Mr. Justice JACKSON delivered the opinion of the Court.

This habeas corpus proceeding involves a single ultimate question — whether administrative hearings in deportation cases must conform to requirements of the Administrative Procedure Act. . . .

Wong Yang Sung, native and citizen of China, was arrested by immigration officials on a charge of being unlawfully in the United States through having overstayed shore leave. . . . A hearing was held before an immigrant inspector who recommended deportation. The Acting Commission approved; and the Board of Immigration Appeals affirmed.

Wong Yang Sung then sought release from custody by habeas corpus proceedings in the District Court for the District of Columbia, upon the sole ground that the administrative hearing was not conducted in conformity with [the separation of functions requirements of] §§554 and 3105 of the Administrative Procedure Act. The Government admitted noncompliance, but asserted that the Act did not apply. . . .

I

. . . Multiplication of federal administrative agencies and expansion of their functions to include adjudications which have serious impact on private rights has been one of the dramatic legal developments of the past half-century. Partly from restriction by statute, partly from judicial self-restraint, and partly by necessity — from the nature of their multitudinous and semilegislative or executive tasks — the decisions of administrative tribunals were accorded considerable finality, and especially with respect to fact finding. The conviction developed, particularly within the legal profession, that this power was not sufficiently safeguarded and sometimes was put to arbitrary and biased use. . . .

[The Court then traced the history of efforts to reform administrative agency procedures from 1929, when Senator Norris proposed an "administrative court," through the 1937 and 1939 presidential studies and congressional hearings to the 1945 McCarran-Sumners bill, which evolved into the APA.]

The Act thus represents a long period of study and strife; it settles long-continued and hard-fought contentions, and enacts a formula upon which opposing social and political forces have come to rest. It contains many compromises and generalities and, no doubt, some ambiguities. Experience may reveal defects. But it would be a disservice to our form of government and to the administrative process itself if the courts should fail, so far as the terms of the Act warrant, to give effect to its remedial purposes where the evils it was aimed at appear.

II

Of the several administrative evils sought to be cured or minimized, [the most relevant is] the purpose to curtail and change the practice of embodying in one person or agency the duties of prosecutor and judge. The President's Committee on Administrative Management voiced in 1937 the theme which, with variations in language, was reiterated through the legislative history of the Act. [It] said:

[Administrations are] obliged to carry on judicial functions under conditions which threaten the impartial performance of that judicial work. The discretionary work of the administrator is merged with that of the judge. Pressures and influences properly enough directed toward officers responsible for formulating and administering policy constitute an unwholesome atmosphere in which to adjudicate private rights. But the mixed duties of the commissions render escape from these subversive influences impossible.

Furthermore, the same men are obliged to serve both as prosecutors and judges. This not only undermines judicial fairness; it weakens public confidence in that fairness. Commission decisions affecting private rights and conduct lie under the suspicion of being rationalizations of the preliminary findings which the commission, in the role of prosecutor, presented to itself.

[Administrative Management in the Government of the United States, Report of the President's Committee on Administrative Management, 36-37 (1937).]

And the Attorney General's Committee on Administrative Procedure, which divided as to the appropriate remedy, was unanimous that this evil existed. Its Final Report said:

These types of commingling of functions of investigation or advocacy with the function of deciding are thus plainly undesirable. But they are also avoidable and should be avoided by appropriate internal division of labor. For the disqualifications produced by investigation or advocacy are personal psychological ones which result from engaging in those types of activity; and the problem is simply one of isolating those who engage in the activity. Creation of independent hearing commissioners insulated from all phases of a case other than hearing and deciding will, the Committee believes, go far toward solving this problem at the level of the initial hearing, provided the proper safeguards are established to assure the insulation. . . .

[Rep. Atty. Gen. Comm. Ad. Proc. 56 (1941), S. Doc. No. 8, 77th Cong., 1st Sess. 56 (1941).]

The Act before us adopts in general this recommended form of remedial action. . . .

III

Turning now to the case before us, we find the administrative hearing a perfect exemplification of the practices so unanimously condemned.

This hearing, which followed the uniform practice of the Immigration Service, was before an immigrant inspector, who, for purposes of the hearing, is called the "presiding inspector." Except with consent of the alien, the presiding inspector may not be the one who investigated the case. . . . But the inspector's duties include investigation of like cases; and while he is today hearing cases investigated by a colleague, tomorrow his investigation of a case may be heard before the inspector whose case he passes on today. . . . The presiding inspector. . . . is required to "conduct the interrogation of the alien and the witnesses in behalf of the Government and shall cross-examine the alien's witnesses and present such evidence as is necessary to support the charges in the warrant of arrest." . . . It may even become his duty to lodge an additional charge against the alien and proceed to hear his own accusation in like manner. . . . Then, as soon as practicable, he is to prepare a summary of the evidence, proposed findings of fact, conclusions of law, and a proposed order. A copy is furnished the alien or his counsel, who may file exceptions and brief, . . . whereupon the whole is forwarded to the Commissioner.

. . . We come, then, to examination of the text of the Act to determine whether the Government is right in its contentions: first, that [§554 of the] Act does not cover deportation proceedings; and, second, that even if it does, the proceedings are excluded from the requirements of the Act by virtue of [§556].

IV

The Administrative Procedure Act, [§554], establishes a number of formal requirements to be applicable "in every case of adjudication required by statute to be determined on the record after opportunity for an agency hearing." The argument here depends upon the words "adjudication required by statute." The Government contends that there is no express requirement for any hearing or adjudication in the statute authorizing deportation, and that this omission shields these proceedings from the impact of [§554]. . . .

[T]he difficulty with any argument premised on the proposition that the deportation statute does not require a hearing is that, without such hearing, there would be no constitutional authority for deportation. The constitutional requirement of procedural due process of law derives from the same source as Congress' power to legislate and, where applicable, permeates every valid enactment of that body. It was under compulsion of the Constitution that this Court long ago held that an antecedent deportation statute must provide a hearing at least for aliens who had not entered clandestinely. . . .

We think that the limitation to hearings "required by statute" in [§554] of the Administrative Procedure Act exempts from that section's application only those hearings which administrative agencies may hold by regulation, rule, custom, or special dispensation; not those held by compulsion. We do not think the limiting words render the Administrative Procedure Act inapplicable to hearings, the requirement for which has been read into a statute by the Court in order to save the statute from invalidity. They exempt hearings of less than statutory authority, not those of more than statutory authority. We would hardly attribute to Congress a purpose to be less scrupulous about the fairness of a hearing necessitated by the Constitution than one granted by it as a matter of expediency. . . .

V

The remaining question is whether the exception of [§556(b)] of the Administrative Procedure Act exempts deportation hearings held before immigrant inspectors. It provides:

> Presiding Officers. — There shall preside at the taking of evidence (1) the agency, (2) one or more members of the body which comprises the agency, or (3) one or more examiners appointed as provided in this Act; but nothing in this Act shall be deemed to supersede the conduct of specified classes of proceedings in whole or part by or before boards or other officers specially provided for by or designated pursuant to statute. . . .[3]

---

3. The text quoted by the Court is that of the APA as it then existed. Because of a later codification, the current APA text is different in certain details but unchanged in substance. — Eds.

The Government argues that immigrant inspectors are "specially provided for by or designated pursuant to" §16 of the Immigration Act, which, in pertinent part, reads

> . . . The inspection . . . of aliens, including those seeking admission or readmission to or the privilege of passing through or residing in the United States, and the examination of aliens arrested within the United States under this Act, shall be conducted by immigrant inspectors. . . .

[8 U.S.C. §152.]

Certainly nothing here specifically provides that immigrant inspectors shall conduct deportation hearings or be designated to do so. [T]hat Congress by grant of these powers has specially constituted them or provided for their designation as hearing officers in deportation proceedings does not appear.

Section [556(b)] qualifies as presiding officers at hearings the agency and one or more of the members of the body comprising the agency, and it also leaves untouched any others whose responsibilities and duties as hearing officers are established by other statutory provisions. But if hearings are to be had before employees whose responsibility and authority derives from a lesser source, they must be examiners whose independence and tenure are so guarded by the Act as to give the assurances of neutrality which Congress thought would guarantee the impartiality of the administrative process.

We find no basis in the purposes, history or text of this Act for judicially declaring an exemption in favor of deportation proceedings from the procedural safeguards enacted for general application to administrative agencies. We hold that deportation proceedings must conform to the requirements of the Administrative Procedure Act if resulting orders are to have validity. Since the proceeding in the case before us did not comply with these requirements, we sustain the writ of habeas corpus and direct release of the prisoner.

Reversed.

Note: Separation of Functions in APA §554

The basic separation of functions provision of the APA is contained in §554(d). To determine when that section applies, however, one must trace through the following labyrinth:

1. Section 554(d) applies to adjudications when an "employee who presides at the reception of evidence pursuant to section 556 . . . make[s] the recommended decision or initial decision required by section 557."
2. Section 557 states that a hearing examiner makes an "initial" or "recommended" decision; and §556(a), (b) provides that he (or a commissioner) shall preside in cases that "section 553 or 554" require "to be conducted in accordance with" §556 unless some statute specifically states that someone else shall preside.
3. Sections 553(c) and 554(a) require that §556 procedures be used when a statute (or, under *Wong Yang Sung*, the Constitution) requires that the rule or order be made "on the record after opportunity for agency hearing."

Thus §554(d) normally applies to adjudications when a hearing examiner presides at a hearing that the underlying substantive statute requires to be held "on the record." (Note that it does not apply to "on-the-record" rulemaking.)

Section 554(d) requires that:

1. The hearing examiner may not "consult a person or party on a fact in issue, unless on notice and opportunity for all parties to participate";
2. The hearing examiner cannot be subject to the direction of an agency employee involved in investigative or prosecuting functions;
3. No agency employee who investigates or prosecutes a case may, in that case "or a factually related case, participate or advise in the decision, recommended decision or agency review pursuant to section 557 . . . except as witness or counsel. . . ."

But the constraints of §554(d) do not apply "in determining applications for initial licenses; . . . . to proceedings involving . . . rates, facilities or practices of public utilities or carriers; or . . . the agency or a member . . . of the body comprising the agency."

At this point, you should look at the full language of these sections contained in Appendix A. In addition, examine 5 U.S.C. §§3105, 7521, 5362, 3344, 1305, which reinforce the independence of the hearing examiner.

Questions: What provisions of the APA did the INS inspector system violate? What intelligible set of policies underlies these sets of provisions and choices?

Problem

Consider the following complaint in an actual FTC case:

FOREVER YOUNG, INC.

Paragraph Two: Respondents advertise, offer for sale, and sell to the general public a medical process called the Forever Young treatment, which is a chemical peeling of the skin on the face and neck for cosmetic purposes. The treatment involves the application of a chemical solution which peels off the outer layers of the skin, producing an alteration in skin appearance as the skin heals. The purported purpose of this treatment is to remove manifestations of aging such as wrinkles, lines, folds, spots, and undesirable features such as blemishes, large pores, and acne marks, in order to make a person appear younger or more attractive. Forever Young, Inc. grants licenses for the purpose of selling the treatment. According to available information, there are presently licensees in Hawaii, California, Washington, Colorado, Virginia, and Oregon.

Paragraph Six: The Nature of the Treatment. Respondents represent the treatment, without any further description, as a technique of facial regeneration which does not involve surgery or abrasions, implying by this and other representations that the treatment is merely a cosmetic process. In fact, the treatment involves application of an abrasive chemical solution (containing phenol, also known as carbolic acid) to the skin, causing a second-degree burn which peels off the outer layers of the skin and produces a change in skin appearance solely by the body's own wound-healing process. The treatment is known as chemosurgery and is a serious medical procedure.

Paragraph Seven: Pain. Respondents advertise the treatment without mentioning the subject of pain or discomfort. One of their brochures represents that the client should not have any pain during the recuperation period and another represents that clients can read, sew, or write letters during the time. In fact, the pain associated with the process can be so severe that respondents' patients are always sedated or anesthetized during the application of acid and may require medication for days, weeks, or months afterward to reduce pain and other discomforts, such as itching and burning. During the treatment, many patients experience such discomforts as the eyes swelling shut and difficulties breathing, and swallowing.

Paragraph Eight: Safety: Systemic Dangers. Respondents represent that the treatment is safe. In fact, the process had, in addition to the pain described above, a number of inherent dangers to the entire body, which respondents do not disclose, including but not limited to:

1. Systemic toxic reaction (poisoning). The chemical used in the Forever Young treatment, phenol, is toxic to kidneys, liver, and other organs of the body when present in sufficient quantities. Phenol can be absorbed through the skin during the treatment in quantities sufficient to cause serious and even fatal illness in some people. One patient died during the Forever Young treatment from this cause. Persons with kidney infections are particularly susceptible to adverse phenol reaction. Yet, Forever Young does perform the treatment on persons with kidney infections. Furthermore, Forever Young does not provide the personnel, facilities, equipment or techniques adequate to prevent or minimize the effects of a systemic toxic reaction.

Assume that this case is now before the ALJ.

(1)(a) If the FTC general counsel has not participated in the case so far, can the ALJ ask him his opinion as to whether the claim that there is no surgery or abrasion is unlawfully deceptive?

(b) If the FTC's staff medical expert in the Bureau of Consumer Protection has not participated in the case, can the ALJ ask her whether Forever Young's treatment is toxic?

(c) Could the ALJ consult, on the same question, a member of the bureau's scientific staff who testified before the ALJ on this question?

(d) May the examiner consult with the bureau staff attorney who prepared the case on questions of either fact or law?

(2) Would it make any difference if, on appeal of the ALJ's decision, one of the commissioners wished to do the consulting described above?

Note: The Coverage of §554(d) and the Aftermath of *Wong Yang Sung*

The "separation of functions" provisions of the APA apply only when an adjudication is required by statute (or, given *Wong Yang Sung*, by the Constitution) to be determined on the record after opportunity for an agency hearing. Recall that United States v. Florida East Coast Ry. Co. involved statutory interpretation to determine if a "hearing . . . on the record" was required for rulemaking. The Court refused to find such a requirement unless the specific words *hearing* and *on the record* appeared in the statute. When the defendant in an adjudication has complained of the lack of an independent hearing examiner, however, the Supreme Court — in decisions antedating *Florida East Coast* — has been willing to infer a statutory requirement of an on-the-record proceeding without those magic words. Thus, in Riss & Co. v. United States, 96 F. Supp. 452 (W.D. Mo.), *rev'd per curiam*, 341 U.S. 906 (1951), the Court apparently found that the statute that authorized the Interstate Commerce Commission (ICC) to issue "certificates of convenience and necessity" to motor carriers required a hearing on the record, even though the statute never mentions either "hearings" or "record." The Court applied a similar analysis to a statute that allowed the postal service to issue mail fraud orders "upon evidence satisfactory to the postal service."[4]

A further question arises if one remembers that the Constitution may require hearings of varying degrees of formality depending on the circumstances. Does *Wong Yang Sung* require an APA-type hearing whenever due process analysis requires a hearing of any sort whatsoever? Courts have been understandably reluctant to extend the holding to the entire spectrum of administrative adjudication. Note that *Wong Yang Sung* involves deportation. Are there many other administrative actions that entrench so drastically on an individual's liberty?

Congress responded to *Wong Yang Sung* by attaching a rider to the Supplemental Appropriations Act of 1951 that explicitly exempted deportation and exclusion hearings from APA requirements. This provision was repealed one year later by the Immigration and Nationality Act, which detailed the procedural requirements for deportation hearings. 8 U.S.C. §1252(b). The "special inquiry officer" can still take the dual role of prosecutor and hearing officer, though he may not hear cases that he has specifically investigated. The special inquiry officer is still subject to supervision and control by the attorney general and district directors of the INS. The Supreme Court upheld these procedures as constitutional, thus suggesting that *Wong Yang Sung* decided as a matter of statutory interpretation, not constitutional law, that APA §554 was meant to apply to hearings required by the Constitution.

For recent cases, see Sheldon v. SEC, 45 F.3d 1515 (11th Cir. 1995); Simpson v. Office of Thrift Supervision, 29 F.3d 1418 (9th Cir. 1994). In *Sheldon*, the court upheld an arrangement by which an agency combined investigative, adjudicative, and adversarial powers, saying that this arrangement was lawful so long as no "employee" served in dual roles. In *Simpson*, the court did not strike down an agency order requiring an executive to pay restitution for breach of fiduciary duties, even though the agency head both authorized the charges and made the ultimate decision about their validity. In the same vein, see Keating v. Office of Thrift Supervision, 45 F.3d 322 (9th Cir. 1995).

b. Separation of Functions in Rulemaking

Hercules Inc. v. EPA
598 F.2d 91 (D.C. Cir. 1978)

TAMM, Circuit Judge. . . .

[Petitioners challenged the Environmental Protection Agency's regulations limiting discharge of toxaphene and endrin into rivers and other waterways. These regulations grew out of §553 notice-and-comment rulemaking proceedings, though it is doubtful that the "rule" applied to anyone other than petitioners. One portion of the case concerned

---

4. See Cates v. Haderlein, 189 F.2d 369 (7th Cir.), *rev'd per curiam*, 342 U.S. 804 (1951). First Amendment considerations may be at work here. See Kirby v. Shaw, 358 F.2d 446, 448 (9th Cir. 1966); Door v. Donaldson, 195 F.2d 764 (D.C. Cir. 1952). Note that even when the statute in question requires that an adjudicatory-style hearing take place on the record, §554(d) may apply only to a later stage in the proceeding. Earlier stages may be viewed as "informal" or preliminary. Thus, in International Tel. & Tel. Corp., Communications Equip. & Systems Div. v. Local 134, Intl. Brotherhood of Elec. Workers, 419 U.S. 428 (1975), the Court held that a §10(k) NLRA proceeding was a "preliminary administrative determination," and did not have the requisite finality for §554(d) to be required.

"separation of functions." The petitioners argued that there had been impermissible contacts between the EPA's staff and the EPA judicial officer who promulgated the rules. The officer reported directly to the EPA administrator and acted as his delegate.]

Before 1976 the EPA's internal procedural rules governing rulemaking barred "the Administrator or the presiding officer [from] consult[ing] with any person or party on a fact at issue." In 1976 EPA changed those rules, deleting this "ex parte" contact rule as unnecessary. Instead, the new EPA rule stated that "the administrator with such staff assistance as he deems necessary and appropriate, shall review the entire record and prepare and file a tentative decision based thereon." The agency justified its action as follows:

> The promulgated standards in turn are to be based solely on that record. Cf., Administrative Procedure Act, 5 U.S.C. Section 556(e). With respect to discussions between the Administrator and Agency staff involved in the presentation of evidence at the hearing, the rule requiring separation of functions which applies in cases of adjudication, 5 U.S.C. Section 554(b), is inapplicable to rulemaking. Hoffmann-La Roche, Inc. v. Kleindienst, 478 F.2d 1 (3d Cir. 1973).
>
> . . . K. Davis, Administrative Law Treatise, Section 13.00 at 453 (1970 Supp.) [discusses] the separation of prosecutorial and decisionmaking functions within an administrative Agency, which is closely related to the ex parte question since the issue with respect to Agency personnel is whether the staff who presents the evidence should be precluded from discussing the regulation with the Administrator out of the presence of the objector's representatives. Although Professor Davis equivocates on what the policy should be, he leaves no doubt about the law: "The conclusion seems to be rather solid that no law requires the Commissioner [of FDA] to separate functions in rulemaking for which on-the-record hearings are required." Id. at p.443.
>
> The rationale for not imposing separation of functions, and the attendant prohibition on communication between those responsible for developing and presenting the proposed rule or standard and the person ultimately charged with promulgation, lies with the nature of rulemaking. The development of a proposed rule or standard includes a number of policy decisions in which many program offices within the agency participate. The Administrator relies on the advice and recommendations of these offices in developing and proposing the standards. At the same time, persons within these offices may well present evidence at rulemaking hearings including information on which the proposed standard was based. It would be counterproductive to reasoned rulemaking if, at the stage of final decision and promulgation, the administrator were isolated from those within the Agency whom he normally consults on policy determinations and whose offices will be charged with implementation and enforcement of the regulations. The institutional nature of the Administrator's decision, as noted previously, is inherent in the very nature of rulemaking, and is normally absent from adjudication.
>
> Because the law clearly does not require the prohibition on ex parte discussions contained in Section 104.16 as originally promulgated, and because nothing in the rulemaking process warrants its retention, it is deleted as proposed.

EPA conducted the proceeding now on review under the new procedural rules. Its chief judicial officer, Ms. Harriet B. Marple, was assigned to aid the Administrator in preparing his final decision. Ms. Marple was confronted with a loosely organized rulemaking record of enormous detail and staggering complexity — thousands of pages of highly technical testimony, affidavits, and studies from a variety of sources — to be considered against an uncertain scientific and legal background. The record had been closed on Oct. 12, 1976. Under the deadline imposed by Section 307(a)(2), the Administrator had two months or less to issue his final standards. . . .

[Marple described her intra-agency contacts as follows: (1) consultation with the administrator, Russell Train; (2) consultation with several EPA attorneys in the Water Quality Division and other EPA attorneys working on the case, for help in locating documents in the record; (3) consultation with an EPA section chief to discuss "toxicological issues . . . raised by the record"; (4) consultation with an EPA expert to discuss "record evidence regarding species diversity"; (5) discussion with Russell Train's executive assistant to explain the issues to him. Marple stated that all these consultations were "for the sole and limited purpose of properly understanding and interpreting . . . the record."]

In *Home Box Office* [v. FCC, 567 F.2d 9 (D.C. Cir. 1977)], this court held that the wide-ranging *private* contacts with the FCC decisionmakers that had occurred were impermissible. . . . Petitioners contend that staff contacts offend the principles underlying the *Home Box Office* decision no less than private contacts. In their view, staff contacts deprive the reviewing court of the full and accurate administrative record, . . . foreclose the opportunity for genuine adversarial discussion among the parties, . . . and, most importantly, are inconsistent with fundamental notions of fairness implicit in due process and with the ideal of reasoned decisionmaking. . . . They stress that this proceeding was more adversarial and formal than the informal rulemaking proceeding reviewed in *Home Box Office*.

EPA responds that, in the APA, Congress expressly sanctioned staff contacts, in contrast to private contacts, because of the quasi-legislative nature of the rulemaking process and the necessities of implementation of administrative policy. 5 U.S.C. §554(d) prohibits staff contacts in adjudication; 5 U.S.C. §§553, 556 & 557 do not express a similar prohibition in rulemaking.

These statutory provisions are discussed in the legislative history, which demonstrates that Congress decided that the strictures of 5 U.S.C. §554(d) should not extend to rulemaking proceedings. . . .[5] This legislative history has been construed consistently to allow the agency's rulemaking staff to assist agency administrators in interpreting the rulemaking record. Further, the Supreme Court's decision in *Vermont Yankee Nuclear Power Corp.* [v. Natural Resources Defense Council, 435 U.S. 519 (1978)], counsels restraint in imposing procedural requirements beyond the letter of the APA. . . .

For two reasons, we have determined that EPA's standards must be upheld in this particular context. . . .

First, both the adoption by EPA of its procedural rules and the issuance of the final decision preceded *Home Box Office.* . . .

Second, the administrative history under section 307(a) created a peculiar context wherein the necessity for staff contacts existed with unusual and compelling force. As we have noted, section 307(a) sets forth rigid and compressed timetables. . . . In view of the extraordinary bulk and complexity of the administrative record, a judicial officer attempting to digest the record and prepare a decision in a matter of weeks would face, at the least, great difficulty in proceeding without staff assistance. Thus, this context invokes the rule of ancient origin that expedition in protecting the public health justifies less elaborate procedure than may be required in other contexts. . . .

---

5. Because the statutory language and legislative history are so unambiguous, we reject petitioners' assertion that 5 U.S.C. §554(d) applies to the decisionmaking stage of the instant proceedings merely because 5 U.S.C. §556(e) requires the decision to be on the record.

Notwithstanding our decision, however, we feel compelled to record our uneasiness with one aspect of this case — the communication between Ms. Marple and EPA staff legal advocates. . . . [The fact that the attorneys who represented the staffs position at the administrative hearing were later consulted by the judicial officer who prepared the final decision possibly gives rise to an appearance of unfairness, even though the consultations did not involve factual or policy issues. During congressional deliberation on the APA, the flexibility of rulemaking procedures was of concern, as the bill's sponsor indicated. . . .

"*The exemption of rule making* and determining applications for licenses, *from provisions of sections* 5(c), [5 U.S.C. §554(d)], 7(c), and 8(a) *may require change if, in practice, it develops that they are too broad.*" . . . 92 Cong. Rec. 2159 (1946) (remarks of Sen. McCarran) (emphasis added).

Amendatory legislation may be justified if agencies do not themselves proscribe post-hearing contacts between staff *advocates* and decisionmakers in formal rulemaking proceedings, lest there be an erosion of public trust and confidence in the administrative process. As we have discussed, until 1976, EPA banned intra-agency contacts in hearings such as these. EPA lifted this ban in 1976 in response to a peculiar situation of past failure and current necessity. Now might be a particularly propitious time for Congress or the agencies to limit or provide disclosure of post-hearing contacts between staff advocates and decision makers. . . .

Notes and Questions

1. In United Steelworkers of America v. Marshall, 647 F.2d 1189 (D.C. Cir. 1981), the D.C. Court of Appeals considered an Occupational Safety and Health Administration (OSHA) rule setting airborne lead exposure standards, a rule derived from the "informal rulemaking" process. The Lead Industry Association pointed out that, during an initial hearing before an ALJ, OSHA staff attorneys acted essentially as advocates for a stringent rule. The leading OSHA lawyer basically organized the hearing, spoke regularly to witnesses, briefed them, explained the parties' various positions to the examiner and to other witnesses, immersed himself in the literature, and conducted much of the questioning. After the hearing was over, he advised the assistant secretary, who had to make the final decision. He prepared summaries of the thousands of record pages, he analyzed the evidence, and he helped draft the final agency statement.

In addition, the secretary relied on reports prepared for her by two outside consultants. The consultants wrote two reports, between 100 and 200 pages each, analyzing critical evidence. The consultants, by the way, happened to be two experts who themselves testified during the hearing. Indeed, they were perhaps the two most important experts testifying in favor of the stringent standard that the industry opposed, and which the secretary eventually adopted. OSHA did not release these two reports publicly.

The court of appeals found that the consultations involved were lawful. It described the basic conclusion in *Hercules* as being that the issue of legal staff participation in the writing of the final decision "was one for Congress or the agencies to resolve." Since informal rulemaking was involved, the APA did not address the problem. Similarly, the court did not see any difference between a *consultant* participating in the creation of a final agency decision and a *staff member* participating in that decision. After all, if the leading agency "advocate" of the stringent standard could privately advise the agency decisionmaker, why couldn't experts, hired as consultants, do the same thing?

Judge McKinnon, dissenting, wrote that "fundamental requirements of fairness and due process in administrative law compel that these outside consultants to whom the agency delegates its obligation to evaluate the evidence must be unbiased and neutral in their evaluation of the record. Just as the actual decision-maker is to be unbiased, so must those to whom such a duty is delegated. No court should condone allowing paid consultants to legally change their hats from expert witnesses subject to cross-examination during the hearings, to 'agency staff, hired after the close of hearings to evaluate the credibility of *their own testimony* and others."

2. Professor Davis criticized the "APA separation of functions" provisions as being both too broad and too narrow. See 3 K. Davis, Administrative Law Treatise ch. 18 (1980). Indeed, one might wonder at the complete exemptions for commissioners and agency heads and for all rulemaking. Are there not some rulemaking occasions, as the *Hercules* court wonders, when agency decisionmakers ought to be forbidden to consult off the record, say, a staff lawyer taking an advocacy role in the case? Are there not other occasions, involving adjudication, when internal communication even with the staff lawyer prosecuting the case is desirable for the agency to discuss, say, a proposed settlement? How is a commissioner to keep control of a case, to narrow its charges, or to drop it where appropriate, unless he can communicate with the staff about it? Yet should he be totally free to talk to all those involved in the adjudication? The considerations are different for the ALJ, but should he not, at least, be able to communicate with his law clerk? What about uninvolved expert staff? See generally Pederson, The Decline of Separation of Functions in Regulatory Agencies, 64 U. Va. L. Rev. 991 (1978).

The Administrative Conference of the United States has considered proposals for reform based on a study by Professor Michael Asimow, The Curtain Falls: Separation of Functions in the Federal Administrative Agencies, 81 Colum. L. Rev. 759 (1981). Asimow surveys practice in the agencies; we recommend his study. For general discussion, see R. Pierce & K. Davis, 2 Administrative Law Treatise 92-102 (1995).

If you could create a rule to change the result in *Steelworkers*, what would it be?

c. The Independence of the Hearing Examiner

Enactment of the APA began a period that has seen the steady increase of the independence, stature, and authority of the hearing examiner. The APA provided that hearing officers were to have no assigned tasks "inconsistent with their duties and responsibilities as hearing examiners," and were in no circumstances to be subject to supervision or direction by anyone "engaged in the performance of investigative or prosecuting functions for an agency." They could not be removed by the agency employing them, but only by the Civil Service Commission (CSC) (now the Merit Systems Protection Board), and then only after notice and a hearing. 5 U.S.C. §7521. Their pay was to be set by the CSC (now the Office of Personnel Management (OPM)) "independently of agency recommendations or ratings," thereby insulating them from agency reprisals for decisions that displeased the agency heads. 5 U.S.C. §5362. The officer who presided over a hearing was expected to render an initial decision that would bind the agency and the parties unless review proceedings were commenced in a timely manner. 5 U.S.C. §557(b).

The initial attempts of the CSC (now the OPM) to select and retain able hearing examiners was somewhat less than successful; in fact, one commentator called it a "fiasco."[6] The commission revised its approach and issued regulations that provided for different grade classifications of hearing examiners within any given agency; opportunities for promotion from one grade to another depended on recommendation of the agency; likewise, assignments were made according to grade ("in rotation to cases of the level of difficulty and importance that are normally assigned to positions of the salary grade they hold"), and tenure for the purposes of layoffs during slack periods was determined under conditions similar to those governing other federal employees. In Ramspeck v. Federal Trial Examiners Conf., 345 U.S. 128 (1953), the Court sustained these regulations. The OPM later amended its regulations to classify hearing examiners in each agency at the same grade, except for the chief in each agency's cadre.

As of 1953, the 294 hearing examiners were distributed broadly among five grade levels, from GS-11 to GS-15. As of 1979, all 1134 ALJs were GS-15s or GS-16s. The accompanying elimination of promotional opportunities, along with discharge only for "cause" and mechanical systems of selection and of work assignment is, in the view of one experienced student of the subject, "a horror story of personnel management which should come to an end. It . . . prevents intelligent selection and adequate compensation of the finest judges, deters voluntary departure of the worst, and erodes incentive all along the way." Scalia, The ALJ Fiasco — A Reprise, 47 U. Chi. L. Rev. 57 (1979). In 1990, Public Law 101-509 replaced the grade system for ALJs with a new system, one that does not cure the problems identified above. See 104 Stat. 1427, 1445 (1990).

Legislative proposals have called for reforming the selection process, making it easier for agencies to choose the ALJs they wish, providing fixed terms of ten years, allowing review of the quality of the ALJs' work at the expiration of the terms, and making removal easier. See, e.g., S. 262, 96th Cong., 2d Sess. (1980). However, the ALJs organized politically and opposed these provisions strongly; the provisions have been dropped from current versions. Some notion of the emotions that are aroused when one begins to examine the "quality of work" is provided by an affidavit of Robert Trachtenberg, director of the Social Security Administration's Bureau of Hearings and Appeals, that was given to a House subcommittee in 1980. He wrote that "[u]pon my appointment as Director in January 1979 I discovered the most lethargic, indifferent, unresponsive and unaccountable organization that I have ever seen in 15 years as a federal employee." In response, a different agency official wrote that Mr. Trachtenberg "grossly exaggerates and flagrantly distorts the truth in his self-serving sworn statement. He appears intoxicated by his own press releases; thereby deluding himself in believing he is the Messiah. . . " Lubbers, Federal Administrative Law Judges: A Focus on Our Invisible Judiciary, 33 Admin. L. Rev. 108 (1981). See also Mans, Selecting the "Hidden Judiciary," 64 Judicature 60, 131 (1976).

The debate on the independence of these officials has not abated. There have been periodic suggestions that the present system of keeping a permanent staff of ALJs affiliated with each agency be abolished, and that a common pool of ALJs for all federal agencies be created, with a director of federal administrative procedure to rotate the examiners among the agencies. These proposals have not yet become law. In 1972, the CSC changed the title of "hearing examiner" to "administrative law judge," as a method of

---

6. Fuchs, The Hearing Examiner Fiasco Under the Administrative Procedure Act, 63 Harv. L. Rev. 737 (1950). See also Note, The Status of the Trial Examiner in Administrative Agencies, 66 Harv. L. Rev. 1065 (1953). The initial Civil Service rules for management of hearing examiners can be found in 5 C.F.R. §§34.1 et seq. (1949).

enhancing their prestige. 37 Fed. Reg. 16787 (1972). Critics of this action have argued that the prestige of the federal judiciary might be eroded if the government confers the title of "judge" on too many non-Article III judges;[7] however, few argue that these officials should be less independent.

Nash v. Bowen
869 F.2d 675 (2d Cir. 1989)

ALTIMARI, Circuit Judge. . . .

Plaintiff-appellant, pro se, Simon Nash is an Administrative Law Judge ("ALJ") with some thirty years experience in the Social Security Administration. In 1967, he became an ALJ in charge ("ALJIC") of the Buffalo, New York field office of hearings and appeals. By 1975, the Social Security Administration (the "agency") was faced with an administrative crisis due to a backlog of over 100,000 cases. In order to eliminate the backlog and the concomitant delays in processing appeals, former director of the Bureau (now "Office") of Hearings and Appeals Robert L. Trachtenberg instituted a series of reforms which appellant contends interfered with the "decisional independence" of ALJs under the APA, the Social Security Act and the due process clause of the fifth amendment. Nash initially protested the new policies within the agency only to be summarily demoted from his position as ALJIC to ALJ. In his original complaint filed May 30, 1978 in the district court, plaintiff alleged, in addition to a claim concerning his demotion which was later dropped, that the Secretary's newly-instituted "Peer Review Program," monthly production goals, and "Quality Assurance System" infringed upon the "quasi-judicial" status of ALJs. . . .

The district court explicitly determined that "[a]lthough the defendants may have engaged in some questionable practices which clearly caused great unrest among ALJs, . . . they did not infringe on the decisional independence of ALJs." . . .

The district court held that the "Peer Review Program" was intended to respond to the "wide disparity in legal and factual determinations among ALJs." Judge Elfvin concluded that various peer review actions constituted "legitimate administrative steps undertaken to enhance the quality and efficiency of the hearing system." Policies designed to insure a reasonable degree of uniformity among ALJ decisions are not only within the bounds of legitimate agency supervision but are to be encouraged. See generally Scalia, The ALJ Fiasco — A Reprise, 47 U. Chi. L. Rev. 57 (1979). In this case, "extra-appellate" review of "dead" cases aimed at improving the quality of ALJ decision-making is entirely consistent with the prerogative of the agency which retains "all the powers which it would have in making the initial decision." 5 U.S.C. §557(b). It is, after all, the Secretary who ultimately is authorized to make final decisions in benefit cases. An ALJ is a creature of statute and, as such, is subordinate to the Secretary in matters of policy and interpretation of law. Thus, the Secretary's efforts through peer review to ensure that ALJ decisions conformed with his interpretation of relevant law and policy were permissible so long as such efforts did not directly interfere with "live" decisions (unless in accordance with the usual administrative review performed by the Appeals

---

7. To "deflate" this criticism, the Office of Personnel Management has also specified that "[e]ach agency . . . may not use the word 'judge' as the title or part of the title for any other position for any purpose." 5 C.F.R. §930. 203a (1977).

Council). . . . The efforts complained of in this case for promoting quality and efficiency do not infringe upon ALJs' decisional independence. . . .

Regarding the Secretary's policy of setting a minimum number of dispositions an ALJ must decide in a month, we agree with the district court that reasonable efforts to increase the production levels of ALJs are not an infringement of decisional independence. In a memorandum dated July 1, 1975, then Director Trachtenberg indicated that while he was opposed to the fixing *of quotas*, he was recommending a *goal* of 26 dispositions per four-week period. When Louis B. Hays became Associate Commissioner of the Office of Hearing and Appeals in 1981, he specifically concerned himself with ALJs whose productivity fell below twenty case dispositions per month. The record also reflects continuing pressure from the agency on ALJs to increase monthly dispositions.

[I]n view of the significant backlog of cases, it was not unreasonable to expect ALJs to perform at minimally acceptable levels of efficiency. Simple fairness to claimants awaiting benefits required no less. Accordingly, we agree with the district court that the decisional independence of ALJs was not in any way usurped by the Secretary's setting of monthly production goals.

The Secretary's "reversal" rate policy embodied in the "Quality Assurance System," however, is cause for concern. To coerce ALJs into lowering reversal rates — that is, into deciding more cases against claimants — would, if shown, constitute in the district court's words "a clear infringement of decisional independence." . . .

The Secretary concedes that he was very concerned about reversal rates, but only to the extent that they *might* indicate errors in the decisionmaking of ALJs. Testimony in the record revealed that reversal rates were used as a benchmark in deciding whether there might be problems in the adjudicatory methods of particularly high (or low) reversal rate ALJs. Statistical record evidence supported the agency's proffered correlation between actual errors of law or policy in ALJs' decisions and extremes in their reversal rates. The agency maintained then, and maintains now, that reducing reversal rates was not the intent of the policy. Indeed, a handwritten notation by Associate Commissioner Hays on a 1982 internal agency memorandum placed the policy in perspective:

> [T]here is *no* goal to reduce reversal rates — there is a goal to improve decisional quality [and] consistency, which is assumed to have as one effect a reduction of the reversal rate.

App. at 2071.

. . . The bottom line in this case is that it was entirely within the Secretary's discretion to adopt reasonable administrative measures in order to improve the decisionmaking process. Since the district court found no direct pressure on ALJs to maintain a fixed percentage of reversals, we conclude that the Secretary's policy in this regard did not infringe upon the "decisional independence" of the ALJs.

Notes and Questions

1. The Bellmon Review Program, at issue in Nash v. Bowen, has been described as follows:

> ALJs with individual allowance rates of 70 percent or higher and ALJs in hearing offices with aggregate allowance rates of 74 percent or higher were targeted for review. Half of the allowance decisions issued by targeted ALJs were evaluated by the Office

of Hearing and Appeals for possible review, and 7 1/2 percent of the allowance decisions issued by these ALJs were formally reviewed by the Appeals Council. On April 1, 1982, the targeted ALJs were divided into four groups based on [certain reversal] rates. Each and every allowance decision by ALJs in the group with the highest [reversal] rates was evaluated for possible review. In the group with the second-highest rates, 75 percent of the ALJs allowance decisions were thus evaluated; in the group with the third-highest rates, 50 percent; and in the group with the lowest rates, 25 percent. In addition, the program was expanded so that 15 percent of all allowance decisions by targeted ALJs were formally reviewed by the Appeals Council. Finally, the program was expanded to provide review of a national random sample of ALJ allowance decisions, ALJ decisions referred from the SSA Office of Disability Operations, and decisions of all new ALJs.

W.C. v. Bowen, 629 F. Supp. 791, 793-794 (W.D. Wash. 1985). See W.C. v. Bowen, 807 F.2d 1592 (9th Cir. 1987) (holding that the review program was a "substantive" rule, promulgated without "notice and comment" and therefore invalid).

Does the court's decision in Nash v. Bowen, read in light of the Bellmon Review Program, convince you?

2. Suppose that the secretary of HHS concluded that ALJs were simply deciding too many cases in favor of the social security claimant. If the secretary had explicitly said that those were her reasons for introducing the programs discussed in Nash v. Bowen, would that case have come out differently? Should the secretary have the right to insist that the ALJs be "tougher" in evaluating the applicants' claims? Should she be able to insist that they treat skeptically, for example, an applicant's contention that he has back pain where medical tests are inconclusive? Could she not promulgate an agency rule that required medical corroboration for reports of such pain? Suppose that she gives reasons for wanting ALJs to be "tougher," for example, people are getting benefits in cases with inadequate proof, the relevant part of the federal budget is unduly strained, resources that should go to old people are going instead to people claiming to be disabled. Compare the treatment of the same problem in a district court case, where the judge expressed considerable skepticism about HHS's performance review program but took no action because HHS had changed its program by the time of the trial. Association of Administrative Law Judges v. Heckler, 594 F. Supp. 1132 (D.C. Cir. 1984).

3. What claims of bias may be brought against an administrative law judge? 5 U.S.C. §556(b) refers to "personal bias" as a ground for "disqualification" of an ALJ. And, of course, due process requires an impartial decisionmaker. But what exactly does this mean?

We may distinguish between (1) *actual* bias, conflict of interest, or impropriety, and (2) an *appearance* of these things. Several circuits have held that the, appearance of impropriety standard does not apply to ALJs. See, e.g., Bunnell v. Barnhart, 336 F.3d 1112 (9th Cir. 2003). These decisions observe that because ALJs work tor their agencies, there would be an appearance of impropriety in every case. Is the latter argument true of Article III judges as well? When a federal judge decides a case against the federal government, her employer, is there always an appearance of impropriety? Are the situations the same?

As to actual bias, even though ALJs are not covered by the Article III statutes that govern bias and recusal on the part of Article III federal judges (discussed infra), courts tend to apply the Article III bias rules by analogy, in order to give content to the due process requirement of an impartial decisionmaker and to §556(b)'s reference to "personal bias." In Liteky v. United States, 510 U.S. 540 (1994), the Court held that as to Article III judges, (1) whether or not the claim of bias has an "extrajudicial source" is an important factor bearing on the propriety of recusal and (2) if there is no extrajudicial source of bias — if the claimed bias raises solely from the adjudicator's previous engagement with the issues or the case, in an official capacity — then recusal is indicated only where there is a "deep-seated favoritism or antagonism that would make fair judgment impossible." *Liteky*, 510 U.S. at 555. Lower court cases have used *Liteky* as the framework for evaluating claims of bias on the part of ALJs. See, e.g., Bieber v. Department of the Army, 287 F.3d 1358 (Fed. Cir. 2002) (no "deep-seated favoritism" when ALJ made disparaging comments about a discharged employee, including asking why the employee didn't "just shut up").

Similar cases, reaching varying results, include Eldeco v. NLRB, 132 F.2d 1007 (6th Cir. 1997) (rejecting challenge of antiemployer bias by an administrative law judge in a labor dispute, even though the ALJ had ruled in favor of the union in 89 percent of cases over 20 years, and had consistently found employer witnesses not credible when their testimony conflicted with that of employees); Miles v. Chater, 84 F.3d 1397 (11th Cir. 1996), finding impermissible bias on the part of an ALJ who said, without any support, that a particular lawyer, hired by one side, "almost invariably concludes that the person being examined is totally disabled."

2. Combination of Functions and Bias at the Agency Head Level

Agency heads typically combine several functions. Although this potentially biases their judgment, there is, unlike conflicts within the agency staff, no easy way to divide functions structurally among commissioners.

a. Combination of Functions

First, consider the fact that most commissions both issue the complaint that initiates the hearing process and decide the resulting case on appeal. Former Trade Commissioner Philip Elman has argued that the combination of these two functions biases commissioners against defendants on appeal because a high dismissal rate on appeal would tend to cast doubt on the commissioners' judgment in having authorized the complaint, would rebuff the staff on which the commission depends, and would tend to encourage disregard of the statute the commission is pledged to enforce. P. Elman, Administrative Reform of the Federal Trade Commission, 59 Geo. L.J. 777, 810 (1971).

Withrow v. Larkin
421 U.S. 35 (1975)

Mr. Justice WHITE delivered the opinion of the Court.

The statutes of the State of Wisconsin forbid the practice of medicine without a license from an Examining Board composed of practicing physicians. The statutes also define and forbid various acts of professional misconduct. . . . To enforce these provisions, the Examining Board is empowered . . . to warn and reprimand, temporarily to suspend the license, and "to institute criminal action or action to revoke license when it finds probable cause therefor under criminal or revocation statute. . . ."

[Larkin practiced medicine in Wisconsin. The board investigated his abortion practices. It first held an "investigative hearing" at which Larkin was present but was not allowed to cross-examine witnesses. It then sent him notice that it would hold a "contested hearing" to determine whether he had practiced under another name, split fees, or allowed unlicensed doctors to perform abortions.

Larkin obtained a federal court injunction against this further "contested hearing" on the ground that it was unfair and unconstitutional to have the investigator make the final decision.

After the court enjoined the "contested hearing," the board held another "investigative hearing." It determined that there was probable cause to believe Larkin had engaged in unprofessional conduct, and it certified his case to the local district attorney for prosecution.

The board here appeals from the lower federal court's decision to enjoin the "contested hearing" — a decision that it based on the unfairness of taking from a doctor "his liberty or property absent the intervention of an independent, neutral and detached decision maker."]

III

. . . We disagree [with the district court]. . . .

Concededly, a "fair trial in a fair tribunal is a basic requirement of due process." In re Murchinson, 349 U.S. 133, 136 (1955). This applies to administrative agencies which adjudicate as well as to courts. Gibson v. Berryhill, 411 U.S. 564, 579 (1973). Not only is a biased decisionmaker constitutionally unacceptable but "our system of law has always endeavored to prevent even the probability of unfairness." In re Murchison, at 136; . . . In pursuit of this end, various situations have been identified in which experience teaches that the probability of actual bias on the part of the judge or decisionmaker is too high to be constitutionally tolerable. Among these cases are those in which the adjudicator has a pecuniary interest in the outcome and in which he has been the target of personal abuse or criticism from the party before him.

The contention that the combination of investigative and adjudicative functions necessarily creates an unconstitutional risk or bias in administrative adjudication has a much more difficult burden of persuasion to carry. It must overcome a presumption of honesty and integrity in those serving as adjudicators; and it must convince that, under a realistic appraisal of psychological tendencies and human weaknesses, conferring investigative and adjudicative powers on the same individuals poses such a risk of actual bias or prejudgment that the practice must be forbidden if the guarantee of due process is to be adequately implemented. . . .

That is not to say that there is nothing to the argument that those who have investigated should not then adjudicate. The issue is substantial, it is not new, and legislators and others concerned with the operations of administrative agencies have given much attention to whether and to what extent distinctive administrative functions should be performed by the same persons. No single answer has been reached. Indeed, the growth, variety, and complexity of the administrative processes have made any one solution highly unlikely. Within the Federal Government itself, Congress has addressed the issue in several different ways, providing for varying degrees of separation from complete separation of functions to virtually none at all. [§554(d) of the APA] provides that no employee engaged in investigating or prosecuting may also participate or advise in the adjudicating function but . . . also expressly exempts from this prohibition "the agency or a member or members of the body comprising the agency."

It is not surprising, therefore, to find that "[t]he case law, both federal and state, generally rejects the idea that the combination [of] judging [and] investigating functions is a denial of due process. . . ." 2 K. Davis Administrative Law Treatise §13.02, p.175 (1958). Similarly, our cases, although they reflect the substance of the problem, offer no support for the bald proposition applied in this case by the District Court that agency members who participate in an investigation are disqualified from adjudicating. The incredible variety of administrative mechanisms in this country will not yield to any single organizing principle. . . .

. . . No specific foundation has been presented for suspecting that the Board had been prejudiced by its investigation or would be disabled from hearing and deciding on the basis of the evidence to be presented at the contested hearing. The mere exposure to evidence presented in nonadversary investigative procedures is insufficient in itself to impugn the fairness of the Board members at a later adversary hearing. Without a showing to the contrary, state administrators "are assumed to be men of conscience and intellectual discipline, capable of judging a particular controversy fairly on the basis of its own circumstances." United States v. Morgan, 313 U.S. 409, 421 (1941).

We are of the view, therefore, that the District Court was in error when it entered the restraining order against the Board's contested hearing and when it granted the preliminary injunction based on the untenable view that it would be unconstitutional for the Board to suspend appellee's license "at its own contested hearing on charges evolving from its own investigation. . . ." The contested hearing should have been permitted to proceed.

IV

Nor do we think the situation substantially different because the Board, when it was prevented from going forward with the contested hearing, proceeded to make and issue formal findings of fact and conclusions of law asserting that there was probable cause to believe that appellee had engaged in various acts prohibited by the Wisconsin statutes. . .

Judges repeatedly issue arrest warrants on the basis that there is probable cause to believe that a crime has been committed and that the person named in the warrant has committed it. Judges also preside at preliminary hearings where they must decide whether the evidence is sufficient to hold a defendant for trial. Neither of these pretrial involvements have been thought to raise any constitutional barrier against the judge's presiding over the trial and, if the trial is without a jury, against making the necessary determination of guilt or innocence. Nor has it been thought that a judge is disqualified from presiding over injunction proceedings because he has initially assessed the facts in issuing or denying a temporary restraining order or a preliminary injunction. It is also very typical for the members of administrative agencies to receive the results of investigations, to approve the filing of charges or formal complaints instituting enforcement proceedings, and then to participate in the ensuing hearings. This mode of procedure does not violate . . . due process of law. We should also remember that it is not contrary to due process to allow judges and administrators who have had their initial decisions reversed on appeal to confront and decide the same questions a second time around. . . .

Here, the Board stayed within the accepted bounds of due process. Having investigated, it issued findings and conclusions asserting the commission of certain acts and ultimately concluding that there was probable cause to believe that appellee had violated the statutes. . . .

That the combination of investigative and adjudicative functions does not, without more, constitute a due process violation, does not, of course, preclude a court from determining from the special facts and circumstances present in the case before it that the risk of unfairness is intolerably high. . . . The judgment of the District Court is reversed and the case is remanded to that court for further proceedings consistent with this opinion.[8]

Note: Agency Bias after Withrow v. Larkin

A number of lower court cases have explored the circumstances under which unacceptable bias has been shown. Some of these cases involve the Constitution; some involve other legal prohibitions on partiality.

In Valley v. Rapides Parish School Board, 118 F.3d 1047 (5th Cir. 1997), a school board discharged a superintendent, after four members had publicly expressed hostility toward the superintendent, and the superintendent had exposed serious wrongdoing by each of them. The court found impermissible bias. In Alpha Epsilon Phi Tau Chapter Housing Assn. v. City of Berkeley, 114 F.3d 840 (9th Cir. 1997), the court refused to find a due process violation, even though the regulatory board's budget was, under the statutory arrangement, increased by the number of regulatees and the penalties imposed on them. The particular issue in the case was whether impermissible bias was shown by the fact that an increase in the board's jurisdiction would increase its budget. Carefully reviewing the record evidence, the court thought that no impermissible bias was shown. Compare Van Harken v. Chicago, 103 F.3d 1346 (7th Cir. 1997), upholding a city's use, for adjudicating disputes involving parking tickets, of part-time, at-will hearing officers. See also Eldeco v. NLRB, 132 F.2d 1007 (6th Cir. 1997) (rejecting challenge of antiemployer bias by an administrative law judge in a labor dispute, even though the ALJ had ruled in favor of the union 89 percent of cases over 20 years, and had consistently found employer witnesses not credible when their testimony conflicted with that of employees).

Note: Empirical Testing of Agency Bias

Judge Richard Posner has tried to investigate empirically the claims of Commissioner Elman and others to the effect that combining prosecution and judging in the commissioners tends to produce unfairness. Posner, The Behavior of Administrative Agencies, 1 J. Legal Stud. 305, 328 (1972). He compared the FTC, which has never delegated its authority over the issuance of complaints, with the NLRB, which has done so.

---

8. See also F. Davis, Case Commentary: Withrow v. Larkin and the "Separation of Functions" Concept in State Administrative Proceedings, 27 Admin. L. Rev. 407 (1975). For various circumstances in which courts have upheld combining adjudication with investigation, see Finer Food Sales Co. v. Block, 708 F.2d 774 (D.C. Cir. 1983) (judicial officer can perform "ministerial act" of issuing complaint in a related proceeding); Gibson v. FTC, 682 F.2d 554 (5th Cir. 1982) (combining investigating and prosecuting "clearly allowed"); Air Products and Chemicals, Inc. v. FERC, 650 F.2d 687 (5th Cir. 1981) (FERC staff presents complaint for issuance, then prosecutes); Grolier, Inc. v. FTC, 699 F.2d 983 (9th Cir. 1983) (ALJ was formerly an advisor to FTC Commissioner but had not "participated in some meaningful way in the events that led to the Agency's decision to prosecute"); see Kroger Co., 98 F.T.C. 939 (1981) (same).

Prior to 1942, all NLRB complaints required board approval. Between 1942 and 1947, regional directors had primary responsibility for their issuance. Since 1947, the board's general counsel — appointed by the president, not the NLRB — makes the decision to issue a complaint independently.

After seeking to measure possible differences in dismissal rates in a variety of ways, Posner found little evidence to support the hypothesis that the combination of functions within an agency leads to agency reluctance to dismiss complaints. His

TABLE 7-1
Dismissal Rate — Significant Dismissals Only

Agency	Period	Total contested cases	Significant dismissals	Significant total dismissals only	% Dismissed	% Dismissed in entirety
NLRB	1938	33	15	5	.45	.15
	1941	18	4	1	.22	.06
	1943	26	14	6	.54	.23
	1945	16	5	4	.31	.25
	1946	27	11	6	.41	.22
	1947	20	10	5	.50	.25
	Total	140	59	27	.42	.19
FTC	1938	60	12	7	.20	.12
	1941	61	17	17	.28	.28
	1943	32	8	7	.25	.22
	1945	32	8	7	.25	.22
	1945	43	11	9	.26	.21
	1946-47	70	18	15	.26	.21
	Total	266	66	55	.25	.21
NLRB	1949	38	26	11	.68	.29
	1950	52	15	9	.29	.17
	1951	57	26	9	.46	.16
	1956	57	30	9	.53	.16
	1960	105	48	22	.46	.21
	1965	103	21	12	.20	.12
	1969	70	29	16	.41	.23
	Total	482	195	88	.40	.18
FTC	1949-50	53	11	9	.21	.17
	1951-52	62	15	12	.24	.19
	1955-56	36	10	7	.28	.19
	1959-60	58	21	7	.36	.12
	1965	34	12	10	.35	.29
Total		243	69	45	.28	.19

findings were based on statistical comparisons such as those presented in Table 7-1 on page 722.

FTC v. CEMENT INSTITUTE, 333 U.S. 683 (1948). The Commission charged producers of Portland cement, including the Marquette Company, with violating §5 of the Federal Trade Commission Act by using a "multiple basing point" pricing system. After all testimony had been taken, Marquette moved that the commissioners disqualify themselves on the grounds of bias and prejudgment, in light of the fact that the commission had previously issued a series of reports condemning the use of multiple basing point pricing systems, particularly in the steel industry, and suggesting that cement was like steel. The commission denied the motion for disqualification; the court of appeals sustained this denial even after assuming that the commission had formed an opinion as to the illegality of the pricing system in the cement industry. The court (relying heavily on the "rule of necessity," which will be discussed below) pointed out that the FTC was "the only tribunal clothed with the power and charged with the responsibility of protecting the public against unfair methods of competition and price discrimination."

In affirming, the Supreme Court said: "In the first place, the fact that the Commission had entertained such views as the result of its prior ex parte investigations did not necessarily mean that the minds of its members were irrevocably closed on the subject of the respondents' basing point practices. Here, in contrast to the Commission's investigations, members of the cement industry were legally authorized participants in the hearings. They produced evidence — volumes of it. They were free to point out to the Commission by testimony, by cross-examination of witnesses, and by arguments, conditions of the trade practices under attack which they thought kept these practices within the range of legally permissible business activities.

"Moreover, Marquette's position, if sustained, would to a large extent defeat the congressional purposes which prompted passage of the Trade Commission Act. Had the entire membership of the Commission been disqualified in the proceedings against these respondents, this complaint could not have been acted upon by the Commission or by any other government agency. Congress has provided for no such contingency. It has not directed that the Commission disqualify itself under any circumstances, has not provided for substitute commissioners should any of its members disqualify, and has not authorized any other government agency to hold hearings, make findings, and issue cease and desist orders in proceedings against unfair trade practices. Yet if Marquette is right, the Commission, by making studies and filing reports in obedience to congressional command, completely immunized the practices investigated, even though they are 'unfair,' from any cease and desist order by the Commission or any other governmental agency.

"There is no warrant in the Act for reaching a conclusion which would thus frustrate its purposes."

AMERICAN CYANAMID CO. v. FTC, 363 F.2d 757 (6th Cir. 1966). As chief counsel of a Senate subcommittee, Paul Rand Dixon helped conduct a broad-ranging investigation into drug industry pricing of broad spectrum antibiotics, including tetracycline, and into the patent office's issuance of the tetracycline patent. Dixon was in charge of the selection of documents; he conducted examination of witnesses, and he worked on the subcommittee report on its investigation. The *Cyanamid* case, which began in 1958, included allegations of collusion in tetracycline pricing and possibly unlawful conduct by the firm in obtaining its patent. The hearing examiner found for the drug companies on all issues. When complaint counsel appealed, the companies moved that Dixon, then chairman of the FTC, disqualify himself. He refused. The commission found against the company. (Chairman Dixon's vote was not critical.) The Sixth Circuit, on appeal, held that Dixon's participation in the hearing "amounted . . . to a denial of due process which invalidated the order under review. . . . It is fundamental that both unfairness and the appearance of unfairness should be avoided. Wherever there may be reasonable suspicion of unfairness, it is best to disqualify." 363 F.2d at 767. The court remanded the case for a de novo consideration of the record without the participation of Chairman Dixon.[9]

CINDERELLA CAREER & FINISHING SCHOOLS v. FTC, 425 F.2d 583 (D.C. Cir. 1970). The FTC brought a complaint against the Cinderella School, alleging that Cinderella had made false claims that its graduates would be able to successfully compete in beauty contests and get better jobs. The hearing examiner dismissed all 13 of the commission's charges. On appeal to the commission, 6 charges were reinstated, and Cinderella was ordered to cease and desist its false advertising. Cinderella appealed. The court held that the FTC had erred in overturning the decision of its hearing examiner without adequate reason. It added:

"An additional ground which requires remand of these proceedings — and which would have required reversal even in the absence of the above-described procedural irregularities — is participation in the proceedings by the then Chairman of the Federal Trade Commission, Paul Rand Dixon.

"Notice that the hearing examiner's dismissal of all charges would be appealed was filed by the Commission staff on February 1, 1968 (Brief for Petitioners at 18). On March 12, 1968, this court's decision was handed down in a prior appeal arising from this same complaint, in which we upheld the Commission's issuance of press releases which called attention to the pending proceedings. Then, on March 15, 1968, while the appeal from the examiner's decision was pending before him, Chairman Dixon made a speech before the Government Relations Workshop of the National Newspaper Association in which he stated:

> What kind of vigor can a reputable newspaper exhibit? . . . How about ethics on the business side of running a paper? What standards are maintained on advertising acceptance? . . . What about carrying ads that offer college educations in five weeks, . . . or becoming an airline's hostess by attending a charm school? . . . Granted that newspapers are not in the advertising policing business, their advertising managers are savvy enough to smell deception when the odor is strong enough. And it is in the public interest, as well as their own, that their sensory organs become more discriminating. The Federal Trade Commission, even where it has jurisdiction, could not protect the public as quickly.

"We indicated in our earlier opinion in this case that 'there is in fact and law authority in the Commission, acting in the public interest, to alert the public to *suspected violations* of the law by *factual press releases* whenever the Commission shall have reason to believe that a respondent is engaged in activities made unlawful by the Act. . . .' This does

---

9. On remand, the FTC again found against the company. The FTC was finally vindicated in Charles Pfizer & Co. v. FTC, 401 F.2d 574 (6th Cir. 1968), *cert. denied*, 394 U.S. 920 (1969) — 11 years after the complaint was first filed.

not give individual Commissioners license to prejudge cases or to make speeches which give the appearance that the case has been prejudged. Conduct such as this may have the effect of entrenching a Commissioner in a position which he has publicly stated, making it difficult, if not impossible, for him to reach a different conclusion in the event he deems it necessary to do so after consideration of the record. . . .

"The test for disqualification has been succinctly stated as being whether 'a disinterested observer may conclude that [the agency] has in some measure adjudged the facts as well as the law of a particular case in advance of hearing it.' Gilligan, Will & Co. v. SEC, 267 F.2d 461, 469 (2d Cir. 1959). . . .

"[T]he United States Court of Appeals for the Sixth Circuit was required to reverse a decision of the FTC because Chairman Dixon refused to recuse himself from the case *even though he had served as Chief Counsel and Staff Director* to the Senate Subcommittee which made the initial investigation into the production and sale of the 'wonder drug' tetracycline. . . . It is appalling to witness such insensitivity to the requirements of due process; it is even more remarkable to find ourselves once again confronted with a situation in which Mr. Dixon, pouncing on the most convenient victim, has determined either to distort the holdings in the cited cases beyond all reasonable interpretation or to ignore them altogether. We are constrained to this harshness of language because of Mr. Dixon's flagrant disregard of prior decisions.

"The rationale for remanding the case despite the fact that former Chairman Dixon's vote was not necessary for a majority is well established: Litigants are entitled to an impartial tribunal whether it consists of one man or twenty and there is no way which we know of whereby the influence of one upon the others can be quantitatively measured. Berkshire Employees Assn. of Berkshire Knitting Mills v. NLRB, 121 F.2d 235, 239 (2d Cir. 1941). . . .

"Vacated and remanded."[10]

Association of National Advertisers v. FTC

627 F.2d 1151 (D.C. Cir. 1979), cert. denied, 447 U.S. 921 (1980)

TAMM, Circuit Judge. . . .

[In 1977, Michael Pertschuk, a new chairman of the FTC, gave a speech in which he strongly suggested that advertising aimed at children harms them. He argued that children do not understand commercials, will fail to distinguish them adequately from other information, and in particular fail to understand how harmful to them advertised sugared foods may be. He outlined a theory under which children's advertising might be legally "deceptive" because it suggests that sugared foods are desirable without explaining the health risks. He suggested that the commission might take action but concluded that it must be "rigorous and open-minded in our analysis of both law and fact." He subsequently repeated these views — often in strong anti-advertising language — in television interviews and in press releases.

In April 1978 the commission issued a notice of proposed rulemaking that considered, among other things, banning televised advertising of sugared products on children's programs. Various advertising associations moved that Pertschuk disqualify himself

---

10. On remand, the FTC went through another round of hearings and entered a cease-and-desist order, In re School Services, Inc., 79 F.T.C. 543 (1971). Reviewing courts tread a fine line in analyzing extramural statements by adjudicatory officials. Compare Kennecott Copper Corp. v. FTC, 467 F.2d 67, 79-80 (10th Cir. 1972), *cert. denied*, 416 U.S. 909 (1974), which carefully distinguished statements about the merits of a pending case from statements about the allegations of the complaint. — ED. NOTE.

and sought court review of his refusal to do so. The district court held that, under the standards of *Cinderella*, Pertschuk should be disqualified. The court of appeals first held that, although §18 of the Magnuson-Moss Act requires hearings with cross-examination for "specific" facts in FTC rulemaking proceedings, these are not "adjudicative" facts. Hence, what is at issue here is "rulemaking," not "adjudication."]

... Had Congress amended section 5 of the FTC Act to declare certain types of children's advertising unfair or deceptive, we would barely pause to consider a due process challenge. . . . Indeed, any suggestion that congressmen may not prejudge factual and policy issues is fanciful. A legislator must have the ability to exchange views with constituents and to suggest public policy that is dependent upon factual assumptions. Individual interests infringed upon by the legislative process are protected, as Justice Holmes wrote, "in the only way that they can be in a complex society, by [the individual's] power, immediate or remote, over those who make the rule." *Bi-Metallic Investment Co. v. State Board of Equalization*, 239 U.S. 441, 445 [(1915)]. . . .

Congress chose, however, to delegate its power to proscribe unfair or deceptive acts or practices to the Commission because "there were too many unfair practices for it to define." S. Rep. No. 597, 63d Cong., 2d Sess. 13 (1914). In determining the due process standards applicable in a section 18 proceeding, we are guided by its nature as rulemaking. When a proceeding is classified as rulemaking, due process ordinarily does not demand procedures more rigorous than those provided by Congress. See Vermont Yankee Nuclear Power Corp. v. NRDC, 435 U.S. 519, 524 & n.1, 542 & n.16 [(1978)]. . . . Congress is under no requirement to hold an evidentiary hearing prior to its adoption of legislation, and "Congress need not make that requirement when it delegates the task to an administrative agency." Bowles v. Willingham, 321 U.S. 503, 519 (1944) (citing *Bi-Metallic*). . . .

We never intended the *Cinderella* rule to apply to a rulemaking procedure such as the one under review. The *Cinderella* rule disqualifies a decisionmaker if "a disinterested observer may conclude that [he] has in some measure adjudged the facts as well as the law of a particular case in advance of hearing it." [L]egislative facts adduced in rulemaking partake of agency expertise, prediction, and risk assessment. In *Cinderella*, the court was able to cleave fact from law in deciding whether Chairman Dixon had prejudged particular factual issues. In the rulemaking context, however, the factual component of the policy decision is not easily assessed in terms of an empirically verifiable condition. Rulemaking involves the kind of issues "where a month of experience will be worth a year of hearings." Application of *Cinderella*'s strict law-fact dichotomy would necessarily limit the ability of administrators to discuss policy questions.

The legitimate functions of a policymaker, unlike an adjudicator, demand interchange and discussion about important issues. We must not impose judicial roles upon administrators when they perform functions very different from those of judges. . . . The *Cinderella* view of a neutral and detached adjudicator is simply an inapposite role model for an administrator who must translate broad statutory commands into concrete social policies. If an agency official is to be effective he must engage in debate and discussion about the policy matters before him. . . .

Accordingly, a Commissioner should be disqualified only when there has been a clear and convincing showing that the agency member has an unalterably closed mind on matters critical to the disposition of the proceeding. The "clear and convincing" test is necessary to rebut the presumption of administrative regularity. . . . The "unalterably closed mind" test is necessary to permit rulemakers to carry out their proper policy-based functions while disqualifying those unable to consider meaningfully a section 18 hearing. . . .

[Reversed.] . . .

LEVENTHAL, Circuit Judge, concurring. . . .

The ultimate test announced by Judge Tamm as to the merits is that disqualification from a rulemaking proceeding results "only when there has been a clear and convincing showing that [the agency member] has an unalterably closed mind on matters critical to the disposition of the [proceeding]." The test reflects a Supreme Court ruling as to administrative agencies.

It is not far removed from the test used in considering challenges to those considered for the duty as jurors quintessentially engaged in specific fact-finding. It is similar to a standard articulated as to recusal of judges.

The application of this test to agencies must take into account important differences in function and functioning between the agencies and court systems. In fulfilling the functions of applying or considering the validity of a statute, or a government program, the judge endeavors to put aside personal views as to the desirability of the law or program, and he is not disqualified because he personally deems the program laudable or objectionable. In the case of agency rulemaking, however, the decisionmaking officials are appointed precisely to implement statutory programs, and with the expectation that they have a personal disposition to enforce them vigilantly and effectively. They work with a combination rather than a separation of functions, in legislative modes, and take action on the basis of information coming from many sources, even though that provides a mind-set before a proceeding is begun, subject to reconsideration in the light of the proceeding. . . .

Consider, for example, the assertions of an agency head that he discerns abuses that may require corrective regulation. One can hypothesize beginning an adjudicatory proceeding with an open mind, indeed a blank mind, a tabula rasa devoid of any previous knowledge of the matter. In sharp contrast, one cannot even conceive of an agency conducting a rulemaking proceeding unless it had delved into the subject sufficiently to become concerned that there was an evil or abuse that required regulatory response. It would be the height of absurdity, even a kind of abuse of administrative process, for an agency to embroil interested parties in a rulemaking proceeding, without some initial concern that there was an abuse that needed remedying, a concern that would be set forth in the accompanying statement of the purpose of the proposed rule.

In its administrative setting an agency's effort is not limited to one type of activity. Investigation and policy-making are integral to the total function just as much as decisionmaking. It is appropriate and indeed mandatory for agency heads and staff to maintain contacts with industry and consumer groups, trade associations and press, congressmen of various persuasions, and to present views in interviews, speeches, meetings, conventions, and testimony. The agency gathers information and perceptions in a myriad of ways and must use it for a myriad of purposes. With capacity and willingness to reconsider there is no basis for disqualification. . . .

MACKINNON, J., (dissenting), [Judge Mackinnon wrote in part that Pertschuk's comments show bias even under the majority's test. He quoted some of those comments:]

[I]n his speech to the Action for Children's Television Research Conference at Boston on November 8, 1977, [Chairman Pertschuk] referred to the "*moral myopia* of children's television advertising." (Emphasis added.) He also stated that "advertisers *seize* on the child's trust and *exploit* it as a weakness for their gain." (Emphasis added.) . . . Later he stated: "Using *sophistication* [sic] techniques like fantasy and animation, they [TV advertisers] *manipulate* children's attitudes." (Emphasis added.) . . .

He then argued: "Why isn't [the] . . . principle [that those responsible for children's well being are entitled to the support of laws designed to aid discharge of that responsibility] applicable to television advertising directed at young children? Why shouldn't established legal precedents embodying this public policy be applied to protect children from this *form of exploitation*? In short, why isn't such advertising unfair within the meaning of the Federal Trade Commission Act and, hence, unlawful?" (Emphasis added.) Can any reasonable person contend that such remarks do not indicate that he has prejudged TV advertising and decided that it *exploits* children? . . .

In a 1978 Newsweek article the Chairman is quoted as follows: "Commercialization of children has crept upon us without scrutiny or action," says Michael Pertschuk, the agency's new chairman. "*It is a major, serious problem.* I am *committed* to taking action." (Emphasis added.) . . .

[Pertschuk also sent several letters to heads of other agencies and to a senator. In content they resembled the following:]

MEMORANDUM
TO: Coleman [*sic*] McCarthy
FROM: Mike Pertschuk

Coleman, I know you share my concern in raising public consciousness to the part we play as a society for permitting children to be made commercial objects. I thought you'd want to see this statement in which I've tried to establish underpinings [*sic*] for a *fundamental assault* on television advertising directed toward young children. (Emphasis added.)

November 17, 1977

Honorable Donald Kennedy
Food and Drug Administration
Parklawn Building
5600 Fishers Lane
Rockville, Maryland 20852

Dear Don:

Setting legal theory aside, the truth is that we've been drawn into this issue because of the *conviction*, which I know you share, that one of the *evils* flowing from the *unfairness* of children's advertising is the resulting distortion of children's perceptions of nutritional values. I see, at this point, our logical process as follows: children's advertising is inherently unfair. [The letter then sets out a plan for an attack on the advertising.]

Sincerely yours,

Michael Pertschuk

(Emphasis added.)

These letters indicate that by November 17, 1977, the Chairman had a "conviction" that there are "*evils* flowing from the *unfairness* of children's advertising . . . " and he had been vigorously marshalling sentiment throughout the nation for a "fundamental assault on television advertising directed toward young children." . . .

Thus, if the Notice of Rulemaking were truthful, so far as Chairman Pertschuk's views were concerned, it would have stated in substance: "The Commission has decided to make a fundamental assault upon Children's Advertising on TV because we are convinced that it is evil, unfair and allowed solely because of the moral myopia of the public and the industry. We solicit comments as to whether it should be prohibited entirely or to some lesser degree."

Questions

1. Do you believe that the bias standards to be applied to an FTC chairman or commissioner ought to be the same as those applied to a member of Congress or other legislator? Note the very fundamental issue at stake here — an issue with ramifications well beyond the narrow area of the "law of bias." A legislator has broad authority to act on the basis of her own views, prejudices, or on any other basis. But a legislator is *elected* — she is held accountable by the voters — and she must persuade a majority of each of two houses of Congress and the president to agree with her. The FTC chairman is not elected and need persuade only two other commissioners to go along. As Chapters 2 and 3 suggest, it used to be argued that this vast power would be held in check by one of the "canons" of the discipline — that is, expertise. That is to say, setting rates (or regulating business?) was a "scientific" matter; therefore experts will carry it out scientifically and will not wield unchecked power. This view is now discredited.

More recently, it has been argued that the regulator's power will be checked by the requirement that decisions are to be made after *public proceedings*, in which a wide range of interest groups participates. This effort — illustrated by hybrid rulemaking requirements — "judicializes" the agency's rulemaking (that is, its "legislative" activity). But if that effort fails to hold the regulator in check — if major legislative decisions are, in fact, made in advance and the record is manipulated — what then is to limit the legislative power of these few appointed officials who are operating under a broad statutory mandate? It is clear that their powers are not minor or interstitial, for very few laws of Congress in any given session are likely to have as broad an impact as the "children's TV" proposals. Is it then so surprising that in 1980 Congress took matters back into its own hands, limited the FTC's rulemaking powers, imposed a legislative veto, and curtailed the children's TV proceedings?

2. Can the opinions in these cases be reconciled?

3. Note the procedure by which the issue of bias is raised. The APA §556(b) states that "[a] presiding or participating employee may at any time disqualify himself. On the filing in good faith of a timely and sufficient affidavit of personal bias or other disqualification of a presiding or participating employee, the agency shall determine the matters as a part of the record and decision in the case."

Does this apply to members of the agency itself? What standard is to be used for determining what is "sufficient"?

Problems

1. Pillsbury, the nation's largest flour company, acquired two small regional flour companies. The FTC issued a complaint, charging a violation of Clayton Act §7. The hearing examiner dismissed the complaint a year later. FTC counsel appealed to the commission, arguing that an acquisition of this sort was per se

illegal. The commission reversed the dismissal but held that no per se doctrine applied under §7.

Soon afterwards, the antitrust subcommittees of both Houses of Congress held hearings and called the chairman of the FTC as a witness. Angry senators and representatives questioned the commission's ruling and expressed their opinions that Congress intended the per se doctrine to apply in just such cases. The questions were so specifically related to the *Pillsbury* case that the FTC chairman announced that he would have to disqualify himself from the pending case. Although two other commissioners were present at various stages of the hearings, they did not testify.

After two more years of hearings, the examiner found no "substantial lessening of competition" and again dismissed the complaint. On appeal, the commission again reversed, finding substantial evidence to support the charges, but again it refused to apply a per se doctrine to §7 acquisition cases. The commission vote was 3-1. The chairman did not participate. The two remaining commissioners who had been exposed to the congressional hearings voted in the majority.

On judicial review, what result?[11]

2. Besides conflicts arising from the combination of adjudication with prosecuting or policymaking, what about conflicts arising from a combination of adjudication with investigation? Is the law applicable to federal agencies more restrictive than in *Withrow* and other constitutional cases? If so, what is the source of this law?

Pangburn was the pilot of a commercial plane that crashed while landing at La Guardia Airport. As required by law, the Civil Aeronautics Board (CAB) began an investigation into the crash. Soon thereafter, independent proceedings were launched by the CAB to suspend Pangburn's pilot's license. Pangburn asked the CAB to refrain from issuing its accident investigation report until after the suspension proceedings were resolved; however, the CAB released its report, which fixed "pilot error" as the cause of the crash, two days before the hearing examiner in the suspension case decided against Pangburn. Pangburn's appeal to the CAB was denied.

On appeal, what result?[12]

b. Other Forms of Bias

Gibson v. Berryhill
411 U.S. 564 (1973)

Mr. Justice WHITE delivered the opinion of the Court.

[The Alabama Board of Optometry, composed solely of optometrists who were independent practitioners not employed by others, brought proceedings in state court against Lee Optical Co. and 13 optometrists employed by Lee, charging unlawful practice of optometry and also instituted disciplinary proceedings against the 13 optometrists for

---

11. See Pillsbury Co. v. FTC, 354 F.2d 952 (5th Cir. 1966). After remand, the FTC entered a final order of dismissal, explaining that the case was then 14 years old and it was impossible to fashion an effective remedy. Pillsbury Mills, Inc., 69 F.T.C. 482 (1966). See Recent Decisions, 52 Va. L. Rev. 946-954 (1966). Compare American Pub. Gas. Assn. v. FPC, 567 F.2d 1016 (D.C. Cir. 1977). See Peter Kiewit Sons' Co. v. Army Corps of Engineers, 714 F.2d 163 (D.C. Cir. 1983) (setting out standards for congressional interference).

12. See Pangburn v. CAB, 311 F.2d 349 (1st Cir. 1962).

unprofessional conduct. The optometrists brought a federal court action to enjoin the board proceeding on the ground that the board was biased and could not provide the plaintiffs with a fair and impartial hearing in conformity with due process of law.]

. . . [The district court noted] that the Board, which acts as both prosecutor and judge in disciplinary proceedings, had previously brought suit against the plaintiffs on virtually identical charges in the state courts and thus might have "preconceived opinions" with regard to the cases pending before them. The court also found as a fact the Lee Optical Co. did a large business in Alabama, and that if it were forced to suspend operations the individual members of the Board, along with other private practitioners of optometry, would fall heir to this business. It also appeared to regard the Board as a suspect adjudicative body in the cases then pending before it because only independently practicing optometrists could be members. . . .

[T]he District Court determined that the aim of the Board was to revoke the licenses of all optometrists in the State who were employed by business corporations such as Lee Optical, and that these optometrists accounted for nearly half of all the optometrists practicing in Alabama. Because the Board of Optometry was composed solely of optometrists in private practice for their own account, the District Court concluded that success in the Board's efforts would possibly redound to the personal benefit of members of the Board, sufficiently so that in the opinion of the District Court the Board was constitutionally disqualified from hearing the charges filed against the appellees.

[W]e affirm [on] the ground of possible personal interest.

It is sufficiently clear from our cases that those with substantial pecuniary interest in legal proceedings should not adjudicate these disputes. Tumey v. Ohio, 273 U.S. 510 (1927). And Ward v. Village of Monroeville, 409 U.S. 57 (1972), indicates that the financial stake need not be as direct or positive as it appeared to be in *Tumey*.[13] It has also come to be the prevailing view that "[m]ost of the law concerning disqualification because of interest applies with equal force to . . . administrative adjudicators." K. Davis, Administrative Law Text §12.04, p.250 (1972), and cases cited. . . . As remote as we are from the local realities underlying this case and it being very likely that the District Court has a firmer grasp of the facts and of their significance to the issues presented, we have no good reason on this record to overturn its conclusion and we affirm it.[14]

Note: Don't Overread *Gibson*

Despite the apparent absolutism of Gibson v. Berryhill, there have been some qualifications in the lower courts. Consider, for example, Stivers v. Pierce, 71 F.3d 732 (9th Cir. 1995), where the court held that an indirect pecuniary interest was simply one factor among many, and that the extent of the risk mattered a great deal. In the case itself,

---

13. Tumey v. Ohio struck down a criminal conviction before a township judge who received his personal salary from the fines he levied on persons convicted in his court. Ward v. Village of Monroeville extended this principle to trials before the mayor of a village that received half of its revenues from fines levied in the mayor's court. In Marshall v. Jerrico, 446 U.S. 238 (1980), the Supreme Court made clear that *Tumey* did not forbid a regional administrator to assess fines for violations of child labor laws simply because the fines collected (after administrative hearings) were used to finance some of the enforcement costs. The administrator is not a judge, and the possibility of bias is removed. — ED. NOTE.

14. The Supreme Court remanded the case to the district court to reconsider the meaning of the Alabama statute in the light of an intervening state court decision interpreting it.

the court held that the risk was too high, but it made clear the need for an individualized assessment. Alpha Epsilon Phi Tau Chapter Housing Assn. v. City of Berkeley, 114 F.3d 840 (9th Cir. 1997), referred to above, upheld a system in which a rent stabilization board seemed to have a financial stake in extending its jurisdiction. In the same vein, see Dool Security Savings Bank v. FDIC, 53 F.3d 1395 (4th Cir. 1995).

From these cases, alongside Gibson v. Berryhill, can you outline some sensible principles to govern this area?

Note: Judicial Disqualification

Consider the following standards for judicial disqualification, 28 U.S.C. §455 as amended Dec. 5, 1974, Pub. L. No. 93-512, §1, 88 Stat. 1609:

> (a) Any justice, judge, magistrate, or referee in bankruptcy of the United States shall disqualify himself in any proceeding in which his impartiality might reasonably be questioned.
> (b) He shall also disqualify himself in the following circumstances:
> (1) Where he has a personal bias or prejudice concerning a party, or personal knowledge of disputed evidentiary facts concerning the proceedings. . . .
> (4) [When he] has a financial interest in the subject matter in controversy . . . or any other interest that could be substantially affected by the outcome of the proceeding. . . .
> (e) No justice . . . shall accept from the parties to the proceeding a waiver of any ground for disqualification enumerated in subsection (b). Where the ground for disqualification arises only under subsection (a), waiver may be accepted provided it is preceded by a full disclosure on the record of the basis for disqualification.

District court proceedings are governed by 28 U.S.C. §144:

> Whenever a party to any proceeding in a district court makes and files a timely and sufficient affidavit that the judge before whom the matter is pending has a personal bias or prejudice either against him or in favor of any adverse party, such judge shall proceed no further therein, but another judge shall be assigned to hear such proceeding.

The American Bar Association Code of Judicial Conduct, adopted in 1972, provides in Canon 3-C that:

> A judge should disqualify himself in a proceeding in which his impartiality might reasonably be questioned. . . .

How do these standards differ? How do they compare with the standards for administrative disqualification?

If a Supreme Court Justice socializes with a government official appearing before the Court in a strictly official capacity, is recusal permissible? Mandatory? Justice Scalia declined to recuse himself from an official-capacity suit against Vice President Cheney. See Cheney v. District Court for the District of Columbia, 124 S. Ct. 1391 (2004). Although the two had been on a hunting trip while the case was pending, Justice Scalia emphasized that under traditional practice, Justices do not recuse based on personal friendship with an official sued in an official capacity; in such cases the suit is against the office, not the person.

c. The "Rule of Necessity"

At common law, the judge was disqualified from participating in any case in which he had a direct pecuniary interest. But the common law courts very early adopted, assimilated, and applied a rule with an opposite effect — "the rule of necessity." It was realistically recognized that the concepts of disqualification and necessity are inseparable, for the object of disqualification is to ensure that, where possible, a judge is disinterested in the matters at issue; its object is not to preclude access to a judicial forum or to bar judicial determination of the legal issues raised. Where the policy of disqualification conflicts with a litigant's rights to obtain a judicial remedy, it has been generally conceded that the former must yield to the latter, trusting the conscience of the court to achieve a just result.

The English courts have traced the history of the "rule of necessity" back to 1430 and the Yearbooks. Parliament in 1743 provided that tax-paying justices of the peace could sit in local government cases, avoiding any need for them to disqualify themselves as taxpayers:

> Thus grew the modern rule of "necessity," that judges should not decline to sit where no substitute was readily available. As Pollock later expressed it, "the settled rule of law is that, although a judge had better not, if it can be avoided, take part in a decision of a case in which he has any personal interest, yet he not only may, but must do so if the case can not be heard otherwise." And this remains the American practice.[15]

The "rule of necessity" has allowed judges to sit on matters involving judicial salaries. In fact, it led Chancellor Kent to decide a case in which his brother was a party. And it applied with equal force to administrative as well as to judicial tribunals.

Problem

The laws of a certain state provide that in any proceeding before the Department of Medical Practice to revoke a doctor's license to practice medicine, the matter shall be referred to a medical committee for hearing and recommendation. A revocation proceeding was initiated against Dr. Walter Evans on the ground that he had made false claims as to the therapeutic value of a treatment for cancer known as the "Koch" treatment.

For 30 years prior to this proceeding, the American Medical Association (AMA) had denounced the Koch treatment as valueless. The *Journal of the American Medical Association* had published over 20 articles condemning it, and the AMA had joined in efforts to revoke the licenses of all doctors who used it. All five of the doctors who were regular members of the medical committee were members and officers of the AMA. One of the five was a cancer specialist who had published several articles saying that the only known methods of fighting most forms of cancer are radium, cobalt treatments, X-rays, and surgery.

Dr. Evans's counsel filed a request with the medical committee and the department that the committee be disqualified for bias and that a new ad hoc committee be named of

---

15. J. Frank, Disqualification of Judges, 56 Yale L.J. 605, 611 (1947). See Brinley v. Hassig, 83 F.2d 351, 357 (10th Cir. 1936).

doctors who were not members of the AMA and who had not prejudged the issues. This request was denied, the hearing was held, and the committee's recommendation that Evans's license be revoked was adopted by the director on behalf of the department.

Should a court on judicial review sustain Dr. Evans's contention that he is entitled to a new hearing because of the bias of the medical committee?

3. Who Decides?

As in most large federal agencies, one of the major problems facing FTC commissioners is finding the time to decide the numerous cases that reach them while also deciding major issues of policy and administering a large agency. Heads of major agencies rely heavily on staff assistance in deciding a case. A commissioner is most unlikely to read the record or even the briefs personally. Staff members probably digest the briefs for him and prepare a memorandum noting the main points of the arguments. Moreover, after reaching a decision, the commissioner probably does not even write his own opinion. That function is given to a special opinion writing section in the general counsel's office or to the commissioner's assistant.

The problem of how a busy administrative official finds time to decide a highly complex adjudication arose in the following case (the first of four Supreme Court opinions in a lengthy and intricate litigation).

Morgan v. United States (Morgan I)
298 U.S. 468 (1936)

Mr, Chief Justice HUGHES delivered the opinion of the Court.

These are fifty suits, consolidated for the purpose of trial, to restrain the enforcement of an order of the Secretary of Agriculture, fixing the maximum rates to be charged by market agencies for buying and selling livestock at the Kansas City Stock Yards. . . .

[The statute that authorizes the secretary of agriculture to fix the rates provides in part: "Whenever after full hearing . . . the Secretary is of the opinion that any rate . . . of a stockyard owner . . . is or will be unjust, unreasonable or discriminatory, the Secretary — (a) May determine and prescribe what will be the just and reasonable rate. . . ."

Plaintiffs alleged in part] [t]hat the Secretary, without warrant of law delegated to Acting Secretaries the determination of issues with respect to the reasonableness of the rates involved. . . . That the Secretary at the time he signed the order in question had not personally heard or read any of the evidence presented at any hearing in connection with the proceeding and had not heard or considered oral arguments relating thereto or briefs submitted on behalf of the plaintiffs, but that the sole information of the Secretary with respect to the proceeding was derived from consultation with employees in the Department of Agriculture out of the presence of the plaintiffs or any of their representatives.

[The district court in which the action was brought struck out these allegations on the ground that they could not state a claim on which relief could be granted. Plaintiffs appealed the dismissal of the claim.]

Certain facts appear of record. The testimony was taken before an examiner. . . . Oral argument upon the evidence was had before the Acting Secretary of Agriculture.

Subsequently, a brief was filed on plaintiff's behalf. Thereafter, reciting "careful consideration of the entire record in this proceeding," findings of fact and conclusions, and an order prescribing rates, were signed by the Secretary of Agriculture. . . .

Second — The outstanding allegation, which the District Court struck out, is that the Secretary made the rate order without having heard or read any of the evidence, and without having heard the oral arguments or having read or considered the briefs which the plaintiff's submitted. That the only information which the Secretary had as to the proceeding was what he derived from consultation with employees of the Department.

[T]he fundamental question [should not] be confused with one of mere delegation of authority. The Government urges that the Acting Secretary who heard the oral argument was in fact the Assistant Secretary of Agriculture. . . . If the Secretary had assigned to the Assistant Secretary the duty of holding the hearing, and the Assistant Secretary accordingly had received the evidence taken by the examiner, had heard argument thereon and had then found the essential facts and made the order upon his findings, we should have had simply the question of delegation. But while the Assistant Secretary heard argument he did not make the decision. The Secretary who, according to the allegation, had neither heard nor read evidence or argument, undertook to make the findings and fix the rates. The Assistant Secretary, who had heard, assumed no responsibility for the findings or order, and the Secretary, who had not heard, did assume that responsibility.[16]

Third — What is the essential quality of the proceeding under review, and what is the nature of the hearing which the statute prescribes?

. . . That duty is widely different from ordinary executive action. It is a duty which carries with it fundamental procedural requirements. There must be a full hearing. There must be evidence adequate to support pertinent and necessary findings of fact. . . .

A proceeding of this sort requiring the taking and weighing of evidences, determinations of fact based upon the consideration of the evidence, and the making of an order supported by such findings, has a quality resembling that of a judicial proceeding. Hence it is frequently described as a proceeding of a quasi-judicial character. The requirement of a "full hearing" has obvious reference to the tradition of judicial proceedings in which evidence is received and weighed by the trier of the facts. The "hearing" is designed to afford the safeguard that the one who decides shall be bound in good conscience to consider the evidence, to be guided by that alone, and to reach his conclusion uninfluenced by extraneous considerations which in other fields might have play in determining purely executive action. The "hearing" is the hearing of evidence and argument. If the one who determines the facts which underlie the order has not considered evidence or argument, it is manifest that the hearing has not been given.

There is thus no basis for the contention that the authority conferred by §310 of the Packers and Stockyards Act is given to the Department of Agriculture, as a department in the administrative sense, so that one official may examine evidence, and another official who has not considered the evidence may make the findings and order. In such a view, it would be possible, for example for one official to hear the evidence and argument and arrive at certain conclusions of fact, and another official who had not heard or considered either evidence or argument to overrule those conclusions and for reasons of policy to announce entirely different ones. It is no answer to say that the question for the court is

16. The power of an official to "subdelegate" his powers to another official when not explicitly given the right to do so by the legislature is analyzed in 1 Davis, Administrative Law §9.01 et seq. (1958); see also Note, Subdelegation by Federal Administrative Agencies, 12 Stan. L. Rev. 808 (1960) — ED. NOTE.

whether the evidence supports the findings and the findings support the order. For the weight ascribed by the law to the findings — their collusiveness when made within the sphere of the authority conferred — rests upon the assumption that the officer who makes the findings has addressed himself to the evidence and upon that evidence has conscientiously reached the conclusions which he deems it to justify. That duty cannot be performed by one who has not considered evidence or argument. It is not an impersonal obligation. It is a duty akin to that of a judge. The one who decides must hear.

This necessary rule does not preclude practicable administrative procedure in obtaining the aid of assistants in the department. Assistants may prosecute inquiries. Evidence may be taken by an examiner. Evidence thus taken may be sifted and analyzed by competent subordinates. Argument may be oral or written. The requirements are not technical. But there must be a hearing in a substantial sense. And to give the substance of a hearing, which is for the purpose of making determinations upon evidence, the officer who makes the determinations must consider and appraise the evidence which justifies them. That duty undoubtedly may be an onerous one, but the performance of it in a substantial manner is inseparable from the exercise of the important authority conferred. . . .

Our conclusion is that the District Court erred in striking out the allegations of Paragraph IV of the bill of complaint with respect to the Secretary's action. The defendants should be required to answer these allegations and the question whether plaintiffs had a proper hearing should be determined.

The decree is reversed and the cause is remanded for further proceedings in conformity with this opinion.

Reversed.

Note: The Ash Council Report

The Ash Council[17] made several specific recommendations designed to free commissioners' time for policymaking:

> If administrative agencies, and particularly regulatory commissions, are to discharge their legislative implementation responsibilities, they should rely less on the case-by-case approach to policy formulation and move increasingly in the direction of rulemaking, especially informal rulemaking, and other expeditious procedures. The disadvantages of the prevailing individual case approach are apparent.
>
> First, commissioners tend to view themselves as judges atop an administrative-judicial hierarchy, with principal responsibility to hear appeals from initial or recommended decisions of hearing examiners acting as finders of fact. They do not, however, accord the usual degree of appellate deference to findings and determinations of the trier of fact and indeed cannot so long as case-by-case review is the predominant vehicle for establishing agency policy.
>
> Second, this preoccupation with quasi-judicial activities has diverted attention and resources away from the more important responsibility of comprehensive and anticipatory policymaking. To the extent that policy is formulated in an adversary context, commissions must fit their policy declarations within the limiting confines of an adversary record. This approach is a barrier to anticipating problems that should be addressed informally without need for, and long before, the culmination of protracted proceedings.

17. The President's Advisory Council on Executive Organization, A New Regulatory Framework; Report on Selected Independent Regulatory Agencies 49-50 (1971).

Third, overjudicialization of the agency review process has a generally debilitating effect on the administrative mechanism. Proceedings before hearing examiners have become more complex as the scope of issues which must be considered has broadened. Rarely is it possible for a hearing examiner to try more than one or two cases simultaneously. Most agencies have three or four examiners for each commissioner and it is becoming commonplace for most decisions to be the subject of administrative appeal.

Consequently, a commission may have before it for resolution at any one time a dozen or more complex proceedings, each the subject of protracted hearings. Obviously, it cannot be expected that every commissioner, indeed that any commissioner, will be able to undertake an independent and full review of the more extensive records. Nor should they in view of the delays that would result. To meet this dilemma, most commissions have established special opinion-writing sections comprised of middle-level staff who review the record and write a draft of the "commission opinion." To a great extent, they define the limits of the commission's sensitivity and its ability to exercise judgment in many cases. Former CAB Member Louis Hector, commenting on this procedure, has noted that: "In the CAB and other regulatory agencies, the members of the agency merely vote on the outcome of a case and the opinion justifying the outcome is written by a professional staff. Members of these opinion-writing staffs explain that they consciously avoid statements of general principle as much as possible in the opinions they write, because they must be able to write an opinion justifying an opposite conclusion the next day, and hence must not be hampered by prior statements of general principles."

As a result, the review function shifts from the commission to a staff group. This in turn relegates the hearing examiner to a subordinate role, which can have detrimental consequences. Hearing examiners may become demoralized and view their function as one of limited utility — an attitude that can encourage appeals, including a multiplicity of interlocutory appeals, which serve to further prevent a commission from directing attention to more important, comprehensive policysetting.

If these serious deficiencies are to be overcome, it will be necessary to place a greater share of the responsibility for individual case determinations on the hearing examiners, leaving the administrator relatively free to concentrate on more appropriate means of formulating broad policy.

We propose that instead of engaging in the systematic review of initial decisions, administrators review, on their own motion, selected cases primarily for consistency with agency policy.

How can the secretary of agriculture or the five FTC commissioners themselves decide the many thousands of matters that come before them? How could they possibly have enough time to do so, particularly in light of the *Morgan I* principle: "He who decides must hear"? The only possible answers to this question are (1) the agency head can formally delegate decisionmaking responsibility to a different official, or (2) the agency head can informally delegate the decision to others who will informally "brief" the agency head on the issues, leaving the agency head to "make" the decision. Whether or not the agency head can take the first course of action depends on the wording of the statute that confers decisionmaking authority. Sometimes, Congress expressly authorizes such subdelegation; sometimes it does not. Of course, when the agency head does delegate, he will lose control of the making of agency policy insofar as that policy is made through adjudication. This fact may help explain why the top management at HHS, in the early 1980s, who wished to adopt a more stringent benefits policy, may have felt frustrated by their inability to force the agency to embody that policy in concrete decisions in individual cases. Whether or not the agency head can take the second course of action depends on how much of a *Morgan I* risk the agency is willing to run.

The agency head's job is primarily one of reviewing decisions made by subordinate officials. Where formal adjudications are involved, those decisions are initially made by ALJs. Section 556 of the APA says that, in formal adjudication or rulemaking, the presiding officer may be "(1) the agency," or "(2) one or more members of the body which comprises the agency," or "(3) one or more administrative law judges." Almost always the agency exercises this choice in favor of having an ALJ preside. Section 557 of the APA says that, when the agency itself does not preside, the presiding employee (that is, the ALJ) will make an initial decision. (The ALJ can also simply take evidence and make a recommended decision, relaying that decision to the agency; or the agency can have the record sent to it and make the decision itself.) When the ALJ makes an initial decision, that decision becomes the agency's decision, unless there is further agency review. Almost every agency provides for some kind of further review, either through an appeal to an appeals board or to the head of the agency, or both. Professor Cass has analyzed the different agency appeals processes. He has found that about 5 percent of all cases are reversed, and that this figure does not differ significantly among the type of appeal provided, that is, whether the appeal goes to an appeals board or to the agency head or to the delegate of an agency head. See Cass, Allocation of Authority Within Bureaucracies: Empirical Evidence and Normative Analysis, 66 Boston U. L. Rev. 1 (1986). By way of comparison, the percentage of district court cases that are reversed in courts of appeals was about 13 percent in 1990. It may be interesting to speculate about the reasons for such different reversal rates.

Pages 739-740 present a chart from Professor Cass's article, which will give you an idea of the number of formal adjudications that agencies handle, their use of ALJs, and the number of appeals.

Note: Probing the Mental Processes of the Decisionmaker

Morgan I is noteworthy not only because of its resounding statement that "the one who decides must hear," but because it seemed to allow the lower courts carte blanche in probing the mental processes of the decisionmaker when evaluating challenged administrative action. Notice that the second holding does not inevitably follow the first: It is possible that a plaintiff who claims that an administrator did not adequately study the evidence may be held to have a perfectly good cause of action, while at the same time, the reviewing court will not allow the plaintiff to gather the evidence he or she needs to prove a claim by interrogating the decisionmaker. There are good reasons why such a doctrine might be adopted: Just as with the doctrine of immunity from personal liability for government officials for acts done in good faith in the course of official duties, the "no probing of the decision process" rule would allow officials to perform their duties without fear of harassment from lawsuits and unseemly probing of their mental operations, thus encouraging efficient administration of the laws. Such a doctrine would then leave the primary checks on undesirable decision processes to the political branches of the government.

In any case, the sweeping *Morgan I* holding was short-lived. Subsequent opinions in the *Morgan I* litigation itself limited the scope of the initial holding.

After *Morgan I*, the Supreme Court remanded the case to the district court, which then took evidence on the question of whether the secretary in fact had "decided" the controversy — issuing the rate order — without having heard or read the evidence or considered the arguments submitted. The secretary and his associates answered interrogatories and testified that: (1) the examiner compiled a record consisting of about 10,000 transcript pages of oral testimony and 1000 pages of statistics exhibits;

Adjudication and Review Data: By Agency

	No. of ALJs	No. of cases	No. of cases completed[1]	No. of cases reviewed	% of cases reviewed	Total time (days)	ALJ time (days)	Review time (days)	No. of cases reversed	% of cases reversed	ALJ caseload
U.S. Dept. of Agriculture	5	705	102	55	7.8%	677.5	435.6	180.7	5	9.1%	47
Bureau of Alcohol, Tobacco & Firearms	1	286	80	47	16.4%	802.1	143.0	145.7	4	8.5%	95.3
Civil Aeronautics Board	11	258	222	203	78.7%	1008.5	262.7	271.8	8	3.9%	7.8
Consumer Products Safety Commission	1	30	9	9	30.0%	1128.2	271.7	401.4	1	11%	10
Drug Enforcement Administration	1	124	44	45	36.2%	309.4	244.0	44.5	2	4.4%	41.3
Environmental Protection Agency	7	381	69	8	2.1%	541.1	221.7	76.1	0	0%	18.1
Federal Communications Commission (1976 Only)	13	132	66	38	28.8%	1384.9	479.4	480.2	6	15.8%	10.2
Federal Energy Regulatory Comm.	22	567	259	248	43.7%	963.7	453.3	306.7	13	5.2%	8.6
Federal Maritime Commission	7	265	152	227	85.7%	539.1	260.2	140.6	13	5.7%	12.6
Federal Trade Commission	12	121	47	56	46.3%	1741.0	720.3	355.7	5	8.9%	3.4
Food and Drug Administration	1	5	4	4	80.0%	1950.4	166.5	611.8	0	0%	11.7
Dept. of Housing & Urban Development	1	638	76	123	19.3%	313.3	161.6	52.7	0	0%	212.7

	No. of ALJs	No. of cases	No. of cases completed[1]	No. of cases reviewed	% of cases reviewed	Total time (days)	ALJ time (days)	Review time (days)	No. of cases reversed	% of cases reversed	ALJ case load
Interstate Commerce Commission	55	4594	1522	847	18.4%	736.0	179.7	297.5	256	30.2%	27.8
Dept. of Labor	66	6172	2925	979	15.9%	764.3	200.4	262.4	38	3.9%	31.2
Maritime Administration	3	36	17	13	36.1%	1266.2	656.8	326.5	5	38.5%	4
NLRB	115	3820	3820	2686	70.3%	386.8	103.8	123.5	125	4.7%	11.1
National Transportation Board	6	1991	848	352	17.7%	389.2	185.4	152.6	23	6.5%	110.6
Nuclear Regulatory Commission	1	30	28	28	93.3%	1482.2	375.7	526.7	0	0%	10
Occupational Safety & Health Rev. Comm. (1977-1978)	48	7642	6762	423	5.5%	*	222.5	422	*	*	79.6
Securities & Exchange Commission	7	275	87	49	17.8%	1352.5	484	409.1	5	10.2%	13.1
Social Security	698	*	631.626	166.312	26.3%	249.2	99.8	40.8	7276	4.4%	301.6
U.S. Coast Guard	16	1937	1672	114	5.9%	391.8	60.2	287.1	21	18.4%	40.4
U.S. International Trade Comm.	2	22	22	22	100.0%	447.8	203.5	76.2	1	4.5%	3.7
U.S. Postal Service	2	566	195	125	22.1%	453.8	209.9	102.3	7	5.6%	94.3
TOTALS			650.654	173.013	26.1%	262.2	101.7	47.2	7814	4.5%	200.5
W/O S.S.A.			19.028	6.701	21.9%	625.4	165.2	250.6	538	8.0%	76.6

[1]Not withdrawn or dismissed.

*Information not available.

Source: Ronald Cass, Allocation of Authority Within Bureaucracies: Empirical Evidence and Normative Analysis, 66 B.U. L. Rev. 1 (1986). Boston University bears no responsibility for any errors that may have occurred in reproduction.

(2) the acting secretary (Mr. Tugwell) held an oral hearing where the argument was general and sketchy; (3) the government did not prepare a brief for, or formulate issues prior to, the oral hearing; (4) the appellants (the market agencies) submitted roughly the same briefs that they had submitted to the examiner; the examiner had prepared no report; (5) after the oral hearing, the bureau staff prepared 180 complex proposed findings, which it did not show to the appellants (the market agencies), but which it did send to the secretary (no longer Mr. Tugwell); and (6) the secretary did not hear the oral argument before Mr. Tugwell, but he dipped into the record that was placed on his desk, he read the briefs of the market agencies, he read the transcript of the oral argument, and he had several conferences with the bureau staff and department lawyers to discuss the proposed findings. With a few changes, he adopted the proposed findings of the bureau. He stated that he had considered the evidence and the order represented his own independent conclusion based on bureau findings; it represented his "own independent reaction to the findings of the men in the Bureau of Animal Industry." The district court sustained the secretary's rate order, holding that the hearing was adequate.

On appeal, in Morgan v. United States, 304 U.S. 1 (1938) (*Morgan II*), the Supreme Court again reversed the district court. Chief Justice Hughes first limited the broad latitude that *Morgan I* apparently gave the lower courts to probe the mind of the administrator. He summarized the testimony of the secretary as set out above and stated:

> In the light of this testimony there is no occasion to discuss the extent to which the Secretary examined the evidence and we agree with the Government's contention that it was not the function of the court to probe the mental processes of the Secretary in reaching his conclusions if he gave the hearing which the law required. The Secretary read the summary presented by appellants' briefs and he conferred with subordinates who had sifted and analyzed the evidence. We assume that the Secretary sufficiently understood its purport. . . .

The Court went on to hold, however, that the hearing was nonetheless inadequate, for the market agencies had not had a "reasonable opportunity" to be "fairly advised of what the Government proposed and to be heard upon" the government's proposals before the government issues its "final command." The Chief Justice wrote that the "right to a hearing embraces not only the right to present evidence but also a reasonable opportunity to know the claims of the opposing party and to meet them." Since there had been no specific complaint when the proceeding began, since there was no tentative report of the hearing examiner, and since the market agencies were not shown the bureau's proposed findings, they did not know precisely what claims they had to meet. "The requirements of fairness are not exhausted in the taking or consideration of evidence but extend to the concluding parts of the procedure as well. . . . " 304 U.S. 1, 20 (1938).

On remand *of Morgan II*, the district court had to decide what to do with funds that the plaintiff Morgan had paid into court — money equal to the difference between the preexisting rates and the new, lower rates in the order that the agencies were protesting. The district court decided that, since the rate order was invalid under *Morgan II*, the funds should be returned to Morgan. The Supreme Court reversed the district court (for the third time). It held in United States v. Morgan, 307 U.S. 183 (1939) (*Morgan III*), that the district court should have impounded the funds, holding them until a new rate was completed. The Court noted that the secretary could order reparations for past years. When the secretary had made his decision on these matters, the district court could dispose of the funds in an appropriate way.

After remand *of Morgan II*, the secretary and the market agencies agreed on a higher rate schedule that would take effect on September 1, 1937. The secretary thereafter made a new decision that the period 1933-1937 (the period for which the funds were impounded) would be governed by precisely the same rate schedule that he had originally promulgated (and which the Supreme Court had set aside in *Morgan II*). The district court refused to apply the secretary's decision to the impounded funds because the decision was based on the test years of 1920, 1930, and 1931, yet costs had gone up between 1933 and 1937. On appeal, in United States v. Morgan, 313 U.S. 409 (1941) (*Morgan IV*), the Supreme Court reversed the district court for the fourth time. Justice Frankfurter wrote that the secretary, in his new order, had heard and considered the relevant arguments. Market conditions were unstable; the proper rate was difficult to determine. "It is not for us to try to penetrate the precise course of the Secretary's reasoning. Our duty is at an end when we find, as we do find, that the Secretary was responsibly conscious of conditions at the market during the years following 1933, that he duly weighed them, and nevertheless concluded that rates similar to those in the 1933 order were proper." Id. at 420.

Justice Frankfurter then turned to the question of probing the mind of the administrator. He wrote:

> Over the Government's objections the district court authorized the market agencies to take the deposition of the Secretary. [Note that this took place after remand *of Morgan III* and concerned the secretary's decision about the impounded money. This is *not* the decision discussed in *Morgan I* and *Morgan II*.] The Secretary thereupon appeared in person at the trial. He was questioned at length regarding the process by which he reached the conclusions of his order, including the manner and extent of his study of the record and his consultation with subordinates. His testimony shows that he dealt with the enormous record in a manner not unlike the practice of judges in similar situations, and that he held various conferences with the examiner who heard the evidence. Much was made of his disregard of a memorandum from one of his officials who, on reading the proposed order, urged considerations favorable to the market agencies. But the [gist] of the business is that the Secretary should never have been subjected to this examination. The proceeding before the Secretary "has adequately [resembled] that of a judicial proceeding." Morgan v. United States, 289 U.S. 468, 480. Such an examination of a judge would be destructive of judicial responsibility. We have explicitly held in this very litigation that "it was not the function of the court to probe the mental processes of the Secretary." 304 U.S. 1, 18. Just as a judge cannot be subjected to such a scrutiny, compare Fayerweather v. Rilch, 95 U.S. 276, 306, 307, so the integrity of the administrative process must be equally respected. . . . It will bear repeating that although the administrative process has had a different development and pursues somewhat different ways from those of courts, they are to be deemed collaborative instrumentalities of justice and the appropriate independence of each should be respected by the other. . . .

Id. at 421-422.

Consider the following case.

National Nutritional Foods Association v. FDA

491 F.2d 1141 (2d Cir. 1974)

[The FDA issued a notice of proposed revision of regulations on food labeling. The statute required their adoption after rulemaking hearings "on the record." The end-product of the subsequent 12-year cycle of rulemaking proceedings was a record consisting of over 32,000 pages of testimony and thousands of pages of exhibits. Based on this material, the FDA drew up and published a set of "tentative final orders." By the time the period for public comment ended, formal exceptions to the proposed rules spread over 1000 pages; there were over 20,000 additional letters. Meanwhile, the commissioner of the FDA, who had overseen this entire proceeding, resigned, and Alexander Schmidt was appointed new chief of the FDA four months later. Within 12 days, he signed 14 final regulations, 13 proposed regulations, and 6 miscellaneous notices. On the thirteenth day after he took office, he signed the rules in question. Plaintiffs petitioned for review of these regulations, contending that it was impossible for Commissioner Schmidt to have reviewed the objections prior to promulgating the rules. The instant opinion derives from the petitioner's motion to depose Commissioner Schmidt and to instigate other discovery devices.]

FRIENDLY, Circuit Judge: . . .

Conceding that it is not the function of this court "to probe the mental processes" of the Commissioner (*Morgan II*), petitioners insist they are entitled to probe whether he exercised his own mental processes at all. More particularly, they claim they are entitled to do this in a situation where two unusual and indisputable facts, namely, the short time between Commissioner Schmidt's assumption of office and his signing of the regulations here at issue, and the large number of other rules promulgated by him in the interval, create more than ordinary basis for doubt as to the extent of his personal reading and consideration.

[Judge Friendly discussed the *Morgan* cases, with particular emphasis on Justice Frankfurter's statements in *Morgan IV*, quoted earlier.]

Subsequent Supreme Court decisions have not detracted from the force of *Morgan IV*. [Petitioners rely on] a portion of Mr. Justice Marshall's opinion in Citizens to Preserve Overton Park, Inc. v. Volpe, [401 U.S. 402 (1971)], stating that on remand the district court "may require the administrative officials who participated in the decision to give testimony explaining their action." But *Overton Park* was a case where the Secretary of Transportation had made no formal findings; the taking of testimony, suggested as being within the range of proper action for the district court on remand, was for the purpose of ascertaining why the highway construction had been authorized, a function performed by the extensive preambles to the regulations here at issue. The Court reaffirmed *Morgan IV*, saying that where findings accompany the decision, "there must be a strong showing of bad faith or improper behavior" before testimony with regard to reasons can be taken. Id. Indeed, the opinion went on to say that testimony might not be required even in *Overton Park* if the Secretary could prepare post hoc findings sufficient to withstand scrutiny. Nothing in the opinion suggests that the Court intended to allow inquiry into the relative participation of the Secretary and his subordinates. Similarly, strong preliminary showings of bad faith have been required in the court of appeals cases cited by petitioners before the taking of testimony has been permitted with regard to internal agency deliberations. See, e.g., Singer Sewing Machine Co. v. NLRB, 329 F.2d 200, 206-208 (4th Cir. 1964).

The facts of this case do not constitute nearly the showing of bad faith necessary to justify further inquiry; indeed they vividly illustrate the necessity of adhering to the presumption of regularity with respect to the participation of the officer authorized to sign administrative orders, especially in the context of the promulgation of legislative rules as distinguished from adjudication. . . . It would suffice under the circumstances that Commissioner Schmidt considered [staff-written] summaries of the objections and of the answers contained in the elaborate preambles and conferred with his staff about them. There is no reason why he could not have done this even in the limited time available. . . .

The motion to take the testimony of the Commissioner and to have other discovery . . . is denied.[18]

Notes

1. In American Fedn. of Govt. Employees v. Reagan, 870 F.2d 723 (D.C. Cir. 1989), the D.C. Circuit considered an order by the president, which simply stated that certain parts of the U.S. marshals service were "excluded" from the list of agencies whose employees were permitted to bargain collectively with the federal government. The relevant statute permitted the president to exclude an agency from "collective bargaining"; "if the president determines" that the agency is primarily involved in "intelligence" or "national security" work, collective bargaining would not be "consistent with national security requirements and considerations." The district court had held that the president had to give reasons for his exclusion of the marshals so that the court could determine whether the act's conditions were met.

The D.C. Circuit reversed. It found that the president had complied with the act on the basis of the "presumption of regularity" (to which Judge Friendly referred in *National Nutritional Foods*). The court referred to the case of Martin v. Mott, 25 U.S. (12 Wheat.) 19 (1827), where a militiaman objected to President Madison's 1812 order calling out the state militia — an order that the president could issue provided that the United States was "invaded or . . . in imminent danger of invasion." The Supreme Court wrote, "It is the opinion of the Court that this objection cannot be maintained. When the President exercises an authority confided to him by law, the presumption is that it is exercised in pursuance of law. Every public official is presumed to act in obedience to his duty, until the contrary is shown; and *a fortiori* this presumption ought to be favourably applied to the chief magistrate of the Union. It is not necessary to aver, that the act which he may rightfully do, was so done."

The D.C. Circuit pointed to many other instances in which this presumption was used to uphold administrative actions; it said that the act "does not itself require or even suggest that any finding be reproduced in the order." It added that no one had "suggested any actual irregularity in the President's factfinding process or activity. In these circumstances, we encounter no difficulty in presuming executive regularity."

2. Why did a "presumption of regularity" not save the SEC in *Chenery I* or the secretary of transportation in *Overton Park*?

---

18. Compare Cinderella Career and Finishing Schools, Inc. v. FTC, where the court set aside the FTC's order partly because the FTC did not give adequate consideration to the record. No "probing of mental processes" was necessary, because the FTC's own opinion said "[I]n view of our decision to independently analyze — and without assistance from consumers or other witnesses — the challenged advertisements and their impact . . . it becomes unnecessary to review the testimony of these expert and consumer witnesses." This was held to be a denial of due process. 425 F.2d at 585, 586. In Public Power Council v. Johnson, 674 F.2d 791 (9th Cir. 1982), the court wrote that "normally there must be a strong showing of bad faith or improper behavior before the court may inquire into the thought processes of administrative decision makers." See also Montrose Chem. Corp. of California v. Train, 491 F.2d 63 (D.C. Cir. 1974), which held that an action under the Freedom of Information Act to obtain internal agency memoranda concerning an agency proceeding in which the plaintiff was interested would fail if the memoranda fell within the category of "probes into the mental process of decision-makers." See also Nathanson, Probing the Mind of the Administrator, 75 Colum. L. Rev. 721 (1975). See generally Gifford, The Morgan Cases: A Retrospective View, 30 Admin. L. Rev. 237 (1978). For a strong rejection of probing mental processes, see National Nutritional Foods Assn. v. Weinberger, 376 F. Supp. 142 (S.D.N.Y. 1974), *rev'd*, 512 F.2d 688 (2d Cir.), *cert. denied sub nom.* National Nutritional Foods Assn. v. Mathews, 423 U.S. 827 (1975). Such probing is also disfavored due to the "post hoc rationalization" nature of the evidence presented. GTE Sylvania, Inc. v. Consumer Prod. Safety Commn., 404 F. Supp. 352, 368-369 n.70 (D. Del. 1975). — ED. NOTE.

3. Assume that the FTC is considering the following plan to lighten the adjudicatory burden on the commissioners: Cases would be categorized as either "major" or "minor" according to the importance of the policy issues they contain. In minor cases, the record from the initial hearing along with briefs and other submissions would be summarized by a member of the opinion writing section. That summary, together with a recommended decision, would be forwarded to the commissioners but not made public. There would be no oral argument. Commissioners would of course remain free to read the briefs or record if they so desired. The relevant statute says that "the Commission" shall decide if the act has been violated. What result?

4. There is some unsettled law involving the extent to which a court, in the process of conducting judicial review, can go beyond the record before the agency. See, e.g., Latecoere International v. U.S. Department of Navy, 19 F.3d 1342 (11th Cir. 1994), in which the court refused to limit itself to the record, because the petitioner had made a strong showing of improper behavior on the agency's part. Several lower court cases seem to have created an "environmental exception" to the rules prohibiting courts from considering only record evidence. See, e.g., National Audubon Society v. Forest Service, 46 F.3d 1437 (9th Cir. 1993); Sierra Club v. Peterson, 185 F.3d 349 (5th Cir. 1999).

8

The Availability and
Timing of Judicial Review

Assume that your client wants to challenge an action of an agency or government official in a court of law. He wishes to argue that the agency is acting unlawfully. How does he get into court? Where does he find a court with jurisdiction? Is the agency action complained of "reviewable"? Does he have "standing"? Is the action "ripe" for review? Has he properly "exhausted his administrative remedies"?

This chapter deals with these questions. We explore the major doctrines of administrative law that govern whether and when a court can consider whether an agency action is unlawful. Technically, of course, these issues are the first ones in an administrative law case; but they are hard to understand without a prior understanding of the doctrines discussed in previous chapters, and hence they are best treated here.

Note also that while some of the relevant issues involve technical matters, they also raise large-scale questions about the relationship between the regulatory state and the common law framework of judicial review and private ordering. In the cases to be discussed here, there are important debates about the New Deal reformation of the system of American public law. To what extent should the interests created by regulatory statutes (to environmental protection, freedom from private discrimination on the basis of race and sex, safe automobiles and workplaces) be conceived as legally cognizable rights? How should courts deal with legal complaints made on the basis of injuries suffered simultaneously by hundreds, thousands, or millions of people? What is the role of judicial restraint in this context? When are the appropriate remedies political rather than legal?

There are intensely pragmatic questions too. Will judicial involvement make things better rather than worse? What are the systemic effects of judicial intervention? If standing, for example, is freely available, will administrative agencies be unable to engage in sensible priority-setting? If standing is not freely available, will administrative agencies be permitted to neglect the problems that they were created to solve?

A. Jurisdiction and Sovereign Immunity

The federal courts are courts of limited jurisdiction. Under article III of the Constitution, Congress must specifically grant lower federal courts jurisdiction to hear cases. Thus, to obtain review of an agency action in a lower federal court, you must find a statute that grants the court jurisdiction to hear your case. If you sue the federal government directly, you must also show that it has waived its "sovereign immunity." And you must show that the particular agency action at issue is "reviewable": that the courts' general power to hear a case has not been explicitly or implicitly precluded by statute.

The first two matters — jurisdiction and sovereign immunity — now generally pose no significant problem for a federal plaintiff seeking to enjoin unlawful federal government action (there are still major obstacles to collecting damages). But this was not always so.

In this section we consider jurisdiction and sovereign immunity, review some history, briefly sketch the evolution of present practice, and describe the current situation. We also examine the availability of federal court remedies against state government actions that violate federal law.

1. History[1]

Historically, plaintiffs did not often need to distinguish among problems of jurisdiction, sovereign immunity, standing, and reviewability. They simply tried to show that a court had the power to review the agency action. They did so by (a) bringing a private law tort or property action against government officials, (b) asking a court to issue one of the special prerogative writs developed by the common law judges to control and review officials' conduct, or (c) defending a criminal prosecution or civil enforcement action brought by the government on the ground that it was unlawful.

a. Private Law Tort Actions

The origins of modern judicial review have been attributed to *Dr. Bonham's Case*, 8 Co. Rep. 107 (C.P. 1610). Bonham, a seventeenth-century English doctor, was fined and imprisoned by the board of censors for practicing medicine in London without a license from the College of Physicians. He brought a tort action for false imprisonment. Lord Coke asserted the court's power to review the findings of the board. He held that the board's power to fine doctors for practicing without a license was void because the board kept half the fine — it was judging where it had self-interest. Such a procedure was "against common right and reason, repugnant or impossible to be performed; the common law will control it, and adjudge such act to be void. . . ." He added that the board could imprison for malpractice, but Dr. Bonham would be allowed to show the court that he was not "inexpert" (he was a Cambridge graduate), for otherwise he would have no remedy since the board "are not made judges."

Dr. Bonham's Case illustrates one method a plaintiff still might have of obtaining court review of the legality of an agency action: She might seek review of an official's enforcement action in a common law suit for damages in tort. (Obviously, to succeed, she must show that a common law tort has been committed.) Alternatively, a plaintiff might seek an injunction in equity against the threatened commission of a tort by a government official, asserting that it would cause irreparable injury and that a later damage action would not provide an adequate remedy.

---

1. This section draws heavily from (and often paraphrases) Jaffe & Henderson, Judicial Review and the Rule of Law: Historical Origins, 72 Law Q. Rev. 345 (1956). See also Jaffe, The Right to Judicial Review, 71 Harv. L. Rev. 401 (1958).

Whether the remedy sought was damages or an injunction, the official would typically assert, as an affirmative defense, that his conduct was authorized by statute. The court would then assess the merits of this defense. In this way, a private law tort action would become the vehicle for determining the legality of officials' conduct. By way of remedy, it would prevent or provide compensation for (and deterrence against) administrative action in excess of or contrary to statutory authority.

This is a private law model of public law. The private law model has been an important historical and conceptual foundation of federal administrative law. It continues to exert an influence, and controversy over private law understandings of public law is an important theme of the modern law of reviewability and standing. As we will see, much of the law of justiciability involves the legitimacy of an independent "public law" model governing judicial review of agency action.

The action of an agency or government official, however, might injure private persons without technically causing a tort. After *Dr. Bonham's Case*, English law saw use of the prerogative "great writs" to provide a method for court review of unlawful administrative behavior. The two most important of the writs were certiorari and mandamus.

b. The Prerogative Writs: England and America

An understanding of the prerogative writs is important to an understanding of the modern law of reviewability and standing. A particular question is how the apparent practice, in both England and early America, of allowing "strangers" to use the writs to enforce public duties bears on the modern law of standing. See Jaffe, Standing to Secure Judicial Review: Private Actions, 75 Harv. L. Rev. 255 (1961); Sunstein, What's Standing After *Lujan*, 91 Mich. L. Rev. 163 (1992); Winter, The Metaphor of Standing and the Problem of Self-Governance, 40 Stan. L. Rev. 1371 (1988).

Certiorari. The *writ of certiorari* first appears in cases about 1275-1280. Before Coke's time it was not used for purposes of review, but rather primarily to obtain a record (or a case) from one court for use in another. After *Dr. Bonham's Case*, however, judges began to use the writ of certiorari to review decisions of the sewer commissions. By the mid-fifteenth century, the sewer commissioners, who included many large landowners, began to undertake huge public works projects. No custom or law of England made clear who was to pay for these projects. The commissioners exercised discretion, and in 1599 the courts began to review the lawfulness of their decisions. Starting in 1643, the judges of the King's Bench used the writ of certiorari to review the sewer commissioners' decisions. This was the beginning of certiorari in the United States.

What is the place of the great writs in the United States? Several state courts built on the English practice, issuing writs of prohibition and established jurisdiction in certiorari — sometimes even allowing strangers to bring suit to enforce the law. See Zylstra v. Corporation of Charlestown, 1 S.C. L. (1 Bay) 382, 398 (1794); State v. Justices of Middlesex, 1 N.J.L. 283, 294 (1794); State v. Corporation of New Brunswick, 1 N.J.L. 450, 451 (1795). In nineteenth-century America, judges used certiorari to review administrative action, in the absence of statutes providing for review. The reviewing court would call on the agency to "certify" the record involved. And in accord with the practice of the King's Bench, certiorari was not available if the agency action challenged by the litigant had not been exclusively on the basis of a record. (This limitation is conventionally expressed through the rule that only "quasi-judicial" and not "legislative" action is reviewable on certiorari.)

At the national level, there is no clear American tradition of reliance on the prerogative writs. According to the Supreme Court's interpretation of the All Writs Act, Congress did not choose, through that act, to create general mandamus, prohibition, and certiorari jurisdiction. See Weston v. City Council of Charleston, 27 U.S. 171 (1829). Congress has never bestowed on the federal district courts the power to issue writs of certiorari, and, since the end of the nineteenth century, certiorari has not been used in the federal courts to obtain review of administrative action. In Degge v. Hitchcock, 229 U.S. 162 (1913), the Supreme Court held that certiorari ran only "from court to court," not from court to agency. Certiorari is still extensively used in the state courts; each jurisdiction subjects its use to myriad statutory and judge-made limitations. See F. Cooper, State Administrative Law 644 (1965).

Mandamus. The writ of *mandamus* is issued to compel an officer to perform a duty required by law. Jaffe and Henderson write:

> [The origin of mandamus] is something of a mystery. For about ten years before *James Bagg's Case* [11 Co. Rep. 94 (1615)] the Court of King's Bench had been granting judgments by which plaintiffs who had been unjustly removed from municipal office were restored to it, but the origin of this rather surprising activity is not at all clear. From this meagre beginning Coke conceived the notion of a sweeping jurisdiction over all errors judicial and extra-judicial. . . . A series of cases in the years 1700-1740 developed the principle that mandamus would not lie where the respondent's function was "judicial" but only where it was "ministerial." . . . Lord Mansfield characterised mandamus with something of Coke's sweep and flourish. "It was introduced," he said, "to prevent disorder from failure of justice and defect of the police. Therefore, it ought to be used for all occasions where the law has established no specific remedy, and where in justice and good government there ought to be one." [In R. v. Barker (1762).]
>
> . . . Mandamus has, however, developed along more modest lines. Nevertheless, . . . throughout the eighteenth century the older tradition prevailed that administration under law was subject to control by the High Court. It is clear that many of the acts and proceedings of the Justices of the Peace were not "judicial," yet all of them were subject to review on certiorari and mandamus.

Jaffe & Henderson, supra, at 359-361.

> Unlike certiorari, the mandamus power has been granted to the federal district courts by statute; it is therefore currently used to check administrative unlawfulness, although its function in the federal system has been superseded in good measure by the general remedy of injunction.

Thus, 28 U.S.C. §1361 provides that the "district courts shall have original jurisdiction of any action in the nature of mandamus to compel an officer or employee of the United States or any agency thereof to perform a duty owed to the plaintiff."

In principle, both mandatory injunctions and mandamus are available to compel "ministerial" acts — where "the duty . . . is so plainly prescribed as to keep from doubt," but not to compel acts that involve "the character of judgment or discretion." Wilbur v. United States, 281 U.S. 206 (1930). This distinction has spawned a host of conflicting and confusing interpretations of the terms *ministerial* and *discretionary*, and has some-times led judges to withhold relief where the action is related to discretionary authority even though the plaintiff claims that the official has exceeded the lawful scope of his discretion. Some leading commentators on the subject have urged the abolition of the distinction, or, at least, a return to the principles enunciated by Chief Justice Taft, who wrote:

> Mandamus issues to compel an officer to perform a purely ministerial duty. It cannot be used to compel or control a duty in the discharge of which by law he is given discretion. The duty may be discretionary within limits. He cannot transgress those limits, and if he does so, he may be controlled by injunction or mandamus to keep within them.

Work v. United States ex rel. Rives, 267 U.S. 175, 177 (1925). So viewed, mandamus would allow a court to grant affirmative injunctive relief to check an administrative abuse of discretion.

There are other technical limitations on the use of mandamus. For example, the issuance of mandamus is controlled by equitable principles. Thus, a court "may refuse to enforce or protect legal rights, the exercise of which may be prejudicial to the public interest." United States ex rel. Greathouse v. Dern, 289 U.S. 352, 360 (1933). Furthermore, mandamus will not lie if the relief requested is negative rather than affir-mative. Aguayo v. Richardson, 473 F.2d 1090 (2d Cir. 1973). Despite these limitations and the confusion surrounding the ministerial-discretionary distinction, mandamus is a useful remedy, and federal jurisdiction is sometimes predicated on the explicit grant of mandamus authority. 28 U.S.C. §1361. See, e.g., Frost v. Weinberger, 515 F.2d 57 (2d Cir. 1975).

The states provide mandamus as a method for review of administrative actions, but its use is the subject of "baffling procedural technicalities. . . . Years of historical develop-ment, in each state, have accumulated intricate age-encrusted filigrees which vary from state to state." 2 F. Cooper, State Administrative Law 653-654 (1965). It is especially notable that the Supreme Court appears, in an early case, to have allowed invocation of a general mandamus statute to enforce "a duty to the public generally" by people having "no interest other than such as belonged to others." Union Pacific Railroad v. Hall, 91 U.S. 343 (1875). This holding bears on the modern law of standing; it suggests that "strangers" may be authorized to bring suit.

Other writs. Other historically based writs include the following: *Prohibition* is used to prevent a "judicial" or "quasi-judicial" body from exercising jurisdiction. Its purpose is to avoid an unnecessary hearing, yet it is not issued if review at a later stage would be adequate. The writ of prohibition to restrain an allegedly unconstitutional tax was treated as a constitutional case in an early decision of the Marshall Court. See Weston v. City of Charleston, 27 U.S. 171 (1829). *Quo warranto* is used to test an office holder's right to his office. *Habeas corpus* is used to test the lawfulness of confinement. The first two of these are used in state, but rarely in federal, proceedings. The last, of course, is well known and used particularly in federal administrative proceedings involving deportation and other immigration matters.

For purposes of understanding American practice, two actions are of special interest; the *qui tam action* and the *informers' action.* The purpose of the qui tam action is to give citizens a right to bring civil suits to help in the enforcement of federal criminal law. Under the qui tam action, a citizen — who might well be a stranger — is permitted to bring suit against offenders of the law. Qui tam actions are familiar to American law. The victor in a qui tam action is ordinarily entitled to recover money to be paid to himself, to the United States, or to both. "Statutes providing for actions by the common informer, who himself has no interest whatever in the controversy other than that given by statute, have been in existence for hundreds of years in England, and in this country ever since the foundation of our Government." United States ex rel. Marcus v. Hess, 317 U.S. 537, 541 n.4 (1943). In the first decade of the nation's existence, Congress created a number of qui tam actions, covering a wide range of prohibited activities. See Krent, Executive Control Over Criminal Law Enforcement: Some Lessons from History, 38 Am. L. Rev. 375, 296-303 (1989). See also Caminker, The Constitutionality of Qui Tam Actions, 99 Yale L.J. 341 (1989). In an important decision, the Supreme Court upheld the qui tam action against article III challenge, in part by emphasizing its historic pedigree. Virginia Agency of Natural Resources v. United States, 529 U.S. 765 (2000).

Through an informers' action, people are allowed to bring suit to enforce public duties, and citizens are permitted to keep a share of the resulting damages or fines. In the states, the informers' action was familiar in the early history of the republic. Early Congresses created several informers' actions to assist in the enforcement of federal law. See Act of July 31, 1789, ch. 5, §29, 1 Stat. 29, 45; Act of May 8, 1792, ch. 36, §5, 1 Stat. 275, 277-278.

You might ask how these historical materials bear on the issue of standing and in particular on Lujan v. Defenders of Wildlife (p. 000).

2. Present Federal Practice: Jurisdiction

With the exception of habeas corpus and mandamus, the common law writs are hardly ever used today to obtain review of federal administrative actions. (They are, however, used in state courts.) In fact, the Administrative Procedure Act (APA) §703 makes clear that a claim need not take the form of such a writ. Plaintiffs typically base their claims on a specific statute that grants a federal court jurisdiction to review a particular agency's decision; or they invoke general "federal question" jurisdiction, 28 U.S.C. §1331, and they plead that they have been (or will be) injured by an unlawful action of an official or agency and seek an injunction, a declaration of illegality, or damages; or they invoke a specialized federal jurisdictional statute, such as the jurisdictional provision of the Civil Rights Act, 28 U.S.C. §1343, that grants jurisdiction to hear particular types of claims. What is important is that some jurisdictional statute must be found.

a. Specific Statutory Review

Judicial review is sometimes authorized by an agency's organic statute that specifically provides how action of that agency is to be reviewed in court. Such a statute is typically taken not only to provide jurisdiction, but also to waive sovereign immunity, and to make "reviewable" the type of agency action to which it refers. Statutes may prescribe review either by an appellate court or by a district court. Most commonly, specific statutory provisions provide that a party may petition the federal court of appeals to have an order set aside; the appeals court forum is appropriate when there is no need to take further evidence and review may proceed on the record made before the agency. Thus, the Communications Act, for example, provides for review of a Federal Communications Commission (FCC) order in the Court of Appeals for the District of Columbia, provided that a notice of appeal is filed within 30 days. 47 U.S.C. §402. But if the record reviewed is inadequate and if there is "a genuine issue of material fact" on which an agency hearing was not required, the court of appeals in some instances is authorized by statute to transfer the case to the district court.

Specific statutory review provisions can also limit the relief judicially available. For example, the 1995 Unfunded Mandate Reform Act requires agency regulations imposing obligations on state, local, or tribal governments to contain a "statement" of the rule's impacts, costs, and benefits. Section 401 of the act provides for judicial review of an agency's failure to complete such a statement; while the court can order a statement to be prepared, an agency's failure to issue the statement cannot be used as a basis for enjoining, invalidating, or otherwise affecting the rule in question.

Less commonly, specific statutes provide for review of certain agency actions in the district courts, where it is easier to develop a record. Moreover, as we shall see below, statutes of general jurisdiction grant that jurisdiction to district courts. Thus, a plaintiff bringing a single case with several different issues may find that statutes provide for jurisdiction over some aspects of his or her case in the district court and over others in the court of appeals. In such circumstances, a single court might take jurisdiction over the whole case on a theory akin to pendent jurisdiction. A plaintiff may also find that the agency action of which he or she complains is not final enough to satisfy a specific statute's grant of authority to a court of appeals to review a "final order." The plaintiff may then obtain review in a district court under a statute of general jurisdiction.

b. Review under Statutes of General or Special Jurisdiction

If no specific statutory review is provided in the relevant organic statute, plaintiffs may seek review under more general principles of administrative law — principles that allow them to prevent unlawful governmental action or to obtain redress when they have been injured. As a result of Erie R.R. v. Tompkins, 304 U.S. 64 (1938), federal courts do not exercise any general common law jurisdiction to redress torts by government officials. But, as we shall see, federal courts have continued the private law model of administrative law by developing special federal law remedies for official activities that would also consti-tute common law torts. Nevertheless, a plaintiff must still find a statute that provides a federal court with jurisdiction to hear his or her claim. The most obvious choice is to proceed under 28 U.S.C. §1331, which grants the federal district courts "original jurisdic-tion of all civil actions arising under the Constitution, laws, or treaties of the United States." Other statutes are also available, which may provide special jurisdiction, specific remedies, or both. For example, a plaintiff can bring a civil rights action against state offi-cials under 42 U.S.C. §1343 (and obtain damages and attorneys' fees); file for habeas corpus under 28 U.S.C. §§2241-2255 or mandamus under 28 U.S.C. §1361; or proceed under statutes such as 28 U.S.C. §1336, which grants jurisdiction in cases involving the regulation of commerce and restraints of trade; or 28 U.S.C. §1339, which grants jurisdiction over actions relating to the postal service; or under other statutes that grant specialized jurisdiction. Despite the existence of many different jurisdictional statutes, note that, when seeking the most commonly desired forms of relief — an injunction and a declaratory judgment — a plaintiff can almost always find jurisdiction under the general federal question provision (28 U.S.C. §1331). When seeking damages for injuries owing to the actions of federal officials, plaintiffs may bring a tort suit against the officers who injured them, based on federal question or diversity jurisdiction, or they may sue the government directly, in which case they can find jurisdiction in the Federal Torts Claims Act (FTCA), 28 U.S.C. §1346(b).

Statutes other than §1331 were more important before 1976 than today. Before then, §1331 applied only to suits where the "matter in controversy" exceeded "the sum or value of $10,000." Plaintiffs who could not meet that requirement argued that the APA, in making agency action reviewable, U.S.C. §§701-706, also granted federal courts jurisdiction to hear plaintiffs seeking review. The Supreme Court firmly rejected this claim, holding that the APA itself bestowed no jurisdiction on the courts. See Califano v. Sanders, 430 U.S. 99 (1977). In 1976 and in 1980, the $10,000 requirement was eliminated with respect to claims against federal and state governmental action, respectively. 90 Stat. 2721; 94 Stat. 2369. Jurisdictional problems in cases involving federal agency review have virtually disappeared.[2]

Accordingly, in the absence of a specific statutory review provision applicable to the agency action in question, a person can now ordinarily obtain review (subject to exceptions of "preclusion" and "commitment to agency discretion" discussed below) by invoking one of the general or special jurisdictional statutes to get into federal district court and invoking the APA as the basis for the court to review the legality of the agency's actions.

c. Defense to Enforcement or Prosecution

Even in the absence of any specific provision in an organic jurisdictional statute, the legality of government action can generally be asserted as a defense to a criminal prosecution or civil enforcement action. If the Government brings a prosecution or enforcement action for violation of a regulation, the invalidity of the regulation can normally be asserted as a defense. (We consider below exceptions to this principle and the constitutional problems that they might raise.)

3. *Present Federal Practice: Sovereign Immunity*

In some cases, a plaintiff seeking an injunction or damages against unlawful federal government action has to consider whether a suit is barred by the doctrine of sovereign immunity. That doctrine holds that the United States cannot be sued without its consent.

---

2. However, organic statutes sometimes limit specific review to certain agency decisions, and then go on to explicitly bar review of other agency decisions under general jurisdictional statutes such as 28 U.S.C. §1331.

A plaintiff who invokes §1331, however, cannot escape problems of sovereign immunity and reviewability as easily as if he or she had invoked a more specific statute. The very breadth of §1331 means that Congress, in enacting it, cannot be taken to have waived immunity or deliberately to have made any particular set of agency actions reviewable.

The jurisdictional amount requirement of §1331 has been eliminated in suits challenging state as well as federal action, but plaintiffs challenging state action generally also invoke the jurisdictional provision of the Civil Rights Act, 28 U.S.C. §1343. Those provisions also do not have a jurisdictional amount requirement. Also, the Act authorizes the award of damages and attorney's fees.

We consider in the next section of this chapter the special problems presented by actions seeking damages against the government (or government officials), and consider here efforts to obtain injunctions or other specific relief.

In most contexts, a plaintiff seeking specific relief has long been allowed to avoid the doctrine of sovereign immunity by suing an officer or employee of the United States instead of the "United States" itself, alleging that the officer was acting contrary to the Constitution or statute, and obtaining an injunction. This remedy reflected the private law model: The official was acting without lawful authority and could be enjoined from committing a common law wrong. But injunction actions against officers — particularly those seeking to control the disposition of government property — were sometimes dismissed on the ground that they were in reality suits against the United States[3] or that the United States was an indispensable party.

The problem of sovereign immunity was largely eliminated for those seeking review of federal agency action by an amendment to APA §702 adopted in 1976. That amendment provides:[4]

> An action in a court of the United States seeking relief other than money damages and stating a claim that an agency or an officer or employee thereof acted or failed to act in an official capacity or under color of legal authority shall not be dismissed nor relief therein be denied on the ground that it is against the United States or that the United States is an indispensable party. The United States may be named as a defendant in any such action, and a judgment or decree may be entered against the United States: Provided, that any mandatory or injunctive decree shall specify the Federal officer or officers (by name or by title), and their successors in office, personally responsible for compliance. Nothing herein (1) affects other limitations on judicial review of the power or the duty of the court to dismiss any action or deny relief on any other appropriate legal or equitable ground; or (2) confers authority to grant relief if any other statute that grants consent to suit expressly or impliedly forbids the relief which is sought.

Note that this statute does *not* apply to actions against the federal government for money damages, where the rules of sovereign immunity still apply, nor does it remove or affect any other doctrines that may limit review. But what is an action for money damages? Bowen v. Massachusetts, 487 U.S. 879 (1988), held that a suit by Massachusetts to challenge a Department of Health and Human Services (HHS) decision denying the state $6 million in federal Medicaid reimbursement was not an action for money damages. In the Court's view, this was an equitable action for specific (monetary) relief. Compare Department of the Army v. Blue Fox, 119 S. Ct. 687 (1999), holding that the waiver of sovereign immunity in the APA does not allow a subcontractor to obtain an equitable lien on funds held by the government for work done on the primary contract. According to the Court, the lien fell within the "money damages" exception, unlike the

---

3. See, e.g., Larson v. Domestic & Foreign Commerce Corp., 337 U.S. 682 (1949). An official cannot raise a defense of sovereign immunity to a claim that he is acting outside statutory authority or unconstitutionally, cf. Ex parte Young, 209 U.S. 123, 160 (1908); but he can raise such a defense to certain other claims of unlawfulness (e.g., a suit based on tort or property law and seeking specific performance).

4. 90 Stat. 2721 (1976). At the same time Congress amended APA §703 to avoid the dismissal of a suit because the plaintiff made a technical mistake in naming the party defendant. The amendment states: "If no special statutory review proceeding is applicable, the action for judicial review may be brought against the United States, the agency by its official title, or the appropriate officer." 90 Stat. 2721 (1976).

claim in *Bowen*, which involved money to which the plaintiff was entitled as a result of enforcing a statutory mandate. See also Hubbard v. EPA, 982 F.2d 531 (D.C. Cir. 1992).

Sovereign immunity is often not a problem in actions to enjoin state government action as contrary to federal law. Ex parte Young, 209 U.S. 123 (1908), following the private law model, held that plaintiff (a regulated railroad) could obtain an injunction against state regulatory officials for threatening to enforce unconstitutional regulations. Because the suit was brought against the officials as individuals, the eleventh amendment imposed no bar. Suit can be brought against the responsible state officials under 28 U.S.C. §1331 or §1343 (the jurisdictional provision of the Civil Rights Act) and an injunction against them obtained.

In some cases — such as those requiring state officials to dispense state monies — the suit may be judicially characterized as one against the state, that is, barred by the eleventh amendment. See, e.g., Edelman v. Jordan, 415 U.S. 65 (1974) (federal court may not order state officials to pay unlawfully withheld welfare benefits). See also Pennhurst State School v. Halderman, 465 U.S. 89 (1984) (sovereign immunity precludes federal court from entering injunction against state official for violation of state law).

In recent years, eleventh amendment litigation has become more frequent and more complex, with growing signs of Supreme Court enthusiasm for finding barriers to federal court review of state activity. Thus, in Seminole Tribe of Florida v. Florida, 517 U.S. 44 (1996), the Supreme Court held, 5-4, that Congress does not have the constitutional power to overcome a state's immunity from suit in federal court, at least if Congress is acting under article I of the Constitution. In the process, the Court overruled its own decision in Pennsylvania v. Union Gas Co., 491 U.S. 1 (1989), and eliminated an enforcement strategy that Congress has frequently attempted to use to overcome state immunity from federal court suits. The extent to which specific relief or damages can be obtained against state or local governmental authorities presents complex questions that will be addressed further in the next section but not fully explored here. A good discussion is Meltzer, The *Seminole* Decision and State Sovereign Immunity, 1996 Sup. Ct. Rev. 1. For other important cases involving sovereign immunity, see Alden v. Maine, 527 U.S. 706 (1999) (barring Congress from requiring state courts to entertain suits by individuals seeking damages for violation of federal law); Florida Prepaid Postsecondary Education Expense Board v. College Savings Bank, 527 U.S. 627 (1999) (striking down federal statute authorizing federal courts to impose monetary liability on states that violated rights conferred by patent laws); Kimel v. Florida Board of Regents, 528 U.S. 62 (2000) (striking down imposition of damage liability on states for violations of Age Discrimination in Employment Act).

4. Present Federal Practice: Venue and Service of Process

Before 1962, the general venue and service of process provisions in title 28 required many plaintiffs seeking judicial review of government actions under general jurisdictional provisions, such as 28 U.S.C. §1331, to file suit in Washington, D.C. — a forum that many potential plaintiffs found inconvenient and expensive. In 1962, Congress liberalized these requirements, enacting the provisions now embodied in 28 U.S.C. §1391(e). Now, unless some other statute specifically provides to the contrary,[5] when one sues an

---

5. Statutes containing specific venue provisions include 7 U.S.C. §608(c)(15) (secretary of agriculture); 15 U.S.C. §45(c) (FTC); 42 U.S.C. §405(g) (HHS); 49 U.S.C. §1486(b)(CAB).

officer or employee of the United States, an agency, or the United States itself, venue is proper "in any judicial district in which (1) a defendant in the action resides, or (2) the cause of action arose, or (3) any real property involved in the action is situated, or (4) the plaintiff resides if no real property is involved in the action." Moreover, §1391(e) provides that service of process is governed by the Federal Rules of Civil Procedure, except that "the delivery of the summons and complaint to the officer or agency . . . may be made by certified mail beyond the territorial limits of the district in which the action is brought." Thus, venue and service requirements do not often inhibit the bringing of a suit challenging agency action.[6]

When two or more petitions for review of the same agency order are brought in different courts of appeals, the agency is required to file the record in the court of first filing.[7] All other courts of appeals must then transfer their petitions to that court. This mechanical "first-filing" rule has led to a "race to the courthouse" among parties with different forum preferences.

Despite the wide range of choice provided by the 1962 venue amendments, many critics claim that too many agency review cases are brought in the District of Columbia Circuit, perhaps because many such cases involve institutional plaintiffs who, along with the agency, "reside" there. They charge that this forum is too distant from those in the country directly affected by many agency decisions. Some of those critics have introduced legislation that would (1) require an agency review proceeding to be brought only in a judicial district where the agency's action "would substantially affect the residents" and (2) require both circuit and district courts to transfer such actions (on request) to a circuit or district "in which the action would have a substantially greater impact" (unless the interests of justice require retention).[8]

B. Damage Actions against Government and Government Officers

When a suit seeking damages is brought against a state or federal government, or their officers and employees, the defendants may assert a defense of sovereign or official immunity. In many instances, the federal government and states have waived or abrogated sovereign immunity, although there are many other cases where damages against the government are not available. In such cases, a plaintiff may seek damages against the responsible officials. But in some cases the courts have created doctrines of official immunity to prevent what they regard as the pernicious side effects of unrestricted damage

---

6. A 1976 amendment makes it clear that a plaintiff can join private parties to his suit against the government, but if he does so, he must comply with whatever venue requirements would apply to a suit against the private party were the government defendants not involved. 90 Stat. 2721 (1976), 28 U.S.C. §1391(e). The Supreme Court has decided that 28 U.S.C. §1391(e) does not grant district courts nationwide jurisdiction over officers sued in their individual capacity. Stafford v. Briggs, 444 U.S. 527 (1980).

7. 28 U.S.C. §2112(a). The court of first filing may later transfer the proceedings to any other court of appeals for "the convenience of the parties in the interests of justice."
Amendment No. 1267 to S. 1080 (Senators DeConcini, Hatch, and Simpson). 128 Cong. Rec. (Feb. 9, 1982). S. 658-659; id., Feb. 10, 1982, S. 755-761.

8. Amendment No. 1267 to S. 1080 (Senators DeConcini, Hatch, and Simpson). 128 Cong. Rec. (Feb. 9, 1982). S. 658–659; id., Feb. 10, 1982, S. 755–761.

liability for individual officials. In reading the materials that follow, you should keep two general questions in mind.

First, when is an after-the-fact (ex post) damage action the appropriate remedy for unlawful government action, and when is the opportunity for a prior (ex ante) agency hearing and judicial review the appropriate remedy? Earlier in this book — when dealing with "emergency" regulatory enforcement, and tort actions against government officials as a substitute for due process hearings in areas such as school discipline — it has been suggested that ex post damages and ex ante hearing and review might be viewed as substitutes. If so, in what situations might damages be the more appropriate remedy?

Take, for example, police arrests at street disturbances or accidents by government employees driving government vehicles on official business. In such cases, a prior hearing and judicial review may not be feasible or appropriate; one may therefore rely on the threat of subsequent damage actions to deter false arrests and careless driving.

Contrast these cases with decisions by regulatory bureaucracies setting railroad rates or determining the design and location of an electric generating facility. In such cases, it may be feasible (though time consuming) to provide a hearing and judicial review before the agency takes action. On the other hand, there would be many problems in relying on ex post damage actions to remedy illegality. In many cases, it would be very difficult to measure, in the context of a pervasively regulated economy, the particular damage suffered by a regulated firm as the result of any single decision. Moreover, such regulatory decisions typically involve a large amount of discretion. To avoid destabilizing uncertainty and unfair second-guessing, courts would probably be very reluctant to award damages unless the illegality was plain. An ex post damage action might thus prove a far less effective check on discretion than a hearing and "hard look" judicial review ex ante.

To what extent can the current pattern in the availability of these two types of remedies — ex ante hearing and review and ex post damages — be explained or justified by considerations of this sort?

A second basic question to keep in mind is whether, if damages are an appropriate remedy, they should be awarded against the government or against the responsible officials. Courts have applied theories of strict "enterprise liability" against private businesses in such areas as products liability and injury from toxic pollutants; these theories may suggest that government should similarly be held liable without regard to fault for the injurious by-products of its activities. But the existing availability of damages against government falls far short of the enterprise liability model. Perhaps this shortfall may be justified in part on the ground that government is not subject to market competition, and therefore that strict enterprise liability may not create incentives for government to reduce the harms it causes. Because it can always raise taxes and stay in business, government may not have a strong incentive to minimize damage liability. An instructive discussion is P. Schuck, Suing Government (1984).

Damage liability against *officers* suffers from other problems. The officers may not have sufficient assets to pay plaintiff's judgments. On the other hand, the threat of damage liability may overdeter, leading officers to be unduly cautious, for example, in making arrests or taking enforcement action. Would the best solution be to impose liability on the government and leave the government free to proceed against the responsible officials by way of an action for indemnity or a disciplinary proceeding?

You should bear *both* questions in mind in reviewing the materials that follow on official immunity. Do the judicial decisions creating immunity for certain officers reflect a determination of the first question — that the case is not one where damages are the appropriate remedy? Or do they reflect a determination of the second question — that even though damages may be an appropriate remedy, subjecting officials to liability creates an excessive risk of overdeterrence? (On this analysis, the appropriate remedy would be damages against the government, but the legislature must waive sovereign immunity to authorize such awards.)

1. Damage Actions against the Government

Suit can be brought against the United States for damages only if there is a statute by which the United States specifically consents to be sued. Since 1946, the United States has consented to many tort claims through the Federal Tort Claims Act.[9] That act, however, constitutes a highly limited waiver of immunity. Its key provision waives sovereign immunity by granting jurisdiction to the district courts:

> The district courts . . . shall have exclusive jurisdiction of civil actions on claims against the United States, for money damages, . . . for injury or loss of property, or personal injury or death caused by the negligent or wrongful act or omission of any employee of the Government while acting within the scope of his . . . employment, under circumstances where the United States, if a private person, would be liable to the claimant. . . .

28 U.S.C. §1346(b).

This grant of jurisdiction has numerous exceptions that are contained in 28 U.S.C. §2680. Immunity is not waived where certain specific agencies or certain specific programs are involved, or if the tort occurs in a foreign country. Moreover, an action of assault, battery, false imprisonment, false arrest, malicious prosecution, or abuse of process can be brought only if a law enforcement officer allegedly committed the tort. Further, no action can be brought for "libel, slander, misrepresentation, deceit, or interference with contract rights." 28 U.S.C. §2680(h).

The most complex exception, however, is that contained in §2680(a), which provides that the waiver of sovereign immunity does not apply to "[a]ny claim based upon an act or omission of an employee of the Government, exercising due care, in the execution of a statute or regulation, whether or not such statute or regulation be valid, or based upon the exercise or performance or the failure to exercise or perform a discretionary function or duty on the part of a federal agency or an employee of the Government, whether or not the discretion involved be abused." See Dalehite v. United States, 346 U.S. 15 (1953); see also United States v. S.A. Empresa de Viacao Aerea Rio Grandense (Varig Airlines), 467 U.S. 797 (1984). In both cases, the Court concluded that the discretionary function or duty "that cannot form a basis for suit under the Tort Claims Act includes more than the initiation of programs and activities. It also includes determinations made by executives or administrators in establishing plans, specifications or schedules of operations. Where there is room for policy judgment and decision there is discretion. It necessarily follows that acts of subordinates in carrying out the operations

---

9. 60 Stat. 842 (1946), now codified in 28 U.S.C. §1346(a) (jurisdiction), §1402(b) (venue), §§1504 and 2110 (Court of Claims review), §2401 (limitation period), §2402 (no jury trial), §2411 (interest), §2412 (costs), §§2671-2680 (procedure and exceptions).

of Government in accordance with official directions cannot be actionable." Consider these cases.

BERKOVITZ v. UNITED STATES, 486 U.S. 531 (1988). The plaintiff, a small child, took a dose of polio vaccine and developed polio. He sued the federal government's Division of Biologic Standards (DBS), claiming (1) that DBS had improperly licensed the laboratory to make the product, called Orimune, and (2) that DBS had improperly permitted the sale of the particular batch of vaccine that the plaintiff took. The Court held that the "discretionary function" exemption did not bar either claim.

The Orimune licensing claim consisted, first, of a charge that DBS had violated a statute or DBS regulation in granting the laboratory a license to produce the vaccine. The relevant statute said that "licenses for [maintaining a polio vaccine laboratory for] preparation of products may be issued only upon a showing that the [laboratory] and the products for which a license is desired meet standards designed to insure the continued safety, priority, and potency of such products, prescribed in regulations. . . ." The regulation said that a "product license shall be issued only upon examination of the product and upon a determination that the product complies with [prescribed] standards," and that an "application for license shall not be considered as filed" until DBS receives information and data about the product that the manufacturer is required to submit. Plaintiff claimed that DBS violated these regulations and the statute by issuing the license without first receiving data that the manufacturer was to submit. Plaintiff's Orimune licensing claim involved another charge, which the Court found "unclear." The Court said that, if the plaintiff meant to charge that DBS licensed Orimune either without determining whether the vaccine complied with regulatory standards or after determining that the vaccine failed to comply, the discretionary function exemption does not bar the claim. That is because the statute imposes a clear duty on DBS to decide whether a vaccine complies with standards and not to license a vaccine that does not comply. If, however, plaintiff meant to claim that DBS's decision was wrong, then the analysis is more complicated.

> In that event, the question turns on whether the manner and method of determining compliance with the safety standards at issue involve agency judgment of the kind protected by the discretionary function exception. [The plaintiff] contend[s] that the determination involves the application of objective scientific standards . . . whereas the Government asserts that the determination incorporates considerable "policy judgment." . . . In making these assertions, the parties have framed the issue appropriately; application of the discretionary function exception to the claim that the determination of compliance was incorrect hinges on whether the agency officials making that determination permissibly exercise policy choice. The parties, however, have not addressed this question in detail. . . . We therefore leave it to the District Court to decide. . . .

The second claim, faulty inspection of the specific vaccine batch, involves a regulatory scheme similar to that in *Varig*. DBS had considerable discretion to decide the extent to which it would examine individual lots. "The discretionary function exception, however, does not apply if the acts complained of do not involve the permissible exercise of policy discretion. Thus, if the Bureau's policy leaves no room for an official to exercise policy judgment in performing a given act, or if the act simply does not involve the exercise of such judgment, the discretionary function exception does not bar a claim that the act was negligent." Here, the plaintiff alleged that DBS "has adopted a policy of testing all vaccine lots for compliance with safety standards and preventing the distribution to the public of any lots that fail to comply." . . . "If [their] allegations are correct — that is, if the Bureau's policy did not allow the official who took the challenged action to release a noncomplying lot on the basis of policy considerations — the discretionary function exception does not bar the claim." The district court must make the relevant determinations.

UNITED STATES v. GAUBERT, 499 U.S. 315 (1991). The Federal Home Loan Bank Board exercised detailed supervisory control over the management of a financially troubled savings bank. The bank's largest shareholder brought suit under the FTCA, claiming that the board's management was negligent and caused him financial loss. The court of appeals denied the government's motion to dismiss. Reversing, the Court first said that where a valid regulation mandates particular conduct, the agency will be sheltered from liability "because the action will be deemed in furtherance of the policies" underlying the regulation, but if it violates such a regulation "there will be no shelter from liability because there is no room for choice and the action will be contrary to policy." Here, relevant law and regulations gave the board discretion to supervise troubled banks through detailed, bold, informal supervision. The board's actions fell within the "discretionary function" exemption from liability, even though the decisions were "made at the operational or management level" and not a "planning" level. Even detailed management decisions "involved the exercise of discretion in furtherance of public policy goals."

There are numerous lower court cases on the scope of the discretionary function exception. See, for example, Irving v. United States, 162 F.3d 154 (1st Cir. 1998), in which a divided en banc court held that OSHA's performance of a workplace inspection qualified for an exception. Shansky v. United States, 164 F.3d 688 (1st Cir. 1999), held that the discretionary function exception applied to the National Park Service, when it failed to place a handrail or warning at a national historic site. GATX/Airlog Co. v. United States, 234 F.3d 1089 (9th Cir. 2000), held that an FAA decision to issue an airworthiness certificate to a kind of aircraft was protected by the exception. See also Demery v. Department of Interior, 357 F.3d 830 (8th Cir. 2004); Macharia v. United States, 334 F.3d 61 (D.C. Cir. 2003); Reed v. Department of Interior, 231 F.3d 501 (9th Cir. 2000); Appley Brothers v. United States, 164 F.3d 1164 (8th Cir. 1999); Aragon v. United States, 146 F.3d 819 (10th Cir. 1998); Rich v. United States, 119 F.3d 447 (6th Cir. 1997).

2. *Traditional Common Law Tort Actions against Government Officers*

A plaintiff barred by sovereign immunity from suing the government for damages might consider suing its officers or employees instead. Under traditional common law principles, those employees would have been exposed to liability to the same extent as their counterparts in the private sector. Indeed, in a famous tort action to recover damages for a horse that a health inspector had destroyed, Justice Holmes held that the inspector was liable unless the horse was *actually* diseased. The health inspector's reasonable belief that the horse was sick was no defense if erroneous, for the statute allowed him to destroy only horses that were *actually* sick, not those he believed so to be. Miller v. Horton, 152 Mass. 540, 26 N.E. 100 (1891).

Such tort actions might be brought against both state and federal officials. Before Erie R.R. v. Tompkins, 304 U.S. 64 (1939), and even afterwards, the federal courts might entertain such suits (particularly those against federal officials) under their diversity jurisdiction or the provision in title 28, §1442, permitting removal of actions against federal officers, without much attention as to whether the law applied was state or federal in origin.

Judges, however, enjoyed an absolute immunity from tort actions unless there was "clear absence of all jurisdiction over the subject-matter." Bradley v. Fisher, 80 U.S. (13 Wall.) 335 (1871). This immunity was needed, according to the Supreme Court, for the judge must be "free to act upon his own convictions, without apprehension of personal consequences to himself." This principle was gradually extended to provide immunity to certain executive branch officials, such as the postmaster general, the secretary of the interior, and the attorney general. Thus, in Gregoire v. Biddle, 177 F.2d 579 (2d Cir. 1949), the Second Circuit considered a suit for damages against the attorney general and other officials based on plaintiff's claim that the defendant had wrongly detained him as an enemy alien on the pretext that he was German, despite a judicial finding that he was French. The court of appeals, in an opinion written by Judge Learned Hand, held that officers of the Department of Justice, in the performance of duties imposed by law, enjoy the same absolute privilege as do judges. The court found that the public interest requires that these officers should speak and act freely and fearlessly in the discharge of their important functions:

> It does indeed go without saying that an official, who is in fact guilty of using his powers to vent his spleen upon others, or for any other personal motive not connected with the public good, should not escape liability for the injuries he may so cause; and, if it were possible in practice to confine such complaints to the guilty, it would be monstrous to deny recovery. The justification for doing so is that it is impossible to know whether the claim is well founded until the case has been tried, and that to submit all officials, the innocent as well as the guilty, to the burden of a trial and to the inevitable danger of its outcome, would dampen the ardor of all but the most resolute, or the most irresponsible, in the unflinching discharge of their duties. Again and again the public interest calls for action which may turn out to be founded on a mistake, in the face of which an official may later find himself hard put to it to satisfy a jury of his good faith. There must indeed be means of punishing public officers who have been truant to their duties; but that is quite another matter from exposing such as have been honestly mistaken to suit by anyone who has suffered from their errors. As is so often the case, the answer must be found in a balance between the evils inevitable in either alternative. In this instance it has been thought in the end better to leave unredressed the wrongs done by dishonest officers than to subject those who try to do their duty to the constant dread of retaliation. Judged as res nova, we should not hesitate to follow the path laid down in the books.
>
> The decisions have, indeed, always imposed as a limitation upon the immunity that the official's act must have been within the scope of his powers; and it can be argued that official powers, since they exist only for the public good, never cover occasions where the public good is not their aim, and hence that to exercise a power dishonestly is necessarily to overstep its bounds. A moment's reflection shows, however, that that cannot be the meaning of the limitation without defeating the whole doctrine. What is meant by saying that the officer must be acting within

his power cannot be more than that the occasion must be such as would have justified the act, if he had been using his power for any of the purposes on whose account it was vested in him. For the foregoing reasons it was proper to dismiss the first count.

The principle enunciated by Judge Hand in *Gregoire* was adopted and extended by four Justices of the Supreme Court in Barr v. Matteo, 360 U.S. 564 (1959). After *Barr*, the extension of immunity continued. Suits were dismissed, for example, alleging that Justice Department officials wrongly had plaintiffs detained and beaten; that an army doctor had negligently left surgical sutures in a patient's kidney; even that a paving maintenance supervisor had negligently allowed an asphalt spreader to run over plaintiff's leg. In each instance, the courts found the official's position sufficiently important and the acts sufficiently related to their duties to warrant application of an absolute privilege in their favor.

In Westfall v. Erwin, 484 U.S. 292 (1988), the Supreme Court held that federal officials are not absolutely immune from liability under state tort law for conduct within the scope of their employment. Within a year of the *Westfall* decision, Congress passed a new law, the Westfall Act, which substantially relieved federal employees of the potential liability that *Westfall* imposed on them. Pub. L. No. 100-694, 102 Stat. 4563, effective Nov. 18, 1988. The act said that its aim was to "protect Federal employees from personal liability for common law torts committed within the scope of their employment, while providing persons injured by the common law torts of Federal employees with an appropriate remedy against the United States." Section 5 of the act provides that the FTCA's remedy against the United States for the negligent or wrongful acts or omissions of any government employee while acting within the scope of his office or employment "is exclusive of any other civil action or proceeding for money damages . . . against the employee whose act of omission gave rise to the claim. . . ." The House Report says that the "availability of suit under the FTCA precludes any other civil action or proceeding of any kind from being brought against an individual Federal employee or his estate if such action or proceeding would sound in common law tort." Section 6 of the law directs the attorney general to defend any tort suit brought against an employee. It authorizes him to certify that "the defendant employee was acting within the scope of his office of employment at the time of the incident." On that certification, any action brought in a state court is removed to the federal district court where it "shall be deemed to be an action or proceeding against the United States."

Suppose that Smith sues a federal employee for, say, slander committed within the scope of his employment. Since the FTCA has an exception forbidding recovery from the government in the case of slander, can Smith sue the employee? The Westfall Act says that remedy against the United States that the FTCA provides "for injury or loss of property or personal injury or death arising or resulting from the negligent *or other wrongful* act or omission of any" federal employee, "is *exclusive* of any other civil action . . ." against the employee. In United States v. Smith, 499 U.S. 160 (1991), the Court held that this language means what it says. The FTCA provides the "exclusive" remedy, even if that remedy is no remedy because of an FTCA exemption (38 U.S.C. §2680). The alternative, rejected by the Court, would be to say that Smith can still sue the employee, who would remain liable unless the act is both (1) within the scope of his employment, and (2) discretionary.

3. *"Public Tort" Actions against Government Officers*

a. §1983 Actions

The Civil Rights Act of 1871, 42 U.S.C. §1983, has proved a fertile source for damage actions against *state* (not federal) officials. It provides:

> Every person who, under color of any [state law, regulation, or custom] subjects . . . any . . . person . . . to the deprivation of any rights, privileges, or immunities secured by the Constitution and laws, shall be liable . . . in an action at law . . . or other proper proceeding for redress.

In Monroe v. Pape, 365 U.S. 167 (1961), the Supreme Court held that plaintiffs could recover damages under the act from police who broke into their homes without a warrant, used physical violence, and illegally detained them in violation of the fourteenth amendment as well as state law. The Court rejected the defense argument that "under color of" state law applies only to action that is authorized by and not forbidden by state law. Thus, all actions of state officials that violate the federal Constitution and harm the plaintiff provide a basis for a damage remedy (as well as for specific relief). A host of civil rights damage actions against state and local officials soon followed.

In Maine v. Thiboutot, 448 U.S. 1 (1980), the Supreme Court, noting the phrase "Constitution and *laws*" in §1983, held that it encompasses virtually all federal laws. Thus, the section encompasses a claim that state officials deprived the plaintiffs of rights granted them under the federal Social Security Act. Justice Powell, dissenting, asked whether the Court seriously meant to apply §1983 to the "literally hundreds of cooperative regulatory and social welfare enactments," covering such diverse subjects as "migrant labor, noxious weeds, historic preservation, wildlife conservation . . . and strip mining." He added that "federal grants and subsidies administered by state and local governments now are available" in such areas as unemployment, food subsidies, welfare, education, transportation, public works, and law enforcement. Are all beneficiaries of such programs potential §1983 plaintiffs who can sue state officials for asserted deprivations?

The Court drew back from the broadest possible implications of *Thiboutot* in Pennhurst State School v. Halderman, 451 U.S. 1 (1981), and Middlesex City Sewerage Auth. v. Sea Clammers, 453 U.S. 1 (1981). In the first of these cases the Court examined a federal "bill of rights" for the mentally retarded; it asked whether Congress intended this federal statute to be privately enforceable and concluded that it did not. In the second case, the Court examined a federal environmental statute that included its own set of administrative enforcement mechanisms; it concluded that the existence of this comprehensive enforcement scheme within the statute showed that Congress did not intend to have §1983 apply and authorized parallel private remedies. When exactly does a comprehensive enforcement scheme preempt the §1983 remedy? For an early discussion, see Sunstein, Section 1983 and the Private Enforcement of Federal Law, 49 U. Ch. L. Rev. 394 (1982). The Supreme Court offered a general framework in Blessing v. Freestone, 520 U.S. 329 (1997). A number of cases explore the question whether a federal statutory program is consistent with an action under §1983; the tendency is to find preemption. See, e.g., Blessing v. Freestone, 520 U.S. 329 (1997); Suter v. Artist M, 503 U.S. 347 (1992); Golden State Transit Corp. v. Los Angeles, 493 U.S. 103 (1989); Smith v. Robinson, 486 U.S. 992 (1984). For lower court decisions, see 31 Foster

Children v. Bush, 329 F.3d 1255 (11th Cir. 2003); Westside Mothers v. Haveman, 289 F.3d 852 (6th Cir. 2002).

If §1983 applies only to those federal statutes that lack a comprehensive enforcement scheme but that Congress wants to be privately enforceable (for example, statutes that create a private right of action themselves), one might ask, What does §1983 add to the statute's own "private right of action"? The first answer is the simplest: Some statutes do not create private rights of action, and here §1983 can be crucial. But §1983 also adds a damage remedy, though it is sometimes difficult to prove the existence of damages that flow from deprivation, for example, of procedural rights. See Carey v. Piphus, 435 U.S. 237 (1978). It also adds the possibility of an award of attorneys' fees. The Civil Rights Attorney's Fees Award Act of 1976, 42 U.S.C. §1988, specifically allows a "court in its discretion [to] allow the prevailing party, other than the United States, a reasonable attorney's fee" in §1983 actions. Can a plaintiff, claiming that a state official has violated a federal statute, then simply add the words "in violation of 42 U.S.C. §1983," to an action brought under the statute itself and thereby obtain attorneys' fees? The question of whether, or when, one may do so has, as yet, no authoritative answer.

b. *Bivens* Actions

The Civil Rights Act §1983 applies only to *state* officials (those who act "under color of state law, regulation or custom"). In Bivens v. Six Unknown Federal Narcotics Agents, 403 U.S. 388 (1971), the Supreme Court held that *federal* officials could be sued for damages flowing from their violation of the plaintiff's fourth amendment rights. The Court implied a cause of action from the Constitution itself. A cause of action based on the Constitution could be found (despite the absence of a statute granting it) if plaintiffs could show (a) a constitutionally protected right, (b) an invasion of that right, and (c) that the requested relief (damages) is appropriate. The Court extended *Bivens* in Davis v. Passman, 442 U.S. 228 (1979), where it held that a former congressional staff employee could sue a congressman for gender discrimination in employment. It implied a cause of action directly from the due process clause of the fifth amendment, interpreted to forbid gender discrimination by a federal official. The Court held a damage remedy "appropriate" because (a) damage relief for invasion of personal interests is traditional, (b) a standard is "judicially manageable," (c) litigation under title VII of the Civil Rights Act (prohibiting employer gender discrimination but *excepting* Congress) has given the courts experience, (d) equitable relief would not necessarily prove sufficient, (e) there is "no *explicit* Congressional declaration" forbidding the remedy, and (f) the courts could deal with any additional problems through other legal devices. The Court's decision may mean that a victim of gender discrimination has at least as good, if not a better, remedy suing under the fifth amendment if his or her employer is a member of Congress (to whom title VII does not apply) as a victim has in the case of an employer who is covered by title VII.

In Carlson v. Green, 446 U.S. 14 (1980), the Court found a direct cause of action under the eighth amendment for prison conditions amounting to cruel and unusual punishment. The Court suggested that there is a private right of action against federal officials for *any* constitutional violation — implied from the Constitution itself — unless (a) there are "special factors counseling hesitation" or (b) "an alternative remedy" is provided by Congress and is "explicitly declared to be a substitute for recovery directly under the Constitution and viewed as equally effective." The fact that Congress had provided an alternative remedy for the type of harm at issue in *Carlson* — by amending the FTCA to cover that harm — was not sufficient, for Congress had not "explicitly declared" it to be a "substitute."

More recent cases have, however, limited *Bivens* actions, generally in cases involving alternative remedies created by law. There is in fact a general trend in this direction. In Bush v. Lucas, 462 U.S. 367 (1983), the Court held that a private action was displaced by an alternative statutory remedy. "Federal civil servants are now protected by an elaborate, comprehensive scheme that encompasses substantive provisions forbidding arbitrary action. . . ." In the same vein, see Chappell v. Wallace, 462 U.S. 296 (1983); Sinclair v. Hawke, 314 F.3d 934 (8th Cir. 2003); Schweicker v. Chillicy, 487 U.S. 412 (1988); Moore v. Glickman, 113 F.3d 98 (9th Cir. 1997); Spanola v. Mathis, 859 F.2d 223 (D.C. Cir. 1988). Correctional Services Corp. v. Malesko, 122 S. Ct. 515 (2001), declined to find a private right of action against corporations contracting to perform traditional governmental functions; the Court emphasized its general unwillingness to extend *Bivens*.

Assar v. Crescent Counties Found. for Med. Care, 13 F.3d 215 (7th Cir. 1993), concluded that Congress's provision of a comprehensive scheme for peer review of decisions affecting participation in the Medicare program precludes a court from providing a *Bivens* remedy for an erroneous decision. See also Bricker v. Rockwell Intl. Corp., 22 F.3d 871 (9th Cir. 1994) (*Bivens* remedy unavailable because implicitly precluded by comprehensive statutory remedial regime, even though remedial regime not available to the petitioner because of a congressional decision to make it prospective only). But see Krueger v. Lyng, 927 F.2d 1050 (8th Cir. 1991) (*Bivens* action not precluded by administratively created remedy of appeal to supervisor of those that fired plaintiff).

The courts have made the *Bivens*-type action an effective way of bringing against federal officials the same type of constitutionally based damage action that §1983 allows against state officials. Not surprisingly the courts have tended to apply §1983-type damage rules to *Bivens*-type actions. See, e.g., Ellis v. Blum, 643 F.2d 68 (2d Cir. 1981); Bishop v. Tice, 622 F.2d 349, 357 (8th Cir. 1980); Halperin v. Kissinger, 606 F.2d 1192, 1207-1208 (D.C. Cir. 1979). And the analysis of whether a comprehensive enforcement scheme preempts the *Bivens* action overlaps with the question whether a comprehensive enforcement scheme preempts a §1983 claim. Can you see any basis for distinguishing between the two kinds of analysis?

c. Official Immunity

Federal courts have granted government employees immunity in §1983 and *Bivens* actions for damages, just as they have in traditional tort actions. Those with absolute immunity include state judges, Stump v. Sparkman, 435 U.S. 349 (1978); prosecutors, Imbler v. Pachtman, 424 U.S. 409 (1976); federal, state, and regional legislators, Lake Country Estates v. Tahoe Regional Planning Agency, 440 U.S. 391 (1979); and the president, Nixon v. Fitzgerald, 457 U.S. 731 (1982). Were we to stop here, it might appear that the scope of immunity in "constitutional tort" actions (§1983 or *Bivens*) was roughly the same as in classical tort actions, see Barr v. Matteo, supra. But this is not the case.

In Scheuer v. Rhodes, 416 U.S. 232 (1974), the Court considered whether a governor and other high state executive officials were immune from a §1983 damage action claiming a violation of constitutionally protected rights. Plaintiffs, who were relations of students killed by National Guard officers in an anti-Vietnam War demonstration at Kent State College, claimed that defendants had failed to properly supervise the guard, amounting to a violation of due process. The Court reasoned that the "official immunity" doctrine was essentially a matter of statutory construction. The doctrine's rationale rested on "(1) the injustice, particularly in the absence of bad faith, of subjecting to liability an officer who is required, by the legal obligation of his position, to exercise discretion; (2) the danger that the threat of such liability would deter his willingness to execute his office with the decisiveness and the judgment required by the public good." The Court concluded that these state officers were not entitled to absolute immunity in a §1983 action but to a "qualified immunity" of "varying scope, . . . the variation being dependent upon the scope of discretion and responsibilities of the office . . . and all the circumstances. . . ." 416 U.S. at 247-248. This qualified immunity covered actions taken in "good faith" and did not protect those who knew or should have known that their actions would deprive the plaintiff of constitutional rights. *Scheuer*, then, breaks radically with *Barr*. And in subsequent cases, the Court has tried to deal with its implications. In Butz v. Economou, 438 U.S. 478 (1978), the Court rejected the claim that the secretary of agriculture was absolutely immune from liability for damages in the context of a claim that the secretary had proceeded against the plaintiff because he had exercised his right to freedom of expression. The Court said that Barr v. Mateo did not "purport to depart from the general rule, which long prevailed, that a federal official may not ignore the limitations which the controlling law has placed on his powers." Thus, the Court held that "in a suit for damages arising from unconstitutional action, federal executive officials exercising discretion are entitled only to the qualified immunity specified in *Scheuer*, subject to those exceptional situations where it is demonstrated that absolute immunity is essential for the conduct of the public business."

In Nixon v. Fitzgerald, 457 U.S. 731 (1982), the Court held that the president enjoyed absolute immunity, even as to constitutional claims. In Harlow v. Fitzgerald, 457 U.S. 800 (1982), the Court held that the president's assistants enjoyed only a "qualified immunity." The Court defined "qualified immunity" as follows:

> Qualified or "good faith" immunity is an affirmative defense that must be pleaded by a defendant official. . . . Decisions of this Court have established that the "good faith" defense has both an "objective" and a "subjective" aspect. The objective element involves a presumptive knowledge of and respect for "basic, unquestioned constitutional rights." Wood v. Strickland, 420 U.S. 308, 322 (1975). The subjective component refers to "permissible intentions." Ibid. Characteristically the Court has defined these elements by identifying the circumstances in which qualified immunity would *not* be available. Referring both to the objective and subjective elements, we have held that qualified immunity would be defeated if an official *"knew or reasonably should have known* that the action he took within his sphere of official responsibility would violate the constitutional rights of the [plaintiff], or if he took the action *with the malicious intention* to cause a deprivation of constitutional rights or other injury. . . .

In FDIC v. Meyer, 510 U.S. 477 (1994), the Court held that a *Bivens* cause of action is not available directly against the Federal Savings and Loan Insurance Corp. (FSLIC), predecessor to FDIC, a federal agency. Meyer, who had been summarily terminated from his job at a thrift when the FSLIC took over the institution, sued the FSLIC official immediately responsible for his termination, Pattullo, for violations of his due process rights. Pattullo successfully asserted a qualified immunity defense. Meyer then sought to assert a *Bivens* constitutional tort claim in damages directly against the FSLIC. The Supreme Court refused to recognize such a right of action. It explained: "Meyer's real complaint is that Pattullo, like many *Bivens* defendants, invoked the protection of qualified immunity. But *Bivens* clearly contemplated that official immunity would be raised. . . . More importantly, Meyer's proposed 'solutions' — essentially the circumvention of qualified immunity — would mean the evisceration of the *Bivens* remedy, rather than its extension. It must be remembered that the purpose of *Bivens* is to deter the *officer*." This deterrent effect would be wholly undermined if *Bivens* actions could be brought directly against the federal agency in question, because plaintiffs would always sue the agency. Moreover, the Court should be especially reluctant to create a damages remedy against the federal government that could result in huge financial liabilities, implicating fiscal issues better left to Congress.

In Clinton v. Jones, 520 U.S. 681 (1997), the Court rejected the president's claim of immunity from suits brought on the basis of allegedly unlawful conduct by the president before he assumed office. The Court concluded that the district court could accommodate the president's schedule without barring the suit while the president remained in office.

Notes

1. Professor Schuck proposed abolition of all governmental immunities while granting complete immunity to all government officials. See P. Schuck, Suing Government (1983). The government would be liable for its officials' behavior on principles of respondeat superior and would not be allowed to assert any immunity defense. Schuck asserts that official liability creates a serious risk of overdeterrence. Officials may be liable if they exercise their authority, for example, to vigorously arrest suspected criminals or to assume government custody of children subject to suspected parental abuse. But no such liability will typically be imposed if they do nothing. Accordingly, damage liability creates asymmetrical incentives that lead to excessive caution. If government agencies bear the liability, they can (Schuck believes) better balance the costs and benefits of zeal as well as take appropriate disciplinary or other corrective action to deal with officials' transgressions. What do you think of this proposal? Reconsider the questions posed at the outset of this section concerning the appropriate use of ex ante hearing and judicial review and ex post damage remedies.

Cleavinger v. Saxner, 474 U.S. 193, 206 (1985), held that members of a prison disciplinary committee have only qualified, as opposed to absolute, immunity, noting that "the line between absolute immunity and qualified immunity is not an easy one to perceive and structure." Federal appellate courts have reached differing results in considering whether agency officials performing adjudicatory functions are entitled to absolute immunity. Compare Watts v. Burkhart, 978 F.2d 269 (6th Cir. 1992) (en banc) (members of state Board of Medical Examiners, sued for suspending or revoking physician's license, protected by absolute quasi-judicial immunity), with Young v. Selsky, 41 F.3d 47 (2d Cir. 1994) (officials deciding prisoners' appeals from disciplinary hearings entitled only to qualified immunity).

2. The Administrative Conference of the United States made the following recommendation. Recommendation 82-6, Dec. 16, 1982. What do you think of it?

RECOMMENDATION

Congress should enact legislation providing that the United States shall be substituted as the exclusive party defendant in all actions for damages for violations of rights secured by the Constitution of the United States committed by federal executive branch officers and employees while acting within the scope of their office or employment. The legislation should provide adequate procedures to ensure that, where a damage action for violation of such rights is brought against an executive branch officer or employee, such action should be deemed to have been brought against the United States upon certification by the Attorney General that the defendant officer or employee was acting within the scope of his office or employment at the time of the incident out of which the suit arose. The Attorney General's failure to make such certification should be judicially reviewable.

Such legislation should provide that, in actions alleging constitutional violations, the United States may assert as a defense any qualified immunity or good faith defense available to the executive branch officer or employee whose conduct gave rise to the claim, or his reasonable good faith belief in the lawfulness of his conduct. The United States should also be free to assert such other defenses as may be available, including the absolute immunity of those officers entitled to such immunity.

The agency that employed the offending official should be responsible for investigation and, where appropriate, for disciplining the official and implementing any other appropriate corrective measures. The Office of Personnel Management should assure, via guidance promulgated through the Federal Personnel Manual and other devices, that agencies are authorized to employ existing mechanisms to impose sanctions on officers and employees who have violated the constitutional rights of any person. Employees should be permitted to assert as a defense in any disciplinary proceeding their good faith in taking the action in question, as well as such other defenses as may be available.

Congressional legislation should preserve the opportunity for jury trial only with respect to claims that arose prior to the effective date of the legislation implementing this recommendation.

C. Reviewability

Even if plaintiff has a claim that a federal government action is unlawful, if a statute (such as 28 U.S.C. §1331) appears to grant jurisdiction, and even if there is no problem of sovereign immunity because only specific relief is sought, the courts may still decline to review the agency's action. How is that possible?

1. The Presumption of Reviewability: Early Law and the New Deal

The English courts often used the prerogative writs to review and to correct improper agency action, but American courts in the nineteenth century took a much narrower view of their power to correct erroneous administrative action. Consider this summary:

Prior to 1887 the fields of federal administration where review proceedings might have been desirable were few, — mainly customs and internal revenue, the regulation of immigration and navigation, and proprietary functions of the Government such as those relating to public lands, patents, postal service, and pensions and other claims. Congress had no considered policy of court review of administrative action and these fields, with few exceptions, were open only to whatever relief common law and equitable remedies afforded.

Among the remedies at law was an action for damages, for money had and received, or for recovery of property. Practically these were of little importance outside of revenue matters. Moreover, review of administrative orders by certiorari was apparently never attempted during this period. In 1913 when the attempt was first made certiorari was held by the Supreme Court to be unavailable for such purposes. [Degge v. Hitchcock, 229 U.S. 162 (1913).]

The Judiciary Act of 1789 gave the federal courts authority to issue "writs not specially provided for by statute, which may be necessary for the exercise of their respective jurisdictions and agreeable to the principles and usages of law." Among such writs was that of mandamus. This authority, however, was inapplicable to review of administrative orders, for it was held to permit use of the writs only as an auxiliary to some suit over which the court had present or prospective jurisdiction original or appellate. The jurisdiction must already exist and could not be conferred by the writ.

Mandamus was, however, available in the courts of the District of Columbia, within whose jurisdiction could be found most of the principal officers of the Government. Also the equitable remedy of injunction was available in all the federal courts including those of the District of Columbia. In most situations these two remedies afforded the only means for judicial consideration of administrative orders but their value was slight. Mandamus would not lie to review an exercise of judgment or discretion by an administrative officer or agency nor to perform a function similar to that of a writ of error. Thus it would not lie to correct errors made by administrative officers or agencies in construing the law, much less to correct discretionary action of the type now dealt with as arbitrary or as being without substantial evidence to support it. The desire to avoid the possibility of conflict between the courts and executive officers ran strong.

When the remedy of injunction was first employed to review administrative action the Supreme Court held that the doctrine of non-reviewability of administrative discretion was as applicable to the writ of injunction as to the writ of mandamus. [Litchfield v. Richards, 5 U.S. (9 Wall.) 575 (1870).]

Lee, The Origins of Judicial Control of Federal Executive Action, 36 Geo. L.J. 287, 295-296 (1948).

An example of the narrow approach toward reviewability is Decatur v. Paulding, 39 U.S. (14 Pet.) 497 (1840). In that case, the widow of the famous naval hero sought a writ of mandamus to compel the secretary of the navy to pay her two pensions — one under a general pension law and the other under a special act of Congress passed for her alone. The Court held the secretary's decision was "discretionary," not "ministerial," because he had to decide (1) whether to reverse a predecessor's decision on the subject, (2) how halfpay should be calculated, and (3) whether there was enough money in the pension fund to satisfy all claims. The Court's attitude is well expressed in its statement that the "interference of the courts with the performance of the ordinary duties of the executive departments of the government, would be productive of nothing but mischief." 14 Pet. at 516.

But the availability of relief was not always as narrow as the Decatur excerpt might suggest. Injunctive relief was often available to control administrative action in excess of "jurisdiction," and the concept of "jurisdiction" was often flexible. The following two cases illustrate an expansive and a restrictive attitude toward review.

American School of Magnetic Healing v. McAnnulty

187 U.S. 94 (1902)

Mr. Justice PECKHAM . . . delivered the opinion of the court.

[Plaintiff ran a mail-order business based in Nevada, Missouri. It taught how to use "the faculty of the brain and mind" to cure sickness. It received about 3000 letters per day containing payments that averaged $1600 per day. The postmaster general, after a hearing, ordered the post office not to deliver plaintiff's mail, but to return it (and all checks) to senders and to mark it "fraudulent" under a statute giving the postmaster general authority to do this "upon evidence satisfactory to him that any person is engaged in any fraudulent . . . scheme for the distribution of money." 28 Stat. 963, 964.]

[T]he questions arising in the case will be limited, (1) to the inquiry as to whether the action of the Postmaster General under the circumstances set forth in the complainants' bill is justified by the statutes; and (2) if not, whether the complainants have any remedy in the courts.

First. As the case arises on demurrer, [i]t is, therefore, admitted that the business of the complainants is founded "almost exclusively on the physical and practical proposition that the mind of the human race is largely responsible for its ills, . . . and that the human race does possess the innate power, through proper exercise of the faculty of the brain and mind, to largely control and remedy the ills that humanity is heir to." . . .

There can be no doubt that the influence of the mind upon the physical condition of the body is very powerful. . . . How far these claims are borne out by actual experience may be a matter of opinion. Just exactly to what extent the mental condition affects the body, no one can accurately and definitely say. . . .

[T]he claim of complainants . . . cannot be proved as a fact to be a fraud . . . nor can it properly be said that those who assume to heal bodily ills or infirmities by a resort to this method of cure are guilty of obtaining money under false pretenses, such as are intended in the statutes, which evidently do not assume to deal with mere matters of opinion upon subjects which are not capable of proof as to their falsity.

Unless . . . the question may be reduced to one of fact as distinguished from mere opinion, we think these statutes cannot be invoked for the purpose of stopping the delivery of mail matter. . . .

That the complainants had a hearing before the Postmaster General . . . cannot affect the case, [for we proceed on demurrer on the basis of undisputed facts]. From these admitted facts it is obvious that complainants in conducting their business, so far as this record shows, do not violate the laws of Congress. The statutes do not as matter of law cover the facts herein.

Second. Conceding . . . the conclusive character of the determination by the Postmaster General of any material and relevant question still of fact . . . the question remains as to the power of the court to grant relief where the Postmaster General . . . has ordered the detention of mail matter when the statutes have not granted him power so to order. Has Congress entrusted the administration of these statutes wholly to the discretion of the Postmaster General, [so] that his determination is conclusive . . . ?

That the conduct of the Post Office is a part of the administrative department of the government is entirely true, but that does not necessarily and always oust the courts of jurisdiction to grant relief to a party aggrieved by any action . . . of that department which is unauthorized by statute. [I]n case an official violates the law . . . the courts generally have jurisdiction to grant relief. . . .

The facts, which are here admitted of record, show that the case is not one which by any construction of those facts is covered or provided for by the statutes under which the Postmaster General has assumed to act, and his determination that those admitted facts do authorize his action is a clear mistake of law, . . . and the courts, therefore, must have power in a proper proceeding to grant relief. Otherwise, the individual is left to the absolutely uncontrolled and arbitrary action of a public and administrative officer, whose action is unauthorized by any law and is in violation of the rights of the individual. Where the action of such an officer is thus unauthorized he thereby violates the property rights of the person whose letters are withheld.

In our view of these statutes the complainants had the legal right under the general acts of Congress relating to the mails to have their letters delivered at the post office as directed. They had violated no law which Congress passed, and their letters contained checks, drafts, money orders and money itself, all of which were their property as soon as they were deposited in the various post offices for transmission by mail. They allege, and it is not difficult to see that the allegation is true, that, if such action be persisted in, these complainants will be entirely cut off from all mail facilities, and their business will necessarily be greatly injured if not wholly destroyed, such business being, so far as the laws of Congress are concerned, legitimate and lawful. In other words, irreparable injury will be done to these complainants by the mistaken act of the Postmaster General in directing the defendant to retain and refuse to deliver letters addressed to them. The Postmaster General's order being the result of a mistaken view of the law could not operate as a defence to this action on the part of the defendant, though it might justify his obedience thereto until some action of the court. In such a case, as the one before us, there is no adequate remedy at law, the injunction to prohibit the further withholding of the mail from complainants being the only remedy at all adequate to the full relief to which the complainants are entitled. . . .

Judgment reversed.

Switchmen's Union v. National Mediation Board

320 U.S. 297 (1943)

Mr. Justice DOUGLAS delivered the opinion of the Court.

This is an action by the petitioners, the Switchmen's Union of North America and some of its members against the National Mediation Board, its members, the Brotherhood of Railroad Trainmen, and the New York Central Railroad Company and the Michigan Central Railroad Company. [The Switchmen and the Brotherhood had disagreed about how yardmen should be classified for purposes of voting in a union election.]

. . . The Brotherhood sought to be the representatives for all the yardmen of the rail lines operated by the New York Central system. The Switchmen contended that yardmen of certain designated parts of the system should be permitted to vote for separate representatives instead of being compelled to take part in a system-wide election.

[T]he board was asked to decide the dispute under §2, Ninth of the Railway Labor Act. The Board designated all yardmen of the carriers as participants in the election. The election was held and the Brotherhood was chosen as the representative. Upon the certification of the result to the carriers, petitioners sought to have the determination by the board cancelled. This suit for cancellation was brought in the district court. That court upheld the decision of the Board. . . . The Circuit Court of Appeals affirmed by a divided vote. The case is here on a petition for a writ of certiorari. . . .

We do not reach the merits of the controversy. For we are of the opinion that the District Court did not have the power to review the action of the National Mediation Board in issuing the certificate.

. . . Generalizations as to when judicial review of administrative action may not be obtained are of course hazardous. Where Congress has not expressly authorized judicial review, the type of problem involved and the history of the statute in question become highly relevant in determining whether judicial review may be nonetheless supplied. [T]he emergence of railway labor problems from the field of conciliation and mediation into that of legally enforceable rights has been quite recent. Until the 1926 Act the legal sanctions of the various acts had been few. The emphas[es] of the legislation were publicity and public opinion. Since 1926 there has been an increasing number of legally enforceable commands incorporated into the Act. And Congress has utilized administrative machinery more freely in the settlement of disputes. But large areas of the first still remain in the realm of conciliation, mediation, and arbitration. On only a few phases of this controversial subject has Congress utilized administrative or judicial machinery and invoked the compulsions of the law. . . .

In that connection the history of §2, Ninth is highly relevant. It was introduced into the Act in 1934 as a device to strengthen and make more effective the processes of collective bargaining. . . . It was aimed not only at company unions which had long plagued labor relations but also at numerous jurisdictional disputes between unions. Commissioner Eastman, draftsman of the 1934 amendments, explained the bill at the Congressional hearings. He stated that whether one organization or another was the proper representative of a particular group of employees was "one of the most controversial questions in connection with labor organization matters." . . . He stated that it was very important "to provide a neutral tribunal which can make the decision and get the matter settled." But the problem was deemed to be so "highly controversial" that it was thought that the prestige of the Mediation Board might be adversely affected by the rulings which it would have to make in these jurisdictional disputes. . . . Accordingly §2, Ninth was drafted so as to give the Mediation Board the power to "appoint a committee of three neutral persons who after hearing shall within ten days designate the employees who may participate in the election." That was added so that the Board's "own usefulness of settling disputes that might arise thereafter might not be impaired." . . . Where Congress took such great pains to protect the Mediation Board in its handling of an explosive problem, we cannot help but believe that if Congress had desired to implicate the federal judiciary and to place on the federal courts the burden of having the final say on any aspect of the problem, it would have made its desire plain.

. . . While the Mediation Board is given specified powers in the conduct of elections, there is no requirement as to hearings. And there is no express grant of subpoena power. The Mediation Board makes no "order." And its only ultimate finding of fact is the certificate. . . . The function of the Board under §2, Ninth is more the function of a referee. To this decision of the referee Congress has added a command enforcible by judicial decree. But the "command" is that "of the statute, not of the Board."

[T]he intent seems plain — the dispute was to reach its last terminal point when the administrative finding was made. There was to be no dragging out of the controversy into other tribunals of law.

That conclusion is reinforced by the highly selective manner in which Congress has provided for judicial review of administrative orders or determinations under the Act. There is no general provision for such review. But Congress has expressly provided for it in two instances. Thus Congress gave the National Railroad Adjustment Board jurisdiction over disputes growing out of "grievances or out of the interpretation or application of agreements concerning rates of pay, rules, or working conditions." §3, First(i). The various divisions of the Adjustment Board have authority to make awards. §3, First(k)-(o). And suits based on those awards may be brought in the federal district courts. §3, First(p). In such suits "the findings and order of the division of the Adjustment Board shall be prima facie evidence of the facts therein stated." The other instance in the Act where Congress provided for judicial review is under §9 [§9 allows the award of an arbitration panel to be "impeached" in court under certain circumstances]. . . . When Congress in §3 and in §9 provided for judicial review of two types of orders or awards and in §2 of the same Act omitted any such provision as respects a third type, it drew a plain line of distinction. And the inference is strong from the history of the Act that that distinction was not inadvertent. The language of the Act read in light of that history supports the view that Congress gave administrative action under §2, Ninth a finality which it denied administrative action under the other sections of the Act.

. . . What is open when a court of equity is asked for its affirmative help by granting a decree for the enforcement of a certificate of the Mediation Board under §2, Ninth raises questions not now before us. . . .

Reversed.

[Justices Reed, Roberts, and Jackson dissented. They pointed out that the board had accepted the Brotherhood's position because it believed that the statute gave it "no discretion to split a single carrier" when determining voting eligibility. The Switchmen claimed that the statute did give the board discretion. Thus, the Switchmen sought to raise on review a pure question of law. "Nothing to which our attention has been called appears in the legislative history indicating a determination of Congress to exclude the courts from their customary power to interpret the laws of the nation in cases or controversies arising from administrative violations of statutory standards." 320 U.S. at 318.]

Switchmen's reflects the New Deal's enthusiasm for administrative autonomy, and the New Deal's suspicion about judicial control of bureaucracies. (Recall that a large part of the New Deal involved an attack on judge-made law in favor of agency-made law — an attack that was accompanied by a belief in agency immunity from judicial control.) Moreover, it has unmistakable echoes in current law, especially with post-1980s skepticism about judicial review of administrative action. Consider *Community Nutrition Institute.* The law of reviewability will inevitably reflect diverse judgments about whether judicial control of administrative action is desirable (as a way of promoting fairness and legality) or undesirable (as a way of producing delay and allowing judicial displacement of political prerogatives). Despite a discernible pro-*Switchmen's* trend, the attitude expressed in *McAnnulty* more often prevails today. Since the 1960s, courts have recognized a "presumption" of reviewability, though since the early 1990s the presumption has been weakened a bit. For an interesting modern debate over the meaning and reach of *Switchmen's*, see Railway Labor Executives' Association v. National Mediation Board, 29 F.3d 655 (D.C. Cir. 1994), where the majority of a divided court held reviewable any Board action that amounted to a "gross violation" of its jurisdictional power.

2. The Modern Presumption — and Its Sources

In the important case of Abbott Laboratories v. Gardner, 387 U.S. 136, 140-141 (1967), which marks the recent era of increased access to judicial review, the Supreme Court wrote:

> [A] survey of our cases shows that judicial review of a final agency action by an aggrieved person will not be cut off unless there is a persuasive reason to believe that such was the purpose of Congress. [T]he Administrative Procedure Act . . . embodies the basic presumption of judicial review to one "suffering legal wrong because of agency action, or adversely affected or aggrieved by agency action within the meaning of a relevant statute," 5 U.S.C. §702, so long as no statute precludes such relief or the action is not one committed by law to agency discretion, 5 U.S.C. §701(a). The Administrative Procedure Act provides specifically not only for review of "[a]gency action made reviewable by statute" but also for review of "final agency action for which there is no other adequate remedy in a court," 5 U.S.C. §704. The legislative material elucidating that seminal act manifests a congressional intention that it cover a broad spectrum of administrative actions, and this Court has echoed that theme by noting that the Administrative Procedure Act's "generous review provisions" must be given a "hospitable" interpretation. . . .

Abbott held that the failure in the Food, Drug and Cosmetic Act to provide for judicial review of the particular type of regulations issued by FDA did not implicitly preclude review under 28 U.S.C. §1331, even though the act did specifically provide for review of other types of FDA regulations. *Abbott* thus rejects the *Switchmen's* logic that selective review provisions in an organic statute impliedly preclude review under general jurisdictional statutes. But see *Community Nutrition Institute*, below, which accepts a version of the logic in *Switchmen's*. In any case, the presumption of review has proved crucial in many cases. See Gutierrez de Martinez v. Lamagno, 515 U.S. 417 (1995); Cherokee Nation v. Babbitt, 117 F.3d 1489 (D.C. Cir. 1997) (relying on presumption to review Department of Interior decision recognizing a group of Native Americans as a "tribe"); Ball, Ball & Brosamer, Inc. v. Reich, 24 F.3d 1447 (D.C. Cir. 1994).

One might well ask about the *source* of the presumption of review. The Court attributes the presumption to the APA. This is not unreasonable; recall that the APA was a compromise between New Deal enthusiasts hostile to judicial control of administrative action and skeptics about agencies who saw judicial control as an indispensable safeguard of rule of law values. In the resulting compromise, a measure of judicial control of administrative action was a prime goal. But could the Court's reasoning be criticized on the ground that there is no presumption of review in the text of the APA itself, but only in the legislative history? Recall the view, asserted vigorously by Justice Scalia, that legislative history is an unreliable guide to statutory meaning.

Could the presumption of review be better based on constitutional considerations? Perhaps the idea is that the exercise of discretion by regulatory agencies is constitutionally troublesome, and that judicial review is necessary to ensure that what might otherwise be open-ended discretion is subject to at least some form of external control. On this view, the presumption of review owes its source to considerations of accountability and legislative supremacy, ideas embodied in article I, and also to rule-of-law considerations, embodied in the due process clause. The presumption of review might then be regarded as a form of constitutionally inspired federal common law, or constitutionally inspired statutory interpretation.

If the APA is unclear, consider whether a presumption of judicial review might be justified not on strictly legal grounds but as an important way of minimizing the costs of error and the costs of decision. Judicial review might be thought important to correct administrative mistakes after the fact, and to deter administrative mistakes before the fact. Thus, there may be more mistakes (of law, policy, fact) if judicial review is unavailable. On the other hand, the existence of judicial review increases the costs of decision, and if courts are likely to make mistakes in certain areas (involving law, policy, or fact), judicial review may increase rather than decrease the costs of errors. Debates over the strength of the presumption of review can therefore be seen as debates over whether judicial involvement is (a) an indispensable safeguard against administrative illegality or arbitrariness, or instead (b) a way of producing delay and allowing the displacement of administrative judgment by judicial judgment.

In particular areas, how might progress be made in resolving a dispute of this kind? Is the dispute mostly an empirical one? Consider this question as you explore the materials to follow.

3. Two Key Exceptions, in Brief

As *Abbott Laboratories* notes, the general rule — reviewability — has two exemptions that are codified in the APA: The APA's review provisions do *not* apply "to the extent that (1) statutes preclude judicial review, or (2) agency action is committed to agency discretion by law." 5 U.S.C. §701.

In asking whether these provisions foreclose judicial review, it is important to keep the following point in mind: Suppose that you are seeking review of an order or an action or an inaction of an agency that you allege is unlawful. Whether you can obtain review depends very much on *what type of claim* you are making. What is the *basis* of your allegation of unlawfulness? That is to say, are you claiming that the agency (1) made an erroneous finding of fact; (2) wrongly applied or violated its own rules and regulations; (3) wrongly applied the statute to a particular set of facts; (4) abused its discretion; (5) wrongly interpreted the statute itself; (6) acted unconstitutionally? The *sort* of claim you are making will have much to do with whether the court reviews your case. Thus, one claim may be reviewable, and another not, under the same basic statute. Court review of an action does not exist "in the air"; review consists of passing on the merits of a specific claim that relates to an agency's action.

4. Preclusion by Statute

APA §701(a)(1) says that the APA's judicial review provisions do not apply "to the extent that . . . statutes preclude review. . . ." As this language suggests, judicial review of the legality of government action *may be made unavailable* because some statute other than the APA (normally the organic statute creating the agency or the administrative program in question) provides that review is not to be had. The statutory preclusion of review might be *explicit* or *implicit*.

As we have seen, courts start with a "presumption of reviewability," which means that they will interpret the asserted preclusive effect of such statutes narrowly. Indeed, the Court in *Abbott Laboratories* said that "only upon a showing of 'clear and convincing evidence' of a contrary legislative intent should the courts restrict access to judicial review." Also, courts frequently interpret language that, on its face, seems explicitly to preclude review not to do so. Implicit preclusion is rare. Legislative silence about the availability of review is normally not construed to show an intent to preclude review.[10] More than occasionally, however, courts have read a statute to preclude review though it says nothing specifically about the matter. Consider the following case.

Block v. Community Nutrition Institute

467 U.S. 340 (1984)

Justice O'CONNOR delivered the opinion of the Court.

[Under the Agricultural Marketing Agreement Act of 1937, the Secretary of Agriculture sets the minimum prices milk handlers (those who process dairy products) must pay to producers (dairy farmers) for their milk. Milk processed for drinking is highest priced; milk used to produce butter, cheese, or milk powder is in a lower class.

Consumers and a nonprofit organization promoting better nutrition for lower income families challenged the Secretary's decision that the higher price applied to reconstituted milk (milk made by adding water to milk powder) not used to manufacture butter or cheese. They argued that this made reconstituted milk uneconomical for handlers to process, and thus deprived consumers of a source of less expensive milk. A milk handler also joined the suit.]

. . . Whether and to what extent a particular statute precludes judicial review is determined not only from its express language, but also from the structure of the statutory scheme, its objectives, its legislative history, and the nature of the administrative action involved. . . .

It is clear that Congress did not intend to strip the judiciary of all authority to review the Secretary's milk market orders. The Act's predecessor, the Agricultural Adjustment Act of 1933, contained no provision relating to administrative or judicial review. In 1935, however, Congress added a mechanism by which dairy handlers could obtain review of the Secretary's market orders. . . . Section 608c(15) requires handlers first to exhaust the administrative remedies made available by the Secretary. . . . These provisions for handler-initiated review make evident Congress' desire that *some* persons be able to obtain judicial review of the Secretary's market orders.

The remainder of the statutory scheme, however, makes equally clear Congress' intention to limit the classes entitled to participate in the development of market orders.

---

10. See, e.g., San Juan Legal Services, Inc. v. Legal Services Corp., 655 F.2d 434, 438 (1st Cir. 1981) ("Statutory silence . . . does not indicate a legislative intent to preclude judicial review"); Kingsbrook Jewish Medical Center v. Richardson, 486 F.2d 663 (2d Cir. 1973). See generally, Note, Reviewability of Administrative Action: The Elusive Search for a Pragmatic Standard, 1974 Duke L.J. 382, 383-388.

The Act contemplates a cooperative venture among the Secretary, handlers, and producers the principal purposes of which are to raise the price of agricultural products and to establish an orderly system for marketing them. Handlers and producers — but not consumers — are entitled to participate in the adoption and retention of market orders. The Act provides for agreements among the Secretary, producers, and handlers[;] for hearings among them[;] and for votes by producers and handlers. Nowhere in the Act, however, is there an express provision for participation by consumers in any proceeding. In a complex scheme of this type, the omission of such a provision is sufficient reason to believe that Congress intended to foreclose consumer participation in the regulatory process. See Switchmen v. National Mediation Board.

To be sure, the general purpose sections of the Act allude to general consumer interests. But the preclusion issue does not only turn on whether the interests of a particular class like consumers are implicated. Rather, the preclusion issue turns ultimately on whether Congress intended for that class to be relied upon to challenge agency disregard of the law. The structure of this Act indicates that Congress intended only producers and handlers, and not consumers, to ensure that the statutory objectives would be realized.

Respondents would have us believe that, while Congress unequivocally directed handlers first to complain to the Secretary that the prices set by milk market orders are too high, it was nevertheless the legislative judgment that the same challenge, if advanced by consumers, does not require initial administrative scrutiny. There is no basis for attributing to Congress the intent to draw such a distinction. The regulation of agricultural products is a complex, technical undertaking. Congress channelled disputes concerning marketing orders to the Secretary in the first instance because it believed that only he has the expertise necessary to illuminate and resolve questions about them. Had Congress intended to allow consumers to attack provisions of marketing orders, it surely would have required them to pursue the administrative remedies provided in §608c(15)(A) as well. The restriction of the administrative remedy to handlers strongly suggests that Congress intended a similar restriction of judicial review of market orders.

Allowing consumers to sue the Secretary would severely disrupt this complex and delicate administrative scheme. It would provide handlers with a convenient device for evading the statutory requirement that they first exhaust their administrative remedies. A handler may also be a consumer and, as such, could sue in that capacity. Alternatively, a handler would need only to find a consumer who is willing to join in or initiate an action in the district court. The consumer or consumer-handler could then raise precisely the same exceptions that the handler must have raised administratively. . . . For these reasons, we think it clear that Congress intended that judicial review of market orders issued under the Act ordinarily be confined to suits brought by handlers in accordance with 7 U.S.C. §608c(15).

The Court of Appeals viewed the preclusion issue from a somewhat different perspective. First, it recited the presumption in favor of judicial review of administrative action that this Court usually employs. It then noted that . . . no legislative history or statutory language directly and specifically supported the preclusion of consumer suits. In these circumstances, the Court of Appeals reasoned that the Act could not fairly be interpreted to overcome the presumption favoring judicial review and to leave consumers without a judicial remedy. We disagree. . . .

The presumption favoring judicial review of administrative action is just that — a presumption. This presumption, like all presumptions used in interpreting statutes, may be overcome by specific language or specific legislative history[, by] contemporaneous judicial construction barring review and the congressional acquiescence in it, or [by] the collective import of legislative and judicial history behind a particular statute. More important for purposes of this case, the presumption favoring judicial review of administrative action may be overcome by inferences of intent drawn from the statutory scheme as a whole. See, e.g., Switchmen v. National Mediation Board. . . .

In this case, the Court of Appeals did not take [a] balanced approach to statutory construction. . . . Rather, it recited this Court's oft-quoted statement that "only upon a showing of 'clear and convincing evidence' of a contrary legislative intent should the courts restrict access to judicial review." Abbott Laboratories v. Gardner. See also Dunlop v. Bachowski. According to the Court of Appeals, the "clear and convincing evidence" standard required it to find unambiguous proof, in the traditional evidentiary sense, of a congressional intent to preclude judicial review at the consumers' behest. Since direct statutory language or legislative history on this issue could not be found, the Court of Appeals found the presumption favoring judicial review to be controlling.

This Court has, however, never applied the "clear and convincing evidence" standard in the strict evidentiary sense the Court of Appeals thought necessary in this case. Rather, the Court has found the standard met, and the presumption favoring judicial review overcome, whenever the congressional intent to preclude judicial review is "fairly discernible in the statutory scheme." In the context of preclusion analysis, the "clear and convincing evidence" standard is not a rigid evidentiary test but a useful reminder to courts that, where substantial doubt about the congressional intent exists, the general presumption favoring judicial review of administrative action is controlling. That presumption does not control in cases such as this one, however, since the congressional intent to preclude judicial review is "fairly discernible" in the detail of the legislative scheme. . . .

[P]reclusion of consumer suits will not threaten realization of the fundamental objectives of the statute. Handlers have interests similar to those of consumers. Handlers, like consumers, are interested in obtaining reliable supplies of milk at the cheapest possible prices. Handlers can therefore be expected to challenge unlawful agency action and to ensure that the statute's objectives will not be frustrated. . . .

Justice STEVENS took no part in the decision of this case.

Bowen v. Michigan Academy of Family Physicians

476 U.S. 667 (1986)

Justice STEVENS delivered the opinion of the Court.

[An association of family physicians, and several individual family physicians, challenged a regulation of the secretary of Health and Human Services setting higher Medicare reimbursement levels for "board certified" family physicians than for identical services performed by non-board certified family physicians. They claimed this distinction violated both the Medicare Act and the fifth amendment.]

I

We begin with the strong presumption that Congress intends judicial review of administrative action. From the beginning "our cases [have established] that judicial review of a final agency action by an aggrieved person will not be cut off unless there is persuasive reason to believe that such was the purpose of Congress."

Abbott Laboratories v. Gardner. In Marbury v. Madison, a case itself involving review of executive action, Chief Justice Marshall insisted that "[t]he very essence of civil liberty certainly consists in the right of every individual to claim the protection of the laws." . . . Committees of both Houses of Congress have endorsed this view. In undertaking the comprehensive rethinking of the place of administrative agencies in a regime of separate and divided powers that culminated in the passage of the Administrative Procedure Act, the Senate Committee on the Judiciary remarked:

> Very rarely do statutes withhold judicial review. It has never been the policy of Congress to prevent the administration of its own statutes from being judicially confined to the scope of authority granted or to the objectives specified. Its policy could not be otherwise, for in such a case statutes would in effect be blank checks drawn to the credit of some administrative officer or board.

The Committee on the Judiciary of the House of Representatives agreed that Congress ordinarily intends that there be judicial review, and emphasized the clarity with which a contrary intent must be expressed:

> The statutes of Congress are not merely advisory when they relate to administrative agencies, any more than in other cases. To preclude judicial review under this bill a statute, if not specific in withholding such review, must upon its face give clear and convincing evidence of an intent to withhold it. The mere failure to provide specially by statute for judicial review is certainly no evidence of intent to withhold review. Taking up the language in the House Committee Report, [*Abbott*] reaffirmed . . . that "only upon a showing of 'clear and convincing evidence' of a contrary legislative intent should the courts restrict access to judicial review."

Subject to constitutional constraints, Congress can, of course, make exceptions to the historic practice whereby courts review agency action. The presumption of judicial review is, after all, a presumption, and "like all presumptions used in interpreting statutes, may be overcome . . ." Block v. Community Nutrition Institute. . . .

II

Section 1395ff[11] on its face is an explicit authorization of judicial review, not a bar. As a general matter, " '[t]he mere fact that some acts are made reviewable should not suffice to support an implication of exclusion as to others. The right to review is too important to be excluded on such slender and indeterminate evidence of legislative intent.' " Abbott Laboratories v. Gardner (quoting L. Jaffe, Judicial Control of Administrative Action 357 (1965)).

---

11. The pertinent text of §1395ff provides:

(a) *Entitlement to and amount of benefits.* The determination of whether an individual is entitled to benefits under part A or part B, and the determination of the amount of benefits under part A, shall be made by the Secretary in accordance with regulations prescribed by him.

(b) *Appeal by individuals.* Any individual dissatisfied with any determination under subsection (a) of this section as to

(A) whether he meets the [eligibility requirements for Part A], or

(B) whether he is eligible to enroll and has enrolled pursuant to the provisions of part B . . . or,

(C) the amount of the benefits under part A (including a determination where such amount is determined to be zero) shall be entitled to a hearing thereon by the Secretary . . . and to judicial review of the Secretary's final decision after such hearing. . . .

In the Medicare program, however, the situation is somewhat more complex. . . . Subject to an amount-in-controversy requirement, individuals aggrieved by delayed or insufficient payment with respect to benefits payable under Part B are afforded an "opportunity for a fair hearing by the *carrier*," §1395u (emphasis added); in comparison, and subject to a like amount-in-controversy requirement, a similarly aggrieved individual under Part A is entitled "to a hearing thereon by the *Secretary* . . . and to judicial review," §1395ff(b). "In the context of the statute's precisely drawn provisions," we held in United States v. Erika, Inc., 456 U.S. 201, 208 (1982), that the failure "to authorize further review for determinations of the amount of Part B awards . . . provides persuasive evidence that Congress deliberately intended to foreclose further review of such claims." Not limiting our consideration to the statutory text, we investigated the legislative history which "confirm[ed] this view," and disclosed a purpose to "'avoid overloading the courts'" with "'trivial matters,'" a consequence which would "'unduly ta[x]'" the federal court system with "'little real value'" to be derived by participants in the program (quoting 118 Cong. Rec. 33992 (1972) (remarks of Sen. Bennett)).

Respondents' federal-court challenge to the validity of the Secretary's regulation is not foreclosed by §1395ff as we construed that provision in *Erika*. The reticulated statutory scheme, which carefully details the forum and limits of review of "any determination . . . of . . . the amount of benefits under part A," §1395ff(b), and of the "amount of . . . payment" of benefits under Part B, §1395u, simply does not speak to challenges mounted against the *method* by which such amounts are to be determined rather than the *determinations* themselves. As the Secretary has made clear, "the legality, constitutional or otherwise, of any provision of the Act or regulations relevant to the Medicare Program" is not considered in a "fair hearing" held by a carrier to resolve a grievance related to a determination of the amount of a Part B award. As a result, an attack on the validity of a regulation is not the kind of administrative action that we described in *Erika* as an "amount determination" which decides "the amount of the Medicare payment to be made on a particular claim" and with respect to which the Act impliedly denies judicial review.

That Congress did not preclude review of the method by which Part B awards are computed (as opposed to the computation) is borne out by the very legislative history we found persuasive in *Erika*. Senator Bennett's introductory explanation to the amendment confirms that preclusion of judicial review of Part B awards — designed "to avoid overloading the courts with quite minor matters" — embraced only "decisions on a claim for payment for a given service." The Senator feared that "[i]f judicial review is made available where any claim is denied, as some court decisions have held, the resources of the Federal court system would be unduly taxed and little real value would be derived by the enrollees. The proposed amendment would merely clarify the original intent of the law and prevent the overloading of the courts with trivial matters because the intent is considered unclear." . . .

Careful analysis of the governing statutory provisions and their legislative history thus reveals that Congress intended to bar judicial review only of determinations of the amount of benefits to be awarded under Part B. Congress delegated this task to carriers who would finally determine such matters in conformity with the regulations and instructions of the Secretary. We conclude, therefore, that those matters which Congress did *not* leave to be determined in a "fair hearing" conducted by the carrier — including challenges to the validity of the Secretary's instructions and regulations — are not impliedly insulated from judicial review by [§1395ff].

III

In light of Congress' express provision for carrier review of millions of what it characterized as "trivial" claims, it is implausible to think it intended that there be no forum to adjudicate statutory and constitutional challenges to regulations promulgated by the Secretary. The Government nevertheless maintains that this is precisely what Congress intended to accomplish [when §1395ii of the Medicare Act incorporates by reference §405(h) of the Social Security Act. Section 405(h) provides:]

FINALITY OF SECRETARY'S DECISION

> The findings and decision of the Secretary after a hearing shall be binding upon all individuals who were parties to such hearing. No findings of fact or decision of the Secretary shall be reviewed by any person, tribunal, or governmental agency except as herein provided. No action against the United States, the Secretary, or any officer or employee thereof shall be brought under section 1331 or 1346 of title 28 to recover on any claim arising under this subchapter.

The Government contends that the third sentence of §405(h) by its terms prevents any resort to the grant of general federal-question jurisdiction contained in 28 U.S.C. §1331. . . . Respondents counter that . . . Congress' purpose was to make clear that whatever specific procedures it provided for judicial review of final action by the Secretary were exclusive, and could not be circumvented by resort to the general jurisdiction of the federal courts.

[W]e need not pass on the meaning of §405(h) in the abstract to resolve this case. Section 405(h) does not apply on its own terms to Part B of the Medicare program, but is instead incorporated *mutatis mutandis* by §1395ii. The legislative history of both the statute establishing the Medicare program and the 1972 amendments thereto provides specific evidence of Congress' intent to foreclose review only of "amount determinations" — i.e., those "quite minor matters" (remarks of Sen. Bennett), remitted finally and exclusively to adjudication by private insurance carriers in a "fair hearing." By the same token, matters which Congress did not delegate to private carriers, such as challenges to the validity of the Secretary's instructions and regulations, are cognizable in courts of law. In the face of this persuasive evidence of legislative intent, we will not indulge the Government's assumption that Congress contemplated review by carriers of "trivial" monetary claims, but intended no review at all of substantial statutory and constitutional challenges to the Secretary's administration of Part B of the Medicare program. This is an extreme position, and one we would be most reluctant to adopt without "a showing of 'clear and convincing evidence,'" Abbott Laboratories v. Gardner, to overcome the "strong presumption that Congress did not mean to prohibit all judicial review" of executive action, Dunlop v. Bachowski. We ordinarily presume that Congress intends the executive to obey its statutory commands and, accordingly, that it expects the courts to grant relief when an executive agency violates such a command. That presumption has not been surmounted here.[12]

The judgment of the Court of Appeals is affirmed.

Justice REHNQUIST took no part in the consideration or decision of this case.

---

12. Our disposition avoids the "serious constitutional question" that would arise if we construed §1395ii to deny a judicial forum for constitutional claims arising under Part B of the Medicare program. . . .

Notes and Questions

1. Should *Community Nutrition Institute* be understood as relaxing the presumption of review? Note that the principal canon of construction used in the case, *expressio unius est exclusio alterius* (to express one thing is to exclude another), can be a hazardous guide to interpretation. The failure to say anything about A, after listing B, C, D, and E, may mean a number of things: that Congress did not think about A; that Congress delegated to courts the decision about the status of A; that members of Congress could not resolve the status of A either way. In *Community Nutrition Institute*, the Court reads silence about consumers to suggest that Congress made an authoritative decision not to allow review at their behest. Why is this a reliable, or the most reliable, inference to draw? Does *Bowen* reject this aspect of *Community Nutrition Institute*? How would you reconcile the two cases?

Consider whether *Community Nutrition Institute* might not be most easily defended as a judicial recognition of the interest-group pressures that are likely to have produced the governing statute. Perhaps judicial review, at the behest of consumers, would have disrupted a legislative compromise. See Easterbrook, Foreword: The Court and the Economic System, 98 Harv. L. Rev. 4 (1984). But compare Macey, Promoting Public-Regarding Legislation Through Statutory Interpretation: An Interest-Group Model, 86 Colum. L. Rev. 223 (1986). Easterbrook's basic suggestion is that courts should be realistic about the interest-group pressures that underlie some statutes and thus interpret statutes realistically; Macey argues that courts should adopt principles of interpretation that will reduce the weight of influence pressure over legislation. How might such a disagreement be mediated?

In light of the foregoing questions — the significance (if any) of statutory silence, and the significance of interest-group theory — should a court find reviewability in a suit brought by milk *producers*, rather than consumers, to challenge marketing orders? Note that, in *Community Nutrition Institute*, the explict provision for review by handlers is in a sense silent about review by producers; perhaps the same *expressio unius* inference that blocked consumer-initiated review should be taken to block producer-initiated review. On the other hand, the opinion states: "Congress intended only producers and handlers, and not consumers, to ensure that the statutory objectives would be realized." *Community Nutrition Institute, supra*. Lower courts have split on the issue. Compare United Dairymen of Arizona v. Veneman, 279 F.3d 1160 (9th Cir. 2002) (statute implicitly precludes review at producers' behest), with Alto Dairy v. Veneman, 336 F.3d 560 (7th Cir. 2003) (no implicit preclusion of review by producers; milk producers were assumed to have a right of review because they were the principal intended beneficiaries of milk marketing orders). On an interest group approach, can any of the three groups — producers, handlers, consumers — be relied upon to indirectly represent the interests of any of the others?

2. *Community Nutrition Institute* is far from the only case finding implicit preclusion of judicial review. Indeed there are many such cases. See, e.g., United States v. Fausto, 484 U.S. 439 (1988), holding that the Civil Service Reform Act implicitly precludes judicial review of adverse personnel actions. The plaintiff sought to use the Tucker Act and the Back Pay Act to obtain monetary relief for an allegedly unlawful discharge. The Court responded that the Civil Service Reform Act had been designed to create a comprehensive system for administrative and judicial review of adverse personnel actions. Hence, the Tucker Act and the Back Pay Act had been preempted. The Court

agreed that there was a presumption in favor of review, but found the presumption overcome by indications of a preclusive intention in the Civil Service Reform Act. Justice Stevens dissented for four members of the Court. For other cases finding implicit preclusion of review, see Dew v. United States, 192 F.3d 366 (2d Cir. 1999) (no review of agency decisions under Uniformed Services Employment and Reemployment Rights Act); Saavedra Bruno v. Albright, 197 F.3d 1153 (D.C. Cir. 1999) (no review of decisions of consuls denying visas).

How important is footnote 12 to the ruling in *Bowen*?

3. Issues of reviewability have arisen under two of the most highly publicized of post-1960s statutes: The Independent Counsel Act and the Voting Rights Act. Suppose that the attorney general refuses to appoint an independent counsel to investigate allegedly unlawful conduct by the president or one of his subordinates. Suppose, for example, that the attorney general concludes that there is insufficient evidence of wrongdoing by the vice president or the secretary of state, but that the attorney general's conclusion seems wrong or improperly motivated. Is the refusal reviewable? In Banzhof v. Smith, 737 F.2d 1167 (D.C. Cir. 1984), a unanimous court found "a specific congressional intent to preclude judicial review" of the attorney general's decision *not* to appoint a special prosecutor to investigate allegations of a high government official's misdeeds. The court examined the history and intent of the Ethics in Government Act, and placed considerable weight on the fact that the act explicitly prohibited such review in a special three-judge court that was to supervise a special prosecutor. This provision said nothing about review in *other* courts, but it would have made little sense to prohibit reviews by this "knowledgeable" court while allowing it elsewhere.

Suppose that the attorney general refuses to veto a plan submitted for approval under the Voting Rights Act. Is the refusal subject to judicial review? In Morris v. Gressette, 432 U.S. 491 (1977), the Court held that it is not. The Court emphasized the short period given to the attorney general to decide whether to veto, and also the existence of alternative remedies, such as a suit against a state in court for putting into effect an unlawful plan. In these circumstances, the Court held that review was implicitly precluded.

4. Normally, silence means "review," for as *Abbott Laboratories* pointed out, there must be "clear and convincing evidence" of a congressional intent to preclude review. In fact, it is common for courts to read statutory language that apparently precludes review so that it does not do so. In Harmon v. Brucker, 355 U.S. 579 (1958), for example, the Supreme Court considered whether or not the secretary of the army could provide a "less than honorable" discharge for a soldier who performed his military service perfectly well but was engaged in allegedly improper activities before he joined the army. The Court held that the secretary was prohibited by statute from using preinduction activity as a basis for denying the soldier an "honorable" discharge; indeed, the solicitor general conceded that the secretary of the army had, in this respect, made a legal mistake. The solicitor general did *not* concede, however, that the courts had the legal power to correct the secretary's mistake. Rather, the relevant statutes established an Army Discharge Review Board with power to review the type of discharge issued and "to change, correct, or modify any discharge. . . ." The act made the findings of the Army Discharge Review Board "final subject only to review by the Secretary of the Army." The Court (per curiam over the dissent of Justice Clark) cryptically stated that (1) it was trying to avoid deciding constitutional questions, (2) judicial review is normally available at the request of a person "who has been injured by an act of a government official which is in excess of his express or implied powers," and (3) the district court could "construe the statutes involved to

determine whether the respondent did exceed his powers," and, if so, "his action would not constitute exercises of his administrative discretion, and, in such circumstances as those before us, judicial relief from this illegality would be available."

The courts' tendency to interpret statutes that apparently preclude review or otherwise restrict its availability to allow review nonetheless is well illustrated in immigration cases. Consider Shaughnessy v. Pedreiro, 349 U.S. 48 (1955). Pedreiro was ordered deported by the attorney general. The 1952 Immigrations Act made the attorney general's decisions "final." The Supreme Court had held that the word *final* in the prior 1951 Immigration Act meant that review was available through habeas corpus and not otherwise. Hiekkila v. Barber, 345 U.S. 229 (1953). Despite the earlier decision, the Court here held that the word *final* in the 1952 act referred "to finality in administrative procedure" not to "cutting off the right of judicial review in whole or in part," for Congress would not have required "a person ordered deported to go to jail in order to obtain review by a court." Thus, review in an action for declaratory and injunctive relief was proper.

When matters less important than citizenship are at stake, the courts have interpreted "finality" clauses less favorably to plaintiffs. But Congress still has had to make its intent to preclude review very specific to be effective. In the Veterans' Benefits Act, for example, Congress wrote that "the decisions of the Administrator on any question of law or fact concerning a claim for benefits or payments under any law administered by the Veterans Administration shall be final and conclusive and no other official or any court of the United States shall have power or jurisdiction to review any such decision." 72 Stat. 1115 (1958).

This section was read to preclude review until the D.C. Circuit held that since the statute used the words *claim for benefits*, it did not apply to administrative action *terminating benefits* correctly paid to the plaintiff. Tracy v. Gleason, 379 F.2d 469 (D.C. Cir. 1967). Congress responded by amending the statute to read:

> [T]he decisions of the Administrator on any question of law or fact under any law administered by the Veterans Administration providing benefits for veterans and their dependants or survivors shall be final and conclusive and no other official or any court shall have power or jurisdiction to review any such decision by an action in the nature of mandamus or otherwise.

38 U.S.C. §211(a) (1970).

What could be more clear? Consider the next case.

Johnson v. Robison
415 U.S. 361 (1974)

Mr. Justice BRENNAN delivered the opinion of the Court:

[Plaintiff, a conscientious objector who served required alternative civilian service, applied for veterans' benefits and was turned down by the administrator, for the statute provided benefits only for veterans of military service. The administrator rejected plaintiff's claim that as so interpreted, the statute was unconstitutional. The Court first decided that the decision of the administrator denying benefits was reviewable.]

. . . We consider first appellant's contention that section 211(a) bars federal courts from deciding the constitutionality of veterans' benefits legislation. Such a construction would, of course, raise serious questions concerning the constitutionality of §211(a) and in such case "it is a cardinal principle that this Court will first ascertain whether a construction of the statute is fairly possible by which the [constitutional] question[s] may be avoided." . . .

Plainly, no explicit provision of §211(a) bars judicial consideration of appellee's constitutional claims. That section provides that "the *decisions* of the Administrator on any question of law or fact *under* any law administered by the Veterans' Administration providing benefits for veterans . . . shall be final and conclusive and no . . . court of the United States shall have power or jurisdiction to review any such decision. . . ." (Emphasis added.) The prohibitions would appear to be aimed at review only of those decisions of law or fact that arise in the *administration* by the Veterans' Administration of a *statute* providing benefits for veterans. A decision of law or fact "under" a statute is made by the Administrator in the interpretation or application of a particular provision of the statute to a particular set of facts. Appellee's constitutional challenge is not to any such decision of the *Administrator*, but rather to a decision of *Congress* to create a statutory class entitled to benefits that does not include I-O conscientious objectors who performed alternative civilian service. Thus, as the District Court stated: "The questions of law presented in these proceedings arise under the Constitution, not under the statute whose validity is challenged." . . .

Nor does the legislative history accompanying the 1970 amendment of §11(a) demonstrate a congressional intention to bar judicial review even of constitutional questions. No-review clauses similar to §211(a) have been a part of veterans' benefits legislation since 1933. While the legislative history accompanying these precursor no-review clauses is almost nonexistent, the Administrator, in a letter written in 1952 in connection with a revision of the clause under consideration by the Subcommittee of the House Committee on Veterans' Affairs, comprehensively explained the policies necessitating the no-review clause and identified two primary purposes: (1) to insure that veterans' benefits claims will not burden the courts and the Veterans' Administration with expensive and time-consuming litigation, and (2) to insure that the technical and complex determinations and applications of Veterans' Administration policy connected with veterans' benefits decisions will be adequately and uniformly made.

The legislative history of the 1970 amendment indicates nothing more than a congressional intent to preserve these two primary purposes. Before amendment, the no-review clause made final "the decisions of the Administrator on any question of law or fact *concerning a claim for benefits or payments* under [certain] law[s] administered by the Veterans' Administration" (emphasis added). . . . In a series of decision . . . the Court of Appeals for the District of Columbia Circuit interpreted the term "claim" as a limitation upon the reach of §211(a), and as a consequence held that judicial review of actions by the Administrator *subsequent* to an original grant of benefits was not barred.

Congress perceived this judicial interpretation as a threat to the dual purposes of the no-review clause. First, the interpretation would lead to an inevitable increase in litigation with consequent burdens upon the courts and the Veterans' Administration. . . .

Second, Congress was concerned that the judicial interpretation of §211(a) would involve the courts in day-to-day determination and interpretation of Veterans' Administration policy. . . .

Thus, the 1970 amendment was enacted to overrule the interpretation of the Court of Appeals for the District of Columbia Circuit, and thereby restore vitality to the two primary purposes to be served by the no-review clause. Nothing whatever in the legislative history of the 1970 amendment, or predecessor no-review clauses, suggests any congressional intent to preclude judicial cognizance of constitutional challenges to veterans' benefits legislation. Such challenges obviously do not contravene the purposes of the no-review clause, for they cannot be expected to burden the courts by their volume, nor do they involve technical considerations of Veterans' Administration policy. We therefore conclude, in agreement with the District Court, that a construction of §211(a) that does not extend the prohibitions of that section to actions challenging the constitutionality of laws providing benefits for veterans is not only "fairly possible" but is the most reasonable construction, for neither the text nor the scant legislative history of §211(a) provides the "clear and convincing" evidence of congressional intent required by this Court before a statute will be construed to restrict access to judicial review. See Abbott Laboratories v. Gardner, 387 U.S. 136, 141 (1967). . . .

For two recent decisions in the same vein, see I.N.S. v. St. Cyr, 33 U.S. 289 (2001); Demore v. Hyung Joon Kim, 510 U.S. 538 (2003). The *St. Cyr* case allowed judicial review at the behest of an alien, partly on the basis of the presumption of review, in the face of a statutory provision saying: "Notwithstanding any other provision of law, no court shall have jurisdiction to review any final order of removal against an alien who is removable by reason of having committed" certain criminal offenses, including the one of which the respondent had been convicted. The Court said that the statute did not eliminate the otherwise-available route of review by petition for habas corpus — even though the title of the relevant provision was "Elimination of Custody Review by Habeas Corpus."

In *Hyung Joon Kim*, the petitioner sought to challenge the constitutionality of a provision of immigration law authorizing the attorney general to detain any alien who is deportable because he committed a specified crime. The provision relevant to reviewability said:

> *Judicial review* — The Attorney General's discretionary judgment regarding the application of this section shall not be subject to review. No court may set aside any action or decision by the Attorney General under this section regarding the detention or release of any alien or the grant, revocation, or denial of bond or parole.

A majority of the Justices, however, said that as in *St. Cyr* nothing in the statute expressly barred review by habeas corpus, and suggested (with a cryptic reference to Johnson v. Robison, supra) that the petitioner's constitutional challenge was to the "statutory framework" rather than to the Attorney General's decision regarding petitioner's "detention" itself. Is this not a false alternative? The challenge is to the detention-as-authorized-by-the-statute. If there were no detention, there would be a serious question about whether a justiciable case or controversy was present; if there were no statutory authorization for the administrative action, a constitutional challenge would be unnecessary.

Having found reviewability, a different majority then went on to hold the statute constitutional in any event. The cynical among us will suspect that the Court, or a decisive coalition of the Justices, is very interested in upholding the abstract principle of reviewability, and that a finding of reviewability is especially likely when the real costs to the government of doing so are low (because the government decision is upheld on the merits). Do the cases fit this theory? Reconsider the question after reading the Note on Reviewability at War, infra.

In Traynor v. Turnage, 485 U.S. 535 (1988), the Supreme Court considered a claim brought by veterans who argued they had been denied educational benefits because they were alcoholics and consequently were unable to use their benefits before those benefits expired. The veterans claimed that the denials violated the Rehabilitation Act of 1973, an act that says that no federal program can discriminate against a handicapped person because of his or her handicap.

The Court reviewed the merits of the veterans' claim (which it rejected). It held that the "no judicial review" statute did not bar review. The Court pointed out that the no-review statute simply "insulated from review decisions of law and fact *under any law administered by the Veterans' Administration*,' that is, decisions made in interpreting or applying a particular provision of that statute to a particular set of facts. . . . But the cases now before us involve the issue whether the law sought to be administered is valid in light of a subsequent statute whose enforcement is not the exclusive domain of the Veterans' Administration. There is no claim that the regulation at issue is inconsistent with the statute under which it was issued and there is no challenge to the Veterans' Administration's construction of any statute dealing with veterans' benefits. . . . Nor is there any reason to believe that the Veterans' Administration has any special expertise in assessing the validity of its regulations construing veterans' benefits statutes under a later-passed statute of general application. . . ." Review of this type of question will not "enmesh the courts in . . . technical and complex determinations and application of Veterans' Administration policy" or "burden the courts" and the agency "with expensive and time consuming litigation."

Congress has enacted the Veterans' Judicial Review Act, 102 Stat. 4105 (1988), which creates a special article I court, a Court of Veterans' Appeals, to review Veterans' Administration benefits decisions. Decisions of that court may be reviewed further in the Court of Appeals for the Federal Circuit (an article III court), but the Federal Circuit's review is limited by provisions that say it cannot review "a challenge to a factual determination" or "a challenge to a law or regulation as applied to the facts of a particular case" (unless the case "presents a constitutional issue").

Consider McNary v. Haitian Refugee Center, 498 U.S. 479 (1991). There, illegal alien farmworkers filed an action in federal district court challenging, as violative of due process, the hearing procedures used by the Immigration and Naturalization Service (INS) in processing their applications for an amnesty program under the Immigration Reform and Control Act of 1956. The Court (6-2) held that the action was not barred by a provision in the act precluding judicial review of a "determination respecting an application" except by a court of appeals on review of an exclusion or deportation order. The reference to "an application" in the statute limits review only with respect to INS decisions on individual claims. Plaintiffs' claim of generic defects in the basic procedures used by the INS was accordingly not affected. See also I.N.S. v. St. Cyr, supra.

In Lindahl v. Office of Personnel Management, 470 U.S. 768 (1985), the Court was asked to consider a denial of a retirement annuity by the Office of Personnel Management (OPM), which alleged that Lindahl had not established that his disability prevented him from doing his job. The Civil Service Retirement Act gives OPM the power to "determine questions of disability and dependency" and says that the "Decisions of the Office concerning these matters are final and conclusive and are not subject to judicial review." The Court held, 5-4, that the statute precludes review only of

OPM's factual determinations about disability. Review would be available to test whether there "has been a substantial departure from important procedural rights, a misconstruction of the governing legislation, or some like error 'going to the heart of the administrative determination.'"

5. *"Committed to Agency Discretion"*

APA §706 states that a reviewing court "shall . . . hold unlawful and set aside agency action . . . found to be . . . an abuse of discretion. . . ." But §701(a)(2) says that the whole chapter, including §706, does not apply to "agency action . . . committed to agency discretion by law." This exception raises several important puzzles. (1) How is this exception at all different from the "statutory preclusion" exception? Isn't a commitment to agency discretion "by law" the same as a "statutory preclusion"? (2) Under APA §706, isn't agency action always reviewable for abuse of discretion? Does this exception mean that there is a class of matters as to which an agency *can* abuse its discretion, and that there is no redress available in a court of law, even though there is no statute precluding review? (3) Why isn't a statutory grant of such broad discretion an unconstitutional delegation of power?

a. Early Lessons

In an early essay, Raoul Berger argued that §701(a)(2) exempts from the review provisions only *lawful* exercise of discretion. Any abuse of discretion would be reviewable unless a statute precludes review. Berger, Administrative Arbitrariness and Judicial Review, 65 Colum. L. Rev. 55 (1965). Louis Jaffe came close to supporting the Berger view when he argued that the discretionary powers granted agencies always have limits, and a court should stand ready to intervene when those limits are overstepped. L. Jaffe, Judicial Control of Administrative Action 359, 375 (1965). Kenneth Culp Davis urged a different interpretation of §701(a)(2). He argued that it means what it says, namely, that an agency might in some instances *abuse* its discretion, yet court review would be precluded. He says that "the presumption of reviewability can be overcome by showing (a) intent of Congress to cut off review, (b) inappropriateness of the subject matter for judicial consideration, or (c) some other reason that a court deems sufficient for unreviewability." K. Davis, Administrative Law of the Seventies 634-635 (1976). The courts determine whether a claim falls within (b) or (c) "on practical grounds in particular cases."

Some support for the Davis position appeared to come from Panama Canal Co. v. Grace Line, Inc., 356 U.S. 309 (1958), in which American shipping companies using the canal sued the Panama Canal Co., a government agency, to set new tolls and for a refund of past overcharges. The applicable statute provided that "tolls shall be prescribed at . . . rates calculated to cover, as nearly as practicable, all costs of maintaining and operating the Panama Canal, together with the facilities and appurtenances related thereto, including interest and depreciation, and an appropriate share of the net costs of operation of the . . . Canal Zone Government." In determining the "appropriate share" the company is to give "substantial weight" to the ratio of canal tolls to its income from various other sources. The Court said that "the initiation of a proceeding for readjustment of the tolls of the Panama Canal is a matter that Congress has left to the discretion of the

Panama Canal Co." It emphasized that "the present conflict rages over questions that at heart involve problems of statutory construction and cost accounting; whether an operating deficit in the auxiliary or supporting activities is a legitimate cost in maintaining and operating the Canal for purpose of the toll formula. These are matters on which experts may disagree; they involve nice issues of judgment and choice, . . . which require the exercise of informed discretion."

There are other early cases in which courts decided *not* to review because of the subject matter at issue or the impact of review on the conduct of government business. In Chicago & Southern Air Lines v. Waterman Steamship Corp., 333 U.S. 103 (1948), Waterman sought judicial review of a CAB order awarding a certificate for an overseas air route to a competitor. The board order, since it involved overseas routes, had the specific approval of the president (as required by Civil Aviation Act §801, 49 U.S.C. §601). The board argued that its order was incomplete and hence not ripe for review prior to presidential review, while afterwards it was, as a presidential action, immune from judicial review. The Supreme Court (dividing 5-4) agreed. The Court wrote, in part:

> While the changes made at direction of the President may be identified, the reasons therefor are not disclosed beyond the statement that "because of certain factors relating to our broad national welfare and other matters for which the Chief Executive has special responsibility, he has reached conclusions which require" changes in the Board's opinion.
>
> The court below considered, and we think quite rightly, that it could not review such provisions of the order as resulted from Presidential direction. The President, both as Commander-in-Chief and as the Nation's organ for foreign affairs, has available intelligence services whose reports are not and ought not to be published to the world. It would be intolerable that courts, without the relevant information, should review and perhaps nullify actions of the Executive taken on information properly held secret. Nor can courts sit in camera in order to be taken into executive confidences. But even if courts could require full disclosure, the very nature of executive decisions as to foreign policy is political, not judicial. Such decisions are wholly confided by our Constitution to the political departments of the government, Executive and Legislative. They are delicate, complex, and involve large elements of prophecy. They are and should be undertaken only by those directly responsible to the people whose welfare they advance or imperil. They are decisions of a kind for which the Judiciary has neither aptitude, facilities nor responsibility and which has long been held to belong in the domain of political power not subject to judicial intrusion or inquiry. . . .
>
> . . . We therefore agree that whatever of this order emanates from the President is not susceptible of review by the Judicial Department.

See also United States ex rel. Schonbrun v. Commanding Officer, 403 F.2d 371 (2d Cir. 1968), *cert. denied*, 394 U.S. 929 (1969); Hahn v. Gottlieb, 430 F.2d 1243 (1st Cir. 1970).

b. Modern Learning: No Law to Apply?

The seminal (and controversial) modern case on the §701(a)(2) exception is *Overton Park*. Reread the relevant passages of the opinion in Chapter 4.

In the key passage, the Supreme Court stated that the §701(a)(2) exception for action "committed to agency discretion" is a "very narrow exception. . . . The legislative history of the Administrative Procedure Act indicates that it is applicable in those rare instances where 'statutes are drawn in such terms that in a given case there is no law to apply.'" This language (the "no law to apply" test) is somewhat opaque, but it suggests that the agency action is immune from review when there exists no legal standard against which its lawfulness can be judged. In other words, a decision is "committed to agency discretion by law" when the governing statute provides no standards against which the plaintiffs claim might be measured. What, precisely, does this mean? A clue comes from considering why the Court found it obvious that there was "law to apply" in *Overton Park* itself. The relevant statute, requiring that parks be protected unless there was no "prudent and feasible alternative," could hardly be read to give the secretary of transportation unfettered discretion.

Note that the *Overton Park* standard appears to resolve several puzzles created by the "committed to agency discretion" exception. The "no law to apply" standard explains why this exception differs from the "preclusion" exemption: the latter refers to congressional foreclosure, the former to an absence of judicially cognizable standards. (Note, however, that the line between implicit preclusion of review and commitment to agency discretion may be thin.) The standard also explains why there may be no review for "abuse of discretion." Sometimes a standard is so open-ended that any exercise of discretion qualifies as legitimate, something other than an abuse.

As we will see, the "no law to apply" test can be understood in several different ways. There are two obvious candidates. First, courts might simply compare the plaintiff's allegation against the governing statute to see whether there are legal standards by which to assess the claim. Here, the "no law to apply" test is the basic one for understanding if a decision has been committed to agency discretion by law. Second, courts might take into account not just whether there is "law to apply," but also such factors as the nature and importance of the interests of the parties, the problems introduced by judicial review, the technical nature or complexity of the issues, and the obviousness of any violations of law. On this view, the "no law to apply" idea is important but only a part of the "committed to agency discretion" inquiry.

c. "No Law to Apply": The Modern Era

Heckler v. Chaney

470 U.S. 821 (1985)

Justice REHNQUIST delivered the opinion of the Court.

This case presents the question of the extent to which a decision of an administrative agency to exercise its "discretion" not to undertake *certain enforcement actions* is subject to judicial review under the Administrative Procedure Act. . . .

I

Respondents have been sentenced to death by lethal injection of drugs under the laws of the States of Oklahoma and Texas. Those States, and several others, have recently adopted this method for carrying out the capital sentence. Respondents first petitioned the FDA, claiming that the drugs used by the States for this purpose, although approved for use by the FDA for the medical purposes stated on their labels, were not approved for use in human executions. They alleged that the drugs had not been tested for the purpose for which they were to be used, and that, given that the drugs would likely be administered by untrained personnel, it was also likely that the drugs would not induce the quick and painless death intended. They urged that use of these drugs for human execution was the "unapproved use of an approved drug" and constituted a violation of the Act's prohibitions against "misbranding." . . . Accordingly, respondents claimed that the FDA was required to approve the drugs as "safe and effective" for human execution before they could be distributed in interstate commerce. See 21 U.S.C. Section 355. They therefore requested the FDA to take various investigatory and enforcement actions to prevent these perceived violations: they requested the FDA to affix warnings to the labels of all the drugs stating that they were unapproved and unsafe for human execution, to send statements to the drug manufacturers and prison administrators stating that the drugs should not be so used, and to adopt procedures for seizing the drugs from state prisons and to recommend the prosecution of all those in the chain of distribution who knowingly distribute or purchase the drugs with intent to use them for human execution.

[The FDA commissioner refused to take the requested enforcement actions. The commissioner was uncertain whether he had jurisdiction to act. Regardless, he wrote:

> Were the FDA clearly to have jurisdiction in the area, moreover, we believe we could be authorized to decline to exercise it under our inherent discretion to decline to pursue certain enforcement matters. The unapproved use of approved drugs is an area in which the case law is far from uniform. Generally, enforcement proceedings in this are initiated only when there is a serious danger to the public health or a blatant scheme to defraud. We cannot conclude that those dangers are present under State lethal injection laws, which are duly authorized statutory enactments in furtherance of proper State functions.

The respondents sought judicial review of the commissioner's decision. The Court of Appeals for the District of Columbia Circuit reviewed this nonenforcement decision. It found "law to apply," see *Overton Park*, page **000**, in an FDA policy statement that indicated the agency was "obligated" to investigate the unapproved use of an approved drug when the use became "widespread" or "endangered the public health." It found the FDA's refusal to act "arbitrary, capricious, or an abuse of discretion."]

II

. . . For us, this case turns on the important question of the extent to which determination by the FDA not to exercise its enforcement authority over the use of drugs in interstate commerce may be judicially reviewed. That decision in turn involves the construction of two separate but necessarily interrelated statutes, the APA and the FDCA [Food, Drug and Cosmetic Act]. . . .

. . . Petitioner urges that the decision of the FDA to refuse enforcement is an action "committed to agency discretion by law" under §701(a)(2).

This Court has not had occasion to interpret this second exception in §701(a) in any great detail. On its face, the section does not obviously lend itself to any particular construction; indeed, one might wonder what difference exists between §(a)(1) and §(a)(2). The former section seems easy in application; it requires construction of the substantive statute involved to determine whether Congress intended to preclude judicial review of certain decisions.

. . . But one could read the language "committed to agency discretion by law" in §(a)(2) to require a similar inquiry. In addition, commentators have pointed out that construction of §(a)(2) is further complicated by the tension between a literal reading of §(a)(2), which exempts from judicial review those decisions committed to agency "discretion," and the primary scope of review prescribed by §706(2)(A) — whether the agency's action was "arbitrary, capricious, or an *abuse of discretion.*" How is it, they ask, that an action committed to agency discretion can be unreviewable and yet courts still can review agency actions for abuse of that discretion? . . .

This Court first discussed §(a)(2) in Citizens to Preserve Overton Park v. Volpe, [401 U.S. 402 (1971)].

[After setting out the language of Section 702, the Court continued:] In this case, there is no indication that Congress sought to prohibit judicial review and there is most certainly no "showing of 'clear and convincing evidence' of a . . . legislative intent" to restrict access to judicial review. Abbott Laboratories v. Garner, 387 U.S. 136, 141 (1967). . . . Similarly, the Secretary's decision here does not fall within the exception for action "committed to agency discretion." This is a very narrow exception. . . . The legislative history of the Administrative Procedure Act indicates that it is applicable in those rare instances where "statutes are drawn in such broad terms that in a given case there is no law to apply." S. Rep. No. 752, 79th Cong., 26 (1945). *Overton Park*, 401 U.S. 402, at 410.

The above quote answers several of the questions raised by the language of §701(a), although it raise[s] others. First, it clearly separates the exception provided by §(a)(1) from the §(a)(2) exception. The former applies when Congress has expressed an intent to preclude judicial review. The latter applies in different circumstances; even where Congress has not affirmatively precluded review, review is not to be had if the statute is drawn so that a court would have no meaningful standard against which to judge the agency's exercise of discretion. In such a case, the statute ("law") can be taken to have "committed" the decisionmaking to the agency's judgment absolutely. This construction avoids conflict with the "abuse of discretion" standard of review in §706 — if no judicially manageable standards are available for judging how and when an agency should exercise its discretion then it is impossible to evaluate agency action for "abuse of discretion." In addition, this construction satisfies the principle of statutory construction mentioned earlier, by identifying a separate class of cases to which §701(a)(2) applies.

To this point our analysis does not differ significantly from that of the Court of Appeals. That court purported to apply the "no law to apply" standard of *Overton Park*. We disagree, however, with that court's insistence that the "narrow construction" of §(a)(2) required application of a presumption of reviewability even to an agency's decision not to undertake certain enforcement actions. Here we think the Court of Appeals broke with tradition, case law, and sound reasoning.

Overton Park did not involve an agency's refusal to take requested enforcement action. It involved an affirmative act of approval under a statute that set clear guidelines for determining when such approval should be given. Refusals to take enforcement steps generally involve precisely the opposite situation, and in that situation we think the presumption is that judicial review is not available. This Court has recognized on several occasions over many years that an agency's decision not to prosecute or enforce, whether through civil or criminal process, is a decision generally committed to an agency's absolute discretion. . . . This recognition of the existence of discretion is attributable in no small part to the general unsuitability for judicial review of agency decisions to refuse enforcement.

The reasons for this general unsuitability are many. First, an agency decision not to enforce often involves a complicated balancing of a number of factors which are peculiarly within its expertise. Thus, the agency must not only assess whether a violation has occurred, but whether agency resources are best spent on this violation or another, whether the agency is likely to succeed if it acts, whether the particular enforcement action requested best fits the agency's overall policies, and indeed, whether the agency has enough resources to undertake the action at all. An agency generally cannot act against each technical violation of the statute it is charged with enforcing. The agency is far better equipped than the courts to deal with the many variables involved in the proper ordering of its priorities. Similar concerns animate the principles of administrative law that courts generally will defer to an agency's construction of the statute it is charged with implementing, and to the procedures it adopts for implementing that statute. See Vermont Yankee Nuclear Power Corp. v. Natural Resources Defense Council, Inc., 435 U.S. 519, 543 [(1978)]. . . .

In addition to these administrative concerns, we note that when an agency refuses to act it generally does not exercise its coercive power over an individual's liberty or property rights, and thus does not infringe upon areas that courts often are called upon to protect. Similarly, when an agency does act to enforce, that action itself provides a focus for judicial review, inasmuch as the agency must have exercised its power in some manner. The action at least can be reviewed to determine whether the agency exceeded its statutory powers. . . .

Finally, we recognize that an agency's refusal to institute proceedings shares to some extent the characteristics of the decision of a prosecutor in the Executive Branch not to indict — a decision which has long been regarded as the special province of the Executive Branch, inasmuch as it is the Executive who is charged by the Constitution to "take Care that the Laws be faithfully executed." U.S. Const., Art. II, §3.

We of course only list the above concerns to facilitate understanding of our conclusion that an agency's decision has traditionally been "committed to agency discretion," and we believe that the Congress enacting the APA did not intend to alter that tradition. Cf. Davis, §28.5 (APA did not significantly alter the "common law" of judicial review of agency action). In so stating, we emphasize that the decision is only presumptively unreviewable; the presumption may be rebutted where the substantive statute has provided guidelines for the agency to follow in exercising its enforcement powers.[13] Thus, in establishing this presumption in the APA, Congress did not set agencies free to disregard legislative direction in this statutory scheme that the agency administers. Congress may limit an agency's exercise of enforcement power if it wishes, either by setting substantive priorities, or by otherwise circumscribing an agency's power to discriminate among issues or cases it will pursue. How to determine when Congress has done so is the question left open by *Overton Park.* . . .

---

13. We do not have in this case a refusal by the agency to institute proceedings based solely on the belief that it lacks jurisdiction. Nor do we have a situation where it could justifiably be found that the agency has "consciously and expressly adopted a general policy" that is so extreme as to amount to an abdication of its statutory responsibilities. See, e.g., Adams v. Richardson, 156 U.S. App. D.C. 267, 480 F.2d 1159 (1973) (en banc). Although we express no opinion on whether such decisions would be unreviewable under §701(a)(2), we note that in those situations the statute conferring authority on the agency might indicate that such decisions were not "committed to agency discretion."

III

[The Court reviewed the FDCA and found nothing in it to rebut "presumption of nonreviewability."]

IV

. . . No colorable claim is made in this case that the agency's refusal to institute proceedings violated any constitutional rights of respondents, and we do not address the issue that would be raised in such a case. . . .

The judgment of the Court of Appeals is reversed.

Justice MARSHALL concurring separately. . . .

I write separately to argue for a different basis of decision: that refusals to enforce, like other agency action, are reviewable in the absence of a "clear and convincing" congressional intent to the contrary, but that such refusals warrant deference when, as in this case, there is nothing to suggest that an agency with enforcement discretion has abused that discretion. . . .

When a statute does not mandate full enforcement, I agree with the Court that an agency is generally "far better equipped than the courts to deal with the many variables involved in the proper ordering of its priorities." As long as the agency is choosing how to allocate finite enforcement resources, the agency's choice will be entitled to substantial deference, for the choice among valid alternative enforcement policies is precisely the sort of choice over which agencies generally have been left substantial discretion by their enabling statutes. *On the merits*, then, a decision not to enforce that is based on valid resource allocation decisions will generally not be "arbitrary, capricious, and [an] abuse of discretion, or otherwise not in accordance with law." 5 U.S.C. §706(A)(2). The decision in this case is no exception to this principle. . . .

The lower courts, facing the problem of agency inaction and its concrete effects more regularly than do we, have responded with a variety of solutions to assure administrative fidelity to congressional objectives: a demand that an agency explain its refusal to act, a demand that explanations given be further elaborated, and injunctions that action "unlawfully withheld or unreasonably delayed," 5 U.S.C. §706, be taken. See generally Stewart & Sunstein, 95 Harv. L. Rev., at 1279. Whatever the merits of any particular solution, one would have hoped the Court would have acted with greater respect for these efforts by responding with a scalpel rather than a blunderbuss.

To be sure, the Court no doubt takes solace in the view that it has created only a "presumption" of unreviewability, and that "this presumption may be rebutted where the substantive statute has provided guidelines for the agency to follow in exercising its enforcement power." But this statement implies far too narrow a reliance on positive law, either statutory or constitutional, as the sole source of limitations on agency discretion not to enforce. In my view, enforcement discretion is also channelled by traditional background understandings against which the APA was enacted and which Congress hardly could be thought to have intended to displace in the APA. [E.g.], a refusal to enforce that stems from a conflict of interest, that is the result of a bribe, vindictiveness or retaliation, or that traces to personal or other corrupt motives ought to be judicially remediable. . . .

Perhaps the Court's reference to guidance from the "substantive statute" is meant to encompass such concerns and to allow the "common law" of judicial review of agency action to provide standards by which inaction can be reviewed. But in that case I cannot fathom what content the Court's "presumption of unreviewability" might have. If inaction can be reviewed to assure that it does not result from improper abnegation of jurisdiction, from complete abdication of statutory responsibilities, from violation of constitutional rights, or from factors that offend principles of rational and fair administrative process, it would seem that a court must always inquire into the reasons for the agency's action before deciding whether the presumption applies. As Judge Friendly said many years ago, review of even a decision over which substantial administrative discretion exists would then be available to determine whether that discretion had been abused because the decision was "made without a rational explanation, inexplicably departed from established policies, or rested . . . on other considerations that Congress could not have intended to make relevant." Wong Wing Hang v. Immigration & Naturalization Service, 360 F.2d 715, 719 (C.A.2 1966). In that event, we would not be finding enforcement decisions unreviewable, but rather would be reviewing them on the merits, albeit with due deference, to assure that such decisions did not result from an abuse of discretion. . . .

Norton v. Southern Utah Wilderness Alliance
542 U.S. 55 (2004)

Justice SCALIA delivered the opinion of the Court.

In this case, we must decide whether the authority of a federal court under the Administrative Procedure Act (APA) to "compel agency action unlawfully withheld or unreasonably delayed," 5 U.S.C. §706(1), extends to the review of the United States Bureau of Land Management's stewardship of public lands under certain statutory provisions and its own planning documents.

I

Almost half the State of Utah, about 23 million acres, is federal land administered by the Bureau of Land Management (BLM), an agency within the Department of Interior. For nearly 30 years, BLM's management of public lands has been governed by the Federal Land Policy and Management Act of 1976 (FLPMA), 90 Stat. 2744, 43 U.S.C. §1701 *et seq.*, which "established a policy in favor of retaining public lands for multiple use management." Lujan v. National Wildlife Federation, 497 U.S. 871, 877 (1990). "Multiple use management" is a deceptively simple term that describes the enormously complicated task of striking a balance among the many competing uses to which land can be put, "including, but not limited to, recreation, range, timber, minerals, watershed, wildlife and fish, and [uses serving] natural scenic, scientific and historical values." 43 U.S.C. §1702(c). . . .

Protection of wilderness has come into increasing conflict with another element of multiple use, recreational use of so-called off-road vehicles (ORVs), which include vehicles primarily designed for off-road use, such as lightweight, four-wheel "all-terrain vehicles," and vehicles capable of such use, such as sport utility vehicles. . . . According to the United States Forest Service's most recent estimates, some 42 million Americans participate in off-road travel each year, more than double the number two decades ago. United States sales of all-terrain vehicles alone have roughly doubled in the past five years, reaching almost 900,000 in 2003. The use of ORVs on federal land has negative environmental consequences, including soil disruption and compaction, harassment of animals, and annoyance of wilderness lovers. Thus, BLM faces a classic land use dilemma of sharply inconsistent uses, in a context of scarce resources and congressional silence with respect to wilderness designation.

In 1999, respondents Southern Utah Wilderness Alliance and other organizations (collectively SUWA) filed this action in the United States District Court for Utah against petitioners BLM, its Director, and the Secretary. In its second amended complaint, SUWA sought declaratory and injunctive relief for BLM's failure to act to protect public lands in Utah from damage caused by ORV use. SUWA made three claims that are relevant here: (1) that BLM had violated its nonimpairment obligation under §1782(a) by allowing degradation in certain WSAs; (2) that BLM had failed to implement provisions in its land use plans relating to ORV use; (3) that BLM had failed to take a "hard look" at whether, pursuant to the National Environmental Policy Act of 1969 (NEPA), 83 Stat. 852, 42 U.S.C. §4321 *et seq.*, it should undertake supplemental environmental analyses for areas in which ORV use had increased. SUWA contended that it could sue to remedy these three failures to act pursuant to the APA's provision of a cause of action to "compel agency action unlawfully withheld or unreasonably delayed." 5 U.S.C. §706(1).

II

All three claims at issue here involve assertions that BLM failed to take action with respect to ORV use that it was required to take. Failures to act are sometimes remediable under the APA, but not always. We begin by considering what limits the APA places upon judicial review of agency inaction.

The APA authorizes suit by "[a] person suffering legal wrong because of agency action, or adversely affected or aggrieved by agency action within the meaning of a relevant statute." 5 U.S.C. §702. Where no other statute provides a private right of action, the "agency action" complained of must be "*final* agency action." §704 (emphasis added). "Agency action" is defined in §551(13) to include "the whole or a part of an agency rule, order, license, sanction, relief, or the equivalent or denial thereof, *or failure to act.*" (Emphasis added.) The APA provides relief for a failure to act in §706(1): "The reviewing court shall . . . compel agency action unlawfully withheld or unreasonably delayed."

Sections 702, 704, and 706(1) all insist upon an "agency action," either as the action complained of (in §§702 and 704) or as the action to be compelled (in §706(1)). The definition of that term begins with a list of five categories of decisions made or outcomes implemented by an agency — "agency rule, order, license, sanction [or] relief." §551(13). All of those categories involve circumscribed, discrete agency actions, as their definitions make clear: "an agency statement of . . . future effect designed to implement, interpret, or prescribe law or policy" (rule); "a final disposition . . . in a matter other than rule making" (order); a "permit . . . or other form of permission" (license); a "prohibition . . . or taking [of] other compulsory or restrictive action" (sanction); or a "grant of money, assistance, license, authority," etc., or "recognition of a claim, right, immunity," etc., or "taking of other action on the application or petition of, and beneficial to, a person" (relief). §§551(4), (6), (8), (10), (11).

The terms following those five categories of agency action are not defined in the APA: "or the equivalent or denial thereof, or failure to act." §551(13). But an "equivalent . . . thereof" must also be discrete (or it would not be equivalent), and a "denial thereof" must be the denial of a discrete listed action (and perhaps denial of a discrete equivalent). The final term in the definition, "failure to act," is in our view properly understood as a failure to take an *agency action* — that is, a failure to take one of the agency actions (including their equivalents) earlier defined in §551(13). Moreover, even without this equation of "act" with "agency action" the interpretive canon of *ejusdem generis* would attribute to the last item ("failure to act") the same characteristic of discreteness shared by all the preceding items. See, e.g., Washington State Dept. of Social and Health Servs. v. Guardianship Estate of Keffeler, 537 U.S. 371, 384-385 (2003). A "failure to act" is not the same thing as a "denial." The latter is the agency's act of saying no to a request; the former is simply the omission of an action without formally rejecting a request — for example, the failure to promulgate a rule or take some decision by a statutory deadline. The important point is that a "failure to act" is properly understood to be limited, as are the other items in §551(13), to a *discrete* action.

A second point central to the analysis of the present case is that the only agency action that can be compelled under the APA is action legally *required*. This limitation appears in §706(1)'s authorization for courts to "compel agency action *unlawfully* withheld."[14] In this regard the APA carried traditional practice prior to its passage, when judicial review was achieved through use of the so-called prerogative writs — principally writs of mandamus under the All Writs Act, now codified at 28 U.S.C. §1651(a). The mandamus remedy was normally limited to enforcement of "a specific, unequivocal command," ICC v. New York, N.H. & H.R. Co., 287 U.S. 178, 204 (1932), the ordering of a " 'precise, definite act . . . about which [an official] had no discretion whatever,' " United States ex rel. Dunlap v. Black, 128 U.S. 40, 46 (1888) (quoting Kendall v. United States ex rel. Stokes, 12 Pet. 524, 613 (1838)). See also ICC v. United States ex rel. Humbolt S.S. Co., 224 U.S. 474, 484 (1912). As described in the Attorney General's Manual on the APA, a document whose reasoning we have often found persuasive, see, e.g., [citations omitted], §706(1) empowers a court only to compel an agency "to perform a ministerial or non-discretionary act," or "to take action upon a matter, without directing *how* it shall act." Attorney General's Manual on the Administrative Procedure Act 108 (1947) (emphasis added).

Thus, a claim under §706(1) can proceed only where a plaintiff asserts that an agency failed to take a *discrete* agency action that it is *required to take*. These limitations rule out several kinds of challenges. The limitation to discrete agency action precludes the kind of broad programmatic attack we rejected in Lujan v. National Wildlife Federation, 497 U.S. 871 (1990). . . .

The limitation to *required* agency action rules out judicial direction of even discrete agency action that is not demanded by law (which includes, of course, agency regulations that have the force of law). Thus, when an agency is compelled by law to act within a certain time period, but the manner of its action is left to the agency's discretion, court can compel the agency to act, but has no power to specify what the action must be. For example. 47 U.S.C. §251(d)(1), which required the Federal Communications Commission "to establish regulations to implement" interconnection requirements "[w]ithin 6 months" of the date of enactment of the Telecommunications Act of 1996, would have supported a judicial decree under the APA requiring the

---

14. Of course §706(1) also authorizes courts to "compel agency action . . . unreasonably delayed" — but a delay cannot be unreasonable with respect to action that is not required.

prompt issuance of regulations, but not a judicial decree setting forth the content of those regulations.

III

A

With these principles in mind, we turn to SUWA's first claim, that by permitting ORV use in certain WSAs [Wilderness Study Areas], BLM violated its mandate to "continue to manage [WSAs] . . . in a manner so as not to impair the suitability of such areas for preservation as wilderness," 43 U.S.C. §1782(c). SUWA relies not only upon §1782(c) but also upon a provision of BLM's Interim Management Policy for Lands Under Wilderness Review, which interprets the nonimpairment mandate to require BLM to manage WSAs so as to prevent them from being "degraded so far, compared with the area's values for other purposes, as to significantly constrain the Congress's prerogative to either designate [it] as wilderness or release it for other uses." App. 65.

Section 1782(c) is mandatory as to the object to be achieved, but it leaves BLM a great deal of discretion in deciding how to achieve it. It assuredly does not mandate, with the clarity necessary to support judicial action under §706(1), the total exclusion of ORV use. SUWA argues that §1782 *does* contain a categorical imperative, namely the command to comply with the nonimpairment mandate. It contends that a federal court could simply enter a general order compelling compliance with that mandate, without suggesting any particular manner of compliance. It relies upon the language from the Attorney General's Manual quoted earlier, that a court can "take action upon a matter, without directing how [the agency] shall act," and upon language in a case cited by the Manual noting that "mandamus will lie . . . even though the act required involves the exercise of judgment and discretion." Safeway Stores v. Brown, 138 F.2d 278, 280 (Emerg. Ct. App. 1943). The action referred to in these excerpts, however, is *discrete* agency action, as we have discussed above. General deficiencies in compliance, unlike the failure to issue a ruling that was discussed in *Safeway Stores*, lack the specificity requisite for agency action.

The principal purpose of the APA limitations we have discussed — and of the traditional limitations upon mandamus from which they were derived — is to protect agencies from undue judicial interference with their lawful discretion, and to avoid judicial entanglement in abstract policy disagreements which courts lack both expertise and information to resolve. If courts were empowered to enter general orders compelling compliance with broad statutory mandates, they would necessarily be empowered, as well, to determine whether compliance was achieved — which would mean that it would ultimately become the task of the supervising court, rather than the agency, to work out compliance with the broad statutory mandate, injecting the judge into day-to-day agency management. To take just a few examples from federal resources management, a plaintiff might allege that the Secretary had failed to "manage wild free-roaming horses and burros in a manner that is designed to achieve and maintain a thriving natural ecological balance," or to "manage the [New Orleans Jazz National] [H]istorical [P]ark in such a manner as will preserve and perpetuate knowledge and understanding of the history of jazz," or to "manage the [Steens Mountain] Cooperative Management and Protection Area for the benefit of present and future generations." 16 U.S.C. §§1333(a), 410bbb-2(a)(1), 460nnn-12(b). The prospect of pervasive oversight by federal courts over the manner and pace of agency compliance with such congressional directives is not contemplated by the APA.

[The remainder of the Court's discussion is omitted.]

Webster v. Doe
486 U.S. 592 (1988)

Chief Justice REHNQUIST delivered the opinion of the Court.

Section 102(c) of the National Security Act [NSA] of 1947, 61 Stat. 498, as amended, provides that:

> [T]he Director of Central Intelligence may, in his discretion, terminate the employment of any officer or employee of the Agency whenever he shall deem such termination necessary or advisable in the interests of the United States. . . .

50 U.S.C. §403(s).

In this case we decide whether, and to what extent, the termination decisions of the Director under §102(c) are judicially reviewable. [The director dismissed the plaintiff from the CIA because he was homosexual. The plaintiff claimed that his dismissal (1) exceeded the director's statutory authority and was an abuse of discretion, and (2) violated the Constitution by depriving him of constitutionally protected liberty, property, and privacy.]

II

[The Court held that the plaintiff's "abuse of discretion" claim was unreviewable because it was "committed to agency discretion by law."] Both *Overton Park* and *Heckler* emphasized that §701(a)(2) requires careful examination of the statute on which the claim of agency illegality is based (the Federal-Aid Highway Act of 1968 in *Overton Park* and the Federal Food, Drug, and Cosmetic Act in *Heckler*). In the present case, respondent's claims against the CIA arise from the Director's asserted violation of §102(c) of the NSA. As an initial matter, it should be noted that §102(c) allows termination of an Agency employee whenever the Director "shall *deem* such termination necessary or advisable in the interest of the United States" (emphasis added), not simply when the dismissal is necessary or advisable to those interests. This standard fairly exudes deference to the Director, and appears to us to foreclose the application of any meaningful judicial standard of review. Short of permitting cross-examination of the Director concerning his views of the Nation's security and whether the discharged employee was inimical to those interests, we see no basis on which a reviewing court could properly assess an Agency termination decision. The language of §102(c) thus strongly suggests that its implementation was "committed to agency discretion by law."

So too does the overall structure of the NSA. Passed shortly after the close of the Second World War, the NSA created the CIA and gave its Director the responsibility "for protecting intelligence sources and methods from unauthorized disclosure." . . . Section 102(c) is an integral part of that statute, because the Agency's efficacy, and the Nation's security, depend in large measure on the reliability and trustworthiness of the Agency's employees. As we recognized in Snepp v. United States, 444 U.S. 507, 510 (1980), employment with the CIA entails a high degree of trust that is perhaps unmatched in Government service. . . .

We thus find that the language and structure of §102(c) indicate that Congress meant to commit individual employee discharges to the Director's discretion, and that §701(a)(2) accordingly precludes judicial review of these decisions under the APA. We reverse the Court of Appeals to the extent that it found such termination reviewable by the courts. . . .

III

[The Court held that the plaintiff's constitutional claims were reviewable. We consider that aspect of the decision at page 0000. The basic idea is that there is a strong presumption in favor of judicial review of constitutional claims, partly because closing off such review may be unconstitutional, and that the Constitution itself supplies "law to apply" in this case.]

[SCALIA, Justice, concurring and dissenting.]

The "no law to apply" test can account for the nonreviewability of certain issues, but falls far short of explaining the full scope of the area from which the courts are excluded. For the fact is that there is no governmental decision that is not subject to a fair number of legal constraints precise enough to be susceptible of judicial application — beginning with the fundamental constraint that the decision must be taken in order to further a public purpose rather than a purely private interest; yet there are many governmental decisions that are not at all subject to judicial review. A United States Attorney's decision to prosecute, for example, will not be reviewed on the claim that it was prompted by personal animosity. Thus, "no law to apply" provides much less than the full answer to whether §701(a)(2) applies.

The key to understanding the "committed to agency discretion by law" provision of §701(a)(2) lies in contrasting it with the "*statutes* preclude judicial review" provision of §701(a)(1). Why "statutes" for preclusion, but the much more general term "law" for commission to agency discretion? The answer is, as we implied in [Heckler v. Chany, 470 U.S. 821 (1985)], that the latter was intended to refer to "the 'common law' of judicial review of agency action." 470 U.S., at 832 — a body of jurisprudence that had marked out, with more or less precision, certain issues and certain areas that were beyond the range of judicial review. That jurisprudence included principles ranging from the "political question" doctrine, to sovereign immunity (including doctrines determining when a suit against an officer would be deemed to be a suit against the sovereign), to official immunity, to prudential limitations upon the courts' equitable power, to what can be described no more precisely than a traditional respect for the functions of the other branches. . . . Only if all the "common law" were embraced within §701(a)(2) could it have been true that, as was generally understood, "[t]he intended result of [§701(a)] is to restate the existing law as to the area of reviewable agency action." Attorney General's Manual on the Administrative Procedure Act 94 (1947). Because that is the meaning of the provision, we have continued to take into account for purposes of determining reviewability, post-APA as before, not only the text and structure of the statute under which the agency acts, but such factors as whether the decision involves "a sensitive and inherently discretionary judgment call," Department of Navy v. Egan, 484 U.S. 518, 427 (1988); whether it is the sort of decision that has traditionally been nonreviewable,

ICC v. Locomotive Engineers, 482 U.S. 270, 282 (1987); *Chaney,* supra, at 832, and whether review would have "disruptive practical consequences," see Southern R. Co. v. Seaboard Allied Milling Corp., 442 U.S. 444, 457 (1979). This explains the seeming contradiction between §701(a)(2)'s disallowance of review to the extent that action is "committed to agency discretion," and §706's injunction that a court shall set aside agency action that constitutes "an abuse of discretion." Since, in the former provision, "committed to agency discretion by law" means "of the sort that is traditionally unreviewable," it operates to keep certain categories of agency action out of the courts; but when agency action is appropriately in the courts, abuse of discretion is of course grounds for reversal.

All this law, shaped over the course of centuries and still developing in its application to new contexts, cannot possibly be contained within the phrase "no law to apply." It is not surprising, then, that although the Court recites the test it does not really apply it. Like other opinions relying upon it, this one essentially announces the test, declares victory and moves on. It is not really true "'that a court would have no meaningful standard against which to judge an agency's exercise of discretion,'" *ante,* at 600, quoting *Chaney,* 470 U.S., at 830. The standard set forth in §102(c) of the National Security Act of 1947, 50 U.S.C. §403(c), "necessary or advisable in the interest of the United States," at least excludes dismissal out of personal vindictiveness, or because the Director wants to give the job to his cousin. Why, on the Court's theory, is respondent not entitled to assert the presence of such excesses, under the "abuse of discretion" standard of §706?

If and when this Court does come to consider the reviewability of a dismissal such as the present one on the ground that it violated the agency's regulation — a question the Court avoids today — the difference between the "no law to apply" test and what I consider the correct test will be crucial. Perhaps a dismissal in violation of the regulations can be reviewed, but not simply because the regulations provide a standard that makes review possible. . . .

For a number of years, the Indian Health Service funded a mental health program for handicapped Indian children, using funds from the service's lump-sum appropriation. The service then cut the program without following rulemaking procedures and allocated the funds to other programs. The court of appeals held that the funding decision was a legislative rule that was subject to notice-and-comment rulemaking, and ordered the program reinstated while the service complied with the procedural requirements of the APA. In Lincoln v. Vigil, 508 U.S. 182 (1993), the Supreme Court reversed on the ground that the service's actions were not reviewable, concluding that the

> allocation of funds from a lump-sum appropriation is [an] administrative decision traditionally regarded as committed to agency discretion. After all, the very point of a lump-sum appropriation is to give an agency the capacity to adapt to changing circumstances and meet its statutory responsibilities in what it sees as the most effective or desirable way. [A] lump-sum appropriation reflects congressional recognition that an agency must be allowed flexibility to shift funds within a particular appropriation account so that the agency can make necessary adjustments for unforeseen developments and changing requirements.

The statute governing applications for an Indian Revolving Fund Loan provides: "Loans may be made only when, in the judgment of the Secretary, there is a reasonable prospect of repayment, and only to applicants who in the opinion of the Secretary are unable to obtain financing from other sources on reasonable terms and conditions." The court held that decisions to grant or deny applications for a loan are committed to agency discretion by law. In so holding, it emphasized the phrases "in the judgment of the Secretary" and "in the opinion of the Secretary." At the same time, the court held that agency action would be reviewable if the agency departed from the statutory criteria. Helgeson v. Bureau of Indian Affairs, 153 F.3d 1000 (9th Cir. 1998). In the same vein, see Ellison v. Connor, 153 F.3d 247 (5th Cir. 1998), holding unreviewable Corps of Engineer decisions to grant or deny permits to use Corps property. The court stressed the open-ended, standardless nature of the statutory terms, which ask whether the property is required for public use and whether the permit would interfere with any operations of the United States.

Note: No Law to Apply — and Prudence

1. Suppose that the defendant had alleged, in Webster v. Doe, that he had been discharged because of his religion. Would the discharge be committed to agency discretion by law? Suppose that the defendant had alleged that he had been discharged because the CIA director was appointing people who had given campaign contributions to the president. Would that discharge be committed to agency discretion by law? What result would have made sense if the plaintiff had contended that the CIA director had made employment decisions as a result of bribes, or that the CIA director was giving an employment preference to his cousins or childhood friends? Consider the view that in at least some such cases, there would have been "law to apply."

Would it be right to say that prudential factors, involving the problems associated with judicial supervision of the CIA, played a role in the *Webster* decision, complementing the "no law to apply" point? Is this true in Lincoln v. Vigil as well? On the implications of Lincoln v. Vigil, see American Medical Association v. Reno, 51 F.3d 1129 (D.C. Cir. 1995) (allowing review of a funding decision on the ground that it was made in violation of APA's procedural requirements for rulemaking); Ramah Navajo School Board v. Babbitt, 87 F.3d 1228 (D.C. Cir. 1996) (allowing review of funding decision because of mandatory criteria found in the statute).

2. Now turn to Heckler v. Chaney. Suppose that the plaintiff had challenged agency inaction on one of the following grounds. (1) A violation of constitutional rights, as in a racially motivated failure to act. (2) An allegedly unlawful conclusion that the agency lacked jurisdiction. (3) A refusal to undertake action that the statute plainly compelled the agency to undertake. (4) A refusal to undertake rulemaking. (5) A refusal to enforce existing rules. (6) A pattern of inaction or a form of statutory abdication. Would inaction be reviewable in any of these cases? See generally Sunstein, Reviewing Agency Inaction after Heckler v. Chaney, 52 U. Chi. L. Rev. 653 (1985); and see Note 3 immediately below this one, on judicial review of agency inaction.

3. Now consider the dispute between Chief Justice Rehnquist and Justice Scalia in Webster v. Doe. Does the Chief Justice really apply a "no law to apply" standard, or does he take account as well of prudential considerations that argue against judicial involvement? Might Justice Scalia be criticized on the ground that there is a danger that a common law of reviewability, founded on such considerations, would become too unruly, too ad hoc? Does Justice Scalia persuasively show that the APA contemplates such a common law of reviewability?

Note in this regard several tendencies in the lower courts. Some courts read *Overton Park* as referring to the need to find "clear and convincing" evidence that Congress intended to grant unreviewable discretion. See, e.g., New York Racing Assn. v. NLRB, 708 F.2d 46 (2d Cir. 1983). This approach tends to collapse §701(a)(2) into §701(a)(1), making all a matter of congressional instructions. And when congressional instructions are unclear, some cases — perhaps including both *Heckler* and *Webster* — suggest that §701(a)(2)'s exception may have a somewhat broader scope in light of the "practical and policy implications of reviewability." See Local 1219, American Fed. of Govt. Employees v. Donovan, 683 F.2d 511, 515 (D.C. Cir. 1982). These factors may, of course, be taken as "evidence" of Congress's "intentions" about reviewability in the particular statutory scheme.

4. Suppose that the "committed to agency discretion of law" exception does mean that there must be "no law to apply." If so, is a decision that an agency action is unreviewable because there is no law to apply identical to a decision that an agency action is lawful because no provision of law bars it? And if this is so, does the "committed to agency discretion by law" exception have just one function: to make agency action *unreviewable* when that agency would otherwise be *lawful*? What purpose, if any, is served by this apparently redundant function? Construct an argument that in *Heckler*, *Webster*, and Lincoln v. Vigil there really was no law to apply to the plaintiffs' particular allegations.

5. Congress has provided that "[t]he Secretary of a military department may correct any military record of the Secretary's department when the Secretary considers it necessary to correct an error or remove an injustice. . . . Such corrections shall be made by the Secretary acting through boards of civilians. . . ." 10 U.S.C. §1551(a)(1). Congress has also provided a limitations period, for a request for such a correction, of three years after the discovery of any error or injustice. But it allows the board to excuse a failure to request correction within the period when "in the interest of justice." In three cases involving former servicemen, heavy drinkers who were discharged under "other than honorable conditions," the board failed to excuse the failure to act within the three-year period. The three former servicemen sought judicial review. Is Webster v. Doe a barrier? In Dickson v. Secretary of Defense, 68 F.3d 1396 (D.C. Cir. 1995), the court held that it was not. *Webster* involved the distinctive security interests of the CIA, and under the relevant statute, the secretary of defense's discretion "is considerably narrower" than the CIA director's. Judge Silberman dissented on the ground that the "interest of justice" standard "is without determinable substantive content." See also Department of the Navy v. Egan, 484 U.S. 518, 528-529 (1988) (holding that there is no judicial review of a decision whether a grant of a security clearance is "clearly consistent with the interests of national security"); Beattie v. Boeing Co., 43 F.3d 559 (10th Cir. 1994) (holding unreviewable an air force decision denying an employee of a government contractor access to Air Force One on grounds of national security).

Compare Madison-Hughes v. Shalala, 80 F.3d 1121 (6th Cir. 1996), in which a patient and a public service brought suit against the secretary of the Department of Health and Human Services (HHS), alleging that they were discriminated against by health care providers in violation of title VI, which prohibits recipients from discriminating on the basis of race, color, or national origin. The governing regulations provide for HHS to collect data and information from recipients of federal funds, sufficient to permit effective enforcement of title VI. The court held that the challenged HHS activities were unreviewable, because "title VI regulations do not include standards for the court to determine the adequacy of HHS's data collection activities. If regulations do not provide guidance about specific legal standards for judicial review, agency action is immune from such review." The court said that "[t]itle VI does not impose on HHS a duty to provide the type of data collection which they allege in their complaint is lacking; it instead imposes a duty on HHS to ensure the compliance of each particular recipient of federal funds through a variety of means, one of which is data collection." The choice among those means, and the mechanisms of enforcement, were within HHS's unreviewable discretion under Heckler v. Chaney. See also Claybrook v. Slater, 111 F.3d 904 (D.C. Cir. 1997), holding unreviewable a decision by an advisory committee to the Federal Highway Administration to pass a resolution criticizing certain inaccuracies in the fund-raising literature of an organization co-chaired by the plaintiff. The plaintiff wanted the agency to adjourn the meeting or otherwise to block the resolution. The court invoked the statutory language, which authorizes the agency "whenever he determines it to be in the public interest, to adjourn" a committee meeting. This language was sufficiently broad, the court said, to preclude review. Compare Clifford v. Pena, 77 F.3d 1414 (D.C. Cir. 1996), allowing review of decisions of the secretary of transportation under an apparently open-ended statute, on the theory that the secretary had built up a series of precedents that could be used to test for arbitrariness.

6. Can you imagine a legal system that would provide a presumption against reviewability, or at least a light, easily rebutted presumption in favor of judicial review? Suppose that a legal system was quite concerned about delay and litigation costs (recall the problem of "ossification" of rulemaking, discussed in Chapter 6); suppose that agencies were, in such a legal system, highly reliable, both democratically accountable and technically expert; and that judges were, in such a legal system, both willful and ignorant of relevant facts, and generally regarded as such. Would it not make sense to create at most a weak presumption in favor of review? If this is so, ask whether different judgments about the appropriate strength of a presumption of review might depend on highly pragmatic and relatively concrete judgments about the risk of agency failure or mistake, the costs and problems introduced by judicial involvement, and the likelihood that courts will perform their jobs poorly or well.

7. There seems to be a modest trend in favor of finding agency decisions committed to agency discretion, see, e.g., Steenholdt v. FAA, 319 F.3d G33 (D.C. Cir. 2003) (FAA decision to renew inspector's license committed to agency's discretion); Friends of Cowlitz v. FERC, 253 F.3d 1161 (9th Cir. 2001) amended at 282 F.3d 609 (2002); American Disabled for Attendant Programs Today v. Department of HUD, 170 F.3d 381 (3d Cir. 1999); South Dakota v. Department of Interior, 69 F.3d 87 (8th Cir. 1995). But the trend remains modest and cautious, and judicial review is the general rule. See, e.g., Kenney v. Glickman, 96 F.3d 1118 (8th Cir. 1996); Head Start Family Educ. Program v. Cooperative Educ. Serv. Agency, 46 F.3d 629 (7th Cir. 1995) (reviewing agency decision to choose a particular Head Start grantee, on ground that statutory provision created "law to apply" by listing nine factors for agency to consider); Brown v. Secretary of HHS, 46 F.3d 102 (1st Cir. 1995) (reviewing an agency's decision not to institute a rulemaking proceeding); Railway Labor Executives' Assn. v. National Mediation Bd., 29 F.3d 655 (D.C. Cir. 1994); Sprague v. King, 23 F.3d 185 (7th Cir. 1994); Ward v. Brown, 22 F.3d 516 (2d Cir. 1994); Monsanto v. EPA, 19 F.3d 1201 (7th Cir. 1994); Mount Evans Co. v. Madigan, 14 F.3d 1444 (10th Cir. 1994) (reviewing a forest service decision not to rebuild a structure that had been destroyed by fire where the agency had received money as settlement of its claim for destruction of the structure, and distinguishing Lincoln v. Vigil on the basis of the distinctive statutory language).

Note: Judicial Review of Agency Inaction

1. Judicial review of agency inaction raises a number of distinctive problems. Perhaps agency inaction is like a prosecutor's failure to act, which is, as the *Heckler* Court said,

traditionally unreviewable. It is possible that article II of the Constitution gives the executive branch immunity from judicial supervision of prosecutorial discretion. Moreover, the private law model of administrative law makes a distinction, as did the Heckler Court, between "coercive" intrusion on common law interests and "noncoercive" failure to act.

On the other hand, as the Court emphasizes in the Norton v. Southern Utah Wilderness Alliance case, the APA does allow judicial review for agency action "unlawfully withheld or unreasonably delayed," §706(1), and it defines action to include "failure to act," §551(13). Moreover, it is possible to question whether a sharp distinction between *action* and *inaction* can be sustained in a regulatory-welfare state. In some sense, the government is always acting (at least through the common law of property, contract, and tort), even if the particular agency at issue appears to be sitting on its hands. Recall the discussion of the New Deal. Mightn't the distinction between action and inaction depend on a form of private law thinking that the rise of that state has repudiated? In this view, the belief that "action" is especially troublesome, or coercive, and that "inaction" is not a proper source of legal concern, depends on pre-New Deal assumptions, to the effect that common law rights are "real" and that new statutory rights are less important or in some sense privileges or gratuities. Perhaps these assumptions have generally been repudiated by the legal culture and should no longer form the basis for judge-made law.

Suppose, for example, that the government refuses to enforce the Animal Protection Act or decides that a certain civil rights statute should lie dormant, or concludes that one of a set of environmental statutes deserves no regulatory activity. Is it obviously "noncoercive" if, in these cases, the government allows private conduct to continue notwithstanding its inconsistency with statute? In any case, mightn't people be injured, and statutes be undone, as much by inaction and nonenforcement as by overzealous action? Would it really be inconsistent with article II for Congress to say that the Environmental Protection Agency (EPA) and the Department of Justice have a nondiscretionary duty to prosecute certain polluters, a duty enforceable in court at the behest of affected citizens?

2. Perhaps the most straightforward argument in Heckler v. Chaney is that agencies have scarce resources and must necessarily act in some cases but not in others. Courts cannot apply "law" to the necessary priority-setting. This argument seems untouched by the considerations just noted. Most agencies are forced, by the simple fact of limited resources, to allow some illegality to continue. The Food and Drug Administration (FDA) is unlikely to be in a position to bring enforcement against every violation of the Food and Drug Act. Indeed, Congress often uses the appropriations process so as to control the extent of agency enforcement activity. In these circumstances, it is hardly unlawful for an agency to fail to act in many cases, and a court will have a very hard time in seeing whether certain kinds of inaction are "arbitrary." For a court to make that determination, it will have to look not only at the particular enforcement action that the plaintiff seeks, but at all or most of the "menu" of enforcement actions before the agency. See Drake v. FAA, 291 F.3d 59 (D.C. Cir. 2002) (FAA may dismiss complaint without hearing; no judicial review); Friends of Cowlitz v. FERC, 253 F.3d 116 (9th Cir. 2001) (decisions whether to enforce licenses committed to agency discretion by law). American Disabled for Attendant Programs Today v. Department of Housing and Urban Development, 170 F.3d 381 (3d Cir. 1999) (refusing to review HUD decisions on whether and how to investigate alleged violations of rules governing housing for the handicapped); Professional Pilots Ass'n. v. FAA, 118 F.3d 758 (D.C. Cir. 1997) (on similar grounds, the court upholds FAA refusal to conduct rulemaking); Sprint Communications v. FCC, 76 F.3d 1221, 1231 (D.C. Cir. 1996) (suggesting that the FCC's failure to investigate a particular matter appears committed to agency discretion by law). This is the principal argument in Heckler v. Chaney; how far does it reach?

There is also a question whether judicial review of agency inaction might not create a system by which private interests are able to dictate public priorities. With all of the possible illegalities that (for example) the EPA might investigate, judicial review of inaction might allow self-interested private groups to conscript enforcement in their preferred direction. See M. Greve, Private Enforcement, Private Rewards: How Environmental Citizen Suits Became an Entitlement Program, in Environmental Politics (M. Greve & F. Lewis eds., 1992); Greve, The Private Enforcement of Environmental Law, 65 Tul. L. Rev. 339 (1990). Such groups may well be in an inferior position to the EPA, which is, perhaps, better able to get a handle on the universe of potential investigations and enforcement proceedings and to set priorities in a sensible manner.

3. Despite these cases courts of appeals do not read Heckler v. Chaney as broadly as possible. A helpful overview is Bhagwat, Three-Branch Monte, 72 Notre Dame L. Rev. 157 (1996). Note first that the D.C. Circuit has held that refusals to institute rulemaking proceedings, unlike isolated cases of enforcement, are not entitled to a "presumption" of nonreviewability. That court, followed elsewhere, has ruled that decisions not to institute rulemaking are likely to be challenged less frequently, that such challenges are likely to turn on issues of law (rather than the issues of fact involved in isolated refusals to enforce), and that the APA itself permits indicated persons to petition for rulemaking and requires the agency to give "a brief statement of the grounds for denial." APA §§553(e), 555(e); National Customs Brokers v. United States, 883 F.2d 93 (D.C. Cir. 1989); American Horse Protection Assn. v. Lyng, 812 F.2d 1 (D.C. Cir. 1987).

Courts have also found that a number of statutes provide sufficient standards to rebut the presumption against review of inaction. See Milk Train, Inc v. Veneman, 310 F.3d 747 (D.C. Cir. 2002); Democratic Congressional Campaign Comm. v. FEC, 831 F.2d 1131 (D.C. Cir. 1987); Doyle v. Brock, 821 F.2d 778 (D.C. Cir. 1987); Shelley v. Brock, 793 F.2d 1368, 1372 (D.C. Cir. 1986). In *Heckler* itself, the Court distinguished Dunlop v. Bachowski, 421 U.S. 560 (1975), on just this ground, claiming that the secretary of labor's failure to set aside union elections was reviewable under the relevant statute. See also the important decision in Federal Election Commission v. Akins, 524 U.S. 11 (1998), and in particular the debate between Justices Breyer and Scalia. So too, courts have reviewed agency inaction when the grounds for inaction were a claim of lack of jurisdiction. In such a case, the apparent argument is that the underlying statute supplies the "law to apply," because an understanding of the statute tells whether the agency has jurisdiction. See Montana Air Chapter No. 29 v. FLRA, 898 F.2d 753 (9th Cir. 1990).

In a prominent pre-*Chaney* case, the D.C. Circuit had held that courts could review the government's alleged failure to enforce title VI of the Civil Rights Acts of 1964, which bans the granting of federal funds to schools that discriminate on the basis of race. *Chaney* suggested that an "abdication" of enforcement responsibilities might be reviewable. This exception — allowing review in the face of an alleged abdication of enforcement responsibilities — appears to survive. See Northern Ind. Public Serv. Co. v. FERC, 782 F.2d 730, 745-746 (7th Cir. 1986). Note, however, that the line between an isolated failure to enforce and an "abdication" seems to be one of degree, and it is easy to imagine cases in which a pattern of inaction is said by the plaintiff to be an "abdication," but is said by the government to be a reasonable allocation of limited resources for enforcement and investigation. Thus, recent decisions are quite skeptical of the "abdication" exception. See, e.g., Riverkeeper v. Collins, 359 F.3d 156 (2d Cir. 2004). The petitioner claimed that the Nuclear Regulatory Commission had abdicated its statutory responsibility to increase security at nuclear power plants after 9/11. The court denied review. It noted that (1) as of yet no court has actually found an abdication sufficient to trigger the exception and (2) adopting an expansive reading of the abdication exception would threaten to swallow up the *Chaney* presumption.

4. How does the Norton v. Southern Utah decision affect these issues? On one reading, *Norton* is an important decision, at least analytically. There is no talk, in *Norton*, of a "presumption of unreviewability for agency inaction." Heckler v. Chaney is not even cited. Rather, the *Norton* Court focuses at all times on the legal merits of the relevant claims. An agency's "failure to act" is an "action" if there is a legal obligation to act, on the merits. If there is such an obligation, then the difference between action and inaction is not legally relevant. The issue, after *Norton*, is not whether the agency was acting or failing to act, but whether the relevant law leaves the agency with discretion as to the relevant issues.

On another view, however, the *Norton* Court should be read merely as saying that where relevant statutes are clear, the presence or absence of a presumption in either direction is irrelevant. If Congress has clearly commanded an agency to do or not do something, and assuming there are no constitutional constraints, then that is what the agency must do (or not do).

6. *The Constitutionality of Preclusion of Review*

The Court in *Robison* and *Webster* said that its finding of reviewability helped to avoid a constitutional question. That question is whether, or when, Congress can constitutionally curtail a right to judicial review. The question was discussed in Crowell v. Benson, in which Justice Brandeis suggested that "under certain circumstances, the constitutional requirement of due process is a requirement of judicial process." When does "due process" include judicial review? Or, put another way, to what extent can Congress constitutionally preclude judicial review of a decision of a government official? The subject is a difficult and intricate one, which we shall only summarize briefly here.

In the case of preclusion of review by federal courts, the problem is founded on article III, section 1 of the Constitution, which states that the "judicial power of the United States, shall be vested in one Supreme Court, and in such inferior courts as the Congress *may* from time to time ordain and establish." This section suggests that Congress may, but need not, establish lower federal courts. The Supreme Court, in Sheldon v. Sill, 49 U.S. (8 How.) 441 (1850), accepted this view and went on to hold that Congress can restrict the jurisdiction of the lower federal courts; it need not grant them full power to hear all federal question cases, "diversity cases," or other sorts of cases that article III lists as within the scope of the federal judicial power. This view was consistent with the position of those who saw article III as a compromise between those who wanted a strong centralizing federal judicial system and those who feared such a system would strip the state courts of their general jurisdiction, which included jurisdiction over federal questions. Under that compromise, Congress would decide the extent to which lower federal courts were needed.

Although article III may give Congress power to limit the jurisdiction of the federal courts, one might ask whether the exercise of that power could, in a given instance, violate the due process clause. Might it, in depriving a litigant of judicial review, say, of a claim that a governmental action was unconstitutional, deprive him or her of life, liberty, or property without due process of law?

This question is the subject of Professor Hart's famous dialogue on the power of Congress to limit the jurisdiction of the federal courts. Bator, Mishkin, Shapiro, and

Wechsler, Hart & Wechsler's The Federal Courts and the Federal System 330 (2d ed. 1973). This dialogue focuses on an act of Congress that would foreclose the federal courts from hearing a claim that the government has denied a litigant an important constitutional right — a claim, for example, that it has deprived him of free speech or his liberty. Professor Hart concludes that as long as *some* judicial forum — state or federal — is available to test the legality of the claim, Congress can constitutionally foreclose access to other forums. If, for example, all federal courts were denied jurisdiction to hear a particular claim (say, that a litigant was denied free speech), that litigant might raise the claim in a state court, and review of that decision could eventually be sought in the Supreme Court. Under these circumstances, the act of Congress limiting or foreclosing access to the federal courts in the first instance would be constitutional. So also may Congress impose reasonable restrictions on the right to review within the federal court system. For example, it may ordinarily direct that review be brought in a specified forum, that a petition to review be filed within 30 days after the challenged agency decision, and so forth.

But suppose that Congress were to enact a statute precluding all review of a particular claim that a federal action was unlawful or unconstitutional. The constitutionality of such an act might depend on several factors, such as the importance of the underlying right of which the litigant was arguably deprived, the government interest in precluding review, and the extent to which the courts are already involved in the litigant's case.

Professor Hart argues that the constitutional problems raised by preclusion of review are especially acute when the courts are asked by the government to enforce coercive orders against persons who claim that the orders are unlawful. Consider Crowell v. Benson (Chapter 2). In that case, a litigant invoked the Court's jurisdiction to obtain a court order transferring to him property (money) belonging to his employer. Under those circumstances, both the Court and Justice Brandeis indicated that some federal court review, at the behest of the employer, of the legal merits of the claim was constitutionally compelled by due process (and, the Court added, by article III as well). But would the Court or Justice Brandeis have reached the same conclusion had the case involved a government benefit to a claimant rather than a coercive order against an individual's property? Consider, in this respect, the relevance of the decisions in Chapter 6 with respect to due process hearing rights. If a person is entitled to some form of administrative hearing where "liberty" or "property" is at stake, should he or she not also be entitled to judicial review, not only to ensure agency conformance with due process requirements, but also to determine the substantive question whether the agency unlawfully deprived that person of "liberty" or "property" in the given circumstances?

The answers to these questions may well depend on the particular type of illegality asserted by the person seeking review. As already noted, claims may run the gamut from a constitutional violation, to abuse of discretion, to factual error.

The courts have not dealt explicitly with the doctrine of a constitutional right to judicial review, nor have they defined its contours. They approached the question tangentially, however, in a series of selective service cases involving the issue of *when* review must take place. In Falbo v. United States, 320 U.S. 549 (1944), the Supreme Court held that a person drafted by his selective service board could not raise questions concerning the legality of his draft classification until after he was inducted; he could raise such issues only as a defense in a criminal trial (for refusing induction) or in a habeas corpus proceeding (after induction). In Wolff v. Selective Serv. Local Bd. No. 16, 372 F.2d 817 (2d Cir. 1967), however, the court of appeals enjoined a draft board from inducting plaintiffs. The court accepted plaintiffs' argument that the board was retaliating against plaintiffs' antiwar demonstration; hence the induction violated first amendment rights, and for that reason a preinduction injunction was proper. Congress responded to *Wolff* by enacting a statute explicitly depriving the courts of power to review "the classification or processing of any registrant . . . except as a defense to a criminal prosecution" after induction. 50 U.S.C. App. §460(b)(3). (This statute was not intended to deprive those drafted of the right to seek habeas corpus.) The Supreme Court, interpreting that statute in Oestereich v. Selective Serv. Sys. Local Bd. No. 11, 393 U.S. 233 (1968), held that it did *not* prevent a court from issuing a preinduction injunction barring the board from drafting a divinity student who had protested against the war. The Court argued that another part of the statute specifically exempts full-time ministry students from the draft; because the exemption is "plain and unequivocal," and because the board's action was clearly wrong, "pre-induction judicial review is not precluded" by the statute. 393 U.S. at 238, 239.

Justice Harlan, concurring, wrote that a failure to interpret the statute to allow him review would deprive petitioner of his liberty "without the prior opportunity to present to any competent forum — agency or court — his substantial claim. . . . Such an interpretation [of the statute] would raise serious constitutional problems." 393 U.S. at 243. Justice Harlan then wrote the following footnote: "It is doubtful whether a person may be deprived of his personal liberty without the prior opportunity to be heard by some tribunal competent fully to adjudicate his claims . . . ," citing, among other cases, Londoner v. Denver, 210 U.S. 373, 385 (1908), with "but cf." citations to North American Cold Storage Co. v. Chicago, 211 U.S. 306 (1908), and Bowles v. Willingham, 321 U.S. 503, 520 (1944). He asserted that the validity of summary administrative deprivation of liberty without a full hearing may turn on the availability of a prompt subsequent hearing, "something not made meaningfully available to petitioner here, either by the option of defending a criminal prosecution for refusing to report for induction . . . or by filing a petition for a writ of habeas corpus after induction. [If petitioner's argument that the board is punishing him by drafting him is correct,] then postponement of a hearing until after induction is tantamount to permitting the imposition of summary punishment, followed by loss of liberty, without possibility of bail, until [habeas corpus can be secured]." Justice Stewart, responding to Justice Harlan, pointed out that persons arrested for criminal offenses are frequently deprived of their liberty prior to a full hearing. 393 U.S. at 250 n.10.

The reach of *Oestereich* was limited by Clark v. Gabriel, 393 U.S. 256 (1968), which held that preinduction review was not proper where plaintiffs' claims to deferment raised issues that were not plain and unequivocal. A majority of the Court held that there was no constitutional objection to this interpretation of the statute. A few weeks after deciding *Clark*, the Court applied it to reject a request for preinduction review of plaintiffs' attack on student deferments based on equal protection grounds. Again, presumably, the Constitution raised no obstacle to postponing review of this constitutional question until after induction.

WEBSTER v. DOE, 486 U.S. 592 (1988).   A CIA employee, discharged by the CIA because he was a homosexual, claimed that his discharge was unlawful both (1) because it exceeded the lawful power to discharge that a statute conferred on the CIA director, and (2) because it violated constitutionally protected rights of privacy, liberty, and property. As you read in the section on *Webster*, the Court held that, in respect to the first of these claims, the CIA's decision was unreviewable; the determination was "committed to agency discretion by law." The Court also held, however, that the employee's constitutional claims were reviewable. Chief Justice Rehnquist wrote, for the Court, that "where

Congress intends to preclude judicial review of constitutional claims its intent to do so must be clear. . . . We require this heightened showing in part to avoid the 'serious constitutional question' that would arise if a federal statute were construed to deny any judicial forum for a colorable constitutional claim. See Bowen v. Michigan Academy of Family Physicians, 476 U.S. 667, 681 n.12 (1986)." The Court could not find a clear congressional intent to prevent judicial review of colorable constitutional claims. It added that the district court could take account of the CIA's special security needs in tailoring discovery and when deciding (should plaintiff win) whether or not an equitable order, such as an injunction requiring reinstatement, is appropriate. Justice Scalia dissented vigorously. He said that it is obvious that the Constitution does not guarantee a judicial forum to consider every constitutional claim; some such claims are fairly trivial; others are clearly committed to the decisionmaking authority of other branches; and Congress must possess some power to decide just which constitutional claims require a judicial remedy. That being so, given the Constitution's delegation to the politically responsive branches of government, of both foreign affairs and national defense powers, and given the especially sensitive and necessary tasks of foreign intelligence, "it is clear that the 'serious constitutional question' feared by the Court is an illusion." At the same time, to permit discharged CIA agents to litigate their dismissals in the court, irrespective of the legal questions at issue, would so seriously harm the intelligence-gathering function (making other nations' intelligence agencies wonder, for example, whether shared information could be kept secret), that the "agent dismissal" decision must be considered one that is "committed to agency discretion by law," precluding judicial review in respect to constitutional, as well as to statutory or other, legal arguments. Justice O'Connor basically agreed with Justice Scalia. She wrote, "Whatever may be the exact scope of Congress' power to close the lower federal courts to constitutional claims in other contexts, I have no doubt about its authority to do so here."

7. *Reviewability at War*

In Chapter 4, in the Note on *Chevron* at War, we considered whether *Chevron* deference is a valid framework for judicial review of presidential determinations of the meaning of statutes. The issue is especially acute under broadly phrased statutes bearing on war, emergencies, and foreign affairs, such as the "Authorization to Use Military Force" (AUMF) against persons or organizations associated with the 9/11 attacks. Here we address the reviewability dimensions of such cases. What is the scope of judicial review when the president makes a determination of fact, or a mixed determination of law and fact, under such statutes?

As we saw in Chapter 4, the APA's provisions for judicial review do not apply in such cases, because the president is not an "agency" within the meaning of the APA. Judicial review in these cases is available (if at all) under the substantive statutes themselves or in the form of "nonstatutory review" — that is, by virtue of common law writs, such as the writ of habeas corpus. In cases such as INS v. St. Cyr, supra, we have seen the Court construe preclusion-of-review provisions in exceptionally narrow fashion, to preserve the possibility of review on habeas corpus. Consider also the following case:

HAMDI v. RUMSFELD, 542 U.S. 507 (2004). After Congress passed a resolution — the Authorization for Use of Military Force (AUMF) — empowering the president to "use all necessary and appropriate force" against "nations, organizations, or persons" that he determines "planned, authorized, committed, or aided" in the September 11, 2001, al Qaeda terrorist attacks, the president ordered the armed forces to Afghanistan to subdue al Qaeda and quell the supporting Taliban regime. Hamdi, an American citizen whom the government classified as an "enemy combatant" for allegedly taking up arms with the Taliban during the conflict, was captured in Afghanistan and detained at a naval brig in Charleston, South Carolina. Hamdi's father filed a habeas petition on his behalf, alleging, among other things, that the government was holding his son in violation of the fifth and fourteenth Amendments. The government attached to its response to the petition a declaration from Michael Mobbs, a Defense Department official. The Mobbs Declaration alleges various details regarding Hamdi's trip to Afghanistan, his affiliation there with a Taliban unit during a time when the Taliban was battling U.S. allies, and his subsequent surrender of an assault rifle. The Government argued that courts should review its determination that a citizen is an enemy combatant under a very deferential "some evidence" standard. (Compare the *Universal Camera* case and the history of the "substantial evidence" standard for review of agency factfinding, discussed in Chapter 4.) Under this review, a court would assume the accuracy of the government's articulated basis for Hamdi's detention, as set forth in the Mobbs Declaration, and assess only whether that articulated basis was a legitimate one.

A plurality (Justice O'Connor and three others) concluded that although Congress had authorized the detention of enemy combatants in the circumstances of the case, due process demands that a citizen held in the United States as an enemy combatant be given a meaningful opportunity to contest the factual basis for that detention before a neutral decisionmaker. The plurality stated that the "ordinary mechanism" for balancing "serious competing interests," and for "determining the procedures that are necessary to ensure that a citizen is not deprived of life, liberty, or property, without due process of law . . . is the test that we articulated in Mathews v. Eldridge." The plurality held that a citizen-detainee seeking to challenge his classification as an enemy combatant must receive notice of the factual basis for his classification, and a fair opportunity to rebut the government's factual assertions before a neutral decisionmaker. The plurality left open the possibility that the neutral decisionmaker could be a military tribunal rather than a federal court.

Justices Souter and Ginsburg, although dissenting on the statutory authorization issue, supplied the votes to make a majority on the due process issue. Justice Scalia, joined by Justice Stevens, dissented on the statutory authorization issue, stating that the government's only options were to charge Hamdi with treason or to obtain from Congress a statute authorizing a formal suspension of the writ of habeas corpus — which the Constitution permits only in cases of "Rebellion or Invasion." U.S. Const., Art. I, Sec. 9. Justice Thomas dissented in the other direction, finding the detention authorized by statute and consistent with due process, even without a further hearing.

1. Observe how many ordinary administrative law concepts and doctrines the Court relies upon in *Hamdi*, even in a case not arising under the APA. These include legal standards for review of fact, Mathews v. Eldridge balancing under procedural due process, and the question whether the president's actions were authorized by statute.

2. What about reviewability? If this were an APA case, would not the government have a powerful case that the enemy-combatant determination is "committed to agency discretion by law" for precisely the reasons Justice Scalia gives in his separate opinion in Webster v. Doe, supra? All sides agreed that the power to determine whether persons

found on a battlefield are "enemy combatants" is one traditionally lodged in the president, under principles of the laws of war and international law, even if those persons are U.S. citizens. Moreover, the "disruptive" institutional and practical consequences that Justice Scalia described as the basis for nonreviewability may well be present in a case like *Hamdi*, as is the idea that the determination at issue involves "a sensitive and inherently discretionary judgment call." Viewed through an administrative law lens, is it odd that Justice Scalia took the position that he did in *Hamdi*?

D. Standing to Secure Judicial Review

1. *Introductory Note*

In addition to establishing that administrative action is reviewable, a litigant must satisfy requirements of standing. These requirements limit the class of persons entitled to secure judicial review.

Organic statutes sometimes spell out, with specificity, who is entitled to seek review. For example, many environmental statutes grant standing to "any person" (such broad grants raise constitutional questions; see Lujan v. Defenders of Wildlife, this chapter). The Federal Communications Act §402(b)(1), 47 U.S.C. §402(b)(1) (1970), provides for review by disappointed applicants for a license. Very frequently, however, such statutes provide generally for review without identifying who is entitled to review. When a litigant seeks review under a general jurisdictional statute such as 28 U.S.C. §1331, the statute does not say who has standing.

What happens when statutes are silent on standing? Historically, the law of standing has been judge-made. Indeed, the roots of standing doctrine lie in the simple idea that a plaintiff must have a cause of action; at common law, the question of standing *is* the question whether a plaintiff has a cause of action. (Consider the law of tort, property, and contract.) By the 1940s, the simple idea had given rise to a complex body of doctrine, produced above all by the confrontation between the administrative state and those who invoked common law ideas of private right to challenge agency action.

APA §702 attempted to codify federal judge-made standing rules by providing for judicial review for a "person suffering legal wrong because of agency action, or adversely affected or aggrieved within the meaning of a relevant statute." As we will see, however, the federal courts have not read the APA as a static codification of standing law as of 1946; on the contrary, they have displayed considerable freedom in modifying judicially formulated standing doctrines in accordance with changing (judicial?) perceptions, values, and needs.

It is important to emphasize that many people have argued that for most of the nation's history there was no separate law of "standing." Whether people could bring suit depended largely on whether they had a cause of action, and whether they had a cause of action depended on positive law. Thus in both England and early America, there was considerable support for the view that if the law said so, anyone might have standing, even strangers; English practice relied on the prerogative writs. See the above discussion of writs; see also Sunstein, What's Standing After *Lujan*? Of Citizen Suits, Injuries, and Article III, 91 Mich. L. Rev. 163 (1992); Winter, The Metaphor of Standing and the

Problem of Self-Governance, 40 Stan. L. Rev. 1371 (1988). Thus, there is some reason to question the idea that the Constitution limits Congress's power to create standing for strangers or citizens, at least as a matter of history. The basic idea of "standing" was that people without a legal right to bring suit had no basis for invoking the jurisdiction of the courts. But for a revisionist view, see Woolhandler & Nelson, Does History Defeat Standing Doctrine? 103 Mich. L. Rev. 689 (2004). The authors contend that although the term "standing" was not used, "there was an active law of standing on the eighteenth and nineteenth centuries," and that body of law disciplined the category of people who had access to federal courts. "Courts regularly designated some areas of litigation as being under public control and others as being under private control."

The history remains controversial. But modern standing doctrine was born in the Progressive and New Deal periods, as judges enthusiastic about modern administration, and unenthusiastic about judicial control of administration, developed devices to limit the role of the judiciary. Justices Brandeis and Frankfurter were especially important in the development of limits on the class of people entitled to bring suit. See Winter, supra. Above all, mere citizens were not permitted to bring suit as such, at least if Congress had not entitled them to do so. It was not clear if these limits depended on statutory interpretation, common law, or an understanding of article III.

Eventually courts insisted on a "private law model" in which standing was ordinarily limited to persons who, because of government action, had suffered specific injury of a type that would be protected at common law if the responsible official had been a private person. For example, if a government official committed what would otherwise be a common law tort, by seizing a person's property to satisfy a tax claim or arresting a person for violation of a cease-and-desist order, the person could seek judicial review to challenge the invasion of his common law rights. The officer would offer as an affirmative defense that the invasion was authorized by statute.

If, however, a government official simply declined to pay a person a welfare benefit or afford her an educational scholarship, no interest protected at common law would be infringed, and she would accordingly lack standing to secure judicial review of the official's conduct, even if it were in flagrant violation of relevant statutes. This limitation of the right to judicial review to instances where common law interests are invaded parallels the "right-privilege" limitation of traditional due process hearing rights.

With the rise of the regulatory welfare state, this private law model of administrative law became increasingly controversial. Why shouldn't those whose interests were protected by statute be entitled to judicial assistance against unlawful or arbitrary agency action? Limiting standing to common law protected interests would effectively immunize from judicial review many activities of contemporary government — including the disposition of advantageous opportunities such as assistance payments, housing, government employment, and the regulatory protection for consumers, workers, and the environment. Eventually "standing" rules tended to shift so as to grant standing to people without common law interests but nonetheless complaining that agencies had acted unlawfully.

In England and in many states, courts recognize a "public action," or action in which any citizen (or, in some contexts, any taxpayer) is recognized as having a sufficient stake in maintaining the rule of law to bring suit challenging assertedly unlawful official action. Modern federal courts have not recognized the "public action." They have insisted that the plaintiff establish that he or she has suffered "injury in fact" as a result of government conduct in order to secure judicial review of its legality.

But why shouldn't anyone be able to complain of government illegality? We will investigate this question in some detail. For the moment consider these possibilities:

1. The question of standing is for congressional resolution. People should not be allowed to bring suit unless Congress has authorized them to do so. There is no "case or controversy" if Congress has not created a cause of action. (This point leaves open the issue whether there are constitutional limits on Congress's power to grant people standing. A possible view is that Congress can grant standing whenever it wants to do so.)

2. Only plaintiffs with a concrete and personal stake will litigate a case with sufficient adversary vigor; otherwise there is a risk of collusive or at least insufficiently enthusiastic litigation.

3. Limitations on standing have democratic goals. They ensure that courts will not undertake to resolve general issues of policy that are better dealt with through the political branches. Courts should only intervene to protect discrete individual interests; otherwise, decisions should be made politically, not judicially. On this view, "the unique advantage of the courts lies in protecting private rights, not in representing the public more wisely than the political branches open." Woolhandler & Nelson, supra, at 733.

4. People whose concrete interests are at stake should have standing to protect their interests; other people are bystanders, or "officious intermeddlers," and they should not be allowed to stop government action that does not bother those directly involved, yet that, for selfish reasons, the intermeddler seeks to hinder.

We shall also consider whether proof by the plaintiff of specific injury is required by article III of the Constitution, which limits the jurisdiction of federal courts to "cases or controversies."

2. The Federal Law of Standing Prior to Data Processing

a. Before the APA

Alabama Power Co. v. Ickes
302 U.S. 464 (1938)

Mr. Justice SUTHERLAND delivered the opinion of the Court. . . .

[Petitioner Alabama Power Co., a privately owned electric power company, brought suit challenging grants by the federal energy administrator of financial aid to municipal electric power companies as part of a federal public works program. Alabama Power contended that it would be competitively injured as a result of the grants and asserted that the grants violated the Constitution and relevant federal statutes.]

Unless a different conclusion is required from the mere fact that petitioner will sustain financial loss by reason of the unlawful competition which will result from the use by the municipalities of the proposed loans and grants, it is clear that petitioner has no such interest and will sustain no such legal injury as enables it to maintain the present suits. Petitioner alleges that it is a taxpayer; but the interest of a taxpayer in the moneys of the federal treasury furnishes no basis for an appeal to the preventive powers of a court of equity. Massachusetts v. Mellon, 262 U.S. 447, 486 et seq. . . .

The claim that the petitioner will be injured, perhaps ruined, by the competition of the municipalities brought about by the use of the moneys . . . presents a clear case of *damnum absque injuria*. Stated in other words, these municipalities have the right under state law to engage in the business in competition with petitioner, since it has been given no exclusive franchise. If its business be curtailed or destroyed by the operations of the municipalities, it will be by lawful competition from which no legal wrong results. . . .

John Doe, let us suppose, is engaged in operating a grocery store. Richard Roe, desiring to open a rival and competing establishment, seeks a loan from a manufacturing concern which, under its charter, is without authority to make the loan. The loan, if made, will be ultra vires. The state or a stockholder of the corporation, perhaps a creditor in some circumstances, may, upon that ground, enjoin the loan. But may it be enjoined at the suit of John Doe, a stranger to the corporation, because the lawful use of the money will prove injurious to him and this result is foreseen and expected both by the lender and the borrower, Richard Roe? Certainly not, unless we are prepared to lay down the general rule that A, who will suffer damage from the lawful act of B, and who plainly will have no case against B, may nevertheless invoke judicial aid to restrain a third party, acting without authority, from furnishing means which will enable B to do what the law permits him to do. Such a rule would be opposed to sound reason, as we have already tried to show, and cannot be accepted.

Note

See also Perkins v. Lukens Steel Co., 310 U.S. 113 (1940): The Walsh-Healy Act requires government suppliers to pay their employees wages not less than those prevailing in the "locality" of employment. The secretary of labor, who was authorized to define geographic localities for purposes of this provision, divided the entire nation into six "localities." The act does not provide specifically for judicial review of the secretary's determinations. A number of suppliers obtained an injunction in federal district court against operation of the minimum-wage requirements, contending that the secretary's definition of "localities" was unduly broad and was contrary to the act. The Supreme Court held that the suppliers' actions should have been dismissed because the suppliers had not shown "an invasion of recognized legal rights" of their own, "as distinguished from the public's interest in the administration of the law." The Court reasoned, "Like private individuals and businesses, the Government enjoys the unrestricted power . . . to determine those with whom it will deal, and to fix the terms and conditions upon which it will make needed purchases."

THE CHICAGO JUNCTION CASE, 264 U.S. 258 (1924). As part of a larger scheme to regulate competition in the railroad industry, the Transportation Act of 1920 amended the Interstate Commerce Act to require ICC approval of railroad consolidations on a determination that such consolidations were in the "public interest." Section 3(3) provided that carriers shall afford "reasonable, proper and equal facilities for the interchange of traffic." The ICC approved the New York Central's acquisition of two terminal railways in Chicago engaged in switching through traffic from one carrier to another. Six carriers who were competitors of the Central sought judicial review of the commission's action, claiming that the acquisition would enable the Central to obtain a disproportionate share of through traffic. The Supreme Court, in an opinion by Justice Brandeis, reversed the district court's dismissal of the competitors' action: "The defendants contend that the plaintiffs have not the legal interest necessary to entitle them to challenge the order. That they have in fact a vital interest is admitted. They are the competitors of the New York Central. [As a result of the ICC's order, a] large volume of traffic has been diverted from their lines to those of the

New York Central. The diversion of traffic has already subjected the plaintiffs to irreparable injury. The loss sustained exceeds $10,000,000. "This loss is not the incident of more
effective competition. . . . It is injury inflicted by denying to the plaintiffs equality of treatment. To such treatment carriers are, under the Interstate Commerce Act, as fully entitled
as any shipper. . . . It is true that, before Transportation Act, 1920, the Interstate Commerce
Act would not have prohibited the owners of the terminal railroads from selling them to
the New York Central. Nor would it have prohibited the latter company from making the
purchase. [T]he purchase might have enabled the New York Central to exclude all other
carriers from use of the terminals. . . . But Transportation Act, 1920, . . . made provision for
securing joint use of terminals; and it prohibited any acquisition of a railroad by a carrier,
unless authorized by the Commission. By reason of this legislation, the plaintiffs, being
competitors of the New York Central and users of the terminal railroads theretofore
neutral, have a special interest in the proposal to transfer the control to that company. . . ."
Justice Sutherland, dissenting, wrote: "It is claimed . . . that Transportation Act, 1920, gives
a right of action to complainants where none existed before. I am unable to perceive any
sound basis for the conclusion. That act, so far as this question is concerned, requires the
carrier, as a prerequisite to an acquisition of the charter here under consideration, to secure
the authorization of the Commission, which that body may grant if 'it will be in the public
interest.' The mere effect of such acquisition upon the business of competing lines is no
more to be considered since the Act of 1920 than it was prior to the passage thereof. It is
the public, not private, interest which is to be considered. "The complainants have no
standing to vindicate the rights of the public, but only to protect and enforce their own
rights. . . . The right of the complainants to sue, therefore, cannot rest upon the alleged
violation of a public interest, but must rest upon some distinct grievance of their own. Loss
of business, or of opportunities to get business, attributable to the activity or increase of
facilities on the part of the competitor is not enough."

FCC v. Sanders Brothers Radio Station
309 U.S. 470 (1940)

[Sanders intervened in an FCC proceeding in opposition to Telegraph Herald's application for a license for a radio station that would compete with Sanders's existing station.
Sanders contended that there was insufficient advertising revenue in the area to sustain two
stations, and that competition between the two stations might drive both of them into bankruptcy, depriving the local public of radio service. The commission granted the license
sought by Telegraph Herald. Sanders sought judicial review of the commission's action,
relying on §402(b) of the Federal Communications Act, which provides for review of FCC
actions by the District of Columbia Circuit Court of Appeals at the behest of a license applicant or "by any other person aggrieved or whose interests are adversely affected by any decision of the Commission granting or refusing [a license application]." The Supreme Court,
in an opinion by Justice Roberts, considered Sanders's standing to secure review. The Court
quoted the Communication Act's "public convenience, interest, or necessity" standard for
licensing decisions, and noted that the licensing system in the act had been established in
response to the chaos resulting from unregulated competition for frequencies.

The Court found that, unlike the Transportation Act administered by the ICC, the
Communications Act was not designed to supplant "free competition," or to create "fair
shares" for industry members. FCC licenses were limited to three years without rights of

renewal. Competition among firms seeking to use the airways was supposed to benefit the public].

We conclude that economic injury to an existing station is not a separate and independent element to be taken into consideration by the Commission in determining whether it shall grant or withhold a license.

It does not follow that, because the licensee of a station cannot resist the grant of a license to another, on the ground that the resulting competition may work economic injury to him, he has no standing to appeal from an order of the Commission granting the application.

Section 402(b) of the Act provides for an appeal to the Court of Appeals of the District of Columbia (1) by an applicant for a license or permit, or (2) "by any other person aggrieved or whose interests are adversely affected by any decision of the Commission granting or refusing any such application."

The petitioner insists that as economic injury to the respondent was not a proper issue before the Commission it is impossible that §402(b) was intended to give the respondent standing to appeal, since absence of right implies absence of remedy. This view would deprive subsection (2) of any substantial effect.

Congress had some purpose in enacting §402(b)(2). It may have been of opinion that one likely to be financially injured by the issue of a license would be the only person having a sufficient interest to bring to the attention of the appellate court errors of law in the action of the Commission in granting the license. It is within the power of Congress to confer such standing to prosecute an appeal.

We hold, therefore, that the respondent had the requisite standing to appeal and to raise, in the court below, any relevant question of law in respect of the order of the Commission.

[On the merits, the Court concluded that the commission had made adequate findings on the financial impact of the license grant as it affected service to the public, and upheld the grant of a license to Telegraph Herald.]

b. The APA

The APA §702 grants standing to any "person suffering legal wrong . . . or adversely affected or aggrieved by agency action within the meaning of a relevant statute." This provision is best understood as codifying the three bases for standing developed in previous judicial decisions. The term *legal wrong* encompasses injuries to interests of plaintiffs protected either by common law or statute, while the phrase *adversely affected or aggrieved . . . within the meaning of a relevant statute* encompasses cases like *Sanders Bros.*, where a specific agency statute granted standing to parties "adversely affected or aggrieved," even though their injury was not otherwise legally protected. Thus, the APA might be understood to recognize, or to establish, that in these classes of cases, plaintiffs have a cause of action against government officials.

Note on Flast v. Cohen and Taxpayer Standing to Enforce the Constitution

Recall our earlier statement that, unlike many states and England, federal courts traditionally do not recognize a "public action" — an action that allows a taxpayer or citizen to complain of "illegality."

Flast v. Cohen, 392 U.S. 83 (1968), presents a partial exception. There, the Court upheld the standing of federal taxpayers to challenge, as a violation of the establishment clause of the first amendment, a federal statute authorizing federal grants for instruction and teaching materials in religious schools. Chief Justice Warren's opinion for the Court held that federal taxpayers must meet a two-part nexus test to attain standing. First, there must be a "logical link" between taxpayer status and the statute challenged; this link is satisfied only if (as here) the statute is an exercise of Congress's taxing and spending power. Second, there must also be a nexus between taxpayer status and the constitutional provision invoked to invalidate the challenged statute. This nexus was satisfied here because the establishment clause was designed to protect taxpayers from paying taxes to support religion. By contrast, this second nexus test had not been met in Frothingham v. Mellon, 262 U.S. 447 (1923), where a federal taxpayer was denied standing to challenge a federal statute authorizing federal grants for infant care as exceeding Congress's "general welfare" authority to tax and spend, and as invading powers reserved to the states by the tenth amendment.

In dissent, Justice Harlan contended that the interest of taxpayers in preventing unconstitutional expenditures of government funds, including expenditures asserted to violate the establishment clause, was no different from that of citizens generally. A taxpayer could hardly establish that her tax liability would be different but for the challenged expenditure, and no taxpayer had any special lien or interest, different from that of citizens generally, on the use of tax monies once paid into the treasury. Justice Harlan stated that article III did not necessarily preclude federal courts from entertaining "public" actions by taxpayers or citizens to redress generalized constitutional grievances. If Congress enacted a statute specifically authorizing a "public action," the courts might entertain it because the statute would represent a judgment by the political branches that exercise of jurisdiction by the courts would not disrupt the allocation of authority among the three branches.

Consider the view that Flast v. Cohen really holds that the establishment clause creates a private cause of action in the particular circumstances of government expenditures. If this is right, Flast v. Cohen is a close cousin of Bivens v. Six Unknown Federal Narcotics Agents, holding that some constitutional provisions create causes of action.

Flast v. Cohen has not been taken to mean that citizens generally have standing to require government to comply with the Constitution. On the contrary, it has been confined to its facts. In Schlesinger v. Reservists Comm. to Stop the War, 418 U.S. 208 (1974), for example, a group of army reserve members sued as "taxpayers" and as "citizens" to stop members of Congress from joining the army reserve. (Article I, §6 of the Constitution forbids members of Congress from holding "any office under the United States.") The Court held the plaintiffs lacked standing as "taxpayers" because there was no "logical nexus" between their status and the constitutional claim they were asserting; they lacked standing as "citizens" because their injury was one suffered by all citizens generally. In United States v. Richardson, 418 U.S. 166 (1974), plaintiffs claimed that the Central Intelligence Agency Act, permitting the CIA to account to Congress for its expenditures "solely on certificate of the Director," violated article I, clause 7 of the Constitution, which requires a regular statement and account of public funds. The Court held that the plaintiffs lacked standing as "taxpayers" and as "citizens" for precisely the same reasons, namely (1) no "logical nexus," and (2) generalized injury.

In Valley Forge Christian College v. Americans United for Separation of Church & State, Inc., 454 U.S. 464 (1982), the plaintiffs sued as "taxpayers" and "citizens," claiming that the government's donation of a military hospital to a church-related college violated the establishment clause. The Court held that the donation did not represent an exercise of the government's article I "spending power" (the power involved in *Flast*), but rather it involved an exercise of the Constitution's article IV, §3 power to administer and to dispose of government property. That being so, there was no "logical nexus" between "taxpayer" status and the relevant constitutional power; hence plaintiffs lacked standing as "citizens." The Court wrote that "the Establishment Clause does not provide a special license to roam the country in search of governmental wrongdoing. . . . The federal courts were simply not constituted ombudsmen of the general welfare."

By contrast, in Michael v. Anderson, 14 F.3d 623, 626 (D.C. Cir. 1994), the court found that voters from each state had standing to assert constitutional challenges to a House of Representatives rule that allowed delegates from a variety of territories and the District of Columbia to vote as members of the Committee of the Whole, because they suffered injury through the dilution of the voting power of their congressperson. The court noted that, even though an injury is widespread, it can form the basis of a federal case as long as each individual can be said to have suffered a distinct and concrete harm.

Note on the Difference between "Constitutional" and "Statutory" Cases

Note that plaintiffs in *Flast* challenged a statute as unconstitutional, while in most administrative law cases plaintiffs challenged a federal agency action as contrary to federal statute. We are primarily concerned with the latter question: Standing in constitutional cases is a complex subject often intertwined with substantive issues of constitutional law. But we deal here with standing in both constitutional and statutory cases. The differences in the considerations underlying standing in the two classes of cases may help in developing appropriate principles of standing in statutory cases (as well as in constitutional cases). Moreover, the Supreme Court has sometimes blurred the differences between the two types of cases and spoken as if the same standards applied to both.

Consider the factors that should determine standing in the two classes of cases. It might be thought that standing should be more liberally granted where constitutional, as opposed to statutory, rights are asserted because constitutional rights are in some sense more "important." But there are strong countervailing considerations.

A constitutional decision allows unelected judges to overrule and displace the political process. In a democratic system, it may be appropriate to limit the occasions for such displacement to cases where the constitutional violation is clear and no remedy is potentially available through the political process. Restrictions on standing — such as denial of standing when a grievance is one shared by citizens at large rather than one borne by an individual or an unpopular and politically weak minority — would be one way to accomplish this objective. Alexander Bickel developed the influential idea of the "passive virtues," exercised when courts decline to hear a constitutional challenge; Bickel's motivation was to show how and why courts use doctrines of justiciability, prominently including doctrines of standing, to limit their intervention in democratic processes. See A. Bickel, The Least Dangerous Branch (1965). See also Sunstein, Leaving Things Undecided, 110 Harv. L. Rev. 4 (1996), for a more recent discussion of judicial "minimalism" under the Constitution.

In statutory cases the analysis might be quite different. In one sense, there is no judicial displacement of the political process at all; courts are being asked to vindicate the political process (in the form of a democratically enacted statute) against an agency, not to displace the political process. Since, under *Chevron*, a plaintiff must show that the agency is plainly wrong, a grant of standing will result in judicial invalidation of agency action only if the plaintiff's argument is very convincing. Could it not be argued that judicial review of administrative action is therefore quite desirable on democratic grounds, and an altogether different issue from that raised by constitutional law? This question might lead a court to allow standing more readily in nonconstitutional cases.

In any case, any judicial displacement of the political process (in the form of agency action or inaction) is, in this setting, only provisional, not final. If Congress believes that a court's construction of a statute is erroneous or unwise, it can amend the statute and effectively overrule the court's action. Of course, Congress might conclude that one good way of ensuring that administrators obey and execute statutory directives is to provide for ready access to court for citizens to challenge agency decisions.

As a practical matter, it is not clear whether courts have interpreted "standing" requirements more strictly when constitutional questions are at issue on the merits of the case. The Court has said that "when a constitutional question is presented . . . , we have strictly adhered to the standing requirement to ensure that our deliberation will have the benefit of adversary presentation and a full development of the relevant facts." Bender v. Williamsport Area School, 475 U.S. 534 (1986) (holding that a party could not claim, on appeal, that he had standing as a "parent" of a child in school because he had not based his standing on that claim in the courts below). In Warth v. Seldin, 422 U.S. 490 (1975), the Court held that a low-income resident of one community, and a builders' association located in that community, could not attack (on constitutional grounds) restrictive zoning ordinances in a nearby, but *different*, community, because they had not shown that they had tried to buy or to build housing in that latter community. But compare Village of Arlington Heights v. Metropolitan Hous. Dev. Corp., 429 U.S. 252 (1977), where, in a very similar case, standing was found because the developer and the low-income person had shown direct interests in building or buying in the community with the restrictive zoning ordinance. Compare, too, Gladstone v. Village of Bellwood, 441 U.S. 91 (1979), and Havens Realty Corp. v. Coleman, 455 U.S. 363 (1982), where the Court seemed to take a broader approach to standing in housing discrimination cases, but in cases that involved a statutory, rather than a constitutional claim.

3. The Data Processing Revolution and the Birth of "Injury in Fact"

Association of Data Processing Service Organizations v. Camp

397 U.S. 150 (1970)

Mr. Justice DOUGLAS delivered the opinion of the Court.

Petitioners sell data processing services to businesses generally. In this suit they seek to challenge a ruling by respondent Comptroller of the Currency that, as an incident to their banking services, national banks, including respondent American National Bank & Trust Company, may make data processing services available to other banks and to bank customers. . . . [The lower federal court found petitioners lacked standing.]

Generalizations about standing to sue are largely worthless as such. One generalization is, however, necessary and that is that the question of standing in the federal courts is to be considered in the framework of Article III which restricts judicial power to "cases" and "controversies." As we recently stated in Flast v. Cohen, 392 U.S. 83, 101: "[I]n terms of Article III limitations on federal court jurisdiction, the question of standing is related only to whether the dispute sought to be adjudicated will be presented in an adversary context and in a form historically viewed as capable of judicial resolution." *Flast* was a *taxpayer's* suit. The present is a *competitor's* suit. And while the two have the same Article III starting point, they do not necessarily track one another.

The first question is whether the plaintiff alleges that challenged action has caused him injury in fact, economic or otherwise. There can be no doubt but that petitioners have satisfied this test. The petitioners not only allege that competition by national banks in the business of providing data processing services might entail some future loss of profits for the petitioners, they also allege that respondent American National Bank & Trust Company was performing or preparing to perform such services for two customers for whom petitioner Data Systems, Inc., had previously agreed or negotiated to perform such services. . . .

The Court of Appeals viewed the matter differently, stating:

> [A] plaintiff may challenge alleged illegal competition when as complainant it pursues (1) a legal interest by reason of public charter or contract, . . . (2) a legal interest by reason of statutory protection, . . . or (3) a "public interest" in which Congress has recognized the need for review of administrative action and plaintiff is significantly involved to have standing to represent the public. . . .

406 F.2d, at 842-843. . . .

The "legal interest" test goes to the merits. The question of standing is different. It concerns, apart from the "case" or "controversy" test, the question whether the interest sought to be protected by the complainant is arguably within the zone of interests to be protected or regulated by the statute or constitutional guarantee in question. Thus the Administrative Procedure Act grants standing to a person "aggrieved by agency action within the meaning of a relevant statute." 5 U.S.C. §702 (1964 ed., Supp. IV). That interest, at times, may reflect "aesthetic, conservational, and recreational" as well as economic values. Scenic Hudson Preservation Conf. v. FPC, 354 F.2d 608, 616 [environmental groups can assert environmental interests of local residents claiming that the FPC disregarded such interests, which the statute required the FPC to consider]; Office of Communication of United Church of Christ v. FCC, 123 U.S. App. D.C. 328, 334-340, 359 F.2d 994, 1000-1006. [Groups representing local viewers have standing as members of the "public" in claiming that the FCC improperly gave a license to a station with discriminatory programming, where the statute required the FCC to protect the public by considering such matters.]

We mention these noneconomic values to emphasize that standing may stem from them as well as from the economic injury on which petitioners rely here. Certainly he who is "likely to be financially" injured, FCC v. Sanders Bros. Radio Station, 309 U.S. 470, 477, may be a reliable private attorney general to litigate the issues of the public interest in the present case.

Apart from Article III jurisdictional questions, problems of standing, as resolved by this Court for its own governance, have involved a "rule of self-restraint." Barrows v. Jackson, 346 U.S. 249, 255. Congress can, of course, resolve the question one way or another, save as the requirements of Article III dictate otherwise. . . .

Where statutes are concerned, the trend is toward enlargement of the class of people who may protest administrative action. The whole drive for enlarging the category of aggrieved "persons" is symptomatic of that trend. In a closely analogous case we held that an existing entrepreneur had standing to challenge the legality of the entrance of a newcomer into the business, because the established business was allegedly protected by a valid city ordinance that protected it from unlawful competition. Chicago v. Atchinson, T. & S.F.R. Co., 357 U.S. 77, 83-84.

It is argued that the Chicago case and the [Environmental Defense Fund v.] *Hardin* case are relevant here because of §4 of the Bank Service Corporation Act of 1962, 76 Sta. 1132, 12 U.S.C. §1864, which provides: "No bank service corporation may engage in any activity other than the performance of bank services for banks."

The Court of Appeals for the First Circuit held in Arnold Tours, Inc. v. Camp, 408 F.2d 1147, 1153, that by reason of §4 a data processing company has standing to contest the legality of a national bank performing data processing services for other banks and bank customers:

> Section 4 had a broader purpose than regulating only the service corporations. It was also a response to the fears expressed by a few senators, that without such a prohibition, the bill would have enabled "banks to engage in a nonbanking activity," S. Rep. No. 2195, [87th Cong., 2d Sess., 7-12] (Supplemental views of Senators Proxmire, Douglas, and Neuberger), and thus constitute "a serious exception to the accepted public policy which strictly limits banks to banking" (Supplemental views of Senators Muskie and Clark). We think Congress has provided the sufficient statutory aid to standing even though the competition may not be the precise kind Congress legislated against.

We do not put the issue in those words, for they implicate the merits. We do think, however, that §4 arguably brings a competitor within the zone of interests protected by it. . . .

[The Court rejected the claim that judicial review of the comptroller's action was precluded.]

Whether anything in the Bank Service Corporation Act or the National Bank Act gives petitioners a "legal interest" that protects them against violations of those Acts, and whether the actions of respondents did in fact violate either of those Acts, are questions which go to the merits and remain to be decided below.

We hold that petitioners have standing to sue and that the case should be remanded for a hearing on the merits.[15]

Notes and Questions

1. In the years before *Data Processing*, a number of influential lower court decisions had read the "legal wrong" standard so as to allow many people affected by agency decisions,

---

15. In a companion case, Barlow v. Collins, 397 U.S. 159 (1970), Justice Douglas used the principles developed in *Data Processing* to sustain the standing of tenant farmers to challenge regulations issued by the Secretary of Labor under the upland cotton programs of the Food and Agriculture Act of 1965, providing for advance payment of federal crop subsidies to farmers. The challenged regulation, which regulated the disposition of such advance payments, permitted their assignment to secure payment of cash rents. The tenant farmers complained that this regulation would permit their landlords to exercise their superior bargaining power to demand, as a condition of lease, assignment of the federal payments to cover rent due. Deprived of the liquidity afforded by government payments, the tenant farmers would also allegedly become dependent on their landlords for advances, at assertedly exorbitant prices, of materials and food during the growing season. The Court held that these allegations demonstrated "injury in fact," and held further that the tenants were "arguably within the zone" of interests protected by the Food and Agriculture Act of 1965; which provides in general terms, without specific reference to the disposition of advance payments, that the Secretary should "provide adequate safeguards to protect the interests of tenants. . . ." — ED. NOTE.

including the beneficiaries of regulatory programs, to bring suit against the government. For example, courts concluded that displaced urban residents, listeners of radio stations, and users of the environment could proceed to challenge an agency's legally insufficient regulatory protection. See Norwalk CORE v. Norwalk Redev. Agency, 395 F.2d 920, 932-937 (2d Cir. 1968); Office of Communication of the Church of Christ v. FCC, 359 F.2d 994, 1000-1006 (D.C. Cir. 1967); Scenic Hudson Preservation Conf. v. FPC, 354 F.2d 608, 615-617 (2d Cir. 1965). In this view, disappointed beneficiaries also suffered a "legal wrong," because the government had failed to do what the law required it to do for their benefit. These cases abandoned the private law model of standing insofar as they suggested that people without a common law interest were entitled to challenge government for failing to protect their statutorily protected interests. Indeed, these cases can be seen as a natural outgrowth of the New Deal itself, insofar as they suggested that the "new" interests recognized by the regulatory state should be entitled to the same kind of legal concern as the "old" interests protected by the common law. These developments inaugurated a "public law model of public law," that is, a model that is independent, or relatively independent, of private law categories. It is especially important that the relevant cases involved an interpretation of the APA's "legal wrong" standard, finding a legal wrong to those whom Congress had sought to benefit via creation of a legal right.

In an important sense, *Data Processing* endorses these decisions. The Court cites several of them, and the "injury in fact" idea appears to break down the distinction between the objects of regulation and the beneficiaries of regulation. Under *Data Processing*, anyone who is harmed is entitled to bring suit. But *Data Processing* also departs dramatically from the lower court cases insofar as it jettisons the whole idea of "legal wrong."

What accounts for this dramatic shift? How can it be legitimate to depart from, or to jettison, the language of the APA? For a suggestion that the shift came from a kind of conceptual revolution, abandoning the pre-New Deal idea that some kind of property interest was a predicate for judicial review, see J. Vining, Legal Identity (1978).

2. In the immediate aftermath of *Data Processing*, courts broke down standing requirements into two parts. First, a plaintiff must satisfy the constitutional requirements — above all, by showing "injury in fact," though the Supreme Court was not entirely clear about the sense in which an "injury in fact" requirement was embedded in the Constitution. Second, the plaintiff must satisfy what have come to be known as the "prudential requirements," most importantly by showing that any injury is "arguably within the zone of interests protected or regulated" by the statute.

All this leaves a large question: What justification does Justice Douglas offer, and what justification might be offered, for his surprising reinterpretation of §702, one that points to "injury in fact" and "arguably within the zone"? The basic idea of "injury in fact" seems to have been spurred by Davis, The Liberalized Law of Standing, 37 U. Chi. L. Rev. 450, 471-473 (1970), which speaks of injury and harm as the basic requirement of the APA. But we have seen reason to doubt this view; the APA appears to have codified the pre-APA grounds for standing, as discussed previously.

3. Does the injury in fact requirement come from article III of the Constitution? It is important to emphasize the novelty of the whole idea of "injury in fact." In the history of the Supreme Court, standing has been discussed in terms of article III on fewer than 180 occasions. Of those occasions, over half occurred after 1980. Of those nearly all occurred since 1965. The first explicit reference to standing as an article III limitation can be found in Stark v. Wickard, 321 U.S. 288 (1944). The "injury in fact" idea was first mentioned in

Barlow v. Collins, 397 U.S. 159 (1970). After 1970, the phrase appears in about 10 cases during each succeeding five-year interval, until a big leap in the 1990s.

If the "injury in fact" terminology was not introduced until 1970, does it follow that it is not in fact a constitutional requirement? The notion of a "case or controversy" seems to impose a limitation on what federal courts can hear. But what kind of limitation? We will return to this question.

4. Consider the view that the "injury in fact" question turns the standing issue into a simple, law-free determination, one that can be made without requiring courts to answer hard questions of statutory construction before they get to the merits. This may have been a goal of *Data Processing* and perhaps helps explain the Court's approach. But later developments raise questions about whether the idea of a simple, law-free determination of whether there is "injury" is right or even coherent. It may be impossible to tell whether injuries qualify as legally cognizable without knowing something about the law. Here is the basic point: Each of us suffers a range of injuries (in fact) every day; whether those injuries are a basis for a suit in federal court depends at least partly on law, not just on whether we are injured (in fact).

Suppose, for example, that a woman complained of sexual harassment in 1945. Would she have suffered injury in fact, when no law recognized her injury as such? It is very likely that a court would deny standing, on the ground that any injury was "purely ideological," or "legally noncognizable." Now suppose that she brings suit in 2002. Would she have injury in fact in 2002, when the law clearly recognized her injury? Of course she would. But is this because she now suffers "injury" when she didn't in 1945? This would be implausible. What has changed is the law, not the question of injury.

At least in most cases, no one thinks that there is a standing problem after the law recognizes a cause of action; and when the law recognizes no cause of action, harms that people experience as "injuries" may well be unlikely sources of legal relief, because such harms seem purely ideological. In the hypothetical in the previous paragraph, it would not be unreasonable to think that she suffered no legally cognizable injury in 1945, not because there was no injury "in fact," but because the law did not recognize her injury as one with which the legal system was concerned. When the legal system recognizes no "injury in fact," isn't it partly because of the law, and not only because of the "facts"? Keep this question in mind as you read the materials that follow. See generally Fletcher, The Structure of Standing, 98 Yale L.J. 221 (1988).

4. "Arguably within the Zone"

Clarke v. Securities Industry Association
479 U.S. 388 (1987)

Justice WHITE delivered the opinion of the Court. . . .

[The plaintiffs, an association of securities dealers, sued the comptroller of the currency claiming that he exceeded his legal authority in permitting two national banks to open offices that sold "discount brokerage services" to the public. In particular, they said that approval violated the McFadden Act, which limits the "general business" of a national bank to its headquarters, basically limits "branches" to those kinds of "in-state" branches that states permit state banks to establish, and which defines a "branch" as "any branch place of business . . . at which deposits are received, or checks paid, or money lent." The comptroller had decided that the "discount brokerage" offices were not "branches" as defined by this statute.]

II

The "zone of interest" formula in *Data Processing* has not proved self-explanatory, but significant guidance can nonetheless be drawn from that opinion. *First*. The Court interpreted the phrase "a relevant statute" in §702 broadly; the data processors were alleging violations of 12 U.S.C. §24 Seventh, yet the Court relied on the legislative history of a much later statute, §4 of the Bank Service Corporation Act of 1962, in holding that the data processors satisfied the "zone of interest" test. *Second*. [T]he Court implicitly recognized the potential for disruption inherent in allowing every party adversely affected by agency action to seek judicial review. The Court struck the balance in a manner favoring review, but excluding those would-be plaintiffs not even "arguably within the zone of interest to be protected or regulated by the statute. . . ."

The reach of the "zone of interest" test, insofar as the class of potential plaintiffs is concerned, is demonstrated by the subsequent decision in Investment Company Institute v. Camp, 401 U.S. 617 (1971). There, an association of open-end investment companies and several individual investment companies sought, among other things, review of a Comptroller's regulation that authorized banks to operate collective investment funds. The companies alleged that the regulation violated the Glass-Steagall Banking Act of 1933, which prohibits banks from underwriting or issuing securities. See 12 U.S.C. §24 Seventh.

Justice Harlan, in dissent, complained that there was no evidence that Congress had intended to benefit the plaintiff's class when it limited the activities permitted national banks. The Court did not take issue with this observation; it was enough to provide standing that Congress, for its own reasons, primarily its concern for the soundness of the banking system, had forbidden banks to compete with plaintiffs by entering the investment company business.

Our decision in Block v. Community Nutrition Institute, 467 U.S. 340 (1984), provides a useful reference point for understanding the "zone of interest" test. There, we held that while milk handlers have the right to seek judicial review of the Agricultural Marketing Agreement Act of 1937, consumers have no such right, because "[a]llowing consumers to sue the Secretary would severely disrupt [the] complex and delicate administrative scheme." We recognized the presumption in favor of judicial review of agency action, but held that this presumption is "overcome whenever the congressional intent to preclude judicial review is 'fairly discernible in the statutory scheme.'" The essential inquiry is whether Congress "intended for [a particular] class [of plaintiffs] to be relied upon to challenge agency disregard of the law." . . .

In cases where the plaintiff is not itself the subject of the contested regulatory action, the [zone of interest] test denies a right of review if the plaintiff's interests are so marginally related to or inconsistent with the purposes implicit in the statute that it cannot reasonably be assumed that Congress intended to permit the suit. The test is not meant to be especially demanding; in particular, there need be no indication of congressional purpose to benefit the would-be plaintiff. . . .

The inquiry into reviewability does not end with the "zone of interest" test. In *Community Nutrition Institute*, the interests of consumers were arguably within the zone of interests meant to be protected by the Act, but the court found that point not dispositive, because at bottom the reviewability question turns on congressional intent, and all indicators helpful in discerning that intent must be weighed. . . .

It is significant for our present inquiry that Congress rejected attempts to allow national banks to branch without regard to state law. There were many among those who supported the McFadden Act, as well as among its opponents. Allusion was made to the danger that national banks might obtain monopoly control over credit and money if permitted to branch. The sponsor of the Act himself stated that "[t]his bill is much more an antibranch-banking bill than a branch-banking bill." In short, Congress was concerned not only with equalizing the status of state and federal banks, but also with preventing the perceived dangers of unlimited branching.

The interest respondent asserts has a plausible relationship to the policies underlying §§36 and 81 of the National Bank Act. Congress has shown a concern over credit and money through unlimited branching. Respondent's members compete with banks in providing discount brokerage services — activities which give banks access to more money, in the form of credit balances, and enhanced opportunities to lend money, viz., for margin purchases. "Congress [has] arguably legislated against the competition that [respondent seeks] to challenge," . . . by limiting the extent to which banks can engage in the discount brokerage business and hence limiting the competitive impact on nonbank discount brokerage houses.

. . . And we see no indication of the kind presented in *Community Nutrition Institute* that make "fairly discernible" a congressional intent to preclude review at respondent's behest. We conclude, therefore, that respondent was a proper party to bring this lawsuit, and we now turn to the merits.

[The Court decided the merits in favor of the comptroller.

Justice Stevens, along with Chief Justice Rehnquist and Justice O'Connor, concurred separately. They stated that one of the purposes of the McFadden Act was to protect potential competitors of banks from too much competition by banks. Their purpose included protecting securities dealers, hence, there was clearly "standing" under traditional analysis and no need for the Court's "exegesis."]

AIR COURIER CONFERENCE v. AMERICAN POSTAL WORKERS UNION, 498 U.S. 517 (1991). A group of statutes known as the Private Express Statutes (PES) grants the postal service a monopoly over the carriage of letters, but allows the service to suspend its restrictions on particular mail routes when "the public interest requires." The Postal Workers Union challenged the service's suspension of its monopoly to allow private couriers to deposit with postal services in other nations letters to be delivered within such nations. In an opinion by Chief Justice Rehnquist, the Court held that the union lacked standing; although the employment opportunities of postal workers might be injured by the ruling, they did not fall within the zone of interest protected by the PES, which, the Court found, was designed not to protect postal workers' jobs but to protect the postal revenues from "cream skimming" by competitors on highly profitable routes, undercutting the service's ability to provide service on other routes. Nor could the zone test be satisfied because a later statute, the Postal Reorganization Act (PRA), which included new provisions designed to protect postal worker interests, also reenacted and recodified the PES and other postal statutes. There was no evidence of linkage between the new provisions of the PRA and the PES provision in issue here. Three justices would have avoided the standing issue by holding that relevant statutes precluded judicial review.

National Credit Union Administration v.
First National Bank & Trust Co.

522 U.S. 479 (1998)

Justice THOMAS delivered the opinion of the Court.

Section 109 of the Federal Credit Union Act (FCUA) provides that "federal credit union membership shall be limited to groups having a common bond of occupation or association, or to groups within a well-defined neighborhood, community, or rural district." Since 1982, the National Credit Union Administration (NCUA), the agency charged with administering the FCUA, has interpreted §109 to permit federal credit unions to be composed of multiple unrelated employer groups, each having its own common bond of occupation. In this case, respondents, five banks and the American Bankers Association, have challenged this interpretation on the ground that §109 unambiguously requires that the same common bond of occupation unite every member of an occupationally defined federal credit union. We granted certiorari to answer two questions. First, do respondents have standing under the Administrative Procedure Act to seek federal court review of the NCUA's interpretation? Second, under the analysis set forth in [Chevron], is the NCUA's interpretation permissible? We answer the first question in the affirmative and the second question in the negative. We therefore affirm.

I

A

In 1934, during the Great Depression, Congress enacted the FCUA, which authorizes the chartering of credit unions at the national level and provides that federal credit unions may, as a general matter, offer banking services only to their members. Section 109 of the FCUA, which has remained virtually unaltered since the FCUA's enactment, expressly restricts membership in federal credit unions. In relevant part, it provides:

"Federal credit union membership shall consist of the incorporators and such other persons and incorporated and unincorporated organizations, to the extent permitted by rules and regulations prescribed by the Board, as may be elected to membership and as such shall each, subscribe to at least one share of its stock and pay the initial installment thereon and a uniform entrance fee if required by the board of directors; except that Federal credit union membership shall be limited to groups having a common bond of occupation or association, or to groups within a well-defined neighborhood, community, or rural district." 12 U.S.C. §1759.

Until 1982, the NCUA and its predecessors consistently interpreted §109 to require that the same common bond of occupation unite every member of an occupationally defined federal credit union. In 1982, however, the NCUA reversed its longstanding policy in order to permit credit unions to be composed of multiple unrelated employer groups. It thus interpreted §109's common bond requirement to apply only to each employer group in a multiple-group credit union, rather than to every member of that credit union. Under the NCUA's new interpretation, all of the employer groups in a multiple-group credit union had to be located "within a well-defined area," but the NCUA later revised this requirement to provide that each employer group could be located within "an area surrounding the [credit union's] home or a branch office that can be reasonably served by the [credit union] as determined by NCUA." Since 1982, therefore, the NCUA has permitted federal credit unions to be composed of wholly unrelated employer groups, each having its own distinct common bond.

B

After the NCUA revised its interpretation of §109, petitioner AT&T Family Federal Credit Union (ATTF) expanded its operations considerably by adding unrelated employer groups to its membership. As a result, ATTF now has approximately 110,000 members nationwide, only 35% of whom are employees of AT&T and its affiliates. The remaining members are employees of such diverse companies as the Lee Apparel Company, the Coca-Cola Bottling Company, the Ciba-Geigy Corporation, the Duke Power Company, and the American Tobacco Company.

In 1990, after the NCUA approved a series of amendments to ATTF's charter that added several such unrelated employer groups to ATTF's membership, respondents brought this action. [R]espondents claimed that the NCUA's approval of the charter amendments was contrary to law because the members of the new groups did not share a common bond of occupation with ATTF's existing members, as respondents alleged §109 required. ATTF and petitioner Credit Union National Association were permitted to intervene in the case as defendants. . . .

[Based] on [our] prior cases finding that competitors of financial institutions have standing to challenge agency action relaxing statutory restrictions on the activities of those institutions, we hold the respondents' interest in limiting the markets that federal credit unions can serve is arguably within the zone of interests to be protected by §109. Therefore, respondents have prudential standing under the APA to challenge the NCUA's interpretation. [The Court discussed *Data Processing, Clarke,* and related holdings.]

Our prior cases, therefore, have consistently held that for a plaintiff's interests to be arguably within the "zone of interests" to be protected by a statute, there does not have to be an "indication of congressional purpose to benefit the would-be plaintiff." The proper inquiry is simply "whether the interest sought to be protected by the complainant is arguably within the zone of interests to be protected . . . by the statute." Hence in applying the "zone of interests" test, we do not ask whether, in enacting the statutory provision at issue, Congress specifically intended to benefit the plaintiff. Instead, we first discern the interests "arguably . . . to be protected" by the statutory provision at issue; we then inquire whether the plaintiff's interests affected by the agency action in question are among them.

Section 109 provides that "federal credit union membership shall be limited to groups having a common bond of occupation or association, or to groups within a well-defined neighborhood, community, or rural district." By its express terms, §109 limits membership in every federal credit union to members of definable "groups." Because federal credit unions may, as a general matter, offer banking services only to members, §109 also restricts the markets that every federal credit union can serve. Although these markets need not be small, they unquestionably are limited. The link between §109's regulation of federal credit union membership and its limitation on the markets that federal credit unions can serve is unmistakable. Thus, even if it cannot be said that Congress had the specific purpose of benefiting commercial banks, one of the interests "arguably . . . to be protected" by §109 is an interest in limiting the markets that federal credit unions can serve. This interest is precisely the interest of respondents affected by the NCUA's interpretation of §109. As competitors of federal credit unions, respondents certainly have an interest in limiting the markets that federal credit unions can serve, and the NCUA's interpretation has affected that interest by allowing federal credit unions to increase their customer bas.[16]

[Petitioners] attempt to distinguish this case principally on the ground that there is no evidence that Congress, when it enacted the FCUA, was at all concerned with the competitive interests of commercial banks, or indeed at all concerned with competition. Indeed, petitioners contend that the very reason Congress passed the FCUA was that "banks were simply not in the picture" as far as small borrowers were concerned, and thus Congress believed it necessary to create a new source of credit for people of modest means.

The difficulty with this argument is that similar arguments were made unsuccessfully in each of *Data Processing* [and] *Clarke*. . . . In each case, we declined to accept the [argument]. We therefore cannot accept petitioners' argument that respondents do not have standing because there is no evidence that the Congress that enacted §109 was concerned with the competitive interests of commercial banks. To accept that argument, we would have to reformulate the "zone of interests" test to require that Congress have specifically intended to benefit a particular class of plaintiffs before a plaintiff from that class could have standing under the APA to sue. We have refused to do this in our prior cases, and we refuse to do so today.

Petitioners also mistakenly rely on our decision in [*Air Courier*]. In *Air Courier*, we held that the interest of Postal Service employees in maximizing employment opportunities was not within the "zone of interests" to be protected by the postal monopoly statutes, and hence those employees did not have standing under the APA to challenge a Postal Service regulation suspending its monopoly over certain international operations. We stated that the purposes of the statute were solely to increase the revenues of the Post Office and to ensure that postal services were provided in a manner consistent with the public interest, see id. Only those interests, therefore, and not the interests of Postal Service employees in their employment, were "arguably within the zone of interests to be protected" by the statute. We further noted that although the statute in question regulated competition, the interests of the plaintiff employees had nothing to do with competition. In this case, not only do respondents have "competitive and direct injury," but, as the foregoing discussion makes clear, they possess an interest that is "arguably . . . to be protected" by §109.

[The Court held that the agency's regulation was impermissible under *Chevron*. It wrote:]

Justice O'CONNOR, with whom Justice STEVENS, Justice SOUTER, and Justice BREYER join, dissenting.

---

16. Contrary to the dissent's contentions, our formulation does not "eviscerate" or "abolish[]" the zone of interests requirement. Nor can it be read to imply that in order to have standing under the APA, a plaintiff must merely have an interest in enforcing the statute in question. The test we have articulated — discerning the interests "arguably . . . to be protected" by the statutory provision at issue and inquiring whether the plaintiff's interests affected by the agency action in question are among them — differs only as a matter of semantics from the formulation that the dissent has accused us of "eviscerating" or "abolishing" (stating that the plaintiff must establish that "the injury he complains of . . . falls within the zone of interests sought to be protected by the statutory provision whose violation forms the legal basis for his complaint") (internal quotations and citation omitted).

Our only disagreement with the dissent lies in the application of the zone of interests test. Because of the unmistakable link between §109's express restriction on credit union membership and the limitation on the markets that federal credit unions can serve, there is objectively "some indication in the statute" that respondents' interest is "arguably within the zone of interests to be protected" by §109. Hence respondents are more than merely incidental beneficiaries of §109's effects on competition.

In determining that respondents have standing under the zone-of-interests test to challenge the National Credit Union Administration's (NCUA's) interpretation of the "common bond" provision of the Federal Credit Union Act (FCUA), 12 U.S.C. §1759, the Court applies the test in a manner that is contrary to our decisions and, more importantly, that all but eviscerates the zone-of-interests requirement. In my view, under a proper conception of the inquiry, "the interest sought to be protected by" respondents in this case is not "arguably within the zone of interests to be protected" by the common bond provision. . . . Accordingly, I respectfully dissent.

The "injury respondents complain of," as the Court explains, is that the NCUA's interpretation of the common bond provision "allows persons who might otherwise be their customers to be . . . customers" of petitioner AT&T Family Federal Credit Union. Put another way, the injury is a loss of respondents' customer base to a competing entity, or more generally, an injury to respondents' commercial interest as a competitor. The relevant question under the zone-of-interests test, then, is whether injury to respondents' commercial interest as a competitor "falls within the zone of interests sought to be protected by the [common bond] provision."

The Court adopts a quite different approach to the zone-of-interests test today, eschewing any assessment of whether the common bond provision was intended to protect respondents' commercial interest. The Court begins by observing that the terms of the common bond provision — "federal credit union membership shall be limited to groups having a common bond of occupation or association, or to groups within a well-defined neighborhood, community, or rural district" — expressly limit membership in federal credit unions to persons belonging to certain "groups." Then, citing other statutory provisions that bar federal credit unions from serving nonmembers, the Court reasons that one interest sought to be protected by the common bond provision "is an interest in limiting the markets that federal credit unions can serve." The Court concludes its analysis by observing simply that respondents, "as competitors of federal credit unions, . . . certainly have [that] interest . . . , and the NCUA's interpretation has affected that interest."

Under the Court's approach, every litigant who establishes injury in fact under Article III will automatically satisfy the zone-of-interests requirement, rendering the zone-of-interests test ineffectual. That result stems from the Court's articulation of the relevant "interest." In stating that the common bond provision protects an "interest in limiting the markets that federal credit unions can serve," the Court presumably uses the term "markets" in the sense of customer markets, as opposed to, for instance, product markets: The common bond requirement and the provisions prohibiting credit unions from serving nonmembers combine to limit the customers a credit union can serve, not the services a credit union can offer.

With that understanding, the Court's conclusion that respondents "have" an interest in "limiting the [customer] markets that federal credit unions can serve" means little more than that respondents "have" an interest in enforcing the statute. The common bond requirement limits a credit union's membership, and hence its customer base, to certain groups, and in the Court's view, it is enough to establish standing that respondents "have" an interest in limiting the customers a credit union can serve. . . .

Our decision in *Air Courier*, likewise cannot be squared with the Court's analysis in this case. . . .

Contrary to the Court's suggestion, its application of the zone-of-interests test in this case is not in concert with the approach we followed in a series of cases in which the plaintiffs, like respondents here, alleged that agency interpretation of a statute caused competitive injury to their commercial interests. In each of those cases, we focused on whether competitive injury to the plaintiff's commercial interest fell within the zone of interests protected by the relevant statute. . . .

It is true, as the Court emphasizes repeatedly, that we did not require in this line of decisions that the statute at issue was designed to benefit the particular party bringing suit. . . . In each of the competitor standing cases, though, we found that Congress had enacted an "anti-competition limitation," or, alternatively, that Congress had "legislated against . . . competition," and accordingly, that the plaintiff-competitor's "commercial interest was sought to be protected by anti-competition limitation" at issue. We determined, in other words, that "the injury [the plaintiff] complained of [fell] within the zone of interest sought to be protected by the [relevant] statutory provision." The Court fails to undertake that analysis here.

Applying the proper zone-of-interest inquiry to this case, I would find that competitive injury to respondents' commercial interests does not arguably fall within the zone of interests sought to be protected by the common bond provision. The terms of the statute do not suggest a concern with protecting the business interests of competitors. The common bond provision limits "federal credit union membership . . . to group having a common bond of occupation or association, or to group within a well-defined neighborhood, community, or rural district." And the provision is framed as an exception to the preceding clause, which confers membership on "incorporators and such other persons and incorporated and unincorporated organizations . . . as may be elected . . . and as such shall each subscribe to at least one share of its stock and pay the initial installment thereon and a uniform entrance fee." The language suggests that the common bond requirement is an internal organizational principle concerned primarily with defining membership in a way that secures a financially sound organization. There is no indication in the text of the provision or in the surrounding language that the membership limitation was even arguably designed to protect the commercial interests of competitors. . . .

In *Data Processing* and *Clarke*, by contrast, the statutes operated against national banks generally, prohibiting all banks from competing in a particular market: Banks in general were barred from providing a specific type of service (*Data Processing*), or from providing services at a particular location (*Clarke*). Thus, whereas in *Data Processing* customers could not obtain data processing services from any national bank, and in *Clarke* customers outside of the permissible branching area likewise could not obtain financial services from any national bank, in this case customers who lack an adequate bond with the members of a particular credit union can still receive financial services from a different credit union. Unlike the statutes in *Data Processing*, *ICI*, and *Clarke*, then, the common bond provision does not erect a competitive boundary excluding credit unions from any identifiable market. . . .

Applying the zone-of-interests inquiry as it has been articulated in our decisions, I conclude that respondents have failed to establish standing. I would therefore vacate the judgment of the Court of Appeals and remand the case with instructions that it be dismissed.

DISMAS CHARITIES, INC. v. U.S. DEPARTMENT OF JUSTICE, 401 F.3d 666 (6th Cir. 2005). Dismas Charities is a nonprofit corporation that owns and operates eighteen community corrections centers in seven states. The Bureau of Prisons altered its interpretation of a statute governing imprisonment policy, thus curtailing the circumstances in which federal prisoners are eligible to serve their sentences in a community correction center. Dismas alleged that the new policy had a severe impact on its operations, drastically reducing the number of offenders housed at community correction centers, and producing a revenue loss of more than $1.2 million. The court concluded that for its principal challenge to the new interpretation, Dismas lacked standing on "zone of interests" grounds.

The relevant statute allows the Bureau to "designate the place of the prisoner's imprisonment," including "any available penal or correctional facility that meets minimum standards of health and habitability." The Bureau is asked to consider a number of factors that bear on the appropriateness and suitability of a facility, including its resources, the nature and circumstances of the offense, and the statement by the court that imposed the sentence. The court concluded that "Dismas fails the zone-of-interests test because the grant of discretion given to the" Bureau to send prisoners to community corrections centers "while arguably intended to help rehabilitate prisoners, was not even arguably intended to provide a benefit to the" community correction centers themselves. The court emphasized that in the case involving competitors, there was reason for treating standing "with particular generosity," in part because "when the government enters the market by chartering specially favored or subsidized market actors, any limit on the activity of such institutions may arguably have, as an implicit purpose, the goal of not distorting the market more than necessary." In this case, that consideration did not apply, and hence Dismas could not challenge the Bureau's decision as violative of the relevant statute.

On the other hand, the court held that Dismas did have standing to challenge the Bureau's alleged failure to comply with §553 of the APA. Community corrections centers "like Dismas are arguably within the zone of interests protected by the notice-and-comment rulemaking requirements protected by the APA." Query: Does this last holding mean that anyone with injury in fact can challenge any agency's failure to comply with the APA?

Notes and Questions

1. The "arguably within the zone" test can be taken as a faint echo of the legal wrong test. The basic idea is similar — the plaintiff's injury must have some connection to the law — but the "arguably within the zone" test is more lenient. It requires a less careful and sustained examination of the governing statute. The underlying issue is whether the statute that the plaintiff invokes was motivated, "arguably" or at all, by a desire to protect people like the plaintiff. If not, there is no standing. But how should a court decide whether a plaintiff is "arguably" within the "zone of interests" that a statute regulates or protects? Were the banking acts in *Data Processing* designed, in part, to protect other firms from competition by banks? Were they designed, in part, to protect fruit and vegetable growers from competition by banks deciding to enter the fruit and vegetable business? How carefully should the Court investigate such questions in deciding whether plaintiffs have standing?

2. Suppose that a particular plaintiff is "arguably" within the "zone of interests" the statute protects, but, after closer analysis, it is clear that he really is *not* within that "zone of interest." Why should this sort of person be permitted to claim that a defendant has violated the statute when other persons whom the statute does not directly protect — say, taxpayers or citizens in general — are not permitted to make that same claim in court?

3. Before *Air Courier*, the Court had never, in the two decades since *Data Processing*, denied someone standing on "zone of interests" grounds. Indeed, *Clarke* was generally understood as an effort to stop lower courts from tightening the zone of interests test. Obviously, *Air Courier* points in a different direction. Is *Air Courier* consistent with

Clarke? Why aren't the interests of postal workers at least arguably part of the "public interest" that the postal service must consider in suspending its monopoly?

After *Air Courier*, there was a modest but noteworthy trend in the direction of tightening the zone of interests test by requiring plaintiffs to show that the statute was in some sense intended to benefit them. This trend suggested a cautious but unambiguous movement back in the direction of old "legal wrong" requirement. An important and representative case is Federation for American Immigration Reform v. Reno, 93 F.3d 897 (D.C. Cir. 1996). The federation is a group of about 1400 dues-paying members who live in the Miami area, where many Cuban immigrants have settled in the past. The federation challenged a new system for the parole and adjustment of status of Cuban nationals. It contended that the result of that system would be to impair the quality of life enjoyed by its members in the area, by, for example, diminishing employment opportunities and crowding public schools. The federation invoked a statute allowing the attorney general to parole "into the United States temporarily . . . for emergent reasons or for reasons deemed strictly in the public interest any alien applying for such admission to the United States, but such parole of such alien shall not be regarded as an admission into the United States." In the view of the federation, the new scheme effectively admitted Cuban nationals "into the Unites States."

The court of appeals held that the federation was not within the zone of interests of the statute. "An intent to protect residents of impacted regions does not appear so plausible from the statute itself that we will infer it without more. . . . Another possibility is that the zone of interests . . . includes the interest that legal residents throughout the United States may have in preventing immigration-related unemployment and stresses. . . . But the widespread nature of this alleged interest, indeed its near universality, suggest to us a negative answer. . . ." Thus there was no standing because Congress had shown no interest in using the relevant immigration laws to protect localities from the various stresses arguably created by increased admissions into the United States. Is this case consistent with *Clarke?*

Compare National Air Traffic Controllers Assn. v. Pena, 1996 U.S. App. LEXIS 8259 (6th Cir. 1996), holding that the national air traffic controllers association is within the zone of interests of the statute governing contracting-out public services, and thus could challenge a decision to contract out, and privatize, certain air traffic control services. Is this decision consistent with *Air Courier?* See also UPS Worldwide Forwarding v. U.S. Postal Service, 66 F.3d 621 (3d Cir. 1995) (allowing a private competitor of the postal service to challenge the international customized mail service of the U.S. Post Office); Schering Corp. v. FDA, 51 F.3d 390 (3d Cir. 1995) (allowing a competing drug manufacturer to bring suit against the FDA on the ground that competitive interests were within the zone of interests). In a similar vein, see Davis v. Philadelphia Housing Auth., 121 F.3d 92 (3d Cir. 1997), where a divided court invoked the "zone of interests" test and granted standing to someone injured by lead poisoning and complaining of a failure of protection under the Lead-Based Paint Poisoning Prevention Act. The court thought it was not dispositive that the plaintiffs were not participants in a low-income rental program under which states were required to comply with the act; in dissent, Judge Cowen argued that the plaintiffs were outside of any "zone."

NCUA seems to reject this trend, and in recent years, there is at most a modest movement in favor of tightening the zone of interests test. But is the *Dismas* case right to suggest that *NCUA* is merely about competitors? Some cases do continue to deny standing on zone of interest grounds. Consider, for example, Courtney v. Smith, 297 F.3d 455

(6th Cir. 2002), in which the court denied standing to federal employees whose jobs were lost as a result of an agency decision to outsource their work. The employees argued that the outsourcing decision was inconsistent with several federal statutes. The Court responded that the plaintiff's interests were not arguably within the zone of interests protected by any of those statutes. See also Cement Kiln Recycling Coalition v. EPA, 255 F.3d 855 (D.C. Cir. 2001), in which the court held that competitors of regulated entities could not challenge agency behavior under environmental statutes: "Petitioner's interest was not in environmental purity, but on increasing the regulatory burden on its competitors. To hold that this satisfied prudential standing would be to create 'a considerable potential for judicial intervention that would distort the regulatory process.'" In the same vein, see Rosebud Sioux Tribe v. McDivit, 286 F.3d 1031 (8th Cir. 2002).

For hard cases, showing some confusion within the lower courts, see Amgen v. Smith, 357 F.3d 103 (D.C. Cir. 2004); National Petrochemical & Refiners Assn. v. EPA, 287 F.3d 1130 (D.C. Cir. 2002); Nevada Land Action Association v. Forest Service, 8 F.3d 713 (9th Cir. 1993) (holding that landowners using federal land for grazing lack standing under the National Environmental Policy Act, because their interest was primarily economic); Liquid Carbonic Industries Corp. v. FERC, 28 F.3d 697 (D.C. Cir. 1994).

4. Evaluate the following view: *Air Courier* and *Dismas* were rightly decided, and they point the way to the future. Hence a trend in the direction of tightening the "zone" test would be a good one. Such a trend would undo the false move in *Data Processing*, by putting judicial attention exactly where it belongs: on the question of whether Congress wanted the plaintiff to be allowed to bring suit. Movement of this kind would have the fortunate effect of pushing the law toward the "legal wrong" idea, which is the language of §706 in any event. Is *NCUA* inconsistent with this view?

5. Assuming that the basic constitutional standing requirement are met (see below), Congress obviously can relax the "prudential" requirements by saying in a statute that any injured person can bring suit. In Bennett v. Spear, 520 U.S. 154 (1996), the Court held that Congress had eliminated the "zone of interests" test through the grant of standing to "any person" to bring suit under the Endangered Species Act. The plaintiffs were immigration districts and ranchers in areas adversely affected by a statement of the secretary of the interior. The court of appeals had held that notwithstanding the grant of standing to "any person," the zone of interests barred the suit because the plaintiffs invoked economic interests unrelated to the environmental goals of the act. Justice Scalia, writing for a unanimous Court, disagreed: "Congress legislates against the background of our prudential standing doctrine, which applies unless it is expressly negated." The Court concluded that the broad grant of standing did expressly negate that doctrine. The Court added: "Our readiness to take the term 'any person' at face value is greatly augmented by two interrelated considerations: that the overall subject matter of this legislation is the environment (a matter in which it is common to think all persons have an interest) and that the obvious purpose of the particular provision in question is to encourage enforcement by so-called 'private attorneys general. . . .'"

5. *What's an Injury, in Fact?*

After *Data Processing*, much of the law of standing has concerned the "injury in fact" test, which the Supreme Court has come to identify as part of the Constitution's requirement that federal courts may hear only "cases or controversies." The Court has concluded that this constitutional requirement has three parts. First, the plaintiff must show "injury in fact." Second, the plaintiff's injury must be caused by the challenged governmental action. Third, it must be possible for a victory on the merits to "redress" the plaintiff's injury. We begin with the first requirement.

a. The Law of Injuries Immediately after *Data Processing*

Sierra Club v. Morton

405 U.S. 727 (1972)

Mr. Justice STEWART delivered the opinion of the Court.

I

The Mineral King Valley is an area of great natural beauty nestled in the Sierra Nevada Mountains in Tulare County, California, adjacent to Sequoia National Park. It has been part of the Sequoia National Forest since 1926. . . .

[The U.S. Forest Service, which is entrusted with the maintenance and administration of national forests, approved a proposal of Walt Disney Enterprises for development of a $35 million ski resort in Mineral King, designed to accommodate 14,000 visitors daily.] To provide access to the resort, the State of California proposes to construct a highway 20 miles in length. A section of this road would traverse Sequoia National Park, as would a proposed high-voltage power line needed to provide electricity for the resort. Both the highway and the power line require the approval of the Department of the Interior. . . .

[The Sierra Club brought suit in federal district court, invoking the APA and claiming violation of several statutes,[17] and seeking a preliminary and permanent injunction. Sierra Club sued as a membership corporation with "a special interest in the conservation and the sound maintenance of the national parks, game refuges and forests of the country," and invoked the judicial-review provisions of the APA, 5 U.S.C. §§701 et seq.

The district court granted a preliminary injunction. The court of appeals reversed, vacating the preliminary injunction. It found that Sierra Club lacked standing to sue and also that it had failed to show sufficient irreparable injury or likelihood success on the merits to justify injunctive relief. Sierra Club based its standing on §702 of the APA. The Supreme Court restated the "injury in fact" and "zone of interests" tests of *Data Processing* and stated: "In deciding this case we do not reach any questions concerning the meaning of the 'zone of interests' test or its possible application to the facts here presented."]

---

17. As analyzed by the District Court, the complaint alleged violations of law falling into four categories. First, it claims that the special-use permit for construction of the resort exceeded the maximum acreage limitation placed upon such permits by 16 U.S.C. §497, and that issuance of a "revocable" use permit was beyond the authority of the Forest Service. Second, it challenged the proposed permit for the highway through Sequoia National Park on the grounds that the highway would not serve any of the purposes of the park, in alleged violation of 16 U.S.C. §1, and that it would destroy timber and other natural resources protected by 16 U.S.C. §§41 and 43. Third, it claims that the Forest Service and the Department of the Interior had violated their own regulations by failing to hold adequate public hearings on the proposed project. Finally, the complaint asserted that 16 U.S.C. §45c requires specific congressional authorization of a permit for construction of a power transmission line within the limits of a national park.

The injury alleged by the Sierra Club will be incurred entirely by reason of the change in the uses to which Mineral King will be put, and the attendant change in the aesthetics and ecology of the area. Thus, in referring to the road to be built through Sequoia National Park, the complaint alleged that the development "would destroy or otherwise adversely affect the scenery, natural and historic objects and wildlife of the park and would impair the enjoyment of the park for future generations." We do not question that this type of harm may amount to an "injury in fact" sufficient to lay the basis for standing under [§702] of the APA. Aesthetic and environmental well-being, like economic well-being, are important ingredients of the quality of life in our society, and the fact that particular environmental interests are shared by the many rather than the few does not make them less deserving of legal protection through the judicial process. But the "injury in fact" test requires more than an injury to a cognizable interest. It requires that the party seeking review be himself among the injured.

The impact of the proposed changes in the environment of Mineral King will not fall indiscriminately upon every citizen. The alleged injury will be felt directly only by those who use Mineral King and Sequoia National Park, and for whom the aesthetic and recreational values of the area will be lessened by the highway and ski resort. The Sierra Club failed to allege that it or its members would be affected in any of their activities or pastimes by the Disney development. Nowhere in the pleadings or affidavits did the Club state that its members use Mineral King for any purpose, much less that they use it in any way that would be significantly affected by the proposed actions of the respondents.[18]

[The Court then discussed its decision is *Sanders Bros.*, which it distinguished from the instant case on the grounds that the competitor there had alleged economic injury from the license grant and that its standing to represent the public interest had been explicitly granted by a congressional statute.]

The trend of cases arising under the APA and other statutes authorizing judicial review of federal agency action has been toward recognizing that injuries other than economic harm are sufficient to bring a person within the meaning of the statutory language, and toward discarding the notion that an injury that is widely shared is ipso facto not an injury sufficient to provide the basis for judicial review. We noted this development

18. The only reference in the pleadings to the Sierra Club's interest in the dispute is contained in paragraph 3 of the complaint, which reads in its entirety as follows:

> Plaintiff Sierra Club is a non-profit corporation organized and operating under the laws of the State of California, with its principal place of business in San Francisco, California since 1892. Membership of the club is approximately 78,000 nationally, with approximately 27,000 members residing in the San Francisco Bay Area. For many years the Sierra Club by its activities and conduct has exhibited a special interest in the conservation and the sound maintenance of the national parks, game refuges and forests of the country, regularly serving as a responsible representative of persons similarly interested. One of the principal purposes of the Sierra Club is to protect and conserve the national recourses of the Sierra Nevada Mountains. Its interests would be vitally affected by the acts hereinafter described and would be aggrieved by those acts of the defendants as hereinafter described and would be aggrieved by those acts of the defendants as hereinafter more fully appears.

In an amici curiae brief filed in this Court by the Wilderness Society and others, it is asserted that the Sierra Club has conducted regular camping trips into the Mineral King area, and that various members of the Club have used and continue to use the area for recreational purposes. These allegations were not contained in the pleadings, nor were they brought to the attention of the Court of Appeals. Moreover, the Sierra Club in its reply brief specifically declines to rely on its individualized interest, as a basis for standing. . . . Our decision does not, of course, bar the Sierra Club from seeking in the District Court to amend its complaint by a motion under Rule 15, Federal Rules of Civil Procedure.

with approval in *Data Processing,* 397 U.S., at 154, in saying that the interest alleged to have been injured "may reflect 'aesthetic, conservational, and recreational' as well as economic values." But broadening the categories of injury that may be alleged in support of standing is a different matter from abandoning the requirement that the party seeking review must himself have suffered an injury.

Some courts have indicated a willingness to take this latter step by conferring standing upon organizations that have demonstrated "an organizational interest in the problem" of environmental or consumer protection. Environmental Defense Fund v. Hardin, 138 U.S. App. D.C. 391, 395, 428 F.2d 1093, 1097. It is clear that an organization whose members are injured may represent those members in a proceeding for judicial review. See, e.g., NAACP v. Button, 371 U.S. 415, 428. But a mere "interest in a problem," no matter how longstanding the interest and no matter how qualified the organization is in evaluating the problem, is not sufficient by itself to render the organization "adversely affected" or "aggrieved" within the meaning of the APA. The Sierra Club is a large and long-established organization, with a historic commitment to the cause of protecting our Nation's natural heritage from man's depredations. But if a "special interest" in this subject were enough to entitle the Sierra Club to commence this litigation, there would appear to be no objective basis upon which to disallow a suit by any other bona fide "special interest" organization, however small or short-lived. And if any group with a bona fide "special interest" could initiate such litigation, it is difficult to perceive why any individual citizen with the same bona fide special interest would not also be entitled to do so.

The requirement that a party seeking review must allege facts showing that he is himself adversely affected does not insulate executive action from judicial review, nor does it prevent any public interests from being protected through the judicial process.[19] It does serve as at least a rough attempt to put the decision as to whether review will be sought in the hands of those who have a direct stake in the outcome. That goal would be undermined were we to construe the APA to authorize judicial review at the behest of organizations or individuals who seek to do no more than vindicate their own value preferences through the judicial process.[20] The principle that the Sierra Club would have us establish in this case would do just that.

[The Court affirmed the dismissal for lack of standing.]

---

19. In its reply brief, after noting the fact that it might gave chosen to assert individualized injury to itself or to its members as a basis for standing, the Sierra Club states:

> The Government seeks to create a "heads I win, tails you lose" situation in which either the courthouse door is barred for lack of assertion of a private, unique injury or a preliminary injunction is denied on the ground that the litigant has advanced private injury which does not warrant an injunction adverse to a competing public interest. Counsel have shaped their case to avoid this trap.

The short answer to this contention is that the "trap" does not exit. The test of injury in fact goes only to the question of standing to obtain judicial review. Once this standing is established, the party may assert the interests of the general public in support of his claims for equitable relief.

20. Every schoolboy may be familiar with Alexis de Tocqueville's famous observation, written in the 1830s, that "[s]carcely any political question arises in the United States that is not resolved, sooner or later, into a judicial question." 1 Democracy in America 280 (1945). Less familiar, however, is de Tocqueville's further observation that judicial reviw is effective largely because it is not available simply at the behest of a partisan faction, but is exercised only to remedy a particular, concrete injury.

"It will be seen, also, that by leaving it to private interest to censure the law, and by intimately uniting the trial of the law with the trial of an individual, legislation is protected from wanton assaults and from the daily aggressions of party spirit. The errors of the legislator are exposed only to meet a real want; and it is always a positive and appreciable fact that must serve as the basis of a prosecution." Id., at 102.

Mr. Justice Powell and Mr. Justice Rehnquist took no part in the consideration or decision of this case.

Mr. Justice DOUGLAS, dissenting. . . .

[Relying on Stone, Should Trees Have Standing? — Toward Legal Rights for Natural Objects, 45 S. Cal. L. Rev. 450 (1972), Justice Douglas would allow actions to be brought in the name of natural objects threatened by development. He would grant standing to hikers, fishermen, zoologists, or others with a "meaningful relation" to a natural object to seek judicial review on its behalf.]

[T]he pressures on agencies for favorable action one way or the other are enormous. The suggestion that Congress can stop action which is undesirable is true in theory; yet even Congress is too remote to give meaningful direction and its machinery is too ponderous to use very often.

The Forest Service — one of the federal agencies behind the scheme to despoil Mineral King — has been notorious for its alignment with lumber companies, although its mandate from Congress directs it to consider the various aspects of multiple use in its supervision of the national forests. . . .

The voice of the inanimate object, therefore, should not be stilled. . . .

Mr. Justice BLACKMUN, dissenting. . . .

1. I would . . . approve the judgment of the District Court which recognized standing in the Sierra Club and granted preliminary relief. I would be willing to do this on condition that the Sierra Club forthwith amend its complaint to meet the specifications the Court prescribes for standing. . . .

2. Alternatively, I would permit an imaginative expansion of our traditional concepts of standing in order to enable an organization such as the Sierra Club, possessed, as it is, of pertinent, bona fide, and well-recognized attributes and purposes in the area of environment, to litigate environmental issues. This incursion upon tradition need not be very extensive. Certainly, it should be no cause for alarm. It is no more progressive than was the decision in *Data Processing* itself. It need only recognize the interests of one who has a provable, sincere, dedicated, and established status. We need not fear that Pandora's box will be opened or that there will be no limit to the number of those who desire to participate in environmental litigation. The courts will exercise appropriate restraints just as they have exercised them in the past. . . .

[A]ny resident of the Mineral King area — the real "user" — is an unlikely adversary for this Disney-governmental project. He naturally will be inclined to regard the situation as one that should benefit him economically. His fishing or camping or guiding or handyman or general outdoor prowess perhaps will find an early and ready market among the visitors. But that glow of anticipation will be short-lived at best. If he is a true lover of the wilderness — as is likely, or he would not be near Mineral King in the first place — it will not be long before he yearns for the good old days when masses of people — that 14,000 influx per day — and their thus far uncontrollable waste were unknown to Mineral King. . . .

The Court chooses to conclude its opinion with a footnote reference to De Tocqueville. In this environmental context I personally prefer the older and particularly pertinent observation and warning of John Donne.[21]

21. "No man is an Iland, intire of itselfe; every man is a peece of the Continent, a part of the maine; if a Clod bee washed away by the Sea, Europe is the lesse, as well as if a Promontorie were, as well as if a Mannor of thy friends or of thine owne were; any man's death diminishes me, because I am involved in Mankinde; And therefore never send to know for whom the bell tolls; it tolls for thee." Devotions XVII.

Note on United States v. SCRAP

In United States v. SCRAP, 412 U.S. 669 (1973), several environmental groups challenged, as a violation of the National Environmental Policy Act (NEPA), the ICC's failure to prepare an environmental impact statement (EIS) before allowing the nation's railroads to institute a general rate increase. Plaintiffs contended that the rate increase would discourage production of recycled as opposed to disposable goods on the theory that more transportation is needed to produce "round trip" recycled goods than "one way" disposables; hence any general rate increase adds more to the cost of recycled than disposable goods. The result, plaintiffs alleged, would be more litter and pollution. An EIS must therefore be prepared to assess the resulting environmental degradation.

The claim of plaintiff Students Challenging Regulatory Agency Procedures (SCRAP) was typical. SCRAP, an unincorporated association of five law students, claimed that its members would suffer harm by being exposed to increased pollution and to increased litter in the forests, rivers, and other natural resources of the Washington, D.C., area used by the students for recreation. The Supreme Court upheld plaintiff's standing but ruled that the ICC's action in refusing to suspend the rate increases was not subject to judicial review and entered judgment for defendants.

The Court found that the environmental interests that SCRAP sought to protect were clearly within the zone protected by NEPA and that SCRAP (unlike Sierra Club) had sufficiently alleged "specific injury" to its members in the form of harm to their use and enjoyment of the natural environment in the Washington, D.C., area. The fact that similar adverse effects would allegedly occur throughout the nation did not deprive plaintiffs of standing:

> To deny standing to persons who are in fact injured simply because many others are also injured, would mean that the most injurious and widespread Government actions could be questioned by nobody. We cannot accept that conclusion.
>
> But the injury alleged here is also very different from that at issue in *Sierra Club* because here the alleged injury to the environment is far less direct and perceptible. . . . The railroads protest that the appellees could never prove that a general increase in rates would have [the environmental effects asserted by plaintiffs], and they contend that these allegations were a ploy to avoid the need to show injury in fact.
>
> Of course, pleadings must be something more than an ingenious academic exercise in the conceivable. A plaintiff must allege that he has been or will in fact be perceptibly harmed by the challenged agency action, not that he can imagine circumstances in which he could be affected by the agency's action. And it is equally clear that the allegations must be true and capable of proof at trial. But we deal here simply with the pleadings in which the appellees alleged a specific and perceptible harm that distinguished them from other citizens who had not used the natural resources that were claimed to be affected.[22] If, as the railroads now assert, these allegations were in fact untrue, then the appellants should have moved for summary judgment on the

---

22. The Government urges us to limit standing to those who have been "significantly" affected by agency action. But, even if we could begin to define what such a test would mean, we think it fundamentally misconceived. "Injury in fact" reflects the statutory requirement that a person be "adversely affected" or "aggrieved," and it serves to distinguish a person with a direct stake in the outcome of a litigation — even though small — from a person with a mere interest in the problem. We have allowed important interests to be vindicated by plaintiffs with no more at stake in the outsome of an action than a fraction of a vote, see Baker v. Carr, 369 U.S. 186; a $5 fine and costs, see McGowan v. Maryland, 366 U.S. 420; and a $1.50 poll tax, Harper v. Virginia Bd. of Elections, 383 U.S. 663. While these cases were not dealing specifically with §10 of the APA, we

standing issue and demonstrated to the District Court that the allegations were sham and raised no genuine issue of fact. We cannot say on these pleadings that the appellees could not prove their allegations which, if proved, would place them squarely among those persons injured in fact by the Commission's action, and entitled under the clear import of Sierra Club to seek review.

Justice White, joined by Chief Justice Burger and Justice Rehnquist, dissented from the Court's disposition of the standing question on the ground that the injuries alleged were too "remote, speculative and insubstantial in fact."

Questions

1. What possible justification is there for denying standing to an established and well-organized California-based environmental group seeking to challenge a particular development in California, while granting standing to an ad hoc group of law students to challenge a nationwide rate increase?

2. Why did the lawyers for Sierra Club decline to allege that members of the club used the Mineral King valley? It is now clear, is it not, that if they had so alleged, the Supreme Court would have upheld Sierra Club's standing? Does the Court's rationale place excessive weight on this pleading issue?

3. Precisely why should "injury in fact" (assuming that this idea is coherent) be a prerequisite for standing? Why shouldn't a person or organization with a demonstrated and sincere interest in an issue be afforded standing so long as the case is vigorously litigated?

Consider Valley Forge Christian College v. Americans United for Separation of Church and State, 454 U.S. 464 (1982):

> The judicial power of the United States defined by Art. III is not an uncondi-tional authority to determine the constitutionality of legislative or executive acts. The power to declare the rights of individuals and to measure the authority of governments, this Court said 90 years ago, "is legitimate only in the last resort, and a necessity in the determination of real, earnest and vital controversy." Chicago & Grand Trunk R. Co. v. Wellman, 143 U.S. 339, 345 (1892). Otherwise, the power "is not judicial . . . in the sense in which judicial power is granted by the Constitution to the courts of the United States." United States v. Ferreira, 13 How. 40, 48 (1852). . . .
>
> The Art. III aspect of standing also reflects a due regard for the autonomy of those persons likely to be most directly affected by a judicial order. The federal courts have abjured appeals to their authority which would convert the judicial process into "no more than a vehicle for the vindication of the value interests of concerned bystanders." United States v. SCRAP, 412 U.S. 669, 687 (1973). Were the federal courts merely publicly funded forums for the ventilation of public grievances or the refinement of jurisprudential understanding, the concept of "standing" would be quite unnecessary. But the "cases and controversies" language of Art. III forecloses the conversion of courts of the United States into judicial versions of college debating forums. . . . The exercise of judicial power, which can so profoundly affect the lives, liberty, and prop-erty of those to whom it extends, is therefore restricted to litigants who can show "injury in fact" resulting from the action which they seek to adjudicate.

---

see no reason to adopt a more restrictive interpretation of "adversely affected" or "aggrieved." As Professor Davis has put it, "The basic idea that comes out in numerous cases is that an identifiable trifle is enough for standing to fight out a question of principle; the trifle is the basis for standing and the principle supplies the motivation." Davis, Standing: Taxpayers and Others, 35 U. Chi. L. Rev. 601, 613.

> The exercise of the judicial power also affects relationships between the coequal branches of the National Government. The effect is, of course, most vivid when a federal court declares unconstitutional an act of the Legislative or Executive Branch. While the exercise of that "ultimate and supreme function". . . is a formidable means of vindicating individual rights, when employed unwisely or unnecessarily it is also the ultimate threat to the continued effectiveness of the federal courts in performing that role. . . .

Are these arguments convincing? Do they have force in the administrative context, when a plaintiff is not attacking a statute on constitutional grounds, but attacking agency action on statutory grounds?

4. What purpose is served by conducting a threshold hearing, directed at the question of standing, on whether the ICC's rate increase will generate more litter in Washington, D.C., parks where plaintiffs are likely to view such litter? Such a procedure might seem bizarre because NEPA has been judicially construed as an essentially procedural statute designed to generate, through an EIS, information of the environmental effects of a proposed action. To require plaintiffs to show what those effects are as a prerequisite to requiring that an EIS be performed seems inconsistent with the basic purpose of NEPA.

In general, lower court cases seem to make an evidentiary hearing quite possible, and sometimes necessary, in disputed cases. See, e.g., Sierra Club v. EPA, 292 F.3d 895 (D.C. Cir. 2002); Public Interest Research Group v. Magnesium Elektron, 123 F.3d 111 (3d Cir. 1997); Florida Audubon Society v. Bentsen, 94 F.3d 658 (D.C. Cir. 1996) (en banc).

5. What kinds of injuries must organizations show? The Washington Apple Advertising Commission is a state commission the members of which are elected by apple growers, and which promoted the development and sale of Washington state apples. It attacked as an unconstitutional burden on interstate commerce a North Carolina law that said all apples sent into North Carolina had to bear "no grade other than the applicable U.S. grade or standard." The Supreme Court held that the commission had standing to raise this claim. In so holding, the Court reviewed cases in which voluntary membership associations had been held to have standing to represent the interests of their members. In Hunt v. Washington Apple Advertising Commn., 432 U.S. 333 (1977), the Court wrote:

> Thus we have recognized that an association has standing to bring suit on behalf of its members when: (a) its members would otherwise have standing to sue in their own right; (b) the interests it seeks to protect are germane to the organization's purpose; and (c) neither the claim asserted not the relief requested requires the participation of individual members in the lawsuit.

The Court concluded that the association satisfied these criteria and that, for standing purposes, the fact that it was a "state" commission was irrelevant. The Court reaffirmed these fairly lenient standards in UAW v. Donovan, 477 U.S. 274 (1986), stating that the "doctrine of associational standing requires that the primary reason people join an organization is often to create an effective vehicle for vindicating interests that they share with others. . . . The very forces that cause individuals to band together in an association will thus provide some guarantee that the association will work to promote their interests."

For a lower court case ruling broadly but in the same vein, see Biodiversity Legal Foundation v. Badgley, 309 F.3d 1166 (9th Cir. 2002), granting standing to organizations challenging a failure to comply with deadline in the Endangered Species Act on the ground that each organization alleged that "its staff, members, and supporters derive scientific, aesthetic, and spiritual benefits from a [species'] continual existence in its natural habitat." See also New York Public Interest Group v. Whitman, 321 F.3d 316 (2d Cir. 2003), 321 F.3d 316 (2d Cir. 2003), allowing an organization to challenge an EPA decision involving alleged deficiencies in a permitting program under the Clean Air Act, when the organization alleged that it had members who live within a few miles of facilities that require permits, and that they were injured by their uncertainty about whether they will be exposed to excess air pollution as a result of the EPA's decision. A different direction is suggested in Sierra Club v. EPA, 292 F.3d 895 (D.C. Cir. 2002), denying standing to an organization's effort to challenge an EPA rule that exempted certain wastewater treatment sludges from regulation, notwithstanding the members' claim that they lived near the sludge facilities and sites.

6. To what extent may public authorities enjoy standing to assert private claims brought under programs that they administer? The director of the Office of Workers' Compensation Programs in the Department of Labor issues and administers regulations for processing workers' compensation claims and assists claimants in asserting such claims. A separate unit in the department — the Benefits Review Board — adjudicates such claims. The director sought judicial review of the board's award of only partial benefits to a claimant; the claimant did not seek review. Director, Office of Workers' Compensation Programs v. Newport News Shipbuilding & Drydock Co., 514 U.S. 122 (1995), held that the director lacked standing because the program statute limited judicial review to "persons adversely affected or aggrieved," which, the Court found, does not ordinarily "refer to an agency acting in its governmental capacity." Justice Scalia's opinion for the Court, states, however, that "Congress could have conferred standing on the Director without infringing Article III of the Constitution." Is this statement consistent with the case that follows? Keep this question in mind as you read the following materials.

b. Injuries in Fact Now

Lujan v. Defenders of Wildlife
504 U.S. 555 (1992)

Justice SCALIA delivered the opinion of the Court with respect to Parts I, II, III-A, and IV, and an opinion with respect to Part III-B, in which THE CHIEF JUSTICE, Justice WHITE, and Justice THOMAS join.

[Section 7(a)(2) of the Endangered Species Act of 1973 divides responsibility for the protection of endangered species between the secretary of the interior and the secretary of commerce. Each federal agency is required to consult with the appropriate secretary to ensure that any action funded by the agency is not likely to jeopardize the continued existence or habitat of any endangered or threatened species. Both secretaries initially promulgated a joint regulation interpreting §7(a)(2) to apply to actions taken in foreign nations; then, they jointly revised the rule to limit the section's geographic scope to the United States and the high seas. Wildlife conservation and other environmental organizations sued, claiming that the revised rule misinterpreted the statute. The court of appeals reversed the district court's dismissal of the suit for lack of standing. On remand, the district court denied the government's motion for summary judgment on standing and granted the plaintiff's cross motion on the merits. It ordered publication of a new rule returning to the original interpretation of §7(a)(2). The court of appeals affirmed.]

II

. . . The party invoking federal jurisdiction bears the burden of establishing [the] elements [of standing]. Since they are not mere pleading requirements but rather an indispensable part of the plaintiff's case, each element must be supported in the same as any other matter on which the plaintiff bears the burden of proof, i.e., with the manner and degree of evidence required at the successive stages of the litigation. . . .

When the suit is one challenging the legality of government action or inaction, the nature and extent of facts that must be averred (at the summary judgment stage) or proved (at the trial stage) in order to establish standing depends considerably upon whether the plaintiff is himself an object of the action (or forgone action) at issue. If he is, there is ordinarily little question that the action or inaction has caused him injury, and that a judgment preventing or requiring the action will redress it. When, however, as in this case, a plaintiff's asserted injury arises from the government's allegedly unlawful regulation (or lack of regulation) of someone else, much more is needed. In that circumstance, causation and redressability ordinarily hinge on the response of the regulated (or regulable) third party to the government action or inaction — and perhaps on the response of others as well. The existence of one or more of the essential elements of standing "depends on the unfettered choices made by independent actors not before the courts and whose exercise of broad and legitimate discretion the courts cannot presume either to control or to predict," and it becomes the burden of the plaintiff to adduce facts showing that those choices have been or will be made in such a manner as to produce causation and permit redressability of injury. Thus, when the plaintiff is not himself the object of the government action or inaction he challenges, standing is not precluded, but it is ordinarily "substantially more difficult" to establish.

III

We think the Court of Appeals failed to apply the foregoing principles in denying the Secretary's motion for summary judgment. . . .

A

Respondents' claim to injury is that the lack of consultation with respect to certain funded activities abroad "increas[es] the rate of extinction of endangered and threatened species." Of course, the desire to use or observe an animal species, even for purely esthetic purposes, is undeniably a cognizable interest for purpose of standing. See, e.g., Sierra Club v. Morton. "But the 'injury in fact' test requires more than an injury to a cognizable interest. It requires that the party seeking review be himself among the injured." Id. . . .

[T]he Court of Appeals focused on the affidavits of two Defenders' members — Joyce Kelly and Amy Skilbred. Ms. Kelly stated that she traveled to Egypt in 1986 and "observed the traditional habitat of the endangered nile crocodile there and intend[s] to do so again, and hope[s] to observe the crocodile directly," and that she "will suffer harm in fact as the result of [the] American . . . role . . . in overseeing the rehabilitation of the

Aswan High Dam on the Nile . . . and [in] develop[ing] . . . Egypt's . . . Master Water Plan." Ms. Skilbred averred that she traveled to Sri Lanka in 1981 and "observed th[e] habitat" of "endangered species such as the Asian elephant and the leopard" at what is now the site of the Mahaweli project funded by the Agency for International Development (AID), although she "was unable to see any of the endangered species"; "this development project," she continued, "will seriously reduce endangered, threatened, and endemic species habitat including areas that I visited[, which] may severely shorten the future of these species"; that threat, she concluded, harmed her because she "intend[s] to return to Sri Lanka in the future and hope[s] to be more fortunate in spotting at least the endangered elephant and leopard." When Ms. Skilbred was asked at a subsequent deposition if and when she had any plans to return to Sri Lanka, she reiterated that "I intend to go back to Sri Lanka," but confessed that she had no current plans: "I don't know [when]. There is a civil war going on right now. I don't know. Not next year, I will say. In the future."

We shall assume for the sake of argument that these affidavits contain facts showing that certain agency-funded projects threaten listed species — though that is questionable. They plainly contain no facts, however, showing how damage to the species will produce "imminent" injury to Mses. Kelly and Skilbred. That the women "had visited" the areas of the projects before the projects commenced proves nothing. As we have said in a related context, "'Past exposure to illegal conduct does not in itself show a present case or controversy regarding injunctive relief . . . if unaccompanied by any continuing, present adverse effects.'" And the affiants' profession of an "inten[t]" to return to the places they had visited before — where they will presumably, this time, be deprived of the opportunity to observe animals of the endangered species — is simply not enough. Such "some day" intentions — without any description of concrete plans, or indeed even any specification of *when* the some day will be — do not support a finding of the "actual or imminent" injury that our cases require. . . .

Besides relying upon the Kelly and Skilbred affidavits, respondents propose a series of novel standing theories. The first, inelegantly styled "ecosystem nexus," proposes that any person who uses any part of a "contiguous ecosystem" adversely affected by a funded activity has standing even if the activity is located a great distance away. This approach, as the Court of Appeals correctly observed, is inconsistent with our opinion in Lujan v. National Wildlife Federation, 497 U.S. 871 (1990), which held that a plaintiff claiming injury from environmental damage must use the area affected by the challenged activity and not an area roughly "in the vicinity" of it. It makes no difference that the general-purpose section of the ESA states that the Act was intended in part "to provide a means whereby the ecosystems upon which endangered species and threatened species depend may be conserved." To say that the Act protects ecosystems is not to say that the Act creates (if it were possible) rights of action in persons who have not been injured in fact, that is, persons who use portions of an ecosystem not perceptibly affected by the unlawful action in question.

Respondents' other theories are called, alas, the "animal nexus" approach, whereby anyone who has an interest in studying or seeing the endangered animals anywhere on the globe has standing; and the "vocational nexus" approach, under which anyone with a professional interest in such animals can sue. Under these theories, anyone who goes to see Asian elephants in the Bronx Zoo, and anyone who is a keeper of Asian elephants in the Bronx Zoo, has standing to sue because the Directory of the Agency for International Development (AID) did not consult with the Secretary regarding the AID-funded project in Sri Lanka. This is beyond all reason. . . .

B

[The Court also concluded that, even if plaintiffs had established injury, they had failed to show that it would be redressed by victory on the merits. The federal agencies supplying funding for the challenged projects had not been made parties to the litigation.]

IV

The Court of Appeals found that respondents had standing for an additional reason: because they had suffered a "procedural injury." The so-called "citizen-suit" provision of the ESA provides, in pertinent part, that "any person may commence a civil suit on his own behalf (A) to enjoin any person, including the United States and any other governmental instrumentality or agency . . . who is alleged to be in violation of any provision of this chapter." 16 U.S.C. §1540(g). The Court held that, because §7(a)(2) requires interagency consultation, the citizen-suit provision creates a "procedure righ[t]" to consultation in all "persons" — so that anyone can file suit in federal court to challenge the Secretary's (or presumably any other official's) failure to follow the assertedly correct consultative procedure, notwithstanding his or her inability to allege any discrete injury flowing from that failure. To understand the remarkable nature of this holding one must be clear about what it does *not* rest upon: This is not a case where plaintiffs are seeking to enforce a procedural requirement the disregard of which could impair a separate concrete interest of theirs (e.g., the procedural requirement for a hearing prior to denial of their license application, or the procedural requirement for an environmental impact statement before a federal facility is constructed next door to them).[23] Nor is it simply a case where concrete injury has been suffered by many persons, as in mass fraud or mass tort situations. Nor, finally, is it the unusual case in which Congress has created a concrete private interest in the outcome of a suit against a private party for the government's benefit, by providing a cash bounty for the victorious plaintiff. Rather, the court held that the injury-in-fact requirement had been satisfied by congressional conferral upon all persons of an abstract, self-contained, noninstrumental "right" to have the Executive observe the procedures required by law. We reject this view.[24]

23. There is this much truth to the assertion that "procedural rights" are special: The person who has been accorded a procedural right to protect his concrete interests can assert that right without meeting all the normal standards for redressability and immediacy. Thus, under our case law, one living adjacent to the site for proposed construction of a federally licensed dam has standing to challenge the licensing agency's failure to prepare an environmental impact statement, even though he cannot establish with any certainty that the statement will cause the license to be withheld or altered, and even though the dam will not be completed for many years. (That is why we do not rely, in the present case, upon the Government's argument that, even if the other agencies were obliged to consult with the Secretary, they might not have followed his advice.) What respondents' "procedural rights" argument seeks, however, is quite different from this: standing for persons who have no concrete interests affected – persons who live (and propose to live) at the other end of the country from the dam.

24. The dissent's discussion of this aspect of the case distorts our opinion. We do not hold that an individual cannot enforce procedural rights; he assuredly can, so long as the procedures in question are designed to protect some threatened concrete interest of his that is the ultimate basis of his standing. The dissent, however, asserts that there exist "classes of procedure duties . . . so enmeshed with the prevention of a substantive, concrete harm that an individual plaintiff may be able to demonstrate a sufficient likelihood of injury just through the breach of that procedural duty." If we understood this correctly, it means that the Government's violation of a certain (undescribed) class of procedural duty satisfies the concrete-injury requirement by itself, without any showing that the procedural violation endangers a concrete interest of the plaintiff (apart from his interest in having the procedure observed). We cannot agree. The dissent is unable to cite a single case in which we actually found standing solely on the basis of a "procedural right" unconnected to the plaintiff's own concrete harm. Its suggestion that we did so in Japan Whaling Assn. v. American Cetacean Soc., 478 U.S. 221 (1986), and

We have consistently held that a plaintiff raising only a generally available grievance about government — claiming only harm to his and every citizen's interest in proper application of the Constitution and laws, and seeking relief that no more directly and tangibly benefits him than it does the public at large — does not state an Article III case or controversy [citing, inter alia, *Richardson, Schlesinger,* and *Valley Forge*]. . . .

To be sure, our generalized-grievances cases have typically involved Government violation of procedures assertedly ordained by the Constitution rather than the Congress. But there is absolutely no basis for making the Article III inquiry turn on the source of the asserted right. Whether the courts were to act on their own, or at the invitation of Congress, in ignoring the concrete injury requirement described in our cases, they would be discarding a principle fundamental to the separate and distinct constitutional role of the Third Branch — one of the essential elements that identifies those "Cases" and "Controversies" that are the business of the courts rather than of the political branches. "The province of the court," as Chief Justice Marshall said in Marbury v. Madison, "is, solely, to decide on the rights of individuals." Vindicating the public interest (including the public interest in Government observance of the Constitution and laws) is the function of Congress and the Chief Executive. The question presented here is whether the public interest in proper administration of the laws (specifically, in agencies' observance of a particular, statutorily prescribed procedure) can be converted into an individual right by a statute that denominates it as such, and that permits all citizens (or, for that matter, a subclass of citizens who suffer no distinctive concrete harm) to sue. If the concrete injury requirement has the separation-of-powers significance we have always said, the answer must be obvious: To permit Congress to convert the undifferentiated public interest in executive officers' compliance with the law into an "individual right" vindicable in the courts is to permit Congress to transfer from the President to the courts the Chief Executive's most important constitutional duty, to "take Care that the Laws be faithfully executed," Art. II, §3. It would enable the courts, with the permission of Congress, "to assume a position of authority over the governmental acts of another and co-equal department," and to become " 'virtually continuing monitors of the wisdom and soundness of Executive action.' " Allen v. Wright. We have always rejected that vision of our role:

> When Congress passes an Act empowering administrative agencies to carry on governmental activities, the power of those agencies is circumscribed by the authority granted. This permits the courts to participate in law enforcement entrusted to administrative bodies only to the extent necessary to protect justiciable individual rights against administrative action fairly beyond the granted powers. . . . This is very far from assuming that the courts are charged more than administrators or legislators with the protection of the rights of the people. Congress and the Executive supervise the acts of administrative agents. . . . But under Article III, Congress established courts to adjudicate cases and controversies as to claims of infringement of individual rights whether by unlawful action of private persons or by the exertion of unauthorized administrative power.

Stark v. Wickard, 321 U.S. 288 (1944).

Robertson v. Methow Valley Citizens Council, 490 U.S. 332 (1989), is not supported by the facts. In the former case, we found that the environmental organizations had standing because the "whale watching and studying of their members w[ould] be adversely affected by continued whale harvesting," and in the latter we did not so much as mention standing, for the very good reason that the plaintiff was a citizens' council for the area in which the challenged construction was to occur, so that its members would obviously be concretely affected.

"Individual rights," within the meaning of this passage, do not mean public rights that have been legislatively pronounced to belong to each individual who forms part of the public.

Nothing in this contradicts the principle that "[t]he . . . injury required by Art. III may exist solely by virtue of 'statutes creating legal rights, the invasion of which creates standing.'" [These other cases] involved Congress' elevating to the status of legally cogniz-able injuries concrete, de facto injuries that were previously inadequate in law. . . . As we said in *Sierra Club*, "[Statutory] broadening [of] the categories of injury that may be alleged in support of standing is a different matter from abandoning the requirement that the party seeking review must himself have suffered an injury." . . .

We hold that respondents lack standing to bring this action and that the Court of Appeals erred in denying the summary judgment motion filed by the United States. The opinion of the Court of Appeals is hereby reversed, and the cause is remanded for proceedings consistent with this opinion.

Justice KENNEDY, with whom Justice SOUTER joins, concurring in part and concur-ring in the judgment.

Although I agree with the essential parts of the Court's analysis, I write separately to make several observations.

I agree with the Court's conclusion in Part III-A that, on the record before us, respondents have failed to demonstrate that they themselves are "among the injured." . . . While it may seem trivial to require that Mses. Kelly and Skilbred acquire airline tickets to the project sites or announce a date certain upon which they will return, this is not a case where it is reasonable to assume that the affiants will be using the sites on a regular basis, see Sierra Club v. Morton, nor do the affiants claim to have visited the sites since the projects commenced. With respect to the Court's discussion of respondents' "ecosys-tem nexus," "animal nexus," and "vocational nexus" theories, I agree that on this record respondents' showing is insufficient to establish standing on any of these bases. I am not willing to foreclose the possibility, however, that in different circumstances a nexus theory similar to those proffered here might support a claim. . . .

I also join Part V of the Court's opinion with the following observations. As Government programs and policies become more complex and far-reaching, we must be sensitive to the articulation of new rights of action that do not have clear analogs in our common-law tradition. Modern litigation has progressed far from the paradigm of Marbury suing Madison to get his commission. . . . In my view, Congress has the power to define injuries and articulate chains of causation that will give rise to a case or controversy where none existed before, and I do not read the Court's opinion to suggest a contrary view. In exercising this power, however, Congress must at the very least identify the injury it seeks to vindicate and relate the injury to the class of persons entitled to bring suit. The citizen-suit provision of the Endangered Species Act does not meet these minimal requirements, because while the statute purports to confer a right on "any person . . . to enjoin . . . the United States and any other governmental instrumentality or agency . . . who is alleged to be in violation of any provision of this chapter," it does not of its own force establish that there is an injury in "any person" by virtue of any "violation."

The Court's holding that there is an outer limit to the power of Congress to confer rights of action is a direct and necessary consequence of the case and controversy limita-tions found in Article III. I agree that it would exceed those limitations if, at the behest of Congress and in the absence of any showing of concrete injury, we were to entertain citizen suits to vindicate the public's nonconcrete interest in the proper administration of the laws. While it does not matter how many persons have been injured by the challenged action, the party bringing suit must show that the action injures him in a concrete and personal way. This requirement is not just an empty formality. It preserves the vitality of the adversarial process by assuring both that the parties before the court have an actual, as opposed to professed, stake in the outcome, and that "the legal questions presented . . . will be resolved, not in the rarified atmosphere of a debating society, but in a concrete factual context conducive to realistic appreciation of the consequences of judicial action." In addition, the requirement of concrete injury confines the Judicial Branch to its proper, limited role in the constitutional framework of Government.

An independent judiciary is held to account through its open proceedings and its reasoned judgments. In this process it is essential for the public to know what persons or groups are invoking the judicial power, the reasons that they have brought suit, and whether their claims are vindicated or denied. The concrete injury requirement helps assure that there can be an answer to these questions; and, as the Court's opinion is careful to show, that is part of the constitutional design. . . .

[Justice Stevens concurred in the judgment on grounds that the new rule correctly interpreted the intended geographical scope of the ESA. He concluded respondents did have standing.]

Justice BLACKMUN, with whom Justice O'Connor joins, dissenting.

I part company with the Court in this case in two respects. First, I believe that respondents have raised genuine issues of fact — sufficient to survive summary judgment — both as to injury and as to redressability. Second, I question the Court's breadth of language in rejecting standing for "procedural" injuries. I fear the Court seeks to impose fresh limitations on the constitutional authority of congress to allow citizen suits in the federal courts for injuries deemed "procedural" in nature. . . .

I think a reasonable finder of fact could conclude from the information in the affidavits and deposition testimony that either Kelly or Skilbred will soon return to the project sites, thereby satisfying the "actual or imminent" injury standard. . . . By requiring a "description of concrete plans" or "specification of when the some day [for a return visit] will be," the Court, in my view, demands what is likely an empty formality. No substantial barriers prevent Kelly or Skilbred fron simply purchasing plane tickets to return to the Aswan and Mahaweli projects. This case differs from other cases in which the imminence of harm turned largely on the affirmative actions of third parties beyond a plaintiff's control. . . .

I fear the Court's demand for detailed descriptions of future conduct will do little to weed out those who are genuinely harmed form those who are not. More likely, it will resurrect a code-pleading formalism in federal court summary judgment practice, as federal courts, newly doubting their jurisdiction, will demand more and more particularized showings of future harm. Just to survive summary judgment, for example, a property owner claiming a decline in the value of his property from governmental action might have to specify the exact date he intends to sell his property and show that there is a market for the property, lest it be surmised he might not sell again. A nurse turned down for a job on grounds of her race had better be prepared to show on what date she was prepared to start work, that she had arranged daycare for her child, and that she would not have accepted work at another hospital instead. . . .

The Court concludes that any "procedural injury" suffered by respondents is insufficient to confer standing. It rejects the view that the "injury-in-fact requirement [is] satisfied by congressional conferral upon all persons of an abstract, self-contained, noninstrumental 'right' to have the Executive observe the procedures required by law." Whatever the Court might mean with that very broad language, it cannot be saying that "procedural injuries" as a class are necessarily insufficient for purposes of Article III standing.

Most governmental conduct can be classified as "procedural." Many injuries caused by governmental conduct, therefore, are categorizable at some level of generality as "procedural" injuries. Yet, these injuries are not categorically beyond the pale of redress by the federal courts. When the Government, for example, "procedurally" issues a pollution permit, those affected by the permittee's pollutants are not without standing to sue. . . .

The Court expresses concern that allowing judicial enforcement of "agencies' observance of a particular, statutorily prescribed procedure" would "transfer from the President to the courts the Chief Executive's most important constitutional duty, to 'take Care that the Laws be faithfully executed.'" In fact, the principal effect of foreclosing judicial enforcement of such procedures is to transfer power into the hands of the Executive at the expense — not of the courts — but of Congress, from which that power originates and emanates.

Under the Court's anachronistically formal view of the separation of powers, Congress legislates pure, substantive mandates and has no business structuring the procedural manner in which the Executive implements these mandates. To be sure, in the ordinary course, Congress does legislate in black-and-white terms of affirmative commands or negative prohibitions on the conduct of officers of the Executive Branch. In complex regulatory areas, however, Congress often legislates, as it were, in procedural shades of gray. That is, it sets forth substantive policy goals and provides for their attainment by requiring Executive Branch officials to follow certain procedures, for example, in the from of reporting, consultation, and certification. . . .

The consultation requirement of §7 of the Endangered Species Act is [such an] action-forcing statute. Consultation is designed as an integral check on federal agency action, ensuring that such action does not go forward without full consideration of its effects on listed species. Once consultation is initiated, the Secretary is under a duty to provide to the action agency "a written statement setting forth the Secretary's opinion, and a summary of the information on which the opinion is based, detailing how the agency action affects the species or its critical habitat." 16 U.S.C. §1536(b)(3)(A). The Secretary is also obligated to suggest "reasonable and prudent alternatives" to prevent jeopardy to listed species. Ibid. The action agency must undertake as well its own "biological assessment for the purpose of identifying any endangered species or threatened species" likely to be affected by agency action. §1536(c)(1). After the initiation of consultation, the action agency "shall not make any irreversible or irretrievable commitment of resources" which would foreclose the "formulation or implementation of any reasonable and prudent alternative measures" to avoid jeopardizing listed species. §1536(d). These action-forcing procedures are "designed to protect some threatened concrete interest," of persons who observe and work with endangered or threatened species. That is why I am mystified by the Court's unsupported conclusion that "[t]his is not a case where plaintiffs are seeking to enforce a procedural requirement the disregard of which could impair a separate concrete interest of theirs."

Congress legislates in procedural shades of gray not to aggrandize its own power but to allow maximum Executive discretion in the attainment of Congress' legislative goals. Congress could simply impose a substantive prohibition on Executive conduct; it could say that no agency action shall result in the loss of more than 5% of any listed species. Instead, Congress sets forth substanive guidelines and allows the Executive within certain procedural constraints, to decide how best to effectuate the ultimate goal. The Court never has questioned Congress' authority to impose such procedural constraints on Executive power. Just as Congress does not violate separation of powers by structuring the procedural manner in which the Executive shall carry out the laws, surely the federal courts do not violate separation of powers when, at the very instruction and command of Congress, they enforce these procedures.

To prevent Congress from conferring standing for "procedural injuries" is another way of saying that Congress may not delegate to the courts authority deemed "executive" in nature. (Congress may not "transfer from the President to the courts the Chief Executive's most important constitutional duty, to 'take Care that the Laws be faithfully executed,' Art. II, §3.") Here Congress seeks not to delegate "executive" power but only to strengthen the procedures it has legislatively mandated. "We have long recognized that the nondelegation doctrine does not prevent Congress from seeking assistance, within proper limits, from its coordinate Branches."

Ironically, this Court has previously justified a relaxed review of congressional delegation to the Executive on grounds that Congress, in turn, has subjected the exercise of that power to judicial review. The Court's intimation today that procedural injuries are not constitutionally cognizable threatens this understanding upon which Congress has undoubtedly relied. In no sense is the Court's suggestion compelled by our "common understanding of what activities are appropriate to legislatures, to executives, and to courts." In my view, it reflects an unseemly solicitude for an expansion of power of the Executive Branch.

It is to be hoped that over time the Court will acknowledge that some classes of procedural duties are so enmeshed with the prevention of a substantive, concrete harm that an individual plaintiff may be able to demonstrate a sufficient likelihood of injury just through the breach of that procedural duty. For example, in the context of the NEPA requirement of environmental-impact statements, this Court has acknowledged "it is now well settled that NEPA itself does not mandate particular results [and] simply prescribes the necessary process," but "these procedures are almost certain to affect the agency's substantive decision." This acknowledgment of an inextricable link between procedural and substantive harm does not reflect improper appellate factfinding. It reflects nothing more than the proper deference owed to the judgment of a coordinate branch — Congress — that certain procedures are directly tied to protection against a substantive harm.

. . . There may be factual circumstances in which a congressionally imposed procedural requirement is so insubstantially connected to the prevention of a substantive harm that it cannot be said to work any conceivable injury to an individual litigant. But, as a general matter, the courts owe substantial deference to Congress' substantive purpose in imposing a certain procedural requirement. In all events, "[o]ur separation-of-powers analysis does not turn on the labeling of an activity as 'substantive' as opposed to 'procedural.'" Mistretta v. United States. There is no room for a per se rule or presumption excluding injuries labeled "procedural" in nature.

In conclusion, I cannot join the Court on what amounts to a slash-and-burn expedition through the law of environmental standing. In my view, "[t]he very essence of civil liberty certainly consists in the right of every individual to claim the protection of the laws, whenever he receives an injury." Marbury v. Madison.

ALLEN v. WRIGHT, 468 U.S. 737 (1984).   A nationwide class action was brought by parents of black school children against the Internal Revenue Service (IRS), contending that the IRS had not carried out its obligation to deny tax-exempt status to private schools that discriminate on the basis of race. The parents claimed that the IRS was allowing many such schools to receive an unlawful tax exemption. They claimed that the IRS's policy amounted to federal support for segregated schools and promoted the organization and expansion of such schools, thus interfering with the efforts of federal agencies and courts to bring about desegregation in school districts that had been suffering from the effects of past segregation. Respondents did not claim that they had applied to the private schools in question but instead that the IRS's unlawful activities had harmed their children, who were attending schools that were undergoing or might undergo desegregation. They claimed that the subsidy to discriminatory private schools decreased the likelihood that desegregation plans would be effective.

The plaintiffs also alleged that the mere fact of government aid to discriminatory private schools was an injury, perhaps one of stigma or denigration. The Court agreed that "this sort of noneconomic injury is one of the most serious consequences of discriminatory government action and is insufficient in some circumstances to support standing." But it said that the plaintiffs would have to show that they had personally been denied equal treatment by the discriminatory conduct. "[I]f the abstract stigmatic injury were cognizable, standing would extend nationwide to all members of the particular racial groups against which the Government was alleged to be discriminating. . . . All such persons could claim the same sort of abstract stigmatic injury. . . . A black person in Hawaii could challenge the grant of a tax exemption to a racially discriminatory school in Maine. Recognition of standing in such circumstances would transform the federal courts into 'no more than a vehicle for the vindication of the value interests of concerned bystanders.'"

NORTHEASTERN FLORIDA CHAPTER OF ASSOCIATED GENERAL CONTRACTORS v. JACKSONVILLE, 508 U.S. 658 (1993).   Jacksonville enacted an ordinance requiring that 10 percent of the money spent on city contracts be "set aside" for minority business enterprises. A contractors' association, consisting mostly of members who would not qualify as minority enterprises, brought suit, claiming that the set-aside violated the equal protection clause. The lower court denies standing on the ground that no member of the association had demonstrated that "but for the program, any AGC member would have bid successfully for any of these contracts." There was, therefore, no injury in fact. The Supreme Court responded:

> When the government erects a barrier that makes it more difficult for members of one group to obtain a benefit than it is for members of another group, a member of the former group seeking to challenge the barrier need not allege that he would have obtained the benefit but for the barrier in order to establish standing. The "injury in fact" in an equal protection case of this variety is the denial of equal treatment resulting from the imposition of the barrier, not the ultimate inability to obtain the benefit. And in the context of a challenge to a set-aside program, the "injury in fact" is the inability to compete on an equal footing in the bidding process, not the loss of a contract. To establish standing, therefore, a party challenging a set-aside program like Jacksonville's need only demonstrate that it is able and ready to bid on contracts and that a discriminatory policy prevents it from doing so on an equal basis.

In an important footnote, the Court added, "It follows from our definition of 'injury in fact' that petitioner has sufficiently alleged both that the city's ordinance is the 'cause' of its injury and that a judicial decree directly to the city to discontinue its program would 'redress' the injury."

Notes and Questions

1. Before Lujan v. Defenders of Wildlife, the Court had not decided a long-disputed question: whether Congress has the constitutional authority to confer standing on citizens generally. Does the Court make a textual argument on behalf of its conclusion? Does it make a historical argument? For a suggestion that there is no historical basis for thinking that Congress may not create citizen suits, see Sunstein, What's Standing After *Lujan?* 91 Mich. L. Rev. 163 (1992); for a careful response, see Woolhandler & Nelson, Does History Defeat Standing Doctrine? 102 Mich. L. Rev. 545 (2004). Try to argue that the textual requirement of a "case" or "controversy" requires a concrete personal stake. Can you meet the view that whether there is a case or controversy depends on whether the plaintiff has a cause of action — and that once Congress has created a cause of action, there is a case or controversy, and hence no article III problem?

Whether or not there is a historical basis for the Court's conclusion, might a structural argument be available? When citizens generally are affected by government action, perhaps the appropriate remedy is political, not legal, even if it can be argued that the agency has violated a statute. Perhaps citizens generally should be required to use their political remedies; the distinctive role of the courts is to protect the concrete rights of individuals, not to vindicate widely diffused interests. Perhaps article III is best taken to incorporate this understanding. Justice Scalia proposes such a view in Scalia, The Doctrine of Standing as an Essential Element of the Separation of Powers, 17 Suffolk U. L. Rev. 881 (1983). On this view, standing limitations are a close cousin of the doctrines governing hearing rights as exemplified by the *Bi-Metallic* case, Chapter 6.

Are there good reasons to think that any violation of the Endangered Species Act, in a case like *Lujan*, is best handled politically, at least if no one has been "injured in fact"? But why isn't that a decision for Congress to make?

2. Note that it is clear that competitors can usually show an "injury in fact"; for example, unsubsidized competitors can be said to be injured by an agency decision that confers subsidies on a competitor, and thus permits it to charge lower prices. See U.S. Telecom Assn. v. FCC, 295 F.3d 1326 (D.C. Cir. 2002). Now suppose that after *Lujan*, Congress amends the EDA to give every American a property interest in the continued existence of current species, and grants every citizen standing to vindicate that property interest in court. Would Justice Scalia vote to uphold that amendment? Would Justice Kennedy? If such a statute would be constitutional, why wouldn't it be right to say that in the EDA provision involved in *Lujan*, Congress effectively gave every citizen just that property interest and thus acted constitutionally? Does Justice Kennedy answer that question?

Suppose that Congress amends the ESA to give a victorious plaintiff, in any citizen suit, a bounty of $200. Would article III be satisfied? Consider in this regard Virginia Agency of Natural Resources v. United States, 529 U.S. 765 (2000). At issue there was the constitutionality of the qui tam action, authorized by the False Claims Act, by which a "relator" can bring an action on behalf of the government against an alleged false claimant. A prevailing plaintiff is allowed to receive a part of the damages owed to the government. The defendant urged that the "relator" lacked standing, because it was not invoking any injury in fact of its own. The Court rejected the argument and upheld the qui tam action, making two points. First, the qui tam action is legitimated by history, since it was common in both England and the colonies, and authorized in many statutes enacted by the first Congress. Second, the relator could be seen as the assignee of the government's claim, and the "assignee of the claim has standing to assert the injury in fact suffered by the assignor." The Court thought it clear that Congress could "define new legal rights, which in turn will confer standing to vindicate an injury caused to the claimant."

Does this decision suggest a possible way for Congress to rewrite the citizen suit provisions without running afoul of *Lujan*?

3. If the plaintiffs in *Lujan* had a plane ticket to visit the places where the relevant species could be found, it seems generally agreed that the injury in fact requirement would have been satisfied. (There is a separate question of redressability, discussed below.) See Bensman v. U.S. Forest Service, 2005 U.S. App. LEXIS 10047 (7th Cir. 2005), granting standing to allow someone to challenge a decision of the Forest Service on the ground that he had "demonstrated both sufficient interest in the Mark Twain National Forest and sufficient possibility of injury to that interest to have constitutional standing. . . . While his past visits are not dispositive, they are sufficient in number and in temporal proximity to lend credence to his plans to return to the forest 'this winter or next spring.' His intention to return is expressed more concretely than the vague plans rejected in *Lujan*."

Compare Japan Whaling Assn. v. American Cetacean Soc., 478 U.S. 221 (1996), which grants standing in a similar setting; there the Court held that an environmental organization could complain of excessive whale harvesting when "whale watching and studying of their members would be adversely affected by continued whale harvesting." But why should so much turn on the existence of a plane ticket? See the note on standing to protect animals, below.

4. It is worthwhile to note that the *Lujan* Court refers not only to the need for an injury in fact but also to the requirement that any injury be "cognizable." Is this a return to the pre-*Data Processing* "legal wrong" standard? See also Raines v. Byrd, 521 U.S. 811 (1997), echoing a statement in Warth v. Seldin, 422 U.S. 490, 500 (1975), that the standing inquiry "often turns on the nature and source of the claim asserted." We will return to this important issue at several points below.

5. In *Northeastern Contractors*, the Court says that the relevant injury involves not the right to receive contracts, but the right to compete on an equal basis with everyone else. This holding suggests that *whether there is an injury in fact depends on how the plaintiff's "harm" is characterized*. This point in turn suggests two questions. First, how does a Court characterize an injury? Second, what constraints does the Constitution impose on the ability of Congress or courts to characterize injuries in certain ways? Consider these problems.

a. An agency in the state of New York makes the requirements for obtaining a drivers' license less severe. Can a driver fearful of more dangerous driving bring suit? With what allegation of injury? Cf. International Bhd. of Teamsters v. Pena, 17 F.3d 1478 (D.C. Cir. 1984) (granting standing to truck drivers fearing greater risk of injury because of driving in the United States by drivers licensed under allegedly more lenient standards of Mexico).

b. A consumer, worried about mad cow disease, can challenge the Department of Agriculture's failure to ban the practice of using "downed cattle" (allegedly at risk of the disease) as food for human consumption. In a case involving these facts, the court held that the increased *risk* of contracting a disease from a potentially dangerous food counted as injury in fact. See Baur v. Veneman, 352 F.3d 625 (2d Cir. 2003). "Although the Supreme Court has yet to speak directly on this issue, the courts of appeals have generally recognized that threatened harm in the form of an increased risk of future injury may serve as injury-in-fact for Article III standing purposes. . . . In this case, we need not decide as a matter of law whether enhanced risk generally qualifies as sufficient injury to confer standing, nor do we purport to imply that we would adopt such a broad view. In the specific context of food and drug safety suits, however, we conclude that such injuries are cognizable for standing purposes, where the plaintiff alleges exposure to potentially harmful products." (Query: Does the court's broad characterization of the injury, as involving a mere risk, run afoul of the idea that generalized grievances are not a legitimate basis for standing? Note that the mere risk of illness from beef, if it exists, is faced by many millions of Americans.)

c. FCC now requires three hours of educational programming for children per week. Can a disappointed viewer, not at all interested in educational programming, attack the requirement? Or suppose that a parent, believing that five or ten hours should be required instead, challenges the FCC's regulation as too lenient. How would you describe the relevant injury?

Are such questions to be answered by reference to the law invoked by the plaintiff, constitutional or statutory? On one view, the only way to characterize the injury is to ask what the law is trying to prevent — a view that fits with the outcomes in (a) and (b) above. See generally Fletcher, supra; Sunstein, Standing Injuries, 1993 Sup. Ct. Rev. 37. But as noted, a broad characterization of the injury threatens to convert it into a generalized grievance. This point is especially important in the cases involving redressability and causation, to which we now turn.

Note: Standing to Protect Animals

As the foregoing discussion suggests, many of the most important standing cases have involved efforts to protect animals, whether endangered or not, from injury at the hands of human beings. Is it possible to come up with generalizations about the circumstances in which these suits can be brought? Should animals have standing as such?

Suppose, for example, that a person who engages in research complains about an agency rule under the Federal Laboratory Animal Welfare Act (FLAWA) on the ground that the agency's failure to include rules with respect to some species left him in doubt about the appropriate treatment of those species. Suppose too that organizations dedicated to protection of animals complain that an inadequate rule under FLAWA injured their interest in improving the treatment of animals and also their interest in obtaining information about the ways in which animals are treated. Is standing available, or is the injury too abstract? The court of appeals denied standing. See Animals Legal Defense Fund v. Espy, 23 F.3d 496 (D.C. Cir. 1994).

But compare Animal Legal Defense Fund v. Glickman, 154 F.3d 426 (D.C. Cir. 1998), in which Marc Jurnove, who frequently visited the Long Island Game Farm Park and Zoo, complained about what he believed to be unlawful treatment of many animals there. A divided court of appeals held that Jurnove had standing, on the ground that Jurnove suffered "aesthetic injury" from the conditions he observed. Can you sketch out a dissenting opinion? Is the argument on Jurnove's behalf weaker or stronger than the argument made by the plaintiffs in *Laidlaw*?

Could animals be given standing to sue in their own name? See Cetacean Community v. Bush, 386 F.3d 1169 (9th Cir. 2004), in which the court denied standing to "all the world's whales, purposes, and dolphins," challenging the United States Navy's use of a certain sonar system during wartime or heightened threat conditions. In the plaintiffs' view, the system violated several statutes, including the Endangered Species Act, the Marine Mammal Protection Act, and the National Environmental Policy Act. The Court held that none of these statutes granted standing to animals. But it held, unambiguously, that "Article III does not prevent Congress from granting standing to an animal by statutorily authorizing a suit in its name." It said, "we see no reason why Article III prevents Congress from authorizing a suit in the name of an animal, any more than it prevents suits brought in the name of artificial persons such as infants, juveniles, and mental incompetents." For discussion of this and related issues, see Sunstein, Standing For Animals, 47 U.C.L.A. L. Rev. 1333 (2000).

6. Nexus, Redressability, and Causation

In Linda R.S. v. Richard D., 410 U.S. 614 (1973), a mother of an illegitimate child complained that the local prosecutor had failed to initiate enforcement proceedings against the father. The mother contended that the prosecutor would have initiated such proceedings if the child had been born within marriage, and that this discriminatory law enforcement policy caused her harm. The Court denied standing on the ground that it was unclear whether a decree in the plaintiff's favor would remedy the plaintiff's injury. "[I]f appellant were granted the requested relief, it would result only in the jailing of the child's father. The prospect that prosecution will, at least in the future, result in payment of support can, at best, be termed only speculative." Id. at 618. This holding helped inaugurate a set of supplemental standing requirements, now understood to be constitutional in character: Any injury must be a result of the defendant's action and likely to be remedied by a decree in the plaintiff's favor.

Simon v. Eastern Kentucky Welfare Rights Organization

426 U.S. 26 (1976)

Mr. Justice POWELL delivered the opinion of the Court.

[Plaintiffs, several indigents and organizations representing indigents, challenged a revenue ruling issued by the IRS modifying the responsibilities of nonprofit hospitals qualifying under §501(c)(3) of the Internal Revenue Code as "charitable" organizations, contributions to which are tax deductible. A 1956 IRS Revenue Ruling, No. 56-185, required that such a hospital must accept some patients in need of hospital services who cannot pay for them, and must do so "to the extent of its financial ability."

In 1969, the IRS issued Revenue Ruling 69-545, describing two hospitals, identified as "A" and "B." The ruling stated that Hospital A, which operated an emergency room open to all but otherwise accepted only paying customers, qualified as a §501(c)(3) charitable organization, even though it did not accept indigents "to the extent of its financial ability."

Each of the individual plaintiffs alleged specific incidents of deprivation, because of their indigency, of medical services by hospitals determined by the IRS to be §501(c)(3) charities. They further alleged that the defendants (the secretary of the treasury and the IRS commissioner), were "encouraging" such hospitals to deny services to indigents through the 1969 revenue ruling. They asserted that the ruling was contrary to the code, claiming that "charitable" in §501(c)(3) means "relief of the poor." They also asserted that as poor persons they were intended beneficiaries of this provision. Finally, they contended that the IRS's failure to afford notice and opportunity for comment in the 1969 ruling violated the APA §553 because the ruling did not fall within the §553 exception for "interpretative" rulemaking.]

In this Court petitioners have argued that a policy of the IRS to tax or not to tax certain individuals or organizations, whether embodied in a Revenue Ruling or otherwise developed, cannot be challenged by third parties whose own tax liabilities are not affected. Their theory is that the entire history of this country's revenue system, including but not limited to the evolution of the Internal Revenue Code, manifests a consistent congressional intent to vest exclusive authority for the administration of the tax laws in the Secretary and his duly authorized delegates, subject to oversight by the appropriate committees of Congress itself. . . .

In addition, petitioners analogize the discretion vested in the IRS with respect to administration of the tax laws to the discretion of a public prosecutor as to when and whom to prosecute. They thus invoke the settled doctrine that the exercise of prosecutorial discretion cannot be challenged by one who is himself neither prosecuted nor threatened with prosecution. See Linda R.S. v. Richard D., [410 U.S. 614, 619 (1973)]. . . . [Putting all such questions aside, the Court held that the petitioners had failed to show the "injury in fact" required by article III.]

. . . The standing question in this suit therefore turns upon whether any individual respondent has established an actual injury, or whether the respondent organizations have established actual injury to any of their indigent members.

The obvious interest of all respondents, to which they claim actual injury, is that of access to hospital services. . . . We . . . assume, for purpose of analysis, that some members have been denied service. But injury at the hands of a hospital is insufficient by itself to establish a case or controversy in the context of this suit, for no hospital is a defendant. The only defendants are officials of the Department of the Treasury, and the only claims of illegal action respondents desire the courts to adjudicate are charged to those officials. "Although the law of standing has been greatly changed in [recent] years, we have steadfastly adhered to the requirement that, at least in the absence of a statute expressly conferring standing, federal plaintiffs must allege some threatened or actual injury resulting from the putatively illegal action before a federal court may assume jurisdiction." Linda R.S. v. Richard D., 410 U.S., at 617. . . .[25] In other words, the "case or controversy" limitation of Art. III still requires that a federal court act only to redress injury that fairly can be traced to the challenged action of the defendant, and not injury that results from the independent action of some third party not before the court.

The complaint here alleged only that petitioners, by the adoption of Revenue Ruling 69-545, had "encouraged" hospitals to deny services to indigents. . . . It is purely speculative whether the denials of service specified in the complaint fairly can be traced to petitioners' "encouragement" or instead result from decisions made by the hospitals without regard to the tax implications.

It is equally speculative whether the desired exercise of the court's remedial powers in this suit would result in the availability to respondents of such services. . . . The Solicitor General states in his brief that, nationwide, private philanthropy accounts for only 4% of private hospital revenues. . . .

Prior decisions of this Court establish that unadorned speculation will not suffice to invoke the federal judicial power.

---

25. The reference in *Linda R.S.* to a "statute expressly conferring standing" was in recognition of Congress' power to create new interests the invasion of which will confer standing. See 410 U.S., at 617 n.3. . . . When Congress has so acted, the requirements of Art. III remain: "[T]he plaintiff still must allege a distinct and palpable injury to himself, even if it is an injury shared by a large class of other possible litigants." Warth v. Seldin, supra, at 501. See also United States v. SCRAP, 412 U.S. 669 (1973); cf. Sierra Club v. Morton, 405 U.S. at 732 n.3.

[In a footnote, the Court asserted that the case at hand was distinguishable from *SCRAP*. Although the line of causation there asserted was "attenuated," the complaint alleged a "specific and perceptible harm" flowing from the agency action. Here the complaint could not survive a motion to dismiss for it failed to allege "an injury that fairly can be traced to petitioners' challenged action." The injury complained of might have occurred even in the absence of the challenged IRS ruling.

The Court ordered that the complaint be dismissed for want of standing.]

Mr. Justice STEWART, concurring.

I join the opinion of the Court holding that the plaintiffs in this case did not have standing to sue. I add only that I cannot now imagine a case, at least outside the First Amendment area, where a person whose own tax liability was not affected ever could have standing to litigate the federal tax liability of someone else.

Mr. Justice BRENNAN, with whom Mr. Justice MARSHALL joins, concurring in the judgment.

[Justice Brennan agreed that plaintiffs lacked standing because they had failed to allege that the hospital that they would use was similar to the hypothetical Hospital A in the IRS ruling. They had therefore failed to allege that the ruling would affect them. Justice Brennan nonetheless thought that tax rulings might well influence a hospital's decision to give free care. Even if the plaintiff could not prove he would receive free care, he should have standing. If a "small but certain" harm, such as that alleged in *SCRAP*, is a sufficient basis for standing, then a lesser probability of suffering a greater harm, such as denial of needed medical care, ought likewise to serve as a basis for standing.]

Of course the most disturbing aspect of today's opinion is the Court's insistence on resting its decision regarding standing squarely on the irreducible Art. III minimum of injury in fact, thereby effectively placing its holding beyond congressional power to rectify. Thus, any time Congress chooses to legislate in favor of certain interests by setting up a scheme of incentives for third parties, judicial review of administrative action that allegedly frustrates the congressionally intended objective will be denied, because any complainant will be required to make an almost impossible showing.

DUKE POWER CO. v. CAROLINA ENVIRONMENTAL STUDY GROUP, 438 U.S. 59 (1978). The plaintiffs, an environmental organization and its members who lived near a nuclear power plant, claimed that the Price-Anderson Act, which limits the liability of privately owned nuclear plants in case of accident (and substitutes a government-sponsored compensation system) violated equal protection and due process by depriving them of common law tort remedies. The Court held that they had standing to make this claim, although it decided against them on the merits of the claim. The Court found "injury in fact" because the plaintiffs suffered from "the environmental and aesthetic consequences of the thermal pollution of the two lakes in the vicinity of the disputed power plants." It found a "causal connection" in testimony that, without the protection from vast liability that the Price-Anderson Act gave the utilities, they might not be able to afford to build the plants. It found "redressability," presumably in its conclusion that, were the courts to declare the act unconstitutional, the plants would not be built and the lakes would not be harmed. Justice Stevens would have denied standing. He wrote, "We are told that but for the Price-Anderson Act there would be no financing of private nuclear plants, no development of those plants by private parties, and hence no present injury to persons such as appellees; we are then asked to remedy an alleged due process violation that may possibly occur at some uncertain time in the future, and may possibly injure the appellees in a way that has no significant connection with any present injury." He said that the "string of contingencies that supposedly holds this case together is too delicate for me."

In Allen v. Wright, cited in *Lujan*, the Court held that one of the plaintiffs' injuries — involving their children's diminished ability to receive education in a racially integrated school — was "beyond, any doubt . . . judicially cognizable." But the Court held that the plaintiffs nonetheless lacked standing "because the injury alleged is not fairly traceable to the Government conduct" challenged as unlawful. The grant of tax exemptions to "some racially discriminatory schools" had only an attenuated causal connection to the desegregation of the schools at issue. "It is, first, uncertain how many racially discriminatory private schools are in fact receiving tax exemptions. Moreover, it is entirely speculative [whether] withdrawal of a tax exemption from any particular school would lead the school to change its policies. . . . It is just as speculative whether any given parent of a child attending such a private school would decide to transfer the child to public school as a result of any changes in educational or financial policy made by the private school once it was threatened with loss of tax-exempt status. It is also pure speculation whether, in a particular community, a large enough number of the numerous relevant school officials would reach decisons that collectively would have a significant impact on the racial composition of the public schools."

The Court concluded that the "chain of causation is even weaker" here than in *Simon*, supra. "It involves numerous third parties (officials of racially discriminatory schools receiving tax exemptions and the parents of children attending such schools) who may not even exist in [plaintiffs'] communities and whose independent decisions may not collectively have a significant effect on the ability of public-school students to receive a desegregated education."

The Court added a reference to the "separation of powers that underlies standing doctrine." The plaintiff's argument "would pave the way generally for suits challenging, not specifically identifiable Government violations of law, but the particular programs agencies establish to carry out their legal obligations. Such suits, even when premised on allegations of several instances of violations of law, are rarely if ever appropriate for federal adjudication. Carried to its logical end, [the plaintiffs'] approach would have the federal courts as virtually continuing monitors of the wisdom and soundness of Executive action; such a role is appropriate for the Congress acting through its committees and the 'power of the purse'; it is not the role of the judiciary, absent actual present or immediately threatened injury resulting from unlawful government action."

The Court concluded that the idea of separation of powers "counsels against recognizing standing in a case brought, not to enforce specific legal obligations whose violation works a direct harm, but to seek a restructuring of the apparatus established by the Executive Branch to fulfill its legal duties. The Constitution, after all, assigns to the Executive Branch, and not to the Judicial Branch, the duty to 'take Care that the Laws be faithfully executed.' We could not recognize . . . standing in this case without running afoul of that structural principle."

Justice Stevens dissented. He wrote that when "a subsidy makes a given activity more or less expensive, injury can be traced to the subsidy for purposes of standing analysis

because of the resulting increase or decrease in the ability to engage in the activity."
Hence "causation analysis is nothing more than a restatement of elementary economics:
when something becomes more expensive, less of it will be purchased." He added,
"Deciding whether the Treasury has violated a specific legal limitation on its enforcement discretion does not intrude upon the prerogatives of the Executive, for in so deciding we are merely saying 'what the law is.'"

At this point you should reread the parts of Lujan v. Defenders of Wildlife
dealing with redressability.

Steel Company v. Citizens for a Better Environment

523 U.S. 83 (1998)

Justice SCALIA delivered the opinion of the Court.

This is a private enforcement action under the citizen-suit provision of the
Emergency Planning and Community Right-To-Know Act of 1986. The case presents
the merits question, answered in the affirmative by the United States Court of Appeals for
the Seventh Circuit, whether EPCRA authorizes suits for purely past violations. It also
presents the jurisdictional question whether respondent, plaintiff below, has standing to
bring this action.

Respondent, an association of individuals interested in environmental protection,
sued petitioner, a small manufacturing company in Chicago, for past violations of
EPCRA. EPCRA establishes a framework of state, regional and local agencies designed to
inform the public about the presence of hazardous and toxic chemicals, and to provide
for emergency response in the event of health-threatening release. Central to its operation are reporting requirements compelling users of specified toxic and hazardous chemicals to file annual "emergency and hazardous chemical inventory forms" and "toxic
chemical release forms," which contain, inter alia, the name and location of the facility,
the name and quantity of the chemical on hand, and, in the case of toxic chemicals, the
waste-disposal method employed and the annual quantity released into each environmental medium. The hazardous-chemical inventory forms for any given calendar year are
due the following March 1st, and the toxic-chemical release forms the following July 1st.

Enforcement of EPCRA can take place on many fronts. The Environmental
Protection Agency (EPA) has the most powerful enforcement arsenal: it may seek criminal,
civil, or administrative penalties. State and local governments can also seek civil penalties,
as well as injunctive relief. For purposes of this case, however, the crucial enforcement
mechanism is the citizen-suit provision, §11046(a)(1), which likewise authorizes civil penalties and injunctive relief, see §11046(c). This provides that "any person may commence a
civil action on his own behalf against . . . an owner or operator of a facility for failure,"
among other things, to "complete and submit an inventory form under section 11022(a) of
this title [and] section 11023(a) of this title." As a prerequisite to bringing such a suit, the
plaintiff must, 60 days prior to filing his complaint, give notice to the Administrator of the
EPA, the State in which the alleged violation occurs, and the alleged violator. The citizen
suit may not go forward if the Administrator "has commenced and is diligently pursuing an

administrative order or civil action to enforce the requirement concerned or to impose a civil penalty."

In 1995 respondent sent a notice to petitioner, the Administrator, and the relevant Illinois authorities, alleging — accurately, as it turns out — that petitioner had failed since 1988, the first year of EPCRA's filing deadlines, to complete and to submit the requisite hazardous-chemical inventory and toxic-chemical release forms under §§11022 and 11023. Upon receiving the notice, petitioner filed all of the overdue forms with the relevant agencies. The EPA chose not to bring an action against petitioner, and when the 60-day waiting period expired, respondent filed suit in Federal District Court. Petitioner promptly filed a motion to dismiss under Federal Rule of Civil Procedure 12(b)(1) and (6), contending that, because its filings were up to date when the complaint was filed, the court had no jurisdiction to entertain a suit for a present violation; and that, because EPCRA does not allow suite for a purely historical violation, respondent's allegation of untimeliness in filing was not a claim upon which relief could be granted. . . .

[The Court concluded that it was appropriate to reach the constitutional issue whether Congress would grant standing in these circumstances.] We turn now to the particulars of respondent's complaint to see how it measures up to Article III's requirements. This case is on appeal from a Rule 12(b) motion to dismiss on the pleadings, so we must presume that the general allegations in the complaint encompass the specific facts necessary to support those allegations. The complaint contains claims "on behalf of both [respondent] itself and its members."[26] It describes respondent as an organization that seeks, uses, and acquires data reported under EPCRA. It says that respondent "reports to its members and the public about storage and release of toxic chemicals into the environment, advocates changes in environmental regulations and statutes, prepares reports for its members and the public, seeks the reduction of toxic chemicals and further seeks to promote the effective enforcement of environmental laws." The complaint asserts that respondent's "right to know about [toxic chemical] releases and its interests in protecting and improving the environment and the health of its members have been, are being, and will be adversely affected by [petitioner's] actions in failing to provide timely and required information under EPCRA." The complaint also alleges that respondent's members, who live in or frequent the area near petitioner's facility, use the EPCRA-reported information "to learn about toxic chemical releases, the use of hazardous substances in their communities, to plan emergency preparedness in the event of accidents, and to attempt to reduce the toxic chemicals in areas in which they live, work and visit." The members' "safety, health, recreational, economic, aesthetic and environmental interests" in the information, it is claimed, "have been, are being, and will be adversely affected by [petitioner's] actions in failing to file timely and required reports under EPCRA."

As appears from the above, respondent asserts petitioner's failure to provide EPCRA information in a timely fashion, and the lingering effects of that failure, as the injury in fact to itself and its members. We have not had occasion to decide whether being deprived of information that is supposed to be disclosed under EPCRA — or at least being deprived

---

26. EPCRA states that "any person may commence a civil action on his own behalf . . ." 42 U.S.C. §11046(1). "Person" includes an association, see §11049(7), so it is arguable that the statute permits respondent to vindicate only its own interests as an organization, and not the interests of its individual members. Since it makes no difference to our disposition of the case, we assume without deciding that the interests of individual members may be the basis of suit.

of it when one has a particular plan for its use — is a concrete injury in fact that satisfies Article III. And we need not reach that question in the present case because, assuming injury in fact, the complaint fails the third test of standing, redressability.

The complaint asks for (1) a declaratory judgment that petitioner violated EPCRA; (2) authorization to inspect periodically petitioner's facility and records (with costs borne by petitioner); (3) an order requiring petitioner to provide respondent copies of all compliance reports submitted to the EPA; (4) an order requiring petitioner to pay civil penalties of $25,000 per day for each violation of §§11022 and 11023; (5) an award of all respondent's "costs, in connection with the investigation and prosecution of this matter, including reasonable attorney and expert witness fees, as authorized by Section 326(f) of [EPCRA]"; and (6) any such further relief as the court deems appropriate. None of the specific items of relief sought, and none that we can envision as "appropriate" under the general request, would serve to reimburse respondent for losses caused by the late reporting, or to eliminate any effects of that late reporting upon respondent.

The first items, the request for a declaratory judgment that petitioner violated EPCRA, can be disposed of summarily. There being no controversy over whether petitioner failed to file reports, or over whether such a failure constitutes a violation, the declaratory judgment is not only worthless to respondent, it is seemingly worthless to all the world.

Items (4), the civil penalties authorized by the statute, see §11045(c), might be viewed as a sort of compensation or redress to respondent if they were payable to respondent. But they are not. These penalties — the only damages authorized by EPCRA — are payable to the United States Treasury. In requesting them, therefore, respondent seeks not remediation of its own injury — reimbursement for the costs it incurred as a result of the late filing — but vindication of the rule of law — the "undifferentiated public interest" in faithful execution of EPCRA. . . .

Item (5), the "investigation and prosecution" costs "as authorized by Section 326(f)," would assuredly benefit respondent as opposed to the citizenry at large. Obviously, however, a plaintiff cannot achieve standing to litigate a substantive issue by bringing suit for the cost of bringing suit. The litigation must give the plaintiff some other benefit besides reimbursement of costs that are a byproduct of the litigation itself. [Respondent] asserts that the "investigation costs" it seeks were incurred prior to the litigation, in digging up the emissions and storage information that petitioner should have filed, and that respondent needed for its own purposes. The recovery of such expenses unrelated to litigation would assuredly support Article III standing, but the problem is that §326(f), which is the entitlement to monetary relief that the complaint invokes, covers only the "costs of litigation." Respondent finds itself, in others words, impaled upon the horns of a dilemma: for the expenses to be reimbursable under the statute, they must be costs of litigation; but reimbursement of the costs of litigation cannot alone support standing.

The remaining relief respondent seeks (item (2), giving respondent authority to inspect petitioner's facility and records, and items (3), compelling petitioner to provide respondent copies of EPA compliance reports) is injunctive in nature. It cannot conceivably remedy any past wrong but is aimed at deterring petitioner from violating EPCRA in the future. The latter objective can of course be "remedial" for Article III purposes, when threatened injury is one of the gravamens of the complaint. If respondent had alleged a continuing violation or the imminence of a future violation, the injunctive relief requested would remedy that alleged harm. But there is no such allegation here — and on the facts of the case, there seems no basis for it. Nothing supports the requested injunctive relief except respondent's generalized interest in deterrence, which is insufficient for purposes of Article III.

The United States, as amicus curiae, argues that the injunctive relief does constitute remediation because "there is a presumption of [future] injury when the defendant has voluntarily ceased its illegal activity in response to litigation," even if that occurs before a complaint is filed. This makes a sword out of a shield. The "presumption" the Government refers to has been applied to refute the assertion of mootness by a defendant who, when sued in a complaint that alleges present or threatened injury, ceases the complained-of activity. It is an immense and unacceptable stretch to call the presumption into service as a substitute for the allegation of present or threatened injury upon which initial standing must be based. . . .

Having found that none of the relief sought by respondent would likely remedy its alleged injury in fact, we must conclude that respondent lacks standing to maintain this suit, and that we and the lower courts lack jurisdiction to entertain it. However desirable prompt resolution of the merits of the EPCRA question may be, it is not as important as observing the constitutional limits set upon courts in our system of separated powers. EPCRA will have to await another day.

The judgment is vacated and the case remanded with instructions to direct that the complaint be dismissed.

It is so ordered.

[Justices O'Connor and Breyer wrote brief concurring opinions.]

Justice STEVENS, with whom Justice SOUTER joins as to Parts I, III, and IV, and with whom Justice GINSBURG joins as to Part III, concurring in the judgment. . . .

II . . .

The Court's conclusion that respondent does not have standing comes from a mechanistic application of the "redressability" aspect of our standing doctrine. "Redressability," of course, does not appear anywhere in the text of the Constitution. Instead, it is a judicial creation of the past 25 years. . . .

In every previous case in which the Court has denied standing because of a lack of redressability, the plaintiff was challenging some governmental action or inaction. None of these cases involved an attempt by one private party to impose a statutory sanction on another private party.

In addition, in every other case in which this Court has held that there is no standing because of a lack of redressability, the injury to the plaintiff by the defendant was indirect (e.g., dependent on the action of a third party). . . .

The Court acknowledges that respondent would have had standing if Congress had authorized some payment to respondent. Yet the Court fails to specify why payment to respondent — even if only a peppercorn — would redress respondent's injuries, while payment to the Treasury does not. Respondent clearly believes that the punishment of the Steel Company, along with future deterrence of the Steel Company and others, redresses its injury, and there is no basis in our previous standing holdings to suggest otherwise.

When one private party is injured by another, the injury can be redressed in at least two ways: by awarding compensatory damages or by imposing a sanction on the wrongdoer that will minimize the risk that the harm-causing conduct will be repeated. Thus, in some cases a tort is redressed by an award of punitive damages; even when such damages are payable to the sovereign, they provide a form of redress for the individual as well.

History supports the proposition that punishment or deterrence can redress an injury. In past centuries in England,[27] in the American colonies, and in the United States,[28] private persons regularly prosecuted criminal cases. The interest in punishing the defendant and deterring violations of law by the defendant and others was sufficient to support the "standing" of the private prosecutor even if the only remedy was the sentencing of the defendant to jail or to the gallows. Given this history, the Framers of Article III surely would have considered such proceedings to be "Cases" that would "redress" an injury even though the party bringing suit did not receive any monetary compensation.[29] . . .

It could be argued that the Court's decision is rooted in another separation of powers concern: that this citizen suit somehow interferes with the Executive's power to "take Care that the Laws be faithfully executed," Art. II, §3. It is hard to see, however, how EPCRA's citizen-suit provision impinges on the power of the Executive. As an initial matter, this is not a case in which respondent merely possesses the "undifferentiated public interest" in seeing EPCRA enforced. Here, respondent — whose members live near the Steel Company — has alleged a sufficiently particularized injury under our precedents. App. 5 (complaint alleges that respondent's members "reside, own property, engage in recreational activities, breathe the air, and/or use areas near [the Steel Company's] facility").

Moreover, under the Court's own reasoning, respondent would have had standing if Congress had authorized some payment to respondent. This conclusion is unexceptional given that respondent has a more particularized interest than a plaintiff in a qui tam suit, an action that is deeply rooted in our history. . . .

Yet it is unclear why the separation of powers question should turn on whether the plaintiff receives monetary compensation. In either instance, a private citizen is enforcing the law. If separation of powers does not preclude standing when Congress creates a legal right that authorizes compensation to the plaintiff, it is unclear why separation of powers should dictate a contrary result when Congress has created a legal right but has directed that payment be made to the federal Treasury. . . .

It is thus quite clear that the Court's holding today represents a significant new development in our constitutional jurisprudence. Moreover, it is equally clear that the Court has the power to answer the statutory question first. It is, therefore, not necessary to reject the Court's

27. "Several scholars have attempted to trace the historical origins of private prosecution in the United States. Without exception, these scholars have determined that the notion of private prosecutions originated in early common law England, where the legal system primarily relied upon the victim or the victim's relatives or friends to bring a criminal to justice. According to these historians, private prosecutions developed in England as a means of facilitating private vengeance." Bessler, The Public Interest and the Unconstitutionality of Private Prosecutors, 47 Ark. L. Rev. 511, 515 (1994) (footnotes omitted).

28. "American citizens continued to privately prosecute criminal cases in many locales during the nineteenth century. In Philadelphia, for example, all types of cases were privately prosecuted, with assault and battery prosecutions being the most common. However, domestic disputes short of assault also came before the court. Thus, 'parents of young women prosecuted men for seduction; husbands prosecuted their wives' paramours for adultery; wives prosecuted their husbands for desertion.' Although many state courts continued to sanction the practice of private prosecutions without significant scrutiny during the nineteenth century, a few state courts outlawed the practice." Id., at 581 (footnotes omitted); A. Steinberg, The Transformation of Criminal Justice: Philadelphia, 1800-1880, p.5 (1989) ("Private prosecution and the minor judiciary were firmly rooted in Philadelphia's colonial past. Both were examples of the creative American adaptation of the English common law. By the seventeenth century, private prosecution was a fundamental part of English common law."); see also F. Goodnow, Principles of the Administrative Law of the United States 412-413 (1905).

29. When such a party obtains a judgment that imposes sanctions on the wrongdoer, it is proper to presume that the wrongdoer will be less likely to repeat the injurious conduct that prompted the litigation. The lessening of the risk of future harm is a concrete benefit.

resolution of the standing issue in order to conclude that it would be prudent to answer the question of statutory construction before announcing new constitutional doctrine.

Justice GINSBURG, concurring in the judgment.

Congress has authorized citizen suits to enforce the Emergency Planning and Community Right-to-Know Act of 1986, 42 U.S.C. §11001 et seq. Does that authorization, as Congress designed it, permit citizen suits for wholly past violations? . . . I agree that the answer is "No." I would . . . resist expounding or offering advice on the constitutionality of what Congress might have done, but did not do.

Friends of the Earth, Inc. v. Laidlaw Environmental Services, Inc.

528 U.S. 167 (2000)

Justice GINSBURG delivered the opinion of the Court.

This case presents an important question concerning the operation of the citizen-suit provisions of the Clean Water Act. Congress authorized the federal district courts to entertain Clean Water Act suits initiated by "a person or persons having an interest which is or may be adversely affected." To impel future compliance with the Act, a district court may prescribe injunctive relief in such a suit; additionally or alternatively, the court may impose civil penalties payable to the United States Treasury. In the Clean Water Act citizen suit now before us, the District Court determined that injunctive relief was inappropriate because the defendant, after the institution of the litigation, achieved substantial compliance with the terms of its discharge permit. The court did, however, assess a civil penalty of $405,800. The "total deterrent effect" of the penalty would be adequate to forestall future violations, the court reasoned, taking into account that the defendant "will be required to reimburse plaintiffs for a significant amount of legal fees and has, itself, incurred significant legal expenses." . . .

I

A

Section 402 of the [Clean Water] Act provides for the issuance, by the Administrator of the Environmental Protection Agency (EPA) or by authorized States, of National Pollutant Discharge Elimination System (NPDES) permits. NPDES permits impose limitations on the discharge of pollutants, and establish related monitoring and reporting requirements, in order to improve the cleanliness and safety of the Nation's waters. Noncompliance with a permit constitutes a violation of the Act.

Under §505(a) of the Act, a suit to enforce any limitation in an NPDES permit may be brought by any "citizen," defined as "a person or persons having an interest which is or may be adversely affected. Sixty days before initiating a citizen suit, however, the would-be plaintiff must give notice of the alleged violation to the EPA, the State in which the alleged violation occurred, and the alleged violator. "[T]he purpose of notice to the alleged violator is to give it an opportunity to bring itself into complete compliance with the Act and thus . . . render unnecessary a citizen suit." Accordingly, we have held that citizens lack statutory standing under §505(a) to sue for violations that have ceased by the time the complaint is filed. . . .

The Act authorizes district courts in citizen-suit proceedings to enter injunctions and to assess civil penalties, which are payable to the United States Treasury. . . .

B

In 1986, defendant-respondent Laidlaw Environmental Services (TOC), Inc., bought a hazardous waste incinerator facility in Roebuck, South Carolina, that included a wastewater treatment plant. [S]hortly after Laidlaw acquired the facility, the South Carolina Department of Health and Environmental Control (DHEC) granted Laidlaw an NPDES permit authorizing the company to discharge treated water into the North Tyger River. The permit, which became effective on January 1, 1987, placed limits on Laidlaw's discharge of several pollutants into the river, including — of particular relevance to this case — mercury, an extremely toxic pollutant. The permit also regulated the flow, temperature, toxicity, and pH of the effluent from the facility, and imposed monitoring and reporting obligations.

Once it received its permit, Laidlaw began to discharge various pollutants into the waterway; repeatedly, Laidlaw's discharges exceeded the limits set by the permit. In particular, despite experimenting with several technological fixes, Laidlaw consistently failed to meet the permit's stringent 1.3 ppb (parts per billion) daily average limit on mercury discharges. The District Court later found that Laidlaw had violated the mercury limits on 489 occasions between 1987 and 1995. . . . On June 12, 1992, FOE filed this citizen suit against Laidlaw under §505(a) of the Act, alleging noncompliance with the NPDES permit and seeking declaratory and injunctive relief and an award of civil penalties. . . .

II

A

Laidlaw contends first that FOE lacked standing from the outset even to seek injunctive relief, because the plaintiff organizations failed to show that any of their members had sustained or faced the threat of any "injury in fact" from Laidlaw's activities. In support of this contention Laidlaw points to the District Court's finding, made in the course of setting the penalty amount, that there had been "no demonstrated proof of harm to the environment" from Laidlaw's mercury discharge violations. . . .

The relevant showing for purposes of Article III standing, however, is not injury to the environment but injury to the plaintiff. To insist upon the former rather than the latter as part of the standing inquiry is to raise the standing hurdle higher than the necessary showing for success on the merits in an action alleging noncompliance with an NPDES permit. Focusing properly on injury to the plaintiff, the District Court found that FOE had demonstrated sufficient injury to establish standing. For example, FOE member Kenneth Lee Curtis averred in affidavits that he lived a half-mile from Laidlaw's facility; that he occasionally drove over the North Tyger River, and that it looked and smelled polluted; and that he would like to fish, camp, swim, and picnic in and near the river between 3 and 15 miles downstream from the facility, as he did when he was a teenager, but would not do so because he was concerned that the water was polluted by Laidlaw's discharges. . . .

Other members presented evidence to similar effect. CLEAN member Angela Patterson attested that she lived two miles from the facility; that before Laidlaw operated the facility, she picnicked, walked, birdwatched, and waded in and along the North Tyger River because of the natural beauty of the area; that she no longer engaged in these activities in or near the river because she was concerned about harmful effects from discharged pollutants; and that she and her husband would like to purchase a home near the river but did not intend to do so, in part because of Laidlaw's discharges. CLEAN member Judy Pruitt averred that she lived one-quarter mile from Laidlaw's facility and would like to fish, hike, and picnic along the North Tyger River, but has refrained from those activities because of the discharges. FOE member Linda Moore attested that she lived 20 miles from Roebuck, and would use the North Tyger River south of Roebuck and the land surrounding it for recreational purposes were she not concerned that the water contained harmful pollutants. . . . These sworn statements, as the District Court determined, adequately documented injury in fact. We have held that environmental plaintiffs adequately allege injury in fact when they aver that they use the affected area and are persons "for whom the aesthetic and recreational values of the area will be lessened" by the challenged activity.

Our decision in Lujan v. National Wildlife Federation, is not to the contrary. We held that the plaintiff could not survive the summary judgment motion merely by offering "averments which state only that one of [the organization's] members uses unspecified portions of an immense tract of territory, on some portions of which mining activity has occurred or probably will occur by virtue of the governmental action." In contrast, the affidavits and testimony presented by FOE in this case assert that Laidlaw's discharges, and the affiant members' reasonable concerns about the effects of those discharges, directly affected those affiants' recreational, aesthetic, and economic interests. These submissions present dispositively more than the mere "general averments" and "conclusory allegations" found in National Wildlife Federation. Nor can the affiants' conditional statements — that they would use the nearby North Tyger River for recreation if Laidlaw were not discharging pollutants into it — be equated with the speculative "'some day' intentions" to visit endangered species halfway around the world that we held insufficient to show injury in fact in Defenders of Wildlife.

Laidlaw argues next that even if FOE had standing to seek injunctive relief, it lacked standing to seek civil penalties. Here the asserted defect is not injury but redressability. Civil penalties offer no redress to private plaintiffs, Laidlaw argues, because they are paid to the government, and therefore a citizen plaintiff can never have standing to seek them.

Laidlaw is right to insist that a plaintiff must demonstrate standing separately for each form of relief sought. But it is wrong to maintain that citizen plaintiffs facing ongoing violations never have standing to seek civil penalties.

We have recognized on numerous occasions that "all civil penalties have some deterrent effect." More specifically, Congress has found that civil penalties in Clean Water Act cases do more than promote immediate compliance by limiting the defendant's economic incentive to delay its attainment of permit limits; they also deter future violations. This congressional determination warrants judicial attention and respect. [It] can scarcely be doubted that, for a plaintiff who is injured or faces the threat of future injury due to illegal conduct ongoing at the time of suit, a sanction that effectively abates that conduct and prevents its recurrence provides a form of redress. Civil penalties can fit that description. To the extent that they encourage defendants to discontinue current violations and deter them from committing future ones, they afford redress to citizen plaintiffs who are injured or threatened with injury as a consequence of ongoing unlawful conduct.

The dissent argues that it is the *availability* rather than the *imposition* of civil penalties that deters any particular polluter from continuing to pollute. This argument misses the mark in two ways. First, it overlooks the interdependence of the availability and the imposition; a threat has no deterrent value unless it is credible that it will be carried out. Second, it is reasonable for Congress to conclude that an actual award of civil penalties does in fact bring with it a significant quantum of deterrence over and above what is achieved by the mere prospect of such penalties. A would-be polluter may or may not be dissuaded by the existence of a remedy on the books, but a defendant once hit in its pocketbook will surely think twice before polluting again.

We recognize that there may be a point at which the deterrent effect of a claim for civil penalties becomes so insubstantial or so remote that it cannot support citizen standing. . . . In this case we need not explore the outer limits of the principle that civil penalties provide sufficient deterrence to support redressability. Here, the civil penalties sought by FOE carried with them a deterrent effect that made it likely, as opposed to merely speculative, that the penalties would redress FOE's injuries by abating current violations and preventing future ones — as the District Court reasonably found when it assessed a penalty of $405,800.

Laidlaw contends that the reasoning of our decision in *Steel Co.* directs the conclusion that citizen plaintiffs have no standing to seek civil penalties under the Act. We disagree. *Steel Co.* established that citizen suitors lack standing to seek civil penalties for violations that have abated by the time of suit. We specifically noted in that case that there was no allegation in the complaint of any continuing or imminent violation, and that no basis for such an allegation appeared to exist. In short, *Steel Co.* held that private plaintiffs, unlike the Federal Government, may not sue to assess penalties for wholly past violations, but our decision in that case did not reach the issue of standing to seek penalties for violations that are ongoing at the time of the complaint and that could continue into the future if undeterred.[30]

---

30. In insisting that the redressability requirement is not met, the dissent relies heavily on Linda R.S. v. Richard D. That reliance is sorely misplaced. In *Linda R.S.*, the mother of an out-of-wedlock child filed suit to force a district attorney to bring a criminal prosecution against the absentee father for failure to pay child support. In finding that the mother lacked standing to seek this extraordinary remedy, the Court drew attention to "the special status of criminal prosecutions in our system," and carefully limited its holding to the "unique context of a challenge to [the non-enforcement of] a criminal statute." Furthermore, as to redressability, the relief sought in *Linda R.S.* — a prosecution which, if successful, would automatically land the delinquent father in jail for a fixed term, with predictably negative effects on his earning power — would scarcely remedy the plaintiff's lack of child support payments. In this regard, the Court contrasted "the civil contempt model whereby the defendant 'keeps the keys to the jail in his own pocket' and may be released whenever he complies with his legal obligations." The dissent's contention, *post* at 716, that "precisely the same situation exists here" as in *Linda R.S.* is, to say the least, extravagant. Putting aside its mistaken reliance on *Linda R.S.*, the dissent's broader charge that citizen suits for civil penalties under the Act carry "grave implications for democratic governance," *post*, at 715-716, seems to us overdrawn. Certainly the federal Executive Branch does not share the dissent's view that such suits dissipate its authority to enforce the law. In fact, the Department of Justice has endorsed this citizen suit from the outset, submitting *amicus* briefs in support of FOE in the District Court, the Court of Appeals, and this Court. As we have already noted, supra, at 701, the Federal Government retains the power to foreclose a citizen suit by undertaking its own action. And if the Executive Branch opposes a particular citizen suit, the statute allows the Administrator of the EPA to "intervene as a matter of right" and bring the Government's views to the attention of the court.

Justice SCALIA, with whom Justice THOMAS joins, dissenting,

[The] plaintiffs in this case fell far short of carrying their burden of demonstrating injury in fact. The Court cites affiants' testimony asserting that their enjoyment of the North Tyger River has been diminished due to "concern" that the water was polluted, and that they "believed" that Laidlaw's mercury exceedances had reduced the value of their homes. These averments alone cannot carry the plaintiffs' burden of demonstrating that they have suffered a "concrete and particularized" injury. General allegations of injury may suffice at the pleading stage, but at summary judgment plaintiffs must set forth "specific facts" to support their claims. [In] this case, the affidavits themselves are woefully short on "specific facts," and the vague allegations of injury they do make are undermined by the evidence adduced at trial.

Typically, an environmental plaintiff claiming injury due to discharges in violation of the Clean Water Act argues that the discharges harm the environment, and that the harm to the environment injures him. This route to injury is barred in the present case, however, since the District Court concluded after considering all the evidence that there had been "no demonstrated proof of harm to the environment," that the "permit violations at issue in this citizen suit did not result in any health risk or environmental harm," that "[a]ll available data . . . fail to show that Laidlaw's *actual* discharges have resulted in harm to the North Tyger River," and that "the overall quality of the river exceeds levels necessary to support . . . recreation in and on the water."

The Court finds these conclusions unproblematic for standing, because "[t]he relevant showing for purposes of Article III standing . . . is not injury to the environment but injury to the plaintiff." This statement is correct, as far as it goes. [In] the normal course, however, a lack of demonstrable harm to the environment will translate, as it plainly does here, into a lack of demonstrable harm to citizen plaintiffs. While it is perhaps possible that a plaintiff could be harmed even though the environment was not, such a plaintiff would have the burden of articulating and demonstrating the nature of that injury. . . . Plaintiffs here have made no attempt at such a showing, but rely entirely upon unsupported and unexplained affidavit allegations of "concern."

Indeed, every one of the affiants deposed by Laidlaw cast into doubt the (in any event inadequate) proposition that subjective "concerns" actually affected their conduct. Linda Moore, for example, said in her affidavit that she would use the affected waterways for recreation if it were not for her concern about pollution. Yet she testified in her deposition that she had been to the river only twice, once in 1980 (when she visited someone who lived by the river) and once after this suit was filed. Similarly, Kenneth Lee Curtis, who claimed he was injured by being deprived of recreational activity at the river, admitted that he had not been to the river since he was "a kid," and when asked whether the reason he stopped visiting the river was because of pollution, answered "no." As to Curtis's claim that the river "looke[d] and smell[ed] polluted," this condition, if present, was surely not caused by Laidlaw's discharges, which according to the District Court "did not result in any health risk or environmental harm." The other affiants cited by the Court were not deposed, but their affidavits state either that they *would* use the river if it were not polluted or harmful (as the court subsequently found it is not. . . . By accepting plaintiffs' vague, contradictory, and unsubstantiated allegations of "concern" about the environment as adequate to prove injury in fact, and accepting them even in the face of a finding that the environment was not demonstrably harmed, the Court makes the injury-in-fact requirement a sham. If there are permit violations, and a member of a plaintiff environmental organization lives near the offending plant, it would be difficult not to satisfy today's lenient standard.

The Court's treatment of the redressability requirement — which would have been unnecessary if it resolved the injury-in-fact question correctly — is equally cavalier. As discussed above, petitioners allege ongoing injury consisting of diminished enjoyment of the affected waterways and decreased property values. They allege that these injuries are caused by Laidlaw's continuing permit violations. But the remedy petitioners seek is neither recompense for their injuries nor an injunction against future violations. Instead, the remedy is a statutorily specified "penalty" for past violations, payable entirely to the United States Treasury. . . .

The Court's opinion reads as though the only purpose and effect of the redressability requirement is to assure that the plaintiff receive *some* of the benefit of the relief that a court orders. That is not so. If it were, a federal tort plaintiff fearing repetition of the injury could ask for tort damages to be paid, not only to himself but to other victims as well, on the theory that those damages would have at least some deterrent effect beneficial to him. Such a suit is preposterous because the "remediation" that is the traditional business of Anglo-American courts is relief specifically tailored to the plaintiff's injury, and not *any* sort of relief that has some incidental benefit to the plaintiff. Just as a "generalized grievance" that affects the entire citizenry cannot satisfy the injury-in-fact requirement even though it aggrieves the plaintiff along with everyone else, so also a generalized remedy that deters all future unlawful activity against all persons cannot satisfy the remediation requirement, even though it deters (among other things) repetition of this particular unlawful activity against these particular plaintiffs.

Thus, relief against prospective harm is traditionally afforded by way of an injunction, the scope of which is limited by the scope of the threatened injury. In seeking to overturn that tradition by giving an individual plaintiff the power to invoke a public remedy, Congress has done precisely what we have said it cannot do: convert an "undifferentiated public interest" into an "individual right" vindicable in the courts. . . .

As I have just discussed, it is my view that a plaintiff's desire to benefit from the deterrent effect of a public penalty for past conduct can never suffice to establish a case or controversy of the sort known to our law. Such deterrent effect is, so to speak, "speculative as a matter of law." Even if that were not so, however, the deterrent effect in the present case would surely be speculative as a matter of fact. . . . If the Court had undertaken the necessary inquiry into whether significant deterrence of the plaintiffs' feared injury was "likely," it would have had to reason something like this: Strictly speaking, no polluter is deterred by a penalty for past pollution; he is deterred by the *fear* of a penalty for *future* pollution. That fear will be virtually nonexistent if the prospective polluter knows that all emissions violators are given a free pass; it will be substantial under an emissions program such as the federal scheme here, which is regularly and notoriously enforced; it will be even higher when a prospective polluter subject to such a regularly enforced program has, as here, been the object of public charges of pollution and a suit for injunction; and it will surely be near the top of the graph when, as here, the prospective polluter has already been subjected to *state* penalties for the past pollution. The deterrence on which the plaintiffs must rely for standing in the present case is the marginal increase in Laidlaw's fear of future penalties that will be achieved by adding federal penalties for Laidlaw's past conduct. . . . I cannot say for certain that this marginal increase is zero; but I can say for certain that it is entirely speculative whether it will make the difference between these plaintiffs' suffering injury in the future and these plaintiffs' going unharmed. In fact, the assertion that it will "likely" do so is entirely farfetched. . . .

Article II of the Constitution commits it to the President to "take Care that the Laws be faithfully executed," Art. II, §3, and provides specific methods by which all persons exercising significant executive power are to be appointed, Art. II, §2. As Justice Kennedy's concurrence correctly observes, the question of the conformity of this legislation with Article II has not been argued — and I, like the Court, do not address it. But Article III, no less than Article II, has consequences for the structure of our government, and it is worth noting the changes in that structure which today's decision allows.

By permitting citizens to pursue civil penalties payable to the Federal Treasury, the Act does not provide a mechanism for individual relief in any traditional sense, but turns over to private citizens the function of enforcing the law. A Clean Water Act plaintiff pursuing civil penalties acts as a self-appointed mini-EPA. Where, as is often the case, the plaintiff is a national association, it has significant discretion in choosing enforcement targets. Once the association is aware of a reported violation, it need not look long for an injured member, at least under the theory of injury the Court applies today. And once the target is chosen, the suit goes forward without meaningful public control. The availability of civil penalties vastly disproportionate to the individual injury gives citizen plaintiffs massive bargaining power — which is often used to achieve settlements requiring the defendant to support environmental projects of the plaintiffs' choosing. See Greve, The Private Enforcement of Environmental Law, 65 Tulane L. Rev. 339, 355-359 (1990). Thus is a public fine diverted to a private interest. . . .

The undesirable and unconstitutional consequence of today's decision is to place the immense power of suing to enforce the public laws in private hands. I respectfully dissent.

Questions

1. What is the purpose of requiring redressability and causation? Consider the view that these requirements are part of the ban on advisory opinions: If the plaintiff has nothing to gain from a decree in his favor, then the court's opinion is essentially an advisory opinion.

What in the text or history of article III forbids Congress from granting standing to Citizens for a Better Environment?

2. Suppose that the plaintiff in *Simon* had alleged that a trustee at a nearby hospital told him the hospital voted to reduce its program to care for indigents as soon as it heard about the revenue ruling. Would the plaintiff then have had standing?

3. Do you think that one person should have standing to litigate the tax liability of another person? Should your cousin be able to sue the IRS to force it to deny you a deduction that you thought you could rightfully take? Should groups of taxpayers be able to sue the IRS to force it to adopt a more restrictive interpretation of the code sections that permit mineral depletion deductions? (If not, why not?) Evaluate the following view: *Simon* and Allen v. Wright really turned, or should have turned, on the long-standing notion that one person has no standing to litigate the tax liability of another. They were not "pure" redressability decisions at all.

4. On one view, the redressability issue is a question of fact, one that is often complex and that must be resolved through factual investigations and possibly evidentiary hearings. See Sierra Club v. EPA, 292 F.3d 895 (D.C. Cir. 2002); Public Interest Research Group v. Magnesium Elektron, 123 F.3d 111 (3d Cir. 1997); Northwest Environmental Defense Center v. Bonneville Power Administration, 117 F.3d 1520 (9th Cir. 1997).

But consider the possibility that whether an injury is redressable depends on how it is characterized. In *Northeastern Contractors*, the Court had no problem with redressability once it characterized the injury as involving the opportunity to compete on an equal basis. If the injury is characterized this way, it becomes unimportant, indeed irrelevant, that the contractors could not show that they would have received the relevant contracts without an affirmative action program. Thus, the *Northeastern Contractors* Court dispensed with the redressability issues in a brief footnote. For one of a number of cases in a similar vein, see International Bhd. of Teamsters v. Pena, 17 F.3d 1478 (D.C. Cir. 1994). There, U.S. truck drivers sought judicial review of a rule that authorized truck drivers licensed in Mexico to drive trucks in the United States; the plaintiffs claimed that the rule would make driving more dangerous. The court suggested that the arguable reduction in safety would probably be sufficient for standing even if truck drivers suffered the same injury as others; but since the truck drivers would be distinctly affected, the increased risk they faced was enough to permit them to bring suit. That is, the injury was an increased risk, not a particular accident. See also Baur v. Veneman, supra, granting standing to a consumer complaining of FDA practices on the ground that the "risk" of mad cow disease was the relevant injury — and that so characterized, the injury would certainly be redressed by a decree in the consumer's favor.

Here is the big question: Why couldn't the injury have been characterized in a similarly broad way in every case? Why couldn't it have been characterized broadly in *Linda R.S.* (an unequal chance at receiving help from the father of one's child), *Simon* (a greater risk of being denied admission to emergency rooms), *Allen v. Wright* (an increased risk of being subject to segregation as a result of noncompliance with the incentives that Congress sought to create), and *Lujan v. Defenders of Wildlife* (a greater risk of loss of species, or a risk of losing species as a result of the unlawful use of federal funds)? Why isn't *Northeastern Contractors* inconsistent with these cases? The largest question is this: How does a court decide whether to characterize an injury broadly or narrowly?

Evaluate the following view: The answer to the last question depends on what the governing law seeks to do, as the *Northeastern Contractors* Court clearly saw. But regulatory statutes are designed generally to combat not particular injuries, but harms that involve opportunities and incentives, or that are probabilistic in character. That's how the court proceeded in Baur v. Veneman, supra. In several of the key cases, the Court has mischaracterized the harm as concrete and particularistic, rather as if it were a common law tort. But this reflects a judicial failure to adapt to the purposes and functions of regulatory statutes. In *Simon*, for example, Congress was not attempting to ensure that particular people would be admitted to emergency rooms. It was attempting to create certain incentives to provide increased likelihood of admission. The same kind of goal was involved in Allen v. Wright and Lujan v. Defenders of Wildlife.

Would it be persuasive to respond that once injuries are characterized broadly, the class of people who suffer them is very large, and large classes of people should resort to the political process rather than the judiciary? On this view, the narrow categorization of the injury is an effort to ensure against generalized grievances — and as *Akins*, below, makes clear, the prohibition on such grievances is part of the prudential law of standing.

5. Is *SCRAP* still good law? Consider Animal Legal Defense Fund v. Espy, 23 F.3d 496 (D.C. Cir. 1994), where a divided court denied standing to a researcher who attacked a regulation under the Federal Laboratory Animal Welfare Act. The researcher claimed that she performed laboratory experiments in the past, was outraged by inhumane treatment in the past and had had bad experiences with supervisors as a result, and expected

to have similar bad experiences in the future because of the agency's failure to cover all of
the species with which she expected to work. The court thought that she could not satisfy
the "imminence" requirement of *Defenders of Wildlife.* Compare Salmon River
Concerned Citizens v. Robertson, 32 F.3d 1346 (9th Cir. 1994), granting standing to
people who alleged that they regularly hiked, fished, and gathered herbs in a forest where
the forest service had decided to use herbicides. (What is their injury, and why would it
be redressed?)

6. The requirements of causation and redressability have created considerable
complexity in the lower courts, partly because they turn standing questions into hard
issues of fact. See Public Interest Research Group v. Magnesium Elekron, 123 F.3d 111
(3d Cir. 1997); Northwest Environmental Defense Center v. Bonneville Power
Administration, 117 F.3d 1520 (9th Cir. 1997). Consider, for example, Center for Auto
Safety v. Thomas, 847 F.2d 843 (D.C. Cir. 1988). Organizations representing purchasers
of cars challenged an EPA rule that compensated manufacturers retroactively for changes
in testing procedures used to measure the fuel economy of each manufacturer's sales
fleet. The retroactive compensation gave General Motors and Ford credits that were
worth hundreds of millions of dollars; the resulting credits could be used to offset penalties incurred in previous years or to produce a cushion against future deficiencies in fuel-
economy standards.

The plaintiffs alleged that as a result of the decision, manufacturers would fail to
develop and use technology that would improve the fuel efficiency of their vehicles, and
hence their members would be less likely to be able to purchase fuel-efficient cars. Their
injury consisted of the diminished availability and increased price of the relevant cars.
Five judges on the D.C. Circuit agreed; they also pointed to a variety of other injuries,
including exposure to increased air pollution, attributable to less conservation of gasoline
than would take place without the challenged rule. Five others disagreed, contending
that "it is not likely that" the plaintiffs' injury, even if it were to occur, "will be caused by
the challenged action, or redressed by a favorable decision." In their view, a change in the
mix of products was not a sufficient injury. Changes in product design qualified as such
an injury, but with respect to these changes, the causation requirements were not met.
This was because a "company cannot be expected to mount a comparable research and
development effort as a short-term response to an unanticipated penalty. . . . Given the
industry's lead times, we also find it unlikely that a reversal of the . . . rule would cause the
manufacturers . . . to redesign their" next two model years "cars to incorporate tested technologies in a broader range of vehicles."

What are the judges on the D.C. Circuit disagreeing about? What concerns would
motivate someone to take one or another side? See also Yessler Terrace Community
Council v. Cisneros, 37 F.3d 442 (9th Cir. 1994); United Transp. Union v. ICC, 891 F.2d
908 (D.C. Cir. 1989); Public Citizen v. FTC, 869 F.2d 1541 (D.C. Cir. 1989);
Dellums v. NRC, 863 F.2d 968 (D.C. Cir. 1988). For an interesting contrast with
Laidlaw, see Public Interest Research Group v. Magnesium Elektron, 123 F.3d 111 (3d
Cir. 1997), disallowing a suit against a polluter on the ground that the plaintiffs could not
show injury as a result of illegal emissions.

Recall Federation for American Immigration Reform v. Reno, 93 F.3d 897 (1996),
supra, where the plaintiffs, residents of Miami, challenged new U.S. policies allowing
more Cubans to stay in, and to come into, the country. As noted above, the court denied
standing on zone of interests grounds; but suppose that Congress clearly intended to grant
standing to the plaintiffs, as, for example, through a new statute. Could the plaintiffs show

an injury in fact that was due to the defendant's action and likely to be redressed by a decree in their favor? Would it be sufficient for them to argue that a new influx of immigrants would produce unemployment and wage reductions and greater burdens on such services as schools and hospitals?

7. Briefly explain what the "injury" was in *Laidlaw*, and why it would be redressed by a decree in the plaintiff's favor. How, on these counts, is the case different from *Steel Company*? Why isn't Justice Scalia correct to urge that no plaintiff, in *Laidlaw*, showed the kind of injury required by the two *Lujan* cases?

7. *Information*

Federal Election Commission v. Akins

524 U.S. 11 (1998)

Justice BREYER delivered the opinion of the Court.

The Federal Election Commission (FEC) has determined that the American Israel Public Affairs Committee (AIPAC) is not "political committee" as defined by the Federal Election Campaign Act of 1971, and, for that reason, the Commission has refused to require AIPAC to make disclosures regarding its membership, contributions, and expenditures that FECA would otherwise require. We hold that respondents, a group of voters, have standing to challenge the Commission's determination in court, and we remand this case for further proceedings.

I

In light of our disposition of this case, we believe it necessary to describe its procedural background in some detail. As commonly understood, the Federal Election Campaign Act seeks to remedy any actual or perceived corruption of the political process in several important ways. The Act imposes limits upon the amounts that individuals, corporations, "political committees" (including political action committees), and political parties can contribute to a candidate for federal political office. The Act also imposes limits on the amount these individuals or entities can spend in coordination with a candidate. (It treats these expenditures as "contributions to" a candidate for purposes of the Act.) As originally written, the Act sets limits upon the total amount that a candidate could spend of his own money, and upon the amounts that other individuals, corporations, and "political committees" could spend independent of a candidate — though the Court found that certain of these last-mentioned limitations violated the First Amendment.

This case concerns requirements in the Act that extend beyond these better-known contribution and expenditure limitations. In particular the Act imposes extensive record-keeping and disclosure requirements upon groups that fall within the Act's definition of a "political committee." Those groups must register with the FEC, appoint a treasurer, keep names and addresses of contributors, track the amount and purpose of disbursements, and file complex FEC reports that include lists of donors giving in excess of $200 per year (often, these donors may be the group's members), contributions, expenditures, and any other disbursements irrespective of their purposes.

The Act's use of the word "political committee" calls to mind the term "political action committee," or "PAC," a term that normally refers to organizations that corporations or trade unions might establish for the purpose of making contributions or expenditures that the Act would otherwise prohibit. But, in fact, the Act's term "political committee" has a much broader scope. The Act states that a "political committee" includes "any committee, club, association or other group of persons which receives" more than $1,000 in "contributions" or "which makes" more than $1,000 in "expenditures" in any given year.

This broad definition, however, is less universally encompassing than at first it may seem, for later definitional subsections limit its scope. The Act defines the key terms "contribution" and "expenditure" as covering only those contributions and expenditures that are made "for the purpose of influencing any election for Federal office." Moreover, the Act sets forth detailed categories of disbursements, loans, and assistance-in-kind that do not count as a "contribution" or an "expenditure," even when made for election-related purposes. In particular, assistance given to help a particular candidate will not count toward the $1,000 "expenditure" ceiling that qualifies an organization as a "political committee" if it takes the form of a "communication" by an organization "to its members" — as long as the organization at issue is a "membership organization or corporation" and it is not "organized primarily for the purpose of influencing the nomination . . . or election, of any individual."

This case arises out of an effort by respondents, a group of voters with views often opposed to those of AIPAC, to persuade the FEC to treat AIPAC as a "political committee." Respondents filed a complaint with the FEC, stating that AIPAC had made more than $1,000 in qualifying "expenditures" per year, and thereby became a "political committee." They added that AIPAC had violated the FEC provisions requiring "political committees" to register and to make public the information about members, contributions, and expenditures to which we have just referred. Respondents also claimed that AIPAC had violated §441b of FECA, which prohibits corporate campaign "contributions" and "expenditures." They asked the FEC to find that AIPAC had violated the Act, and, among other things, to order AIPAC to make public the information that FECA demands of a "political committee."

AIPAC asked the FEC to dismiss the complaint. AIPAC described itself as an issue-oriented organization that seeks to maintain friendship and promote goodwill between the United States and Israel. AIPAC conceded that it lobbies elected officials and disseminates information about candidates for public office. But in responding to the §441b charge, AIPAC denied that it had made the kinds of "expenditures" that matter for FECA purposes (i.e., the kinds of election-related expenditures that corporations cannot make, and which count as the kind of expenditures that, when they exceed $1,000, qualify a group as a "political committee").

To put the matter more specifically: AIPAC focused on certain "expenditures" that respondents had claimed were election-related, such as the costs of meetings with candidates, the introduction of AIPAC members to candidates, and the distribution of candidate position papers. AIPAC said that its spending on such activities, even if election-related, fell within a relevant exception. They amounted, said AIPAC, to communications by a membership organization with its members, which the Act exempts from its definition of "expenditures," §431(9)(B)(iii). In AIPAC's view, these communications therefore did not violate §441b's corporate expenditure prohibition. (And, if AIPAC was right, those expenditures would not count towards the $1,000 ceiling on "expenditures" that might transform an ordinary issue-related group into a "political committee.")

The FEC's General Counsel concluded that, between 1983 and 1988, AIPAC had indeed funded communications of the sort described. The General Counsel said that those expenditures were campaign related, in that they amounted to advocating the election or defeat of particular candidates. He added that these expenditures were "likely to have crossed the $1,000 threshold." At the same time, the FEC closed the door to AIPAC's invocation of the "communications" exception. The FEC said that, although it was a "close question," these expenditures were not membership communications, because that exception applies to a membership organization's communications with its members, and most of the persons who belonged to AIPAC did not qualify as "members" for purposes of the Act. Still, given the closeness of the issue, the FEC exercised its discretion and decided not to proceed further with respect to the claimed "corporate contribution" violation.

The FEC's determination that many of the persons who belonged to AIPAC were not "members" effectively foreclosed any claim that AIPAC's communications did not count as "expenditures" for purposes of determining whether it was a "political committee." Since AIPAC's activities fell outside the "membership communications" exception, AIPAC could not invoke that exception as a way of escaping the scope of the Act's term "political committee" and the Act's disclosure provisions, which that definition triggers.

The FEC nonetheless held that AIPAC was not subject to the disclosure requirements, but for a different reason. In the FEC's view, the Act's definition of "political committee" includes only those organizations that have as a "major purpose" the nomination or election of candidates. Cf. Buckley v, Valeo, 424 U.S. at 79. AIPAC, it added, was fundamentally an issue-oriented lobbying organization, not a campaign-related organization, and hence AIPAC fell outside the definition of a "political committee" regardless. The FEC consequently dismissed respondents' complaint.

Respondents filed a petition in Federal District Court seeking review of the FEC's determination dismissing their complaint. . . .

II

The Solicitor General argues that respondents lack standing to challenge the FEC's decision not to proceed against AIPAC. He claims that they have failed to satisfy the "prudential" standing requirements upon which this Court has insisted. He adds that respondents have not shown that they "suffer injury in fact," that their injury is "fairly traceable" to the FEC's decision, or that a judicial decision in their favor would "redress" the injury. In his view, respondents' District Court petition consequently failed to meet Article III's demand for a "case" or "controversy."

We do not agree with the FEC's "prudential standing" claim. Congress has specifically provided in FECA that "any person who believes a violation of this Act . . . has occurred, may file a complaint with the Commission." It has added that "any party aggrieved by an order of the Commission dismissing a complaint filed by such party . . . may file a petition" in district court seeking review of that dismissal. History associates the word "aggrieved" with a congressional intent to cast the standing net broadly — beyond the common-law interests and substantive statutory rights upon which "prudential" standing traditionally rested.

Moreover, prudential standing is satisfied when the injury asserted by a plaintiff "'arguably [falls] within the zone of interests to be protected or regulated by the statute . . . in question.'" The injury of which respondents complain — their failure to obtain relevant information — is injury of a kind that FECA seeks to address. We have found nothing in the

Act that suggests Congress intended to exclude voters from the benefits of these provisions, or otherwise to restrict standing, say, to political parties, candidates, or their committees.

Given the language of the statute and the nature of the injury, we conclude that Congress, intending to protect voters such as respondents from suffering the kind of injury here at issue, intended to authorize this kind of suit. Consequently, respondents satisfy "prudential" standing requirements.

Nor do we agree with the FEC or the dissent that Congress lacks the constitutional power to authorize federal courts to adjudicate this lawsuit. . . . In our view, respondents here have suffered a genuine "injury in fact."

The "injury in fact" that respondents have suffered consists of their inability to obtain information — lists of AIPAC donors (who are, according to AIPAC, its members), and campaign-related contributions and expenditures — that, on respondents' view of the law, the statute requires that AIPAC make public. There is no reason to doubt their claim that the information would help them (and others to whom they would communicate it) to evaluate candidates for public office, especially candidates who received assistance from AIPAC, and to evaluate the role that AIPAC's financial assistance might play in a specific election. Respondents' injury consequently seems concrete and particular. Indeed, this Court has previously held that a plaintiff suffers an "injury in fact" when the plaintiff fails to obtain information which must be publicly disclosed pursuant to a statute. Public Citizen v. Department of Justice, 491 U.S. 440, 449 (1989) (failure to obtain information subject to disclosure under Federal Advisory Committee Act "constitutes a sufficiently distinct injury to provide standing to sue"). See also Havens Realty Corp. v. Coleman, 455 U.S. 363, 373-374 (1982) (deprivation of information about housing availability constitutes "specific injury" permitting standing).

The dissent refers to United States v. Richardson, 418 U.S. 166 (1974), a case in which a plaintiff sought information (details of Central Intelligence Agency expenditures) to which, he said, the Constitution's Accounts Clause, Art. I, §9, cl. 7, entitled him. The Court held that the plaintiff there lacked Article III standing. The dissent says that Richardson and this case are "indistinguishable." But as the parties' briefs suggest — for they do not mention Richardson — that case does not control the outcome here.

Richardson's plaintiff claimed that a statute permitting the CIA to keep its expenditures nonpublic violated the Accounts Clause, which requires that "a regular Statement and Account of the Receipts and Expenditures of all public Money shall be published from time to time." The Court held that the plaintiff lacked standing because there was "no 'logical nexus' between the [plaintiffs'] asserted status of taxpayer and the claimed failure of the Congress to require the Executive to supply a more detailed report of the [CIA's] expenditures." Id., at 175.

In this case, however, the "logical nexus" inquiry is not relevant. Here, there is no constitutional provision requiring the demonstration of the "nexus" the Court believed must be shown in Richardson and Flast. Rather, there is a statute which, as we previously pointed out, does seek to protect individuals such as respondents from the kind of harm they say they have suffered, i.e., failing to receive particular information about campaign-related activities.

The fact that the Court in Richardson focused upon taxpayer standing, not voter standing, places that case at still a greater distance from the case before us. We are not suggesting, as the dissent implies, that Richardson would have come out differently if only the plaintiff had asserted his standing to sue as a voter, rather than as a taxpayer. Faced with such an assertion, the Richardson Court would simply have had to consider whether "the Framers . . . ever imagined that general directives [of the Constitution] would be subject to enforcement by an individual citizen." *Richardson*, supra, at 178, n.11. But since that answer (like the answer to whether there was taxpayer standing in *Richardson*) would have rested in significant part upon the Court's view of the Accounts Clause, it still would not control our answer in this case. All this is to say that the legal logic which critically determined *Richardson*'s outcome is beside the point here.

The FEC's strongest argument is its contention that this lawsuit involves only a "generalized grievance." The Solicitor General points out that respondents' asserted harm (their failure to obtain information) is one which is "'shared in substantially equal measure by all or a large class of citizens.'" This Court, he adds, has often said that "generalized grievances" are not the kinds of harms that confer standing. [*Lujan*; Allen v. Wright; *Valley Forge*]. Whether styled as a constitutional or prudential limit on standing, the Court has sometimes determined that where large numbers of Americans suffer alike, the political process, rather than the judicial process, may provide the more appropriate remedy for a widely shared grievance.

The kind of judicial language to which the FEC points, however, invariably appears in cases where the harm at issue is not only widely shared, but is also of an abstract and indefinite nature — for example, harm to the "common concern for obedience to law." L. Singer & Sons v. Union Pacific R. Co., 311 U.S. 295, 303 (1940). The abstract nature of the harm — for example, injury to the interest in seeing that the law is obeyed — deprives the case of the concrete specificity that characterized those controversies which were "the traditional concern of the courts at Westminster"; and which today prevents a plaintiff from obtaining what would, in effect, amount to an advisory opinion.

Often the fact that an interest is abstract and the fact that it is widely shared go hand in hand. But their association is not invariable, and where a harm is concrete, though widely shared, the Court has found "injury in fact." See *Public Citizen*, 491 U.S. at 449-450 ("The fact that other citizens or groups of citizens might make the same complaint after unsuccessfully demanding disclosure . . . does not lessen [their] asserted injury."). Thus the fact that a political forum may be more readily available where an injury is widely shared (while counseling against, say, interpreting a statute as conferring standing) does not, by itself, automatically disqualify an interest for Article III purposes. Such an interest, where sufficiently concrete, may count as an "injury in fact." This conclusion seems particularly obvious where (to use a hypothetical example) large numbers of individuals suffer the same common-law injury (say, a widespread mass tort), or where large numbers of voters suffer interference with voting rights conferred by law. We conclude that similarly, the informational injury at issue here, directly related to voting, the most basic of political rights, is sufficiently concrete and specific such that the fact that it is widely shared does not deprive Congress of constitutional power to authorize its vindication in the federal courts.

Respondents have also satisfied the remaining two constitutional standing requirements. The harm asserted is "fairly traceable" to the FEC's decision about which respondents complain. Of course, as the FEC points out, it is possible that even had the FEC agreed with respondents' view of the law, it would still have decided in the exercise of its discretion not to require AIPAC to produce the information. But that fact does not destroy Article III "causation," for we cannot know that the FEC would have exercised its prosecutorial discretion in this way. Agencies often have discretion about whether or not to take a particular action. Yet those adversely affected by a discretionary agency decision generally have standing to complain that the agency based its decision upon an improper legal ground. If a reviewing court agrees that the agency misinterpreted the law, it will set aside the agency's action and remand the case — even though the agency (like a new jury after a mistrial) might later, in the exercise of its lawful discretion, reach the same result for a different reason. Thus respondents' "injury in fact" is "fairly traceable" to the FEC's decision not to issue its complaint, even though the FEC might reach the same result exercising its discretionary powers lawfully. For similar reasons, the courts in this case can "redress" respondents' "injury in fact."

Finally, the FEC argues that we should deny respondents standing because this case involves an agency's decision not to undertake an enforcement action — an area generally not subject to judicial review. . . . This Court [had] noted that agency enforcement decisions "have traditionally been 'committed to agency discretion,'" and concluded that Congress did not intend to alter that tradition in enacting the APA. We deal here with a statute that explicitly indicates the contrary.

In sum, respondents, as voters, have satisfied both prudential and constitutional standing requirements. They may bring this petition for a declaration that the FEC's dismissal of their complaint was unlawful. . . .

For these reasons, the decision of the Court of Appeals is vacated, and the case is remanded for further proceedings consistent with this opinion.

It is so ordered.

Justice SCALIA, with whom Justice O'CONNOR and Justice THOMAS join, dissenting.

The provision of law at issue in this case is an extraordinary one, conferring upon a private person the ability to bring an Executive agency into court to compel its enforcement of the law against a third party. Despite its liberality, the Administrative Procedure Act does not allow such suits, since enforcement action is traditionally deemed "committed to agency discretion by law." If provisions such as the present one were commonplace, the role of the Executive Branch in our system of separated and equilibrated powers would be greatly reduced, and that of the Judiciary greatly expanded.

Because this provision is so extraordinary, we should be particularly careful not to expand it beyond its fair meaning. In my view the Court's opinion does that. Indeed, it expands the meaning beyond what the Constitution permits.

I

It is clear that the Federal Election Campaign Act does not intend that all persons filing complaints with the Commission have the right to seek judicial review of the rejection of their complaints. This is evident from the fact that the Act permits a complaint to be filed by "[a]ny person who believes a violation of this Act . . . has occurred," but accords a right to judicial relief only to "any party aggrieved by an order of the Commission dismissing a complaint filed by such party." The interpretation that the Court gives the latter provision deprives it of almost all its limiting force. Any voter can sue to compel the agency to require registration of an entity as a political committee, even though the "aggrievement" consists of nothing more than the deprivation of access to information whose public availability would have been one of the consequences of registration.

This seems to me too much of a stretch. It should be borne in mind that the agency action complained of here is not the refusal to make available information in its possession that the Act requires to be disclosed. A person demanding provision of information that the law requires the agency to furnish — one demanding compliance with the Freedom of Information Act or the Advisory Committee Act, for example — can reasonably be described as being "aggrieved" by the agency's refusal to provide it. What the respondents complain of in this suit, however, is not the refusal to provide information, but the refusal (for an allegedly improper reason) to commence an agency enforcement action against a third person. That refusal itself plainly does not render respondents "aggrieved" within the meaning of the Act, for in that case there would have been no reason for the Act to differentiate between "person" and "party aggrieved." Respondents claim that each of them is elevated to the special status of a "party aggrieved" by the fact that the requested enforcement action (if it was successful) would have had the effect, among others, of placing certain information in the agency's possession, where respondents, along with everyone else in the world, would have had access to it. It seems to me most unlikely that the failure to produce that effect — both a secondary consequence of what respondents immediately seek, and a consequence that affects respondents no more and with no greater particularity than it affects virtually the entire population — would have been meant to set apart each respondent as a "party aggrieved" (as opposed to just a rejected complainant) within the meaning of the statute.

This conclusion is strengthened by the fact that this citizen-suit provision was enacted two years after this Court's decision in United States v. Richardson, 418 U.S. 166 (1974), which, as I shall discuss at greater length below, gave Congress every reason to believe that a voter's interest in information helpful to his exercise of the franchise was constitutionally inadequate to confer standing. Richardson had said that a plaintiff's complaint that the Government was unlawfully depriving him of information he needed to "properly fulfill his obligations as a member of the electorate in voting" was "surely the kind of a generalized grievance" that does not state an Article III case or controversy.

And finally, a narrower reading of "party aggrieved" is supported by the doctrine of constitutional doubt, which counsels us to interpret statutes, if possible, in such fashion as to avoid grave constitutional questions. As I proceed to discuss, it is my view that the Court's entertainment of the present suit violates Article III. Even if one disagrees with that judgment, however, it is clear from Richardson that the question is a close one, so that the statute ought not be interpreted to present it.

II

In Richardson, we dismissed for lack of standing a suit whose "aggrievement" was precisely the "aggrievement" respondents assert here: the Government's unlawful refusal to place information within the public domain. The only difference, in fact, is that the aggrievement there was more direct, since the Government already had the information within its possession, whereas here the respondents seek enforcement action that will bring information within the Government's possession and then require the information to be made public. The plaintiff in Richardson challenged the Government's failure to disclose the expenditures of the Central Intelligence Agency (CIA), in alleged violation of the constitutional requirement, Art. I, §9, cl. 7, that "a regular Statement and Account of the Receipts and Expenditures of all public Money shall be published from time to time." We held that such a claim was a nonjusticiable "generalized grievance" because "the impact on [plaintiff] is plainly undifferentiated and common to all members of the public."

It was alleged in *Richardson* that the Government had denied a right conferred by the Constitution, whereas respondents here assert a right conferred by statutes — but of course "there is absolutely no basis for making the Article III inquiry turn on the source of the asserted right." [*Lujan*]. The Court today distinguishes *Richardson* on a different basis — a basis that reduces it from a landmark constitutional holding to a curio. According to the Court, "*Richardson* focused upon taxpayer standing, . . . not voter standing." In addition to being a silly distinction, given the weighty governmental purpose underlying the "generalized grievance" prohibition — viz., to avoid "something in the nature of an Athenian democracy or a New England town meeting to oversee the conduct of the National Government by means of lawsuits in federal courts" — this is also a distinction that the Court in *Richardson* went out of its way explicitly to eliminate. It is true enough that the narrow question presented in *Richardson* was " 'whether a federal taxpayer has standing.' " But the *Richardson* Court did not hold only, as the Court today suggests, that the plaintiff failed to qualify for the exception to the rule of no taxpayer standing established by the "logical nexus" test of Flast v. Cohen, 392 U.S. 83 (1968). The plaintiff's complaint in *Richardson* had also alleged that he was " 'a member of the electorate,' " and he asserted injury in that capacity as well. The *Richardson* opinion treated that as fairly included within the taxpayer-standing question, or at least as plainly indistinguishable from it:

> The respondent's claim is that without detailed information on CIA expenditures — and hence its activities — he cannot intelligently follow the actions of Congress or the Executive, nor can he properly fulfill his obligations as a member of the electorate in voting for candidates seeking national office.
> This is surely the kind of a generalized grievance described in both *Frothingham* and *Flast* since the impact on him is plainly undifferentiated and common to all members of the public.

[The] Court's opinion asserts that our language disapproving generalized grievances "invariably appears in cases where the harm at issue is not only widely shared, but is also of an abstract and indefinite nature." [If] that is so — if concrete generalized grievances (like concrete particularized grievances) are OK, and abstract generalized grievances (like abstract particularized grievances) are bad — one must wonder why we ever developed the superfluous distinction between generalized and particularized grievances at all. But of course the Court is wrong to think that generalized grievances have only concerned us when they are abstract. One need go no further than *Richardson* to prove that — unless the Court believes that deprivation of information is an abstract injury, in which event this case could be disposed of on that much broader ground.

What is noticeably lacking in the Court's discussion of our generalized-grievance jurisprudence is all reference to two words that have figured in it prominently: "particularized" and "undifferentiated." See *Richardson*, supra, at 177; *Lujan*, 504 U.S. at 560, 560, n.1. "Particularized" means that "the injury must affect the plaintiff in a personal and individual way." Id., at 560, n.1. If the effect is "undifferentiated and common to all members of the public," Richardson, the plaintiff has a "generalized grievance" that must be pursued by political rather than judicial means. These terms explain why it is a gross oversimplification to reduce the concept of a generalized grievance to nothing more than "the fact that [the grievance] is widely shared," thereby enabling the concept to be dismissed as a standing principle by such examples as "large numbers of individuals suffering the same common-law injury (say, a widespread mass tort), or . . . large numbers of voters suffering interference with voting rights conferred by law," ibid. The exemplified injuries are widely shared, to be sure, but each individual suffers a particularized and differentiated harm. One tort victim suffers a burnt leg, another a burnt arm — or even if both suffer burnt arms they are different arms. One voter suffers the deprivation of his franchise, another the deprivation of hers. With the generalized grievance, on the other hand, the injury or deprivation is not only widely shared but it is undifferentiated. The harm caused to Mr. Richardson by the alleged disregard of the Statement-of-Accounts Clause was precisely the same as the harm caused to everyone else: unavailability of a description of CIA expenditures. Just as the (more indirect) harm caused to Mr. Akins by the allegedly unlawful failure to enforce FECA is precisely the same as the harm caused to everyone else: unavailability of a description of AIPAC's activities.

The Constitution's line of demarcation between the Executive power and the judicial power presupposes a common understanding of the type of interest needed to sustain a "case or controversy" against the Executive in the courts. A system in which the citizenry at large could sue to compel Executive compliance with the law would be a system in which the courts, rather than the President, are given the primary responsibility to "take Care that the Laws be faithfully executed." We do not have such a system because the common understanding of the interest necessary to sustain suit has included the requirement, affirmed in *Richardson*, that the complained-of injury be particularized and differentiated, rather than common to all the electorate. When the Executive can be directed by the courts, at the instance of any voter, to remedy a deprivation which affects the entire electorate in precisely the same way — and particularly when that deprivation (here, the unavailability of information) is one inseverable part of a larger enforcement scheme — there has occurred a shift of political responsibility to a branch designed not to protect the public at large but to protect individual rights. "To permit Congress to convert the undifferentiated public interest in executive officers' compliance with the law into an 'individual right' vindicable in the courts is to permit Congress to transfer from the President to the courts the Chief Executive's most important constitutional duty. . . ." *Lujan*, 504 U.S. at 577. If today's decision is correct, it is within the power of Congress to authorize any interested person to manage (through the courts) the Executive's enforcement of any law that includes a requirement for the filing and public availability of a piece of paper. This is not the system we have had, and is not the system we should desire.

Because this statute should not be interpreted to confer upon the entire electorate the power to invoke judicial direction of prosecutions, and because if it is so interpreted the statute unconstitutionally transfers from the Executive to the courts the responsibility to "take Care that the Laws be faithfully executed," Art. II, §3, I respectfully dissent.

Note on Procedural Injuries, Information, Article II, and Beneficiaries of Regulatory Statutes

1. Often an administrative law case involves a "procedural" injury, that is, an agency's failure to follow the required procedures. Lujan v. Defenders of Wildlife offered a suggestive footnote — see above — on this question, and *Akins* offers an important discussion. But mysteries remain. In particular, the whole question of procedural injuries has a complex relationship to issues of redressability and causation.

Suppose that an object of regulation — a company, for example — contends that an agency has failed to comply with the procedural requirements of §553 of the APA. A gasoline producer might complain, for example, that the EPA has imposed a regulatory requirement without giving adequate notice in the *Federal Register*. Is there a problem of redressability if the agency can claim, with reason, that it is "purely speculative" whether the agency's behavior would have been changed by compliance with the procedural requirement? The general answer appears to be entirely clear — there is no standing problem in such cases — but under the Court's cases, it is not clear why the redressability requirement does not raise an issue. Does *Akins* provide an adequate answer?

In the key footnote in Lujan v. Defenders of Wildlife, the Court suggests that a properly supported claim of a purely procedural injury supports standing to challenge a violation of a procedural requirement, such as the procedures required by the APA or NEPA. Thus the rise of causation requirements is not meant to bar objects of regulation from challenging procedural illegality. But why, exactly, is someone who lives near a project entitled to challenge the failure to prepare an environmental impact statement? Does it help to characterize the injury not as the environmental harm, but as the failure to subject the project to the process of public supervision that Congress sought to create?

For discussion, see Sugar Cane Growers Cooperative v. Veneman, 289 F.3d 89 (D.C. Cir. 2002). There the Cooperative contended that the Department of Agriculture violated the APA by taking certain actions without going through notice-and-comment proceedings. The government contended that standing was unavailable, because the Department might have made the decision even if it had followed any notice-and-comment requirements. The court responded: "A plaintiff who alleges deprivation of a procedural protection to which he is entitled never has to prove that if he had received the procedure the substantive result would have been altered. All that is necessary is to show that the procedural step was connected to the substantive result." All courts seem to agree on this point, but again: Why?

2. You may have noticed that in several of the post-1980s standing cases, the Court has referred not only to article III but also to article II. This is a prominent theme in *Akins*, Allen v. Wright, and Lujan v. Defenders of Wildlife. What is the role of article II concerns in these cases? Would standing for people without a concrete and personal harm endanger the president's constitutional prerogatives? Would those prerogatives be less endangered if, in *Lujan*, the plaintiffs had purchased plane tickets? Justice Stevens's argument in Allen v. Wright seems to be that article II makes faithful execution of the law a duty, not a license. If this is so, is the Court's analysis wrong?

3. Many statutes, like that in *Akins* and *Citizens for a Better Environment*, call for the provision of information. After *Akins*, are there *any* limitations on Congress's power to grant people standing to vindicate an interest in receiving information? Note that the Freedom of Information Act allows "any person" to obtain information that is supposed to be publicly available, even if that person is simply curious and has no obvious personal stake. Lower courts have held that the grant of standing to "any person" under FOIA is constitutional, and *Akins* appears to support this view. But how is this consistent with Lujan v. Defenders of Wildlife? See the lower court's statement in Akins v. FEC, 101 F.3d 731 (D.C. Cir. 1996): "Congress can create a legal right (and, typically, a cause of action to protect that right) the interference with which will create an Article III injury. Such a legal right can be given to all persons in the country. In that event, an individual whose individual right has been frustrated or interfered with has standing to sue, even though all other persons have the same right, without the claim being regarded as a generalized grievance. That is why anyone

denied information under [FOIA] has standing to sue regardless of his or her reasons for suing."

Is this what the Supreme Court means to say in *Akins*? See also Lepelletier v. FDCI, 164 F.3d 37 (D.C. Cir. 1999), allowing standing to review a denial of information under FOIA, but stressing that the information was relevant to the litigant's business relationships. In American Canoe Association v. City of Louisa, 389 F.3d 536 (6th Cir. 2004), the American Canoe Association and the Sierra Club complained of a violation of the National Pollutant Discharge Elimination System permit issued to the city with respect to a river. The Sierra Club complained of certain reporting violations, which, it said, produced "informational injuries," with one of its members stating that "the lack of information deprived him of the ability to make choices about whether it was 'safe to fish, paddle, and recreate in this waterway.'" The court held that this allegation was enough for standing.

Suppose that a public interest group seeks to obtain information involving (for example) campaign contributions and receipts, discharges of toxic substances, services to the elderly, or public health. For general discussion, see Sunstein, Informational Regulation and Informational Standing, 147 U. Pa. L. Rev. 613 (1999). What must the public interest group show? Must it show that the failure to disclose the relevant information "injures" its members? What did the *Akins* plaintiff need to show? See Common Cause v. FEC, 108 F.3d 413 (D.C. Cir. 1997). Consider the view that *Akins* allows Congress to give any citizen the right to obtain information. Is this an excessive reading of the case? See Byrd v. EPA, 174 F.3d 239 (D.C. Cir. 1999), where the court held that an environmental consultant could challenge an EPA decision refusing to treat a peer review panel as an Advisory Committee. According to the court, the consultant suffered informational injury, because he was deprived of timely access to the panel's written comments. See also Chiron Corp. v. NTSB, 198 F.3d 935 (D.C. Cir. 1999), refusing to recognize informational standing on the ground that the relevant source of law did not confer a legal right to the information in question. And in Bensman v. U.S. Forest Service, 2005 U.S. App. LEXIS 10047 (7th Cir. 2005), the court denied informational standing to people seeking information pursuant to the Appeals Reform Act. According to the court, the ARA did not provide a right to information, and was in this sense very different from FOIA or the statute involved in *Akins*.

4. In several of the key cases, the Court has explicitly or implicitly drawn a distinction between the "objects" of regulation (those against whom an agency is proceeding) and the "beneficiaries" of regulation (those for whom a statute was created). The distinction is most explicit in Lujan v. Defenders of Wildlife, where the Court says that an object ordinarily has standing, but that "When . . . a plaintiff's asserted injury arises from the government's allegedly unlawful regulation (or lack of regulation) of someone else, much more is needed." This is a theme of Allen v. Wright as well; it links the developing law of standing with Heckler v. Chaney, holding that agency inaction is presumed unreviewable. What, exactly, is the basis for this distinction between objects and beneficiaries? Why should courts favor the former over the latter? Is this the legacy of the old private law model of standing? Would such a distinction have desirable or undesirable incentive effects on administrators? For discussion, see Fallon, Of Justiciability, Remedies, and Public Law Litigation, 59 N.Y.U. L. Rev. 1 (1984); Scalia, The Doctrine of Standing as an Essential Element of the Separation of Powers, 17 Suffolk L. Rev. 881 (1983); Sunstein, Standing and the Privatization of Public Law, 88 Colum. L. Rev. 1432 (1988).

Note on Congressional Standing

May members of Congress bring suit when some law or action seems to affect their official responsibilities? In Raines v. Byrd, 521 U.S. 811 (1997), the Supreme Court offered some guidance on this much-disputed question. Individual members of Congress brought suit to challenge on constitutional grounds the Line Item Veto Act, which gives the president the authority to "cancel" certain spending and tax benefit measures after he has signed them into law. The act also expressly granted standing to members of Congress. The lower court held that the claim that the act diluted their voting power under article I of the Constitution was sufficient for standing. The Supreme Court reversed. The Court emphasized the need for a "personal injury" that was "legally and judicially cognizable," a need that would be especially insistent in a dispute that "would force us to decide whether an action taken by one of the other two branches of government was constitutional."

The Court said that no case had recognized standing for members of Congress, and also that history "appears to cut against them as well," since "no suit was brought on the basis of claimed injury to official authority" in past contexts in which members of Congress might have found a legal assault on their constitutional powers.

> In sum, appellees have alleged no injury to themselves as individuals (contra Powell [v. McCormack, 395 U.S. 486 (1969), where the Court allowed a member of Congress to challenge his exclusion from the House of Representatives]), the institutional injury they allege is wholly abstract and widely dispersed (contra Coleman [v. Miller, 307 U.S. 433 (1939), where the Court allowed state legislators to attack the official record of a vote appearing to ratify a constitutional amendment]), and their attempt to litigate this dispute at this time and in this form is contrary to historical experience.

The Court said that *Coleman* stood "at most" for "the proposition that legislators whose votes would have been sufficient to defeat (or enact) a specific legislative act have standing to sue if that legislative act goes into effect (or does not go into effect), on the ground that their votes have been completely nullified."

Justice Souter, joined by Justice Ginsburg, concurred, suggesting that it was "fairly debatable" whether the injury in fact requirement was satisfied by the injury of depriving the plaintiffs "of their official role in voting on the provisions that became law." In this case, the more general separation of powers principles argued in favor of "waiting for a private suit." Justice Stevens dissented on the ground that "the opportunity to cast" the relevant votes "is a right guaranteed by the text of the Constitution," and it was "clear that the persons who are deprived of that right by the Act have standing to challenge its constitutionality." Justice Breyer, also dissenting, emphasized Congress's grant of standing and said that *Coleman* was controlling authority on behalf of the plaintiffs. In *Coleman*, as here, the representatives' votes were "threatened with nullification."

Question: Does *Raines* foreclose standing for representatives in all cases in which they are complaining of adverse effects on their constitutional voting authority? Why, precisely, would it be bad if little or nothing remains of *Coleman*?

Problems

1. The Toxic Chemical Act requires EPA to promulgate rules that govern the treatment of hazardous wastes, such as oil residues, buried in toxic waste dumps. EPA promulgates a

regulation that requires soil that contains any benzene to be "reprocessed" to the point where the soil contains fewer than five parts benzene per million parts soil. The Waste Reprocessing Company, your client, believes that the standard is too lenient, and that it therefore violates that statute's mandate that EPA make waste dumps "safe" for the general public. Your client points out that, if EPA would reduce the standard to three parts per million, it could make a lot more money selling its special soil reprocessing machine that releases oil residues harmlessly into the air.

Do you think your client has standing to make this claim? What will you argue?

2. The Federal Housing Act, 42 U.S.C. §§1441-1490C, originally enacted in 1949 and frequently amended, gives the secretary of the Department of Housing and Urban Development (HUD) authority to make capital grants to local public agencies for urban renewal projects. Many limitations and conditions are placed on the making of such grants, including the following (42 U.S.C. §1456(g)):

> No provision permitting the new construction of hotels or other housing for transient use in the re-development of any urban renewal area under this Act shall be included in the urban renewal plan unless the community in which the project is located, under regulations prescribed by the Secretary, has caused to be made a competent independent analysis of the local supply of transient housing and as a result thereof has determined that there exists in the area a need for additional units of such housing.

The act contains no provisions for judicial review.

Among the projects formulated under this act was one for Utica, New York. The plan drawn up by the local public agencies, and approved by the secretary for the award of a grant, included in the project area a new hotel for transients. The owners of the Hotel Utica, a large hotel in the city located near the project area, have brought an action in a federal court against the secretary of HUD, the regional administrator of HUD, and certain local officials, to enjoin the use of any local or federal funds for the erection of hotels or other transient housing in the project area. The owners allege (1) that they would suffer severe economic loss from the erection of transient housing; (2) that the competent, independent study required by law has not been made; and (3) that there is already a substantial surplus of transient housing in the Utica metropolitan area.

Defendants have moved to dismiss on the grounds that plaintiffs lack standing to maintain the action and that judicial review of the plan on the basis alleged may not be had. What result?

Concluding Note on Standing

Consider whether one can describe the law of standing as follows:

First, there are three constitutional requirements: (1) injury in fact — concrete and particularized, and actual or imminent; (2) the injury must have been caused by the defendant's allegedly unlawful conduct; and (3) the injury must be redressable by a decree in the plaintiff's favor. Second, there are several "prudential" requirements: (1) the injury must be arguably within the statute's zone of interests; (2) the injury must not be that of a third party; (3) the injury must not be broadly generalized. Third, if the plaintiff is an organization, there are three more requirements: (1) the members would have standing; (2) the interests at stake are germane to the organization's purpose; and (3) individual member's participation in the suit is not needed.

If this is a correct statement of black letter law, consider what purpose these rules serve. What is the *meaning* of each? The *point* of each?

Would it be better if the Court focused the standing inquiry on the following question: Does any source of law give the plaintiff a right to bring suit? See International Primate Protection League v. Administrators of Tulane Educ. Fund, 500 U.S. 72, 77 (1994), where the Court said that "standing is gauged by the specific common law, statutory or constitutional claims that a party presents," and noted that standing "should be seen as a question of substantive law, answerable by reference to the statutory and constitutional provision whose protection is invoked." Is the Court heading in that direction? When it forbids Congress from granting standing, does it have a constitutional basis, textual or historical, for doing so?

E. The Timing of Review: Ripeness, Finality, and Exhaustion

We discuss here three closely related doctrines relating to timing. For all of them, the basic concern is that judicial intervention is *premature*. There is considerable confusion in the cases, however, about how to separate the three — ripeness, finality, and exhaustion — and sometimes courts mix them together.

The APA contains no explicit ripeness requirement, nor does it require litigants to exhaust their administrative remedies. It does, however, authorize review only of "final agency action" under §704. When an agency's action is not "final," it is not reviewable under the APA. See, e.g., American Airlines v. Herman, 176 F.3d 283 (5th Cir. 1999), where the court held an agency's action "nonfinal" when the agency had rejected American Airlines' defenses against a claim of unlawful discrimination, but had not yet ruled on whether American had engaged in that discrimination. In that very case, the court also held that the agency's decision was not "ripe" for review and that administrative remedies had not been exhausted.

The requirements of ripeness and exhaustion of administrative remedies might be seen as *part* of the requirement of finality under §704; they are more often seen as independent and longstanding common law principles, always understood to be part of the law of judicial review of agency action. The exhaustion requirement is perhaps the easiest to distinguish and to understand as a wholly separate idea: Here the problem is that the plaintiff is going to court where the agency is entirely available to hear the claim. But when the plaintiff has not exhausted his administrative remedies, there is a good chance that the case is also not ripe, and that the agency action is not final. When administrative remedies have not been exhausted, the case might seem not to be ripe for that very reason.

On the other hand, it is easy to imagine ripeness problems where there is no administrative remedy to exhaust, and where agency action seems entirely final: Imagine that an agency has issued a rule, but has not yet enforced it against anyone. To understand the law, the first step is to see how one might argue that there is a problem in terms of any one of the doctrines.

1. Ripeness

Our emphasis in this section is on ripeness, which may be taken to be a subset of the requirement of "final agency action." But we shall also mention cases that rely solely on the rubric of finality (taken up shortly in its own right), rather than ripeness.

a. Ripeness: The Old Learning

Columbia Broadcasting System v. United States

316 U.S. 407 (1942)

[CBS's radio network comprised 123 stations, 7 of which were owned by CBS and 1 of which was leased by it. The remaining 115 affiliated stations had entered into contracts with CBS, usually for five-year periods, under which the stations agreed to broadcast, on demand from CBS, specified numbers of hours of network programming weekly. Stations affiliated with CBS agreed not to broadcast the programs of any other network.

The FCC is given statutory authority to issue and renew broadcast licenses for individual stations but has no statutory authority to regulate networks as such. In 1941, the commission promulgated "Chain Broadcasting Regulations," which provided for nonrenewal or cancellation of the license of any station having network affiliation contracts that prohibited a local station from carrying programs of another network or required stations to carry network programs except under narrowly specified conditions. Many of the provisions in the existing contracts between CBS and its affiliates were proscribed by the regulations. The commission argued that the regulations were necessary to enhance competition in the broadcast industry.

CBS sought immediate judicial review of the regulations pursuant to §402(a) of the Federal Communications Act and the Urgent Deficiencies Act (since repealed), which authorized three-judge district courts to entertain suits "to enforce, enjoin, set aside, annul, or suspend any order of the Commission."]

Mr. Chief Justice STONE delivered the opinion of the Court.

[CBS] allege[d] that since the stations fear the loss of their licenses, as a result of the regulations, they will not negotiate for or renew affiliation contracts containing such provisions. And because they fear the loss of their licenses, the stations have threatened to cancel and repudiate their affiliation contracts, and many have notified appellant that they will not be bound by their contracts after the regulations become effective. As a consequence, appellant's ability to conduct its business and maintain its public broadcasting service is seriously impaired. . . .

[The day after the suit was filed, the FCC issued a supplemental "Minute" stating that stations, in a renewal proceeding, might contest the validity of the regulations without fear of nonrenewal if they agreed to comply with the regulations in the future if they were held valid. CBS then submitted an affidavit asserting, despite the "Minute," that stations had continued to threaten cancellation or nonrenewal of their contracts; it submitted additional affidavits to that effect by five affiliated stations.

The three-judge district court dismissed the suit for want of jurisdiction. The Supreme Court reversed, holding that the issuance of the regulations constituted a reviewable "order" within the meaning of §402(a) of the Communications Act and the Urgent Deficiencies Act, and that the complaint demonstrated equitable grounds for immediate review. Enforcement of the regulations had been stayed pending the resolution of the litigation.]

The regulations here prescribe rules which govern the contractual relationships between the stations and the networks. If the applicant for a license has entered into an affiliation contract, the regulations require the Commission to reject his application. If a licensee renews his contract, the regulations . . . authorize the Commission to cancel his license. . . . The regulations are not any the less reviewable because their promulgation did not operate of their own force to deny or cancel a license. It is enough that failure to comply with them penalizes licensees, and appellant, with whom they contract. If an administrative order has that effect it is reviewable and it does not cease to be so merely because it is not certain whether the Commission will institute proceedings to enforce the penalty incurred under its regulations for noncompliance. . . .

Most rules of conduct having the force of law are not self-executing but require judicial or administrative action to impose their sanctions with respect to particular individuals. [A] valid exercise of the rule-making power is addressed to and sets a standard of conduct for all to whom its terms apply. It operates as such in advance of the imposition of sanctions upon any particular individual. It is common experience that men conform their conduct to regulations by governmental authority so as to avoid the unpleasant legal consequences which failure to conform entails. And in this case it is alleged without contradiction that numerous affiliated stations have conformed to the regulations to avoid loss of their licenses with consequent injury to appellant.

Such regulations have the force of law before their sanctions are invoked as well as after. When, as here, they are promulgated by order of the Commission and the expected conformity to them causes injury cognizable by a court of equity, they are appropriately the subject of attack under the provisions of §402(a) and the Urgent Deficiencies Act. [Citing cases.] . . .

Of course, the Commission was at liberty to follow a wholly different procedure. Instead of proclaiming general regulations applicable to all licenses, in advance of any specific contest over a license, it might have awaited such a contest to declare that the policy which these regulations embody represents its concept of the public interest. . . . Having adopted this order under its rulemaking power, the Commission cannot insist that the appellant be relegated to that judicial review which would be exclusive if the rule-making power had never been exercised and consequently had never subjected appellant to the threatened irreparable injury.

The Commission argues that, since its Report characterized the regulations as announcements of policy, the order promulgating them is no more subject to review than a press release similarly announcing its policy. Undoubtedly, regulations adopted in the exercise of the administrative rule-making power, like laws enacted by legislatures, embody announcements of policy. But they may be something more. When, as here, the regulations are . . . couched in terms of command and accompanied by an announcement of the Commission that the policy is one "which we will follow in exercising our licensing power," they must be taken by those entitled to rely upon them as what they purport to be — an exercise of the delegated legislative power — which, until amended, are controlling alike upon the Commission and all others whose rights may be affected by the Commission's execution of them. The Commission's contention that the regulations are no more reviewable than a press release is hardly reconcilable with its own recognition that the regulations afford legal basis for cancellation of the license of a station if it renews its contract with appellant. . . .

[T]he allegations of the complaint and . . . the effect of the Commission's order if those allegations are sustained upon the trial, [are] enough to establish the threat of irreparable injury to appellant's business and to show also that the injury can not be avoided, as the Commission suggests, by appellant's intervention in proceedings upon applications for renewal of licenses by its affiliates or in proceedings to cancel their licenses, if and when such proceedings are instituted. . . .

Nor does the Commission's minute, filed after the present suit was brought, afford an adequate basis for requiring appellant to seek relief by intervention in a proceeding on application for a license reviewable under §402(b). . . . Without full exploration of the subject, such as can be had only at the trial, we cannot say that the minute will afford a sufficient inducement to persuade the affiliated stations to cease cancellations and assume the initiative in litigating the validity of the regulations and of the contracts which they undertake to condemn. The affidavit filed in the court below on the application for a stay is to the contrary. . . .

Reversed.

Mr. Justice FRANKFURTER, dissenting: . . .

In promulgating these regulations the Communications Commission merely announced its conception of one aspect of the public interest, namely, the relationship of certain provisions in network-affiliation contracts to the obligation of a station licensee to render the most effective service to the listening public. The regulations themselves determine no rights. They alter the status of neither the networks nor licensees. As such they require nobody — neither the networks, the licensees, nor the Commission — to do anything. They are merely an announcement to the public of what the Commission intends to do in passing upon future applications for station licenses. No action of the stations or the networks can violate the regulations, for there is nothing the regulations require them to do or refrain from doing. . . .

The regulations do not . . . commit the Commission to any definitive course of action in passing upon applications for licenses. Consistent with the regulations . . . the Commission is free to dilute them with amendments and exceptions. The construction of the regulations and their application to particular situations is still in the hands of the Commission. Administrative adjudication is still open. Before its completion it is not ripe for judicial review. . . .

This leaves only the suggestion that since the action taken by the Commission, although not the completion of its adjudicatory process, nevertheless drastically affects substantial business interests, it is proper for the courts to intercede at this stage. . . . As a practical matter, the impact upon the business operations of the network and their affiliated stations would probably be as disturbing as if the policies formulated in the regulations had been expressed through a press release. . . . But assume that the greater formality given to the announcement of the Commission's statement of policy through the regulations intensified the practical business consequences. Congress has not conferred upon the district courts jurisdiction over "practical business consequences." They can review action of administrative agencies only when there is an "order," and when Congress in §402(a) made only an "order" of the Communications Commission reviewable, it incorporated the settled doctrine established by an unbroken series of decisions in this Court that the courts could review only a final determination by an agency whereby its administrative process has been concluded. . . .

. . . While formally we may appear to be dealing with technicalities, behind these considerations lie deep issues of policy in the division of authority as between administrative agencies and courts in carrying out the constitutional will of Congress. . . .

. . . If threatened damage through general pronouncement of policy for future administrative action, even if cast in the formal language of a regulation, is to give rise to equitable review, . . . the same basis of irreparable harm which is here equated to jurisdiction will bear rich litigious fruit in the case of "regulations" issued by the Securities and Exchange Commission which are damaging in their immediate repercussions to stock exchange and holding companies, or regulations announced by the Treasury for the guidance of taxpayers but which adversely affect business interests, or regulations by the Federal Power Commission, etc. . . .

Hardship there may well come through action of an administrative agency. But to slide from recognition of a hardship to assertion of jurisdiction is once more to assume that only the courts are the guardians of the rights and liberties of the people. . . .

Mr. Justice REED and Mr. Justice DOUGLAS join in this dissent.

Notes and Questions

1. Justice Frankfurter rested his dissent on Justice Brandeis's classic exposition of the "finality" doctrine in United States v. Los Angeles & Salt Lake R.R., 273 U.S. 299, 308-310 (1927). The Court there held that the ICC's "final" evaluation of a railroad's property, which would be used for ratemaking and other regulatory purposes, was not a final "order" subject to review either under the Urgent Deficiencies Act or general federal jurisdictional statutes. Justice Brandeis wrote, for the Court:

> The so-called order here complained of is one which does not command the carrier to do, or to refrain from doing anything; which does not grant or withhold any authority, privilege or license; which does not extend or abridge any power or facility; which does not subject the carrier to any liability, civil or criminal; which does not change the carrier's existing or future status or condition; which does not determine any right or obligation. This so-called order is merely the formal record of conclusions reached after a study of data collected in the course of research conducted by the Commission, through its employees.

Are *Los Angeles Railroad* and *CBS* consistent?

2. What is the basis for CBS's standing to bring suit?

3. In United States v. Storer Broadcasting Co., 351 U.S. 192 (1956), the Court allowed Storer to obtain review of an FCC regulation limiting to five the number of stations one person might own. The majority, citing *CBS*, reasoned that the regulations "now operate to control the business affairs" of Storer, because Storer, which owned five stations already, was planning to ask for FCC approval to acquire a sixth station. The regulations also exposed Storer to the risk of a license forfeiture if its stocks were bought up by a person controlling another station. It was accordingly a reviewable "order" under §402(a) of the Communications Act.[31]

Frozen Foods Express v. United States, 351 U.S. 40 (1956), held to be a reviewable order a 71-page ICC report setting forth the commission's very narrow interpretations of a statutory provision exempting the carriage of "agricultural commodities (not including manufactured products thereof)" from the general requirements of ICC licensure for interstate transport. The application of the exemption with respect to dozens of partially processed commodities (for example, frozen chickens) had long been disputed. Reviewability was found on the ground that carriers who disagreed with the commission's

---

31. Note that *CBS*, which arose after enactment of the APA, held that the FCC's issuance of regulations was an "order" reviewable under the provisions of the Urgent Deficiencies Act and the Communications Act providing for review of an ICC "order." Under the APA, the regulations, issued through rulemaking, would not be an "order" because under the definitional provisions in Sec. 501 of the APA, that term is limited to the final disposition of a matter other than rulemaking — i.e., adjudication. This reflects the familiar circumstance that words must be construed in relation to their legal context and governing interpretive methods and purposes.

narrow construction of the exemption were subject to cease-and-desist orders and possible criminal penalties if they continued to carry, without an ICC permit, products that the commission had ruled not exempt. Justice Harlan, dissenting, pointed out that the ICC had stated that it would not regard its report as binding in the decision of particular cases.

Is either *Storer* or *Frozen Foods* compelled by *CBS*?[32]

b. Modern Ripeness Doctrine: *Abbott Laboratories* and Beyond

In addition to insisting on finality, courts applying the ripeness requirement have considered whether the agency's resolution of the relevant legal issues is sufficiently focused and concrete to make judicial review appropriate. Further, some courts have also considered whether denial of review would subject the party seeking review to "hardship." In reviewing the materials that follow, consider the role of these various elements of ripeness, and the extent to which the ripeness requirement is judge-made administrative law, a principle of interpretation of the APA and other statutes, or an article III constitutional requirement.

Abbott Laboratories v. Gardner
387 U.S. 136 (1967)

[As part of the 1962 amendments to the Food, Drug and Cosmetic Act, Congress, in §502(e)(1)(B) of the act, required prescription drug manufacturers to print on labels, advertising, and other printed materials the "established name" of a drug "prominently and in type at least half as large as that used thereon for the proprietary name or designation for such drug" every time the proprietary name appeared. The "proprietary" name was the trademarked or brand name established by a particular manufacturer of a given drug, while the "established" name was a generic name (designated by the FDA) for all drugs of the same chemical composition, regardless of the various brand names under which they were sold. The purpose of this requirement was to encourage price competition among manufacturers in marketing chemically identical generic drugs by alerting physicians, patients, and pharmacists to the identity, and by discouraging manufacturers from advertising to promote a brand name for a drug.

Pursuant to statutory authority to issue regulations for the "efficient enforcement" of the act, the commissioner of the FDA, following APA rulemaking procedures of notice and opportunity for comment, issued regulations requiring the established name of a drug to "accompany each appearance" of the drug's proprietary name in all labels, enclosures, advertising, and promotional literature for the drug.

The Pharmaceutical Manufacturers' Association and 37 of its members promptly brought an injunction action in district court, invoking general federal jurisdictional statutes and asserting that the regulation's requirement that the established name of the

---

32. For a more restrictive approach to preenforcement review, see International Longshoremen's & Warehousemen's Union v. Boyd, 347 U.S. 222 (1954), declining to entertain a challenge by a union and several of its members who traveled to Alaska every summer for employment to an announced policy of the Seattle District Director of Immigration and Naturalization to treat aliens returning from Alaskan summer employment as if they were aliens entering the United States for the first time. Justice Frankfurter, for the Court, warned that a legal ruling "in advance of . . . immediate adverse effect in the context of a concrete case involves too remote and abstract an inquiry for the proper exercise of the judicial function." 347 U.S. at 224.

drug accompany the proprietary name every time the latter is used exceeded the authority granted to the FDA by the 1962 amendments.

The district court ruled for plaintiffs on the merits. On appeal, the Third Circuit Court of Appeals reversed on jurisdictional grounds, holding that the act precluded court review of the regulations prior to their enforcement, and that no justiciable "case or controversy" was presented.]

Mr. Justice HARLAN delivered the opinion of the Court: . . .

The first question we consider is whether Congress by the Federal Food, Drug and Cosmetic Act intended to forbid pre-enforcement review of this sort of regulation promulgated by the Commissioner. The question is phrased in terms of "prohibition" rather than "authorization" because a survey of our cases shows that judicial review of a final agency action by an aggrieved person will not be cut off unless there is persuasive reason to believe that such was the purpose of Congress. . . . The Administrative Procedure Act provides specifically not only for review of "[a]gency action made reviewable by statute" but also for review of "final agency action for which there is no other adequate remedy in a court," 5 U.S.C. §704. The legislative material elucidating that seminal act manifests a congressional intention that it cover a broad spectrum of administrative actions.[33] [O]nly upon a showing of "clear and convincing evidence" of a contrary legislative intent should the courts restrict access to judicial review. See also Jaffe, Judicial Control of Administrative Action 336-359 (1965).

Given this standard, we are wholly unpersuaded that the statutory scheme in the food and drug area excludes this type of action. The Government relies on no explicit statutory authority for its argument that pre-enforcement review is unavailable, but insists instead that because the statute includes a specific procedure for such review of certain enumerated kinds of regulations,[34] not encompassing those of the kind involved here, other types were necessarily meant to be excluded from any pre-enforcement review. The issue, however, is not so readily resolved; we must go further and inquire whether in the context of the entire legislative scheme the existence of that circumscribed remedy evinces a congressional purpose to bar agency action not within its purview from judicial review. As a leading authority in this field has noted, "The mere fact that some acts are made reviewable should not suffice to support an implication of exclusion as to others. The right to review is too important to be excluded on such slender and indeterminate evidence of legislative intent." Jaffe, supra, at 357.

[The Court then reviewed in detail the structure and legislative history of the act.]

We conclude that nothing in the Food, Drug and Cosmetic Act itself precludes this action. . . .

A further inquiry must, however, be made. The injunctive and declaratory judgment remedies are discretionary, and courts traditionally have been reluctant to apply them to administrative determinations unless these arise in the context of a controversy "ripe" for judicial resolution. Without undertaking to survey the intricacies of the ripeness doctrine it is fair to say that its basic rationale is to prevent the courts, through avoidance of premature

---

33. See H.R. Rep. No. 1980, 79th Cong., 2d Sess. 41 (1946): "To preclude judicial review under this bill a statute, if not specific in withholding such review, must upon its face give clear and convincing evidence of an intent to withhold it. The mere failure to provide specially by statute for judicial review is certainly no evidence of intent to withhold review." See also S. Rep. No. 752, 79th Cong., 1st Sess. 26 (1945).

34. Section 701(e) [of the Food, Drug and Cosmetic Act] provides a procedure for the issuance of regulations under certain specifically enumerated statutory sections. Section 701(f) establishes a procedure for direct review by a court of appeals of a regulation promulgated under §701(e).

adjudication, from entangling themselves in abstract disagreements over administrative policies, and also to protect the agencies from judicial interference until an administrative decision has been formalized and its effects felt in a concrete way by the challenging parties. The problem is best seen in a twofold aspect requiring us to evaluate both the fitness of the issues for judicial decisions and the hardship to the parties of withholding court consideration.

As to the former factor, we believe the issues presented are appropriate for judicial resolution at this time. First, all parties agree that the issue tendered is a purely legal one: whether the statute was properly construed by the Commissioner to require the established name of the drug to be used every time the proprietary name is employed. Both sides moved for summary judgment in the District Court, and no claim is made here that further administrative proceedings are contemplated. It is suggested that the justification for this rule might vary with different circumstances, and that the expertise of the Commissioner is relevant to passing upon the validity of the regulation. This of course is true, but the suggestion overlooks the fact that both sides have approached this case as one purely of congressional intent, and that the Government made no effort to justify the regulation in factual terms.

Second, the regulations in issue we find to be "final agency action" within the meaning of §10 of the Administrative Procedure Act, 5 U.S.C. §704, as construed in judicial decisions. An "agency action" includes any "rule," defined by the Act as "an agency statement of general or particular applicability and future effect designed to implement, interpret, or prescribe law or policy," §§2(c), 2(g), 5 U.S.C. §§551(4), 551(13). The cases dealing with judicial review of administrative actions have interpreted the "finality" element in a pragmatic way.

[The Court cited *CBS, Frozen Foods Express,* and *Storer Broadcasting.*]

The Government argues, however, that the present case can be distinguished from cases like *Frozen Foods Express* on the ground that in those instances the agency involved could implement its policy directly, while here the Attorney General must authorize criminal and seizure actions for violations of the statute. In the context of this case, we do not find this argument persuasive. These regulations are not meant to advise the Attorney General, but purport to be directly authorized by the statute. Thus, if within the Commissioner's authority, they have the status of law and violations of them carry heavy criminal and civil sanctions. Also, there is no representation that the Attorney General and the Commissioner disagree in this area; the Justice Department is defending this very suit. It would be adherence to a mere technicality to give any credence to this contention.

This is also a case in which the impact of the regulations upon the petitioners is sufficiently direct and immediate as to render the issue appropriate for judicial review at this stage. These regulations purport to give an authoritative interpretation of a statutory provision that has a direct effect on the day-to-day business of all prescription drug companies; its promulgation puts petitioners in a dilemma that it was the very purpose of the Declaratory Judgment Act to ameliorate. As the District Court found on the basis of uncontested allegations, "Either they must comply with the every time requirement and incur the costs of changing over their promotional material and labeling or they must follow their present course and risk prosecution." 228 F. Supp. 855, 861. The regulations are clear-cut, and were made effective immediately upon publication; as noted earlier the agency's counsel represented to the District Court that immediate compliance with their terms was expected. If petitioners wish to comply they must change all their labels, advertisements, and promotional materials; they must destroy stocks of printed matter;

and they must invest heavily in new printing type and new supplies. The alternative to compliance — continued use of material which they believe in good faith meets the statutory requirements, but which clearly does not meet the regulation of the Commissioner — may be even more costly. That course would risk serious criminal and civil penalties for the unlawful distribution of "misbranded" drugs.

It is relevant at this juncture to recognize that petitioners deal in a sensitive industry, in which public confidence in their drug products is especially important. To require them to challenge these regulations only as a defense to an action brought by the Government might harm them severely and unnecessarily. Where the legal issue presented is fit for judicial resolution, and where a regulation requires an immediate and significant change in the plaintiffs' conduct of their affairs with serious penalties attached to noncompliance, access to the courts under the Administrative Procedure Act and the Declaratory Judgment Act must be permitted, absent a statutory bar or some other unusual circumstance, neither of which appears here. . . .

Finally, the Government urges that to permit resort to the courts in this type of case may delay or impede effective enforcement of the Act. We fully recognize the important public interest served by assuring prompt and unimpeded administration of the Pure Food, Drug and Cosmetic Act, but we do not find the Government's argument convincing. First, in this particular case, a pre-enforcement challenge by nearly all prescription drug manufacturers is calculated to speed enforcement. If the Government prevails, a large part of the industry is bound by the decree; if the Government loses, it can more quickly revise its regulation.

The Government contends, however, that if the Court allows this consolidated suit, then nothing will prevent a multiplicity of suits in various jurisdictions challenging other regulations. The short answer to this contention is that the courts are well equipped to deal with such eventualities. . . .

[The opinion noted the power of federal courts to transfer venue in order to consolidate related litigation, or to enjoin multiple or harassing lawsuits.]

In addition to all these safeguards against what the Government fears, it is important to note that the institution of this type of action does not by itself stay the effectiveness of the challenged regulation. There is nothing in the record to indicate that petitioners have sought to stay enforcement of the "every time" regulation pending judicial review. See 5 U.S.C. §705. If the agency believes that a suit of this type will significantly impede enforcement or will harm the public interest, it need not postpone enforcement of the regulation and may oppose any motion for a judicial stay on the part of those challenging the regulation. Ibid. It is scarcely to be doubted that a court would refuse to postpone the effective date of an agency action if the Government could show, as it made no effort to do here, that delay would be detrimental to the public health or safety. . . .

Reversed and remanded.

Decided the same day as *Abbott Laboratories* were Toilet Goods Assn. v. Gardner, 387 U.S. 158 (1967), and Gardner v. Toilet Goods Assn., 387 U.S. 167 (1967), both of which arose out of a preenforcement district court action by a cosmetic manufacturers' trade association and its members, seeking declaratory and injunctive relief against various regulations issued by FDA under the 1960 Color Additives Amendments to the Food, Drug and Cosmetic Act, expanding FDA's authority to regulate color additives. The district court held that the regulations were subject to preenforcement review.

The Second Circuit reversed the district court's jurisdictional ruling with respect to one regulation (the access regulation) that provided that if a manufacturer refused to permit duly authorized FDA employees "free access" to all "manufacturing facilities, processes, and formulae" involved in the manufacture of color additives, the FDA would suspend batch certification service of additives (a prerequisite to their subsequent marketing) until access was permitted.

In Toilet Goods Assn. v. Gardner, the Supreme Court, in an opinion by Justice Harlan, agreed with the court of appeals that the validity of this regulation was not ripe for review. The regulation, it conceded, represented the FDA's "considered and formalized determination" and also presented a pure issue of law under the statute, which specifically grants FDA inspection authority for prescription drugs but does not grant such authority for color additives. The Court (over the dissent of Justice Douglas) nonetheless concluded that the issues were not ripe for review:

> The regulation serves notice only that the Commissioner *may* under certain circumstances order inspection of certain facilities and data, and that further certification of additives *may* be refused to those who decline to permit a duly authorized inspection until they have complied in that regard. At this juncture we have no idea whether or when such an inspection will be ordered and what reasons the Commissioner will give to justify his order. [The issue of the regulations' validity] will depend not merely on an inquiry into statutory purpose, but concurrently on an understanding of what types of enforcement problems are encountered by the FDA, the need for various sorts of supervision in order to effectuate the goals of the Act, and the safeguards devised to protect legitimate trade secrets (see 21 CFR §130.14(c)). We believe that judicial appraisal of these factors is likely to stand on a much surer footing in the context of a specific application of this regulation than could be the case in the framework of the generalized challenge made here. . . .
>   . . . Moreover, no irremediable adverse consequences flow from requiring a later challenge to this regulation by a manufacturer who refuses to allow this type of inspection. Unlike the other regulations challenged in this action, in which seizure of goods, heavy fines, adverse publicity for distributing "adulterated" goods, and possible criminal liability might penalize failure to comply, . . . a refusal to admit an inspector here would at most lead only to a suspension of certification services to the particular party, a determination that can then be promptly challenged through an administrative procedure, which in turn is reviewable by a court. Such review will provide an adequate forum for testing the regulation in a concrete situation.

The companion case, Gardner v. Toilet Goods Assn., reviewed the Second Circuit's affirmance of the district court's ruling in favor of preenforcement review of a number of other FDA color additive regulations (the definitional regulations), amplifying the statutory definition of color additives to include diluents, including certain cosmetics, within the scope of color additives, and narrowly construing the statutory exemption for hair dyes. The Supreme Court affirmed this aspect of the court of appeals' ruling, concluding that the regulations' reviewability was established by *Abbott Laboratories*.

The effect of the regulations in question was to expand the FDA's preexisting definition of color additives. Under the act, manufacture and distribution of color additives is prohibited and subject to criminal sanctions unless the color additive is approved by FDA as safe, and particular batches of the additive have been certified by FDA. The Court reasoned that the regulations represented the FDA's considered view; that their validity involved a pure question of statutory construction that could be resolved now; and that issuance of the regulations placed the manufacturers in the dilemma of acquiescing in the regulations and complying, at substantial expense, with FDA clearance procedures, or defying the regulations at the risk of incurring serious sanctions.

Justice Fortas, joined by Chief Justice Warren and Justice Clark, issued an opinion dissenting in Gardner v. Toilet Goods Assn. (the definitional regulations) and *Abbott Laboratories*:

> With all respect, I submit that established principles of jurisprudence, solidly rooted in the constitutional structure of our Government, require that the courts should not intervene in the administrative process at this stage, under these facts and in this gross, shotgun fashion. . . .
>
> The Court, by today's decisions, . . . has opened Pandora's box. Federal injunctions will now threaten programs of vast importance to the public welfare. The Court's holding here strikes at programs for the public health. The dangerous precedent goes even further. It is cold comfort — it is little more than delusion — to read in the Court's opinion that "It is scarcely to be doubted that a court would refuse to postpone the effective date of an agency action if the Government could show . . . that delay would be detrimental to the public health or safety." Experience dictates, on the contrary, that it can hardly be hoped that some federal judge somewhere will not be moved as the Court is here, by the cries of anguish and distress of those regulated, to grant a disruptive injunction. . . .
>
> In evaluating the destructive force and effect of the Court's action in these cases, it is necessary to realize that it is arming each of the federal district judges in this Nation with power to enjoin enforcement of regulations and actions under the federal law designed to protect the people of this Nation against dangerous drugs and cosmetics. Restraining orders and temporary injunctions will suspend application of these public safety laws pending years of litigation — a time schedule which these cases illustrate.[35] They are disruptive enough, regardless of the ultimate outcome. The Court's validation of this shotgun attack upon this vital law and its administration is not confined to these suits, these regulations, or these plaintiffs — or even this statute. It is a general hunting license; and I respectfully submit, a license for mischief because it authorizes aggression which is richly rewarded by delay in the subjection of private interests to programs which Congress believes to be required in the public interest. . . .
>
> Actually, if the Court refused to permit this shotgun assault, experience and reasonably sophisticated common sense show that there would be orderly compliance without the disaster so dramatically predicted by the industry, reasonable adjustments by the agency in real hardship cases, and where extreme intransigence involving substantial violations occurred, enforcement actions in which legality of the regulation would be tested in specific, concrete situations. . . .

Questions

1. Was Justice Harlan correct in arguing that *Abbott Laboratories* follows a fortiori from *CBS* and *Storer*? From *Frozen Food Express*? Are the Court's rulings in *Abbott Laboratories* and Gardner v. Toilet Goods Assn. (definitional regulations) consistent with its rationale in Toilet Goods Assn. v. Gardner (access regulations)?

2. Justice Fortas is evidently concerned about the substantive impact of the Court's procedural ruling. What is that impact likely to be? Isn't Justice Fortas arguing, in effect,

---

35. The "every time" regulation was published about four years ago, on June 20, 1963, 28 Fed. Reg. 6375. As a result of litigation begun in September of 1963, it has not yet been put into force. The "definition" regulations and the "access" regulation with respect to color additives were published on June 22, 1963, 28 Fed. Reg. 6439, 6446. Litigation was begun in November of 1963, and the regulations are not yet operative.

that it is proper and legitimate to permit agencies to threaten regulated firms with enforcement of illegal regulations in order to coerce settlements more favorable to the agency?

3. Before *Abbott Laboratories*, the courts typically reviewed the lawfulness of an agency's rule, not when the agency promulgated the rule, but when the agency enforced the rule. Why? After *Abbott Laboratories*, reviewing practice changed. Now, courts often find that an agency's rule is "ripe" for review when it is promulgated, and review of its lawfulness takes place at that time. (You have seen examples of such review, for example, in Chapter 6.) See, for example, American Forest and Paper Assn. v. EPA, 137 F.3d 291 (5th Cir. 1998), which involved a challenge to a rule requiring a state, before issuing a permit under the Clean Air Act, to consult with federal agencies with respect to potential harmful effects on endangered species. The court said that the issue involved was purely one of law and that deferring review would impose an "immediate significant burden on the petitioner," through "delays in the permitting process and the added risk that an application will be denied." In the same vein, see Minnesota Citizens Concerned for Life v. Federal Election Commission, 113 F.2d 129 (8th Cir. 1997), allowing preenforcement review of a narrow interpretation of the "qualified nonprofit corporations" allowed to make exempt "independent expenditures" during political campaigns. For other relevant cases, see Chamber of Commerce v. Federal Election Commission, 69 F.3d 600 (D.C. Cir. 1995) (also allowing preenforcement review of FEC rule); Nationwide Mutual Insurance Co. v. Cisneros, 52 F.3d 1351 (6th Cir. 1995); Allsteel v. EPA, 25 F.3d 312 (6th Cir. 1994); Southern Ohio Coal v. Office of Surface Mining, 20 F.3d 1418 (6th Cir. 1994). Note, however, that there appears to be a more recent trend in favor of questioning preenforcement review, as discussed below.

Query: Should the same presumption of reviewability applicable to legislative rules, like those in *Abbott Laboratories*, also apply to interpretive and procedural rules?

The shift toward greater preenforcement review reflects changes in the judge-made law of reviewability, as in *Abbott Laboratories*. It also reflects statutory changes. Congress during the past several decades has enacted many statutes authorizing, and in many cases requiring, agencies to use rulemaking to implement statutory programs that provide specifically for judicial review of rules on promulgation.

Is this shift to preenforcement review, especially of regulations, desirable as a public policy matter? Consider the arguments of Justice Harlan in favor of such review; those arguments have received increasing attention in recent years. Jerry Mashaw and David Harfst, reviewing the experience of the National Highway Transportation Safety Administration's (NHTSA) regulatory experience with respect to regulating auto and highway safety, conclude that preenforcement review has tended to overburden rulemaking by "frontloading" an adversary overlay to the development of agency policy and introducing undue delay, impeding timely and effective highway safety regulation. They find that, as a result, NHTSA has shifted regulatory measures to case-by-case adjudicatory measures (such as recalls of auto models for safety defects) that overall may be less desirable than regulation. Echoing Justice Harlan, they concede that there are good arguments for preenforcement review of regulations:

> Costs of compliance with invalid rules are saved, uncertainty about the legality of regulation is more quickly removed, all affected parties receive similar treatment and regulators are held strictly accountable because they cannot suppress legal contests through enforcement compromises.

J. Mashaw & D. Harfst, The Struggle for Auto Safety 246-247 (1990).

On the other hand, they believe that giving manufacturers the freedom to escape the "dilemma" of complying with regulations claimed to be unlawful or defying them and facing enforcement sanctions tends to promote manufacturer incentives for noncompliance; precludes or postpones the development of practical experience with implementing regulatory requirements that can generate information to test their feasibility and appropriateness and instead leads to abstract court litigation over requirements that have never been implemented; and cuts off the possibility of ongoing negotiation and compromise between the regulatory agency and those regulated in light of practical experience with implementation. Compare the views expressed by Justice Fortas in *Abbott Laboratories.*

To what extent can one generalize from the NHTSA experience? Consider that NHTSA regulation of auto safety is directed at a very small number of manufacturers. What if preenforcement review of EPA regulations, some of which affect tens or hundreds of thousands of regulated entities, were eliminated? How would such a change affect the position of environmental groups, which now regularly challenge EPA regulations as inadequate? Should preenforcement review of regulations be eliminated?

Richard J. Pierce, Jr., Seven Ways to Deossify Agency Rulemaking, 47 Admin. L. Rev. 59 (1995), finds that preenforcement review has contributed to "ossification" of the rulemaking process by promoting "hard look" judicial review of regulations and giving agencies and interested industry and other interests incentives to load the rulemaking record with massive analysis and data about the cost, feasibility, and appropriateness of a rule whose validity is contested and resolved before it is ever applied. On balance, are these problems outweighed by the advantages of a regulatory regime built on widespread use of rulemaking that is subject to prompt review by all of the many parties that participated in the rulemaking process? If judicial review were postponed to the implementation and enforcement stage, how would that affect the incentives of different interests to participate in the rulemaking process? How would it affect democratic dialogue and accountability? The rule of law? Are there better ways of addressing the problems identified by Mashaw and Harfst than eliminating preenforcement review of regulations?

c. The Relationship between Preenforcement and Postenforcement Judicial Review

Some statutes simply authorize review of a promulgated rule prior to the time it is enforced. See, e.g., Occupational Safety and Health Act, §6(f), 29 U.S.C. §655(f) (1975). Other statutes go further, not only authorizing preenforcement review, but also forbidding review of the lawfulness of the rule when the rule later is enforced. The Clean Water and Clean Air Acts, for example, state that persons seeking review of the lawfulness of rules promulgated under those acts must do so within 60 or 90 days of the promulgation of the rules. These acts go on to say that rules in respect to which preenforcement review "could have been" obtained "shall not be subject to judicial review in civil or criminal proceedings for enforcement."

Some courts have interpreted the first kind of statute as simply providing an additional permissive method for review. These courts have not considered whether or the extent to which the opportunity for review before enforcement precludes review after enforcement. Other courts have found in the statute's authorization for preenforcement review a limitation on the kinds of review that a litigant may seek at the enforcement stage. Compare, for example, Commonwealth Edison Co. v. Nuclear Regulatory Commn., 830 F.2d 610 (7th Cir. 1987) (finding no intent in the statute permitting preenforcement review to cut off later, enforcement-stage, review), with RSR Corp. v. Donovan, 747 F.2d 294 (5th Cir. 1984) (finding just such an intent but in a different statute). In the following case, the District of Columbia Circuit summarizes its standards for providing "enforcement-stage" review of a rule that might have been reviewed at the "pre-enforcement" stage.

NLRB Union v. FLRA
834 F.2d 191 (D.C. Cir. 1987)

A final order of the FLRA [Federal Labor Relations Authority] must be appealed within sixty days. 5 U.S.C. §7123(a). The FLRA's promulgation of final rules or regulations constitutes a final order marking the commencement of the sixty-day limitation period. The regulations the Union seeks to amend were issued in final form on January 17, 1980. The FLRA argues that, while it was obliged to respond to the Union's petition to amend the rules, see 5 U.S.C. §§553e(e), 7134 (1987), its [negative] response is not an appealable final order under 5 U.S.C. §7123(a). Because the Union's appeal appears to be an attack on regulations adopted almost seven years before that appeal was filed, the FLRA submits that judicial review should be barred by the sixty-day statute of limitations.

The FLRA's contention ignores the settled law of this circuit. In a long line of cases stretching back to Functional Music Inc. v. FCC, 274 F.2d 543 (D.C. Cir. 1958), *cert. denied*, 361 U.S. 813 (1959), this court has repeatedly distinguished indirect attacks on the substantive validity of regulations initiated more than sixty days after their promulgation from like attacks on their procedural lineage. It has also noted that the scope of appellate review varies with the nature of the substantive attack. To avoid further confusion on this score, we offer a brief summary of prior holdings.

An agency's regulations may be attacked in two ways once the statutory limitations period has expired. First, a party who possesses standing may challenge regulations directly on the ground that the issuing agency acted in excess of its statutory authority in promulgating them. A challenge of this sort might be raised, for example, by way of defense in an enforcement proceeding.[36] Thus, suppose that the FLRA adopted a regulation prohibiting unions from representing women; suppose further, that the regulation went unchallenged during the statutory limitations period; finally, suppose that the General Counsel filed [unfair labor practice] charges against a union for failure to execute a negotiated collective bargaining agreement because the employer refused to extend coverage of the agreement to female employees. Under such circumstances, the union could clearly challenge the validity of the regulation on which the employer and the FLRA were relying, even if that regulation went uncontested throughout the applicable statutory limitations period. . . .

The second method of obtaining judicial review of agency regulations once the limitations period has run is to petition the agency for amendment or rescission of the regulations and then to appeal the agency's decision. We have distinguished three types of challenges on appeal.

---

36. See, e.g., Geller v. FCC, 610 F.2d 973, 978 (D.C. Cir. 1979) ("Had the Commission applied one or more of the 1972 regulations [which were not attacked during the statutory limitations period] to the detriment of some individual, he would clearly have been in a position to complain of the order doing so.") . . .

(a) A petitioner's contention that a regulation suffers from some *procedural* infirmity, such as an agency's unjustified refusal to allow affected parties to comment on a rule before issuing it in final form, will not be heard outside of the statutory limitations period. . . . Countenancing such challenges . . . would on balance waste administrative resources and unjustifiably impair the reliance interests of those who conformed their conduct to the contested regulation. . . .

(b) A petitioner's claim that a regulation suffers from some *substantive* deficiency *other than the agency's lack of statutory authority* to issue that regulation may be brought by petitioning the agency for amendment or rescission and then appealing the denial of that petition. . . . An appellate court's review in cases of this kind, however, is limited to the *"narrow issues as defined by the denial of the petition for rulemaking,"* and does not extend to a challenge of the agency's original action in promulgating the disputed rule. . . . Furthermore, review of an agency's decision not to promulgate a rule proposed by the petitioner is extremely limited. . . .

(c) Finally, a petitioner's contention that a regulation should be amended or rescinded because it *conflicts with the statute* from which its authority derives is reviewable outside of a statutory limitations period. . . .

Notes

1. *NLRB Union* is distinguished in Cronin v. FAA, 73 F.3d 1126 (D.C. Cir. 1996), in which pilots and their union challenged FAA regulations establishing procedures for testing and punishing employees for use of alcohol. The court ruled that the procedural due process challenge was not ripe for review, relying on *Abbott Labs*. (Can you see how the two-part inquiry into ripeness might not permit this challenge?) But in a footnote, the court added that the action might also be barred by the requirement that a challenge be filed within sixty days, which the petitioners failed to do. The court said, "We doubt that ALPA can escape the 60-day filing deadline that began running on February 15, as it seeks to do, merely by relying on NLRB Union v. FLRA. In that case, we observed that, in some circumstances, a viable 'method of obtaining judicial review of agency regulations once the limitations period has run is to petition the agency for amendment or rescission of the regulations and then to appeal the agency's decision.' However, it is far from clear that, in the present situation, ALPA's petition to modify the alcohol testing regulations brings this case within the reasoning of *NLRB Union*. For example, although this court permitted the NLRB Union to appeal the FLRA's response to the union's untimely petition for amendment, the opinion in *NLRB Union* took pains to note that such an appeal was 'the only remaining path to judicial consideration of the substantive validity of the FLRA's regulations.' (emphasis added). The same situation does not exist here, for . . . affected employees may challenge the legality of the regulations in an enforcement action."

2. Suppose the statute in question, unlike the FLRA statute, specifically says that "enforcement-stage" review is *not* available. The Clean Air Act, for example, says that such review is not available where preenforcement review "could have been" obtained. Of course, such a statute, in "precluding" review, will be open to the same kinds of restrictive interpretations (thereby permitting review) that we have seen, for example, in Johnson v. Robison, supra. In particular, the words *could have been* are subject to interpretation. At the least, a rule could not have been subject to review at the earlier preenforcement stage when the legal issue was not yet "ripe" for review. This fact apparently means that courts will sometimes have to conduct a "retrospective ripeness" analysis,

asking whether the issue was "ripe" earlier, with a positive answer now leading, not to judicial review, but, ironically, to the preclusion of judicial review, for, if the matter was "ripe" earlier, it cannot be reviewed now (perhaps at the request of a litigant who was not earlier aware of the rule's existence and therefore did not challenge it; now the agency has decided to enforce the rule against him, at which point he has become very much aware of it). See Diamond Shamrock Corp. v. Costle, 580 F.2d 670 (D.C. Cir. 1978). In Eagle-Picher Indus. v. EPA, 759 F.2d 950 (D.C. Cir. 1985), the court said that it had "entertained untimely claims only in a limited number of exceptional circumstances where the petitioner lacked a meaningful opportunity to challenge the agency action during the review period due to, for example, inadequate notice that the petitioner would be affected by the action, confusion in the law as to the proper forum for review, and lack of ripeness during the review period. Proferred excuses for late filing are carefully scrutinized. . . ."

3. In Northwest Tissue Center v. Shalala, 1 F.3d 522 (7th Cir. 1993), the plaintiffs brought an action challenging FDA regulations governing replacement heart valves. FDA had issued a regulation in 1980 classifying replacement heart valves as Class III devices, subject to significant marketing restrictions. In 1987, FDA promulgated a second regulation subjecting replacement heart valves to premarket approval. In 1991, FDA issued a Notice of Applicability of a Final Rule ("NAFR"), which informed manufacturers that allografts, which are human heart valves recovered from deceased human donors that are preserved and stored for transplantation, were subject to the 1980 and 1987 regulations. Allografts had been distributed commercially for years with no indication from FDA that they were subject to the replacement heart valve regulations.

The plaintiffs claimed, among other things, that FDA wrongfully denied the plaintiffs the right to comment on the 1980 and 1987 regulations in violation of the APA and the Food, Drug, and Cosmetic Act, because nothing in the regulations or administrative record provided notice that the regulations would apply to allografts. They argued that judicial review of their claim was not foreclosed by the statutory 30-day limitations period for review of final FDA regulations requiring premarket approval of medical devices because there was no indication when FDA promulgated the regulations that allografts were to be deemed "replacement heart valves."

The court held that the plaintiffs could be forgiven for failing to file a timely challenge to the 1980 and 1987 regulations if they had not received adequate notice of the potential application of the regulations to their products. The court remanded the case to the district court for an examination of whether the agency had provided adequate notice of its intention to regulate allografts under the replacement valve regulations.

4. Suppose the company against which the EPA has enforced its rule was not in business at the time the rule was promulgated. Can it challenge the rule's procedural, or its substantive, legality? Suppose other firms raised challenges at the time? Suppose no other firm was in quite the same position as the present challenger?

d. Statutory Preclusion of Preenforcement Review

As we have seen, *Abbott Laboratories* created a strong presumption in favor of the availability of preenforcement review under general federal jurisdictional statutes and the APA; such review is presumed to be available even though Congress did not provide for it in the specific statute governing the agency's action but instead provided only for postenforcement review. As we have also seen, Congress has in recent years often provided for preenforcement review in the relevant statute, and in some cases made preenforcement review exclusive, cutting off possible postenforcement review. But the converse is also possible; Congress may preclude preenforcement review and make postenforcement review exclusive. It may do so explicitly. And, despite the prescription established in *Abbott Laboratories*, courts have sometimes found implied preclusion.

The Comprehensive Environmental Response, Compensation and Liability Act (CERCLA, popularly known as Superfund), authorizes EPA to (a) issue administrative orders requiring responsible parties to clean up toxic wastes, and (b) initiate enforcement actions in federal district court to require such a party to comply with the order and to collect substantial civil penalties (up to $5,000 per day) for disregarding it. EPA can also recover three times the amount of income that EPA expended for cleanup as a result of noncompliance with the order unless the party establishes that its failure to comply was "substantially justified." Wagner Seed Co.'s warehouse was struck by lightning; the resulting fire and efforts to douse it resulted in widespread contamination of the surrounding soil by chemicals stored in the warehouse. EPA issued an administrative order requiring Wagner to clean up the contamination. Invoking 28 U.S.C. §1331 and the APA, Wagner sought judicial review of the order, claiming that it exceeds EPA's authority because Wagner is entitled to a statutory defense to liability for releases of chemicals caused by an "act of God." *Held:* The review sought by Wagner is impliedly precluded by the Superfund statute, which provides only for jurisdiction over enforcement actions initiated by EPA, Wagner must wait to present any defenses to liability until such time as an enforcement action is brought; to allow preenforcement review would unduly hobble EPA's flexibility to ensure prompt cleanup of hazardous wastes. Wagner Seed Co. v. Daggett, 800 F.2d 310 (2d Cir. 1986).

What dilemma does this place Wagner in? Is the decision consistent with current law on implied preclusion of review? Does Wagner have any constitutional arguments against preclusion?[37]

Preenforcement review was also denied in Thunder Basin Coal v. Reich, 510 U.S. 200 (1994). The Federal Mine Safety and Health Amendments Act of 1977 provides that representatives of the mine operator and of the mine workers shall be entitled to accompany federal mine safety inspectors during mine inspections. The mine operator must post at the mine the names of the workers' designated representatives. The workers at a Thunder Basin mine who were not unionized but were the target of organizing efforts by the United Mine Workers (UMW) selected two employees of the UMW, who were not employees of Thunder Basin. Despite a letter from federal Mine Safety and Health Administration (MSHA) officials instructing it to do so, Thunder Basin refused to post their names and instead brought suit in federal district court to enjoin enforcement of the posting requirement, contending that in this case it would lead to infringement of its rights under the National Labor Relations Act, including the right to exclude union organizers from its property. The Mine Act authorizes MSHA to issue citations for violation of Mine Act requirements and provides a process for administrative and judicial review if the citation is contested. Although the Mine Act did not preclude preenforcement review, the Court found such review implicitly precluded on the ground that it would hamper effective administration and enforcement of the Mine Act.

Why doesn't *Abbott Laboratories* require preenforcement review in this case? Is it relevant that Thunder Basin claimed that its rights under another statute were being infringed?

37. Congress in 1986 amended CERCLA to explicitly preclude preenforcement review of such orders.

National Automatic Laundry & Cleaning Council v. Shultz

443 F.2d 689 (D.C. Cir. 1971)

LEVENTHAL, Circuit Judge:

[Counsel for the National Automatic Laundry & Cleaning Council (NALCC), a trade association for the coin-operated laundry and dry cleaning industry, wrote the Federal Wage and Hour Administration concerning the applicability to coin-operated laundry employees of the maximum hour and minimum wage provisions of the Fair Labor Standards Act. The question of coverage was posed in the context of three representative factual situations specified in the letter. In a reply letter, the administrator stated his view that in each situation the employees would be covered by the act, which would require the employers to pay a specified minimum wage, and time-and-a-half for overtime, or face awards for back pay, attorneys' fees, and (potentially) civil or criminal sanctions. NALCC brought an action against the secretary of labor in district court, contending that the administration's interpretation was erroneous, and seeking declaratory and injunctive relief. The district court dismissed for want of jurisdiction. The court of appeals reversed on the jurisdictional issue, but ruled in favor of the government on the merits. An excerpt from the court's opinion summarizing its discussion of the reviewability issue follows:]

. . . The ultimate question is whether the problems generated by pre-enforcement review are of such a nature that, taken together, they outweigh the hardship and interest of plaintiff's members and establish that judicial review of the interpretative ruling should be deferred. To some extent a balancing is involved. . . .

Plainly there is a need for advisory interpretations by agency officials. The overwhelming bulk of these are not given by the agency head, and are not within the scope of our ruling announced today. When a general, interpretative ruling signed by the head of an agency has been crystallized following reflective examination in the course of the agency's interpretative process, and is accordingly entitled to deference not only as a matter of fact from staff and citizenry expected to conform but also as a matter of law from a court reviewing the question, there coexist both multiple signposts of authoritative determination, finality and ripeness, and a concomitant indication that the resultant pointing toward prompt judicial review will benefit the total administrative process by resolving uncertainties without intolerable burden or disruption. In the last analysis the Administrator will have latitude to restrict the rulings he signs. There is warrant, then, for discerning at least a limited presumption of pre-enforcement judicial review in the case of authoritative interpretative rulings.

There is the possibility that judicial review at too early a stage removes the process of agency refinement, including give-and-take with the regulated interests, that is an important part of the life of the agency process. The considerations developed in the dissent of Justice Fortas in *Abbott Laboratories* describe realities of the administrative process that must be taken into account.

They can be taken into account under our decision. As we have indicated, an affidavit by the agency head — not a mere argument by its court counsel — that a matter is still under meaningful refinement and development, will likely provide the element of tentativeness and reconsideration that should negative finality, or in any event ripeness. . . .

The overruling of threshold objections does not necessarily portend the propriety of a court ruling on the merits. A declaratory judgment, like other forms of equitable relief, is granted only as a matter of judicial discretion, exercised in the public interest. . . . Public

Affairs Associates v. Rickover,369 U.S. 111 (1962); Lampkin v. Connors, 123 U.S. App. D.C. 371, 360 F.2d 505 (1966). In *Rickov*, the Court exercised its discretion and remanded for amplification of the record, saying, "These are delicate problems. . . . Adjudication of such problems, certainly by way of resort to a discretionary declaratory judgment, should rest on an adequate and full-bodied record. The record before us is woefully lacking in these requirements." 369 U.S. at 113. But that kind of discretion is more soundly exercised after the court has probed the merits, and not by way of a threshold consideration.

[Judge Leventhal then acknowledged the government's potential interest in avoiding multiple preenforcement litigation and in binding all members of a regulated industry to the outcome of a preenforcement challenge. He suggested that these interests could be satisfied by insisting on maintenance of a preenforcement challenge as a class action, an alternative that probably would be feasible where the challenge was brought by a trade association.]

In the course of time other problems of administration or litigation may emerge. We anticipate that they can be managed by reference to doctrines that govern the conduct of litigation, or the scope of relief granted. We find no threshold obstacle that requires dismissal of the action before us merely because it seeks judicial review of the "agency action" of interpretation prior to the institution of an agency action for enforcement.

Notes and Questions

1. What is left of traditional principles of ripeness after *NALCC*? Recall that in *CBS*, Justice Frankfurter in dissent had jocularly argued that the Chain Broadcasting Regulations had no greater legal effect than an FCC press release, implying that since a press release certainly would not be judicially reviewable, neither were the regulations. Is it entirely clear today that a press release would not be judicially reviewable?[38]

2. While *NALCC*'s "functional" approach has been emulated by other courts in finding assertedly nonfinal agency action ripe for review, see Arch Mineral Corp. v. Babbitt, 104 F.3d 660 (4th Cir. 1997); Student Loan Marketing Assn. v. Riley, 104 F.3d 397 (D.C. Cir. 1997); Continental Airlines v. CAB, 522 F.2d 107 (D.C. Cir. 1975), ripeness limitations on reviewability still exist, and *NALCC* might well be seen as a high-water mark for refusal to insist on those limitations — as we shall soon see in more detail. Indeed, it is not at all clear that *NALCC* would be decided the same way today. See, e.g., Air Brake Systems v. Mineta, 357 F.3d 632 (6th Cir. 2005), in which the court of appeals

---

38. See A. E. Staley Mfg. Co. v. United States, 310 F. Supp. 485 (D. Minn. 1970). Compare Independent Broker-Dealers' Trade Assn. v. SEC, 442 F.2d 132 (D.C. Cir.), *cert. denied*, 404 U.S. 828 (1971), sustaining the general equity jurisdiction of a federal district court to review a written request from the SEC to the New York Stock Exchange asking for a particular change of Exchange rules. The Exchange, with the subsequent acquiescence of the Commission, adopted a modified version of the requested change, which assertedly worked injury to plaintiffs. The Securities Exchange Act authorized the SEC to require, after notice and hearing, modifications in exchange rules if SEC requests for such changes were not heeded.

As Judge Leventhal points out in NALCC, a ruling that an issue is ripe for review does not necessarily establish that a litigant in a district court action will be entitled to relief if she prevails on the merits, because a court may still refuse to exercise its equitable discretion to award declaratory or injunctive relief. See, e.g., A. O. Smith v. FTC, 530 F.2d 515 (3d Cir. 1976), sustaining the district court's ruling that a challenge by business firms to the breadth of the FTC's "line of business" requirements for reporting corporate data was ripe for review, but overturning the district court's grant of a preliminary injunction against the requirements on the ground that the firms had not shown either that the expenses of compliance or the civil fines to which they would be subjected if they chose not to comply were so grave as to constitute "irreparable injury" warranting relief. Is the issue of irreparable injury distinct from the issue of ripeness?

was presented with letters posted on the National Highway Safety Commission Web site. The letters, from the Chief Counsel of the agency, said that certain brake systems do not comply with the relevant agency standard. The court found judicial review premature, emphasizing that the letters were based on hypothetical facts, did not bind the agency or regulated persons, and were tentative.

In the early case of New York Stock Exch. v. Bloom, 562 F.2d 736 (D.C. Cir. 1977), an informal opinion letter signed by the comptroller general, which stated that proposed investment services by a national bank would not violate relevant statutes, was held not ripe for review at the behest of the New York Stock Exchange, seeking to protect its member firms from bank competition. NALCC was distinguished on the ground that here the comptroller had explicitly reserved the possibility of a change of views if further facts were presented. Moreover, unlike the plaintiffs in *Abbott Laboratories* and *NALCC*, the stock exchange was not put to the Hobson's choice of complying with an assertedly illegal agency policy or defying it and running the risk of serious sanctions. Also, the stock exchange could protect its interests by a private suit against the banks to enjoin their competition as illegal. In the same vein, see DRG Funding Corp. v. Secretary of Housing and Urban Development, 76 F.3d 1212 (D.C. Cir. 1996); Amalgamated Clothing & Textile Workers v. SEC, 15 F.3d 254 (2d Cir. 1994). We take up this question at various points below.

3. Why should an agency be able to escape judicial review of its legal position by the refusal of the agency head to sign a formal letter of advice or clarification? Given bureaucratic realities, won't the staff's formally expressed position have nearly as much impact on private conduct as that of an agency head? See Kixmiller v. SEC, 492 F.2d 641 (D.C. Cir. 1974), using the distinction between advice from staff and advice from agency heads to deny review of staff advice. Compare NRDC v. EPA, 22 F.3d 1125 (D.C. Cir. 1994), holding reviewable an EPA position on approval of state implementation plans under the Clean Air Act that was reflected in three documents: a "supplement" to its *Federal Register* statement justifying its adoption of applicable regulations, an internal memorandum to EPA regional directors, and a letter (written by a subordinate EPA official) to an environmental organization opposed to EPA's position. The court stated that the test is whether "the agency views its deliberative process as sufficiently final to demand compliance with its announced position." The "absence of a formal statement of the agency's position, as here, is not dispositive." See also HRI v. EPA, 198 F.3d 1224 (10th Cir. 2000), holding that an EPA letter was ripe for review.

RENO v. CATHOLIC SOCIAL SERVICES, 509 U.S. 43 (1993).   In 1986, Congress authorized a major amnesty program for aliens residing illegally in the United States. Aliens had a period of one year from enactment to apply for amnesty under the program. Among the many requirements for naturalization in the 1986 act was the requirement that applicants prove "continuous physical presence" in the United States since November 6, 1986, except for "brief, casual and innocent" absences. An INS regulation narrowly interpreted this last provision to require that an illegal alien have obtained INS permission, termed "advance parole," before leaving the United States. In the absence of advance parole, an absence would not be treated as brief, casual, and innocent. A class of illegal aliens had brought suit challenging the regulation, claiming that it was based on an impermissible construction of the statute. Some number of the plaintiff class allegedly knew of the unlawful regulation of the INS and had concluded that they were ineligible for legalization and for that reason failed to file an application within the one-year period.

They sought a declaration and injunction that the one-year limitation period for legalization applications should not apply to them.

The Court held, in an opinion by Justice Souter, that the claims were not ripe: "The regulations . . . impose no penalties for violating any newly imposed restriction, but limit access to a benefit created by the Reform Act but not automatically bestowed on eligible aliens. Rather, the Act requires each alien desiring the benefit to take further affirmative steps, and to satisfy criteria beyond those addressed in the disputed regulations. [A] class member's claim would ripen only once he took the affirmative steps that he could take before the INS blocked his path by applying the regulation to him." Accordingly, individuals would have to file applications and challenge their denial by the INS before obtaining judicial review. Justice O'Connor, concurring in the result, criticized the majority's "reliance on a categorical rule that would-be beneficiaries cannot challenge benefit-conferring regulations until they apply for benefits." Justice Stevens, dissenting, found the claims ripe: "[O]fficial advice that specified aliens were ineligible for amnesty was certain to convince those aliens to retain their 'shadow' status rather than come forward. At the moment that decision was made — at the moment respondents conformed their behavior to the invalid regulations — those regulations concretely and directly affected respondents, consigning them to the shadow world from which the [amnesty program] was designed to deliver them, and threatening to deprive them of the statutory entitlement that would otherwise be theirs."

Notes and Questions

1. Is *Catholic Social Services* consistent with *Abbott Laboratories*? Does the difference in result turn on the interests at stake: traditional common law rights (the right to make and sell a product) on the one hand, and the interest in a government benefit on the other? If so, is the privileging of traditional common law rights justified? See Sunstein, Standing and the Privatization of Public Law, 88 Colum. L. Rev. 1432 (1988). Or is the difference in result justified because the manufacturers in *Abbott Laboratories* faced a dilemma of either making costly changes in their business practices to conform to an assertedly unlawful regulation or violate the regulation and risk sanctions, whereas the plaintiffs in *Catholic Social Services* faced no analogous dilemma?

2. What ripeness principles apply to an agency's failure to issue a rule? The Heckler v. Chaney presumption against reviewability, in the absence of relevant discretion-limiting statutory provisions, of an enforcement agency's failure to take enforcement action in a particular case does not extend, as a general matter, to an agency's failure to issue regulations. APA §553(e) provides for petitions to agencies for issuance of rules; an agency's denial of such a petition is presumably "final" and ripe for review.[39] But what if the agency defers action on a petition for a considerable period of time, claiming that it is still studying the issue of whether to issue rules — such as rules sought by the environmental group to deal with a particular environmental problem that the group claims to be very serious, more serious than other problems that are higher on the agency's current regulatory agenda? At what point is delay equivalent to denial of the petition?

---

39. On the merits, however, courts will, in the absence of relevant statutory mandates, "defer" to agency decisions about the best use of its limited resources and the desirability and priority to be accorded a given voluntary regulatory initiative. See, e.g., National Association of Regulated Utility Commissioners v. Department of Energy, 851 F.2d 124 (D.C. Cir. 1988).

See Gordon v. Norton, 322 F.3d 1213 (10th Cir. 2003). In that case, a rancher objected to a program of the Fish & Wildlife Service, one that reintroduced wolves into the northern Rocky Mountains. The agency responded via letter, and the rancher brought suit, seeking to challenge the letter, the relevant agency rules, and the agency's inaction. The court held both that the agency decision was not final and that the dispute was not ripe for review. It emphasized that the agency had not completed its decision-making process (as the letter indicated), that it had not engaged in unreasonable delay, and that its refusal to designate certain "kills" as "wolf kills" had no immediate impact. See also Fox Television Stations v. FCC, 280 F.3d 1027 (D.C. Cir. 2002), finding an agency's failure to repeal two rules to be subject to review.

To what extent should a court, in applying ripeness analysis to an agency's failure to issue a rule, apply the benefit-burden distinction enunciated in *Catholic Social Services*? If it does, how should the distinction be applied? Can't regulatory beneficiaries contend that nonenforcement subjects them to a continuing burden? Moreover, if the regulatory agency fails to regulate, they have no subsequent legal remedy; those subject to regulation can always avail themselves of postenforcement review.

3. Why should the plaintiff's hardship — whether in the form of being subject to an assertedly unlawful imposition of duties or an unlawful denial of benefits — play any role at all in ripeness determinations? Chief Judge Edwards recently summarized pertinent rulings of the D.C. Circuit as follows: "[O]nce we have determined that an issue is clearly fit for review, there is no need to consider 'the hardship to the parties of withholding review' [citing *Abbott Laboratories*] because there would be no advantage to be had from delaying review.'" Action for Children's Television v. FCC, 59 F.3d 1249, 1258 (D.C. Cir. 1995) (Opinion of Edwards, C.J.). Subsequent cases draw this statement into question, as we shall now see.

e. A Change in Course for Ripeness?

There are many recent indications of some dissatisfaction with *Abbott Laboratories*, at least insofar as it authorizes preenforcement review of regulations. Recall the arguments by Pierce and by Mashaw and Harfst, supra, to the effect that preenforcement review can have perverse effects, partly by discouraging agencies from issuing rules, partly because of getting courts into the picture at a stage when defending the rule might not be easy.

Contemporary cases have raised questions about preenforcement review. *Thunder Basin Coal Co.*, supra, is in some tension with *Abbott Laboratories*. In *Thunder Basin*, the Court did not make much of any presumption in favor of preenforcement review and found, as sufficient evidence to preclude such review, that the statute explicitly authorized review in an enforcement proceeding. In Shalala v. Illinois Council on Long Term Care, 529 U.S. 1 (2000), the Court found that under the Medicaid Act, a litigant could not mount a pre-application challenge to agency rules. The Court said that any presumption in favor of preenforcement review "must be far weaker than a presumption against all such review. . . ." The dissenting opinions also raised questions about the strength of the presumption. For varying cases on preenforcement review, see Clean Air Implementation Project v. EPA, 150 F.3d 1200 (D.C. Cir. 1998); Firemen's Fund Insurance Co. v. Quankenbush, 87 F.3d 290 (9th Cir. 1996); American Forest and Paper Assn. v. EPA, 137 F.3d 291 (5th Cir. 1998).

In Ohio Forestry Assn. v. Sierra Club, 523 U.S. 733 (1998), the Court held unripe a dispute involving a Forest Service resource management plan adopted for a national forest. The Court emphasized that additional steps had to be taken before any tree could be cut in the forest; it also said that the petitioners would have an opportunity to challenge the validity of the actions ultimately taken. In the same vein, see Wilderness Society v. Alcock, 83 F.3d 386 (11th Cir. 1996). Consider the following case.

National Park Hospitality Association v. Department of the Interior

538 U.S. 803 (2003)

Justice THOMAS delivered the opinion of the Court.

Petitioner, a nonprofit trade association that represents concessioners doing business in the national parks, challenges a National Park Service (NPS) regulation that purports to render the Contract Disputes Act of 1978 (CDA), 92 Stat. 2383, 41 U.S.C. §601 *et seq.*, inapplicable to concession contracts. We conclude that the controversy is not yet ripe for judicial resolution.

The CDA establishes rules governing disputes arising out of certain Government contracts. The statute provides that these disputes first be submitted to an agency's contracting officer. A Government contractor dissatisfied with the contracting officer's decision may seek review either from the United States Court of Federal Claims or from an administrative board in the agency. Either decision may then be appealed to the United States Court of Appeals for the Federal Circuit.

Since 1916 Congress has charged NPS to "promote and regulate the use of the Federal areas known as national parks," "conserve the scenery and the natural and historic objects and the wild life therein," and "provide for [their] enjoyment [in a way that] will leave them unimpaired for the enjoyment of future generations." An Act To establish a National Park Service, 39 Stat. 535, 16 U.S.C. §1. To make visits to national parks more enjoyable for the public, Congress authorized NPS to "grant privileges, leases, and permits for the use of land for the accommodation of visitors." Such "privileges, leases, and permits" have become embodied in national parks concession contracts.

The specific rules governing national parks concession contracts have changed over time. In 1998, however, Congress enacted the National Parks Omnibus Management Act of 1998 (1998 Act or Act), Pub. L. 105-391, 112 Stat. 3497 (codified with certain exceptions in 16 U.S.C. §5951-5966), establishing a new and comprehensive concession management program for national parks. The 1998 Act authorizes the Secretary of the Interior to enact regulations implementing the Act's provisions.

NPS, to which the Secretary has delegated her authority under the 1998 Act, promptly began a rulemaking proceeding to implement the Act. After notice and comment, final regulations were issued in April 2000. 65 Fed. Reg. 20630 (2000) (codified in 36 CFR pt. 51). The regulations define the term "concession contract" as follows:

> A *concession contract (or contract)* means a binding written agreement between the Director and a concessioner. . . . Concession contracts are not contracts within the meaning of 41 U.S.C. 601 *et seq.* (the Contract Disputes Act) and are not service or procurement contracts within the meaning of statutes, regulations or policies that apply only to federal service contracts or other types of federal procurement actions. 3 36 CFR §51.3 (2002). . . .

Determining whether administrative action is ripe for judicial review requires us to evaluate (1) the fitness of the issues for judicial decision and (2) the hardship to the parties of withholding court consideration. *Abbott Laboratories*, supra, at 149. "Absent [a statutory provision providing for immediate judicial review], a regulation is not ordinarily considered the type of agency action 'ripe' for judicial review under the [Administrative Procedure Act (APA)] until the scope of the controversy has been reduced to more manageable proportions, and its factual components fleshed out, by some concrete action applying the regulation to the claimant's situation in a fashion that harms or threatens to harm him. (The major exception, of course, is a substantive rule which as a practical matter requires the plaintiff to adjust his conduct immediately. . . .)" Lujan v. National Wildlife Federation, 497 U.S. 871, 891 (1990). Under the facts now before us, we conclude this case is not ripe.

We turn first to the hardship inquiry. The federal respondents concede that, because NPS has no delegated rulemaking authority under the CDA, the challenged portion of §51.3 cannot be a legislative regulation with the force of law. They note, though, that "agencies may issue interpretive rules 'to advise the public of the agency's construction of the statutes and rules *which it administers*,'" and seek to characterize §51.3 as such an interpretive rule.

We disagree. [NPS] is not empowered to administer the CDA. Rather, the task of applying the CDA rests with agency contracting officers and boards of contract appeals, as well as the Federal Court of Claims, the Court of Appeals for the Federal Circuit, and, ultimately, this Court. Moreover, under the CDA, any authority regarding the proper arrangement of agency boards belongs to the Administrator for Federal Procurement Policy. . . . Consequently, we consider §51.3 to be nothing more than a "general statemen[t] of policy" designed to inform the public of NPS' views on the proper application of the CDA. . . .

Viewed in this light, §51.3 does not create "adverse effects of a strictly legal kind," which we have previously required for a showing of hardship.

Moreover, §51.3 does not affect a concessioner's primary conduct. Unlike the regulation at issue in *Abbott Laboratories*, which required drug manufacturers to change the labels, advertisements, and promotional materials they used in marketing prescription drugs on pain of criminal and civil penalties, the regulation here leaves a concessioner free to conduct its business as it sees fit. See also Gardner v. Toilet Goods Assn., Inc., 387 U.S. 167, 171 (1967) (regulations governing conditions for use of color additives in foods, drugs, and cosmetics were "self-executing" and had "an immediate and substantial impact upon the respondents").

We have previously found that challenges to regulations similar to §51.3 were not ripe for lack of a showing of hardship. In *Toilet Goods Assn.*, for example, the Food and Drug Administration (FDA) issued a regulation requiring producers of color additives to provide FDA employees with access to all manufacturing facilities, processes, and formulae. We concluded the case was not ripe for judicial review because the impact of the regulation could not "be said to be felt immediately by those subject to it in conducting their day-to-day affairs" and "no irremediabl[y] adverse consequences flow[ed] from requiring a later challenge." Indeed, the FDA regulation was more onerous than §51.3 because failure to comply with it resulted in the suspension of the producer's certification and, consequently, could affect production. Here, by contrast, concessioners suffer no practical harm as a result of §51.3. All the regulation does is announce the position NPS will take with respect to disputes arising out of concession contracts. While it informs the public of NPS' view that concessioners are not entitled to take advantage of the provisions of the CDA, nothing in the regulation prevents concessioners from following the procedures set forth in the CDA once a dispute over a concession contract actually arises. . . .

Petitioner contends that delaying judicial resolution of this issue will result in real harm because the applicability *vel non* of the CDA is one of the factors a concessioner takes into account when preparing its bid for NPS concession contracts. Petitioner's argument appears to be that mere uncertainty as to the validity of a legal rule constitutes a hardship for purposes of the ripeness analysis. We are not persuaded. If we were to follow petitioner's logic, courts would soon be overwhelmed with requests for what essentially would be advisory opinions because most business transactions could be priced more accurately if even a small portion of existing legal uncertainties were resolved. In short, petitioner has failed to demonstrate that deferring judicial review will result in real hardship.

We consider next whether the issue in this case is fit for review. Although the question presented here is "a purely legal one" and §51.3 constitutes "final agency action" within the meaning of §10 of the APA, we nevertheless believe that further factual development would "significantly advance our ability to deal with the legal issues presented." While the federal respondents generally argue that NPS was correct to conclude that the CDA does not cover concession contracts, they acknowledge that certain types of concession contracts might come under the broad language of the CDA. Similarly, while petitioner and respondent Xanterra Parks & Resorts, LLC, present a facial challenge to §51.3, both rely on specific characteristics of certain types of concession contracts to support their positions. In light of the foregoing, we conclude that judicial resolution of the question presented here should await a concrete dispute about a particular concession contract.

For the reasons stated above, we vacate the judgment of the Court of Appeals insofar as it addressed the validity of §51.3 and remand with instructions to dismiss the case with respect to this issue.

Justice STEVENS, concurring in the judgment.

Petitioner seeks this Court's resolution of the straightforward legal question whether the Contract Disputes Act of 1978 (CDA, 41 U.S.C. §601 et seq., applies to concession contracts with the National Park Service. Though this question is one that would otherwise be appropriate for this Court to decide, in my view petitioner has not satisfied the threshold requirement of alleging sufficient injury to invoke federal-court jurisdiction. If such allegations of injury were present, however, this case would not raise any of the concerns that the ripeness doctrine was designed to avoid.

. . . In the view of the Park Service, a procurement contract is one that obligates the Government to pay for goods and services that it receives, whereas concession contracts authorize third parties to provide services to park area visitors. Petitioner, on the other hand, argues that the contracts provide for the performance of services that discharge a public duty even though the Government does not pay the concessionaires. Whichever view may better reflect the intent of the Congress that enacted the CDA, it is perfectly clear that this question of statutory interpretation is as "fit" for judicial decision today as it will ever be. Even if there may be a few marginal cases in which the applicability of the CDA may depend on unique facts, the regulation's blanket exclusion of concession contracts is either a correct or an incorrect interpretation of the statute. The issue has been fully briefed and argued and, in my judgment, is ripe for decision.

The second aspect of the ripeness inquiry is less clear and less important. If there were reason to believe that further development of the facts would clarify the legal question, or that the agency's view was tentative or apt to be modified, only a strong showing of hardship to the parties would justify a prompt decision. In this case, it is probably correct that the hardship associated with a delayed decision is minimal. On the other hand, as the Park Service's decision to promulgate the regulation demonstrates, eliminating the present uncertainty about the applicable dispute resolution procedures will provide a benefit for all interested parties. If petitioner had alleged sufficient injury arising from the Park Service's position, I would favor the exercise of our discretion to consider the case ripe for decision. Because such an allegation of injury is absent, however, petitioner does not have standing to have this claim adjudicated.

. . . Though some of petitioner's members may well have suffered some sort of injury from the Park Service's regulation, neither the allegations of the complaint nor the evidence in the record identifies any specific injury that would be redressed by a favorable decision on the merits of the case. Accordingly, petitioner has no standing to pursue its claim. For this reason, I concur in the Court's judgment.

Justice BREYER, with whom Justice O'CONNOR joins, dissenting.

Like the majority, I believe that petitioner National Park Hospitality Association has standing here to pursue its legal claim, namely, that the dispute resolution procedures set forth in the Contract Disputes Act of 1978 (CDA), apply to national park concession contracts. But, unlike the majority, I believe that the question is ripe for our consideration.

I cannot agree with Justice Stevens that the trade association lacks Article III standing to bring suit on behalf of its members. In my view, the National Park Service's definition of "concession contract" to exclude the CDA's protections (a definition embodied in the regulation about which the Association complains, see 36 CFR §51.3 (2002)) causes petitioner and its members "injury in fact."

For one thing, many of petitioner's members are parties to, as well as potential bidders for, park concession contracts. Lodging for Federal Respondents 6 (listing 590 concession contracts in 131 parks). Those members will likely find that disputes arise under the contracts. And in resolving such disputes, the Park Service, following its regulation, will reject the concessioners' entitlement to the significant protections or financial advantages that the CDA provides. In the circumstances present here, that kind of injury, though a future one, is concrete and likely to occur.

For another thing, the challenged Park Service interpretation causes a present injury. If the CDA does not apply to concession contract disagreements, as the Park Service regulation declares, then some of petitioner's members must plan now for higher contract implementation costs. . . .

These circumstances make clear that petitioner's members will likely suffer a concrete monetary harm, either now or in the foreseeable future. Such a showing here is sufficient to satisfy the Constitution's standing requirements. . . .

Given this threat of immediate concrete harm (primarily in the form of increased bidding costs), this case is also ripe for judicial review. As Justice Stevens explains in Parts I and II of his opinion, the case now presents a legal issue — the applicability of the CDA to concession contracts — that is fit for judicial determination. That issue is a purely legal one, demanding for its resolution only use of ordinary judicial interpretive techniques. . . .

The Park Service's interpretation is definite and conclusive, not tentative or likely to change; as the majority concedes, the Park Service's determination constitutes "final agency action" within the meaning of the Administrative Procedure Act.

The only open question concerns the nature of the harm that refusing judicial review at this time will cause the Association's members. See *Abbott Laboratories*, supra, at 149. The fact that concessioners can raise the legal question at a later time, after a specific contractual dispute arises, militates against finding this case ripe. So too does a precedential concern: Will present review set a precedent that leads to premature challenges in other cases where agency interpretations may be less formal, less final, or less well suited to immediate judicial determination?

But the fact of immediate and particularized (and not totally reparable) injury during the bidding process offsets the first of these considerations. And the second is more than offset by a related congressional statute that specifies that prospective bidders for Government contracts can obtain immediate judicial relief from agency determinations that unlawfully threaten precisely this kind of harm. See 28 U.S.C. §1491(b)(1) (allowing prospective bidder to object, for instance, to "solicitation by a Federal agency for bids . . . for a proposed contract" and permitting review of related allegation of "any . . . violation of statute or regulation in connection with a procurement or a proposed procurement"). . . .

In sum, given this congressional policy, the concrete nature of the injury asserted by petitioner, and the final nature of the agency action at issue, I see no good reason to postpone review. I would find the issue ripe for this Court's consideration.

Notes and Questions

1. *Nationality Park Hospitality Association* is part of new ferment in the law of ripeness — accompanied by parallel ferment in the law of finality. A relatively conventional decision is Flue-Cured Tobacco Cooperative Stabilization Corp. v. EPA, 313 F.3d 852 (4th Cir. 2002), in which the court found that a report characterizing second-hand smoke as a "carcinogen" was not ripe for review, because it did not have a concrete effect on anyone. A more controversial decision is Atlantic States Legal Foundation v. EPA, 325 F.3d 281 (D.C. Cir. 2003), where the court refused to review an EPA rule that allowed New York State to approve pilot programs governing hazardous waste — programs that allowed utilities to accumulate, in central collection facilities, wastes produced at remote locations. The court emphasized that it needed to know more about the question of implementation in order to resolve the legal issue; it also said that waiting would not harm the plaintiff. In the same general vein, see AT&T Corp. v. FCC, 349 F.3d 692 (D.C. Cir. 2003), holding that a declaratory order is not ripe for review; Sprint Corp. v. FCC, 331 F.3d 952 (D.C. Cir. 2003), holding that an FCC order, allowing initiation of a new method for allocating telephone numbers, was not ripe, because the court could not tell whether the method was unduly discriminatory until it was implemented; NRDC v. FAA, 292 F.3d 875 (D.C. Cir. 2002), holding that three letters were not ripe because they depended on hypothetical facts and because they did not affect those regulated but instead affected only members of the general public; Gordon v. Norton, 322 F.3d 1213 (10th Cir. 2003), similarly holding that a letter from the Fish & Wildlife Service was not reviewable.

Consider an evident issue beneath some of these decisions: Some agency actions do not affect regulated persons immediately, but they do affect the general public, in the sense that their interests are not protected. Why should decisions that have such effects be deemed not to be ripe for review?

2. What, exactly, underlies the Court's decision in *Nationality Park Hospitality Association*? The Court's decision does appear to be in some tension with *Abbott Labs* — and certainly with several of the cases that followed it. Is the Court's concern limited to premature interventions that are made before an adequate record has been developed?

Problems

1. International Rightswatch Committee, which holds several shares of stock in Megacorp, requested that the company include in management's proxy solicitation materials for its annual meeting a proposed resolution that Megacorp dedicate "all reasonable efforts" to preventing human rights abuses in all of the many countries in which it does business. Section 14(a) of the Securities and Exchange Act prohibits registered companies such as Megacorp from soliciting proxies in contravention of regulations issued by the Securities and Exchange Commission (SEC). The SEC's §14(a) regulations require management to include shareholder proposals in management proxy solicitations but contain an exception for proposals "primarily for the purpose of promoting general economic, political, racial, religious, social or similar causes." Megacorp refused to include the committee's proposal in its proxy materials, invoking the quoted exception. As required by the regulations, it filed with the commission the proposal and a statement of reasons for its conclusion. The committee wrote to the SEC protesting Megacorp's actions.

The commission's division of corporate finance advised Megacorp and the committee that it objected to the omission of the proposal from Megacorp's proxy material. Megacorp asked members of the commission to review this determination. Thereafter, the secretary of the commission (who is charged with official correspondence on the SEC's behalf) wrote Megacorp a letter stating that the commission agreed with its corporate finance division that omission of the proposal was not consistent with file regulations. No reasons for the conclusion were given by either the division or the commission itself. (The commission staff reviews thousands of proxy statements each year, most of them in the spring months.) If a company that has violated §14(a) is listed on an exchange (as Megacorp is), the commission may institute administrative proceedings of a disciplinary nature for an unlawful omission from a proxy solicitation, and may even use a violation of §14a as a basis for delisting the security. It may ask the attorney general to institute a criminal prosecution against a willful violation. Finally, it may in its discretion (under §21(e) of the Securities Exchange Act) bring a federal court action to enjoin the company from engaging in a violation of §14(a). As of this date, no enforcement action has been brought, and the commission has not indicated whether it intends to bring one. Megacorp's annual meeting is scheduled to be held in a few weeks.

Section 25(a) of the Securities Exchange Act provides that "any person aggrieved by an order issued by the Commission in a proceeding under this Act to which such person is a party may obtain a review of such order in the . . . United States Court of Appeals for the District of Columbia."

a. In what court should Megacorp seek review? What are its chances of obtaining review of the SEC's position?

b. Suppose that the commission had concluded that omission of the proposal was consistent with the commission's regulations and the committee seeks review. What result? (N.B. The courts have implied a private right of action on behalf of a shareholder whose proposal is improperly omitted by management; thus the committee could always bring its own suit against Megacorp.)

2. The Dietary Supplement Commission (DSC), an association of dietary supplement manufacturers, brings an action in federal district court under 28 U.S.C. §§1331, 1361 and the APA, seeking declaratory and injunctive relief against the FDA's position regarding the classification of dietary supplement CQ10, which is manufactured by DSC's members. FDA enforcement officials have asserted, in letters sent to a number of DSC members, that CQ10 is a "food additive" because it is mixed by users with their foods, that there are no FDA regulations prescribing the conditions under which CQ10 may be safely used, and that therefore under the Food, Drug, and Cosmetic Act its sale is unlawful unless and until manufacturers of CQ10 petition FDA and FDA adopts such regulations. FDA officials have also initiated administrative proceedings to seize bottles of HyperTonic, a version of CQ10 manufactured by one of DSC's members. DSC contends that CQ10 is a "food" rather than a "food additive" and, that even if it is a "food additive," it is "generally recognized as safe" within the meaning of the act and therefore may be marketed without FDA regulations prescribing the conditions under which it may be safely used. Should the court entertain DSC's claims?

2. Finality

APA §704 can be understood to have codified the "ripeness" requirement. It states that the agency action that is "subject to judicial review" is (1) that action made reviewable by a specific organic statute, or (2) "final agency action for which there is no other adequate remedy in a court" (in the latter case review would be obtained under a general jurisdictional statute such as 28 U.S.C. §1331). The latter half of §704 refers to "final" agency action, and many specific review provisions in organic statutes also speak of an agency order or other action that is "final."

Accordingly, the courts must consider "finality," which is typically treated independently of ripeness. See, e.g., Dalton v. Specter, 511 U.S. 462 (1994) (holding that a report of the Defense Base Closure and Realignment Commission, listing the bases it recommends for closure, is not final); Bennett v. Spear, 520 U.S. 154 (1997) (holding that a biological opinion by the Fish & Wildlife Service is final, because it is the "consummation" of the agency's decisionmaking process, and because the action is one from which legal consequences "will flow"); Sierra Club v. Gorsuch, 715 F.2d 653 (D.C. Cir. 1983).

For an agency action to be "final" the agency decisionmaking process must have reached a resolution and come to a halt, at least for the present. As a standard example, see Reliable Automatic Sprinkler Co. v. CPSC, 324 F.3d 726 (D.C. Cir. 2003). There the court was confronted with a statement containing a preliminary determination, by the CPSC, that a manufacturer's product constituted a substantial hazard and also containing a request that the manufacturer take voluntary actions to eliminate the hazard. The court found the agency's decision to be too preliminary to count as a final, particularly because there was no imposition of a duty or denial of a right. For a more controversial question, consider an effort to require the United States Trade Representative to prepare an environmental impact statement before sending a proposed treaty to the president for approval. In an important case, a lower court held that the agency's decision to send the proposed treaty to the president does not count as "final agency action." See Public Citizen v. U.S. Trade Representative, 5 F.3d 549 (D.C. Cir. 1993). It is worth emphasizing here the two separate points mentioned in Bennett v. Spear: consummation of the agency's decisionmaking process and an action determining rights or from which legal consequences will follow. There is an evident connection between this two-part inquiry and the two-part inquiry in *Abbott Labs* — but note that they are not identical.

Consider Western Illinois Home Health Care v. Herman, 150 F.3d 659 (7th Cir. 1998), finding that the finality requirement was met by a letter sent by an Assistant District Director of the agency. The court emphasized that the relevant letter was not tentative or interlocutory; that it established a legal duty; that its receipt subjected the petititioner to a risk of civil penalties; and that there were no mechanisms for an internal appeal. These points might well be taken as the start of a general account of the finality of agency letters. In the same vein, see the holdings about the arguable finality of an agency letter in Gordon v. Norton, 322 F.3d 1213 (10th Cir. 2003); AT&T v. EEOC, 270 F.3d 923 (D.C. Cir. 2001); Arch Mineral Corp. v. Babbitt, 104 F.3d 660 (4th Cir. 1997); Student Loan Marketing Assn. v. Riley, 104 F.3d 397 (D.C. Cir. 1997). See also Puget Sound Energy v. U.S., 310 F.3d 613 (9th Cir. 2002) (finding "final" a letter denying a demand for refunds in a ratemaking dispute); DRG Funding Corp. v. Secretary of Housing and Urban Development, 76 F.3d 1212 (D.C. Cir. 1996); Amalgamated Clothing & Textile Workers v. SEC, 15 F.3d 254 (2d Cir. 1994).

See also Role Models America v. White, 317 F.3d 327 (D.C. Cir. 2003), holding final a "record of decision" by the Department of Defense about the disposition of the property of a closed defense base. So too, the court found the finality requirement met in a case in which the FCC declined to repeal two rules. Fox Television Stations v. FCC, 280 F.3d 1027 (D.C. Cir. 2002). The court said that the FCC's decision was "final as a matter of law" and that it amounted to "the Commission's last word on whether, as of 1998, the Rules were still" necessary.

Note: Special Issues of Reviewability of Articles Involving the President

In Franklin v. Massachusetts, 505 U.S. 788 (1992), Massachusetts brought an action challenging aspects of the 1990 census as arbitrary and capricious under the APA. Pursuant to the relevant statutory scheme, the secretary of commerce is required to take the census, after which the data are "reported by the Secretary to the President of the United States." 13 U.S.C. §141(a). Thereafter, the president "shall transmit to the Congress a statement showing the whole number of persons in each State. . . ." 2 U.S.C. §2a(a). The Court concluded that, although the secretary had reported the census data to the president, and the president had transmitted to Congress the "statement," there was no final agency action reviewable under the APA and that the courts accordingly could not entertain Massachusetts' claims of deficiencies in the conduct of the census by the

Commerce Department. The secretary's action was not "final" for APA purposes. Justice O'Connor wrote for the majority:

> To determine when an agency action is final, we have looked to, among other things, whether its impact is sufficiently direct and immediate and has a direct effect on day-to-day business. An agency action is not final if it is only the ruling of a subordinate official, or tentative. The core question is whether the agency has completed its decisionmaking process, and whether the result of that process is one that will directly affect the parties. In this case, the action that creates an entitlement to a particular number of Representatives and has a direct effect on the reapportionment is the President's statement to Congress, not the Secretary's report to the President.

The president's transmission of the statement was final but not reviewable because the president is not an "agency" for APA purposes. See also Dalton v. Specter, 511 U.S. 462 (1994) (reports submitted by the secretary of defense to an independent commission to recommend military base closings and to Congress and subject to presidential certification are not final agency actions within the meaning of 5 U.S.C. §704 because they "carry no direct consequences" and are "more like a tentative recommendation than a final and binding determination"). Compare Japan Whaling Assn. v. American Cetacean Socy., 478 U.S. 221 (1986) (secretary of commerce's certification to president that Japanese nationals' activities were endangering fisheries reviewable; secretary's certification automatically triggered sanctions regardless of president's subsequent action).

3. Exhaustion

One often reads court opinions stating that a party must "exhaust administrative remedies" before challenging an administrative action in court. But there are many exceptions to this general rule. We shall distinguish here among three sets of circumstances in which an "exhaustion" question might arise. First, a litigant may seek court review of a claim that he or she has never submitted to the agency. This is the classical situation of exhaustion, where the litigant seeks to avoid the administrative process altogether. It is presented in *Bethlehem*, the first case below. Second, a litigant may seek court review of a claim that he or she has presented to the agency, which has rejected it. However, the controversy includes other claims that are the subject of ongoing agency proceedings and have not yet been decided. This is the problem of interlocutory review. Third, a litigant may seek court review of a claim when agency proceedings are over, and where he or she did not raise (or did not pursue) the claim before the agency. This is the problem of waiver. We shall consider each of these three situations in turn.

a. The Classical Exhaustion Requirement

Myers v. Bethlehem Shipbuilding Corp.

303 U.S. 41 (1938)

Mr. Justice BRANDEIS delivered the opinion of the Court.

The question for decision is whether a federal district court has equity jurisdiction to enjoin the National Labor Relations Board from holding a hearing upon a complaint filed by it against an employer alleged to be engaged in unfair labor practices prohibited by National Labor Relations Act. . . .

The declared purpose of the National Labor Relations Act is to diminish the causes of labor disputes burdening and obstructing interstate and foreign commerce; and its provisions are applicable only to such commerce. . . .

[On April 13, 1936, the board filed an administrative complaint against Bethlehem Shipbuilding, asserting that it was engaging in unfair labor practices at its Fore River Plant in Quincy, Massachusetts, and that the plant was engaged in interstate commerce. The board notified Bethlehem of the time and date of an administrative hearing at which Bethlehem could introduce evidence and argument in opposition to the complaint's allegations. On the day of the scheduled hearing, Bethlehem filed a bill in equity in the United States District Court for Massachusetts to enjoin the board proceedings, asserting that it had not committed any unfair labor practice, that its plant was not engaged in interstate commerce, and that the board had no jurisdiction to proceed. The district court granted a temporary restraining order and, subsequently, a preliminary injunction against the proceedings. The latter was affirmed by the court of appeals.]

We are of the opinion that the District Court was without power to enjoin the Board from holding the hearings.

First. There is no claim by the Corporation that the statutory provisions and the rules of procedure prescribed for such hearings are illegal; or that the Corporation was not accorded ample opportunity to answer the complaint of the Board; or that opportunity to introduce evidence of the allegations made will be denied. The claim is that the provisions of the Act are not applicable to the Corporation's business at the Fore River Plant, because the operations conducted there are not carried on, and the products manufactured are not sold, in interstate or foreign commerce, that, therefore, the Corporation's relations with its employees at the plant cannot burden or interfere with such commerce; that hearings would, at best, be futile; and that the holding of them would result in irreparable damage to the Corporation, not only by reason of their direct cost and the loss of time of its officials and employees, but also because the hearings would cause serious impairment of the good will and harmonious relations existing between the Corporation and its employees, and thus seriously impair the efficiency of its operations.

Second. The District Court is without jurisdiction to enjoin hearings because the power "to prevent any person from engaging in any unfair practice affecting commerce," has been vested by Congress in the Board and the Circuit Court of Appeals, and Congress has declared: "The power shall be exclusive, and shall not be affected by any other means of adjustment or prevention that has been or may be established by agreement, code, law, or otherwise." The grant of that exclusive power is constitutional, because the Act provided for appropriate procedure before the Board and in the review by the Circuit Court of Appeals an adequate opportunity to secure judicial protection against possible illegal action on the part of the Board. No power to enforce an order is conferred upon the Board. To secure enforcement, the Board must apply to a Circuit Court of Appeals for its affirmance. And until the Board's order has been affirmed by the appropriate Circuit Court of Appeals, no penalty accrues for disobeying it. . . .

It is true that the Board has jurisdiction only if the complaint concerns interstate or foreign commerce. Unless the Board finds that it does, the complaint must be dismissed. And if it finds that interstate or foreign commerce is involved, but the Circuit Court of Appeals concludes that such finding was without adequate evidence to support it, or otherwise contrary to law, the Board's petition to enforce it will be dismissed, or the employer's petition to have it set aside will be granted. . . .

Third. The Corporation contends that, since it denies that interstate or foreign commerce is involved and claims that a hearing would subject it to irreparable damage, rights guaranteed by the Federal Constitution will be denied unless it be held that the District Court has jurisdiction to enjoin the holding of a hearing by the Board. So to hold would, as the Government insists, in effect substitute the District Court for the Board as the tribunal to hear and determine what Congress declared the Board exclusively should hear and determine in the first instance. The contention is at war with the long settled rule of judicial administration that no one is entitled to judicial relief for a supposed or threatened injury until the prescribed administrative remedy has been exhausted. That rule has been repeatedly acted on in cases where, as here, the contention is made that the administrative body lacked power over the subject matter.

Obviously, the rule requiring exhaustion of the administrative remedy cannot be circumvented by asserting that the charge on which the complaint rests is groundless and that the mere holding of the prescribed administrative hearing would result in irreparable damage. Lawsuits also often prove to have been groundless; but no way has been discovered of relieving a defendant from the necessity of a trial to establish the fact. . . .

Notes and Questions: *Bethlehem Shipbuilding* and Different Versions of the Exhaustion Requirement

1. The second reason given by Justice Brandeis for precluding judicial review of the labor board's proceeding until it is complete is that the National Labor Relations Act vests exclusive jurisdiction in the courts of appeals to review board decisions, and that a district court action, brought under general jurisdictional statutes, to enjoin NLRB proceedings prior to their completion is thereby precluded by the act. In light of *Abbott Laboratories* and other more recent cases establishing a strong presumption in favor of review, is this part of the *Bethlehem* opinion still good law? Has this aspect of *Bethlehem* been overruled by enactment of APA §703, which provides for review in "the special statutory review proceeding relevant to the subject matter in a court specified by statute, or, in the absence or inadequacy thereof, any applicable form of legal action, including actions for declaratory judgments or writs of prohibitory or mandatory injunction," and further provides, in §704, for review of "[a]gency action made reviewable by statute and final agency action for which there is no other adequate remedy in a court. . . ."? Recall, however, that the reach of these provisions is limited by §701(a), which excepts situations where "statutes preclude judicial review."

2. Apart from the argument of implied statutory preclusion, what other reasons does Justice Brandeis present for denying judicial review prior to completion of the agency's proceedings? How persuasive do you find them, assuming that Bethlehem's claim of lack of jurisdiction is a strong one and that the administrative proceedings will be protracted and expensive? Should the result turn on how strong the court believes the lack of jurisdiction claim to be? Does it matter whether the claim is factually embedded (as in *Bethlehem*) or not?

Note that in a few cases, courts decide whether the agency has jurisdiction even before the target of a subpoena obtains an agency decision on that question. See, e.g., EEOC v. Karuk Tribe Housing Authority, 260 F.3d 1071 (9th Cir. 2001). The court there stated that "judicial intervention prior to an agency's initial determination of its jurisdiction is appropriate only where: (1) there is clear evidence that exhaustion of administrative remedies will result in irreparable injury; (2) the agency's jurisdiction is plainly lacking; and (2) the agency's special expertise will be of no help on the question of jurisdiction." The court concluded that the Tribe's sovereignty would be irreparably injured by enforcement of the subpoena and that the EEOC plainly lacked jurisdiction over an internal dispute between a Tribe and one of its members.

Can you think of hypothetical cases in which this exception would also be found?

3. The D.C. Circuit has typically required a party seeking review of the lawfulness of agency rules to have participated in agency rulemaking proceedings. See, e.g., Environmental Defense Fund v. EPA, 595 F.2d 62, 91 (D.C. Cir. 1978). It has, however, "excused litigants from their exhaustion obligations as to a particular issue so long as the agency, in fact, considered the issue. [C]ourts have waived exhaustion requirements if the agency 'has had an opportunity to consider the identical issues [presented to the court] but which were raised by other parties.'" Natural Resources Defense Council v. EPA, 804 F.2d 710, 714 (D.C. Cir. 1986). See, to the same effect, American Forest and Paper Assn. v. EPA, 137 F.3d 291 (5th Cir. 1998).

4. Is the requirement of exhaustion different from the requirement of ripeness? If so, what is the difference? Consider the *Catholic Social Services* case, below, and the "food additives" problem, below. Should review have been denied in those cases on exhaustion grounds?

b. Interlocutory Review

A litigant who has presented one claim to an agency and had it rejected by the agency but has other claims pending for agency decision may assert that an immediate court ruling in her favor as the decided claim will moot the entire controversy and relieve her of the burden of participating in further agency proceedings. Review may nonetheless be refused for reasons that traditionally apply where interlocutory review by appellate courts of trial court ruling is at issue: Piecemeal appeals will delay trial court resolution of the case; and, in their absence, a trial court may reach a decision on other grounds in favor of the person seeking interlocutory review, eliminating the need for any review.

Consider the following case.

FTC v. Standard Oil Co. of California
449 U.S. 232 (1980)

[The Federal Trade Commission Act authorizes the FTC to initiate by complaint administrative proceedings if it has "reason to believe" that respondents are engaged in unfair methods of competition. The act provides that if the proceedings eventuate in a cease-and-desist order, respondents may obtain judicial review thereof in a court of appeals. The FTC issued a complaint against eight major oil companies, asserting that they had engaged in unfair methods of competition in connection with the OPEC oil boycott during the late 1970s, exacerbating domestic shortages and high prices. The respondents moved the commission to dismiss the complaint, asserting that it had been filed as a result of political pressure by Congress, that the commission had failed to develop information that might sustain its charges, and that the charges had no basis in fact, and that accordingly the statutory "reason to believe" requirement for the issuance of a complaint had not been satisfied. The commission denied the motion on the merits and denied it again on respondents' motion for reconsideration. Respondents thereupon sought judicial review of the commission's refusal to dismiss the complaint. The Court, per Justice Powell, held that the commission's denial of the motion to dismiss was not "final agency action" and was accordingly not presently subject to judicial review.]

Serving only to initiate the proceedings, the issuance of the complaint averring reason to believe has no legal force comparable to that of the regulation at issue in *Abbott Laboratories*, nor any comparable effect upon Socal's daily business. The regulations in *Abbott Laboratories* forced manufacturers to "risk serious criminal and civil penalties" for noncompliance, . . . or "change all their labels, advertisements, and promotional materials; . . . destroy stocks of printed matter; and . . . invest heavily in new printing type and new supplies." . . . Socal does not contend that the issuance of the complaint had any such legal or practical effect, except to impose upon Socal the burden of responding to the charges made against it. Although this burden certainly is substantial, it is different in kind and legal effect from the burdens attending what heretofore has been considered to be final agency action.

In contrast to the complaint's lack of legal or practical effect upon Socal, the effect of the judicial review sought by Socal is likely to be interference with the proper functioning of the agency and a burden for the courts. Judicial intervention into the agency process denies the agency an opportunity to correct its own mistakes and to apply its expertise. . . . Intervention also leads to piecemeal review which at the least is inefficient and upon completion of the agency process might prove to have been unnecessary. . . .

Furthermore, unlike the review in *Abbott Laboratories*, judicial review to determine whether the Commission decided that it had the requisite reason to believe would delay resolution of the ultimate question whether the Act was violated. Finally, every respondent to a Commission complaint could make the claim that Socal had made. Judicial review of the averments in the Commission's complaints should not be a means of turning prosecutor into defendant before adjudication concludes.

[Socal argues] that it will be irreparably harmed unless the issuance of the complaint is judicially reviewed immediately. Socal argues that the expense and disruption of defending itself in protracted adjudicatory proceedings constitutes irreparable harm. As indicated above, we do not doubt that the burden of defending this proceeding will be substantial. But "the expense and annoyance of litigation is 'part of the social burden of living under government.'" . . .

Notes and Questions

1. Sometimes courts deny interlocutory review of a single issue on the ground that it is not "ripe"; sometimes review is also denied on "exhaustion" grounds. Is not the claim presented for review in *Standard Oil* "ripe"? Has not the litigant exhausted his agency remedies on that issue? If so, how can the Court deny review? What are the practical consequences for agency administration of allowing review? For discussion, see Thermal Science v. Nuclear Regulatory Commission, 184 F.3d 803 (8th Cir. 1999), refusing to review a civil penalty proceeding on the ground that the petitioner had available remedies before the NRC.

2. The APA §704 provides for review of "final agency action." The APA says nothing about exhaustion. If an agency action is ripe and "final," for example in definitely reject-ing a claim made by a party, what is the source of the courts' authority to deny review by insisting that that party exhaust other claims?

3. Consider the following effort to summarize the relevant considerations for requir-ing exhaustion in Roosevelt Campobello Intl. Park Commn. v. EPA, 684 F.2d 1034 (1st Cir. 1982):

> From the court's perspective, premature review not only can involve judges in deciding issues in a context not sufficiently concrete to allow for focus and intelligent analysis, but it also can involve them in deciding issues unnecessarily, wasting time and effort. From the agency's perspective, premature review not only can deprive the agency of the opportunity to refine, revise or clarify the particular rule or other matter at issue, but it also can deprive it of the opportunity to resolve the underlying contro-versy on other grounds, thus creating a consensus among the parties or avoiding the need for court proceedings.

4. In some cases, the agency has definitively rejected the claim on which review is sought. But the situation may be more complex. The litigant's claim may have been rejected by the agency in the first instance, but an administrative appeal may be sought. (But the appellate agency authority may have consistently rejected similar claims in the past.) In either situation, courts have developed exceptions to the "rule" that administra-tive procedures with respect to remaining claims must first be exhausted before any review is available.

That there should be exceptions that allow "interlocutory" review is not surprising. After all, federal courts of appeals *must* hear certain interlocutory appeals from district courts (appeals from orders granting or denying injunctions for instance), and they *may* hear certain others (when the district court certifies the question as important). See 28 U.S.C. §§1291, 1292 (1975). The policy against "piecemeal" review is sometimes over-come by the need to obtain speedy appellate guidance. There are no statutes available telling courts how to balance similar interests in the agency context, however. Thus, in a set of decisions that commentators have criticized as inconsistent and "uninspiring,"[40] courts have developed an ad hoc series of exceptions.

a. *Social security claims.* One approach to creating exceptions is exemplified by Mathews v. Eldridge, 424 U.S. 319 (1976), where the Court allowed an SSD claimant to obtain immediate review of his claim that pretermination SSD administrative procedures were constitutionally inadequate without having exhausted all available agency proce-dures with respect to his claims on the merits. The Supreme Court, considering the Social Security Act's requirement that courts review only "final" agency decisions, divided "finality" into two elements. The requirement that a claim for social security benefits be first presented to the agency is "nonwaivable." However, the requirement that "the admin-istrative remedies prescribed" by the agency "be exhausted" is "waivable." The agency might "waive" its procedures by not objecting to court review on exhaustion grounds. More important, a court may insist on a "waiver" over the agency's objection, that is, it may create an exception to the "exhaustion" rule.

---

[40]. See K. Davis, Administrative Law of the Seventies 449 (1976). See also the discussion of exhaustion in Fuchs, Prerequisites to Judicial Review of Administrative Agency Action, 51 Ind. L.J. 817, 859-911 (1976).

But when does such an "exception" come into play? Judge Becker argues that in the social security context the following requirements must be met: "(1) the unexhausted claim must be at least substantially collateral to the question whether plaintiffs should continue to receive disability benefits; (2) the [agency] must have taken a fixed and final position on the unexhausted claim, thereby rendering exhaustion futile; and (3) requiring exhaustion must impose substantial hardship on, or cause irreparable harm to, the plaintiffs." Kuehner v. Schweiker, 717 F.2d 813, 822-823 (3d Cir. 1983). *Mathews* met all three requirements.

Bowen v. City of New York, 476 U.S. 467 (1986), allowed immediate review by a group of disability claimants whose claims were pending before SSA; they sought to challenge a restrictive SSA definition of "mental illness" as unlawful. The Court held that it would require the agency to waive exhaustion because the claimants' judicial challenge presented a pure issue of law that was collateral to their administrative claims for benefits; that SSA's position on the definition of mental illness was fixed; and that requiring exhaustion would cause severe hardship. "The ordeal of having to go through the administrative appeal process may trigger a severe medical setback." *Query:* Was the issue that claimants raised in court collateral to their benefits claims?

Another exception to exhaustion, as well as the convoluted law of "finality" in the social security context, is illustrated in Ryan v. Bensten, 12 F.3d 245 (D.C. Cir. 1993). A regional SSA office had denied Ryan's claim for retirement benefits because he was a prisoner and the Social Security Act prohibits payment of benefits to incarcerated felons. Ryan contended that the prohibition was unconstitutional. After unsuccessfully seeking reconsideration from the regional office, he filed a court challenge without seeking an ALJ hearing followed by appeal to the appeals council — the normal administrative procedures for challenging an initial denial of benefits. The district court dismissed Ryan's action on the ground that there was not yet a "final" agency decision. The court of appeals affirmed.

> [T]he Supreme Court has found waiver appropriate . . . when the Secretary determines that the only issue before him is one of the constitutionality of a provision of the Act and that he cannot allow or disallow benefits on any ground other than the constitutional ground. Because the constitutionality of a statutory provision is an issue beyond his competence to decide, exhaustion is futile. Weinberger v. Salfi, 422 U.S. 749 (1975). Further agency review would not serve the purposes of exhaustion, namely, "preventing premature interference with agency processes, . . . afford[ing] the parties and the courts the benefit of [the agency's] experience and expertise, [or] compil[ing] a record which is adequate for judicial review." Id. at 765. When exhaustion is futile, the Salfi Court held, the Secretary may waive the exhaustion requirement. The Court further indicated that "[t]he term 'final decision' is not only left undefined by the Act, but its meaning is left to the Secretary to flesh out by regulation." Id. at 766. The Secretary heeded the Court and has by regulation enabled a benefit claimant to bypass the final two stages of administrative review by creating an expedited appeals process (EAP) the claimant can use if he contends, and the SSA agrees, that the only obstacle preventing him from receiving benefits is a provision of the Act he alleges is unconstitutional. See 20 C.F.R. §§404.923-404.924. Agreement to use the EAP constitutes a "final decision" for the purpose of judicial review. 20 C.F.R. §404.926(e). . . .
>
> [T]he only issue is [Ryan's] constitutional challenge to section 402(x) and his benefits cannot be suspended or continued on the basis of any other section of the Act. Thus, exhaustion would appear to be futile. Nevertheless, the Secretary has not

waived the exhaustion requirement. We must consider therefore whether we may effectively waive the requirement and, if so, whether we should. . . .

[The court held that it would not insist on waiver of the exhaustion requirement in this case.]

The EAP procedure benefits both the parties and the court. First, it allows the claimant to circumvent full Department review. At the same time, when a claimant has availed himself of the EAP, the parties come to court in agreement as to the facts and the applicable law; only the statute's constitutionality remains in dispute. This means that when the case reaches the district court there will be no question regarding exhaustion of remedies or applicability of the futility doctrine. Nor will either party be faced with novel legal or factual claims beyond the constitutional question. Hence, the constitutional issue will be isolated for thorough analysis. . . .

Compliance with the EAP, it should be emphasized, is not another wall constructed to stymie a claimant's efforts to obtain judicial review of his claim. Indeed, the EAP is an "expedited" procedure. It merely requires a claimant to agree with the SSA in writing that no facts are in dispute, and to allege that the provision of the Act prohibiting his receipt of benefits is unconstitutional and that he does not otherwise challenge the SSA's interpretation of the Act.

b. *Issues of "jurisdiction" and procedure.* Federal courts, in waiving exhaustion, sometimes stress the "jurisdictional" nature of the claim at issue. Thus, the Supreme Court has said that immediate judicial review is available when the agency plainly exceeds its statutory or constitutional authority. Skinner & Eddy Corp. v. United States, 249 U.S. 557, 562-563 (1919). See also Allen v. Grand Central Aircraft Co., 347 U.S. 535 (1954). Judge Friendly analyzed APA §§703 and 704, concluding that immediate judicial review is available if an agency "refuses to dismiss a proceeding that is plainly beyond its jurisdiction as a matter of law." PepsiCo, Inc. v. FTC, 472 F.2d 179, 187 (2d Cir. 1972). There the court allowed immediate judicial review of the FTC's refusal to join PepsiCo bottlers in a proceeding against PepsiCo challenging its franchise agreements with the bottlers; PepsiCo contended that the bottlers were indispensable parties.

The D.C. Circuit reviewed and upheld a claim that the Consumer Products Safety Commission lacked the statutory authority to assess civil penalties in an administrative proceeding, and enjoined a proceeding to assess such penalties. Athlone Indus. v. CPSC, 707 F.2d 1485 (D.C. Cir. 1983). On the other hand, in General Fin. Corp. v. FTC, 700 F.2d 366 (7th Cir. 1983), several insurance companies sought an injunction against an ongoing FTC investigation. They pointed to a statute forbidding FTC investigations of the business of insurance. The court held that the proceeding was not yet "ripe" for review. The companies could oppose the investigation when, and if, the FTC sought to enforce subpoenas.

Judge Friendly also argued in *PepsiCo* that the exhaustion doctrine should not apply when the agency proceeding is "being conducted in a manner that cannot result in a valid order." In Yanish v. Wixon, 81 F. Supp. 499 (N.D. Cal. 1948), *aff'd*, 181 F.2d 492 (9th Cir. 1950), the court accepted an interlocutory challenge to an immigration deportation proceeding based on the claim that the agency failed to use required APA procedures. Cf. Goldberg v. Kelly. It may be relevant that agency procedural issues involve less comparative agency expertise or that the agency is less likely to change its mind about the validity of established procedures. In other cases, courts have insisted on exhaustion of procedural claims. See, e.g., Allen v. Grand Central Aircraft, supra; Beard v. Stahr, 370

U.S. 41 (1962). The differences in results may reflect differences in practical features of the cases making "interlocutory" review more, or less, sensible in the circumstances.[41]

c. *"Pragmatism"?* Should federal courts more explicitly take a "pragmatic" approach to interlocutory review, long followed by the state courts? See, e.g., Ward v. Keenan, 70 A.2d 77 (N.J. 1949); Nolan v. Fitzpatrick, 89 A.2d 13 (N.J. 1952). Where the courts do not require exhaustion, they typically refer to factors such as the following: Is the agency's mind closed in respect to the issue? See, e.g., Kuehner v. Schweiker, supra. Is the question "legal" in nature, that is, is the agency comparatively less "expert" in answering it than the court? See, e.g., Athlone Industries v. CPSC, 707 F.2d 1485 (D.C. Cir. 1983). Is the plaintiff likely to suffer serious injury in the absence of prompt judicial intervention? See, e.g., Southeast Alaska Conservation Council v. Watson, 697 F.2d 1305 (9th Cir. 1983) (injunction against agency allowing mining exploration in an environmentally sensitive area issued despite availability of further agency remedies). Of course, if a court's invocation of the exhaustion requirement is "discretionary" one would expect to see it invoked when the court believes further agency proceedings will help reach a sensible resolution of the controversy. See Ezratty v. Commonwealth of Puerto Rico, 648 F.2d 770 (1st Cir. 1981) (specifically invoking this rationale).

Thus far, we have focused on exceptions to the exhaustion requirement in the context of interlocutory review. To what extent should a "pragmatic" approach to exhaustion allow for review in situations like *Bethlehem Shipbuilding*, where a litigant seeks review of a claim that was neither presented to nor ruled on by an agency? Was it not clear that the NLRB would have flatly rejected a claim by Bethlehem Shipbuilding that its plant was not engaged in interstate commerce? If so, why automatically require that the claim be presented to the board before judicial review can be sought?

c. Waiver of Unpresented or Unexhausted Claims

A court of appeals typically will not address an issue that the appellant did not raise in the district court below. The reasons are partly practical. (The reviewing court would likely benefit from the district court's judgment.) And they are partly institutional. (A system that forces consideration of all issues at the earlier stage is more manageable.)

---

41. In Amos Treat & Sons v. SEC, 306 F.2d 260 (D.C. Cir. 1962), immediate review was permitted of a claim by respondent in a disciplinary proceeding that an SEC commissioner should be disqualified from participating because of his prior involvement, as SEC staff member, in the issues. But SEC v. R. A. Holman & Co., 323 F.2d 284 (D.C. Cir.), *cert. denied*, 375 U.S. 943 (1963), refused to hear a similar claim prior to completion of the administrative proceedings where (unlike *Amos Treat*) the facts relating to the prior involvement in the case as staff members of commissioners were disputed by the SEC, the court voicing fear that judicial pursuit of the claim in the midst of an agency proceeding "could lead to a breakdown in the administrative process which has long been criticized for its slow pace." 323 F.2d at 287.

See also Smith v. Illinois Bell Tel. Co., 270 U.S. 587 (1926), where exhaustion was not required when the relevant agency had lain "dormant" for two years; Walker v. Southern Ry. Co., 385 U.S. 196 (1966) (administrative delay of up to 10 years). Where the National Railway Adjustment Board, for example, was deadlocked and could not decide whether yard-masters were "yard service employees," the Court decided the issue. Railway Conductors v. Swan, 329 U.S. 520 (1947). (Justice Frankfurter wrote separately: If "thus far deadlock has resulted, it does not follow that it will continue, if the Court keeps hands off."). See Goldman, Administrative Delay and Judicial Relief, 66 Mich. L. Rev. 1423 (1968). Note that APA §706(1) allows courts to "compel agency action unlawfully withheld or unreasonably delayed."

Exceptions, however, will be made "in the interests of justice" — a standard that gives the appeals court discretion to waive the requirement to prevent serious hardship or injustice.

Similar considerations have led courts to refuse to hear issues that the parties did not raise or that they did not "exhaust" before administrative agencies. If it is too late to return to the agency, the party will have lost the issue. This is the practical "bite" of this component of the exhaustion doctrine. It has particular importance in the administrative area, where, as *Chenery* so well illustrates (see Chapter 5), courts have stressed the importance of ensuring that agencies bring their discretion and expertise to bear in resolving all issues before the courts conduct review. Yet, here too, occasionally the reasons for enforcing this requirement seem weak and the hardship great. The courts may create a narrow "exception," similar to those described in the previous section, to prevent this hardship.

McKart v. United States
395 U.S. 185 (1969)

Mr. Justice MARSHALL delivered the opinion of the Court.

[Petitioner was convicted for willfully failing to report for induction into the armed forces. He had originally been classified 4-A by his local draft board, exempt from induction because he was the sole surviving son in a family whose head had been killed in World War II. However, when petitioner's mother died, the local board, after consulting with the state director, reclassified him 1-A on the theory that the family unit had ceased to exist and that the statutory exemption for sole surviving sons therefore no longer applied. The petitioner failed to avail himself of the opportunity, provided by selective service regulations, to appear before the local board to contest reclassification and to appeal the reclassification through the selective service system. He also failed to report for induction when ordered to do so.

The Court first concluded, in a review of the relevant statute and its legislative history, that petitioner was entitled to a sole surviving son exemption even after his mother's death, and that the local board had therefore erred in reclassifying him as eligible for induction.

The Court then considered and rejected the government's claim that petitioner was precluded from raising the defense of erroneous classification in his criminal prosecution because he had failed to exhaust administrative remedies on the reclassification issue.]

Perhaps the most common application of the exhaustion doctrine is in cases where the relevant statute provides that certain administrative procedures shall be exclusive. See Myers v. Bethlehem Shipbuilding Corp. . . . The reasons for making such procedures exclusive, and for the judicial application of the exhaustion doctrine in cases where the statutory requirement of exclusivity is not so explicit, are not difficult to understand. A primary purpose is, of course, the avoidance of premature interruption of the administrative process. The agency, like a trial court, is created for the purpose of applying a statute in the first instance. Accordingly, it is normally desirable to let the agency develop the necessary factual background upon which decisions should be based. And since agency decisions are frequently of a discretionary nature and frequently require expertise, the agency should be given the first chance to exercise that discretion or to apply that expertise. And of course it is generally more efficient for the administrative process to go forward without interruption than it is to permit the parties to seek aid from the courts at various intermediate stages. The very same reasons lie behind judicial rules sharply limiting interlocutory appeals.

Closely related to the above reason is a notion peculiar to administrative law. The administrative agency is created as a separate entity and invested with certain powers and duties. The courts ordinarily should not interfere with an agency until it has completed its action, or else has clearly exceeded its jurisdiction. As Professor Jaffe puts it, "[t]he exhaustion doctrine is, therefore, an expression of executive and administrative autonomy."[42] This reason is particularly pertinent where the function of the agency and the particular decision sought to be reviewed involve exercise of discretionary powers granted the agency by Congress, or require application of special expertise.

Some of these reasons apply equally to cases like the present one, where the administrative process is at an end and a party seeks judicial review of a decision that was not appealed through the administrative process. Particularly, judicial review may be hindered by the failure of the litigant to allow the agency to make a factual record, or to exercise its discretion or apply its expertise. Certain very practical notions of judicial efficiency come into play as well. A complaining party may be successful in vindicating his rights in the administrative process. If he is required to pursue his administrative remedies, the courts may never have to intervene. And notions of administrative autonomy require that the agency be given a chance to discover and correct its own errors. Finally, it is possible that frequent and deliberate flouting of administrative processes could weaken the effectiveness of an agency by encouraging people to ignore its procedures.

[I]t is well to remember that use of the exhaustion doctrine in criminal cases can be exceedingly harsh. The defendant is often stripped of his only defense; he must go to jail without having any judicial review of an assertedly invalid order. This deprivation of judicial review occurs not when the affected person is affirmatively asking for assistance from the courts but when the Government is attempting to impose criminal sanctions on him. Such a result should not be tolerated unless the interests underlying the exhaustion rule clearly outweigh the severe burden imposed upon the registrant if he is denied judicial review. The statute as it stood when petitioner was reclassified said nothing which would require registrants to raise all their claims before the appeal boards. We must ask, then, whether there is in this case a governmental interest compelling enough to outweigh the severe burden placed on petitioner. Even if there is no such compelling interest when petitioner's case is viewed in isolation, we must also ask whether allowing all similarly situated registrants to bypass administrative appeal procedures would seriously impair the Selective Service System's ability to perform its functions.

The question of whether petitioner is entitled to exemption as a sole surviving son is, as we have seen, solely one of statutory interpretation. The resolution of that issue does not require any particular expertise on the part of the appeal board; the proper interpretation is certainly not a matter of discretion. In this sense, the issue is different from many Selective Service classification questions which do involve expertise or the exercise of discretion, both by the local boards and the appeal boards.[43] Petitioner's failure to take his

---

42. L. Jaffe, Judicial Control of Administrative Action 425 (1965).

43. Conscientious objector claims, Military Selective Service Act of 1967, §6(j), 81 Stat. 104, 50 U.S.C. App. §456(j) (1964 ed., Supp. III), or deferments for those engaged in activities deemed "necessary to the maintenance of the national health, safety, or interest," id., §6(h)(2), 81 Stat. 102, 50 U.S.C. App. §456(h)(2) (1964 ed., Supp. III), would appear to be examples of questions requiring the application of expertise or the exercise of discretion.

claim through all administrative appeals only deprived the Selective Service System of the opportunity of having its appellate boards resolve a question of statutory interpretation. Since judicial review would not be significantly aided by an additional administrative decision of this sort, we cannot see any compelling reason why petitioner's failure to appeal should bar his only defense to a criminal prosecution. . . .

We are thus left with the Government's argument that failure to require exhaustion in the present case will induce registrants to bypass available administrative remedies. The Government fears an increase in litigation and a consequent danger of thwarting the primary function of the Selective Service System, the rapid mobilization of manpower. . . .

We do not, however, take such a dire view of the likely consequences of today's decision. At the outset, we doubt whether many registrants will be foolhardy enough to deny the Selective Service System the opportunity to correct its own errors by taking their chances with a criminal prosecution and a possibility of five years in jail. The very presence of the criminal sanction is sufficient to ensure that the great majority of registrants will exhaust all administrative remedies before deciding whether or not to continue the challenge to their classifications. And, today's holding does not apply to every registrant who fails to take advantage of the administrative remedies provided by the Selective Service System. For, as we have said, many classifications require exercise of discretion or application of expertise; in these cases, it may be proper to require a registrant to carry his case through the administrative process before he comes into court. . . .

We hold that petitioner's failure to appeal his classification and failure to report for his preinduction physical do not bar a challenge to the validity of his classification as a defense to his criminal prosecution for refusal to submit to induction. We also hold that petitioner was entitled to exemption from military service as a sole surviving son. Accordingly, we reverse the judgment of the court below and remand the case for entry of a judgment of acquittal.

It is so ordered.

[Justice White entered an opinion concurring in the result. He disagreed with the Court's conclusion that exhaustion should not be required because the case turned on an issue of statutory construction, asserting that the courts frequently defer to agencies' interpretation of statutes and that reviewing courts should have the benefit of such interpretations. However, he believed that the essentials of the exhaustion requirement had been satisfied because petitioner had presented his claim for exemption to the local board, and the local board had consulted with higher authorities within the Selective Service System before rejecting it.]

Note

McKart is a most unusual ruling. Courts more frequently take an approach opposite to that of *McKart* and enforce the doctrine of "waiver." Explaining this more typical view, the Second Circuit stated:

> We perceive no reason peculiar to this appeal to depart from the general rule that all issues which a party contests on appeal must be raised [before the agency first]. The rule serves many beneficial purposes which are fully applicable here. In particular, it allows the issues involved in litigation to be narrowed and a proper record to be developed so the issues actually raised are well framed for review.

Franklin County Employment and Training Admin. v. Donovan, 707 F.2d 41 (2d Cir. 1982). Similarly, in McGee v. United States, 402 U.S. 479 (1971), in which a registrant, convicted for failure to report for induction, had failed to exhaust administrative remedies on claims of exemption as a conscientious objector and theology student, the Court ruled that there were "factual issues which should have been fully pursued before and resolved by the agency." Decision of the registrant's claim to exemption was said to depend on "the application of expertise by administrative bodies in resolving underlying issues of fact," subject to quite limited judicial review. In these circumstances, exhaustion should be required in order to permit the agency "to make a factual record, or to exercise its discretion or apply its expertise. . . ." Are due process problems raised by barring the assertion of a defense to a criminal prosecution unless defendant has earlier raised the defense in an administrative proceeding? Cf. Yakus v. United States, 321 U.S. 414 (1944).

Lower court cases refusing to enforce a sanction of waiver include Etelson v. Office of Personnel Management, 684 F.2d 918 (D.C. Cir. 1982). The litigant challenged OPM rules governing the evaluation of candidates for ALJ positions. The challenge was before the agency for several years. The court allowed Etelson to assert an issue that he had raised several years earlier before the agency but had not pursued there more recently. The court reasoned that the agency had been on notice, its position was firmly fixed, and Etelson had not had enough information until recently to know how important the issue was. See also Sierra Club v. ICC, 1978 Fed. Carr. Cas. (CCH) ¶82,768 (D.C. Cir. 1978), in which the court allowed a litigant to raise for the first time on appeal the inadequacy of an environmental impact statement. The court reasoned that the "marginal protection to the integrity of the administrative process" was outweighed by the public interest in ensuring adequate consideration of environmental concerns. (Are there, then, special rules for the environment?) Courts have also refused to enforce a "waiver" rule where the issues involved were strictly legal and did not call for agency expertise, such as a constitutional issue. See Atlantic Richfield v. Department of Energy, 769 F.2d 771 (D.C. Cir. 1984); Reid v. Department of Energy, 765 F.2d 147 (9th Cir. 1985).

May courts require litigants to exhaust internal agency review procedures that are discretionary in character? In Darby v. Cisneros, 509 U.S. 137 (1993), Darby had received an adverse judgment from a hearing officer at HUD. HUD regulations provided that the hearing officer's decision would be final unless the secretary, "as a matter of discretion" decided to review the decision. Although the regulation further provided that "[a]ny party may request such review," the parties conceded that pursuit of the remedy was not required by any agency rule. Darby did not request review by the secretary, instead bringing an action in district court. The court of appeals held that the action should be dismissed because Darby had failed to exhaust his administrative remedies. The Supreme Court held that "with respect to actions brought under the APA, Congress effectively codified the doctrine of exhaustion of administrative remedies in §[704, citing the third sentence thereof]. [W]here the APA applies, an appeal to 'superior agency authority' is a prerequisite to judicial review only when expressly required by statute or when an agency rule requires appeal before review and the administrative action is made inoperative pending that review. Courts are not free to impose an exhaustion requirement as a rule of judicial administration where the agency action has already become 'final' under §[704]."

The Court in Darby rejected the government's claim that §704 addressed only the question of finality for ripeness purposes and did not cut off the courts' discretion in applying the exhaustion requirement. Does Darby establish one set of exhaustion rules for cases brought under the APA and another for cases brought under specific statutory review provisions that lack a provision similar to the last sentence in §554? What if an agency adopts a regulation requiring parties who lose at a lower level in the administrative process to petition for discretionary review at a higher level, and providing that the lower-level decision is not final until the petition is either denied or granted and a higher-level decision reached?

Questions

1. Consider the following statement: "There is no single exhaustion doctrine! There are doctrines of (a) 'ripeness,' (b) 'interlocutory review,' and (c) 'waiver of issues not raised below.' The label 'exhaustion' is simply misleading." Do you agree or disagree? Why?

2. In considering questions of interlocutory review and waiver, we have pointed to the appellate court-trial court analogy. How do considerations for and against review differ in the reviewing court-agency context? Does *Chevron* undercut *McKart*'s suggestion that there is less reason to require exhaustion on an issue of statutory interpretation?

d. Alternative Judicial and Administrative Remedies

In some cases there may be two different potentially available remedies for assertedly unlawful agency action. One remedy may be available through the administrative process; if the agency denies relief, its action can then be judicially reviewed. Alternatively, a remedy against the unlawful action may be immediately available through an action in court — such as a *Bivens* action for damages against an official. Must a claimant follow the first remedy? In the following case, the Court invoked the concept of "exhaustion" to resolve the issue. Consider whether the case really turns on the principle of exhaustion — which traditionally has been thought to relate to the *timing of judicial review* of administrative decisions. Rather, it would seem to turn on the proper relations between two different and independent sets of remedial schemes, one administrative and the other judicial, an issue that we discuss in the following section on primary jurisdiction.

McCARTHY v. MADIGAN, 503 U.S. 140 (1992).   A federal prisoner, McCarthy, brought a *Bivens* action for damages in federal court against various prison officials, alleging eighth amendment violations. He did not pursue remedies provided by the Federal Bureau of Prisons ("BOP") grievance procedures, adopted by BOP pursuant to its general statutory authority to control and manage the federal prison system. In an opinion by Justice Blackmun, the Supreme Court held that "exhaustion" was not required:

> This Court long has acknowledged the general rule that parties exhaust prescribed administrative remedies before seeking relief from the federal courts. See, e.g., Myers v. Bethlehem Shipbuilding Corp. . . . Exhaustion is required because it serves the twin purposes of protecting administrative agency authority and promoting judicial efficiency. . . . Notwithstanding these substantial institutional interests, federal courts are vested with a virtually unflagging obligation to exercise the jurisdiction given them. . . . Administrative remedies need not be pursued if the litigant's interests in immediate judicial review outweigh the government's interests in the efficiency or administrative autonomy that the exhaustion doctrine is designed to further. . . .

This Court has recognized at least three broad sets of circumstances in which the interests of the individual weigh heavily against requiring administrative exhaustion. First, requiring resort to the administrative remedy may occasion undue prejudice to subsequent assertion of a court action. Such prejudice may result, for example, from an unreasonable or indefinite timeframe for administrative action. Even where the administrative decisionmaking schedule is otherwise reasonable and definite, a particular plaintiff may suffer irreparable harm if unable to secure immediate judicial consideration of his claim.

Second, an administrative remedy may be inadequate because of some doubt as to whether the agency was empowered to grant effective relief. For example, an agency [may not hold unconstitutional a statute under which it operates].

Third, an administrative remedy may be inadequate where the administrative body is shown to be biased or has otherwise predetermined the issue before it.

In light of these general principles, we conclude that petitioner McCarthy need not have exhausted his constitutional claim for money damages. As a preliminary matter, we find the Congress has not meaningfully addressed the appropriateness of requiring exhaustion in this context. [T]he general grievance procedure was neither enacted nor mandated by Congress. . . . Because Congress has not required exhaustion of a federal prisoner's *Bivens* claim, we turn to an evaluation of the individual and institutional interests at stake in this case. The general grievance procedure heavily burdens the individual interests of the petitioning inmate [by imposing short procedural deadlines and by failing to authorize an award of money damages]. . . . [Nor do we] find the interests of the [BOP] to weigh heavily in favor of exhaustion in view of the remedial scheme and particular claim presented here.

Chief Justice Rehnquist, joined by Justices Scalia and Thomas, concurred in the judgment solely on the ground of the inadequacy of the administrative remedy. "[I]n cases such as this one where prisoners seek monetary relief, the [BOP's] administrative remedy furnishes no effective remedy at all, and it is therefore improper to impose an exhaustion requirement."

Problems

1. The Federal Trade Commission Act authorizes the FTC to institute administrative proceedings and eventually issue cease-and-desist orders against firms engaged in "unfair or deceptive acts or practices." By unanimous vote of its five commissioners, the FTC institutes such a proceeding against television networks and advertisers, arguing that their advertising practices with respect to children's television programs are deceptive and unfair. The case is referred to one of the commission's ALJs for a hearing. The respondent networks and advertisers file a motion with the commission to disqualify the commission chairman on grounds of prejudgment; they attach to the complaint numerous public statements by the chairman that, they assert, demonstrate disqualifying bias and prejudgment. They also allege that the chairman caused the commission to institute the proceedings against them and request that they be discontinued. The commission (with the chairman participating) unanimously denies the motion. The respondents promptly institute suit against the commission and the individual commissioners in federal district court, invoking federal question jurisdiction under 28 U.S.C. §1331, repeating their allegations, and requesting disqualification of the chairman and dismissal of the administrative proceedings against them.

The Federal Trade Commission Act provides that any person subject to an FTC cease-and-desist order "may obtain a review of such order" by filing a petition for review in an appropriate court of appeals within 60 days after the service of such order.

The defendants (the commission and the commissioners) move to dismiss the suit instituted by the networks and advertisers, asserting that their claims are not subject to review at this time, and that the district court lacks jurisdiction over them.

a. What result?

b. Suppose that respondents instead move for dismissal of the proceedings on the ground that the Federal Trade Commission Act is unconstitutional because it gives article II law enforcement powers to an independent federal agency outside of the direct control and supervision of the president?

2. One Howell, an alien, entered the United States illegally and was therefore subject to deportation. In accordance with immigration statutes and regulations, she petitioned for classification as an immediate relative because she was the spouse of a U.S. citizen, and applied for adjustment of her status to that of permanent resident. The INS denied her application for adjustment of status, and gave her 60 days to leave the country voluntarily. She did not leave within 60 days. Thereafter, she filed an action in federal district court for review of the decision denying her adjustment of status. Shortly after her action was filed, the INS ordered her deported. INS regulations provide: "No appeal lies from the denial of an application by the director, but the applicant retains the right to renew his or her application in [deportation] proceedings." 8 C.F.R. §245.2(a)(5)(ii). In addition, 8 C.F.R. §245.2(a)(1) provides that "[a]fter an alien has been served with an order to show cause or warrant of arrest, his application for adjustment of status . . . shall be made and considered only in [deportation] proceedings." The INS moves to dismiss Howell's district court action on grounds that she has failed to exhaust her administrative remedies in deportation proceedings. What result? Suppose the INS had ordered her deported before she filed her court action?

4. Judicial Stay of Administrative Action Pending Review or Grants of Interim Relief

Courts generally have authority to stay administrative action until judicial review of that action has been completed. Both 28 U.S.C. §2349 and 5 U.S.C. §705 of the APA itself so provide. In any case, in Scripps-Howard Radio v. FCC, 316 U.S. 4 (1942), Justice Frankfurter strongly implied that the power to issue such stays was inherent in the federal courts, independent of statutory authorization. The traditional considerations to be weighed in granting a stay were articulated in the oft-cited decision of Virginia Petroleum Jobbers' Assn. v. FPC, 259 F.2d 921, 925 (D.C. Cir. 1959):

> (1) Has the petitioner made a strong showing that he is likely to prevail on the merits of his appeal? (2) Has the petitioner shown that without such relief he will be irreparably injured? (3) Would the issuance of a stay substantially harm other parties interested in the proceedings? (4) Where lies the public interest?

However, the scope of the power of the federal courts to issue stays was thrown into doubt by the Court's decision in Sampson v. Murray, 415 U.S. 61 (1974). Respondent, who had been discharged from probationary government employment, contended that the administrative procedures afforded her were inadequate because the discharge was based in part on her previous government employment, and therefore procedures more elaborate than those normally afforded probationary employees applied. After her request for additional procedures was denied, she filed an administrative appeal to the Civil Service Commission; if successful on appeal, she would be entitled to full back pay, but not necessarily to reinstatement. While the appeal was pending, she successfully sought an order from the district court enjoining her discharge until the administrative appeal was exhausted. The court of appeals affirmed, pointing out that the Civil Service Commission had no authority to order a stay of discharge pending administrative appeals, and finding that the interim injury to respondent's reputation and loss of earnings constituted irreparable injury. The Supreme Court reversed, noting that the statutes governing the civil service system did not explicitly authorize judicial relief of the sort afforded by the courts below; that, unlike *Scripps-Howard*, administrative proceedings had not yet been completed; that the relief afforded was the equivalent of a total victory for respondent; and that the government should enjoy broad latitude in personnel matters. The Court concluded that these considerations did not altogether deprive the district court of inherent authority to issue stays of administrative action pending judicial review, but they did require that such authority be exercised only to prevent serious irreparable injury. It found injury to reputation from discharge and interim loss of earnings to fall far short of the necessary showing of irreparable injury. Justices Douglas, Brennan, and Marshall dissented.

Compare the "irreparable injury" issue in *Murray* with the comparable issue in the context of predischarge hearing rights in Arnett v. Kennedy (Chapter 6). Consider also *Murray*'s reliance in part on the circumstance that the discharged employee had not yet exhausted her administrative remedies. Does this whipsaw litigants between the exhaustion requirement and *Murray*'s reluctance for courts to grant relief during the pendency of administrative proceedings that might vindicate the litigant? On the other hand, consider the concerns expressed by Justice Fortas in *Abbott Laboratories* about the disruptive effects of judicial stays. Should the Court try to deal with this problem through preclusive requirements of ripeness and exhaustion, or by limiting the availability of stays?

Courts occasionally confront a situation the converse of *Murray*, in which an agency asks a court to grant interim relief in favor of the agency pending completion of agency proceedings. Agencies sometimes obtain interim relief through self-help, such as seizure of "misbranded" drugs.[44] In other instances, statutes authorize agencies (such as the Labor Board) to apply to courts for interim relief. In the absence of such enabling statutes, however, courts have often held that they are without jurisdiction to grant relief. But in FTC v. Dean Foods Co., 384 U.S. 597 (1966), the Court held that the courts of appeals have jurisdiction to enjoin a merger pending the resolution of a suit filed by the FTC.

---

44. See, e.g., North Am. Cold Storage Co. v. Chicago; Ewing v. Mytinger & Casselberry. However, as the materials in Chapter 6 illustrate, due process may require that an administrative hearing be afforded before action is taken. In other instances, statutes may provide for prompt judicial review of summary administrative action; the statute involved in *Ewing* so provided. Also, summary action may be subject to later review in a tort suit against the responsible officials.

F. Primary Jurisdiction

Under the doctrine of primary jurisdiction a party is likely to have begun an action in court, possibly seeking relief against another private party; however, the court will withhold relief because the case involves an issue that might be decided by an administrative agency. It is desirable, in the court's view, that the agency decide that issue before the court reaches its own decision. Thus the court may hold the case on its docket and refer the party to the agency. Sometimes, the court will add that once the agency reaches its decision, the matter is at an end; it will not hold the case on its docket. In this case, the agency has not only "primary" but also "exclusive" jurisdiction.

The notion of "primary jurisdiction" is sometimes traced to Texas & Pacific R.R. Co. v. Abilene Cotton Oil Co., 204 U.S. 426 (1907). The statutory scheme involved there was unusual. Before the Interstate Commerce Act, a shipper who believed that a railroad had overcharged him could sue in court for the difference between the charge and a "reasonable rate." The Interstate Commerce Act, however, gave the ICC the power to hear a shipper's claim that a particular rate was unreasonable, and to order reparations for an overcharge. The Act prohibited not only unreasonably high rates but also unreasonable discrimination among shippers. Section 22 of the Act stated that "nothing in this Act . . . shall in any way abridge or alter the remedies now existing at common law or by statute but the provisions of this Act are in addition to such remedies."

A cotton oil company sued the railroad, in a district court, for an overcharge. The Supreme Court held, despite the language of §22, that the Interstate Commerce Act required a shipper to bring his claim for an overcharge before the ICC as an initial matter. Any other result, in the Court's view, could lead to a hodgepodge of railroad rates contrary to the expressed intent of the Act. Mr. Justice White wrote:

> [I]f, without previous action by the Commission, power might be exerted by courts and juries generally to determine the reasonableness of an established rate, it would follow that unless all courts reached an identical conclusion a uniform standard of rates in the future would be impossible, as the standard would fluctuate and vary, depending upon the divergent conclusions reached as to the reasonableness by the various courts called upon to consider the subject as an original question. Indeed, the recognition of such a right is wholly inconsistent with the administrative power conferred upon the Commission and with the duty, which the statute casts upon that body, of seeing to it that the statutory requirement as to the uniformity and equality of rates is observed. Equally obvious is it that the existence of such a power in the courts, independent of prior action by the Commission, would lead to favoritism, to the enforcement of one rate in one jurisdiction and a different one in another, would destroy the prohibition against preferences and discrimination, and afford, moreover, a ready means by which, through collusive proceedings, the wrongs which the statue was intended to remedy could be successfully inflicted.

204 U.S. at 440-441.

As to §22, the Court wrote, "This clause, however cannot be construed as continuing in shippers a common law right, the continued existence of which would be absolutely inconsistent with the provisions of the act. In other words, the act cannot be held to destroy itself." 204 U.S. at 446.

The Court's opinion suggests that the Act simply abolished a preexisting common law remedy and created a new one, which the Commission was to enforce (despite the statutory disclaimer). But, whether the ICC's jurisdiction was in fact "exclusive" is not clear, since the statute required a shipper, who had been awarded reparations by the ICC, to sue in district court to collect the reparations from the railroad. Thus, as a practical matter, the opinion requires the shipper to go *first* to the ICC to obtain an opinion about a rate's reasonableness and *then* to go to the district court (if necessary) to collect an overcharge. Insofar as the later court action takes the form of ordinary review of an agency decision, one might say the Commission had "exclusive" jurisdiction. Insofar as the later action was de novo, the effect of the *Abilene* decision was to give the courts the benefit of the agency's views concerning an issue that the courts might later decide. Then one might call the ICC's jurisdiction "primary" but not "exclusive."

In a later case, Great Northern Ry. Co. v. Merchants Elevator Co., 259 U.S. 285 (1922), a shipper sued to recover a small overcharge. The railroad claimed the charge was proper under its tariffs. The issue turned on the construction of the tariffs. Justice Brandeis, for the Court, wrote that "the task to be performed is to determine the meaning of words of the tariff which were used in their ordinary sense, and to apply that meaning to the undisputed facts." 259 U.S. at 294. Hence, the shipper need not go to the Commission for relief but can apply directly to the courts.

> Preliminary resort to the Commission is necessary where the inquiry is essentially one of fact and of discretion in technical matters and uniformity can be secured only if its determination is left to the Commission. Moreover, that determination is reached ordinarily upon voluminous and conflicting evidence, for the adequate appreciation of which acquaintance of many intricate facts of transportation is indispensable; and such acquaintance is commonly to be found only in a body of experts.

259 U.S. at 291.

United States v. Western Pacific R.R.
352 U.S. 59 (1956)

[The Government shipped napalm bombs on the Western Pacific Railroad. It was charged the high tariff rate applicable to "incendiary bombs." The Government stated that, since the bombs contained no "burster charge" or fuse, they could not explode. Hence the lower tariff rate for "gasoline in steel drums" should apply. The Government refused to pay the high rate; the railroad sued in the Court of Claims. The Court of Claims itself construed the tariffs and held that the high tariff for "incendiary bombs" applied. The court also rejected the Government's claim that ICC should (as a matter of primary jurisdiction) pass on whether the tariff was "reasonable."]

Mr. Justice HARLAN delivered the opinion of the Court:

We are met at the outset with question of whether the Court of Claims properly applied the doctrine of primary jurisdiction in this case; that is, whether it correctly allocated the issues in the suit between the jurisdiction of the Interstate Commerce Commission and that of the court. In the view of the court below, the case presented two entirely separate questions. One was the question of the construction of the tariff — whether Item 1820 [governing "incendiary bombs"] was applicable to these shipments.

The second was the question of the reasonableness of that tariff, if so applied. The Court of Claims assumed . . . that the first of these — whether the "1820" rate applied — was a matter simply of tariff construction and thus properly within the initial cognizance of the court. The second — the reasonableness of the tariff as applied to these shipments — it seemed to regard as being within the initial competence of the Interstate Commerce Commission. Before this Court neither side has questioned the validity of the lower court's views in these respects. Nevertheless, because we regard the maintenance of a proper relationship between the courts and the Commission in matters affecting transportation policy to be of continuing public concern, we have been constrained to inquire into this aspect of the decision. We have concluded that in the circumstances here presented the question of tariff construction, as well as that of the reasonableness of the tariff as applied, was within the exclusive primary jurisdiction of the Interstate Commerce Commission.

The doctrine of primary jurisdiction, like the rule requiring exhaustion of administrative remedies, is concerned with promoting proper relationships between the courts and administrative agencies charged with particular regulatory duties. "Exhaustion" applies where a claim is cognizable in the first instance by an administrative agency alone; judicial interference is withheld until the administrative process has run its course. "Primary jurisdiction," on the other hand, applies where a claim is originally cognizable in the courts, and comes into play whenever enforcement of the claim requires the resolution of issues which, under a regulatory scheme, have been placed within the special competence of an administrative body; in such a case the judicial process is suspended pending referral of such issues to the administrative for its views. . . .

No fixed formula exists for applying the doctrine of primary jurisdiction. In every case the question is whether the reasons for the existence of the doctrine are present and whether the purposes it serves will be aided by its application in the particular litigation. These reasons and purposes have often been given expression by this Court. In the earlier cases emphasis was laid on the desirable uniformity which would obtain if initially a specialized agency passed on certain types of administrative questions. See Texas & Pacific R. Co. v. Abilene Cotton Oil Co., 204 U.S. 426. More recently the expert and specialized knowledge of the agencies involved has been particularly stressed. See Far East Conference v. United States, 342 U.S. 570. The two factors are part of the same principles,

> now firmly established, that in cases [of] issues of fact not within the conventional experience of judges or cases requiring the exercise of administrative discretion, agencies created by Congress for regulating the subject matter should not be passed over. This is so even though the facts after they have been appraised by specialized competence serve as a premise for legal consequences to be judicially defined. Uniformity and consistency in the regulation of business entrusted to a particular agency are secured, and the limited functions of review by the judiciary are more rationally exercised, by preliminary resort for ascertaining and interpreting the circumstances underlying legal issues to agencies that are better equipped than courts by specialization, by insight gained through experience, and by more flexible procedures.

Id., at 574-575.

The doctrine of primary jurisdiction thus does "more than prescribe the mere procedural time table of the lawsuit. It is a doctrine allocating the lawmaking power over certain aspects" of commercial relations. "It transfers from court to agency the power to determine" some of the incidents of such relations.

Thus the first question presented is whether effectuation of the statutory purposes of the Interstate Commerce Act requires that the Interstate Commerce Commission should first pass on the construction of the tariff in dispute here; this, in turn, depends on whether the question raises issues of transportation policy which ought to be considered by the Commission in the interests of a uniform and expert administration of the regulatory scheme laid by that Act. . . .

[The Court went on to hold that to decide whether the term *incendiary bomb* applied to these shipments was a complex matter, requiring considerable expertise. Does the higher rate reflect only the risk of an explosion, or are there other commercial factors at work? Moreover, one cannot readily separate the question of the tariff's construction from its reasonableness. Both call for the Commission's expertise.]

. . . We say merely that where, as here, the problem of cost allocation is relevant, and where therefore the questions of construction and reasonableness are so intertwined that the same factors are determinative on both issues, then it is the Commission which must first pass on them. [Reversed and remanded.]

Notes

1. The Court in *Western Pacific* apparently reached the primary jurisdiction issue even though the parties themselves did not raise it. "It is now well established that the doctrine is not waived by the failure of the parties to present it in the trial court, or on appeal, since the doctrine exists for the proper distribution of power between judicial and administrative bodies and not for the convenience of the parties." Distrigas v. Boston Gas Co., 693 F.d 1113, 1117 (1st Cir. 1982).[45]

2. One basic purpose underlying the doctrine of primary jurisdiction is that of permitting the courts "to make a workable allocation of business between themselves and the agencies." CAB v. Modern Air Transp. Inc., 179 F.2d 622, 625 (2d Cir. 1950). In many cases, the allocation reflects the court's need to obtain the "expert" views of the agency, particularly on matters such as ratemaking. See, e.g., Burlington Northern, Inc. v. United States, 459 U.S. 131 (1982). One court has looked to the following factors to determine whether the doctrine should be invoked: "(1) Whether the agency determination lay at the heart of the task assigned the agency by Congress; (2) whether agency expertise was required to unravel intricate, technical facts; and (3) whether, though perhaps not determinative, the agency determination would materially aid the court." Mashpee Tribe v. New Seabury Corp., 592 F.2d 575, 580-581 (1st Cir. 1979).

3. In *Abilene Cotton* and several other of the preceding cases, agency action may completely dispose of the entire controversy. Often, however, agency action may dispose of, or help to clarify, only one issue in a complex case. In such a case, a district court might hold the case on its docket until after the agency has acted. Consider the following example:

In General American Tank Car Corp. v. El Dorado Terminal Co., 308 U.S. 422 (1940), a shipper of coconut oil leased railroad cars from a private leasing company, filled them with oil, and gave them to the railroad to transport. The oil company paid the railroad the ordinary coconut oil rate, but, because the oil company supplied its own cars, the railroad paid this sum (1.5 cents per mile) not to the oil company directly but to the leasing

---

45. See also Nader v. Allegheny Airlines, 512 F.2d 527, 542 n.37 (D.C. Cir. 1975).

company that rented its cars to the oil company. The leasing company was supposed to deduct the 1.5 cents per mile from the rental fee that the oil company owed it. This amount turned out to be greater than the rental fee. The leasing company refused to give the extra sum to the oil company on the ground that doing so would effectively make the oil company's shipping charge lower than its competitors', thus constituting an illegal transportation rebate. The oil company sued for the sum in an ordinary contract action in district court. The ICC filed an amicus brief arguing for primary jurisdiction and maintaining, in any event, that the payment would constitute an illegal rebate. The Supreme Court wrote:

> The action was an ordinary one . . . on a written contract. The court had jurisdiction of the subject matter and of the parties. But it appeared here . . . that the question of the reasonableness and legality of the practices of the parties was subjected by the Interstate Commerce Act to the administrative authority of the Interstate Commerce Commission. The policy of the Act is that reasonable allowances and practices . . . are to be fixed and settled after full investigation by the Commission, and that there is remitted to the courts only the function of enforcing claims arising out of the failure to comply with Commission's lawful orders.
>
> When it appeared in the course of the litigation that an administrative problem, committed to the Commission, was involved, the court should have stayed its hand pending the Commission's determination of the lawfulness and reasonableness of the practices under the terms of the Act. There should not be a dismissal, but, . . . the cause should be held pending the conclusion of an appropriate administrative proceeding. Thus any defense the petitioner may have will be saved to it. . . .

308 U.S. at 432-433.

Nader v. Allegheny Airlines

426 U.S. 290 (1976)

[Ralph Nader held a confirmed reservation on Allegheny's Washington/Hartford 10:15 A.M. flight. He was "bumped" because Allegheny had sold more confirmed reservations than there were seats on the plane. In fact, Allegheny deliberately and secretly overbooked the flight (as do all airlines on many flights) because it knew from statistical studies that some confirmed passengers would not show up. The practice of "deliberate overbooking" tends to prevent airplanes from leaving with empty seats; on the other hand, it can severely inconvenience the passengers who are bumped. These latter, under CAB rules, receive "denied boarding compensation" equal roughly to the price of their ticket.

Nader refused the offer of denied boarding compensation and sued in federal district court for compensatory and punitive damages. His case rested in part on a common law claim of fraudulent misrepresentation. He argued that he should, at least, have been told by the airline about its overbooking practice so that he could plan accordingly.]

Mr. Justice POWELL delivered the opinion of the Court.

The only issue before us concerns the Court of Appeals' disposition on the merits of petitioner's claim of fraudulent misrepresentation. . . . [Section 411 of the Civil Aeronautics Act provides that the Board may "determine whether any air carrier . . . is engaged in unfair or deceptive practices" and, if so, issue a "cease and desist" order. The Court of Appeals] held that a determination by the Board that a practice is not deceptive within the meaning of §411 would, as a matter of law, preclude a common-law tort action seeking damages for injuries caused by that practice. Therefore, the court held that the Board must be allowed to determine in the first instance whether the challenged practice (in this case, the alleged failure to disclose the practice of overbooking) falls within the ambit of §411. The court took judicial notice that a rulemaking proceeding concerning possible changes in reservation practices in response to the 1973-1974 fuel crisis was already underway and that a challenge to the carrier's overbooking practices had been raised by an intervenor in that proceeding. The District Court was instructed to stay further action on petitioner's misrepresentation claim pending the outcome of the rulemaking proceeding. The Court of Appeals characterized its holding as "but another application of the principles of primary jurisdiction, a doctrine whose purpose is the coordination of the workings of agency and court." . . .

The question before us, then, is whether the Board must be given an opportunity to determine whether respondent's alleged failure to disclose its practice of deliberate overbooking is a deceptive practice under §411 before petitioner's common-law action is allowed to proceed. The decision of the Court of Appeals requires the District Court to stay the action brought by petitioner in order to give the Board an opportunity to resolve the question. If the Board were to find that there had been no violation of §411, respondent would be immunized from common-law liability.

Section 1106 of the Act, 49 U.S.C. §1506, provides that "[n]othing contained in this chapter shall in any way abridge or alter the remedies now existing at common law or by statute, but the provisions of this chapter are in addition to such remedies." The Court of Appeals found that "although the saving clause of §1106 purports to speak in absolute terms it cannot be read so literally." 167 U.S. App. D.C., at 367, 512 F.2d, at 544. In reaching this conclusion, it relied on Texas & Pacific R. Co. v. Abilene Cotton Oil Co., 204 U.S. 426 (1907).

In this case, unlike *Abilene*, we are not faced with an irreconcilable conflict between the statutory scheme and the persistence of common-law remedies. In *Abilene* the carrier, if subject to both agency and court sanctions, would be put in an untenable position when agency and court disagreed on the reasonableness of a rate. The carrier could not abide by the rate filed with the Commission, as required by statute, and also comply with a court's determination that the rate was excessive. The conflict between the court's common-law authority and the agency's ratemaking power was direct and unambiguous. The court in the present case, in contrast, is not called upon to substitute its judgment for the agency's on the reasonableness of a rate — or, indeed, on the reasonableness of any carrier practice. There is no Board requirement that air carriers engage in overbooking or that they fail to disclose that they do so. And any impact on rates that may result from the imposition of tort liability or from practices adopted by a carrier to avoid such liability would be merely incidental. Under the circumstances, the common-law action and the statute are not "absolutely inconsistent" and may coexist, as contemplated by §1106.

. . . The Court of Appeals . . . also held . . . that the Board has the power in a §411 proceeding to approve practices that might otherwise be considered deceptive and thus to immunize carriers from common-law liability. . . .

We cannot agree. No power to immunize can be derived from the language of §411. And where Congress has sought to confer such power it has done so expressly, as in §414 of the Act, 49 U.S.C. §1384, which relieves those affected by certain designated orders (not including orders issued under §411) "from the operations of the 'antitrust laws.'" . . .

Section 411, in contrast, is purely restrictive. It contemplates the elimination of "unfair or deceptive practices" that impair the public interest. Its role had been described in American Airlines, Inc. v. North American Airlines, Inc., supra, at 85:

> "Unfair or deceptive practices or unfair methods of competition," as used in §411, are broader concepts than the common-law idea of unfair competition. . . . The section is concerned not with punishment of wrongdoing or protection of injured competitors, but rather with protection of the public interest.

As such, §411 provides an injunctive remedy for vindication of the public interest to supplement the compensatory common-law remedies for private parties preserved by §1106. . . .

Section 411 is both broader and narrower than the remedies available at common law. A cease-and-desist order may issue under §411 merely on the Board's conclusion, after an investigation determined to be in the public interest, that a carrier is engaged in an "unfair or deceptive practice." No findings that the practice was intentionally deceptive or fraudulent or that it in fact has caused injury to an individual are necessary. . . . On the other hand, a Board decision that a cease-and-desist order is inappropriate does not represent approval of the practice under investigation. It may merely represent the Board's conclusion that the serious prohibitory sanction of a cease-and-desist order is inappropriate, that a more flexible approach is necessary. A wrong may be of the sort that calls for compensation to an injured individual without requiring the extreme remedy of a cease-and-desist order. . . .

In sum, §411 confers upon the Board a new and powerful weapon against unfair and deceptive practices that injure the public. But it does not represent the only, or best, response to all challenged carrier actions that result in private wrongs.

. . . Even when common-law rights and remedies survive and the agency in question lacks the power to confer immunity from common-law liability, it may be appropriate to refer specific issues to an agency for initial determination where that procedure would secure "[u]niformity and consistency in the regulation of business entrusted to a particular agency" or where "the limited functions of review by the judiciary [would be] more rationally exercised, by preliminary resort for ascertaining and interpreting the circumstances underlying legal issues to agencies that are better equipped than courts by specialization by insight gained through experience, and by more flexible procedure." Fair East Conference v. United States, 342 U.S., at 574-575. . . .

The doctrine has been applied, for example, when an action otherwise within the jurisdiction of the court raises a question of the validity of a rate or practice included in a tariff filed with an agency, . . . particularly when the issue involves technical questions of fact uniquely within the expertise and experience of an agency — such as matters turning on an assessment of industry conditions. . . . In this case, however, considerations of uniformity in regulation and of technical expertise do not call for prior reference to the Board.

Petitioner seeks damages for respondent's failure to disclose its overbooking practices. He makes no challenge to any provision in the tariff, and indeed there is no tariff provision of Board regulation applicable to disclosure practices. . . .

Referral of the misrepresentation issue to the Board cannot be justified by the interest in informing the court's ultimate decision with "the expert and specialized knowledge" . . . of the Board. The action brought by petitioner does not turn on a determination of the reasonableness of a challenged practice — a determination that could be facilitated by an informed evaluation of the economics or technology of the regulated industry. The standards to be applied in an action for fraudulent misrepresentation are within the conventional competence of the courts, and the judgment of a technically expert body is not likely to be helpful in the application of these standards to the facts of this case.

We are particularly aware that, even where the wrong sought to be redressed is not misrepresentation but bumping itself, which has been the subject of Board consideration and for which compensation is provided in carrier tariffs, the Board has contemplated that there may be individual adjudications by courts in common-law suits brought at the option of the passenger. The present regulations dealing with the problems of overbooking [provide] . . . that the bumped passenger will have a choice between accepting denied boarding compensation as "liquidated damages for all damages incurred . . . as a result of the carrier's failure to provide the passenger with confirmed reserved space," or pursuing his or her common-law remedies. . . .

We conclude that petitioner's tort action should be stayed pending reference to the Board and accordingly the decision of the Court of Appeals on this issue is reversed. The Court of Appeals did not address the question whether petitioner had introduced sufficient evidence to sustain his claim. We remand the case for consideration of that question and for further proceedings consistent with this opinion.

It is so ordered.

Mr. Justice WHITE, concurring.

I join the court's opinion with these additional words. . . . [T]here is not present here the additional consideration that a §411 proceeding would be helpful in resolving, or affecting in some manner, the state-law claim for compensatory and punitive damages, Cf. Ricci v. Chicago Mercantile Exchange, 409 U.S. 289 (1973); Chicago Mercantile Exchange v. Deaktor, 414 U.S. 113 (1973). I seriously doubt that any pending or future §411 case would reveal anything relevant to this case about the Board's view of the propriety of overbooking and of overselling that is not already apparent from prior proceedings concerning those subjects.

Questions

1. For an effort to clarify the law, see Ricci v. Chicago Mercantile Exchange, 409 U.S. 289 (1973). There the Court said that the idea of primary jurisdiction applies when conduct at issue in court "is . . . at least arguably protected or regulated by . . . [a] regulatory statute." Primary jurisdiction would be invoked when the agency's decision may well be a "material aid" to the judicial judgment. See in this vein Brown v. MCI Worldcom Network Services, 277 F.3d 1166 (9th Cir. 2002), where the court refused to apply primary jurisdiction in a case involving tariff enforcement, an issue that can be resolved by the FCC or in district court. The court said that "primary jurisdiction is properly invoked when a case presents a far-reaching question that 'requires expertise or uniformity in administration.' . . . If resolution of [the[] claim involves a straightforward interpretation of [defendant's] filed tariff, the district court will be competent to resolve it without resort to [the agency]."

2. The following situation occurs from time to time throughout the law: Rights and duties of large numbers of people are created by a statute or a common law system, which we shall call General Scheme A. Congress then enacts a new statute, say Regulatory Statute B, which governs a smaller group of people. Congress might state in Statute B

that a portion of A does not apply to the smaller group. Congress may have provided a roughly equivalent substitute for A in B, but it need not have done so; Congress may have said *expressly* that A does not apply, but it also may say it only through *implication*. Suppose that Congress, in enacting B, provides such an exemption from A, and suppose further that B is enforced by an agency, not a court. Then, if a plaintiff sues in court under A, but asserts a cause of action that falls within the exemption provided by B, it is hardly surprising that the court will dismiss the action, for statute A simply does not apply. Thus, if Congress implies in the Civil Aviation Act that the antitrust laws do not apply to certain airline practices, a court will dismiss an antitrust case attacking them. Similarly, if the Aviation Act supersedes state tort law, a state court will dismiss a tort claim. In either case, the Act might give plaintiffs a related cause of action before the agency itself.

(a) Does this describe *Abilene? Western Pacific? American Tank Car?*

(b) The above description may account for "exclusive jurisdiction," but it certainly does not account for the whole of the doctrine of primary jurisdiction. Of what else does that doctrine consist?

3. In *American Tank Car*, the ICC submitted an amicus brief to the court setting forth its position. Why then was there any need to refer the case to the agency? Indeed, given the power of the courts to request amicus briefs and the agency's ability to supply them on matters it deems important, what need is there for the doctrine of primary jurisdiction?

4. The modern cases have continued the pragmatic use of the primary jurisdiction doctrine, which often involves a degree of balancing. When the issue is highly technical, or when a high degree of uniformity is necessary, the court is likely to say that the agency has primary jurisdiction over it. On the other hand, the court is more likely to decide the issue if use of the doctrine would result in significant, and harmful, delay, or if the underlying statute reflects a judgment, implicit or explicit, that judicial judgment is acceptable. One new theme has also emerged: There is an evident connection between the old primary jurisdiction doctrine and the principle of deference to agency interpretations announced in Chevron v. NRDC, supra. If the statutory provision is ambiguous, and if the dispute arises in court, perhaps the agency should be said to have primary jurisdiction, on the ground that the agency decision will be binding if reasonable.

Consider American Automobile Manufacturers Association v. Massachusetts Department of Environmental Protection, 163 F.3d 74 (1st Cir. 1998). A central issue in the case was the status of a Memorandum of Agreement (MOA) between California and automobile makers; the MOA involved an agreement, by the makers, to sell a specified percentage of low-emission vehicles in California, beginning in 1998. If the MOA was a "standard" within the meaning of the Clean Air Act, other states, including Massachusetts, could include it in their own low-emission vehicle program. The automobile makers objected that the MOA was not a standard; Massachusetts contended that it was. The court held that this issue was within the primary jurisdiction of the EPA. It emphasized that the term "standard" was ambiguous and that under *Chevron*, courts should defer to the EPA interpretation. The court also emphasized the institutional advantages of the EPA, which has "deep familiarity with the CAA and the public policy considerations that underlie these statutory provisions." It added that the EPA was in a good position to ensure "a uniform answer" and to "provide a nationwide answer."

In a similar vein, see Access Telecommunications v. Southwestern Bell Telephone Co., 137 F.3d 605 (8th Cir. 1998), where the court held that alleged overcharges by a firm subject to FCC regulation should be referred to the FCC, because of the presence of technical issues more suitable for FCC resolution. See also Massachusetts v. Blackstone Valley Electric Co., 67 F.3d 981 (1st Cir. 1995), invoking the interest in uniformity and application of technical expertise to conclude that the EPA had primary jurisdiction over the question of whether ferric ferrocyanide qualified as a hazardous substance within the meaning of CERCLA.

But pragmatic considerations are sometimes taken to counsel against invocation of the primary jurisdiction doctrine. Consider United States v. Haun, 124 F.3d 745 (6th Cir. 1997), where the court held that the Department of Agriculture did not have primary jurisdiction over an issue involving a violation of the Packers and Stockyards Act. The court emphasized that the dispute did not involve issues of uniformity, discretion, or "intricate fact." To the same effect, see National Communications Association v. AT&T, 46 F.3d 220 (2d Cir. 1995), holding that tariff interpretation should not be deferred to the agency because technical and policy issues were not involved and because of the problem of delay. In PHC, Inc. v. Pioneer Healthcare, Inc., 75 F.3d 75 (1st Cir. 1995), the court acknowledged that the validity of a trademark raises issues calling for uniformity and application of expertise, but nonetheless held that primary jurisdiction should not be invoked, because it would produce delay, and because the U.S. Patent and Trademark Office could not provide either damages or injunctive relief.

For a discussion from the Supreme Court, see Marquez v. Screen Actors Guild, 525 U.S. 33 (1998). At issue was whether, in the unusual context of a claim that the union violated its duty of fair representation, the NLRB had primary jurisdiction over legal issues relating to the interpretation of the National Labor Relations Act. There was a reasonable argument that the NLRB did have primary jurisdiction, because interpretation of the NLRA was necessary to evaluate a claim of a violation of the duty of fair representation. The Court concluded that the NLRB would have primary jurisdiction if the plaintiff's claim was only of a breach of the NLRA, and did not include allegations of arbitrary, discriminatory, or bad faith union conduct. But if the plaintiff did make such allegations, and if the issue of statutory interpretation was "collateral" to them, the court could resolve the case on its own.

For the view that primary jurisdiction can never be invoked when the agency is a plaintiff, see United States v. Any and All Radio Station Transmission Equipment, 204 F.3d 658 (6th Cir. 2000). The court said that the "agency's decision to pursue a judicial remedy rather than an administrative remedy speaks volumes about its views regarding the necessity of administrative expertise." For other cases, see In re Starnet, 355 F.3d 634 (7th Cir. 2004); Baker v. IBP, 357 F.3d 685 (7th Cir. 2004); Rymes Heating Oils v. Springfield Terminal Railway Co., 358 F.3d 91 (1st Cir. 2004).

Appendix A:
Selected Provisions from the Federal Administrative Procedure Act

Chapter 5, Subchapter II — Administrative Procedure

§551. *Definitions*

For the purpose of this subchapter —

(1) "agency" means each authority of the Government of the United States, whether or not it is within or subject to review by another agency, but does not include —

(A) the Congress;

(B) the courts of the United States;

(C) the governments of the territories or possessions of the United States;

(D) the government of the District of Columbia; or except as to the requirements of section 552 of this title —

(E) agencies composed of representatives of the parties or of representatives of organizations of the parties to the disputes determined by them;

(F) courts martial and military commissions;

(G) military authority exercised in the field in time of war or in occupied territory; or

(H) functions conferred by sections 1738, 1739, 1743, and 1744 of title 12; chapter 2 of title 41; subchapter II of chapter 471 of title 49; or sections 1884, 1891-1902, and former section 1641(b)(2), of title 50, appendix;

(2) "person" includes an individual, partnership, corporation, association, or public or private organization other than an agency;

(3) "party" includes a person or agency named or admitted as a party, or properly seeking and entitled as of right to be admitted as a party, in an agency proceeding, and a person or agency admitted by an agency as a party for limited purposes;

(4) "rule" means the whole or a part of an agency statement of general or particular applicability and future effect designed to implement, interpret, or prescribe law or policy or describing the organization, procedure, or practice requirements of an agency and includes the approval or prescription for the future of rates, wages, corporate or financial structures or reorganizations thereof, prices, facilities, appliances, services or allowances therefor or of valuations, costs, or accounting, or practices bearing on any of the foregoing;

(5) "rule making" means agency process for formulating, amending, or repealing a rule;

(6) "order" means the whole or a part of a final disposition, whether affirmative, negative, injunctive, or declaratory in form, of an agency in a matter other than rule making but including licensing;

(7) "adjudication" means agency process for the formulation of an order;

(8) "license" includes the whole or a part of an agency permit, certificate, approval, registration, charter, membership, statutory exemption or other form of permission;

(9) "licensing" includes agency process respecting the grant, renewal, denial, revocation, suspension, annulment, withdrawal, limitation, amendment, modification, or conditioning of a license;

(10) "sanction" includes the whole or a part of an agency —

(A) prohibition, requirement, limitation, or other condition affecting the freedom of a person;

(B) withholding of relief;

(C) imposition of penalty or fine;

(D) destruction, taking, seizure, or withholding of property;

(E) assessment of damages, reimbursement, restitution, compensation, costs, charges, or fees;

(F) requirement, revocation, or suspension of a license; or

(G) taking other compulsory or restrictive action;

(11) "relief" includes the whole or a part of an agency —

(A) grant of money, assistance, license, authority, exemption, exception, privilege, or remedy;

(B) recognition of a claim, right, immunity, privilege, exemption, or exception; or

(C) taking of other action on the application or petition of, and beneficial to, a person;

(12) "agency proceeding" means an agency process as defined by paragraphs (5), (7), and (9) of this section;

(13) "agency action" includes the whole or a part of an agency rule, order, license, sanction, relief, or the equivalent or denial thereof, or failure to act; and

(14) "ex parte communication" means an oral or written communication not on the public record with respect to which reasonable prior notice to all parties is not given, but it shall not include requests for status reports on any matter or proceeding covered by this subchapter.

§552. *Public Information; Agency Rules, Opinions, Orders, Records, and Proceedings*

(a) Each agency shall make available to the public information as follows;

(1) Each agency shall separately state and currently publish in the Federal Register for the guidance of the public —

(A) descriptions of its central and field organization and the established places at which, the employees (and in the case of a uniformed service, the members) from whom, and the methods whereby, the public may obtain information, make submittals or requests, or obtain decisions;

(B) statements of the general course and method by which its functions are channeled and determined, including the nature and requirements of all formal and informal procedures available;

(C) rules of procedure, descriptions of forms available or the places at which forms may be obtained, and instructions as to the scope and contents of all papers, reports, or examinations;

(D) substantive rules of general applicability adopted as authorized by law, and statements of general policy or interpretations of general applicability formulated and adopted by the agency; and

(E) each amendment, revision, or repeal of the foregoing.

Except to the extent that a person has actual and timely notice of the terms thereof, a person may not in any manner be required to resort to, or be adversely affected by, a matter required to be published in the Federal Register and not so published. For the purpose of this paragraph, matter reasonably available to the class of persons affected thereby is deemed published in the Federal Register when incorporated by reference therein with the approval of the Director of the Federal Register.

(2) Each agency, in accordance with published rules, shall make available for public inspection and copying —

(A) final opinions, including concurring and dissenting opinions, as well as orders, made in the adjudication of cases;

(B) those statements of policy and interpretations which have been adopted by the agency and are not published in the Federal Register; and

(C) administrative staff manuals and instructions to staff that affect a member of the public;

(D) copies of all records, regardless of form or format, which have been released to any person under paragraph (3) and which, because of the nature of their subject matter; the agency determines have become or are likely to become the subject of subsequent requests for substantially the same records; and

(E) a general index of the records referred to under subparagraph (D);

unless the materials are promptly published and copies offered for sale. For records created on or after November 1, 1996, within one year after such date, each agency shall make such records available, including by computer telecommunications or, if computer telecommunications means have not been established by the agency, by other electronic means. To the extent required to prevent a clearly unwarranted invasion of personal privacy, an agency may delete identifying details when it makes available or publishes an opinion, statement of policy, interpretation, staff manual, instruction, or copies of records referred to in subparagraph (D). However, in each case the justification for the deletion shall be explained fully in writing, and the extent of such deletion shall be indicated on the portion of the record which is made available or published, unless including that indication would harm an interest protected by the exemption in subsection (b) under which the deletion is made. If technically feasible, the extent of the deletion shall be indicated at the place in the record where the deletion was made. Each agency shall also maintain and make available for public inspection and copying current indexes providing identifying information for the public as to any matter issued, adopted, or promulgated after July 4, 1967, and required by this paragraph to be made available or published. Each agency shall promptly publish, quarterly or more frequently, and distribute (by sale or otherwise) copies of each index or supplements thereto unless it determines by order published in the Federal Register that the publication would be unnecessary and impracticable, in which case the agency shall nonetheless provide copies of such index on request at a cost not to exceed the direct cost of duplication. Each agency shall make the index referred to in subparagraph (E) available by computer telecommunications by December 31, 1999. A final order, opinion, statement of policy, interpretation, or staff manual or instruction that affects a member of the public may be relied on, used, or cited as precedent by an agency against a party other than an agency only if —

(i) it has been indexed and either made available or published as provided by this paragraph; or

(ii) the party has actual and timely notice of the terms thereof.

(3)(A) Except with respect to the records made available under paragraphs (1) and (2) of this subsection, each agency, upon any request for records which (i) reasonably describes such records and (ii) is made in accordance with published rules stating the time, place, fees (if any), and procedures to be followed, shall make the records promptly available to any person.

(B) In making any record available to a person under this paragraph, an agency shall provide the record in any form or format requested by the person if the record is readily reproducible by the agency in that form or format. Each agency shall make reasonable efforts to maintain its records in forms or formats that are reproducible for purposes of this section.

(C) In responding under this paragraph to a request for records, an agency shall make reasonable efforts to search for the records in electronic form or format, except when such efforts would significantly interfere with the operation of the agency's automated information system.

(4) (A)(i) In order to carry out the provisions of this section, each agency shall promulgate regulations, pursuant to notice and receipt of public comment, specifying the schedule of fees applicable to the processing of requests under this section and establishing procedures and guidelines for determining when such fees should be waived or reduced. Such schedule shall conform to the guidelines which shall be promulgated, pursuant to notice and receipt of public comment, by the Director of the Office of Management and Budget and which shall provide for a uniform schedule of fees for all agencies.

(ii) Such agency regulations shall provide that —

(I) fees shall be limited to reasonable standard charges for document search, duplication, and review, when records are requested for commercial use;

(II) fees shall be limited to reasonable standard charges for document duplication when records are not sought for commercial use and the request is made by an educational or noncommercial scientific institution, whose purpose is scholarly or scientific research; or a representative of the news media; and

(III) for any request not described in (I) or (II), fees shall be limited to reasonable standard charges for document search and duplication.

(iii) Documents shall be furnished without any charge or at a charge reduced below the fees established under clause (ii) if disclosure of the information is in the public interest because it is likely to contribute significantly to public understanding of the operations or activities of the government and is not primarily in the commercial interest of the requester.

(iv) Fee schedules shall provide for the recovery of only the direct costs of search, duplication, or review. Review costs shall include only the direct costs incurred during the initial examination of a document for the purposes of determining whether the documents must be disclosed under this section and for the purposes of withholding any portions exempt from disclosure under this section. Review costs may not include any costs incurred in resolving issues of law or policy that may be raised in the course of processing a request under this section. No fee may be charged by an agency under this section —

(I) if the costs of routine collection and processing of the fee are likely to equal or exceed the amount of the fee; or

(II) for any request described in clause (ii)(II) or (III) of the subparagraph for the first two hours of search time or for the first one hundred pages of duplication.

(v) No agency may require advance payment of any fee unless the requester has previously failed to pay fees in a timely fashion, or the agency has determined that the fee will exceed $250.

(vi) Nothing in this subparagraph shall supersede fees chargeable under a statute specifically providing for setting the level of fees for particular types of records.

(vii) In any action by a requester regarding the waiver of fees under this section, the court shall determine the matter de novo: Provided, that the court's review of the matter shall be limited to the record before the agency.

(B) On complaint, the district court of the United States in the district in which the complainant resides, or has his principal place of business, or in which the agency records are situated, or in the District of Columbia, has jurisdiction to enjoin the agency from withholding agency records and to order the production of any agency records improperly withheld from the complainant. In such a case the court shall determine the matter de novo, and may examine the contents of such agency records in camera to determine whether such records or any part thereof shall be withheld under any of the exemptions set forth in subsection (b) of this section, and the burden is on the agency to sustain its action. In addition to any other matters to which a court accords substantial weight, a court shall accord substantial weight to an affidavit of an agency concerning the agency's determination as to technical feasibility under paragraph (2)(C) and subsection (b) and reproducibility under paragraph (3)(B).

(C) Notwithstanding any other provision of law, the defendant shall serve an answer or otherwise plead to any complaint made under this subsection within thirty days after service upon the defendant of the pleading in which such complaint is made, unless the court otherwise directs for good cause shown.

[(D) Repealed. Pub.L. 98-620, Title IV, §402(2), Nov. 8, 1984, 98 Stat. 3357]

(E) The court may assess against the United States reasonable attorney fees and other litigation costs reasonably incurred in any case under this section in which the complainant has substantially prevailed.

(F) Whenever the court orders the production of any agency records improperly withheld from the complainant and assesses against the United States reasonable attorney fees and other litigation costs, and the court additionally issues a written finding that the circumstances surrounding the withholding raise questions whether agency personnel acted arbitrarily or capriciously with respect to the withholding, the Special Counsel shall promptly initiate a proceeding to determine whether disciplinary action is warranted against the officer or employee who was primarily responsible for the withholding. The Special Counsel, after investigation and consideration of the evidence submitted, shall submit his findings and recommendations to the administrative authority of the agency concerned and shall send copies of the findings and recommendations to the officer or employee or his representative. The administrative authority shall take the corrective action that the Special Counsel recommends.

(G) In the event of noncompliance with the order of the court, the district court may punish for contempt the responsible employee, and in the case of a uniformed service, the responsible member.

(5) Each agency having more than one member shall maintain and make available for public inspection a record of the final votes of each member in every agency proceeding.

(6) (A) Each agency, upon any request for records made under paragraph (1), (2), or (3) of this subsection shall —

(i) determine within 20 days (excepting Saturdays, Sundays, and legal public holidays) after the receipt of any such request whether to comply with such request and shall immediately notify the person making such request of such determination and the reasons therefor, and of the right of such person to appeal to the head of the agency any adverse determination; and

(ii) make a determination with respect to any appeal within twenty days (excepting Saturdays, Sundays, and legal public holidays) after the receipt of such appeal. If on appeal the denial of the request for records is in whole or in part upheld, the agency shall notify the person making such request of the provisions for judicial review of that determination under paragraph (4) of this subsection.

(B)(i) In unusual circumstances as specified in this subparagraph, the time limits prescribed in either clause (i) or clause (ii) of subparagraph (A) may be extended by written notice to the person making such request setting forth the unusual circumstances for such extension and the date on which a determination is expected to be dispatched. No such notice shall specify a date that would result in an extension for more than ten working days, except as provided in clause (ii) of the subparagraph.

(ii) With respect to a request for which a written notice under clause (i) extends the time limits prescribed under clause (i) of subparagraph (A), the agency shall notify the person making the request if the request cannot be processed within the time limit specified in that clause and shall provide the person an opportunity to limit the scope of the request so that it may be processed within that time limit or an opportunity to arrange with the agency an alternative time frame for processing the request or a modified request. Refusal by the person to reasonably modify the request or arrange such an alternative time frame shall be considered as a factor in determining whether exceptional circumstances exist for purposes of subparagraph (C).

(iii) As used in this subparagraph, "unusual circumstances" means, but only to the extent reasonably necessary to the proper processing of the particular requests —

(I) the need to search for and collect the requested records from field facilities or other establishments that are separate from the office processing the request;

(II) the need to search for, collect, and appropriately examine a voluminous amount of separate and distinct records which are demanded in a single request; or

(III) the need for consultation, which shall be conducted with all practicable speed, with another agency having a substantial interest in the determination of the request or among two or more components of the agency having substantial subject-matter interest therein.

(iv) Each agency may promulgate regulations, pursuant to notice and receipt of public comment, providing for the aggregation of certain requests by the same requestor, or by a group of requestors acting in concert, if the agency reasonably believes that such requests actually constitute a single request, which would otherwise satisfy the unusual circumstances specified in this subparagraph, and the requests involve clearly related matters. Multiple requests involving unrelated matters shall not be aggregated.

(C)(i) Any person having a request to any agency for records under paragraph (1), (2), or (3) of this subsection shall be deemed to have exhausted his administrative remedies with respect to such request if the agency fails to comply with the applicable time limit provisions of this paragraph. If the Government can show exceptional circumstances exist and that the agency is exercising due diligence in responding to the request, the court may retain jurisdiction and allow the agency additional time to complete its review of the records. Upon any determination by an agency to comply with a request for records, the records shall be made promptly available to such person making such request. Any notification of denial of any request for records under this subsection shall set forth the names and titles or positions of each person responsible for the denial of such request.

(ii) For purposes of this subparagraph, the term "exceptional circumstances" does not include a delay that results from a predictable agency workload of requests under this section, unless the agency demonstrates reasonable progress in reducing its backlog of pending requests.

(iii) Refusal by a person to reasonably modify the scope of a request or arrange an alternative time frame for processing a request (or a modified request) under clause (ii) after being given an opportunity to do so by the agency to whom the person made the request shall be considered as a factor in determining whether exceptional circumstances exist for purposes of this subparagraph.

(D)(i) Each agency may promulgate regulations, pursuant to notice and receipt of public comment, providing for multitrack processing of requests for records based on the amount of work or time (or both) involved in processing requests.

(ii) Regulations under this subparagraph may provide a person making a request that does not qualify for the fastest multitrack processing an opportunity to limit the scope of the request in order to quality for faster processing.

(iii) This subparagraph shall not be considered to affect the requirement under subparagraph (C) to exercise due diligence.

(E)(i) Each agency shall promulgate regulations, pursuant to notice and receipt of public comment, providing for expedited processing of requests for records —

(I) in cases in which the person requesting the records demonstrates a compelling need; and

(II) in other cases determined by the agency.

(ii) Notwithstanding clause (i), regulations under this subparagraph must ensure —

(I) that a determination of whether to provide expedited processing shall be made, and notice of the determination shall be provided to the person making the request, within 10 days after the date of the request; and

(II) expeditious consideration of administrative appeals of such determinations of whether to provide expedited processing.

(iii) An agency shall process as soon as practicable any request for records to which the agency has granted expedited processing under this subparagraph. Agency action to deny or affirm denial of a request for expedited processing pursuant to this subparagraph, and failure by an agency to respond in a timely manner to such a request shall be subject to judicial review under paragraph (4), except that the judicial review shall be based on the record before the agency at the time of the determination.

(iv) A district court of the United States shall not have jurisdiction to review an agency denial of expedited processing of a request for records after the agency has provided a complete response to the request.

(v) For purposes of this subparagraph, the term "compelling need" means —

(I) that a failure to obtain requested records on an expedited basis under this paragraph could reasonably be expected to pose an imminent threat to the life or physical safety of an individual; or

(II) with respect to a request made by a person primarily engaged in disseminating information, urgency to inform the public concerning actual or alleged Federal Government activity.

(vi) A demonstration of a compelling need by a person making a request for expedited processing shall be made by a statement certified by such person to be true and correct to the best of such person's knowledge and belief.

(F) In denying a request for records, in whole or in part, an agency shall make a reasonable effort to estimate the volume of any requested matter the provision of which is denied, and shall provide any such estimate to the person making the request, unless providing such estimate would harm an interest protected by the exemption in subsection (b) pursuant to which the denial is made

(b) This section does not apply to matters that are —

(1)(A) specifically authorized under criteria established by an Executive order to be kept secret in the interest of national defense or foreign policy and (B) are in fact properly classified pursuant to such Executive order;

(2) related solely to the internal personnel rules and practices of an agency;

(3) specifically exempted from disclosure by statute (other than section 552b of this title), provided that such statute (A) requires that the matters be withheld from the public in such a manner as to leave no discretion on the issue, or (B) establishes particular criteria for withholding or refers to particular types of matters to be withheld;

(4) trade secrets and commercial or financial information obtained from a person and privileged or confidential;

(5) inter-agency or intra-agency memorandums or letters which would not be available by law to a party other than an agency in litigation with the agency;

(6) personnel and medical files and similar files the disclosure of which would constitute a clearly unwarranted invasion of personal privacy;

(7) records or information compiled for law enforcement purposes, but only to the extent that the production of such law enforcement records or information (A) could reasonably be expected to interfere with enforcement proceedings, (B) would deprive a person of a right to a fair trial or an impartial adjudication, (C) could reasonably be expected to constitute an unwarranted invasion of personal privacy, (D) could reasonably

be expected to disclose the identity of a confidential source, including a State, local, or foreign agency or authority or any private institution which furnished information on a confidential basis, and, in the case of a record or information compiled by criminal law enforcement authority in the course of a criminal investigation or by an agency conducting a lawful national security intelligence investigation, information furnished by a confidential source, (E) would disclose techniques and procedures for law enforcement investigations or prosecutions, or would disclose guidelines for law enforcement investigations or prosecutions if such disclosure could reasonably be expected to risk circumvention of the law, or (F) could reasonably be expected to endanger the life or physical safety of any individual;

(8) contained in or related to examination, operating, or condition reports prepared by, on behalf of, or for the use of an agency responsible for the regulation or supervision of financial institutions; or

(9) geological and geophysical information and data, including maps, concerning wells.

Any reasonably segregable portion of a record shall be provided to any person requesting such record after deletion of the portions which are exempt under this subsection. The amount of information deleted shall be indicated on the released portion of the record, unless including that indication would harm an interest protected by the exemption in this subsection under which the deletion is made. If technically feasible, the amount of the information shall be indicated at the place in the record where such deletion is made.

(c)(1) Whenever a request is made which involves access to records described in subsection (b)(7)(A) and —

(A) the investigation or proceeding involves a possible violation of criminal law; and

(B) there is reason to believe that (i) the subject of the investigation or proceeding is not aware of its pendency, and (ii) disclosure of the existence of the records could reasonably be expected to interfere with enforcement proceedings, the agency may, during only such time as that circumstance continues, treat the records as not subject to the requirements of this section.

(2) Whenever informant records maintained by a criminal law enforcement agency under an informant's name or personal identifier are requested by a third party according to the informant's name or personal identifier, the agency may treat the records as not subject to the requirements of this section unless the informant's status as an informant has been officially confirmed.

(3) Whenever a request is made which involves access to records maintained by the Federal Bureau of Investigation pertaining to foreign intelligence or counterintelligence, or international terrorism, and the existence of the records is classified information as provided in subsection (b)(1), the Bureau may, as long as the existence of the records remains classified information, treat the records as not subject to the requirements of this section.

(d) This section does not authorize withholding of information or limit the availability of records to the public, except as specifically stated in this section. This section is not authority to withhold information from Congress.

(e)(1) On or before February 1 of each year, each agency shall submit to the Attorney General of the United States a report which shall cover the preceding fiscal year and which shall include —

(A) the number of determinations made by the agency not to comply with requests for records made to such agency under subsection (a) and the reasons for each such determination;

(B)(i) the number of appeals made by persons under subsection (a)(6), the result of such appeals, and the reason for the action upon each appeal that results in a denial of information; and

(ii) a complete list of all statutes that the agency relies upon to authorize the agency to withhold information under subsection (b)(3), a description of whether a court has upheld the decision of the agency to withhold information under each such statute, and a concise description of the scope of any information withheld;

(C) the number of requests for records pending before the agency as of September 30 of the preceding year, and the median number of days that such requests had been pending before the agency as of that date;

(D) the number of requests for records received by the agency and the number of requests which the agency processed;

(E) the median number of days taken by the agency to process different types of requests;

(F) the total amount of fees collected by the agency for processing requests; and

(G) the number of full-time staff of the agency devoted to processing requests for records under this section, and the total amount expended by the agency for processing such requests.

(2) Each agency shall make each such report available to the public including by computer telecommunications, or if computer telecommunications means have not been established by the agency, by other electronic means.

(3) The Attorney General of the United States shall make each report which has been made available by electronic means available at a single electronic access point. The Attorney General of the United States shall notify the Chairman and ranking minority member of the Committee on Government Reform and Oversight of the House of Representatives and the Chairman and ranking minority member of the Committees on Governmental Affairs and the Judiciary of the Senate, no later than April 1 of the year in which each such report is issued, that such reports are available by electronic means.

(4) The Attorney General of the United States, in consultation with the Director of the Office of Management and Budget, shall develop reporting and performance guidelines in connection with reports required by this subsection by October 17, 1997, and may establish additional requirements for such reports as the Attorney General determines may be useful.

(5) The Attorney General of the United States shall submit an annual report on or before April 1 of each calendar year which shall include for the prior calendar year a listing of the number of cases arising under this section, the exemption involved in each case, the disposition of such case, and the cost, fees, and penalties assessed under subparagraphs (E), (F), and (G) of subsection (a)(4). Such report shall also include a description of the efforts undertaken by the Department of Justice to encourage agency compliance with this section.

(f) For purposes of this section, the term —

(1) "agency" as defined in section 551(1) of this title includes any executive department, military department, Government corporation, Government controlled corporation, or other establishment in the executive branch of the Government (including the Executive Office of the President), or any independent regulatory agency; and

[§§552a (dealing with protection of individual privacy) and 552b (dealing with open government meetings) are omitted.]

§553. Rulemaking

(a) This section applies, accordingly to the provisions thereof, except to the extent that there is involved —

(1) a military or foreign affairs function of the United States; or

(2) a matter relating to agency management or personnel or to public property, loans, grants, benefits, or contracts.

(b) General notice of proposed rulemaking shall be published in the Federal Register, unless persons subject thereto are named and either personally served or otherwise have actual notice thereof in accordance with law. The notice shall include —

(1) a statement of the time, place, and nature of public rulemaking proceedings.

(2) reference to the legal authority under which the rule is proposed; and

(3) either the terms or substance of the proposed rule or a description of the subjects and issues involved.

Except, when notice or hearing is required by statute, this subsection does not apply —

(A) to interpretative rules, general statements of policy, or rules of agency organization, procedure, or practice; or

(B) when the agency for good cause finds (and incorporates the finding and a brief statement of reasons therefor in the rules issued) that notice and public procedure thereon are impracticable, unnecessary, or contrary to the public interest.

(c) After notice required by this section, the agency shall give interested persons an opportunity to participate in the rulemaking through submission of written data, views, or arguments with or without opportunity for oral presentation. After consideration of the relevant matter presented, the agency shall incorporate in the rules adopted a concise general statement of their basis and purpose. When rules are required by statute to be made on the record after opportunity for an agency hearing, sections 556 and 557 of this title apply instead of this subsection.

(d) The required publication or service of a substance rule shall be made not less than 30 days before its effective date, except —

(1) a substantive rule which grants or recognizes an exemption or relieves a restriction;

(2) interpretative rules and statements of policy; or

(3) as otherwise provided by the agency for good cause found and published with the rule.

(e) Each agency shall give an interested person the right to petition for the issuance, amendment, or repeal of a rule.

§554. Adjudications

(a) This section applies, according to the provisions thereof, in every case of adjudication required by statute to be determined on the record after opportunity for an agency hearing, except to the extent that there is involved —

(1) a matter subject to a subsequent trial of the law and the facts de novo in a court;

(2) the selection or tenure of an employee, except an administrative law judge appointed under section 3105 of this title;

(3) proceedings in which decisions rest solely on inspections, tests, or elections;

(4) the conduct of military or foreign affairs functions;

(5) cases in which an agency is acting as an agent for a court; or

(6) the certification of worker representatives.

(b) Persons entitled to notice of an agency hearing shall be timely informed of —

(1) the time, place, and nature of the hearing;

(2) the legal authority and jurisdiction under which the hearing is to be held; and

(3) the matters of fact and law asserted.

When private persons are the moving parties, other parties to the proceeding shall give prompt notice of issues controverted in fact or law; and in other instances agencies may by rule require responsive pleading. In fixing the time and place for hearings, due regard shall be had for the convenience and necessity of the parties or their representatives.

(c) The agency shall give all interested parties opportunity for —

(1) the submission and consideration of facts, arguments, offers of settlement, or proposals of adjustment when time, the nature of the proceeding, and the public interest permit; and

(2) to the extent that the parties are unable so to determine a controversy by consent, hearing and decision on notice and in accordance with sections 556 and 557 of this title.

(d) The employee who presides at the reception of evidence pursuant to section 556 of this title shall make the recommended decision or initial decision required by section 557 of this title, unless he becomes unavailable to the agency. Except to the extent required for the disposition of ex parte matters as authorized by law, such an employee may not —

(1) consult a person or party on a fact in issue, unless on notice and opportunity for all parties to participate; or

(2) be responsible to or subject to the supervision or direction of an employee or agent engaged in the performance of investigative or prosecuting functions for an agency. An employee or agent engaged in the performance of investigative or prosecuting functions for an agency in a case may not, in that or a factually related case, participate or advise in the decision, recommended decision, or agency review pursuant to section 557 of this title, except as witness or counsel in public proceedings. This subsection does not apply —

(A) in determining applications for initial licenses;

(B) to proceedings involving the validity or application of rates, facilities, or practices of public utilities or earners; or

(C) to the agency or a member or members of the body comprising the agency.

(e) The agency, with like effect as in the case of other orders, and in its sound discretion, may issue a declaratory order to terminate a controversy or remove uncertainty.

§555.   *Ancillary Matters*

(a) This section applies, according to the provisions thereof, except as otherwise provided by this subchapter.

(b) A person compelled to appear in person before an agency or representative thereof is entitled to be accompanied, represented, and advised by counsel or, if permitted by the agency, by other qualified representative. A party is entitled to appear in person or by or with counsel or other duly qualified representative in an agency proceeding. So far as the orderly conduct of public business permits, an interested person may appear before an agency or its responsible employees for the presentation, adjustment, or determination of an issue, request, or controversy in a proceeding, whether interlocutory summary, or otherwise, or in connection with an agency function. With due regard for the convenience and necessity of the parties or their representatives and within a reasonable time, each agency shall proceed to conclude a matter presented to it. This subsection does not grant or deny a person who is not a lawyer the right to appear for or represent others before an agency or in an agency proceeding.

(c) Process, requirement of a report, inspection, or other investigative act or demand may not be issued, made, or enforced except as authorized by law. A person compelled to submit data or evidence is entitled to retain or, on payment of lawfully prescribed costs, procure a copy or transcript thereof, except that in a nonpublic investigator proceeding the witness may for good cause be limited to inspection of the official transcript of his testimony.

(d) Agency subpenas authorized by law shall be issued to a party on request and, when required by rules of procedure, on a statement or showing of general relevance and reasonable scope of the evidence sought. On contest, the court shall sustain the subpena or similar process or demand to the extent that it is found to be in accordance with law. In a proceeding for enforcement, the court shall issue an order requiring the appearance of the witness or the production of the evidence or data within a reasonable time under penalty of punishment for contempt in case of contumacious failure to comply.

(e) Prompt notice shall be given of the denial in whole or in part of a written application, petition, or other request of an interested person made in connection with any agency proceeding. Except in affirming a prior denial or when the denial is self-explanatory, the notice shall be accompanied by a brief statement of the grounds for denial.

§556. Hearings; Presiding Employees; Powers and Duties; Burden of Proof; Evidence; Record as Basis of Decision

(a) This section applies, according to the provisions thereof, to hearings required by section 553 or 554 of this title to be conducted in accordance with this section.

(b) There shall preside at the taking of evidence —

    (1) the agency;

    (2) one or more members of the body which comprises the agency; or

    (3) one or more administrative law judges appointed under section 3105 of this title.

This subchapter does not supersede the conduct of specified classes of proceedings, in whole or in part, by or before boards or other employees specially provided for by or designated under statute. The functions of presiding employees and of employees participating in decisions in accordance with section 557 of this title shall be conducted in an impartial manner. A presiding or participating employee may at any time disqualify himself. On the filing in good faith of a timely and sufficient affidavit of personal bias or other disqualification of a presiding or participating employee, the agency shall determine the matters as a part of the record and decision in the case.

(c) Subject to published rules of the agency and within its powers, employees presiding at hearing may —

(1) administer oaths and affirmations;

(2) issue subpenas authorized by law;

(3) rule on offers of proof and receive relevant evidence;

(4) take depositions or have depositions taken when the ends of justice would be served;

(5) regulate the course of the hearing;

(6) hold conferences for the settlement or simplification of the issues by consent of the parties or by the use of alternative means of dispute resolution as provided in subchapter IV of this chapter;

(7) inform the parties as to the availability of one or more alternative means of dispute resolution, and encourage use of such methods;

(8) require the attendance at any conference held pursuant to paragraph (6) of at least one representative of each party who has authority to negotiate concerning resolution of issues in controversy;

(9) dispose of procedural requests or similar matters;

(10) make or recommend decisions in accordance with section 557 of this title; and

(11) take other action authorized by agency rules consistent with this subchapter.

(d) Except as otherwise provided by statute, the proponent of a rule or order has the burden of proof. Any oral or documentary evidence may be received, but the agency as a matter of policy shall provide for the exclusion of irrelevant, immaterial, or unduly repetitious evidence. A sanction may not be imposed or rule or order issued except on consideration of the whole record or those parts thereof cited by a party and supported by and in accordance with the reliable, probative, and substantial evidence. The agency may, to the extent consistent with the interests of justice and the policy of the underlying statutes administered by the agency, consider a violation of section 557(d) of this title sufficient grounds for a decision adverse to a party who has knowingly committed such violation or knowingly caused such violation to occur. A party is entitled to present his case or defense by oral or documentary evidence, to submit rebuttal evidence, and to conduct such cross-examination as may be required for a full and true disclosure of the facts. In rule making or determining claims for money or benefits or applications for initial licenses an agency may, when a party will not be prejudiced thereby, adopt procedures for the submission of all or part of the evidence in written form.

(e) The transcript of testimony and exhibits, together with all papers and requests filed in the proceeding, constitutes the exclusive record for decision in accordance with section 557 of this title and, on payment of lawfully prescribed costs, shall be made available to the parties. When an agency decision rests on official notice of a material fact not appearing in the evidence in the record, a party is entitled, on timely request, to an opportunity to show the contrary.

§557. *Initial Decisions; Conclusiveness; Review by Agency; Submissions by Parties; Contents of Decisions; Record*

(a) This section applies, according to the provision thereof, when a hearing is required to be conducted in accordance with section 556 of this title.

(b) When the agency did not preside at the reception of the evidence, the presiding employee or, in cases not subject to section 554(d) of this title, an employee qualified to preside at hearings pursuant to section 556 of this title, shall initially decide the case unless the agency requires, either in specific cases or by general rule, the entire record to be certified to it for decision. When the presiding employee makes an initial decision, that decision then becomes the decision of the agency without further proceedings unless there is an appeal to, or review on motion of, the agency within the time provided by rule. On appeal from or review of the initial decision, the agency has all the powers which it would have in making the initial decision except as it may limit the issues on notice or by rule. When the agency makes the decision without having presided at the reception of the evidence, the presiding employee or an employee qualified to preside at hearings pursuant to section 556 of this title shall first recommend a decision, except that in rule making or determining application of initial licenses —

(1) instead thereof the agency may issue a tentative decision or one of its responsible employees may recommend a decision; or

(2) this procedures may be omitted in a case in which the agency finds on the record that due and timely execution of its functions imperatively and unavoidably so requires.

(c) Before a recommended, initial, or tentative decision, or a decision on agency review of the decision of subordinate employees, the parties are entitled to a reasonable opportunity to submit for the consideration of the employees participating in the decisions —

(1) proposed findings and conclusions; or

(2) exceptions to the decisions or recommended decisions of subordinate employees or to tentative agency decisions; and

(3) supporting reasons for the exceptions or proposed findings or conclusions.

The record shall show the ruling on each finding, conclusion, or exception presented. All decisions, including initial, recommended, and tentative decisions, are a part of the record and shall include a statement of —

(A) findings and conclusions, and the reasons or basis therefor, on all the material issues of fact, law, or discretion presented on the record; and

(B) the appropriate rule, order, sanction, relief, or denial thereof.

(d)(1) In any agency proceeding which is subject to subsection (a) of this section, except to the extent required for the disposition of ex parte matters as authorized by law —

(A) no interested person outside the agency shall make or knowingly cause to be made to any member of the body comprising the agency, administrative law judge, or other employee who is or may reasonably be expected to be involved in the decisional process of the proceeding, an ex parte communication relevant to the merits of the proceeding;

(B) no member of the body comprising the agency, administrative law judge, or other employee who is or may reasonably be expected to be involved in the decisional process of the proceeding, shall make or knowingly cause to be made to any interested person outside the agency an ex parte communication relevant to the merits of the proceeding;

(C) a member of the body comprising the agency, administrative law judge, or other employee who is or may reasonably be expected to be involved in the decisional process of such proceeding who receives, or who makes or knowingly causes to be made, a communication prohibited by this subsection shall place on the public record of the proceeding:

(i) all such written communications;

(ii) memoranda stating the substance of all such oral communications; and

(iii) all written responses, and memoranda stating the substance of all oral responses, to the materials described in clauses (i) and (ii) of this subparagraph;

(D) upon receipt of a communication knowingly made or knowingly caused to be made by a party in violation of this subsection, the agency, administrative law judge, or other employee presiding at the hearing may, to the extent consistent with the interests of justice and the policy of the underlying statutes, require the party to show cause why his claim or interest in the proceeding should not be dismissed, denied, disregarded, or otherwise adversely affected on account of such violation; and

(E) the prohibitions of this subsection shall apply beginning at such time as the agency may designate, but in no case shall they begin to apply later than the time at which a proceeding is noticed for hearing unless the person responsible for the communication has knowledge that it will be noticed, in which case the prohibitions shall apply beginning at the time of his acquisition of such knowledge.

(2) This subsection does not constitute authority to withhold information from Congress.

§558. Imposition of Sanctions; Determination of Applications for Licenses; Suspension, Revocation, and Expiration of Licenses

(a) This section applies, according to the provisions thereof, to the exercise of a power or authority.

(b) A sanction may not be imposed or a substantive rule of order issued except within jurisdiction delegated to the agency and as authorized by law.

(c) When application is made for a license required by law, the agency, with due regard for the rights and privileges of all interested parties or adversely affected persons and within a reasonable time, shall set and complete proceedings required to be conducted in accordance with sections 556 and 557 of this title or other proceedings required by law and shall make its decision. Except in cases of willfulness or those in which public health, interest, or safety requires otherwise, the withdrawal, suspension, revocation, or annulment of a license is lawful only if, before the institution of agency proceedings therefor, the licensee has been given —

(1) notice by the agency in writing of the facts or conduct which may warrant the action; and

(2) opportunity to demonstrate or achieve compliance with all lawful requirements.

When the licensee has made timely and sufficient application for a renewal or a new license in accordance with agency rules, a license with reference to an activity of a continuing nature does not expire until the application has been finally determined by the agency.

§559. Effect on Other Laws; Effect of Subsequent Statute

This subchapter, chapter 7, and sections 1305, 3105, 3344, 4301(2)(E), 5372, and 7521, and the provisions of section 5335(a)(B) of this title that relate to administrative law judges, do not limit or repeal additional requirements imposed by statute or otherwise recognized by law. Except as otherwise required by law, requirements or privileges relating to evidence or procedure apply equally to agencies and persons. Each agency is granted the authority necessary to comply with the requirements of this subchapter through the issuance of rules or otherwise. Subsequent statute may not be held to supersede or modify this subchapter, chapter 7, sections 1305, 3105, 3344, 4301(2)(E), 5372, or 7521 of this title, or the provisions of section 5335(a)(B) of this title that relate to administrative law judges, except to the extent that it does so expressly.

Chapter 7 — Judicial Review

§701. Application; Definitions

(a) This chapter applies, according to the provisions thereof, except to the extent that —

(1) statutes preclude judicial review; or

(2) agency action is committed to agency discretion by law.

(b) For the purpose of this chapter —

(1) "agency" means each authority of the Government of the United States, whether or not it is within or subject to review by another agency, but does not include —

(A) the Congress;

(B) the courts of the United States;

(C) the governments of the territories or possessions of the United States;

(D) the government of the District of Columbia;

(E) agencies composed of representatives of the parties or of representatives of organizations of the parties to the disputes determined by them;

(F) courts martial and military commissions;

(G) military authority exercised in the field in time of war or in occupied territory; or

(H) functions conferred by sections 1738, 1739, 1743, and 1744 of title 12; chapter 2 of title 41; subchapter II of chapter 471 of title 49; or sections 1884, 1891-1902, and former section 1641(b)(2), of title 50, appendix; and

(2) "person," "rule," "order," "license," "sanction," "relief," and "agency action" have the meanings given them by section 551 of this title.

§702. Right of Review

A person suffering legal wrong because of agency action, or adversely affected or aggrieved by agency action within the meaning of a relevant statute, is entitled to judicial review thereof. An action in a court of the United States seeking relief other than money damages and stating a claim that an agency or an officer or employee thereof acted or failed to act in an official capacity or under color of legal authority shall not be dismissed nor relief therein be denied on the ground that it is against the United States or that the United States is an indispensable party. The United States may be named as a defendant in any such action, and a judgment or decree may be entered against the United States: Provided, That any mandatory or injunctive decree shall specify the Federal officer or officers (by name or by title), and their successors in office, personally responsible for compliance. Nothing herein (1) affects other limitations on judicial review or the power or duty of the court to dismiss any action or deny relief on any other appropriate legal or equitable ground; or (2) confers authority to grant relief if any other statute that grants consent to suit expressly or impliedly forbids the relief which is sought.

§703. Form and Venue of Proceeding

The form of proceeding for judicial review is the special statutory review proceeding relevant to the subject matter in a court specified by statute or, in the absence or inadequacy thereof, any applicable form of legal action, including actions for declaratory judgments or writs of prohibitory or mandatory injunction or habeas corpus, in a court of competent jurisdiction. If no special statutory review proceeding is applicable, the action for judicial review may be brought against the United States, the agency by its official title, or the appropriate officer. Except to the extent that prior, adequate, and exclusive opportunity for judicial review is provided by law, agency action is subject to judicial review in civil or criminal proceedings for judicial enforcement.

§704. Actions Reviewable

Agency action made reviewable by statute and final agency action for which there is no other adequate remedy in a court are subject to judicial review. A preliminary, procedural, or intermediate agency action or ruling not directly renewable is subject to review on the review of the final agency action. Except as otherwise expressly required by statute, agency action otherwise final is final for the purposes of this section whether or not there has been presented or determined an application for a declaratory order, for any form of reconsideration, or unless the agency otherwise requires by rule and provides that the action meanwhile is inoperative, for an appeal to superior agency authority.

§705. Relief Pending Review

When an agency finds that justice so requires, it may postpone the effective date of action taken by it, pending judicial review. On such conditions as may be required and to the extent necessary to prevent irreparable injury, the reviewing court, including the court to which a case may be taken on appeal from or on application for certiorari or other writ to a reviewing court, may issue all necessary and appropriate process to postpone the effective date of an agency action or to preserve status or rights pending conclusion of the review proceedings.

§706. Scope of Review

To the extent necessary to decision and when presented, the reviewing court shall decide all relevant questions of law, interpret constitutional and statutory provisions, and determine the meaning or applicability of the terms of an agency action. The reviewing court shall —

(1) compel agency action unlawfully withheld or unreasonably delayed; and

(2) hold unlawful and set aside agency action, findings, and conclusions found to be —

(A) arbitrary, capricious, an abuse of discretion, or otherwise not in accordance with law;

(B) contrary to constitutional right, power, privilege, or immunity;

(C) in excess of statutory jurisdiction, authority, or limitations, or short of statutory right;

(D) without observance of procedure required by law;

(E) unsupported by substantial evidence in a case subject to sections 556 and 557 of this title or otherwise reviewed on the record of an agency hearing provided by statute; or

(F) unwarranted by the facts to the extent that the facts are subject to trial de novo by the reviewing court.

In making the foregoing determinations, the court shall review the whole record or those parts of it cited by a party, and due account shall be taken of the rule of prejudicial error.

Administrative Law Judges

§3105. Appointment of Administrative Law Judges

Each agency shall appoint as many administrative law judges as are necessary for proceedings required to be conducted in accordance with sections 556 and 557 of this title. Administrative law judges shall be assigned to cases in rotation so far as practicable, and may not perform duties inconsistent with their duties and responsibilities as administrative law judges.

§7521. Actions against Administrative Law Judges

(a) An action may be taken against an administrative law judge appointed under section 3105 of this title by the agency in which the administrative law judge is employed only for good cause established and determined by the Merit Systems Protection Board on the record after opportunity for hearing before the Board.

(b) The actions covered by this section are —

(1) a removal;

(2) a suspension;

(3) a reduction in grade;

(4) a reduction in pay; and

(5) a furlough of 30 days or less;

but do not include —

(A) a suspension or removal under section 7532 of this title;

(B) a reduction-in-force action under section 3502 of this title; or

(C) any action initiated under section 1215 of this title.

§5372. *Administrative Law Judges*

(a) For the purposes of this section, the term "administrative law judge" means an administrative law judge appointed under section 3105.

(b)(1)(A) There shall be 3 levels of basic pay for administrative law judges (designated as AL-1, 2, and 3, respectively), and each such judge shall be paid at 1 of those levels, in accordance with the provisions of this section.

(B) Within level AL-3, there shall be 6 rates of basic pay, designated as AL-3, rates A through F, respectively. Level AL-2 and level AL-1 shall each have 1 rate of basic pay.

(C) The rate of basic pay for AL-3, rate A, may not be less than 65 percent of the rate of basic pay for level IV of the Executive Schedule, and the rate of basic pay for AL-1 may not exceed the rate for level IV of the Executive Schedule.

(2) The Office of Personnel Management shall determine, in accordance with procedures which the Office shall by regulation prescribe, the level in which each administrative-law-judge position shall be placed and the qualifications to be required for appointment to each level.

(3)(A) Upon appointment to a position in AL-3, an administrative law judge shall be paid at rate A of AL-3, and shall be advanced successively to rates B, C, and D of that level at the beginning of the next pay period following completion of 52 weeks of service in the next lower rate, and to rates E and F of that level at the beginning of the next pay period following completion of 104 weeks of service in the next lower rate.

(B) The Office of Personnel Management may provide for appointment of an administrative law judge in AL-3 at an advanced rate under such circumstances as the Office may determine appropriate.

(4) Subject to paragraph (1), effective at the beginning of the first applicable pay period commencing on or after the first day of the month in which an adjustment takes effect under section 5303 in the rates of basic pay under The General Schedule, each rate of basic pay for administrative law judges shall be adjusted by an amount determined by the President to be appropriate.

(c) The Office of Personnel Management shall prescribe regulations necessary to administer this section.

§3344. *Details; Administrative Law Judges*

An agency as defined by section 551 of this title which occasionally or temporarily is insufficiently staffed with administrative law judges appointed under section 3105 of this title may use administrative law judges selected by the Office of Personnel Management from and with the consent of other agencies.

§1305.   *Administrative Law Judges*

For the purpose of sections 3105, 3344, 4301(2)(D), and 5372 of this title the provisions of section 5335(a)(B) of this title that relate to administrative law judges, the Office of Personnel Management may, and for the purpose of section 7521 of this title, the Merit Systems Protection Board may, investigate, prescribe regulations, appoint advisory committees as necessary, recommend legislation, subpena witnesses and records, and pay witness fees as established for the courts of the United States.

Appendix B: Selected Provisions from the Unfunded Mandates Reform Act

§1501. Purposes

The purposes of this chapter are —

(1) to strengthen the partnership between the Federal Government and State, local, and tribal governments;

(2) to end the imposition, in the absence of full consideration by Congress, of Federal mandates on State, local, and tribal governments without adequate Federal funding, in a manner that may displace other essential State, local, and tribal governmental priorities;

(3) to assist Congress in its consideration of proposed legislation establishing or revising Federal programs containing Federal mandates affecting State, local, and tribal governments, and the private sector by —

    (A) providing for the development of information about the nature and size of mandates in proposed legislation; and

    (B) establishing a mechanism to bring such information to the attention of the Senate and the House of Representatives before the Senate and the House of Representatives vote on proposed legislation;

(4) to promote informed and deliberate decisions by Congress on the appropriateness of Federal mandates in any particular instance;

(5) to require that Congress consider whether to provide funding to assist State, local, and tribal governments in complying with Federal mandates, to require analyses of the impact of private sector mandates, and through the dissemination of that information provide informed and deliberate decisions by Congress and Federal agencies and retain competitive balance between the public and private sectors;

(6) to establish a point-of-order vote on the consideration in the Senate and House of Representatives of legislation containing significant Federal intergovernmental mandates without providing adequate funding to comply with such mandates;

(7) to assist Federal agencies in their consideration of proposed regulations affecting State, local, and tribal governments, by —

    (A) requiring that Federal agencies develop a process to enable the elected and other officials of State, local, and tribal governments to provide input when Federal agencies are developing regulations; and

    (B) requiring that Federal agencies prepare and consider estimates of the budgetary impact of regulations containing Federal mandates upon State, local, and tribal governments and the private sector before adopting such regulations, and ensuring that small governments are given special consideration in that process; and

967

(8) to begin consideration of the effect of previously imposed Federal mandates, including the impact on State, local, and tribal governments of Federal court interpretations of Federal statutes and regulations that impose Federal intergovernmental mandates.

§1502. Definitions

For purposes of this chapter —

(1) except as provided in section 1555 of this title, the terms defined under section 658 of this title shall have the meanings as so defined; and

(2) the term "Director" means the Director of the Congressional Budget Office.

§1503. Exclusions

This chapter shall not apply to any provision in a bill, joint resolution, amendment, motion, or conference report before Congress and any provision in a proposed or final Federal regulation that —

(1) enforces constitutional rights of individuals;

(2) establishes or enforces any statutory rights that prohibit discrimination on the basis of race, color, religion, sex, national origin, age, handicap, or disability;

(3) requires compliance with accounting and auditing procedures with respect to grants or other money or property provided by the Federal Government;

(4) provides for emergency assistance or relief at the request of any State, local, or tribal government or any official of a State, local, or tribal government;

(5) is necessary for the national security or the ratification or implementation of international treaty obligations;

(6) the President designates as emergency legislation and that the Congress so designates in statute; or

(7) relates to the old-age, survivors, and disability insurance program under title II of the Social Security Act (including taxes imposed by sections 3101(a) and 3111(a) of Title 26 (relating to old-age, survivors, and disability insurance)).

§1511. Cost of Regulations

(a) Sense of the Congress. It is the sense of the Congress that Federal agencies should review and evaluate planned regulations to ensure that the cost estimates provided by the Congressional Budget Office will be carefully considered as regulations are promulgated.

(b) Statement of cost. At the request of a committee chairman or ranking minority member, the Director shall, to the extent practicable, prepare a comparison between —

(1) an estimate by the relevant agency, prepared under section 1532 of this title, of the costs of regulations implementing an Act containing a Federal mandate; and

(2) the cost estimate prepared by the Congressional Budget Office for such Act when it was enacted by the Congress.

(c) **Cooperation of Office of Management and Budget.** At the request of the Director of the Congressional Budget Office, the Director of the Office of Management and Budget shall provide data and cost estimates for regulations implementing an Act containing a Federal mandate covered by part B of title IV of the Congressional Budget and Impoundment Control Act of 1974.

§1513.   *Impact on Local Governments*

(a) **Findings.** The Senate finds that —

(1) the Congress should be concerned about shifting costs from Federal to State and local authorities and should be equally concerned about the growing tendency of States to shift costs to local governments;

(2) cost shifting from States to local governments has, in many instances, forced local governments to raise property taxes or curtail sometimes essential services; and

(3) increases in local property taxes and cuts in essential services threaten the ability of many citizens to attain and maintain the American dream of owning a home in a safe, secure community.

(b) **Sense of the Senate.** It is the sense of the Senate that —

(1) the Federal government should not shift certain costs to the State, and States should end the practice of shifting costs to local governments, which forces many local governments to increase property taxes;

(2) States should end the imposition, in the absence of full consideration by their legislatures, of State issued mandates on local governments without adequate State funding, in a manner that may displace other essential government priorities; and

(3) one primary objective of this Act and other efforts to change the relationship among Federal, State, and local governments should be [to] reduce taxes and spending at all levels and to end the practice of shifting costs from one level of government to another with little or no benefit to taxpayers.

§1532.   *Statements to Accompany Significant Regulatory Actions*

(a) **In general.** Unless otherwise prohibited by law, before promulgating any general notice of proposed rulemaking that is likely to result in promulgation of any rule that includes any Federal mandate that may result in the expenditure by State, local, and tribal governments, in the aggregate, or by the private sector, of $100,000,000 or more (adjusted annually for inflation) in any 1 year, and before promulgating any final rule for which a general notice of proposed rulemaking was published, the agency shall prepare a written statement containing —

(1) an identification of the provision of Federal law under which the rule is being promulgated;

(2) a qualitative and quantitative assessment of the anticipated costs and benefits of the Federal mandate, including the costs and benefits to State, local, and tribal governments or the private sector, as well as the effect of the Federal mandate on health, safety, and the natural environment and such an assessment shall include —

(A) an analysis of the extent to which such costs to State, local, and tribal governments may be paid with Federal financial assistance (or otherwise paid for by the Federal Government); and

(B) the extent to which there are available Federal resources to carry out the intergovernmental mandate;

(3) estimates by the agency, if and to the extent that the agency determines that accurate estimates are reasonably feasible, of —

(A) the future compliance costs of the Federal mandate; and

(B) any disproportionate budgetary effects of the Federal mandate upon any particular regions of the nation or particular State, local, or tribal governments, urban or rural or other types of communities, or particular segments of the private sector;

(4) estimates by the agency of the effect on the national economy, such as the effect on productivity, economic growth, full employment, creation of productive jobs, and international competitiveness of United States goods and services, if and to the extent that the agency in its sole discretion determines that accurate estimates are reasonably feasible and that such effect is relevant and material; and

(5)(A) a description of the extent of the agency's prior consultation with elected representatives (under section 1534 of this title) of the affected State, local, and tribal governments;

(B) a summary of the comments and concerns that were presented by State, local, or tribal governments either orally or in writing to the agency; and

(C) a summary of the agency's evaluation of those comments and concerns.

(b) Promulgation. In promulgating a general notice of proposed rulemaking or a final rule for which a statement under subsection (a) is required, the agency shall include in the promulgation a summary of the information contained in the statement.

(c) Preparation in conjunction with other statement. Any agency may prepare any statement required under subsection (a) in conjunction with or as a part of any other statement or analysis, provided that the statement or analysis satisfies the provisions of subsection (a) of this section.

§1534.   State, Local, and Tribal Government Input

(a) In general. Each agency shall, to the extent permitted in law, develop an effective process to permit elected officers of State, local, and tribal governments (or their designated employees with authority to act on their behalf) to provide meaningful and timely input in the development of regulatory proposals containing significant Federal intergovernmental mandates.

(b) Meetings between State, local, tribal and Federal officers. The Federal Advisory Committee Act (5 U.S.C. App.) shall not apply to actions in support of intergovernmental communications where —

(1) meetings are held exclusively between Federal officials and elected officers of State, local and tribal governments (or their designated employees with authority to act on their behalf) acting in their official capacities; and

(2) such meetings are solely for the purposes of exchanging views, information, or advice relating to the management or implementation of Federal programs established pursuant to public law that explicitly or inherently share intergovernmental responsibilities or administration.

(c) **Implementing guidelines.** No later than 6 months after March 22, 1995, the President shall issue guidelines and instructions to Federal agencies for appropriate implementation of subsections (a) and (b) of this section consistent with applicable laws and regulations.

§1535.   Least Burdensome Option or Explanation Required

(a) **In general.** Except as provided in subsection (b) of this section, before promulgating any rule for which a written statement is required under section 1532 of this title, the agency shall identify and consider a reasonable number of regulatory alternatives and from those alternatives select the least costly, most cost-effective or least burdensome alternative that achieves the objectives of the rule, for —

(1) State, local, and tribal governments, in the case of a rule containing a Federal intergovernmental mandate; and

(2) the private sector, in the case of a rule containing a Federal private sector mandate.

(b) **Exception.** The provisions of subsection (a) of this section shall apply unless —

(1) the head of the affected agency publishes with the final rule an explanation of why the least costly, most cost-effective or least burdensome method of achieving the objectives of the rule was not adopted; or

(2) the provisions are inconsistent with law.

(c) **OMB certification.** No later than 1 year after March 22, 1995, the Director of the Office of Management and Budget shall certify to Congress, with a written explanation, agency compliance with this section and include in that certification agencies and rulemakings that fail to adequately comply with this section.

§1536.   Assistance to Congressional Budget Office

The Director of the Office of Management and Budget shall —

(1) collect from agencies the statements prepared under section 1532 of this title; and

(2) periodically forward copies of such statements to the Director of the Congressional Budget Office on a reasonably timely basis after promulgation of the general notice of proposed rulemaking or of the final rule for which the statement was prepared.

§1538.   Annual Statements to Congress on Agency Compliance

No later than 1 year after March 22, 1995, and annually thereafter, the Director of the Office of Management and Budget shall submit to the Congress, including the Committee on Governmental Affairs of the Senate and the Committee on Government Reform and Oversight of the House of Representatives, a written report detailing compliance by each agency during the preceding reporting period with the requirements of this subchapter.

§1551. Baseline Study of Costs and Benefits

(a) **In general.** No later than 18 months after March 22, 1995, the Advisory Commission on Intergovernmental Relations (hereafter in this subchapter referred to as the "Advisory Commission"), in consultation with the Director, shall complete a study to examine the measurement and definition issues involved in calculating the total costs and benefits to State, local, and tribal governments of compliance with Federal law.

(b) **Considerations.** The study required by this section shall consider —

(1) the feasibility of measuring indirect costs and benefits as well as direct costs and benefits of the Federal, State, local, and tribal relationship; and

(2) how to measure both the direct and indirect benefits of Federal financial assistance and tax benefits to State, local, and tribal governments.

§1571. Judicial Review

(a) **Agency statements on significant regulatory actions.** (1) In general. Compliance or noncompliance by any agency with the provisions of sections 1532 and 1533(a)(1) and (2) of this title shall be subject to judicial review only in accordance with this section.

(2) Limited review of agency compliance or noncompliance. (A) Agency compliance or noncompliance with the provisions of sections 1532 and 1533(a)(1) and (2) of this title shall be subject to judicial review only under section 706(1) of Title 5, and only as provided under subparagraph (B).

(B) If an agency fails to prepare the written statement (including the preparation of the estimates, analyses, statements, or descriptions) under section 1532 of this title or the written plan under section 1533(a)(1) and (2) of this title, a court may compel the agency to prepare such written statement.

(3) Review of agency rules. In any judicial review under any other Federal law of an agency rule for which a written statement or plan is required under sections 1532 and 1533(a)(1) and (2) of this title, the inadequacy or failure to prepare such statement (including the inadequacy or failure to prepare any estimate, analysis, statement or description) or written plan shall not be used as a basis for staying, enjoining, invalidating or otherwise affecting such agency rule.

(4) Certain information as part of record. Any information generated under sections 1532 and 1533(a)(1) and (2) of this title that is part of the rulemaking record for judicial review under the provisions of any other Federal law may be considered as part of the record for judicial review conducted under such other provisions of Federal law.

(5) Application of other federal law. For any petition under paragraph (2) the provisions of such other Federal law shall control all other matters, such as exhaustion of administrative remedies, the time for and manner of seeking review and venue, except that if such other Federal law does not provide a limitation on the time for filing a petition for judicial review that is less than 180 days, such limitation shall be 180 days after a final rule is promulgated by the appropriate agency.

(6) Effective date. This subsection shall take effect on October 1, 1995, and shall apply only to any agency rule for which a general notice of proposed rulemaking is promulgated on or after such date.

(b) Judicial review and rule of construction. Except as provided in subsection (a) of this section —

(1) any estimate, analysis, statement, description or report prepared under this chapter, and any compliance or noncompliance with the provisions of this chapter, and any determination concerning the applicability of the provisions of this chapter shall not be subject to judicial review; and

(2) no provision of this chapter shall be construed to create any right or benefit, substantive or procedural, enforceable by any person in any administrative or judicial action.

Appendix C:
Negotiated Rulemaking and Alternative Dispute Resolution Act

§561. *Purpose*

The purpose of this subchapter is to establish a framework for the conduct of negotiated rulemaking, consistent with section 553 of this title, to encourage agencies to use the process when it enhances the informal rulemaking process. Nothing in this subchapter should be construed as an attempt to limit innovation and experimentation with the negotiated rulemaking process or with other innovative rulemaking procedures otherwise authorized by law.

§562. *Definitions*

For the purposes of this subchapter the term —
(1) "agency" has the same meaning as in section 551(1) of this title;
(2) "consensus" means unanimous concurrence among the interests represented on a negotiated rulemaking committee established under this subchapter unless such committee —
(A) agrees to define such term to mean a general but not unanimous concurrence; or
(B) agrees upon another specified definition;
(3) "convener" means a person who impartially assists an agency in determining whether establishment of a negotiated rulemaking committee is feasible and appropriate in a particular rulemaking;
(4) "facilitator" means a person who impartially aids in the discussions and negotiations among the members of a negotiated rulemaking committee to develop a proposed rule;
(5) "interest" means, with respect to an issue or matter, multiple parties which have a similar point of view or which are likely to be affected in a similar manner;
(6) "negotiated rulemaking" means rulemaking through the use of a negotiated rulemaking committee;
(7) "negotiated rulemaking committee" or "committee" means an advisory committee established by an agency in accordance with this subchapter and the Federal Advisory Committee Act to consider and discuss issues for the purpose of reaching a consensus in the development of a proposed rule;
(8) "party" has the same meaning as in section 551(3) of this title;
(9) "person" has the same meaning as in section 551(2) of this title;

(10) "rule" has the same meaning as in section 551(4) of this title; and

(11) "rulemaking" means "rule making" as that term is defined in section 551(5) of this title.

§563. *Determination of Need for Negotiated Rulemaking Committee*

(a) Determination of need by the agency. An agency may establish a negotiated rulemaking committee to negotiate and develop a proposed rule, if the head of the agency determines that the use of the negotiated rulemaking procedure is in the public interest. In making such a determination, the head of the agency shall consider whether —

(1) there is a need for a rule;

(2) there are a limited number of identifiable interests that will be significantly affected by the rule;

(3) there is a reasonable likelihood that a committee can be convened with a balanced representation of persons who —

(A) can adequately represent the interests identified under paragraph (2); and

(B) are willing to negotiate in good faith to reach a consensus on the proposed rule;

(4) there is a reasonable likelihood that a committee will reach a consensus on the proposed rule within a fixed period of time;

(5) the negotiated rulemaking procedure will not unreasonably delay the notice of proposed rulemaking and the issuance of the final rule;

(6) the agency has adequate resources and is willing to commit such resources, including technical assistance, to the committee; and

(7) the agency, to the maximum extent possible consistent with the legal obligations of the agency, will use the consensus of the committee with respect to the proposed rule as the basis for the rule proposed by the agency for notice and comment.

(b) Use of conveners. (1) Purposes of conveners. An agency may use the services of a convener to assist the agency in —

(A) identifying persons who will be significantly affected by a proposed rule, including residents of rural areas; and

(B) conducting discussions with such persons to identify the issues of concern to such persons, and to ascertain whether the establishment of a negotiated rulemaking committee is feasible and appropriate in the particular rulemaking.

(2) Duties of conveners. The convener shall report findings and may make recommendations to the agency. Upon request of the agency, the convener shall ascertain the names of persons who are willing and qualified to represent interests that will be significantly affected by the proposed rule, including residents of rural areas. The report and any recommendations of the convener shall be made available to the public upon request.

§564. *Publication of Notice; Applications for Membership on Committees*

(a) Publication of notice. If, after considering the report of a convener or conducting its own assessment, an agency decides to establish a negotiated rulemaking committee, the agency shall publish in the *Federal Register* and, as appropriate, in trade or other specialized publications, a notice which shall include —

(1) an announcement that the agency intends to establish a negotiated rulemaking committee to negotiate and develop a proposed rule;

(2) a description of the subject and scope of the rule to be developed, and the issues to be considered;

(3) a list of the interests which are likely to be significantly affected by the rule;

(4) a list of the persons proposed to represent such interests and the person or persons proposed to represent the agency;

(5) a proposed agenda and schedule for completing the work of the committee, including a target date for publication by the agency of a proposed rule for notice and comment;

(6) a description of administrative support for the committee to be provided by the agency, including technical assistance;

(7) a solicitation for comments on the proposal to establish the committee, and the proposed membership of the negotiated rulemaking committee; and

(8) an explanation of how a person may apply or nominate another person for membership on the committee, as provided under subsection (b).

(b) Applications for membership or committee. Persons who will be significantly affected by a proposed rule and who believe that their interests will not be adequately represented by any person specified in a notice under subsection (a)(4) may apply for, or nominate another person for, membership on the negotiated rulemaking committee to represent such interests with respect to the proposed rule. Each application or nomination shall include —

(1) the name of the applicant or nominee and a description of the interests such person shall represent;

(2) evidence that the applicant or nominee is authorized to represent parties related to the interests the person proposes to represent;

(3) a written commitment that the applicant or nominee shall actively participate in good faith in the development of the rule under consideration; and

(4) the reasons that the persons specified in the notice under subsection (a)(4) do not adequately represent the interests of the person submitting the application or nomination.

(c) Period for submission of comments and applications. The agency shall provide for a period of at least 30 calendar days for the submission of comments and applications under this section.

§565. *Establishment of Committee*

(a) **Establishment.** (1) Determination to establish committee. If after considering comments and applications submitted under section 564, the agency determines that a negotiated rulemaking committee can adequately represent the interests that will be significantly affected by a proposed rule and that it is feasible and appropriate in the particular rulemaking, the agency may establish a negotiated rulemaking committee. In establishing and administering such a committee, the agency shall comply with the Federal Advisory Committee Act with respect to such committee, except as otherwise provided in this subchapter.

(2) Determination not to establish committee. If after considering such comments and applications, the agency decides not to establish a negotiated rulemaking committee,

the agency shall promptly publish notice of such decision and the reasons therefor in the *Federal Register* and, as appropriate, in trade or other specialized publications, a copy of which shall be sent to any person who applied for, or nominated another person for membership on the negotiating rulemaking committee to represent such interests with respect to the proposed rule.

(b) **Membership.** The agency shall limit membership on a negotiated rulemaking committee to 25 members, unless the agency head determines that a greater number of members is necessary for the functioning of the committee or to achieve balanced membership. Each committee shall include at least one person representing the agency.

(c) **Administrative support.** The agency shall provide appropriate administrative support to the negotiated rulemaking committee, including technical assistance.

§566. *Conduct of Committee Activity*

(a) **Duties of committee.** Each negotiated rulemaking committee established under this subchapter shall consider the matter proposed by the agency for consideration and shall attempt to reach a consensus concerning a proposed rule with respect to such matter and any other matter the committee determines is relevant to the proposed rule.

(b) **Representatives of agency on committee.** The person or persons representing the agency on a negotiated rulemaking committee shall participate in the deliberations and activities of the committee with the same rights and responsibilities as other members of the committee, and shall be authorized to fully represent the agency in the discussions and negotiations of the committee.

(c) **Selecting facilitator.** Notwithstanding section 10(e) of the Federal Advisory Committee Act, an agency may nominate either a person from the Federal Government or a person from outside the Federal Government to serve as a facilitator for the negotiations of the committee, subject to the approval of the committee by consensus. If the committee does not approve the nominee of the agency for facilitator, the agency shall submit a substitute nomination. If a committee does not approve any nominee of the agency for facilitator, the committee shall select by consensus a person to serve as facilitator. A person designated to represent the agency in substantive issues may not serve as facilitator or otherwise chair the committee.

(d) **Duties of facilitator.** A facilitator approved or selected by a negotiated rulemaking committee shall —

(1) chair the meetings of the committee in an impartial manner;

(2) impartially assist the members of the committee in conducting discussions and negotiations; and

(3) manage the keeping of minutes and records as required under section 10(b) and (c) of the Federal Advisory Committee Act, except that any personal notes and materials of the facilitator or of the members of a committee shall not be subject to section 552 of this title.

(e) **Committee procedures.** A negotiated rulemaking committee established under this subchapter may adopt procedures for the operation of the committee. No provision of section 553 of this title shall apply to the procedures of a negotiated rulemaking committee.

(f) **Report of committee.** If a committee reaches a consensus on a proposed rule, at the conclusion of negotiations the committee shall transmit to the agency that established the committee a report containing the proposed rule. If the committee does not reach a consensus on a proposed rule, the committee may transmit to the agency a report specifying any areas in which the committee reached a consensus. The committee may include in a report any other information, recommendations, or materials that the committee considers appropriate. Any committee member may include as an addendum to the report additional information, recommendations, or materials.

(g) **Records of committee.** In addition to the report required by subsection (f), a committee shall submit to the agency the records required under section 10(b) and (c) of the Federal Advisory Committee Act.

§567. *Termination of Committee*

A negotiated rulemaking committee shall terminate upon promulgation of the final rule under consideration, unless the committee's charter contains an earlier termination date or the agency, after consulting the committee, or the committee itself, specifies an earlier termination date.

§568. *Services, Facilities, and Payment of Committee Member Expenses*

(a) **Services of conveners and facilitators.** (1) In general. An agency may employ or enter into contracts for the services of an individual or organization to serve as a convener or facilitator for a negotiated rulemaking committee under this subchapter, or may use the services of a Government employee to act as a convener or a facilitator for such a committee.

(2) Determination of conflicting interests. An agency shall determine whether a person under consideration to serve as convener or facilitator of a committee under paragraph (1) has any financial or other interest that would preclude such person from serving in an impartial and independent manner.

(b) **Services and facilities of other entities.** For purposes of this subchapter, an agency may use the services and facilities of other Federal agencies and public and private agencies and instrumentalities with the consent of such agencies and instrumentalities, and with or without reimbursement to such agencies and instrumentalities, and may accept voluntary and uncompensated services without regard to the provisions of section 1342 of title 31. The Federal Mediation and Conciliation Service may provide services and facilities, with or without reimbursement, to assist agencies under this subchapter, including furnishing conveners, facilitators, and training in negotiated rulemaking.

(c) **Expenses of committee members.** Members of a negotiated rulemaking committee shall be responsible for their own expenses of participation in such committee, except that an agency may, in accordance with section 7(d) of the Federal Advisory Committee Act, pay for a member's reasonable travel and per diem expenses, expenses to obtain technical assistance, and a reasonable rate of compensation, if —

(1) such member certifies a lack of adequate financial resources to participate in the committee; and

(2) the agency determines that such member's participation in the committee is necessary to assure an adequate representation of the member's interest.

(d) **Status of member as Federal employee.** A member's receipt of funds under this section or section 569 shall not conclusively determine for purposes of sections 202 through 209 of title 18 whether that member is an employee of the United States Government.

§569. *Encouraging Negotiated Rulemaking*

(a) The President shall designate an agency or designate or establish an interagency committee to facilitate and encourage agency use of negotiated rulemaking. An agency that is considering, planning, or conducting a negotiated rulemaking may consult with such agency or committee for information and assistance.

(b) To carry out the purposes of this subchapter, an agency planning or conducting a negotiated rulemaking may accept, hold, administer, and utilize gifts, devises, and bequests of property, both real and personal if that agency's acceptance and use of such gifts, devises, or bequests do not create a conflict of interest. Gifts and bequests of money and proceeds from sales of other property received as gifts, devises, or bequests shall be deposited in the Treasury and shall be disbursed upon the order of the head of such agency. Property accepted pursuant to this section, and the proceeds thereof, shall be used as nearly as possible in accordance with the terms of the gifts, devises, or bequests.

§570. *Judicial Review*

Any agency action relating to establishing, assisting, or terminating a negotiated rule-making committee under this subchapter shall not be subject to judicial review. Nothing in this section shall bar judicial review of a rule if such judicial review is otherwise provided by law. A rule which is the product of negotiated rulemaking and is subject to judicial review shall not be accorded any greater deference by a court than a rule which is the product of other rulemaking procedures.

§571. *Definitions*

For the purposes of this subchapter, the term —

(1) "agency" has the same meaning as in section 551(1) of this title;

(2) "administrative program" includes a Federal function which involves protection of the public interest and the determination of rights, privileges, and obligations of private persons through rule making, adjudication, licensing, or investigation, as those terms are used in subchapter II of this chapter;

(3) "alternative means of dispute resolution" means any procedure that is used to resolve issues in controversy, including, but not limited to, conciliation, facilitation, mediation, factfinding, minitrials, arbitration, and use of ombuds, or any combination thereof;

(4) "award" means any decision by an arbitrator resolving the issues in controversy;

(5) "dispute resolution communication" means any oral or written communication prepared for the purposes of a dispute resolution proceeding, including any memoranda, notes or work product of the neutral parties or nonparty participant; except that

a written agreement to enter into a dispute resolution proceeding, or final written agreement or arbitral award reached as a result of a dispute resolution proceeding, is not a dispute resolution communication;

(6) "dispute resolution proceeding" means any process in which an alternative means of dispute resolution is used to resolve an issue in controversy in which a neutral is appointed and specified parties participate;

(7) "in confidence" means, with respect to information, that the information is provided —

(A) with the expressed intent of the source that it not be disclosed; or

(B) under circumstances that would create the reasonable expectation on behalf of the source that the information will not be disclosed;

(8) "issue in controversy" means an issue which is material to a decision concerning an administrative program of an agency, and with which there is disagreement —

(A) between an agency and persons who would be substantially affected by the decision; or

(B) between persons who would be substantially affected by the decision;

(9) "neutral" means an individual who, with respect to an issue in controversy, functions specifically to aid the parties in resolving the controversy;

(10) "party" means —

(A) for a proceeding with named parties, the same as in section 551(3) of the title; and

(B) for a proceeding without named parties, a person who will be significantly affected by the decision in the proceeding and who participates in the proceeding;

(11) "person" has the same meaning as in section 551(2) of this title; and

(12) "roster" means a list of persons qualified to provide services as neutrals.

§572. *General Authority*

(a) An agency may use a dispute resolution proceeding for the resolution of an issue in controversy that relates to an administrative program, if the parties agree to such proceeding.

(b) An agency shall consider not using a dispute resolution proceeding if —

(1) a definitive or authoritative resolution of the matter is required for precedential value, and such a proceeding is not likely to be accepted generally as an authoritative precedent;

(2) the matter involves or may bear upon significant questions of Government policy that require additional procedures before a final resolution may be made, and such a proceeding would not likely serve to develop a recommended policy for the agency;

(3) maintaining established policies is of special importance, so that variations among individual decisions are not increased and such a proceeding would not likely reach consistent results among individual decisions;

(4) the matter significantly affects persons or organizations who are not parties to the proceeding;

(5) a full public record of the proceeding is important, and a dispute resolution proceeding cannot provide such a record; and

(6) the agency must maintain continuing jurisdiction over the matter with authority to alter the disposition of the matter in the light of changed circumstances, and a dispute resolution proceeding would interfere with the agency's fulfilling that requirement.

(c) Alternative means of dispute resolution authorized under this subchapter are voluntary procedures which supplement rather than limit other available agency dispute resolution techniques.

§573.   Neutrals

(a) A neutral may be a permanent or temporary officer or employee of the Federal Government or any other individual who is acceptable to the parties to a dispute resolution proceeding. A neutral shall have no official, financial, or personal conflict of interest with respect to the issues in controversy, unless such interest is fully disclosed in writing to all parties and all parties agree that the neutral may serve.

(b) A neutral who serves as a conciliator, facilitator, or mediator serves at the will of the parties.

(c) The President shall designate an agency or designate or establish an interagency committee to facilitate and encourage agency use of dispute resolution under this subchapter. Such agency or interagency committee, in consultation with other appropriate Federal agencies and professional organizations experienced in matters concerning dispute resolution, shall —

(1) encourage and facilitate agency use of alternative means of dispute resolution; and

(2) develop procedures that permit agencies to obtain the services of neutrals on an expedited basis.

(d) An agency may use the services of one or more employees of other agencies to serve as neutrals in dispute resolution proceedings. The agencies may enter into an interagency agreement that provides for the reimbursement by the user agency or the parties of the full or partial cost of the services of such an employee.

(e) Any agency may enter into a contract with any person for services as a neutral, or for training in connection with alternative means of dispute resolution. The parties in a dispute resolution proceeding shall agree on compensation for the neutral that is fair and reasonable to the Government.

§574.   Confidentiality

(a) Except as provided in subsections (d) and (e), a neutral in a dispute resolution proceeding shall not voluntarily disclose or through discovery or compulsory process be required to disclose any dispute resolution communication or any communication provided in confidence to the neutral, unless —

(1) all parties to the dispute resolution proceeding and the neutral consent in writing, and, if the dispute resolution communication was provided by a nonparty participant, that participant also consents in writing;

(2) the dispute resolution communication has already been made public;

(3) the dispute resolution communication is required by statute to be made public, but a neutral should make such communication public only if no other person is reasonably available to disclose the communication; or

(4) a court determines that such testimony or disclosure is necessary to —

(A) prevent a manifest injustice;

(B) help establish a violation of law; or

(C) prevent harm to the public health or safety, of sufficient magnitude in the particular case to outweigh the integrity of dispute resolution proceedings in general by reducing the confidence of parties in future cases that their communications will remain confidential.

(b) A party to a dispute resolution proceeding shall not voluntarily disclose or through discovery or compulsory process be required to disclose any dispute resolution communication, unless —

(1) the communication was prepared by the party seeking disclosure;

(2) all parties to the dispute resolution proceeding consent in writing;

(3) the dispute resolution communication has already been made public;

(4) the dispute resolution communication is required by statute to be made public;

(5) a court determines that such testimony or disclosure is necessary to —

(A) prevent a manifest injustice;

(B) help establish a violation of law; or

(C) prevent harm to the public health and safety, of sufficient magnitude in the particular case to outweigh the integrity of dispute resolution proceedings in general by reducing the confidence of parties in future cases that their communications will remain confidential;

(6) the dispute resolution communication is relevant to determining the existence or meaning of an agreement or award that resulted from the dispute resolution proceeding or to the enforcement of such an agreement or award; or

(7) except for dispute resolution communications generated by the neutral, the dispute resolution communication was provided to or was available to all parties to the dispute resolution proceeding.

(c) Any dispute resolution communication that is disclosed in violation of subsection (a) or (b), shall not be admissible in any proceeding relating to the issues in controversy with respect to which the communication was made.

(d)(1) The parties may agree to alternative confidential procedures for disclosures by a neutral. Upon such agreement the parties shall inform the neutral before the commencement of the dispute resolution proceeding of any modifications to the provisions of subsection (a) that will govern the confidentiality of the dispute resolution proceeding. If the parties do not so inform the neutral, subsection (a) shall apply.

(2) To qualify for the exemption established under subsection (j), an alternative confidential procedure under this subsection may not provide for less disclosure than the confidential procedures otherwise provided under this section.

(e) If a demand for disclosure, by way of discovery request or other legal process, is made upon a neutral regarding a dispute resolution communication, the neutral shall make reasonable efforts to notify the parties and any affected nonparty participants of the demand. Any party or affected nonparty participant who receives such notice and within 15 calendar days does not offer to defend a refusal of the neutral to disclose the requested information shall have waived any objection to such disclosure.

(f) Nothing in this section shall prevent the discovery or admissibility of any evidence that is otherwise discoverable, merely because the evidence was presented in the course of a dispute resolution proceeding.

(g) Subsections (a) and (b) shall have no effect on the information and data that are necessary to document an agreement reached or order issued pursuant to a dispute resolution proceeding.

(h) Subsections (a) and (b) shall not prevent the gathering of information for research or educational purposes, in cooperation with other agencies, governmental entities, or dispute resolution programs, so long as the parties and the specific issues in controversy are not identifiable.

(i) Subsections (a) and (b) shall not prevent use of a dispute resolution communication to resolve a dispute between the neutral in a dispute resolution proceeding and a party to or participant in such proceeding, so long as such dispute resolution communication is disclosed only to the extent necessary to resolve such dispute.

(j) A dispute resolution communication which is between a neutral and a party and which may not be disclosed under this section shall also be exempt from disclosure under section 552(b)(3).

§575. *Authorization of Arbitration*

(a)(1) Arbitration may be used as an alternative means of dispute resolution whenever all parties consent. Consent may be obtained either before or after an issue in controversy has arisen. A party may agree to —

(A) submit only certain issues in controversy to arbitration; or

(B) arbitration on the condition that the award must be within a range of possible outcomes.

(2) The arbitration agreement that sets forth the subject matter submitted to the arbitrator shall be in writing. Each such arbitration agreement shall specify a maximum award that may be issued by the arbitrator and may specify other conditions limiting the range of possible outcomes.

(3) An agency may not require any person to consent to arbitration as a condition of entering into a contract or obtaining a benefit.

(b) An officer or employee of an agency shall not offer to use arbitration for the resolution of issues in controversy unless such officer or employee —

(1) would otherwise have authority to enter into a settlement concerning the matter; or

(2) is otherwise specifically authorized by the agency to consent to the use of arbitration.

(c) Prior to using binding arbitration under this subchapter, the head of an agency, in consultation with the Attorney General and after taking into account the factor in section 572(b), shall issue guidance on the appropriate use of binding arbitration and when an officer or employee of the agency has authority to settle an issue in controversy through binding arbitration.

§576. *Enforcement of Arbitration Agreements*

An agreement to arbitrate a matter to which this subchapter applies is enforceable pursuant to section 4 of title 9, and no action brought to enforce such an agreement shall be dismissed nor shall relief therein be denied on the grounds that it is against the United States or that the United States is an indispensable party.

§577. *Arbitrators*

(a) The parties to an arbitration proceeding shall be entitled to participate in the selection of the arbitrator.

(b) The arbitrator shall be a neutral who meets the criteria of section 573 of this title.

§578. *Authority of the Arbitrator*

An arbitrator to whom a dispute is referred under this subchapter may —

(1) regulate the course of and conduct arbitral hearings;

(2) administer oaths and affirmations;

(3) compel the attendance of witnesses and production of evidence at the hearing under the provisions of section 7 of title 9 only to the extent the agency involved is otherwise authorized by law to do so; and

(4) make awards.

§579. *Arbitration Proceedings*

(a) The arbitrator shall set a time and place for the hearing on the dispute and shall notify the parties not less than 5 days before the hearing.

(b) Any party wishing a record of the hearing shall —

(1) be responsible for the preparation of such record;

(2) notify the other parties and the arbitrator of the preparation of such record;

(3) furnish copies to all identified parties and the arbitrator; and

(4) pay all costs for such record, unless the parties agree otherwise or the arbitrator determines that the costs should be apportioned.

(c)(1) The parties to the arbitration are entitled to be heard, to present evidence material to the controversy, and to cross-examine witnesses appearing at the hearing.

(2) The arbitrator may, with the consent of the parties, conduct all or part of the hearing by telephone, television, computer, or other electronic means, if each party has an opportunity to participate.

(3) The hearing shall be conducted expeditiously and in an informal manner.

(4) The arbitrator may receive any oral or documentary evidence, except that irrelevant, immaterial, unduly repetitious, or privileged evidence may be excluded by the arbitrator.

(5) The arbitrator shall interpret and apply relevant statutory and regulatory requirements, legal precedents, and policy directives.

(d) No interested person shall make or knowingly cause to be made to the arbitrator an unauthorized ex parte communication relevant to the merits of the proceeding, unless the parties agree otherwise. If a communication is made in violation of this subsection, the arbitrator shall ensure that a memorandum of the communication is prepared and made a part of the record, and that an opportunity for rebuttal is allowed. Upon receipt of a communication made in violation of this subsection, the arbitrator may, to the extent consistent with the interests of justice and the policies underlying this subchapter, require the offending party to show cause why the claim of such party should not be resolved against such party as a result of the improper conduct.

(e) The arbitrator shall make the award within 30 days after the close of the hearing, or the date of the filing of any briefs authorized by the arbitrator, whichever date is later, unless —

(1) the parties agree to some other time limit; or

(2) the agency provides by rule for some other time limit.

§580. Arbitration Awards

(a)(1) Unless the agency provides otherwise by rule, the award in an arbitration proceeding under this subchapter shall include a brief, informal discussion of the factual and legal basis for the award, but formal findings of fact or conclusions of law shall not be required.

(2) The prevailing parties shall file the award with all relevant agencies, along with proof of service on all parties.

(b) The award in an arbitration proceeding shall become final 30 days after it is served on all parties. Any agency that is a party to the proceeding may extend this 30-day period for an additional 30-day period by serving a notice of such extension on all other parties before the end of the first 30-day period.

(c) A final award is binding on the parties to the arbitration proceeding, and may be enforced pursuant to sections 9 through 13 of title 9. No action brought to enforce such an award shall be dismissed nor shall relief therein be denied on the grounds that it is against the United States or that the United States is an indispensable party.

(d) An award entered under this subchapter in an arbitration proceeding may not serve as an estoppel in any other proceeding for any issue that was resolved in the proceeding. Such an award also may not be used as precedent or otherwise be considered in any factually unrelated proceeding, whether conducted under this subchapter, by an agency, or in a court, or in any other arbitration proceeding.

§581. Judicial Review

(a) Notwithstanding any other provision of law, any person adversely affected or aggrieved by an award made in an arbitration proceeding conducted under this subchapter may bring an action for review of such award only pursuant to the provisions of sections 9 through 13 of title 9.

(b) A decision by an agency to use or not to use a dispute resolution proceeding under this subchapter shall be committed to the discretion of the agency and shall not be subject to judicial review, except that arbitration shall be subject to judicial review under section 10(b) of title 9.

Table Correlating Provisions of the Administrative Procedure Act as Presently Codified in 5 U.S.C. and Sections of the Act as Originally Enacted in 1946

5 U.S.C.	1946 Administrative Procedure Act
§551(1)	Sec. 2(a)
§551(2), (3)	Sec. 2(b)
§551(4), (5)	Sec. 2(c)
§551(6), (7)	Sec. 2(d)
§551(8), (9)	Sec. 2(e)
§551(10), (11)	Sec. 2(f)
§551(12), (13)	Sec. 2(g)
§552(a)-(e)	Sec. 3
§552(a)	Sec. 4
§553(b)	Sec. 4(a)
§553(c)	Sec. 4(b)
§553(d)	Sec. 4(c)
§553(e)	Sec. 4(d)
§554(a)	Sec. 5
§554(b)	Sec. 5(a)
§554(c)	Sec. 5(b)
§554(d)	Sec. 5(c)
§554(e)	Sec. 5(d)
§555(a)	Sec. 6
§555(b)	Sec. 6(a)
§555(c)	Sec. 6(b)
§555(d)	Sec. 6(c)
§555(e)	Sec. 6(d)
§556(a)	Sec. 6
§556(b)	Sec. 7(a)
§556(c)	Sec. 7(b)
§556(d)	Sec. 7(c)
§556(e)	Sec. 7(d)
§557(a)	Sec. 8
§557(b)	Sec. 8(a)
§557(c)	Sec. 8(b)
§558(a)	Sec. 9
§558(b)	Sec. 9(a)

§558(c)	Sec. 9(b)
§559	Sec. 12
§701(a)	Sec. 10
§701(b)(1), (2)	Sec. 2(a)-(g)
§702	Sec. 10(a)
§703	Sec. 10(b)
§704	Sec. 10(c)
§705	Sec. 10(d)
§706(1), (2)	Sec. 10(e)
§3105	Sec. 11 (1st sentence)
§7521	Sec. 11 (2nd sentence)
§5362	Sec. 11 (3rd sentence)
§3344	Sec. 11 (4th sentence)
§1305	Sec. 11 (5th sentence)

Table of Cases

Index